American Casebook Series
Hornbook Series and Basic Legal Texts
Nutshell Series

of

WEST PUBLISHING COMPANY
P.O. Box 64526
St. Paul, Minnesota 55164–0526

ACCOUNTING

Faris' Accounting and Law in a Nutshell, 377 pages, 1984 (Text)

Fiflis, Kripke and Foster's Teaching Materials on Accounting for Business Lawyers, 3rd Ed., 838 pages, 1984 (Casebook)

Siegel and Siegel's Accounting and Financial Disclosure: A Guide to Basic Concepts, 259 pages, 1983 (Text)

ADMINISTRATIVE LAW

Davis' Cases, Text and Problems on Administrative Law, 6th Ed., 683 pages, 1977 (Casebook)

Davis' Basic Text on Administrative Law, 3rd Ed., 617 pages, 1972 (Text)

Davis' Police Discretion, 176 pages, 1975 (Text)

Gellhorn and Boyer's Administrative Law and Process in a Nutshell, 2nd Ed., 445 pages, 1981 (Text)

Mashaw and Merrill's Cases and Materials on Administrative Law–The American Public Law System, 2nd Ed., 975 pages, 1985 (Casebook)

Robinson, Gellhorn and Bruff's The Administrative Process, 2nd Ed., 959 pages, 1980, with 1983 Supplement (Casebook)

ADMIRALTY

Healy and Sharpe's Cases and Materials on Admiralty, 875 pages, 1974 (Casebook)

Maraist's Admiralty in a Nutshell, 390 pages, 1983 (Text)

Sohn and Gustafson's Law of the Sea in a Nutshell, 264 pages, 1984 (Text)

AGENCY—PARTNERSHIP

Fessler's Alternatives to Incorporation for Persons in Quest of Profit, 258 pages, 1980 (Casebook)

AGENCY—PARTNERSHIP—Continued

Henn's Cases and Materials on Agency, Partnership and Other Unincorporated Business Enterprises, 2nd Ed., 733 pages, 1985 (Casebook)

Reuschlein and Gregory's Hornbook on the Law of Agency and Partnership, 625 pages, 1979, with 1981 pocket part (Text)

Seavey, Reuschlein and Hall's Cases on Agency and Partnership, 599 pages, 1962 (Casebook)

Selected Corporation and Partnership Statutes and Forms, approximately 555 pages, 1985

Steffen and Kerr's Cases and Materials on Agency-Partnership, 4th Ed., 859 pages, 1980 (Casebook)

Steffen's Agency-Partnership in a Nutshell, 364 pages, 1977 (Text)

AGRICULTURAL LAW

Meyer, Pedersen, Thorson and Davidson's Agricultural Law: Cases and Materials, 931 pages, 1985 (Casebook)

AMERICAN INDIAN LAW

Canby's American Indian Law in a Nutshell, 288 pages, 1981 (Text)

Getches, Rosenfelt and Wilkinson's Cases on Federal Indian Law, 660 pages, 1979, with 1983 Supplement (Casebook)

ANTITRUST LAW

Gellhorn's Antitrust Law and Economics in a Nutshell, 2nd Ed., 425 pages, 1981 (Text)

Gifford and Raskind's Cases and Materials on Antitrust, 694 pages, 1983 with 1985 Supplement (Casebook)

Hovenkamp's Economics and Federal Antitrust Law, Student Ed., 414 pages, 1985 (Text)

List current as of April, 1985

T7202—1g

I

LAW SCHOOL PUBLICATIONS—Continued

ANTITRUST LAW—Continued

Oppenheim, Weston and McCarthy's Cases and Comments on Federal Antitrust Laws, 4th Ed., 1168 pages, 1981 with 1985 Supplement (Casebook)

Posner and Easterbrook's Cases and Economic Notes on Antitrust, 2nd Ed., 1077 pages, 1981, with 1984–85 Supplement (Casebook)

Sullivan's Hornbook of the Law of Antitrust, 886 pages, 1977 (Text)

See also Regulated Industries, Trade Regulation

ART LAW

DuBoff's Art Law in a Nutshell, 335 pages, 1984 (Text)

BANKING LAW

Lovett's Banking and Financial Institutions in a Nutshell, 409 pages, 1984 (Text)

Symons and White's Teaching Materials on Banking Law, 2nd Ed., 993 pages, 1984 (Casebook)

BUSINESS PLANNING

Epstein and Scheinfeld's Teaching Materials on Business Reorganization Under the Bankruptcy Code, 216 pages, 1980 (Casebook)

Painter's Problems and Materials in Business Planning, 2nd Ed., 1008 pages, 1984 (Casebook)

Selected Securities and Business Planning Statutes, Rules and Forms, 470 pages, 1985

CIVIL PROCEDURE

Casad's Res Judicata in a Nutshell, 310 pages, 1976 (text)

Cound, Friedenthal, Miller and Sexton's Cases and Materials on Civil Procedure, 4th Ed., approximately 1147 pages, 1985 with 1985 Supplement (Casebook)

Ehrenzweig, Louisell and Hazard's Jurisdiction in a Nutshell, 4th Ed., 232 pages, 1980 (Text)

Federal Rules of Civil-Appellate-Criminal Procedure—West Law School Edition, approximately 500 pages, 1985

Friedenthal, Kane and Miller's Hornbook on Civil Procedure, Student Edition, approximately 870 pages, 1985 (Text)

Hodges, Jones and Elliott's Cases and Materials on Texas Trial and Appellate Procedure, 2nd Ed., 745 pages, 1974 (Casebook)

Hodges, Jones and Elliott's Cases and Materials on the Judicial Process Prior to Trial in Texas, 2nd Ed., 871 pages, 1977 (Casebook)

Kane's Civil Procedure in a Nutshell, 271 pages, 1979 (Text)

CIVIL PROCEDURE—Continued

Karlen's Procedure Before Trial in a Nutshell, 258 pages, 1972 (Text)

Karlen, Meisenholder, Stevens and Vestal's Cases on Civil Procedure, 923 pages, 1975 (Casebook)

Koffler and Reppy's Hornbook on Common Law Pleading, 663 pages, 1969 (Text)

Marcus and Sherman's Complex Litigation—Cases and Materials on Advanced Civil Procedure, approximately 900 pages, 1985 (Casebook)

Park's Computer-Aided Exercises on Civil Procedure, 2nd Ed., 167 pages, 1983 (Coursebook)

Siegel's Hornbook on New York Practice, 1011 pages, 1978 with 1985 Pocket Part (Text)

See also Federal Jurisdiction and Procedure

CIVIL RIGHTS

Abernathy's Cases and Materials on Civil Rights, 660 pages, 1980 (Casebook)

Cohen's Cases on the Law of Deprivation of Liberty: A Study in Social Control, 755 pages, 1980 (Casebook)

Lockhart, Kamisar and Choper's Cases on Constitutional Rights and Liberties, 5th Ed., 1298 pages plus Appendix, 1981, with 1985 Supplement (Casebook)—reprint from Lockhart, et al. Cases on Constitutional Law, 5th Ed., 1980

Vieira's Civil Rights in a Nutshell, 279 pages, 1978 (Text)

COMMERCIAL LAW

Bailey's Secured Transactions in a Nutshell, 2nd Ed., 391 pages, 1981 (Text)

Epstein and Martin's Basic Uniform Commercial Code Teaching Materials, 2nd Ed., 667 pages, 1983 (Casebook)

Henson's Hornbook on Secured Transactions Under the U.C.C., 2nd Ed., 504 pages, 1979 with 1979 P.P. (Text)

Murray's Commercial Law, Problems and Materials, 366 pages, 1975 (Coursebook)

Nordstrom and Clovis' Problems and Materials on Commercial Paper, 458 pages, 1972 (Casebook)

Nordstrom and Lattin's Problems and Materials on Sales and Secured Transactions, 809 pages, 1968 (Casebook)

Nordstrom, Murray and Clovis' Problems and Materials on Sales, 515 pages, 1982 (Casebook)

Selected Commercial Statutes, 1389 pages, 1985

Speidel, Summers and White's Teaching Materials on Commercial and Consumer Law, 3rd Ed., 1490 pages, 1981 (Casebook)

Stockton's Sales in a Nutshell, 2nd Ed., 370 pages, 1981 (Text)

COMMERCIAL LAW—Continued

Stone's Uniform Commercial Code in a Nutshell, 2nd Ed., 516 pages, 1984 (Text)

Uniform Commercial Code, Official Text with Comments, 994 pages, 1978

UCC Article 9, Reprint from 1962 Code, 128 pages, 1976

UCC Article 9, 1972 Amendments, 304 pages, 1978

Weber and Speidel's Commercial Paper in a Nutshell, 3rd Ed., 404 pages, 1982 (Text)

White and Summers' Hornbook on the Uniform Commercial Code, 2nd Ed., 1250 pages, 1980 (Text)

COMMUNITY PROPERTY

Mennell's Community Property in a Nutshell, 447 pages, 1982 (Text)

Verrall and Bird's Cases and Materials on California Community Property, 4th Ed., 549 pages, 1983 (Casebook)

COMPARATIVE LAW

Barton, Gibbs, Li and Merryman's Law in Radically Different Cultures, 960 pages, 1983 (Casebook)

Glendon, Gordon and Osakive's Comparative Legal Traditions: Text, Materials and Cases on the Civil Law, Common Law, and Socialist Law Traditions, approximately 1190 pages, 1985 (Casebook)

Glendon, Gordon, and Osakwe's Comparative Legal Traditions in a Nutshell, 402 pages, 1982 (Text)

Langbein's Comparative Criminal Procedure: Germany, 172 pages, 1977 (Casebook)

COMPUTERS AND LAW

Mason's An Introduction to the Use of Computers in Law, 223 pages, 1984 (Text)

CONFLICT OF LAWS

Cramton, Currie and Kay's Cases-Comments-Questions on Conflict of Laws, 3rd Ed., 1026 pages, 1981 (Casebook)

Scoles and Hay's Hornbook on Conflict of Laws, Student Ed., 1085 pages, 1982 (Text)

Scoles and Weintraub's Cases and Materials on Conflict of Laws, 2nd Ed., 966 pages, 1972, with 1978 Supplement (Casebook)

Siegel's Conflicts in a Nutshell, 469 pages, 1982 (Text)

Engdahl's Constitutional Power in a Nutshell: Federal and State, 411 pages, 1974 (Text)

Lockhart, Kamisar and Choper's Cases-Comments-Questions on Constitutional Law, 5th Ed., 1705 pages plus Appendix, 1980, with 1985 Supplement (Casebook)

CONFLICT OF LAWS—Continued

Lockhart, Kamisar and Choper's Cases-Comments-Questions on the American Constitution, 5th Ed., 1185 pages plus Appendix, 1981, with 1985 Supplement (Casebook)—reprint from Lockhart, et al. Cases on Constitutional Law, 5th Ed., 1980

Manning's The Law of Church-State Relations in a Nutshell, 305 pages, 1981 (Text)

Miller's Presidential Power in a Nutshell, 328 pages, 1977 (Text)

CONSTITUTIONAL LAW

Nowak, Rotunda and Young's Hornbook on Constitutional Law, 2nd Ed., Student Ed., 1172 pages, 1983 (Text)

Rotunda's Modern Constitutional Law: Cases and Notes, 2nd Ed., approximately 1055 pages, 1985, with 1985 Supplement (Casebook)

Williams' Constitutional Analysis in a Nutshell, 388 pages, 1979 (Text)

See also Civil Rights

CONSUMER LAW

Epstein and Nickles' Consumer Law in a Nutshell, 2nd Ed., 418 pages, 1981 (Text)

McCall's Consumer Protection, Cases, Notes and Materials, 594 pages, 1977, with 1977 Statutory Supplement (Casebook)

Selected Commercial Statutes, 1389 pages, 1985

Spanogle and Rohner's Cases and Materials on Consumer Law, 693 pages, 1979, with 1982 Supplement (Casebook)

See also Commercial Law

CONTRACTS

Calamari & Perillo's Cases and Problems on Contracts, 1061 pages, 1978 (Casebook)

Calamari and Perillo's Hornbook on Contracts, 2nd Ed., 878 pages, 1977 (Text)

Corbin's Text on Contracts, One Volume Student Edition, 1224 pages, 1952 (Text)

Fessler and Loiseaux's Cases and Materials on Contracts, 837 pages, 1982 (Casebook)

Freedman's Cases and Materials on Contracts, 658 pages, 1973 (Casebook)

Friedman's Contract Remedies in a Nutshell, 323 pages, 1981 (Text)

Fuller and Eisenberg's Cases on Basic Contract Law, 4th Ed., 1203 pages, 1981 (Casebook)

Hamilton, Rau and Weintraub's Cases and Materials on Contracts, 830 pages, 1984 (Casebook)

Jackson and Bollinger's Cases on Contract Law in Modern Society, 2nd Ed., 1329 pages, 1980 (Casebook)

Keyes' Government Contracts in a Nutshell, 423 pages, 1979 (Text)

CONTRACTS—Continued

Reitz's Cases on Contracts as Basic Commercial Law, 763 pages, 1975 (Casebook)

Schaber and Rohwer's Contracts in a Nutshell, 2nd Ed., 425 pages, 1984 (Text)

COPYRIGHT

See Patent and Copyright Law

CORPORATIONS

Hamilton's Cases on Corporations—Including Partnerships and Limited Partnerships, 2nd Ed., 1108 pages, 1981, with 1981 Statutory Supplement and 1985 Supplement (Casebook)

Hamilton's Law of Corporations in a Nutshell, 379 pages, 1980 (Text)

Henn's Cases on Corporations, 1279 pages, 1974, with 1980 Supplement (Casebook)

Henn and Alexander's Hornbook on Corporations, 3rd Ed., Student Ed., 1371 pages, 1983 (Text)

Jennings and Buxbaum's Cases and Materials on Corporations, 5th Ed., 1180 pages, 1979 (Casebook)

Selected Corporation and Partnership Statutes, Regulations and Forms, 555 pages, 1985

Solomon, Stevenson and Schwartz' Materials and Problems on Corporations: Law and Policy, 1172 pages, 1982 with 1984 Supplement (Casebook)

CORPORATE FINANCE

Hamilton's Cases and Materials on Corporate Finance, 895 pages, 1984 (Casebook)

CORRECTIONS

Krantz's Cases and Materials on the Law of Corrections and Prisoners' Rights, 2nd Ed., 735 pages, 1981, with 1982 Supplement (Casebook)

Krantz's Law of Corrections and Prisoners' Rights in a Nutshell, 2nd Ed., 384 pages, 1983 (Text)

Popper's Post-Conviction Remedies in a Nutshell, 360 pages, 1978 (Text)

Robbins' Cases and Materials on Post Conviction Remedies, 506 pages, 1982 (Casebook)

Rubin's Law of Criminal Corrections, 2nd Ed., 873 pages, 1973, with 1978 Supplement (Text)

CREDITOR'S RIGHTS

Bankruptcy Code, Rules and Forms, Law School and C.L.E. Ed., 602 pages, 1984

Epstein's Debtor-Creditor Law in a Nutshell, 2nd Ed., 324 pages, 1980 (Text)

Epstein and Landers' Debtors and Creditors: Cases and Materials, 2nd Ed., 689 pages, 1982 (Casebook)

CREDITOR'S RIGHTS—Continued

Epstein and Sheinfeld's Teaching Materials on Business Reorganization Under the Bankruptcy Code, 216 pages, 1980 (Casebook)

LoPucki's Player's Manual for the Debtor-Creditor Game, 123 pages, 1985 (Coursebook)

Riesenfeld's Cases and Materials on Creditors' Remedies and Debtors' Protection, 3rd Ed., 810 pages, 1979 with 1979 Statutory Supplement and 1981 Case Supplement (Casebook)

White's Bankruptcy and Creditor's Rights: Cases and Materials, 812 pages, 1985 (Casebook)

CRIMINAL LAW AND CRIMINAL PROCEDURE

Cohen and Gobert's Problems in Criminal Law, 297 pages, 1976 (Problem book)

Davis' Police Discretion, 176 pages, 1975 (Text)

Dix and Sharlot's Cases and Materials on Criminal Law, 2nd Ed., 771 pages, 1979 (Casebook)

Federal Rules of Civil-Appellate-Criminal Procedure—West Law School Edition, approximately 500 pages, 1985

Grano's Problems in Criminal Procedure, 2nd Ed., 176 pages, 1981 (Problem book)

Israel and LaFave's Criminal Procedure in a Nutshell, 3rd Ed., 438 pages, 1980 (Text)

Johnson's Cases, Materials and Text on Substantive Criminal Law in its Procedural Context, 3rd Ed., approximately 750 pages, 1985 (Casebook)

Kamisar, LaFave and Israel's Cases, Comments and Questions on Modern Criminal Procedure, 5th ed., 1635 pages plus Appendix, 1980 with 1985 Supplement (Casebook)

Kamisar, LaFave and Israel's Cases, Comments and Questions on Basic Criminal Procedure, 5th Ed., 869 pages, 1980 with 1985 Supplement (Casebook)—reprint from Kamisar, et al. Modern Criminal Procedure, 5th ed., 1980

LaFave's Modern Criminal Law: Cases, Comments and Questions, 789 pages, 1978 (Casebook)

LaFave and Israel's Hornbook on Criminal Procedure, Student Ed., 1142 pages, 1985 (Text)

LaFave and Scott's Hornbook on Criminal Law, 763 pages, 1972 (Text)

Langbein's Comparative Criminal Procedure: Germany, 172 pages, 1977 (Casebook)

Loewy's Criminal Law in a Nutshell, 302 pages, 1975 (Text)

CRIMINAL LAW AND CRIMINAL PROCEDURE—Continued

Saltzburg's American Criminal Procedure, Cases and Commentary, 2nd Ed., 1193 pages, 1985 with 1985 Supplement (Casebook)

Uviller's The Processes of Criminal Justice: Investigation and Adjudication, 2nd Ed., 1384 pages, 1979 with 1979 Statutory Supplement and 1983 Update (Casebook)

Uviller's The Processes of Criminal Justice: Adjudication, 2nd Ed., 730 pages, 1979. Soft-cover reprint from Uviller's The Processes of Criminal Justice: Investigation and Adjudication, 2nd Ed. (Casebook)

Uviller's The Processes of Criminal Justice: Investigation, 2nd Ed., 655 pages, 1979. Soft-cover reprint from Uviller's The Processes of Criminal Justice: Investigation and Adjudication, 2nd Ed. (Casebook)

Vorenberg's Cases on Criminal Law and Procedure, 2nd Ed., 1088 pages, 1981 with 1985 Supplement (Casebook)

See also Corrections, Juvenile Justice

DECEDENTS ESTATES

See Trusts and Estates

DOMESTIC RELATIONS

Clark's Cases and Problems on Domestic Relations, 3rd Ed., 1153 pages, 1980 (Casebook)

Clark's Hornbook on Domestic Relations, 754 pages, 1968 (Text)

Krause's Cases and Materials on Family Law, 2nd Ed., 1221 pages, 1983 (Casebook)

Krause's Family Law in a Nutshell, 400 pages, 1977 (Text)

Krauskopf's Cases on Property Division at Marriage Dissolution, 250 pages, 1984 (Casebook)

ECONOMICS, LAW AND

Goetz' Cases and Materials on Law and Economics, 547 pages, 1984 (Casebook)

Manne's The Economics of Legal Relationships—Readings in the Theory of Property Rights, 660 pages, 1975 (Text)

See also Antitrust, Regulated Industries

EDUCATION LAW

Alexander and Alexander's The Law of Schools, Students and Teachers in a Nutshell, 409 pages, 1984 (Text)

Morris' The Constitution and American Education, 2nd Ed., 992 pages, 1980 (Casebook)

EMPLOYMENT DISCRIMINATION

Player's Cases and Materials on Employment Discrimination Law, 2nd Ed., 782 pages, 1984 (Casebook)

Player's Federal Law of Employment Discrimination in a Nutshell, 2nd Ed., 402 pages, 1981 (Text)

See also Women and the Law

ENERGY LAW

Rodgers' Cases and Materials on Energy and Natural Resources Law, 2nd Ed., 877 pages, 1983 (Casebook)

Selected Environmental Law Statutes, 786 pages, 1985

Tomain's Energy Law in a Nutshell, 338 pages, 1981 (Text)

See also Natural Resources Law, Environmental Law, Oil and Gas, Water Law

ENVIRONMENTAL LAW

Bonine and McGarity's Cases and Materials on the Law of Environment and Pollution, 1076 pages, 1984 (Casebook)

Findley and Farber's Cases and Materials on Environmental Law, 2nd Ed., approximately 800 pages, 1985 (Casebook)

Findley and Farber's Environmental Law in a Nutshell, 343 pages, 1983 (Text)

Rodgers' Hornbook on Environmental Law, 956 pages, 1977 with 1984 pocket part (Text)

Selected Environmental Law Statutes, 786 pages, 1985

See also Energy Law, Natural Resources Law, Water Law

EQUITY

See Remedies

ESTATES

See Trusts and Estates

ESTATE PLANNING

Kurtz' Cases, Materials and Problems on Family Estate Planning, 853 pages, 1983 (Casebook)

Lynn's Introduction to Estate Planning, in a Nutshell, 3rd Ed., 370 pages, 1983 (Text)

See also Taxation

EVIDENCE

Broun and Meisenholder's Problems in Evidence, 2nd Ed., 304 pages, 1981 (Problem book)

Cleary and Strong's Cases, Materials and Problems on Evidence, 3rd Ed., 1143 pages, 1981 (Casebook)

Federal Rules of Evidence for United States Courts and Magistrates, 337 pages, 1984

Graham's Federal Rules of Evidence in a Nutshell, 429 pages, 1981 (Text)

LAW SCHOOL PUBLICATIONS—Continued

EVIDENCE—Continued

Kimball's Programmed Materials on Problems in Evidence, 380 pages, 1978 (Problem book)

Lempert and Saltzburg's A Modern Approach to Evidence: Text, Problems, Transcripts and Cases, 2nd Ed., 1296 pages, 1983 (Casebook)

Lilly's Introduction to the Law of Evidence, 486 pages, 1978 (Text)

McCormick, Elliott and Sutton's Cases and Materials on Evidence, 5th Ed., 1212 pages, 1981 (Casebook)

McCormick's Hornbook on Evidence, 3rd Ed., Student Ed., 1155 pages, 1984 (Text)

Rothstein's Evidence, State and Federal Rules in a Nutshell, 2nd Ed., 514 pages, 1981 (Text)

Saltzburg's Evidence Supplement: Rules, Statutes, Commentary, 245 pages, 1980 (Casebook Supplement)

FEDERAL JURISDICTION AND PROCEDURE

Currie's Cases and Materials on Federal Courts, 3rd Ed., 1042 pages, 1982 (Casebook)

Currie's Federal Jurisdiction in a Nutshell, 2nd Ed., 258 pages, 1981 (Text)

Federal Rules of Civil-Appellate-Criminal Procedure—West Law School Edition, approximately 500 pages, 1985

Forrester and Moye's Cases and Materials on Federal Jurisdiction and Procedure, 3rd Ed., 917 pages, 1977 with 1981 Supplement (Casebook)

Redish's Cases, Comments and Questions on Federal Courts, 878 pages, 1985 (Casebook)

Vetri and Merrill's Federal Courts, Problems and Materials, 2nd Ed., 232 pages, 1984 (Problem Book)

Wright's Hornbook on Federal Courts, 4th Ed., Student Ed., 870 pages, 1983 (Text)

FUTURE INTERESTS

See Trusts and Estates

IMMIGRATION LAW

Aleinikoff and Martin's Immigration Process and Policy, approximately 950 pages, 1985 (Casebook)

Weissbrodt's Immigration Law and Procedure in a Nutshell, 345 pages, 1984 (Text)

INDIAN LAW

See American Indian Law

INSURANCE

Dobbyn's Insurance Law in a Nutshell, 281 pages, 1981 (Text)

Keeton's Cases on Basic Insurance Law, 2nd Ed., 1086 pages, 1977

INSURANCE—Continued

Keeton's Basic Text on Insurance Law, 712 pages, 1971 (Text)

Keeton's Case Supplement to Keeton's Basic Text on Insurance Law, 334 pages, 1978 (Casebook)

Keeton's Programmed Problems in Insurance Law, 243 pages, 1972 (Text Supplement)

York and Whelan's Cases, Materials and Problems on Insurance Law, 715 pages, 1982, with 1985 Supplement (Casebook)

INTERNATIONAL LAW

Henkin, Pugh, Schachter and Smit's Cases and Materials on International Law, 2nd Ed., 1152 pages, 1980, with Documents Supplement (Casebook)

Jackson's Legal Problems of International Economic Relations, 1097 pages, 1977, with Documents Supplement (Casebook)

Kirgis' International Organizations in Their Legal Setting, 1016 pages, 1977, with 1981 Supplement (Casebook)

Weston, Falk and D'Amato's International Law and World Order—A Problem Oriented Coursebook, 1195 pages, 1980, with Documents Supplement (Casebook)

Wilson's International Business Transactions in a Nutshell, 2nd Ed., 476 pages, 1984 (Text)

INTERVIEWING AND COUNSELING

Binder and Price's Interviewing and Counseling, 232 pages, 1977 (Text)

Shaffer's Interviewing and Counseling in a Nutshell, 353 pages, 1976 (Text)

INTRODUCTION TO LAW

Dobbyn's So You Want to go to Law School, Revised First Edition, 206 pages, 1976 (Text)

Hegland's Introduction to the Study and Practice of Law in a Nutshell, 418 pages, 1983 (Text)

Kinyon's Introduction to Law Study and Law Examinations in a Nutshell, 389 pages, 1971 (Text)

See also Legal Method and Legal System

JUDICIAL ADMINISTRATION

Carrington, Meador and Rosenberg's Justice on Appeal, 263 pages, 1976 (Casebook)

Nelson's Cases and Materials on Judicial Administration and the Administration of Justice, 1032 pages, 1974 (Casebook)

JURISPRUDENCE

Christie's Text and Readings on Jurisprudence—The Philosophy of Law, 1056 pages, 1973 (Casebook)

LAW SCHOOL PUBLICATIONS—Continued

JUVENILE JUSTICE

Fox's Cases and Materials on Modern Juvenile Justice, 2nd Ed., 960 pages, 1981 (Casebook)

Fox's Juvenile Courts in a Nutshell, 3rd Ed., 291 pages, 1984 (Text)

LABOR LAW

Gorman's Basic Text on Labor Law—Unionization and Collective Bargaining, 914 pages, 1976 (Text)

Leslie's Labor Law in a Nutshell, 403 pages, 1979 (Text)

Nolan's Labor Arbitration Law and Practice in a Nutshell, 358 pages, 1979 (Text)

Oberer, Hanslowe and Andersen's Cases and Materials on Labor Law—Collective Bargaining in a Free Society, 2nd Ed., 1168 pages, 1979, with 1979 Statutory Supplement and 1982 Case Supplement (Casebook)

See also Employment Discrimination, Social Legislation

LAND FINANCE

See Real Estate Transactions

LAND USE

Hagman's Cases on Public Planning and Control of Urban and Land Development, 2nd Ed., 1301 pages, 1980 (Casebook)

Hagman's Hornbook on Urban Planning and Land Development Control Law, 706 pages, 1971 (Text)

Wright and Gitelman's Cases and Materials on Land Use, 3rd Ed., 1300 pages, 1982 (Casebook)

Wright and Wright's Land Use in a Nutshell, 2nd Ed., approximately 350 pages (Text)

LEGAL HISTORY

Presser and Zainaldin's Cases on Law and American History, 855 pages, 1980 (Casebook)

See also Legal Method and Legal System

LEGAL METHOD AND LEGAL SYSTEM

Aldisert's Readings, Materials and Cases in the Judicial Process, 948 pages, 1976 (Casebook)

Berch and Berch's Introduction to Legal Method and Process, 550 pages, 1985 (Casebook)

Bodenheimer, Oakley and Love's Readings and Cases on an Introduction to the Anglo-American Legal System, 161 pages, 1980 (Casebook)

Davies and Lawry's Institutions and Methods of the Law—Introductory Teaching Materials, 547 pages, 1982 (Casebook)

Dvorkin, Himmelstein and Lesnick's Becoming a Lawyer: A Humanistic Perspective on Legal Education and Professionalism, 211 pages, 1981 (Text)

LEGAL METHOD AND LEGAL SYSTEM—Continued

Fryer and Orentlicher's Cases and Materials on Legal Method and Legal System, 1043 pages, 1967 (Casebook)

Greenberg's Judicial Process and Social Change, 666 pages, 1977 (Coursebook)

Kelso and Kelso's Studying Law: An Introduction, 587 pages, 1984 (Coursebook)

Kempin's Historical Introduction to Anglo-American Law in a Nutshell, 2nd Ed., 280 pages, 1973 (Text)

Kimball's Historical Introduction to the Legal System, 610 pages, 1966 (Casebook)

Murphy's Cases and Materials on Introduction to Law—Legal Process and Procedure, 772 pages, 1977 (Casebook)

Reynolds' Judicial Process in a Nutshell, 292 pages, 1980 (Text)

See also Legal Research and Writing

LEGAL PROFESSION

Aronson, Devine and Fisch's Problems, Cases and Materials on Professional Responsibility, 745 pages, 1985 (Casebook)

Aronson and Weckstein's Professional Responsibility in a Nutshell, 399 pages, 1980 (Text)

Mellinkoff's The Conscience of a Lawyer, 304 pages, 1973 (Text)

Mellinkoff's Lawyers and the System of Justice, 983 pages, 1976 (Casebook)

Pirsig and Kirwin's Cases and Materials on Professional Responsibility, 4th Ed., 603 pages, 1984 (Casebook)

Schwartz and Wydick's Problems in Legal Ethics, 285 pages, 1983 (Casebook)

Selected Statutes, Rules and Standards on the Legal Profession, 276 pages, Revised 1984

Smith's Preventing Legal Malpractice, 142 pages, 1981 (Text)

Wolfram's Hornbook on Professional Responsibility, Student Edition, approximately 950 pages (Text)

LEGAL RESEARCH AND WRITING

Cohen's Legal Research in a Nutshell, 4th Ed., 450 pages, 1985 (Text)

Cohen and Berring's How to Find the Law, 8th Ed., 790 pages, 1983. Problem book by Foster and Kelly available (Casebook)

Cohen and Berring's Finding the Law, 8th Ed., Abridged Ed., 556 pages, 1984 (Casebook)

Dickerson's Materials on Legal Drafting, 425 pages, 1981 (Casebook)

Felsenfeld and Siegel's Writing Contracts in Plain English, 290 pages, 1981 (Text)

Gopen's Writing From a Legal Perspective, 225 pages, 1981 (Text)

Mellinkoff's Legal Writing—Sense and Nonsense, 242 pages, 1982 (Text)

LAW SCHOOL PUBLICATIONS—Continued

LEGAL RESEARCH AND WRITING—
Continued

Rombauer's Legal Problem Solving—Analysis, Research and Writing, 4th Ed., 424 pages, 1983 (Coursebook)

Squires and Rombauer's Legal Writing in a Nutshell, 294 pages, 1982 (Text)

Statsky's Legal Research, Writing and Analysis, 2nd Ed., 167 pages, 1982 (Coursebook)

Statsky's Legislative Analysis: How to Use Statutes and Regulations, 2nd Ed., 217 pages, 1984 (Text)

Statsky and Wernet's Case Analysis and Fundamentals of Legal Writing, 2nd Ed., 441 pages, 1984 (Text)

Teply's Programmed Materials on Legal Research and Citation, 334 pages, 1982. Student Library Exercises available (Coursebook)

Weihofen's Legal Writing Style, 2nd Ed., 332 pages, 1980 (Text)

LEGISLATION

Davies' Legislative Law and Process in a Nutshell, 279 pages, 1975 (Text)

Nutting and Dickerson's Cases and Materials on Legislation, 5th Ed., 744 pages, 1978 (Casebook)

Statsky's Legislative Analysis: How to Use Statutes and Regulations, 2nd Ed., 217 pages, 1984 (Text)

LOCAL GOVERNMENT

McCarthy's Local Government Law in a Nutshell, 2nd Ed., 404 pages, 1983 (Text)

Michelman and Sandalow's Cases-Comments-Questions on Government in Urban Areas, 1216 pages, 1970, with 1972 Supplement (Casebook)

Reynolds' Hornbook on Local Government Law, 860 pages, 1982 (Text)

Valente's Cases and Materials on Local Government Law, 2nd Ed., 980 pages, 1980 with 1982 Supplement (Casebook)

MASS COMMUNICATION LAW

Gillmor and Barron's Cases and Comment on Mass Communication Law, 4th Ed., 1076 pages, 1984 (Casebook)

Ginsburg's Regulation of Broadcasting: Law and Policy Towards Radio, Television and Cable Communications, 741 pages, 1979, with 1983 Supplement (Casebook)

Zuckman and Gayne's Mass Communications Law in a Nutshell, 2nd Ed., 473 pages, 1983 (Text)

MEDICINE, LAW AND

King's The Law of Medical Malpractice in a Nutshell, 340 pages, 1977 (Text)

Shapiro and Spece's Problems, Cases and Materials on Bioethics and Law, 892 pages, 1981 (Casebook)

MEDICINE, LAW AND—Continued

Sharpe, Fiscina and Head's Cases on Law and Medicine, 882 pages, 1978 (Casebook)

MILITARY LAW

Shanor and Terrell's Military Law in a Nutshell, 378 pages, 1980 (Text)

MORTGAGES

See Real Estate Transactions

NATURAL RESOURCES LAW

Laito's Cases and Materials on Natural Resources Law, approximately 930 pages, 1985 (Casebook)

See also Energy Law, Environmental Law, Oil and Gas, Water Law

NEGOTIATION

Edwards and White's Problems, Readings and Materials on the Lawyer as a Negotiator, 484 pages, 1977 (Casebook)

Williams' Legal Negotiation and Settlement, 207 pages, 1983 (Coursebook)

OFFICE PRACTICE

Hegland's Trial and Practice Skills in a Nutshell, 346 pages, 1978 (Text)

Strong and Clark's Law Office Management, 424 pages, 1974 (Casebook)

See also Computers and Law, Interviewing and Counseling, Negotiation

OIL AND GAS

Hemingway's Hornbook on Oil and Gas, 2nd Ed., Student Ed., 543 pages, 1983 (Text)

Huie, Woodward and Smith's Cases and Materials on Oil and Gas, 2nd Ed., 955 pages, 1972 (Casebook)

Lowe's Oil and Gas Law in a Nutshell, 443 pages, 1983 (Text)

See also Energy and Natural Resources Law

PARTNERSHIP

See Agency—Partnership

PATENT AND COPYRIGHT LAW

Choate and Francis' Cases and Materials on Patent Law, 2nd Ed., 1110 pages, 1981 (Casebook)

Miller and Davis' Intellectual Property—Patents, Trademarks and Copyright in a Nutshell, 428 pages, 1983 (Text)

Nimmer's Cases on Copyright and Other Aspects of Entertainment Litigation, 3rd Ed., approximately 1000 pages, 1985 (Casebook)

POVERTY LAW

Brudno's Poverty, Inequality, and the Law: Cases-Commentary-Analysis, 934 pages, 1976 (Casebook)

LAW SCHOOL PUBLICATIONS—Continued

POVERTY LAW—Continued

LaFrance, Schroeder, Bennett and Boyd's Hornbook on Law of the Poor, 558 pages, 1973 (Text)

See also Social Legislation

PRODUCTS LIABILITY

Noel and Phillips' Cases on Products Liability, 2nd Ed., 821 pages, 1982 (Casebook)

Noel and Phillips' Products Liability in a Nutshell, 2nd Ed., 341 pages, 1981 (Text)

PROPERTY

Aigler, Smith and Tefft's Cases on Property, 2 volumes, 1339 pages, 1960 (Casebook)

Bernhardt's Real Property in a Nutshell, 2nd Ed., 448 pages, 1981 (Text)

Boyer's Survey of the Law of Property, 766 pages, 1981 (Text)

Browder, Cunningham and Smith's Cases on Basic Property Law, 4th Ed., 1431 pages, 1984 (Casebook)

Bruce, Ely and Bostick's Cases and Materials on Modern Property Law, 1004 pages, 1984 (Casebook)

Burby's Hornbook on Real Property, 3rd Ed., 490 pages, 1965 (Text)

Burke's Personal Property in a Nutshell, 322 pages, 1983 (Text)

Chused's A Modern Approach to Property: Cases-Notes-Materials, 1069 pages, 1978 with 1980 Supplement (Casebook)

Cohen's Materials for a Basic Course in Property, 526 pages, 1978 (Casebook)

Cunningham, Stoebuck and Whitman's Hornbook on the Law of Property, Student Ed., 916 pages, 1984 (Text)

Donahue, Kauper and Martin's Cases on Property, 2nd Ed., 1362 pages, 1983 (Casebook)

Hill's Landlord and Tenant Law in a Nutshell, 319 pages, 1979 (Text)

Moynihan's Introduction to Real Property, 254 pages, 1962 (Text)

Uniform Land Transactions Act, Uniform Simplification of Land Transfers Act, Uniform Condominium Act, 1977 Official Text with Comments, 462 pages, 1978

See also Real Estate Transactions, Land Use

PSYCHIATRY, LAW AND

Reisner's Law and the Mental Health System, Civil and Criminal Aspects, 696 pages, 1985 (Casebooks)

REAL ESTATE TRANSACTIONS

Bruce's Real Estate Finance in a Nutshell, 2nd Ed., 262 pages, 1985 (Text)

Maxwell, Riesenfeld, Hetland and Warren's Cases on California Security Transactions in Land, 3rd Ed., 728 pages, 1984 (Casebook)

REAL ESTATE TRANSACTIONS—Continued

Nelson and Whitman's Cases on Real Estate Transfer, Finance and Development, 2nd Ed., 1114 pages, 1981, with 1983 Supplement (Casebook)

Nelson and Whitman's Hornbook on Real Estate Finance Law, 2nd Ed., Standard Ed., approximately 900 pages, 1985 (Text)

Osborne's Cases and Materials on Secured Transactions, 559 pages, 1967 (Casebook)

REGULATED INDUSTRIES

Gellhorn and Pierce's Regulated Industries in a Nutshell, 394 pages, 1982 (Text)

Morgan, Harrison and Verkuil's Cases and Materials on Economic Regulation of Business, 2nd Ed., 670 pages, 1985 (Casebook)

Pozen's Financial Institutions: Cases, Materials and Problems on Investment Management, 844 pages, 1978 (Casebook)

See also Mass Communication Law, Banking Law

REMEDIES

Dobbs' Hornbook on Remedies, 1067 pages, 1973 (Text)

Dobbs' Problems in Remedies, 137 pages, 1974 (Problem book)

Dobbyn's Injunctions in a Nutshell, 264 pages, 1974 (Text)

Friedman's Contract Remedies in a Nutshell, 323 pages, 1981 (Text)

Leavell, Love and Nelson's Cases and Materials on Equitable Remedies and Restitution, 3rd Ed., 704 pages, 1980 (Casebook)

McCormick's Hornbook on Damages, 811 pages, 1935 (Text)

O'Connell's Remedies in a Nutshell, 2nd Ed., 325 pages, 1985 (Text)

York, Bauman and Rendleman's Cases and Materials on Remedies, 4th Ed., approximately 1025 pages, 1985 (Casebook)

REVIEW MATERIALS

Ballantine's Problems

Black Letter Series

Smith's Review Series

West's Review Covering Multistate Subjects

SECURITIES REGULATION

Hazen's Hornbook on The Law of Securities Regulation, Student Ed., 739 pages, 1985 (Text)

Ratner's Securities Regulation: Materials for a Basic Course, 2nd Ed., 1050 pages, 1980 with 1982 Supplement (Casebook)

Ratner's Securities Regulation in a Nutshell, 2nd Ed., 322 pages, 1982 (Text)

LAW SCHOOL PUBLICATIONS—Continued

SECURITIES REGULATION—Continued

Selected Securities and Business Planning Statutes, Rules and Forms, 470 pages, 1985

SOCIAL LEGISLATION

Hood and Hardy's Workers' Compensation and Employee Protection Laws in a Nutshell, 274 pages, 1984 (Text)

LaFrance's Welfare Law: Structure and Entitlement in a Nutshell, 455 pages, 1979 (Text)

Malone, Plant and Little's Cases on Workers' Compensation and Employment Rights, 2nd Ed., 951 pages, 1980 (Casebook)

See also Poverty Law

TAXATION

Dodge's Cases and Materials on Federal Income Taxation, approximately 825 pages, 1985 (Casebook)

Dodge's Federal Taxation of Estates, Trusts and Gifts: Principles and Planning, 771 pages, 1981 with 1982 Supplement (Casebook)

Garbis and Struntz' Cases and Materials on Tax Procedure and Tax Fraud, 829 pages, 1982 with 1984 Supplement (Casebook)

Gunn's Cases and Materials on Federal Income Taxation of Individuals, 785 pages, 1981 with 1985 Supplement (Casebook)

Hellerstein and Hellerstein's Cases on State and Local Taxation, 4th Ed., 1041 pages, 1978 with 1982 Supplement (Casebook)

Kahn and Gann's Corporate Taxation and Taxation of Partnerships and Partners, 2nd Ed., 1204 pages, 1985 (Casebook)

Kragen and McNulty's Cases and Materials on Federal Income Taxation: Individuals, Corporations, Partnerships, 4th Ed., approximately 1200 pages, 1985 (Casebook)

McNulty's Federal Estate and Gift Taxation in a Nutshell, 3rd Ed., 509 pages, 1983 (Text)

McNulty's Federal Income Taxation of Individuals in a Nutshell, 3rd Ed., 487 pages, 1983 (Text)

Posin's Hornbook on Federal Income Taxation of Individuals, Student Ed., 491 pages, 1983 with 1985 pocket part (Text)

Rice and Solomon's Problems and Materials in Federal Income Taxation, 3rd Ed., 670 pages, 1979 (Casebook)

Rose and Raskind's Advanced Federal Income Taxation: Corporate Transactions—Cases, Materials and Problems, 955 pages, 1978 (Casebook)

Selected Federal Taxation Statutes and Regulations, approximately 1300 pages, 1985

Soboloff and Weidenbruch's Federal Income Taxation of Corporations and Stockholders in a Nutshell, 362 pages, 1981 (Text)

TORTS

Christie's Cases and Materials on the Law of Torts, 1264 pages, 1983 (Casebook)

Dobbs' Torts and Compensation—Personal Accountability and Social Responsibility for Injury, 955 pages, 1985 (Casebook)

Green, Pedrick, Rahl, Thode, Hawkins, Smith and Treece's Cases and Materials on Torts, 2nd Ed., 1360 pages, 1977 (Casebook)

Green, Pedrick, Rahl, Thode, Hawkins, Smith, and Treece's Advanced Torts: Injuries to Business, Political and Family Interests, 2nd Ed., 544 pages, 1977 (Casebook)—reprint from Green, et al. Cases and Materials on Torts, 2nd Ed., 1977

Keeton, Keeton, Sargentich and Steiner's Cases and Materials on Torts, and Accident Law, 1360 pages, 1983 (Casebook)

Kionka's Torts in a Nutshell: Injuries to Persons and Property, 434 pages, 1977 (Text)

Malone's Torts in a Nutshell: Injuries to Family, Social and Trade Relations, 358 pages, 1979 (Text)

Prosser and Keeton's Hornbook on Torts, 5th Ed., Student Ed., 1286 pages, 1984 (Text)

Shapo's Cases on Tort and Compensation Law, 1244 pages, 1976 (Casebook)

See also Products Liability

TRADE REGULATION

McManis' Unfair Trade Practices in a Nutshell, 444 pages, 1982 (Text)

Oppenheim, Weston, Maggs and Schechter's Cases and Materials on Unfair Trade Practices and Consumer Protection, 4th Ed., 1038 pages, 1983 (Casebook)

See also Antitrust, Regulated Industries

TRIAL AND APPELLATE ADVOCACY

Appellate Advocacy, Handbook of, 249 pages, 1980 (Text)

Bergman's Trial Advocacy in a Nutshell, 402 pages, 1979 (Text)

Binder and Bergman's Fact Investigation: From Hypothesis to Proof, 354 pages, 1984 (Coursebook)

Goldberg's The First Trial (Where Do I Sit?, What Do I Say?) in a Nutshell, 396 pages, 1982 (Text)

Haydock, Herr and Stempel's, Fundamentals of Pre-Trial Litigation, 768 pages, 1985 (Casebook)

Hegland's Trial and Practice Skills in a Nutshell, 346 pages, 1978 (Text)

Hornstein's Appellate Advocacy in a Nutshell, 325 pages, 1984 (Text)

Jeans' Handbook on Trial Advocacy, Student Ed., 473 pages, 1975 (Text)

McElhaney's Effective Litigation, 457 pages, 1974 (Casebook)

LAW SCHOOL PUBLICATIONS—Continued

TRIAL AND APPELLATE ADVOCACY—
Continued

Nolan's Cases and Materials on Trial Practice, 518 pages, 1981 (Casebook)

Parnell and Shellhaas' Cases, Exercises and Problems for Trial Advocacy, 171 pages, 1982 (Coursebook)

Sonsteng, Haydock and Boyd's The Trialbook: A Total System for Preparation and Presentation of a Case, Student Ed., 404 pages, 1984 (Coursebook)

TRUSTS AND ESTATES

Atkinson's Hornbook on Wills, 2nd Ed., 975 pages, 1953 (Text)

Averill's Uniform Probate Code in a Nutshell, 425 pages, 1978 (Text)

Bogert's Hornbook on Trusts, 5th Ed., 726 pages, 1973 (Text)

Clark, Lusky and Murphy's Cases and Materials on Gratuitous Transfers, 3rd Ed., approximately 1200 pages, 1985 (Casebook)

Gulliver's Cases and Materials on Future Interests, 624 pages, 1959 (Casebook)

Gulliver's Introduction to the Law of Future Interests, 87 pages, 1959 (Casebook)—reprint from Gulliver's Cases and Materials on Future Interests, 1959

McGovern's Cases and Materials on Wills, Trusts and Future Interests: An Introduction to Estate Planning, 750 pages, 1983 (Casebook)

Mennell's Cases and Materials on California Decedent's Estates, 566 pages, 1973 (Casebook)

Mennell's Wills and Trusts in a Nutshell, 392 pages, 1979 (Text)

TRUSTS AND ESTATES—Continued

Powell's The Law of Future Interests in California, 91 pages, 1980 (Text)

Simes' Hornbook on Future Interests, 2nd Ed., 355 pages, 1966 (Text)

Turrentine's Cases and Text on Wills and Administration, 2nd Ed., 483 pages, 1962 (Casebook)

Uniform Probate Code, 5th Ed., Official Text With Comments, 384 pages, 1977

Waggoner's Future Interests in a Nutshell, 361 pages, 1981 (Text)

WATER LAW

Getches' Water Law in a Nutshell, 439 pages, 1984 (Text)

Trelease's Cases and Materials on Water Law, 3rd Ed., 833 pages, 1979, with 1984 Supplement (Casebook)

See also Energy Law, Natural Resources Law, Environmental Law

WILLS

See Trusts and Estates

WOMEN AND THE LAW

Kay's Text, Cases and Materials on Sex-Based Discrimination, 2nd Ed., 1045 pages, 1981, with 1983 Supplement (Casebook)

Thomas' Sex Discrimination in a Nutshell, 399 pages, 1982 (Text)

See also Employment Discrimination

WORKERS' COMPENSATION

See Social Legislation

IMMIGRATION:
PROCESS AND POLICY

By

Thomas Alexander Aleinikoff
Professor of Law
University of Michigan Law School

and

David A. Martin
Professor of Law
University of Virginia School of Law

AMERICAN CASEBOOK SERIES

WEST PUBLISHING CO.
ST. PAUL, MINN., 1985

COPYRIGHT © 1985 By WEST PUBLISHING CO.
            50 West Kellogg Boulevard
            P.O. Box 64526
            St. Paul, Minnesota 55164–0526

Library of Congress Cataloging in Publication Data

Aleinikoff, Thomas Alexander, 1952–
  Immigration, process and policy.

  (American casebook series)
  Includes index.

  1. Emigration and immigration law—United States—Cases.
I. Martin, David A., 1948–   . II. Title. III. Series.
KF4818.A43 1985   342.73'082   85–8996
                  347.30282

ISBN 0–314–90039–X

A. & M.–Immigration Law ACB

To the Aleinikoffs, Marrows, Mays, and Wises
  And for Rachel

To the Martins, Meekers, Johnstons, and Bowmans
  And for Cyndy, Amy, and Jeff

*

Preface

For decades, immigration and nationality law has been something of a neglected stepchild in the law schools. Most schools offer no immigration course at all. Where courses exist, they typically focus on the practical business of learning a complex statute and preparing students for careers as immigration attorneys, often finding little time to devote to larger issues of policy and principle.

Immigration law has suffered from the lack of sustained academic attention. All too often, instead of measured policy debate, one encounters in this field merely the polarized confrontation of charge and counter-charge: government supporters reflexively advocating a hard-line response; government opponents reflexively assuming that maximum advocacy for the particular aliens involved will bring about the best public policy. We don't deny that the issues are the kind that stir—and ought to stir—deep feelings. But we believe there is far more room for careful and balanced study of long-term policy options, even among those who care passionately about the ultimate values at stake. Law schools should serve as one important forum for such exploration.

As law students, we too enjoyed little exposure to the subject. Later, during stints in government service in Washington, each of us found himself dealing occasionally with immigration matters, but we discovered our mutual interest in the subject only when the Cuban boatlift of 1980 brought lawyers from the Departments of Justice and State together. There is nothing like a full-fledged crisis—especially one offering no satisfactory solutions—to cement an appreciation of the subject's fascinations and frustrations. We carried that interest with us when we moved into the academy, along with vague intentions to teach immigration law, but with little idea of just what was in store.

Now, after teaching and writing in the field for several years, we have come to wonder how the intrinsic attractions of the subject for classroom teaching have gone so widely unnoticed. Immigration law, we have learned, can be one of the richest and most rewarding subjects for both students and professors. It is redolent of our national history, reflecting both successes that are the legitimate source of national pride, and disspiriting failures. Major public policy issues appear repeatedly, posing deeper questions concerning national identity, membership, moral philosophy, constitutional interpretation, public law, public administration, international relations, and the limits of practical politics. Immigration law also furnishes a vital setting for studying the interaction of our three branches of government. Indeed, we have been struck by how many major Supreme Court decisions on larger questions of administrative and constitutional law have been decided in immigration cases—the legislative veto case, *INS v. Chadha*, 103 S.Ct. 2764 (1983), being only the latest example.

An immigration course, however, need not always keep the student at the heights occupied by great questions of philosophy, public policy, and constitutional interpretation. Immigration law also provides a worthy vehicle for refining basic lawyering skills, especially the capacity for close reading of an intricate statute and the discipline of mastering a specialized technical vocabulary. One judge who had just struggled through a complex interpretive task reflected on his experience:

> Whatever guidance the regulations furnish to those cognoscenti familiar with [immigration] procedures, this court, despite many years of legal experience, finds that they yield up meaning only grudgingly and that morsels of comprehension must be pried from mollusks of jargon.

Dong Sik Kwon v. INS, 646 F.2d 909, 919 (5th Cir. 1981). Students ought to learn how to wield their *escargot* forks expertly, and then they should be inspired to ask whether the food could not be prepared in a more sensible way.

Beyond this, the student of immigration law must develop an awareness of how legislation evolves and an ability to make use of the materials of legislative history—for today's Immigration and Nationality Act (INA) is the product of over a hundred years of congressional efforts to fashion laws that regulate immigration. There are also thousands of administrative and judicial precedents, often in remarkable conflict with one another in both holding and spirit. These provide excellent raw materials for practice in the art of advocacy, hypothetically representing either a private client or a government agency.

There may be many reasons for immigration law's historical insularity. But we wrote this book with the conviction that a lack of good teaching materials has played a role—materials with which nonspecialists might feel comfortable but which specialists might also find challenging. (In this respect, we remember well our own problems when we first taught the course.) When we began our work on this book, there was no casebook at all on the subject of immigration law. Treatises existed, and various kinds of manuals that have been used as the basis for the course by practitioners of many year's experience. But it is a daunting prospect for nonspecialists to put together workable supplemental materials on their own, especially if they aspire to teaching more than just the technical details.

We hope this book will contribute toward ending the law schools' neglect and the subject's insularity. We have consciously sought to make the reader aware of the broader dimensions of the subject, but without ignoring the nuts-and-bolts foundation that a novice practitioner in the field would find necessary. We don't spend time, for example, exploring all 19 grounds for deportation appearing in INA § 241(a). We do devote enough attention to selected grounds, however, as well as the basic structure of those provisions, so that a student would know where to turn for answers to the detailed questions that might arise in practice. We have aimed, above all, at recapturing immigration law as a worthy and exciting area for academic study, without losing sight of the basic learning a student must master if he or she chooses to open an immigration practice the following year. Whether we have succeeded in these aims remains to be seen, but we invite users of this book—instructors and students—to write us with their reactions and suggestions for expanded or reduced coverage.

We have also consciously tried to avoid the polarities that often beset the field. It is easy to develop sympathy for the individual alien involved in a particular case, and to strive to mold the legal doctrine to bring about a warm-hearted result for that person. Too many law review notes, and often judges as well, succumb to this temptation, neglecting to take adequate account of the long-term implications for an immigration system that must cope with millions of applications each year. We try to keep the reader aware of that larger systemic perspective—without suggesting that systems should always prevail over warm-heartedness, of course.

This book is selective. Our guiding principle has been to choose items we think will prove useful in the classroom setting, to serve the pedagogical objectives we have outlined. The book therefore makes no pretense of serving as a treatise giving a practitioner comprehensive guidance to all the relevant decisions touching on a particular issue. There are several other works in the field that meet that need. Nevertheless, within these guidelines, we have sought to take account of relevant cases and administrative actions through July 1984. In addition, we have found it possible to incorporate several important developments that have occurred since then.

We could not have completed this book without support, assistance, and encouragement from numerous friends—faculty colleagues, practitioners, government officials, students, and others—and especially from our families. It is not possible to list all whose help has been valuable, but a few deserve particular mention. Excellent research assistance was provided by Karen Baril, Asli Basgoz, Cynthia Battles, Andrew Chaikovsky, Megan Dorsey, Charles Meyer, Gretchen Miller, Harry Newman, Celia Roth, David Schrumpf, Carla Schwartz, Keith Shandalow, Kimery Shelton, Barbara Strack and Rafael Villarruel at Michigan, and by Katharine Bunn, Wanda Hagan, Stephen Wood, and especially Matt Nydell, John Quarterman, and Dean Strang at Virginia. Faculty colleagues who were quite helpful (sometimes when they were unaware of the project we had in mind) include Vincent Blasi, Richard Bonnie, Harold Bruff, David Chambers, Tom Gerety, Louis Henkin, Jerold Israel, Douglas Kahn, Yale Kamisar, Douglas Leslie, Richard Lillich, Sallyanne Payton, Glen Robinson, Stephen Saltzburg, Terrance Sandalow, Joseph Sax and Joseph Vining. Beyond the law schools, we owe thanks to Arthur Helton, David North, Alex Stepick, and Kim Wallace who supplied valuable information and source materials. We express our special gratitude to Patty Blum, Paul Schmidt, Terry Sandalow and Stephen Legomsky, who read portions of the manuscript and supplied us with useful suggestions. Paul Schmidt deserves particular mention for all the time he took from a crowded schedule at the Immigration and Naturalization Service (where he is Deputy General Counsel) to apply his encyclopedic knowledge of immigration law toward helping us make fewer mistakes than we otherwise would have. A final word of deepest thanks to Donna Moses, Marian Ryerson, and Lisa Skrzycki, whose dedication to the preparation of draft after draft of these materials went far beyond the call of duty.

ALEX ALEINIKOFF
DAVID MARTIN

November 30, 1984

Technical Matters

A few technical matters require further explanation. In editing cases and other materials reprinted here, we have marked textual deletions with asterisks, but we have often omitted simple citations to cases or other authorities without any printed indication. Similarly, we have deleted footnotes from reprinted materials without signalling the omission. Where we chose to retain a footnote, however, we have maintained the original numbering. Our own footnotes appearing in the midst of reprinted materials are marked with alphabetical superscripts; they also end with the notation "— eds." When we drop footnotes to text that we wrote ourselves, we have used the ordinary numerical designations.

INA CITATIONS

How to cite the sections of the Immigration and Nationality Act (INA) posed a special problem. Most—but by no means all—court decisions refer to INA provisons by means of the numbers employed in Title 8 of the U.S. Code, where the Act is codified. This is understandable, even though the system used to translate Act numbers into U.S. Code numbers strikes us as eccentric and unpredictable. Doubtless most nonspecialists find it easier to refer to the U.S.C.A. on their shelves rather than having to hunt down a specially printed copy of the Act itself, employing the original numbering.

Nevertheless, we decided ultimately to use the section numbers of the Act consistently throughout this book, to the exclusion of the U.S. Code numbers—and not only because we expect our readers to count themselves as specialists before they are finished. The administrative framework for Regulations and Operations Instructions is intimately linked to the numbering scheme of the original Act. For example, regulations implementing the exclusion provisions, § 212 of the INA, appear in Part 212 of 8 C.F.R. Operations Instructions are similarly coded. Anyone even minimally active in the field therefore will profit from acquaintance with this fundamental numbering scheme.

Consequently, we have excised references to the Act using the U.S. Code numbering system from all cases and materials, and substituted direct INA section references, without expressly indicating where such substitutions have occurred. Readers who must know the corresponding U.S. Code number will find a conversion chart below. In addition, Appendix A reprints the text of the important sections of the INA. Each section reprinted there begins with a parallel reference to the corresponding section of 8 U.S.C.

Recent Immigration Reform Efforts

Since at least the early 1970's, Congress has considered various proposals to reform the INA in order to deal with the problem of illegal migration to the United States. Because initial proposals bogged down in controversy and division, in 1978 Congress established a blue-ribbon commission to carry out comprehensive studies and offer recommendations that might furnish a basis for eventual consensus on the necessary reform measures. Act of October 5, 1978, § 4, Pub. L. No. 95–412, 92 Stat. 907. The statute created the Select Commission on Immigration and Refugee Policy (SCIRP), composed of four public members appointed by the President, four Cabinet officers, four Senators, and four Representatives. The Commission issued its final report in March 1981, with wide-ranging recommendations for changes in the Act and its administration. It also published as a separate volume a lengthy staff report on the matters within its mandate, accompanied by separate volumes that were appendices to the staff report. Each appendix represents an important compilation of research materials on the subject of the volume, sometimes reprinting previous studies, often reporting on studies newly chartered by the Commission.

After the Commission reported, Congress returned to the reform debate. The most important legislation introduced on these subjects came to be known as the Simpson-Mazzoli bill, after its chief legislative sponsors, the chairmen of the key subcommittees having jurisdiction over immigration matters (Sen. Alan Simpson (R.–Wyo.) and Rep. Romano Mazzoli (D.–Ky.)). It began life as a single proposal, but took on somewhat disparate forms as it moved through the legislative process in the two chambers. The Senate passed a bill in 1982, but the House failed to act before the 97th Congress expired. The battle was taken up again in the 98th Congress. Both houses passed versions of Simpson-Mazzoli, but the House did not act until June 1984, and the margin of passage was only 5 votes. In the charged atmosphere of an impending election, the conference committee was unable to resolve the differences before adjournment.

We will often refer to these measures, as they represent the most current legislative thinking on a host of difficult public policy questions. We use the abbreviated citation "S. 529" for the bill the Senate passed in 1983, and "H.R. 1510" for the one that passed the House, using the bill numbers originally attached when Simpson and Mazzoli introduced their measures during the 98th Congress. (This involves some slight terminological inaccuracy in referring to the bill the House voted for in June 1984, as the House technically passed its own version of S. 529—substituting for the Senate provisions the wording it had developed in debates on H.R. 1510. We preserve the original numbering for ease of reference, but use it to refer to the version that passed the full House.)

ABBREVIATED CITATION FORMS

Most citations in the book conform to *A Uniform System of Citation*, customarily used by law journals. For a few items that are cited frequently, however, we have abbreviated even further:

"Developments"

Note, *Developments in the Law—Immigration Policy and the Rights of Aliens*, 96 Harv.L.Rev. 1286 (1983).

"G & R"

C. Gordon and H. Rosenfield, Immigration Law and Procedure (rev. ed. 1984). (The leading treatise in the field, available now as an eight-volume looseleaf set, with frequent updating. We cite it by topical section number, in accordance with the organizational scheme of the treatise.)

"INA"

The Immigration and Nationality Act. (Passed in 1952, Pub. L. No. 82–414, 66 Stat. 163, as a comprehensive codification replacing earlier immigration and nationality laws, and frequently amended since then. The Act itself is codified, according to an idiosyncratic numbering scheme, in Title 8 of the United States Code; a conversion chart, showing corresponding section numbers, appears below. We cite by INA section number, *not* U.S.C. section number, to the current amended statute.)

"H.R. 1510"

H.R. 1510, 98th Cong., 2d Sess., as passed by the House, 130 Cong. Rec. H6166 (daily ed. June 20, 1984). (See above for more complete explanation.)

"Interp.Rel."

Interpreter Releases. (The leading reporting service on administrative, legislative and judicial developments in the immigration field. It is published 50 times a year by the American Council for Nationalities Service.)

"O.I."

Operations Instructions. (The manual of detailed guidelines and policy statements issued by the Immigration and Naturalization Service and used by immigration officers in implementing the statute and the regulations. Those Instructions which have been released to the public are reprinted in volume 4 of the G & R treatise.)

"S. 529"

S. 529, 98th Cong., 1st Sess., as passed by the Senate, 129 Cong. Rec. S6970 (daily ed. May 18, 1983).

"SCIRP, Final Report"

"SCIRP, Staff Report"

"SCIRP, Appendix A, . . ., etc."

Select Commission on Immigration and Refugee Policy, U.S. Immigration Policy and the National Interest, Final Report and Recommendations (1981); id., Staff Report, Supplement to the Final Report and Recommendations of [SCIRP]; id., Appendix A to the Staff Report, etc. (Each lettered appendix is published as a separate volume.)

Acknowledgments

The authors wish to express their thanks to copyright holders for permission to reprint excerpts from the following materials.

Ackerman, Bruce, Social Justice in the Liberal State, pp. 89–95. Copyright © 1980 by the Yale University Press. Reprinted by permission of the publisher.

Aleinikoff, T. Alexander, Aliens, Due Process and "Community Ties": A Response to Martin, 44 University of Pittsburgh Law Review 237 (1983). Copyright © 1983. Reprinted by permission.

Aleinikoff, T. Alexander, Political Asylum in the Federal Republic of Germany and the Republic of France: Lessons for the United States, 17 University of Michigan Journal of Law Reform 183 (1984). Copyright © 1984. Reprinted by permission.

Arendt, Hannah, The Origins of Totalitarianism, pp. 293–302 (2d ed. 1962). Copyright © 1958 by Hannah Arendt. Reprinted by permission of the publisher, George Allen & Unwin, Ltd.

Bickel, Alexander, The Morality of Consent, ch. 2. Copyright © 1975 by the Yale University Press. Reprinted by permission of the publisher.

Briggs, Vernon M., Jr., "Foreign Labor Programs as an Alternative to Illegal Immigration: A Dissenting View," in Peter G. Brown and Henry Shue, eds., The Border that Joins: Mexican Migrants and U.S. Responsibility (Totowa, N.J.: Rowman and Littlefield © 1983), pp. 235–243. Reprinted by permission.

Bruck, Connie, Springing the Haitians, The American Lawyer, September 1982, pp. 36–39. Copyright © 1982. Reprinted by permission.

Cohen, Julius, Judicial "Legisputation" and the Dimensions of Legislative Meaning, 36 Indiana Law Journal 414 (1961). Copyright © 1961. Reprinted by the permission of the Indiana Law Journal and Fred B. Rothman & Co.

Cornelius, Wayne, Mexican Migration to the United States: The Limits of Government Intervention (1981) (Working Paper No. 5 in U.S.-Mexican Studies). Copyright © 1981 by the Center for U.S.-Mexican Studies, University of California, San Diego. Reprinted by permission.

Crewdson, John, The Tarnished Door: The New Immigrants and the Transformation of America. Copyright © 1983 by John Crewdson.

Harper, Elizabeth and Chase, Roland, Immigration Laws of the United States (3rd ed. 1975). Copyright © 1975 by the Bobbs-Merrill Company, Inc. Reprinted with permission.

Hart, Henry, The Power of Congress to Limit the Jurisdiction of the Federal Courts: An Exercise in Dialectic, 66 Harvard Law Review 1362 (1953). Copyright © 1953 by the Harvard Law Review Association. Reprinted by permission.

Helton, Arthur, Political Asylum under the 1980 Refugee Act: An Unfulfilled Promise, 17 University of Michigan Journal of Law Reform 243 (1984). Copyright © 1984. Reprinted by permission.

Henkin, Louis, Foreign Affairs and the Constitution. Copyright © 1972 by the Foundation Press, Inc. Reprinted by permission.

Higham, John, Strangers in the Land: Patterns of American Nativism. Copyright © 1955 by the Trustees of Rutgers College in New Jersey. Reprinted by permission.

Interpreter Releases, vol. 57, p. 80 (1980); vol. 59, pp. 144–45 (1982); vol. 60, p. 844 (1983); vol. 61, pp. 378, 442, 462 (1984). Copyright © 1980, 1982, 1983 and 1984 by the American Council for Nationalities Service. Reprinted by permission.

King, Timothy, Immigration from Developing Countries: Some Philosophical Issues, 93 Ethics 525 (1983). Copyright © 1983 by the University of Chicago. All rights reserved. Reprinted by permission.

Kirmeyer, Sharon, There's No 'Safe Haven' in El Salvador, The Washington Post, July 14, 1984. Copyright © 1984. Reprinted by permission.

Landis, James M., A Note on "Statutory Interpretation," 46 Harvard Law Review 886 (1930). Copyright © 1930 by the Harvard Law Review Association. Reprinted by permission.

Lopez, Gerald P., Undocumented Mexican Migration: In Search Of a Just Immigration Law and Policy, 28 UCLA Law Review 615 (1981). Copyright © 1981, The Regents of the University of California. All rights reserved. Reprinted by permission of the author and the Regents of the University of California.

Martin, David A., Due Process and Membership in the National Community: Political Asylum and Beyond, 44 University of Pittsburgh Law Review 165 (1983). Copyright © 1983. Reprinted by permission.

Martin, David A., The Refugee Act of 1980: Its Past and Future, 1982 Michigan Yearbook of International Legal Studies 91. Copyright © 1982 by the Clark Boardman Company. Reprinted by permission.

Weissbrodt, David, Immigration Law and Procedure in a Nutshell (1984). Copyright © 1984. Reprinted by permission of the author and the West Publishing Company.

Wildes, Leon, The Nonpriority Program of the Immigration and Naturalization Service Goes Public: The Litigative Uses of the Freedom of Information Act, 14 San Diego Law Review 42 (1976). Copyright © 1976, 1977 by the San Diego Law Review Association. Reprinted by permission.

Summary of Contents

Table of Contents

APPENDICES

Table of Cases

The principal cases are in Italic type. Cases cited or discussed are in Roman type. References are to Pages.

*

Table of Authorities

*

Table of Statutes, Rules and Regulations

References are to pages.

STATUTES AT LARGE

STATUTES AT LARGE

*

Conversion Chart

CORRESPONDENCE OF SECTIONS OF THE IMMIGRATION AND NATIONALITY ACT AND SECTIONS OF TITLE 8, UNITED STATES CODE

INA §	8 U.S.C. §	INA §	8 U.S.C. §	INA §	8 U.S.C. §
101	1101	246	1256	289	1359
102	1102	247	1257	290	1360
103	1103	248	1258	291	1361
104	1104	249	1259	292	1362
105	1105	250	1260	301	1401
106	1105a	251	1281	302	1402
201	1151	252	1282	303	1403
202	1152	253	1283	304	1404
203	1153	254	1284	305	1405
204	1154	255	1285	306	1406
205	1155	256	1286	307	1407
206	1156	257	1287	308	1408
211	1181	261	1301	309	1409
212	1182	262	1302	310	1421
213	1183	263	1303	311	1422
214	1184	264	1304	312	1423
215	1185	265	1305	313	1424
221	1201	266	1306	314	1425
222	1202	271	1321	315	1426
223	1203	272	1322	316	1427
224	1204	273	1323	317	1428
231	1221	274	1324	318	1429
232	1222	275	1325	319	1430
233	1223	276	1326	320	1431
234	1224	277	1327	321	1432
235	1225	278	1328	322	1433
236	1226	279	1329	323	1434
237	1227	280	1330	324	1435
238	1228	281	1351	325	1436
239	1229	282	1352	326	1437
240	1230	283	1353	327	1438
241	1251	284	1354	328	1439
242	1252	285	1355	329	1440
243	1253	286	1356	330	1441
244	1254	287	1357	331	1442
245	1255	288	1358	332	1443

INA §	8 U.S.C. §	INA §	8 U.S.C. §	INA §	8 U.S.C. §
333	1444	344	1455	356	1488
334	1445	346	1457	357	1489
335	1446	347	1458	358	1501
336	1447	348	1459	359	1502
337	1448	349	1481	360	1503
338	1449	350	1482	411	1521
339	1450	351	1483	412	1522
340	1451	352	1484	413	1523
341	1452	353	1485	414	1524
342	1453	354	1486		
343	1454	355	1487		

IMMIGRATION:
PROCESS AND POLICY

*

Chapter One

FOUNDATIONS OF THE IMMIGRATION POWER

SECTION A. THE SOURCES OF THE FEDERAL IMMIGRATION POWER

This casebook will attempt to familiarize you with an exceedingly complex statute, the Immigration and Nationality Act, as well as expose you to current debates on American immigration and refugee policy. These debates are largely about how many and what kind of immigrants the United States should permit to enter each year. What the debates take for granted is the power of the Congress to enact laws that regulate which aliens may enter the United States and under what conditions those that enter may remain. It is with this issue—the source of Congress' immigration power—that we begin this book.

You may find it curious that the source of Congress' power could be an interesting question. Surely the Founding Fathers would have endowed Congress explicitly with a power as important as that of controlling immigration. Yet the Constitution of the United States includes no language that expressly grants Congress such authority.

The Supreme Court did not address the question until the second century of this country's existence. This was primarily due to the fact that Congress did not enact significant limits on immigration until the 1880's. For most of the nineteenth century, Congress permitted open borders in an attempt to provide the developing nation with labor and capital.

Chinese Immigration

The first immigration statutes to be subjected to judicial scrutiny were the so-called "Chinese exclusion laws," passed in 1882, 1884, 1888 and 1892.[1] These statutes—like many later immigration laws—were the product of economic and political concerns laced with racism and nativism.

---

1. The first federal statutes limiting immigration, enacted in 1875 and 1882, prohibited the entry of criminals, prostitutes, idiots, lunatics, and persons likely to become a public charge. Act of March 3, 1875, Ch. 141, 18 Stat. 477; Act of August 3, 1882, Ch. 376, 22 Stat. 214.

Large-scale Chinese immigration into the United States began during the California gold rush of 1848. Chinese laborers were also sought to help construct the Central Pacific Railroad, built between 1864 and 1869. In a time of labor shortage, the Chinese were welcomed on the West Coast.

With the end of the gold rush and the arrival of European immigrants in California due to the completion of the transcontinental railroad, the demand for, and toleration of, Chinese laborers declined. The Panic of 1873, drought and the depression of 1877 fostered extreme anti-alien fervor in the West. Nativist groups demanded legislation to force the Chinese out of California. Of particular note was the Workingmen's Party of California, led by fireballer Dennis Kearney. The Party's Manifesto, published in 1876, stated:

> To an American death is preferable to a life on a par with the Chinaman * * *. Treason is better than to labor beside a Chinese slave * * *. The people are about to take their own affairs into their own hands and they will not be stayed either by * * * state militia, [or] United States Troops.

Throughout the 1870's the Chinese were subject to virulent and often violent attacks. The Chinese were accused of being criminals, prostitutes and opium addicts, while at the same time they were assailed for their willingness to perform hard work at low wages. Justice Field, who had served as a Justice on the California Supreme Court before joining the United States Supreme Court in 1863, described the prevailing view of Chinese laborers as follows:

> [The Chinese laborers] were generally industrious and frugal. Not being accompanied by families, except in rare instances, their expenses were small; and they were content with the simplest fare, such as would not suffice for our laborers and artisans. The competition between them and our people was for this reason altogether in their favor, and the consequent irritation, proportionately deep and bitter, was followed, in many cases, by open conflicts, to the great disturbance of the public peace.

> The differences of race added greatly to the difficulties of the situation. * * * [T]hey remained strangers in the land, residing apart by themselves, and adhering to the customs and usages of their own country. It seemed impossible for them to assimilate with our people or to make any change in their habits or modes of living. As they grew in numbers each year the people of the coast saw, or believed they saw, in the facility of immigration, and in the crowded millions of China, where population presses upon the means of subsistence, great danger that at no distant day that portion of our country would be overrun by them unless prompt action was taken to restrict their immigration.

The Chinese Exclusion Case, 130 U.S. 581, 595, 9 S.Ct. 623, 626, 32 L.Ed. 1068 (1889).

The Chinese had been the victims of discriminatory legislation in California since the 1850's. They were subjected to entry, license and occupation taxes, originally to raise money for the California treasury and later as a means to deter immigration. Chinese were not allowed to vote, denied the right to testify in court and prohibited from attending public schools with white children. Most of these statutes were declared invalid, either as a violation of the Fourteenth Amendment or as conflicting with federal treaties.[2]

Federal Regulation of Chinese Immigration

At first, the federal government had welcomed Chinese immigration. Based on the desires to improve trade with China and provide cheap labor for completion of the railroads, the United States negotiated the Burlingame Treaty. July 28, 1868, United States-China, 16 Stat. 739, T.S. No. 48.[3] The Treaty recognized "the inherent and inalienable right of man to change his home and allegiance, and also the mutual advantage of free migration and emigration of [American and Chinese] citizens * * * for purposes of curiosity, of trade or as permanent residents." It therefore guaranteed citizens of one country visiting or residing in the other "the same privileges, immunities and exemptions * * * as may be enjoyed by the citizens or subjects of the most favored nation."

The restrictionist and racist tide in California began to have an impact in national politics by the mid-1870's.[4] The demand for federal legislation was due, in part, to the court decisions that had struck down California statutes as unlawful discrimination against the Chinese. Adopting restrictionist legislation, however, would have threatened a breach of the spirit, if not the letter, of the Burlingame Treaty. Accordingly, Congress authorized a diplomatic trip to China to renegotiate the Treaty. A supplemental treaty was signed in November 1880. Treaty of November 17, 1880, United States-China, 22 Stat. 826, T.S. No. 49.

The Treaty of 1880 authorized the United States to "regulate, limit or suspend" immigration of Chinese laborers whenever their entry or residence in the United States "affects or threatens to affect the interests of that country, or to endanger the good order of [the United States] or of

---

2. See, e.g., Ho Ah Kow v. Nunan, 5 Sawyer 552 (C.C.D.Cal.1879) (Mr. Justice Field on circuit) (invalidating San Francisco's "Queue Ordinance" which required that all prisoners have their hair cut to a maximum length of one inch); People v. Downer, 7 Cal. 170 (1857) (invalidating $50 tax on Chinese passengers); Ling Sing v. Washburn, 20 Cal. 534 (1862) (voiding capitation tax on Chinese). See generally M. Coolidge, Chinese Immigration (1909); McClain, The Chinese Struggle for Civil Rights in Nineteenth Century America: The First Phase, 1850–1870, 72 Cal.L.Rev. 529 (1984).

3. Anson Burlingame, for whom the Treaty was named, had served as the American Minister to China for six years. He resigned from his position to represent the Chinese Government in the United States.

4. While federal legislation grew increasingly restrictionist in the last quarter of the nineteenth century, it is interesting that the Reconstruction Congress enacted legislation that extended protection to Chinese immigrants against discrimination. Section 16 of the Voting Rights Act of 1870, 16 Stat. 144, guaranteed "all persons" the "same right to make and enforce contracts, to sue, be parties, give evidence, and to the full and equal benefits of all laws and proceedings for the security of persons and property as is enjoyed by white citizens * * *." Other provisions in the civil rights laws had defined the protected class simply as "citizens." The use of the phrase "all persons" was intended to bring Chinese aliens within the law's protection. See McClain, supra note 2; Runyon v. McCrary, 427 U.S. 160, 195–201, 96 S.Ct. 2586, 2606–09, 49 L.Ed.2d 415 (1976) (White, J., dissenting).

any locality within the territory thereof." The Treaty expressly stated that the authority to suspend immigration applied only to *Chinese laborers,* and that the suspension power did not include the authority to "absolutely prohibit" immigration. Importantly, the Treaty preserved the right of Chinese laborers already within the United States "to go and come of their own free will and accord."

Within a year of the ratification of the Treaty, Congress enacted the first of the Chinese exclusion laws. The Act of May 6, 1882, Ch. 126, 22 Stat. 58, suspended the immigration of Chinese laborers for 10 years. The statute did not alter the right of Chinese laborers who were residing in the United States at the time the Treaty was signed to leave and return to the United States. To help effectuate the suspension of new immigration without limiting the ability of resident Chinese to leave and return, the Act established a procedure for the issuance of "certificates of identity" which would entitle Chinese laborers to re-enter the United States after a trip abroad.

The certificate system created by the 1882 Act was not mandatory and led to dissatisfaction. It was claimed that Chinese arriving for the first time persuaded officials that they were returning to a prior lawful residence in the United States. Congress sought to prevent evasion of the 1882 Act by enacting legislation in 1884 which rendered the certificate "the only evidence permissible to establish [the alien's] right of entry."

The federal legislation did not end anti-Chinese agitation in the West. In 1885 and 1886, brutal violence against Chinese occurred in California, Washington and Oregon. In Rock Spring, Wyoming, a mob of white miners attacked Chinese who had refused to join a strike; 28 Chinese were killed.

The United States government again sought to modify the Burlingame Treaty, signing a treaty in 1888 which would have prohibited the immigration of Chinese laborers for an additional twenty years. When rumors reached Washington that China was not likely to ratify the treaty,[5] Congress passed a statute on October 1, 1888, that prohibited the return of all Chinese laborers who had left the United States *even if they had obtained a certificate before their departure under the procedure established by the 1882 and 1884 Acts.* It further provided that no more certificates would be issued. The statute stranded Chinese in China who had been residents of the United States. It also effectively prevented Chinese then residing in the United States from returning home for a visit: since no more certificates would be issued, once they left the United States they would not be able to re-enter. The statute thus conflicted with the provisions of the Burlingame Treaty and the Treaty of 1880 which had guaranteed the right of aliens "to go and come of their own free will."

Chae Chan Ping was a Chinese laborer who had entered the United States in 1875. He lived in San Francisco until 1887, when he left for a visit to China. Before departing, he obtained a certificate pursuant to the

---

5. *See* Tien-La Li, Congressional Policy of Chinese Immigration 53–66 (1916).

1882 and 1884 Acts.   He returned to California shortly after passage of the 1888 Act and was denied re-admission to the United States even though he possessed a certificate.   Chae Chan Ping brought suit, alleging that the 1888 Act violated the Constitution and conflicted with the Burlingame and 1880 Treaties.   The opinion of Justice Field, writing for a unanimous Supreme Court, follows.

THE CHINESE EXCLUSION CASE
(CHAE CHAN PING v. UNITED STATES)

Supreme Court of the United States, 1889.
130 U.S. 581, 9 S.Ct. 623, 32 L.Ed. 1068.

Mr. JUSTICE FIELD delivered the opinion of the Court.

* * *

* * * It must be conceded that the act of 1888 is in contravention of express stipulations of the [Burlingame] treaty of 1868 and of the supplemental treaty of 1880, but it is not on that account invalid or to be restricted in its enforcement.   The treaties were of no greater legal obligation than the act of Congress.   By the Constitution, laws made in pursuance thereof and treaties made under the authority of the United States are both declared to be the supreme law of the land, and no paramount authority is given to one over the other.   A treaty, it is true, is in its nature a contract between nations and is often merely promissory in its character, requiring legislation to carry its stipulations into effect.   Such legislation will be open to future repeal or amendment.   If the treaty operates by its own force, and relates to a subject within the power of Congress, it can be deemed in that particular only the equivalent of a legislative act, to be repealed or modified at the pleasure of Congress.   In either case the last expression of the sovereign will must control.

* * *

There being nothing in the treaties between China and the United States to impair the validity of the act of Congress of October 1, 1888, was it on any other ground beyond the competency of Congress to pass it?   If so, it must be because it was not within the power of Congress to prohibit Chinese laborers who had at the time departed from the United States, or should subsequently depart, from returning to the United States.   Those laborers are not citizens of the United States; they are aliens.   That the government of the United States, through the action of the legislative department, can exclude aliens from its territory is a proposition which we do not think open to controversy.   Jurisdiction over its own territory to that extent is an incident of every independent nation.   It is a part of its independence.   If it could not exclude aliens it would be to that extent subject to the control of another power.   As said by this court in the case of *The Exchange,* 7 Cranch, 116, 136, speaking by Chief Justice Marshall: "The jurisdiction of the nation within its own territory is necessarily exclusive and absolute.   It is susceptible of no limitation not imposed by itself.   Any restriction upon it, deriving validity from an external source, would imply a diminution of its sovereignty to the extent of the restriction, and an investment of that sovereignty to the same extent in that power which could impose such restriction. All exceptions, therefore, to the full and complete power of a nation within its own territories, must be traced up to the consent of the nation itself. They can flow from no other legitimate source."

While under our Constitution and form of government the great mass of local matters is controlled by local authorities, the United States, in their relation to foreign countries and their subjects or citizens are one nation, invested with powers which belong to independent nations, the exercise of which can be invoked for the maintenance of its absolute independence and security throughout its entire territory. The powers to declare war, make treaties, suppress insurrection, repel invasion, regulate foreign commerce, secure republican governments to the States, and admit subjects of other nations to citizenship, are all sovereign powers, restricted in their exercise only by the Constitution itself and considerations of public policy and justice which control, more or less, the conduct of all civilized nations.   * * *

The control of local matters being left to local authorities, and national matters being entrusted to the government of the Union, the problem of free institutions existing over a widely extended country, having different climates and varied interests, has been happily solved. For local interests the several States of the Union exist, but for national purposes, embracing our relations with foreign nations, we are but one people, one nation, one power.

To preserve its independence, and give security against foreign aggression and encroachment, is the highest duty of every nation, and to attain these ends nearly all other considerations are to be subordinated. It matters not in what form such aggression and encroachment come, whether from the foreign nation acting in its national character or from vast hordes of its people crowding in upon us. The government, possessing the powers which are to be exercised for protection and security, is clothed with authority to determine the occasion on which the powers shall be called forth; and its determination, so far as the subjects affected are concerned, are necessarily conclusive upon all its departments and officers. If, therefore, the government of the United States, through its legislative department, considers the presence of foreigners of a different race in this country, who will not assimilate with us, to be dangerous to its peace and security, their exclusion is not to be stayed because at the time there are no actual hostilities with the nation of which the foreigners are subjects. The existence of war would render the necessity of the proceeding only more obvious and pressing. The same necessity, in a less pressing degree, may arise when war does not exist, and the same authority which adjudges the necessity in one case must also determine it in the other. In both cases its determination is conclusive upon the judiciary. If the government of the country of which the foreigners excluded are subjects is dissatisfied with this action it can make complaint to the executive head of our government, or resort to any other measure which, in its judgment, its interests or dignity may demand; and there lies its only remedy.

* * *

The exclusion of paupers, criminals and persons afflicted with incurable diseases, for which statutes have been passed, is only an application of the same power to particular classes of persons, whose presence is deemed injurious or a source of danger to the country. As applied to them, there has never been any question as to the power to exclude them. The power is constantly exercised; its existence is involved in the right of self-preservation.   * * *

The power of exclusion of foreigners being an incident of sovereignty belonging to the government of the United States, as a part of those sovereign powers delegated by the Constitution, the right to its exercise at any time when, in the judgment of the government, the interests of the country require it, cannot be granted away or restrained on behalf of any one.   The powers of government are delegated in trust to the United States, and are incapable of transfer to any other parties. They cannot be abandoned or surrendered. Nor can their exercise be hampered, when needed for the public good, by any considerations of private interest. The exercise of these public trusts is not the subject of barter or contract. Whatever license, therefore, Chinese laborers may have obtained, previous to the act of October 1, 1888, to return to the United States after their departure, is held at the will of the government, revocable at any time, at its pleasure. Whether a proper consideration by our government of its previous laws, or a proper respect for the nation whose subjects are affected by its action, ought to have qualified its inhibition and made it applicable only to persons departing from the country after the passage of the act, are not questions for judicial determination. If there be any just ground of complaint on the part of China, it must be made to the political department of our government, which is alone competent to act upon the subject.

* * *

Order affirmed.

Discussion: Sources of the Immigration Power

1. Delegated Powers

A fundamental principle of American constitutional law is that the federal government "is one of enumerated powers"; it can exercise "only the powers granted to it" and powers "necessary and proper" to the execution of delegated powers. *McCulloch v. Maryland,* 17 U.S. (4 Wheat.) 316, 324, 4 L.Ed. 579 (1819).

What delegated powers does Justice Field rely upon to support the conclusion that Congress had the authority to pass the Chinese exclusion laws? To what other powers explicit in Article I of the Constitution might he have appealed? Consider the following in responding.

a. *The Commerce Power.*   Art. I, § 8, cl. 3, of the Constitution authorizes Congress "to regulate Commerce with foreign Nations, and among the several States." In the mid-1800's, the Supreme Court invalidated a number of state statutes that sought to regulate immigration through the imposition of taxes or other regulations on carriers. *See Chy Lung v. Freeman,* 92 U.S. (2 Otto) 275, 23 L.Ed. 550 (1876), discussed *infra; Henderson v. New York,* 92 U.S. (2 Otto) 259, 23 L.Ed. 543 (1876) (striking down New York requirement that ship masters pay $1.50 tax per passenger brought to New York or provide $300 bond to indemnify city for relief expenses for four years); *The Passenger Cases,* 48 U.S. (7 How.) 283, 12 L.Ed. 702 (1849) (invalidating Massachusetts and New York taxes on immigrants). *The Passenger Cases* yielded a 5–4 decision in which eight Justices wrote opinions. While it is difficult to discover a ground for the decision that a majority of the Court agreed upon, the commerce power received prominent attention in the opinions of Justices McLean, Wayne, Catron and Grier.

If state laws were void as an invasion of Congress' commerce powers, then it is not surprising that the Court upheld a *federal* statute, enacted in 1882, that imposed a tax of fifty cents on every alien arriving in the United States. *Head Money Cases,* 112 U.S. 580, 5 S.Ct. 247, 28 L.Ed. 798 (1884). Said the Court: "Congress [has] the power to pass a law regulating immigration as a part of commerce of this country with foreign nations." *Id.* at 600, 5 S.Ct. at 254.

Can the commerce power be relied upon to uphold the regulation of aliens who do not come to the United States for commercial purposes? Is the migration of children, refugees, poor people, or spouses of resident aliens "commerce"? The Supreme Court, in at least one case, has concluded that migration is commerce. In *Edwards v. California,* 314 U.S. 160, 62 S.Ct. 164, 86 L.Ed. 119 (1941), a California statute that made it a crime to bring an indigent person into the state was struck down as an unconstitutional interference with Congress' power to regulate interstate commerce. The Court, through Justice Byrnes, stated that "it is settled beyond question that the transportation of persons is 'commerce.'" In a footnote, he added: "It is immaterial whether or not the transportation is commercial in character." *Id.* at 172 n. 1, 62 S.Ct. at 166 n. 1.[6] Four Justices concurred in the result of the Court on other grounds, including Justice Jackson who believed that the California statute violated the "privileges or immunities" clause of the Fourteenth Amendment. He expressed the following concern over the majority's reliance on the commerce clause: "[T]he migrations of a human being, of whom it is charged that he possesses no thing that can be sold and has no wherewithal to buy, do not fit easily into my notions of what is commerce. To hold that the measure of his rights is the commerce clause is likely to result eventually either in distorting the commercial law or in denaturing human rights." *Id.* at 182, 62 S.Ct. at 171.

b. *The Naturalization Power.* Art. I, § 8, cl. 4 of the Constitution grants Congress the power to "establish an uniform Rule of Naturalization." This power was expressly delegated to Congress to prevent the

---

6. *See also Caminetti v. United States,* 242 U.S. 470, 37 S.Ct. 192, 61 L.Ed. 442 (1917) (upholding convictions under the White Slave Traffic Act of men who had transported their mistresses across state lines, even though it was neither charged nor proved at trial that the transportation was for commercial purposes).

confusion and controversy that could arise from separate state laws bestowing citizenship. *See* J. Kettner, The Development of American Citizenship, 1608–1870, at 224–25 (1978).

Does the power to naturalize necessarily imply the power to regulate the admission of aliens who may eventually be eligible for naturalization? Not obviously. One might well distinguish between regulation of the *physical entry* of aliens into the *territory* of the United States and regulation of the entry into the *political community* of the United States through the extension of full political rights to naturalized citizens. Can the Constitution be read as granting Congress only the latter power while reserving the former power to the States?

Interestingly, in the early years of the Republic, Congress viewed the naturalization power as a way to regulate immigration. In most states, aliens could not own or inherit land, vote or hold office—disabilities that were removed upon naturalization. Congress could thus encourage or discourage immigration by altering the prerequisites (such as length of residence) for naturalization. *See, e.g.,* 1 Annals of Cong. 1109–1125 (1790) (debate on Naturalization Act of 1790).

c. *The War Power.* Art. I, § 8, cl. 11 grants Congress the power "to declare War." It is beyond dispute that the war power gives the federal government the authority to stop the entry of enemy aliens and to expel enemy aliens residing in the United States. This power was first granted to the President by one of the Alien and Sedition Acts and remains on the books today. *See* 50 U.S.C.A. §§ 21–23. The constitutionality of this provision has been consistently upheld. *See, e.g., Ludecke v. Watkins,* 335 U.S. 160, 68 S.Ct. 1429, 92 L.Ed. 1881 (1948). But is it possible to view the war power as authorizing the mass of statutes that presently regulate immigration—or even the statute challenged in *The Chinese Exclusion Case?*

d. *The Migration and Importation Clause.* Art. I, § 9, cl. 1 of the Constitution provides:

> The Migration or Importation of such Persons as any of the States now existing shall think proper to admit, shall not be prohibited by the Congress prior to the Year one thousand eight hundred and eight.

The denial of power to Congress *before* 1808 seems to imply the existence of such power *after* that year. Thus, this clause, at first reading, appears to authorize congressional power to *prohibit* immigration after 1808, and probably—by reasonable implication—to regulate it as well.

Unfortunately things are not as clear as they seem. This clause is almost assuredly a veiled reference to an institution that the Founding Fathers could not bring themselves, in a charter of fundamental law, to recognize by name: slavery. *The Passenger Cases,* 48 U.S. (7 How.) 283, 512–13, 12 L.Ed. 702 (1849) (opinion of Justice Daniel). Thus this clause has generally been interpreted as prohibiting congressional attempts to stop the slave trade before 1808.[7] *See generally,* D.B. Davis, The Problem

---

7. Congress passed a law prohibiting the importation of slaves on March 2, 1807, Ch. 22, 2 Stat. 426, which took effect January 1, 1808.

of Slavery in the Age of Revolution, 1770–1823, at 119–31 (1975); Berns, *The Constitution and the Migration of Slaves,* 78 Yale L.J. 198 (1968).

Even recognizing that protection of the slave trade was the primary motivation for the clause, is there any good reason for so limiting its application? Note in particular that the clause refers to *"the migration and importation"* of persons. One might well ask why the Constitution would include the word "migration"—which sounds like voluntary movement of people—if the clause were intended to apply only to the slave trade. At least three answers are possible, each of which stops short of finding in the clause a general power to regulate immigration. The first two restrict the clause to regulation of the slave trade: (1) "migration" was intended to refer to movement of slaves among the States, while importation referred to the initial entrance of the slave into the United States; or (2) "migration" was used in addition to "importation" "to prevent * * * cavils" over whether slaves were persons or property. *The Passenger Cases,* 48 U.S. (7 How.) 283, 476, 12 L.Ed. 702 (1849) (opinion of Chief Justice Taney). The third interpretation, offered in a dictum by the Supreme Court in 1883, goes beyond the slave trade but limits the clause to the regulation of immigration of blacks:

> There has never been any doubt that this clause had exclusive reference to persons of the African race. The two words "migration" and "importation" refer to the different conditions of this race as regards freedom and slavery. When the free black man came here, he migrated; when the slave came, he was imported.

People v. Compagnie Générale Transatlantique, 107 U.S. (17 Otto) 59, 62, 2 S.Ct. 87, 27 L.Ed. 383 (1883) (striking down New York State tax on immigrants).

The interpretation of the "migration and importation" clause arose in the debate over the Alien and Sedition Acts, passed by a Federalist Congress in 1798. The Alien Act authorized the President "to *order* all such *aliens* as he shall judge dangerous to the peace and safety of the United States * * * to depart out of the territory of the United States." Act of June 25, 1798, 1 Stat. 571 (emphasis in original). Jeffersonians opposed to the Act argued that the "migration and importation" clause granted a general power over immigration, not just the slave trade, and that such power could not be exercised until 1808—some ten years in the future. The Speaker of the House, Jonathan Dayton of New Jersey, who had been present at the Constitutional Convention, responded as follows:

> Mr. Dayton (the Speaker) commenced his observations with declaring that he should not have risen on this occasion, if no allusion had been made to the proceedings in the Federal Convention which framed the Constitution of the United States, or if the representation which was given of what passed in that body, had been a perfectly correct and candid one. He expressed his surprise at what had fallen from the gentleman from Georgia (Mr.

Baldwin) relatively to that part of the Constitution, which had been selected as the text of opposition to the bill under consideration, *viz*:

"The migration or importation of such persons as any of the States now existing shall think proper to admit, shall not be prohibited by Congress, prior to the year 1808." He could only ascribe either to absolute forgetfulness, or to willful misrepresentation, the assertion of the member from Georgia, that it was understood and intended by the General Convention that the article in question should extend to the importation or introduction of citizens from foreign countries. As that gentleman and himself were the only two members of the House of Representatives who had the honor of a seat in that body, he deemed it his indispensable duty to correct the misstatement that had thus been made. He did not therefore, hesitate to say, in direct contradiction to his novel construction of the article (made as it would seem to suit the particular purposes of the opponents of the Alien bill) that the proposition itself was originally drawn up and moved in the Convention, by the deputies from South Carolina, for the express purpose of preventing Congress from interfering with the introduction of slaves into the United States, within the time specified. He recollected also, that in the discussion of its merits, no question arose, or was agitated respecting the admission of foreigners, but, on the contrary, that it was confined simply to slaves, and was first voted upon and carried with that word expressed in it, which was afterwards upon reconsideration changed for "such persons," as it now stands, upon the suggestion of one of the Deputies from Connecticut. The sole reason assigned for changing it was, that it would be better not to stain the Constitutional code with such a term, since it could be avoided by the introduction of other equally intelligible words, as had been done in the former part of the same instrument, where the same sense was conveyed by the circuitous expression of "three fifths of all other persons."

8 Annals of Cong. 1992–93 (1798).

e. *The Foreign Affairs Power.* In *The Chinese Exclusion Case*, Justice Field sought to associate the power to regulate immigration with the power to conduct foreign affairs: "[T]he United States, in their relation to foreign countries and their subjects or citizens, are one nation, invested with powers which belong to independent nations * * *. * * * [F]or national purposes, *enforcing our relations with foreign nations,* we are but one people, one nation, one power." (Emphasis supplied.)

In modern constitutional terms, these words would be seen as an appeal to the foreign affairs power of the federal government. But like the immigration power, the foreign affairs power receives no explicit mention in the Constitution. Finding the constitutional basis of the power to conduct foreign relations has proven a vexing task, as Professor

Louis Henkin, a leading scholar on foreign affairs and the Constitution, has described:

> The Constitution does not delegate a "power to conduct foreign relations" to the federal government or confer it upon any of its branches. Congress is given power to regulate commerce with foreign nations, to define offenses against the law of nations, to declare war, and the President the power to make treaties and send and receive ambassadors, but these hardly add up to the power to conduct foreign relations. Where is the power to recognize other states or governments, to maintain or break diplomatic relations, to open consulates elsewhere and permit them here, to acquire or cede territory, to give or withhold foreign aid, to proclaim a Monroe Doctrine or an Open-Door Policy, indeed to determine all the attitudes and carry out all the details in the myriads of relationships with other nations that are "the foreign policy" and "the foreign relations" of the United States? * * * Congress can regulate foreign commerce but where is the power to make other laws relating to our foreign relations—to regulate immigration, or the status and rights of aliens, or activities of citizens at home or abroad affecting our foreign relations? These "missing" powers, and a host of others, were clearly intended for and have always been exercised by the federal government, but where does the Constitution say that it shall be so?

> * * *

> The attempt to build all the foreign affairs powers of the federal government with the few bricks provided by the Constitution has not been accepted as successful. It requires considerable stretching of language, much reading between lines, and bold extrapolation from "the Constitution as a whole," and that still does not plausibly add up to all the power which the federal government in fact exercises.

L. Henkin, Foreign Affairs and the Constitution 16–18 (1972).[8]

Does Justice Field adequately describe how the immigration power may be inferred from the (somewhat tenuously inferred) power to conduct foreign relations? Moreover, are all regulations of immigration intended as acts of foreign policy? See Legomsky, *Immigration Law and the Principle of Plenary Congressional Power*, 1984 Sup.Ct.Rev. 255, 261–69. Were the Chinese exclusion laws? Or were they passed *despite* foreign policy objectives of the United States?[9]

---

8. As Henkin further notes, the difficulty of locating a constitutional source for the foreign affairs power probably produced the unique theory expressed by the Court in *United States v. Curtiss-Wright Export Corp.,* 299 U.S. 304, 57 S.Ct. 216, 81 L.Ed. 255 (1936): that the foreign affairs powers derive not from the Constitution at all, but rather are inherent in the notion of a sovereign nation. We will discuss a similar justification for the immigration power below.

9. Some immigration decisions are clearly part of the conduct of American foreign policy. For example, during the Iranian Hostage crisis of 1980–81, President Carter ordered all Iranian students in the United States to report to INS offices and demon-

The federal government's power to conduct foreign affairs, whether or not it justifies federal regulation of immigration, has led the courts to invalidate *state* statutes that attempt to regulate immigration. The classic statement of this position occurs in *Chy Lung v. Freeman,* 92 U.S. (2 Otto) 275, 23 L.Ed. 550 (1875). The case involved, in the Court's words, "a most extraordinary statute" that authorized the California Commissioner of Immigration to inspect aliens seeking to enter the United States. For any alien determined by the Commissioner to be deaf, dumb, blind, crippled, infirm, or a lunatic, idiot, pauper, convicted criminal or lewd or debauched woman, the master of the vessel was required to give a bond or pay an amount determined by the Commissioner to be sufficient to provide for the alien's care. In striking the statute down, the Court, through Justice Miller, relied in large part on the impact that such a regulation could have on American foreign policy.

Individual foreigners, however distinguished at home for their social, their literary, or their political character, are helpless in the presence of this potent commissioner. Such a person may offer to furnish any amount of surety on his own bond, or deposit any sum of money; but the law of California takes no note of him. It is the master, owner, or consignee of the vessel alone whose bond can be accepted; and so a silly, an obstinate, or a wicked commissioner may bring disgrace upon the whole country, the enmity of a powerful nation, or the loss of an equally powerful friend.

While the occurrence of the hypothetical case just stated may be highly improbable, we venture the assertion, that, if citizens of our own government were treated by any foreign nation as subjects of the Emperor of China have been actually treated under this law, no administration could withstand the call for a demand on such government for redress.

Or, if this plaintiff and her twenty companions had been subjects of the Queen of Great Britain, can any one doubt that this matter would have been the subject of international inquiry, if not of a direct claim for redress? Upon whom would such a claim be made? Not upon the State of California; for, by our Constitution, she can hold no exterior relations with other nations. It would be made upon the government of the United States. If that government should get into a difficulty which would lead to war, or to suspension of intercourse, would California alone suffer, or all the Union? If we should conclude that a pecuniary indemnity was proper as a satisfaction for the injury, would California pay it, or the Federal government? If that government has forbidden the States to hold negotiations with any foreign nations, or to declare war, and has taken the whole subject of these relations upon herself, has the Constitution, which provides for this, done so foolish a thing as to leave it in

strate the lawfulness of their presence in the country. *See Narenji v. Civiletti,* 617 F.2d 745 (D.C.Cir.1979), cert. denied 446 U.S. 957, 100 S.Ct. 2928, 64 L.Ed.2d 815 (1980).

the power of the States to pass laws whose enforcement renders the general government liable to just reclamations which it must answer, while it does not prohibit to the States the acts for which it is held responsible?

The Constitution of the United States is no such instrument. The passage of laws which concern the admission of citizens and subjects of foreign nations to our shores belongs to Congress, and not to the States. It has the power to regulate commerce with foreign nations: the responsibility for the character of those regulations, and for the manner of their execution, belongs solely to the national government. If it be otherwise, a single State can, at her pleasure, embroil us in disastrous quarrels with other nations.

Id. at 279–80.[10]

2.   Inherent Power

Justice Field writes in *The Chinese Exclusion Case* that "[t]he power of exclusion of foreigners [is] an incident of sovereignty belonging to the government of the United States, as a part of those sovereign powers delegated by the Constitution." Earlier in the opinion he states:

That the government of the United States * * * can exclude aliens from its territories is a proposition which we do not think open to controversy. Jurisdiction over its own territory to that extent is an incident of every independent nation. It is a part of its independence. If it could not exclude aliens, it would be to that extent subject to the control of another power.

Three years later in *Nishimura Ekiu v. United States,* 142 U.S. 651, 12 S.Ct. 336, 35 L.Ed. 1146 (1892),[11] Justice Gray, writing for the court, stated:

It is an accepted maxim of international law, that every sovereign nation has the power, as inherent in sovereignty, and essential to preservation, to forbid the entrance of foreigners within its dominions, or to admit them only in such cases and upon such conditions as it may see fit to prescribe. In the United States, this power is vested in the national government, to which the Constitution has committed the entire control of international relations, in peace as well as in war.

These powerful and oft-cited passages mask deep and unanswered puzzles. If the federal government is one of delegated powers, how can it possess "inherent powers" that seem to owe their existence to sources outside the Constitution? Why should "maxims of international law"

10. *See also Hines v. Davidowitz,* 312 U.S. 52, 61 S.Ct. 399, 85 L.Ed. 581 (1941), which involved the validity of Pennsylvania's Alien Registration Act. Although the Court struck down the statute as conflicting with federal legislation, it discussed at length the impact that local legislation regulating aliens could have on the conduct of foreign relations.

11. *Nishimura Ekiu* upheld the immigration act of 1891 which codified existing exclusion laws and provided for exclusive inspection of aliens by the federal government.

define the power of Congress? Isn't that what a (or at least our) Constitution is for? Even if we accept the idea that an attribute of sovereignty is the power to regulate immigration, why don't we discover that power in the States, which, under the Tenth Amendment, retain all powers not delegated to the federal government?

The Supreme Court has answered these questions in a different context in a manner that might surprise. In *United States v. Curtiss-Wright Export Co.*, 299 U.S. 304, 57 S.Ct. 216, 81 L.Ed. 255 (1936), the Court, through Justice Sutherland, expounded at length upon the source of the federal government's foreign affairs power. Oddly enough, it found the power to derive, not from the Constitution, but from the fact of independence itself:

> The broad statement that the federal government can exercise no power except those specifically enumerated in the Constitution, and such implied powers as are necessary and proper to carry into effect the enumerated powers, is categorically true only in respect of our internal affairs.

> * * *

> As a result of the separation from Great Britain by the colonies acting as a unit, the powers of external sovereignty passed from the Crown not to the colonies severally, but to the colonies in their collective and corporate capacity as the United States of America.

> * * *

> The Union existed before the Constitution, which was ordained and established among other things to form "a more perfect Union."

> * * *

> It results that the investment of the federal government with the powers of external sovereignty did not depend upon the affirmative grants of the Constitution.

299 U.S. at 315–18, 57 S.Ct. at 218–20.

Under the reasoning of *Curtiss-Wright*, we need no longer scrutinize the Constitution to find the immigration powers. We need simply conclude that the power to regulate the flow of aliens over our borders is inherent in the concept of sovereignty.[12]

Curtiss-Wright has been seriously questioned on logical and historical grounds.[13] Its theory is particularly troubling in the immigration area. If the power to regulate immigration is extra-constitutional, is it subject to

12. Indeed, Professor Henkin believes that *Curtiss-Wright* goes beyond *The Chinese Exclusion Case*. He asserts that the latter case did not view the immigration power as extra-constitutional, but rather as supplementary to those granted. Henkin, *supra*, at 22. Do you agree?

13. *See* Henkin, *supra*, at 23–26; Lofgren, *United States v. Curtiss-Wright Export Co.: An Historical Reassessment*, 83 Yale L.J. 1 (1973); Note, *Constitutional Limits on the Power to Exclude Aliens*, 82 Col.L.Rev. 995 (1982).

any limits within the Constitution? May aliens be excluded without a guarantee of due process? Are aliens living in the United States not entitled to the protections of the First, Fourth, Fifth and Sixth Amendments? The Supreme Court has repeatedly stated that they are.[14] But how can these constitutional limits be applied to a power that exists outside the Constitution?

3. Constructional and Structural Arguments

Perhaps there is some source of power between delegated powers and extra-constitutional powers. Let us suggest two.

a. *The Rule of Necessity.* Judge Learned Hand has written:

> For centuries it has been an accepted canon in interpretation of documents to interpolate into the text such provisions, though not expressed, as are essential to prevent the defeat of the venture at hand; and this applies with special force the interpretation of constitutions, which, since they are designed to cover a great multitude of necessarily unforeseen occasions, must be cast in general language, unless they are constantly amended.

L. Hand, The Bill of Rights 14 (1958).

Is it possible to infer the immigration power using Hand's reasoning—"not [as] a logical deduction from the structure of the Constitution but only as a practical condition upon its successful operation"? *Id.* at 15. Justice Field hints at such a justification when he argues that if the federal government were not able to control immigration, the United States "would be to that extent subject to the control of another power." Unfriendly nations could send *agents provocateurs* to disrupt American institutions; developing nations could send workers to take advantage of American jobs; other countries could seek to solve their problems of overpopulation by "exporting" people to the United States. Perhaps to lose control of one's borders is to "defeat the venture at hand" by losing our ability to achieve the objects for which the Constitution was established: "to insure domestic Tranquility, provide for the common defense, promote the general Welfare."

How far can the Rule of Necessity take us? Must the government demonstrate some serious threat to the security or integrity of the nation before aliens may be excluded? Is this a question a court should answer, or is it one to be left to the political branches of government?

b. *A Structural Justification.* Charles Black, a leading constitutional scholar, has suggested that much of our constitutional law may be seen not as "the explication or exegesis of [a] particular textual passage," but rather as an "inference from the structures and relationships created by the constitution." C. Black, Structure and Relationship in Constitutional Law 7 (1964). Under this view, one does not focus on isolated clauses in

---

14. *See, e.g., Bridges v. Wixon,* 326 U.S. 135, 65 S.Ct. 1443, 89 L.Ed. 2103 (1945); *United States v. Brignoni-Ponce,* 422 U.S. 873, 95 S.Ct. 2574, 45 L.Ed.2d 607 (1975); *Wong Yang Sung v. McGrath,* 339 U.S. 33, 70 S.Ct. 445, 94 L.Ed. 616 (1950); *Wong Wing v. United States,* 163 U.S. 228, 16 S.Ct. 977, 41 L.Ed. 140 (1896).

the document; instead, the interpreter takes a step back and examines the shape of the Constitution as a whole: the institutions it creates and the relationships between those institutions.

The primary purpose of the Constitution is to establish a system of government for a nation, a nation encompassing territory and members ("citizens"). A system of government is the process by which citizens establish rules of conduct for persons within the territory. From these premises, two sorts of structural arguments may follow. First, borrowing from the previous discussion, to be a sovereign nation, a people must have control over their territory. A nation of open borders runs the risk of not being able to govern itself because its sovereignty, to some extent, is in the hands of the other nations of the world. It seems reasonable to believe that the persons who wrote and ratified the Constitution thought (or hoped) they were creating a nation that would be able to take its place among other nations as an equal; one that would possess the powers of sovereignty generally possessed by all other nations. If, as the Supreme Court stated in 1876, it was a well-established "maxim of international law" that all sovereign states had the power to regulate immigration, it is nearly inconceivable that such a power could not have been a part of the Founding Fathers' concept of "nationhood." One might almost conclude that the power was so plain it did not even need to be enumerated; it followed from the very act of creating a sovereign nation.[15] Certainly the powers written into the document support such a conclusion; the power to regulate foreign commerce, prohibit the slave trade after 1808, enter into treaties, and establish a uniform rule of naturalization may all be viewed as manifestations of an underlying principle that one aspect of the sovereign nation created by the Constitution is the power to regulate the admission of aliens.

A second structural argument may be based on the notion of citizenship and the relationship of the citizen to the nation. Citizens, through the process of government, argue about, protect and further values. This discussion of values is essentially a process of national self-definition. The regulation of immigration may be crucial to the process of self-definition. Not only do immigration decisions give citizens the ability to regulate who the participants in the discussion will be, such decisions themselves are an act of self-definition. By deciding whom we permit to enter the country, we say much about who we are as a nation. As the Chinese exclusion laws demonstrate, the process of self-definition can be ugly, racist, short-sighted, wrong. But it is one that every people must possess to be a sovereign people. As Michael Walzer has written:

> [T]he right to choose an admissions policy is * * * not merely a matter of acting in the world, exercising sovereignty, and pursuing national interests. At stake here is the shape of the community that acts in the world, exercises sovereignty, and so on.

---

15. Compare the statement of Justice Holmes that: "It is admitted that sovereign states have inherent power to deport aliens, and seemingly that Congress is not deprived of this power by the Constitution of the United States." *Tiaco v. Forbes,* 228 U.S. 549, 557, 33 S.Ct. 585, 586, 57 L.Ed. 960 (1913).

Admission and exclusion are at the core of communal independence. They suggest the deepest meaning of self-determination.

M. Walzer, *Spheres of Justice: A Defense of Pluralism and Equality* 61–62 (1983). Thus we have identified two kinds of structural arguments to justify the immigration power: one based on *self-preservation,* the other on *self-definition.*[16]

The Chinese Exclusion Laws and Equal Protection

In its first major examination of the Fourteenth Amendment, the Supreme Court stated that it "doubt[ed] very much whether any action of a state not directed by way of discrimination against the negroes as a class, or on account of their race, will ever be held to come within the purview of [the equal protection clause]." *Slaughter-House Cases,* 83 U.S. (16 Wall.) 36, 21 L.Ed. 394 (1873). Yet in a case of major importance, decided thirteen years later—and three years before *The Chinese Exclusion Case*—the court held that the equal protection clause protected Chinese against discriminatory enforcement of a San Francisco ordinance regulating laundries. Based on evidence that 200 Chinese laundries had been ordered closed while 80 similar laundries operated by non-Chinese had not, the Court concluded that "no reason for [the discrimination] exists except hostility to the race and nationality to which the petitioners belong." *Yick Wo v. Hopkins,* 118 U.S. 356, 374, 6 S.Ct. 1064, 1073, 30 L.Ed. 220 (1886).

If the Fourteenth Amendment protected Chinese citizens operating laundries in San Francisco, why were not the Chinese exclusion laws similarly invalid—evidencing, as they did, hostility based on race and nationality?

The quick answer is that the Fourteenth Amendment applies only to the actions of the States, and not to the federal government. This formalistic answer, perhaps obvious in the late nineteenth century, may explain why an equal protection challenge was not made in *The Chinese Exclusion Case.*

That answer, while perhaps adequate in 1889, cannot suffice today. In *Bolling v. Sharpe,* 347 U.S. 497, 74 S.Ct. 693, 98 L.Ed. 884 (1954), a companion case to *Brown v. Board of Education,* the court held that segregated schools in the District of Columbia violated the due process clause of the Fifth Amendment. Since *Bolling,* it has been taken as given that "[e]qual protection analysis in the Fifth Amendment area is the same as that under the Fourteenth Amendment."[17] Does this mean that the

16. Neither the necessity nor the structural arguments, at least so far as we have pursued them, have gotten us to a *federal* immigration power. We may be able to justify the existence of such a power somewhere in these United States, but why is it not lodged in those political units with general sovereign powers—the States? A short answer is that the idea of fifty states carrying on fifty immigration policies not controllable by the federal government cannot be supported, at least in the twentieth century. The interference that such policies would have with the established authority of Congress to regulate the economy and conduct foreign affairs is apparent.

17. *Buckley v. Valeo,* 424 U.S. 1, 93, 96 S.Ct. 612, 670, 46 L.Ed.2d 659 (1976) (per curiam). *See generally* Edward S. Corwin's The Constitution and What It Means Today,

Chinese exclusion laws would be invalid today? Not quite. The Supreme Court has made clear that the equal protection component of the Fifth Amendment is only a modest restraint on the federal immigration power. While the Supreme Court has vigorously scrutinized most state legislation that discriminates against aliens, *see, e.g., Graham v. Richardson,* 403 U.S. 365, 91 S.Ct. 1848, 29 L.Ed.2d 534 (1971), it has permitted Congress to "make rules that would be unacceptable if applied to citizens." *Mathews v. Diaz,* 426 U.S. 67, 80, 96 S.Ct. 1883, 1891, 48 L.Ed.2d 478 (1976). This is not to say that notions of equal protection do not apply at all to federal regulations of immigration. It simply means that the Court is not likely to demand that Congress provide a compelling justification for immigration laws that discriminate on the basis of nationality or alienage.

If Congress were to re-enact the Chinese exclusion laws today, could they survive even this lower level of scrutiny? Recall Justice Field's description of the American perceptions of the Chinese as unassimilable and a threat to American workers and political institutions. Are these adequate justifications for the laws? Or, do they represent precisely the kind of racism and stereotyping that the Fourteenth Amendment (as now reflected in the Fifth Amendment) was intended to prevent?

From Exclusion to Deportation

The Chinese Exclusion Case answered the question of whether Congress could *exclude* aliens from the United States. "Exclusion," in immigration law, refers to the process of preventing aliens from making a formal entry into the country. The Chinese exclusion laws not only prevented new Chinese laborers from entering the United States, but also prohibited the *return* of Chinese who had been residents of the United States and had left with certificates valid under 1882 and 1884 laws. Aliens, like these Chinese, who have lawfully obtained permanent residence in this country and have left for a short period of time, are usually referred to as "returning residents" when they seek to re-enter the United States.[18] Does the exclusion of first-time entrants raise distinct constitutional issues from the exclusion of returning residents? It is clear that the court did not think so in *The Chinese Exclusion Case.*

In 1892, Congress again addressed the issue of Chinese immigration. Act of May 5, 1892, Ch. 60, 27 Stat. 25. The 1882 statute had imposed a 10 year "temporary suspension" of the immigration of laborers. The 1892 statute extended the suspension for another 10 years. More importantly, the 1892 Act provided for the *deportation* of aliens residing in the United States. ["Deportation" has two meanings in the immigration laws. Here, it means the removal of aliens already within the United States—in contrast to the "exclusion" of aliens at the border who are seeking entry. "Deportation," in this context, is often referred to as "expulsion." "Deportation" may also be used to mean the physical removal to another

370 (H. Chase and C. Ducat, eds., 14th ed. 1978).

18. The status of "permanent resident alien"—and the right to return—may be lost by an alien who stays outside the United States too long, thereby indicating an intent to abandon residence here. *See* C. Gordon & H. Rosenfield, *Immigration Law and Procedure* § 2.19 [hereinafter cited as "G & R"].

country of any alien whether inside or at the border of the United States. Thus it is sometimes said that aliens who arrive at a port of entry in the United States are "excluded and deported." To avoid confusion, in this book we will use "exclusion" to refer to a denial of entry and "deportation" or "expulsion" to refer to the removal of an alien who has entered the United States.]

The 1892 Act authorized the deportation of any Chinese alien unlawfully in the United States. It further required all Chinese laborers then living in the United States to acquire a "certificate of residence" from the Collector of Internal Revenue within one year after passage of the Act. An alien who failed to do so could "be arrested * * * and taken before a United States judge, whose duty it shall be to order that he be deported from the United States." He could escape deportation only upon a demonstration "that by reason of accident, sickness or other unavoidable cause, he has been unable to procure his certificate, * * * and by at least one credible white witness, that he was a resident of the United States at the time of the passage of [the Act]." 27 Stat. 25–26.

This statute was challenged on numerous constitutional grounds. The Supreme Court's decision follows.

FONG YUE TING v. UNITED STATES

Supreme Court of the United States, 1893.
149 U.S. 698, 13 S.Ct. 1016, 37 L.Ed. 905.

[Three Chinese laborers who were arrested and held by Federal authorities for not having certificates of residence petitioned for writs of habeas corpus. The Circuit Court for the Southern District of New York denied relief, and the Supreme Court consolidated the cases on appeal. The facts of one of the cases are stated.]

* * * On April 11, 1893, the petitioner applied to the collector of internal revenue for a certificate of residence; the collector refused to give him a certificate, on the ground that the witnesses whom he produced to prove that he was entitled to the certificate were persons of the Chinese race and not credible witnesses, and required of him to produce a witness other than a Chinaman to prove that he was entitled to the certificate, which he was unable to do, because there was no person other than one of the Chinese race who knew and could truthfully swear that he was lawfully within the United States on May 5, 1892, and then entitled to remain therein; and because of such unavoidable cause he was unable to produce a certificate of residence, and was now without one. The petitioner was arrested by the marshal, and taken before the judge; and clearly established, to the satisfaction of the judge, that he was unable to procure a certificate of residence, by reason of the unavoidable cause aforesaid; and also established, to the judge's satisfaction, by the testimony of a Chinese resident of New York, that the petitioner was a resident of the United States at the time of the passage of the act; but having failed to establish this fact clearly to the satisfaction of the court by at least one credible white witness, as required by the statute, the judge ordered the

petitioner to be remanded to the custody of the marshal, and to be deported from the United States, as provided in the act.

* * *

MR. JUSTICE GRAY, after stating the facts, delivered the opinion of the court.

The general principles of public law which lie at the foundation of these cases are clearly established by previous judgments of this court, and by the authorities therein referred to.

* * *

The right of a nation to expel or deport foreigners, who have not been naturalized or taken any steps towards becoming citizens of the country, rests upon the same grounds, and is as absolute and unqualified as the right to prohibit and prevent their entrance into the country.

* * *

The statements of leading commentators on the law of nations are to the same effect.

Vattel says: "Every nation has the right to refuse to admit a foreigner into the country, when he cannot enter without putting the nation in evident danger, or doing it a manifest injury. What it owes to itself, the care of its own safety, gives it this right; and in virtue of its natural liberty, it belongs to the nation to judge whether its circumstances will or will not justify the admission of the foreigner." "Thus, also, it has a right to send them elsewhere, if it has just cause to fear that they will corrupt the manners of the citizens; that they will create religious disturbances, or occasion any other disorder, contrary to the public safety. In a word, it has a right, and is even obliged, in this respect, to follow the rules which prudence dictates." Vattel's Law of Nations, lib. 1, c. 19, §§ 230, 231.

Ortolan says: "The government of each state has always the right to compel foreigners who are found within its territory to go away, by having them taken to the frontier. This right is based on the fact that, the foreigner not making part of the nation, his individual reception into the territory is matter of pure permission, of simple tolerance, and creates no obligation. The exercise of this right may be subjected, doubtless, to certain forms by the domestic laws of each country; but the right exists none the less, universally recognized and put in force. In France, no special form is now prescribed in this matter; the exercise of this right of expulsion is wholly left to the executive power." Ortolan, Diplomatie de la Mer, lib. 2, c. 14, (4th ed.) p. 297.

* * *

The right to exclude or to expel all aliens, or any class of aliens, absolutely or upon certain conditions, in war or in peace, being an inherent and inalienable right of every sovereign and independent nation, essential to its safety, its independence and its welfare, the question now before the court is whether the manner in which Congress has exercised this right in * * * the act of 1892 is consistent with the Constitution.

The United States are a sovereign and independent nation, and are vested by the Constitution with the entire control of international relations, and with all the powers of government necessary to maintain that control and to make it effective. The only government of this country, which other nations recognize or treat with, is the government of the Union; and the only American flag known throughout the world is the flag of the United States.

The Constitution of the United States speaks with no uncertain sound upon this subject. That instrument, established by the people of the United States as the fundamental law of the land, has conferred upon the President the executive power; has made him the commander-in-chief of the army and navy; has authorized him, by and with the consent of the Senate, to make treaties, and to appoint ambassadors, public ministers and consuls; and has made it his duty to take care that the laws be faithfully executed. The Constitution has granted to Congress the power to regulate commerce with foreign nations, including the entrance of ships, the importation of goods and the bringing of persons into the ports of the United States; to establish a uniform rule of naturalization; to define and punish piracies and felonies committed on the high seas, and offences against the law of nations; to declare war, grant letters of marque and reprisal, and make rules concerning captures on land and water; to raise and support armies, to provide and maintain a navy, and to make rules for the government and regulation of the land and naval forces; and to make all laws necessary and proper for carrying into execution these powers, and all other powers vested by the Constitution in the government of the United States, or in any department or officer thereof. And the several States are expressly forbidden to enter into any treaty, alliance or confederation; to grant letters of marque and reprisal; to enter into any agreement or compact with another State, or with a foreign power; or to engage in war, unless actually invaded, or in such imminent danger as will not admit of delay.

In exercising the great power which the people of the United States, by establishing a written Constitution as the supreme and paramount law, have vested in this court, of determining, whenever the question is properly brought before it, whether the acts of the legislature or of the executive are consistent with the Constitution, it behooves the court to be careful that it does not undertake to pass upon political questions, the final decision of which has been committed by the Constitution to the other departments of the government.

* * *

The power to exclude aliens and the power to expel them rest upon one foundation, are derived from one source, are supported by the same reasons, and are in truth but parts of one and the same power.

* * *

Chinese laborers * * * like all other aliens residing in the United States for a shorter or longer time, are entitled, so long as they are permitted by the government of the United States to remain in the country, to the safeguards of the Constitution, and to the protection of the laws, in regard to their rights of person and of property, and to their civil and criminal responsibility. But they continue to be aliens, having taken no steps towards becoming citizens, and incapable of becoming such under the naturalization laws; and therefore remain subject to the power of Congress to expel them, or to order them to be removed and deported from the country, whenever in its judgment their removal is necessary or expedient for the public interest.

* * *

* * * Congress, under the power to exclude or expel aliens, might have directed any Chinese laborer, found in the United States without a certificate of residence, to be removed out of the country by executive officers, without judicial trial or examination, just as it might have authorized such officers absolutely to prevent his entrance into the country. But Congress has not undertaken to do this.

The effect of the provisions of * * * the act of 1892 is that, if a Chinese laborer, after the opportunity afforded him to obtain a certificate of residence within a year, at a convenient place, and without cost, is found without such a certificate, he shall be so far presumed to be not entitled to remain within the United States, that an officer of the customs, or a collector of internal revenue, or a marshal, or a deputy of either, may arrest him, not with a view to imprisonment or punishment, or to his immediate deportation without further inquiry, but in order to take him before a judge, for the purpose of a judicial hearing and determination of the only facts which, under the act of Congress, can have a material bearing upon the question whether he shall be sent out of the country, or be permitted to remain.

* * *

If no evidence is offered by the Chinaman, the judge makes the order of deportation, as upon a default. If he produces competent evidence to explain the fact of his not having a certificate, it must be considered by the judge; and if he thereupon appears to be entitled to a certificate, it is to be granted to him. If he proves that the collector of internal revenue has unlawfully refused to give him a certificate, he proves an "unavoidable cause," within the meaning of the act, for not procuring one. If he proves that he had procured a certificate which has been lost or destroyed, he is to be allowed a reasonable time to procure a duplicate thereof.

The provision which puts the burden of proof upon him of rebutting the presumption arising from his having no certificate, as well as the requirement of proof, "by at least one credible white witness, that he was a resident of the United States at the time of the passage of this act," is within the acknowledged power of every legislature to prescribe the evidence which shall be received, and the effect of that evidence, in the courts of its own government. * * * The competency of all witnesses, without regard to their color, to testify in the courts of the United States, rests on acts of Congress, which Congress may at its discretion modify or repeal. Rev.Stat. §§ 858, 1977. The reason for requiring a Chinese alien, claiming the privilege of remaining in the United States, to prove the fact of his residence here, at the time of the passage of the act, "by at least one credible white witness," may have been the experience of Congress, as mentioned by Mr. Justice Field in *Chae Chan Ping's case,* that the enforcement of former acts, under which the testimony of Chinese persons was admitted to prove similar facts, "was attended with great embarrassment, from the suspicious nature, in many instances, of the testimony offered to establish the residence of the parties, arising from the loose notions entertained by the witnesses of the obligation of an oath." 130 U.S. 598, 9 S.Ct. 627. And this requirement, not allowing such a fact to be proved solely by the testimony of aliens in a like situation, or of the same race, is quite analogous to the provision, which has existed for seventy-seven years in the naturalization laws, by which aliens applying for naturalization must prove their residence within the limits and under the jurisdiction of the United States, for five years next preceding, "by the oath or affirmation of citizens of the United States."   * * *

The proceeding before a United States judge * * * is in no proper sense a trial and sentence for a crime or offence. It is simply the ascertainment, by appropriate and lawful means, of the fact whether the conditions exist upon which Congress has enacted that an alien of this class may remain within the country. The order of deportation is not a punishment for crime. It is not a banishment, in the sense in which that word is often applied to the expulsion of a citizen from his country by way of punishment. It is but a method of enforcing the return to his own country of an alien who has not complied with the conditions upon the performance of which the government of the nation, acting within its constitutional authority and through the proper departments, has determined that his continuing to reside here shall depend. He has not, therefore, been deprived of life, liberty or property, without due process of law; and the provisions of the Constitution, securing the right of trial by jury, and prohibiting unreasonable searches and seizures, and cruel and unusual punishments, have no application.

The question whether, and upon what conditions, these aliens shall be permitted to remain within the United States being one to be determined by the political departments of the government, the judicial department cannot properly express an opinion upon the wisdom, the policy or the justice of the measures enacted by Congress in the exercise of the powers confided to it by the Constitution over this subject.

* * *

In the [case stated above], the petitioner had, within the year, applied to a collector of internal revenue for a certificate of residence, and had been refused it, because he produced and could produce none but Chinese witnesses to prove the residence necessary to entitle him to a certificate. Being found without a certificate of residence, he was arrested by the marshal, and taken before the United States District Judge, and established to the satisfaction of the judge, that, because of the collector's refusal to give him a certificate of residence he was without one by unavoidable cause; and also proved, by a Chinese witness only, that he was a resident of the United States at the time of the passage of the act of 1892. Thereupon the judge ordered him to be remanded to the custody of the marshal, and to be deported from the United States, as provided in that act.

It would seem that the collector of internal revenue, when applied to for a certificate, might properly decline to find the requisite fact of residence upon testimony which, by an express provision of the act, would be insufficient to prove that fact at a hearing before the judge. But if the collector might have received and acted upon such testimony, and did, upon any ground, unjustifiably refuse a certificate of residence, the only remedy of the applicant was to prove by competent and sufficient evidence at the hearing before the judge the facts requisite to entitle him to a certificate. To one of those facts, that of residence, the statute, which, for the reasons already stated, appears to us to be within the constitutional authority of Congress to enact, peremptorily requires at that hearing the testimony of a credible white witness. And it was because no such testimony was produced, that the order of deportation was made.

Upon careful consideration of the subject, the only conclusion which appears to us to be consistent with the principles of international law, with the Constitution and laws of the United States, and with the previous decisions of this court, is that in each of these cases the judgment of the Circuit Court, dismissing the writ of *habeas corpus,* is right and must be

Affirmed.

MR. JUSTICE BREWER dissenting.

I dissent from the opinion and judgment of the court in these cases, and the questions being of importance, I deem it not improper to briefly state my reasons therefor.

I rest my dissent on three propositions: First, that the persons against whom the penalties of * * * the act of 1892 are directed are persons lawfully residing within the United States; secondly, that as such they are within the protection of the Constitution, and secured by its guarantees against oppression and wrong; and, third, that [the Act] deprives them of liberty and imposes punishment without due process of law, and in disregard of constitutional guarantees, especially those found in the Fourth, Fifth, Sixth, and Eighth Articles of the Amendments.

And, first, these persons are lawfully residing within the limits of the United States. [Justice Brewer then discusses the Burlingame Treaty and the 1880 Treaty.]

* * *

While subsequently to [these treaties], Congress passed several acts to restrict the entrance into this country of Chinese laborers, and while the validity of this restriction was sustained in the *Chinese Exclusion case,* 130 U.S. 581, 9 S.Ct. 633, 32 L.Ed. 1068, yet no act has been passed denying the right of those laborers who had once lawfully entered the country to remain, and they are here not as travellers or only temporarily. We must take judicial notice of that which is disclosed by the census, and which is also a matter of common knowledge. There are 100,000 and more of these persons living in this country, making their homes here, and striving by their labor to earn a livelihood. They are not travellers, but resident aliens.

But, further, [the Act] recognizes the fact of a lawful residence, and only applies to those who have such; for the parties * * * to be reached by its provisions, are "Chinese laborers within the limits of the United States at the time of the passage of this act, and who are entitled to remain in the United States." These appellants, therefore, are lawfully within the United States, and are here as residents, and not as travellers. They have lived in this country, respectively, since 1879, 1877, and 1874—almost as long a time as some of those who were members of the Congress that passed this act of punishment and expulsion.

That those who have become domiciled in a country are entitled to a more distinct and larger measure of protection than those who are simply passing through, or temporarily in it, has long been recognized by the law of nations. * * *

* * *

* * * [W]hatever rights a resident alien might have in any other nation, here he is within the express protection of the Constitution, especially in respect to those guarantees which are declared in the original amendments. It has been repeated so often as to become axiomatic, that this government is one of enumerated and delegated powers, and, as declared in Article 10 of the amendments, "the powers not delegated to the United States by the Constitution, nor prohibited by it to the States, are reserved to the States respectively, or to the people."

It is said that the power here asserted is inherent in sovereignty. This doctrine of powers inherent in sovereignty is one both indefinite and dangerous. Where are the limits to such powers to be found, and by whom are they to be pronounced? Is it within legislative capacity to declare the limits? If so, then the mere assertion of an inherent power creates it, and despotism exists. May the courts establish the boundaries? Whence do they obtain the authority for this? Shall they look to the practices of other nations to ascertain the limits? The governments of other nations have elastic powers—ours is fixed and bounded by a written constitution. The expulsion of a race may be within the inherent powers of a despotism. History, before the adoption of this Constitution, was not destitute of examples of the exercise of such a power; and its framers were familiar with history, and wisely, as it seems to me, they gave to this government no general power to banish. Banishment may be resorted to as punishment for crime; but among the powers reserved to the people and not delegated to the government is that of determining whether whole classes in our midst shall, for no crime but that of their race and birthplace, be driven from our territory.

Whatever may be true as to exclusion, * * * I deny that there is any arbitrary and unrestrained power to banish residents, even resident aliens. What, it may be asked, is the reason for any difference? The answer is obvious. The Constitution has no extraterritorial effect, and those who have not come lawfully within our territory cannot claim any protection from its provisions. And it may be that the national government, having full control of all matters relating to other nations, has the power to build, as it were, a Chinese wall around our borders and absolutely forbid aliens to enter. But the Constitution has potency everywhere within the limits of our territory, and the powers which the national government may exercise within such limits are those, and only those, given to it by that instrument. Now, the power to remove resident aliens is, confessedly, not expressed. Even if it be among the powers implied, yet still it can be exercised only in subordination to the limitations and restrictions imposed by the Constitution. * * *

* * *

* * * [The Act] deprives of "life, liberty, and property without due process of law." It imposes punishment without a trial, and punishment cruel and severe. It places the liberty of one individual subject to the unrestrained control of another. Notice its provisions: It first commands all to register. He who does not register violates that law, and may be punished; and so the section goes on to say that one who has not complied with its requirements, and has no certificate of residence, "shall be deemed and adjudged to be unlawfully within the United States," and then it imposes as a penalty his deportation from the country. Deportation is punishment. It involves first an arrest, a deprival of liberty; and, second, a removal from home, from family, from business, from property. * * *

* * * [I]t needs no citation of authorities to support the proposition that deportation is punishment. Every one knows that to be forcibly taken away from home, and family, and friends, and business, and property, and sent across the ocean to a distant land, is punishment; and that oftentimes most severe and cruel. * * *

But punishment implies a trial: "No person shall be deprived of life, liberty, or property, without due process of law." Due process requires that a man be heard before he is condemned, and both heard and condemned in the due and orderly procedure of a trial as recognized by the common law from time immemorial. * * * And no person who has once come within the protection of the Constitution can be punished without a trial. It may be summary, as for petty offences and in cases of contempt, but still a trial, as known to the common law. * * * But here, the Chinese are * * * arrested and, without a trial, punished by banishment.

Again, it is absolutely within the discretion of the collector to give or refuse a certificate to one who applies therefor. Nowhere is it provided what evidence shall be furnished to the collector, and nowhere is it made mandatory upon him to grant a certificate on the production of such evidence. It cannot be due process of law to impose punishment on any person for failing to have that in his possession, the possession of which he can obtain only at the arbitrary and unregulated discretion of any official. It will not do to say that the presumption is that the official will act reasonably and not arbitrarily. When the right to liberty and residence is involved, some other protection than the mere discretion of any official is required. * * *

Again, a person found without such certificate may be taken before a United States Judge. What judge? A judge in the district in which the party resides or is found? There is no limitation in this respect. A Chinese laborer in San Francisco may be arrested by a deputy United States marshal, and taken before a judge in Oregon; and when so taken before that judge, it is made his duty to deport such laborer unless he proves his innocence of any violation of the law, and that, too, by at least one credible white witness. And how shall he obtain that witness? No provision is made in the statute therefor. Will it be said that [the Sixth Amendment] * * * gives to the accused a right to have a compulsory process for obtaining witnesses in his favor? The reply is, that if he is entitled to one part of that article, he is entitled to all; and among them is the right to a speedy and public trial by an impartial jury of the State and district. The only theory upon which this proceeding can be sustained is that he has no right to any benefits of [the Sixth Amendment] * * *; and if he has no right thereto, and the statute has made no provision for securing his witnesses or limiting the proceeding to a judge of the district where he resides, the result follows inevitably, as stated, that he may be arrested by any one of the numerous officials named in the statute, and carried before any judge in the United States that such official may select, and, then, unless he proves that which he is given no means of proving, be punished by removal from home, friends, family, property, business, to another country.

It is said that these Chinese are entitled, while they remain, to the safeguards of the Constitution and to the protection of the laws in regard to their rights of person and of property; but that they continue to be aliens, subject to the absolute power of Congress to forcibly remove them. In other words, the guarantees of "life, liberty, and property," named in the Constitution, are theirs by sufferance and not of right. Of what avail are such guarantees?

Once more: Supposing a Chinaman from San Francisco, having obtained a certificate, should go to New York or other place in pursuit of work, and on the way his certificate be lost or destroyed. He is subject to arrest and detention, the cost of which is in the discretion of the court, and judgment of deportation will be suspended a reasonable time to enable him to obtain a duplicate from the officer granting it. In other words, he cannot move about in safety without carrying with him this certificate. The situation was well described by Senator Sherman in the debate in the Senate: "They are here ticket-of-leave men; precisely as, under the Australian law, a convict is allowed to go at large upon a ticket-of-leave, these people are to be allowed to go at large and earn their livelihood, but they must have their tickets-of-leave in their possession." And he added: "This inaugurates in our system of government a new departure; one, I believe, never before practised, although it was suggested in conference that some such rules had been adopted in slavery times to secure the peace of society."

It is true this statute is directed only against the obnoxious Chinese; but if the power exists, who shall say it will not be exercised to-morrow against other classes and other people? If the guarantees of these amendments can be thus ignored in order to get rid of this distasteful class, what security have others that a like disregard of its provisions may not be resorted to? * * *

* * *

In view of this enactment of the highest legislative body of the foremost Christian nation, may not the thoughtful Chinese disciple of Confucius fairly ask, Why do they send missionaries here?

MR. JUSTICE FIELD dissenting.

I also wish to say a few words upon these cases and upon the extraordinary doctrines announced in support of the orders of the court below.

* * *

I had the honor to be the organ of the court in announcing [the] opinion and judgment [of the Court in *The Chinese Exclusion Case*]. I still adhere to the views there expressed in all particulars; but between legislation for the exclusion of Chinese persons—that is, to prevent them from entering the country—and legislation for the deportation of those who have acquired a residence in the country under a treaty with China, there is a wide and essential difference. The power of the government to exclude foreigners from this country, that is, to prevent them from entering it, whenever the public interests in its judgment require such exclusion, has been repeatedly asserted by the legislative and executive departments of our government and never denied; but its power to deport from the country persons lawfully domiciled therein by its consent, and engaged in the ordinary pursuits of life, has never been asserted by the legislative or executive departments except for crime, or as an act of war in view of existing or anticipated hostilities * * *.

[Justice Field then discusses the Alien and Sedition Acts of 1798, which among other things, authorized the President to remove aliens adjudged to be dangerous to the peace and safety of the United States.]

* * *

The duration of the act was limited to two years, and it has ever since been the subject of universal condemnation. In no other instance, until the law before us was passed, has any public man had the boldness to advocate the deportation of friendly aliens in time of peace. I repeat the statement, that in no other instance has the deportation of friendly aliens been advocated as a lawful measure by any department of our government. And it will surprise most people to learn that any such dangerous and despotic power lies in our government—a power which will authorize it to expel at pleasure, in time of peace, the whole body of friendly foreigners of any country domiciled herein by its permission, a power which can be brought into exercise whenever it may suit the pleasure of Congress, and be enforced without regard to the guarantees of the Constitution intended for the protection of the rights of all persons in their liberty and property. Is it possible that Congress can, at its pleasure, in disregard of the guarantees of the Constitution, expel at any time the Irish, German, French, and English who may have taken up their residence here on the invitation of the government, while we are at peace with the countries from which they came, simply on the ground that they have not been naturalized?

* * *

The purpose of [the 1892 law] was to secure the means of readily identifying the Chinese laborers present in the country and entitled to remain, from those who may have clandestinely entered the country in violation of its laws. Those entitled to remain, by having a certificate of their identification, would enable the officers of the government to readily discover and bring to punishment those not entitled to enter but who are excluded. To procure such a certificate was not a hardship to the laborers, but a means to secure full protection to them, and at the same time prevent an evasion of the law.

This object being constitutional, the only question for our consideration is the lawfulness of the procedure provided for its accomplishment, and this must be tested by the provisions of the Constitution and laws intended for the protection of all persons against encroachment upon their rights. Aliens from countries at peace with us, domiciled within our country by its consent, are entitled to all the guaranties for the protection of their persons and property which are secured to native-born citizens. The moment any human being from a country at peace with us comes within the jurisdiction of the United States, with their consent—and such consent will always be implied when not expressly withheld, and in the case of the Chinese laborers before us was in terms given by the treaty referred to—he becomes subject to all their laws, is amenable to their punishment and entitled to their protection. Arbitrary and despotic power can no more be exercised over them with reference to their persons and property, than over the persons and property of native-born citizens. They differ only from citizens in that they cannot vote or hold any public office. As men having our common humanity, they are protected by all the guaranties of the Constitution. To hold that they are subject to any different law or are less protected in any particular than other persons, is in my judgment to ignore the teachings of our history, the practice of our government, and the language of our Constitution. Let us test this doctrine by an illustration. If a foreigner who resides in the country by its consent commits a public offence, is he subject to be cut down, maltreated, imprisoned, or put to death by violence, without accusation made, trial had, and judgment of an established tribunal following the regular forms of judicial procedure? If any rule in the administration of justice is to be omitted or discarded in his case, what rule is it to be? If one rule may lawfully be laid aside in his case, another rule may also be laid aside, and all rules may be discarded. In such instances a rule of evidence may be set aside in one case, a rule of pleading in another; the testimony of eye-witnesses may be rejected and hearsay adopted, or no evidence at all may be received, but simply an inspection of the accused, as is often the case in tribunals of Asiatic countries where personal caprice and not settled rules prevail. That would be to establish a pure, simple, undisguised despotism and tyranny with respect to foreigners resident in the country by its consent, and such an exercise of power is not permissible under our Constitution.   Arbitrary and tyrannical power has no place in our system.   * * *

I utterly dissent from and reject the doctrine expressed in the opinion of the majority, that "Congress, under the power to exclude or expel aliens, might have directed any Chinese laborer found in the United States without a certificate of residence to be removed out of the country by executive officers, without judicial trial or examination, just as it might have authorized such officers absolutely to prevent his entrance into the country."   An arrest in that way for that purpose would not be a reasonable seizure of the person within the meaning of the Fourth Article of the amendments to the Constitution.   It would be brutal and oppressive.   The existence of the power thus stated is only consistent with the admission that the government is one of unlimited and despotic power so far as aliens domiciled in the country are concerned.   According to its theory, Congress might have ordered executive officers to take the Chinese laborers to the ocean and put them into a boat and set them adrift; or to take them to the borders of Mexico and turn them loose there; and in both cases without any means of support; indeed, it might have sanctioned towards these laborers the most shocking brutality conceivable.   I utterly repudiate all such notions, and reply that brutality, inhumanity, and cruelty cannot be made elements in any procedure for the enforcement of the laws of the United States.

The majority of the court have, in their opinion, made numerous citations from the courts and the utterances of individuals upon the power of the government of an independent nation to exclude foreigners from entering its limits, but none, beyond a few loose observations, as to its power to expel and deport from the country those who are domiciled therein by its consent.   * * *

The government of the United States is one of limited and delegated powers.   It takes nothing from the usages or the former action of European governments, nor does it take any power by any supposed inherent sovereignty.   There is a great deal of confusion in the use of the word "sovereignty" by law writers.   Sovereignty or supreme power is in this country vested in the people, and only in the people.   By them certain sovereign powers have been delegated to the government of the United States and other sovereign powers reserved to the States or to themselves.   This is not a matter of inference and argument, but is the express declaration of the Tenth Amendment to the Constitution, passed to avoid any misinterpretation of the powers of the general government.   That amendment declares that "The powers not delegated to the United States by the Constitution, nor prohibited by it to the States, are reserved to the States, respectively, or to the people."   When, therefore, power is exercised by Congress, authority for it must be found in express terms in the Constitution, or in the means necessary or proper for the execution of the power expressed.   If it cannot be thus found, it does not exist.

It will be seen by its provisions that the [Act] recognizes the right of certain Chinese laborers to remain in the United States, but to render null that right it declares that if within one year after the passage of the act any Chinese laborer shall have neglected, failed, or refused to comply with the provisions of the act to obtain a certificate of residence, or shall be found within the jurisdiction of the United States without a certificate of residence, he shall be deemed and adjudged to be unlawfully within the United States, and may be arrested by any United States customs official, collector of internal revenue or his deputies, a United States marshal or his deputies, and taken before a United States judge, whose duty it shall be to order that he be deported from the United States, unless he shall establish clearly to the satisfaction of the judge that by reason of accident, sickness, or other unavoidable cause he has been unable to secure his certificate, and to the satisfaction of the judge by at least one credible white witness that he was a resident of the United States at the time of the passage of the act. His deportation is thus imposed for neglect to obtain a certificate of residence, from which he can only escape by showing his inability to secure it from one of the causes named. That is the punishment for his neglect, and that being of an infamous character can only be imposed after indictment, trial, and conviction. If applied to a citizen, none of the justices of this court would hesitate a moment to pronounce it illegal. Had the punishment been a fine, or anything else than of an infamous character, it might have been imposed without indictment; but not so now, unless we hold that a foreigner from a country at peace with us, though domiciled by the consent of our government, is withdrawn from all the guaranties of due process of law prescribed by the Constitution, when charged with an offence to which the grave punishment designated is affixed.

The punishment is beyond all reason in its severity. It is out of all proportion to the alleged offence. It is cruel and unusual. As to its cruelty, nothing can exceed a forcible deportation from a country of one's residence, and the breaking up of all the relations of friendship, family, and business there contracted. The laborer may be seized at a distance from his home, his family and his business, and taken before the judge for his condemnation, without permission to visit his home, see his family, or complete any unfinished business. Mr. Madison well pictures its character in his powerful denunciation of the alien law of 1798 in his celebrated report upon the resolutions, from which we have cited, and concludes, as we have seen, that *if a banishment of the sort described be not a punishment, and among the severest of punishments, it will be difficult to imagine a doom to which the name can be applied.*

Again, when taken before a United States judge, he is required, in order to avoid the doom declared, to establish clearly to the satisfaction of the judge that by reason of accident, sickness, or other unavoidable cause, he was unable to secure his certificate, and that he was a resident of the United States at the time, *by at least one credible white witness.* Here the government undertakes to exact of the party arrested the testimony of a witness of a particular color, though conclusive and incontestible testimony from others may be adduced. The law might as well have said, that unless the laborer should also present a particular person as a witness who could not be produced, from sickness, absence, or other cause, such as the archbishop of the State, to establish the fact of residence, he should be held to be unlawfully within the United States.

There are numerous other objections to the provisions of the act under consideration. Every step in the procedure provided, as truly said by counsel, tramples upon some constitutional right. Grossly it violates the Fourth Amendment * * *.

* * *

I will not pursue the subject further. The decision of the court and the sanction it would give to legislation depriving resident aliens of the guaranties of the Constitution fills me with apprehensions. Those guaranties are of priceless value to every one resident in the country, whether citizen or alien. I cannot but regard the decision as a blow against constitutional liberty, when it declares that Congress has the right to disregard the guaranties of the Constitution intended for the protection of all men, domiciled in the country with the consent of the government, in their rights of person and property. How far will its legislation go? The unnaturalized resident feels it to-day, but if Congress can disregard the guaranties with respect to any one domiciled in this country with its consent, it may disregard the guaranties with respect to naturalized citizens. What assurance have we that it may not declare that naturalized citizens of a particular country cannot remain in the United States after a certain day, unless they have in their possession a certificate that they are of good moral character and attached to the principles of our Constitution, which certificate they must obtain from a collector of internal revenue upon the testimony of at least one competent witness of a class or nationality to be designated by the government?

What answer could the naturalized citizen in that case make to his arrest for deportation, which cannot be urged in behalf of the Chinese laborers of to-day?

I am of the opinion that the orders of the court below should be reversed, and the petitioners should be discharged.

Mr. Chief Justice Fuller dissenting.

I also dissent from the opinion and judgment of the court in these cases.

If the protection of the Constitution extends to Chinese laborers who are lawfully within and entitled to remain in the United States under previous treaties and laws, then the question whether this act of Congress so far as it relates to them is in conflict with that instrument, is a judicial question, and its determination belongs to the judicial department.

However reluctant courts may be to pass upon the constitutionality of legislative acts, it is of the very essence of judicial duty to do so when the discharge of that duty is properly invoked.

* * *

The argument is that friendly aliens, who have lawfully acquired a domicil in this country, are entitled to avail themselves of the safeguards of the Constitution only while permitted to remain, and that the power to expel them and the manner of its exercise are unaffected by that instrument. It is difficult to see how this can be so in view of the operation of the power upon the existing rights of individuals; and to say that the residence of the alien, when invited and secured by treaties and laws, is held in subordination to the exertion against him, as an alien, of the absolute and unqualified power asserted, is to import a condition not recognized by the fundamental law. Conceding that the exercise of the power to exclude is committed to the political department, and that the denial of entrance is not necessarily the subject of judicial cognizance, the exercise of the power to expel, the manner in which the right to remain may be terminated, rest on different ground, since limitations exist or are imposed upon the deprivation of that which has been lawfully acquired. And while the general government is invested, in respect of foreign countries and their subjects or citizens, with the powers necessary to the maintenance of its absolute independence and security throughout its entire territory, it cannot, in virtue of any delegated power, or power implied therefrom, or of a supposed inherent sovereignty, arbitrarily deal with persons lawfully within the peace of its dominion. But the act before us is not an act to abrogate or repeal treaties or laws in respect of Chinese laborers entitled to remain in the United States, or to expel them from the country, and no such intent can be imputed to Congress. As to them, registration for the purpose of identification is required, and the deportation denounced for failure to do so is by way of punishment to coerce compliance with that requisition. No euphuism can disguise the character of the act in this regard. It directs the performance of a judicial function in a particular way, and inflicts punishment without a judicial trial. It is, in effect, a legislative sentence of banishment, and, as such, absolutely void. Moreover, it contains within it the germs of the assertion of an unlimited and arbitrary power, in general, incompatible with the immutable principles of justice, inconsistent with the nature of our government, and in conflict with the written Constitution by which that government was created and those principles secured.[a]

Notes

1.   Are Exclusion and Deportation Two Sides of the Same Coin?

Justice Gray states that "[t]he right of a nation to expel or deport foreigners, who have not been naturalized or taken any steps towards becoming citizens of the country, rests upon the same ground, and is as absolute and unqualified as the right to prohibit and prevent their entrance into the country." The dissents of Justices Brewer, Field and Fuller argue that the Constitution imposes limits on the *exercise* of the deportation power—limits that may not apply to the exclusion power. But do these Justices doubt the *existence* of the power to deport aliens? *Do* the constitutional sources of the exclusion power equally support a power to deport aliens who have entered the country?

a.   The exclusion of Chinese was extended several times and not repealed until 1943. *See generally* F. Riggs, Pressures on Congress: A Study of Repeal of Chinese Exclusion (1950).

Under the current law, aliens may be deported (1) for conduct occurring prior to their entry (*e.g.*, INA § 241(a)(19) (Nazis)); (2) if they were excludable at time of entry (INA § 241(a)(1)); and (3) for conduct occurring after a lawful entry (*e.g.*, INA § 241(a)(4) (conviction of a crime involving moral turpitude)). Does an adequate description of the basis for the power to exclude aliens necessarily provide a basis for the deportation of the aliens in the third category?

2.   The Dissenters

Justice Field wrote the opinion for the Court in *The Chinese Exclusion Case*—an opinion joined by Justice Brewer. (Chief Justice Fuller joined the Court after *The Chinese Exclusion Case* was decided.) On what grounds were these Justices not convinced that the exclusion case controlled the deportation case?

For Justice Brewer the answer was "obvious": "The Constitution has no extraterritorial effect, and those who have not come lawfully within our territory cannot claim any protection from its provisions. * * * But the Constitution has potency elsewhere within the limits of our territory * * *." Does this adequately distinguish *The Chinese Exclusion Case?* The alien in that case was detained upon a steamship within the port of San Francisco. How can he not be deemed to have been "within our territory"? Nor does Brewer's second ground (unlawful entry) appear persuasive. Chae Chan Ping was a returning resident who had attained prior lawful residence in this country.

Chief Justice Fuller seems to view deportation as different from exclusion because the former entails "deprivation of that which has been lawfully acquired." Does this adequately distinguish *The Chinese Exclusion Case*, which involved the exclusion of a returning resident? Was not Chae Chan Ping being deprived of that which he had lawfully acquired?

We will see repeated efforts to draw a line between exclusion and deportation based on the *location* (Brewer's ground) or *stake* (Fuller's ground) of the alien. To foreshadow what will be a major theme of this book, we do not believe that the "location argument" makes sense. Furthermore, if one takes the "stake argument" seriously—which we do—it will require a fundamental rethinking of both *The Chinese Exclusion Case* and *Fong Yue Ting*. We will address these issues more fully after we have considered the current statutory provisions regarding exclusion and deportation.

3.   Deportation and Punishment: *Wong Wing v. United States*

The majority opinion holds that an "order of deportation is not a punishment for crime"; therefore, "the provisions of the Constitution, securing the right of trial by jury, and prohibiting unreasonable searches and seizures, and cruel and unusual punishments, have no application." Does this mean that Congress could imprison aliens unlawfully residing in the United States without providing them the protections mandated by the Constitution in criminal proceedings?

The Supreme Court answered this question in the landmark case of *Wong Wing v. United States*, 163 U.S. 228, 16 S.Ct. 977, 41 L.Ed. 140

(1896), which examined a section of the 1892 immigration act not considered in *Fong Yue Ting*. The challenged section provided that any Chinese citizen judged to be in the United States illegally "shall be imprisoned at hard labor for a period of not exceeding one year and thereafter removed from the United States." Act of May 5, 1892, Ch. 60, 27 Stat. 25. The Court struck down the provision:

The Chinese exclusion acts operate upon two classes—one consisting of those who came into the country with its consent, the other of those who have come into the United States without their consent and in disregard of the law. Our previous decisions have settled that it is within the constitutional power of Congress to deport both of these classes, and to commit the enforcement of the law to executive officers.

The question now presented is whether Congress can promote its policy in respect to Chinese persons by adding to its provisions for their exclusion and expulsion punishment by imprisonment at hard labor, to be inflicted by the judgment of any justice, judge or commissioner of the United States, without a trial by jury. * * *

We think it clear that detention, or temporary confinement, as part of the means necessary to give effect to the provisions for the exclusion or expulsion of aliens would be valid. Proceedings to exclude or expel would be vain if those accused could not be held in custody pending the inquiry into their true character and while arrangements were being made for their deportation. Detention is a usual feature of every case of arrest on a criminal charge, even when an innocent person is wrongfully accused; but it is not imprisonment in a legal sense.

So, too, we think it would be plainly competent for Congress to declare the act of an alien in remaining unlawfully within the United States to be an offence, punishable by fine or imprisonment, if such offence were to be established by a judicial trial.

But the evident meaning of the section in question, and no other is claimed for it by the counsel for the Government, is that the detention provided for is an imprisonment at hard labor, which is to be undergone before the sentence of deportation is to be carried into effect, and that such imprisonment is to be adjudged against the accused by a justice, judge or commissioner, upon a summary hearing. * * *

* * *

Our views, upon the question thus specifically pressed upon our attention, may be briefly expressed thus: We regard it as settled by our previous decisions that the United States can, as a matter of public policy, by Congressional enactment, forbid aliens or classes of aliens from coming within their borders, and expel aliens or classes of aliens from their territory, and can, in order to make effectual such decree of exclusion or expulsion, devolve the power and duty of identifying and arresting the persons included in such decree, and causing their deportation, upon executive or subordinate officials.

But when Congress sees fit to further promote such a policy by subjecting the persons of such aliens to infamous punishment at hard labor, or by confiscating their property, we think such legislation, to be valid, must provide for a judicial trial to establish the guilt of the accused.

No limits can be put by the courts upon the power of Congress to protect, by summary methods, the country from the advent of aliens whose race or habits render them undesirable as citizens, or to expel such if they have already found their way into our land and unlawfully remain therein. But to declare unlawful residence within the country to be an infamous crime, punishable by deprivation of liberty and property, would be to pass out of the sphere of constitutional legislation, unless provision were made that the fact of guilt should first be established by a judicial trial. It is not consistent with the theory of our government that the legislature should, after having defined an offence as an infamous crime, find the fact of guilt and adjudge the punishment by one of its own agents.

Id. at 234–37, 16 S.Ct. 979–81.[19]

SECTION B.   A BRIEF HISTORY OF IMMIGRATION TO THE UNITED STATES

Writing in the Federalist Papers, John Jay observed: "Providence has been pleased to give this one connected country to one united people—a people descended from the same ancestors, speaking the same language, professing the same religion, attached to the same principles of government, very similar in their manners and customs." The Federalist No. 2. This statement, clearly false when written in 1787, cannot begin to describe the ethnic, racial, religious and political richness that two hundred years of immigration have brought the United States.

Our immigration history has shown America at its best and worst. Literally tens of millions of aliens have been welcomed to our shores. The United States has accepted more refugees for permanent settlement than any other country in the world. Even today, in a time of growing restrictionism here and abroad, the United States admits for permanent residence approximately half a million aliens a year. Unlike many of the Western industrialized nations, it is relatively easy for lawfully admitted aliens to attain citizenship; and any person born in the United States is an American citizen, irrespective of the nationality of her parents.[20]

---

19. As the Court notes, Congress could achieve the same *end* by simply making illegal entry a crime. (Indeed, it has. INA § 275.) But this would clearly invoke a pan-oply of constitutional rights available to defendants in criminal prosecutions.

20. "All persons born or naturalized in the United States, and subject to the jurisdiction thereof, are citizens of the United

But there is also a darker side to the history of American immigration policy—one that often has overshadowed the national symbol of the Statue of Liberty. "The image of the golden door," the United States Commission on Civil Rights has written, "is a tarnished one." United States Commission on Civil Rights, The Tarnished Golden Door: Civil Rights Issues in Immigration 1 (1981). Some federal laws have been blatantly racist, prohibiting immigration from China and Japan and favoring northern and western Europeans over southern and eastern Europeans. Persons have been excluded or deported for their political beliefs. Enforcement of the immigration laws has, at times, violated fundamental notions of fairness and decency.[21] Aliens continue to be scapegoats for many of the problems of American society.[22]

We will explore these conflicting perspectives in the chapters ahead. What follows is a brief history of American immigration. Note particularly the role that economic, political, and international events have played in the formulation of immigration policy.

SELECT COMMISSION ON IMMIGRATION AND REFUGEE POLICY [SCIRP], U.S. IMMIGRATION POLICY AND THE NATIONAL INTEREST

Staff Report 92, 93, 161–216 (1981).

IMMIGRATION AND U.S. HISTORY—THE EVOLUTION OF THE OPEN SOCIETY *

* * * The first inhabitants to the New World, scientists believe, came when the last great Ice Age lowered the level of the Pacific Ocean sufficiently to expose a land bridge between Asia and North America, enabling people to cross the ocean from Asia. Recent evidence suggests that the ancestors of the present-day native Americans settled in North America more than 30,000 years ago and by about 10,000 B.C. had expanded their settlement as far as the tip of South America.

Some 116 centuries later, migration to America occurred again, this time coming from the opposite direction. European monarchs and merchants—whether Spanish, Portuguese, French, English or Dutch—encouraged exploration and then settlement of the newly "discovered" lands of the Americas. The descendants of the occupants of these lands, native American Indians, sometimes joke that the "Indians had bad immigration

States and of the State wherein they reside." U.S. Const. Amend. 14, § 1. The section's reference to "subject to the jurisdiction thereof" is intended to except from citizenship children born to representatives of foreign countries residing in this country. See United States v. Wong Kim Ark, 169 U.S. 649, 18 S.Ct. 456, 42 L.Ed. 890 (1898).

21. See generally J.R. Garcia, Operation Wetback: The Mass Deportation of Mexican Undocumented Workers in 1954 (1980); W. Preston, Jr., Aliens and Dissenters: Federal Suppression of Radicals, 1903–1933, at 208–37 (1965) (describing the Palmer Raids of 1919–20).

22. In April 1982, the INS launched "Operation Jobs," an enforcement program aimed at removing undocumented workers from blue-collar and service jobs in order to provide work for unemployed American workers. Over 5,000 aliens were arrested around the nation. The obvious message was that undocumented alien workers were responsible for high levels of unemployment in the United States.

* Lawrence H. Fuchs and Susan S. Forbes, principal authors. [The footnotes have been renumbered—eds.]

laws." In fact, there were a variety of responses. In some cases, Indian tribes welcomed the new settlers, negotiating treaties, many of which were abrogated by the colonists. In other instances, the Indians fought newcomers who encroached upon their lands. Whatever the response, though, most tribes found themselves overwhelmed by the better-armed Europeans.

The continents of the Western Hemisphere soon became a microcosm of the European continent, peopled in the north by northern and western Europeans and in the south by the Spanish and Portuguese.

Because of the diversity of national origins, it was by no means certain at the time of English settlement that those who spoke the English language would dominate the development of the area that eventually became the United States. To the south of the British-occupied territories were Spanish colonies, to the north were the French, between were Dutch and Swedish settlements. By the second half of the eighteenth century, though, the French had been defeated and had withdrawn from Canada, a modus vivendi of sorts had been established with Spain and the small Dutch and Swedish settlements had been incorporated into the middle colonies of New York, New Jersey, Pennsylvania and Delaware. Hence, it was a certainty by the time of the Revolution that the newly formed republic would be one in which the English influence would prevail.

Despite Anglo-American dominance, however, the colonial period saw the establishment of a tendency towards ethnic pluralism that also was to become a vital part of U.S. life. At least a dozen national groups found homes in the area. Most came in search of religious toleration, political freedom and/or economic opportunity. Many, particularly some ancestors of those who later thought of themselves as "the best people," came as paupers, or as bond servants and laborers who paid for their passage by promising to serve employers, whom they could not leave for a specified number of years. Not all came of their own free will. Convicts and vagrants were shipped from English jails in the seventeenth century. Beginning in Virginia in 1619, some 350,000 slaves were brought from Africa until the end of the slave trade in 1807.

Non-English arrivals were treated with ambivalence, whether they were Dutch, German or even Scotch-Irish Presbyterians from Great Britain. The Germans who came to Pennsylvania, for example, had first learned of the colony through an advertising campaign designed by William Penn to attract their attention and migration. The earliest German settlers came in the hopes of finding liberty of conscience, and once their glowing reports were sent back to Germany, others of their nationality—seeking not only religious toleration but economic opportunity—followed. They were welcomed by many English colonists who applauded their industry and piety. Yet, they were attacked by others who questioned if they would ever assimilate.

This question asked about each successive wave of immigrants was to become a familiar refrain in U.S. history, but the ambivalence towards foreigners was by no means great enough during the colonial period to cause restrictions on immigration. In fact, the Declaration of Indepen-

A. & M.–Immigration Law ACB—5

dence cites as one of the failings of King George III, and thus a justification for revolution, that "He has endeavored to prevent the Population of these States; for that purpose obstructing the Laws for Naturalization of Foreigners; refusing to pass others to encourage their migrations hither, and raising the conditions of new Appropriations of Lands."

After the revolution and the creation of a new government, Americans kept the gates of their new country open for several reasons. The land was vast, relatively rich and sparsely settled. At the time of the first census, taken in 1790, America had a recorded population of 3,227,000— all immigrants or descendants of seventeenth and eighteenth century arrivals.[1] The population density at that time was about 4.5 persons per square mile. Labor was needed to build communities as well as to clear farms on the frontier and push back the Indians. People were needed to build a strong country, strong enough to avoid coming once again under the rule of a foreign power. Moreover, many U.S. citizens thought of their new nation as an experiment in freedom—to be shared by all people, regardless of former nationality, who wished to be free.

Despite all of these reasons for a liberal immigration policy, some doubts still remained about its wisdom. Although people were needed to build the new nation, some feared that the entry of too many aliens would cause disruptions and subject the United States to those foreign influences that the nation sought to escape in independence.

With the signing of the Treaty of Paris in 1783, the United States was officially recognized as an independent nation and the history of official U.S. immigration policy began. * * *

Beginning in 1790, Congress passed a series of acts regulating naturalization. The first act permitted the liberal granting of citizenship to immigrants. After a heated debate—in which the losing side argued not only for strict naturalization requirements but also for barriers against the admission of "the common class of vagrants, paupers and other outcasts of Europe"—Congress required a two-year period of residence and the renunciation of former allegiances before citizenship could be claimed.

By 1795, though, the French Revolution, and the ensuing turmoil in Europe, had raised new fears about foreign political intrigue and influence. A new naturalization act, passed in 1795, imposed more stringent requirements including a five-year residency requirement for citizenship and the renunciation of not only allegiances but titles of nobility. Still, some thought U.S. standards for naturalization were too liberal, and, in 1798, another law was passed that raised the residency requirement to fourteen years. At the same time, the Alien Enemies Act and the Alien Friends Act gave the president powers to deport any alien whom he considered dangerous to the welfare of the nation. One proponent of these laws explained his support: "If no law of this kind was passed, it would be in the power of an individual State to introduce such a number

1. More than 75 percent of this population was of British origin, another eight percent was German and the rest were mainly Dutch, French or Spanish. In addition, approximately a half million black slaves and perhaps as many Native Americans lived within the borders of the United States.

of aliens into the country, as might not only be dangerous, but as might be sufficient to overturn the Government, and introduce the greatest confusion in the country."

The xenophobia that gave rise to the Alien Acts of 1798 passed with the transfer of power from the Federalist to the Republican Party in 1800. The [Alien Friends Act was] permitted to expire,[a] and, in 1802, a new Naturalization Act re-established the provisions of the 1795 Act—what was to become a permanent five-year residency requirement for citizenship. While the Republicans were by no means free of suspicion of foreigners, they were not sufficiently fearful of the consequences of immigration to impose any restraints on the entry or practices of the foreign born. Instead, they pursued a policy that has been aptly described by Maldwyn Allen Jones in his history, *American Immigration:*

> Americans had to some degree reconciled the contradictory ideas that had influenced the thinking of the Revolutionary generation and had developed a clearly defined immigration policy. All who wished to come were welcome to do so; but no special inducements or privileges would be offered them.

For the next 75 years, the federal government did little about the regulation of immigration. It did establish procedures that made the counting of a portion of all immigrants possible. In 1819 Congress passed a law requiring ship captains to supply to the Collector of Customs a list of all passengers on board upon arrival at U.S. ports. This list was to indicate their sex, occupation, age and "country to which they severally belonged." At first only Atlantic and Gulf port information was collected; Pacific ports were added after 1850. Immigration information from Hawaii, Puerto Rico and Alaska dates only from the beginning of the twentieth century, as does the recording of information across land borders with Canada and Mexico.

Although a fully accurate picture of the level of all immigration cannot be made, the data available have enabled historians to sketch the general composition and trend of U.S. immigration. These data show a steadily increasing level of immigration. Immigrants arriving between the end of the Revolutionary War and the passage of the 1819 act are estimated to have totaled about 250,000. During the next ten years, over 125,000 came, and between 1830 and 1860, almost 4.5 million European immigrants arrived in the United States. Never before had the United States had to incorporate so large a number of newcomers into its midst. At first, the new arrivals were greeted with enthusiasm. With a nation to be built, peasants from Norway were as welcome as skilled craftsmen from Great Britain and experienced farmers from western, Protestant Germany. The novelist Herman Melville characterized this spirit:

> There is something in the contemplation of the mode in which America has been settled, that, in a noble breast, should forever extinguish the prejudices of national dislikes.

---

a. The Alien Enemies Act is still on the books. 50 U.S.C. §§ 21–23—eds.

Settled by the people of all nations, all nations may claim her for their own. You cannot spill a drop of American blood without spilling the blood of the whole world....

We are the heirs of all time, and with all nations, we divide our inheritance. On this Western Hemisphere all tribes and people are forming into one federate whole; and there is a future which shall see the estranged children of Adam restored as to the old hearthstone in Eden.

Beginning in the 1830s, though, the composition of the groups entering the United States began to change, and few U.S. residents thought so romantically about the new immigrants.

Waves of Irish during the potato famines and German Catholic immigrants flowed into the country during the European depressions of the 1840s. These Catholics entered a country that was not only overwhelmingly Protestant, but that had been settled by some of the most radical sectarians, who prided themselves on their independence from the Pope's authority as well as from any king's. To begin with, U.S. residents had brought with them from Europe centuries of memories of the Catholic-Protestant strife that had so long dominated that continent's social and political life. Much anti-Irish feeling arose from these roots and was nourished by an oversimplified view of Catholicism which saw Catholics as unable to become good citizens—that is, independent and self-reliant—since they were subject to orders from the church. Even before the mass immigration of Catholics during the 1840s and 1850s, the xenophobic inventor Samuel F.B. Morse warned his fellow Americans:

> How is it possible that foreign turbulence imported by shiploads, that riot and ignorance in hundreds of thousands of human priest-controlled machines should suddenly be thrown into our society and not produce turbulence and excess? Can one throw mud into pure water and not disturb its clearness?

It was easy to blame these new immigrants for many of the problems of the rapidly changing, increasingly urban nineteenth century U.S. society. Hostility against immigrants grew as they were accused of bringing intemperance, crime and disease to the new world. The first Select Committee of the House of Representatives to study immigration concluded:

> that the number of emigrants from foreign countries into the United States is increasing with such rapidity as to jeopardize the peace and tranquility of our citizens, if not the permanency of the civil, religious, and political institutions of the United States....
> Many of them are the outcasts of foreign countries; *paupers, vagrants,* and *malefactors* ... sent hither at the expense of foreign governments, to relieve them from the burden of their maintenance.

A Protestant magazine sounded a further alarm by suggesting that "the floodgates of intemperance, pauperism and crime are thrown open by [immigrants], and if nothing be done to close them, they will carry us back to all of the drunkenness and evil of former times.["]

Out of these fears arose an alliance of those committed to saving the United States from the alleged dangers of immigration. Composed of social reformers who hoped to preserve the nation's institutions, some Protestant evangelicals who hoped to preserve the nation's morals and nativists who hoped to preserve the nation's ethnic purity, they formed associations, such as the secret Order of the Star-Spangled Banner, and political parties, such as the Know-Nothing Party.

These groups were committed to placing a curb on immigration itself and to ensuring that foreigners not be permitted to participate in the nation's political affairs. The naturalization statutes were a principal target of their concern. A pamphlet of the Know-Nothing Party warned of the inadequacy of these laws in protecting the nation against fraud:

> It is notorious that the grossest frauds have been practiced on our naturalization laws, and that thousands and tens of thousands have every year deposited votes in the ballot box, who could not only not read them, and knew nothing of the nature of the business in which they were engaged, but who had not been six months in the country, and, in many cases,. hardly six days.

The party hoped to avoid these problems by eliminating the participation of even naturalized immigrants in the political process.

At its most vitriolic, nativism manifested itself in anti-Catholic riots against the Irish. New York, Philadelphia and Boston all saw such violence. Exposes revealing the "truth" about Catholic nunneries—that they were dens of iniquity and vice—precipitated the burning of convents and Catholic churches.[2] Although strident, nativist voices did not prevail. Attacks on ethnic groups usually came from a small, but vocal portion of the population that by no means represented the wishes of all Americans. Even during the times in which nativism reached its peak, there continued to be a variety of potent support for unlimited immigration. Economic needs, reinforced by the ideals of opportunity and freedom that were more deeply rooted in the country than was the anti-Catholic heritage or fears of foreign takeover, worked against restricting immigration or making requirements for citizenship or voting more stringent.

After the Civil War, the country's desire for immigrants seemed insatiable * * *. Railroads were being laid across the nation, thus opening vast lands for settlement. Labor was needed to gouge the earth for coal and iron, to work in rapidly developing mills and to build cities.

As demand for labor increased, so too did the number of immigrants. From 1860 to 1880, about 2.5 million Europeans entered this country each decade; during the 1880s the number more than doubled to 5.25 million. Another 16 million immigrants entered during the next quarter century, with 1.25 million entering in 1908.

---

2. Not all convent-burning was indicative of anti-Catholicism per se. The burning of the Ursuline Convent at Charlestown, Massachusetts was due mainly to the local brickmakers' resentment of Irish economic competition.

Because the numbers of immigrants were so large, it appeared as if the United States had never before experienced immigration of this sort. Not only was there a change in the size of the flow, there was also a change, once more, in the source of immigration. The migration before the 1880s had been overwhelmingly from northern and western Europe. Even the hated Irish Catholics had come from a country where English was generally spoken and Irish immigration was now traditional. Less than three percent of the foreign-born population of the country had come from eastern or southern Europe. During the 1890s that pattern began to reverse itself, and during the first decade of the twentieth century, about 70 percent came from the new areas.

Just as the Irish and Germans had appeared to Americans to be more "foreign" than English Protestants, so too did the new immigrants appear to be more "foreign" than the old ones. In what may be an inevitable process, the old immigrants had become familiar and, therefore, respectable while the new ones were put under the closest possible scrutiny for signs of dissimilitude. And, alien characteristics are exactly what many Americans found—strange coloring, strange physiques, strange customs and strange languages.

The new immigrants were disliked and feared. They were considered culturally different and incapable of this country's version of self-government, and not because of their backgrounds but because they were thought to be biologically and inherently inferior. Influential professors of history, sociology and eugenics taught that some races could never become what came to be called "100 percent American."

A leading academic proponent of nativism, Edward Ross, wrote of Jews that they are "the polar opposite of our pioneer breed. Undersized and weak muscled, they shun bodily activity and are exceedingly sensitive to pain." He also lamented that it was impossible to make Boy Scouts out of them. Italians, he noted, "possess a distressing frequency of low foreheads, open mouths, weak chins, poor features, skewed faces, small or knobby crania and backless heads." According to Ross, Italians "lack the power to take rational care of themselves." He concluded that the new immigrants in general were undesirable because they "are beaten men from beaten races, representing the worst failures in the struggle for existence."

Even though * * * mortality statistics do not support the contention that the new immigrants were inherently diseased or biologically inferior, such sentiments began to take their toll. In 1882 the United States passed its first racist, restrictionist immigration law, the Chinese Exclusion Act. From 1860 to 1880, Chinese immigration had grown from 40,000 to over 100,000. Chinese labor had been welcomed to lay railway lines and work in mining. However, with the completion of the transcontinental railroad, which was followed by a depression in the 1870s, intense anti-Chinese feelings developed, particularly in the West, where hardworking and ambitious Chinese had made lives for themselves.

The attacks upon the Chinese often focused upon their inability, in the eyes of their opponents, to assimilate. In 1876, a California State Senate Committee described the Chinese as follows:

> They fail to comprehend our system of government; they perform no duties of citizenship.... They do not comprehend or appreciate our social ideas.... The great mass of the Chinese ... are not amenable to our laws.... They do not recognize the sanctity of an oath.

The supposed criminality of the Chinese was of particular concern. Although the crime statistics of the period do not bear out the accusations, the Chinese were believed to be criminals nevertheless. The state senate committee complained that "the Pacific Coast has become a Botany Bay to which the criminal classes of China are brought in large numbers and the people of this coast are compelled to endure this affliction." The Chinese were especially accused of bringing gambling and prostitution to the region. In 1876, *Scribner's Magazine* noted that "no matter how good a Chinaman may be, ladies never leave their children with them, especially little girls." The legislative committee concluded that "the Chinese are inferior to any race God ever made ... [and] have no souls to save, and if they have, they are not worth saving."

Restrictionists—looking for justifications for closing other types of immigration—also eyed European immigrants as criminally inclined. The Police Commissioner of New York, Theodore Bingham, wrote in the *North American Review* that ["]85 percent of New York criminals were of exotic origin and half of them were Jewish." The author of an article in *Collier's Magazine* labeled Italians as "the most vicious and dangerous" criminals, and he suggested that "80 percent of the limited number of clever thieves" were Jewish.

Again, the crime statistics do not bear out the accusations. * * * The majority of immigrants were arrested for the petty crimes—vagrancy, disorderly conduct, breach of the peace, drunkenness—associated with poverty and difference in values. Immigrants were statistically more likely to commit minor offenses than were the native born who tended to commit property crimes and crimes of personal violence. According to the statistics, there was only one real cause for concern as far as immigrant crime was concerned. The children of the foreign born were the most likely group of all to commit crimes. Their crimes more often resembled those of the native born, though, than those of immigrants. This pattern indicates, more than anything else, that acculturation occurred even in the area of crime.

Despite the known evidence that immigrants were neither inherently criminal nor diseased, nativist arguments emphasizing the inferiority of immigrants were widely accepted. Restrictionists called for legislation that would decide whether the United States would be, as some put it, peopled by British, German and Scandinavian stock, or the new immigrants, "beaten men from beaten races; representing the worst failures in the struggle for existence."

Earlier, nativism had been offset by confidence that the United States had room for all, by a tradition of welcoming the poor and the oppressed and by belief that life in the New World would transform all comers into new Adams and Eves in the American Eden. At the end of the century, however, these ideas were affected by four historical developments:

- The official closing of the U.S. frontier;

- Burgeoning cities and increasing industrialization;

- The persistence of immigrants from southern and eastern Europe in maintaining their traditions; and

- The Catholic or Jewish religion of most of the new immigrants.

In the light of these developments, many Americans began to doubt the country's capacity to welcome and absorb the ever-increasing waves of new immigrants.

Evidence of this new feeling about European immigration could be seen as early as 1891. There had been earlier attempts at controlling the entry of immigrants to the United States—in the Act of 1875 that excluded prostitutes and alien convicts and in the Act of 1882 that barred the entry of lunatics, idiots, convicts and those liable to become a public charge—but these were not as comprehensive as the measure debated that year. One of the principal spokesmen for the bill, Henry Cabot Lodge, of Massachusetts, urged his fellow congressmen to establish new categories of admission to the United States in order to "sift ... the chaff from the wheat" and prevent "a decline in the quality of American citizenship." The 1891 bill added new categories of exclusion that mirrored the concerns about the biological inferiority of immigrants. Those suffering from loathsome or contagious diseases and aliens convicted of crimes involving moral turpitude were barred from entry. The bill also provided for the medical inspection of all arrivals.[3]

Both houses of Congress quickly passed the measure; in the Senate, noted the *New York Times,* "the matter did not even occupy ten minutes." The measure did not go far enough for the quantitative restrictionists, though, since it did not succeed in stemming the flow of new entrants. In their efforts to change immigration policy, these restrictionists began to center their arguments upon one area of regulation—literacy.

As early as 1887, economist Edward W. Bemis gave a series of lectures in which he proposed that the United States prevent the entry of all male adults who were unable to read and write their own language. He argued that such a regulation would reduce by half or more those who were poor and undereducated. As awareness of the nature of the new immigration grew, nativists realized that a literacy test would also discriminate between desirable and undesirable nationalities, not just individuals. The proponents of the test saw it as an effective method of nationality restriction because, unlike the other "proofs" of cultural inferiority, literacy could easily and readily be measured.

---

3. Further grounds of exclusion similar in intent were added in 1903 and 1907.

The new immigrants were often attacked for their attachments to their native languages and what was perceived to be a failure to learn English. In an editorial, the *Nation* magazine proposed that a literacy test was insufficient and that English-language ability should be a requirement of entry. Recognizing that a proposal to make English a requirement of entry would effectively limit immigration to residents of the British Isles, the *Nation* declared in 1891 what other restrictionists believed—that "we are under no obligation to see that all races and nations enjoy an equal chance of getting here."

A literacy bill was first introduced in the Congress in 1895, and under the leadership of Senator Lodge passed both houses. In the last days of his administration, President Cleveland vetoed it, suggesting that the test was hypocritical. The House overrode his veto, but the Senate took no action and the proposal died. In a new wave of xenophobia that followed the assassination of President McKinley by an anarchist mistakenly believed to be an immigrant, a new bill passed the House. Despite the support of the new president, Theodore Roosevelt, the bill's sponsors were unable to gain a favorable vote in the Senate, and it too died.

In 1906, new, comprehensive legislation was proposed that included a literacy test for admission and both a literacy and an English-language requirement for naturalization. The restrictionists, now aided by labor unions wary of competition, were opposed in their endeavors by newly organized ethnic groups as well as business leaders opposed to any elimination of new labor sources. In all but one area, the restrictionists were triumphant. Once again, though, they were unsuccessful in gaining passage of a literacy requirement for either entry or naturalization. English-language proficiency was made a basis for citizenship, though, since most congressmen agreed with Representative Bonynge that "history and reason alike demonstrate that you cannot make a homogeneous people out of those who are unable to communicate with each other in one common language."

In 1907, after the restrictionist attempt to impose a literacy requirement failed, immigration to the United States reached a new high—with the arrival of 1,285,000 immigrants—and an economic depression hit the country. That same year, Congress passed legislation to establish a joint congressional presidential Commission to study the impact of immigrants on the United States. Its members appointed in 1909, the Dillingham Commission, as it is usually known, began its work convinced that the pseudoscientific racist theories of superior and inferior peoples were correct and that the more recent immigrants from southern and eastern Europe were not capable of becoming successful Americans. Although their own data contradicted these ideas, the Commission nevertheless held on to them. The Commission's recommendations were published in 1911 with 41 volumes of monographs on specific subjects, including discussions of immigrants and crime, changes in the bodily form of immigrants and the industrial impact of immigration. In the view of the Commission, their findings all pointed to the same conclusions:

- Twentieth century immigration differed markedly from earlier movements of people to the United States;

- The new immigration was dominated by the so-called inferior peoples—those who were physically, mentally and linguistically different, and, therefore, less desirable than either the native-born or early immigrant groups; and

- Because of the inferiority of these people, the United States no longer benefited from a liberal immigration admissions policy and should, therefore, impose new restrictions on entry.

The Commission endorsed the literacy test as an appropriate mechanism to accomplish its ends.

The demand for large-scale restriction still did not succeed, though, because of the continuing demand for labor, the growing political power of the new immigrant groups and the commitment of the nation's leaders to preserving the tradition of free entry.   In 1912, Congress once more passed a literacy test, but President Taft successfully vetoed it, extolling the "sturdy but uneducated peasantry brought to this country and raised in an atmosphere of thrift and hard work" where they have "contributed to the strength of our people and will continue to do so."   Another veto, this time by President Woodrow Wilson, defeated the work of the restrictionists in 1915.   According to Wilson, the literacy test "seeks to all but close entirely the gates of asylum which have always been open to those who could find nowhere else the right and opportunity of constitutional agitation for what they conceived to be the natural and inalienable rights of men."

After the United States entered World War I in 1917, Congress finally overrode the presidential veto and enacted legislation that made literacy a requirement for entry.   The bill also codified the list of aliens to be excluded, and it virtually banned all immigration from Asia.   The efforts of the restrictionists were finally successful, in large measure because World War I brought nervousness about the loyalty and assimilability of the foreign born to a fever pitch.   The loyalty of immigrants became a hot political issue.   Theodore Roosevelt, for example, stormed against "hyphenated Americans," as he voiced his concern that the country was becoming little more than a "poly-glot boarding house."   A frenzy of activity against German Americans (who only a short while before were thought, along with the English, Scots and Scandinavians to be the best qualified to enter) led to the closing of thriving German-language schools, newspapers and social clubs.   The Governor of Iowa took what may have been the strongest measures; he decreed that the use of any language other than English in public places or over the telephone would be prohibited.

This agitation against the foreign born culminated in two efforts: a movement to "Americanize" immigrants and the development of immigration restrictions based on national origins quotas.   The Americanization movement had had its start in 1915 when two government agencies, operating independently of each other, began assessing the number and efficacy of immigrant education programs operating in the country.   One of these agencies, the Bureau of Naturalization, undertook a letter-writing campaign aimed at learning the degree to which such programs existed. The following summer, the Bureau held a conference in Washington to discuss the information it collected and propose plans for speeding the acculturation of immigrants. In the meantime, though, the Bureau of Education convened its own conference, out of which came the National Committee of One Hundred—prominent citizens organized "for the purpose of assisting in a national campaign for the education of immigrants to fit them for American life and citizenship." With the efforts of these two agencies for guidance, hundreds of communities, private organizations and businesses embarked upon their own programs of Americanization. * * * Lobbying efforts by the Bureau of Education led many states—twenty between 1919 and 1921—to pass legislation establishing Americanization programs to ensure that all immigrants would learn English, the "language of America," as a California commission called it.

Industry also joined the movement. It was frequently asserted that "ignorance of English is a large factor in [job] turnover" and similarly that "there is an important connection between ignorance of English and illiteracy to economic loss." The National Association of Manufacturers encouraged Americanization programs among its members. Henry Ford set up classes within his plants and required attendance of his 5,000 non-English-speaking employees. The International Harvester Company produced its own lesson plans for the non-English-speaking workers in its plants. They clearly taught more than English itself. The first plan read:

I hear the whistle. I must hurry.

I hear the five minute whistle.

It is time to go into the shop....

I change my clothes and get ready to work....

I work until the whistle blows to quit.

I leave my place nice and clean.

I put all my clothes in the locker.

I must go home.

By 1923, the Bureau of Naturalization announced it had 252,808 immigrants in 6,632 citizenship-training courses around the nation. Of these, 4,132 were conducted in public school buildings, 1,256 in homes, 371 in factories and 873 at other locations.

The success of the Americanization program in enrolling immigrants was not enough to satisfy the opponents of immigration. Still convinced that racial differences precluded the full assimilation of the new immigrants, some nativists doubted the ability of Americanization classes to transform immigrants into "100 percent Americans." Some were convinced that all immigrants should be compelled to learn English, and if they could not, should be subject to deportation. Theodore Roosevelt proclaimed that "I would have the government provide that every immigrant be required to learn English, with instruction furnished free. If after five years he has not learned it let him be returned to the country from which he came." To Roosevelt and other nativists, failure to learn English represented some sort of disloyalty or a failure of will; both were clearly reasons for expelling the alien.

As the movement to compel assimilation of those already here progressed, those fearful of the consequences of immigration also sought new restrictions on entry. Restrictionists had learned that the literacy requirement which they believed held so much promise was not succeeding as had been expected. Immigration from southern and eastern Europe continued. The literacy rates of European countries showed increasing numbers eligible for entry; Italy even established schools in areas of high emigration to teach peasants to be literate so that they could pass the new U.S. test for entry.

To quantitative restrictionists, new measures were needed. The suspension of all immigration—an idea never before of any great appeal in U.S. immigration history—began to gain support. The two groups most associated with it, organized labor and "100 percenters", had little else in common. Labor supported suspension of immigration because of the competition for jobs that occurred with the entry of aliens.

The 100 percenters feared that European people and ideas—whether "bestial hordes" from conquered Germany or the "red menace" of Bolshevism—would contaminate U.S. institutions and culture.

The extreme form of restrictionism proposed by those wishing to ban all immigration gained some support in the House of Representatives, where arguments that postwar immigration was composed largely of Jews who were "filthy, un-American, and often dangerous in their habits" were particularly effective, but failed to pass the Senate Committee on Immigration, which was dominated by easterners with large businesses and ethnic constituencies favorable to immigration.

Instead, the Senate proposed its own legislation to reduce overall immigration and to change the ethnic composition of those permitted entry. The goal of the bill—similar to one originally proposed by Senator Dillingham of the earlier Immigration Commission—was to ensure that northern and western Europeans still had access to the United States while southern and eastern European immigration would be restricted. In 1921, Congress passed and President Harding signed into law the Senate-proposed legislation—a provisional measure which introduced the concept of national origins quotas. This act established a ceiling on European immigration and limited the number of immigrants of each nationality to three percent of the number of foreign-born persons of that nationality resident in the United States at the time of the 1910 census.

This first quota act was extended for two more years, but in 1924 came the passage of what was heralded as a permanent solution to U.S. immigration problems. The Johnson-Reed measure, more commonly known as the National Origins Act,—provided for an annual limit of 150,000 Europeans, a complete prohibition on Japanese immigration, the issuance and counting of visas against quotas abroad rather than on arrival, and the development of quotas based on the contribution of each nationality to the overall U.S. population rather than on the foreign-born population. This law was designed to preserve, even more effectively than the 1921 law, the racial and ethnic status quo of the United States. The national origins concept was also designed, as John Higham wrote in his study of U.S. nativism, *Strangers in the Land,* to give "comfort to the democratic conscience" by counting everyone's ancestors and not just the foreign born themselves.

Recognizing that it would take some time to develop the new quotas, as a stopgap measure the bill provided for the admission of immigrants according to annual quotas of two percent of each nationality's proportion of the foreign-born U.S. population in 1890 until 1927—amended to 1929—when the national origins quotas were established. The use of the 1890 census had been criticized as a discriminatory measure since it seemed to change the rules of European entry solely to lower the number of the so-called "new" immigrants. Use of the 1890 census instead of that of 1910 meant a reduction in the Italian quota from 42,000 to about 4,000, in the Polish quota from 31,000 to 6,000 and in the Greek quota from 3,000 to 100. The proponents of the new legislation argued, however, that use of the 1910 Census was what was really discriminatory since it underestimated the number of visas that should go to those from northern and western Europe.

In preparing its report on the new legislation, the House Committee on Immigration relied heavily on an analysis prepared by John B. Trevor, an aide to Representative Johnson, which gave an estimated, statistical breakdown of the origins of the U.S. population. Trevor also calculated the quotas that would be derived from the use of the 1890 and 1910 census figures on the foreign born. He found that the 1890 census better approximated the national origins of the overall population. Trevor argued that about 12 percent of the U.S. population in 1890 derived from eastern and southern Europe, but on the basis of the 1910 census they were given about 44 percent of the total quota. Using the 1890 census they would have 15 percent of the immigrant numbers. The restrictionists were thus able to turn around the criticism aimed against them by arguing that previous policy favored the "new" immigrants at the expense of the older U.S. stock.

Despite the rhetoric of its supporters—and the exemption of members of the Western Hemisphere from its quotas—the Immigration Act of 1924 clearly represented a rejection of one of [the] longest-lived democratic traditions of the United States, represented by George Washington's view that the United States should ever be "an asylum to the oppressed and the needy of the earth." It also represented a rejection of cultural pluralism as a U.S. ideal. The Commissioner of Immigration could report, one year after this legislation took effect, that virtually all immigrants now "looked" exactly like Americans. Abraham Lincoln's fear that when the nativists gained control of U.S. policy they would rewrite the Declaration of Independence to read: "All men are created equal, except Negroes, and foreigners, and Catholics" seemed to be coming true.

Immigration to the United States suffered still another blow with the Great Depression. During the 1930s, only 500,000 immigrants came to the United States, less than one-eighth of the number that had arrived in the previous decade. Most reduced in number were members of those nations jointly affected by the national origins quotas, and by economic conditions that made impossible their usual pattern of temporary migration for the purposes of work. Temporary migration was a familiar pattern before the imposition of the new legislation. In fact, the prevalence among the "new" immigrants of "birds of passage"—accused of being unstable forces in society, prone to crime and disease and displacing U.S. citizens from jobs—had been one reason for passing restrictive legislation. Temporary migration can be measured through data on emigration, the number of immigrants who leave the country some time after arrival. Throughout most of the early twentieth century, according to official statistics that were collected beginning in 1908, emigration stood at a minimum of 20 percent of immigration and, more commonly, at 30 to 40 percent. In times of depression, the proportion of those who left the country as opposed to those who arrived increased still further; the temporary migrants returned home until conditions in this country improved. In 1932, at the height of the Great Depression, the emigration figure stood at 290 percent of legal immigration. While 35,576 entered the country, over 100,000 left.

Those most tragically affected by the U.S. policy of restrictive immigration (and the economic problems that made U.S. citizens unwilling to alter it) were the refugees who tried to flee Europe before the outbreak of World War II. Although some efforts were made to accommodate them—in 1940 the State Department permitted consuls outside of Germany to issue visas to German refugees because the German quota sometimes remained unfilled—these measures were too few and came too late to help most of the victims of Nazi persecution. In what may be the cruelest single action in U.S. immigration history, the U.S. Congress in 1939 defeated a bill to rescue 20,000 children from Nazi Germany, despite the willingness of U.S. families to sponsor them, on the grounds that the children would exceed the German quota. Those refugees who were able to come in under existing quotas were still subject to all of the other requirements of entry, and a significant number were refused visas because of the public charge provisions in the grounds for exclusion.

Although the quota system of the 1920s stood substantially intact until 1965, U.S. immigration policy was affected by the events of World War II—in particular the shock this country received when it learned most graphically of the fate of the refugees refused entry. Even before that knowledge came, the war challenged long-held notions about U.S. traditions and needs. The United States realized that it once more needed the labor of aliens, for example. This country and Mexico then negotiated a large-scale temporary worker program—the bracero program—designed to fill the wartime employment needs of the United States. Also, in large part because of the alliance of the United States with China, Congress repealed the ban on all Chinese immigration, making it possible for a small number of Chinese once again to enter the country as legal immigrants. Notions of the inherent inferiority of certain groups [were] dispelled when those same groups became allies in the fight against other groups that were proving to be much stronger enemies than expected.

For a short period, the atmosphere was right for a liberalization of immigration policy. At the close of the war, especially after Americans learned of the Nazi atrocities, they seemed united in their appreciation of democracy and their commitment to renewing the U.S. role as a haven for the oppressed. An important first step was taken by President Harry S. Truman who issued a directive in December 1945 admitting 40,000 war refugees. Responding to the plight of U.S. soldiers who had married overseas, Congress passed the "War Brides Act" in 1946, which permitted 120,000 alien wives, husbands and children of members of the armed forces to immigrate to the United States.

In the years following the war, the executive branch continued to take an active role in reshaping immigration policy, even after the advent of the Cold War when public attitudes towards the issue turned more conservative. Most of these efforts, though, were in the area of refugee admissions and did not change the basic structure of U.S. immigration law. President Truman prodded the Congress to pass the Displaced Persons Act in 1948. After its expiration, Congress passed the Refugee Relief Act, under which 214,000 persons were admitted. Designed principally to expedite the admission of refugees fleeing Iron Curtain countries, the Act incorporated safeguards to prevent the immigration of undesirable aliens. Additional measures were passed in 1956 and 1957 to facilitate the entry of Hungarians displaced by the revolution in that country and "refugee-escapees" fleeing Communist or Communist-occupied or dominated countries and countries in the Middle East. In 1960, the Refugee Fair Share Law was passed to provide a temporary program for the admission of World War II refugees and displaced persons who remained in camps under the mandate of the United Nations High Commissioner for Refugees. This legislation gave the Attorney General a specific mandate to use his parole authority to admit eligible refugee-escapees. Although the statute was for a limited period of time, it was more comprehensive than other refugee admission programs and provided an ongoing mechanism to assist refugees.

Despite these strides in developing a policy that permitted refugees to escape from some of the restrictions of the national origins quota requirements, little else in the way of progress occurred in the immigration area until the 1960s. In fact the determination to preserve the quota system was so strong that the refugee measures provided that those entering under those provisions were to be charged to future quotas of their country of origin, as long as these did not exceed 50 percent of the quota of any one year. The refugee acts were seen as complements to the national origins policy; they made the 1924 law more responsive to emergencies but did not significantly alter immigration policy itself.

During the early 1950s, the climate was not ripe for any major liberalizing changes. Concern with communist expansion dominated U.S.

thinking in the early 1950s, and the stand against communism often took the form of opposition to anything foreign. It was a period in which ethnic customs and values could easily be defined as "un-American."

It was in such an atmosphere that congressional hearings on a new immigration law took place. They were conducted under the leadership of Senator Patrick A. McCarran who, with his followers, believed that there were in the United States what he called "indigestible blocks" which would not assimilate into the American way of life. In 1952, the McCarran-Walter bill—passed into law as the Immigration and Nationality Act—consolidated previous immigration laws into one statute, but, in so doing, it preserved the national origins quota system. The Act also established a system of preferences for skilled workers and the relatives of U.S. citizens and permanent resident aliens, and tightened security and screening procedures.

It established a 150,000 numerical limitation on immigration from the Eastern Hemisphere; most Western Hemisphere immigration remained unrestricted, although it established a subquota for immigrants born in the colonies or dependent areas of the Western Hemisphere. Finally, the Act repealed Japanese exclusion and established a small quota for the Asia-Pacific Triangle under which Orientals would be charged.

Congress passed the McCarran-Walter Act over the veto of President Truman who favored the liberalization of the immigration statutes and the elimination of national origins quotas. In his veto message, he strongly reaffirmed U.S. ideals.

> Such a concept [national origins quota] is utterly unworthy of our traditions and ideals. It violates the great political doctrine of the Declaration of Independence that "all men are created equal." It denies the humanitarian creed inscribed beneath the Statue of Liberty proclaiming to all nations: "Give me your tired your poor, your huddled masses, yearning to breathe free...."

President Truman on September 4, 1952 appointed a commission to study and evaluate the immigration and naturalization policies of the United States. On January 1, 1953 the Commission issued its report, *Whom We Shall Welcome,* a statement of support for a nondiscriminatory, liberal immigration policy. The Commission summarized its findings:

> The Commission believes that our present immigration laws—
>
>> flout fundamental American traditions and ideals, display a lack of faith in America's future, damage American prestige and position among other nations, ignore the lessons of the American way of life.
>
> The Commission believes that laws which fail to reflect the American spirit must sooner or later disappear from the statute books.
>
> The Commission believes that our present immigration laws should be completely rewritten.

It was not until 1965 that major changes—some urged as early as the Truman Commission—were actually made in the Immigration and Nationality Act. The election of John F. Kennedy, a descendent of Irish immigrants and the first Catholic president of the United States, marked a turning point in immigration history and focused attention again on immigration policy. As a senator, Kennedy had written *A Nation of Immigrants,* a book denouncing the national origins quota system. Now, as President, he introduced legislation to abolish the 40-year-old formula.

That a Catholic could be elected president signified the extent to which the United States had changed since the 1920s. Across the country came a lessening in anti-Catholic, anti-Asian and anti-Semitic sentiment, in part the result of a new tolerance of racial and ethnic differences stimulated by the civil rights movement. By the mid-1960s, Congress was ready for proposals to liberalize immigration policy, particularly after the assassination of President Kennedy and the Lyndon Johnson presidential landslide of 1964. The effort to eliminate the national origins quotas—begun many years earlier—culminated in the passage of the Immigration and Nationality Act Amendments of 1965.

The amendments accomplished the following:

- Abolished the national origins formula, replacing it with a per-country limit of 20,000 on every country outside the Western Hemisphere, and an overall ceiling of 160,000 for those countries;

- Placed a ceiling of 120,000 on immigration from the Western Hemisphere with no country limits; and

- Established Eastern Hemisphere preferences for close relatives, as well as those who had occupational skills needed in the United States under a seven-category preference system.

In signing the new bill, President Lyndon Johnson said:

from this day forth, those wishing to emigrate into America shall be admitted on the basis of their skills and their close relationship to those already here.

The fairness of this standard is so self-evident ... yet the fact is that for over four decades the immigration policy of the United States has been twisted and has been distorted like a harsh injustice of the national origins quota system ... families were kept apart because a husband or a wife or a child had been born in the wrong place. Men of needed skill and talent were denied entrance because they came from southern or eastern Europe or from one of the developing continents. The system violated the basic principle of American democracy—the principle that values and rewards each man on the basis of his merit ... it has been un-American.

The new amendments, as the President suggested, heralded in a new era in U.S. immigration policy. No longer would one nationality be given a larger quota than another in the Eastern Hemisphere. Preference would be given to reuniting families and to bringing those who had certain desirable or needed abilities. These were to be the goals of immigration policy, and the goal of preserving the racial and ethnic domination of northern and western Europe would no longer be an explicit part of U.S. immigration law.

The United States was, of course, far from free of prejudice at that time, and one part of the 1965 law reflected a change in policy that was in part due to antiforeign sentiments. Prejudice against dark-skinned people, particularly in social and economic life, remained strong. In the years after World War II, as the proportion of Spanish-speaking residents increased, much of the lingering nativism in the United States was directed against those from Mexico and Central and South America. The 1952 law—in keeping with the "Good Neighbor" policy, as it was described by Franklin Delano Roosevelt—had not placed any limitations on immigration from these regions, but by 1965 the pressure for such restrictions had mounted. Giving in to these pressures as a price to be paid for abolishing the national origins system, Congress put into the 1965 amendments a ceiling on immigration from the Western Hemisphere that was designed to close the last remaining open door of U.S. policy. This provision went into effect on July 1, 1968.

The legislation did not accomplish its goal regarding Western Hemisphere immigration without substantial costs. In 1976, the House Judiciary Committee reported on the effect of ending the Good Neighbor open door: a steadily increasing backlog of applicants from Latin America, with prospective immigrants waiting two years for a visa. The Committee, recognizing that the ceiling on Western Hemisphere migration had been part of a compromise in the passage of the 1965 amendments, noted:

> When repealing the national origins quota system, the 89th Congress did not provide an adequate mechanism for implementing the Western Hemisphere ceiling.... The result, completely unforeseen and unintended, has been considerable hardship for intending immigrants from this hemisphere who until 1968 enjoyed the privilege of unrestricted immigration.

In 1976 a new law was passed to make regulations regarding immigration the same for both hemispheres, applying to countries of the Western Hemisphere the 20,000-per-country limit and the preference system that was in effect in the Eastern Hemisphere. The only provision to cause any controversy in the 1976 Act was the application of the per-country ceiling provision to Mexico, which had exceeded the 20,000 limit every year since the enactment of the 1965 amendments. There was considerable support for the idea that special provisions should be permitted for contiguous countries, particularly Mexico, because of the special relationship that had developed as a result of shared borders. President Gerald Ford noted in his statement on signing the 1976 amendments into law that he would submit legislation to Congress to increase the immigration quotas for Mexicans desiring to come to the United States, and President Jimmy Carter endorsed similar legislation in 1977. No action, however, was taken to provide this special treatment for Mexico.

The 1976 law maintained two last vestiges of differential geographic treatment—the separate annual ceilings of 170,000 for the Eastern and

120,000 for the Western Hemisphere and the special ceiling (600 visas per year) assigned to colonies and dependencies. In 1978, new legislation combined the ceilings for both hemispheres into a worldwide total of 290,000 with the same seven-category preference system and per-country limits applied to both.[4] Senator Edward Kennedy described the benefits accruing from the 1978 legislation:

> The establishment of a worldwide ceiling corrects an anomaly in the law, and is a logical step in consequence of the major immigration reforms Congress enacted in 1965—on which I served as floor manager at the time.

> In the long term, this reform makes more flexible the provisions of the preference system, and in the short run it has the likely effect of allowing the use of more nonpreference visas next year for the backlog in the Western Hemisphere and the use of more conditional entry visas for Indochina refugees—a need that is extraordinarily urgent in Southeast Asia today. All this will not involve, however, any increase in the total annual immigration authorized under the law.

Concern about Indochinese conditional entries was an important consideration in the establishment of a worldwide ceiling. The 1965 amendments to the Immigration and Nationality Act had included a permanent statutory authority for the admission of refugees, called the conditional entry provision, patterned after earlier legislation, especially the Fair Share Refugee Act of 1960. The seventh preference category was designated for these admissions and was allocated six percent of the Eastern Hemisphere ceiling of 170,000 visas, one-half of which could be used for aliens in the United States who were adjusting their status. In 1976 the preference system was extended to the Western Hemisphere, under a separate numerical ceiling with its own proportion of seventh-preference slots. At the time of Senator Kennedy's remarks, it was apparent that Western Hemisphere seventh-preference numbers—applicable only to Cubans who were then unable to leave in sizeable numbers—were unused whereas Eastern Hemisphere demand was great. A worldwide ceiling would permit the visas to go where the refugee need was greatest without reference to hemisphere.

The 1978 amendments did not address the full range of issues raised by U.S. refugee policy, nor were they intended to do so. The working definition of a refugee—originally developed during the Cold War—still included considerations of national origins, even though the rest of immigration policy had dismissed this criteria.

In the Immigration and Nationality Act of 1952, a refugee was defined as a person [sic] who:

> (i) because of persecution or fear of persecution on account of race, religion, or political opinion * * * have fled (I) from any Communist or Communist-dominated country or area, or (II) from any country within the general area of the Middle East, and (ii)

---

4. The colony/dependency ceiling is still in force.

are unable or unwilling to return to such country or area on account of race, religion, or political opinion, and (iii) are not nationals of the countries or areas in which their application for conditional entry is made; or (B) that they are persons uprooted by catastrophic natural calamity as defined by the President who are unable to return to their usual place of abode.

This definition did not permit the entry of those fleeing noncommunist persecution unless they came from the Middle East.

Problems also arose because of the inadequacy of the conditional-entry provisions in dealing with large-scale emergencies. Although when these provisions were enacted Congress intended that they would be the means through which most refugees would be admitted, the parole provision of the Immigration and Nationality Act was actually the major authority for the entrance of large groups of refugees. Under the parole authority, the Attorney General has the discretion to parole any alien into the United States temporarily, under such conditions as the Attorney General may prescribe, in emergencies or for reasons deemed strictly in the public interest. During the 1960s, Cuban refugees were paroled into the United States; between 1962 and the end of May 1979, over 690,000 Cubans entered this country under that authority. In 1975, two parole programs were adopted to aid the resettlement of refugees from Indochina. Other major programs permitted the parole of still more Indochinese between 1976 and 1979. In June 1979 President Carter announced that the number of Indochinese paroled into the country would be set at 14,000 per month. During the same period, the parole of about 35,000 Soviet refugees for the year was also authorized as was the entry of slightly more than a thousand Chilean and Lebanese parolees.

The parole authority had been used in these cases because the conditional entry provisions were too limited to deal with emergencies. Yet reliance on the parole authority seemed to be an inappropriate response to what were recurring situations. Attorney General Griffin B. Bell described one of the major problems with the use of the parole authority in refugee crises: "This . . . has the practical effect of giving the Attorney General more power than the Congress in determining limits on the entry of refugees into the country." He also noted that the use of parole authority prevented the country from giving clear signals to other nations about the extent of U.S. willingness and ability to respond to world refugee needs. Because of the absence of an ongoing policy for refugee admissions, the United States was unable to plan effectively, and, as Bell concluded, "individual refugees [were] hostage to a system that necessitates that their plight build to tragic proportions so as to establish the imperative to act."

The concerns about refugees led to legislative action in 1979 and 1980. The Refugee Act of 1980 was designed to correct the deficiencies of U.S. refugee policy by providing ongoing mechanisms for the admission and aid of refugees. The legislation broadened the definition of refugee by removing the geographic and ideological limitations of the earlier conditional-entry provisions. It also established an allocation of 50,000 for normal refugee admissions, through 1982, and provided procedures through which the President in consultation with Congress could increase this number annually in response to unforeseen circumstances. It further provided for a special conditional entry status with adjustment to permanent resident alien status after one year in the United States.

In addition to making changes in admissions policy, the Refugee Act of 1980 also established the ongoing responsibility of the federal government for the resettlement of refugees accepted under the Act. The legislation included provision for up to 100 percent reimbursement to states for cash and medical assistance provided to refugees during their first 36 months in this country and for grants to voluntary agencies for some of their costs incurred in resettlement.[b]

b. For further general discussion of American immigration history, *see* J. Higham, Strangers in the Land: Patterns of American Nativism, 1860–1925 (1955); M.A. Jones, American Immigration (1960); O. Handlin, The Uprooted (2d ed. 1973); Schuck, *The Transformation of Immigration Law*, 84 Colum.L.Rev. 1 (1984).—eds.

LEVELS AND RATES OF U.S. IMMIGRATION, 1870–1979 [23]

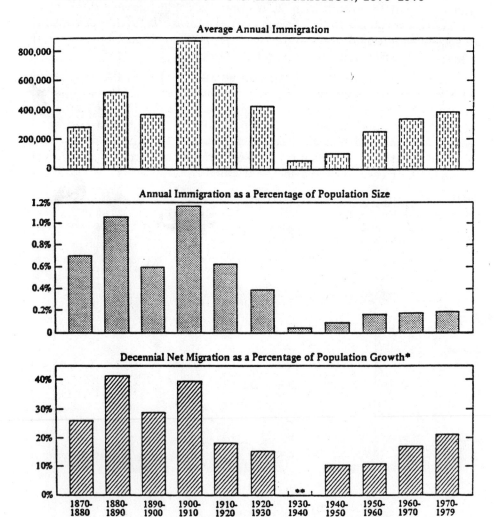

*Decennial net migration as a percentage of population growth equals total decennial population increase minus natural population increase (births and deaths) divided by total population increase.

**Emigration exceeded immigration by 85,000.

SOURCE: "Immigrants: How Many?" Select Commission on Immigration and Refugee Policy, January 1980.

[D2304]

23.   SCIRP, Staff Report 28.

U.S. GROSS IMMIGRATION, 1976–1981 [24]

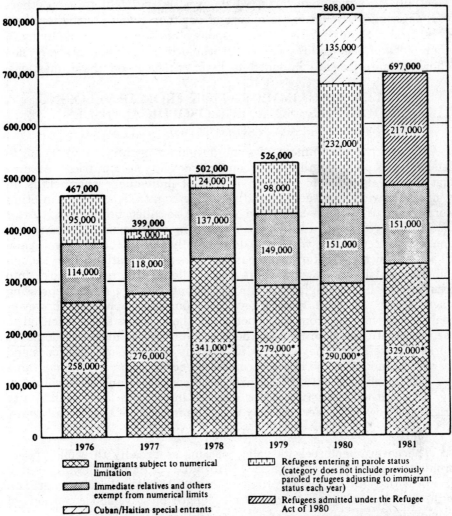

Immigrants subject to numerical limitation

Immediate relatives and others exempt from numerical limits

Cuban/Haitian special entrants

Refugees entering in parole status (category does not include previously paroled refugees adjusting to immigrant status each year)

Refugees admitted under the Refugee Act of 1980

SOURCES: U.S. Immigration and Naturalization Annual Reports, 1976-78 and unpublished INS data, 1979; INS reports of aliens paroled and special entrants admitted, 1976-80; State Department field visa issuance reports and projections based on previous totals in certain categories for 1980 and 1981.

* Includes part of the 145,000 extra numerically limited visas issued as a result of the Silva v. Levi court decision.

[D2305]

SECTION C.   THE EXERCISE OF THE IMMIGRATION POWER: THE MORAL CONSTRAINTS

Having read *The Chinese Exclusion Case* and *Fong Yue Ting*, you are aware that Congress has the constitutional authority to regulate immigration to the United States. This conclusion probably comes as little surprise to you. A much more difficult issue is how Congress should use its power. In beginning to answer that question we believe that it is

24. SCIRP, Staff Report 29.

important first to explore possible moral bases for, or constraints upon, exercise of the immigration power. If our presence in the United States is essentially an accident of birth, what gives us the right to keep others from entering? [25] What is the nature of our moral claim to the territory of the United States? What is our responsibility to needy people living in other parts of the world? To needy people in the United States? The following materials are intended to help you focus on these questions.

TIMOTHY KING, IMMIGRATION FROM DEVELOPING COUNTRIES: SOME PHILOSOPHICAL ISSUES
Ethics, April 1983, 525–31.

Suppose the government of some developed country to be trying to determine its policies on immigration from developing countries. Assume that the immigration in question is that of individuals whose skills, in comparison with both sending and receiving countries, are low—in other words, that we are not concerned with the so-called brain-drain. After inquiry, the government reaches the following conclusions: (1) the migration is into occupations which are domestically among the least well paid; (2) some domestic workers will remain in these occupations even though the incomes they now earn there have fallen. Others will move into occupations slightly higher up the premigration wage scale, depressing wages there; (3) most members of the domestic population, however, benefit economically from migration since they possess skills essential to their occupations which neither the migrants nor the displaced domestic workers possess, and they are now able to buy more cheaply the goods and services produced in the migrant-competing occupations; (4) the migrants are well informed about working and social conditions and come voluntarily; and (5) their departure raises average incomes in their countries of origin and does not lower and may raise the incomes of the poorest there.

* * *

The government sees its policy options as broadly threefold: (1) to prohibit immigration altogether; (2) to allow unlimited flows of immigrants with right to long-term residence; (3) to allow limited migration with tight control over its magnitude, length of stay, and conditions of employment.

Believing that these questions raise philosophical as well as practical administrative and political issues, the government has formed a committee of philosophers to advise it. I shall summarize their discussion * * *.

---

25. "The parents of most individuals who are United States citizens by birth were themselves United States citizens and contributed to the development of the society we currently enjoy. Thus, it may be argued that citizens by birth have a greater entitlement than naturalized citizens and noncitizens to participate in the society their parents created. Yet one cannot accept uncritically the morality of confining people, simply because of the decisions of their ancestors, to the abhorrent conditions prevalent in much of the third world. * * * One's moral doubt grows when one realizes that racist immigration laws in large part determined whose ancestors had the opportunity to enter the United States in the past, * * * and that the disparity in wealth between developed nations and the third world may be due in part to the exploitative economic and military policies pursued by developed nations in the past."

Developments in the Law—Immigration Policy and the Rights of Aliens, 96 Harv.L.Rev. 1286, 1465 n. 13 (1983) [hereinafter cited as *Developments*].

For Philosopher A, the issue was essentially one of global utilitarianism. He argued that once a reasoning human being lifted her sights above pure egoism and recognized the interests of others as well as of herself, she must eventually accept that all of humankind had equal claim to be considered.[3] There could be no objective reason for giving priority to the interests of a particular family, tribe, or nation. If this were accepted there could be little doubt that, however utilities were weighted and aggregated, the consequences of unrestricted immigration were superior to any alternative. It was clear that the number of people gaining from such a policy exceeded those who lost from it, and that while the gainers included some of the rich of the world, the poorest groups also gained.

B said that although he did not regard himself as a utilitarian, he came to the same conclusion. The issue was one of global social justice. Rawls had argued that social justice required maximizing the welfare of the least well-off (subject to the requirement of equal liberty), and although he had confined this principle to justice within nations, suggesting that the principles for international relations would be differently determined, B could see no justification for this.[4] If the [Rawlsian] "veil of ignorance" approach to questions of social justice was an attempt to eliminate morally arbitrary factors from judgments about the justice of particular social arrangements, there could be nothing more arbitrary than the wealth of the society in which one happened to have been born. Representatives of all societies meeting behind such a veil of ignorance would presumably adopt a global "maximin" principle on the same reasoning that Rawls had applied to national questions. Applying such a principle on a global basis, it was clear that the least well-off would benefit most from unrestricted migration.

C agreed that the right policy was unrestricted migration, though he considered the arguments advanced for this by A and B to be unacceptable. Both assumed that government policies could be selected simply by comparing the outcomes of policies in the light of some a priori criterion. But such an approach could lead to the unjustified disregard of the rights of individuals and minorities. In addition it involved looking at a snapshot of the current situation without consideration of the historical processes which had brought it about. Rather, the state should be seen as a protective association for a particular territory with a monopoly over the use of force in that territory and the obligation to protect the rights of everybody there.[5] This did not give it justification to interfere with the rights of individuals to trade with each other, including trade in labor services, even when their trading partners were members of other protective associations. Unrestricted migration ought therefore to be permitted.

---

3. *See, e.g.,* Peter Singer, *The Expanding Circle* (New York: Farrar, Strauss & Giroux, 1980), p. 131. It should be noted, however, that Singer later cautions against making the ethical code of society too heavily dependent on abstract moral reasoning.

4. John Rawls, *A Theory of Justice* (Cambridge, Mass.: Harvard University Press,

1971), pp. 377–79; Brian Barry, *The Liberal Theory of Justice* (Oxford: Oxford University Press, 1973), pp. 128–33; Charles Beitz, *Political Theory and International Relations* (Princeton, N.J.: Princeton University Press, 1979), pp. 127–76.

5. Robert Nozick, *Anarchy, State and Utopia* (New York: Basic Books, 1974).

D came to the same practical conclusion as the three preceding speakers but disagreed with all the arguments so far put forward. All had spoken as though national boundaries were irrelevant to the choice of policy and had maintained that the government should adopt principles which made no distinction between the welfare of its own citizens and those of other countries (except in the case of C, who had argued that it had to protect certain rights of its citizens). This was both unjustifiable and unrealistic. In the first place, it was natural for one to feel a diminishing level of concern for the welfare of others as they became increasingly remote from one's family and immediate friends.[6] Not only did this appeal to intuition; it was also efficient since it often meant that assistance could be given to the needy without cumbersome and expensive schemes of social welfare. A sense of family responsibility, a sense of attachment to small community groups, and beyond these, loyalty to the nation were things to be encouraged rather than opposed.

Second, the question of the extent to which an individual had any moral obligation to come to the assistance of others at some cost to himself was a very difficult one. National boundaries were one contrivance for helping to define this. In general he believed that a nation had a duty to refrain from directly harming another nation but no obligation to assist it if this was detrimental to its own interests.

Third, national governments had responsibilities to their constituents, to consider their welfare rather than to pursue some abstract and little accepted ideals. There could be no doubt that there was nearly universal acceptance of the idea that a nation-state had a right to determine its own immigration policy. Although states had no right to coerce potential emigrants into remaining, they had no duty to admit emigrants from other states. In these circumstances, citizens had a right to expect that the government to which they gave allegiance would promote their own interests, rather than some global ideal.

D therefore argued that the issue collapsed into one of national economic policy. The total income of citizens would be higher with a policy of unrestricted immigration; those who gained, could, in principle, compensate those who lost, and they could not be bribed not to make the change. If the government wished to use fiscal mechanisms to make such transfers, it could. As an aside, however, he noted that he did not favor such transfers. Economic life, he observed, was unfair; trying to compensate piecemeal for some aspects of unfairness while others inevitably remained led governments arbitrarily to favor some individuals compared to others no less deserving.

E accepted most of what D had said but did not think that the issue should be judged by purely economic criteria. These gave greatest weight to those with the greatest economic strength, which was unjust. E would simply submit the issue to a referendum. Since those who gained from

6. Henry Sidgwick, *Methods of Ethics* (1907; reprint ed., London: Macmillan, 1962), p. 246.

the policy of unrestricted migration greatly outnumbered those who lost, one might expect a referendum to reflect this.

F agreed that the interests of the inhabitants of the nation-state rather than the world as a whole should be decisive. In contrast to D, however, this led him to uncompromising opposition to all immigration of the type in question. He argued that membership in a human community was a primary good of the first importance.[7] This carried with it both a degree of security and some mutual obligation to assist fellow members. The world as a whole was not yet such a community; indeed it showed few tendencies in this direction. To foster cohesion within such a community, membership could not simply be kept open to anybody who wished to apply.[8] In the first place, this might destroy the loyalty of those who were hurt by immigration. Second, it would change the character of the community in ways that might be unattractive to existing members even if it was economically advantageous to many of them. It was not certain that a referendum would favor immigration at all, and certainly not unrestricted immigration. In Britain and the United States, there was considerable evidence that continued immigration was unpopular and that the arguments were not simply economic. But in any case a referendum was not the right way to settle the issue, since those who would be hurt by immigration had some right to protection by the rest of the community. Since he did not feel that the world economy could seriously be regarded as the sort of scheme of social cooperation which underlay Rawls's approach to social justice, Rawlsian arguments should be applied at a national level. This would favor a policy of no immigration at all, unless there was a cast-iron policy of redistributing the gains from migration to the losers. Knowing how little income or wealth is actually redistributed by the fiscal system in practice in most countries, he found this highly implausible.

He also pointed out that population growth was much higher in developing countries than in developed countries, and that this contributed to employment problems, low wages, and pressures to migrate. Such population growth was thus imposing a cost to the societies in which it was occurring. Emigration let them pass some of this cost on to the rest of the world. Although many developing countries had policies to try to reduce population growth, these were not universal, and even where they existed on paper, they were often not vigorously implemented. Emigration reduced the pressure on governments to take action, and so increased the burden of population growth for the world as a whole.

Population growth in developing countries raised a practical question which it was impossible to ignore. Seventy-five percent of the world's population lived in developing countries, and it was impossible to reduce significantly population pressure in most countries by emigration from them, no matter how generous developed countries were in allowing immigration. Sooner or later every country would have to control immi-

---

7. Michael Walzer, "The Distribution of Membership," in *Boundaries: National Autonomy and Its Limits*, pp. 1–35.

8. Henry Sidgwick, *The Elements of Politics* (London: Macmillan, 1897), pp. 307–9.

gration; virtually all now do so. Permitting immigration even for a short period meant increasing family ties across national boundaries, and growing expectations of future migration—ties which, sooner or later, would have to be weakened, expectations which would have to be dashed. Those suffering the severance of family ties and dashed expectations might well exceed the number of people benefiting from the migration. But in any case the number of people who could benefit from migration was trivially small in relation to those in need.

G was disturbed by the tendency of previous speakers to take an "all or nothing" stance on the issue. He felt that a good case could be made for limited, but not unrestricted, immigration. He would favor some sort of "guest-worker" program, admitting limited numbers of immigrants on a temporary basis into specific occupations. Although this would have an adverse economic effect on some people, their numbers would be limited, and the community could take steps to help and compensate them. Retraining and other assistance could be provided. In this way the rest of the community could obtain many of the benefits of unlimited immigration, while retaining control over the process. In other words, by permitting discrimination between citizens and noncitizens in the labor market, the country might obtain its goods and services at lower cost, while limiting the harm done to citizens.

H also favored limited migration. He agreed with F on the importance of community membership as a primary good. It was incorrect to see the state as simply an association to provide public goods—a better analogy was a club, or even an extended family. The decision to admit to membership was not to be taken lightly. But having taken it, immigrants should be admitted to full membership, not simply as live-in servants. Otherwise one had an exploited, disenfranchised class of individuals in the community, denied political rights and civil liberties, and subject to continual threat of deportation. But if human rights were truly universal, they should apply to everybody everywhere, not simply in their country of permanent citizenship. Furthermore, the need to enforce two classes of community members, through the actions of both the police and private employers, was bound to invade the privacy of all residents, including citizens. In addition the guest worker was separated from his dependents for long periods of time, causing considerable hardship to both. If guest workers were doing socially necessary work, they should be given the potential to become full members of society.

G retorted that giving full economic rights to immigrants would eliminate many of the alleged gains from migration. One might agree that aliens had a right to due process and basic liberties, without holding that they had the right to vote, or to equality with respect to labor legislation and social security. The economic and social rights set out in the Universal Declaration of Human Rights were much more controversial than, for example, the right not to be tortured.

A, the global utilitarian, said he was particularly disturbed by two of the arguments of later speakers. The notion of the modern nation state as a private club or a tightly knit scheme of social cooperation was absurd.

National boundaries had often been arbitrarily determined by historical events and frequently failed to respect cultural or linguistic groupings. Nations differed enormously in size, power, wealth, and social cohesion. Not infrequently, national legislation forbade local communities, and possibly even private clubs, from discriminating on the basis of race, or national origin. Yet here it was being suggested that it was permissible for a nation, which was a much less tightly knit grouping, to do just that. This sort of argument had frequently been used to justify immigration policies that blatantly discriminated among different ethnic groups—for example White Australia policies, U.S. immigration quotas before 1965, and de facto immigration restrictions in Britain.

The other argument concerned the disparity of population growth rates in developed or developing countries and the inevitability of immigration restrictions. More immigration was not likely to lead to faster growth in the place of origin. There was plenty of evidence that the level of development was a very significant determinant of population growth rates, along with government population policy.[9] So if the effect of migration was to lead to more rapid development of the countries of emigration, this would have a favorable effect on population growth. In either case, this was not likely to be very large in relation to the whole population problem.

However, the fact that the beneficiaries from migration were few in comparison with the size of the world's population and poverty problem was not a good argument for doing nothing. The fact that rescuers at a fire may be only able to rescue 1 percent of those caught in it is not an argument for failing to rescue that 1 percent. The fact that one could not give enough foreign assistance to eliminate world poverty was not an argument for giving none at all. Even if generous immigration policies imposed a cost on every citizen of the host country, he believed that their much more comfortable position would justify the imposition of the cost. But this was not even at issue here, since in general citizens of the host country would be better-off.

BRUCE ACKERMAN, SOCIAL JUSTICE IN THE LIBERAL STATE

89–95 (1980)

[In this work of political philosophy, Professor Ackerman defends modern liberalism as having "its own inner coherence when understood as a sustained effort to achieve a power structure in which all members of a political community can engage in a distinctive form of dialogue with one another." (P. 30.) That "distinctive dialogue," which Ackerman refers to as "Neutral Dialogue," is characterized by several principles, two of which are relevant here: (1) The Rationality Principle: "Whenever anybody questions the legitimacy of another's power, the power holder must respond not by suppressing the questioner but by giving a reason that explains why he is more entitled to the resource than the questioner is."

---

9. *See, e.g.,* Ronald G. Ridker, ed., *Population and Development: The Search for Selec-* *tive Interventions* (Baltimore: Johns Hopkins University Press, 1976).

(P. 4.)   (2) The Neutrality Principle: "No reason is a good reason if it requires the power holder to assert: (a) that his conception of the good is better than that asserted by any of his fellow citizens, *or* (b) that, regardless of his conception of the good, he is intrinsically superior to one or more of his fellow citizens." (P. 11.)   Ackerman uses the device of the Neutral Dialogue—in which power holders are forced to provide neutral and consistent reasons for their control of resources—to generate principles of social justice.   The dialogues below concern the first question that Ackerman must consider: who is entitled to participate in the Neutral Dialogue?   Or, to put the matter more concretely, what moral claims does an individual have to membership (or citizenship) in a liberal society?]

Imagine * * * that there are two spaceships—Explorer and Apollo— engaged in the task of discovery.   * * * The Explorer, however, lands first, and the Commander of that ship gives each member of her landing party a single grain of manna [a] with which to begin life.   A split second later, the Apollonians arrive and demand equal standing in the burgeoning liberal polity:

Apollonian: I want half your manna.

Explorer: Sorry, but I need all of it—and more—if I am to attain my ends in life.

Apollonian: But I need it too!   If personal need is a good reason for your getting manna, why shouldn't it count in my case as well?

Explorer: Do I have to answer that question?

Apollonian: Absolutely.   Rationality requires power wielders to answer the question of legitimacy whenever it is raised.

Explorer: But I want nothing from you!

Apollonian: That doesn't mean you're not exercising power over me. I want half the manna and you're trying to stop me.   That's enough to establish a power relationship requiring justification.

Explorer: Look, I didn't ask you to come.   Why don't you just go away?

Apollonian: I didn't ask you to come either.   Why isn't that an equally good reason for you to go away and leave all the manna for me?

Explorer: Well, if you really must know, I'll come up with a serious answer.

Apollonian: I'm waiting.

Explorer: I should get the manna because I'm a citizen of the liberal state we Explorers have established, and you're not.

Apollonian: Progress at last.   There's only one problem.

Explorer: What's that?

---

a.   "Manna", according to Ackerman's fantasy, is a resource that is "infinitely divisible and malleable, capable of transformation into any physical object a person may desire."   However, "it is impossible to squeeze an infinite quantity of a desired good from a single grain of the miracle substance." (P. 31.)—eds.

Apollonian: * * * [W]hy do you think you qualify as a citizen and I do not?

Explorer: Easy. I landed on the Explorer, hence I must be a citizen of the liberal state we Explorers have established.

Apollonian: That can't be right. After all, there are lots of things that landed on the Explorer that don't qualify as citizens. That hunk of metal, for example. (*Pointing to the spaceship.*)

Explorer: But I'm different from the hunk because I can justify my claims to power.

Apollonian: So can I. Why then don't I qualify as a citizen along with you?

* * *

Explorer: Because I landed in the hunk and you didn't!

Apollonian: Awfully mysterious. This metal hunk doesn't even qualify as a citizen and yet it constitutes the decisive difference between you and me.

Explorer: But you don't deny the fact that, thanks to the Explorer, I got here ahead of you.

Apollonian: I don't deny the fact. I just want to know why the fact should count as a reason justifying your superior power position.

Explorer: Because people who arrive first are better than people who arrive second.

Apollonian: Reason at last! But this would plainly be an un-Neutral reason if given to a citizen of the liberal state.

Explorer: An irrelevant objection. I'm giving this as a reason for *denying* you citizenship. No Neutrality objections please; by its own terms, the [Neutrality] principle limits its protections to "citizens."

Apollonian: And what about your children? Will they ever qualify as citizens?

Explorer: Of course.

Apollonian: But they will arrive even later than I have.

Explorer: Do I have to respond to this point?

Apollonian: Absolutely. * * *

Explorer: Well, if you insist, I declare that the special superiority that I possess by virtue of my first arrival is passed down to my descendants forever and ever, while the special inferiority you possess taints your descendants as well.

Apollonian: And suppose that I deny your claim, asserting instead that true moral superiority resides with those with a high IQ or those with a particularly beautiful body or those who are born black or those—

Explorer: Then what you'd say would simply be wrong. True moral superiority resides with the first inhabitants and their descendants. Only a fool would think otherwise!

Apollonian: Aren't you troubled by the kinds of answers you're giving?

Explorer: An irrelevant question. * * * You've asked some hard questions, but I've answered them. Have I satisfied you?

Apollonian: Not at all. * * *

* * * [D]on't you agree that citizenship is the most fundamental right a person could have in a liberal state?

Explorer: Why do you think so?

Apollonian: After all, it is nothing less than to have conversational rights * * *. And what could be more fundamental than that?

Explorer: A good point.

* * *

Apollonian: If citizenship is the most fundamental right in liberal theory, how can you allow this right to be assigned for reasons you would never tolerate on less important questions?

* * *

Explorer: You know, I really *do* wish you'd go away.

Apollonian: I realize that. But I'm *not* going away. Like it or not, you are exercising power over me, and I shall continue to press my question of legitimacy. So tell me, isn't it obvious that citizenship *is* the most fundamental status question; after all, you're using it as the reason for denying me *all* my rights!

Explorer: Really, I have more important things to do with my time and manna than engage in such twaddle.

Apollonian: *More* important things! Do you imagine that you are some divinity whose claim to dominion over me is self-evident? Why don't you answer my question?

Explorer: Well, frankly, I do find it difficult to deny that citizenship is central. After all, in order to establish my own rights to scarce resources, I am constantly relying on my citizenship status.

Apollonian: Then you must concede the same to me.

Explorer: And if I do not?

Apollonian: Then you must abandon the claim that you Explorers have established an ideal liberal state. For the first principle of such a polity requires each of its citizens to provide rational and consistent answers to the question of legitimacy whenever asked. And you have just failed this minimal test.

* * *

* * * We can make sense of citizenship only by rooting it in more fundamental ideas of political community. In liberal theory, the polity

achieves its distinctiveness by a commitment to a process by which questions are, in principle, followed by rational answers. Nor can answers take any form the power wielders find convenient. Instead, when faced with the question of legitimacy, *the challenged party cannot respond by asserting the moral inferiority of the questioner.* It is this basic idea that is particularized by Neutrality's guarantee to all "citizens" of the liberal state. Yet this basic idea also applies to the conversation that determines the citizenship status of persons capable of participating in a liberal polity. The liberal state is not a private club; it is rather a public dialogue by which each person can gain social recognition of his standing as a free and rational being. I cannot justify my power to exclude you without destroying my own claim to membership in an ideal liberal state.

* * *

But it is time to descend to earth. Quite unthinkingly, we have come to accept the idea that we have the right to exclude nonresidents from our midst. Yet, unless something further can be said, the dialogue between Explorer and Apollonian applies equally to the conversation between a rich American and an impoverished Mexican who swims over the border for a talk. The American can no more declare the intrinsic superiority of the first occupant than the Explorer can. Instead, it is only a very strong empirical claim that can permit the American to justify exclusion of the foreign-born from "his" liberal state.

To simplify the argument, divide the world into two nation-states, the poor East and the rich West. Assume further that Western domestic institutions are organized in a liberalish way while the East is an authoritarian dictatorship in which a small elite explicitly declares its superiority over the masses they exploit. Assume, finally, that as part of its second-best response to this dark reality, the West has adopted a forthcoming immigration policy, admitting a large number, Z, of Easterners on a first-come, first-served basis. Indeed, Z is so large that it strains the capacity of Western institutions to sustain a liberal political conversation. Any more than Z and the West's standing as a liberal society will be endangered; the presence of so many alien newcomers will generate such anxiety in the native population that it will prove impossible to stop a fascist group from seizing political power to assure native control over the immigrant underclass. Nonetheless, the Easterners keep coming at an awesome rate; the scene takes place at the armed Western border:

Easterner: I demand recognition as a citizen of this liberal state.

Western Statesman: We refuse.

Easterner: What gives you the right to refuse me? Do you think I would fail to qualify as a citizen of an ideal liberal state?

Westerner: Not at all.

Easterner: Do you imagine you're better than me simply because you've been born west of this frontier?

Westerner: No. If that were all, I would not hesitate before admitting you.

Easterner: Well, then, what's the trouble?

Westerner: The fact is that we in the West are far from achieving a perfect technology of justice; if we admit more than Z newcomers, our existing institutions will be unable to function in anything but an explicitly authoritarian manner.

Easterner: But why am I being asked to bear the costs of imperfection?

Westerner: Sorry, we're doing everything we can. But Z is the limit on immigrants.

Easterner: But you're not doing *everything*. Why not expel some of your native-born Westerners and make room for me? Do you think they're better than I am?

Westerner: Z is the limit on our assimilative capacity only on the assumption that there exists a cadre of natives familiar with the operation of liberal institutions. If some of the natives were removed from the population, even Z would be too many.

Easterner: So what am I to do? I'll be dead before I get to the front of the line of immigrants.

Westerner: Go back among your own people and build your own liberal state. We'll try to help you out as best we can.

* * *

The *only* reason for restricting immigration is to protect the ongoing process of liberal conversation itself. Can our present immigration practices be rationalized on this ground?

MICHAEL WALZER, SPHERES OF JUSTICE: A DEFENSE OF PLURALISM AND EQUALITY
31–34, 37–40, 45, 47–49, 61–62 (1983)*

The idea of distributive justice presupposes a bounded world within which distributions [take] place: a group of people committed to dividing, exchanging, and sharing social goods, first of all among themselves. That world * * * is the political community, whose members distribute power to one another and avoid, if they possibly can, sharing it with anyone else. When we think about distributive justice, we think about independent cities or countries capable of arranging their own patterns of division and exchange, justly or unjustly. We assume an established group and a fixed population, and so we miss the first and most important distributive question: How is that group constituted?

I don't mean, How *was* it constituted? I am concerned here not with the historical origins of the different groups, but with the decisions they make in the present about their present and future populations. The

* (New York, N.Y.: Basic Books, Inc., 1983). Revised from Michael Walzer, *The Distribution of Membership*, in Peter G. Brown and Henry Shue, eds., Boundaries: National Autonomy and its Limits (Totowa, N.J.: Rowman and Littlefield © 1981). Reprinted by permission.

primary good that we distribute to one another is membership in some human community. And what we do with regard to membership structures all our other distributive choices: it determines with whom we make those choices, from whom we require obedience and collect taxes, to whom we allocate goods and services.

* * *

* * * Since human beings are highly mobile, large numbers of men and women regularly attempt to change their residence and their membership, moving from unfavored to favored environments. Affluent and free countries are, like élite universities, besieged by applicants. They have to decide on their own size and character. More precisely, as citizens of such a country, we have to decide: Whom should we admit? Ought we to have open admissions? Can we choose among applicants? What are the appropriate criteria for distributing membership?

The plural pronouns that I have used in asking these questions suggest the conventional answer to them: we who are already members do the choosing, in accordance with our own understanding of what membership means in our community and of what sort of a community we want to have. Membership as a social good is constituted by our understanding; its value is fixed by our work and conversation; and then we are in charge (who else could be in charge?) of its distribution. But we don't distribute it among ourselves; it is already ours. We give it out to strangers. Hence the choice is also governed by our relationships with strangers—not only by our understanding of those relationships but also by the actual contacts, connections, alliances we have established and the effects we have had beyond our borders. * * *

* * * In a number of ancient languages, Latin among them, strangers and enemies were named by a single word. We have come only slowly, through a long process of trial and error, to distinguish the two and to acknowledge that, in certain circumstances, strangers (but not enemies) might be entitled to our hospitality, assistance, and good will. This acknowledgment can be formalized as the principle of mutual aid, which suggests the duties that we owe, as John Rawls has written, "not only to definite individuals, say to those cooperating together in some social arrangement, but to persons generally." Mutual aid extends across political (and also cultural, religious, and linguistic) frontiers. The philosophical grounds of the principle are hard to specify (its history provides its practical ground). * * *

It is the absence of any cooperative arrangements that sets the context for mutual aid: two strangers meet at sea or in the desert or, as in the Good Samaritan story, by the side of the road. What precisely they owe one another is by no means clear, but we commonly say of such cases that positive assistance is required if (1) it is needed or urgently needed by one of the parties; and (2) if the risks and costs of giving it are relatively low for the other party. Given these conditions, I ought to stop and help the injured stranger, wherever I meet him, whatever his membership or my own. This is our morality; conceivably his, too. It is, moreover, an obligation that can be read out in roughly the same form at the collective level. Groups of people ought to help necessitous strangers whom they somehow discover in their midst or on their path. But the limit on risks and costs in these cases is sharply drawn. I need not take the injured stranger into my home, except briefly, and I certainly need not care for him or even associate with him for the rest of my life. My life cannot be shaped and determined by such chance encounters. Governor John Winthrop, arguing against free immigration to the new Puritan common-wealth of Massachusetts, insisted that this right of refusal applies also to collective mutual aid: "As for hospitality, that rule does not bind further than for some present occasion, not for continual residence." Whether Winthrop's view can be defended is a question that I shall come to only gradually. Here I only want to point to mutual aid as a (possible) external principle for the distribution of membership, a principle that doesn't depend upon the prevailing view of membership within a particu-lar society. The force of the principle is uncertain, in part because of its own vagueness, in part because it sometimes comes up against the internal force of social meanings. And these meanings can be specified, and are specified, through the decision-making processes of the political community.

   * * * [S]o long as members and strangers are, as they are at present, two distinct groups, admissions decisions have to be made, men and women taken in or refused. Given the indeterminate requirements of mutual aid, these decisions are not constrained by any widely accepted standard. That's why the admissions policies of countries are rarely criticized, except in terms suggesting that the only relevant criteria are those of charity, not justice. It is certainly possible that a deeper criticism would lead one to deny the member/stranger distinction. But I shall try, nevertheless, to defend that distinction and then to describe the internal and the external principles that govern the distribution of mem-bership.

* * *

   * * * The same writers who defended free trade in the nineteenth century also defended unrestricted immigration. They argued for perfect freedom of contract, without any political restraint. International society, they thought, should take shape as a world of neighborhoods, with individuals moving freely about, seeking private advancement. In their view, as Henry Sidgwick reported it in the 1890s, the only business of state officials is "to maintain order over [a] particular territory . . . but not in any way to determine who is to inhabit this territory, or to restrict the enjoyment of its natural advantages to any particular portion of the human race." Natural advantages (like markets) are open to all comers, within the limits of private property rights; and if they are used up or devalued by overcrowding, people presumably will move on, into the jurisdiction of new sets of officials.

   Sidgwick thought that this is possibly the "ideal of the future," but he offered three arguments against a world of neighborhoods in the present. First of all, such a world would not allow for patriotic sentiment, and so the "casual aggregates" that would probably result from the free movement of individuals would "lack internal cohesion." Neighbors would be strangers to one another. Second, free movement might interfere with efforts "to raise the standard of living among the poorer classes" of a particular country, since such efforts could not be undertaken with equal energy and success everywhere in the world. And, third, the promotion of moral and intellectual culture and the efficient working of political institutions might be "defeated" by the continual creation of heterogeneous populations. Sidgwick presented these three arguments as a series of utilitarian considerations that weigh against the benefits of labor mobility and contractual freedom. But they seem to me to have a rather different character. The last two arguments draw their force from the first, but only if the first is conceived in non-utilitarian terms. It is only if patriotic sentiment has some moral basis, only if communal cohesion makes for obligations and shared meanings, only if there are members as well as strangers, that state officials would have any reason to worry especially about the welfare of their own people (and of *all* their own people) and the success of their own culture and politics. For it is at least dubious that the average standard of living of the poorer classes throughout the world would decline under conditions of perfect labor mobility. Nor is there firm evidence that culture cannot thrive in cosmopolitan environments, nor that it is impossible to govern casual aggregations of people. As for the last of these, political theorists long ago discovered that certain sorts of regimes—namely, authoritarian regimes—thrive in the absence of communal cohesion. That perfect mobility makes for authoritarianism might suggest a utilitarian argument against mobility; but such an argument would work only if individual men and women, free to come and go, expressed a desire for some other form of government. And that they might not do.

Perfect labor mobility, however, is probably a mirage, for it is almost certain to be resisted at the local level. Human beings, as I have said, move about a great deal, but not because they love to move. They are, most of them, inclined to stay where they are unless their life is very difficult there. They experience a tension between love of place and the discomforts of a particular place. While some of them leave their homes and become foreigners in new lands, others stay where they are and resent the foreigners in their own land. Hence, if states ever become large neighborhoods, it is likely that neighborhoods will become little states. Their members will organize to defend the local politics and culture against strangers. Historically, neighborhoods have turned into closed or parochial communities (leaving aside cases of legal coercion) whenever the state was open: in the cosmopolitan cities of multinational empires, for example, where state officials don't foster any particular identity but permit different groups to build their own institutional structures (as in ancient Alexandria), or in the receiving centers of mass immigration movements (early twentieth century New York) where the country is an open but also an alien world—or, alternatively, a world full of aliens. The case is similar where the state doesn't exist at all or in areas where it doesn't function. Where welfare monies are raised and spent locally, for example, as in a seventeenth-century English parish, the local people will seek to exclude newcomers who are likely welfare recipients. It is only the nationalization of welfare (or the nationalization of culture and politics) that opens the neighborhood communities to whoever chooses to come in.

Neighborhoods can be open only if countries are at least potentially closed. Only if the state makes a selection among would-be members and guarantees the loyalty, security, and welfare of the individuals it selects, can local communities take shape as "indifferent" associations, determined solely by personal preference and market capacity. Since individual choice is most dependent upon local mobility, this would seem to be the preferred arrangement in a society like our own. The politics and the culture of a modern democracy probably require the kind of largeness, and also the kind of boundedness, that states provide. I don't mean to deny the value of sectional cultures and ethnic communities; I mean only to suggest the rigidities that would be forced upon both in the absence of inclusive and protective states. To tear down the walls of the state is not, as Sidgwick worriedly suggested, to create a world without walls, but rather to create a thousand petty fortresses.

The fortresses, too, could be torn down: all that is necessary is a global state sufficiently powerful to overwhelm the local communities. Then the result would be the world of the political economists, as Sidgwick described it—a world of radically deracinated men and women. Neighborhoods might maintain some cohesive culture for a generation or two on a voluntary basis, but people would move in, people would move out; soon the cohesion would be gone. The distinctiveness of cultures and groups depends upon closure and, without it, cannot be conceived as a stable feature of human life. If this distinctiveness is a value, as most people (though some of them are global pluralists, and others only local loyalists) seem to believe, then closure must be permitted somewhere. At some level of political organization, something like the sovereign state must take shape and claim the authority to make its own admissions policy, to control and sometimes restrain the flow of immigrants.

* * *

* * * To say that states have a right to act in certain areas is not to say that anything they do in those areas is right. One can argue about particular admissions standards by appealing, for example, to the condition and character of the host country and to the shared understandings of those who are already members. * * * Decisions of this sort are subject to constraint, but what the constraints are I am not yet ready to say. It is important first to insist that the distribution of membership in American society, and in any ongoing society, is a matter of political decision. The labor market may be given free rein, as it was for many decades in the United States, but that does not happen by an act of nature or of God; it depends upon choices that are ultimately political. What kind of community do the citizens want to create? With what other men and women do they want to share and exchange social goods?

* * *

Can a political community exclude destitute and hungry, persecuted and stateless—in a word, necessitous—men and women simply because they are foreigners? Are citizens bound to take in strangers? Let us assume that the citizens have no formal obligations; they are bound by nothing more stringent than the principle of mutual aid. The principle must be applied, however, not to individuals directly but to the citizens as a group, for immigration is a matter of political decision. Individuals participate in the decision making, if the state is democratic; but they decide not for themselves but for the community generally. And this fact has moral implications. It replaces immediacy with distance and the personal expense of time and energy with impersonal bureaucratic costs. Despite John Winthrop's claim, mutual aid is more coercive for political communities than it is for individuals because a wide range of benevolent actions is open to the community which will only marginally affect its present members * * *. * * * These actions probably include the admission of strangers, for admission to a country does not entail the kinds of intimacy that could hardly be avoided in the case of clubs and families. Might not admission, then, be morally imperative, at least for *these* strangers, who have no other place to go?

* * *

* * * [Wealth, resources and territory] can be superfluous, far beyond what the inhabitants of a particular state require for a decent life (even as they themselves define the meaning of a decent life). Are those inhabitants morally bound to admit immigrants from poorer countries for as long as superfluous resources exist? Or are they bound even longer than that, beyond the limits of mutual aid, until a policy of open admissions ceases to attract and benefit the poorest people in the world? Sidgwick seems to have opted for the first of these possibilities; he proposed a primitive and parochial version of Rawls's difference principle: immigration can be restricted as soon as failure to do so would "interfere materially ... with the efforts of the government to maintain an adequately high standard of life among the members of the community generally—especially the poorer classes." But the community might well decide to cut off immigration even before that, if it were willing to export (some of) its superfluous wealth. * * * [T]hey could share their wealth with necessitous strangers outside their country or with necessitous strangers inside their country. But just how much of their wealth do they have to share? Once again, there must be some limit, short (and probably considerably short) of simple equality, else communal wealth would be subject to indefinite drainage. The very phrase "communal wealth" would lose its meaning if all resources and all products were globally common. * * *

If we stop short of simple equality, there will continue to be many communities, with different histories, ways of life, climates, political structures, and economies. Some places in the world will still be more desirable than others, either to individual men and women with particular tastes and aspirations, or more generally. Some places will still be uncomfortable for at least some of their inhabitants. Hence immigration will remain an issue even after the claims of distributive justice have been met on a global scale—assuming, still, that global society is and ought to be pluralist in form and that the claims are fixed by some version of collective mutual aid. The different communities will still have to make admissions decisions and will still have a right to make them. If we cannot guarantee the full extent of the territorial or material base on which a group of people build a common life, we can still say that the common life, at least, is their own and that their comrades and associates are theirs to recognize or choose.

There is, however, one group of needy outsiders whose claims cannot be met by yielding territory or exporting wealth; they can be met only by taking people in. This is the group of refugees whose need is for membership itself, a non-exportable good. The liberty that makes certain countries possible homes for men and women whose politics or religion isn't tolerated where they live is also non-exportable: at least we have found no way of exporting it. These goods can be shared only within the protected space of a particular state. At the same time, admitting refugees doesn't necessarily decrease the amount of liberty the members enjoy within that space. The victims of political or religious persecution, then, make the most forceful claim for admission. If you don't take me in, they say, I shall be killed, persecuted, brutally oppressed by the rulers of my own country. What can we reply?

* * *

The distribution of membership is not pervasively subject to the constraints of justice. Across a considerable range of the decisions that are made, states are simply free to take in strangers (or not)—much as they are free, leaving aside the claims of the needy, to share their wealth with foreign friends, to honor the achievements of foreign artists, scholars, and scientists, to choose their trading partners, and to enter into collective security arrangements with foreign states. But the right to choose an admissions policy is more basic than any of these, for it is not merely a matter of acting in the world, exercising sovereignty, and pursuing national interests. At stake here is the shape of the community that acts in the world, exercises sovereignty, and so on. Admission and exclusion are at the core of communal independence. They suggest the deepest meaning of self-determination. Without them, there could not be *communities of character,* historically stable, ongoing associations of men and women with some special commitment to one another and some special sense of their common life.

But self-determination in the sphere of membership is not absolute. It is a right exercised, most often, by national clubs or families, but it is held in principle by territorial states. Hence it is subject both to internal decisions by the members themselves (*all* the members, including those who hold membership simply by right of place) and to the external principle of mutual aid. Immigration, then, is both a matter of political choice and moral constraint.   * * *

Discussion

1. In Professor Ackerman's first dialogue, do you think the Explorer has made her best argument in responding to the Apollonian's demand for manna? Imagine a different version of the dialogue.

Apollonian: I want half your manna.

Explorer: Sorry. In order to attain our goals in life, it is necessary for Explorers to adopt an admissions policy that preserves and furthers our culture and political institutions.

Apollonian: But I would like to join your community. Just give me some manna, and I'll show you what a productive member I can be.

Explorer: We Explorers are aware that you might well put the manna to good use. Nor do we question the moral worthiness of your goals. In fact, we might even export some manna to your home country to help you achieve your life plans. But your conception of the good may not be our conception of the good. Communities are more than distribution centers for resources. They are "ongoing associations of men and women with some special commitment to one another and some special sense of their common life." [Walzer, *Spheres of Justice, supra,* at 62.] Thus, while your need for manna is moving, it can grant you no right to enter our community.

Apollonian: But what did you do to deserve the manna you are keeping from me? You did not create it. By refusing me entry to your community you are saying I am not worthy of being a member. You are thus violating a basic tenet of liberalism by denying that I am at least as good as you.

Explorer: Not at all. We respect your right to establish and live in your own community according to whatever principles of membership you agree upon. But surely you can have no right to destroy our right of self-determination simply because your ship got you to our community. In a few years—once we have multiplied our manna and created the society we desire—we will take applications from Apollonians, Centaurians, Venutians, and other foreigners. Apply and we shall see what happens.

Apollonian: You are no liberal.

Explorer: But your liberalism appears inherently contradictory. You are violating your own rules by insisting that we run our community according to your principles. Are you not asserting that your idea of the good is better than ours? Are you not denying us the right to choose the kind of people and community we would like to be?

Does the Explorer sound more persuasive here? Persuasive enough?

2. The Apollonian-Explorer debates may seem a bit artificial because they concern a situation that we rarely see today: the settlement of newly discovered, unoccupied land. Suppose the Apollonians arrived several

generations after the Explorers and in that time the Explorers had developed a thriving economy and rich culture. What different arguments might the Explorers make? Would they be more compelling? Would such arguments support a policy of the Explorers that gave preference to Explorers emigrating from the "old country" over the Apollonians? [26]

Note an ambiguity in Professor Ackerman's dialogue. Do the Apollonians wish to settle on the planet—and join the Explorer community—or simply take some of the manna back to their home country? Is the moral claim to manna (essentially a question of distributive justice) different than the moral claim to membership? Or, to put the question in more practical terms, what is and should be the relationship between American immigration and foreign aid policies? [27]

3. Ackerman asserts that "[t]he *only* reason for restricting immigration is to protect the ongoing process of liberal conversation itself." Would Walzer agree? Do you? To what extent are the positions of Ackerman and Walzer reflected in the earlier discussion of the source of congressional authority to restrict immigration? (Consider particularly the structural justifications based on self-preservation and self-determination.)

26. Consider the defense of the Senate Judiciary Committee for retention of the national origins quota system in the McCarran-Walter Act of 1952:

Without giving credence to any theory of Nordic Superiority, the subcommittee believes that the adoption of the national origins formula was a rational and logical method of numerically restricting immigration in such a manner as to best preserve the sociological and cultural balance in the population of the United States. There is no doubt that it favored the peoples of the countries of northern and western Europe over those of southern and eastern Europe, but the subcommittee holds that the peoples who had made the greatest contribution to the development

of this country were fully justified in determining that the country was no longer a field for further colonization, and henceforth, further immigration would not only be restricted but directed to admit immigrants considered to be more readily assimilable because of the similarity of their cultural background to those of the principal components of our population.

S.Rep. No. 1515, 81st Cong., 2d Sess. 455 (1950).

27. For discussions of normative principles in foreign policy and international distributive justice, *see* C. Beitz, *Political Theory and International Relations* (1979); H. Shue, *Basic Rights: Subsistence, Affluence, and U.S. Foreign Policy* (1980).

Chapter Two

FEDERAL AGENCIES

A person who decides she wants to immigrate to the United States may well start the process by visiting the American official most easily accessible: the consular officer posted to her home country. If she looks carefully at the signs around the entrance of the consulate, she may learn that consuls are officers of the Department of State. And, in short order, if she pursues her application, she will come into contact with a rather bewildering variety of other U.S. agencies.

She will almost surely need an approved visa petition from the Immigration and Naturalization Service (INS), through a process initiated by a close family member already in the United States, or by a prospective employer. If an employer is involved, the Department of Labor will play an important role. If a family member's petition is denied, an appeal may take the case before the Board of Immigration Appeals (BIA), which is not part of INS, but is, like INS, located within the Department of Justice. Once a petition is approved, the action shifts back to the consulate for thorough screening before a visa issues. At the port of entry, she will again encounter the INS in the person of the immigration inspector, who is entitled to rethink the screening determination of the consul. At that stage, a representative of the Public Health Service might perform medical reviews. And there are several other potential governmental players, as well.

In light of these complexities, we will detour briefly before launching our examination of the substantive provisions of the Immigration and Nationality Act (INA), in order to describe the agencies that administer those provisions. You may wish to refer back to this general map later, to help in determining why an issue was decided initially by one agency rather than another, for example, or why a dispute now in the courts went through the particular forms and stages of administrative and judicial review that it followed.

SECTION A. THE DEPARTMENT OF JUSTICE

Take a careful look at section 103 of the INA. That basic enabling provision places the principal authority for administering the Act, as well as enforcing its provisions against lawbreakers, in the Attorney General.

81

But note that administering and enforcing can be quite different under-takings, each calling for distinct skills and orientation. Administering any complex statute (think of the Social Security Act or other public assistance measures) often requires the administrators to counsel affected individuals regarding their possible rights, liabilities and future actions— what forms to file, what benefits or exemptions to seek—and help guide them through the process. In large measure, these functions involve service to the public. Enforcement of a statute, however, particularly one that is frequently violated, might properly call forth an attitude of tough-mindedness and suspicion on the part of the officials involved. The two functions can coexist if the agency is carefully organized and the administrators are sensitive, skillful and well-trained, but there is inevitably tension between the tasks. And since the INA is both highly complex and notoriously violated on a broad scale, the tension here becomes particularly acute. The possibilities for (and reality of) conflicts and confusion of roles based upon these potentially incompatible tasks will often be apparent in the materials we consider throughout this book.[1]

1. THE IMMIGRATION AND NATURALIZATION SERVICE

A few powers relating to immigration are split off and reserved for the Secretary of State and for diplomatic and consular officers under section 104, but the Attorney General retains all residual authority under the statute and is plainly the key figure in its implementation. The Attorney General is authorized under section 103—and inescapably required—to delegate responsibilities to officers of "the Service" (meaning the Immigration and Naturalization Service, INS) and also to other officers or employees of the Department of Justice.[2] The Service, headed by the Commissioner of Immigration and Naturalization, is therefore expressly established by statute, but the INA says little about which of the Attorney General's delegated immigration powers must be lodged there, rather than in other units of the Justice Department. Although most such powers in fact have been delegated to the Service, this statutory flexibility, permitting delegation to subordinates who are not part of INS, has led to some important recent changes, to be discussed below.

Organizationally, INS is a constituent part of the Department of Justice, roughly equivalent, on the organization charts, to the Civil Rights or Antitrust Division, for example, or the Bureau of Prisons. The Com-

---

1. For further exploration of these problems, with recommended changes, see SCIRP, Final Report 238–44 (1981); U.S. Commission on Civil Rights, The Tarnished Golden Door: Civil Rights Issues in Immigration 40–43 (1980).

2. The Service has been part of the Justice Department only since 1940. Early federal regulation of immigration was under the authority of the Secretary of the Treasury, who initially had to act through State officials, usually designated by State governors. In 1891, Congress decided that the divided authority under this scheme was unworkable. Legislation that year created the federal post of Superintendent of Immigration within the Treasury Department. In 1903, these functions were transferred to the Department of Commerce and Labor. When that Department was split in 1913, immigration functions moved to the new Department of Labor. There they remained until a general reorganization plan of 1940 transferred the Immigration and Naturalization Service (as it had been known since 1933) to the Department of Justice. A complete account appears in Congressional Research Service, 96th Cong., 2d Sess., History of the Immigration and Naturalization Service (Comm. Print 1980).

missioner is assisted by four Associate Commissioners, a General Counsel, and a host of other officers located in the INS Central Office in Washington, D.C. That central office is set up to deal almost exclusively with budgetary matters and with broad questions of policy, law, and administration.

INS was once respected as a relatively well-run and efficient administrative agency, even by those who disagreed with many of the policies carried out. But those days are long in the past. As its tasks expanded and the statute and regulations became more complex, the agency's budget and staffing levels did not keep pace. Management systems became badly outmoded, and tales of long delays on routine matters, lost files, and poor morale among employees—often accompanied by testiness (and worse) toward the agency's clientele—became distressingly common.[3] Although INS has introduced several promising improvements in recent years (especially to automate records and rationalize the adjudication system), it still rarely receives the benefit of the doubt in its many controversies—from the public, the Congress, the courts, or even from other parts of the executive branch.

A lawyer handling a matter involving an individual alien almost certainly would not go to the central office in Washington. Such questions are dealt with in the district offices, the basic operating units of the Service. There are thirty-four such offices in this country and three located overseas, each headed by a district director. (The overseas offices have a limited and carefully defined set of functions; most overseas activity relating to immigration falls to the Department of State.) The thirty-four basic district offices cover all the territory of the United States, and there exist suboffices within many of the districts. These U.S. district offices are grouped together into four regions, each headed by a regional commissioner. The regional offices constitute a middle level in the INS hierarchy, and they now primarily carry certain budgeting and administrative responsibilities.

Each district office is divided into units, some concerned principally with enforcement, others with adjudication and related service functions. For example, the investigations staff, consisting of about 1000 non-uniformed officers throughout the 34 districts, concentrates on enforcement in the interior of the country—locating aliens who are illegally present, detecting fraud, investigating smuggling operations, and the like. In addition, there are some 1500 immigration inspectors stationed at roughly 200 ports of entry, about half of these land border posts and the rest international airports and seaports. Their function is to examine the documents, or other evidence of entitlement to enter, presented by arriving aliens and citizens alike. In fiscal year 1978, over 277 million persons were inspected and admitted, 61 percent of them aliens. The number doubtless includes multiple counting of people who made multiple entries.

3. *See* SCIRP, Final Report 238–44; *The Tarnished Golden Door, supra* note 1, at 31–34; General Accounting Office, *Prospects* *Dim for Effectively Enforcing Immigration Laws* 19–24 (1980).

Another key enforcement arm is the Border Patrol, staffed by about 2800 officers as of 1983. It is a component part of INS, but Border Patrol officers are not under the supervision of the district directors. The Border Patrol has its own distinctive geographic and bureaucratic organization pattern, broken down into twenty "sectors" that ring the country. Although the sectors cooperate closely with the district offices, they report to the higher levels of the service through the regional commissioners. The Border Patrol performs enforcement functions exclusively, nearly all of its work focusing on locations between and around designated ports of entry.[4]

As we indicated, much of the district office staff devotes its time to adjudication functions. But in most cases, this is not the kind of "adjudication" that lawyers tend to think of—a formal hearing involving two contestants battling out the issues before a detached decisionmaker. For example, when a grandfather from the old country who has come to visit decides he would like to stay a bit longer with his granddaughter, he must apply to the district office for an extension of stay as a tourist or, to use the technical term, a "temporary visitor for pleasure." If a student here on an F–1 visa wishes to change schools, he must obtain INS approval. The district office is where such approval is sought. When an alien who has come to this country as a nonimmigrant marries a citizen or permanent resident alien and decides to settle here (a frequent occurrence), she must apply to the district office for adjustment of her status to that of a lawful permanent resident. And when a citizen decides to help her brother come from abroad to resettle here as an immigrant, the process does not start overseas where the brother is located. It begins instead with the citizen's filing of a visa petition in the district office having jurisdiction over the citizen's place of residence. The district director will review the petition in order to verify the claimed family relationship and establish prima facie qualification for preference immigration, but of course several other steps must be completed—many of them by U.S. consular officials in the brother's home country—before an immigrant visa will issue.

In each such case (and there are many other examples in the district office), the officer who passes on the petition or request must decide whether the application is complete and bona fide, whether it meets the requirements set forth in the statute and the regulations, and in many cases whether the application further merits a favorable exercise of the discretion that the law vests in the Attorney General, or, by his delegation, in the district director. (Although we will often speak of "the district director" as the decisionmaker on such matters, in fact most such adjudications are further delegated and are actually decided by lower-level immigration examiners.) These decisions amount to adjudication, but much of the time the applicant does not even see in person the officer who will make the decision. The case must instead be made in writing on one of dozens of prescribed forms that work their way through the INS

---

4. For a more complete description of enforcement staffing and operations, including many of the statistics used in the text, *see* SCIRP, Appendix G, at 69–85; Immigration and Naturalization Service, 1982 Annual Report 12–14; G & R § 3.14.

bureaucracy by the thousands each day. In 1982, the adjudications divisions in the district offices received over two million applications and petitions for benefits under the INA.[5]

An article from *The New Yorker* provides some penetrating insights into the operations of an INS district office and the day-to-day practice of immigration law.

CALVIN TRILLIN, MAKING ADJUSTMENTS

The New Yorker, May 28, 1984, at 50–52, 56–57.

[T]he agreement of May 17, 1982 * * * gave immigration lawyers their own line, on one side of the entrance [to the building housing the Houston District Office of INS.] Before that, they had to stand in line with the general public, across from the fish wholesaler. That line is let inside the gate in gulps of twenty or so; on mornings when it happened to have a couple of hundred people in it, a lawyer who hadn't arrived before dawn could spend most of his day outside the building.

* * *

Under the agreement of May 17, 1982, a lawyer can use the special lawyers' line and file papers with a special clerk on one predetermined day of the week, according to the first letter of his last name. Wednesday is for people whose names begin with letters "H" through "P." On Wednesdays, Frank Halim, who studied law in Bombay as well as in New York, is almost always at Immigration. So is Patrick Murphy, a former English professor, who handles immigration matters for Fulbright & Jaworski, one of Houston's huge downtown firms. His business usually concerns the non-immigrant visas available for intracompany transfers— what I heard referred to at times as fat-cat visas. The Wednesday crowd also includes Richard Prinz, one of the few immigration lawyers in Houston who regularly go to court—defending someone accused of smuggling aliens into the country, for instance, or someone the I.N.S. is trying to deport under a provision of the law that permits the deportation of permanent residents who have been convicted of a serious crime.

* * *

A lawyer who has come to Immigration to accompany a client at an interview has another wait ahead of him inside the building, but that wait may be enlivened by the opportunity to buttonhole a passing immigration examiner and press for information on some other case. An immigration lawyer often has a case that he is particularly eager to have moved along quickly. An immigration lawyer always has a case that has been maddeningly, inexplicably delayed. The Houston office is thought of as more efficient than most I.N.S. district offices, but, considering the reputation of most I.N.S. district offices, that is not the sort of compliment that someone might be tempted to frame and hang on the wall. When people who deal regularly with the I.N.S. try to illustrate the depths of its inefficiency and obduracy, they often find themselves at a loss for American institutions to compare it with, and turn to foreign examples—the South Vietnamese

5. 1982 Annual Report, *supra* note 4, at 16.

Army, maybe, or the Bolivian Foreign Service. About the kindest remark that is ever made concerning the efficiency level of the Immigration and Naturalization Service is that the agency has been chronically underfinanced and overworked, and that is a remark usually made by an I.N.S. official.

Simply finding out, through the device of a shrewdly timed buttonholing, which examiner is handling which sort of visa applications is valuable in the immigration practice. So is knowing how to find him. * * * [Patrick Murphy] still carries among the papers in his briefcase a blueprint of the Houston District Office of the Immigration and Naturalization Service. "A blueprint of the building is the key to the practice of immigration law," he told me that rainy Wednesday.

"I beg to differ," a colleague said. "The key to the practice of immigration law is knowing that an immigration examiner who wants to go to the bathroom has to pass through the waiting room to get there."

* * *

"Have you ever won a suspension case?" I asked an immigration lawyer in Houston.

"It depends on what you mean by winning," he said.

Immigration lawyers win time. Given calendar delays and court appeals and bureaucratic lethargy, a suspension-of-deportation action might take years. The immigration judges in Houston have almost never granted asylum to a Salvadoran, so, strictly speaking, lawyers in Houston have almost never won a Salvadoran-asylum case. On the other hand, there is a backlog of eight thousand asylum cases to be heard in Houston, there are only two immigration judges to hear them, and there are three levels of appeal—so, speaking not very strictly, lawyers have won a lot of time in Salvadoran-asylum cases. In time, as immigration lawyers say, "something good could happen." The client might marry a citizen—giving him permanent-resident status unless Immigration decides that the marriage is a sham. The client might find a job that makes it possible to get permanent residence through labor certification. Congress might pass the Simpson-Mazzoli bill, which would legalize the presence of any alien who can demonstrate that he has lived in this country since before some specified date. The I.N.S. might lose the file. Meanwhile, the client is in the United States, and that is what he wanted in the first place. Nothing good is likely to happen to someone who is hanging around the American consulate in Karachi or Salonika waiting for an immigrant visa—one reason that, in the words of George Sellnau, "any immigration lawyer worth his salt would say, 'Get here first!' " [a]

The fact that an alien has been living in the United States for months, or even years, with no more documentation than an expired

a. Is this sound advice? Is it consistent with an attorney's ethical obligations?

To secure a nonimmigrant visa, an applicant must normally satisfy the consul that he has "a residence in a foreign country which he has no intention of abandoning." INA § 101(a)(15). For a discussion of the ethical constraints on advising a client about the INA provision regarding a fixed intent to immigrate, see D. Weissbrodt, Immigration Law and Procedure in a Nutshell 286–89 (1984).—eds.

student visa does not prevent him from getting a green card [*i.e.*, obtaining permanent resident status] if, say, he manages to get labor certification before Immigration manages to deport him. One reason that lawyers are so eager to grab an immigration examiner as he walks through the waiting room is that they are often trying to juggle matters in a way that makes something good happen before something bad happens. Immigration lawyers are people who have an interest in seeing that some folders are on the top of the pile and some folders are on the bottom of the pile.

2. SPECIAL INQUIRY OFFICERS, a/k/a IMMIGRATION JUDGES

You may have noticed that we have not yet mentioned the kind of adjudication that probably generates the most drama and draws the greatest attention. Certainly it has the highest potential for an immediate impact on the right of an alien physically present in this country to remain. We are speaking, of course, of exclusion and deportation decisions.

Under the statute, proceedings to exclude or deport aliens must be conducted by "special inquiry officers," officials designated by the Attorney General as "specially qualified" to carry out this role. See INA § 101(b)(4) (definition); § 235(b), § 236(a) (exclusion proceedings); § 242(b) (deportation proceedings). Throughout most of our history, such officers were simply experienced or senior immigration officers, designated to hold such hearings as part—but only part—of a range of responsibilities to administer and enforce the immigration laws. On one day they might have examined aliens at the border, on another investigated violations, on yet another marshalled the case against a deportable alien, and on still another served as a special inquiry officer to adjudicate the deportation of other aliens who had been investigated by their colleagues.

This mixture of roles prompted court challenges alleging that the use of adjudicators so closely involved in enforcement functions violated due process rights to a fair hearing. In 1950, the Supreme Court seemed to bring down the curtain on this practice and to require that officers conducting the hearing be separated from enforcement responsibilities. *Wong Yang Sung v. McGrath*, 339 U.S. 33, 70 S.Ct. 445, 94 L.Ed. 616 (1950). But while the Court's opinion hinted that such separation might be required by the Constitution, its holding rested squarely only on the (then relatively new) Administrative Procedure Act (APA). Congress reacted quickly, attaching to an appropriations bill a rider that exempted immigration proceedings from the separation-of-functions requirements in the APA. Two years later, when earlier immigration laws were comprehensively revised and codified to create the Immigration and Nationality Act of 1952, Congress preserved the possibility that enforcement officials could serve as special inquiry officers. In the congressional debates on the INA, supporters of the *Wong Yang Sung* decision argued for a more rigid separation of functions on due process grounds. In the end, however, they could not prevail against widespread congressional concerns about the expense and potential complications if the proceedings became more judicial in nature. A few of their opponents also suggested that the political and diplomatic implications of immigration policy precluded the use of fully insulated, quasi-judicial adjudicating officers. The congressional majority, however, did concede a few points to the critics. The INA expressly precludes any special inquiry officer from adjudicating the case of an alien as to whom he had earlier undertaken investigatory or prosecutorial functions. INA § 242(b). When the Supreme Court considered these new, watered-down separation-of-functions provisions contained in the INA, it found no due process violation. *Marcello v. Bonds,* 349 U.S. 302, 311, 75 S.Ct. 757, 762, 99 L.Ed. 1107 (1955).

The current *statutory* provisions governing the role of special inquiry officers in exclusion and deportation proceedings (INA §§ 236(a), 242(b)), bear two striking features, largely unchanged since 1952. (Current practice is a different matter, but we will come to that in a moment.) First, as we have noted, is the decided statutory tolerance for officers who sometimes adjudicate and sometimes enforce. And second, the statutory framework for the hearings to be conducted by these special inquiry officers also departs significantly from the adversarial model familiar to Anglo-American practice. *See generally* Damaska, *Evidentiary Barriers to Conviction and Two Models of Criminal Procedure: A Comparative Study,* 121 U.Pa.L.Rev. 506, 554–89 (1973) (usefully describing and comparing adversarial and nonadversarial models of procedure). These officers not only preside over the proceedings like judges, but the statute also expressly authorizes them to present or receive evidence, and also to interrogate, examine, and cross-examine witnesses, including the alien respondent. This broad authority for an active or "inquisitorial" role is based, at least in part, on a desire to permit a full development of the record even when neither party—the government or the alien—is represented by counsel. Such a statutory framework, however, has drawn frequent condemnation, not only because it departs from the adversarial model but particularly because it does so in a setting where the decisionmaker, by training and background, may be biased toward enforcement and skeptical of the alien's claims.[6]

Due process arguments of this type failed to carry the day in Congress in 1952. But where individual rights arguments failed to alter the system, over the years bureaucratic imperatives—including the division of labor, the felt need for increasing professionalization, and the Central Office's drive for more rational and predictable decisionmaking—have largely succeeded in securing both types of changes the due process advocates had urged. Commingling of roles for these adjudicators is a thing of the past, and regulations have engrafted most features of trial-type hearings onto procedures that one would expect to be quite different, if one looked only at the bare provisions of the statute. The statute itself has not been changed. It merely *permitted* the old arrangements; it did

---

6. *See* The Tarnished Golden Door, *supra* note 1, at 37–43; *Developments,* 96 Harv.L. Rev. 1286, 1363–66 (1983); *Whom We Shall Welcome: Report of the President's Commission on Immigration and Naturalization* 152–167 (1953). *See generally* Roberts, *The Exercise of Administrative Discretion under the Immigration Laws,* 13 San Diego L.Rev. 144, 147–48 (1975).

not require them. And regulations have now accomplished some major alterations.

The seeds of this evolution were sown in the statute itself. In deportation proceedings, section 242(b) authorizes the Attorney General, if he finds it useful, to provide for the presence of another immigration officer to present the evidence on behalf of the government and to carry out cross-examination—thus freeing the special inquiry officer for a more passive, judge-like, decisionmaking role. In 1956, the Service began to use this procedure regularly for contested cases. And beginning with administrative changes in 1962, INS has developed a specialized staff of "trial attorneys" to fulfill this function. The regulations now require that the government case in deportation proceedings be presented by a trial attorney unless the alien concedes deportability, 8 C.F.R. § 242.16(c), and in practice a trial attorney or other INS officer appears in virtually all deportation and exclusion proceedings, whatever the issues. *See id.* §§ 236.2(c), 242.9; G & R § 5.7c.

Parallel specialization and professionalization have taken place among the special inquiry officers themselves. Since 1956, INS has required that special inquiry officers have law degrees, and the Service generally has insulated them from other enforcement functions. Beginning in 1973, as a sign of their evolving status within the agency, a new regulation was promulgated changing the designation of these officials to "immigration judges." *See* 8 C.F.R. § 1.1(*l*), G & R § 5.7b. (Do not be confused by this title. The statute still refers to these officials as "special inquiry officers"; the terms are fully synonymous.) Gradually a stronger *esprit de corps* developed among the immigration judges, who increasingly took their quasi-judicial role seriously and resisted what were regarded as efforts to hinder or control their functions emanating from elsewhere in the Service.

Nevertheless, through the early 1980's, immigration judges remained subordinate in a significant way to the district directors in charge of the district where they held court—especially in matters of budget and administrative support. If the district director did not place a high priority on the adjudicative functions of the immigration judge, the judge might go for weeks without adequate secretarial services, and the tapes of deportation or exclusion hearings might languish for months before a typist was made available to transcribe the proceedings. These developments obviously magnified the possibility of delay, and they drew criticism from many quarters, including the Select Commission on Immigration and Refugee Policy. *See* SCIRP, Final Report 246.

In January of 1983, the Department of Justice took important steps to remedy several of these problems. New regulations separated the corps of immigration judges from the Immigration and Naturalization Service and placed them in a new unit, known as the Executive Office of Immigration Review (EOIR), located in the Department of Justice and directly accountable to the Associate Attorney General. *See* 48 Fed.Reg. 8038, 8056 (1983) (amending 8 C.F.R. Parts 1, 3, 100, and 28 C.F.R. Pt. 0). This does not mean that all the immigration judges moved to Washington; most remain physically in their old offices located in various INS facilities throughout the country. Nevertheless, it is clear that EOIR now controls the budget available to immigration judges and provides directly for support services. Today, no immigration judge is answerable to anyone in the Service, and this different line of accountability provides an improved structural assurance of adjudicative neutrality.

It would be neater if immigration judges conducted only exclusion and deportation proceedings, and if all other adjudications were the responsibility of the district directors and their delegates. But the jurisdictional distribution is unfortunately not so straightforward. Immigration judges also play a role, for example, in proceedings to rescind an admitted immigrant's adjustment of status under INA § 246, in proceedings to withdraw the approval of schools previously authorized for attendance by nonimmigrant students, 8 C.F.R. § 214.4, and in hearing challenges brought by aliens ordered *not* to leave the country under the departure control provisions of 8 C.F.R. § 215.5. By far the largest portion of their work, however, remains the hearing of exclusion and deportation cases—including passing upon a wide variety of applications for relief that may be made in such proceedings by aliens who concede that they are formally excludable or deportable.

As of late 1983, position ceilings in the Department of Justice authorized a maximum of 55 immigration judges. The magnitude of the adjudicative responsibilities they face is reflected in the following excerpt from a recent petition for certiorari filed by the Solicitor General:

> Projections for fiscal year 1983 are 92,643 deportation cases received and 62,523 adjudicated; 7,620 exclusion cases received and 5,886 adjudicated; and 2,484 motions to reopen received and 2,241 adjudicated. This will amount to 70,650 completed adjudications for the year, or 5.35 adjudications *per day* per immigration judge. By way of contrast, 6,023 criminal defendants were actually tried in the United States district courts during fiscal year 1982 * * * by 484 district judges. This averages out to 12.44 criminal trials *per year* per judge.

Quoted in 60 Interp.Rel. 844 (1983).

The new structural separation of adjudication from enforcement functions is of course an important element of real independence and neutrality on the part of immigration judges, but it is not the only test. The types of training and working instructions such officials receive are also significant, as are long-term career patterns. That is, if a government employee could become an immigration judge only by serving several years in the Border Patrol or the enforcement units of the INS—or even several years as an INS attorney (historically a more common pattern)—then one would expect a quite different orientation on the part of the adjudicators, compared to a system where recruiting was more broadly based. Critics have charged that an enforcement mentality pervades immigration-related agencies, including those separate from INS. They have also argued that even structural independence like that now enjoyed by EOIR is inadequate, as immigration judges and the BIA remain ultimately answerable to the Attorney General, and he in turn remains the chief enforcement officer under the statute.[7]

As a result, arguments are frequently heard for a wholly separate adjudicative agency, divorced from the Department of Justice and perhaps set up as an Article I court. *See, e.g.,* Roberts, *Proposed: A Specialized Statutory Immigration Court,* 18 San Diego L.Rev. 1 (1980); Levinson, *A Specialized Court for Immigration Hearings and Appeals,* 56 Notre Dame Law. 644 (1981). But in its consideration of immigration reform bills in the early 1980's, Congress remained noticeably cool to these proposals for complete independence. Why should this be so? Are there good arguments for keeping a higher degree of political sensitivity and accountability or control, in light of the nature of immigration adjudications and their possible links to foreign policy decisions?

To shift the focus, consider whether the mere fact of a formal chain of command running from adjudicators up to a Cabinet-level official who retains enforcement responsibilities (as is the case under the 1983 regulations) substantially undermines independence and neutrality. The answer probably cannot be given in the abstract, simply by consulting tables of organization. Instead it depends significantly on the conception of their own role that the adjudicating officers develop and how they reinforce and protect that conception (for example, through training, publications, and union or professional organizations). It may also depend on how the supervisory officer exercises his or her authority. *See generally* J. Mashaw, Bureaucratic Justice 41–44 (1983). (The Mashaw book contains an excellent and thorough discussion of the often contradictory demands and expectations associated with any system requiring "mass justice" adjudications. Though the book's focus is the Social Security disability insurance system, many of its insights are useful for understanding immigration decisions.)

3. APPEALS

The Act expressly gives aliens ruled excludable by immigration judges a right of appeal to the Attorney General (INA § 236(b)), and deportable aliens have equivalent appeal rights by regulation. 8 C.F.R. § 242.21. Naturally a Cabinet officer cannot hear such pleas personally. In practice, therefore, appeals are heard by the Board of Immigration Appeals (BIA), a five-member review body appointed by the Attorney General. Although the Board has existed since immigration responsibilities were first given to the Attorney General in 1940, it has never been recognized by statute; it is entirely a creature of the Attorney General's regulations.[8]

---

7. *See Developments, supra* note 6, at 1363–66; *The Tarnished Golden Door, supra* note 1, at 42–43. Recent hirings by EOIR, however, reveal an effort at broader-based recruiting. *See* 61 Interp.Rel. 81–82 (1984) (announcing hiring of five new immigration judges, only one of whom had worked in INS; one had been a municipal court judge in Arizona and another an administrative law judge for the state of Missouri).

8. Since 1921, a Board of Review had existed in the Department of Labor, empowered to make recommendations to the Secretary regarding the disposition of appeals in exclusion and deportation cases. In 1940, following the transfer of immigration functions to the Department of Justice, new regulations changed the name of the Board and vested in it authority to issue final orders in such matters.

Nevertheless, it is important to recognize that the Board has never been a part of INS. Instead, it has always been accountable directly to the Attorney General through a separate chain of command. Under the 1983 reorganization, the BIA is one of two constituent units of the Executive Office for Immigration Review in the Department of Justice (the other is the corps of immigration judges).

The staple of the Board's jurisdiction consists of appeals from immigration judge decisions in exclusion and deportation cases. 8 C.F.R. § 3.1(b)(1), (2). But the Board also hears appeals, for example, from decisions relating to bonds, parole, and detention of deportable aliens, and from decisions imposing administrative fines and penalties on aircraft and vessels. *Id.* § 3.1(b)(4), (7). The Board also reviews determinations on visa petitions for intending immigrants, but only if the basis for the petition is a family relationship, *id.* § 3.1(b)(5); petitions based on occupational preferences follow a different avenue of appeal. As you may have noted, not all adjudications reviewed by the Board come from immigration judges. Several provisions of the regulations authorize Board review of decisions made by district directors on matters that have never been before an immigration judge. *See, e.g., id.* § 3.1(b)(3), (5), (6).[9]

What about all the other adjudications not reviewable by the BIA? A few are simply not appealable administratively—such as denials by district directors of applications to change from one nonimmigrant status to another (say, from student to tourist, or vice versa). *Id.* § 248.3(f). But a majority of decisions issued by district directors are in fact appealable. For example, if the district director denies a visa petition based on occupational grounds—for permanent workers under the third or sixth preference or for temporary workers in nonimmigrant categories H and L—such decisions are reviewable within the INS hierarchy, and not by immigration judges or the Board. *Id.* § 103.1(f)(2)(ii), (x).[10]

For many years, such internal appeals went to the four regional commissioners of INS. This appeal structure, however, provided problems, equivalent to a split among federal circuit courts, as different regional commissioners sometimes reached contradictory results on the same legal question. In September 1983, INS therefore centralized all appellate authority previously vested in the regional commissioners. Such appeals now go directly from the district director's office to the Associate Commissioner for Examinations, located in Washington, where they are initially screened and processed by a centralized Administrative

9. The workload of the BIA is reflected in these statistics: In fiscal year 1983, the Board docketed 3,630 cases involving 4,110 individuals. Meantime, it entered orders in 4,068 cases involving 4,511 individuals. 61 Interp.Rel. 277 (1984). Only a fraction of the Board's decisions result in opinions officially published as "precedent decisions."

10. In addition, a few district director decisions are not subject to administrative appeal, but the alien may renew the application once exclusion or deportation proceedings have begun, and the immigration judge

then considers the application *de novo. See, e.g.,* 8 C.F.R. §§ 208.8(c), 208.9 (applications for asylum); *id.* § 245.2(a)(4) (application for adjustment of status to lawful permanent resident). Other such decisions are appealable within INS and subsequently can be renewed before the immigration judge, whose decision can be appealed to the BIA. *See, e.g., id.* §§ 103.1(f)(2)(vi), 212.7(a); *Matter of Sanchez,* 17 I & N Dec. 218 (BIA 1980) (review of waivers of excludability under INA § 212(h)).

Appeals Unit. *See* 48 Fed.Reg. 43160 (1983) (amending 8 C.F.R. Pt. 103). The Associate Commissioner also has appellate authority over a minute slice of decisions initially made by immigration judges.

Thus two main appellate tribunals or decisionmakers now exist within the Department of Justice: the BIA and the Associate Commissioner for Examinations.[11] We would like to present a rule of thumb that would allow an easy differentiation between the two zones of appellate jurisdiction, but we cannot. Although there are rough patterns, the actual line drawn between the categories seems to defy theory. Especially mystifying is the distinction between visa petitions based on family ties and those based on occupational grounds. Although both types of petitions are decided originally by the same adjudicating officers exercising the authority of district directors, appeals in occupational cases go to the INS central office, in family cases to the BIA (except petitions for orphans filed by adoptive parents, which go to the central office!).

We are therefore reduced to this advice: If you want to appeal an exclusion or deportation order issued by an immigration judge, go to the BIA. Beyond this, in order to appeal an adverse determination, consult the regulations to determine the forum. Do not assume you can guess which route is correct. But at the same time, you need not despair. It is not excessively difficult to determine the appropriate forum once you realize that you should scout the regulations to find a reference to the precise determination you wish to have reviewed. Title 8 C.F.R. §§ 3.1(b) and 103.1(f) are the most important such regulations.

A large quantity of appellate decisions are handed down each month. Only a fraction of these are officially reported. These latter have been designated as "precedent decisions," 8 C.F.R. § 103.3(e), and they are published in the multi-volume set known as "Administrative Decisions Under Immigration and Nationality Laws of the United States" (I & N Dec.). *Id.* § 103.9(a). You will find there reported decisions from the BIA and the Associate Commissioner, and also some decided by the Commissioner, the Deputy Commissioner, Regional Commissioners, and occasionally the Attorney General.[12]

---

11. There are also possibilities for "certification" of the case to the Commissioner, the Deputy Commissioner, or other appellate authority for an authoritative decision by one of those high officials, at the initiative of the reviewing official, or of the initial decisionmaker, if the question is a complex or novel one. 8 C.F.R. § 103.4. In addition, cases before the BIA are "referred" to the Attorney General for a final authoritative decision by that Cabinet officer, either before or after an initial ruling by the Board, in three circumstances: when the Attorney General so directs; when the Chairman or a majority of the BIA decides that the case should be referred; or when the Commissioner requests referral. *Id.* § 3.1(h).

12. Immigration regulations are published by the INS (and to a much lesser extent by other Justice Department units) in Title 8 of the Code of Federal Regulations, usually after notice-and-comment rulemaking procedures in accordance with the Administrative Procedure Act, 5 U.S.C.A. §§ 552–553. For guidance, INS officers also rely significantly on what are known as Operations Instructions, compiled in a thick volume updated and supplemented periodically without going through the APA rulemaking procedures. Although many OI's read like regulations, INS treats them more like an internal operating manual; there have been controversies over their exact function and status within the administrative scheme. *See* G & R § 1.18b. For many years, the OI's were not released, but beginning in 1972, and in compliance with the Freedom of Information Act, 5 U.S.C.A. § 552, INS made nearly all

SECTION B.   THE DEPARTMENT OF STATE

For the last 60 years, nearly all persons wishing to travel to the United States, even for a short visit, have been required to secure preliminary documents known as visas from a U.S. official overseas.[13] State Department officials, called consular officers, are stationed at over 200 offices throughout the world to decide on applications for visas. *See* INA §§ 221, 222.

Securing a visa, as arduous a process as it may be for some, does not guarantee admission—and the relevant documents bear a warning to this effect.   Visas do not constitute permission to enter the United States. They are more in the nature of permission to travel to the United States and apply for admission at the border.   In other words, the admitting immigration officer is entitled to disagree with the consular officer and thus to detain a properly documented alien for an exclusion hearing. Fortunately, this disagreement does not happen often.   Indeed, the system would break down if visas did not usually function to secure entry.   But because airlines and other carriers are subject to substantial fines and other penalties if they bring aliens here without proper documents, INA §§ 233, 273, they are often quite demanding that the papers presented by a traveller at the foreign ticket counter are all in order.   A visa therefore constitutes an indispensable document for most aliens wishing to come here from another country.

Although section 104 of the INA places these documentation responsibilities in officials of the Department of State, the formal authority of the Secretary of State is circumscribed.   Note the curious language of § 104(a)(1), giving the Secretary broad authority, but excepting from his control "those powers, duties, and functions conferred upon the consular officers relating to the granting or refusal of visas."   Can it really be intended to give consular officers autocratic power, immune to the supervision of their nominal superiors, to decide whether to issue documents indispensable to aliens who wish to come to this country?   Critics have often charged that this is the way the system operates.   *See, e.g., Whom We Shall Welcome: Report of the President's Commission on Immigration and Naturalization* 147 (1953).   But there is a different theory that underlies this provision: namely, that such separation insulates what are meant to be routine bureaucratic decisions on admissibility from the high politics that are the stock-in-trade of the Secretary of State and his subordinates on the diplomatic side of the Department.[14]

of them public. The current version appears as Volume 4 of the G & R treatise. INS also communicates guidance to its offices by means of a variety of policy wires, cables, and memoranda that are not necessarily incorporated into the OI's. The important ones, however, are carried in reporting services like Interpreter Releases, published by the American Council for Nationalities Service, or the Federal Immigration Law Re-porter, published by the Washington Service Bureau.

13. Exceptions to the visa requirement are described in Chapter Three, p. 271 n. 10.

14. *See* Simpson, *Policy Implications of U.S. Consular Operations* in The Consular Dimension of Diplomacy 11 (M. Herz ed. 1983).

To be sure, this provision may occasionally function to fortify an American ambassador when she is explaining why the generalissimo's dissolute nephew was denied a visa and will not receive one whatever foreign policy consequences are threatened. But it remains a fair question whether this statutory explanation is convincing to the generalissimo or to the ambassador. Consular officers are members of the foreign service, dependent on their superiors for advancement in their profession. Indeed, many of the officers issuing visas are foreign service officers on their first assignment with the Department, hoping to move out of consular work and into future assignments as political officers.

What this putative insulating measure does accomplish is to complicate moderately the normal bureaucratic business of review and supervision to assure timeliness, consistency of outcomes, and compliance with the statute and the regulations. Nevertheless, these bureaucratic imperatives have still found expression. The State Department has developed informal review mechanisms, crafted with delicate attention to § 104(a)(1). All visa refusals are followed by review of the papers, carried out by a second consular officer, who may raise questions with the first. If the reviewing officer remains convinced that a visa should be issued, she may issue it herself. But she lacks authority, no matter how far she outranks the initial officer, to order the subordinate to issue that visa under his own name. Differences of opinion may also be referred to the Visa Office in Washington for what is labelled an "advisory opinion" on the dispute. Technically such opinions are binding only on legal questions, while the determination of facts remains fully the responsibility of the consular officer.[15] Visa Office advice, however, is usually followed. Although denial of a visa may totally prevent an alien from travelling to the United States, courts almost uniformly deny judicial review of such decisions—especially at the behest of the alien.

As the statute indicates, visa issuance falls under the general responsibility of the Bureau of Consular Affairs, headed by an Assistant Secretary of State. Although the statute specifically mentions a Visa Office and Passport Office within the Bureau, a 1979 reorganization created within the Bureau three divisions, each headed by a Deputy Assistant Secretary: Visa Services, Passport Services, and Overseas Citizens Services. Indeed, the life of a consular officer in a foreign country consists of more than simply issuing and denying visas. It also involves considerable assistance to U.S. citizens—those who have lost passports, those who have been arrested and incarcerated in a foreign jail, those who need certain documents issued or certified, and those who have met other difficulties. Consular officers also participate in the process of passing on claims by persons abroad who assert that they are United States citizens and should

---

15. Consider whether other arrangements for administrative review, including the possibility of explicitly binding rulings by an appellate administrative tribunal, would improve the functioning of the system. For various suggestions along these lines, *see* SCIRP, Final Report 253–55 (1981) (rejecting proposals for a formal and independent review mechanism but suggesting improvements in the current informal system); Note, *Consular Discretion in the Immigrant Visa Issuing Process,* 16 San Diego L.Rev. 87, 151–58 (1978). *See also* G & R §§ 3.8b, 3.11b.

receive benefits and papers accordingly.[16] *See generally* G & R §§ 1.11–1.-12.

SECTION C. OTHER FEDERAL AGENCIES

1. THE DEPARTMENT OF LABOR

The statute requires the Department of Justice to cooperate with the Labor Department in the process that leads to the granting of visas to persons who are subject to the labor certification requirement. Before such documents can be issued, the Labor Department, through its Employment and Training Administration, must certify that American workers in the applicant's field are unavailable in the locality of the applicant's destination and that the applicant's employment will not adversely affect wages and working conditions of American workers. The labor certification requirement primarily applies to third- and sixth-preference immigrants, but similar labor certification (where Labor plays an advisory role) is also necessary for nonimmigrants in certain business-related categories.

We will examine the complicated and specialized process of labor certification in some detail in Chapter Three.

2. THE PUBLIC HEALTH SERVICE

The Public Health Service (PHS), headed by the Surgeon General, is an agency in the Department of Health and Human Services. Because several grounds of exclusion relate to medical conditions, PHS doctors and other authorized medical officials play a role under the Immigration and Nationality Act, both at ports of entry and overseas. PHS doctors conduct medical examinations of arriving aliens, and some of their determinations are unreviewable by INS or any other body, save a special medical review panel established pursuant to the statute. *See* INA §§ 234, 236(d).

---

16. The State Department issues a Foreign Affairs Manual (FAM), certain chapters of which are devoted to interpretations and instructions relating to immigration and nationality questions, and amplifying the regulations appearing in 22 C.F.R. Parts 41–53. Portions of the Manual have been released to the public, and are now available in Volume 6 of the G & R treatise. Many of the documents and records involved in visa processing, however, are confidential under specific statutory direction. INA § 222(f). *See Medina-Hincapie v. Department of State,* 700 F.2d 737 (D.C.Cir.1983).

Chapter Three

ADMISSION AND EXCLUSION

The American immigration system allows for the admission of two broad categories of aliens: immigrants and nonimmigrants. An alien in either group must show initially that he or she qualifies for admission by meeting certain categorical qualifying requirements, and must also demonstrate that none of the multiple grounds for exclusion appearing in § 212(a) of the INA renders him or her ineligible for entry.

In this chapter, we will examine first the qualifying categories and then the exclusion provisions. We will also consider "parole," an administrative device that may permit the physical presence of an alien despite a failure to qualify otherwise for admission. And we conclude by studying the procedures used to decide the applicability of these various substantive provisions. Along the way a host of statutory, regulatory, and constitutional issues will also attract our attention.

SECTION A. CATEGORICAL QUALIFICATIONS

1. NONIMMIGRANTS

A nonimmigrant, generally speaking, is an alien who seeks entry to the United States for a specific purpose to be accomplished during a temporary stay. The qualifying categories for nonimmigrants are set forth, rather surprisingly, as part of the statutory definition of "*immigrant*." INA § 101(a)(15). But a close examination of § 214, which is captioned "Admission of nonimmigrants," will reveal the reason for this placement.

Section 214(b) establishes a presumption that is fundamental to the workings of the admission process. Under that section, any alien who wishes to come to the United States is presumed to be an "immigrant"— and therefore subject to the more restrictive requirements applicable to the latter category.[1] The alien applicant, then, must shoulder the burden

---

1. Note that not only are aliens presumed to be immigrants, but they are also presumed to be nonpreference immigrants— thus falling within the least favorable category for permanent immigration—until they establish that they are entitled to be considered in one of the preference categories or to be exempt from numerical restrictions as a "special immigrant" or "immediate relative." INA § 203(d). We will explore the

of demonstrating that he or she is entitled to nonimmigrant status. Section 101(a)(15) simply mirrors this basic presumption in definitional form. It defines "immigrant," without further embellishment, as "every alien except" those who happen to fall within one of the carefully defined categories of nonimmigrants which § 101(a)(15) then proceeds to list.

The nonimmigrant categories range from tourists, who are now generally granted an entry period of six months (even if they intend a shorter visit); through students and various business-related categories, which may allow entry for longer periods; to diplomats and employees of foreign countries or affiliated with international organizations, whose stay may be extended indefinitely and who are exempted from several other requirements because of their official status. *See, e.g.,* INA § 102. The Visa Office has developed a set of visa symbols for the various nonimmigrant categories, generally tracking the alphabetical subparagraphs in § 101(a)(15), and sometimes subdividing the categories even further than is suggested by the statutory language. For example, a tourist enters as a "temporary visitor for pleasure" on a B–2 visa. An alien here temporarily on business, perhaps to negotiate a contract with an American supplier, will enter on a B–1 visa, as a "temporary visitor for business." A student headed for an academic institution receives an F–1 visa; the student's spouse and children receive F–2 visas. INS employs the same symbols for nonimmigrant admission categories.[2] You can gain a sense of the diversity of the nonimmigrant categories by examining the following chart.

NONIMMIGRANT CLASSES [3]

Visa Symbol	Class	Relevant INA Section
A–1	Ambassador, public minister, career diplomat or consular officer, and members of immediate family	101(a)(15)(A)(i)
A–2	Other foreign government official or employee, and members of immediate family	101(a)(15)(A)(ii)
A–3	Attendant, servant, or personal employee of alien classified A–1 or A–2, and members of immediate family	101(a)(15)(A)(iii)
B–1	Temporary visitor for business	101(a)(15)(B)
B–2	Temporary visitor for pleasure	101(a)(15)(B)
C–1	Alien in transit	101(a)(15)(C)
C–2	Alien in transit to United Nations	101(a)(15)(C)

meaning of all these terms later in this section.

2. As Section D will develop in greater detail, visas serve to authorize travel to the United States in order to apply for admission at the port of entry. After entry, however, the category and expiration date shown in the admission documents issued at the border, or later modified in the INS district office, provide the important determinants of the rights and limitations attached to the nonimmigrant entry, whatever might have been shown on the visa.

3. In addition to the categories shown, the Visa Office has developed seven nonimmigrant visa categories for persons coming to the United States in accordance with the NATO treaties.

Visa Symbol	Class	Relevant INA Section
	Headquarters District under Headquarters Agreement	
C–3	Foreign government official, members of immediate family, attendant, servant, or personal employee, in transit	212(d)(8)
D	Crewman (seaman or airman)	101(a)(15)(D)
E–1	Treaty trader, spouse, and children (under a "treaty of commerce and navigation" between the U.S. and the alien's country)	101(a)(15)(E)(i)
E–2	Treaty investor, spouse, and children	101(a)(15)(E)(ii)
F–1	Student attending academic institution	101(a)(15)(F)(i)
F–2	Spouse or child of F–1 student	101(A)(15)(F)(ii)
G–1	Principal resident representative of recognized foreign member government to international organization, his or her staff, and members of immediate family	101(a)(15)(G)(i)
G–2	Other representative of recognized foreign member government to international organization, and members of immediate family	101(a)(15)(G)(ii)
G–3	Representative of nonrecognized or nonmember foreign government to international organization, and members of immediate family	101(a)(15)(G)(iii)
G–4	International organization officer or employee, and members of immediate family	101(a)(15)(G)(iv)
G–5	Attendant, servant, or personal employee of alien classified G–1, G–2, G–3, or G–4, and members of immediate family	101(a)(15)(G)(v)
H–1	Temporary worker of distinguished merit and ability	101(a)(15)(H)(i)
H–2	Temporary worker performing services unavailable in the U.S.	101(a)(15)(H)(ii)
H–3	Trainee	101(a)(15)(H)(iii)
H–4	Spouse or child of alien classified H–1, H–2, or H–3	101(a)(15)(H)
I	Representative of foreign information media, spouse, and children	101(a)(15)(I)
J–1	Exchange visitor (in the U.S. for teaching, research, or study under specially designated programs like the Fulbright Scholar program) [4]	101(a)(15)(J)

4. Most exchange visitors are ineligible to become permanent residents, or to change to any other nonimmigrant status except A and G, unless they first return to their home countries for two years. INA § 212(e). Congress adopted this strict requirement (subject to waiver in narrow circumstances, *id.*, see *Slyper v. Attorney General*, 576 F.Supp. 559 (D.D.C.1983)), to ameliorate the risk of "brain drain" from less developed countries as a result of exchange programs. *See Newton v. INS*, 736 F.2d 336 (6th Cir.1984); *Mendez v. Major*, 340 F.2d 128 (8th Cir.1965); G & R § 6.8g.

Visa Symbol	Class	Relevant INA Section
J–2	Spouse or child of exchange visitor	101(a)(15)(J)
K–1	Fiancee or fiance of U.S. citizen	101(a)(15)(K)
K–2	Child of fiancee or fiance of U.S. citizen	101(a)(15)(K)
L–1	Intracompany transferee	101(a)(15)(L)
L–2	Spouse or child of alien classified L–1	101(a)(15)(L)
M–1	Student in vocational or other recognized non-academic institution	101(a)(15)(M)(i)
M–2	Spouse or child of M–1 student	101(a)(15)(M)(ii)

The statute places no fixed numerical limits on nonimmigrant admissions. Control is maintained through the qualitative requirements reflected in the categorical qualification provisions, and by application of the grounds for exclusion appearing in INA § 212(a). The most important determination with respect to many of the nonimmigrant categories consists of a finding that the alien "has a residence in a foreign country which he has no intention of abandoning." *See, e.g.,* INA § 101(a)(15)(B), (F), (H), (J). Because a significant percentage of the "illegal alien" population in this country consists not of people who sneaked across a land border, but of those who overstayed nonimmigrant visas, *see* SCIRP, Appendix E, at 30–34, consular officers tend to be especially careful about these matters, particularly in certain countries known for a high incidence of visa abuse.

The relative demand for the respective nonimmigrant classifications is reflected in these admissions figures for fiscal year 1981:

Foreign government officials	84,710
Temporary visitors for business	1,135,422
Temporary visitors for pleasure	9,515,170
Transit aliens	214,218
Treaty traders and investors	80,802
Students	240,805
Spouses and children of students	31,056
International representatives	54,223
Temporary workers and trainees	44,770
Spouses and children of temporary workers and trainees	10,110
Representatives of foreign information media	16,708
Exchange visitors	80,230
Spouses and children of exchange visitors	27,793
Fiances or fiancees of U.S. citizens	5,456
Children of fiances and fiancees	742
Intracompany transferees	38,595
Spouses and children of intracompany transferees	26,449
NATO officials	7,124
Total	11,614,383

Source: 1981 Statistical Yearbook of the Immigration and Naturalization Service, Table 64.

We will not explore the requirements for the various nonimmigrant categories in any detail in this book, but those desiring more information can find useful treatments in G & R §§ 2.6–2.16B, and National Lawyers Guild, Immigration Law and Defense, Chapter 3 (1983).

2. IMMIGRANTS: OVERVIEW

Immigrants, as the name suggests, are coming here for permanent residence.[5] Not surprisingly, the law imposes more demanding requirements—both substantively and procedurally—on persons relocating permanently. In addition, since 1921, the law has imposed annual numerical limitations on most such immigration. The character of those limitations, as we have seen, changed considerably in 1965, when Congress abandoned the former national-origins quota system in favor of a more neutral preference system. Currently, the preference provisions of the law allow the immigration of 270,000 individuals annually, with these numbers allocated among six basic categories. Eighty percent of these numbers are reserved for family reunification preference categories, and twenty percent are granted to persons based on the employment needs of the United States. If aliens in the preference categories do not use all of the 270,000 available admission slots, the remainder is open for "nonpreference" admissions. INA § 203(a)(7). But nonpreference admission numbers have not been available since 1978 for distribution to people on the visa waiting lists. Moreover, because many preference categories have built up a considerable backlog, there is no realistic prospect that such numbers will become available in the future.

The preference categories, subject to fixed numerical limits, provide only part of the picture of legal, permanent immigration. Over and above these 270,000 admission spaces, the law also allows for the admission, wholly unconstrained by numerical limitations, of "immediate relatives" of United States *citizens*. That term is defined to include spouses, parents (if the petitioning citizen is over 21), and unmarried minor children. INA § 201(b). In 1979, there were about 138,000 such immigrants; in 1980, 151,000; in 1981, 147,000. The number rises and falls depending entirely upon demand by qualified individuals, but in recent years the trend has been generally upward. The law also provides equivalently for a relative handful of first-time admissions, free of numerical ceilings, for specialized categories of persons labelled "special immigrants." INA §§ 101(a)(27), 201(a). These admissions—for example, ministers of religion and longtime foreign-national employees of the U.S. government—do not exceed a few thousand each year.[6]

---

5. After admission, immigrants are also often referred to as lawful permanent residents (LPR's) or permanent resident aliens (PRA's), until they obtain citizenship through naturalization. PRA status means quite simply that they may stay as long as they wish (provided they do not engage in certain post-entry activities that render them deportable). Most immigrants who choose to apply for naturalization after meeting the residence requirement—ordinarily five years—qualify rather routinely, but there is no obligation to apply for naturalization. One may remain in PRA status indefinitely.

6. INA § 101(a)(27)(A) also treats as "special immigrants" lawful permanent residents "returning from a temporary visit abroad." There are several hundred thousand admissions each year in this category,

As a further addition to the 270,000 ceiling figure, the law permits the admission of refugees screened and selected abroad. Unlike "immediate relatives," however, this category is not entirely free of numerical constraints. Although the statute does not set a uniform ceiling to be observed each year, it does spell out a careful procedure whereby the President, in consultation with Congress, will establish such a ceiling at the beginning of each fiscal year, based on the best available predictions about refugee needs over the coming 12 months. The refugee provisions will receive closer attention in Chapter Eight.[7]

As you read through the following material, be ready to consult the following sections of the INA: in connection with nonimmigrants, § 101(a)(15) (basic categories), and §§ 214 and 248 (procedures for admission and for change of nonimmigrant categories); with respect to immigrants, § 101(a)(27) (definition of "special immigrant"), § 101(b)(1), (2) (definition of "child" and "parent"), § 201 (numerical limitations and provisions regarding "immediate relatives"), § 202 (other numerical limitations), § 203 (setting forth the basic preference scheme), and §§ 204–206 and 245 (basic procedures for admission and for adjustment of status from nonimmigrant to immigrant).

but these are all readmissions of persons who went through the full immigrant screening process in the past. This rather anomalous designation is made necessary because the law presumes that entering aliens are all immigrants subject to numerical limitation, *see* note 1 *supra*, absent proof of exemption. If it were not for the escape hatch provided by § 101(a)(27)(A), then, many LPR's would have difficulty gaining reentry after a trip abroad, and in any event many would be double-counted against the immigration quotas.

Returning resident aliens also receive certain other benefits, such as exemption from some documentary requirements. But they nonetheless can be excluded when attempting reentry; the exclusion grounds of INA § 212(a) apply anew each time they cross the border. *See* G & R § 2.19; Chapter Four *infra*.

7. We will not be discussing in this chapter other significant components of *de facto* immigration to this country. The most important such group consists of "illegal aliens" or "undocumented workers." All statements of the total of illegal aliens in this country involve guesswork, but the Select Commission on Immigration and Refugee Policy estimated their numbers at 3.5 to 6 million in 1978. Mexican nationals probably make up less than half the total; Jamaica, the Dominican Republic, Haiti, El Salvador, South America and various countries in Asia apparently contribute large numbers, most of the latter being visa overstays. SCIRP, Final Report, at 36; Appendix E, at 13–34. *See* Chapter Nine, *infra*.

In addition, at times the United States has allowed large groups into the country under the Attorney General's parole power—primarily refugees before the passage of the Refugee Act of 1980 (*See* Chapter Eight *infra*), but also some 150,000 "Cuban-Haitian Entrants" given this parole designation during the Mariel boatlift crisis in the spring of 1980. *See* G & R § 2.54. Technically, people in parole status have not made an entry into this country—the law treats them as though they were still at the border applying for entry—but nearly all the parolees in the categories mentioned here are expected to stay indefinitely. They probably will eventually adjust status to lawful permanent residence under special legislative provisions.

Finally, we mention in passing the situation of so-called *Silva* class members. From 1968 through 1976, the Visa Office reduced the number of visas available to Western Hemisphere immigrants each year to reflect the number of Cuban refugees already in this country granted permanent resident status under the Cuban Adjustment Act of 1966. In 1976 the Office of Legal Counsel in the Department of Justice ruled that this practice was inconsistent with the law. Soon thereafter, a federal court held that the error had to be corrected retroactively to the benefit of the plaintiff class members in a case called *Silva v. Levi,* and a complicated procedure was developed to make 144,946 recaptured nonpreference admission numbers available to Western Hemisphere aliens who had applied for nonpreference immigration before January 1, 1977. *See Silva v. Bell,* 605 F.2d 978 (7th Cir.1979); G & R § 7.8e.

CHARLES GORDON & ELLEN GITTEL GORDON
IMMIGRATION AND NATIONALITY LAW:
STUDENT EDITION*

§§ 2.5, 2.18, 2.23–2.24 (1984).

§ 2.5 Terms of Admission of Nonimmigrants

The Attorney General is empowered to prescribe conditions for the admission of nonimmigrants, including the furnishing of a bond when deemed appropriate to insure the alien's departure from the United States upon the expiration of his alloted time or upon his failure to maintain status. An applicant for entry or extension of stay as a nonimmigrant must establish that he is admissible to the United States or that a ground for inadmissibility has been waived, and that he has any necessary passport and visa, unless such documents have been waived.

The following conditions apply generally to all nonimmigrants:

(1) Time limits. The admitting immigration officer fixes the maximum span for which the nonimmigrant is admitted, making allowance for the time needed to accomplish this temporary purpose of the entry.

(2) Conditions of stay. After admission to the United States as a nonimmigrant the alien is permitted to remain in the United States only upon the following conditions.

That he *will maintain the nonimmigrant status under which he was admitted* or which he subsequently may have been accorded.

That he *will depart from the United States* within the period of his admission or any authorized extension, or on abandonment of his authorized nonimmigrant status.

That he *will not engage in employment or activity in the United States inconsistent with his status* unless permission is first obtained from the district director at the place of the alien's temporary residence in the United States.

That he *will fulfill other conditions* imposed by the admitting immigration officer to assure his maintenance of status and timely departure.

There is no authority to revoke nonimmigrant status, and violations of such status can be challenged only in deportation proceedings.

(3) Extensions of temporary stay. Any nonimmigrant, other than one admitted in transit (C), fiancee (K), or as an alien crewman (D), who has not violated his status or overstayed his allotted time may be granted an extension or extensions of his temporary stay. However, extensions of stay are subject to the same conditions as the original admission; the applicant must show compliance with previous conditions and agree to comply with further conditions that may be imposed.

A nonimmigrant who violates his status or overstays his authorized period of stay is subject to deportation. However, an alien admitted as a nonimmigrant is eligible to apply for adjustment to permanent residence status.

*   *   *

IMMIGRANTS EXEMPT FROM GENERAL NUMERICAL RESTRICTIONS

Immediate Relatives

§ 2.18   Spouse, Child or Parent of United States Citizen

The present statute excludes from numerical restrictions the "immediate relatives" of American citizens. This term is defined to include the spouses, children and parents of American citizens.

§ 2.18a   Spouse of United States citizen

The Act of 1952 grants immediate relative status to the alien spouse of a United States citizen. This dispensation is more generous than prior law, since it gives equal benefits to the husbands and wives of American citizens.

(1) Valid and subsisting marriage as prerequisite. In order to obtain exempt status, or to obtain other immigration benefits available to a "spouse," [t]here must, of course, be a valid and subsisting marriage between the parties. The validity of a marriage ordinarily will be judged by the law of the place where it is celebrated.

*   *   *

§ 2.18b   Child of United States citizen

The Act of 1952 awards exemption from numerical restrictions, as an "immediate relative," to the alien child of a United States citizen. Definitions in the Act of 1952 and in its amendments have delineated a broad connotation of "child" under the immigration laws in order to preserve the family unit.

(1) Age and marital status. By definition a child includes only an unmarried person under the age of 21. A child excluded from immediate relative status by these limitations may be eligible for first or for fourth preference classification.

(2) Stepchild. The 1952 Act defines a child for immigration purposes as including a stepchild, if the child was under 18 at the time the marriage creating the status of stepchild occurred. The alien stepchild of a United States citizen thus is entitled to preferred status.

Congress in 1957 adopted a "clarifying" amendment specifying that the 1952 Act's definition of stepchild applies whether or not the child was born out of wedlock.

(3) Legitimate child. The definition for immigration purposes of child also embraces a child born out of wedlock who is legitimated under the law of the child's or the father's residence or domicile, whether in or outside the United States, if such legitimation occurs while the child is under 18 and in the legal custody of the legitimating parent or parents.

Legitimation means the grant of full legal status as a child, and usually is accomplished by marriage of the child's natural parents.

(4) Illegitimate child.   For immigration purposes an illegitimate child is to be regarded as the "child" of its natural mother.   Consequently the alien illegitimate child of a United States citizen mother now is entitled to preferred status.   An illegitimate child can claim no benefits through its father unless the child is legitimated.   The constitutionality of this exclusion has been upheld, in rejecting a contention that it constitutes an invidious and irrational discrimination, and thus denies due process of law.

(5) Adopted child.   Under the amended statute, the definition of "child" has also been expanded to include a child adopted while under the age of 16, if the child thereafter has been in the legal custody of, and has resided with, the adopting parent or parents for at least 2 years.   An alien child who meets these requirements can claim immediate relative status through an adopting parent who is a citizen of the United States.   It should be noted that the natural parents of a child which qualifies as an adopted child or an orphan are precluded from claiming immigration benefits on the basis of such relationship.

Adoption must conform with the law of the applicable place of residence or domicile.   In such situations, the immigration authorities frequently solicit advice from the Library of Congress regarding the legal requirements in particular countries, and rely on such advice in the absence of a persuasive showing to the contrary by the petitioner.

* * *

§ 2.18c   Parents of United States citizen

The third segment of the "immediate relative" category, now entitled to enter without regard to the numerical limitations, are the parents of United States citizens, such citizens being at least 21 years of age.

"Parent" is a defined term and means a parent who is such by reason of relationship to a "child" within the statutory contemplation.   Thus it may include a stepparent, the mother of a child born out of wedlock, or an adoptive parent, if the statutory prerequisites are met.   However, in order to be a "parent" within the contemplation of the statute his "child" must have qualified as such within the statutory definition at the time their relationship was established.   The parent is not disqualified because the child is now married and over 21 if the child satisfied the statutory definition at the time the relationship was established.

§ 2.18d   Preliminary petition requirement

A person claiming to be the spouse, parent, or child of an American citizen cannot obtain preferred status unless a petition for issuance of an immigration visa (Form I–130) is filed on his behalf with the Attorney General by the United States citizen parent, child, or spouse and is approved by the Attorney General on a finding that the beneficiary is entitled to preferred status.

* * *

IMMIGRANTS SUBJECT TO GENERAL NUMERICAL LIMITATIONS

§ 2.23 Annual Immigration Allotments

§ 2.23a The worldwide annual quota

Before 1978 there were separate immigration quotas for the Eastern and Western Hemispheres. A 1978 statutory amendment combined these separate quotas into a single worldwide annual ceiling of 290,000, which was reduced to 270,000 when a separate allocation for refugees was made in 1980. As amended, the statute directs that not more than 72,000 of this number shall be issued in each of the first three quarters of each fiscal year. * * *

§ 2.23b Modifications of normal selection pattern

(1) General preclusion of discrimination.

The statute, as amended in 1965, prohibits discriminations against immigrants because of race, sex, nationality, place of birth, or place of residence.

(2) Significance of place of origin.

The 1965 amendments discarded the previous national origins formula. Therefore the immigrant's country of origin usually is no longer relevant in the selection process. However, it should be noted that a limitation of 20,000 is placed upon the number of immigrant visas and of conditional entries made available, exclusive of special immigrants and immediate relatives, to natives of any single country in any fiscal year. The general rule is that place of birth determines the immigrant's chargeability, but special rules are prescribed to promote unity of families. Special rules are also prescribed for colonial possessions.

§ 2.24 Priorities Within Worldwide Annual Quota

§ 2.24a First preference: Unmarried sons and daughters of United States citizens

The first preference of 20%, a total of 54,000 visas, is made available to qualified immigrants who are the unmarried sons and daughters of United States citizens. The statute's use of "sons and daughters" is designed to avoid its definition of "child," since those who qualify as "children" of American citizens are entitled to exempt status as immediate relatives. Thus the first preference is applicable only to adult, unmarried children of American citizens. Married children may fall within the fourth preference.

§ 2.24b Second preference: Spouses and unmarried sons and daughters of lawfully resident aliens

The second preference of 26%, a total of 70,200 plus any visas not used by the first-preference group, is made available to qualified immigrants who are the spouses or the unmarried sons or daughters of an alien lawfully admitted for permanent residence. Here too the statute's use of "unmarried sons or daughters" is intended to avoid its definition of child. We note that although a resident alien's married child is not within the second-preference group, such a child may qualify for the fourth preference if his parent becomes a citizen. Moreover, the statute gives no preference to the parents of a lawfully resident alien.

§ 2.24c   Third preference: Professionals, scientists and artists

The third preference of 10%, a total of 27,000 visas, is made available to:

> "qualified immigrants who are members of the professions, or who because of their exceptional ability in the sciences or arts will substantially benefit prospectively the national economy, cultural interests, or welfare of the United States, and whose services in the professions, sciences or arts are sought by an employer in the United States."

The statute defines "profession" to "include but not be limited to architects, engineers, lawyers, physicians, surgeons, and teachers in the elementary or secondary schools, colleges, academies, or seminaries." This statutory reference to physicians and surgeons in effect is modified by 1976 legislation which radically curtailed the immigration opportunities for foreign doctors.

The statutory listing manifestly is by no means exclusive, and the designation of occupations which may be regarded as professions within the third preference is proceeding by the familiar process of inclusion and exclusion.

It should be noted that, unlike the preferences based on relationship, the ceiling for the third preference is fixed, and this category does not inherit the visa numbers unused by higher priority groups.

A number of significant features should be noted. First, there is no qualifying requirement for professionals, whose professional status in itself entitles them to the third preference. The aliens who comprise the second segment of the third preference must show, however, that their exceptional ability in the sciences or arts promises substantial benefit for the national economy, cultural interests, or welfare of the United States. Second, as the result of a 1976 statutory amendment, the third-preference alien must now be coming to a particular employer in the United States. Third, all aliens in the third preference must obtain a certification from the Secretary of Labor that their coming to the United States will not adversely affect American labor. It is also important to note that an alien who does not meet the criteria for the third preference may seek sixth preference classification.

§ 2.24d   Fourth preference: Married sons and daughters of United States citizens

The fourth preference of 10%, a total of 27,000 visas, plus any visas not used by the first three preference groups, is made available to qualified immigrants who are the married sons or daughters of United States citizens.

§ 2.24e Fifth preference: Brothers and sisters of United States citizens

The fifth preference of 24%, a total of 64,800 visas, plus any visas not used by the first four preference groups, is made available to qualified immigrants who are the brothers or sisters of United States citizens, provided such citizens are at least 21 years of age. In referring to "brothers" and "sisters," Congress again has used undefined terms, with a manifest design for flexibility. However, the statutory definition of "child" is followed in determining whether the prospective immigrant qualifies as a brother or sister.

§ 2.24f Sixth preference: Immigrants coming to perform labor

The sixth preference of 10%, a total of 27,000 visas, is made available:

"to qualified immigrants who are capable of performing specified skilled or unskilled labor, not of a temporary or seasonal nature, for which a shortage of employable and willing persons exists in the United States."

Like the third preference (and unlike the preferences based on relationship), the sixth preference has a fixed ceiling and does not inherit the visa numbers unused by higher priority groups. In addition, it must satisfy the special labor certification requirements. The statute requires that the alien must be capable of performing "specified" labor, that the labor must not be of a temporary or seasonal nature, and that there must be a shortage of persons in the United States able and willing to perform such labor.

§ 2.24g Nonpreference immigrants

Any portion of the annual quotas which is not used by the six preference groups is made available to other qualified immigrants. * * * The nonpreference group thus includes all immigrants who are not entitled to immediate relative or special immigrant status and who are not within one of the [six] preference categories. Every immigrant is presumed to be a nonpreference immigrant unless he establishes to the satisfaction of the consular officer and the immigration officer that he is entitled to preference or exempt status. Moreover, the nonpreference immigrant who is subject to the labor certification requirement must obtain a certification from the Secretary of Labor that his coming to the United States will not adversely affect American labor.

§ 2.24h Spouses and children of preference or nonpreference immigrants

The spouse or child of a preference or nonpreference immigrant, accompanying or following to join him, is entitled to the same status and the same order of consideration as the principal immigrant, if an immigrant visa or conditional entry is not otherwise immediately available. The regulations regard the family members as "accompanying" the preference alien, without the need for a visa petition on their behalf, if they receive immigrant visas within 4 months after the principal obtains an immigrant visa or adjustment of status, or within 4 months after his departure from a foreign country to which he traveled in order to confer his foreign state chargeability upon them. The "following to join" language is construed even more generously, and permits the grant of derivative status, without the need for a visa petition on behalf of the family of preference immigrants, if they come to join the preference immigrant in the United States at any time after his acquisition of lawful residence status. But a spouse or child acquired after the grant of permanent residence to the principal alien is not regarded as accompanying or following to join him.

§ 2.24i Preliminary petition requirement

Priority as a member of the six preference groups can be procured only by filing a petition for such preferred status on behalf of the prospective immigrant and obtaining the Attorney General's approval.

§ 2.24j Preliminary certification from Department of Labor

Immigrants in the third and sixth preferences or in the nonpreference category who seek to enter the United States for the purpose of performing skilled or unskilled labor are barred from entry unless they first obtain a certification from the Secretary of Labor that (1) there is a shortage of qualified and available workers in the United States to perform such labor; and (2) the immigrant's employment will not adversely affect wages and working conditions in the United States.

§ 2.24k Timing of allocations from worldwide quota

Demand for immigration may be in excess of the available supply of allocations. The general rule is that allocations are made first to the preference classes in their numerical order of priority, with the prescribed numerical limitations for each class. Within the nonpreference group the rule of first come, first served, is followed, and qualified immigrants within that category are assigned visas strictly in the order in which they qualify. The visa priority date of an immigrant with an individual labor certification is the date a valid application for such certification was received in the appropriate State Employment Service office. In regard to the six preference groups immigrant visas within each group are issued to eligible aliens in the order in which the visa petitions on their behalf are filed, except when third or sixth preference immigrants are entitled to an earlier priority date on the basis of an approved labor certification.

――――

Problems

To sharpen your initial familiarity with the functioning of these preference categories, and your understanding of who may petition and who may benefit from a petition, work through the following problems. (As to some, you should remember that a lawful permanent resident qualifies for naturalization, in most cases, after five years' residence in this country.) In each, assume you are an attorney approached for advice. What do you recommend? What additional information must you develop, if any? There may be many ways to accomplish the client's aims; try to find the most expeditious one. (You might also reconsider your suggestions after reviewing the information on backlogs in several preference categories, appearing in the Notes immediately following these problems.)

1. Your client has been a lawful permanent resident of the United States since 1976. Last month in Nairobi he married a national of Kenya who has a six-year-old child by a previous marriage (which was properly terminated by a valid divorce action), and naturally he wants to bring his wife and her child to this country as soon as possible.

2. Your client is a lawful permanent resident alien who entered this country in that status in 1977. He wants to bring his brother here from Greece.

3. Your client, a citizen of the Philippines, entered as a lawful permanent resident alien two years ago under the fourth preference. At the time he brought with him his wife and three of his four children, leaving behind an 18-year-old daughter. This daughter had already entered college and believed at the time that she did not want to emigrate. Now she has changed her mind, and would like to come to the United States and take up studies in this country as soon as possible.

4. You have been contacted by a 20-year-old Swiss national who wishes to immigrate to the United States. He has heard that family ties are the key to immigration, and he reports that he has an uncle in Chicago who is a U.S. citizen and would be willing to do any necessary paperwork.

Notes

1. The following chart, one of a series published monthly by the Visa Office, suggests the complexity of the administrative system for managing numerically limited immigration, as well as the long backlogs that have developed in many preference categories. The dates appearing on the chart indicate visa allocation priority dates. No immigrant subject to the numerical quotas may receive a visa until his or her priority date has been reached. The immigrant's priority date is the date when the first relevant document was filed with the appropriate administrative agency (visa petition for the family categories; application for labor certification for the third and sixth preferences). Note that this is a date many months in advance of any determination by those agencies that the alien is in fact eligible. Naturally no visa will issue until all the eligibility determinations are concluded. On the chart, "C" indicates that a category is current; "U" indicates that visas are unavailable for that category. For a more complete description of the administrative scheme, *see The*

Operation of the Immigrant Numerical Control System, 61 Interp.Rel. 718 (1984) (reprinting account published in the Visa Office Bulletin).

VISA PREFERENCE NUMBERS FOR JULY 1984

CHARGE ABILITY	1ST	2ND	3RD	4TH	5TH	6TH	NONPREF- ERENCE
All chargeability areas except those listed below	C	8–15–83	C	C	12–15–80	12–15–82	U
CHINA-mainland born	C	8–15–83	C	C	5–8–79	U	U
INDIA	C	8–15–83	8–1–83	C	11–1–80	12–15–82	U
KOREA	C	8–15–83	C	C	1–15–80	12–15–82	U
MEXICO	C	1–22–77	U	U	U	U	U
PHILIPPINES	C	12–22–79	10–1–70	12–22–77	7–1–73	12–15–82	U
HONG KONG	C	4–22–78	11–2–82	6–22–79	12–8–72	2–22–79	U

Source: 61 Interp.Rel. 462 (1984).

2. Some countries are listed separately on the preceding chart because they are at or near the per-country limits established by INA § 202 (20,000 per year for most countries; 600 per year for colonies). If all 20,000 admission numbers are used in a given year, then under § 202(e) special allocation rules come into effect for the following year. That is why a country like the Philippines has numbers left over for the lower preferences, even though demand there for the second and third preferences is so high that people in those categories could easily fill the 20,000 annual quota.

The wording of § 202(e) has been construed by the Visa Office in a highly technical way, however, so that with some countries, in some years, the section does not accomplish its evident purpose. For example, in fiscal year 1983, demand for sixth preference visas from Mexico fell just short of the 2,000 available under § 202(e). Thus Mexico claimed something less than the full 20,000 allocation for that year. Under the Visa Office interpretation, the special allocation rules could not be applied to Mexico for 1984 because of this shortfall, even though total demand from Mexico obviously exceeds 20,000 annually, by a large margin. As a result, on the chart you see that no admissions were available to Mexicans who qualified under the third through sixth preferences; demand for the first and second preferences alone was expected to use the full 20,000 quota. Of course, this pattern makes it virtually certain that § 202(e) will once again apply in fiscal year 1985. The courts have sustained this Visa Office approach. *See, e.g., Angco v. Haig,* 514 F.Supp. 1328 (E.D.Pa.1981).

Western Hemisphere countries were not subject to per-country ceilings until 1976. As the chart reflects, the change that year had a highly disadvantageous impact on applicants from Mexico—the country with the highest demand for immigrant visas (slightly ahead of the Philippines). Several proposals have appeared in Congress since then to open the doors wider to migration from Mexico, and each house actually voted in favor of such an increase during the 98th Congress, as part of the Simpson-Mazzoli immigration reform bills. The Senate version would have raised the ceiling for "any foreign state contiguous to the United States," meaning Canada and Mexico, to 40,000 each, and if one country failed to use its full quota, extra admission numbers equal to the shortfall would be provided to the other contiguous country in the following fiscal year. Because Canadian immigration has been running well below 10,000 annually in recent years, in practice this change probably would have made over 50,000 numbers available annually for intending immigrants chargeable to Mexico, once the system became fully operational. S. 529, § 201. The House bill did not raise the 20,000 ceiling, but allowed equivalent shifting of unused Canadian numbers to Mexico (and theoretically in the other direction, if Mexican immigration were ever to fall short of the ceiling)—thus envisioning a rise in Mexican immigration to over 30,000 annually. H.R. 1510, § 201. Because the conference committee was unable to resolve other differences between the two bills before the 98th Congress ended, no change has yet been enacted.

3. The following information provided by the Visa Office provides a further indication of the backlog problem. The chart below shows active registrations known to consular officers at overseas posts as of January 1984—essentially the number in each category who had completed all but the last step in the qualifying process, and who were then on the consulate's waiting list:

	Number	% of Total Registrants
1st preference:	7,686	.5%
2nd preference:	286,045	18.0%
3rd preference:	25,697	1.6%
4th preference:	70,506	4.4%
5th preference:	1,025,664	64.6%
6th preference:	38,635	2.5%
nonpreference:	133,127	8.4%
Total	1,587,360	100.0%

Source: 61 Interp.Rel. 399 (1984).

In providing these figures, the Visa Office noted that total active registrations had increased at the time by a total of 12.5% over comparable figures one year earlier, with most of this increase occurring in the fifth preference category. The two leading chargeability areas, Mexico and the Philippines, together account for 39% of the total: 313,496 registrants in Mexico and 306,261 in the Philippines.

The Visa Office also pointed out that these figures understate total demand, because they include only those cases handled by Foreign Service posts. Cases pending before the INS in the United States requesting adjustment of status were not included in the figures. This is a significant omission, because in recent years adjustments of status have accounted for over 20 percent of all numerically limited immigration. (Adjustment of status, to be considered in detail later in this Chapter, permits qualified nonimmigrants in the United States to acquire status as immigrants without ever leaving the country or receiving immigrant visas. Such aliens must prove their qualifications by petitioning INS; the State Department is not directly involved.)

4. Do these backlogs suggest that the purposes behind adoption of the preference system in 1965 are no longer being served? Several observers have reached such a conclusion and have suggested various changes. *See, e.g.* SCIRP, Appendix D, at 47–54 (views of Charles Keely, who, among other suggestions, would shift to a true preference system for family reunification—meeting all demand in the highest category before admitting any in the second, and so on.)

The fifth preference, for brothers and sisters of U.S. citizens, has come in for special scrutiny, because of its alleged "visa multiplier" effect.

> Unlike the other categories, the allotment of visas based on "sibship" potentially leads to an unlimited demand for visas by *new* qualified applicants. For example, the admission of one immigrant who has foreign-born siblings or who marries an individual with foreign-born siblings automatically creates additional potentially qualified visa applicants, who, when admitted, can petition for the siblings of their spouses. Indeed, if the immigrant's parents are admitted, they can in turn petition for *their* brothers and sisters resulting potentially in the addition of the brother and sister in-laws, uncles, cousins, etc. of the original immigrant.

The Preference System: Hearings Before the Subcomm. on Immigration and Refugee Policy of the Sen. Comm. on the Judiciary, 97th Cong., 1st Sess. 213 (1981) (testimony of Professor Mark R. Rosenzweig). Others testifying at the same hearing countered that, for many ethnic groups, "brothers and sisters, whether or not they are married, are an integral part of the family reunion concept. Elimination of this preference category would violate a sacrosanct human right of an American citizen to live with his family according to his own traditional life-style." *Id.* at 170 (testimony of Rev. Joseph A. Cogo).

In its consideration of immigration reform legislation in 1982, the Senate decided that the fifth preference, for brothers and sisters of U.S. citizens, should be eliminated altogether. S.2222, 97th Cong., 2d Sess., § 202. In 1983, examining the same issue, the Senate voted to make such immigration available only to *unmarried* brothers and sisters. S.529, § 202. The House has firmly resisted any changes in fifth preference immigration, but all the same, it has not voted to increase the allocation of numbers to the fifth preference. This ignoring of the backlog problem cannot last indefinitely. How would you solve it?

5. A related issue concerns the growing numbers of immediate relatives to whom no numerical ceiling applies. In fiscal year 1970, 79,213 people were admitted in this category. By 1975, the number had grown to 91,504, and it has continued to rise: in 1976, 102,019; in 1977, 105,957; in 1978, 125,819; in 1979, 138,178; and in 1980, 151,131. Statistical Abstract of the United States: 1984, Table No. 124. Several critics, especially those who advocate curbs on overall U.S. population growth,

find this a serious defect. The 1983 Senate bill would have made significant changes along these lines, setting an annual ceiling of 350,000 on the family reunification preference categories and deducting from that number, each year, the previous year's total of "immediate relative" immigration. S.529, § 201. Should demand for the latter ever reach 350,000, then, all other family immigration would cease. Is this sound policy?

6. Nonpreference immigration, as originally conceived, was meant in large part to fulfill the American tradition of openness to those who simply had the determination and fortitude to make it on their own in a new land—"new seed" immigrants, as they have often been called. But with the apparent demise of nonpreference immigration, these purposes are no longer met. Family reunification accounts for the overwhelmingly dominant proportion of current immigration—eighty percent of numerically limited immigration, and a growing number of "immediate relatives." U.S. employment needs occupy the only other secure niche in the system. Certainly, family reunification and the supplying of labor needs represent important ends to be served by our immigration laws, but are they *this* important—to the exclusion of most other goals?

Furthermore, the dominance of the family factor may favor certain countries, because it "excludes significant immigration from those countries without a base for family reunification. This includes some countries from which immigration was previously nominal or nonexistent, from new countries, and from countries whose base has been eroded because immigration from them was historic rather than recent." SCIRP, Appendix D, at 55 (staff paper).

In light of these changes, should the law be amended to assure at least some access for "new seed" immigrants? How would you design such a system? For one such proposal, based roughly on Canada's system which assigns points for various desirable characteristics (including family ties, employment skills, intended locality for resettlement, and many other factors), *see id.* at 55–61.

Changing Patterns of American Immigration

The national-origins quota system, adopted in the 1920's, was an effort to freeze the ethnic composition of the American population. As the following graph indicates, it was not entirely successful in meeting this professed goal, largely because of the provisions allowing numerically unconstrained immigration from Western Hemisphere countries.

THE ORIGINS OF U.S. IMMIGRATION, BY REGION, 1821–1979

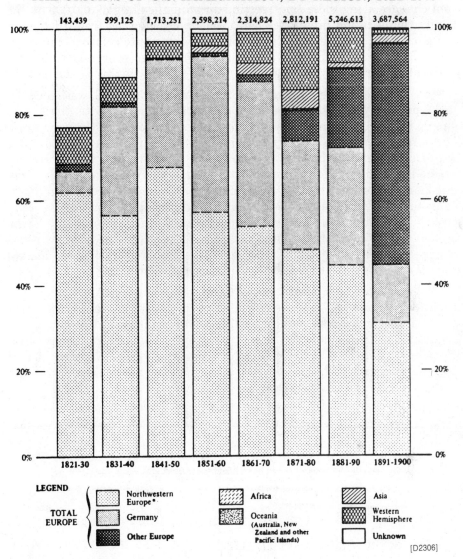

LEGEND

TOTAL EUROPE {
- Northwestern Europe*
- Germany
- Other Europe

- Africa
- Oceania (Australia, New Zealand and other Pacific Islands)

- Asia
- Western Hemisphere
- Unknown

[D2306]

[Graph continues on the next page.]

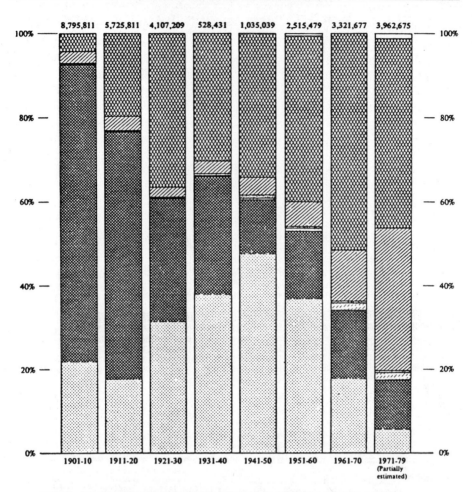

SOURCES: 1821-1970– U.S. Bureau of the Census, Historical Statistics of the United States, Colonial Times to 1970.
2 vols. Washington, D.C.: U.S. Government Printing Office, 1975.
1971-1979–U.S. Immigration and Naturalization Service, Table 13, Annual Reports, and unpublished data.

*Includes immigration from Germany, 1901-79.   [D2307]

Source: SCIRP, Staff Report 172–173.

After the national origins system was abolished in 1965, some observers worried that its discriminatory effects would continue in a more
disguised form, owing to the strong preference given to family reunification categories. Such immigration, after all, requires the presence in this
country of family members who gained admission under the old system to
initiate the process. If particular countries or ethnic groups were excluded earlier, there will be no base for using the family reunification
provisions of the new, ostensibly more neutral system.

The graph indicates, however, that the worst fears of perpetuating a
blatantly discriminatory system have not been realized. For example,
Asians, heavily disfavored under the Chinese exclusion acts, the "Gentleman's Agreement" with Japan, and the national origins laws, now fill a
very large proportion of immigration slots. Of course, there remain
particular countries with low totals because of the absence of a family

reunification base, and immigration from Africa still claims only a small proportion of annual numbers. But overall, the abolition of the national origins system, combined with significant refugee admission programs, has altered the racial and ethnic composition of immigration to the United States in the last several decades. Once again, as they did in a much different context around the turn of the century (when pressure was mounting for ethnically based immigration restrictions), social scientists are beginning to speak of "the new immigration"—and so are politicians.

DOUGLAS S. MASSEY, DIMENSIONS OF THE NEW IMMIGRATION TO THE UNITED STATES AND THE PROSPECTS FOR ASSIMILATION

7 Ann.Rev. of Sociology 57–63, 77–79 (1981).

Over the past two decades, immigration to the United States has sharply increased to levels not seen since the great immigrant years before 1920. During the 1960's, legal immigration exceeded three million persons for the first time in 30 years, and during the 1970s it easily surpassed four million. Making fairly conservative allowances for illegal migration, the total figure for the past decade approaches the all-time high of 8.8 million immigrants recorded between 1900 and 1909. * * *

WHO ARE THE NEW IMMIGRANTS?

Since 1960, immigration to the United States has been shaped by three developments. First was the passage of the 1965 Amendments to the Immigration and Nationality Act, which abolished the discriminatory national origins quota system and replaced it with an ethnic-blind preference system. Second was the fall of U.S.-backed governments in Cuba and Indochina, producing large numbers of refugees seeking entry to the United States. Third was the emergence during the 1960s of a world-wide pattern of international labor migration between low and high income countries. Each of these developments has produced a characteristic stream of immigrants to the United States.

LEGAL IMMIGRANTS: NEW AND OLD

By raising the annual ceiling from 158,000 to 290,000 immigrants and expanding the classes exempt from numerical limitation, the 1965 Amendments substantially increased the volume of legal U.S. immigration. In the years since 1968 (when the Amendments took effect), immigration averaged 416,000 annually, compared to 282,000 in the decade prior to 1965. * * * In 1978, legal immigration topped 600,000 for the first time since 1924.

Elimination of the quota system also caused a rapid shift in immigrants' ethnic origins away from Europe and into Asia and the Western Hemisphere. Between 1900 and 1965, 75% of all immigrants to the United States were of European extraction. Since 1968, 62% have been from Asia or Latin America (29% and 33%, respectively). In Asia, prominent contributors have been China (Hong Kong, Taiwan, and China), Japan, the Philippines, Korea, and India. In the Western Hemisphere salient sources have been Mexico, the Dominican Republic, Jamaica, Haiti, and Colombia.

As the geographic origins of the new immigrants differ from the old, so too do their destinations in the United States. Immigration is no longer directed primarily to the northeastern states, as it was before 1920. To traditional immigrant receiving states such as New York, New Jersey, Illinois, and Pennsylvania, new states have been added in the south and west. By 1978, the four largest alien populations were located in California, New York, Texas, and Florida.

Demographically, U.S. immigration policies have produced an immigrant population much more like the native population than was the case historically. Whereas immigrants before 1920 were predominantly male and single, today's immigrants closely resemble the U.S. population with respect to age, sex, and marital status. Socioeconomically, the new immigrants display a much broader mix than in earlier times. While the vast majority of immigrants before 1920 were unskilled blue-collar workers, the occupational distribution of immigrants is now bimodal, with clusters in both white- and blue-collar categories. This aggregate bimodality results from a preponderance of Asians in white-collar occupations. Among Hispanics, Mexicans tend to be of somewhat lower socioeconomic status than migrants from other regions of the Western Hemisphere.

REFUGEES: 1960–1980

Although the 1965 Amendments provided for the annual admission of 17,400 refugees, the vast majority have entered the United States outside of this statutory provision, either through special legislation or under the parole authority granted the Attorney General.[a] As a result, there are now close to one million Cubans in the United States; and by the end of the fiscal year 1980, over 400,000 Indochinese had been admitted. While there are other smaller refugee populations (e.g. Soviet Jews), the vast majority of refugees since 1960 have been Cuban or Indochinese.

Like legal immigrants, the age-sex composition of Cuban exiles and their children roughly corresponds to that of the U.S. population; and Cuban refugees have similarly come from both ends of the socioeconomic ladder. While early refugee cohorts were made up disproportionately of well-educated, white-collar individuals, recent exiles have been drawn increasingly from the less well-educated Cuban working class. Whites are substantially overrepresented in all refugee cohorts, compared to the racial composition of the island population.

Indochinese refugees similarly display a relatively balanced age and sex distribution. Although males and children do predominate to a degree, this can be explained by the absence of people above age 45 (due to the hardships involved in leaving Vietnam) and by the large number of men of military age (former soldiers in the South Vietnamese army). The vast majority of refugees came to this country in family groups. Socioeconomically, high status occupations and advanced educations were overrep-

a. The refugee admission provisions were changed significantly by the Refugee Act of 1980. *See* Chapter Eight, *infra* —eds.

resented. Of those arriving in 1975, 47% of household heads came from a white-collar background, and over 70% had at least some high school education. Finally, Indochinese—and Cubans—have tended to settle in the same areas as legal migrants, reinforcing the more balanced regional distribution of the new immigration.

Migrant Workers: Undocumented Aliens and Others

Over the past two decades, a widespread pattern of international labor migration has developed between low and high income countries.

In the United States, this development has led to a marked increase in undocumented migration, and intense interest has generated a burgeoning research literature on this topic.   * * *

There has been considerable controversy over the true extent of undocumented migration to the United States. More conjectural figures have put the number of illegal migrants at eight million and even as high as 12 million. However, such estimates have been severely criticized and are in disrepute. Three studies using different statistical methods have each suggested undocumented populations in the range of 3–6 million as of 1975, with four million commonly taken as a rule of thumb.   * * *

While the undocumented population tends to be predominantly male, females nonetheless comprise a significant and apparently growing part. For a variety of reasons, females are systematically underrepresented in apprehensions statistics. However, samples of unapprehended migrants indicate a clear female participation. Among such samples, the percentage of women varies between 20% and 56%, with a mean value of around 33%. There is also evidence that female migration is on the increase.

As might be expected, undocumented migrant populations exhibit a tendency to cluster in the labor force ages. Nonetheless, studies indicate that children often accompany undocumented parents to the United States. Family migration appears to be more common among Western Hemisphere nations other than Mexico.

In general, undocumented migrants come from the lower middle ranges of the socioeconomic ladder, although undocumented Mexicans tend to be of a somewhat lower status than migrants from the rest of the Western Hemisphere. Both Mexican and non-Mexican undocumented workers are concentrated primarily in the secondary labor market in unskilled blue-collar or service positions. However, compared to Mexicans, other Western Hemisphere migrants display a somewhat greater tendency to hold skilled or semi-skilled jobs.

* * *

The New Immigrants: A Composite Picture

During the past decade, approximately four million visas were issued for immigrants to the United States. If we accept three million as a lower-bound estimate of illegal aliens in 1975, and assume a new annual inflow of 200,000 since that time, the undocumented population in 1980 would exceed four million persons. Allowing for the emigration of one million legal immigrants, discounting for the presence of one million undocumented aliens in the country before 1970, and adding in about one million refugees, total net immigration during the 1970s probably exceeded seven million persons. The vast majority of these immigrants were either Hispanic or Asian. Included in all three groups—legals, illegals, and refugees—were large numbers of women and children immigrating to this country as members of family groups. Compared to earlier immigrants, today's migrants comprise a broader mix of socioeconomic backgrounds, drawing on both ends of the educational and occupational spectrums, and are dispersed more widely throughout the country. Thus the new immigration is likely to be widely felt at all levels of society and in all regions of the country. * * *

SUMMARY AND CONCLUSION

* * *

On the whole, the new immigrants appear to be well-launched on the path to assimilation within the core of American life. With exposure to U.S. society over the generations, and socioeconomic advancement, traditional family orientations change to accommodate life in an urban industrial society. Sex roles become less circumscribed and kinship is focused increasingly on the nuclear family.

Taken as a whole, total fertility of the new immigrants is lower than that of the native U.S. population. High fertility groups like Mexicans are effectively counterbalanced by groups with very low fertility, such as the Japanese, Chinese, Cubans, and South and Central Americans. Even among Mexicans, fertility falls sharply with exposure to U.S. society and rising socioeconomic status. Thus the new immigration should not lead to a long-term increase in total U.S. fertility.

Although little is known about residential segregation of Asian groups in the United States, Hispanics show a clear trend toward spatial assimilation with increasing time in the United States and socioeconomic advancement. Unlike blacks, there is little evidence of widespread and systematic discrimination in housing. In general, there seems to be little likelihood that Hispanic populations will develop a ghetto-like spatial distribution analogous to that of the U.S. black population.

There is no information on patterns of Asian political participation. Among Hispanics, this is the dimension on which the least assimilation has occurred. Hispanics generally display a level of political participation considerably below that of Anglos and blacks. While low rates of voting can be attributed to class factors, Hispanics of all classes are unlikely to take an active role in politics. The middle class is particularly reluctant to assume a leadership position. Thus socioeconomic mobility may increase Hispanic power at the ballot box, but is unlikely to dramatically alter the political status quo.

With respect to the ultimate indicator of social integration, both Hispanics and Asians appear to be moving rapidly toward marital assimilation. Intermarriage increases sharply over the generations and with rising socioeconomic status. Among Asians, exogamy by individuals is currently above 50% overall, and Hispanics generally surpass this figure after the first generation. On this acid test of assimilation, the new immigrants thus appear to be following in the footsteps of the old in merging into the core of U.S. society.

In large measure, the trends toward assimilation just described are predicated on the assumption of continued social mobility. In each case, degree of assimilation varies directly with socioeconomic status. Should social mobility be blocked or disrupted, the process of immigrant assimilation could be considerably slowed.

Overall, studies from the past two decades indicate that, if anything, socioeconomic opportunity in the United States has increased. Thus all the new immigrant groups experienced upward mobility over time and across generations. Among Asian and Cuban populations, upward mobility has been quite rapid in recent years, while among Puerto Ricans and Mexicans it has been slower. To some extent, these differences in rates of mobility can be attributed to differences in socioeconomic background between groups.

Against this generally sanguine assessment of prospects for the new immigrants in this country, three potentially serious social problems loom. First is the possibility that U.S. society is in the process of creating a new, quasi-racial underclass out of the Puerto Rican population. With respect to patterns of assimilation, this group resembles the U.S. black population more than other Hispanic groups. It is spatially isolated from the mainstream of U.S. society by a high degree of residential segregation and is socially confined by low rates of intermarriage, even with other Hispanic groups. There is some evidence that Puerto Ricans are having difficulty breaking out of the secondary labor market, further accentuating their isolation in society. For some reason, possibly because of their partially black ancestry, Puerto Ricans appear to suffer a greater degree of prejudice and discrimination than other Hispanic or Asian groups in the United States.

A second problem is the relative lack of economic progress exhibited by Mexican Americans over the last two decades. Even controlling for social background, their performance falls below that of other minorities. Indeed, controlling for background variables, Mexicans [are] less able than blacks to translate their human capital into achievements. Several researchers have suggested that Mexican Americans are also having problems moving out of the secondary labor market and into more rewarding jobs. An important task for future research will thus be to sort out why Mexican income remains so low, and why returns to human capital are below those of other groups.

Finally, the undocumented population represents a potentially serious exception to the smooth assimilation of Hispanics into U.S. society. The lack of a legal right to employment and residence in the United States clearly represents a barrier to upward mobility among illegal immigrants, and for their children it can only represent an additional handicap to the many they already possess. If the status quo is maintained, undocumented immigrants have the potential to develop into a significant underclass, not without hope of advancement, but certainly hindered.

STATEMENT OF SENATOR ALAN K. SIMPSON, COMMISSIONER,
SELECT COMMISSION ON IMMIGRATION
AND REFUGEE POLICY

SCIRP, Final Report 409–13 (1981).

Numbers. New *legal* entries of immigrants and refugees for fiscal years 1977–1980 totaled, respectively, about 400,000; 500,000; 525,000; 675,000. Emigration may be as high as 30% of the number of new immigrants (not counting refugees). Although the exact figure is unknown, net *illegal* immigration may well number in the hundreds of thousands per year.

In a 1980 study by Dr. Leon F. Bouvier, who served as research demographer on the Select Commission staff and now is with the Population Reference Bureau, Washington, D.C., "The Impact of Immigration on the Size of the U.S. Population," he estimates that even if (a) net immigration, illegal as well as legal, equals 750,000 per year; (b) the fertility rate of the existing population and its descendants remains at its present low level (which seems unlikely); and (c) the fertility rate of new immigrants and their descendants immediately declines to that of the present population as a whole (which seems even less likely); then the U.S. population in the year 2080 will be 300,000,000, one-third of which will consist of post-1979 immigrants and their descendants.

* * *

Ethnic Patterns.

* * *

The present immigration flow differs from past flows in [a] * * * significant way. Immigration to the United States is now dominated to a high degree by persons speaking a single foreign language, Spanish, when illegal immigration is considered. The assimilation of the English language and other aspects of American culture by Spanish-speaking immigrants appears to be less rapid and complete than for other groups. A desire to assimilate is often reflected by the rate at which an immigrant completes the naturalization process necessary to become a U.S. citizen. A study by the Select Commission staff indicates that immigrants from Latin America naturalize to a lesser extent than those from other regions.* In part the apparently lower degree of assimilation may be due to the proximity to and the constant influx of new Spanish-speaking illegal immigrants from Latin America, many of whom regard their stay as only "temporary" and thus may not feel the need or desire to learn English or otherwise assimilate; and finally the greater tolerance for bilingualism and "biculturalism" in recent years, at least among a majority of legislators, who have adopted government policies which seem actually to promote linguistic and cultural separatism, policies such as the promotion of bilingual/"bicultural" education and foreign language ballots.

* A sample of those granted permanent resident status in 1971 was examined. Of those of Mexican origin who remained in the U.S. at the end of 7 years, only 5% had naturalized. For the entire region of South America the rate was 24.6%, for Europe 42.6%, and for Asia 80.3% (excluding China, India, Korea, and the Philippines, whose rates were, respectively, 73.8%, 67.8%, 80.9%, and 67.6%). [Note that Canadians had naturalized at a rate of 5–6%—eds.]

Under existing law and policies such patterns are likely to continue to be accentuated since the pressures for international migration are likely to increase over the coming decades, especially from regions which already dominate U.S. immigration flows.

Assimilation. Although the subject of the immediate economic impact of immigration receives great attention, assimilation to fundamental American public values and institutions may be of far more importance to the future of the United States. If immigration is continued at a high level and yet a substantial portion of the newcomers and their descendants do not assimilate, they may create in America some of the same social, political and economic problems which existed in the country which they have chosen to depart. Furthermore, as previously mentioned, a community with a large number of immigrants who do not assimilate will to some degree seem unfamiliar to longtime residents. Finally, if linguistic and cultural separatism rise above a certain level, the unity and political stability of the nation will in time be seriously eroded.

Questions

What does Senator Simpson mean by "assimilation"? Is the rate at which aliens naturalize a good measure? (Mexican and Canadians naturalize at rates far below most other nationalities. Does this indicate lack of assimilation?) Should he distinguish among economic, political, social and cultural assimilation? How do Massey's data and conclusions affect your evaluation of Senator Simpson's comments?

————

Linguistic assimilation remains a sensitive issue. Consider the various additional views reported in the following article.

JAMES FALLOWS, IMMIGRATION: HOW IT'S AFFECTING US

The Atlantic Monthly, November 1983, at 88–89.

Hispanics are more acutely aware than most Anglos that, as a practical reality, English is the national language of commerce, government, and mobility. But some have suggested that, in principle, it should not be this way.

They invoke the long heritage of Mexican-Americans in the Southwest. As "Californios" or "Tejanos," the ancestors of some of these families lived on and owned the territory before the Anglo settlers. Others came across at the turn of the century, at a time of Mexican upheaval; still others came during the forties and fifties, as workers. They have paid taxes, fought in wars, been an inseparable part of the region's culture. Yet they were also subject to a form of discrimination more casual than the segregation of the Old South, but having one of the same effects. Because of poverty or prejudice or gerrymandered school districts, many Mexican-Americans were, in effect, denied education. One result is that many now in their fifties and sixties do not speak English well. Still, they are citizens, with the right of citizens to vote. How are

they to exercise their right if to do so requires learning English? Do they
not deserve a ballot printed in a language they can understand?

* * *

[As a result of court decisions and legislation during the 1970's,]
ballots in parts of the country are printed in Spanish, or Chinese, or
Tagalog, along with English. This is true even though anyone applying
for naturalization must still pass an English-proficiency test, which consists of questions such as "What are the three branches of government?"
and "How long are the terms of a U.S. Senator and member of Congress?"
The apparent inconsistency reflects the linguistic reality that many native-born citizens have not learned the national language.

* * *

But there are those who feel that even the present arrangement is too
onerous. Rose Matsui Ochi, an assistant to the mayor of Los Angeles,
who served on the Select Commission, dissented from the commission's
recommendation to keep the English-language requirement for citizenship. She wrote in her minority opinion, "Abolishing the requirement
recognizes the inability of certain individuals to learn English." Cruz
Reynoso, the first Mexican-American appointee to the California Supreme
Court, was also on the Select Commission, and he too dissented. "America is a *political* union—not a cultural, linguistic, religious or racial
union," he wrote. "Of course, we as individuals would urge all to learn
English, for that is the language used by most Americans, as well as the
language of the marketplace. But we should no more demand English-
language skills for citizenship than we should demand uniformity of
religion. That a person wants to become a citizen and will make a good
citizen is more than enough."

Some Chicano activists make the same point in less temperate terms.
Twice I found myself in shouting matches with Mexican-Americans who
asked me who I thought I was to tell them—after all the homeboys who
had died in combat, after all the insults they'd endured on the playground
for speaking Spanish—what language they "should" speak.

That these arguments were conducted in English suggests the theoretical nature of the debate. Still, in questions like this, symbolism can
be crucial. "I have sympathy for the position that the integrating
mechanism of a society is language," Henry Cisneros [mayor of San
Antonio] says, "The U.S. has been able to impose fewer such integrating
mechanisms on its people than other countries, but it needs some tie to
hold these diverse people, Irish, Jews, Czechs, together as a nation.
Therefore, I favor people learning English and being able to conduct
business in the official language of the country."

"The *unum* demands only certain things of the *pluribus*," Lawrence
Fuchs [Executive Director of the Select Commission] says. "It demands
very little. It demands that we believe in the political ideals of the
republic, which allows people to preserve their ethnic identity. Most
immigrants come from repressive regimes; we say, we're asking you to
believe that government should *not* oppress you. Then it only asks one

other thing: that in the wider marketplace and in the civic culture, you use the official language. No other society asks so little.

"English is not just an instrument of mobility. It is a sign that you really are committed. If you've been here five years, which you must to be a citizen, and if you are reasonably young, you should be able to learn English in that time. The rest of us are entitled to that."

3. FAMILY REUNIFICATION CATEGORIES

The dominant feature of current arrangements for permanent immigration to the United States is family reunification. Immediate relatives of U.S. citizens, as we have seen, can immigrate without numerical limitation, and up to eighty percent of the numerically limited immigration spaces are reserved for family members who qualify under the 1st, 2nd, 4th, or 5th preference. The next three cases address the extent of Congress' power to define a "family" for immigration purposes, and the extent of any similar authority in the Immigration Service as it implements the broad definitions that Congress has adopted.

FIALLO v. BELL

Supreme Court of the United States, 1977.
430 U.S. 787, 97 S.Ct. 1473, 52 L.Ed.2d 50.

MR. JUSTICE POWELL delivered the opinion of the Court.

This case brings before us a constitutional challenge to §§ 101(b)(1)(D) and 101(b)(2) of the Immigration and Nationality Act of 1952 (Act).

I

The Act grants special preference immigration status to aliens who qualify as the "children" or "parents" of United States citizens or lawful permanent residents. Under § 101(b)(1), a "child" is defined as an unmarried person under 21 years of age who is a legitimate or legitimated child, a stepchild, an adopted child, or an illegitimate child seeking preference by virtue of his relationship with his natural mother. The definition does not extend to an illegitimate child seeking preference by virtue of his relationship with his natural father. Moreover, under § 101(b)(2), a person qualifies as a "parent" for purposes of the Act solely on the basis of the person's relationship with a "child." As a result, the natural father of an illegitimate child who is either a United States citizen or permanent resident alien is not entitled to preferential treatment as a "parent."

The special preference immigration status provided for those who satisfy the statutory "parent-child" relationship depends on whether the immigrant's relative is a United States citizen or permanent resident alien. A United States citizen is allowed the entry of his "parent" or "child" without regard to *either* an applicable numerical quota *or* the labor certification requirement. On the other hand, a United States permanent resident alien is allowed the entry of the "parent" or "child" subject to numerical limitations but without regard to the labor certification requirement.[a]

a. Before the 1976 amendments to the INA, most Western Hemisphere immigration was subject to an annual ceiling of 120,000, but the preference system did not

Appellants are three sets of unwed natural fathers and their illegitimate offspring who sought, either as an alien father or an alien child, a special immigration preference by virtue of a relationship to a citizen or resident alien child or parent. In each instance the applicant was informed that he was ineligible for an immigrant visa unless he qualified for admission under the general numerical limitations and, in the case of the alien parents, received the requisite labor certification.

* * *

At the outset, it is important to underscore the limited scope of judicial inquiry into immigration legislation. This Court has repeatedly emphasized that "over no conceivable subject is the legislative power of Congress more complete than it is over" the admission of aliens. Our cases "have long recognized the power to expel or exclude aliens as a fundamental sovereign attribute exercised by the Government's political departments largely immune from judicial control." *Shaughnessy v. Mezei*, 345 U.S. 206, 210, 73 S.Ct. 625, 628, 97 L.Ed. 956 (1953). Our recent decisions have not departed from this long-established rule. Just last Term, for example, the Court had occasion to note that "the power over aliens is of a political character and therefore subject only to narrow judicial review." *Hampton v. Mow Sun Wong*, 426 U.S. 88, 101 n. 21, 96 S.Ct. 1895, 1904–1905, 48 L.Ed.2d 495 (1976); accord, *Mathews v. Diaz*, 426 U.S. 67, 81–82, 96 S.Ct. 1883, 1892, 48 L.Ed.2d 478 (1976). And we observed recently that in the exercise of its broad power over immigration and naturalization, "Congress regularly makes rules that would be unacceptable if applied to citizens." *Id.*, at 80, 96 S.Ct., at 1891.

Appellants apparently do not challenge the need for special judicial deference to congressional policy choices in the immigration context,[5] but instead suggest that a "unique coalescing of factors" makes the instant case sufficiently unlike prior immigration cases to warrant more searching judicial scrutiny.

Appellants first observe that since the statutory provisions were designed to reunite families wherever possible, the purpose of the statute was to afford rights not to aliens but to United States citizens and legal permanent residents. Appellants then rely on our border-search decisions in *Almeida-Sanchez v. United States*, 413 U.S. 266, 93 S.Ct. 2535, 37 L.Ed.2d 596 (1973), and *United States v. Brignoni-Ponce*, 422 U.S. 873, 95 S.Ct. 2574, 45 L.Ed.2d 607 (1975), for the proposition that the courts must scrutinize congressional legislation in the immigration area to protect

apply. Aliens who were not excludable simply queued up for available numbers. All were subject to the labor certification requirement, however, unless it was waived because of specified family relationships. The Court treats the *Fiallo* case under pre-1976 law, but you should keep in mind that parents of permanent resident aliens—unlike parents of American citizens—no longer receive any special immigration benefits. —eds.

5. The appellees argue that the challenged sections of the Act, embodying as

they do "a substantive policy regulating the admission of aliens into the United States, [are] not an appropriate subject for judicial review." Our cases reflect acceptance of a limited judicial responsibility under the Constitution even with respect to the power of Congress to regulate the admission and exclusion of aliens, and there is no occasion to consider in this case whether there may be actions of the Congress with respect to aliens that are so essentially political in character as to be nonjusticiable.

against violations of the rights of citizens. At issue in the border-search cases, however, was the nature of the protections mandated by the Fourth Amendment with respect to Government procedures designed to stem the illegal entry of aliens. Nothing in the opinions in those cases suggests that Congress has anything but exceptionally broad power to determine which classes of aliens may lawfully enter the country.

Appellants suggest a second distinguishing factor. They argue that none of the prior immigration cases of this Court involved "double-barreled" discrimination based on sex and illegitimacy, infringed upon the due process rights of citizens and legal permanent residents, or implicated "the fundamental constitutional interests of United States citizens and permanent residents in a familial relationship." But this Court has resolved similar challenges to immigration legislation based on other constitutional rights of citizens, and has rejected the suggestion that more searching judicial scrutiny is required. In *Kleindienst v. Mandel*, [408 U.S. 753 (1972), considered below, page 194], for example, United States citizens challenged the power of the Attorney General to deny a visa to an alien who, as a proponent of "the economic, international, and governmental doctrines of World communism", was ineligible to receive a visa under INA § 212(a)(28)(D) absent a waiver by the Attorney General. The citizen-appellees in that case conceded that Congress could prohibit entry of all aliens falling into the class defined by [that section]. They contended, however, that the Attorney General's statutory discretion to approve a waiver was limited by the Constitution and that their First Amendment rights were abridged by the denial of Mandel's request for a visa. The Court held that "when the Executive exercises this [delegated] power negatively on the basis of a facially legitimate and bona fide reason, the courts will neither look behind the exercise of that discretion, nor test it by balancing its justification against the First Amendment interests of those who seek personal communication with the applicant." 408 U.S., at 770, 92 S.Ct., at 2585. We can see no reason to review the broad congressional policy choice at issue here under a more exacting standard than was applied in *Kleindienst v. Mandel*, a First Amendment case.[6]

---

6. The thoughtful dissenting opinion of our Brother Marshall would be persuasive if its basic premise were accepted. The dissent is grounded on the assumption that the relevant portions of the Act grant a "fundamental right" to American citizens, a right "given only to the citizen" and not to the putative immigrant. The assumption is facially plausible in that the families of putative immigrants certainly have an interest in their admission. But the fallacy of the assumption is rooted deeply in fundamental principles of sovereignty.

We are dealing here with an exercise of the Nation's sovereign power to admit or exclude foreigners in accordance with perceived national interests. Although few, if any, countries have been as generous as the United States in extending the privilege to immigrate, or in providing sanctuary to the oppressed, limits and classifications as to who shall be admitted are traditional and

necessary elements of legislation in this area. It is true that the legislative history of the provision at issue here establishes that congressional concern was directed at "the problem of keeping families of United States citizens and immigrants united." H.R.Rep. No. 1199, 85th Cong., 1st Sess., 7 (1957), U.S.Code Cong. & Admin.News, 1957, pp. 2016, 2020. See also H.R.Rep. No. 1365, 82d Cong., 2d Sess., 29 (1952), U.S.Code Cong. & Admin.News 1952, pp. 1653, 1680 (statute implements "the underlying intention of our immigration laws regarding the preservation of the family unit"). To accommodate this goal, Congress has accorded a special "preference status" to certain aliens who share relationships with citizens or permanent resident aliens. But there are widely varying relationships and degrees of kinship, and it is appropriate for Congress to consider not only the nature of these relationships but also problems of identification,

Finally, appellants characterize our prior immigration cases as involving foreign policy matters and congressional choices to exclude or expel groups of aliens that were "specifically and clearly perceived to pose a grave threat to the national security," * * * "or to the general welfare of this country." * * * We find no indication in our prior cases that the scope of judicial review is a function of the nature of the policy choice at issue. To the contrary, "[s]ince decisions in these matters may implicate our relations with foreign powers, and since a wide variety of classifications must be defined in the light of changing political and economic circumstances, such decisions are frequently of a character more appropriate to either the Legislature or the Executive than to the Judiciary," and "[t]he reasons that preclude judicial review of political questions also dictate a narrow standard of review of decisions made by the Congress or the President in the area of immigration and naturalization." *Mathews v. Diaz,* 426 U.S., at 81–82, 96 S.Ct., at 1892.

* * *

III

As originally enacted in 1952, § 101(b)(1) of the Act defined a "child" as an unmarried legitimate or legitimated child or stepchild under 21 years of age. The Board of Immigration Appeals and the Attorney General subsequently concluded that the failure of this definition to refer to illegitimate children rendered ineligible for preferential nonquota status both the illegitimate alien child of a citizen mother, and the alien mother of a citizen born out of wedlock. The Attorney General recommended that the matter be brought to the attention of Congress, and the Act was amended in 1957 to include what is now § 101(b)(1)(D). Congress was specifically concerned with the relationship between a child born out of wedlock and his or her natural mother, and the legislative history of the 1957 amendment reflects an intentional choice not to provide preferential immigration status by virtue of the relationship between an illegitimate child and his or her natural father.

This distinction is just one of many drawn by Congress pursuant to its determination to provide some—but not all—families with relief from various immigration restrictions that would otherwise hinder reunification of the family in this country. In addition to the distinction at issue here, Congress has decided that children, whether legitimate or not, cannot qualify for preferential status if they are married or are over 21 years of age. Legitimated children are ineligible for preferential status unless their legitimation occurred prior to their 18th birthday and at a time when they were in the legal custody of the legitimating parent or

administration, and the potential for fraud. In the inevitable process of "line drawing," Congress has determined that certain classes of aliens are more likely than others to satisfy national objectives without undue cost, and it has granted preferential status only to those classes.

As Mr. Justice Frankfurter wrote years ago, the formulation of these "[p]olicies pertaining to the entry of aliens . . . is entrusted exclusively to Congress". *Galvan v. Press,* 347 U.S., at 531, 74 S.Ct., at 743. This is not to say, as we make clear in n. 5, *supra,* that the Government's power in this area is never subject to judicial review. But our cases do make clear that despite the impact of these classifications on the interests of those already within our borders, congressional determinations such as this one are subject only to limited judicial review.

parents. Adopted children are not entitled to preferential status unless they were adopted before the age of 14 and have thereafter lived in the custody of their adopting or adopted parents for at least two years. And stepchildren cannot qualify unless they were under 18 at the time of the marriage creating the stepchild relationship.

With respect to each of these legislative policy distinctions, it could be argued that the line should have been drawn at a different point and that the statutory definitions deny preferential status to parents and children who share strong family ties. But it is clear from our cases that these are policy questions entrusted exclusively to the political branches of our Government, and we have no judicial authority to substitute our political judgment for that of the Congress.

Appellants suggest that the distinction drawn in § 101(b)(1)(D) is unconstitutional under any standard of review since it infringes upon the constitutional rights of citizens and legal permanent residents without furthering legitimate governmental interests. Appellants note in this regard that the statute makes it more difficult for illegitimate children and their natural fathers to be reunited in this country than for legitimate or legitimated children and their parents, or for illegitimate children and their natural mothers. And appellants also note that the statute fails to establish a procedure under which illegitimate children and their natural fathers could prove the existence and strength of their family relationship. Those are admittedly the consequences of the congressional decision not to accord preferential status to this particular class of aliens, but the decision nonetheless remains one "solely for the responsibility of the Congress and wholly outside the power of this Court to control." *Harisiades v. Shaughnessy,* 342 U.S., at 597, 72 S.Ct., at 522 (Frankfurter, J., concurring). Congress obviously has determined that preferential status is not warranted for illegitimate children and their natural fathers, perhaps because of a perceived absence in most cases of close family ties as well as a concern with the serious problems of proof that usually lurk in paternity determinations.[8] In any event, it is not the judicial role in cases of this sort to probe and test the justifications for the legislative decision.[9] *Kleindienst v. Mandel,* 408 U.S., at 770, 92 S.Ct., at 2585.

8. The inherent difficulty of determining the paternity of an illegitimate child is compounded when it depends upon events that may have occurred in foreign countries many years earlier. Congress may well have given substantial weight, in adopting the classification here challenged, to these problems of proof and the potential for fraudulent visa applications that would have resulted from a more generous drawing of the line. Moreover, our cases clearly indicate that legislative distinctions in the immigration area need not be as " 'carefully tuned to alternative considerations,' " * * * as those in the domestic area.

9. Appellants insist that the statutory distinction is based on an overbroad and outdated stereotype concerning the relationship of unwed fathers and their illegitimate children, and that existing administrative procedures, which had been developed to deal with the problems of proving paternity, maternity, and legitimation with respect to statutorily recognized "parents" and "children," could easily handle the problems of proof involved in determining the paternity of an illegitimate child. We simply note that this argument should be addressed to the Congress rather than the courts. Indeed, in that regard it is worth noting that a bill introduced in the 94th Congress would have eliminated the challenged distinction. H.R. 10993, 94th Cong., 1st Sess. (1975).

IV

We hold that §§ 101(b)(1)(D) and 101(b)(2) of the Immigration and Nationality Act of 1952 are not unconstitutional by virtue of the exclusion of the relationship between an illegitimate child and his natural father from the preferences accorded by the Act to the "child" or "parent" of a United States citizen or lawful permanent resident.

Affirmed.

MR. JUSTICE MARSHALL, with whom MR. JUSTICE BRENNAN joins, dissenting.

Until today I thought it clear that when Congress grants benefits to some citizens, but not to others, it is our duty to insure that the decision comports with Fifth Amendment principles of due process and equal protection. Today, however, the Court appears to hold that discrimination among citizens, however invidious and irrational, must be tolerated if it occurs in the context of the immigration laws. Since I cannot agree that Congress has license to deny fundamental rights to citizens according to the most disfavored criteria simply because the Immigration and Nationality Act is involved, I dissent.

* * *

The definitions [in § 101(b)] cover virtually all parent-child relationships except that of biological father-illegitimate child. Thus while all American citizens are entitled to bring in their alien children without regard to either the numerical quota or the labor certification requirement, fathers are denied this privilege with respect to their illegitimate children. Similarly, all citizens are allowed to have their parents enter without regard to the labor certification requirement, and, if the citizen is over 21, also without regard to the quota. Illegitimate children, however, are denied such preferences for their fathers.

The unfortunate consequences of these omissions are graphically illustrated by the case of appellant Cleophus Warner. Mr. Warner is a naturalized citizen of the United States who * * * petitioned the Attorney General for an immigrant visa for his illegitimate son Serge, a citizen of the French West Indies. Despite the fact that Mr. Warner acknowledged his paternity and registered as Serge's father shortly after his birth, has his name on Serge's birth certificate, and has supported and maintained Serge since birth, the special dispensation from the quota and labor certification requirements was denied because Serge was not a "child" under the statute. It matters not that, as the Government concedes, Serge's mother has abandoned Serge to his father and has, by marrying another man, apparently rendered impossible, under French West Indies law, Mr. Warner's ever legitimating Serge. Mr. Warner is simply not Serge's "parent."

* * *

This case, unlike most immigration cases that come before the Court, directly involves the rights of citizens, not aliens. "[C]oncerned with the problem of keeping families of United States citizens and immigrants united", H.R.Rep. No. 1199, 85th Cong., 1st Sess., 7 (1957), U.S.Code Cong. & Admin.News 1957, p. 2020, Congress extended to American citizens the right to choose to be reunited in the United States with their immediate families. The focus was on citizens and their need for relief from the hardships occasioned by the immigration laws. The right to seek such relief was given only to the citizen, not the alien. INA § 204. If the citizen does not petition the Attorney General for the special "immediate relative" status for his parent or child, the alien, despite his relationship, can receive no preference. It is irrelevant that aliens have no constitutional right to immigrate and that Americans have no constitutional right to compel the admission of their families. The essential fact here is that Congress did choose to extend such privileges to American citizens but then denied them to a small class of citizens. When Congress draws such lines among citizens, the Constitution requires that the decision comport with Fifth Amendment principles of equal protection and due process. The simple fact that the discrimination is set in immigration legislation cannot insulate from scrutiny the invidious abridgment of citizens' fundamental interests.

* * *

Once it is established that this discrimination among citizens cannot escape traditional constitutional scrutiny simply because it occurs in the context of immigration legislation, the result is virtually foreordained. One can hardly imagine a more vulnerable statute.

The class of citizens denied the special privilege of reunification in this country is defined on the basis of two traditionally disfavored classifications—gender and legitimacy. Fathers cannot obtain preferred status for their illegitimate children; mothers can. Conversely, every child except the illegitimate—legitimate, legitimated, step-, adopted—can obtain preferred status for his or her alien father. The Court has little tolerance for either form of discrimination.

* * *

In view of the legislation's denial of this right to these classes, it is clear that, whatever the verbal formula, the Government bears a substantial burden to justify the statute.

* * *

The legislative history, however, gives no indication of why these privileges were absolutely denied illegitimate children and their fathers. The Government suggests that Congress may have believed that "such persons are unlikely to have maintained a close personal relationship with their offspring." If so, Congress' chosen shorthand for "closeness" is obviously overinclusive. No one can dispute that there are legitimate, legitimated, step-, and adoptive parent-child relationships and mother-illegitimate child relationships that are not close and yet are accorded the preferential status. Indeed, the most dramatic illustration of the overinclusiveness is the fact that while Mr. Warner can never be deemed a "parent" of Serge, nevertheless, if he should marry, his wife could qualify as a stepparent, entitled to obtain for Serge the preferential status that Mr. Warner cannot obtain. *Andrade v. Esperdy*, 270 F.Supp. 516 (S.D. N.Y.1967); *Nation v. Esperdy*, 239 F.Supp. 531 (S.D.N.Y.1965). Similarly, a man who, in an adulterous affair, fathers a child outside his marriage cannot be the "parent" of that child, but his wife may petition as stepparent. *Matter of Stultz*, 15 I & N Dec. 362 (1975).

That the statute is underinclusive is also undisputed. Indeed, the Government could not dispute it in view of the close relationships exhibited in appellants' cases, recognized in our previous cases, and established in numerous studies.

The Government suggests that Congress may have decided to accept the inaccurate classifications of this statute because they considered a case-by-case assessment of closeness and paternity not worth the administrative costs. This attempted justification is plainly inadequate. In *Stanley v. Illinois*, [405 U.S. 645, 92 S.Ct. 1208, 31 L.Ed.2d 551 (1972)], we expressed our low regard for the use of "administrative convenience" as the rationale for interfering with a father's right to care for his illegitimate child.

> "Procedure by presumption is always cheaper and easier than individualized determination. But when, as here, the procedure forecloses the determinative issues of competence and care, when it explicitly disdains present realities in deference to past formalities, it needlessly risks running roughshod over the important interests of both parent and child. It therefore cannot stand." 405 U.S., at 656–657, 92 S.Ct., at 1215.

This Court has been equally intolerant of the rationale when it is used to deny rights to the illegitimate child. While we are sensitive to " 'the lurking problems with respect to proof of paternity,' " we are careful not to allow them to be " 'made into an impenetrable barrier that works to shield otherwise invidious discrimination.' " We require, at a minimum, that the statute [be] " 'carefully tuned to alternative considerations' ", and not exclude all illegitimates simply because some situations involve difficulties of proof.

Given such hostility to the administrative-convenience argument when invidious classifications and fundamental rights are involved, it is apparent that the rationale is inadequate in the present case. As I observed earlier, since Congress gave no indication that administrative costs were its concern we should scrutinize the hypothesis closely. The likelihood of such a rationale is diminished considerably by the comprehensive and elaborate administrative procedures already established and employed by the INS in passing on claims of the existence of a parent-child relationship. All petitions are handled on a case-by-case basis with the petitioner bearing the burden of proof. Moreover, the INS is no stranger to cases requiring proof of paternity. When, for example, a citizen stepmother petitions for the entrance of her husband's illegitimate child, she must necessarily prove that her husband is the child's father. Indeed, it is ironic that if Mr. Warner marries and his wife petitions for Serge, her proof will, in fact, be one step more complex than his would be—not only must she prove his paternity, but she must also prove their marriage. Nevertheless, she would be entitled to an opportunity to prove those facts; he is not.

Nor is a fear of involvement with foreign laws and records a persuasive explanation of the omission. In administering the Act with respect to legitimated children, for example, the critical issue is whether the steps undertaken are adequate under local law to render the child legitimate, and the INS has become expert in such matters. I note, in this connection, that where a child was born in a country in which all children are legitimate, proof of paternity is the critical issue and the proof problems are identical to those involved with an illegitimate child.

Given the existence of these procedures and expertise, it is difficult indeed to give much weight to the hypothesized administrative-convenience rationale. Moreover, as noted previously, this Court will not allow concerns with proof to justify "an impenetrable barrier that works to shield otherwise invidious discrimination." As the facts of this case conclusively demonstrate, Congress has "failed to consider the possibility of a middle ground between the extremes of complete exclusion and case-by-case determination of paternity." Mr. Warner is a classic example of someone who can readily prove both paternity and closeness. Appellees concede this. The fact that he is **denied the** opportunity demonstrates beyond peradventure that Congress has failed to " 'carefully tun[e] [the statute] to alternative considerations.' " That failure is fatal to the statute.

When Congress grants a fundamental right to all but an invidiously selected class of citizens, and it is abundantly clear that such discrimination would be intolerable in any context but immigration, it is our duty to strike the legislation down. Because the Court condones the invidious discrimination in this case simply because it is embedded in the immigration laws, I must dissent.

Mr. JUSTICE WHITE also dissents, substantially for the reasons stated by Mr. JUSTICE MARSHALL in his dissenting opinion.

Notes

1. Justice Marshall's dissent seems to suggest that the Court can apply more rigorous constitutional review to the classifications in *Fiallo* without necessarily having to apply such scrutiny in most other immigration cases. "This case," he writes, "unlike most immigration cases that come before the Court, directly involves the rights of citizens." He supports this claim by citing passages in the legislative history which demonstrate that Congress paid particular attention to citizens' interests in family reunification.

But does this factor really distinguish most immigration cases? Nearly all permanent immigration today, except for refugees, begins with a petition filed with the INS by a U.S. citizen. (For the second preference, the petitioner need not be a citizen. That preference allows a permanent resident alien to petition, but the category of beneficiaries is more limited: spouse or unmarried son or daughter.) Even the employment-based preferences usually begin in this way, with a petition filed by the prospective American employer. Several nonimmigrant classifications follow a similar procedure. Moreover, do you doubt that the legislative history of most immigration provisions will contain speeches by members of Congress emphasizing their solicitude for the interests of *citizens?*

2. After *Fiallo,* could Congress amend the INA to make all but members of the Caucasian race ineligible for immigration? What standard should a court use in considering an equal protection challenge to such a statute? Cf. *Dunn v. INS,* 499 F.2d 856 (9th Cir.1974), cert. denied 419 U.S. 1106, 95 S.Ct. 776, 42 L.Ed.2d 801 (1975) (using the "rational basis" test in denying an equal protection challenge to a provision rendering Mexican nationals ineligible to adjust status from nonimmigrant to immigrant while within the United States; the INA was later amended to remove this preclusion). Before the 1965 INA amendments abolished the national-origins quota system, courts rather easily disposed of constitutional challenges to the lines Congress had drawn. *See, e.g., Hitai v. INS,* 343 F.2d 466 (2d Cir.1965). *Hitai* even presented an aggravated example of purely racial theories as manifested in the INA at that time. Hitai was born in Brazil to naturalized Brazilian citizens. But because his parents had been born Japanese citizens, he came within the small Japanese quota under the INA as then written, rather than being treated like other citizens of Brazil. Even in this setting, the court sustained the constitutionality of the statute.

Against the background of cases like *Hitai,* it is somewhat surprising that the Supreme Court in *Fiallo* goes so far as to state (in footnote 5) that "[o]ur cases reflect acceptance of a limited judicial responsibility" to review Congress's line-drawing, rather than no responsibility at all. Perhaps the Court speaks of a "limited responsibility" precisely to preserve the possibility that it might strike down any modern immigration legislation that established preference categories based explicitly on racial distinctions.

Still, we need to consider the underlying question regarding the judicial role more carefully. It is virtually inconceivable in the 1980's that a statute drawing explicit racial lines that disadvantage nonwhite groups would issue forth from Congress. But arguably analogous provisions are within the realm of possibility in forms that might present knottier problems. Suppose, for example, that Congress responded to a new crisis in the Middle East by providing that no nationals of the following countries could be admitted to the United States: Morocco, Algeria, Libya, Egypt, Jordan, Syria, Saudi Arabia, Kuwait, and Iraq. If you were the judge, how would you analyze a case wherein the plaintiffs allege that the statute violates equal protection principles because it constitutes discrimination against Arabs as a racial group? In one sense of the term, the statute is based on "national origin" discrimination. Should such distinctions in the immigration sphere be considered wholly equivalent to "racial" discrimination and thus subject to "strict scrutiny"? Or is the statute to be upheld if it rests on a "rational basis" or—perhaps even less demanding—a "facially legitimate and bona fide reason"?

If the government claims that foreign policy concerns justify the use of these immigration restrictions, how should a court evaluate the genuineness and strength of such factors? Are courts institutionally capable of handling such review? *See Narenji v. Civiletti,* 617 F.2d 745 (D.C.Cir. 1979), cert. denied 446 U.S. 957, 100 S.Ct. 2928, 64 L.Ed.2d 815 (1980) (reversing a district court decision that struck down, on equal protection grounds, an INS regulation imposing special reporting and review requirements solely on Iranian students, adopted in wake of the seizure of U.S. diplomats in Tehran); *Jean v. Nelson,* 727 F.2d 957, 978 & n. 30 (11th Cir.1984) (en banc), *cert granted,* ___ U.S. ___, 105 S.Ct. 563, 83 L.Ed.2d 504 (1984) (ruling that at least Congress and high-level executive branch officials may constitutionally discriminate among aliens on the basis of national origin; the en banc court carefully avoided any phrasing that might suggest approval of discrimination based on "race," even though an earlier panel decision, vacated by the en banc court, had ruled against the government based precisely on its finding of racial—not national-origin—discrimination against the plaintiff Haitians).

3. Justice Marshall states that if Cleophus Warner were now to marry, his wife could petition to bring in Serge Warner as her stepchild, citing *Andrade v. Esperdy,* 270 F.Supp. 516 (S.D.N.Y.1967). Some cases have indeed held that the statutory definition of stepchild, INA § 101(b)(1)(B), is to be applied in this literal fashion. But the Board of Immigration Appeals has resisted such an interpretation, arguing that the statutory purpose could be fulfilled by granting petitions for stepchildren only where there is evidence of a pre-existing family unit or equivalent ties. In *Matter of Moreira,* 17 I & N Dec. 41, 46–47 (BIA 1979), the Board stated its approach as follows:

> [A] steprelationship will be recognized for immigration purposes only where the stepparent has shown an interest in the step-child's welfare prior to that child's eighteenth birthday, either by permitting the child to live in the family home and caring for him as a parent, or, if the child did not live with the stepparent, by demonstrating an active parental interest in the child's support, instruction, and general welfare.

In *Palmer v. Reddy,* 622 F.2d 463 (9th Cir.1980), the court explicitly rejected the *Moreira* standards and directed that "stepchild" be construed literally. For the Board's agonized response to *Palmer, see Matter of Bonnette,* 17 I & N Dec. 587 (BIA 1980). Which approach is more consistent with the congressional plan? Which makes more sense to you?

DE LOS SANTOS v. INS

United States Court of Appeals, Second Circuit, 1982.
690 F.2d 56.

KEARSE, CIRCUIT JUDGE:

Plaintiff Domingo Antonio de los Santos ("Domingo"), a citizen of the Dominican Republic and a lawful permanent resident of the United States, appeals from a final judgment of the United States District Court for the Southern District of New York, Robert J. Ward, *Judge,* dismissing his complaint seeking reversal of a ruling by defendant Immigration and Naturalization Service ("INS") that denied preferential immigration status for Enmanuel de los Santos ("Enmanuel") as Domingo's son under §§ 101(b)(1)(C) and 203(a)(2) of the Immigration and Nationality Act ("Act"). Section 203(a)(2) grants preferential status to, *inter alios,* the legitimate and legitimated children of lawful permanent residents of the United States. Enmanuel, a citizen and resident of the Dominican Republic, was born in 1957 out of wedlock. On the basis of undisputed facts, the district court concluded that Enmanuel had not been legitimated within the meaning of § 101(b)(1)(C) of the Act and granted summary judgment dismissing Domingo's complaint. We affirm substantially for the reasons stated in the opinion of the district court, reported at 525 F.Supp. 655.

BACKGROUND

Under the complex statutory scheme governing the admission of aliens seeking to immigrate to the United States, one of the groups given immigration priority is composed of "the spouses, unmarried sons or unmarried daughters of an alien lawfully admitted for permanent residence." INA § 203(a)(2). Although the Act contains no definition of "son" or "daughter," these terms are construed to mean that the prospective immigrant must be the "child" of the permanent resident alien. *See, e.g., Lau v. Kiley,* 563 F.2d 543, 545 (2d Cir.1977). The statutory definition of "child" includes certain illegitimate offspring. Section 101(b)(1)(C) of the Act provides that an individual born out of wedlock is a "child" if he or she has been

> legitimated under the law of the child's residence or domicile, or under the law of the father's residence or domicile, whether in or outside the United States, if such legitimation takes place before the child reaches the age of eighteen years and the child is in the legal custody of the legitimating parent or parents at the time of such legitimation.

INS [sic] has interpreted the word "legitimated" to refer to a child born out of wedlock who has been accorded legal rights that are identical to those enjoyed by a child born in wedlock. *See, e.g., Matter of Reyes,* Interim Decision No. 2822 (BIA 1980); *Matter of Clahar,* Interim Decision No. 2643, 16 I & N 484 (BIA 1978); *Matter of Remy,* Interim Decision No. 2160, 14 I & N 183 (BIA 1972).

The law of the Dominican Republic provides two means by which the illegitimate status of a child born out of wedlock may be altered. First, in a process called "legitimate filiation," the child may be legitimated by the subsequent marriage of his parents if they have acknowledged the child prior to or in the act of their marriage:

> Children born out of wedlock who are not the offspring of incestuous or adulterous unions, may be legitimated by the subsequent marriage of their parents in the cases where they have legally acknowledged them prior to or in the act of their marriage.

Dominican Civil Code [DCC] art. 331. DCC art. 333 provides that children legitimated in this fashion "shall enjoy the same rights and benefits of legitimate children." Second, an illegitimate child may be "naturally filiated":

> With respect to the mother a natural filiation is established by the sole fact of birth.

> With respect to the father, it is established by acknowledgment or by judicial decision.

Law 985 of Aug. 1, 1945, art. 2. However, Law 985 art. 1 provides as follows:

Natural filiation established pursuant to the provisions of the law produces the same effects as legitimate filiation *with the exception of the distinction made in matters concerning successions.*

(Emphasis added.)   The exception referred to provides that in the event the parent also has a legitimate child or children and dies intestate, the naturally filiated child will inherit only one half the share attributable to a legitimate child.   Law 985 art. 10.

In the present case, Domingo and Enmanuel's mother have never been married to each other, and Domingo does not contend that Enmanuel has been legitimated under DCC art. 331.   Rather, he asserts that he "acknowledged" Enmanuel eight days after Enmanuel was born, thereby naturally filiating Enmanuel under Law 985 art. 1, and that Enmanuel was thus legitimated under Dominican law for purposes of the United States immigration laws.

INS rejected Domingo's petition, concluding, as it had previously in *Matter of Reyes, supra,* that natural filiation under Dominican law does not establish rights identical to those enjoyed by legitimate children, and hence a "naturally filiated" Dominican child cannot be deemed "legitimated" within the meaning of § 101(b)(1)(C) of the Act.   Domingo challenges here, as he did in the district court, INS's interpretation of legitimation as unreasonable and unduly narrow.

DISCUSSION

We affirm the judgment dismissing Domingo's complaint substantially for the reasons given in Judge Ward's thorough opinion, reported at 525 F.Supp. 655, and add only the following observations.

First, there is no serious question of Dominican law that is unresolved in any material respect.   The district court implicitly construed Dominican law as according to children naturally filiated under Law 985 rights that are less extensive than those of legitimate children and children legitimated under DCC art. 331.   This determination, which we review as a question of law, Fed.R.Civ.P. 44.1, was eminently correct.   Domingo recognizes that under Dominican law naturally filiated children do not enjoy inheritance rights as extensive as those of legitimate children.   The only serious question he poses is whether the naturally filiated child's lesser right of inheritance is a permissible basis for INS's refusal to deem such a child legitimated within the meaning of the immigration laws.

As to the matter of the correct interpretation of § 101(b)(1)(C), while this too is a question of law subject to full review by the appellate court, in general we must give deference to the construction accorded to a statute by the agency charged with its administration.   Thus, if INS's interpretation is reasonable, in that it is consistent with the statutory language, legislative history, and purpose of the statute, we will not invalidate it.

We agree with the district court that INS's interpretation of "legitimated" as requiring the acquisition of rights coextensive with those of a legitimate child is consistent with the language of the Act.   The plain meaning of the word is discussed in greater detail in the district court's opinion, and need not be explored further here.   The district court also reviewed at length the legislative history of the Act and of related statutes, to determine whether INS's interpretation is consistent with Congress's intent. Although the legislative history is not dispositive, we see in it no indication that Congress intended the word "legitimated" to denote the acquisition of fewer rights than those enjoyed by a legitimate son or daughter. Accordingly, the history, to the extent that it sheds light on this question, supports the view that INS's interpretation is not inconsistent with Congress's intent.

The closest question is whether INS's interpretation, as applied in the present case, is consistent with the purpose of the statutory scheme. Immigration preference categories were created as a means of allocating visas when the demand for them exceeds the number lawfully available. In general, insofar as is pertinent here, the Act grants preferential status to close relatives of United States citizens and permanent residents in order to facilitate the reunification of families.

INS contends that since the number of available visas is limited, the goal of family reunification requires that the Act be strictly interpreted in order to minimize the number of successful fraudulent claims. INS's narrow interpretation is thus based on the belief that a claimant will be less likely to claim as his child a person with whom he does not have a bona fide parent/child relationship if he must confer full filial rights on that person than if he may successfully assert such a claim while conferring fewer rights. We think this belief farfetched as it is applied to the provisions of Dominican law at issue here. Here the difference between the rights of naturally filiated children and legitimate children is slight: if the parent of a naturally filiated child dies intestate, and if there are legitimate children, the naturally filiated child will inherit only half the share attributable to a legitimate child. It hardly seems likely that a rule based solely on such a small difference—especially one that disappears if the parent dies testate or without legitimate children—would have any efficacy in deterring fraud. *See, e.g., Reyes v. INS,* 478 F.Supp. 63, 66 (E.D.N.Y.1979); *Delgado v. INS,* 473 F.Supp. 1343, 1348 (S.D.N.Y.1979). INS's interpretation of "legitimated," however, is a general one requiring complete identity of rights, not one focusing solely on rights of inheritance. Further, the rule is designed for worldwide application; it has not been fashioned with reference to particular distinctions drawn by the laws of any one country. In the context of rights such as financial support and use of the family name, and indeed in the context of other differences in rights of inheritance, INS's interpretation may well have the effect of reducing fraud.

It is not the province of the courts to insist that INS's interpretations of the Act result in the perfect immigration scheme, or even that they be the best interpretations possible. Rather INS is given a fair amount of latitude to exercise its judgment as to what interpretations will best effectuate the goals of the Act. * * * Since INS's strict interpretation is consistent with the language and history of the Act and is, as a general matter, reasonably calculated to serve the purposes of the Act, it is entitled to deference, and we will not invalidate it because in the present instance its usefulness may be tenuous.

CONCLUSION

The judgment of the district court is affirmed.

Notes

1.   In many countries, legitimation can occur only by the marriage of the natural father and the natural mother.   Such a marriage is sometimes impossible—either because one party is unwilling or because of legal impediments—despite genuinely close ties between the father and the child.   Having in mind barriers like this, as well as the relatively trivial inheritance differences under the law of the Dominican Republic, an earlier court decision on facts like those in *de los Santos* was highly critical of the Board's rule requiring full equality of rights:

> The rule adopted has no reasonable relation to preventing fraud, and it ignores "the foremost policy underlying the granting of preference visas under our immigration laws, the reunification of families * * * ".

Delgado v. INS, 473 F.Supp. 1343, 1348 (S.D.N.Y.1979), quoting *Lau v. Kiley,* 563 F.2d 543 (2d Cir.1977).

To say that the Board's rule interferes with family reunification is a powerful charge.   But is this really an objection to the *Board's* interpretation?   Recall that the district court found, after lengthy inquiry, that the plain meaning of "legitimated" connotes full equality of rights; Webster's Dictionary strongly supports this understanding.   *See* 525 F.Supp. at 661–662.   Isn't *Delgado* objecting to the underlying *statutory* policy that restricts the recognition of certain close ties which fathers may develop with their natural children?   The Board has answered these questions this way:

> Where Congress has specified those father-child relationships which should be recognized for immigration purposes using terms of commonly understood legal meaning, the Board cannot "redefine" those terms based on their own views as to how the purposes underlying the immigration laws might be better achieved.   In interpreting the language of § 101(b), although one must be mindful of the purpose of the immigration laws to preserve the family unit, it must also be recognized that § 101(b) in fact embodies the congressional conclusions as to which familial relationships warrant recognition.   See *Fiallo v. Bell* * * *.

Matter of Reyes, 17 I & N Dec. 512, 516 (B.I.A. 1980).

2.   Besides relying on plain meanings, the Board, as the principal case shows, also justified its rule by reference to the statutory purpose of deterring fraud.   The Second Circuit found this a close question, but ultimately deferred to the Board's judgment that a fixed rule requiring full equality of rights was best suited for worldwide application.   If one assumes that Congress has left the agency some discretion, should the Board be so wedded to its bright-line test, or should it consider the likelihood of fraudulent claims case by case?   Case-by-case consideration might involve developing, over time, a list of countries where the differ-

ences in rights between legitimate children and illegitimate children formally acknowledged are so trivial as not to give rise to a significant risk of fraud. Alternatively, case-by-case determination might be done on an individual basis rather than country-by-country. For example, the Board (or the initial adjudicating officer) might simply require proof of some procedure formally acknowledging paternity, as well as other evidence demonstrating genuine family relationships between the father and child, sufficient to show that the acknowledgement was not meant for the sole (and hence fraudulent) purpose of conferring immigration benefits.

If we adopt this latter stance, we come near to the position Justice Marshall seemed to advocate in *Fiallo,* requiring the recognition of a relation for immigration purposes whenever the petitioner "can readily prove both paternity and closeness." But if we have come this far, why should we stop there? Why should *both* factors be required? Why shouldn't closeness alone be sufficient? After all, Justice Marshall is elsewhere quite critical of "Congress' chosen shorthand for 'closeness,'" finding the definitions used both overinclusive and underinclusive. Why shouldn't aunts, uncles, or cousins be given family reunification immigration benefits if the petitioner shows that in his ethnic group—or perhaps only in his particular family—such ties are as close as the average ties among members of the usual suburban American nuclear family? See SCIRP, Staff Report, at 371 (quoting the testimony of Father Joseph A. Cogo, urging immigration benefits for grandparents and "fireside relatives like an aunt who's not married * * * and living with the family. * * * [T]hey should not be subjected to a definition by other ethnic groups just because other ethnic groups have different definitions in their tradition.")

Indeed, why require biological relationships at all? Why not adopt a system allowing family reunification-type immigration benefits based on closeness alone—that is, based on proof of functional family ties, whatever the biological relationship? *See Antoine-Dorcelli v. INS,* 703 F.2d 19 (1st Cir.1983) (requiring the BIA to consider "family" ties between the Haitian housekeeper and an American family she has lived with for over 30 years, for purposes of determining whether deportation would cause "extreme hardship" within the meaning of § 244); *cf. Adams v. Howerton,* 673 F.2d 1036 (9th Cir.1982) *cert. denied* 458 U.S. 1111, 102 S.Ct. 3494, 73 L.Ed.2d 1373 (1982) (refusing to extend immigration benefits based on a homosexual marriage, even though the court assumed that the marriage was valid under state law).

3. Once we work our way through to these possible alternative schemes, however, we should pause to take stock of the administrative implications. Under the rule approved in *de los Santos,* immigration examiners considering petitions for allegedly legitimated children usually need only consult BIA decisions to see whether the particular procedure (such as natural filiation) in the country at issue has been held to constitute "legitimation" under the INA. Even if the petitioner is from a country whose legitimation laws have not been reviewed yet by the BIA, the issue remains fairly clearcut for the immigration examiner. Does the procedure result in *full* equality of rights? The inquiry is directed toward the legal system of the country, not into the details of family relationships. Thus the examiner has no substantial discretion, and is not

required to make judgment calls about whether seemingly minor differences are so significant in the actual practice of the foreign country that they should result in disqualification from immigration benefits.

At the opposite extreme falls the hypothetical proposal allowing preferential treatment whenever the petitioner shows family-like "closeness." How would such a scheme be implemented? What kinds of evidence would be relevant in proving closeness? Do we want INS agents or consular officers asking about the intimate details of life around the family fireside in order to decide whether the relationship to an aunt is close enough to merit immigration benefits? Remember that most immigration examiners are relatively low-level bureaucrats, many of them lacking a full four-year college degree. They are not psychologists or sociologists. Vast changes in recruitment patterns, compensation, training and regular duties would be required to create a system wherein examiners had such a background. These staffing realities may help account for decisions by the INS and the BIA to use bright-line tests (despite occasional outcomes that may seem arbitrary), rather than employ vague criteria expanding the inquiry into other areas. Case-by-case judgments of "closeness" or other elusive concepts (like the likelihood of fraud in the use of a particular legitimation procedure) would give rise to a related concern. They are much harder for supervisors—ultimately running all the way up to the Attorney General—to monitor, in order to assure that like cases are treated alike, and even to detect whether an officer has issued a decision in a given case because of corruption or other improper favoritism.

Of course, the question remains whether these benefits to sound administration from the use of bright-line tests are outweighed by the inevitability of arbitrary outcomes and their impact in the particular setting. Judging that balance can be a difficult task, and administrators may have incentives for erring in favor of fixed rules. But judges may similarly be too quick to dismiss as "administrative convenience" certain concerns that are far more complex than simply adding to the annual agency appropriation. A most useful discussion of these issues appears in Diver, *The Optimal Precision of Administrative Rules*, 93 Yale L.J. 65 (1983).

4. The court seems to suggest, in the second paragraph in *de los Santos*, that "son" or "daughter" means the same thing as "child" under the statute. This is not quite accurate. A "child" must be under 21 and unmarried; the statute refers to "son" or "daughter" when Congress wishes to include people enjoying the same basic familial relationship, but who may be over that age or married. The other stipulations of INA § 101(b)(1) do apply, however, in deciding whether or not an individual is a son or daughter.

> While neither of the terms "sons" or "daughters" is defined in the Act, it seems well established that in order to qualify as a "son" or "daughter" for the purposes of obtaining visa preference, one must once have qualified as a "child" under § 101(b)(1) of the Act * * *.

Lau v. Kiley, 563 F.2d 543, 545 (2d Cir.1977). *See also Nazareno v. Attorney General,* 512 F.2d 936 (D.C.Cir.1975) *cert. denied* 423 U.S. 832, 96 S.Ct. 53, 46 L.Ed.2d 49 (1975) (reviewing the complicated statutory history to decide that the age ceiling on adoptions appearing in INA § 101(b)(1) applies in deciding whether an alien qualifies as a son or daughter; persons adopted at age 32 do not qualify).

5. As is evident, family relationship questions will often turn on foreign law, the law of petitioner's or beneficiary's domicile at the time of birth or other relevant event. This may present unique difficulties:

> Foreign law, and particularly the kind of nonstatutory, custom law with which this Board must often deal, is sometimes hard to ascertain. It is particularly difficult for the alien, who frequently finds that local consulates, or even his embassy, do not have appropriate legal help or may even be unsympathetic to his claims and hence not disposed to be helpful.

Matter of Lee, 16 I & N Dec. 305, 308 (BIA 1977) (Appleman, Member, dissenting).

The BIA has held that foreign law is a question of fact, and that the petitioner has the burden of proving any point of foreign law on which he relies to establish eligibility for an immigration benefit. *Matter of Annang,* 14 I & N Dec. 502 (BIA 1973). *Cf.* Fed.R.Civ.P. 44.1 (allowing for determination of foreign law through any relevant source, including testimony, but treating the determination as a ruling on a question of law); *Crespo v. United States,* 185 Ct.Cl. 127, 399 F.2d 191, 192 (1968) ("Although the law of a foreign jurisdiction may be proved as a fact, it is the function of the court and not that of a jury to determine the state of the foreign law from the proof presented on the issue."). But INS personnel and the Board of Immigration Appeals frequently resort as well to expert advice from the staff of the Library of Congress. *See, e.g., Matter of Lee, supra,* at 305; *id.* at 308 (Appleman, Member, dissenting) (suggesting that the petitioner should have been given an opportunity to comment on the Library of Congress memorandum before the Board relied on it).

In this process, mistakes are not unknown. *See, e.g., Matter of Hann,* Interim Dec. No. 2867 (BIA 1981) (modifying three earlier cases on the effect of divorces in the Dominican Republic, because the earlier decisions were based on a faulty translation of a Dominican statute). The *Hann* decision itself had to be modified two years later when the Board's attention was drawn to the effect of yet another provision of the Dominican Civil Code. *Matter of Zorilla,* Interim Dec. No. 2937 (BIA 1983). See also *Lau v. Kiley,* 563 F.2d 543 (2d Cir.1977) (lengthy and scholarly inquiry into the question of legitimacy of children born out of wedlock in the People's Republic of China).

———

Application of the family reunification provisions can be complicated not only by the need to interpret foreign law. It may also require difficult determinations about the interaction of state family law and federal immigration law, as the following case demonstrates.

KALISKI v. DISTRICT DIRECTOR

United States Court of Appeals, Ninth Circuit, 1980.
620 F.2d 214.

SOLOMON, DISTRICT JUDGE.

The Immigration and Naturalization Service (INS) appeals from the judgment of the district court approving a preferential visa petition filed by appellee Vasa Kaliski on behalf of his son Milivoj who was born out of wedlock in Yugoslavia in 1934. We affirm.

In January 1973, Kaliski filed a petition for a preferential immigrant visa for his son. INS rejected the petition because Milivoj was born out of wedlock, and because there was no evidence that he was legitimated under Yugoslav law before his eighteenth birthday as required by the Immigration and Nationality Act. The Board of Immigration Appeals (Board) affirmed the rejection. The district court, on a petition for review, reversed the decision of the INS on the ground that Milivoj was legitimated under California law before his eighteenth birthday.

Section 201 of the Act sets a quota on the number of immigrant visas allowed for each fiscal year. Within the quota are seven categories of persons entitled to preferential treatment. One such preference is for "qualified immigrants who are the married sons or married daughters of citizens of the United States." INA § 203(a)(4).

To qualify as a married son or daughter, an immigrant must have qualified as a "child" under INA § 101(b)(1)(C). *Nazareno v. Attorney General*, 512 F.2d 936 (2nd Cir.), *cert. denied*, 423 U.S. 832, 96 S.Ct. 53, 46 L.Ed.2d 49 (1975). A "child" is defined as:

(1) . . . an unmarried person under twenty-one years of age who is—

. . . . .

(C) a child legitimated under the law of the child's residence or domicile, or under the law of the father's residence or domicile, whether in or outside the United States, if such legitimation takes place before the child reaches the age of eighteen years and the child is in the legal custody of the legitimating parent or parents at the time of such legitimation.

There are [two major] issues presented here: (1) Was California law applicable in this case when neither Kaliski nor his son had any contact with California before the son's eighteenth birthday? (2) Was Kaliski's son legitimated under California law before his eighteenth birthday, as required by section 101(b)(1)(C)? * * *

FACTS

Vasa Kaliski was born in Yugoslavia in 1908. Between 1932 and 1941, he lived with but never married Magdelena Rotsenk because she was Catholic and he was Greek Orthodox. In 1934, Magdelena gave birth to their son Milivoj who lived with them until 1941. In that year, while serving in the Yugoslav army, Kaliski was taken prisoner by the Germans and was interned in a prisoner-of-war camp in Germany until his release in 1945. He lived in resettlement camps in Germany until 1951 when he emigrated to the United States. He established domicile in California in 1953 and became a citizen in 1971.

On January 3, 1973, Kaliski filed a petition with INS to obtain a preferential immigrant visa for his son who still lives in Yugoslavia. INS and the Board rejected the petition because Milivoj was not legitimated under Yugoslav law before his eighteenth birthday. The district court reviewed the decision of the INS and held that Milivoj is entitled to a preferential visa because he was legitimated under California law before his eighteenth birthday.[1]

APPLICABILITY OF CALIFORNIA LAW

Under section 230 of the California Civil Code,[2] the father of an illegitimate child may legitimate the child by receiving the child into his family and acknowledging the child as his own. The California Supreme Court, in *In re Lund's Estate,* 26 Cal.2d 472, 159 P.2d 643 (1945), held that an illegitimate child was legitimated by the father under section 230 even if the legitimating acts occurred before either the father or the son had any contact with California, as long as the father later established his domicile in California.

The district court held that Kaliski legitimated Milivoj under California law by raising him during the first seven years of his life. California law was held to be applicable because Kaliski later established his domicile in California.

INS contends that California law should not be applied here because neither the father nor the son had any contact with the state before the son's eighteenth birthday and the legitimating acts did not occur in California. The INS contends that a state law affecting the distribution of property is not determinative in citizenship or immigration cases.

In our view, the INS interpreted the law incorrectly. Under § 101(b)(1)(C), an immigrant qualifies as a "child" by being legitimated under the law of the father's domicile. The only restrictions are that the child must be under the age of eighteen when legitimated and the child must reside with the father at the time of legitimation. Both of these events occurred here. The fact that a state's legitimation statute is intended only to determine property distribution is irrelevant because that is the primary purpose of all such statutes. We hold that a state law which recognizes legitimating acts which occur before the father and child have any contact with the state is applicable in immigration cases.

AGE LIMIT

INS contends that even if California law applies, Milivoj was not legitimated under California law before his eighteenth birthday because

---

1. A federal court may review the denial of the INS of a preferential visa petition to determine if the denial was an abuse of discretion. Abuse of discretion may be found if there is no evidence to support the decision or if the decision is based on an improper understanding of the law. *Song Jook Suh v. Rosenberg,* 437 F.2d 1098, 1102 (9th Cir.1971). Here, the district court ruled that the INS applied erroneous legal standards in denying the petition.

2. Section 230 was repealed by enactment of the 1976 Uniform Parentage Act, California Civil Code, §§ 7000–7018.

his father did not establish domicile in California until Milivoj was nineteen years old.

INS argues that the Act requires the father or child to reside in a jurisdiction recognizing the child's legitimacy before the child is eighteen years old. Kaliski argues that the Act only requires that the legitimating acts occur before the child is eighteen years old, and that the father and child need not reside in the jurisdiction which subsequently recognizes the legitimating acts before the child's eighteenth birthday.

The age limit requirement is designed to prevent fraud. Without the limitation, persons of any age could enter the United States by being "legitimated" by bogus parents, thereby encouraging the kind of immigrant traffic now prevalent because of sham marriages between American citizens and foreigners.

Nevertheless, the possibility of fraud is no greater if the less stringent requirement urged by Kaliski is adopted. The petitioner must establish that (1) he is the natural father of the child; (2) that he performed legitimating acts while the child was in his custody and before the child was eighteen years old; and (3) that, at the time of the petition to the INS, the father or son lived in a jurisdiction recognizing the legitimating acts as sufficient to make the child legitimate.

Furthermore, the humane purpose of the Act—to reunite families— would be frustrated by the strict interpretation urged by the INS. An illegitimate child born in Yugoslavia is disadvantaged because the legitimation requirements in that country are strict. However, a child born out of wedlock in the Peoples Republic of China has an advantage because that country has abolished any distinctions between legitimate and illegitimate children. *See Lau v. Kiley,* 563 F.2d 543 (2d Cir.1977). There is no rational basis for such an arbitrary distinction, particularly where that distinction does not further, and may detract from, the purpose of the Act which is to prevent continued separation of families.

The district court correctly ruled that California law was applicable and that Milivoj was legitimated under the law of California before his eighteenth birthday.

* * *

The judgment of the district court is affirmed.

Questions

1. What is the *Kaliski* court saying in the third-to-last paragraph of the opinion as excerpted? Has the decision of the People's Republic of China to abolish distinctions between legitimate and illegitimate children rendered unconstitutional (because "irrational") all denials of U.S. immigration benefits to illegitimate children?

2. Could Cleophus Warner, one of the plaintiffs in *Fiallo v. Bell* (his situation is described in some detail in Justice Marshall's dissenting opinion there), now obtain a visa for his son by moving to California?

Problems

1. (a) B was born out of wedlock in 1940 and adopted into another family at the age of one year. P was born in 1945 to the natural parents

of B, who by then had married. P immigrated to the United States, with her parents, in 1955. Now an American citizen, P petitions in 1980 to bring in her "sister" B, whose existence she discovered only in 1976, but whom she has visited frequently and with whom she has developed close and affectionate ties. Should this petition for fifth preference benefits be granted? Suppose B had not been adopted until 1950. Should this make a difference in the outcome?

(b) X was born in 1960 and Y in 1962, both to the same natural parents, who were validly married at the time. In 1973, X was adopted by family A, who immigrated to America in 1975, bringing X as their child. In 1981, shortly after reaching the age of 21, X petitioned for a fifth preference visa for Y. Should the visa petition be approved? Should this case be treated differently from problem (a)?

See generally Matter of Gur, 16 I & N Dec. 123 (BIA 1977); *Matter of Garner,* 15 I & N Dec. 215 (BIA 1975); *Matter of Fujii,* 12 I & N Dec. 495 (Dist.Dir.1967).

2. Z was abandoned by his natural parents in 1951, when he was only a few days old. H and W, nationals of Italy, took him into their home in Verona and considered Z a part of their family from that time forward. They could not afford formal adoption proceedings, however, until late 1955. A few months later, their quota number was reached after many years on the American immigration waiting list. They decided to fulfill their longstanding desire to migrate to the United States, even though they could not bring Z with them because the laws at the time made no provision for adopted children. When they departed in mid-1956, they left Z in the care of W's sister. In 1957, the law was amended to add language essentially in the form that now appears in INA § 101(b)(1)(E). They immediately petitioned for a visa that would permit Z to join them. Under that section, can Z be considered their "child"? *See Matter of M,* 8 I & N Dec. 118 (BIA 1958, Atty Gen 1959).

Immigration Based on Marriage

Nonpreference immigration has been unavailable since 1978. Third- and sixth-preference immigration requires proper contacts with a willing employer, and probably has become more difficult to secure with higher levels of unemployment in the United States. If an alien lacks family members in this country already in position to file a visa petition, marriage to a U.S. citizen or permanent resident may appear as the only available option for securing admission as an immigrant. We will consider here a few of the problems that may result.

BARK v. INS

United States Court of Appeals, Ninth Circuit, 1975.
511 F.2d 1200.

HUFSTEDLER, CIRCUIT JUDGE:

Petitioner was denied adjustment of status from student visitor to permanent resident, pursuant to section 245 of the Immigration and Nationality Act ("the Act"), and he seeks review. Respondent has conceded that the denial was based solely on the Immigration Judge's conclusion, affirmed by the Board of Immigration Appeals, that petitioner was ineligible for adjustment of status because the marriage upon which he based his application was a sham.

Petitioner and his wife had been sweethearts for several years while they were living in their native Korea. She immigrated to the United States and became a resident alien. Petitioner came to the United States in August, 1968, initially as a business visitor and then as a student. They renewed their acquaintance and were married in Hawaii in May 1969. Petitioner's wife filed a petition on his behalf to qualify him for status as the spouse of a resident alien pursuant to sections 203(a)(2) and 204 of the Act. Petitioner thereafter filed his own application for adjustment of status under section 245 of the Act.

Petitioner and his wife testified at the hearing on his application that they married for love and not for the purpose of circumventing the immigration laws; they admitted quarreling and separating. Their testimony about the time and extent of their separation was impeached by evidence introduced by the Service. The Immigration Judge discredited their testimony and held that the marriage was a sham, relying primarily (perhaps solely), on the evidence of their separation. In affirming the Immigration Judge's decision, the Board of Immigration Appeals stated: "Investigation revealed that [petitioner] and his wife lived in separate quarters. While both testified that their marriage was 'a good marriage,' their testimony as to how much time they actually spent together was conflicting."

Petitioner's marriage was a sham if the bride and groom did not intend to establish a life together at the time they were married. The concept of establishing a life as marital partners contains no federal dictate about the kind of life that the partners may choose to lead. Any attempt to regulate their life styles, such as prescribing the amount of time they must spend together, or designating the manner in which either partner elects to spend his or her time, in the guise of specifying the requirements of a bona fide marriage would raise serious constitutional questions. (*Cf.* Roe v. Wade (1973) 410 U.S. 113, 93 S.Ct. 705, 35 L.Ed.2d 147; Graham v. Richardson (1971) 403 U.S. 365, 91 S.Ct. 1848, 29 L.Ed.2d 534; Griswold v. Connecticut (1965) 381 U.S. 479, 85 S.Ct. 1678, 14 L.Ed.2d 510.) Aliens cannot be required to have more conventional or more successful marriages than citizens.

Conduct of the parties after marriage is relevant only to the extent that it bears upon their subjective state of mind at the time they were married. (Lutwak v. United States (1953) 344 U.S. 604, 73 S.Ct. 481, 97 L.Ed. 593.) Evidence that the parties separated after their wedding is relevant in ascertaining whether they intended to establish a life together when they exchanged marriage vows. But evidence of separation, standing alone, cannot support a finding that a marriage was not bona fide when it was entered. The inference that the parties never intended a bona fide marriage from proof of separation is arbitrary unless we are reasonably assured that it is more probable than not that couples who separate after marriage never intended to live together. Common experience is directly to the contrary. Couples separate, temporarily and permanently, for all kinds of reasons that have nothing to do with any preconceived intent not to share their lives, such as calls to military service, educational needs, employment opportunities, illness, poverty, and domestic difficulties. Of course, the time and extent of separation, combined with other facts and circumstances, can and have adequately supported the conclusion that a marriage was not bona fide.[1]

The administrative record discloses that the Immigration Judge and Board of the Immigration Appeals did not focus their attention on the key issue: Did the petitioner and his wife intend to establish a life together at the time of their marriage? The inquiry, instead, turned on the duration of their separation, which, as we have pointed out, is relevant to, but not dispositive of the intent issue. Moreover, the determination may have been influenced by the irrelevant fact, cited by respondent to support the Service, that "the wife could and did leave as she pleased when they were together." The bona fides of a marriage do not and cannot rest on either marital partner's choice about his or her mobility after marriage.

We decline to speculate about the conclusion that would have been reached if the Service had confined itself to evidence relevant to the parties' intent at the time of their marriage. The Service will have an opportunity on remand to develop the record in accordance with the views herein expressed.

Reversed and remanded.

CALVIN TRILLIN, MAKING ADJUSTMENTS
The New Yorker, May 28, 1984, at 65, 71.

One of the procedures that Beaumont Martin often tells potential clients that they can carry out themselves is filing for a green card on the basis of having married an American citizen. If they are good at English and uncowed by bureaucrats, they might indeed file the papers themselves— although they might stand in line for hours, present documents to the clerk at the counter, and be told, perhaps not terribly politely, that some mistake or omission means that they have to go through the process all over again another day. Also, immigration lawyers can predict a good number of the questions an immigration examiner is likely to ask if he has reason to suspect that the marriage is a sham: Where does she put her shoes at night? What do his parents do for a living? What's his favorite food? Where did you meet her?

---

1. *E.g.,* Lutwak v. United States, *supra,* 344 U.S. 604, 73 S.Ct. 481, 97 L.Ed. 593, which involved criminal prosecutions stemming from an elaborate scheme to secure entry into the United States for two brothers and the former wife of one of them under the "War Brides Act." Female veterans were hired to marry the brothers, and the brothers' nephew (also a veteran) married the former wife. The parties agreed beforehand to separate as soon as possible, and none of them ever cohabited.

In United States v. Sacco (9th Cir.1970) 428 F.2d 264 the defendant claimed derivative citizenship based on his mother's marriage to a citizen. His mother's marriage was found a sham because she married solely to legitimate a child. She did not marry to circumvent the immigration laws, but the evidence was clear that she and her husband never intended to live together after marriage.

* * *

A lawyer is not allowed to coach his clients during the interview, but his presence can provide not just a sense of security but a sort of implied character witness. An immigration lawyer's practice depends to some extent on his reputation at Immigration, so it is obviously not in his best interest to become known as someone who shows up in the company of couples he suspects are attached only by the requirements necessary for a green card. Immigration examiners, many of whom began their career as border patrolmen, tend to be suspicious by nature, and most of them have seen their suspicions confirmed any number of times. True love hit Iranian students with a peculiar frequency a few years ago, when a lot of them had visa problems; Nigerian students are also known for being quick down the aisle. Any couple who seem far apart culturally or ethnically or linguistically obviously raise suspicions, even if they are accompanied by a pillar of the immigration bar. When the Turkish waiter Beaumont Martin was representing showed up with his new American wife outside Immigration one Wednesday, she turned out to be a nice-looking, exceedingly dark-skinned black woman. Ed Prud'homme looked the couple over, turned to Martin, and said, in the shorthand that allows old acquaintances to place bets with each other without much elaboration, "Three dollars."

* * *

At [a Houston immigration lawyers'] gathering I attended, Ed Prud'homme found out that he had not in fact won three dollars on the outcome of the Turkish waiter's interview. Beaumont Martin acknowledged, though, that the questioning had been unusually prolonged. The waiter, he reported, had almost destroyed his own case when he seemed to avoid giving a specific answer about the last gift he had received from his wife. Before the waiter was in the room, his wife had answered the same question by saying that she had given him some undershorts; apparently, he was embarrassed to mention such intimate apparel before strangers. "I finally started laughing," Martin said. "So did the examiner. It was so much like 'The Newlywed Game.' "

Sham Marriages and the Ethical Responsibilities of An Attorney

The discovery of fraudulent marriages is a difficult and time-consuming process for the INS, and investigation practices vary from district to district. *See* Leidigh, *Defense of Sham Marriage Deportations,* 8 U.C.–Davis L.Rev. 309, 315–16 (1975). Does an attorney who is representing an alien claiming to be married to a United States citizen have an ethical obligation to determine the *bona fides* of the client's marriage? Does the lawyer have some responsibility to help enforce the immigration laws? Consider the following letter, reprinted in 59 Interp.Rel. 144–45 (1982).

> The firm at which I now work as an associate handles on the average about 100 spousal I–130's per year. Like any sensible practitioners, we do not induce clients to commit fraud; nor do we receive confessions from clients on the subject. Thus, in any given case, we never "know" that a sham marriage is involved. Yet, we are all quite certain that between 90 and 95% of these

cases involve sham marriages. The circumstances make it completely obvious.

It is our experience that INS will never detect a sham marriage unless one of the parties to the conspiracy actually tells them outright that the marriage was contracted for immigration purposes (as, for revenge) or unless the client handles his arrangements in a completely idiotic fashion (*e.g.,* he fails to learn the name of his "wife," he gets an accomplice who is twice his age and can't speak his language, etc.). The record is fairly clear: in about 3 years, roughly 250 sham marriages have gone through this office. INS has detected nothing despite the fact that these clients have not taken extraordinary precautions to avoid detection and despite the fact that many secure dissolutions almost immediately after the Green Card issues.

So beneficial is the status of "spouse of a U.S. citizen," so simple is the procedure, so high the success rate, that it becomes more and more difficult to dissuade clients from taking this route to a Green Card. Recently, there is even a trend in the direction of respectable clients, who might well obtain labor certificates, going the marriage route simply for convenience and speed. Where an alien has little chance of qualifying for Permanent Residence in any other way, it is no easy matter to persuade them that a method that works well over 99% of the time should not be resorted to.

(This letter almost surely exaggerates the prevalence of marriage fraud in immigration proceedings. For example, preliminary results of an INS pilot study done at the Boston district office found reasons to suspect fraud in 30% of the spouse petitions intensively reviewed—far below 90%, but hardly a statistic to inspire confidence.)

What would you do if you were in the position of the attorney who wrote the letter? The immigration regulations allow the Department of Justice to suspend or disbar any attorney "[w]ho willfully misinforms or deceives an officer or employee of the Department of Justice concerning any material and relevant fact in connection with a case." 8 C.F.R. § 292.3(3). Would an attorney have an affirmative duty to disclose information suggesting a sham marriage? Or would disclosure jeopardize the lawyer-client relationship?

Rule 1.6 of the Model Rules of Professional Conduct (as adopted by the American Bar Association in 1983) states: "A lawyer shall not reveal information relating to representation of a client unless the client consents after consultation"—with certain narrow exceptions. The Comment to this rule makes clear that it "applies not merely to matters communicated in confidence by the client but also to all information relating to the representation, whatever its source." An earlier draft of the Model Rules permitted a lawyer to reveal information "to rectify the consequences of a client's criminal or fraudulent act in the commission of which the lawyer's services had been used." Model Rules of Professional Conduct, Rule 1.6(b)(3) ("final" draft, 1981). This language was deleted, however, from the version adopted by the ABA in 1983. The 1981 draft of Rule 1.2(d) of the Model Rules prohibited a lawyer from assisting a client "in conduct that the lawyer knows or reasonably should know is criminal or fraudulent." The final approved version, however, deletes the words "or reasonably should know" from the rule. Model Rules of Professional Conduct, Rule 1.2(d) (1983).

Despite the obvious effort of the ABA in 1983 to strengthen client confidentiality and reduce attorney obligations unilaterally to reveal or rectify questionable practices, some state bars seem to enforce a conception of ethical responsibility more in line with the 1981 draft. The following appeared in the Texas Bar Journal, and is reprinted from 61 Interp.Rel. 442 (1984):

> The District 10 Grievance Committee issued a private reprimand to an attorney of San Antonio on Dec. 22, 1983. The committee found that the attorney failed to undertake an adequate investigation into the marital status of his client before assisting him in an application for temporary status with the Immigration and Naturalization Service. The attorney knew, or should have known, that his client's marital status was questionable. Also, the attorney failed to timely advise the Immigration and Naturalization Service as to false information given to it at the time of the application for temporary status. Shortly thereafter, the attorney knew that false information had been given.

See also United States v. Maniego, 710 F.2d 24 (2d Cir.1983) (per curiam) (sustaining lawyers' convictions on fraud charges growing out of major sham marriage operation).

DABAGHIAN v. CIVILETTI

United States Court of Appeals, Ninth Circuit, 1975.
607 F.2d 868.

CHOY, CIRCUIT JUDGE:

Dabaghian appeals from the district court's judgment upholding a decision of the Immigration and Naturalization Service ("INS") which stripped him of permanent-resident status. We reverse and remand with instruction to enter judgment for Dabaghian.

Dabaghian is a native and citizen of Iran. He entered the United States as a visitor in 1967 and obtained student status in 1968. In September 1971 he married a United States citizen. In October 1971 he applied for adjustment of status to "alien lawfully admitted for permanent residence" under § 245 of the Immigration and Nationality Act. The adjustment of status was granted on January 13, 1972, a date on which there is contested evidence to show that he was separated from his wife. On January 28, 1972, Dabaghian filed for divorce, which was granted seven months later. In September 1973 he married an Iranian citizen.

In August 1974 the Attorney General moved under § 246 of the Act, to rescind the adjustment of status on the ground that Dabaghian had not in fact been eligible for it at the time it was granted. The Immigration Judge revoked Dabaghian's status as a permanent resident; a split Board of Immigration Appeals dismissed Dabaghian's appeal. His action for review and relief in the district court was then dismissed on summary judgment.

The INS, it is important to note, never has claimed or proved that Dabaghian's first marriage was a sham or fraud when entered. Instead, the INS moved to rescind on the ground that on January 13, 1972, when the adjustment of status was granted, his marriage was dead in fact even though it was still legally alive. Thus, says the INS, he was not the "spouse" of a United States citizen and was ineligible for the adjustment of status.

We reject the INS' legal position. If a marriage is not sham or fraudulent from its inception, it is valid for the purposes of determining eligibility for adjustment of status under § 245 of the Act until it is legally dissolved.

The INS contention has no support in any statute or federal decision. Indeed, it has been rejected time and again in recent immigration cases.

* * *

[After discussing *Bark* and other Ninth Circuit precedents, the court continued:]

In *Chan v. Bell,* 464 F.Supp. 125 (D.D.C.1978), the INS rejected an American wife's petition under § 204 of the Act to classify her alien husband as a "spouse" under § 201(b) of the Act. Such petitions are to establish eligibility, as in the present case, for an application for adjustment of status to that of a permanent resident. The INS denied the petition solely because the spouses had separated; the INS admitted the marriage was legally valid and not sham. The court rejected the INS position, noting that even the relevant INS regulation "quite appropriately conditions the revocation of a petition merely upon the 'legal termination' of the relationship of husband and wife, not upon any assumed dissolution of the marriage by reference to a standard not known to the law of domestic relations." 464 F.Supp. at 128.

The court in *Chan* stated that the INS "has no expertise in the field of predicting the stability and growth potential of marriages—if indeed anyone has—and it surely has no business operating in that field." *Id.* at 130. Moreover, the very effort to apply the "factually-dead" test would trench on constitutional values; it "would inevitably lead the INS into invasions of privacy which even the boldest of government agencies have heretofore been hesitant to enter." *Id.* at 130 n. 13.

* * *

Dabaghian's purported ineligibility turns upon whether he was the "spouse" of an American citizen at the time of adjustment of status. If he was, he was eligible then to receive permanent-resident status, not subject to any quota. The word "spouses" in § 201(b) includes the parties to all marriages that are legally valid and not sham. There is no exception for marriages that the INS thinks are "factually dead" at the time of adjustment. For the INS to give such an interpretation to "spouses" and for the Attorney General to be satisfied that Dabaghian was not a "spouse" are abuses of discretion. Since no other reason for ineligibility under § 245 of the Act has been alleged or proven, there can be no rescission of Dabaghian's permanent-resident status.

Reversed and Remanded to the district court with instruction to enter a judgment directing the INS to reinstate Dabaghian as a permanent resident.

Notes

1. INS and the Board have traditionally sought to deny visa petitions for alleged spouses in two distinct situations: (1) when the underlying marriage is sham or fraudulent—that is, when the parties "did not intend to establish a life together at the time they were married," *Bark v. INS, supra*—and (2) when the underlying marriage is nonviable or "factually dead" at the time when the immigration benefit is sought. The agencies persisted in using both grounds for denial for many years after the first court decisions ruling use of the second test invalid. In 1980, the Board finally capitulated and ruled that, in the future, visa petitions will not be denied based solely on a finding that the underlying marriage is not viable. *Matter of McKee*, 17 I & N Dec. 332 (BIA 1980). It emphasized, however, that it still will scrutinize evidence of current separation in order to determine whether the initial marriage was sham or fraudulent; this position is consistent with *Bark* and *Dabaghian*. The Board has also stressed that petitions may not be granted on the basis of marriages *legally* terminated as of the date that the immigration benefit is to be conferred. *Matter of Boromand*, 17 I & N Dec. 450, 453 (BIA 1980). Nor may immigration benefits be granted when the spouses have legally separated under a formal, written separation agreement. *Matter of Lenning*, 17 I & N Dec. 476 (1980). *See generally* G & R § 2.18a; *Benefits for Spouses Under the Immigration and Nationality Act*, 1 Imm. Law Rep. 121 (1982).

2. All of 15 days elapsed between Dabaghian's adjustment of status and his filing for divorce from the U.S.-citizen wife who had petitioned for his adjustment. If the "foremost policy" of our permanent immigration provisions is family reunification, as the court stated in *Lau v. Kiley*, 563 F.2d 543, 547 (2d Cir.1977), why should Dabaghian benefit when his family manifestly has no interest in unifying? In other words, isn't the "factually dead" standard a sound way of implementing the statute, in light of Congress's overriding purpose?

3. One reason for the court's rejection of the "factually dead" test in *Dabaghian* appears to be the court's concern about the potential intrusiveness of the questioning INS might conduct to see if the marriage were still "alive." Yet, is not a similarly intrusive inquiry necessary to determine whether a marriage is a "sham"?

4. The BIA has also encountered sham divorces—formal dissolution of marriage bonds for the sole purpose of claiming benefits that are available only to unmarried persons, such as second preference visas for sons and daughters. Some Nevada officials fear that the practice is relatively common among aliens who file for divorce under that state's liberal divorce laws. *See Sham Divorces Still Stump Judges*, Las Vegas Sun, Dec. 10, 1982, at 21, col. 1.

In *Matter of Aldecoaotalora,* Interim Dec. No. 2948 (BIA 1983), the Board ruled that such a divorce would not be recognized for immigration purposes, where the former spouses continued to live together and to hold property jointly. It based this conclusion on its view that "the intent of Congress in providing for preference status for unmarried sons and daughters of lawful permanent residents was to reunite with their parents unmarried children who, although not minors, were still part of a family unit. * * * By her own admissions, the beneficiary has established that, although divorced from her husband, she has neither severed her relationship with him nor returned to the family unit of her parents." Is this an accurate reading of congressional intent? Could INS deny second preference benefits to otherwise eligible persons who have never been married on the grounds that they have long lived apart from the parents' family unit?

4. OCCUPATIONAL CATEGORIES AND LABOR CERTIFICATION

The impulse to protect American workers against allegedly unfair competition from immigrant laborers has long played a role in the shaping of our immigration laws. As we have seen, the first federal immigration controls were imposed in 1875. Just ten years later Congress adopted the first labor-related immigration measure, the Contract Labor Law of 1885. Act of February 26, 1885, Ch. 164, 23 Stat. 332. Its enforcement provisions were strengthened two years later. Act of Feb. 23, 1887, Ch. 220, 24 Stat. 414. As described by a later congressional committee, this law

> was aimed at the practice of certain employers importing cheap labor from abroad. This importation practice began in 1869. Advertisements were printed offering inducements to immigrants to proceed to this country, particularly to the coal fields, for employment. Many advertisements asserted that several hundred men were needed in places where there were actually no vacancies. The object was to oversupply the demand for labor so that the domestic laborers would be forced to work at reduced wages. * * *
>
> The alien contract labor law made it unlawful to import aliens or assist in importation or migration of aliens into the United States, its Territories, or the District of Columbia under contract, made previous to the importation or migration, for the performance of labor or service of any kind in the United States. The law made such contracts void [with certain exceptions] and provided certain penalties.

H.R.Rep. No. 1365, 82d Cong., 2d Sess. 12–13 (1952) (footnote omitted).

These provisions remained on the books until the major restructuring and codification of our immigration laws that took place with passage of the McCarran-Walter Act in 1952. By then, opinion concerning foreign labor recruitment had changed considerably. In the view of many, the country needed at least selective efforts to fill gaps in the U.S. personnel pool with immigrant workers. And it was thought that other measures, such as the National Labor Relations Act and the Fair Labor Standards Act, afforded adequate protection against the earlier employer abuses. *See generally* Rodino, *The Impact of Immigration on the American Labor Market,* 27 Rutgers L.Rev. 245 (1974); G & R § 2.40. The 1952 Act therefore repealed the 1885 law and adopted in its place § 212(a)(14) of the INA. In its initial form, operative until 1965, this section permitted the Secretary of Labor to block the entry of aliens seeking to enter for the purpose of skilled or unskilled labor upon a finding that such entry would displace U.S. workers or "adversely affect" the wages and working conditions of U.S. workers similarly employed. The initiative rested with the Secretary of Labor to declare an occupation oversupplied, and he rarely bestirred himself to invoke the provision.

In 1965, responding to effective lobbying pressure led by the A.F.L.–C.I.O., Congress reversed the operation of § 212(a)(14). The law now essentially presumes that foreign workers are not needed; the alien and his intending employer must take the initiative to secure affirmative certification. As it currently reads, that section now excludes from admission:

> Aliens seeking to enter the United States, for the purpose of performing skilled or unskilled labor, unless the Secretary of Labor has determined and certified to the Secretary of State and the Attorney General that (A) there are not sufficient workers who are able, willing, qualified (or equally qualified in the case of aliens who are members of the teaching profession or who have exceptional ability in the sciences or the arts), and available at the time of application for a visa and admission to the United States and at the place where the alien is to perform such skilled or unskilled labor, and (B) the employment of such aliens will not adversely affect the wages and working conditions of the workers in the United States similarly employed. The exclusion of aliens under this paragraph shall apply to preference immigrant aliens described in section 203(a)(3) and (6), and to nonpreference immigrant aliens described in section 203(a)(7)[.]

Although this provision appears in § 212, as part of the lengthy list of grounds for exclusion, it is more usefully conceptualized as a provision setting forth one of the initial grounds of qualification that an intending immigrant must fulfill. Indeed, the third sentence of § 203(a)(7) makes this conceptual linkage more explicit. As that sentence indicates, the labor certification requirement applies to every entering immigrant in the two preference categories that are based on occupational skills, the third and sixth preferences. INA § 203(a)(3), (6). The Act reserves up to 20% of the numerically limited immigration to this country for such immigrants. And although the point is now largely academic in light of the over-subscription of the preference categories, labor certification was also designed as a check on nonpreference immigration. See INA § 203(a)(7). Before an alien can obtain approval of a visa petition in any of these categories, he or she must secure a labor certification from the Department of Labor. (There are limited exceptions. See 8 C.F.R. § 212.8.) In sharp contrast, immigrants entering by virtue of a family relationship, either as "immediate relatives," or under the first, second, fourth, or fifth preference, are exempted from the labor certification requirement, even if they intend to work.

The Department of Labor was not initially well-equipped to handle the new responsibility imposed in 1965; years passed before the agency developed detailed and well-structured procedures and regulations to implement these provisions. We will be examining these below, primarily in the context of *individual* labor certification—a procedure whereby a single employer, having a particular alien in mind, takes steps to secure the necessary Labor Department approval. But, to place these cases in context, you should understand that the Department of Labor has also managed to avoid the need for that complicated individual process with respect to several occupations by means of certain broad determinations embodied in the Department's Schedule A and Schedule B.

Schedule A lists occupations judged chronically short of qualified U.S. workers. It amounts to a blanket determination that anyone seeking that kind of work in the United States will not displace U.S. workers or adversely affect wages and working conditions. The Schedule, as of this writing, includes licensed nurses, physical therapists, certain scientists and artists "of exceptional ability," certain executive and managerial positions, and other occupations. *See* 20 C.F.R. § 656.10. A qualified alien seeking to come to this country to work in those occupations can avoid processing at the Department of Labor altogether. He or she may file other relevant papers directly with the consular officer overseas, or with the INS if the applicant is already in this country and seeks adjustment of status from nonimmigrant to immigrant. *See* 20 C.F.R. § 656.22.

In contrast, Schedule B lists occupations in which the Department of Labor considers there are sufficient U.S. workers throughout the country and for which a labor certification will not be issued. Current examples include parking lot attendants, bartenders, cashiers, keypunch operators, truck drivers, and many others. There are provisions for waivers of this Schedule B preclusion, but waivers are rare. *See* 20 C.F.R. §§ 656.11, 656.23.

If the alien's occupation does not appear on either schedule, then the employer must initiate the individual certification process by filing Form ETA 750 and demonstrating that the manifold requirements for individual labor certification have been fulfilled. 20 C.F.R. §§ 656.20–656.21. (Many of the details of these requirements are reflected in the *Production Tool* case, below.) Initial processing is carried out in the local Job Service office, an arm of the state government, but the actual determinations are made by a regional "certifying officer," who is a federal official employed by the Employment and Training Administration of the Department of Labor. In fiscal year 1981, approximately 33,000 applications for labor certification were filed; 25,763 were approved. *Industrial Holographics, Inc. v. Donovan,* 722 F.2d 1362, 1367 n. 8 (7th Cir.1983).

If the certifying officer believes that the employer's application does not meet the requirements, he or she issues a Notice of Findings—essentially, a preliminary determination that the certification should be denied. The employer may contest this preliminary determination and file additional information or take new steps to meet the objections. If these are unsuccessful, the certifying officer issues a Final Determination denying certification. 20 C.F.R. §§ 656.24–656.25. The employer is entitled to another round of administrative review, adjudicated by administrative law judges within the Department of Labor. *Id.* §§ 656.26–656.27. Judicial review of a labor certification denial is available in federal district court under the Administrative Procedure Act, after the employer has exhausted the administrative remedies. *See e.g., Reddy, Inc. v. Department of Labor*, 492 F.2d 538, 542–44 (5th Cir.1974).[8]

If the certifying officer approves, he or she issues the formal labor certification, and the papers proceed to the INS for consideration of the employer's actual visa petition (Form I–140). INS approval is not pro forma. Under current regulations, the Department of Labor's certification is conclusive regarding labor market conditions, but INS is entitled to question the alien's qualifications for the certified job, or otherwise investigate fraud or misrepresentation by the alien or the employer, and to deny a visa petition on such grounds despite labor certification. *See, e.g., K.R.K. Irvine, Inc. v. Landon*, 699 F.2d 1006 (9th Cir.1983); *Madany v. Smith*, 696 F.2d 1008 (D.C.Cir.1983); *Joseph v. Landon*, 679 F.2d 113 (7th Cir.1982). If INS detects no such defects, its approval of the visa petition is then communicated to a consular officer in the alien's country for the ultimate processing of the immigrant visa.

PESIKOFF v. SECRETARY OF LABOR

United States Court of Appeals, District of Columbia Circuit, 1974.
501 F.2d 757, cert. denied 419 U.S. 1038, 95 S.Ct. 525, 42 L.Ed.2d 315.

J. Skelly Wright, Circuit Judge:

Appellants seek review of a decision of the Secretary of Labor denying certification for appellant Quintero to enter the United States as an alien seeking to perform skilled or unskilled labor. Appellants filed in the District Court a complaint requesting, pursuant to 28 U.S.C. § 2201 (1970) and 5 U.S.C. § 704 (1970), a declaratory judgment that the Secretary's decision was an unlawful exercise of his authority under Section 212(a)(14) of the Immigration and Nationality Act. The District Court dismissed the complaint for failure to state a cause of action, and this appeal followed. We find that the Secretary, in declining to grant certification, did not abuse the discretion vested in him by Section 212(a)(14) and affirm.

I

Appellant Pesikoff is a Houston child psychiatrist. His wife was a law student when this action was commenced. They are the parents of two preschool-age children. Because of the time demands on him and his wife, Dr. Pesikoff felt it important that he obtain help in caring for his

8. For a more complete description of the Department of Labor's processes for considering applications for labor certification, *see* G & R §§ 2.40, 3.6; *Labor Certification Procedures*, 1 Imm.L.Rep. 1 (1981).

household.   He states he attempted to find such assistance through newspaper advertisements, employment agencies, and inquiries with friends.   He learned from the latter source that appellant Quintero, a citizen of Mexico with experience in caring for children, was available to work as a live-in maid.   Dr. Pesikoff entered into a contract with Ms. Quintero under which she was to be paid $70 per week plus room and board for providing washing, ironing, cooking, and care for the two Pesikoff children.   Though Ms. Quintero was to live in, Dr. Pesikoff represented to the Secretary that her work day was to have been only from 8:00 a.m. to 12:00 noon and from 2:00 p.m. to 6:00 p.m.

On or about July 20, 1971 appellants submitted a request to the Department of Labor that the Secretary, pursuant to Section 212(a)(14), certify Ms. Quintero for immigration into this country for the purpose of being employed by the Pesikoffs as a live-in maid.

* * *

* * * A Department of Labor Manpower Administration officer in Dallas, Texas, to whom the Secretary's authority under this provision had been delegated, informed Dr. Pesikoff on July 28, 1971 that the Secretary could not issue for Ms. Quintero the certification required by Section 212(a)(14) because available job market information did not show that United States workers were unavailable for the job Ms. Quintero was to perform.   Before denying Dr. Pesikoff's request the certifying officer had been advised by the Texas Employment Commission that there were approximately 180 maids registered in the Commission's Houston office. The Employment Commission also advised that inquiries of employers and perusals of newspaper advertisements enabled it to estimate that in excess of 100 maids were available for work.   The Commission indicated, however, that very few of the registered workers would accept jobs that required cooking and that none were willing to live in.

In affirming the certifying officer's decision, the Labor Department's Assistant Regional Manpower Administrator in Texas cited the Employment Commission's report on the general availability of maids in Houston. The Administrator stated that the absence in Houston of maids willing to live in was irrelevant to the Pesikoff application because "based on the job described and hours of work, the live-in requirement is a personal preference and not a necessity in the performance of the job."   In March 1972 appellants filed in the District Court their complaint against the Secretary, dismissal of which we now review.

[The Court held that Dr. Pesikoff had standing to obtain judicial review of the Secretary's decision under the Administrative Procedure Act.]

* * *

* * * Dr. Pesikoff asserts that the Secretary's denial constituted an abuse of his discretion under Section 212(a)(14) because it was based on insufficient evidence.   More specifically, Dr. Pesikoff argues that the Secretary should have presented evidence sufficient to prove that there were particular workers available, willing, able, and qualified to perform all the tasks Ms. Quintero had contracted to perform and to live in with the Pesikoffs while doing so.

Our evaluation of Dr. Pesikoff's position must commence with an analysis of the section and its legislative history. We first stress that the section is written so as to set up a presumption that aliens should not be permitted to enter the United States for the purpose of performing labor because of the likely harmful impact of their admission on American workers. This presumption, the statutory language makes clear, can be overcome only if the Secretary of Labor has determined that the two conditions set forth in parts (A) and (B) of the subsection are met. This structuring of the statute strongly indicates that the Secretary is not obligated to prove in the case of every alien seeking entry to perform labor that the conditions are not met. Given the presumption of the statute against admission, if the Secretary's consultation of the general labor market data readily available to him suggests that there is a pool of potential workers available to perform the job which the alien seeks, the burden should be placed on the alien or his putative employer to prove that it is not possible for the employer to find a qualified American worker.

This interpretation of the statute is supported by its legislative history. Before enactment of the 1965 amendments to the Immigration and Nationality Act, Section 212(a)(14) was structured to permit entry to aliens seeking to perform labor in the United States unless the Secretary of Labor certified that there were sufficient American workers available to perform such labor or that the employment of the aliens would adversely affect the wages and working conditions of American workers. The Senate and House reports on the 1965 amendments to the Act make clear that Congress, by restructuring Section 212(a)(14) to exclude such aliens unless the Secretary certified that there were *not* sufficient American workers available, intended to reverse the prior presumption favoring admission to strengthen the protection of the American labor market and to reduce the burden on the Secretary in implementing this protection.

* * *

In light of our interpretation of Section 212(a)(14) and the legislative history supporting this interpretation, we conclude that the Secretary's denial of Ms. Quintero's certification did not constitute an abuse of discretion. First, we find proper the Secretary's treatment of Dr. Pesikoff's live-in requirement for his maid as a personal preference irrelevant to determination of whether there was in Houston a pool of potential workers willing to perform the Pesikoffs' domestic tasks. If the Secretary were required to find an individual American worker who met all the personal specifications of the prospective employer of each alien seeking Section 212(a)(14) certification, the burden on him in performing his statutory duty to protect the American labor market would be much greater than Congress intended in passing the 1965 amendments to the Act. It is well within the Secretary's discretion to ignore employer specifications which he deems, in accordance with his labor market expertise, to be irrelevant to the basic job which the employer desires performed. The Secretary may, therefore, survey the available labor market for a class of workers who, while possibly not meeting the prospective employer's personalized job description, do provide the employer with the potential for getting his job accomplished. The Secretary's treatment and classification of Dr. Pesikoff's employee request as one for a general maid who could live in or out was an appropriate exercise of the above described discretion. Dr. Pesikoff's statement to the Labor Department that Ms. Quintero would work only from 8:00 a.m. to 12:00 noon and 2:00 p.m. to 6:00 p.m. indicates that her need to live in is not significantly different from that of millions of American workers who readily and adequately perform their duties without living at their employment site.

We think the Secretary's treatment of Dr. Pesikoff's live-in preference was appropriate for an additional reason. As set forth above, Section 212(a)(14) provides that in order to grant an alien labor certification the Secretary must determine, not only that there are not American workers available, but also that employment of the alien will not adversely affect American wages and working conditions. The Secretary could well predict that the wages and working conditions of American maids would be adversely affected if Americans seeking domestic help could import, at the prevailing wage for live-out daily maids, aliens to work as live-in maids who are almost continuously on call. There is nothing in the record which moves us to question Dr. Pesikoff's representation that Ms. Quintero would have limited working hours. However, if the Secretary were to deem relevant to his survey of the available American work force a live-in preference of an employer who represents that his maid will work limited daytime hours, an American employer intending to work an alien at least intermittently around the clock could, by simple misrepresentation, defeat one of the primary purposes of Section 212(a)(14). Our analysis above of the section and its legislative history indicates that the Secretary has discretion to protect the American labor market against such employers with prophylactic procedures such as the employer personal preference disposition he made here.

* * *

Affirmed.

[A separate opinion by Judge MacKinnon, dissenting as to the "personal preference" issue, is omitted.]

Notes

1. The *Pesikoff* majority recognizes substantial discretion in the Secretary of Labor to determine what constitutes "the basic job" that the employer seeks to have accomplished, and then to decide, in light of that judgment, whether the specific requirements set forth in the employer's job description are excessive. But how does one decide what constitutes the "basic job" and what constitutes mere "personal preference"? Isn't the employer in a far better position to know in detail what the job requires? Won't employers suffer whenever the Department decides to treat a newly developed line of work or specialty as merely something

that ought to be shoehorned into one of its standardized categories of "basic jobs"? Does the statute authorize—or, on the other hand, require—such an intrusive role for the agency? Why or why not?

Several other courts have been far less deferential than *Pesikoff* to the Secretary of Labor on these issues. *Ratnayake v. Mack,* 499 F.2d 1207 (8th Cir.1974), is illustrative. In that case, the operators of a school devoted to the Montessori method of teaching sought labor certification for two well-trained Montessori-method teachers from Ceylon. The Department's denial was based on labor market data showing a surplus of college-trained teachers who could, in the Department's view, do the essential job with a minimum of training in the Montessori method. The court ruled for the employer:

> In reviewing the job requirements established by appellant schools, the mere fact that the prerequisite for employment is a lengthy and extensive training period does not automatically give the Secretary the power to disregard them as unreasonable. There must be some deference accorded employment qualifications for "[e]very employer is entitled to hire persons who have qualifications that can be utilized in a manner that will contribute to the efficiency and quality of the business." Acupuncture Center of Washington v. Brennan, 364 F.Supp. 1038, 1042 (D.D.C. 1973). In *Acupuncture Center,* the court held that it was not unreasonable for the employer to demand that applicants speak three dialects of Chinese as well as have an understanding of acupuncture terminology and science. The First Circuit has recently asserted that the Secretary "should not have the privilege of determining the qualifications of any particular applicant for the job to be filled. Nor without proof, should he have the right to attack the good faith of an employer's personnel procedures." Digilab, Inc. v. Secretary of Labor, 495 F.2d 323, at 326 [(1st Cir.) cert. denied, 419 U.S. 840, 95 S.Ct. 70, 42 L.Ed.2d 67 (1974)]. The job requirements of an employer are not to be set aside if they are shown to be reasonable and tend to contribute to or enhance the efficiency and quality of the business.

499 F.2d, at 1212.

The *Ratnayake* case, on its facts, is not difficult to swallow. The Labor Department had decided, in essence, that the basic job was simply that of school teacher, and it apparently was not willing to allow the development of a new and separate job classification—Montessori teachers—at least not with the two-year training requirements that the school envisioned. But the standard the court employed to overturn the agency's ruling is quite broad. In this court's view, the employer's job requirements should be upheld if they are "reasonable and tend to contribute to or enhance the efficiency and quality of the business." Can't a clever lawyer always draft job specifications tailored so precisely to the background of the alien intended as a beneficiary that they exclude all other persons in the world, and then successfully defend such requirements as reasonably calculated to "enhance" the employer's business? (Consider in this connection the facts of the *Acupuncture Center* case, summarized in the *Ratnayake* excerpt above.)

2. The Labor Department's current approach has been described as follows:

> One of the factors to be considered by the certifying officer is whether the skills listed by the employer are unduly restrictive, and in reaching this conclusion a certifying officer refers to a Dictionary of Occupational Titles which describes the "specific vocational preparation" needed for various occupations. If the applicant prescribes qualifications which are more restrictive than those listed in the Dictionary of Occupational Titles for the occupation in question, the burden is on the employer to prove the business necessity for more rigorous requirements by adequate documentation.

Oriental Rug Importers, Limited v. Employment and Training Administration, 696 F.2d 47, 48 (6th Cir.1982). *See also* Bodin, *Developments at the U.S. Department of Labor,* 60 Interp.Rel. 809 (1983).

3. Consider other possible incentives created by the intricate provisions for individual labor certification.

> In order to obtain a labor certification, the alien, [generally] must have a specific job offer from a prospective employer. * * * Obviously, it is not easy for an alien to learn of a job opening, and to obtain an offer for it, while abroad. Still less likely is it that the prospective employer will be willing to file a set of papers with the Labor Department—and possibly haggle with them over job requirements and wages—on behalf of an alien whom he has never met, for a job to be taken two or three years later when the alien is finally admitted. As a result, * * * aliens by the thousands enter the United States with visitors' visas forbidding them to work, and then seek and obtain job offers and illegally fill those jobs while awaiting their immigrant visas. When the visa is available, they return home briefly to receive it from the consul, and are back at work here in the United States soon after. It therefore appears that the requirement that the alien have a specific job offer (rather than simply be qualified in a job area known to be short of personnel) and the long delays in obtaining a visa combine to make illegal immigration and employment helpful if not necessary steps in the pursuit of permanent residence in the United States.

Abrams & Abrams, *Immigration Policy—Who Gets In and Why?,* 38 The Pub.Int. 3, 14–15 (1975).

———

Some idea of how the labor certification process looks from the perspective of the immigration bar can be derived from the following reading. It is reprinted from *The New Yorker* article excerpted previously, an account of the author's experiences spending a few weeks examining the practice of immigration law in Houston.

CALVIN TRILLIN, MAKING ADJUSTMENTS
The New Yorker, May 28, 1984, at 61–62, 65–66.

The process of getting labor certification amounts to staging a sort of sham employment offer. The lawyer writes a job description that complies with the Department of Labor's standards, and the potential employer of the alien actually advertises such a job through the state employment commission. If someone shows up who is a citizen and has the qualifications outlined in the ad and is willing to work for the stated wage, the labor certification is not granted—although the employer has no obligation to give the citizen a job. If the lawyer who wrote the job description has been skillful, there is a good chance that no qualified citizen will show up. Writing job descriptions that pass the Department of Labor but attract no other potential employees is what Ed Prud'homme calls "one of the few art forms in the business," and Beaumont Martin is considered one of the artists. One of the Chinese students had managed to get a job in the accounting department of a small oil company, and, since the job required some computer expertise, Martin decided to write a job description that nudged her over a bit from accounting to computer analysis. ("There are a lot of people running around with accounting degrees.") When he had typed it up, he handed it to her:

SYSTEMS ANALYST 020.067–018

Conduct analyses of accounting, management, and operational problems and formulate mathematical models for solution by IBM computer system, using FORTRAN, COBOL, and PASCAL. Analyze problems in terms of management information. Write computer programs and devise and install accounting system and related procedures. Masters or equal in management information systems. $1667/month.

She read it over. "It's beautiful," she said.

* * *

Along with the forms and folders on the floor next to Beaumont Martin's lounge chair was a worn copy of a fourteen-hundred-page government book called Dictionary of Occupational Titles—known to immigration lawyers as the D.O.T. For anyone who wants to make labor certification into an art form, the D.O.T. is an essential piece of equipment. It contains one-paragraph descriptions of virtually every occupation practiced by anybody in the United States. It describes the task of a neurosurgeon and it describes the task of a fibre-glass-container-winding operator. In a consistently direct style, it says what a leak hunter does ("Inspects barrels filled with beer or whisky to detect and repair leaking barrels") and what a sponge buffer does ("Tends machine that buffs edges of household sponges to impart rounded finish") and what an airline pilot does ("Pilots airplane"). Using the D.O.T. as a guide, an immigration lawyer tries to give the client an occupational title in the least crowded field available and then describe the job in a paragraph that sounds pretty much like a paragraph in the D.O.T. but happens to describe almost nobody but the client in question. "Immigration law is taking a short-order cook and making him into an executive chef," Pete Williamson told me. "What we're talking about here is a matter of focus."

When I was discussing labor certification with Pete Williamson one afternoon, he mentioned a young woman he had seen that day who wanted to stay in the country but did not fall into any of the categories of family reunification. She obviously did not qualify for any of the non-immigrant visas available to businessmen or investors. She was already married—to someone who, as it happened, had more or less the same visa problems that she did. Her only hope for a green card was labor certification. Her only occupation was looking after the children of a neighbor.

I said that it didn't sound promising. A few days with immigration lawyers had greatly broadened my view of how the employment sections of the immigration law were actually used. I was no longer under the delusion that the law worked to bring to this country people who had rare skills or worked in fields where there were serious shortages of American workers. "It's a matter of nudging the client's situation over a bit one way or another in order to make it fit into a category that's eligible," one lawyer had told me. "And sometimes, if you want to stay in the United States, you have to shape your career to fit the immigration law." Williamson had explained that it was possible for, say, a South American shirt manufacturer who wanted to resettle here to come in on a visitor's visa or a business visa, establish a corporation, have the personnel department of the corporation file an application to have him labor-certified as the president of a shirt firm doing business with Latin America ("Must know Spanish. Must be familiar with South American cottons . . ."), apply for a green card through the labor certification, and settle in for life. Still, it seemed unlikely that being a mother's helper in Texas was a job "for which a shortage of employable and willing persons exists."

There were two other important elements in the case, Williamson said. The young woman in question was a college graduate. Also, both she and the children she looked after were Muslims—all from Pakistan. Williamson intended to nudge her over from a nanny to a tutor—a tutor qualified to instruct the children in their own culture and religion. He thought it unlikely that any citizen with similar qualifications would respond to the ad. Williamson takes some satisfaction in such focussing—enough, he says, to offset the repetitiousness of certain aspects of the practice and the frustrations of dealing with the Immigration and Naturalization Service. "It's a competent, involved, technical job in which, if you're successful, you can see the consequences of your actions," he told me when I asked what appealed to him about practicing immigration law. "Also, I don't like the government."

Ever since *Pesikoff*, courts have differed on who bears the ultimate burden of proof in a labor certification case, the employer or the Department of Labor. The following case seeks to establish a middle ground, building on important changes that the Department made in its regulations in 1977—regulations meant in part to address the judicial criticism of Labor Department practices that had been rather common before that time.

PRODUCTION TOOL CORP. v. EMPLOYMENT TRAINING ADMINISTRATION

United States Court of Appeals, Seventh Circuit, 1982.
688 F.2d 1161.

HARLINGTON WOOD, JR., CIRCUIT JUDGE.

Production Tool Corp. and Kenall Manufacturing Co. appeal from separate orders affirming final decisions of the United States Department of Labor denying their applications for permanent alien labor certifications as provided for by the Immigration and Nationality Act, § 212(a)(14), and the regulations promulgated thereunder, 20 C.F.R. Pt. 656 (1980). Appellants challenge the validity and application of those regulations. For the following reasons, we affirm.

I

* * *

In 1977, the Secretary of Labor promulgated new regulations setting forth the procedures "whereby such immigrant labor certifications may be applied for, and given or denied." 20 C.F.R. Pt. 656. In applying for certification on behalf of an alien, the employer must submit various documents which show the employer's efforts to fill the job vacancy with a United States worker. *Id.* § 656.21(b). The provision at issue requires documentation which "clearly shows" that:

(9)(i) The employer has advertised and is still advertising the job opportunity without success in such media as newspapers of general circulation, and ethnic and professional publications;

(ii) The employer's advertising offers prevailing working conditions and requirements and the prevailing wage for the occupation calculated pursuant to § 656.40 of this Part, states the rate of pay, offers training if the job opportunity is the type for which the employer customarily provides training, and offers wages, terms and conditions of employment which are no less favorable than those offered to the alien;

(iii) The employer's advertising describes the job opportunity with particularity; the documentation shall include a copy of at least one advertisement placed by the employer;

(iv) The employer's advertising has produced no satisfactory results.

Id. § 656.21(b)(9). The regulations require the certifying officer, in judging whether a United States worker is "willing" to take the job opportunity, to examine the results of the employer's recruitment efforts and to "determine if there are other appropriate sources of workers where the employer should have recruited or might be able to recruit U.S. workers." *Id.* § 656.24(b)(2)(i). Failure by the employer to comply with the application procedures constitutes a separate ground for denying certification. *Id.* § 656.24(b)(1).

If the certifying officer determines that the applicant has not met the requirements of 20 C.F.R. § 656.21 or that there is a United States worker who is "able, willing, qualified, and available" for the job, the officer issues a Notice of Findings setting forth the specific basis for the decision. *Id.* § 656.25. The employer or the alien may then submit rebuttal evidence, which the certifying officer must review. A final determination to grant or deny is then made, and if certification is denied, the employer may request administrative-judicial review by a hearing officer. *Id.* § 656.26.

II

On May 3, 1977, Production Tool filed an application for labor certification on behalf of its employee Manuel Aguilar. The certifying officer denied that application in part for the stated reason that Production Tool "elected not to comply" with the advertising requirements of 20 C.F.R. § 656.21(b)(9). The hearing officer affirmed and the district court denied relief on the same ground. Production Tool admits that it did not comply with that regulation.

On June 13, 1977, Kenall filed an application on behalf of Blanca Fabian. Kenall had advertised the position in the *Reader* at a wage rate of $4.00. The Certifying Officer, after receiving Kenall's rebuttal evidence, denied certification on the ground, *inter alia,* that Kenall's newspaper advertisements did not satisfy 20 C.F.R. § 656.21(b)(9) because they did not offer the prevailing wage of $4.70 and were not placed in a newspaper of "general circulation." The Hearing Officer affirmed, noting that counsel for Kenall had conceded, and the record showed, that the advertising did not fully comply with the regulations: "This undisputed fact together with the unacceptable advertising in the *Reader* establishes a sufficient basis for affirming the denial." The district court entered summary judgment for appellees.

Production Tool and Kenall contend that the Secretary of Labor was without statutory authority to promulgate the regulations at issue and that, even if authorized, the regulations are invalid because they are inconsistent with the command and purpose of § 212(a)(14). Kenall separately argues that the denial of labor certification constituted an abuse of discretion because 1) it had offered to pay and advertise the prevailing wage and 2) the *Reader,* under Illinois law, is considered a newspaper of general circulation.

III

The validity of the advertising regulation, according to appellants, turns on the distinction between "legislative" and "interpretive" rules. Appellants assert that the regulation at issue is legislative because it "creates or changes existing rights and obligations" and, as such, "require[s] specific statutory authorization." In both decisions, the district courts found that promulgation of the advertising regulation was a valid exercise of the Secretary of Labor's inherent authority to adopt interpretive rules.

After examining the relevant case law, we believe that the distinction between legislative and interpretive rules is of little, if any, value in determining whether the Secretary must have a specific grant of rule making authority to promulgate the regulation at issue. That distinction nonetheless becomes important when reviewing the regulation to determine whether it constitutes a proper exercise of rule making authority.

* * *

It is well established that an agency charged with a duty to enforce or administer a statute has inherent authority to issue interpretive rules informing the public of the procedures and standards it intends to apply in exercising its discretion. It is clear that § 212(a)(14) vests the Secretary of Labor with substantial discretion to receive and grant or deny applications for labor certification. *Silva v. Secretary of Labor,* 518 F.2d 301, 310 (1st Cir.1975). In particular, that provision delegates to the Secretary "the determination of whether the factual circumstances underlying any particular application for certification satisfy the [two] substantive requirements of subsection 212(a)(14) ...." *Castaneda-Gonzalez v. INS,* 564 F.2d 417, 423 (D.C.Cir.1977). While the Secretary is charged with the duty to exercise this discretion, the statute does not specify the procedures to be followed or the standards to be applied. Section 212(a)(14) sets forth two substantive requirements—unavailability and lack of adverse effect—but those terms offer little guidance to the certifying officer and prospective applicants. Thus we may reasonably assume that Congress contemplated that the Secretary would issue regulations filling in the essential details. Indeed, Senator Kennedy, the floor manager and a major proponent of the 1965 amendment to § 212(a)(14), stated on the Senate floor: "there will be cases where the Secretary will be expected to ascertain in some detail the need for the immigrant in this country under the provisions of the law. In any event we would expect the Secretary of Labor to devise workable rules and regulations by which he would carry out his responsibilities under the law without unduly interrupting or delaying immigration to this country." 111 Cong.Rec. 24227 (1965). *See also id.* 21758 ("The bill provides for regulatory discretion which resides with the Secretary of Labor in imposing conditions to keep out immigrants who would take work away ....") (remarks of Rep. Celler). Moreover, the court in *Silva* sternly criticized the Secretary for failing to "promulgate suitable regulations": "in an area where the Secretary has considerable power under general statutory standards and must decide numerous cases in a routine fashion, the clarification of policy through rules or published pronouncements would protect against arbitrary action." 518 F.2d at 311. The absence of an express delegation of legislative power does not itself render the advertising regulation void.[1]

---

1. We decide only that promulgation of the advertising requirement was a valid exercise of the Secretary's inherent rule making power. We therefore need not determine whether Congress intended to delegate "legislative" authority under § 212(a)(14), though other courts apparently have assumed such a grant. *See, e.g., Lewis-Mota v. Secretary of Labor,* 469 F.2d 478 (2d Cir. 1972); *Trimble House Corp. v. Marshall,* 497 F.Supp. 546 (N.D.Ga.1980).

Appellants also contend that the advertising regulation shifts the burden of proving unavailability of domestic workers to the employer-applicant. This, they say, is contrary to the intent of Congress and to the greater weight of judicial decisions construing § 212(a)(14). Appellants' argument is not without merit, but we agree with the district court that the regulation constitutes a valid exercise of the Secretary's inherent authority to promulgate rules governing the administration of § 212(a)(14).

The interpretation of a statute by the agency charged with enforcement or administration is entitled to great deference provided it is consistent with the congressional purpose. "[W]e need not find that [the agency's] construction is the only reasonable one, or even that it is the result we would have reached had the question arisen in the first instance in judicial proceedings." *Udall v. Tallman,* 380 U.S. 1, 16, 85 S.Ct. 792, 801, 13 L.Ed.2d 616 (1965), *quoting Unemployment Commission v. Aragan,* 329 U.S. 143, 153, 67 S.Ct. 245, 250, 91 L.Ed. 136 (1946). "[T]he rulings, interpretations and opinions [of the agency], while not controlling upon the courts by reason of their authority, do constitute a body of experience and informed judgment to which courts and litigants may properly resort for guidance." *Skidmore* [*v. Swift & Co.,* 323 U.S. 134, 140, 65 S.Ct. 161, 164, 89 L.Ed. 124 (1944)]. Deference is especially appropriate where, as here, the rule was adopted only after all interested persons were given notice and an opportunity to comment pursuant to § 553 procedures.

Congress enacted § 212(a)(14) to protect the domestic labor force from job competition and adverse working conditions as a result of foreign workers entering the labor market. * * * The labor market findings the Secretary must make are designed to effectuate that purpose. The 1952 version of § 212(a)(14) provided that aliens will not be permitted to enter to perform work "*if* the Secretary of Labor has determined and certified ... that (A) sufficient workers in the United States who are able, willing, and qualified *are available* ... or (B) the employment of such aliens *will* adversely affect the wages and working conditions ...." Act of June 27, 1952, ch. 477, § 212(a)(14), 66 Stat. 183 (emphasis added). In 1965 Congress sought to strengthen the protection of United States workers by amending § 212(a)(14) to require exclusion *unless* the Secretary affirmatively finds that there are *not* sufficient domestic workers available and that entry of the foreign worker will *not* adversely affect working conditions. Pub.L. No. 89–236, § 10(a), 79 Stat. 917. As the Senate Report stated, "Under the instant bill, [the present] procedure is substantially changed. The primary responsibility is placed upon the intending immigrant to obtain the Secretary of Labor's clearance prior to issuance of a visa establishing" the two statutory prerequisites. 1965 U.S.Code Cong. & Ad.News 3333–34. *See* H.R.Rep. No. 745, 89th Cong., 1st Sess. 14 (1965). Whereas the 1952 Act opened the door to immigrant workers unless the Secretary acted to exclude them, the 1965 amendment closed that door and placed direct responsibility on the alien to petition the Secretary to open it. *See* 1 C. Gordon & H. Rosenfield, Immigration Law & Procedure § 2.40a at 2–290 (1982).

* .* *

Implicit in this court's reasoning [in earlier cases] is the premise that labor certification must be granted under § 212(a)(14) unless the Secretary affirmatively determines that able, qualified, and willing United States workers *are* available or that employment of the alien *will* have an adverse effect. Appellants therefore contend that, under the law of this circuit, the burden of proof rests with the Secretary.

While this court has never addressed the statutory basis for that unstated assumption, we need not defend it here, for we believe that the advertising rule, as written, is not inconsistent with Seventh Circuit precedent.

* * *

An applicant-employer does not bear the ultimate burden of persuasion. The regulations require the certifying officer to look to various sources in determining whether a United States worker is available, able, and qualified and whether employment of the alien will have an adverse effect on wages and working conditions. 20 C.F.R. §§ 656.24(b)(2)(ii)–(iv), (b)(3). The documented results of the employer's recruitment efforts are considered only to determine whether a United States worker is *willing* to take the job opportunity. *Id.* § 656.24(b)(2)(i). Even on that inquiry, the certifying officer must also look to the Employment Service Office's recruitment efforts and, presumably, may consider any other sources that may be appropriate. Moreover, the regulations parallel this circuit's position that certification may be denied only upon an affirmative finding of availability and adverse effect. *Id.* § 656.24(b)(2).

We believe that Seventh Circuit precedent does not preclude the imposition of a "burden of production" that is well-defined, very specific, and not unduly burdensome. Rather, documentation of the employer's recruitment efforts will enable the Secretary to make an *informed* decision on the basis of *reliable* evidence. This was our primary concern in [our earlier cases]. Indeed, the regulations may be viewed as a reaction to strong criticism by this and other circuits of the data upon which determinations had been made and the failure to determine the subsidiary questions of whether the available worker is able, qualified, and willing. In particular, the Secretary has found it a difficult task to establish that an available worker is "willing." These regulations seem reasonably designed to gather the most reliable information on that requirement. Finally, by specifying the information to be relied upon in determining whether a worker is willing, the regulations reduce the potential for arbitrariness, a major point of criticism under the prior regulations. *See Silva*, 518 F.2d at 311. *See also Alschuler v. HUD*, 686 F.2d 472, 482 (7th Cir.1982) (agency must "adopt some adequate institutional means for marshalling the appropriate legislative facts"). Given the strong congressional intent to protect American workers and the statutory duty of the Secretary to determine worker availability and labor conditions, we find the Secretary's advertising regulation to be a reasonable exercise of rule making authority.

IV

Having determined the advertising requirement to be a valid rule, it follows that the Secretary must be permitted to give effect to that rule by making substantial compliance a prerequisite to approval of an application. *See Morrison & Morrison, Inc. v. Secretary of Labor,* 626 F.2d 771 (10th Cir.1980). Production Tool admits that it did not comply. Kenall, however, argues in the alternative that the certifying officer abused his discretion by ruling that the *Reader* is not a newspaper of general circulation.

An agency's interpretation of its own regulation is controlling unless "plainly erroneous or inconsistent." We agree with the district court that the certifying officer's construction must stand.

Under the regulations, an employer must advertise the job opportunity "in such media as newspapers of general circulation, and ethnic and professional publications." The obvious purpose of that requirement is, as the hearing officer noted, to test adequately the labor market in the area of intended employment. The statute itself refers to workers who are available "at the place" of the job opportunity. The hearing officer, however, found Kenall's advertisement deficient under the regulation since the *Reader* is a neighborhood weekly with a circulation of 92,000 in only a limited area of Chicago.

The Tenth Circuit upheld a requirement that a Denver employer advertise in the eastern edition of the *Wall Street Journal* for a foreign investment representative. *Morrison & Morrison,* 626 F.2d at 773–74. In view of the sophisticated nature of the job sought, the court concluded that "[a] requirement that does not involve a significant expenditure of money which is likely to reach the pool of U.S. citizen prospects, is not inconsistent with the law or the regulations promulgated thereunder." *Id.* at 774.

Here, the job opportunity—quality control inspector—is centrally located in the city of Chicago. It is entirely reasonable for the Secretary to require advertisement for such a job to be run in one of the two major Chicago newspapers which circulate in the entire metropolitan area. The Illinois cases Kenall cites define "newspaper of general circulation" only for the purpose of publishing legal notices and have very little bearing on whether a job advertisement in the *Reader* adequately tests the relevant labor market. What constitutes the relevant labor market is a question that falls squarely within the Secretary's realm of expertise. Thus we are especially hesitant to second-guess that judgment.

V

Failure on the part of appellants substantially to comply with the Secretary of Labor's valid advertising regulation precluded the certifying officer from being able to determine whether any available United States worker was "willing" to take the job opportunities which appellants sought to fill with alien labor. The decisions of the district courts therefore are Affirmed.

The Prevailing Wage Requirement

In *Production Tool,* Kenall's initial application was found defective in part because the employer was not offering the "prevailing wage." (For the Labor Department's current regulations on this question, *see* 20 C.F.R. § 656.40.) The Department of Labor insists on payment of prevailing wages in order to implement the statutory directive that employment of the alien not "adversely affect the wages and working conditions of the workers in the United States similarly employed." But what wage level is "prevailing"? What is the relevant group for comparison, and how much discretion should the Secretary have in making such decisions? The question is analogous to determining what constitutes the "basic job."

Golabek v. Regional Manpower Administration, 329 F.Supp. 892 (E.D. Pa.1971) involved an application for labor certification for an art teacher in a parochial school. The Department denied certification in part because the wage offered was below comparable wages paid in the local public schools. The district court reversed the determination, holding that parochial school wages should have been the standard for comparison. The court explained—rather unhelpfully—that the "classroom and school situation is different and there may be any number of reasons why a teacher would prefer to work in one school system rather than the other." *Id.* at 896. How should such issues be resolved in a way that affords reasonable protection against erosion of wage scales for U.S. workers?

The Department's "prevailing wage" approach raises deeper issues as well. Insisting on such wages prevents a *deterioration* of pay scales as currently provided in the relevant industry. But deterioration is not the only possible adverse effect that wages might suffer. Should the Department be equally concerned about retarding increases in wages that might otherwise occur in times of labor shortage?

Consider a concrete example. Professional nurses are in such short supply that licensed nurses are exempt from individual labor certification, under the provisions of Schedule A. In fact, however, there are large numbers of trained U.S. workers in the field who simply do not practice that profession; wages have traditionally been low, and many trained nurses find better opportunities for higher pay in other fields. Indeed, some claim that wages have remained low in the nursing field because it has traditionally been regarded as "women's work." *See Women's Work—and Wages,* Newsweek, July 9, 1984, at 22; *Lemons v. City and County of Denver,* 17 FEP Cas. 906 (D.Colo.1978), affirmed 620 F.2d 228 (10th Cir.1980), cert. denied 449 U.S. 888, 101 S.Ct. 244, 66 L.Ed.2d 114 (1980) (plaintiffs asserted that the city engaged in forbidden sex discrimination by paying nurses less than workers in male-dominated occupations; court refused to accept this "comparable worth" theory and ruled for defendants). *See generally Women and the Workplace: The Implications of Occupational Segregation* (M. Blaxall & B. Reagan eds. 1976). If hospitals were unable to hire alien nurses at current wage scales, what would be likely to happen? If you conclude that employers would bid up wages, drawing many qualified workers back into the labor pool, and inducing more people to develop the necessary skills and training, consider what other conditions must hold for this conclusion to be sound. Would the same results occur in the restaurant or hotel business, in factories, in marginal small businesses?

The relatively easy availability of foreign nurses under Schedule A may well interfere with improvements in wages. Should this result be considered an adverse effect? In other words, is the Department of Labor's time horizon too short or vision too restricted in light of the fundamental workings of a free-market system? On the other hand, should the Department's approach be seen instead as a valid measure to keep down hospital costs or to keep marginally profitable hospitals open and functioning? Is the Labor Department the appropriate agency to carry out this function?

YUI SING TSE v. INS

United States Court of Appeals, Ninth Circuit, 1979.
596 F.2d 831.

BROWNING, CIRCUIT JUDGE:

[The petitioner had sought adjustment of status under INA § 245, see p. 282 *infra,* from nonimmigrant student to sixth preference immigrant based on a labor certification for a job as Chinese specialty cook. INS denied adjustment.]

At a hearing held July 24, 1975, petitioner disclosed that he had applied and been accepted for admission to dental school, and would enroll in the fall. He testified it would require four years to complete dental school, and that he intended to continue working as a full-time Chinese specialty cook to support himself and his family while attending school.

The immigration judge denied petitioner's request for an adjustment of status and ordered petitioner deported. The Board affirmed on the ground that petitioner was ineligible for an adjustment of status because he planned to become a dentist rather than to continue to work as a cook.

* * *

Taken together, sections 212(a)(14) and 203(a)(6) are designed to permit aliens capable of performing jobs for which American workers are not available to come to this country, while protecting American workers from the competition of aliens entering the United States to take jobs American workers could fill. *See Maceren v. District Director,* 509 F.2d 934, 936 n. 2 (9th Cir.1974); [G & R] §§ 2.27g, 2.40(a), at 2–210, 2–289; *Matter of Poulin,* 13 I & N 264, 266 (1969).

The second and potentially conflicting interest involved is the interest of an alien granted permanent resident status in the opportunity to earn a living, to improve his economic circumstances, and to engage in common occupations, without unreasonable limitation or invidious discrimination. *Cf.* [G & R] §§ 1.34, 3.6g, at 3–93–4. This interest was reflected in a regulation of the Department of Labor in effect when the Board rendered its decision in this case which provided that "[t]he terms and conditions of the labor certificate shall not be construed as preventing an immigrant properly admitted to the United States from subsequently changing his occupation, job, or area of residence." 29 C.F.R. § 60.5(f) (1976). Addressing the question of an alien's freedom to change occupations, the court in *Castaneda-Gonzalez v. INS,* 183 U.S.App.D.C. 396, 412, 564 F.2d 417, 433 n. 36 (1977), noted the previous existence of this regulation and said: "[a]ny other interpretation could raise serious constitutional issues as to the extent to which employment opportunities may be restricted on the basis of alienage."

In the present case, the Board looked solely to whether at the moment of entry the alien intended to change from the certificated employment, and concluded that petitioner was not entitled to preference as an immigrant because his intention at "entry" was to change employment, though only in the distant future and upon a condition that might not be satisfied. The standard applied by the Board was entirely subjective. It was both too narrow and too rigid to accommodate the interests to be protected.

It is appropriate to require that the alien intend to occupy the certificated occupation for a period of time that is reasonable in light both of the interest served by the statute and the interest in freedom to change employment. But to hold, as the Board did in this case, that an alien is not eligible for admission as a preference immigrant when his intention at entry is to engage in the certified employment unless and until he can complete the educational and other requirements for advancement to the profession of dentistry, a period of four years, fails to recognize that both the interest underlying the grant of preference and the interest in freedom of opportunity for self-improvement would be substantially served by petitioner's admission.

The Board's approach is not required either by the statute or by the Board's regulations.

* * *

Reversed and remanded.

WALLACE, CIRCUIT JUDGE, dissenting:

I respectfully dissent.

* * *

[The] question most emphatically is not whether an immigrant alien, once properly admitted, may change jobs. Rather, the question is whether an alien who applies for immigrant status, and who is thus considered as if he were initially entering the country, *see, e.g., Campos v. INS,* 402 F.2d 758, 760 (9th Cir.1968), may definitely intend, at the time that he makes his application, to change employment from that for which he acquires his labor certificate.

The Board did not forbid an immigrant alien from changing his mind in the future and improving his employment situation. The Board simply held that at the specific time the petitioner submits his application, he must have made a choice to work in the specific area for which he received the work certificate. When the petitioner admits that his desire to do that type of work is merely temporary (i.e., until he can secure some other type of work), he does not qualify.

* * *

The protection of the American work force, as underscored by section 212(a)(14), specifically has to do with where an alien will compete in the job market. The ultimate intent of petitioner is not to work as a Chinese food cook but to work as a dentist. Granting him a labor certificate for what is obviously only temporary employment and closing the Board's eyes to his eventual employment desire would merely frustrate the basic purposes of the statute and prevent the Board from performing its statutorily mandated duty of protecting American labor.

* * *

Notes

1. Similar questions to those presented in the principal case arise when an alien enters under a third- or sixth-preference visa, and either works for a very short time at the certified employment or fails to report for that job at all. The courts have generally been insistent that aliens are not deportable on such facts alone. The government must go further and prove that the alien willfully misrepresented his intent to take the certified work at the time of his entry. *See, e.g., Jang Man Cho v. INS,* 669 F.2d 936 (4th Cir.1982) (reversing and remanding deportation order for further proceedings, even though the alien never even reported for the certified employment); Annotation, 62 A.L.R.Fed. 402 (1983).

2. Suppose Congress explicitly rewrote the statute to require, as a prerequisite to visa issuance, a commitment from third- and sixth-preference immigrants that they remain in the certified employment for a minimum of, say, five years. Consider the majority's dictum in *Yui Sing Tse.* Would there be constitutional problems with such a provision, given Congress's broad authority over entry? Would such a change constitute sound policy?

3. Many studies of the labor certification provisions suggest that the entire system (including the provisions for certification of "H–2" temporary workers, to be considered in the next reading) is virtually ignored in certain portions of the country and in certain employment sectors. This is especially true of agricultural employment in the southwestern United States, apparently because needs for foreign labor can be filled outside legal channels through the employment of undocumented workers. *See* Chapter Nine, *infra.* Moreover, under cases like *Yui Sing Tse* and *Jang Man Cho,* an alien may be able to secure labor certification and then, after a token stay in the certified employment—long enough to defeat deportation or prosecution based on bad faith or willful misrepresentation—enter any field of employment he wishes. That is, there is little guarantee that even those who do enter after complying with the complicated requirements of the occupational preferences will refrain from

competing with American workers in fields where there is no labor shortage.

In light of these problems, is labor certification worth the trouble? *See, e.g.,* G & R § 2.40d (suggesting that "the labor certification program in its present form is a failure"). Should Congress give up on preference provisions tied so closely to specific job requirements? Should all immigration for permanent residence be based on family reunification or other personal characteristics specific to the alien, no matter what field of work he or she may ultimately choose? How would you craft such requirements? *See* SCIRP, Appendix D, at 57–61 (proposal for a category of "new seed" or "independent" immigrants to be selected under a point system modeled on the Canadian experience; the Select Commission rejected this idea in favor of continuing a system based on U.S. needs for labor); Chiswick, *An Alternative Approach to Immigration Policy: Rationing by Skill*, 2 Population Research & Policy Rev. 21 (1983) (another proposal for a point system).

Temporary Workers

CONGRESSIONAL RESEARCH SERVICE, TEMPORARY WORKER PROGRAMS: BACKGROUND AND ISSUES

Senate Committee on the Judiciary, 96th Cong., 2d Sess.
58–64, 70, 74–78 (Comm.Print 1980).

C. ADMISSION OF TEMPORARY WORKERS UNDER THE IMMIGRATION AND NATIONALITY ACT

With the exception of the Mexican bracero workers,[a] all other temporary alien workers have been admitted under the terms of * * * the Immigration and Nationality Act of 1952, as amended, since it went into effect on December 24, 1952. By definition, aliens entering for the express purpose of performing temporary labor are nonimmigrants, as opposed to immigrants, who are admitted permanently and are free to change occupations upon entry, even if they entered under one of the occupational preferences.

1. The H–2 Temporary Worker Provision

Although aliens entering under some of the other nonimmigrant classifications may also accept employment under specified conditions, as discussed below, the temporary admission of most foreign workers under

---

a. "Bracero" literally means one who works with his arms; the closest English equivalent is probably "field hand." Beginning in 1942 the United States entered into a series of agreements with Mexico for the employment of temporary agricultural workers, under a variety of statutes authorizing the practice. Between 4 and 5 million Mexican workers were employed under this "Bracero Program" before the special statutory authority was allowed to lapse in 1964. A more complete description appears in this Committee Print, at 15–58; and in Cardenas, *United States Immigration Policy Toward Mexico: An Historical Perspective*, 2 Chicano L.Rev. 66 (1975). Many observers believe that the bracero program contributed significantly to today's illegal immigration because the migration patterns established under the bracero program simply continued even after the legal authority ended. *See* Committee Print, at 58; Cardenas, *supra*, at 79–80. —eds.

the Immigration and Nationality Act is governed by section 101(a)(15)(H) and section 214(c).

Section 101(a)(15)(H) is one of the 12 categories of nonimmigrants defined by the Immigration and Nationality Act. It provides for the entry of three subcategories of temporary workers, as follows: (i) persons of distinguished merit and ability, (ii) other temporary workers, and (iii) trainees. The second subcategory, the so-called H–2 provision, is the most frequently used and is the primary subject of the following discussion. It reads as follows:

> (H) an alien having a residence in a foreign country which he has no intention of abandoning * * * (ii) who is coming temporarily to the United States to perform other temporary services or labor, if unemployed persons capable of performing such services or labor cannot be found in this country, but this clause shall not apply to graduates of medical schools coming to the United States to perform services as members of the medical profession * * *.

Section 214(c) authorizes the Attorney General to make determinations regarding the importation of aliens under section 101(a)(15)(H), upon petition from the importing employers. "Consultation with appropriate agencies of the Government" is also required. The statutory language, unamended since 1952, follows:

> (c) The question of importing any alien as a nonimmigrant under section 101(a)(15)(H) in any specific case or specific cases shall be determined by the Attorney General, after consultation with appropriate agencies of the Government, upon petition of the importing employer. Such petition shall be made and approved before the visa is granted. The petition shall be in such form and contain such information as the Attorney General shall prescribe. The approval of such a petition shall not, of itself, be construed as establishing that the alien is a nonimmigrant.

In the case of the H–2 worker, a reasonably formalized procedure for Justice Department consultation with the Department of Labor has been set forth with varying degrees of detail in the regulations intermittently since 1953.

* * *

According to the usual procedures now and in the past, the initial action on the H–2 employer's application is made by the local office of the State employment service. This includes a recommendation regarding the availability or unavailability of domestic workers. This action must be approved by the U.S. Labor Department, and may be overruled by the Department of Justice, since the Attorney General has final authority regarding the admission of H–2 workers.

Of the 46,675 "H" entries in fiscal year 1977, 15,702 were "H–1's", 27,760 were "H–2's", and 3,213 were "H–3's". Regarding countries of origin in fiscal year 1977, the single largest number of H–2 entries came from Jamaica—10,650, followed by 4,493 from Canada, and 2,070 from the

Philippines. * * * Mexican H–2 entries were 1,089 in fiscal year 1978, up from 977 in fiscal year 1977, and 761 in fiscal year 1976.

H–2's enter temporarily for jobs which are themselves temporary in nature. Because they cannot be employed in jobs which are of an ongoing nature, they are not surprisingly heavily concentrated in seasonal agricultural activities and in show business and professional sports. The single largest group of H–2's admitted in fiscal year 1977 were farm laborers—11,421.

These were followed by writers, artists, and entertainers (5,479), a classification which, when combined with the H–1 entries (6,709), outnumbered farmworkers. Other major occupational categories accounting for H–2 entries in fiscal year 1977 were musicians and composers (3,586), athletes (1,385), and lumbermen (1,121).

While the number of H–2 entries is not large, their impact tends to be concentrated in certain areas and occupations—for instance, apple picking on the east coast, sugar cane cutting in Florida, and construction work in Guam.

* * *

Many of the arguments about the impact of H–2's in the areas and industries in which they are concentrated closely resemble those of the bracero era. The employers argue that a genuine shortage of domestic workers exists, which the Labor Department is often reluctant to acknowledge because of its institutional concern with unemployment. On the other hand, critics of the H–2 provision and its administration, particularly as it pertains to agricultural workers, argue that H–2 workers depress wages, cause some displacement of resident workers due in part to employer preference, and result in an inherently undemocratic two-class labor force. Regarding this latter point, it has been observed that "the mass-admitted nonimmigrant workers have the same general characteristics of the braceros of our past and the European guest workers of today, in that they are legal alien workers with some rights but with considerably fewer rights than those of citizens and resident alien workers."

The major differences between the H–2 provision and the bracero program are that the H–2 provision is a permanent part of the law, not intended to meet a specific national manpower shortage; that the numbers admitted under the provision have been significantly smaller—27,760 H–2's in fiscal year 1977, compared to 436,049 braceros 20 years earlier in 1957; that, while it is limited to temporary employment, it is not specifically limited to agricultural work; and that it is not reinforced by international treaty, as was the bracero program.

Another significant difference has been that a relatively small number of Mexicans has been admitted under the H–2 provision; this is despite the fact that * * * the H–2 provision has no geographic restrictions. The limited number of Mexican H–2's has been partly the result of administrative determinations by the U.S. Labor Department, either that domestic workers have been available in the areas and occupations for which Mexican workers have been requested, or that employers have failed to meet the requirements of the regulations governing the importation of H-2's. Thus, the decision to admit Mexican onion pickers into Presidio, Tex., in June 1977, reportedly at the urging of President Carter, was contrary to the recommendation of the Labor Department.

Apart from the ongoing controversy which has surrounded the H-2 provision in recent years, particularly regarding the admission of Jamaicans to pick apples on the east coast, the provision is of particular interest at this time because its expansion is one of the options under consideration as an alternative to illegal migration for temporary employment. * * * [I]t should be noted at the outset that greatly increasing the number of H-2 admissions would require fundamental changes in both the assumptions which govern the admission of the workers, and the administration of the provision. Thus, it is difficult to predict from past experience what future experience under a significantly enlarged program would be likely to be because, by definition, it would be a significantly different program.

* * *

a. Overview: Legislative and administrative history of the H-2 provision

The H-2 provision evolved from a combination of the fourth and ninth provisos to section 3 of the Immigration Act of 1917. Section 3 sets forth a list of inadmissible aliens, including contract laborers. The fourth proviso authorized the Attorney General to grant waivers of the exclusion clause regarding skilled contract laborers upon a finding that "labor of like kind unemployed can not be found in this country." The ninth proviso allowed for a waiver of excludability for inadmissible aliens, including contract laborers, for temporary entry, and was the principal authority for the admission of agricultural worker[s] during the periods before and after the enactment of special legislation for that purpose during World War II. Administrative procedures developed jointly in 1948 by the Commissioner of the Immigration and Naturalization Service and the Director of the U.S. Employment Service required that before such a waiver could be issued, the need for the workers had to be investigated by INS and certified by the U.S. Employment Service; and it had to be shown that their admission would not displace or otherwise detrimentally affect labor in this country.

In 1950 the Senate Judiciary Committee considered temporary agricultural workers in its comprehensive report entitled "The Immigration and Naturalization Systems of the United States." The committee found "that the agricultural labor supply in the United States, particularly in the Southwestern States, requires supplementation," and made the following recommendation:

> * * * provisions should be made in permanent legislation which would permit the admission of temporary agricultural labor in a nonimmigrant classification when like labor cannot be found in this country. The determination of the necessity for the importation of such labor in any particular instance should be made by the Commissioner of Immigration and Naturalization upon appli-

cation by the interested employer before the importation and after a full investigation of the facts and consultation with appropriate agencies.

This recommendation was essentially enacted into law as the H–2 provision of the Immigration and Nationality Act of 1952—and remains in effect today—with the very important omission of the Mexican agricultural labor program. Beginning in 1951 the Mexican program was authorized by separate legislation, Public Law 78, until its expiration on December 31, 1964.

Regulations published by the Justice Department's Immigration and Naturalization Service require Labor Department certification of the unavailability of domestic workers as a prerequisite for admitting H–2 workers, thus following the pattern established during the initial period of the temporary foreign labor programs, and after 1947. Labor Department certifications in the case of H–2 workers are advisory only, and may be overridden by the Justice Department, which has final authority. The H–2 provision differed in this respect from those governing the bracero program, under which the role of the Labor Department was considerably more extensive.

* * *

The history of the administration of the H–2 provision has been a fairly turbulent one, particularly in recent years in reaction to rising unemployment. The Labor Department has been alternatively accused of certifying too few and too many alien workers.

* * *

b. Overview of H–2 operations

H–2 temporary workers are as closely linked to their employers as were braceros. They are petitioned for by their prospective employers; approval of the petition is automatically terminated in the event that the employer dies, goes out of business, or files a written withdrawal of the petition before the beneficiary arrives in the United States; and in the event that an alien wishes to change employers, a new petition must be submitted by the prospective new employer.

The admission process is initiated by the employer, who files a petition with the Attorney General, usually as represented by the INS district director who has jurisdiction over the area where the services are to be performed. The law requires approval by the Attorney General, after consultation with the appropriate agencies, which in practice has been limited to the Labor Department and takes the form of labor certification. Regulations issued by INS require that, "either a certification from the Secretary of Labor or his designated representative stating that qualified persons in the United States are not available and that the employment of the beneficiary will not adversely affect the wages and working condition of workers in the United States similarly employed, or a notice that such a certification cannot be made, shall be attached to every nonimmigrant visa petition to accord an alien a classification under section 101(a)(15)(H)(ii) of the Act."

The Department of Labor's Employment and Training Administration, in turn, has issued regulations governing the labor certification process. The H–2 petitioning employer is required to file an application for labor certification with the local office of the State Employment Service, which reports its findings to the regional office of the U.S. Department of Labor's Employment and Training Administration (ETA). The final decision on certification is made by the ETA.

Detailed requirements are set forth in the regulations pertaining to the labor certification process for temporary agricultural and logging employment. The application for certification submitted to the local office of the State Employment Service is required to include a job offer for U.S. workers and to meet specified standards regarding wages, working conditions, housing, transportation, and workers' rights and benefits. Quoting from the preamble to the regulations, "In short, the regulations provide, with respect not only to transportation and subsistence costs but also with respect to all wages, benefits, and working conditions, that employers must offer and provide U.S. workers with at least the same level of wages, benefits and working conditions offered or provided to foreign workers."

Adverse effect rates for agricultural and logging employment in certain States are published annually by the Labor Department, most recently on June 5, 1979. "Adverse effect rates" are defined in the regulations as the—

> wage rate which the Administrator has determined must be offered and paid to foreign and U.S. workers for a particular occupation and/or area so that the wages of similarly employed U.S. workers will not be adversely affected. The Administrator may determine that the prevailing wage rate in the area and/or occupation is the adverse effect rate, if the use (or non-use) of aliens has not depressed the wages of similarly employed U.S. workers. The Administrator may determine that a wage rate higher than the prevailing wage rate is the adverse effect rate if the Administrator determines that the use of aliens has depressed the wages of similarly employed U.S. workers.

* * *

The regulations governing the admission of H–2 agricultural workers may be interpreted as a belated battle won by those who argued during the bracero years, first, that domestic workers should be guaranteed the same benefits as those guaranteed the Mexican foreign workers by the international treaties and individual contracts; and, second, that the requirement that foreign workers be paid the prevailing wage provided no protection to domestic workers in areas and occupations so dominated by foreign workers that their wage became the prevailing wage. As such, the regulations derive directly from those issued by Secretary of Labor Wirtz in December 1964 which were specifically intended not only to prevent the resurfacing of the bracero program under the authority of [the INA,] but also to decrease and perhaps end the dependence of U.S. employers on foreign labor, in part by raising the cost of using them. On the other hand, it should be noted that employers of H–2 agricultural workers are exempted from paying social security and unemployment taxes, which lowers the cost of their employment compared to domestic workers.

Petitions for the issuance of H–2 nonimmigrant visas and the accompanying labor certification are filed with INS. Although the role of the Labor Department is advisory, and the Attorney General is required by law to make the final determination, INS "will in most cases abide by the decision of the Labor Department."

In the event that the petition is granted, it is transmitted to the consul for the issuance of a visa. If a time period is specified in the labor certification, the validity of the visa petition cannot exceed that time period. In the event that no time period is specified, the visa petition is valid for 1 year from the date of the labor certification. Extensions may be requested in increments of 1 year each, not exceeding 3 years of uninterrupted stay. Each request for an extension must be accompanied by a labor certification.

Notes

1. For a recent summary of current procedures and the evolving substantive requirements for temporary foreign workers, *see The H–2 Category for Temporary Workers*, 3 Imm.L.Rep. 1 (1984). The Labor Department has also published additional guidelines explaining its role and the necessary procedures. 49 Fed.Reg. 25837–45 (1984).

2. The H–2 temporary worker program remains controversial. Some claim that it is too slow and cumbersome to meet the needs of U.S. employers. *See Proposals to Amend the Immigration and Nationality Act: Hearings Before the Subcommittee on Labor Standards of the House Committee of Education and Labor*, 98th Cong., 1st Sess. 17–18 (1983) (testimony of Steven Karalekas). Many studies indicate that far more foreign workers than have ever been included in the H–2 program simply enter illegally each year to take temporary jobs in this country, especially in the Southwest. Others believe that any use of temporary foreign employees undermines the wages and working conditions of U.S. workers. *See* Staff of Senate Committee on the Judiciary, 96th Cong., 2d Sess., Temporary Worker Programs: Background and Issues 62, 100–101 (Comm.Print 1980). Still others object on ethical grounds to the idea of importing people solely for their labor, without offering them full membership rights. *See* M. Walzer, Spheres of Justice: A Defense of Pluralism and Equality 56–61 (1983). We will examine these controversies more closely in Chapter Nine.

3. Other nonimmigrants may secure permission to work in certain limited circumstances. *See* 8 C.F.R. § 109.1.

Alien Commuters

One other category—a rather anomalous one—deserves mention here. Beginning in 1927, U.S. immigration authorities began to permit the entry *as immigrants* of certain commuting workers who maintain their actual residences across the border in Canada or Mexico, provided they meet the other general qualifications for immigrant status. Some commute daily; others commute on a seasonal basis. The Congressional Research Service Study, *supra,* at 82–83, describes this group as follows:

> Commuter aliens, or "green card commuters," are aliens who have been admitted as immigrants, for permanent residence, and who live in either Canada or Mexico and commute to the United States for daily or seasonal employment. The number of commuters was reported at the end of fiscal year 1978 at 57,268, of whom 49,290 commuted across the Mexican border.

> The card used by the commuter to enable him to pass freely across the U.S. border as an immigrant legally entitled to work in this country is no longer the green special border crossing identification card once used (hence the colloquial name "green carder"), but the Alien Registration Receipt Card (Form I–151 or I–551) issued to registered immigrants. Under present law and regulations, this card entitles any alien admitted for permanent residence the right to reenter the country following a temporary absence of less than a year. The significance of the commuter status is that the alien must meet the conditions for entry into the United States, particularly that of labor certification, only at the time of his first admission; thereafter, he is considered as returning to his residence in the United States. Commuter status for alien employment purposes is dependent on the alien's having a permanent and stable job in this country when he is first admitted; and, in the event that he loses that job subsequent to obtaining commuter status, on his not remaining unemployed for a period exceeding 6 months. [*See* 8 C.F.R. § 211.5.]

* * *

> The commuter system differs in significant respects from the bracero and H–2 programs. The workers are not specifically tied to individual employers; they are not limited to agriculture or any other specific employment; they are not limited to occupations and areas where there is a labor shortage except by the availability of employment; and they are subject to all of the labor laws which apply to U.S. citizens and permanent resident aliens. In short, with the exceptions of the fact that they are tied to a rather limited geographic region by virtue of the fact that they commute across the Mexican or Canadian border, they are subject only to the fairly minimal restraints on immigrants in the U.S. labor market.

How can commuters be considered as returning from a "temporary visit abroad" (and thus entitled to "special immigrant" status under INA § 101(a)(27)(A)) when they make no pretense of having a residence within our borders? The question arose most pointedly after the 1965 amendments required affirmative labor certification for persons entering in order to work, since those who qualify as commuters do not obtain subsequent labor certification even when they change jobs. Labor organizations persisted in raising these issues and particularly in challenging INS's perpetuation of the commuter status after enactment of the 1965 legislation. But when the question finally reached the Supreme Court, in a suit brought by the United Farm Workers Organizing Committee, a narrow majority sustained the administrative practice, citing its lengthy history and the possible foreign policy consequences if it were terminated. *Saxbe v. Bustos,* 419 U.S. 65, 95 S.Ct. 272, 42 L.Ed.2d 231 (1974). The four dissenters argued vigorously that commuter status contravened the plain language of the INA. *Id.* at 80–89 (White, J., dissenting).

SECTION B.   GROUNDS FOR EXCLUSION

1. OVERVIEW

With the practical demise of nonpreference immigration in 1978, all who wish to come to this country must first fit themselves within one of the qualifying categories canvassed in the preceding sections. But that is only part of the story. They must also avoid any determination of excludability under INA § 212(a). Both consular officers asked to issue visas and immigration inspectors at the port of entry will consider the applicability of these provisions.

Section 212(a) lists classes of aliens who "shall be ineligible to receive visas and shall be excluded from admission into the United States." There are 33 such classes and numerous detailed subclasses—all addressed to qualitative characteristics that are considered for various reasons to be undesirable. As one court commented, these provisions constitute "a magic mirror, reflecting the fears and concerns of past Congresses." *Lennon v. INS,* 527 F.2d 187, 189 (2d Cir.1975). They cover quite a range, from clearly understandable and legitimate requirements to others of dubious heritage. Many of them surely would not be included by modern Congresses—at least not in anything like their current form— if somehow all present immigration provisions were to disappear from the books and today's Congress had to sit down to create a new code from scratch. Yet the list has stubbornly resisted reform, much less comprehensive revision. Even the Select Commission on Immigration and Refugee Policy, which carried out an otherwise comprehensive study of immigration laws from 1978 through 1981, ducked the thorny political controversies that might be involved in recasting the grounds of exclusion. Although it went on record as believing "that the present exclusionary grounds should not be retained," the Commission did not provide particulars. Rather it simply urged Congress to reexamine the grounds for exclusion now set forth in the INA, SCIRP, Final Report 282–83, to the chagrin of some of its members who had urged the Commission to tackle the issue directly, *see, e.g., id.* at 346–52 (views of Rep. Holtzman).

Section 212(a)—one of the lengthiest subsections in the whole INA— hardly makes for easy reading. The rest of section 212 is equally daunting. It consists primarily of exemption and waiver provisions that cut back in intricate and hard-to-catalogue ways on the exclusion grounds in subsection (a). Some of the later subsections provide across-the-board exemptions in specified circumstances; others stipulate situations in which the Attorney General is granted discretion to waive exclusion grounds following case-by-case inquiry.

You are not expected to commit the exclusion grounds to memory, but you should become familiar with the general structure of § 212 and its provisions. Toward that end, we begin here with a general treatment that furnishes a kind of map for the section. Before reading it or § 212, however, you might find it useful to skip ahead to the problems on page 192, so as to have a few concrete fact situations in mind as you read. You may find it easier to become acquainted with Section 212 by dipping into it for the answers to specific questions, rather than simply plodding through it from start to finish.

After this general review, we will then consider in depth a few selected exclusion grounds.

NATIONAL LAWYERS GUILD, IMMIGRATION LAW AND DEFENSE

§§ 5.1–5.3 (2d ed. 1983).

§ 5.1. Introduction

The issue of exclusion may arise in four contexts:

1. Prior to entry, when a consul overseas denies a visa application based upon one of the grounds for exclusion. * * *

2. At the border, when, even though the alien has been issued a visa, the immigration inspectors nevertheless find the alien excludable and deny admission.

3. After entry, when an alien who has been legally admitted into the country is subjected to deportation proceedings on the basis that he or she was excludable at the time of entry (or reentry). *See* § 241(a)(1).

4. When an alien applies for permanent residency while in the United States through the adjustment of status procedures, * * * the applicant is also subject to possible denial of his or her application based upon one of the grounds of exclusion.[a]

* * *

§ 5.2. Grounds for Exclusion

This section discusses the qualitative restrictions upon the entry of noncitizens into the United States. These restrictions which forbid

---

a. There are two other settings where the issue of excludability may also arise. First, when a lawful permanent resident returns to the United States after a trip abroad, the exclusion grounds are often applied anew. *See* Chapter Four. Second, in naturalization proceedings, the applicant for citizenship may have to show that his admission as a lawful permanent resident many years earlier was proper, including compliance with the exclusion grounds. *See Matter of Longstaff,* 716 F.2d 1439 (5th Cir.1983, cert. denied ___ U.S. ___, 104 S.Ct. 2668, 81 L.Ed.2d 373 (1984), excerpted later in this Section.—eds.

classes of "undesirable" noncitizens from entry are based principally on health, moral, criminal, political, and economic grounds.

Since 1875, when the first restrictions were enacted to bar convicts and prostitutes from entry, there has been a tradition of growth in the number of grounds for exclusion. The statute lists thirty-three separate categories of noncitizens who are barred from entry. § 212(a).

Technically, every time a noncitizen, whether a permanent resident or nonimmigrant, applies for admission, even on a return to the United States after a temporary visit abroad, he or she is excludable if he or she falls within one of the thirty-three classes of excludable aliens.

Certain grounds of excludability will not apply to aliens previously admitted as refugees or asylees pursuant to the Refugee Act of 1980. Section 209(c) provides that such grounds as likelihood of becoming a public charge, lack of appropriate entry documents, literacy, and the two-year foreign residence requirement for foreign medical graduates shall not bar adjustment of status under this section; with certain exceptions, the Attorney General may, in his discretion, waive any other ground of excludability for refugee or asylee applicants for adjustment of status.

§ 5.2(a). Economic Grounds

The following classes of aliens are barred from entering the United States because of their economic situation:

1. *Persons who are paupers, professional beggars, or vagrants.* § 212(a)(8).

2. *Persons who, in the opinion of consular or immigration officials, are likely at any time to become public charges.* § 212(a)(15). A person likely to become a public charge is "one who by reason of poverty, insanity, disease, or disability will probably become a charge upon the public." *Gegiow v. Uhl,* 239 U.S. 3 (1915).

* * *

3. *Persons who are seeking entry for the purpose of performing skilled or unskilled labor,* unless the Secretary of Labor certifies that there are not enough workers who are able, willing, qualified, and available to perform such labor, and that wages and working conditions of workers in the United States similarly employed will not be adversely affected by the employment of such aliens. § 212(a)(14). This exclusion provision applies to the third and sixth preference and nonpreference immigrant applicants.

* * *

§ 5.2(b). Health Grounds

The following classes of noncitizens are barred entry because of mental conditions:

1. *Persons who are mentally retarded.* § 212(a)(1).

2. *Persons who are insane.* § 212(a)(2).

3. *Persons who have had one or more attacks of insanity.* § 212(a)(3).

4. *Persons afflicted with psychopathic personalities, or with sexual deviation, or with a mental defect.* § 212(a)(4).

In *Fleuti v. Rosenberg,* 302 F.2d 652 (9th Cir.1962), *aff'd on other grounds,* 374 U.S. 449 (1963), the Ninth Circuit held that this section was unconstitutionally vague in requiring the deportation of a sexual deviate who returned to his residence in this country after a temporary absence. As a result, the specific language requiring exclusion of "sexual deviates" was added to overcome the *Fleuti* problems. H.R.Rep. No. 11101, 89th Cong., 1st Sess. 18 (1965). In 1967 the Supreme Court upheld the constitutionality of the exclusion of a homosexual noncitizen under these provisions. *Boutilier v. INS,* 387 U.S. 118 (1967).

* * *

5. *Persons who are narcotic drug addicts.* [§ 212(a)(5).]

6. *Persons who are chronic alcoholics.* § 212(a)(5).

A waiver may be obtained by a person excludable on the grounds of mental retardation, or who has suffered one or more attacks of insanity, if the person has a spouse, son, daughter, or parent (if the noncitizen is unmarried and, if adopted, is under twenty-one years old) who is a citizen, a lawfully admitted resident of the United States, or an alien who has been issued an immigrant visa, § 212(g). An application for this waiver is filed on Form I–601, either by the noncitizen seeking the waiver or by the family member. The procedure to be followed in submitting this waiver application is set forth in 8 C.F.R. § 212.7(b)(2).

* * *

The following classes of noncitizens are barred entry because of physical conditions:

1. *Persons afflicted with any dangerous contagious disease.* § 212(a)(6). The Public Health Service has designated the following as dangerous contagious diseases within the contemplation of the statute: actinomycosis; amebiasis; blastomycosis; chancroid; favus; filariasis; gonorrhea; granuloma inquinale; keratoconjunctivitis infectious; leishmaniasis; leprosy; lymphogranuloma venereum; mycetoma; paragonimiasis; ringworm of the scalp; shistosomiasis; syphillis, infectious stage; trachoma; trypanosomiasis; tuberculosis; yaws. 42 C.F.R. § 34.2(b).

A waiver may be secured by a noncitizen with active tuberculosis who has a spouse, son, daughter, or parent (if the noncitizen is unmarried, and if adopted, is under twenty-one) who is a citizen, a lawful permanent resident, or an alien issued an immigrant visa. § 212(g). An application for this waiver is filed on Form I–601 either with the consul or the INS. 8 C.F.R. § 212.7(b). Persons applying for this must consult the special instructions in Form I–601.

2. *Persons certified by the examining medical officer as having a physical defect, disease, or disability* which the consul or immigration

officer determines may affect their ability to earn a living, unless they prove that they do not have to earn a living.

Waivers may be secured by persons excludable for physical defects (other than tuberculosis, leprosy, or a dangerous contagious disease) upon posting of a bond guaranteeing that they will not become public charges. § 213.

§ 5.2(c). Criminal Grounds

One of the earliest motivations for restrictions on the entry of noncitizens into the United States was to keep out criminals. At one time, of course, the American colonies were populated by convicts, and there was no bar to their entry in large numbers. Now, however, the following criminal classes of noncitizens are barred:

1. *Persons who have been convicted of a crime involving moral turpitude.*[b] In certain instances noncitizens who are convicted or admit the essential elements of crimes involving moral turpitude are not subject to exclusion: (a) if the crime is a "purely political" offense; (b) if the crime was committed more than five years prior to the application for a visa by a noncitizen under age eighteen, provided that the noncitizen has been released from prison for at least five years; or (c) if the crime was the only one committed by the noncitizen and is a misdemeanor classifiable as a petty offense. [§ 212(a)(9).]

2. *Persons who admit having committed a crime involving moral turpitude* or the acts constituting the essential elements of such crime. § 212(a)(9).

3. *Persons who have been convicted of two crimes* (other than political offenses) for which the sentences to confinement actually imposed aggregate five years or more. [§ 212(a)(10).]

Waivers may be obtained by noncitizens seeking entry who are excludable on the above three criminal grounds if they establish that their exclusion would result in extreme hardship to a spouse, parent (if the noncitizen is a child), son, or daughter who is a citizen or lawful permanent resident. § 212(h).

* * *

4. *Persons who have been convicted of any law or regulation relating to the illicit possession of, or trafficking in, narcotics, drugs, or marijuana.* § 212(a)(23).

Waiver of excludability for simple possession of less than thirty grams of marijuana is available under § 212(h). * * * The relationship to citizen or resident alien spouse, parent or child, and extreme hardship must be shown, as with other (h) waivers.

b. Commission of a crime involving moral turpitude can also be a ground for deportation. We will consider carefully various questions concerning these provisions in Chapter Five.—eds.

§ 5.2(d). Quasi-Criminal and Moral Grounds

The following noncitizen classes are barred entry into the United States upon moral grounds:

1. *Persons who are polygamists* or who practice or advocate polygamy. [§ 212(a)(11).]

2. *Persons who are* (a) *prostitutes* or who have engaged in prostitution; (b) seeking to enter for the purpose of prostitution or for other immoral purpose, or for commercialized vice even though unrelated to prostitution; or (c) procurers, or are supported by proceeds of prostitution. [§ 212(a)(12).]

A waiver of excludability may be obtained by persons excludable on grounds related to prostitution when their exclusion would result in extreme hardship to a citizen or lawful permanent resident spouse, parent (if the noncitizen is a child), son, or daughter. * * *

3. *Persons who are coming to the United States to engage in any immoral sexual act.* [§ 212(a)(13).]

4. *Persons who have at any time knowingly and for gain assisted another noncitizen to enter in violation of law.* § 212(a)(31).

5. *Persons who have sought to procure a visa or other documentation by fraud* or willful misrepresentation of a material fact. § 212(a)(19).

* * *

This ground for exclusion may be waived for aliens with permanent resident or citizen spouses, parents, or children in the United States. § 212(i). * * *

§ 5.2(e). Entry and Documentary Grounds

All noncitizens must comply with prescribed documentary requirements before entry to the United States is allowed. Generally, they must present valid unexpired visas and passports. §§ 211(a) and 212(a)(20). This is a condition for entry whether the noncitizen is seeking to enter permanently as an immigrant or temporarily as a nonimmigrant.

Unless the documentary requirements have been waived, by regulation, the consul abroad has plenary power over whether a visa is issued. In order to receive a visa the noncitizen must submit a number of supporting documents. 22 C.F.R. § 42.111. The consul is authorized to refuse to issue a visa if it appears that the noncitizen has not supplied all of the necessary supporting documents with the visa application, or that he or she appears inadmissible for any of the other exclusionary provisions. § 221(g). There is no review of a refusal of the consul to grant a visa. The courts have not recognized a right to review consular decisions in this area.

Although passports valid for sixty days are required for all arriving immigrants, the requirement may be waived by the Immigration Service for an immigrant who (a) is the parent, spouse, or unmarried son or daughter of a citizen or resident; (b) is the child born to a citizen or resident temporarily abroad; (c) is a returning resident temporarily abroad; (d) is stateless, or, because of opposition to Communism, is unwilling to obtain a passport, or is the accompanying spouse or unmarried son or daughter of such immigrant; (e) is a third preference quota immigrant; (f) is a member of the Armed Forces of the United States; or (g) has satisfied the district director that there is good cause for failure to present the document. 8 C.F.R. § 211.2.

The Immigration Service may waive the visa requirement for (a) a child born subsequent to the issuance of a visa to the accompanying parent; (b) a child born to a citizen or resident abroad on a temporary visit; and (c) a returning resident in possession of [an alien registration receipt card]. 8 C.F.R. § 211.1.[16]

Additionally, visas and passports may be waived in individual cases by joint action of the Immigration Service and the State Department on the basis of unforeseen emergency or on the basis of reciprocity with respect to nationals of a foreign contiguous territory or adjacent [islands.] § 212(d)(4). Form I–193 is used and a $10 fee is paid.

The Immigration Service may grant a waiver of a passport or visa requirement of a nonimmigrant only after a favorable recommendation from the consul or the State Department.[17]

§ 5.2(f). Technical Grounds

The following additional classes of noncitizens are barred from entering the United States:

1. *Persons who have been previously excluded* and who seek reentry within one year without obtaining the permission of the Attorney General prior to reembarkation. § 212(a)(16). Request for permission to reapply is made on Form I–212, and a fee must be paid. Reentry in violation of this section is a criminal offense. § 276.

2. *Persons who have been previously deported,* who have been removed at government expense pursuant to § 242(b) of the Act, 8 U.S.C. § 1252(b), or who have been removed as distressed aliens under prior laws, and who seek admission within five years of the date of such deportation or removal, unless the Attorney General has granted his consent to a

---

16. Aliens lawfully admitted for permanent residence who temporarily proceed abroad voluntarily, who are not under any order of deportation, and who are returning to a lawful unrelinquished domicile of seven consecutive years may be admitted in the discretion of the Immigration Service when the alien is excludable for any ground other than those relating to disloyalty or subversive political activity. § 212(c). * * * [We will consider § 212(c) at length in Chapter Six.—eds.]

17. § 212(d)(3) of the Act, 8 U.S.C. § 1182(d)(3). The INS may grant waivers of inadmissibility to nonimmigrant applicants for all grounds except on the grounds that the entry would be prejudicial to the best interests of the United States, or that applicants would probably engage in subversive conduct after entry.

A § 212(d)(3) waiver is available to aliens excludable under § 212(a)(28) unless the Secretary of State determines that admissibility is contrary to security interests; or unless the alien is a member of the Palestine Liberation Organization, a representative of a labor organization in a country where it is an instrument of the state, or a native of a country failing to comply with the Helsinki Final Act. P.L. 96–60, amending 22 U.S.C. § 2691 (1979).

readmission application prior to embarkation. § 212(a)(17). * * * [Reentry] without permission is a criminal offense, § 276. Permission to reapply should be sought on Form I–212. Factors to be considered in making a determination on such an application are: the applicant's moral character, the recency of his deportation, whether his services are needed in the United States, and his length of residence in the United States. Remedial relief is the intent of these provisions.

3. *Aliens who are draft evaders* (during time of war or national emergency). § 212(a)(22). Exclusion for evasion of military service during the war in Vietnam has been specifically pardoned by President Carter.

* * *

4. *Aliens who are ineligible for citizenship.*[18]

5. *Aliens who accompany an excluded alien* helpless because of infancy, sickness, or physical or mental disability. § 212(a)(30).

6. *Aliens who cannot read thirty to forty words in any language or dialect.* § 212(a)(25).

The following are exempt from the literacy requirement:

a. any noncitizen sixteen years of age and under;

b. any noncitizen physically incapable of reading;

c. any noncitizen lawfully admitted for permanent residence who is returning from a temporary visit abroad;

d. any noncitizen who is the parent, grandparent, spouse, daughter, or son of an admissible alien, or of an alien lawfully admitted for permanent residence, or of a citizen of the United States, if the illiterate alien is accompanying or coming to join such relative in the United States, § 212(b);

e. any noncitizen who is seeking to enter the United States to escape religious persecution in the country of last permanent residence, § 212(b)[;]

f. any noncitizen seeking entry as a nonimmigrant, § 212(d)(1).

§ 5.2(g). Political Grounds

The following classes of noncitizens are barred from entering the United States on grounds of subversion:

1. *Persons whom the consular officer or Attorney General believes seek to enter* to engage in *activities which would be prejudicial to the* best interests, welfare, safety, or *security of the United States.* [§ 212(a)(27).]

2. *Persons who are anarchists.* § 212(a)(28)(A).

---

18. § 212(a)(22). This provision covers noncitizens—except nonimmigrants—who are ineligible for citizenship by reason of draft exemption claims filed as aliens under the Selective Service Act. *See Ceballos y Arboleda v. Shaughnessy,* 352 U.S. 599 (1957); *McGrath v. Kristensen,* 340 U.S. 162 (1950).

3. *Persons who are advocates of opposition to organized government.* § 212(a)(28)(B).

4. *Persons who are members of, or affiliated with, organizations advocating opposition to organized government.* § 212(a)(28)(B).

5. *Persons who are members of, or those affiliated with, the Communist Party* or any other totalitarian party, its affiliates, direct predecessors, or successors in the United States or abroad.[21]

6. *Persons who are advocates of doctrines of World Communism* or totalitarian dictatorship in the United States, or members of, or affiliated with, organizations advocating such doctrines. § 212(a)(28)(D).

7. *Persons who are members of, or affiliated with, organizations required to be registered* under the Subversive Activities Control Act of 1950 (ch. 1024, § 7, 64 Stat. 993). § 212(a)(28)(E).[21.1]

8. *Persons who are advocates of violent or unconstitutional overthrow of the government* of the United States or all forms of law, and who are members of, or affiliated with, organizations advocating such doctrines. § 212(a)(28)(F).

9. *Persons who are advocates of the unlawful killing or assaulting of officers of the United States* government or of any other organized government, who are advocates of the unlawful destruction of property, or of sabotage, and who are members of, or affiliated with, organizations advocating such doctrines. § 212(a)(28)(F).

10. *Persons who are writers or publishers of subversive literature.* § 212(a)(28)(G).

11. *Persons who are distributors, printers, and displayers of subversive literature,* with knowledge of its subversive character. § 212(a)(28)(G).

12. *Persons who are members of, or those affiliated with,* organizations writing, printing, distributing, or possessing for circulation subversive literature.

13. *Persons whom consular or immigration officers believe would probably engage in subversive activities* or join a subversive organization.

21. § 212(a)(28)(C). Exempt from all provisions of (a)(28), except the anarchist class, are those who establish the following:

1. Membership or affiliation has ended before reaching one's sixteenth birthday.

2. Membership or affiliation is or was by operation of law, *i.e.,* without acquiescence, as in the case of a person who automatically became a member or affiliate "by official act, proclamation, order, edict, or decree."

3. Membership or affiliation is or was involuntary.

4. Membership or affiliation is or was for the purpose of obtaining employment, food rations, or other essentials of living, and was necessary for such purposes.

5. Membership or affiliation was terminated, and there has been an active opposition to the doctrines of the subversive organization for at least five years prior to the date of visa application. § 212(a)(28)(I).

Active opposition shall be construed as embracing speeches, writings, and other overt or covert activities. 22 C.F.R. § 42.-91(a)(28)(vii). In addition, it must be established that the alien's entry will be in the public interest. The Attorney General is required to report to Congress the cases of all persons admitted under this provision. § 212(a)(28)(I).

21.1. Section 7 of the Subversive Activities Control Act of 1950 was repealed by the Act of Jan. 2, 1968, 81 Stat. 766.

§ 212(a)(29). This provision may not be waived even for nonimmigrants. § 212(d)(3).

14. *Persons who were Nazis* or Nazi collaborators, or who worked for Nazi allies, and who "ordered, incited, assisted, or otherwise participated in the persecution of any person because of race, religion, national origin, or political opinion." § 212(a)(33). This ground for exclusion, added by P.L. 95–549, effective October 1, 1978, is not waivable under § 212(d).

§ 5.3. Waivers of Excludability

Under certain circumstances, the Attorney General is authorized to exercise discretion in favor of waiving one of the grounds for exclusion when aliens meet specified statutory standards. These grounds for waivers of excludability are discussed generally in § 212(b)–(i). Two points must be noted regarding the grounds for waiver generally:

First, the exercise of discretion by the Attorney General is not mandatory, and cases in which an alien is statutorily eligible for a waiver may not necessarily result in one being granted. While judicial review is available generally regarding abuse of discretionary powers, since the issue of waivers will almost uniformly arise when the alien is not present in the country (*i.e.*, at the border or overseas), the right to judicial review of the decision to deny discretionary relief is practically nonexistent. *See Kleindienst v. Mandel*, 408 U.S. 753 (1972).

Second, waiver is not permitted when exclusion is premised upon § 212(a)(27), (a)(29), and (a)(33) of the Act. Under these grounds for exclusion, which relate to national security and being a Nazi collaborator, discretion may not be exercised in favor of admission.

* * *

Regarding nonimmigrants, waivers of excludability are available for substantive grounds as well as for documentary deficiencies. § 212(d)(3) and (d)(4). If a waiver is granted, often a bond will be required, especially if the nonimmigrant has not satisfied the consul or immigration authorities that he or she will not become a public charge.

Problems

Section 212 is extraordinarily long and complex. Test your initial ability to find your way through it by hunting down the answers to the following questions. In each one, what paragraphs of § 212(a) might apply? What waiver provisions from the later subsections might relieve the alien of the application of such exclusion grounds? What other factual information might you need to develop? What other statutory provisions or case law might you have to consult to arrive at an answer?

1. Your client qualifies for the first preference, but was convicted of petty larceny seven years ago and sent to prison for a total of three months. Is she excludable? What if she had been convicted of two counts

of petty larceny? What if the conviction was for grand theft? What if it was for possession of 150 grams of marijuana?

2.   A consular officer considering the issuance of a student visa under section 101(a)(15)(F) is told by the CIA of solid intelligence information linking the alien to a terrorist organization responsible for recent bombings. A check with local police authorities in the alien's home country, however, reveals no convictions or even arrests for any offenses. Can this alien be excluded? On what ground?

3.   A national of Colombia is apprehended on the beach at night, tugging a small boat up away from the waterline. Undaunted, he tells the Border Patrol officers that he is glad to see them and wishes to apply for admission as a tourist. He has a passport. Is he excludable? On what ground?

4.   Your client wishes to bring his father in for a three-month visit from his home in Yugoslavia, but the father is illiterate. Will he be able to secure a nonimmigrant visa? What if the father is literate but was convicted of narcotics trafficking and served a two-year sentence, ending 15 years ago? What if the conviction was for burglary? Under each factual assumption—illiteracy, narcotics trafficking, burglary—could the father secure entry as an immigrant?

2. EXCLUSION OF SUBVERSIVES AND THE SEARCH FOR SUBSTANTIVE CONSTITUTIONAL CONSTRAINTS ON EXCLUSION GROUNDS

In 1903, in the wake of the 1901 assassination of President McKinley, Congress added to the grounds of exclusion a provision rendering anarchists ineligible for admission. See pp. 351–52 *infra.* In succeeding years, and particularly during times of war or other national emergency, Congress expanded and elaborated the grounds of exclusion based on activities, beliefs, and affiliations which it viewed as subversive. *See* E. Hutchinson, Legislative History of American Immigration Policy 1798–1965, at 423–27 (1981).

By 1952, the list was quite lengthy. Although some people made an effort to cut back on these provisions in the debate that year over the proposed Immigration and Nationality Act, Congress chose to perpetuate them in the prolix and expansive form now found in § 212(a)(27)–(29). They have remained part of the law, unchanged, since 1952, though they are used less frequently now than they were in the Cold War years immediately after their passage.

Take a look at paragraphs (27) through (29) of § 212(a). Are these provisions consistent with the First Amendment? The Supreme Court considered the constitutional validity of some of them in 1971, in the *Mandel* case, which follows. Keep in mind certain background information as you read *Mandel.* The Court has long struggled to fashion doctrines for judging what limits the First Amendment places on government efforts to restrict or punish subversive activities or advocacy of unlawful action. *See* P. Brest & S. Levinson, Processes of Constitutional Decisionmaking 1111–34 (2d ed. 1983). Justice Holmes' "clear and present danger" test, first announced in *Schenck v. United States,* 249 U.S. 47, 39 S.Ct. 247, 63 L.Ed. 470 (1919), was one such attempt.   Just two years before *Mandel,* however, the court seemed to have reached an important landmark clarifying applicable doctrine and providing the tightest limits yet on government action in this realm.   In *Brandenburg v. Ohio,* 395 U.S. 444, 89 S.Ct. 1827, 23 L.Ed.2d 430 (1969) (per curiam), the court ruled that the First Amendment forbids government action proscribing unlawful advocacy "except where such advocacy is directed to inciting or producing imminent lawless action and is likely to incite or produce such action."   This doctrinal evolution caused some to think that the court was prepared to make substantial inroads into § 212(a)(28) when the *Mandel* case appeared on its docket.

KLEINDIENST v. MANDEL

Supreme Court of the United States, 1972.
408 U.S. 753, 92 S.Ct. 2576, 33 L.Ed.2d 683.

MR. JUSTICE BLACKMUN delivered the opinion of the Court.

[Ernest Mandel was a well-known Belgian author who described himself as "a revolutionary Marxist" but not a member of the Communist party.   His writings and activities rendered him excludable under INA §§ 212(A)(28)(D) and (G)(v), as one who advocates or teaches "the economic, international, and governmental doctrines of world communism."   He had visited the United States twice before filing the unsuccessful visa application that led to this litigation.   Both times, apparently unbeknownst to him, he was the beneficiary of a waiver, in accordance with INA § 212(d)(3), of his excludability under § 212(a)(28).   In 1969, he applied for a non-immigrant visa to attend several conferences in the United States.   He was informed of his excludability, and after several rounds of correspondence, he was told that the Attorney General would not grant a waiver this time, because, in the Attorney General's view, he had violated the terms of his earlier admissions by deviating from the stated purposes of those trips.   Mandel and several of those who had invited him to this country filed suit.   The District Court ruled for the plaintiffs.]

* * *

II

Until 1875 alien migration to the United States was unrestricted. The Act of March 3, 1875, 18 Stat. 477, barred convicts and prostitutes. Seven years later Congress passed the first general immigration statute. Act of Aug. 3, 1882, 22 Stat. 214.   Other legislation followed.   A general revision of the immigration laws was effected by the Act of Mar. 3, 1903, 32 Stat. 1213.   Section 2 of that Act made ineligible for admission "anarchists, or persons who believe in or advocate the overthrow by force or violence of the Government of the United States or of all government or of all forms of law."   By the Act of Oct. 16, 1918, 40 Stat. 1012, Congress expanded the provisions for the exclusion of subversive aliens. Title II of the Alien Registration Act of 1940, 54 Stat. 671, amended the

1918 Act to bar aliens who, at any time, had advocated or were members of or affiliated with organizations that advocated violent overthrow of the United States Government.

In the years that followed, after extensive investigation and numerous reports by congressional committees, see *Communist Party v. Subversive Activities Control Board,* 367 U.S. 1, 94 n. 37, 81 S.Ct. 1357, 1409 n. 37, 6 L.Ed.2d 625 (1961), Congress passed the Internal Security Act of 1950, 64 Stat. 987. This Act dispensed with the requirement of the 1940 Act of a finding in each case, with respect to members of the Communist Party, that the party did in fact advocate violent overthrow of the Government. These provisions were carried forward into the Immigration and Nationality Act of 1952.

We thus have almost continuous attention on the part of Congress since 1875 to the problems of immigration and of excludability of certain defined classes of aliens. The pattern generally has been one of increasing control with particular attention, for almost 70 years now, first to anarchists and then to those with communist affiliation or views.

III

It is clear that Mandel personally, as an unadmitted and nonresident alien, had no constitutional right of entry to this country as a nonimmigrant or otherwise. *United States ex rel. Turner v. Williams,* 194 U.S. 279, 292, 24 S.Ct. 719, 723, 48 L.Ed. 979 (1904); *United States ex rel. Knauff v. Shaughnessy,* 338 U.S. 537, 542, 70 S.Ct. 309, 312, 94 L.Ed. 317 (1950); *Galvan v. Press,* 347 U.S. 522, 530–532, 74 S.Ct. 737, 742–743, 98 L.Ed. 911 (1954); *see Harisiades v. Shaughnessy,* 342 U.S. 580, 592, 72 S.Ct. 512, 520, 96 L.Ed. 586 (1952).

The appellees concede this. Indeed, the American appellees assert that "they sue to enforce their rights, individually and as members of the American public, and assert none on the part of the invited alien." "Dr. Mandel is in a sense made a plaintiff because he is symbolic of the problem."

The case, therefore, comes down to the narrow issue whether the First Amendment confers upon the appellee professors, because they wish to hear, speak, and debate with Mandel in person, the ability to determine that Mandel should be permitted to enter the country or, in other words, to compel the Attorney General to allow Mandel's admission.

IV

In a variety of contexts this Court has referred to a First Amendment right to "receive information and ideas":

> "It is now well established that the Constitution protects the right to receive information and ideas. 'This freedom [of speech and press] ... necessarily protects the right to receive ....'"

* * *

In the present case, the District Court majority held:

> "The concern of the First Amendment is not with a non-resident alien's individual and personal interest in entering and being heard, but with the rights of the citizens of the country to have the alien enter and to hear him explain and seek to defend his views; that, as *Garrison* [*v. Louisiana,* 379 U.S. 64, 85 S.Ct. 209, 13 L.Ed.2d 125 (1964)] and *Red Lion* [*Broadcasting Co. v. FCC,* 395 U.S. 367, 89 S.Ct. 1794, 23 L.Ed.2d 371 (1969)] observe, is of the essence of self-government." 325 F.Supp., at 631.

The Government disputes this conclusion on two grounds. First, it argues that exclusion of Mandel involves no restriction on First Amendment rights at all since what is restricted is "only action—the action of the alien in coming into this country." Principal reliance is placed on *Zemel v. Rusk,* 381 U.S. 1, 85 S.Ct. 1271, 14 L.Ed.2d 179 (1965), where the Government's refusal to validate an American passport for travel to Cuba was upheld. The rights asserted there were those of the passport applicant himself. The Court held that his right to travel and his asserted ancillary right to inform himself about Cuba did not outweigh substantial "foreign policy considerations affecting all citizens" that, with the backdrop of the Cuban missile crisis, were characterized as the "weightiest considerations of national security." *Id.,* at 13, 16, 85 S.Ct., at 1279. The rights asserted here, in some contrast, are those of American academics who have invited Mandel to participate with them in colloquia debates, and discussion in the United States. In light of the Court's previous decisions concerning the "right to receive information," we cannot realistically say that the problem facing us disappears entirely or is nonexistent because the mode of regulation bears directly on physical movement.

* * *

The Government also suggests that the First Amendment is inapplicable because appellees have free access to Mandel's ideas through his books and speeches, and because "technological developments," such as tapes or telephone hook-ups, readily supplant his physical presence. This argument overlooks what may be particular qualities inherent in sustained, face-to-face debate, discussion and questioning. While alternative means of access to Mandel's ideas might be a relevant factor were we called upon to balance First Amendment rights against governmental regulatory interests—a balance we find unnecessary here in light of the discussion that follows in Part V—we are loath to hold on this record that existence of other alternatives extinguishes altogether any constitutional interest on the part of the appellees in this particular form of access.

V

Recognition that First Amendment rights are implicated, however, is not dispositive of our inquiry here. In accord with ancient principles of the international law of nation-states, the Court in *The Chinese Exclusion Case,* 130 U.S. 581, 609, 9 S.Ct. 623, 631, 32 L.Ed. 1068 (1889), and in *Fong Yue Ting v. United States,* 149 U.S. 698, 13 S.Ct. 1016, 37 L.Ed. 905 (1893), held broadly, as the Government describes it, that the power to exclude aliens is "inherent in sovereignty, necessary for maintaining normal international relations and defending the country against foreign encroachments and dangers—a power to be exercised exclusively by the political branches of government ...." Since that time, the Court's general reaffirmations of this principle have been legion. The Court without exception has sustained Congress' "plenary power to make rules for the admission of aliens and to exclude those who possess those characteristics which Congress has forbidden." *Boutilier v. Immigration and Naturalization Service,* 387 U.S. 118, 123, 87 S.Ct. 1563, 1567, 18 L.Ed.2d 661 (1967). "[O]ver no conceivable subject is the legislative power of Congress more complete than it is over" the admission of aliens. *Oceanic Navigation Co. v. Stranahan,* 214 U.S. 320, 339, 29 S.Ct. 671, 676, 53 L.Ed. 1013 (1909).

* * *

We are not inclined in the present context to reconsider this line of cases. Indeed, the appellees, in contrast to the *amicus,* do not ask that we do so. The appellees recognize the force of these many precedents. In seeking to sustain the decision below, they concede that Congress could enact a blanket prohibition against entry of all aliens falling into the class defined by §§ 212(a)(28)(D) and (G)(v), and that First Amendment rights could not override that decision. But they contend that by providing a waiver procedure, Congress clearly intended that persons ineligible under the broad provision of the section would be temporarily admitted when appropriate "for humane reasons and for reasons of public interest." S.Rep.No. 1137, 82d Cong., 2d Sess., 12 (1952). They argue that the Executive's implementation of this congressional mandate through decision whether to grant a waiver in each individual case must be limited by the First Amendment rights of persons like appellees. Specifically, their position is that the First Amendment rights must prevail, at least where the Government advances no justification for failing to grant a waiver. They point to the fact that waivers have been granted in the vast majority of cases.[7]

Appellees' First Amendment argument would prove too much. In almost every instance of an alien excludable under § 212(a)(28), there are

---

7. The Government's brief states:

"The Immigration and Naturalization Service reports the following with respect to applications to the Attorney General for waiver of an alien's ineligibility for admission under Section 212(a)(28):

"Year	Total Number of Applications for Waiver of Section 212(a) (28)	Number of Waivers Granted	Number of Waivers Denied
1971	6210	6196	14
1970	6193	6189	4
1969	4993	4984	9
1968	4184	4176	8
1967	3860	3852	8 "

Brief for Appellants 18 n. 24. These cases, however, are only those that, as § 212(d)(3)(A) provides, come to the Attorney General with a positive recommendation from the Secretary of State or the consular officer. The figures do not include those cases where these officials had refrained from making a positive recommendation.

probably those who would wish to meet and speak with him. The ideas of most such aliens might not be so influential as those of Mandel, nor his American audience so numerous, nor the planned discussion forums so impressive. But the First Amendment does not protect only the articulate, the well known, and the popular. Were we to endorse the proposition that governmental power to withhold a waiver must yield whenever a bona fide claim is made that American citizens wish to meet and talk with an alien excludable under § 212(a)(28), one of two unsatisfactory results would necessarily ensue. Either every claim would prevail, in which case the plenary discretionary authority Congress granted the Executive becomes a nullity, or courts in each case would be required to weigh the strength of the audience's interest against that of the Government in refusing a waiver to the particular alien applicant, according to some as yet undetermined standard. The dangers and the undesirability of making that determination on the basis of factors such as the size of the audience or the probity of the speaker's ideas are obvious. Indeed, it is for precisely this reason that the waiver decision has, properly, been placed in the hands of the Executive.

Appellees seek to soften the impact of this analysis by arguing, as has been noted, that the First Amendment claim should prevail, at least where no justification is advanced for denial of a waiver. The Government would have us reach this question, urging a broad decision that Congress has delegated the waiver decision to the Executive in its sole and unfettered discretion, and any reason or no reason may be given. This record, however, does not require that we do so, for the Attorney General did inform Mandel's counsel of the reason for refusing him a waiver. And that reason was facially legitimate and bona fide.

* * *

In summary, plenary congressional power to make policies and rules for exclusion of aliens has long been firmly established. In the case of an alien excludable under § 212(a)(28), Congress has delegated conditional exercise of this power to the Executive. We hold that when the Executive exercises this power negatively on the basis of a facially legitimate and bona fide reason, the courts will neither look behind the exercise of that discretion, nor test it by balancing its justification against the First Amendment interests of those who seek personal communication with the applicant. What First Amendment or other grounds may be available for attacking exercise of discretion for which no justification whatsoever is advanced is a question we neither address or decide in this case.

Reversed.

Mr. Justice Douglas, dissenting.

Under *The Chinese Exclusion Case*, 130 U.S. 581, 9 S.Ct. 623, 32 L.Ed. 1068, rendered in 1889, there could be no doubt but that Congress would have the power to exclude any class of aliens from these shores. The accent at the time was on race. Mr. Justice Field, writing for the Court, said: "If, therefore, the government of the United States, through its legislative department, considers the presence of foreigners of a different race in this country, who will not assimilate with us, to be dangerous to its peace and security, their exclusion is not to be stayed because at the time there are no actual hostilities with the nation of which the foreigners are subjects." *Id.*, at 606, 9 S.Ct., at 630.

An ideological test, not a racial one, is used here. But neither, in my view, is permissible, as I have indicated on other occasions. Yet a narrower question is raised here.

* * *

As a matter of statutory construction, I conclude that Congress never undertook to entrust the Attorney General with the discretion to pick and choose among the ideological offerings which alien lecturers tender from our platforms, allowing those palatable to him and disallowing others. The discretion entrusted to him concerns matters commonly within the competence of the Department of Justice—national security, importation of drugs, and the like.

I would affirm the judgment of the three-judge District Court.

MR. JUSTICE MARSHALL, with whom MR. JUSTICE BRENNAN joins, dissenting.

* * *

I * * * am stunned to learn that a country with our proud heritage has refused Dr. Mandel temporary admission. I am convinced that Americans cannot be denied the opportunity to hear Dr. Mandel's views in person because their Government disapproves of his ideas. Therefore, I dissent from today's decision and would affirm the judgment of the court below.

* * *

Today's majority apparently holds that Mandel may be excluded and Americans' First Amendment rights restricted because the Attorney General has given a "facially legitimate and bona fide reason" for refusing to waive Mandel's visa ineligibility. I do not understand the source of this unusual standard. Merely "legitimate" governmental interests cannot override constitutional rights. Moreover, the majority demands only "facial" legitimacy and good faith, by which it means that this Court will never "look behind" any reason the Attorney General gives. No citation is given for this kind of unprecedented deference to the Executive, nor can I imagine (nor am I told) the slightest justification for such a rule.

Even the briefest peek behind the Attorney General's reason for refusing a waiver in this case would reveal that it is a sham. The Attorney General informed appellees' counsel that the waiver was refused because Mandel's activities on a previous American visit "went far beyond the stated purposes of his trip ... and represented a flagrant abuse of the opportunities afforded him to express his views in this country." But, as the Department of State had already conceded to appellees' counsel, Dr. Mandel "was apparently not informed that [his previous] visa was issued only after obtaining a waiver of ineligibility and therefore [Mandel] may not have been aware of the conditions and limitations attached to the [previous] visa issuance." There is *no* basis in the present record for concluding that Mandel's behavior on his previous visit was a "flagrant abuse"—or even willful or knowing departure—from visa restrictions. For good reason, the Government in this litigation has *never* relied on the Attorney General's reason to justify Mandel's exclusion. In these circumstances, the Attorney General's reason cannot possibly support a decision for the Government in this case. But without even remanding for a factual hearing to see if there is *any* support for the Attorney General's determination, the majority declares that his reason is sufficient to override appellees' First Amendment interests.

Even if the Attorney General had given a compelling reason for declining to grant a waiver under § 212(d)(3)(A), this would not, for me, end the case. As I understand the statutory scheme, Mandel is "ineligible" for a visa, and therefore inadmissible, solely because, within the terms of § 212(a)(28), he has advocated communist doctrine and has published writings advocating that doctrine. The waiver question under § 212(d)(3)(A) is totally secondary and dependent, since it is triggered here only by a determination of (a)(28) ineligibility.

* * *

Accordingly, I turn to consider the constitutionality of the sole justification given by the Government here and below for excluding Mandel—that he "advocates" and "publish[es] ... printed matter ... advocating ... doctrines of world communism" within the terms of § 212(a)(28).

Still adhering to standard First Amendment doctrine, I do not see how (a)(28) can possibly represent a compelling governmental interest that overrides appellees' interests in hearing Mandel. Unlike (a)(27) or (a)(29), (a)(28) does not claim to exclude aliens who are likely to engage in subversive activity or who represent an active and present threat to the "welfare, safety, or security of the United States." Rather, (a)(28) excludes aliens solely because they have advocated communist doctrine. Our cases make clear, however, that government has no legitimate interest in stopping the flow of ideas. It has no power to restrict the mere advocacy of communist doctrine, divorced from incitement to imminent lawless action. *Noto v. United States,* 367 U.S. 290, 297–298, 81 S.Ct. 1517, 1520–1521, 6 L.Ed.2d 836 (1961); *Brandenburg v. Ohio,* 395 U.S. 444, 447–449, 89 S.Ct. 1827, 1829–1831, 23 L.Ed.2d 430 (1969). For those who are not sure that they have attained the final and absolute truth, all ideas, even those forcefully urged, are a contribution to the ongoing political dialogue. The First Amendment represents the view of the Framers that "the path of safety lies in the opportunity to discuss freely supposed grievances and proposed remedies; and that the fitting remedy for evil counsels is good ones"—"more speech." *Whitney v. California,* 274 U.S., at 375, 377, 47 S.Ct., at 648, 649, 71 L.Ed. 1095 (Brandeis, J., concurring).

* * *

The heart of Appellants' position in this case * * * is that the Government's power is distinctively broad and unreviewable because "[t]he regulation in question is directed at the admission of aliens." Thus, in the appellants' view, this case is no different from a long line of cases holding that the power to exclude aliens is left exclusively to the "political" branches of Government, Congress, and the Executive.

These cases are not the strongest precedents in the United States Reports, and the majority's baroque approach reveals its reluctance to rely on them completely. They include such milestones as *The Chinese Exclusion Case*, 130 U.S. 581, 9 S.Ct. 623, 32 L.Ed. 1068 (1889), and *Fong Yue Ting v. United States*, 149 U.S. 698, 13 S.Ct. 1016, 37 L.Ed. 905 (1893), in which this Court upheld the Government's power to exclude and expel Chinese aliens from our midst.

But none of these old cases must be "reconsidered" or overruled to strike down Dr. Mandel's exclusion, for none of them was concerned with the rights of American citizens. All of them involved only rights of the excluded aliens themselves. At least when the rights of Americans are involved, there is no basis for concluding that the power to exclude aliens is absolute. "When Congress' exercise of one of its enumerated powers clashes with those individual liberties protected by the Bill of Rights, it is our 'delicate and difficult task' to determine whether the resulting restriction on freedom can be tolerated." *United States v. Robel*, 389 U.S. 258, 264, 88 S.Ct. 419, 424, 19 L.Ed.2d 508 (1967).

* * *

I do not mean to suggest that simply because some Americans wish to hear an alien speak, they can automatically compel even his temporary admission to our country. Government may prohibit aliens from even temporary admission if exclusion is necessary to protect a compelling governmental interest.[6] Actual threats to the national security, public health needs, and genuine requirements of law enforcement are the most apparent interests that would surely be compelling. But in Dr. Mandel's case, the Government has, and claims, no such compelling interest. Mandel's visit was to be temporary. His "ineligibility" for a visa was based solely on § 212(a)(28). The only governmental interest embodied in that section is the Government's desire to keep certain ideas out of circulation in this country. This is hardly a compelling governmental interest. Section (a)(28) may not be the basis for excluding an alien when Americans wish to hear him. Without any claim that Mandel "live" is an actual threat to this country, there is no difference between excluding Mandel because of his ideas and keeping his books out because of their ideas. Neither is permitted.

* * *

Notes

1. Some commentators treat *Mandel* as deciding only the applicability of the First Amendment to the waiver scheme. In this view, the case leaves open the constitutional validity of § 212(a)(28) itself. *See, e.g.,* Note, *Judicial Review of Visa Denials: Reexamining Consular Nonreview-*

---

6. I agree with the majority that courts should not inquire into such things as the "probity of the speaker's ideas." Neither should the Executive, however. Where Americans wish to hear an alien, and their claim is not a demonstrated sham, the crucial question is whether the *Government's* interest in excluding the alien is compelling.

ability, 52 N.Y.U.L.Rev. 1137, 1149 (1977); Committee on Immigration and Nationality Law of the Association of the Bar of the City of New York, Visa Denials on Ideological Grounds: An Update 15–16 (mimeo, March 1984). Is this an accurate reading of the somewhat elliptical treatment of First Amendment issues in Part V of the majority opinion? Isn't Justice Marshall correct when he states that the waiver question "is totally secondary and dependent"—meaning that the majority, despite the way it avoids direct discussion of the issue, has inescapably decided that paragraph (28) is consistent with the First Amendment?

Part of the difficulty stems from the curious construction, to say the least, of the majority opinion. The court seems to go out of its way to find that a First Amendment issue exists, only to reach an ultimate result extremely deferential to the political branches of the government, an outcome hardly characteristic of most other First Amendment cases. The majority finds a free speech issue despite its apparent acceptance of the notion that *Mandel,* "as an unadmitted and nonresident alien," would have no First Amendment rights to assert. But even on the majority's view that the First Amendment grants the other plaintiffs a right to "receive information and ideas," aren't the government defendants correct that information and ideas are not restricted by the visa denial—that the denial does not abridge speech, for it merely affects conduct or action?

The court's answer to this question is not entirely straightforward. But in any event, the majority does refuse to use the defendants' suggested analysis as a way of evading the free speech issues. Having decided to confront such issues, however, the court then resolves them by sustaining government immigration decisions whenever they are based on "a facially legitimate and bona fide reason." Is this outcome functionally similar to saying that there will be no First Amendment scrutiny in the immigration field?

2. If we are to be critical of the majority opinion, however, perhaps we should also cast a critical eye on the dissents. Justice Douglas would overturn the visa denial based solely on his reading of the statute and the underlying congressional intent. Apparently he would find that the Attorney General, under the statute, *must* waive excludability unless he finds that the alien's presence would raise concerns "commonly within the competence of the Department of Justice—national security, importation of drugs, and the like." Can this possibly have been the intent of Congress in enacting paragraph (28) and making it waivable under subsection (d)(3)? Why would Congress even add paragraph (28) when other subsections address security and criminal concerns directly (for example, paragraphs 9, 10, 23, 27 and 29)?

3. Justice Marshall does not pretend to find such an improbable congressional intent, but instead bases his dissent squarely on constitutional grounds. He believes he can distinguish all the "old cases" recognizing plenary power in the political branches over the exclusion of aliens, because none of those cases, he says, involved the rights of citizens. But isn't this fact a mere accident of litigation? If Justice Marshall's views became the governing doctrine, wouldn't nearly every excluded alien be in

a position to find U.S. citizens who wish to speak with him or her and who could join as co-plaintiffs? Naturally, not all excluded individuals would find so distinguished a group as Mandel found, but Marshall surely would agree with the majority that First Amendment rights do not depend on the stature or number of the would-be listeners.

Justice Marshall goes on to remind us that not all plaintiffs who wish to speak with an alien denied a visa would win under his test. But if the government must show a *compelling* interest to sustain any particular exclusion, perhaps Marshall's opinion portends far wider consequences than just an occasional overturning of denials under paragraph (28). Is there a compelling interest, tied to the factors Marshall lists—national security, public health, or law enforcement—in excluding people a consul believes are likely to become public charges? People who plan to work but have not secured labor certification? Who are illiterate? Who don't have passports good for six months? What compelling interest supports a numerical ceiling of 270,000 annually, if the ceiling is challenged by an alien who could show that he would be admitted this year under a ceiling set at 350,000? We assume of course, that he is supported by citizens who want to hear him speak—or perhaps more potently, supported by lawful permanent resident family members who want to reunite the family as well as engage in political discussions. *See Moore v. East Cleveland,* 431 U.S. 494, 503–505, 97 S.Ct. 1932, 1937–38, 52 L.Ed.2d 531 (1977) (plurality opinion) ("the Constitution protects the sanctity of the family," including the extended family). Does Marshall's theory leave any room at all for numerical ceilings? At what number do the interests supporting ceilings become compelling?

Later Developments

If *Mandel* is properly read as holding that the Constitution places few, if any, constraints on the choice of substantive exclusion grounds, that is hardly the end of the issue. It simply means that any objections to such grounds will have to be pressed in a political forum, rather than the judicial forum. Amelioration might come either through executive action—widely employing available waiver provisions—or through legislative action to amend the statute.

In 1977, Congress took a small step toward cutting back the application of INA § 212(a)(28). Inspired by the freedom-of-movement provisions of the Helsinki Accords, Congress adopted the so-called McGovern Amendment. 22 U.S.C.A. § 2691. Its key language states:

> [T]he Secretary of State should, within 30 days of receiving an application for a nonimmigrant visa by any alien who is excludible [sic] from the United States by reason of membership in or affiliation with a proscribed organization but who is otherwise admissible to the United States, recommend that the Attorney General grant the approval necessary for the issuance of a visa to such alien, unless the Secretary determines that the admission of such alien would be contrary to the security interests of the United States and so certifies to the Speaker of the House of

Representatives and the Chairman of the Committee on Foreign Relations of the Senate.

Id. § 2691(a).

Note that the provision is not coextensive with paragraph (28). It deals only with exclusions based on membership or affiliation with certain organizations, and later amendments have even cut back somewhat on those applications—for example, by removing members of the Palestine Liberation Organization and of labor organizations which are "in fact instruments of a totalitarian state." *Id.* § 2691(b)–(d). Nevertheless, when it applies, the section essentially creates a presumption of admissibility despite the proscribed membership or affiliation, and it improves the chances that denials will receive widespread publicity, because of the reporting requirements.

After the Reagan Administration took office in 1981, it began using paragraphs (27) through (29) of INA § 212(a) on a wider scale. Visas were denied to Hortensia Allende, the widow of Salvador Allende, a Marxist and former President of Chile; Tomas Borge, Interior Minister of Nicaragua under the Sandinista government; Roberto d'Aubuisson, the right-wing President of the Salvadoran Constitutional Assembly; General Nino Pasti, a former member of the Italian Senate and critic of U.S. deployment of nuclear missiles in Europe; and many others. *See* Note, *First Amendment and the Alien Exclusion Power—What Standard of Review?*, 4 Cardozo L.Rev. 457 (1983); Dionne, *Issue and Debate: Barring Aliens for Political Reasons,* The New York Times, Dec. 8, 1983. Administration officials cited "foreign policy reasons," and occasionally stated they did not want to provide "a propaganda platform" in the United States for the excluded individuals. Secretary of State George Shultz remarked on the Borge visa denial: "As a general proposition I think we have to favor freedom of speech, but it can get abused by people who do not wish us well, and I think we have to take some reasonable precautions about that." Atkinson, *Congressmen, Others Denounce Denial of Visas to U.S. Critics,* The Washington Post, Dec. 3, 1983, at A12.

Some of these denials were carried out under paragraph (28), but the Administration made increasing use of paragraph (27), which provides for exclusion of persons seeking to enter "to engage in activities which would be prejudicial to the public interest, or endanger the welfare, safety, or security of the United States." Indeed, paragraph (27) was used in several instances where paragraph (28) might also have been available—leading some critics to charge that the former section was employed in order to avoid the reporting requirements imposed by the McGovern Amendment. Lawsuits have been filed challenging most of these visa denials. They have raised constitutional issues and also have asserted that a denial under paragraph (27) that is based on the expected speech of the individual after admission goes beyond the original congressional intent in enacting that paragraph.[9] Some members of Congress have also shown a

---

9. In *Abourezk v. Reagan,* 592 F.Supp. 880 (D.D.C.1984), the court upheld the visa denials at issue under § 212(a)(27). It insist- ed, however, that visa denials would not be proper if based solely on "the content of whatever communication [the alien] might

renewed interest in legislative efforts to amend these grounds of exclusion.

What should U.S. policy be? How can we provide adequate protection against genuine dangers (for example, from terrorist organizations) and yet remain consistent in our admission policies with the values that underlie the First Amendment? *See generally* Committee on Immigration and Nationality Law of the Assoc. of the Bar of the City of New York, Visa Denials on Ideological Grounds: An Update (1984) (urging substantive modification of § 212(a)(27)–(29)); and *id.* (dissent of J. Philip Anderegg) (arguing that Committee's alternatives were plainly inadequate to safeguard U.S. interests).

3. A BRIEF DIGRESSION: JUDICIAL REVIEW OF CONSULAR VISA DENIALS

In cases construing and applying the Administrative Procedure Act, 5 U.S.C.A. §§ 701–706, the Supreme Court has held that, under modern concepts, agency action today is presumptively reviewable in the courts, absent clear signals from the Congress making judicial review inapplicable. *See Abbott Laboratories v. Gardner,* 387 U.S. 136, 140–41, 87 S.Ct. 1507, 1510–12, 18 L.Ed.2d 681 (1967); 2 K.C. Davis, Administrative Law Treatise § 9.6, at 244 (2d ed. 1980). But consular decisions made overseas are still generally held to be beyond the reach of judicial review, largely because of the way that lower courts have construed the holding of *Mandel.* This doctrine applies not only to a person seeking a visa for a short vacation in the United States, but also to a person seeking an immigration visa based on his or her relation to a U.S. citizen or permanent resident alien.

PENA v. KISSINGER

United States District Court, Southern District of New York, 1976.
409 F.Supp. 1182.

POLLACK, DISTRICT JUDGE.

Plaintiff seeks review of the allegedly capricious decision of the American Consul in Santo Domingo denying an immigrant visa to her husband, Francisco A. Pena, a Dominican Republic, Western Hemisphere citizen who intends to work in the United States. Plaintiff is also a native and citizen of the Dominican Republic, but is a lawful permanent resident of the United States.

Mr. Pena applied for the visa as the spouse of a lawful permanent resident of the United States. The Consul, a defendant herein, denied his application on the ground that Pena's marriage to the plaintiff was a sham and undertaken to facilitate his immigration to the United States.

make while in this country." It also held that the conclusory assertion of foreign policy interests underlying the denials, made in a nonconfidential affidavit filed with the court by the Undersecretary of State, was inadequate to establish a "facially legitimate and bona fide reason" that would sustain the decision. Only after examining *in camera* a further classified affidavit submitted by the government was the court satisfied that the *Mandel* standard had been met.

Plaintiff sues for a declaratory judgment that her marriage to Pena is a valid one, and for a direction to the Consul to process Pena's visa application on that basis. * * *

The defendants, officials of the State Department and a consulate employee, have moved pursuant to Fed.R.Civ.P. 56 for summary judgment on the grounds that the plaintiff lacks standing to sue, that a consul's denial of a visa application is not subject to judicial review, and that mandamus jurisdiction may not be invoked against consular officials in regard to the processing of visas.

While the outcome might be different if this Court were "writing on a clean slate," *Galvan v. Press,* 347 U.S. 522, 530, 74 S.Ct. 737, 742, 98 L.Ed. 911, 921 (1954) (Frankfurter, J.), the defendants' motion for summary judgment must be granted partially and the complaint dismissed insofar as it seeks declaratory and injunctive relief.

* * *

C. JUDICIAL REVIEW

Notwithstanding plaintiff's standing to bring suit, the government maintains that the decision of an American consul to deny a visa to an alien is not subject to review in the courts. The precedents do appear to distinguish between a decision to deport an alien who is already in the United States and a decision to exclude or deny admission to an alien who remains outside; review is permitted of the former even where the alien initially gained admission illegally, but denied of the latter. *See, e.g., United States ex rel. Knauff v. Shaughnessy,* 338 U.S. 537, 543, 70 S.Ct. 309, 312, 94 L.Ed. 317, 324 (1950); *Shaughnessy v. United States ex rel. Mezei,* 345 U.S. 206, 73 S.Ct. 625, 97 L.Ed. 956 (1953).

Thus, there is substantial support in the cases for the government's position that consular decisions in regard to the issuance of visas are unreviewable. In *United States ex rel. London v. Phelps,* 22 F.2d 288 (2d Cir.1927), *cert. denied,* 276 U.S. 630, 48 S.Ct. 324, 72 L.Ed. 741 (1928), the Second Circuit declared:

> Whether the consul has acted reasonably or unreasonably is not for us to determine. Unjustifiable refusal to visé a passport may be ground for diplomatic complaint by the nation whose subject has been discriminated against. ... It is beyond the jurisdiction of the court. 22 F.2d at 290.

A similar view was expressed in *United States ex rel. Ulrich v. Kellogg,* 58 App.D.C. 360, 30 F.2d 984, *cert. denied,* 279 U.S. 868, 49 S.Ct. 482, 73 L.Ed. 1005 (1929). These cases have been cited as authority in more recent decisions which find such consular decision-making immune from judicial scrutiny. *See Loza-Bedoya v. INS,* 410 F.2d 343 (9th Cir.1969); *Licea-Gomez v. Pilliod,* 193 F.Supp. 577 (N.D.Ill.1960).

As a consequence, American Consuls appear free to act arbitrarily or even maliciously in their conduct toward foreign nationals seeking entrance into the United States. This result has been labelled "brutal," and a "trivializ[ation] [of] the great guarantees of due process," Hart, *The*

Power of Congress to Limit the Jurisdiction of Federal Courts: An Exercise in Dialectic, 66 Harv.L.Rev. 1362, 1395 (1953), as well as "an astonishing anomaly in American jurisprudence," Rosenfield, *Consular Non-Reviewability: A Case Study in Administrative Absolutism,* 41 Amer.Bar Assoc.J. 1109, 1110 (1955).

The law has undergone considerable change since the decisions were rendered in *London, Ulrich, Knauff* and *Mezei.* The rights afforded to aliens have been expanded, whether they are in the United States lawfully, or interacting with American officials outside the United States. Similarly, the Courts have adopted a more favorable attitude to the reviewability of administrative action under the Administrative Procedure Act. Since that Act applies to action by the State Department involving immigration matters, *see Rusk v. Cort,* 369 U.S. 367, 82 S.Ct. 787, 7 L.Ed.2d 809 (1962), it might have been expected that the "astonishing anomaly" of consular non-reviewability would also undergo change.

Indeed, while the Supreme Court asserted in *Knauff* that "it is not within the province of any court, *unless expressly authorized by law,* to review the determination of the political branch of the Government to exclude a given alien," 338 U.S. at 543, 70 S.Ct. at 312 (emphasis added), it subsequently declared in *Rusk v. Cort, supra,* that exceptions to the APA's presumption of reviewability of decisions made under the Immigration and Nationality Act would not be made "in the absence of clear and convincing evidence that Congress so intended." 369 U.S. at 380, 82 S.Ct. at 794. Thus, it appears true that "the courts have liberalized the standard governing reviewability" of administrative action in the immigration area.

Nonetheless, the Supreme Court in *Kleindienst v. Mandel,* 408 U.S. 753, 92 S.Ct. 2576, 33 L.Ed.2d 683 (1972), has recently reaffirmed the older authorities which restrict the reviewability of decisions by immigration officials. It appears that if plaintiff's claim to review here is controlled by *Mandel,* the defendants are entitled to summary judgment on the issue discussed.

* * *

[In *Mandel,* the] Supreme Court recognized that "First Amendment rights are implicated," but held that judicial review was unavailable where the government had acted on "the basis of a facially legitimate and bona fide reason." In reaching that conclusion the Court relied upon— and explicitly declined to reconsider—an 1895 opinion in which the Court had declared:

> The power of congress to exclude aliens altogether from the United States, or to prescribe the terms and conditions upon which they may come to this country, and to have its declared policy in that regard enforced exclusively through executive officers, *without judicial intervention,* is settled by our previous adjudications. 408 U.S. at 766, 92 S.Ct. at 2583 (emphasis added), citing *Lem Moon Sing v. United States,* 158 U.S. 538, 547, 15 S.Ct. 967, 970, 39 L.Ed. 1082, 1085.

Consequently, the Court concluded that it was unnecessary to balance the plaintiffs' First Amendment rights against the government's interest in excluding Mandel.

In holding that the Courts may not "look behind the exercise" of an official's discretionary authority to deny admission to an alien, the *Mandel* Court has seemingly precluded Mrs. Pena's ability to invoke judicial scrutiny of the Consul's denial of a visa to her husband. That result might be different were it possible to characterize the review sought here as involving only the Consul's decision concerning the *bona fides* of plaintiff's marriage, and not the visa denial. Such a characterization would be disingenuous, however, since the status of the marriage is merely an element in Mr. Pena's eligibility for a visa. The Consul's determination regarding the marriage is the "facially legitimate and bona fide reason" which is the basis for the discretionary decision on the visa application; as such, *Mandel* interdicts Court examination of the Consul's determination.

This result may seem anomalous, since the Courts are not reluctant to review the validity of marriages, even in the immigration context, where the challenged decision has been made by an official of the Immigration and Naturalization Service as distinguished from a Consul in the employ of the State Department. Moreover, judicial review is common of agency determinations—involving the denial of a labor certification—made pursuant to [INA § 212(a)(14)], the very statute under which the defendants here acted when they determined that Mr. Pena was subject to the labor requirement because his marriage was spurious.

It is thus arguable that the plaintiff should nonetheless be entitled to judicial review here to assure, at a minimum, that her constitutional right to procedural due process has been satisfied by the Consul's decision-making procedures. As a resident legal alien, plaintiff is entitled to the full panoply of constitutional protection. Consequently, while "[w]hatever the procedure authorized by Congress is, it is due process as far as an alien denied entry is concerned," *United States ex rel. Knauff v. Shaughnessy, supra,* 338 U.S. at 544, 70 S.Ct. at 313, 94 L.Ed. at 325, it may not be due process as far as it affects an American citizen or permanent resident alien who has standing, as does the plaintiff here, to challenge it. Furthermore, it is settled that agency action which is committed to the agency's discretion and thus otherwise foreclosed from judicial review is nevertheless reviewable if it allegedly exceeds constitutional bounds. * * * Accordingly, this analysis suggests that Mrs. Pena is entitled to a review of the Consul's assessment of the status of her marriage to determine if his decision was reached so arbitrarily and capriciously as to violate her right to procedural due process.

However appealing this argument may be, it appears to run afoul of *Mandel.* In that case, the plaintiffs were Americans who sought to interpose the Constitution between themselves and a discretionary exercise of power by the Attorney General which affected them while acting directly upon an alien abroad; the Supreme Court decided that the constitutional interests recognized there were not susceptible of judicial protection in the face of the "plenary congressional power to make policies and rules for exclusion of aliens ...." 408 U.S. at 769, 92 S.Ct. at 2585, 33 L.Ed.2d at 696. Since it would be outside the province of a District Court to disregard this lesson from the High Court, *but see Hart, supra,* 66 Harv.L.Rev. at 1396 ("when justices ... write opinions in behalf of the Court which ignore the painful forward steps of a whole half century of adjudication, making no effort to relate what then is being done to what the Court has done before, they write without authority for the future"), plaintiff is not entitled to judicial review of the Consul's decision.

* * *

Notes

1. Despite Judge Pollack's obvious reluctance to reach this result, hasn't he misread *Mandel*? Here he concludes that Ms. Pena "is not entitled to judicial review of the Consul's decision," but isn't this quite different from the outcome in *Mandel*? Didn't Mandel or, more precisely, Mandel's U.S. citizen coplaintiffs, obtain judicial review of that consular decision—simply losing on the merits according to a test that is highly favorable to the government? Of course, Judge Pollack also observes that the consul's stated ground for decision here was facially legitimate and bona fide, but he still casts his ultimate ruling as a judgment that he lacks jurisdiction to review the consul's action.

Perhaps it makes little difference to losing plaintiffs whether they lose "on the merits" according to a test that provides so little penetration of the government's stated justification or lose instead because the courts consider themselves without jurisdiction to hear the case. But it may make some difference to the ultimate development of a sound body of law. Consider this: Some observers have regarded the *Mandel* case as significant not for its deference to the government but rather for suggesting, for the first time, that the courts might have any role at all in reviewing immigration decisions of this type. *See, e.g.,* Note, *Judicial Review of Visa Denials: Reexamining Consular Nonreviewability,* 52 N.Y.U.L.Rev. 1137, 1148–49 (1977). (This view was given a mild boost in 1977, in an analogous setting, when the Court stated in *Fiallo v. Bell,* 430 U.S. 787, 793 n. 5, 97 S.Ct. 1473, 1478 n. 5, 52 L.Ed.2d 50 (1977) that past cases "reflect acceptance of a limited judicial responsibility under the Constitution even with respect to the power of Congress to regulate the admission and exclusion of aliens.")

If the courts are at least hearing the cases, perhaps further progress could be made in refining the substantive test without intruding unduly on immigration decisions or upsetting U.S. foreign relations. Even the "facially legitimate and bona fide reason" test contains the seeds of growth. Dissenting in *Fiallo,* Justice Marshall read *Mandel* as rejecting a government claim of "unfettered discretion" in visa decisions. He went on to restate the *Mandel* review standard as follows: There must be a finding that the denial "was based on a 'legitimate and bona fide' reason." *Id.* at 807, 97 S.Ct. at 1486. Consider the impact such a slight amendment of the formula would have on the role of reviewing courts. Indeed, would such an amendment go too far?

In any event, the *Mandel* substantive test, deferential as it is, at least seems to place on the government the burden of coming forth with some statement of reasons for visa denials. *Burrafato v. Department of State,* 523 F.2d 554, 556 (2d Cir.1975), *cert. denied* 424 U.S. 910, 96 S.Ct. 1105, 47 L.Ed.2d 313 (1976), illustrates how the court's understanding of *Mandel* might be decisive for the outcome of the case. The court there relied on *Mandel* in holding that the district court lacked subject matter jurisdiction, even though the State Department, contrary to its own regulations, had failed to state any reasons for denying a visa to the citizen plaintiff's husband.

2. Even if *Mandel* permits Congress to exempt visa decisions (and indeed all denials of admission, whether taking place in a consulate overseas or at the border) from judicial review, has Congress chosen to do so? Where is that choice expressed?

Recall from Chapter Two that an unusual provision in § 104 of the INA exempts individual visa determinations from the supervision and control of the Secretary of State. Doesn't it follow, *a fortiori,* that Congress also wanted such determinations insulated from the review of the courts? Or, on the contrary, should we find that the case for judicial review is made even stronger by § 104? Since there is no administrative appeal from visa denials, isn't it plausible that Congress either would have left open the chance for judicial review or would have denied such review explicitly? After all, § 104 says nothing expressly, one way or the other, about review by any governmental official or body except the Secretary of State. *See* Gotcher, *Review of Consular Visa Determinations,* 60 Interp. Rel. 247 (1983) (arguing that the doctrine of consular nonreviewability is unfounded). Is this second argument undercut by the existence of the de facto State Department review mechanism described in Chapter Two?

In any event, whatever problems we might have with *Pena's* reading of *Mandel,* its conclusion that consular decisions are unreviewable has been widely accepted. *See, e.g., Ventura-Escamilla v. INS,* 647 F.2d 28, 30 (9th Cir.1981); *Rivera de Gomez v. Kissinger,* 534 F.2d 518 (2d Cir.1976) (*per curiam*), *cert. denied* 429 U.S. 897, 97 S.Ct. 262, 50 L.Ed.2d 181; *Hermina Sague v. United States,* 416 F.Supp. 217 (D.Puerto Rico 1976). Some courts have found jurisdiction, however, to consider underlying questions regarding the constitutionality of the statute under which the consul acted, despite the consular nonreviewability doctrine. *Martinez v. Bell,* 468 F.Supp. 719 (S.D.N.Y.1979) (sustaining the government on the merits). *See also Abourezk v. Reagan,* 592 F.Supp. 880, 883–84 n. 10 (D.D.C.1984) (approving visa denial under the "facially legitimate and bona fide" standard, but upholding judicial review because of First Amendment issues and because denial decision was made by high officials in Washington, not consular officer stationed abroad).

3. In many settings, courts have used a different basis—standing doctrine—for refusing to reach the merits of challenges to immigration decisions, including visa denials, filed by aliens who are not present in the

United States. (Aliens in the United States, even after an illegal entry, have usually had little trouble securing judicial review of immigration decisions affecting them, see G & R § 8.23, either under the Administrative Procedure Act, *see Reddy, Inc. v. Department of Labor,* 492 F.2d 538 (5th Cir.1974), or under the special provisions for judicial review set forth in the INA and examined in Chapter Seven below.)

Several cases outside the immigration field have established "the general rule that non-resident aliens have no standing to sue in United States Courts." *Berlin Democratic Club v. Rumsfeld,* 410 F.Supp. 144, 152 (D.D.C.1976). Although there are exceptions to this rule (and a possible trend toward relaxing these standing limitations), *see Cardenas v. Smith,* 733 F.2d 909 (D.C.Cir.1984), standing remains a major obstacle to the hearing of challenges to visa denials. *See* G & R § 8.3; *Chinese American Civic Council v. Attorney General,* 396 F.Supp. 1250 (D.D.C.1975), *affirmed on other grounds* 566 F.2d 321 (D.C.Cir.1977). There are a few cases that recognize standing in nonresident aliens outside the United States to challenge immigration decisions, but they involved alien plaintiffs who had been in the United States shortly before bringing the lawsuit, *Estrada v. Ahrens,* 296 F.2d 690 (5th Cir.1961); *Jaimez-Revolla v. Bell,* 598 F.2d 243 (D.C.Cir.1979), or aliens who were part of a plaintiff class composed primarily of aliens present in the country, *see Silva v. Bell,* 605 F.2d 978 (7th Cir.1979).

Standing determinations involve both constitutional limitations and prudential considerations tied to conceptions about the appropriate role of the courts. *See Warth v. Seldin,* 422 U.S. 490, 498, 95 S.Ct. 2197, 2204, 45 L.Ed.2d 343 (1975). Clearly most aliens outside the United States challenging visa denials or other negative immigration decisions would satisfy the constitutional requirements. They can demonstrate "injury in fact" fairly traceable to the actions of the United States government, giving them the necessary personal stake in the controversy. *See id.* at 498–99, 95 S.Ct. at 2204–05; *Larson v. Valente,* 456 U.S. 228, 238–39, 102 S.Ct. 1673, 1680, 72 L.Ed.2d 33 (1982).

Denial of standing to nonresident aliens not physically present thus rests on prudential considerations. As one court phrased the matter: denial of standing is based on "the policy reasons against affording a Federal forum for a person anywhere in the world challenging denial of entry or immigration status." *Chinese-American Civic Council, supra,* at 1251. Consular officers worldwide received 6,315,000 applications for nonimmigrant visas in fiscal year 1983 (a decline of ten percent from the previous year) and over 400,000 applications for immigrant visas. At least 700,000 applications overall were denied. (The statistics are derived from numbers provided in Goelz, *Current Overview of Developments at the Dept. of State,* 61 Interp.Rel. 542 (1984).) There are only 507 federal district court judges.

Are judges justified on prudential grounds in fearing a flood of litigation if review of visa determinations were allowed? Is this the real concern underlying the strained readings of *Mandel* to find that jurisdiction is lacking? If so, shouldn't courts be more candid about the real reasons—especially when those reasons carry some genuine persuasive power? Finally, if we are relying on counsels of prudence in limiting the judicial review of visa denials, would it be possible to provide review of applications for immigrant visas, where the stakes are higher, even while denying review in the more numerous nonimmigrant cases? (If so, Ms. Pena's case was much more deserving of review than was Mandel's.)

4. THE PUBLIC CHARGE PROVISION

Concern about an influx of paupers underlay many of the earliest attempts—then carried out by the state governments—to impose broad-scale restrictions on immigration. *See, e.g., Mayor of the City of New York v. Miln,* 36 U.S. (11 Pet.) 102, 9 L.Ed. 648 (1837); *The Passenger Cases,* 48 U.S. (7 How.) 283, 12 L.Ed. 702 (1849). In 1882, Congress enacted the first federal provision barring from entry "any person unable to take care of himself or herself without becoming a public charge." Act of Aug. 3, 1882, Ch. 376, § 2, 22 Stat. 214.

The Supreme Court considered the public charge provision in *Gegiow v. Uhl,* 239 U.S. 3, 36 S.Ct. 2, 60 L.Ed. 114 (1915). There the immigration commissioner had initially excluded certain Russian immigrants on this ground, reciting these reasons for the exclusion: "That they arrived here with very little money, * * * and are bound for Portland, Oregon, where the reports of industrial conditions show that it would be impossible for these aliens to obtain employment; that they have no one legally obligated here to assist them." *Id.* at 8, 36 S.Ct. at 2. The Supreme Court struck down this attempt to make the public charge provision a crude form of labor certification.

> The single question on this record is whether an alien can be declared likely to become a public charge on the ground that the labor market in the city of his immediate destination is overstocked. In the [statute] determining who shall be excluded, 'Persons likely to become a public charge' are mentioned between paupers and professional beggars, and along with idiots, persons dangerously diseased, persons certified by the examining surgeon to have a mental or physical defect of a nature to affect their ability to earn a living, convicted felons, prostitutes and so forth. The persons enumerated in short are to be excluded on the ground of permanent personal objections accompanying them irrespective of local conditions unless the one phrase before us is directed to different considerations than any other of those with which it is associated. Presumably it is to be read as generically similar to the others mentioned before and after.

Id. at 9–10, 36 S.Ct. at 3.

As thus limited, this venerable provision of the statutes continues to play an important role in excluding applicants for visas. A recent study describes its significance as follows:

> The public charge provision of the Act is responsible for the greatest number of immigrant visa refusals. In 1975, after taking into account refusals overcome, consular officers relied on the

public charge provision to deny visas in almost sixty percent of all refusals. During the period from July, 1976, through June, 1977, the public charge provision accounted for sixty-one percent of all initial refusals in Mexico but only eleven percent of all initial refusals in Canada.

On its face, the public charge provision of the Act represents a broad grant of discretion. Ineligibility includes "[a]liens who, *in the opinion of the consular officer* at the time of application for a visa, . . . are likely at any time to become public charges."

[State Department] regulations attempt to structure this discretion. A sworn job offer from an employer in the United States, for example, may establish eligibility. However, these regulations provide that consular officers must presume ineligible aliens who rely solely on expected income that falls below the income poverty guidelines.

The interpretative and procedural notes to the Departmental regulations attempt more detailed structuring of the public charge provision. These notes contain Departmental policy governing acceptable types of public charge evidence. A partial list of such evidence includes bank deposits, pre-arranged employment, affidavits of support, and bonds posted.

Departmental policy places a high priority on flexibility in the evaluation of evidence regarding sufficient funds to meet the public charge provision. According to the *Foreign Affairs Manual,* consular officers should consider a variety of factors, including the applicant's age, his physical condition, his family status, and economic conditions in the United States. Moreover, stated policy prohibits consular officers from using "a fixed sum of money as the sole criterion for judging a prospective immigrant's ability to meet the public charge requirement of the law."

Comment, *Consular Discretion in Immigrant Visa-Issuing Process,* 16 San Diego L.Rev. 87, 113–14 (1978) (emphasis in original).

MATTER OF KOHAMA

Associate Commissioner, Examinations, 1978.
17 I & N Dec. 257

This matter is before the Associate Commissioner, Examinations on certification as provided by 8 C.F.R. 103.4 for review of the District Director's decision denying the motion to reconsider his previous decision denying the applications for status as permanent residents under section 245 of the Immigration and Nationality Act.

The applicants are husband and wife, natives and citizens of Japan, 73 and 65 years of age. They last entered the United States as nonimmigrant visitors for pleasure on December 10, 1975, and were authorized to remain until March 16, 1976.

On March 23, 1976, immediate relative visa petitions were filed in their behalf by their naturalized United States citizen daughter. Concurrent with these petitions, the applicants filed applications to adjust their status to that of permanent residents pursuant to section 245 of the Immigration and Nationality Act, as amended. Satisfactory evidence of the claimed daughter-parent relationship was presented and the petitions were approved May 1976. By virtue of their approved visa petitions and their admission to the United States as nonimmigrant visitors, they were statutorily eligible to file the application for adjustment of status.

The applicants are unemployed and do not have savings or independent means of support. They rely, instead, on support from their daughter and son-in-law, both of whom are employed. As evidence of this support they presented affidavits executed by the daughter and son-in-law, along with evidence of their combined income of approximately $34,000 per year.

Following interviews in connection with the pending applications for adjustment of status on June 22, 1976, the applicants were advised that it would be necessary for them to post bonds each in the amount of $5,000 in order to insure that they would not become public charges. The applicants' son-in-law advised the Service by letter dated September 15, 1976, that it would be difficult for him and his spouse to post the bonds due to the charges imposed by the bonding company. In this letter the Service was requested to grant a period of 2 or 3 months to allow for the location of a suitable bonding company.

The record contains no evidence that the bonds were posted, and on March 17, 1977, the applications were denied by the District Director on the grounds that the applicants were likely to become public charges, pursuant to section 212(a)(15) of the Act. In his decision the District Director concluded that the affidavits of support presented by the daughter and son-in-law were not acceptable and bases this conclusion on two court decisions, *County of San Diego* [*v. Viloria*, 276 Cal.App.2d 350, 80 Cal.Rptr. 869 (1969)] and *Department of Mental Hygiene of California v. Renal*, 173 N.Y.S.2d 231 (1957). The District Director states that these court decisions hold that the affidavit of support is a moral obligation and does not create any legal obligation to support the beneficiaries of the affidavit. The District Director also relied upon the *Matter of Harutunian*, 14 I&N Dec. 583 (R.C.1974). This decision also related to an applicant for adjustment of status pursuant to section 245 who was of advanced age, without means of support and with no one responsible for her support. This decision set forth criteria to be taken into consideration in determining the applicability of section 212(a)(15). The alien's age, incapability of earning a livelihood, a lack of sufficient funds for self-support, and a lack of persons in this country willing and able to assure that the alien will not need public support.

Following the denial of the applications, a motion to reopen and reconsider was filed April 22, 1977. The motion, which was prepared by the son-in-law set forth the following facts: He and his wife, the applicants' daughter, have been responsible for virtually all the wife's family's support since 1961. The motion describes a closely knit family, each doing their portion to see that the others did not want for the necessities of life. Three other children, one of whom is now married, are now employed and self-sufficient and also able to provide support to their parents. Attached to the motion are copies of numerous checks as well as bank records which reflect that the applicants' daughter and son-in-law have contributed several thousands of dollars to the parents' support over the last 10 or more years.

The motion to reopen and reconsider was considered by the District Director on June 10, 1977, who concluded that no new facts or evidence had been presented and accordingly affirmed his previous denial.

Despite the two State court decisions cited by the District Director, it is not believed the affidavits of support, although not legal obligations, are without weight in determining whether a person is likely to become a public charge. 8 C.F.R. 103.2(b)(1), which sets forth the requirement of evidence in support of applications, states in part: "Form I–34 may be used if an affidavit of support would be helpful in resolving any public charge aspect." In light of this regulation, the Service must give the affidavits due consideration consistent with the deponents' ability to provide the promised support. In the case at hand, the deponents have presented evidence of support over the past several years, as well as their ability to do so into the foreseeable future.

In the matter of *Harutunian, supra,* cited by the District Director, the circumstances are not parallel to the case at hand. In *Harutunian, supra,* the applicant was without any evidence of support, either of her own or by another person. In addition, she had a history of being dependent on the State of California for old age assistance; in the contrast, the present applicants have not received public assistance.

It is my conclusion that the applicants, although not self-supporting, have presented sufficient evidence that they will be supported if granted permanent resident status in the United States and are not likely to become public charges and are not, therefore, subject to the exclusion provisions of section 212(a)(15) of the Immigration and Nationality Act, as amended.

In view of the foregoing, it is determined that the record establishes the applicants' eligibility for the benefits sought under section 245 of the Act. Accordingly, the District Director's decision to deny the motion to reopen and reconsider is hereby withdrawn and the motion is granted.

* * *

Note

Congress has manifested some concern over the possible implications of state court decisions holding that affidavits of support are not legally enforceable. In 1980 it amended the statute establishing Supplemental Security Income (a federal program for the aged, blind, and disabled) to provide that, for three years after entry, the income and assets of the sponsor signing such an affidavit shall be deemed to be available to the alien beneficiaries, for purposes of determining eligibility for SSI. There are exemptions for refugees and for those whose disability necessitating assistance developed only after arrival in the United States. 42 U.S.C.A. § 1382j. In succeeding years, similar "deeming" provisions were added to the legislation governing other assistance programs. *See, e.g.,* 42 U.S.C.A. § 615 (Aid to Families with Dependent Children); 7 U.S.C.A. § 2014(i) (food stamp program).

With regard to the SSI program, the bill that initially passed the Senate in 1980 would have made affidavits of support legally enforceable as a matter of federal law. The conference committee decided against that approach, however, substituting instead the deeming provisions (and also providing for notification to potential sponsors that their income would be deemed to the aliens in this fashion and that they would have to provide information on their assets and income when aliens applied for public assistance). *See* H.R.Conf.Rep. No. 96–944, 96th Cong., 2d Sess., at 70–72 (1980); 1980 U.S.Code Cong. & Ad.News 1392, 1417–19. Why would Congress have chosen the deeming approach? Which should it have chosen? What recourse does an alien denied public assistance now have if her sponsor has lost interest?

5. THE EXCLUSION OF HOMOSEXUALS

The first legislation imposing federal immigration controls focused on characteristics Congress deemed objectionable on moral grounds (although these concerns also overlapped with interests in public safety). The law made unlawful the immigration of convicts and of "women imported for the purposes of prostitution." Act of March 3, 1875, Ch. 141, 18 Stat. 477. In 1882 and 1891, Congress added medical grounds to the list. Act of Aug. 3, 1882, Ch. 376, 22 Stat. 214; Act of March 3, 1891, Ch. 551, 26 Stat. 1084. The latter statute rendered excludable, among other classes, "idiots, insane persons, * * * [and] persons suffering from a loathsome or contagious disease."

Both concerns, medical and moral, still find expression in § 212(a). Persons who are mentally retarded, insane, or afflicted with dangerous contagious disease are medically excludable. INA § 212(a)(1), (2), (6). Polygamists, prostitutes, and aliens intending "to engage in any other unlawful commercialized vice" are excludable on what we may characterize fairly as moral grounds. INA § 212(a)(11), (12). Since at least 1952, Congress has also sought to exclude homosexuals under INA § 212(a)(4), which, as amended in 1965, applies to aliens "afflicted with psychopathic personality, sexual deviation, or a mental defect." Although encompassed within a medical ground of exclusion, the exclusion of homosexuals appears to have been based on both medical and moral grounds. *See Developments,* 96 Harv.L.Rev. 1286, 1344–46 (1983).

Since 1965, however, both medical and moral views have evolved considerably. Authoritative medical diagnostic manuals no longer treat homosexuality per se as a form of mental illness. But the change in society's thinking about the morality of homosexuality is less clearcut. Is the exclusion still enforceable on moral grounds despite the medical changes, and despite the growth, at least in some sectors of the population, of tolerance or support for homosexual lifestyles? The materials that follow reflect the attempts of all three branches of government to deal with these volatile and politically charged questions.

NOTE, THE PROPRIETY OF DENYING ENTRY TO HOMOSEXUAL ALIENS: EXAMINING THE PUBLIC HEALTH SERVICE'S AUTHORITY OVER MEDICAL EXCLUSIONS

17 Mich.J.L.Ref. 331, 332–38 (1984)

I. HISTORY OF THE EXCLUSION OF HOMOSEXUAL ALIENS

Since the late nineteenth century, Congress has enacted a number of statutes containing provisions that have excluded aliens afflicted with mental disabilities from admission into the United States. Congress initially sought to stem the influx of aliens likely to become dependents of the states, and consequently limited the purview of its first Act to "lunatics" and "idiots." Subsequent statutes, however, excluded aliens on the basis of mental disability, without relating the disability to the alien's capability of self-support. In order to achieve this broader objective, Congress expanded its formulation of mental disabilities by including within it "persons of constitutional psychopathic inferiority." Although no court ever determined that the expression "constitutional psychopathic inferiority" encompassed homosexuality, this expression acted as the precursor of the terms "psychopathic personality" and "sexual deviation," which immigration officials and courts have employed to exclude homosexual aliens from admission.

A. Legislative History of the Immigration and Nationality Act

In 1947, the Senate undertook a comprehensive investigation of the immigration system. This investigation culminated in the release of a Judiciary Committee Report, which recommended the addition of "homosexuals and other sex perverts" to the class of medically excludable aliens. A bill incorporating these recommendations accompanied the report.

To aid its deliberation, Congress asked the Public Health Service (PHS) to comment on the medical aspects of the proposed legislation. The PHS responded, but the meaning and implications of its response remain unclear. Unlike its analyses of the other medical classifications set forth by the bill, the PHS's comments on "homosexuals and sex perverts" included no specific recommendation. Instead, the PHS addressed the difficulty encountered in substantiating the diagnosis of homosexuality and sexual perversion, and added that, in "instances where the disturbance in sexuality [might] be difficult to uncover, a more obvious disturbance in personality [might] be encountered which would warrant a classification of psychopathic personality or mental defect."

The Senate Judiciary Committee reformulated the immigration bill to reflect both the PHS report and testimony presented in joint hearings. This new bill eliminated "homosexuals and sex perverts" as an exclusionary category. The report accompanying the bill maintained that the Senate made this change in response to the PHS assertion that "the provision for the exclusion of aliens afflicted with psychopathic personality or a mental defect ... [was] sufficiently broad to provide for the exclusion of homosexuals and sex perverts." The report further specified that the "change in nomenclature [was] not to be construed in any way as modifying the intent to exclude all aliens who are sexual deviates." The revised bill passed Congress to become the Immigration and Nationality Act (INA).

B. Judicial Interpretation of the INA

The first significant issue to arise from the application of section 212(a)(4) of the INA concerned whether the expression "psychopathic personality" included "homosexuality." Initially there was little doubt that it did. Following a number of administrative decisions, the Second Circuit in *Quiroz v. Neelly* [43] looked to the legislative history of the Act and concluded that, regardless of the medical profession's understanding of the term "psychopathic personality," Congress intended it to include homosexuality.[44]

In *Fleuti v. Rosenberg*,[45] however, the Ninth Circuit disrupted this consensus. *Fleuti* involved the deportation of an allegedly homosexual alien under section 241(a)(1) of the INA, a provision requiring the deportation of any alien who, though excludable at the time of entry, had somehow gained admission. The Ninth Circuit objected to the use of postentry behavior in determining the excludability of an alien, and maintained that evidence of homosexual activity subsequent to entry was irrelevant to the decision of whether immigration officials should have admitted an alien in the first place. Unfortunately, the Ninth Circuit's determination that, in the context of postentry behavior, the expression "psychopathic personality" was void for vagueness led some courts to misunderstand the case * * *.

In *Boutilier v. INS*,[52] the Supreme Court eliminated the confusion surrounding the validity of using the expression "psychopathic personality" to exclude homosexual aliens. The Court held that Congress intended the expression "psychopathic personality" to include homosexuality and, furthermore, that the phrase is not used as a clinical term, but as an expression designed to achieve Congress's goal of excluding homosexual aliens. The Court also rejected the void-for-vagueness argument, asserting that, with regard to preentry behavior, Congress's plenary power to

43. 291 F.2d 906 (5th Cir.1961).

44. We find it unnecessary "to embark" ... "on an amateur's voyage on the fog-enshrouded sea of psychiatry." ... The legislative history is clear as to the meaning to be given to ["psychopathic personality"]. ... Whatever the phrase ... may mean to the psychiatrist, to Congress it was intended to include homosexuals and sex perverts. It is that intent which controls here. *Id.* at 907.

45. 302 F.2d 652 (9th Cir.1962), *vacated and remanded on other grounds,* 374 U.S. 449 (1963).

52. 387 U.S. 118 (1967). Justice Brennan dissented for the same reasons Judge Moore did in the lower court opinion. Justices Douglas and Fortas dissented because they found "psychopathic personality" too vague a term to be employed as a criterion for imposition of penalties or punishment and that "affliction" conveyed the idea of an accustomed pattern of conduct, or a way of life, which had not been demonstrated in this case. *Id.* at 125–35.

make rules for the admission of aliens was not subject to any constitutional requirement of fair warning.

C. 1965 Amendment

In 1965, Congress substantially revised immigration policy. One change made was the addition of the term "sexual deviation" to section 212(a)(4) of the INA in response to its understanding of the Ninth Circuit's decision in *Fleuti*. The report accompanying this legislation first reiterated the Judiciary Committee's 1952 position that the "change in nomenclature" resulting from the elimination of homosexuality and sexual perversion as explicit exclusionary categories was "not to be construed in any way as modifying the intent to exclude all aliens who are sexual deviates." The report then explained that the committee specifically had added the medical term "sexual deviation" as a ground of exclusion to resolve any remaining doubt.

Later Developments

The inspection and exclusion of homosexual aliens—until 1979—was carried out jointly by the INS and PHS. The INS would refer aliens suspected of being homosexuals to the PHS for examination, just as it would any alien believed to be excludable for a physical or mental defect. If PHS determined that an alien was excludable as a homosexual, it would issue a "Class A certificate." INA § 234. The statute provides that in any case in which a certificate is issued, "the decision of the [immigration judge] shall be based solely upon such certification." INA § 236(d).

This procedure was scuttled following an announcement by the PHS that it would no longer play a part in the exclusion of aliens suspected of being homosexuals. A court decision described the sequence of events:

> On August 2, 1979 the Surgeon General of the United States announced a new policy for the Public Health Service. As part of this policy, PHS personnel were ordered not to issue medical certificates solely because an alien is suspected of being homosexual. The old policy was revised for two reasons. First, according to "current and generally accepted canons of medical practice", homosexuality *per se* is no longer considered to be a mental disorder.[3] Second, "the determination of homosexuality is not made through a medical diagnostic procedure." 56 Interpreter Releases 387, 398 (1979).

3. In making this determination, the Surgeon General placed great weight on the fact that, according to the comprehensive listing of currently recognized psychiatric diagnoses in the 1974 revised edition and the 1979 edition of the Diagnostic and Statistical Manual of Mental Disorders published by the American Psychiatric Association, homosexuality is not considered to be a psychiatric disorder. The Surgeon General was also influenced by the fact that the American Psychiatric Association's position had been officially endorsed by the American Psychological Association, the American Public Health Association, the American Nurses' Association, and the Council of Advanced Practitioners in Psychiatric and Mental Health Nursing of the American Nurses' Association. The PHS has traditionally relied on these organizations for their "professional expertise ... [and] for advice and information on a wide variety of physical and mental health issues." 56 Interpreter Releases 387, 398 (1979).

In response, the INS initially allowed suspected homosexuals to enter the country conditionally under parole status, deferring their medical examinations pending resolution of this dispute with the PHS. N.Y.Times, Aug. 15, 1979, at A14, col. 1. The Assistant Attorney General, Office of Legal Counsel of the Department of Justice, acknowledged that the Immigration and Nationality Act granted the Surgeon General "discretion to promulgate policies regarding the description and diagnosis of disease," but found that this discretion was limited by Congress' specific intent to bar homosexuals, and suggested that the INS promulgate a uniform policy for investigating suspected homosexuals. 56 Interpreter Releases 569, 572 (1979).

On September 9, 1980, the INS adopted "Guidelines and Procedures for the Inspection of Aliens Who Are Suspected of Being Homosexual", which provide that an arriving alien will not be asked any questions regarding his or her sexual preference. If an alien "makes an unambiguous oral or written admission of homosexuality" or if a third person who is also presenting himself or herself for inspection "voluntarily states, without prompting or prior questioning, that an alien who arrived in the United States at the same time ... is a homosexual," the alien may be examined privately by an immigration official and asked to sign a statement declaring he or she is homosexual. A hearing is held before an Immigration Judge and the alien is excluded based on his admissions. No medical certificate is obtained under the new guidelines. 57 Interpreter Releases 440 (1980).

Hill v. INS, 714 F.2d 1470, 1472–73 (9th Cir.1983).

The change in policy by the PHS raised two distinct issues. First, does INS have the authority to exclude aliens for being homosexuals if PHS has not issued a Class A certificate—that is, does the INA mandate that a medical determination be made by a government doctor before an alien may be excluded on medical grounds? The Ninth Circuit ruled against the INS in *Hill v. INS, supra,* concluding that the statute requires the INS to obtain a medical certificate before excluding "self-declared homosexuals" from the United States. (This conclusion is challenged in the case that follows and in Note, *Homosexual Aliens, supra,* at 347–49.)

The second issue is whether, following PHS's announcement, homosexuals are still excludable from the United States. The district court in the *Hill* case had held that the PHS's conclusion that homosexuality should not now be considered a psychopathic condition meant that the statute no longer excluded homosexuals:

Plaintiffs first contend that by section 212(a)(4) Congress did not intend to exclude alien homosexuals from admission into the United States once it was medically determined that homosexuality per se was no longer considered to be a mental disorder or sexual deviation. Thus as the INS policy excludes homosexuals per se, it violates Congressional intent and so is invalid. Plaintiffs argue that Congress intended to exclude homosexuals as having a sexual deviation or mental disorder based upon medical authority at that time that viewed homosexuality as a medical illness, specifically a mental disorder classified as sexual deviance. If medical authority changed, and no longer considered homosexuality to be a medical illness at all, then Congress intended that the INS could no longer exclude homosexuals from entry under the medical exclusion set forth in § 212(a)(4) as sexual deviants. In support of its interpretation of Congressional intent plaintiffs make two assertions. First, Congress required medical certification of persons excludable under section 212(a)(4) This evidences Congress' intent to rely upon current medical opinion in determining whether an alien is excludable from entry into the United States. Thus, the term sexual deviation as it appears in section 212(a)(4) is not to be an inelastic exclusion of homosexuals. Second, plaintiffs assert that if Congress intended to exclude homosexuals from entry irrespective of medical opinion as to whether homosexuality was considered to be a mental disorder, it would have specifically stated that homosexuals were a class of aliens excludable from entry into the United States.

The assertion that the term "sexual deviation" was not to be an inelastic opinion, but rather expands and contracts to current medical opinion, cannot be fully accepted due to the decision of the Supreme Court in *Boutilier*. The Supreme Court there decided that Congressional use of the term 'psychopathic personality' was not to invoke a "clinical" test. *Boutilier,* 387 U.S. at 123. Therefore a change in medical thinking that homosexual persons were no longer considered to be afflicted with a "psychopathic personality," but were considered to be afflicted with a "sexual deviation," would not affect the exclusion from admission of homosexual aliens. *Id.* The same congressional intent was evidenced in Congress' amendment to the Act in 1965. In the House and Senate Reports, S.Rep. 748, 89th Cong., 1st Sess., H.Rep. 745, 89th Cong., 1st Sess., reprinted in 1965 U.S.Code Cong. & Ad. News 3328, 3337, Congress indicated that because there was question whether homosexuality was encompassed within the term "psychopathic personality," the term "sexual deviation" was added as a ground of exclusion. Thus, *Boutilier* authority precludes ascribing to Congress the intent that the term "sexual deviance" will not apply to exclude homosexual aliens if medical opinion determines that homosexuality per se is no longer considered to be a sexual deviation, but is considered to be some other form of mental illness.

However, *Boutilier* authority is not controlling where the medical profession has not changed the medical illness label applied to a homosexual, (the situation in *Boutilier*), but rather has determined that homosexuality is no longer a medical illness, mental disorder, or a sexual deviation at all. * * * [M]edical authorities now have determined that homosexuality per se is not a mental disorder or sexual deviation. * * * Section 212(a)(4) is a *medical* exclusion to admission to the United States. Once medical authorities decided that homosexuality per se was no longer a medical problem of any type, the court cannot ascribe to Congress an intention that homosexuals still be excluded from entry due solely to their homosexuality as the reason Congress originally intended to exclude them no longer exists.

When *Boutilier* was decided there was no dispute among medical authorities that homosexuality was a mental disorder; the only dispute was in classifying which disorder homosexuality came within. The *Boutilier* Court apparently recognized that homosexuals were to be excluded from entry into the United States for medical reasons by its use of medical terms in its opinion. And importantly, the problem presented by plaintiffs herein is not the problem of a "clinical" definition of homosexuality, *see Boutilier,* 387 U.S. at 123, 87 S.Ct. at 1566, but rather whether a "clinical" problem exists at all. *Boutilier* does not preclude the Court from finding that Congress did not intend that homosexuals be excluded from entry into the United States solely because they are homosexuals once medical authorities have determined that homosexuality is not a medical illness, mental disorder, or sexual deviation, and the Court so finds this to be the congressional intent.

Lesbian/Gay Freedom Day Committee, Inc. v. USINS, 541 F.Supp. 569, 583–85 (N.D.Cal.1982). (The Court of Appeals did not reach this issue because of its conclusion that exclusion required a medical certificate from the PHS. *See Hill v. INS,* 714 F.2d at 1472 n. 1.)

Consider the views of the Fifth Circuit on these issues.

MATTER OF LONGSTAFF

United States Court of Appeals, Fifth Circuit, 1983.
716 F.2d 1439, cert. denied ___ U.S. ___, 104 S.Ct. 2668, 81 L.Ed.2d 373 (1984).

ALVIN B. RUBIN, CIRCUIT JUDGE:

May a resident alien be denied naturalization because he was a homosexual at the time he was admitted to the United States? The district court, 538 F.Supp. 589, answered this question in the affirmative. We affirm its judgment that the petitioner is ineligible for naturalization because, being excludable on the ground of his homosexuality when he arrived here, he was not lawfully admitted to the United States.

I.

Richard John Longstaff, now forty-three, is a native and citizen of the United Kingdom of Great Britain and Northern Ireland. On November 14, 1965, he was admitted to the United States as a permanent resident. Before he arrived in the United States, Longstaff filled out a form entitled "Application for Immigrant Visa and Alien Registration." To the question:

3(b) Are you now or have you ever been afflicted with psychopathic personality, epilepsy, mental defect, fits, fainting spells, convulsions or a nervous breakdown?

Longstaff answered, "No." The question was based on a provision of the Immigration & Nationality Act (the Act), § 212(a), excluding persons thus "afflicted." Congress intended the term "psychopathic personality" to designate homosexuals as well as persons having psychopathic disorders, as that term is generally understood. However, no evidence suggests that Longstaff knew or had reason to know that "psychopathic personality" was a term of art that included homosexuals and consequently excluded them from admission to the United States.[1]

Longstaff eventually settled in Texas, where he established himself in business. He owns two shops, operated under the trade name Union Jack, selling clothing and offering hairdressing services to both men and women. He has never been charged with any offense other than traffic violations. Reputable witnesses testified that they believe him to be a person of good moral character.

In his fifteenth year of residence, Longstaff sought naturalization as a citizen of the United States. * * *

* * * [A]n examiner for the Immigration and Naturalization Service (the INS) interrogated Longstaff. The examiner concluded that Longstaff had met his burden of establishing good moral character; nevertheless, he recommended denial of the petition because Longstaff had engaged in homosexual activity before entering the United States in 1965. He concluded that Longstaff (1) had been excludable under the Act; (2) had not been "lawfully admitted," as the Act requires for naturalization, and (3) could not be naturalized. After a trial de novo, the district court again denied Longstaff's petition for naturalization on this basis.

II.

No person may be naturalized unless he has been lawfully admitted to the United States for permanent residence in accordance with all applicable provisions of the Act. The applicant has the burden of proving that he entered the United States lawfully. * * *

* * *

III.

Among the classes of aliens ineligible to receive visas and excluded from lawful admission to the United States by the Act are "aliens afflicted with psychopathic personality." * * *

* * * [Longstaff] contends that the Act does not exclude homosexuals on the basis that they are determined judicially to have such a sexual preference or even on the basis that they state that they have this preference, but that it is designed to exclude only those persons declared by a Public Health Service (PHS) medical officer to be "afflicted" with "psychopathic personality" or "sexual deviation." He premises his argu-

---

1. Indeed, Longstaff had reason to anticipate progressive social tolerance toward homosexuality. Private homosexual activity between consenting adults had recently been decriminalized in Great Britain in accordance with the recommendations of the 1963 Report of the Great Britain Committee on Homosexual Offenses and Prostitution, known as the Wolfenden Report.

ment on the Act's separation of medical from other reasons for exclusion. Because the exclusion of those afflicted with psychopathic personality is contained in a clause enumerating medical bases for exclusion, Longstaff argues, excludibility for homosexuality must be determined in the same fashion and by the same procedures as excludability for affliction with a mental defect or a dangerous contagious disease. Because these conditions are "subject to medical determination," he contends that only a medical officer has the power to determine whether any of them exists.

* * *

The Act provides that arriving aliens may be detained at the border while immigration and medical officers examine them for "physical and mental defects or disabilities" that warrant exclusion. [INA § 232.] It also requires that the physical and mental examination of arriving aliens be conducted by medical officers of the United States Public Health Service or if PHS officers are unavailable, by civil surgeons employed on terms prescribed by the Attorney General. [INA § 234.] These physicians "shall conduct all medical examinations and shall certify, for the information of the immigration officers and the special inquiry officers, any physical and mental defect or disease observed by such medical officers in any such alien." [*Id.*]

Longstaff urges the court to infer from the use of the word "shall" that an applicant may not be excluded for medical reasons unless the basis for exclusion is determined by a physician. He supports this argument by reference both to the past administrative practice and to the Act's declaration that a medical certificate is conclusive evidence of medical excludability. Accordingly, he argues, a medical certificate is the sole type of evidence an immigration judge may consider. He adds that the 1917 Act, which the 1952 Act replaced, was also construed to give conclusive effect to a medical certificate of excludability. To evaluate this argument, we examine the history and structure of the Act and the procedure that must be followed by an alien who seeks to immigrate to the United States.

IV.

* * *

When a visa was issued to Longstaff, the procedure employed, which appears not to have changed substantially, was as follows: an alien seeking admission for permanent residence in the United States was required to apply to a consular official outside of the United States for a visa. Issuing visas was the responsibility of the State Department, while examining aliens for admissibility to the United States was the duty of the INS, an arm of the Justice Department. Before the consular officer could issue the visa, the alien was required to complete an application form and to submit to physical and mental examination by a PHS officer or a designated physician.

The consular officer was forbidden to issue a visa if it appeared from statements in the alien's application or from the papers submitted with it that the alien was ineligible to receive a visa, hence excludable, or if the consular officer knew or had reason to believe that this was the case. Thus, in the usual course of events, an alien who was excludable never received a visa. Presumably, if an applicant for a visa answered "yes" to the psychopathic personality question, he would be denied a visa. If he answered "no" but were found by the PHS officer conducting the pre-visa physical and mental examination to have such a personality, he would also be denied a visa.

Because the immigrant visa was valid for only four months, the PHS officer at the port of entry usually did not make another physical or mental examination. Unless there was some reason to suspect that the alien had suffered a change in health or that the prior examination was erroneous, the domestic PHS officer merely reviewed the medical report attached to the visa. An immigration officer inspected the visa and determined whether the alien was to be admitted. Unless his decision was challenged by another immigration officer, the alien was admitted. The immigration officer might require the alien's sworn statements and other evidence regarding "any matter which is material and relevant to the enforcement of [the Act]," including the production of books, papers, and documents; and the testimony, under subpoena, of witnesses. Any alien who "may not appear to the examining immigration officer at the point of arrival to be clearly and beyond a doubt entitled to land shall be detained for further inquiry to be conducted by [an immigration judge]." That judge made the decision concerning admission.

Former INS immigration officers testified that, because of the procedure for issuing visas, they made no inquiry about the sexual preference of aliens arriving with a visa. One former immigration officer testified that they spent an average of only 38 seconds examining each alien and his papers and that ordinarily the PHS officers merely inspected the pre-visa medical certificate to be certain that it was in order.

There is no evidence in the record regarding the procedure followed when an alien who arrived in the United States with a visa affirmatively disclosed at that time that he was a homosexual. Presumably, such a person would have been referred to a PHS medical officer for a determination of his admissibility.

As Longstaff asserts, the statute provides that the medical officer's certification of "any mental disease, defect, or disability which would bring such alien within any of the classes excluded from admission" is conclusive evidence of excludability. [INA § 236(d).] This does not necessarily mean, however, that the absence of certification is conclusive evidence of admissibility. The Act also requires that medical officers be provided with suitable facilities for the detention and examination of all arriving aliens who are suspected of being excludable on the basis of physical or mental condition. [INA § 234.] But this does not necessarily mean that such an examination is ordinarily conducted or that aliens may be excluded for medical reasons only after such an examination.

* * *

If only certification of homosexuality by a medical officer could warrant exclusion of homosexuals, then the Surgeon General [by announcing that PHS would no longer examine aliens suspected of being homosexuals] would have effectively checkmated Congressional policy. Confronted with the problem raised by the Surgeon General's abdication of the power he had sought from Congress, the INS initially allowed all suspected homosexuals to enter the United States under parole status while it sought counsel from the Justice Department's Office of Legal Counsel on whether it was still obligated to exclude homosexuals. The Office of Legal Counsel informed the INS that it was still required to do so. The opinion of the Ninth Circuit in [*Hill v. INS, supra,*] reads the Act as requiring it to do so only when homosexuality is certified by a medical officer. Because the statute requires medical examination to be conducted by medical officers of the Public Health Service, the Surgeon General's refusal to allow these officers to make such certification precludes the exclusion of anyone for homosexuality. We cannot, however, conclude that a medical certificate was indispensable to bar a professed homosexual from entry to the United States in 1965 or that obtaining such a certificate now is a prerequisite to denying naturalization.

Although the term "homosexual" is not a scientific designation, and studies indicate that many males have homosexual experiences, there can be no doubt that Longstaff both knew what the term meant and was not uncertain about his sexual preferences. He stated that he had been a homosexual "as far back as [he could] remember in [his] life." He testified that he had engaged in "homosexual activities" before his entry into the United States. He defined a homosexual experience as "going to bed with a person of the same sex, ... in other words, sexual relations." He admitted having "deviate sexual intercourse" as defined in the Texas statute "at least a dozen times in the State of Texas." He had previously lived in Oklahoma and said he had "committ[ed] homosexual activity in Oklahoma." When asked "when did you first enter into such activities?" he answered, "I've always been a homosexual, ... from birth." He considers himself "now a known homosexual in the community."

A certificate that an alien is suffering from a medical condition that requires him to be excluded is conclusive. * * * The statute and these decisions might well lead to the conclusion that a medical determination by a PHS officer that the alien is not suffering from such a condition is also conclusive. But neither the premise nor the inference leads to the conclusion that non-excludability is conclusively established by the absence of any examination at all.

The procedural protections built into the exclusion process demonstrate Congress's intent that only competent evidence of medical excludability be adduced in exclusion proceedings. But there is no reason why an informed applicant's admission that he falls within an excludable class is not competent evidence on which to base an exclusion decision. INA § 236(d) is not to the contrary. That section specifies that, if an immigration judge in an exclusion hearing is presented with a medical certificate "that an alien is afflicted ... with any mental disease, defect, or disability," his decision "shall be based solely on such certification." It merely makes clear that the petitioner has no right to introduce evidence rebutting the certificate. It does not expressly forbid an immigration judge to find an applicant excludable on the basis of evidence other than a medical certificate.

* * *

To remand the case for a medical determination of homosexuality would appear to be to ask for a certification of the obvious. It is patent that sexual preference cannot be determined by blood test or physical examination; even doctors must reach a decision by interrogation of the person involved or of others professing knowledge about that person. To require the INS to disregard the most reliable source of information, the statements of the person involved, would be to substitute secondary evidence for primary.

* * *

In response to the refusal of the PHS to make medical determinations of homosexuality and the determination of the office of legal counsel that the INS was nonetheless obliged to exclude homosexuals, the INS has adopted a new policy, "Guidelines and Procedures for the Inspection of Aliens Who Are Suspected of Being Homosexual." This statement provides that an arriving alien will not be asked any questions regarding his sexual preference. If an alien "makes an unambiguous oral or written admission of homosexuality" (which does not include exhibition of buttons, literature, or other similar material), or if a third person who is also presenting himself for inspection "voluntarily states, without prompting or prior questioning, that an alien who arrived in the United States at the same time . . . is a homosexual," the alien may be examined privately by an immigration officer and asked to sign a statement that he is a homosexual. That statement forms the evidentiary basis for exclusion.

Thus, the administrative agency charged with enforcement of the Act has interpreted it as not requiring a medical certificate as a condition for the exclusion of homosexuals. This interpretation is entitled to deference.

That homosexuality is no longer considered a psychopathic condition is established by the opinion of the government's highest medical officer, the Surgeon General. We are bound, nonetheless, by *Boutilier's* ruling that the phrase "psychopathic personality," is a term of art, not dependent on medical definition,[56] and by the congressional bar against persons "afflicted with . . . sexual deviation." Homosexuality can now be demon-

---

56. Judge Aguilar concluded in *Lesbian/Gay Freedom Day Committee, Inc.*, 541 F.Supp. at 585, that, "*Boutilier* does not preclude the Court from finding that Congress did not intend that homosexuals be excluded from entry into the United States solely because they are homosexuals once medical authorities have determined that homosexuality is not a medical illness, mental disorder, or sexual deviation, and the Court so finds this to be the congressional intent." We disagree with this interpretation of *Boutilier* and of Congressional intent. *Quiroz v. Neelly*, 291 F.2d 906, 907 (5th Cir.1961). Like the Supreme Court, we look behind the technical phrases in the Act to the purpose of its drafters. Congress clearly intended to exclude homosexuals from entry into the United States and its use of medical language to describe the excludable class was not intended to lay down a clinical test for exclusion, dependent on the vicissitudes of medical opinion. *Boutilier*, 387 U.S. at 122, 87 S.Ct. at 1566, 18 L.Ed.2d at 665. Indeed, although Congress employed medical terminology to describe the excludable class, it is evident that moral as well as medical reasons underlay the congressional decision to exclude homosexuals. *Developments in the Law—Immigration Policy and the Rights of Aliens*, 96 Harv.L.Rev. 1286, 1346 & nn. 92–94 (1983). * * *

strated in INS proceedings only by an alien's unambiguous admission or by the voluntary statement of a third person, made without either prompting or questioning. Longstaff is thus barred from naturalization by his own truthful statements that he was excludable as a homosexual at the time of his entry, and, therefore, was not lawfully admitted for permanent residence. There is no evidence that, when he sought a visa eighteen years ago, he was asked any question that would indicate to him or to any other intelligent layman that his sexual preferences might affect the issuance of a visa, or that he knowingly gave a false answer to any question asked of him. In the eighteen years of his residence, he has led a constructive life. We are, however, bound to decide according to a law made in the exercise of a power that is plenary. If Congress's policy is misguided, Congress must revise that policy. If the result achieved by the policy is unfair to a deserving person who desires to become a citizen, the injustice must be corrected by lawmakers.

Based on the finding that Longstaff was a homosexual when he entered the United States, the district court correctly decided that he was then excludable, that his excludability may now be proved, and that, being excludable, he may not be naturalized. Therefore, its judgment is Affirmed.

TATE, CIRCUIT JUDGE, dissenting:

The majority has certainly reached a logical conclusion, based upon its intelligent analysis of applicable legislation and jurisprudential authority, that the petitioner Longstaff may be denied naturalization in 1983 because, when he was admitted to the United States in 1965 (following which he has led a constructive life), he was a homosexual and thus could have been excluded from admission to the United States. The majority therefore concludes that Longstaff was not "lawfully admitted" to the United States, a prerequisite for naturalization.

I respectfully dissent. For the reasons extensively detailed by the Ninth Circuit recently in *Hill v. United States Immigration and Naturalization Service*, 714 F.2d 1470 (9th Cir.1983), I would conclude that a homosexual may not lawfully be denied admission in the absence of a medical certificate to that effect.

I premise my conclusion on the peculiar statutory framework at issue in this case. As the majority states, Congress listed "psychopathic personality" and "sexual deviation" as causes for exclusion in a list of seven medical bases for exclusion. This list of medical causes for exclusion is further supplemented by twenty-six other non-medical bases for exclusion. Furthermore, INA § 234 provides that either medical officers of the Public Health Service or civil surgeons employed by the United States *"shall"* conduct the physical and mental examination of all aliens suspected of being medically excludable under INA § 212(a)(1)–(5) (thus including the grounds of psychopathic personality and sexual deviation). These medical personnel and surgeons are the only persons authorized by the Act to certify the existence of *"any"* medical condition permitting exclusion.

Therefore, the statutory scheme contemplates that medical personnel will diagnose and certify any *medical* cause for deportation or exclusion. Moreover, as the majority concedes, the apparent practice of the Immigration and Naturalization Service (the "INS") has been "to exclude for homosexuality only those persons for whom a [medical] certificate was issued."

Nonetheless, the majority concludes that Congress did not intend for a medical certificate attesting to an individual's homosexuality to be the only competent evidence for exclusion on the basis of "psychopathic personality" or "sexual deviation." To the contrary, however, I do not believe that it is overly formalistic to find that Congress did intend in its statutory scheme to *require* medical certification, and only medical certification, of any "medical" cause for exclusion. In this context, it must be remembered that the statute provides that an alien in the United States may be deported if he "at the time of entry was within one or more of the classes of aliens excludable by the law existing at the time of [his] entry" into the United States. INA § 241(a)(1).

In my view, Congress intended to avoid not only an initial exclusion from admission, but also an ex post facto determination for deportation purposes, from being based solely on the non-medical judgment of bureaucratic agencies that a "medical" cause for exclusion existed at the time of a person's admission, when that determination is unsupported by a professional judgment by a member of the medical profession. This interpretation is further supported when, as here, the medical condition is indefinite and arguable (or, *e.g.,* where a condition was latent at the time of entry and undiscoverable *then* by a medical examination); then, medical conditions that allegedly existed at the time of presumably lawful admission could later be administratively misused to deport persons unpopular in actuality for non-medical reasons. Thus, I believe that Congress intended the medical certification procedure to be interposed as an important safeguard against abusive "medical" exclusions or deportations by introducing the independent factor of a professional medical examination into this aspect of the exclusion and deportation process.

Nor does my reading of Congress' intent differ because homosexuality is no longer recognized by medical experts to be a psychopathic condition. As the majority notes, we are bound by the Supreme Court's ruling in *Boutilier v. Immigration and Naturalization Service,* 387 U.S. 118, 87 S.Ct. 1563, 18 L.Ed.2d 661 (1967), to the effect that homosexuality is a "medical" condition then included within the phrase "psychopathic personality." *Id.* And since this ruling is apparently not dependent on current medical opinion, *Boutilier, supra,* 387 U.S. at 124, 87 S.Ct. at 1567, I can see no reason to treat homosexuality differently from the other grounds for medical exclusion.

Thus, exclusion or deportation on grounds of homosexuality must be subject to the same safeguards of medical certification as exclusion or deportation on other medical grounds such as "mental retardation" or "mental defect." Just as Congress was unwilling to rely on a bureaucratic determination that a person has a "mental defect",[2] the *statute* clearly

---

2. No more, I believe, did Congress intend to allow agents of the Immigration and Naturalization Service to exclude or deport aliens solely on the basis of a self-admission

suggests that Congress was equally unwilling to accept a non-medical determination that a person has a "psychopathic personality" because of homosexuality (the test of lawful admission at the time of Longstaff's entry). The importance of adhering to the congressional intent that only professional medical determinations be made, so as to avoid the improper non-medical administrative classification of a person as "medically" excludable or deportable, requires that the courts respect these stringent statutory standards by not creating procedural exceptions only for certain "medical" conditions.

The INS argues that it should not be required to produce medical certification of homosexuality for exclusion or deportation purposes since such certification is now difficult to obtain. In particular, the INS contends that it should be allowed to rely on other forms of evidence under the statute, because the PHS, pursuant to an order by the Surgeon General, has refused since 1979 to medically diagnose and certify that an individual is a homosexual.

It is basic, however, that this court is without authority to ignore the mandate of Congress' statutory scheme merely because there is an inter-agency dispute over the mechanics of statutory enforcement. If this administrative dispute renders the exclusion of homosexuals under the statute ineffective, then it is for Congress, not this court, to alter its statutory scheme requiring medical certification. Absent such congressional intervention, I am unwilling to infer that Congress intended to allow the non-medical personnel of an administrative agency to use "medical" classifications—as is the practice in present-day Russia—to exile persons for newly-discovered mental defects or other "medical conditions."

Thus, I agree with the Ninth Circuit in *Hill, supra,* that Congress did so intend to treat medical causes for exclusion or deportation differently from non-medical causes for denial of lawful admission to the United States, and that we must respect the intended illogic of Congress in according such talismanic significance to the presence or absence of a conclusive medical certification as determinative of admissibility or deportability.

* * *

Notes

1. It is usual, in interpreting a statute, to look to the purpose of the statute and the intent of the drafters at the time the legislation was enacted. Which of the following statements better states the "legislative intent" of the enacting Congress regarding the exclusion of homosexuals:

(1) homosexuals are excludable;

that "I have a mental defect" or "I have had an attack of insanity" or "I am a moron", which are some of the other causes for medical exclusion under the Act. Under the statutory scheme, Congress simply did not intend to permit a non-medical determination as to the existence of "medical" causes for exclusion or deportation, including "psychopathic personality" and "sexual deviation."

    (2) persons suffering from mental illness or sexual deviance are excludable; and so long as homosexuality is considered pathological, homosexuals are excludable;

    (3) Congress delegated authority to PHS to determine what conditions should be considered to be mental illness or sexual deviance within the purview of INA § 212(a)(4).

How would each characterization of congressional intent affect the decisions in the *Hill* and *Longstaff* cases?

The statements above look to the intent of the Congress that passed the statute. Should that be the relevant intent? The 1952 and 1965 Congresses are long gone, and it may or may not be true that their judgments accurately reflect moral or medical views of most Americans (or the medical community) on homosexuality. Should courts act under the guise of "interpretation" to bring older statutes into line with what they judge to be more modern views? How should a court discover the modern thinking on such a subject (either of the current Congress or of the public)? Of what relevance is the fact that legislation to remove this exclusion ground has been introduced in several recent sessions, but has made little headway? *See* Note, *The Propriety of Denying Entry to Homosexual Aliens,* 17 Mich.J.L.Ref. 331, 358 (1984).

Both Judge Rubin and Judge Tate in *Longstaff* recognize that Congress could act to clarify its current intent in light of changes in medical and ethical thinking since 1965, especially since neither opinion writer bases his conclusions on the Constitution. But it is not easy to get a legislature to take up such a controversial topic. The majority and minority in *Longstaff* essentially differ, then, only as to what rule should prevail in the meantime, until Congress chooses to legislate anew (if it ever does). Or to put the matter another way, they differ over which side in the ongoing policy debate over exclusion of homosexuals should bear the burden of overcoming legislative inertia—and which side's views will be implemented in default of new congressional action.

For a sensitive discussion of the way that courts have often made creative, or even farfetched, use of "interpretation" to reallocate the burden of legislative inertia when statutes no longer "fit," coupled with a controversial proposal to make judicial updating of such statutes more candid and systematic, *see* G. Calabresi, *A Common Law for the Age of Statutes* (1982). Professor Calabresi would permit courts to treat old statutes the way they have traditionally treated old common-law doctrines: judges could modify them in light of later changes in the legal landscape rendering the old statutes plainly obsolete. He also suggests that the absence of such an updating mechanism often tempts courts to dispose of ill-fitting statutes by stretching the application of constitutional provisions. But constitutional rulings have a significant disadvantage. They are far more resistant to later legislative revision than common-law-type judicial correctives would be, should the judges happen to misconstrue current thinking on the subject.

    2. The government did not petition for certiorari in the *Hill* case. Instead, the Acting Deputy Attorney General wrote the Assistant Secre-

tary for Health in the Department of Health and Human Services, directing that the Public Health Service change its practices. He wrote:

> As you know, Congress intended homosexuality to be one of the grounds for exclusion under [§ 212(a)(4)] of the Immigration and Nationality Act. Even though the Immigration and Naturalization Service does not question entrants about their sexual preference, it has a statutory responsibility to exclude self-proclaimed homosexuals.
>
> Accordingly, in order for the Immigration and Naturalization Service to carry out its congressionally mandated responsibility in the Ninth Circuit, you are required to instruct the Public Health Service to resume the process for issuance of the certificate referred to in [INA § 234] for self-proclaimed homosexual aliens seeking admission in the Ninth Circuit who are referred by the Immigration and Naturalization Service to a Public Health Service officer for examination. We do not read the law to require, in such circumstances, that the certificate be based on anything other than the alien's own statement of homosexuality.

61 Interp.Rel. 378 (1984). INS follows *Hill* only in the Ninth Circuit. See 62 Interp.Rel. 166–67 (1985).

SECTION C. PAROLE

Suppose an intending immigrant is detained at the border and ultimately ruled excludable on a ground that is not waivable under § 212. What happens if she becomes gravely ill before removal can be effected? Can the district director send her to the hospital without permitting an entry and thus violating the Act? Must the district director condemn a portion of the hospital and make it a part of the INS detention facility?

Not surprisingly, immigration authorities early found ways to cope with such circumstances without initiating costly condemnation proceedings and without directly violating the exclusion laws. They developed the concept of parole, under which an alien is allowed to travel away from the border and the detention facilities and yet remain subject to exclusion proceedings, rather than the more cumbersome and protective deportation proceedings, when it comes time to test out the alien's ultimate right to remain. In the eyes of the law, an alien paroled into the country near San Diego remains constructively at the border, even if she is authorized to travel all the way to Omaha in the center of the country. Technically, a parolee has made no "entry." (We will explore the intricacies of entry and its consequences in Chapter Four.) In a way, then, parole would serve to make the hospital bed of the gravely ill alien mentioned above a functional extension of the border detention facilities, but without having to transfer title to the hospital into the government's name.

At first, parole "was fashioned by administrative ingenuity" alone, without statutory sanction. G & R § 2.54. But the 1952 Act codified the practice in § 212(d)(5). The Attorney General is now expressly authorized to parole aliens "temporarily under such conditions as he may prescribe for emergent reasons or reasons deemed strictly in the public interest." The statute also makes clear that at the end of the parole the alien returns "to the custody from which he was paroled and thereafter his case shall continue to be dealt with in the same manner as that of any other applicant for admission to the United States."

A 1952 congressional committee report explained the intent of this provision:

> The provision in the instant bill represents an acceptance of the recommendation of the Attorney General with reference to this form of discretionary relief. The committee believes that the broader discretionary authority is necessary to permit the Attorney General to parole inadmissible aliens into the United States in emergency cases, such as the case of an alien who requires immediate medical attention before there has been an opportunity for an immigration officer to inspect him, and in cases where it is strictly in the public interest to have an inadmissible alien present in the United States, such as, for instance, a witness or for purposes of prosecution.

H.R.Rep. No. 1365, 82nd Cong., 2d Sess., at 52; 1952 U.S.Code Cong. & Ad.News 1653, 1706. Congress plainly contemplated that parole might be used either before or after a final determination of excludability.

When the Justice Department decided to close Ellis Island and other border processing and detention facilities in 1954, see T. Pitkin, *Keepers of the Gate: A History of Ellis Island* 176–77 (1975), parole thereafter was used primarily to permit the temporary release of aliens in exclusion processing, pending a final decision on their admissibility. As it happened, some aliens might be on parole in this fashion for several years, establishing equities that made their case for remaining more sympathetic. Long-time parolees also began to assert an entitlement based on their lengthy physical presence, free of restraints, to certain forms of relief technically available under the INA only to aliens in deportation rather than exclusion proceedings. The Supreme Court ultimately held that such benefits are not available to parolees, in a case that discusses the history and policy underlying parole. *Leng May Ma v. Barber,* 357 U.S. 185, 78 S.Ct. 1072, 2 L.Ed.2d 1246 (1958). Excerpts follow:

> [O]ur immigration laws have long made a distinction between those aliens who have come to our shores seeking admission, such as petitioner, and those who are within the United States after an entry, irrespective of its legality. In the latter instance the Court has recognized additional rights and privileges not extended to those in the former category who are merely "on the threshold of initial entry."

> * * *

> For over a half century this Court has held that the detention of an alien in custody pending determination of his admissibility does not legally constitute an entry though the alien is

physically within the United States. * * * Our question is whether the granting of temporary parole somehow effects a change in the alien's legal status. In § 212(d)(5) of the Act, generally a codification of the administrative practice pursuant to which petitioner was paroled, the Congress specifically provided that parole "shall not be regarded as an admission of the alien," and that after the return to custody the alien's case "shall *continue* to be dealt with in the same manner as that of any other applicant for admission to the United States." (Emphasis added.)
* * *

The Court previously has had occasion to define the legal status of excluded aliens on parole. In *Kaplan v. Tod,* 1925, 267 U.S. 228, 45 S.Ct. 257, 258, 69 L.Ed. 585 (1925), an excluded alien was paroled to a private Immigrant Aid Society pending deportation. The questions posed were whether the alien was "dwelling in the United States" within the meaning of a naturalization statute, and whether she had "entered or [was] found in the United States" for purpose of limitations. Mr. Justice Holmes disposed of the problem by explicitly equating parole with detention:

> "The appellant could not lawfully have landed in the United States * * *, and until she legally landed 'could not have dwelt within the United States.' Moreover while she was at Ellis Island she was to be regarded as stopped at the boundary line and kept there unless and until her right to enter should be declared. When her prison bounds were enlarged by committing her to the custody of the Hebrew Society, the nature of her stay within the territory was not changed. She was still in theory of law at the boundary line and had gained no foothold in the United States." 267 U.S. at page 230, 45 S.Ct., at page 257.

* * *

The parole of aliens seeking admission is simply a device through which needless confinement is avoided while administrative proceedings are conducted. It was never intended to affect an alien's status, and to hold that petitioner's parole placed her legally "within the United States" is inconsistent with the congressional mandate, the administrative concept of parole, and the decisions of this Court. Physical detention of aliens is now the exception, not the rule, and is generally employed only as to security risks or those likely to abscond. Certainly this policy reflects the humane qualities of an enlightened civilization. The acceptance of petitioner's position in this case, however, with its inherent suggestion of an altered parole status, would be quite likely to prompt some curtailment of current parole policy—an intention we are reluctant to impute to the Congress.

357 U.S. at 187–90, 78 S.Ct. at 1073–75. (The "humane" and "enlightened" policy favoring release while exclusion proceedings were underway
came to an end in 1981, principally because the executive branch believed
the release policy attracted too many asylum-seekers who could usually
avoid detention and accept employment here while adjudication of asylum
dragged on. We will consider the detention controversy later in this
Chapter.)

As it had evolved, parole thus became an outstandingly flexible tool
in the hands of the executive branch, permitting the physical presence of
selected aliens despite other disqualifications—whether those be the application of the exclusion grounds of § 212(a) or the lack of an admission
number under the national-origins quotas, or later, under the preference
system. Presidents eventually began to take vigorous—and controversial—advantage of this flexibility, to bring in large groups of aliens in
compelling circumstances. The first such episode occurred when the
Soviet Union sent tanks into Hungary to put down a revolution there in
1956. Hungarian quotas were full, but the Eisenhower administration
came under increasing pressure to admit large numbers of Hungarian
refugees. The President ultimately decided to make innovative use of the
parole power to bring some 30,000 refugees to this country.

Thus began a long and controversial practice of paroling in refugees
when ordinary statutory provisions proved inadequate. People fleeing
Cuba and Indochina, among others, were later beneficiaries. Many in
Congress protested. Parole, they insisted, was supposed to be temporary,
whereas the refugees were clearly here for an indefinite stay, and it was
supposed to be used in individual cases, not for large groups. Nevertheless, the practice continued until Congress rewrote the refugee provisions
comprehensively in the Refugee Act of 1980. When Congress did so, it
closed the refugee-parole loophole permanently by adding subparagraph
(B) to § 212(d)(5). That provision forbids the paroling of refugees except
in isolated individual cases for individually compelling reasons. (Chapter
Eight traces these developments in more detail.)

But that amendment did not spell the end of paroles of large groups.
Soon after enactment of the Refugee Act, approximately 125,000 Cubans
arrived directly—and chaotically—by boat in south Florida in the span of
a few months, after Cuban Premier Fidel Castro opened the port of Mariel
to permit their exit. The arriving Marielitos were excludable for lack of
documents (and many on other grounds), and the political asylum claims
most of them were filing would take months or years to process. But INS
was obviously unable to detain such a large number. The answer?
Parole, freeing most of the arrivals to sponsors. This release was technically consistent with § 212(d)(5)(B) because the aliens had not been determined to be refugees when they were paroled, and they were not being
paroled as part of an official refugee program. Indeed, especially because
Cuba adamantly refused, for over three years, to cooperate in the return
of any of the Marielitos, there really was no alternative to a parole on this
scale. Later the Attorney General formalized the parole category used for
this group (as well as that of some 30,000 Haitians who arrived during
this period) with the label "Cuban/Haitian entrant—status pending."

Congress acquiesced by providing funding to assist the parolees (again, there was no realistic alternative). Over a thousand of the Marielitos, however, remained in detention several years after arrival, largely because of criminal activity either in the United States or in Cuba before their departure. Their cases have posed difficult due process questions to be considered later in this Chapter.

Parole can thus be used for a wide variety of purposes, either before or after an administrative finding of excludability: to permit medical treatment, to allow appearance in litigation or a criminal prosecution, to prevent inhumane separation of families or for other humanitarian reasons, or to permit release pending adjudication of an exclusion case. *See* G & R § 2.54. But parole may be granted only by the Attorney General and a rather select list of his delegates, principally the district directors. Neither immigration judges nor the BIA have authority to order parole. *Matter of Conceiro,* 14 I & N Dec. 278 (BIA 1973), *petition for habeas corpus dismissed, Conceiro v. Marks,* 360 F.Supp. 454 (S.D.N.Y.1973). A district director's denial of parole is judicially reviewable for abuse of discretion, but courts have generally been quite deferential in reviewing the exercise of such discretion. *See, e.g., Bertrand v. Sava,* 684 F.2d 204 (2d Cir.1982). *But see Moret v. Karn,* 746 F.2d 989 (3d Cir.1984) (reversing parole revocation where INS failed to follow its own internal procedures).

SECTION D. PROCEDURES

The efforts of agencies and courts to implement the complicated substantive provisions outlined in the earlier sections of this chapter have resulted in an elaborate set of admission and exclusion procedures and a distinctive due process jurisprudence. No doubt you have gained some acquaintance with the procedures from the previous readings. Here we will set forth those procedures more comprehensively, first as applied to nonimmigrants and then as applied to immigrants. We begin, however, by considering the constitutional framework for admission procedures.

1. DUE PROCESS IN EXCLUSION PROCEEDINGS

Since 1950, the due process rights of aliens in exclusion proceedings might well be summarized in one famous (and rather chilling) sentence written by Justice Minton: "Whatever the procedure authorized by Congress is, it is due process as far as an alien denied entry is concerned." *United States ex rel. Knauff v. Shaughnessy,* 338 U.S. 537, 544, 70 S.Ct. 309, 313, 94 L.Ed. 317 (1950). *Knauff* has never been overruled; hence you might expect this section of the casebook to be exceedingly short. Instead we will spend several pages examining *Knauff* and a 1953 case, *Mezei,* which accomplished the improbable task of rendering the *Knauff* outcome even more severe. We do so precisely because we view the *Knauff-Mezei* doctrine as extreme. It has provoked a steady stream of critical academic commentary, and there are now signs in some decisions, including the Supreme Court's *Plasencia* opinion, reprinted below, that the time has come for some modification of the doctrine.

Part of the criticism rests on the way the doctrine assigns excludable aliens to constitutional limbo. Part of it also rests on the odd way the court of the 1950's seemed to draw the lines between the aliens who fall into this disfavored class and those who manage to get more complete due process protection (traditionally, those who are in deportation rather than exclusion proceedings). We will introduce these due process questions here, but we will still be discussing them at various places through Chapters Four and Five, as we move away from the border and consider constitutional limitations on deportation proceedings.

UNITED STATES ex rel. KNAUFF v. SHAUGHNESSY

Supreme Court of the United States, 1950.
338 U.S. 537, 70 S.Ct. 309, 94 L.Ed. 317.

MR. JUSTICE MINTON delivered the opinion of the Court.

May the United States exclude without hearing, solely upon a finding by the Attorney General that her admission would be prejudicial to the interests of the United States, the alien wife of a citizen who had served honorably in the armed forces of the United States during World War II? The District Court for the Southern District of New York held that it could, and the Court of Appeals for the Second Circuit affirmed. We granted certiorari to examine the question especially in the light of the War Brides Act of December 28, 1945.

Petitioner was born in Germany in 1915. She left Germany and went to Czechoslovakia during the Hitler regime. There she was married and divorced. She went to England in 1939 as a refugee. Thereafter she served with the Royal Air Force efficiently and honorably from January 1, 1943, until May 30, 1946. She then secured civilian employment with the War Department of the United States in Germany. Her work was rated "very good" and "excellent." On February 28, 1948, with the permission of the Commanding General at Frankfurt, Germany, she married Kurt W. Knauff, a naturalized citizen of the United States. He is an honorably discharged United States Army veteran of World War II. He is, as he was at the time of his marriage, a civilian employee of the United States Army at Frankfurt, Germany.

On August 14, 1948, petitioner sought to enter the United States to be naturalized. On that day she was temporarily excluded from the United States and detained at Ellis Island. On October 6, 1948, the Assistant Commissioner of Immigration and Naturalization recommended that she be permanently excluded without a hearing on the ground that her admission would be prejudicial to the interests of the United States. On the same day the Attorney General adopted this recommendation and entered a final order of exclusion. To test the right of the Attorney General to exclude her without a hearing for security reasons, *habeas corpus* proceedings were instituted in the Southern District of New York, based primarily on provisions of the War Brides Act. The District Court dismissed the writ, and the Court of Appeals affirmed.

The authority of the Attorney General to order the exclusion of aliens without a hearing flows from the Act of June 21, 1941, amending § 1 of the Act of May 22, 1918 (55 Stat. 252, 22 U.S.C. § 223). By the 1941 amendment it was provided that the President might, upon finding that the interests of the United States required it, impose additional restrictions and prohibitions on the entry into and departure of persons from the United States during the national emergency proclaimed May 27, 1941. Pursuant to this Act of Congress the President on November 14, 1941, issued Proclamation 2523. This proclamation recited that the interests of the United States required the imposition of additional restrictions upon the entry into and departure of persons from the country and authorized the promulgation of regulations jointly by the Secretary of State and the Attorney General. It was also provided that no alien should be permitted to enter the United States if it were found that such entry would be prejudicial to the interests of the United States.

Pursuant to the authority of this proclamation the Secretary of State and the Attorney General issued regulations governing the entry into and departure of persons from the United States during the national emergency. Subparagraphs (a) to (k) of § 175.53 of these regulations specified the classes of aliens whose entry into the United States was deemed prejudicial to the public interest. Subparagraph (b) of § 175.57 provided that the Attorney General might deny an alien a hearing before a board of inquiry in special cases where he determined that the alien was excludable under the regulations on the basis of information of a confidential nature, the disclosure of which would be prejudicial to the public interest.

It was under this regulation § 175.57(b) that petitioner was excluded by the Attorney General and denied a hearing. We are asked to pass upon the validity of this action.

At the outset we wish to point out that an alien who seeks admission to this country may not do so under any claim of right. Admission of aliens to the United States is a privilege granted by the sovereign United States Government. Such privilege is granted to an alien only upon such terms as the United States shall prescribe. It must be exercised in accordance with the procedure which the United States provides. *Nishimura Ekiu* v. *United States,* 142 U.S. 651, 659, 12 S.Ct. 336, 338, 35 L.Ed. 1146; *Fong Yue Ting* v. *United States,* 149 U.S. 698, 711, 13 S.Ct. 1016, 1021, 37 L.Ed. 905.

Petitioner contends that the 1941 Act and the regulations thereunder are void to the extent that they contain unconstitutional delegations of legislative power. But there is no question of inappropriate delegation of legislative power involved here. The exclusion of aliens is a fundamental act of sovereignty. The right to do so stems not alone from legislative power but is inherent in the executive power to control the foreign affairs of the nation. When Congress prescribes a procedure concerning the admissibility of aliens, it is not dealing alone with a legislative power. It is implementing an inherent executive power.

Thus the decision to admit or to exclude an alien may be lawfully placed with the President, who may in turn delegate the carrying out of this function to a responsible executive officer of the sovereign, such as the Attorney General. The action of the executive officer under such authority is final and conclusive. Whatever the rule may be concerning deportation of persons who have gained entry into the United States, it is not within the province of any court, unless expressly authorized by law, to review the determination of the political branch of the Government to exclude a given alien. *Nishimura Ekiu* v. *United States,* 142 U.S. 651, 659–660, 12 S.Ct. 336, 338, 35 L.Ed. 1146; *Fong Yue Ting* v. *United States,* 149 U.S. 698, 713–714, 13 S.Ct. 1016, 1022, 37 L.Ed. 905; *Ludecke* v. *Watkins,* 335 U.S. 160, 68 S.Ct. 1429, 92 L.Ed. 1881. *Cf. Yamataya* v. *Fisher,* 189 U.S. 86, 101, 23 S.Ct. 611, 614, 47 L.Ed. 721. Normally Congress supplies the conditions of the privilege of entry into the United States. But because the power of exclusion of aliens is also inherent in the executive department of the sovereign, Congress may in broad terms authorize the executive to exercise the power, *e.g.,* as was done here, for the best interests of the country during a time of national emergency. Executive officers may be entrusted with the duty of specifying the procedures for carrying out the congressional intent. What was said in *Lichter* v. *United States,* 334 U.S. 742, 785, 68 S.Ct. 1294, 1316, 92 L.Ed. 1694, is equally appropriate here:

> "It is not necessary that Congress supply administrative officials with a specific formula for their guidance in a field where flexibility and the adaptation of the congressional policy to infinitely variable conditions constitute the essence of the program.... Standards prescribed by Congress are to be read in the light of the conditions to which they are to be applied. 'They derive much meaningful content from the purpose of the Act, its factual background and the statutory context in which they appear.'"

Whatever the procedure authorized by Congress is, it is due process as far as an alien denied entry is concerned. *Nishimura Ekiu* v. *United States, supra; Ludecke* v. *Watkins, supra.*

In the particular circumstances of the instant case the Attorney General, exercising the discretion entrusted to him by Congress and the President, concluded upon the basis of confidential information that the public interest required that petitioner be denied the privilege of entry into the United States. He denied her a hearing on the matter because, in his judgment, the disclosure of the information on which he based that opinion would itself endanger the public security.

We find no substantial merit to petitioner's contention that the regulations were not "reasonable" as they were required to be by the 1941 Act. We think them reasonable in the circumstances of the period for which they were authorized, namely, the national emergency of World War II. * * * We reiterate that we are dealing here with a matter of *privilege.* Petitioner had no vested *right* of entry which could be the subject of a prohibition against retroactive operation of regulations affecting her status.

Affirmed.

Mr. Justice Jackson, whom Mr. Justice Black and Mr. Justice Frankfurter join, dissenting.

I do not question the constitutional power of Congress to authorize immigration authorities to turn back from our gates any alien or class of aliens. But I do not find that Congress has authorized an abrupt and brutal exclusion of the wife of an American citizen without a hearing.

* * *

[JUSTICE FRANKFURTER'S dissenting opinion is omitted. JUSTICE DOUGLAS and JUSTICE CLARK took no part in deciding the case.]

SHAUGHNESSY v. UNITED STATES ex rel. MEZEI

Supreme Court of the United States, 1953.
345 U.S. 206, 73 S.Ct. 625, 97 L.Ed. 956.

MR. JUSTICE CLARK delivered the opinion of the Court.

This case concerns an alien immigrant permanently excluded from the United States on security grounds but stranded in his temporary haven on Ellis Island because other countries will not take him back. The issue is whether the Attorney General's continued exclusion of respondent without a hearing amounts to an unlawful detention, so that courts may admit him temporarily to the United States on bond until arrangements are made for his departure abroad. After a hearing on respondent's petition for a writ of habeas corpus, the District Court so held and authorized his temporary admission on $5,000 bond. The Court of Appeals affirmed that action, but directed reconsideration of the terms of the parole. Accordingly, the District Court entered a modified order reducing bond to $3,000 and permitting respondent to travel and reside in Buffalo, New York. Bond was posted and respondent released. Because of resultant serious problems in the enforcement of the immigration laws, we granted certiorari.

Respondent's present dilemma springs from these circumstances: Though, as the District Court observed, "[t]here is a certain vagueness about [his] history", respondent seemingly was born in Gibraltar of Hungarian or Rumanian parents and lived in the United States from 1923 to 1948. In May of that year he sailed for Europe, apparently to visit his dying mother in Rumania. Denied entry there, he remained in Hungary for some 19 months, due to "difficulty in securing an exit permit." Finally, armed with a quota immigration visa issued by the American Consul in Budapest, he proceeded to France and boarded the *Ile de France* in Le Havre bound for New York. Upon arrival on February 9, 1950, he was temporarily excluded from the United States by an immigration inspector acting pursuant to the Passport Act as amended and regulations thereunder [the same statute and regulations applied in the *Knauff* case].

Pending disposition of his case he was received at Ellis Island. After reviewing the evidence, the Attorney General on May 10, 1950, ordered the temporary exclusion to be made permanent without a hearing before a board of special inquiry, on the "basis of information of a confidential nature, the disclosure of which would be prejudicial to the public interest." That determination rested on a finding that respondent's entry would be prejudicial to the public interest for security reasons. But thus far all attempts to effect respondent's departure have failed: Twice he shipped out to return whence he came; France and Great Britain refused him permission to land. The State Department has unsuccessfully negotiated with Hungary for his readmission. Respondent personally applied for entry to about a dozen Latin American countries but all turned him down. So in June 1951 respondent advised the Immigration and Naturalization Service that he would exert no further efforts to depart. In short, respondent sat on Ellis Island because this country shut him out and others were unwilling to take him in.

Asserting unlawful confinement on Ellis Island, he sought relief through a series of habeas corpus proceedings. After four unsuccessful efforts on respondent's part, the United States District Court for the Southern District of New York on November 9, 1951, sustained the writ. The District Judge, vexed by the problem of "an alien who has no place to go", did not question the validity of the exclusion order but deemed further "detention" after 21 months excessive and justifiable only by affirmative proof of respondent's danger to the public safety. When the Government declined to divulge such evidence, even *in camera,* the District Court directed respondent's conditional parole on bond. By a divided vote, the Court of Appeals affirmed. Postulating that the power to hold could never be broader than the power to remove or shut out and that to "continue an alien's confinement beyond that moment when deportation becomes patently impossible is to deprive him of his liberty", the court found respondent's "confinement" no longer justifiable as a means of removal elsewhere, thus not authorized by statute, and in violation of due process. Judge Learned Hand, dissenting, took a different view: The Attorney General's order was one of "exclusion" and not "deportation"; respondent's transfer from ship to shore on Ellis Island conferred no additional rights; in fact, no alien so situated "can force us to admit him at all."

* * *

It is true that aliens who have once passed through our gates, even illegally, may be expelled only after proceedings conforming to traditional standards of fairness encompassed in due process of law. The Japanese Immigrant Case (Kaoru Yamataya v. Fisher), 1903, 189 U.S. 86, 100–101, 23 S.Ct. 611, 614, 47 L.Ed. 721; Wong Yang Sung v. McGrath, 1950, 339 U.S. 33, 49–50, 70 S.Ct. 445, 453–454, 94 L.Ed. 616; Kwong Hai Chew v. Colding, 1953, 344 U.S. 590, 598, 73 S.Ct. 472, 478. But an alien on the threshold of initial entry stands on a different footing: "Whatever the procedure authorized by Congress is, it is due process as far as an alien denied entry is concerned." United States ex rel. Knauff v. Shaughnessy, *supra.* And because the action of the executive officer under such authority is final and conclusive, the Attorney General cannot be compelled to disclose the evidence underlying his determinations in an exclusion case; "it is not within the province of any court, unless expressly authorized by law, to review the determination of the political branch of the Government". United States ex rel. Knauff v. Shaughnessy. In a case such as this, courts cannot retry the determination of the Attorney General.

Neither respondent's harborage on Ellis Island nor his prior residence here transforms this into something other than an exclusion proceeding. Concededly, his movements are restrained by authority of the United States, and he may by habeas corpus test the validity of his exclusion. But that is true whether he enjoys temporary refuge on land, or remains continuously aboard ship. In sum, harborage at Ellis Island is not an entry into the United States. For purposes of the immigration laws, moreover, the legal incidents of an alien's entry remain unaltered whether he has been here once before or not. He is an entering alien just the same, and may be excluded if unqualified for admission under existing immigration laws.

To be sure, a lawful resident alien may not captiously be deprived of his constitutional rights to procedural due process. Kwong Hai Chew v. Colding, 1953, 344 U.S. 590, 601, 73 S.Ct. 472, 479; Cf. Delgadillo v. Carmichael, 1947, 332 U.S. 388, 68 S.Ct. 10, 92 L.Ed. 17. Only the other day we held that under some circumstances temporary absence from our shores cannot constitutionally deprive a returning lawfully resident alien of his right to be heard. Kwong Hai Chew v. Colding, supra. Chew, an alien seaman admitted by an Act of Congress to permanent residence in the United States, signed articles of maritime employment as chief steward on a vessel of American registry with home port in New York City. Though cleared by the Coast Guard for his voyage, on his return from four months at sea he was "excluded" without a hearing on security grounds. On the facts of that case, including reference to § 307(d)(2) of the Nationality Act of 1940, we felt justified in "assimilating" his status for constitutional purposes to that of continuously present alien residents entitled to hearings at least before an executive or administrative tribunal. Accordingly, to escape constitutional conflict we held the administrative regulations authorizing exclusion without hearing in certain security cases inapplicable to aliens so protected by the Fifth Amendment.

But respondent's history here drastically differs from that disclosed in Chew's case. Unlike Chew who with full security clearance and documentation pursued his vocation for four months aboard an American ship, respondent, apparently without authorization or reentry papers,[9] simply left the United States and remained behind the Iron Curtain for 19 months. Moreover, while § 307 of the 1940 Nationality Act regards maritime service such as Chew's to be continuous residence for naturalization purposes, that section deems protracted absence such as respondent's a clear break in an alien's continuous residence here. In such circumstances, we have no difficulty in holding respondent an entrant alien or "assimilated to [that] status" for constitutional purposes. That being so, the Attorney General may lawfully exclude respondent without a hearing as authorized by the emergency regulations promulgated pursuant to the Passport Act. Nor need he disclose the evidence upon which that deter-

9. * * * Of course, neither a reentry permit, issuable upon proof of prior lawful admission to the United States, nor an immigration visa entitles an otherwise inadmissible alien to entry. An immigrant is not unaware of this; [the statute] directs those facts to be "printed conspicuously upon every immigration visa." * * *

mination rests. United States ex rel. Knauff v. Shaughnessy, 1950, 338 U.S. 537, 70 S.Ct. 309, 94 L.Ed. 317.

There remains the issue of respondent's continued exclusion on Ellis Island. Aliens seeking entry from contiguous lands obviously can be turned back at the border without more. While the Government might keep entrants by sea aboard the vessel pending determination of their admissibility, resulting hardships to the alien and inconvenience to the carrier persuaded Congress to adopt a more generous course. By statute it authorized, in cases such as this, aliens' temporary removal from ship to shore. But such temporary harborage, an act of legislative grace, bestows no additional rights. Congress meticulously specified that such shelter ashore "shall not be considered a landing" nor relieve the vessel of the duty to transport back the alien if ultimately excluded. And this Court has long considered such temporary arrangements as not affecting an alien's status; he is treated as if stopped at the border.

Thus we do not think that respondent's continued exclusion deprives him of any statutory or constitutional right. It is true that resident aliens temporarily detained pending expeditious consummation of deportation proceedings may be released on bond by the Attorney General whose discretion is subject to judicial review. Carlson v. Landon, 1952, 342 U.S. 524, 72 S.Ct. 525, 96 L.Ed. 547. By that procedure aliens uprooted from our midst may rejoin the community until the Government effects their leave. An exclusion proceeding grounded on danger to the national security, however, presents different considerations; neither the rationale nor the statutory authority for such release exists. Ordinarily to admit an alien barred from entry on security grounds nullifies the very purpose of the exclusion proceeding; Congress in 1950 declined to include such authority in the statute. That exclusion by the United States plus other nations inhospitality results in present hardship cannot be ignored. But, the times being what they are, Congress may well have felt that other countries ought not shift the onus to us; that an alien in respondent's position is no more ours than theirs. Whatever our individual estimate of that policy and the fears on which it rests, respondent's right to enter the United States depends on the congressional will, and courts cannot substitute their judgment for the legislative mandate.

Reversed.

MR. JUSTICE BLACK, with whom MR. JUSTICE DOUGLAS concurs, dissenting.

Mezei came to this country in 1923 and lived as a resident alien in Buffalo, New York, for twenty-five years. He made a trip to Europe in 1948 and was stopped at our shore on his return in 1950. Without charge of or conviction for any crime, he was for two years held a prisoner on Ellis Island by order of the Attorney General. Mezei sought habeas corpus in the District Court. He wanted to go to his wife and home in Buffalo. The Attorney General defended the imprisonment by alleging that it would be dangerous to the Nation's security to let Mezei go home even temporarily on bail. Asked for proof of this, the Attorney General answered the judge that all his information was "of a confidential nature" so much so that telling any of it or even telling the names of any of his secret informers would jeopardize the safety of the Nation. Finding that Mezei's life as a resident alien in Buffalo had been "unexceptional" and that no facts had been proven to justify his continued imprisonment, the District Court granted bail. The Court of Appeals approved. Now this Court orders Mezei to leave his home and go back to his island prison to stay indefinitely, maybe for life.

MR. JUSTICE JACKSON forcefully points out the danger in the Court's holding that Mezei's liberty is completely at the mercy of the unreviewable discretion of the Attorney General. I join MR. JUSTICE JACKSON in the belief that Mezei's continued imprisonment without a hearing violates due process of law.

* * *

MR. JUSTICE JACKSON, whom MR. JUSTICE FRANKFURTER joins, dissenting.

Fortunately it still is startling, in this country, to find a person held indefinitely in executive custody without accusation of crime or judicial trial. Executive imprisonment has been considered oppressive and lawless since John, at Runnymede, pledged that no free man should be imprisoned, dispossessed, outlawed, or exiled save by the judgment of his peers or by the law of the land. The judges of England developed the writ of habeas corpus largely to preserve these immunities from executive restraint.

Under the best tradition of Anglo-American law, courts will not deny hearing to an unconvicted prisoner just because he is an alien whose keep, in legal theory, is just outside our gates. Lord Mansfield, in the celebrated case holding that slavery was unknown to the common law of England, ran his writ of habeas corpus in favor of an alien, an African Negro slave, and against the master of a ship at anchor in the Thames.

I.

What is our case?[2] In contemplation of law, I agree, it is that of an alien who asks admission to the country. Concretely, however, it is that of a lawful and law-abiding inhabitant of our country for a quarter of a century, long ago admitted for permanent residence, who seeks to return home. After a foreign visit to his aged and ailing mother that was prolonged by disturbed conditions of Eastern Europe, he obtained a visa for admission issued by our consul and returned to New York. There the Attorney General refused to honor his documents and turned him back as a menace to this Nation's security. This man, who seems to have led a life of unrelieved insignificance, must have been astonished to find himself suddenly putting the Government of the United States in such fear that it was afraid to tell him why it was afraid of him. He was shipped and reshipped to France, which twice refused him landing. Great Britain declined, and no other European country has been found willing to open

---

2. I recite facts alleged in the petition for the writ. Since the Government declined to try the case on the merits, I think we must consider the question on well-pleaded allegations of the petition. Petitioner might fail to make good on a hearing; the question is, must he fail without one?

its doors to him. Twelve countries of the American Hemisphere refused his applications. Since we proclaimed him a Samson who might pull down the pillars of our temple, we should not be surprised if peoples less prosperous, less strongly established and less stable feared to take him off our timorous hands. With something of a record as an unwanted man, neither his efforts nor those of the United States Government any longer promise to find him an abiding place. For nearly two years he was held in custody of the immigration authorities of the United States at Ellis Island, and if the Government has its way he seems likely to be detained indefinitely, perhaps for life, for a cause known only to the Attorney General.

Is respondent deprived of liberty? The Government answers that he was "transferred to Ellis Island on August 1, 1950 for safekeeping," and "is not being detained in the usual sense, but is in custody solely to prevent him from gaining entry into the United States in violation of law. He is free to depart from the United States to any country of his choice." Government counsel ingeniously argued that Ellis Island is his "refuge" whence he is free to take leave in any direction except west. That might mean freedom, if only he were an amphibian! Realistically, this man is incarcerated by a combination of forces which keeps him as effectually as a prison, the dominant and proximate of these forces being the United States immigration authority. It overworks legal fiction to say that one is free in law when by the commonest of common sense he is bound. Despite the impeccable legal logic of the Government's argument on this point, it leads to an artificial and unreal conclusion. We must regard this alien as deprived of liberty, and the question is whether the deprivation is a denial of due process of law.

The Government on this point argues that "no alien has any constitutional right to entry into the United States"; that "the alien has only such rights as Congress sees fit to grant in exclusion proceedings"; that "the so-called detention is still merely a continuation of the exclusion which is specifically authorized by Congress"; that since "the restraint is not incidental to an order [of exclusion] but is itself the effectuation of the exclusion order, there is no limit to its continuance" other than statutory, which means no limit at all. The Government all but adopts the words of one of the officials responsible for the administration of this Act who testified before a congressional committee as to an alien applicant, that "He has no rights."

The interpretations of the Fifth Amendment's command that no person shall be deprived of life, liberty or property without due process of law, come about to this: reasonable general legislation reasonably applied to the individual. The question is whether the Government's detention of respondent is compatible with these tests of substance and procedure.

II. SUBSTANTIVE DUE PROCESS

* * *

Due process does not invest any alien with a right to enter the United States, nor confer on those admitted the right to remain against the national will. Nothing in the Constitution requires admission or sufferance of aliens hostile to our scheme of government.

Nor do I doubt that due process of law will tolerate some impounding of an alien where it is deemed essential to the safety of the state.

* * *

I conclude that detention of an alien would not be inconsistent with substantive due process, provided—and this is where my dissent begins— he is accorded procedural due process of law.

III. PROCEDURAL DUE PROCESS

Procedural fairness, if not all that originally was meant by due process of law, is at least what it most uncompromisingly requires. Procedural due process is more elemental and less flexible than substantive due process. It yields less to the times, varies less with conditions, and defers much less to legislative judgment. Insofar as it is technical law, it must be a specialized responsibility within the competence of the judiciary on which they do not bend before political branches of the Government, as they should on matters of policy which compromise substantive law.

If it be conceded that in some way this alien could be confined, does it matter what the procedure is? Only the untaught layman or the charlatan lawyer can answer that procedures matter not. Procedural fairness and regularity are of the indispensable essence of liberty. Severe substantive laws can be endured if they are fairly and impartially applied. Indeed, if put to the choice, one might well prefer to live under Soviet substantive law applied in good faith by our common-law procedures than under our substantive law enforced by Soviet procedural practices. Let it not be overlooked that due process of law is not for the sole benefit of an accused. It is the best insurance for the Government itself against those blunders which leave lasting stains on a system of justice but which are bound to occur on *ex parte* consideration. Cf. United States ex rel. Knauff v. Shaughnessy, 338 U.S. 537, 70 S.Ct. 309, 94 L.Ed. 317, which was a near miss, saved by further administrative and congressional hearings from perpetrating an injustice. *See* Knauff, *The Ellen Knauff Story* (New York) 1952.

Our law may, and rightly does, place more restrictions on the alien than on the citizen. But basic fairness in hearing procedures does not vary with the status of the accused. If the procedures used to judge this alien are fair and just, no good reason can be given why they should not be extended to simplify the condemnation of citizens. If they would be unfair to citizens, we cannot defend the fairness of them when applied to the more helpless and handicapped alien. This is at the root of our holdings that the resident alien must be given a fair hearing to test an official claim that he is one of a deportable class. Wong Yang Sung v. McGrath, 339 U.S. 33, 70 S.Ct. 445, 94 L.Ed. 616.

The most scrupulous observance of due process, including the right to know a charge, to be confronted with the accuser, to cross-examine informers and to produce evidence in one's behalf, is especially necessary where the occasion of detention is fear of future misconduct, rather than crimes committed.

* * *

Because the respondent has no right of entry, does it follow that he has no rights at all? Does the power to exclude mean that exclusion may be continued or effectuated by any means which happen to seem appropriate to the authorities? It would effectuate his exclusion to eject him bodily into the sea or to set him adrift in a rowboat. Would not such measures be condemned judicially as a deprivation of life without due process of law? Suppose the authorities decide to disable an alien from entry by confiscating his valuables and money. Would we not hold this a taking of property without due process of law? Here we have a case that lies between the taking of life and the taking of property; it is the taking of liberty. It seems to me that this, occurring within the United States or its territorial waters, may be done only by proceedings which meet the test of due process of law.

Exclusion of an alien without judicial hearing, of course, does not deny due process when it can be accomplished merely by turning him back on land or returning him by sea. But when indefinite confinement becomes the means of enforcing exclusion, it seems to me that due process requires that the alien be informed of its grounds and have a fair chance to overcome them. This is the more due him when he is entrapped into leaving the other shore by reliance on a visa which the Attorney General refuses to honor.

It is evident that confinement of respondent no longer can be justified as a step in the process of turning him back to the country whence he came. Confinement is no longer ancillary to exclusion; it can now be justified only as the alternative to normal exclusion. It is an end in itself.

The Communist conspiratorial technique of infiltration poses a problem which sorely tempts the Government to resort to confinement of suspects on secret information secretly judged. I have not been one to discount the Communist evil. But my apprehensions about the security of our form of government are about equally aroused by those who refuse to recognize the dangers of Communism and those who will not see danger in anything else.

Congress has ample power to determine whom we will admit to our shores and by what means it will effectuate its exclusion policy. The only limitation is that it may not do so by authorizing United States officers to take without due process of law the life, the liberty or the property of an alien who has come within our jurisdiction; and that means he must meet a fair hearing with fair notice of the charges.[9]

9. The trial court sought to reconcile due process for the individual with claims of security by suggesting that the Attorney General disclose *in camera* enough to enable a judicial determination of the legality of the confinement. The Attorney General re- fused. I do not know just how an *in camera* proceeding would be handled in this kind of case. If respondent, with or without counsel, were present, disclosures to them might well result in disclosures by them. If they are not allowed to be present, it is hard to

It is inconceivable to me that this measure of simple justice and fair dealing would menace the security of this country. No one can make me believe that we are that far gone.

HENRY HART, THE POWER OF CONGRESS TO LIMIT THE JURISDICTION OF THE FEDERAL COURTS: AN EXERCISE IN DIALECTIC

66 Harv.L.Rev. 1362, 1389–96 (1953).

* * *

Q. How then can aliens have any rights to assert in habeas corpus? I thought they came and stayed only at the pleasure of Congress.

A. The Supreme Court seemed to think so, too, at first. In its earliest decisions the Court started with the premise of plenary legislative power and on that basis seemed to be prepared to take the word "final" in the statutes literally and to decline any review whatever, even in deportation cases.[84]

Before long, however, it began to see that the premise needed to be qualified—that a power to lay down general rules, even if it were plenary, did not necessarily include a power to be arbitrary or to authorize administrative officials to be arbitrary. It saw that, on the contrary, the very existence of a jurisdiction in habeas corpus, coupled with the constitutional guarantee of due process, implied a regime of law. It saw that in such a regime the courts had a responsibility to see that statutory authority was not transgressed, that a reasonable procedure was used in exercising the authority, and—seemingly also—that human beings were not unreasonably subjected, even by direction of Congress, to an uncontrolled official discretion.[85]

see how it would answer the purpose of testing the Government's case by cross-examination or counter-evidence, which is what a hearing is for. The questions raised by the proposal need not be discussed since they do not call for decision here.

84. The Chinese Exclusion Case, 130 U.S. 581 (1889) (admission); Nishimura Ekiu v. United States, 142 U.S. 651 (1892) (admission); Fong Yue Ting v. United States, 149 U.S. 698 (1893) (deportation); Lem Moon Sing v. United States, 158 U.S. 538 (1895) (admission); Li Sing v. United States, 180 U.S. 486 (1901) (deportation); Fok Yung Yo v. United States, 185 U.S. 296 (1902) (admission); Lee Lung v. Patterson, 186 U.S. 168 (1902) (admission).

85. The turning point was the Japanese Immigrant Case (Yamataya v. Fisher), 189 U.S. 86 (1903), involving an immigrant taken into custody for deportation four days after her landing. After referring to earlier cases cited in note 84, *supra*, the Court said:

But this court has never held, nor must we now be understood as holding, that administrative officers, when executing the provisions of a statute involving the liberty of persons, may disregard the fundamental principles that inhere in "due process of law" as understood at the time of the adoption of the Constitution. One of these principles is that no person shall be deprived of his liberty without opportunity, at some time, to be heard, before such officers, in respect of the matters upon which that liberty depends. . . . No such arbitrary power can exist where the principles involved in due process of law are recognized.

This is the reasonable construction of the acts of Congress here in question, and they need not be otherwise interpreted. . . . An act of Congress must be taken to be constitutional unless the contrary plainly and palpably appears. *Id.* at 100–01.

Compare Justice Holmes' formulation in *Chin Yow* [*v. United States,* 208 U.S. 8, 12 (1908),] an admission case: "The decision of the Department is final, but that is on the presupposition that the decision was after a

Under the benign influence of these ideas, the law grew and flourished, like Egypt under the rule of Joseph. Thousands of cases were decided whose presence in the courts cannot be explained on any other basis. But what the status of many of these cases is now is not altogether clear.

Q. Why?

A. There arose up new justices in Washington which knew not Joseph. Citing only the harsh precepts of the very earliest decisions, they began to decide cases accordingly, as if nothing had happened in the years between.

In the *Knauff* case, Justice Minton said that, "Whatever the rule may be concerning deportation of persons who have gained entry into the United States, it is not within the province of any court, unless expressly authorized by law, to review the determination of the political branch of the Government to exclude a given alien." Since Congress has never expressly authorized any court to review an exclusion order, this statement either ignores or renders obsolete every habeas corpus case in the books involving an exclusion proceeding.

On the procedural side, Justice Minton went so far as to say that, "Whatever the procedure authorized by Congress is, it is due process as far as an alien denied entry is concerned," a patently preposterous proposition.

Justice Clark repeated and applied both statements in the *Mezei* case.

Q. Then we're back where we started half a century ago?

A. Oh no. The aberrations have been largely confined to admission cases. In deportations, for the most part, the Court has adhered to the sound and humane philosophy of the middle period. In some respects it has even extended its applications.

What is happening is what so often happens when there has been a development in the law of which the judges are incompletely aware. Some decisions follow the earlier precedents and some the later, until the conflict of principle becomes intolerable, and it gets ironed out.

Q. Do you mean to say that you don't think there are any material differences between the case of an alien trying to get into the country and the case of one whom the Government is trying to put out?

A. No. Of course there are differences in these alien cases—not only those simple ones but many others.[92] But such differences are

hearing in good faith, however summary in form."

* * *

92. For example, if the alien is applying for admission, the force of his claim may vary according to whether he is coming for the first time or seeking to resume a permanent residence previously authorized. If he is coming for the first time, it may make a difference whether he is a stowaway or in possession of a duly authorized visa. If he has a visa, it may make a difference whether it is one for permanent residence or only for a temporary visit. If he is seeking to resume a previously authorized residence, it may make a difference whether he carries a reentry permit, border crossing card, or other document purporting to facilitate reentry.

Similarly, if the alien is resisting expulsion, the force of his claim may vary according to whether he entered legally or illegal-

material only in determining the content of due process in the particular situation. What process is due always depends upon the circumstances, and the Due Process Clause is always flexible enough to take the circumstances into account.

The distinctions the Court has been drawing recently, however, are of a different order. They are distinctions between when the Constitution applies and when it does not apply at all. Any such distinction as that produces a conflict of basic principle, and is inadmissible.

Q. What basic principle?

A. The great and generating principle of this whole body of law— that the Constitution always applies when a court is sitting with jurisdiction in habeas corpus. For then the court has always to inquire, not only whether the statutes have been observed, but whether the petitioner before it has been "deprived of life, liberty, or property, without due process of law," or injured in any other way in violation of the fundamental law.

That is the premise of the deportation cases, and it applies in exactly the same way in admission cases. The harsh early decisions announcing a contrary premise applied such a contrary premise without distinction in both deportations and admissions. Indeed, Justice Minton cited early admission and deportation precedents indiscriminately in *Knauff,* without noticing that the principle which had compelled repudiation of the deportation precedents required repudiation also of the others.

That principle forbids a constitutional court with jurisdiction in habeas corpus from ever accepting as an adequate return to the writ the mere statement that what has been done is authorized by act of Congress. The inquiry remains, if *Marbury v. Madison* still stands, whether the act of Congress is consistent with the fundamental law. Only upon such a principle could the Court reject, as it surely would, a return to the writ which informed it that the applicant for admission lay stretched upon a rack with pins driven in behind his finger nails pursuant to authority duly conferred by statute in order to secure the information necessary to determine his admissibility. The same principle which would justify rejection of this return imposes responsibility to inquire into the adequacy of other returns.

Granting that the requirements of due process must vary with the circumstances, and allowing them all the flexibility that can conceivably be claimed, it still remains true that the Court is obliged, by the presuppositions of its whole jurisdiction in this area, to decide whether what has been done is consistent with due process—and not simply pass back the buck to an assertedly all-powerful and unimpeachable Congress.

Q. Would it have made any difference in *Knauff* and *Mezei* if the Court had said that the aliens were entitled to due process and had got it, instead of saying that they weren't entitled to it at all?

---

ly. If he entered legally, it may make a difference whether he was duly admitted for permanent residence or came in only as a   seaman, student, or other temporary visitor for business or pleasure.

A.   At least the opinions in that case might have been intellectually respectable. Whether the results would have been different depends upon subtler considerations. Usually, however, it *does* make a difference whether a judge treats a question as not properly before him at all, or as involving a matter for decision.

Take *Knauff,* for example. Remember that the War Brides Act was highly ambiguous on the point in issue of whether exclusion without a hearing was authorized. If one approaches such a question on the assumption that it is constitutionally neutral, as Justice Minton declared it to be, it is at least possible to resolve the doubt as he resolved it. But if one sees constitutional overtones, the most elementary principles of interpretation call for the opposite conclusion. Note how crucially important constitutional assumptions have been in the interpretation of statutes throughout this whole area.

Again, take the facts of *Mezei,* in comparison with its *dicta.* The *dicta* say, in effect, that a Mexican wetback who sneaks successfully across the Rio Grande is entitled to the full panoply of due process in his deportation. But the holding says that a duly admitted immigrant of twenty-five years' standing who has married an American wife and sired American children, who goes abroad as the law allows to visit a dying parent, and who then returns with passport and visa duly issued by an American consul, is entitled to nothing—and, indeed, may be detained on an island in New York harbor for the rest of his life if no other country can be found to take him.

I cannot believe that judges adequately aware of the foundations of principle in this field would permit themselves to trivialize the great guarantees of due process and the freedom writ by such distinctions. And I cannot believe that judges taking responsibility for an affirmative declaration that due process has been accorded would permit themselves to arrive at such brutal conclusions.

Q.   But that is what the Court has held. And so I guess that's that.

A.   No, it isn't.

The deepest assumptions of the legal order require that the decisions of the highest court in the land be accepted as settling the rights and wrongs of the particular matter immediately in controversy. But the judges who sit for the time being on the court have no authority to remake by fiat alone the fabric of principle by which future cases are to be decided. They are only the custodians of the law and not the owners of it. The law belongs to the people of the country, and to the hundreds of thousands of lawyers and judges who through the years have struggled, in their behalf, to make it coherent and intelligible and responsive to the people's sense of justice.

And so, when justices of the Supreme Court sit down and write opinions in behalf of the Court which ignore the painful forward steps of a whole half century of adjudication, making no effort to relate what then is being done to what the Court has done before, they write without authority for the future. The appeal to principle is still open and, so long as courts of the United States sit with general jurisdiction in habeas corpus, that means an appeal to them and their successors.

* * *

T. ALEXANDER ALEINIKOFF, ALIENS, DUE PROCESS AND "COMMUNITY TIES": A RESPONSE TO MARTIN

44 U.Pitt.L.Rev. 237, 258–59 (1983).

It is not hard to imagine the potential harshness that *Knauff* and *Mezei* can work on the alien at the border. But I would argue that it has been the immigration policymakers and enforcement officials who have suffered the most under the hands-off approach of *Knauff* and *Mezei* in recent years.

In most areas of law, constitutional due process has developed as a dialogue between the courts and the other branches of government. As notions of what constitutes fundamental fairness have evolved over time, the courts have "persuaded" legislators and administrators to add procedural protections when important liberty or property interests are at stake. Even in immigration law, the Court's demand for due process in deportation hearings has produced a steady conversation between the Congress and the courts.

This growth of process is less likely when the Supreme Court announces that it has no role to play. Such is the situation of the alien at the border. The clear signal of *Knauff* and *Mezei* is that the government is free—at least as to initial entrants and undocumented aliens at the border—to provide the procedures it deems appropriate. Given the perceived crush of aliens at the gates, the cost of process, and the difficulty of patrolling tens of thousands of miles of land and sea borders, it is not unreasonable to assume that Congress will opt for less rather than more process. More importantly, the border officials will search for ways to avoid the procedures that Congress mandates.

Recent cases involving the deportation, exclusion and detention of aliens from Haiti and El Salvador indicate that this predictable response to a hands-off approach from the courts has in fact occurred. Not only has due process, up until now, withered on the vine at the border, but the government in such cases continues to argue that the courts have no authority to intervene at all because the cases involve "political questions" and issues of international relations.

Lower courts will obey *Knauff* and *Mezei* for a long time, leading government officials down the garden path. But when the government conduct becomes so outrageous, so obviously unfair, federal judges will put a stop to it. In attempting to do so, however, they will not be able to simply add another flower in the garden of due process, because due process has never taken root at the border. Thus the courts are forced to leap in with both feet, demanding costly and intrusive procedures that make control of the borders and deportation of aliens considerably more difficult.

This is hardly a healthy way for due process to grow; and the results have ramifications beyond the domain of immigration law. If notions of due process reflect judgments of our society about fairness and the importance of procedural regularity, these norms should have their source in as broad a range of human experience as possible. * * *

Notes

1. Congressional and public pressure eventually secured the release of both Knauff and Mezei. Ellen Knauff was ultimately granted a full hearing at which the adverse information was revealed. Although the special inquiry officer ruled against her, the BIA reversed that result on appeal and admitted her to the United States, in a lengthy opinion setting forth in detail the slender evidence that had formed the basis for the Justice Department's initial judgment that she was dangerous. The BIA opinion is reprinted as an appendix to the book she wrote about her experience. E. Knauff, *The Ellen Knauff Story* (1952). Ignatz Mezei secured his release under a special clemency measure after he had spent nearly four years in detention on Ellis Island. Unlike Knauff, he was paroled rather than formally admitted. *See Trop v. Dulles*, 356 U.S. 86, 102 n. 36, 78 S.Ct. 590, 599 n. 36, 2 L.Ed.2d 630 (1957); Davis, *The Requirements of a Trial-Type Hearing*, 70 Harv.L.Rev. 193, 251 (1956).

2. In 1952, Congress provided explicit statutory authority for the kinds of secret procedures that were employed against Knauff and Mezei on the authority of regulations alone. Section 235(c) of the INA, unchanged since 1952, now permits the Attorney General to order exclusion without a hearing if he acts on the basis of "information of a confidential nature, the disclosure of which * * * would be prejudicial to the public interest, safety, or security." It is invoked far less frequently today than it was in the 1950's, but it is still employed on occasion. *See, e.g., El-Werfalli v. Smith* 547 F.Supp. 152 (S.D.N.Y.1982) (court sustains exclusion under § 212(a)(27), based on confidential information, of Libyan student coming to attend classes in aircraft training).

3. Professor Hart reads *Mezei* as stating, in dicta, that clandestine entrants ("Mexican wetbacks") receive the full panoply of due process rights in deportation proceedings. If so, the case creates an obvious inducement to enter without inspection, for the alien then winds up in a better constitutional position than the unfortunate soul who does as he is supposed to do and presents himself for inspection at the port of entry. Such a result is at best ironic, as several courts have noted. *See, e.g., Louis v. Nelson*, 544 F.Supp. 973, 977 (S.D.Fla.1982), *affirmed in part sub nom. Jean v. Nelson*, 727 F.2d 957 (11th Cir.1984), *cert. granted,* ___ U.S. ___, 105 S.Ct. 563, 83 L.Ed.2d 504 (1984); *Fernandez v. Wilkinson*, 505 F.Supp. 787, 790 (D.Kan.1980), *affirmed on other grounds sub nom. Rodriguez-Fernandez v. Wilkinson*, 654 F.2d 1382 (10th Cir.1981); *Sannon v. United States*, 427 F.Supp. 1270, 1276 (S.D.Fla.1977), vacated and remanded on other grounds 566 F.2d 104 (5th Cir.1978).

But does *Mezei* have to be read that way? The Court describes the constitutionally preferred class as "aliens who have once passed through our gates, even illegally." Aliens who enter without inspection would seem to have jumped the fence, rather than passing through the gates. Maybe the Court meant to protect only those who were inspected at entry and who are later brought into deportation proceedings because of some defect—some illegality—that comes to light thereafter, revealing that the original entry was illegal, despite compliance with the formalities of inspection. The *Yamataya* and *Wong Yang Sung* cases cited in *Mezei* right after the quoted line can be read as supporting such a distinction. *See* Martin, *Due Process and Membership in the National Community: Political Asylum and Beyond,* 44 U.Pitt.L.Rev. 165, 231–32 n. 234 (1983). Should such a distinction be made?

In any event, the traditional understanding of *Mezei* has read the case as Hart read it in 1953. See the lower court cases cited earlier in this note. Under that understanding, an alien's entitlement to due process is to be determined by whether she stands at the border trying to get in (even if she has been here before), or instead has already made an entry and must be removed. In other words, due process depends on whether the alien is in exclusion or deportation proceedings—on location, rather than on the stakes involved for the alien. We ask you to consider, both here and in later chapters, whether this application of the Constitution makes sense, and—a more difficult and important question—what alternative due process doctrines might be more satisfactory.

4. *Kwong Hai Chew v. Colding,* 344 U.S. 590, 73 S.Ct. 472, 97 L.Ed. 576 (1953), decided only a few months before *Mezei* and described therein, presents an odd contrast with the latter case. How should the dividing line be drawn between protected permanent resident aliens like Chew and unprotected aliens like Mezei—length of absence, nature of activities while outside the United States, types of preclearance before departure? Justice Clark's opinion in *Mezei* refers to several factors but fails to reveal which was decisive. The BIA ultimately decided that, at least for purposes of allocating the burden of proof in removal proceedings of any kind, an alien would be treated like Chew whenever he presented "a colorable claim to returning lawful resident alien status." *Matter of Kane,* 15 I & N Dec. 258, 264 (BIA 1975), relying on *Chew v. Rogers,* 257 F.2d 606 (D.C.Cir.1958) (upon remand after the Supreme Court's decision). *See also Matter of Becerra-Miranda,* 12 I & N Dec. 358 (BIA 1967); *Matter of B.,* 5 I & N Dec. 712 (BIA 1954). Is this a reasonable reading? Can it possibly account for what happened to Mezei?

5. In his footnote 9 in *Mezei,* Justice Jackson suggests that *in camera* revelation of the evidence would afford no solution to the underlying problem. Do you agree? In many settings, Congress evidently does not. In statutes passed during the 1970's, it often provided for *in camera* court review of sensitive information, as a kind of substitute for the full adversarial testing process. *See Ray v. Turner,* 587 F.2d 1187 (D.C.Cir. 1978) (discussing *in camera* review procedures under the Freedom of Information Act) and *United States v. Belfield,* 692 F.2d 141 (D.C.Cir.1982) (discussing similar procedures under the Foreign Intelligence Surveillance Act). Furthermore, in sharp contrast to its practices during the 1950's, the Justice Department now appears willing to share with the court *in*

camera the sensitive information on which exclusion decisions are based, in those infrequent instances when INA § 235(c) is employed to bar a full hearing. *See El-Werfalli v. Smith,* 547 F.Supp. 152 (S.D.N.Y.1982); *Abourezk v. Reagan,* 592 F.Supp. 880 (D.D.C.1984), where the courts suggested that the information on the public record might not sustain the exclusion order or visa denial, but went on to approve the government decisions after reviewing confidential information *in camera.*

6. Justice Jackson's resistance to *in camera* procedures may stem from his uniquely inflexible view of the requirements of procedural due process. As part III of his *Mezei* dissent reveals, he seems to regard due process requirements as a rather fixed set, apparently defined by the usual elements of the traditional adversarial model familiar to us from its use, for example, in criminal trials. Whatever the merits of this view, the Supreme Court has not accepted it. Modern due process cases stress the flexibility of the concept; procedures acceptable in some settings may be wholly unacceptable in others. What process is due now depends on the interests at stake for the government and the individual, to be judged according to a test described in the landmark case of *Mathews v. Eldridge,* 424 U.S. 319, 96 S.Ct. 893, 47 L.Ed.2d 18 (1976). The *Plasencia* case, reprinted below, discusses *Eldridge* and reflects the current approach.

The following case amounts to a potentially significant retrenchment on the reach of *Mezei* and *Knauff.* Ask yourself, as you read, just how much of the earlier doctrine survives.

LANDON v. PLASENCIA

Supreme Court of the United States, 1982.
459 U.S. 21, 103 S.Ct. 321, 74 L.Ed.2d 21.

JUSTICE O'CONNOR delivered the opinion of the Court.

* * *

I

Respondent Maria Antonieta Plasencia, a citizen of El Salvador, entered the United States as a permanent resident alien in March, 1970. She established a home in Los Angeles with her husband, a United States citizen, and their minor children. On June 27, 1975, she and her husband travelled to Tijuana, Mexico. During their brief stay in Mexico, they met with several Mexican and Salvadoran nationals and made arrangements to assist their illegal entry into the United States. She agreed to transport the aliens to Los Angeles and furnished some of the aliens with alien registration receipt cards that belonged to her children. When she and her husband attempted to cross the international border at 9:27 on the evening of June 29, 1975, an INS officer at the port of entry found six nonresident aliens in the Plasencias' car. The INS detained the respondent for further inquiry pursuant to § 235(b) of the Immigration and

Nationality Act of 1952.[1] In a notice dated June 30, 1975, the INS charged her under § 212(a)(31) of the Act, which provides for the exclusion of any alien seeking admission "who at any time shall have, knowingly and for gain, encouraged, induced, assisted, abetted, or aided any other alien to enter or to try to enter the United States in violation of law," and gave notice that it would hold an exclusion hearing at 11:00 a.m. on June 30, 1975.[2]

An immigration law judge conducted the scheduled exclusion hearing. After hearing testimony from the respondent, her husband, and three of the aliens found in the Plasencias' car, the judge found "clear, convincing and unequivocal" evidence that the respondent did "knowingly and for gain encourage, induce, assist, abet, or aid nonresident aliens" to enter or try to enter the United States in violation of law.

* * *

[The Court ruled initially that she was properly placed in exclusion rather than deportation proceedings—an issue we will treat in Chapter Four.]

IV

* * * Plasencia [also] argued * * * that she was denied due process in her exclusion hearing. We agree with Plasencia that under the circumstances of this case, she can invoke the Due Process Clause on returning to this country, although we do not decide the contours of the process that is due or whether the process accorded Plasencia was insufficient.

This Court has long held that an alien seeking initial admission to the United States requests a privilege and has no constitutional rights regarding his application, for the power to admit or exclude aliens is a sovereign prerogative. See, *e.g., United States ex rel. Knauff v. Shaughnessy*, 338 U.S. 537, 542, 70 S.Ct. 309, 312, 94 L.Ed. 317 (1950); *Nishimura Ekiu v. United States*, 142 U.S. 651, 659–660, 12 S.Ct. 336, 338, 35 L.Ed. 1146

---

1. Section 235, 8 U.S.C. § 1225, provides in part:

"(a) The inspection ... of aliens (including alien crewmen) seeking admission or readmission to ... the United States shall be conducted by immigration officers, except as otherwise provided in regard to special inquiry officers. All aliens arriving at ports of the United States shall be examined by one or more immigration officers at the discretion of the Attorney General and under such regulations as he may prescribe. ...

"(b) Every alien ... who may not appear to the examining immigration officer at the port of arrival to be clearly and beyond a doubt entitled to land shall be detained for further inquiry to be conducted by a special inquiry officer."

2. The hearing was authorized by § 236, which provides in part:

"(a) A special inquiry officer shall conduct proceedings under this section, administer oaths, present and receive evidence, and in-

terrogate, examine, and cross-examine the alien or witnesses. He shall have authority in any case to determine whether an arriving alien who has been detained for further inquiry under section [235] shall be allowed to enter or shall be excluded and deported. The determination of such special inquiry officer shall be based only on the evidence produced at the inquiry. ... Proceedings before a special inquiry officer under this section shall be conducted in accordance with this section, the applicable provisions of sections [235 and 287(b),] and such regulations as the Attorney General shall prescribe, and shall be the sole and exclusive procedure for determining admissibility of a person to the United States under the provisions of this section. ... A complete record of the proceedings and of all testimony and evidence produced at such inquiry, shall be kept."

(1892). Our recent decisions confirm that view. See, *e.g., Fiallo v. Bell,* 430 U.S. 787, 792, 97 S.Ct. 1473, 1477, 52 L.Ed.2d 50 (1977); *Kleindienst v. Mandel,* 408 U.S. 753, 92 S.Ct. 2576, 33 L.Ed.2d 683 (1972). As we explained in *Johnson v. Eisentrager,* 339 U.S. 763, 770, 70 S.Ct. 936, 939, 94 L.Ed. 1255 (1950), however, once an alien gains admission to our country and begins to develop the ties that go with permanent residence his constitutional status changes accordingly. Our cases have frequently suggested that a continuously present resident alien is entitled to a fair hearing when threatened with deportation, and, although we have only rarely held that the procedures provided by the executive were inadequate, we developed the rule that a continuously present permanent resident alien has a right to due process in such a situation.

The question of the procedures due a returning resident alien arose in *Kwong Hai Chew v. Colding,* [344 U.S. 590, 73 S.Ct. 472, 97 L.Ed. 576 (1953)]. There, the regulations permitted the exclusion of an arriving alien without a hearing. We interpreted those regulations not to apply to Chew, a permanent resident alien who was returning from a five-month voyage abroad as a crewman on an American merchant ship. We reasoned that, "For purposes of his constitutional right to due process, we assimilate petitioner's status to that of an alien continuously residing and physically present in the United States." Then, to avoid constitutional problems, we construed the regulation as inapplicable. Although the holding was one of regulatory interpretation, the rationale was one of constitutional law. Any doubts that *Chew* recognized constitutional rights in the resident alien returning from a brief trip abroad were dispelled by *Rosenberg v. Fleuti,* [374 U.S. 449, 83 S.Ct. 1804, 10 L.Ed.2d 1000 (1963),] where we described *Chew* as holding "that the returning resident alien is entitled as a matter of due process to a hearing on the charges underlying any attempt to exclude him."

If the permanent resident alien's absence is extended, of course, he may lose his entitlement to "assimilat[ion of his] status," *Kwong Hai Chew v. Colding, supra,* 344 U.S., at 596, 73 S.Ct., at 477, to that of an alien continuously residing and physically present in the United States. In *Shaughnessy v. United States ex rel. Mezei,* 345 U.S. 206, 73 S.Ct. 625, 97 L.Ed. 956 (1953), this Court rejected the argument of an alien who had left the country for some twenty months that he was entitled to due process in assessing his right to admission on his return. We did not suggest that no returning resident alien has a right to due process, for we explicitly reaffirmed *Chew.* We need not now decide the scope of *Mezei;* it does not govern this case, for Plasencia was absent from the country only a few days, and the United States has conceded that she has a right to due process.

The constitutional sufficiency of procedures provided in any situation, of course, varies with the circumstances. * * * In evaluating the procedures in any case, the courts must consider the interest at stake for the individual, the risk of an erroneous deprivation of the interest through the procedures used as well as the probable value of additional or different procedural safeguards, and the interest of the government in using the current procedures rather than additional or different procedures. *Mathews v. Eldridge,* 424 U.S. 319, 334–335, 96 S.Ct. 893, 902–903, 47 L.Ed.2d 18 (1976). Plasencia's interest here is, without question, a weighty one. She stands to lose the right "to stay and live and work in this land of freedom." Further, she may lose the right to rejoin her immediate family, a right that ranks high among the interests of the individual. The government's interest in efficient administration of the immigration laws at the border also is weighty. Further, it must weigh heavily in the balance that control over matters of immigration is a sovereign prerogative, largely within the control of the executive and the legislature. The role of the judiciary is limited to determining whether the procedures meet the essential standard of fairness under the Due Process Clause and does not extend to imposing procedures that merely displace congressional choices of policy. Our previous discussion has shown that Congress did not intend to require the use of deportation procedures in cases such as this one. Thus, it would be improper simply to impose deportation procedures here because the reviewing court may find them preferable. Instead, the courts must evaluate the particular circumstances and determine what procedures would satisfy the minimum requirements of due process on the re-entry of a permanent resident alien.

Plasencia questions three aspects of the procedures that the government employed in depriving her of these interests. First, she contends that the immigration law judge placed the burden of proof upon her. In a later proceeding in *Chew,* the Court of Appeals for the District of Columbia Circuit held, without mention of the Due Process Clause, that, under the law of the case, Chew was entitled to a hearing at which the INS was the moving party and bore the burden of proof. *Kwong Hai Chew v. Rogers,* 257 F.2d 606 (CADC 1958). The BIA has accepted that decision, and although the Act provides that the burden of proof is on the alien in an exclusion proceeding, § 291, the BIA has followed the practice of placing the burden on the government when the alien is a permanent resident alien. *See, e.g., In re Salazar,* [17 I & N Dec. 167, 169 (BIA 1979);] *In re Kane,* 15 I & N Dec. 258, 264 (BIA 1975); *In re Becerra-Miranda,* 12 I & N Dec. 358, 363–364, 366 (BIA 1967). There is no explicit statement of the placement of the burden of proof in the Attorney General's regulations or in the immigration law judge's opinion in this case and no finding on the issue below.

Second, Plasencia contends that the notice provided her was inadequate. She apparently had less than eleven hours' notice of the charges and the hearing. The regulations do not require any advance notice of the charges against the alien in an exclusion hearing, and the BIA has held that it is sufficient that the alien have notice of the charges at the hearing, *In re Salazar, supra,* at 169. The United States has argued to us that Plasencia could have sought a continuance. It concedes, however, that there is no explicit statutory or regulatory authorization for a continuance.

Finally, Plasencia contends that she was allowed to waive her right to representation,[8] without a full understanding of the right or of the

---

8. The statute provides a right to representation without expense to the government. Section 292. Plasencia has not suggested that she is entitled to free counsel.

consequences of waiving it. Through an interpreter, the immigration law judge informed her at the outset of the hearing, as required by the regulations, of her right to be represented. He did not tell her of the availability of free legal counsel, but at the time of the hearing, there was no administrative requirement that he do so. 8 CFR § 236.2(a) (1975). The Attorney General has since revised the regulations to require that, when qualified free legal services are available, the immigration law judge must inform the alien of their existence and ask whether representation is desired. 44 Fed.Reg. 4654 (Jan. 23, 1979) (codified at 8 CFR § 236.2(a) (1982)). As the United States concedes, the hearing would not comply with the current regulations.

If the exclusion hearing is to ensure fairness, it must provide Plasencia an opportunity to present her case effectively, though at the same time it cannot impose an undue burden on the government. It would not, however, be appropriate for us to decide now whether the new regulation on the right to notice of free legal services is of constitutional magnitude or whether the remaining procedures provided comport with the Due Process Clause. Before this Court, the parties have devoted their attention to the entitlement to a deportation hearing rather than to the sufficiency of the procedures in the exclusion hearing.[9] Whether the several hours' notice gave Plasencia a realistic opportunity to prepare her case for effective presentation in the circumstances of an exclusion hearing without counsel is a question we are not now in a position to answer. Nor has the government explained the burdens that it might face in providing more elaborate procedures. Thus, although we recognize the gravity of Plasencia's interest, the other factors relevant to due process analysis—the risk of erroneous deprivation, the efficacy of additional procedural safeguards, and the government's interest in providing no further procedures—have not been adequately presented to permit us to assess the sufficiency of the hearing. We remand to the Court of Appeals to allow the parties to explore whether Plasencia was accorded due process under all of the circumstances.

Accordingly, the judgment of the Court of Appeals is

Reversed and remanded.

JUSTICE MARSHALL, concurring in part and dissenting in part.

I agree that the Immigration and Nationality Act permitted the INS to proceed against respondent in an exclusion proceeding. The question

9. Thus, the question of Plasencia's entitlement to due process has been briefed and argued, is properly before us, and is sufficiently developed that we are prepared to decide it. Precisely what procedures are due, on the other hand, has not been adequately developed by the briefs or argument. The dissent undertakes to decide these questions, but, to do so, must rely heavily on an argument not raised by Plasencia: to wit, that she was not informed at the hearing that the alleged agreement to receive compensation and the meaningfulness of her departure were critical issues. Also, the dissent fails to discuss the interests that the government may have in employing the procedures that it did. The omission of arguments raised by the parties is quite understandable, for neither Plasencia nor the government has yet discussed what procedures are due. Unlike the dissent, we would allow the parties to explore their respective interests and arguments in the Court of Appeals.

then remains whether the exclusion proceeding held in this case satisfied the minimum requirements of the Due Process Clause. While I agree that the Court need not decide the precise contours of the process that would be constitutionally sufficient, I would not hesitate to decide that the process accorded Plasencia was insufficient.

The Court has already set out the standards to be applied in resolving the question. Therefore, rather than just remand, I would first hold that respondent was denied due process because she was not given adequate and timely notice of the charges against her and of her right to retain counsel and to present a defense.[2]

While the type of hearing required by due process depends upon a balancing of the competing interests at stake, due process requires "at a minimum ... that deprivation of life, liberty or property by adjudication be preceded by notice and opportunity for hearing." *Mullane v. Central Hanover Bank & Trust Co.*, 339 U.S. 306, 313, 70 S.Ct. 652, 656, 94 L.Ed. 865 (1950). Permanent resident aliens who are detained upon reentry into this country clearly are entitled to adequate notice in advance of an exclusion proceeding.

To satisfy due process, notice must "clarify what the charges are" in a manner adequate to apprise the individual of the basis for the government's proposed action. Notice must be provided sufficiently in advance of the hearing to "give the charged party a chance to marshal the facts in his defense." * * *

Respondent was not given notice sufficient to afford her a reasonable opportunity to demonstrate that she was not excludable. The immigration judge's decision to exclude respondent was handed down less than 24 hours after she was detained at the border on the night of June 29, 1975. By notice in English dated June 30, 1975, she was informed that a hearing would be conducted at eleven o'clock on the morning of that same day, and that the government would seek to exclude her on the ground that she had "wilfully and knowingly aided and abetted the entry of illegal aliens into the United States in violation of the law and for gain." It was not until the commencement of the hearing that she was given notice in her native language of the charges against her and of her right to retain counsel and to present evidence.

The charges against Plasencia were also inadequately explained at the hearing itself. The immigration judge did not explain to her that she would be entitled to remain in the country if she could demonstrate that she had not agreed to receive compensation from the aliens whom she had driven across the border. Nor did the judge inform respondent that the meaningfulness of her departure was an issue at the hearing.

These procedures deprived Plasencia of a fair opportunity to show that she was not excludable under the standards set forth in the Immigration and Nationality Act. Because Plasencia was not given adequate notice of the standards for exclusion or of her right to retain counsel and

---

2. Because Plasencia did not receive constitutionally sufficient notice, I find it unnecessary to address the other constitutional deficiencies she asserts.

present a defense, she had neither time nor opportunity to prepare a response to the government's case. The procedures employed here virtually assured that the Government attorney would present his case without factual or legal opposition.

When a permanent resident alien's substantial interest in remaining in this country is at stake, the Due Process Clause forbids the Government to stack the deck in this fashion. Only a compelling need for truly summary action could justify this one-sided proceeding. In fact, the Government's haste in proceeding against Plasencia could be explained only by its desire to avoid the minimal administrative and financial burden of providing her adequate notice and an opportunity to prepare for the hearing. Although the various other government interests identified by the Court may be served by the exclusion of those who fail to meet the eligibility requirements set out in the Immigration and Nationality Act, they are not served by procedures that deny a permanent resident alien a fair opportunity to demonstrate that she meets those eligibility requirements.

I would therefore hold that respondent was denied due process.

Notes

1. *Plasencia* distinguishes *Mezei;* it does not purport to overrule the latter case. But at least the Court has now removed much of the threat that *Mezei* seemed to pose to permanent resident aliens who travel. Henceforth, full due process entitlement seems to be the norm for nearly all such persons, even if they are validly placed in exclusion proceedings, and *Mezei* marks out an ill-defined exception.

But how should we go about drawing the line that distinguishes these exceptional cases? The Court says only that an alien may lose her protected status if her "absence is extended." In future cases should the one-year rule that governs for some purposes under the immigration laws be employed? For example, a returning resident loses the right to rely on her Alien Registration Receipt Card (familiarly known as the "green card") as a reentry permit if her absence extends beyond one year. 8 C.F.R. § 211.1(b). Or should the test take more subjective factors into account? That is, rather than relying mechanically on length of absence, should a court try to determine whether the alien *intended* to abandon his residence status? (The BIA now uses a multiple factor test to determine whether an alien has intended to abandon residence here and thus no longer qualifies as a special immigrant under INA § 101(a)(27)(A). *See Matter of Kane,* 15 I & N Dec. 258, 262–64.)

If any subjective intent test is ultimately employed, the Court probably could not avoid a de facto overruling of *Mezei.* According to the facts as Mezei pleaded them, he had no intention of making a lengthy journey, much less of abandoning his U.S. home. And the fact that his family remained behind in Buffalo while he travelled lends a strong measure of plausibility to Mezei's argument.

2. The Court has often proclaimed the death of the old right-privilege distinction that used to play a major role in deciding due process

controversies. *See, e.g., Goldberg v. Kelly,* 397 U.S. 254, 262, 90 S.Ct. 1011, 1017, 25 L.Ed.2d 287 (1970); *Board of Regents v. Roth,* 408 U.S. 564, 571, 92 S.Ct. 2701, 2706, 33 L.Ed.2d 548 (1972). But the Court in *Plasencia* explains the denial of due process rights to first-time applicants for admission by asserting that such a person "requests a privilege and has no constitutional rights regarding his application." Is this an accurate characterization? Should any government action be free of due process scrutiny? *See generally* Smolla, *The Re-emergence of the Right-Privilege Distinction in Constitutional Law: The Price of Protesting Too Much,* 35 Stan.L.Rev. 69 (1982).

In *Roth, supra,* the court placed new emphasis on a careful threshold assessment of the nature of the individual interest at stake. The Due Process Clause protects only against deprivations of "life, liberty, or property," the Court stressed, and not all government actions negatively affecting individuals deprive them of such interests.

> To have a property interest in a benefit, a person clearly must have more than an abstract need or desire for it. He must have more than a unilateral expectation of it. He must, instead, have a legitimate claim of entitlement to it. * * *
>
> Property interests, of course, are not created by the Constitution. Rather, they are created and their dimensions are defined by existing rules or understandings that stem from an independent source like state law * * *.

408 U.S. at 577, 92 S.Ct. 2709.

Liberty, according to *Roth,* enjoys a more expansive conception. (Later cases may have cut back on its extent, however. *See* G. Gunther, *Constitutional Law: Cases and Materials* 661–66 (10th ed. 1980); *Connecticut Board of Pardons v. Dumschat,* 452 U.S. 458, 101 S.Ct. 2460, 69 L.Ed.2d 158 (1981); *Arnett v. Kennedy,* 416 U.S. 134, 94 S.Ct. 1633, 40 L.Ed.2d 15 (1974) (opinion of Rehnquist, J.).) *Roth* states: "In a Constitution for a free people, there can be no doubt that the meaning of 'liberty' must be broad indeed." 408 U.S. at 572, 92 S.Ct. at 2707. *Roth* also quotes from *Meyer v. Nebraska,* 262 U.S. 390, 399, 43 S.Ct. 625, 626, 67 L.Ed. 1042 (1923):

> Without doubt [liberty] denotes not merely freedom from bodily restraint but also the right of the individual to contract, to engage in any of the common occupations of life, to acquire useful knowledge, to marry, establish a home and bring up children, to worship God according to the dictates of his own conscience, and generally to enjoy those privileges long recognized ... as essential to the orderly pursuit of happiness by free men.

If you are beginning to think that *Knauff* was wrongly decided, ask yourself just what sort of a liberty or property interest Ellen Knauff had at stake there. In other words, can her claim, as a first-time applicant for admission, be brought within the *Roth* framework? To be sure, exclusion imposed bodily restraints on her freedom of movement, but do all aliens in the world who might happen to present themselves at our borders for the first time have a legitimate claim of entitlement to free movement in this very potent sense? If we think of Knauff's claim under the "property" rubric, did she have more than a unilateral expectation or hope that she would be permitted to enter the United States? If you think the War Brides Act provides the independent source for a "legitimate claim of entitlement," would that approach permit us to distinguish Knauff's situation from the case of any other first-time applicant for admission who has a visa and believes that he meets the admission requirements set forth in the INA, but nonetheless finds himself enmeshed in exclusion proceedings upon arrival at the port of entry? Can we afford to provide due process to everyone in the world who simply presents himself or herself at a port of entry? If so, how much process? If not, how do we decide when due process rights attach?

2. ADMISSION PROCEDURES: A GLANCE BACKWARD

Ellis Island, for many years the principal port of entry for immigrants to the United States, has become a fixture in American folklore. Before we examine modern procedures, it may be worthwhile to look closely at the procedures employed at that facility.

The following passages paint a composite picture of immigrant processing at Ellis Island in 1907, the year that still holds the record for the highest number of immigrants admitted. Keep in mind that this was before the national-origins quotas were adopted. Indeed, no numerical ceilings applied at all, but each alien had to satisfy various qualitative exclusion criteria.

ANN NOVOTNY, STRANGERS AT THE DOOR: ELLIS ISLAND, CASTLE GARDEN, AND THE GREAT MIGRATION TO AMERICA
10–23 (1971).

Soon after dawn the next day, there was a sudden change in the ship's motion and a different sound from the engine. The harbor pilot from Ambrose Lightship had just come aboard. Early risers up on deck cried out in different languages as they caught sight of a gray strip of land (the Long Island, someone said it was called) emerging on the horizon as the sun burned off the morning mist. One word was the same on all tongues: "America!" Many of those peering at the coast broke into tears. Down in steerage there was frenzied excitement as immigrants jostled around bunks, arranging bundles for the last time, washing hands and faces in basins of cold, salty water, combing unwashed hair or smoothing creases out of the prettiest apron, saved for this occasion—all in an attempt to look their best for the American inspectors. Money was counted for the hundredth time, then secreted away in some safe inner pocket. The deck became more and more crowded as baggage was carried up and added to the mounting piles of battered suitcases, wicker baskets, cooking pots tied in old blankets and bulky goose-feather pillows bound together with thin rope. Then there was nothing to do for a while except find a place to sit and rehearse once again the best answers to all the questions the inspectors might ask about health, money, work and friends.

* * *

Heads on deck turned as a small cutter came alongside. A ladder was raised against the ship's rail, and two men and a woman in uniforms climbed aboard and pushed their way quickly through the crowd of immigrants toward the second cabin-class area. A murmur of apprehension ran through the watching crowd, but the officers barely glanced at the immigrants. Their business was with cabin-class passengers only, and the immigrants' turn would come later, at Ellis Island. In the saloon, the immigration inspector asked two or three brief questions of each waiting second-cabin passenger, while the other man, a doctor from the U.S. Public Health Service, looked quickly at their eyes as they filed past. Full information about these travelers was listed, as required by law, on the ship's official passenger list or "manifest." Because the shipping companies had made a great fuss when regular inspections in this class had begun about five years earlier, the inspector did his job as quickly as possible. He hardly looked at a small hunchbacked Polish woman from Danzig, who said that her husband and children would meet her at the pier; he did not know or care that this woman had been deported from Ellis Island because of her deformity two years earlier, when the whole family had arrived in steerage, and that her husband had finally saved enough money to bring her into the country this easy way. If the woman could afford to travel in style, she would obviously never become a public charge. When the last second-cabin passenger had been passed, the inspector ran his eyes down the first-cabin list of Americans and wealthy foreign visitors who were coming to tour or settle in this country (no one ever called *them* "immigrants"), and simply muttered, "Okay, that'll do." The Public Health Service officer was chatting with the ship's doctor, making sure that there had been no cases of epidemic diseases such as cholera, yellow fever or typhoid. If any serious contagious illnesses had been reported, the patients would have been taken at once on the quarantine boat, the *James W. Wadsworth,* to hospital wards on Hoffman Island, while other passengers would have been held in strict isolation on nearby Swinburn Island until the danger of their developing symptoms had passed. As it was, the doctor said the ship's hospital contained only one second-cabin woman with suspected appendicitis. This patient, in the care of the matron, was led down to the cutter and the small launch headed straight for Ellis Island's hospital.

The liner had been moving slowly north into the Upper Bay while this inspection was taking place. As the enormous harbor came into view, expressions of wonder and awe could be heard on the steerage deck, and people in the center pushed and craned to get a better look at the spectacular sight. Mothers lifted small children into the air to see. There on the left was the towering Statue of Liberty, lifting her torch of freedom to the sky. The bay itself was filled with other steamships, tugs and paddle-wheeled ferries crossing in all directions; an excursion boat passed, carrying a happy crowd to Coney Island. Rising on the skyline five miles away were the office buildings of lower Manhattan, taller than anything in Hamburg; so tall, in fact, that they looked like a ridge of small hills. The highest one of all, the new Singer Building, would reach forty-seven stories when it was finished the next year. Also on the left of their view, just beyond the Statue of Liberty, were the red brick buildings of Ellis Island where the immigrants would be taken. They had all heard of the Island and knew its name. That was the famous Island of Tears— *Tranen Insel* to the Germans, *Isola delle Lacrime* to the Italians—where those whom the inspectors judged too weak, old or poor to support themselves would be detained, then deported back to Europe to rebuild a broken life there.

* * *

[The steamer discharged its passengers at a pier in Manhattan. Cabin-class passengers were allowed to proceed to their destination, but the other immigrants were ushered onto a tightly packed ferry-boat or barge for the trip to Ellis Island. They might spend several hours aboard, waiting just off the crowded docks at the island before landing space became available. After disembarking, there was more waiting, in groups clustered according to big numbers on the tags tied to their coats.]

* * * Then the shouting began once more and, one by one, groups of thirty people at a time moved slowly forward, through the big door into dark tiled corridors, then—jostling two or three abreast—up a steep flight of stairs.

Their eyes blinking in the sudden bright light, they paused for a moment at the top. Sunshine streamed through the arched windows of the largest room they had ever seen. An unbelievable crowd of men, women and children was on all sides—enough to populate ten villages back home—and the hall was so huge that it might have contained their farm animals as well.

* * *

The immigrants at the top of the stairs were not given any more time to stand and stare. "This way! Hurry up!" an interpreter shouted in several languages, and they were pushed along one of the dozens of metal railings which divided the whole floor into a maze of open passageways. Although they did not realize it, they were already passing their first test as they hastened down the row in single file. Twenty-five feet away a doctor, in the smart blue uniform of the U.S. Public Health Service, was watching them carefully as they approached him. All children who looked over two years old were taken from their mothers' arms and made to walk.

It took only a few moments for the immigrants to reach the doctor, but that was time enough for his sharp eyes to notice one man who was breathing too heavily, a woman who was trying to hide her limp behind a big bundle, and a young girl whose shuffle and bewildered gaze might have been symptoms of a feeble mind. As each immigrant paused in front of him, the doctor looked hard at his face, hair, neck and hands; at the same time, with an interpreter at his side to help, he asked short questions about the immigrant's age or work to test his alertness. When a mother came up with children, each child in turn, starting with the oldest, was asked his name to make sure that he was not deaf or dumb.

In the doctor's hand was a piece of chalk; on the coats of about two out of every ten or eleven immigrants who passed him he scrawled a large white letter—"H" for possible heart trouble, "L" for lameness, a circled "X" for suspected mental defects, or "F" for a bad rash on the face. Then the immigrants filed on to a second doctor who was looking for diseases specifically mentioned in the law as reasons for deportation: signs of tuberculosis, leprosy, or a contagious skin disease of the scalp called *favus*.

* * *

At the end of the aisle interpreters waved immigrants whose coats were unmarked back toward the main part of the Registry Hall. But those whose coats bore chalk letters were pushed aside into a "pen," an area enclosed by a wire screen, to wait for more detailed medical examinations by other doctors. If they had any of the diseases proscribed by the immigration laws, or seemed too ill or feeble-minded to earn their living, they would be deported. One sobbing mother was pushed into the enclosure to wait with her little girl of eight or nine. The law said a parent had to accompany any very young child who was deported; but children of ten or older were sent back to Europe alone and simply released in the port from which they had sailed. Several weeping families in the hall were trying to make a terrible decision—"Shall we all go back together? Who will stay?"

Those immigrants waiting on benches for their final test talked anxiously and rehearsed for the last time their answers to probable questions about jobs, cash and relatives. Some said it was best to answer questions as fully as possible. Others said that inspectors were just like lawyers, always trying to trip you up, and it was best to keep your mouth shut and just say "Yes" and "No" so they couldn't muddle you. Could American officials be bribed with a gold coin or two? You had to be very, very careful. You had to show some money, but perhaps it wasn't safe to show it all. The waiting time, often an hour or two on busy days like these, seemed endless to the nervous immigrants; many of them leaned against their bundles in exhaustion and tried to sleep.

At last an interpreter moved them into the adjoining row. He made sure that they all had the same big number pinned on their coats. At the end of the aisle sat an inspector, on whose desk lay the manifest headed by that number. This large sheet of paper had been prepared by the shipping company and contained answers to questions about each of the thirty immigrants listed on it. As the first immigrant from the group approached the high desk, the inspector peered at the tag on his coat, noted the smaller "1" in its bottom corner, put his finger against that man's name on the first line of the form, and wearily prepared to start the questioning again.

* * *

* * * Before this long day was over, the interpreter would have helped the inspector question between four and five hundred immigrants, so that between them the two officials had only about two minutes in which to decide whether each immigrant was "clearly and beyond a doubt entitled to land," as the law specified. Every doubtful case was detained for further questioning.

The rapid queries, designed to verify the most important of the twenty-nine bits of information about each immigrant on the manifest, began: "What work do you do? " "Do you have a job waiting for you? " "Who paid for your passage here? " "Is anyone meeting you? " "Where are you going? " "Can you read and write? " "Have you ever been in prison? " "How much money do you have? " "Show it to me now." "Where did you get it? "

Nearly all of the immigrants quickly got curt nods from the inspector, who handed them landing cards, and sudden friendly smiles from the interpreter. They were in! "Praise God," murmured an elderly Ruthenian farmer, bending suddenly over the desk and kissing the back of the inspector's hand in gratitude. For most of the group, the ordeal was over. After only three or four hours on Ellis Island, they were free to go.

* * *

But the beginning was delayed, perhaps forever, for the unfortunate immigrants who were kept behind at Ellis Island. As one manifest group passed, for example, the inspector singled out a pretty Swedish girl who said she was going to Chicago alone to get married; he ordered her detained until her fiancé or a representative from the Lutheran Pilgrim House came to get her. Immigration officials refused to send single women alone into the streets of strange cities. If the Swedish girl's boy friend came East to meet her, an interpreter would probably escort the young couple to City Hall to be married on the spot to prevent any deception (in earlier days hundreds of marriages were performed on Ellis Island itself to combat "white slavery"). A second detained immigrant was an old Russian Jew whose threadbare pockets contained only seventy-five cents. His American relatives in Rhode Island would send him money for a train ticket, he said. Terrified that the inspector was not going to admit him, he began to sob out the story of his family's murder in the 1905 *pogrom,* wailing that the Americans might as well kill him then and there as send him back. A man from the Hebrew Immigrant Aid Society came running up at the sound of the commotion. He soothed the old man, saying that he would send a telegram at once to his relatives, and that the old man would be well looked after on the Island until the money arrived. A few minutes later, a nervous young Italian, sweating with excitement, answered pressing questions about the work he could do by waving a well-thumbed letter under the inspector's nose. An Italian uncle in Pittsfield—"See, right here"—had promised him a job on a construction gang. A frown passed over the inspector's face as he ordered the young man detained for the Board of Special Inquiry. "But why? Why? " the young man shouted. As the interpreter said that the Contract Labor Law would be explained at the hearing, the young man's heart sank. He had forgotten! He had been warned to lie about this! Immigrants had to show that they were strong and clever enough to find work easily, but it was against the law for them to have agreed before they left home to take a specific job in exchange for their passage. This law had been in effect for over twenty years. It was meant to protect immigrants from slave-like labor, and to protect American workers from gangs of European laborers imported by a "boss" to break strikes or keep wages low. If this young man had sailed with several friends, all of whom were bound for Pittsfield, the inspector would have felt sure that the padrone system was at work, and the whole group would probably have been sent back to Italy together.

The Swedish girl, the old Russian and the unlucky Italian were typical of those immigrants (about two out of every ten) who were held at the Island for more than a few hours. More than half of them, like the girl and the old man, were detained for two or three days for their own protection. The others, such as the young Italian, who faced more questioning before a Board of Special Inquiry, rarely numbered more than one out of every ten people admitted. Immigrants were brought before the board for many different reasons, including violations of the Contract Labor Law. A telegram from Europe might have brought word that an immigrant was a criminal wanted by the police in his own country; perhaps a man's wife had reported that he was deserting her. Sometimes inspectors felt that an immigrant was really a pauper who had been given a steamship ticket and a suit of clothes by a foreign government eager to get him off its charity rolls. Unfortunate people physically or mentally handicapped in earning a living would be deported if they seemed "likely to become public charges." The law ordered deportation for anyone who was a criminal, a prostitute, or suffering from insanity or a contagious disease. A few immigrants were sent back because of their political or religious beliefs: they were usually anarchists who wanted to overthrow organized government, or polygamists who believed that a man should have several wives.

A detained immigrant went into a small side office to face the Board of Special Inquiry, made up of three inspectors and an interpreter sitting behind a long desk. He swore on the Bible or a crucifix to tell the truth, then answered questions about his right to land, as a stenographer recorded his words. No lawyers were present, but an immigrant's friends and relatives were often brought to the Island to testify in his behalf. The votes of two out of the three inspectors decided a case, but if the third inspector or the immigrant himself felt that a sentence of deportation was unfair, he could appeal the decision to the Secretary of Commerce and Labor in Washington. At this stage, the immigrant was allowed to hire a lawyer to help him. In fact, the secretary often sustained an immigrant's appeal, or ordered a new hearing to be held if fresh evidence was presented. Sometimes the immigrant would be admitted after a bond was posted guaranteeing that he would not become dependent on public charity. Inspectors who were chosen by Ellis Island's commissioner to serve on the Boards of Special Inquiry, like their colleagues in the Registry Hall, worked under great pressure in these busy years and had to rely mainly on their common sense. In a single year, seventy thousand or more cases would be heard. The system was not too cruel: about five out of every six immigrants whose cases were heard were admitted by the boards after careful questioning. The greatest number of exclusions happened in 1911, when about thirteen thousand immigrants (just over two per cent of the 650,000 who arrived that year) were sent back to their homelands.

* * *

The shipping companies, who were supposed to screen out all "undesirables" in Europe, had to transport the immigrants home without charge and to pay for the cost of keeping them on the Island until their next ships arrived.

The job of housing and feeding all the detained immigrants was almost too much for the officials at Ellis Island. There wasn't enough room even for the immigrants who passed through without delay. The architects who designed the buildings in 1897 had planned them to accommodate no more than 500,000 foreigners in one year—they had believed that the flood tide of immigration was over. No one guessed that the high point of the greatest mass movement in history was just about to begin. For inspectors and immigrants alike, it was a nightmare * * *.

———

Seven years later the outbreak of World War I slowed the immigrant flow to a mere trickle. After the war immigration picked up again, but in 1921 Congress changed the legal requirements significantly. Enormous confusion resulted, as administrators struggled to make a system that was designed to perform qualitative screening serve also to impose quantitative ceilings. The Novotny book describes the transition (*id.* at 127–130):

> The First Quota Law, or Johnson Act, which went into effect on June 3, 1921, specified that no more than twenty per cent of a nation's quota could be filled in any one month. Officials of the shipping companies were close to panic; during the last few days of grace they organized a mad dash to land thousands of immigrants in American ports before the deadline. Any ship that could make the transatlantic passage was crammed with passengers and some vessels racing through the Narrows actually collided in their haste. During June, once the new system was in effect, steamships still raced to land their passengers on Ellis Island as soon as possible, and within the first few days of the month the specified twenty per cent of all national quotas had been filled. Then the first scenes of a human tragedy began. Some ten thousand aliens arrived at Ellis Island to be told that their quotas had been filled for June—there was no room for them in America. It was an impossible situation that no one, apparently, had foreseen. Puzzled officials held the surplus immigrants on their ships and asked Washington for instructions; the answer came back that the immigrants were to be admitted on bond, and their numbers subtracted from July's quotas.

But in July, and during the first days of every succeeding month, the same thing happened, as the steamships continued their race to grab as large a share as possible of the quotas for their own passengers. Whole shiploads of immigrants were now turned back to Europe in scenes of terrible anguish described by one Public Health Service doctor as "one of my most painful reminiscences of service at the Island." She recalled one particular group of five hundred southeastern Europeans who had sold their homes and possessions and traveled four thousand miles to start a new life, only to hear after they had passed the Statue of Liberty that they were inadmissible. "They screamed and bawled and beat about like wild animals, breaking the waiting-room furniture and attacking the attendants, several of whom were severely hurt. It was a pitiful spectacle. ..." The immigrants were helpless victims of the steamship lines, and the immigration inspectors were helpless too, in the face of the new law. Commissioner Wallis complained bitterly to Washington in October, 1921, that "our nation is committing a gross injustice." He urged that immigrants be examined by American consuls in European ports, to save all this "indescribable" suffering "that would melt a heart of granite."

* * *

* * * The restrictive law and the sad tales of rejection which were taken back to Europe reduced the volume of arrivals; physical improvements were made; and the staff was better organized. The First Quota Law, never intended to be more than a temporary measure, was replaced in July, 1924, by a second, more restrictive, act based on the same principle. The basis for the quotas was moved back from the population census of 1910 to that of 1890—cutting still further the proportion of "new" immigrants (who in 1890 were just starting to arrive). The percentage of admissible immigrants from any nation was reduced from three per cent to two per cent of its population in this older census, and the overall ceiling was slashed from 358,000 to 164,000 people a year. Italy's quota, under this arrangement, was cut from 42,057 under the First Quota Law to a mere 3,845 per year. The second law's most important provision, as far as Ellis Island's history is concerned, was a rule that all immigrants were to be inspected at the American consular offices in Europe, where visas would be issued to those found acceptable. Consuls would slowly fill the national quotas, issuing no more than ten per cent of the available visas in one month, in an attempt to end the first-come-first-served system used by the steamships and the inevitable disappointments in American ports.

As soon as the second law went into effect, the Secretary of Labor visited Ellis Island and boasted that the place looked "like a 'deserted village'." Immigrants were still examined there, but they arrived in an evenly-spaced flow over the months, and very few of those who had been judged acceptable by the consuls had to be detained. There was now enough time and space for physical conditions on the Island to be rapidly improved: iron bunks were moved out to make room for proper beds with mattresses, and modern plumbing replaced what one magazine writer called the "ancient exhibits." Ellis Island looked like a different place—and it was, because its role was completely changing. In 1926 and 1927, immigration inspectors and Public Health Service doctors were stationed at American consulates over most of Europe, and the primary inspection of the immigrants—once the Island's function—was finished before the immigrants even set sail. Possession of an American visa was almost a guarantee of admission. Inspectors in New York needed only to make a final check of all passengers as the ships sailed into the Upper Bay, and they held only a few doubtful cases—eventually about one per cent of all arrivals—for questioning before Boards of Inquiry or for medical treatment. By 1926, much of Ellis Island's staff had been disbanded. Dust began to settle in the empty rooms. In 1928 officials in Washington were acknowledging it to be "something of an economic problem."

Other useful accounts of Ellis Island appear in D. Brownstone, I. Franck, D. Brownstone, Island of Hope, Island of Tears (1979); T. Pitkin, Keepers of the Gate: A History of Ellis Island (1975); and The New Immigration (J. Appel ed. 1971) (reprinting an essay by Jacob Riis reporting on his 1903 visit to Ellis Island; the essay is notable for the intriguing mixture of sympathy and aversion toward the immigrants displayed by Riis, a former immigrant himself, who had passed through Castle Garden, Ellis Island's predecessor, many years earlier). Procedures at San Francisco's equivalent of Ellis Island, known as Angel Island, are movingly reflected in H. Lai, G. Lim, J. Yung, Island: Poetry and History of Chinese Immigrants on Angel Island 1910–1940 (1980).

3. MODERN PROCEDURES

a. Nonimmigrants

Those who want to come to the United States for a temporary stay must first secure, in nearly every case,[10] a nonimmigrant visa from a U.S.

---

10. The exceptions are described in G & R § 2.31c. To take a few of the important examples, Mexican nationals who have a border crossing card on Form I–186 or I–586 do not need to present a passport and visa at the border to gain admission. The card is valid for visits of up to 72 hours within 25 miles of the border. A supplemental form (I–444) can be obtained to authorize visits up to 30 days anywhere in Arizona, California, Nevada, New Mexico, or Texas. G & R § 6.16a; 8 C.F.R. §§ 212.6, 235.1(f), (g).

In addition, the visa requirement is waived altogether for Canadian nationals provided they are entering for a temporary stay. 8 C.F.R. § 212.1(a). If you have traveled to Europe in recent years, you probably realize that many other Western countries waive their visa requirements for U.S. citizens, and for other nationals, on a far wider scale than is possible under U.S. law for citizens of those countries. This lack of reciprocity has been a sore spot for some European governments, and the Select Commission on Immigration and Refugee Policy recommended a broader visa waiver program for tourists and business travelers coming from countries with low visa abuse rates. SCIRP, Final Report 217–18 (1981). All immigration reform bills passed by either house from 1982 through 1984 contained au-

consular officer in a foreign country. Application is usually made in person at the American consulate, but the personal appearance requirements can be waived for a range of categories. Most of the time such a visa application can be processed immediately. During fiscal year 1983, U.S. consuls processed a total of 6,315,000 nonimmigrant visa applications, issuing 5,576,000 visas. Applications were down about 10 percent from the previous year. Goelz, *Current Overview of Developments at the Department of State,* 61 Interp.Rel. 542, 543 (1984).

The alien bears the burden of proving qualification for the visa, and the most important issue is usually whether the alien truly has a home in the foreign country to which he or she intends to return. The consular officer has discretion to require any kind of documentary support deemed necessary. A few of the nonimmigrant categories, such as H, L, and K, require advance clearance from INS, secured by means of a petition filed by the alien's expected employer or intended spouse, as the case may be.

If the visa application is approved, the consular officer stamps a visa into the applicant's passport. The stamp will show a visa number, date and place of issue, expiration date, and visa classification. Unless otherwise specified, the visa is good for any number of entries before its expiration. In some countries, on a reciprocal basis, the visa can be issued to temporary visitors for business or pleasure (the B–1 and B–2 categories) without time limitation.

Without such a visa, the alien probably cannot gain permission to board a plane or other vessel for the United States; carriers are subject to fines and other expenses for bringing aliens without adequate documentation. *See* INA §§ 233, 273. But the visa does not guarantee admission. Immigration officers at the border are not bound by the consul's decisions on admissibility and may seek to exclude an alien despite the possession of the visa. INA § 221(h).

Aliens admitted as nonimmigrants will receive from the admitting officer an endorsed Form I–94, the Arrival-Departure Record, which is usually stapled into the passport, and is meant to be surrendered upon departure from the United States. This Form specifies the nonimmigrant admission classification, the time allowed for the alien to remain in the United States, and any other specific conditions of entry. For example, if a nonimmigrant has received INS's permission to work, this permission will be registered by an appropriate stamp or endorsement on the I–94. A "green card," which is a document issued only to lawful permanent residents, is thus not the only valid proof of work authorization, but nonimmigrants are not permitted to be employed without specific INS permission. Most nonimmigrants do not receive it.

Although people commonly speak of an alien's being here "on a tourist visa" or "on a student visa," this usage is technically incorrect— and potentially misleading. The visa serves only to help move the alien to the port of entry. The type and length of her actual entry are controlled by the I–94. If the I–94 states admission until March 1, 1984,

thorization for such measures on a pilot program basis, but subject to rather exacting conditions. *See, e.g.,* S.2222, 97th Cong., 2d Sess. § 213 (1982).

the alien must leave by then (or apply to INS on the appropriate form and secure an extension). On March 2, it will do no good to point to a visa expiration date of September 1, 1984. Of course, she could leave in late February and use the visa to journey back to the United States on August 30. If the admitting officer determines that the new visit is bona fide, she may then receive a new I–94 valid, for example, for another six months' visit here. After her entry, the visa's expiration makes no difference to her continued right to stay. She may also apply to INS to change from one nonimmigrant classification to another—for example, from B–2 tourist to F–1 student—under INA § 248. If permission is granted, she need not have the visa amended. The change will be reflected adequately on the I–94. You may wish to read through § 248 now, and also the other most important statutory provisions relating to nonimmigrant admission procedures (INA §§ 214; 221(a)–(b), (f)–(h); and 222(c)–(f)) to confirm your understanding of how the procedures operate.

b. Immigrants

The process of securing status as a lawful permanent resident alien in the United States is more elaborate and time-consuming than what is involved in securing nonimmigrant admission. In this section we will look first at the visa process, then consider procedures at the border, and finally examine adjustment of status under § 245.

Visas and Visa Petitions

In connection with the following materials, you will want to review INA §§ 104, 204, 211, 221, and 222.

AUSTIN T. FRAGOMEN, JR., THE PERMANENT RESIDENCY PROCESS, IN 15TH ANNUAL IMMIGRATION AND NATURALIZATION INSTITUTE

473–76 (Practicing Law Institute 1982).

VI. *Visa Processing.* As opposed to adjustment of status, which is a privilege accorded under the Act, the normal procedure provided for becoming a permanent resident is to apply for and obtain an immigrant visa at a U.S. consulate outside of the United States. A visa must be obtained through visa processing at a U.S. consulate abroad when the beneficiary is located abroad, and when the beneficiary, although in the United States, is not eligible for adjustment of status. Aliens who enter the United States without inspection and aliens who work without authorization must visa process, since adjustment in their cases is barred.[a]

A. Petition Requirements—In order for an alien to submit a visa application, he must first obtain an approved petition to classify himself in a preference classification or as an immediate relative of a U.S. citizen. Only if the alien qualifies for permanent residence in some other manner,

a. See INA § 245(a), (c)(2) for the language barring adjustments in such circumstances.—eds.

such as under a "special immigrant" category or as a nonpreference investor, may the alien forego the prerequisite of an approved petition. When the petitioner, either the family member or employer, dependent on the type of petition, is in the U.S., the petition must be submitted directly to the appropriate INS district office in the U.S. Once the petition is approved by the INS, it will be forwarded to the U.S. consulate designated by the petitioner on the petition. When the petitioner is outside of the U.S., the petition can be submitted to the U.S. consulate which will forward it for adjudication to the INS office overseas with jurisdiction. U.S. consular officials have some authority to adjudicate petitions for immediate relatives of U.S. citizens. All other petitions must be ruled on by the INS. Once the approved petition is received by the consulate, the visa application process can go forward.

B. Visa Availability—Once the petition is received by the consulate, the process of issuing a visa will only go forward if a visa is immediately available for the alien in the preference category for which the petition was approved, and from the home country to which the alien is charged. The priority date established for the alien's visa case will be clearly indicated to the consulate on the transmittal notice with the petition. If the priority date is not current, the alien will be notified that the petition has been received and will be held pending availability of a visa. If the priority date is current, or when it becomes current, the alien will be sent Packet III.

C. Packet III—The first step in visa processing once the approved petition has a current priority date, is the issuance of "Packet III" to the alien. This packet contains the basic biographical forms and information on necessary documentation that is required in order for an immigrant visa to be issued. The alien is advised to return the biographical data sheet immediately. Once he has gathered all of the documents required, such as police certificates, any relevant criminal records, birth and marriage documents, etc., he must return to the consulate notification that all documentation has been obtained. Until this notification is received, no further steps will be taken by the consulate.

D. Visa Appointment—Once the consulate has been notified that all documents have been obtained and it has received any police clearances it has solicited on its own, the alien will be notified of an appointment date at the consulate, when the actual application for an immigrant visa will be made. At the same time the alien is notified of the requirement for a medical examination by a doctor in the country where the consulate is located. Generally, an appointment with the doctor is established by the consulate, either on the same date or a few days before the visa appointment. At the interview with the consular official, the alien's case is scrutinized to determine that the alien is admissible. This scrutiny involves an evaluation of the 33 grounds for exclusion to determine whether any of these grounds apply to the alien. If the alien is found excludable, his visa application can be denied at this stage. If a waiver of the relevant ground for exclusion is available, a waiver application can be made at the interview, to be forwarded by the consular official to the INS for adjudication. The consular official will then conduct an interview of the parties in furtherance of the waiver application, and the results of the interview will also be forwarded to the INS.

E. Visa Issuance and Denial—A visa, when issued, is valid for four months. The visa permits the alien to travel to the United States to apply for entry as a lawful permanent resident. Upon admission by the INS officers at the border, a record of admission as a permanent resident is made, and an application for issuance of the appropriate documentation (Alien Registration Receipt Card or "green" card) is forwarded to the card-issuing facility. The alien's file is sent on to the INS office with jurisdiction over the alien's place of residence in the U.S. A visa can only be denied for reasons set out in the statute or regulations. Review of a denial, however, is extremely limited, and the State Department will only issue advisory opinions when a denial is based on an issue of law. Although theoretically the consul need not follow the advisory opinion, in practice the consul is likely to follow the State Department's opinion. No federal court review from a denial of a visa application is permitted.

––––––––––

The process of securing an immigrant visa usually begins with the filing of a visa petition at the INS district office. This petition is meant to verify the family or employment relationship that underlies the alien's claim to preference or immediate relative status. Family petitions are filed on Form I–130. Petitions for occupational preference are filed on Form I–140, and the employer generally must have secured labor certification from the Labor Department before presenting the I–140 to the district office. Upon approval, INS endorses the visa petition and forwards it to the U.S. consul in the country where the alien is expected to complete the rest of the processing. Approval does not mean that INS has found the alien generally admissible; that issue must be decided by the consul. *See De Figueroa v. INS,* 501 F.2d 191 (7th Cir.1974).

The family member or employer who files the request is known as the petitioner; the alien overseas who wants to immigrate is known as the beneficiary. The labels indicate who remains in command of the process at this stage: the petitioner. That individual can withdraw the petition at any time, without the beneficiary's consent, and certain events, such as the petitioner's death, result in automatic revocation. 8 C.F.R. § 205.1. The beneficiary receives no vested rights based merely on the approval of a petition. If, at the time of revocation, the beneficiary has not already traveled to the United States under the immigrant visa, or been accorded an adjustment of status based on the petition, the revocation will be effective to block the beneficiary's immigration. *See Wright v. INS,* 379 F.2d 275 (6th Cir.1967); *Amarante v. Rosenberg,* 326 F.2d 58 (9th Cir.1964).

The immigrant visa is not stamped into the alien's passport. It is a separate document, with attachments, meant to be presented in its special envelope to the admitting immigration officer at the port of entry. If that officer finds no disqualifications upon his inspection, he will keep the immigrant visa, make a notation of admission as a lawful permanent resident in the alien's passport, and forward the necessary papers for ultimate issuance of the Alien Registration Receipt Card, Form I–551. Issuance may take up to six months.

The I–551 is the celebrated "green card," although in recent years it has been issued in a version nearly white in color. Before 1976, a truly green card, Form I–151, was used as the alien registration receipt card. That version was replaced with the current, machine-readable I–551 when new technology became available, but resident aliens who received the old form on arrival may still use it for all the same purposes as the I–551. The green card is usually thought of as a permit for employment in the United States. It does fulfill that purpose and also many others, but as its official name suggests, it was adopted principally to serve as evidence of compliance with the alien fingerprinting and registration requirements of INA §§ 261–266. *See* especially § 264(d) and 8 C.F.R. Pt. 264. (The I–94 usually serves a similar function for nonimmigrants, evidencing compliance with applicable registration provisions, although many nonimmigrants are exempt from fingerprinting under reciprocal arrangements with their countries of nationality. *See* 8 U.S.C.A. § 1201a.) When the federal government adopted its comprehensive alien registration scheme in 1940, its action served to preempt similar requirements then being imposed by the states. *See Hines v. Davidowitz,* 312 U.S. 52, 61 S.Ct. 399, 85 L.Ed. 581 (1941). For more on the background of federal alien registration provisions, *see* G & R § 6.10.

If a permanent resident alien plans to leave this country temporarily, he may do so and then return as a "special immigrant" under INA §§ 101(a)(27)(A), 211(b). (Make sure you understand why such aliens are treated as special immigrants under the Act.) But for purposes of return, it is important for the alien to take along documentation clearly demonstrating that he or she is a returning resident. In most instances, the I–551, the Alien Registration Receipt Card, serves as the needed re-entry permit. 8 C.F.R. § 211.1(b). *See* INA § 223, governing reentry permits. But as we will examine later, in nearly all circumstances such a return to the United States constitutes a new "entry" under the Act, making all the exclusion grounds of § 212(a) applicable afresh. Possession of a green card thus will not *assure* re-entry; it merely dispenses with certain documentary requirements.

At the Border

After securing a visa and traveling to the United States, intending immigrants and nonimmigrants will encounter an immigration inspector at the border checkpoint or port of entry. Most will be admitted after a few quick and routine questions. A small percentage will undergo more thorough processing, and perhaps will be placed in exclusion proceedings before an immigration judge, the ultimate forum (subject to administrative and judicial review) for testing the applicant's right to enter.

In connection with the following material, you should review INA §§ 231–240 and read §§ 235 and 236 with care.

ELIZABETH J. HARPER, IMMIGRATION LAWS OF
THE UNITED STATES

487–92 (3d ed. 1975).

§ 1. Summary

Whether an alien is admissible to the United States when he arrives
at a port of entry is determined by the Immigration and Naturalization
Service. The fact that an alien is in possession of an immigrant or
nonimmigrant visa in itself does not entitle him to enter the United
States if he is found inadmissible by the Immigration and Naturalization
Service. (Sections 221(h), 235). The burden of proof that he is admissible
rests upon the applicant for admission. (Section 291).

The initial examination of an arriving alien, called primary inspection, is conducted by an inspecting immigration officer. He can admit but
not exclude the alien. If the inspecting immigration officer, also referred
to as primary inspector, believes that the cause of the alien's excludability
can be readily removed by the exercise of discretionary authority he may
refer the case to the district director. If the district director exercises
discretionary authority the primary inspector may admit the alien. However, if an alien is not clearly entitled to land he must be detained and the
case referred for further inquiry to a special inquiry officer. The special
inquiry officer conducts a formal hearing. The decision of the special
inquiry officer must be based on the evidence of record and, with certain
exceptions, may be appealed to the Board of Immigration Appeals. Special rules apply if an alien is excluded on physical or mental grounds.
Limited judicial review of the final administrative decision in exclusion
proceedings is available by habeas corpus.

§ 2. Inspection and Admission of Aliens

(A) INSPECTION AT PORTS OF ENTRY

Every alien, whether immigrant or nonimmigrant, arriving at a port
of the United States, is examined by one or more immigration officers in
order to determine whether he is entitled to land. Immigration officers
are authorized to board and search any vessel, aircraft, railway car or
other vehicle in which they believe aliens are being brought into the
United States. (Section 235(a))

(B) PRE-EXAMINATION IN UNITED STATES TERRITORIES AND POSSESSIONS

In the case of any aircraft proceeding from Guam, Puerto Rico, or the
Virgin Islands of the United States directly to any other of such places or
to the continental United States, the examination may be made immediately prior to the departure of the aircraft. (8 CFR 235.5(a))

(C) PRE-EXAMINATION IN CONTIGUOUS TERRITORY AND ADJACENT ISLANDS

In the case of any aircraft or vessel proceeding directly from foreign
contiguous territory or adjacent islands to the continental United States,
the examination may be made immediately prior to the departure of the

aircraft or vessel. The examination of aliens under these circumstances has the same effect as though made at the destined port of entry into the United States. (8 CFR 235.5(b))

(D) GENERAL QUALIFICATIONS

Every alien asking admission into the United States may be required to state under oath the purpose for which he comes and the length of time he intends to remain in the United States. He can be required to give any other information necessary for determining whether he belongs to any of the excludable classes. The following general qualifications and requirements must be met by any alien seeking to enter the United States as an immigrant or nonimmigrant:

(1) He must apply for admission in person at a place designated as a port of entry for aliens;

(2) He must apply for admission at a time the immigration office at the port is open for inspection;

(3) He must make his application in person to an immigration officer;

(4) He must present whatever documents are required, and

(5) He has to establish that he is not subject to exclusion under the immigration laws, Executive orders or Presidential proclamations. (8 CFR 235.1)

(E) ADMISSION

If the inspecting immigration officer finds an alien admissible he will insert in the alien's passport, if one is required, the word "admitted" and the date and place of admission. The same information will be inserted on the immigrant visa, re-entry permit, or the Arrival-Departure Card (Form I–94), presented by, or prepared for, an alien who is admitted. (8 CFR 235.4)

(F) DETENTION AND REFERRAL

If the examining immigration officer finds that an alien is not clearly entitled to land, or if his decision to admit him is challenged by another immigration officer, the alien is detained for further inquiry by a special inquiry officer. However, if the examining officer has reason to believe that the cause of an alien's excludability can readily be removed by:

(1) the posting of a bond,

(2) the exercise of discretionary authority vested in the Attorney General to waive certain grounds of ineligibility or to waive jointly with the Secretary of State certain documentary requirements, or

(3) the exercise of discretionary authority by the Attorney General for the admission of otherwise inadmissible returning resident aliens,

he may, instead of detaining the alien, refer his case to the district director within whose district the port is located. In such case further examination is deferred until the district director has decided whether the alien should be admitted by granting administrative relief as indicated above. (Section 236(a); 8 CFR 235.7)

If the examining immigration officer detains the alien for further inquiry before a special inquiry officer, the alien must be promptly informed by the delivery of Form I–122, "Notice to Alien detained for Hearing by Special Inquiry Officer." (8 CFR 235.6)

§ 3. Special Inquiry

(A) SPECIAL INQUIRY OFFICER

A special inquiry officer, also referred to as an immigration judge (8 CFR § 1.1(1)), is an immigration officer whom the Attorney General deems specially qualified to conduct special inquiries and who is designated and selected by the Attorney General individually or by regulations to conduct such proceedings. No immigration officer is permitted to act as a special inquiry officer in any case in which he has engaged in investigative or prosecuting functions. (Sections 101(b)(4), 236(a))

(B) RESPONSIBILITIES

The special inquiry officer determines whether an alien detained on inspection is to be excluded and deported from the United States or whether he will be permitted to enter. Hearings before the special inquiry officer are not open to the public unless the alien requests that the public, including the press, be admitted and states for the record that he is waiving the requirement that the hearing be closed. The decision of a special inquiry officer in exclusion proceedings must be rendered only on the evidence produced in the hearing and is final unless it is reversed on appeal. (Section 236(a), (b)). In exclusion proceedings the special inquiry officer rules on objections, introduces material and relevant evidence on behalf of the Government and the alien and regulates the course of the hearing. (8 CFR 236.2(b))

(C) HEARING

In exclusion proceedings the alien may be represented by an attorney or representative who is permitted to examine the alien. The attorney or representative or the alien himself is permitted to examine any witness offered in the alien's behalf and to cross-examine any witness called by the Government, to offer evidence and to make objections. (8 CFR 236.2)

(D) TRIAL ATTORNEY

The district director may assign an immigration officer to the exclusion proceedings as a trial attorney for the Government. The responsibilities of a trial attorney include the presentation of evidence and the interrogation, examination, and cross-examination of the applicant and other witnesses. (8 CFR 236.2(c))

(E) RECORD OF HEARING

Exclusion hearings are recorded verbatim except for statements made off the record with the permission of the special inquiry officer. The record of the hearing including the testimony and exhibits, the special inquiry officer's decision and all written orders, motions, and appeals constitute the record in the case. (8 CFR 236.2(e))

(F) DECISION

The special inquiry officer will either admit or exclude the alien. His decision may be oral or written. If made orally the alien, at his request, is furnished with a transcript of the decision. (8 CFR [236.5])

(G) APPEAL

(1) Appeal by Alien

The decision of the special inquiry officer excluding the alien may be appealed to the Board of Immigration Appeals. If the decision is made orally, the alien who wishes to appeal must file immediately Form I–290A, "Notice of Appeal to the Board of Immigration Appeals." He is given ten days to file a brief. An appeal from a written decision must be taken within thirteen days after mailing. (8 CFR [236.7(b)]).

(2) Appeal by District Director

An order admitting the alien may be appealed by the district director within five days from the day of decision. In such case the alien is advised that he may make representations to the Board including the filing of a brief. (8 CFR [236.7(c)]).

————

Notes

1. As is evident from this reading, in the ordinary case an alien held for exclusion proceedings has fairly extensive procedural rights under the statute and implementing regulations. The alien enjoys a right to counsel (at no expense to the government), an opportunity to present his case by written or oral evidence, as he chooses, and the chance to cross-examine opposing witnesses. The decision must be based exclusively on the record compiled in the administrative proceedings, and the immigration judge must set forth the reasons for the decision, which is then subject to both administrative and judicial review.

The Simpson-Mazzoli bills would have cut back, however, on the procedural entitlements of one class of excludable aliens, those who arrive without documents. The Senate bill was the more restrictive. S. 529, § 121, would have replaced the first sentence of INA § 235(b) with, *inter alia,* the following:

(b)(1) If an examining immigration officer at the port of arrival determines that an alien does not have the documentation required to obtain entry into the United States, does not have any reasonable basis for legal entry into the United States, and has not applied for asylum under section 208, such alien shall not be admissible and shall be excluded from entry into the United States without further inquiry or hearing.

Section 123(b) of the bill ostensibly precluded judicial review of such summary exclusion decisions.

What exactly would this change accomplish? Would it be constitutional under the tests the Supreme Court developed in *Mathews v. Eldridge?* In your view, does the Constitution require some avenue of appeal? Or is the summary procedure appropriately tailored in light of the very limited range of factual issues an alien subject to it under S.529 could be expected to raise? *Cf. Califano v. Yamasaki*, 442 U.S. 682, 696–97, 99 S.Ct. 2545, 2555–56, 61 L.Ed.2d 176 (1979). Would the proposed change be good policy in light of the increase in undocumented migration in recent years?

2. As Harper points out, the possession of a visa does not guarantee that the alien will be admitted. The immigration inspector may reach his own conclusions about the alien's admissibility. (Indeed, even if he decides to admit, the government may still retry the question of admissibility years later, by bringing deportation proceedings alleging that the alien was excludable at the time of entry. INA § 241(a)(1), to be discussed in Chapter Five.) Why should this be so? Hasn't the U.S. consul, a government official sworn to uphold the laws and expert in the application of the immigration provisions, already determined, after inquiry, that the alien meets the requirements for admission to the United States? Shouldn't principles of *res judicata* or estoppel prevent such redeterminations?

Part of the answer lies in the explicit directive from Congress that admissibility is to remain open to wholesale reconsideration. INA §§ 204(e), 221(h). But the Supreme Court also held, relatively early in the history of federal immigration controls, that principles of *res judicata* did not have to be applied in such proceedings. *Pearson v. Williams*, 202 U.S. 281, 26 S.Ct. 608, 50 L.Ed. 1029 (1906). *See* Gordon, *Finality of Immigration and Nationality Decisions: Can the Government Be Estopped?*, 31 U.Chi.L.Rev. 433 (1964). In any event, significant practical problems would arise if administrative *res judicata* were held to apply here, for in that event the agencies would doubtless develop procedures far more cumbersome and painstaking than anything we now experience. Most border processing can be quick and routine, even perfunctory, precisely because an admission decision is not binding on the government for the indefinite future.

For an account of the growing acceptance of administrative *res judicata* in some settings, and a suggestion, in dictum, that it might apply to some determinations under the immigration and nationality laws, *see Cartier v. Secretary of State*, 506 F.2d 191, 195–98 (D.C.Cir.1974), *cert. denied* 421 U.S. 947, 95 S.Ct. 1677, 44 L.Ed.2d 101 (1975).

3. Section 235(b) provides that every alien who does not appear to be "clearly and beyond a doubt entitled to land" shall receive an exclusion hearing. But there are two exceptions enumerated there. The first we have already encountered. It precludes a hearing when an alien is deemed excludable based on confidential information, in accordance with § 235(c). The second is based on § 273(d), and it allows for summary exclusion of stowaways, without a hearing before an immigration judge. *See* G & R § 3.23a. But, as you might expect, there are also exceptions to this exception. Stowaways who appear to be returning residents may be entitled to a full hearing. *Matter of B.,* 5 I & N Dec. 712 (BIA 1954). And it has been held that stowaways who apply for political asylum must be given a full hearing on the asylum issue, under the Refugee Act of 1980. *Yiu Sing Chun v. Sava,* 708 F.2d 869 (2d Cir.1983).

Adjustment of Status

For many years, the only avenue for gaining immigrant status required the issuance of an immigrant visa, and visas were not—and still are not—issued in the United States. They must be obtained from U.S. consular officers posted abroad, usually in the country of the alien's nationality or residence. The Immigration Service found itself faced increasingly with aliens in this country in nonimmigrant status, however, who could show that they qualified for permanent immigration and who wished to avoid a costly trip overseas. One might easily say that such "nonimmigrants" deserve no special favors, as their new immigration plans reveal that they were not legitimate nonimmigrants from the start. Suspicion about such concealed intentions remains of real concern, but the administrators eventually concluded that many who sought an easier way to change status had honestly undergone a change of heart after arrival here—usually associated with marriage to a U.S. citizen or permanent resident.

In 1935 the agency therefore developed a "pre-examination" process that simplified matters somewhat. Under it, clearly qualified aliens could complete most of the necessary paperwork while in this country, and then travel briefly (and less expensively) to a U.S. consulate in Canada to secure the actual immigrant visa. This administrative reform built pressure for Congress to amend the statute and allow even greater simplification.

In 1952, with the new Immigration and Nationality Act, Congress finally made the change. It adopted § 245, which authorizes "adjustment of status" from nonimmigrant to immigrant for aliens who meet certain requirements. This whole process can be carried out by the INS, and the alien need never leave the United States. Congress periodically has changed the qualifications—sometimes loosening them, sometimes tightening them, in response to increasing or declining concern about possible abuses by the nonimmigrants who might seek those benefits. Indeed, controversy continues over whether the availability of the adjustment option encourages fraud by nonimmigrant visa applicants. Some claim that this mechanism induces people to conceal their intent to immigrate in order to secure nonimmigrant admission and then, after entry, establish the family ties or employment relationships necessary to adjust status. *See, e.g.*, SCIRP, Appendix G 35–38, 47.

JAIN v. INS

United States Court of Appeals, Second Circuit, 1979.
612 F.2d 683.

FEINBERG, CIRCUIT JUDGE:

Om Prakash Jain, a citizen of India in this country on a nonimmigrant business visa, petitions for review of a decision of the Board of Immigration Appeals, which denied his application for adjustment of status under section 245 of the Immigration and Nationality Act. The Board based its denial, in the exercise of its discretion, on a finding that petitioner entered the United States with a preconceived intent to remain permanently in this country. Petitioner's principal claim is that this is an improper reason for denying relief under section 245. For reasons given below, we reject this contention, along with petitioner's other arguments. We therefore deny the petition for review and affirm the decision of the Board.

I

The facts, as they appear in the record before us, may fairly be summarized as follows. This is petitioner Jain's third stay in the United States. The first began in June 1974, when he was 23 years old and was admitted on a nonimmigrant visa as a visitor for business. Jain had obtained that visa as the proprietor and business representative of a company located in Jaipur, India, which exported gems, beads and semi-precious stones. Jain remained here for four to five weeks looking for customers, but left without success. A little over a year later, Jain returned in the same capacity as before, and again found no customers. After staying in this country a month, Jain again departed. While he was here, however, Jain apparently conceived the idea of creating a company within the United States to import beads and jewelry from India and keep an inventory here. This would allow Jain to guarantee quick delivery to potential customers, thus overcoming the difficulty he had earlier encountered in seeking to sell his goods. Before he left this country on this second visit, Jain retained an attorney, created a new import company supposedly located in the room at the hotel where he stayed, filed a certificate of doing business under the assumed name of Asian Imports and obtained a social security number for himself.

Upon his return to India, Jain quickly liquidated his export firm in Jaipur by turning it over to his brother. Thereafter, he reentered the United States in January 1976 on a nonimmigrant business visa good for four months, as the representative of his former export business. The true reason for his return, however, was to run Asian Imports, his newly established enterprise here. Within a month, Jain also applied to the Immigration and Naturalization Service for adjustment of his status to that of permanent resident alien. The basis of the application was his alleged status as an investor, a term of art in this context more fully described below.[a]

Two years later, the District Director of the Service denied Jain's application for adjustment of status because of his lack of good faith in applying for his nonimmigrant visa abroad. After Jain failed to depart voluntarily, the Service began deportation proceedings. Before an immigration judge, Jain conceded his deportability, but again sought adjustment of status as an investor and, in the alternative, applied for reinstatement of voluntary departure status. After a hearing, the immigration judge held in August 1978 that Jain did not qualify as an investor and, alternatively, that even if he did, his application would be denied on discretionary grounds because Jain last entered this country with a preconceived intent to remain permanently. On appeal, the Board in July 1979 affirmed the decision of the immigration judge on the second, discretionary ground, and granted Jain again the privilege of voluntary departure. Jain's petition to us for review allows him to enjoy the automatic stay of deportation that accompanies such action, and almost four years have now elapsed since Jain's entry in January 1976 on a four-month business visa.

II

* * *

The Act presumes that entering aliens seek to do so as immigrants. Consequently, nonimmigrants—those aliens seeking entry only for a limited time and purpose—bear the burden of demonstrating to the United States consular officials abroad and the immigration authorities in this country that they are bona fide nonimmigrants. Jain, like many nonimmigrants, obtained entry under a nonimmigrant visa for business. Such a visa allows an alien to conduct business in the United States for a foreign employer for a limited period. 8 C.F.R. 214.2(b). However, in order to establish his bona fide nonimmigrant status and thereby qualify for such a visa, a nonimmigrant is required to demonstrate to the satisfaction of the immigration authorities that he has a foreign residence that he has no intention of abandoning and that he will depart voluntarily at the end of his authorized stay.

Under earlier versions of the Act, nonimmigrant aliens who sought to adjust their status to that of immigrants were required to leave the country and seek reentry as immigrants. To ameliorate this hardship, the Immigration and Naturalization Service devised an administrative procedure, known as pre-examination, under which nonimmigrant aliens were examined by immigration officials in the United States and were issued an immigrant visa by the consular office in Canada if their admissibility as immigrants was established. This procedure was used extensively for many years. In 1952, Congress enacted section 245 of the

a. There is no preference under § 203 for investors, but in 1976 an adequate investment might exempt a non-preference alien from the labor certification requirement. See the note on Investors as Immigrants, following this case.—eds.

Act, to obviate the need for the pre-examination procedure. The current version of the statute provides in pertinent part:

> (a) The status of an alien, other than an alien crewman, who was inspected and admitted or paroled into the United States may be adjusted by the Attorney General, in his discretion and under such regulations as he may prescribe, to that of an alien lawfully admitted for permanent residence if (1) the alien makes an application for such adjustment, (2) the alien is eligible to receive an immigrant visa and is admissible to the United States for permanent residence, and (3) an immigrant visa is immediately available to him at the time his application is approved.[b]

Thus, a nonimmigrant alien may now adjust his status to that of an immigrant without leaving the country if he is admissible for permanent residence and is eligible for an immigrant visa, which is "immediately available" to him. However, even if the nonimmigrant satisfies these express statutory requirements, the Service has discretion under section 245 to deny the application for adjustment of status. Furthermore, the alien bears the burden of persuading the Service to exercise its discretion favorably, since adjustment of status under section 245 is considered to be extraordinary relief.

The deceptively brief statutory requirements of section 245 nonetheless pose complex administrative problems. One major obstacle facing section 245 applicants is to demonstrate that an immigrant visa is "immediately available." The law governing the availability of visas is complicated, and if a nonimmigrant cannot establish an exemption from the numerical limitations applicable to certain categories of immigrant visas, he must await the chronological distribution of such visas. Furthermore, certain categories of immigrant visas are unavailable unless the applicant either obtains a certification from the Secretary of Labor that his employment in this country will not affect the American labor market adversely or establishes an exemption from this certification requirement. Jain apparently was eligible only for this type of visa and therefore attempted to establish an exemption from the certification requirement as an investor in a domestic enterprise. The investor exemption, at the time Jain applied, allowed waiver of the certification requirement if the alien had invested over $10,000 in an enterprise that he managed and that directly created domestic job opportunities. *Mehta v. Immigration and Naturalization Service,* 574 F.2d 701 (2d Cir.1978). While Jain's investment in Asian Imports apparently satisfied the requisite amount, the immigration judge found that Jain was ineligible for the investor exemption because his enterprise had "failed to expand job opportunities for anyone in this country." Relying on the authority of *Mehta,* supra, the judge therefore found that Jain had failed to demonstrate that an immigrant visa was "immediately available." Although this determination of statutory ineligibility seems amply supported by the record, the Board of

---

b. An amendment in 1976 changed the last word to "filed." For a discussion of its significance, *see* G & R § 7.7b(4).—eds.

Immigration Appeals affirmed the denial of section 245 relief on the second rationale offered by the immigration judge—that Jain's application did not warrant a favorable exercise of discretion. We now turn to this issue.

III

The immigration judge ruled that even if Jain were "statutorily eligible" for adjustment of status, relief would be denied as a discretionary matter. Because Jain had already liquidated his business in India and made plans to operate Asian Imports in this country, the judge concluded that Jain had "not been candid" with the immigration authorities when he last entered the country on a nonimmigrant visa for business and that his application presented no "outstanding or unusual equities" warranting a favorable exercise of discretion. The Board of Immigration Appeals adopted this ground for decision, holding that the evidence supported "the immigration judge's conclusion that [Jain] entered the United States with a preconceived intent to remain permanently" and that such a finding would support a discretionary denial of status adjustment.

Petitioner now argues that his preconceived intent to remain permanently in this country after entering on a temporary nonimmigrant visa was an improper basis for denying discretionary relief. The issue is an important one, and apparently has not been addressed in a published opinion of this court. However, a number of other circuits have considered whether the good faith of an alien's entry as a nonimmigrant is a proper consideration in the exercise of discretion under section 245. The most extensive discussion of the issue is by the Third Circuit, sitting en banc in *Ameeriar v. Immigration and Naturalization Service,* 438 F.2d 1028 (3d Cir.1971). Both the majority opinion and the dissent of Judge Gibbons rely heavily upon the legislative history of section 245, although their interpretations differ. The original version of section 245 enacted in 1952 to replace the pre-examination procedure authorized the Attorney General, through the Service, to grant relief "under such regulations as he may prescribe to insure the application of this paragraph solely to the cases of aliens who entered the United States in good faith as nonimmigrants." 66 Stat. 217. Therefore, good faith entry as a nonimmigrant was apparently regarded as a condition precedent to the favorable exercise of discretion. This requirement was deleted in the 1960 amendments to the Act in order to enlarge the Service's discretion to act favorably on behalf of nonimmigrants who were otherwise eligible for admission as immigrants. However, the Service thereafter took the position that the absence of good faith entry, even though no longer a statutory bar to section 245 relief, was nonetheless a factor relevant to the favorable exercise of discretion. See Sofaer, The Change of Status Adjudication: A Case Study of the Informal Agency Process, 1 J. Legal Studies 349, 374–76 (1972). The majority in *Ameeriar,* as well as the other circuits that have considered the issue, adopted this view.

* * *

While the statutory question is not free from doubt, we nonetheless believe that the majority view is more persuasive.

* * *

Furthermore, allowing the Service the discretion to deny section 245 relief to nonimmigrant aliens who enter in bad faith appears to comport with the proper administration of the statute. As previously noted, the Act distinguishes between immigrants and nonimmigrants and specifically requires those seeking nonimmigrant status to establish that they have no intention of abandoning their foreign residence and that they will depart voluntarily at the end of their authorized stay. We do not know whether Jain would have received an immigrant visa had he applied for one in India with a true statement of his intent. But had the true facts been known, he clearly would not have received a nonimmigrant visa because he would not have been entitled to one. Jain did not seek entry into the United States to represent a foreign employer for a limited period; he instead sought entry to remain permanently and to run his own business here. To require the Service to disregard this misrepresentation by Jain would effectively undercut the Act's requirement that nonimmigrants demonstrate their bona fide status. In contrast, permitting the Service to deny section 245 relief based on the nonimmigrant's lack of good faith protects the integrity of the consular procedures established by the Act.

Finally, it should be noted that denial of section 245 relief, when coupled with a grant of voluntary departure, is a lenient disposition of what might possibly be regarded as fraud. Although denied an adjustment of status, Jain is not precluded from seeking entry as an immigrant through the normal process established by the Act.

* * *

Thus, we are content to adopt the majority view espoused in *Ameeriar,* knowing full well that in this area Congress legislates frequently and can correct us if we are wrong. On this reading of section 245, it is clear that the Board's decision was not an abuse of discretion.

* * *

IV

Jain also argues on appeal that he was denied due process because he was unable to appeal the original denial of his section 245 application directly and could only do so in the context of deportation proceedings. We find this argument to be without merit. Although the regulations do preclude a direct administrative appeal from the denial by a district director of a section 245 application, 8 C.F.R. § 245.2(a)(4), the alien is entitled to a de novo review of his application in the context of deportation proceedings. *Id.* We consider this dual opportunity to present a section 245 application to provide ample process, particularly in light of the discretionary nature of section 245 relief. The fact that the second consideration of the application takes place within the context of a deportation proceeding is irrelevant. Petitioner's argument to the contrary assumes that Jain could have avoided deportation proceedings simply by choosing not to renew his section 245 application. However, since Jain's deportability as an overstay was clear, the initiation of deportation proceedings was a matter over which he had no control.

Accordingly, the petition for review is denied.

Notes on Adjustment of Status

1. Adjustment of status has become increasingly popular over the years since its adoption in 1952. Although the year-to-year totals have fluctuated up and down, the general trend is decidedly upward. Here are the totals for the first six preference categories and for immediate relatives during the four most recent years for which data are available. (These statistics focus on immediate relatives and the six preference categories in order to gain usefully comparable figures. They avoid lumping in adjustments of status for refugees and certain other categories to which other, special adjustment provisions apply.)

	FY 1978	FY 1979	FY 1980	FY 1981
Adjustments stated preference categories	47,985	45,323	45,460	47,583
immediate relatives	41,741	43,129	58,127	52,398
Total adjustments	89,726	88,452	103,587	99,981
Total permanent resident admissions for the year (stated preference categories and immediate relatives)	346,993	389,616	412,356	418,035
Adjustments as percentage of total admissions	25.9%	22.7%	25.1%	23.9%

Source: 1981 Statistical Yearbook of the Immigration and Naturalization Service, Table 4A.

The largest single group of adjustments under § 245 traditionally consists of new spouses of United States citizens, who can come in without numerical limitation as immediate relatives. In 1978, 33,066 aliens secured adjustment of status on this basis; in 1979, 33,023 did so; in 1980, 44,389; and in 1981, 40,419. *Id.*

2. The *Jain* case sketches the applicable procedures for adjustment of status. In its purest form, adjustment simply provides a replacement for traveling overseas to obtain an immigrant visa in the classic fashion, from a consular officer. Adjustment does not supersede the need for a visa petition in those immigration categories to which the petition requirement applies, but often those petitions (on Form I–130 for family preferences and I–140 for occupational preferences) can be submitted simultaneously with the application for adjustment on Form I–485. Both the petition and the adjustment application will be adjudicated by the

same agency, INS, and usually by the same examinations officer in the INS district office. The consular process, in contrast, will not start until the consul receives an approved visa petition from INS.

In passing on the actual application for adjustment of status based on the information supplied on the I–485 (as distinguished from deciding the merits of the accompanying visa petition), the INS examiner makes all the same determinations as a consular officer. She must assure that the applicant is qualified for the immigrant category claimed, and must go on to judge whether any of the grounds of exclusion might apply. For purposes of this process, the applicant for adjustment, although physically within the United States, is considered exactly as though he were at the border applying for initial entry. *See Yui Sing Tse v. INS,* 596 F.2d 831, 834 (9th Cir.1979).

3. As the *Jain* case also makes clear, the district director's delegate considering an adjustment application has to make several determinations beyond those required of a consular officer. In particular, the INS officer must decide whether the applicant meets the special requirements imposed by § 245. The most important are the following: (1) The alien must have been inspected and admitted or paroled. INA § 245(a). This means that adjustment is available almost exclusively to people present in the United States on nonimmigrant visas; it cannot under any circumstances be claimed by those who entered without inspection. Note, however, that the alien need not necessarily have complied with all the conditions of the nonimmigrant admission in order to qualify for adjustment. In other words, visa overstays and certain other such violators are statutorily eligible. But such noncompliance—especially serious noncompliance—may have an important bearing on the exercise of the district director's discretion. (2) The alien must have been admitted in some status other than that of alien crewman (§ 245(c)(1)), "transit without visa" (§ 245(c)(3)), or exchange visitor under admission category J (§ 212(e), which provides that exchange visitors, in most circumstances, must agree to return to their home countries for two years after completion of the visit). (3) The alien must not have worked without INS authorization as a nonimmigrant, after the effective date of the statutory amendment that added this requirement, January 1, 1977. *See Pei-Chi Tien v. INS,* 638 F.2d 1324 (5th Cir.1981). This final limitation, imposed under § 245(c)(2), does not apply, by its terms, to adjustment applicants who are the immediate relatives of U.S. citizens.

Beyond these preclusions, the district director must be sure that an immigrant visa is immediately available to the applicant as of the date when the Form I–485 is filed. If the applicant seeks to qualify in one of the six numerically limited preference categories, availability can usually be determined by consulting the chart in the most recent Visa Office Bulletin—*see* page 111, *supra,* for a sample. In short, if there is a two year backlog for aliens in this applicant's preference category, the theory of § 245 is that the alien should pass that time in his home country and eventually come in, if he is still interested, through the regular immigrant visa process. But occasionally it has proved possible either through administrative grace or tenacious litigation for an alien to string out his stay until the priority date, which is fixed as of the filing of a successful visa petition or labor certification, is finally reached. For an example of the intricacies that may be involved in such processing, and in the determination whether or not an immigrant visa is "immediately available" at the relevant time, *see Dong Sik Kwon v. INS,* 646 F.2d 909 (5th Cir.1981). *See generally* G & R § 7.7c.

One last factor is vitally important in § 245 adjudications: the application of the "Attorney General's" discretion. *Jain* suggests the difficulties in managing such discretion and in submitting it to meaningful judicial review. *See Matter of Blas,* 15 I & N. Dec. 626 (BIA 1974, AG 1976). Such issues will be examined at length in Chapter Six where we consider various provisions providing relief from deportation, most of which call upon INS to make a similar exercise of discretion.

4. It is important to remember that an alien denied adjustment on one of the grounds described in the previous note is not necessarily disqualified from permanent resident alien status; he will simply have to use the usual immigrant visa process if he wishes to obtain permanent residence. For example, if an adjustment application is denied because the alien entered without inspection, he can probably return to his home country and apply for an immigrant visa from there. Earlier clandestine entries do not bar the issuance of an immigrant visa if all the other qualifications are met—at least if the applicant left this country voluntarily and not under a deportation order (*see* INA § 212(a)(17)).

Moreover, remarkably enough, INS and the State Department have found it useful to develop a simplified procedure, called "Stateside Criteria Processing," which is very much like the old "pre-examination" described in *Jain.* See O.I. § 212.11; 9 FAM § 42.110, Note 2.2. This has developed even though the enactment of § 245 was probably expected to eliminate arrangements of this type. Under Stateside Criteria Processing, certain carefully selected categories of aliens who are disqualified from the benefits of § 245 but who are clearly eligible for immigrant visas (such as beneficiaries of approved immediate relative petitions who originally entered without inspection) are permitted to go to Mexico or Canada to secure their immigrant visas from our consulates there, rather than make the more expensive journey back to their home countries. Intricate arrangements have been worked out with those two governments in order to make this system function, by guaranteeing that the United States will accept the return of the alien, on parole, if for some reason the U.S. consul does not issue the expected visa. *See* G & R § 7.3b; 59 Interp.Rel. 496 (1983) (latest Visa Office guidelines for such cases).

5. Adjustment of status for one who qualifies in one of the preference categories is not a numerical add-on; it counts against the annual total in the same fashion as would admission under an immigrant visa for the same category. For this reason, adjustment will not be granted in the numerically limited preference categories until INS has contacted the Visa Office at the State Department and secured an immigrant visa number for the appropriate preference classification.

6. If the applicant is denied adjustment of status by the district director, as Jain was, on either statutory or discretionary grounds, no administrative appeal is allowed. 8 C.F.R. § 245.2(a)(4). Instead, the regulations provide that the application for adjustment may be renewed before the immigration judge conducting the alien's deportation proceedings. The immigration judge is not bound in any way by the earlier adjudication in the district office, but instead applies the statutory grounds and exercises the Attorney General's discretion anew, based on any information in the appropriate forms or developed at the deportation hearing. In this latter setting, adjustment functions more like the other provisions for relief from deportation to be covered in Chapter Six, rather than as the replacement for immigrant visa processing we have been examining in this chapter.

Ordinarily there is no judicial review of a denial of adjustment until after a renewal in the deportation hearing has proved unsuccessful. In that event, review is sought directly in the court of appeals as part of the statutory review procedure under INA § 106(a), which brings to the court all issues tried in the actual deportation proceedings. The *Jain* case exemplifies this avenue of review. But occasionally an alien has secured immediate judicial review in the district court, under § 279, of the district director's denial of adjustment, without waiting for the commencement of a deportation proceeding. *See Nasan v. INS*, 449 F.Supp. 244 (N.D.Ill. 1978).

7. For a thorough description and critique of adjustment procedures and requirements, based on detailed studies of adjudications in the New York District Office in 1967–68, *see* Sofaer, *The Change-of-Status Adjudication: A Case Study of the Informal Agency Process*, 1 J. Legal Stud. 349 (1972). This study contains several suggestions for procedural improvements that still remain cogent. *See also* G & R § 7.7.

Rescission of Adjustment of Status

The last sentence of INA § 246(a) provides for rescission of adjustment of status acquired under § 245 if "it shall appear to the satisfaction of the Attorney General that the person was not in fact eligible for such adjustment of status." *See generally Zaoutis v. Kiley*, 558 F.2d 1096 (2d Cir.1977). Contested rescission actions are heard by immigration judges, and are appealable to the BIA. 8 C.F.R. Part 246 (1984).

Note that § 246 rescissions are subject to a five-year statute of limitations. This is a curious provision, because in 1952, when the adjustment procedure was created, along with § 246, Congress was busy *removing* nearly all statutes of limitation that had previously restricted the deportation of aliens whose initial entry was later revealed to be defective. *See* H.R.Rep. No. 2096, 82d Cong., 2d Sess. 129 (1952); 98 Cong.Rec. 4302 (1952) (remarks of Rep. Walter). The five-year limitation in § 246(a) is so curious, in fact, that the Justice Department has tried to explain it away as "a historical anomaly or the result of an accident in the legislative process." Quoted in *Oloteo v. INS*, 643 F.2d 679, 683 n. 8 (9th Cir.1981). (We will examine the broader issue of statutes of limitation for deportation more closely in Chapter Five.)

Is there any reason why an alien whose status was adjusted should enjoy greater immunity after five years than does an alien who entered on an immigrant visa? We are hard put to come up with a policy justification. Nevertheless, the Board of Immigration Appeals, in various encounters with § 246(a), has steadfastly attempted to give real meaning to the apparent congressional choice to favor adjustment beneficiaries. In two significant cases, the Board read the section as providing, in essence, immunity to removal for an adjusted alien after five years had passed. In both instances, however, the Attorney General took referral of the cases and reversed the Board's decision. *Matter of S.,* 9 I & N Dec. 548 (BIA 1961; AG 1962), and *Matter of Belenzo,* 17 I & N Dec. 374 (BIA 1980; AG 1981). The Attorney General held that even after the five years have passed, the alien remains fully subject to deportation (or exclusion if he has traveled abroad and seeks readmission), whether the ground for deportation or exclusion relates to a defect in the original entry prior to adjustment (*Matter of S.*) or to a defect in the adjustment itself (*Matter of Belenzo*). As a result, if INS seeks to remove an adjusted alien *within* five years, it must always commence rescission proceedings first and then, if successful, launch deportation proceedings. *See Matter of Saunders,* 16 I & N Dec. 326 (BIA 1977). After five years, INS may go directly to deportation proceedings. The lapse of time furnishes no immunity on the bottom-line issue of removal. *See* Orlow, *Rescission—Rationalizing the Irrational,* 6 Immig.J. 6 (1983).

Doesn't this approach effectively read the five-year limitation out of the statute? The Attorney General believed that he had not wholly transgressed the congressional intent: "the limitations period is designed to assure that, if no other action to obtain rescission is taken within 5 years, the Attorney General may not use the procedural mechanism for rescission, but must instead seek deportation, a route that offers special statutory safeguards to the alien." *Belenzo, supra,* at 383–84. Do you find this a convincing explanation?

Given the absence of statutes of limitation applicable to most immigrants, probably either outcome—the Board's or the Attorney General's—leads to unsatisfactory and distasteful results. In light of this dilemma, do you regard the Attorney General's decisions as a creative response to a congressional accident, assuring equal treatment of two classes of aliens (those who adjust and those who enter on an immigrant visa) who are similarly situated in every functional respect? Or do these decisions amount to a flouting of congressional intent to treat adjusted aliens as a preferred class, a choice which, however hard to justify, is evident from the plain language of the statute?

Investors as Immigrants

The current statute provides no immigration preference for prospective investors. When nonpreference numbers were still available, however, aliens could use their investment plans to secure one of those admission spots, because a prospective investment was held to exempt the alien from the labor certification requirement under INS regulations.

The magnitude of the required investment has varied, but the most recent regulations mandate commitment of $40,000 and a demonstration that the enterprise will employ at least one U.S. citizen or permanent resident other than the applicant and his or her family members. 8 C.F.R. § 212.8. With the unavailability of nonpreference immigration since 1978, these opportunities have disappeared. *See generally Foreign Investors: Strategies for Obtaining Residence,* 4 Imm.Law Rep. 97–102 (1985); Note, *Immigration for Investors: A Comparative Analysis of U.S., Canadian, and Australian Policies,* 7 B.C. Int'l & Comp.L.Rev. 113 (1984).

Should our laws encourage the immigration of investors? We provide a preference for those who come to *fill* jobs for which American workers are insufficient; should we provide a preference for aliens who would come to *create* jobs for American workers? The Select Commission on Immigration and Refugee Policy, which issued its report in 1981, was persuaded that we should. It recommended reserving a small number of spaces for substantial investors, and it suggested that a minimum investment of $250,000 might be an appropriate requirement. SCIRP, Final Report 131–32. Father Theodore M. Hesburgh dissented from this recommendation, commenting that "the rich should not be able to buy their way into this country." *Id.* at 336.

In 1982 the Senate passed an immigration reform bill containing the recommended preference for investors proposing to commit $250,000 and employ at least four U.S. workers. S. 2222, § 202, 97th Cong., 2d Sess. (1982). That bill did not reach the House floor. In 1983, when the reform battle was renewed in the 98th Congress, Senator Bumpers led a fight against this provision on the floor of the Senate. Sounding the same theme Father Hesburgh had pressed in 1981, he argued that the provision "is odious, it is offensive, it flies right in the face of the national character of this country." 129 Cong.Rec. S6738 (daily ed. May 16, 1983). Evidently he persuaded a majority of his colleagues, because the provision was deleted from the 1983 Senate bill by a vote of 51–46. House versions of the recent immigration reform bills have not contained an investor preference.

SECTION E.   DUE PROCESS REVISITED: DETENTION OF EXCLUDABLE ALIENS

In *Shaughnessy v. United States ex rel. Mezei,* 345 U.S. 206, 73 S.Ct. 625, 97 L.Ed. 956 (1953), the Supreme Court clearly approved indefinite detention of an excludable alien, without any judicial testing of the substantive merits or even the procedural validity of the detention order. The decision provoked harsh criticism in the press and in academic commentary, as we have seen. But succeeding years presented few opportunities to rethink the result in that case.

In part, the absence of such opportunities reflects the relative rarity of a case like Mezei's; most of the time an excludable alien has somewhere to go. Indeed, it is usually recognized under international law that a nation has an obligation to permit the return of its nationals. *See, e.g.,* A. Roth, *International Law Applied to Aliens* 39–44 (1949); *Universal Declaration of Human Rights,* Article 13(2) ("Everyone has the right to leave any country, including his own, and to return to his country."). And beyond this, the government simply began to detain aliens less frequently. Not only was the McCarthy era subsiding (bringing a reduction in security-based exclusions), but perhaps more importantly, the Justice Department decided to close Ellis Island and other detention facilities in 1954, largely as an economy measure. Thereafter, the overwhelming majority of aliens in exclusion proceedings were freed on parole, unless there was some significant reason to regard them as dangerous or as likely to abscond before the hearing.

In 1980 this situation changed. Beginning in April of that year, thousands of undocumented Cubans arrived directly in the United States from the port of Mariel, opened by the Cuban government with an invitation to relatives in the United States to come pick up their family members. But the returning boats brought not only relatives. Cuban officials also forced them to carry thousands of others whom the Cubans wished to remove. As it turned out, a small percentage (but a sizable number) of the 125,000 Marielitos had criminal records in Cuba. For this reason, although the vast majority of the Cubans were paroled shortly after arrival, the government chose to detain many based on their criminal records. A few others committed criminal offenses after arrival, leading to a revocation of the initial parole. The detainees were given hearings and nearly all were held excludable. But the Cuban government refused to take them back. Not wishing to incur the expense of lengthy detentions, but also not wanting to release dangerous criminals, the government undertook various screening measures to decide who among this riskier group could be released.

At about the same time, a boat flow of longer standing was beginning to peak. Since the early 1970's, Haitians had been coming to Florida by small boat and very often filing for political asylum upon encountering INS. The numbers of Haitian asylum applicants exceeded 1000 per month during much of 1980. These numbers were low compared to the Cuban flow at the time, but they did place additional strain on INS resources and on several agencies of the state of Florida, where most of them landed. Shortly after taking office, the Reagan administration began extensive review of the problem of immigration control. The release policy followed since 1954 came to be seen as one cause of the increase in the number of asylum-seekers, making it more attractive for excludable aliens to come to the United States. Even if meritless, an asylum claim would purchase several months or years in this country, free of restraints and usually with permission to work. After mid-1981, the 1954 release policy was ended, although there is some controversy about when and how the new detention policy came into existence. Detention pending exclusion hearings became the norm thereafter, at least for aliens who arrived without documents. Several lawsuits challenged these new detention practices. The most important cases involved Haitians, even though other groups, such as Salvadorans and Guatemalans, were also affected. (The Cuban flow had been cut off in September 1980.)

Detention thus posed due process questions in two different but related settings, and it is hard to know which is the more poignant. Cubans believed to have criminal records faced confinement of indefinite duration; for all anyone could tell at the time, it might be permanent. The prospects for release seemed to be entirely dependent on the uncertainties of diplomacy between two feuding and mutually suspicious nations.[a] On the other hand, restrictive measures of some sort are more easily justified in the case of individuals who have committed serious crimes in the past. Moreover, these Cuban detainees had been ruled excludable, and most of those exclusion orders were final by the time the due process litigation reached decision in the courts.

The Haitians were in a different situation. Any who found confinement intolerable did not have to await the outcome of diplomatic maneuvering to secure release. They could simply return to Haiti. But of course, most were resisting such return based on the claim that they would be persecuted if they did so. Moreover, they had not yet been ruled excludable; asylum applications were still pending in the administrative system or in the courts. Some might yet prove to have perfectly valid entitlements to remain. Nevertheless, unlike the Cubans, they did not face the prospect of endless confinement. One way or another, detention would end, either with deportation to Haiti or release into the United States with status as an asylee, as soon as the asylum claims were finally adjudicated.

The first significant ruling on detention was issued in one of the Cuban cases.

RODRIGUEZ–FERNANDEZ v. WILKINSON

United States Court of Appeals, Tenth Circuit, 1981.
654 F.2d 1382.

LOGAN, CIRCUIT JUDGE.

This is an appeal from a decision of the district court granting a writ of habeas corpus, ordering immediate release of Pedro Rodriguez-Fernandez to the custody of an American citizen upon such conditions as the Attorney General of the United States may impose. Rodriguez-Fernandez is a Cuban national who arrived in the United States aboard the so-called Freedom Flotilla which carried approximately 125,000 people from Cuba to Key West, Florida. Petitioner arrived at Key West on June 2, 1980, seeking admission to this country as a refugee.

---

a. In December 1984, however, the two countries finally agreed to the phased return of 2746 Marielitos, in return for the resumption of regular immigration processing in Havana. The White House announcement of the accord specified that the returnees would be individuals who had committed serious crimes in Cuba or the United States, or who "suffer from severe mental disor- ders." Court cases were filed on behalf of prospective returnees, but the actual removals nonetheless began in early 1985. See 61 Interp. Rel. 1080–85 (1984); *Garcia-Mir v. Smith*, ___ U.S. ___, 105 S.Ct. 948, 83 L.Ed.2d 901 (1985) (Rehnquist, J., denying stay of circuit court order that permitted initial returns).

Acting pursuant to INA § 233(a), immigration officials permitted Rodriguez-Fernandez to leave the boat and placed him in custody pending a determination of his eligibility for admission. In an interview with immigration officials, Rodriguez-Fernandez admitted that at the time he left Cuba he was a prisoner serving a sentence in a Cuban prison for attempted burglary and escape. He denied being guilty of the attempted burglary, for which he was tried by a military revolutionary court. But he confessed that he had prior convictions in 1959 and 1964, in each case for the theft of a suitcase from a bus or train station, and that while serving an eight year term for the second theft he escaped from prison. In 1973, at the time of his conviction, he received a four year sentence for the attempted burglary and an added three year term for the escape. He testified he was scheduled for release from prison on June 27, 1981, apparently at the expiration of the terms imposed in 1973. Based upon his criminal record and lack of immigration documents, the officers found that Rodriguez-Fernandez was not clearly entitled to land. He was then detained pending an exclusion hearing pursuant to INA §§ 212(a)(9), (20), and 235(b). Following a brief stay at a processing camp in Wisconsin, petitioner was transferred to the federal penitentiary at Leavenworth, Kansas.

In a formal exclusion hearing held July 21, 1980, an immigration hearing officer determined that Rodriguez-Fernandez was an excludable alien and ordered him deported to Cuba pursuant to INA § 237(a). Petitioner does not challenge the lawfulness of the exclusion order; that is not an issue in this appeal. The Immigration and Naturalization Service on August 28, 1980, requested the State Department to arrange petitioner's deportation to Cuba. Cuba, however, has refused all requests to accept petitioner and other members of the Freedom Flotilla. The trial court found,

> "Cuba has either not responded or responded negatively to six diplomatic notes transmitted by the United States. Thus, the Government has been unable to expeditiously carry out the order of deportation and cannot even speculate as to a date of departure. No other country has been contacted about possibly accepting petitioner."

Fernandez v. Wilkinson, 505 F.Supp. 787, 789 (D.Kan.1980). Upon Cuba's refusal to accept petitioner, the Attorney General ordered his continued detention in the federal penitentiary at Leavenworth. He was incarcerated there in September 1980, when he filed the instant petition for a writ of habeas corpus. Thereafter, he was transferred to the United States Penitentiary in Atlanta, Georgia, where he is currently held with approximately 1,700 other excludable Cubans similarly situated.

By an order dated December 31, 1980, the district court held that Rodriguez-Fernandez has no rights to avoid detention under either the Fifth or Eighth Amendments to the United States Constitution. However, it held that the Attorney General's actions under the circumstances were arbitrary and an abuse of his discretion. It found that although the Attorney General's actions did not offend any statute, they violated principles of customary international law which create a right to be free from such detention.   The order gave the government ninety days to release Rodriguez-Fernandez.   The court later denied a government motion to reopen based upon the transfer of petitioner to Atlanta.   On April 22, 1981, a compliance hearing was held with respect to its earlier order. The government reported that, exercising the discretionary parole power, representatives of the Attorney General determined Rodriguez-Fernandez to be releasable pursuant to INA § 212(d)(5).   He had not been released, however, because of a suspension imposed by the new national administration of President Reagan to permit a reconsideration of government policies.   The court was informed that the President had appointed a special task force due to file a report May 4, 1981, discussing, *inter alia,* what should be done with the excluded Cubans still being detained.   It requested an additional sixty days to effect either the deportation or parole of Rodriguez-Fernandez.   On April 23, 1981, the district court denied the government's request and ordered petitioner's release within twenty-four hours to the sponsorship of an American citizen living in Kansas City.   From these orders the government has appealed.

* * *

Rodriguez-Fernandez has committed no offense against the United States; he has merely appeared on our shores as a member of the Freedom Flotilla seeking permission to immigrate.   Yet, he has been confined in a maximum security federal prison, some of the time in solitary confinement, for more than a year.

The case presents unusual difficulties.   The applicable statutes are vague with regard to the problem facing this Court.   Also, the case law generally recognizes almost absolute power in Congress concerning immigration matters, holding that aliens in petitioner's position cannot invoke the Constitution to avoid exclusion and that detention pending deportation is only a continuation of exclusion rather than "punishment" in the constitutional sense.

In the instant case the detention is imprisonment under conditions as severe as we apply to our worst criminals.   It is prolonged; perhaps it is permanent.   At least six times Cuba has been approached to take back petitioner and others in his status; Cuba has consistently refused or failed to acknowledge the request.   The last attempt to effect a return was apparently in August 1980, many months ago.   Thus it appears detention is here used as an alternative to exclusion rather than a step in the process of returning petitioner to his native Cuba.   Petitioner testified he is willing to go to another country, "anywhere in the world where I'll not be a prisoner unjustly or unfairly."   Under the statute, however, he may not specify a place of deportation; it states that he is to be deported to the country from whence he came.   INA § 237(a).[a]

We dispose of the appeal by construing the applicable statutes to require Rodriguez-Fernandez' release at this time.   Nevertheless, it seems important to discuss the serious constitutional questions involved if the statute were construed differently.

---

a. This provision was amended in late 1981 to afford the Attorney General greater flexibility in selecting the country to which an excludable alien will be sent.—eds.

It is clear Rodriguez-Fernandez can invoke no constitutional protection against his exclusion from the United States. He may be excluded for considerations of race, politics, activities, or associations that would be constitutionally prohibited if he were a citizen. *See Kleindienst v. Mandel,* 408 U.S. 753, 92 S.Ct. 2576, 33 L.Ed.2d 683 (1972).

* * *

Nevertheless, if an alien in Rodriguez-Fernandez' position should be accused of committing a crime against the laws of this country, he would be entitled to the constitutional protections of the Fifth and Fourteenth Amendments. *Yick Wo v. Hopkins,* 118 U.S. 356, 6 S.Ct. 1064, 30 L.Ed. 220 (1886), stated,

> "The Fourteenth Amendment to the Constitution is not confined to the protection of citizens. It says: 'Nor shall any State deprive any person of life, liberty or property without due process of law; nor deny to any person within its jurisdiction the equal protection of the laws.' These provisions are universal in their application, to all persons within the territorial jurisdiction, without regard to any difference of race, of color, or of nationality; and the equal protection of the laws is a pledge of the protection of equal laws."

118 U.S. at 369, 6 S.Ct. at 1070. In *Wong Wing v. United States,* 163 U.S. 228, 16 S.Ct. 977, 41 L.Ed. 140 (1896), the Court extended this concept.

> "Applying this reasoning to the 5th and 6th Amendments, it must be concluded that all persons within the territory of the United States are entitled to the protection guaranteed by those amendments, and that even aliens shall not be held to answer for a capital or other infamous crime, unless on a presentment or indictment of a grand jury, nor be deprived of life, liberty, or property without due process of law."

163 U.S. at 238, 16 S.Ct. at 981. The Court there struck down as unconstitutional a statute allowing administrative officials to arrest and imprison for up to one year Chinese found to be illegally within the country. The opinion quoted with apparent approval language from *Fong Yue Ting v. United States,* 149 U.S. 698, 13 S.Ct. 1016, 37 L.Ed. 905 (1893), which declared orders of deportation are not punishment for crime, but distinguished "those provisions of the statute which contemplate only the exclusion or expulsion of Chinese persons and those which provide for their imprisonment at hard labor, pending which their deportation is suspended." 163 U.S. at 236, 16 S.Ct. at 980.

Thus, it would appear that an excluded alien in physical custody within the United States may not be "punished" without being accorded the substantive and procedural due process guarantees of the Fifth Amendment.[3] Surely Congress could not order the killing of Rodriguez-Fernandez and others in his status on the ground that Cuba would not

---

3. We agree with *United States v. Henry,* 604 F.2d 908 (5th Cir.1979), that no distinction can be drawn in application of these rules between an alien, like Rodriguez-Fernandez, who is regarded as standing at the border and one who is a resident in the United States. * * *

take them back and this country does not want them. Even petitioner's property cannot be taken without just compensation, absent the existence of a state of war between the United States and his country. *Russian Volunteer Fleet v. United States,* 282 U.S. 481, 51 S.Ct. 229, 75 L.Ed. 473 (1931). Certainly imprisonment in a federal prison of one who has been neither charged nor convicted of a criminal offense is a deprivation of liberty in violation of the Fifth Amendment, except for the fiction applied to these cases that detention is only a continuation of the exclusion. This euphemistic fiction was created to accommodate the necessary detention of excludable and deportable aliens while their cases are considered and arrangements for expulsion are made. Detention pending deportation seems properly analogized to incarceration pending trial or other disposition of a criminal charge, and is, thus, justifiable only as a necessary, temporary measure. Obviously detention pending trial assumes a different status if there is to be no trial. If, in this case, administrative officials ordered penitentiary confinement for life or a definite term because Cuba would not accept petitioner, it seems certain the courts would apply *Wong Wing* and hold that such imprisonment is impermissible punishment rather than detention *pending* deportation. Logic compels the same result when imprisonment is for an indefinite period, continued beyond reasonable efforts to expel the alien.

Federal circuit and district courts have long held deportable aliens in custody more than a few months must be released because such detention has become imprisonment.

* * *

The linchpin of the government's case is *Shaughnessy v. United States ex rel. Mezei,* 345 U.S. 206, 73 S.Ct. 625, 97 L.Ed. 956 (1953). There an alien was confined to Ellis Island for twenty-one months before his case was decided by the Supreme Court. The Court refused to require his release within the United States. It may be, as Judge McWilliams states in his dissent, that a fair reading of that case supports the view that no constitutional infirmity exists in the continuing incarceration of Rodriguez-Fernandez, who has been in custody only a year. Nevertheless, differences exist between that case and this one which we think are significant. First, the primary focus of *Mezei* was upon the excluded alien's right to a due process hearing concerning his right of reentry into this country. Also, he was excluded as a security risk and the Korean War was in progress; security risks and enemy aliens during wartime have always been treated specially. The conditions of Mezei's confinement on Ellis Island do not appear to be comparable to Rodriguez-Fernandez' imprisonment in two maximum security prisons. In *Mezei* there were continuing efforts to deport. Twice the alien was shipped out to other countries which refused to permit him to land; he applied for entry to other countries and thereafter voluntarily terminated his efforts to find a new home. His petition for relief sought not only release from confinement but also admission to the United States.

Even with these special facts *Mezei* has been criticized as the nadir of the law with which the opinion dealt. *See* Hart, *The Power of Congress to*

Limit the Jurisdiction of Federal Courts: An Exercise in Dialectic, 66 Harv.L.Rev. 1362, 1387–1396 (1953). In more recent cases, the Supreme Court has expanded the constitutional protections owed aliens apart from the right to enter or stay in this country. *See e.g., Hampton v. Mow Sun Wong,* 426 U.S. 88, 96 S.Ct. 1895, 48 L.Ed.2d 495 (1976); *Graham v. Richardson,* 403 U.S. 365, 91 S.Ct. 1848, 29 L.Ed.2d 534 (1971). Due process is not a static concept, it undergoes evolutionary change to take into account accepted current notions of fairness. Finally, we note that in upholding the plenary power of Congress over exclusion and deportation of aliens, the Supreme Court has sought support in international law principles. *E.g., Fong Yue Ting v. United States,* 149 U.S. 698, 13 S.Ct. 1016, 37 L.Ed. 905 (1893). It seems proper then to consider international law principles for notions of fairness as to propriety of holding aliens in detention. No principle of international law is more fundamental than the concept that human beings should be free from arbitrary imprisonment. *See* Universal Declaration of Human Rights, Arts. 3 and 9, U.N. Doc. A/801 (1948); The American Convention on Human Rights, Part I, ch. II, Art. 7, 77 Dept. of State Bull. 28 (July 4, 1977). For these several reasons, we believe *Mezei* does not compel the conclusion that no constitutional problems inhere in petitioner's detention status.

When it passed the Internal Security Act of 1950 and its successor, the Immigration and Naturalization Act of 1952, 8 U.S.C. § 1101 *et seq.,* Congress was painfully aware of more than 3,000 warrants of deportation made unenforceable by the refusals of the countries of origin to grant passports for these persons' return. *See e.g.,* H.R.Rep. No. 1192, 81st Cong., 1st Sess. 7–10 (1949). Most were nationals of iron-curtain countries and aliens residing in the United States. Despite these facts, or perhaps because of them, the Act provides for detention no longer than six months in deportation cases. INA § 242(c). Further detention is permitted only after conviction for violation of restrictions imposed upon release on parole, or after conviction for willfully refusing to depart or to cooperate in securing departure. *Id.* § 1252(e).

Provisions relating to excludable aliens seeking entry are not as specific. They provide for "temporary removal" from the transportation vehicle or vessel to a place of "detention, pending a decision on the aliens' eligibility to enter the United States and until they are either allowed to land or returned to the care of the transportation line or to the vessel or aircraft which brought them." Temporary parole into the United States is permitted in the discretion of the Attorney General, but is not to be regarded as admission of the alien into the country.

Are we to read these provisions to permit indefinite detention as an alternative to exclusion, in view of the fact that Congress imposed a specific time limitation on holding resident aliens but none as to those "standing at the border"? We do not. There is no evidence to suggest that prior to the instant case a significant number of excludable aliens have been physically detained for periods of long duration. Justice Tom Clark, who was Attorney General during the formation of the presently effective immigration laws, stated in *Leng May Ma v. Barber,* 357 U.S. 185, 190, 78 S.Ct. 1072, 1075, 2 L.Ed.2d 1246 (1958), "[p]hysical detention of aliens is now the exception, not the rule, and is generally employed only as to security risks or those likely to abscond."

Neither will we read into the statute a specific time limit for detention. Rather, since the statute contemplates temporary detention, we hold that detention is permissible during proceedings to determine eligibility to enter and, thereafter, during a reasonable period of negotiations for their return to the country of origin or to the transporter that brought them here. After such a time, upon application of the incarcerated alien willing to risk the possible alternatives to continued detention, the alien would be entitled to release. This construction is consistent with accepted international law principles that individuals are entitled to be free of arbitrary imprisonment. It is also consistent with the statutory treatment of deportable resident aliens and with the constitutional principles outlined above.

We do not construe the Act to require release within the United States. The statute appears to contemplate that parole is to be in the absolute discretion of the Attorney General, at least as to aliens in Rodriguez-Fernandez' position, convicted of crimes involving moral turpitude. Parole within the country is one option available to the government, and we note that, under procedures approved by the predecessor to the present Attorney General, this petitioner was found to be qualified for such parole. But other options exist. He can be returned to the transportation vessel which brought him to the American shore, if it exists. INA § 233. We would not read INA § 237 to preclude his being sent to a country other than Cuba, if Cuba will not take him.

When an excludable alien in custody tests the detention by writ of habeas corpus, * * * we hold that the burden is upon the government to show that the detention is still temporary pending expulsion, and not simply incarceration as an alternative to departure. Information on this issue is more readily available to the government. On the record before us, it appears there are no current negotiations with Cuba or any other country to take petitioner and there is no reason for his continued incarceration other than the fact that no country has agreed to take him. That is insufficient reason to hold him further.

Since our interpretation of the applicable law and the relief ordered differs somewhat from that of the district court, we give the government thirty days in which to effectuate his release in a manner consistent with this opinion. It is so ordered.

McWILLIAMS, CIRCUIT JUDGE, dissenting:

* * *

The determination as to whether a particular excludable alien is to be detained or released on parole, pending deportation, rests within the sound discretion of the Attorney General. In the instant case, the Attorney General in the exercise of that discretion declined to release Rodriguez-Fernandez on parole and ordered him detained in a maximum security penal institution. Under the circumstances, I find no abuse of discretion on the part of the Attorney General. Rodriguez-Fernandez has a long record of criminality. In fact, he was in prison serving a sentence at the very time he was allowed by Cuban authorities to go to Florida.

* * *

The flaw in the majority opinion, as I see it, is that it attempts to deal with the fate of all 125,000 Cuban refugees in this one case. We are here concerned with one individual, Rodriguez-Fernandez. Perhaps my rule, if it were the rule of the majority, would apply to others similarly situated to Rodriguez-Fernandez, but it would of course not apply to others who are dissimilarly situated. For example, the indefinite detention in a maximum security institution of a true Cuban political refugee with no history of criminality, who is nonetheless determined to be an excludable alien, would in my view, constitute an abuse of discretion by the Attorney General.

* * *

Notes

The majority in *Rodriguez-Fernandez* distinguishes the *Mezei* case on the ground that Mezei was a security risk. But isn't someone with a criminal record also a security risk, even if in a more mundane fashion? The majority also suggests that the petitioner need not be released into the United States. Are any of its suggested alternatives realistic?

Later Developments

Following the principal case, other courts considered similar issues and reached disparate results. In *Palma v. Verdeyen,* 676 F.2d 100 (4th Cir.1982), the court found that the statute authorized the indefinite detention of excludable aliens. It pointed in particular to the absence from INA § 237 of any language limiting the length of detention that would be comparable to the limitations imposed in the deportation setting by § 242(c). Citing *Knauff* and *Mezei,* the court also found few constitutional limitations on such detention. Nevertheless, it insisted that the Attorney General had to abide faithfully by the limitations Congress imposed, and it went on to review the denial of parole under an abuse-of-discretion standard. Because of the petitioner's serious record of misbehavior in the detention facilities, in addition to his conviction of theft offenses in Cuba, the court found no abuse of discretion. It authorized continued detention, "pending further review of his suitability for parole in accordance with the Justice Department's plan." The Second Circuit reached a similar result, reversing a district court decision that ordered release of several detained Haitians. *Bertrand v. Sava,* 684 F.2d 204 (2d Cir.1982) (emphasizing the narrow scope of judicial review of the district director's parole decisions).

The next important decision occurred in a case brought by Haitian detainees who still had asylum claims pending. In *Louis v. Nelson,* 544 F.Supp. 973 (S.D.Fla.1982), the court ruled that the new detention policy put into effect in 1981 was invalid for failure to comply with the notice-and-comment rulemaking procedures required by the Administrative Procedure Act (APA). It also held, after lengthy consideration, that the plaintiffs' claim of national-origin discrimination, allegedly committed by INS and directed invidiously against black Haitians, could be heard under the Constitution, despite their excludable status. But it found against the plaintiffs on the facts of the case, ruling that intentional discrimination had not been proven.

The Justice Department responded to the APA-based ruling with quick promulgation of interim detention regulations, published "under protest" for notice and comment, but made effective immediately. 47 Fed.Reg. 30044 (July 9, 1982) (amending 8 C.F.R. §§ 212.5, 235.3). The notice stated: "The Administration has determined that a large number of Haitian nationals and others are likely to attempt to enter the United States illegally unless there is in place a detention and parole regulation meeting the approval of the District Court. Such a large scale influx would clearly be contrary to the public interest." The notice emphasized the drafters' belief that the statutory mandate makes detention the norm (quoting the language of INA § 235(b)), and went on to summarize the only exceptions for undocumented aliens awaiting an exclusion hearing. The new regulations permit release under these circumstances: "(1) serious medical conditions; (2) pregnant women; (3) certain juveniles; (4) aliens with close family relatives in the United States; (5) other unusual situations warranting parole." A later notice responded to comments received from the public, and made the interim rules final, with minor wording changes. 47 Fed.Reg. 46493 (Oct. 19, 1982).

Meanwhile, both sides sought review of the district court's decision in *Louis v. Nelson*. In 1982, a panel of the Eleventh Circuit affirmed the APA ruling, and went ahead to reverse the finding of no discrimination. *Jean v. Nelson*, 711 F.3d 1455 (11th Cir.1983). But the panel's ruling was shortly vacated when the entire court agreed to rehear the case en banc. 714 F.2d 96 (11th Cir.1983).

In the meantime, important developments had occurred in the Cuban cases. In *Fernandez-Roque v. Smith*, 567 F.Supp. 1115 (N.D.Ga.1983), *reversed* 734 F.2d 576 (11th Cir. 1984), the court issued the most ambitious decision yet, protecting the due process rights of excludable aliens. The case was a habeas corpus class action brought on behalf of over 1000 Marielitos detained in the Atlanta Federal Penitentiary. By this time, INS had developed a well-defined Status Review Plan for considering the release of the detained Cubans:

> The plan created a review panel selected from officials of the different divisions of the Department of Justice. Under the plan, the panel initially examines the file of the detainee. To recommend release, the panel must conclude that "(1) the detainee is presently a nonviolent person, (2) the detainee is likely to remain nonviolent, and (3) the detainee is unlikely to commit any criminal offenses following his release." If the panel decides in favor of parole, its recommendation is forwarded to the Commissioner of the Immigration and Naturalization Service (Commissioner) for approval.

If the Commissioner rejects the panel's recommendation or if the panel is unable to make a determination based solely on the detainee's file, the alien is personally interviewed by the panel. Written notice of the interview is furnished to the alien at least seven days in advance. At the interview, the detainee may be assisted by a person of his choice. He may examine the documents and may submit either written or oral information supporting his release.

After the interview, the panel forwards its recommendation to the Commissioner. If the Commissioner grants release, he may impose "such special conditions as considered appropriate by the Commissioner." If parole is denied, the alien remains in custody. In either case, the detainee is notified of the Commissioner's final decision in English and Spanish. The plan provides for at least annual reviews of an alien's case as long as he remains in detention.

Parole may be revoked if the alien is convicted in the United States of a felony or a serious misdemeanor. An alien who poses a clear and imminent danger to the community or himself may also be returned to custody. Finally, parole may be revoked if an alien released to a special placement project violates the conditions of his parole. Upon revocation of parole, the alien is returned to detention and any further petition for release is processed under the plan.

Fernandez-Roque v. Smith, 734 F.2d 576, 579 (11th Cir.1984).

At the trial level in *Fernandez-Roque,* the district court first determined, in disagreement with *Rodriguez-Fernandez,* that the INA granted authority to the Attorney General to detain excludable aliens indefinitely. But the court went on to rule that the Constitution places potent limitations on the exercise of that authority:

Once an excludable alien's detention can no longer be justified merely as a means to his exclusion, *i.e.,* once detention is no longer justifiable simply on the basis of excludability, then a legitimate expectation arises that the detention will end unless some new justification for continuing the detention is established. The basis for this expectation is simply the fundamental principle inherent in our constitutional system that all persons are entitled to their liberty absent some legally sufficient reason for detaining them. An alien's excludability provides such a reason so long as the detention reasonably serves as an aid to the alien's exclusion. After this initial period of time, however, the individual's basic entitlement to liberty once again comes to the fore. Thus, even though the government is authorized to detain excludable aliens indefinitely where immediate exclusion is impracticable, the excludability determination itself provides the essential predicate for the exercise of this authority only for an initial, temporary period of time. Thereafter, a liberty interest arises on behalf of the alien detainee requiring that the continued exercise of the detention power be justified on the basis of a procedurally adequate finding that the detainee, if released, is likely to abscond, to pose a risk to the national security, or to pose a serious and significant threat to persons or property within the United States.

567 F.Supp. at 1128. The court distinguished *Mezei* on the grounds that Mezei's detention was founded on a wartime emergency measure, and also based on its reading that Mezei sought formal admission to the country, not parole. *Id.* at 1129. In this latter understanding, the court relied on the exact wording of a passage from *Landon v. Plasencia,* 459 U.S. 21, 103 S.Ct. 321, 329, 74 L.Ed.2d 21 (1982), which stated that "an alien seeking initial admission to the United States requests a privilege and has no constitutional rights *regarding his application*" (emphasis supplied). Since petitioners here were not seeking formal admission, they were not asking a court to find constitutional rights regarding an application for admission. Instead, they sought only parole pending arrangements for return to Cuba.

Having found a cognizable liberty interest, the court went on to spell out what process was due the petitioners. Although the court acknowledged the "superficial adequacy" of exclusion hearings in procedural terms, it nevertheless suggested that the procedural safeguards are "largely illusory." *Id.* at 1128, quoting from *Developments,* 96 Harv.L.Rev. 1286, 1364 (1983). Moreover, it considered the Status Review Plan inadequate, even though the procedures were similar to those judged acceptable by the Supreme Court for use by a state parole board deciding on the release of those serving criminal sentences. Such procedures might be adequate in that setting, the district court ruled, because the original deprivation of liberty was based on a criminal trial with a wide range of procedural protections not accorded in a determination of excludability. *Id.* at 1131–32.

Although the court rejected the petitioners' claim that they were entitled to procedures equivalent to those available at a criminal trial, it went on to mandate a lengthy list of procedural protections: (1) prior written notice of the factual allegations supporting continued detention, and access to the underlying information in government files; (2) right to compulsory attendance of witnesses; (3) right to confrontation and cross-examination of adverse witnesses, unless good cause related to prison discipline is shown; (4) a neutral decisionmaker who will decide based solely on the evidence adduced at the hearing and who will produce a written statement of the reasons for his decision (and whose decision would not be reviewable by any other government official); (5) protection against self-incrimination; (6) counsel provided at government expense; and (7) a requirement that the government carry the burden of proof, according to a "clear and convincing evidence" standard, that the detainee "will be likely to abscond, to pose a risk to the national security, or to pose a serious threat to persons or property in the United States." *Id.* at 1145.

What is the source of the liberty interest the court discovers? What are its contours? Notice that the ruling here covers more than merely *procedural* due process. The court would not consider adequate a jury trial with full safeguards if the only factual determination leading to continued incarceration were whether the alien arrived without documents. The court requires certain substantive findings. What is the source of these latter requirements?

The district court's decision in *Fernandez-Roque* was reversed by the Court of Appeals, holding that "excludable aliens cannot challenge either admission *or parole* decisions under a claim of constitutional right." *Fernandez-Roque v. Smith,* 734 F.2d 576, 582 (11th Cir.1984) (emphasis supplied). But this reversal was clearly foreshadowed a few months earlier when the higher court, sitting en banc, issued its decision in *Jean v. Nelson,* the Haitian detainee litigation:

JEAN v. NELSON

United States Court of Appeals, Eleventh Circuit, en banc, 1984.
727 F.2d 957, cert. granted, ___ U.S. ___, 105 S.Ct. 563, 83 L.Ed.2d 504 (1984).

VANCE, CIRCUIT JUDGE:

[The court first vacated, on the grounds of mootness, that portion of the district court's judgment finding noncompliance with the APA, owing to the release of most of the original class members and the promulgation of the 1982 regulations.]

* * *

B. THE CONSTITUTIONAL RIGHTS OF EXCLUDABLE ALIENS

Any analysis of the constitutional rights of aliens in the immigration context must begin by taking note of the fundamental distinction between the legal status of excludable or unadmitted aliens and aliens who have succeeded in effecting an "entry" into the United States, even if their presence here is completely illegal. The Supreme Court originally indicated that the powers of the political branches with respect to the exclusion and expulsion of aliens are equally broad, *see Fong Yue Ting,* 149 U.S. at 713–14, 13 S.Ct. at 1022, but it soon recognized that "an alien who has entered the country, and has become subject in all respects to its jurisdiction, and a part of its population" is entitled to due process under the fifth amendment and cannot be deported "without giving him all opportunity to be heard upon the questions involving his right to be and remain in the United States." *Kaoru Yamataya v. Fisher [The Japanese Immigrant Case],* 189 U.S. 86, 101, 23 S.Ct. 611, 615, 47 L.Ed. 721 (1903). While resident aliens, regardless of their legal status, are therefore entitled to at least limited due process rights, aliens "who have never been naturalized, nor acquired any domicile of residence within the United States, nor even been admitted into the country pursuant to law" stand in a very different posture: "As to such persons, the decisions of executive or administrative officers, acting within powers expressly conferred by congress, are due process of law." *Nishimura Ekiu,* 142 U.S. at 660, 12 S.Ct. at 339.

In the eighty years since the Court first recognized this distinction between the rights of excludable and deportable aliens, it has become engrained in our law. * * *

* * *

This principle was reiterated by the Court last Term in *Landon v. Plasencia,* 459 U.S. 21, 32, 103 S.Ct. 321, 329, 74 L.Ed.2d 21 (1982), in which Justice O'Connor noted that

> an alien seeking admission to the United States requests a privilege and has no constitutional rights regarding his application, for the power to admit or exclude aliens is a sovereign prerogative.... [H]owever, once an alien gains admission to our country and begins to develop the ties that go with permanent residence his constitutional status changes accordingly.

Aliens seeking admission to the United States therefore have no constitutional rights with regard to their applications and must be content to accept whatever statutory rights and privileges they are granted by Congress. The INA does in fact contain a number of provisions that collectively guarantee at least limited due process protection for excludable aliens. Under § 236(a), an alien seeking entry is entitled to a hearing on the validity of his application for admission before an immigration judge. At the hearing the alien is permitted the assistance of counsel, § 292, and has the right to present evidence in his own behalf, to examine and object to evidence against him, and to cross-examine witnesses presented by the government. 8 C.F.R. § 236.2(a). If the immigration judge determines that the alien is not entitled to admission, this decision may be appealed to the Board of Immigration Appeals (BIA). INA § 236(b); 8 C.F.R. § 236.7. An alien may also challenge a final order of exclusion in the federal courts by filing a petition for a writ of habeas corpus. INA § 106(b).

* * *

There is no question that the Haitian plaintiffs in this case are excludable aliens and have not been formally admitted into the United States. Since an alien's legal status is not altered by detention or parole under the entry doctrine fiction, it seems clear that plaintiffs here can claim no greater rights or privileges under our laws than any other group of aliens who have been stopped at the border. The district court, however, concluded that the entry doctrine and the precedents cited above were inapplicable because the Haitian plaintiffs here are challenging their continued incarceration *pending* a determination of admissibility, rather than seeking to compel the government to grant them admission in a legal sense. Likewise, the panel distinguished *Mezei* and other immigration decisions on the grounds that those cases concerned "immigration procedures" rather than "the discretionary exercise of the Executive's parole power." *Jean,* 711 F.2d at 1484–85. The panel also considered the entry doctrine inapplicable because "its purpose [is] to limit the procedural rights of an excludable alien 'regarding his application' for admission," *id.* at 1484 (quoting Plasencia, 459 U.S. at ___, 103 S.Ct. at 329), and therefore concluded that the Haitian plaintiffs had equal protection rights on the basis of their physical presence within the territorial limits of the United States. *See id.* 1484–85.

Although the distinction between parole and admission drawn by the panel and the district court is not an implausible one, we conclude that it cannot be reconciled with the Supreme Court's jurisprudence in this area. In particular, we believe that the Court's decision in *Mezei* is controlling on this issue and that a close examination of the facts at issue in *Mezei* forecloses us from relying on the arguments that the panel and the district court found persuasive. Thus, we cannot accept appellees' argument that *Mezei* is not on point because "the alien was challenging non-admissibility, not incarceration." The gravamen of Mezei's complaint was clearly not the government's right to exclude him—a permanent exclusion order had already been entered in his case, and he did not contest it in his habeas petition—but the power of the government to continue to detain him without a hearing pending his deportation. *See Mezei*, 345 U.S. at 207, 73 S.Ct. at 627. Justice Clark stated explicitly in his majority opinion that "[t]he issue is whether the Attorney General's continued exclusion of respondent without a hearing *amounts to an unlawful detention,* so that courts may admit him *temporarily* to the United States on bond until arrangements are made for his departure abroad." *Id.* (emphasis added).

* * * We therefore conclude that *Mezei* compels us to hold that the Haitian plaintiffs in this case cannot claim equal protection rights under the fifth amendment, even with regard to challenging the Executive's exercise of its parole discretion.

We realize, of course, that *Mezei*—like its predecessor, *Knauff*—has been heavily criticized by academic commentators. As an intermediate appellate court, however, we cannot properly question the continued authority of this Supreme Court precedent—a precedent that the Court cited without reconsideration as recently as last Term. *See Plasencia*, 459 U.S. at 32, 103 S.Ct. at 329. With regard to the key issue here—whether the grant or denial of parole is an integral part of the admissions process—*Mezei* is fully in accord with other, less controversial precedents. * * *

These decisions reflect policy imperatives and fundamental principles of national sovereignty that cannot be easily dismissed, regardless of the individual merits of the Court's decisions in *Knauff* and *Mezei*.[19] The reason that Congress has passed legislation regulating the admission of aliens is its concern about how their entry will affect the economic, political, and social well-being of this nation. The grant of parole is subject to certain restrictions and is theoretically of a short-term character, but it does permit the physical entry of the alien into the midst of our society and implicates many of the same considerations—such as employ-

---

19. It is worth pointing out in this context that much of the criticism of *Mezei* and *Knauff* has focussed on the fact that the aliens who were ordered excluded without a hearing in those cases had strong personal or family ties to the United States. *See Mezei*, 345 U.S. at 216–17, 73 S.Ct. at 631–32 (Black, J., dissenting); *Knauff*, 338 U.S. at 539, 70 S.Ct. at 310. Most excludable aliens have far weaker claims to enjoying the benefits of admission into this country, however, and the harsh results of *Knauff* and *Mezei* should not obscure the compelling policy justifications that support the entry doctrine fiction and the general principle that excludable aliens have no rights with regard to their applications for admission or parole.

ment and national security concerns—that justify restrictions on admission. Parole is an act of extraordinary sovereign generosity, since it grants temporary admission into our society to an alien who has no legal right to enter and who would probably be turned away at the border if he sought to enter by land, rather than coming by sea or air.   * * *

* * *

Of course, there are certain circumstances under which even excludable aliens are accorded rights under the Constitution.

* * *

For example, those with the status of deportable aliens are constitutionally entitled to rights in the deportation context that are inapplicable to exclusion proceedings. Illegal or resident aliens may also claim other rights under the fifth and fourteenth amendments. *See, e.g., Plyler v. Doe,* 457 U.S. 202, 102 S.Ct. 2382, 72 L.Ed.2d 786 (1982); *Hampton v. Mow Sun Wong,* 426 U.S. 88, 96 S.Ct. 1895, 48 L.Ed.2d 495 (1976); *Graham v. Richardson,* 403 U.S. 365, 91 S.Ct. 1848, 29 L.Ed.2d 534 (1971); *Yick Wo v. Hopkins,* 118 U.S. 356, 6 S.Ct. 1064, 30 L.Ed. 220 (1886).

The courts have also recognized that aliens can raise constitutional challenges to deprivations of liberty or property outside the context of entry or admission, when the plenary authority of the political branches is not implicated. Aliens seized by United States officials for suspected involvement in criminal activity are entitled to the same constitutional rights that normally apply in such proceedings. *See, e.g., Wong Wing,* 163 U.S. at 238, 16 S.Ct. at 981 ("[A]liens shall not be held to answer for a capital or other infamous crime, unless on a presentment or indictment of a grand jury, nor be deprived of life, liberty, or property without due process of law."); *United States v. Henry,* 604 F.2d 908, 914 (5th Cir.1979) ("[A]n alien who is within the territorial jurisdiction of this country, whether it be at the border or in the interior, in a proper case and at the proper time, is entitled to those protections guaranteed by the Fifth Amendment in criminal proceedings which would include the *Miranda* warning."). The courts have further ruled that aliens who are the victims of unconstitutional government action abroad are protected by the Bill of Rights if the government seeks to exploit fruits of its unlawful conduct in a criminal proceeding in the United States. *United States v. Demanett,* 629 F.2d 862, 866 (3d Cir.), *cert. denied,* 450 U.S. 910, 101 S.Ct. 1347, 67 L.Ed.2d 333 (1980); *United States v. Toscanino,* 500 F.2d 267, 280 (2d Cir.1974); *cf. United States v. Tiede,* 86 F.R.D. 227, 242–44 (U.S. Ct. for Berlin 1979) (protections of Bill of Rights apply to friendly aliens in the American sector of West Berlin). The Supreme Court has also recognized that even non-resident aliens are entitled to the protection of the fifth amendment's prohibition on unlawful takings. *Russian Volunteer Fleet v. United States,* 282 U.S. 481, 489, 491–92, 51 S.Ct. 229, 232, 75 L.Ed. 473 (1931).

These authorities, however, do not mandate the conclusion that excludable aliens such as the Haitian plaintiffs can claim equal protection rights under the fifth amendment with regard to parole. *Russian Volunteer Fleet* can be distinguished because it clearly does not implicate in any way the powers of the national government over immigration. When the government seizes the property of foreign nationals within this country, its actions do not fall within a sphere of plenary executive and legislative authority, and it therefore cannot claim that the aliens involved are entitled only to the degree of due process that Congress is prepared to extend them as a matter of grace.

Similar considerations apply in the context of criminal prosecutions. When the government subjects an alien to the criminal process it is plainly no longer seeking to effectuate its power to control admission into the United States by removing the alien from this country. The arrests of the aliens in *Wong Wing* and *Henry* may have grown out of the Executive's efforts to control the entry of foreigners into the United States, but the decision by government officials to subject them to criminal prosecution or punishment, rather than deportation, completely changed the nature of the proceedings. From that point forward any action taken by the government derived not from its power to control admission into this country, but from the powers of the Executive over law enforcement. The government's actions in prosecuting Henry and imprisoning Wong Wing therefore fell outside the plenary power to control immigration that justifies the extraordinary executive and congressional latitude in that area.

* * *

Some courts and commentators have suggested that when an exercise of the government's power to exclude results in an indefinite detention of an excludable alien, at some point the continued imprisonment becomes punishment, regardless of the legal justifications or fictions involved. These authorities contend that at this juncture the government should be required to make some justification to continue to detain the alien. *See, e.g., Rodriguez-Fernandez v. Wilkinson,* 654 F.2d 1382, 1387 (10th Cir. 1981); *Soroa-Gonzalez v. Civiletti,* 515 F.Supp. 1049, 1056 n. 6 (N.D.Ga. 1981); *Fernandez-Roque v. Smith,* 91 F.R.D. 239, 243 (N.D.Ga.1981), *appeal dismissed,* 671 F.2d 426 (11th Cir.1982); Note, *Constitutional Limits on the Power to Exclude Aliens,* 82 Colum.L.Rev. 957, 980 (1982); Note, *The Constitutional Rights of Excluded Aliens: Proposed Limitations on the Indefinite Detention of the Cuban Refugees,* 70 Geo.L.J. 1303, 1306 (1982).

* * *

We could distinguish *Rodriguez-Fernandez* from this case on the grounds that the former involved an alien against whom an exclusion order had already been entered and who was clearly unable to return to his country of origin.[26] Indeed, the tenth circuit placed no time limits on the government's ability to detain excludable aliens pending the admission decision. *Id.* at 1389. Nevertheless, we detect two significant problems that prevent us from endorsing the tenth circuit's reasoning. The first—which is controlling from our point of view—is that it cannot be reconciled with the Supreme Court' decision in *Mezei,* which held that an

---

26. Haiti has indicated that it is willing to accept the return of these aliens. Although plaintiffs contend that they fear prosecution if they return to Haiti, its government has denied that they would be subject to any reprisals.

excludable alien could not challenge his continued detention without a hearing. The second difficulty is that if the prospect of indefinite detention is held to be sufficient to require the government to meet some judicially-imposed standard to continue to detain an alien, the plenary authority of the political branches in the exclusion area is largely rendered nugatory. The prospect of indefinite confinement, after all, can be raised by the refusal of an excludable alien to return home, or the refusal of his country of origin or any other country to accept him.

This is the critical flaw with the second circuit's decision in *Mezei* and the tenth circuit's decision in *Rodriguez-Fernandez*, each of which based the alien's right to challenge his continued confinement on whether or not he had a foreseeable chance of being able to go elsewhere. At first glance, this is an attractive solution. It seems both humane and eminently realistic, because it does not turn on legal fictions and distinctions that appear to lack practical substance. Unfortunately, this approach would ultimately result in our losing control over our borders. A foreign leader could eventually compel us to grant physical admission via parole to any aliens he wished by the simple expedient of sending them here and then refusing to take them back. In the probable absence of any reliable information about such aliens beyond what they cared to provide, could the government meet its burden under some judicially-imposed standard of showing that indefinite detention was justified? It seems unlikely.

Mindful of the Supreme Court's warning that "[a]ny rule of constitutional law that would inhibit the flexibility of the political branches of government to respond to changing world conditions should be adopted only with the greatest caution," *Mathews v. Diaz*, 426 U.S. 67, 81, 96 S.Ct. 1883, 1892, 48 L.Ed.2d 478 (1976), we conclude that we must resist the temptation to tamper with the authority of the Executive by ruling that excludable aliens have constitutional rights in this area, even with regard to their applications for parole.

C. JUDICIAL REVIEW OF EXECUTIVE DISCRETION

Although we hold that the Haitian plaintiffs cannot challenge the refusal of executive officials to parole them on the basis of the fifth amendment's equal protection guarantee, this is not the end of our inquiry. That the authority of the political branches in this area is plenary does not mean that it is wholly immune from judicial review. As two leading commentators have noted, the Executive's discretionary authority concerning parole decisions "is broad, but not unlimited. It may be subjected to judicial scrutiny on a charge that discretion was arbitrarily exercised or withheld." 1 C. Gordon & H. Rosenfield, *supra*, at § 2.54. This principle has been recognized by our colleagues on the second and fourth circuits, who have held that an executive official's decision to deny parole to an unadmitted alien may be subject to judicial review for abuse of discretion. *Bertrand v. Sava*, 684 F.2d 204, 210 (2d Cir.1982); *Palma v. Verdeyen*, 676 F.2d 100, 105 (4th Cir.1982).

* * *

The discretionary decisions of executive officials in the immigration area are therefore subject to judicial review, but the scope of that review is extremely limited. . * * *

* * *

Thus, under the approach taken by the Supreme Court in *Kleindienst v. Mandel* and adopted by the second circuit in *Bertrand,* the critical question a court must answer when reviewing an alien's challenge to the denial of his request for parole is whether the immigration officials involved were acting within the scope of their delegated powers. * * * Congress has delegated remarkably broad discretion to executive officials under the INA, and these grants of statutory authority are particularly sweeping in the context of parole. * * * In view of these provisions, immigration officials clearly have the authority to deny parole to unadmitted aliens if they can advance "a facially legitimate and bona fide reason" for doing so.

The Haitian plaintiffs contend that such a reason was lacking in this case, submitting that they were the victims of national origin discrimination. Plaintiffs and the district court both stressed that the challenged actions here were those of executive officials rather than Congress, apparently believing that the Executive is clearly prohibited from adopting policies on its own motion that discriminate on the basis of national origin in the immigration field while Congress is just as clearly permitted to do so. Because the government has contended throughout this case that its new detention policy does not discriminate on the basis of national origin, resolution of this question is not essential to our holding; however, we believe that responsible executive officials such as the President or Attorney General possess this authority under the INA.[30] Nevertheless, since the discretion of lower-level immigration officials is circumscribed not

---

30. In view of the Supreme Court's repeated emphasis on the concurrent nature of executive and legislative power in this area and the sweeping congressional delegations of discretionary authority to the Executive under the INA, there is little question that the Executive has the power to draw distinctions among aliens on the basis of nationality. This issue was squarely presented to the D.C. Circuit in *Narenji v. Civiletti,* 617 F.2d 745 (D.C.Cir.1979), *cert. denied,* 446 U.S. 957, 100 S.Ct. 2928, 64 L.Ed.2d 815 (1980), in which the court upheld a regulation requiring nonimmigrant alien post-secondary school students of Iranian citizenship or birth to provide information to the INS concerning their residence and academic status. The court held that the challenged regulation was within the Attorney General's authority under INA § 103(a), which permits the Attorney General to "perform such other acts as he deems necessary" for carrying out his responsibility to administer and enforce the immigration laws, and concluded that "[d]istinctions on the basis of nationality may be drawn in the immigration field by

the Congress or the Executive. [Citations omitted]. So long as such distinctions are not wholly irrational they must be sustained." 617 F.2d at 747.

Although Congress significantly altered the system of nationality-based quotas for the issuance of immigration visas in 1965, *see* 1 C. Gordon & H. Rosenfield, *supra,* at § 1.4c, it has not disturbed a variety of administrative provisions that distinguish among aliens on the basis of national origin. *See, e.g.,* 8 C.F.R. § 101.1 (presumption of lawful admission for certain national groups); *id.* § 212.1 (documentary requirements for nonimmigrants of particular nationalities); *id.* § 252.1 (relaxation of inspection requirements for certain British and Canadian crewmen). The courts have generally viewed such classifications as within the permissible scope of executive discretion. *See, e.g., Nademi v. INS,* 679 F.2d 811 (10th Cir.), *cert. denied* ___ U.S. ___, 103 S.Ct. 161, 74 L.Ed.2d 134 (1982); *Malek-Marzban v. INS,* 653 F.2d 113 (4th Cir.1981); *Yassini v. Crosland,* 618 F.2d 1356 (9th Cir.1980).

only by legislative enactments but also by the instructions of their superiors in the executive branch, our conclusion that the Executive's policy is consistent with the power delegated by Congress does not end the process of judicial inquiry here. The district court must still determine whether the actions of lower-level officials in the field conform to the policy statements of their superiors in Washington. For as the second circuit correctly noted in *Bertrand:*

> [T]he constitutional authority of the political branches of the federal government to adopt immigration policies based on criteria that are not acceptable elsewhere in our public life would not permit an immigration official, in the absence of such policies, to "apply neutral regulations to discriminate on [the basis of race and national origin]."

684 F.2d at 212 n. 12 (quoting *Vigile v. Sava*, 535 F.Supp. 1002, 1016 (S.D.N.Y.1982)).

The district court on remand should conduct such proceedings as are necessary to determine whether there exists a facially legitimate and bona fide reason for the government's decision to deny parole to the class members presently in detention, remembering that it is not the court's proper role "to disregard the [stated criteria employed] or to substitute its own policy preferences for those of the official vested by law with discretionary authority to act on requests for parole." *Id.* at 217. The district court should consider (1) whether local immigration officials in fact exercised their discretion under § 212(d)(5)(A) to make individualized determinations and (2) whether the criteria employed in making those determinations were consistent with the statutory grant of discretion by Congress, the regulations promulgated by the agencies involved, and the policies which had been established by the President and the Attorney General. If the court should find that low-level immigration officials have discriminated on the basis of national origin despite the adoption of a contrary policy by their superiors in the executive branch, such conduct would constitute an abuse of discretion that would justify appropriate relief. Without expressing any opinion on this score, we note that the district court may wish to reconsider whether class treatment is still an appropriate vehicle for making the determinations set forth above. We therefore remand for further proceedings in light of this opinion.

TJOFLAT, concurring in part and dissenting in part: [omitted]

KRAVITCH, CIRCUIT JUDGE, specially concurring in part and dissenting in part with whom JOHNSON, HATCHETT and CLARK, CIRCUIT JUDGES, join.

* * *

* * * My objection to the majority's reading of the INA is the conclusion that the Attorney General may invidiously discriminate in the granting of parole merely because the Executive decides, without rational reason, that aliens from a certain country should be denied temporary parole.

Nor does such a view create the possibility that the United States would "lose control over our borders." The scenario that the majority describes of a foreign leader sending over citizens of his country and "compel[ling] us to grant physical admission via parole ...," is both irrelevant to the holding and unnecessarily alarmist.

First, here we are concerned only with the discriminatory denial of temporary parole prior to deportation or exclusion proceedings; hence, the constitutionality of "indefinite detention" is not properly before us. Second, to the extent pre-deportation parole is relevant, such a de facto invasion envisioned by the majority would present a rational basis for the Attorney General to deny temporary parole. Third, the President has the capability of preventing any such crisis under INA § 212(f) (cited by the majority as an example of the Executive's broad powers) and § 215(a), which gives the President broad powers to act during a national emergency or time of war; moreover, such an "attack" on our borders would likely fall under the Executive's foreign affairs power. Finally, the majority's prime concern—ensuring that excludable aliens could be detained indefinitely *without a justifiable reason*—would extend the holdings of those cases cited by the majority beyond their intended scope and meaning.

* * *

Notes

How should the cases in this Section of the Chapter have been decided? Would it have been possible to reverse the district court's procedurally demanding decision in *Fernandez-Roque* without declaring excludable aliens so far beyond the reach of the Fifth Amendment? Has the *Jean* court properly understood what the Supreme Court intended in *Plasencia?*

Is it appropriate to detain asylum applicants at all? What if they arrive in exceedingly large numbers, as they did in Florida in mid-1980? How long may such detention last? Is detention permissible if it is adopted for deterrent purposes, that is, explicitly to discourage more asylum-seekers from coming by making more severe the conditions experienced by the first arrivals? How does a court develop standards for judging when conditions permit—or require—release? We shall return to some of these questions when we consider the law of political asylum in Chapter Eight.

For a sampling of the voluminous commentary on the detention of excludable aliens, *see* Note, *The Indefinite Detention of Excludable Aliens: Statutory and Constitutional Justifications and Limitations,* 82 Mich.L. Rev. 61 (1983); Note, *The Constitutional Rights of Excluded Aliens: Proposed Limitations on the Indefinite Detention of the Cuban Refugees,* 70 Geo.L.J. 1303 (1982); Note, *Statutory and Constitutional Limitations on the Indefinite Detention of Excluded Aliens,* 62 B.U.L.Rev. 553 (1982); Note, *Constitutional Limits on the Power to Exclude Aliens,* 82 Colum.L. Rev. 957 (1982).

Chapter Four

ENTRY

SECTION A. THE DEFINITION OF "ENTRY" AND ITS RELEVANCE

The concept of "entry" into the United States plays a crucial, and somewhat curious, role in immigration law. For an alien whom the government seeks to send home, "entry" is the difference between exclusion and deportation: aliens who have "entered" the United States are entitled to deportation hearings; aliens who have not "entered" are placed in exclusion hearings. (This distinction is not made explicit in the statute. From what provisions of the INA may it be inferred? Hint: *See* §§ 235, 236 and 291.) Furthermore, numerous grounds of deportation are keyed to "entry," *see* INA § 241(a)(1); and illegal entry is the core of several criminal provisions in the statute. *See* INA §§ 274–77.

"Entry" is defined in § 101(a)(13) of the INA as:

[A]ny coming of an alien into the United States, from a foreign port or place or from an outlying possession, whether voluntarily or otherwise, except that an alien having a lawful permanent residence in the United States shall not be regarded as making an entry into the United States for the purposes of the immigration laws if the alien proves to the satisfaction of the Attorney General that his departure to a foreign port or place or to an outlying possession was not intended or reasonably to be expected by him or his presence in a foreign port or place or in an outlying possession was not voluntary: *Provided*, That no person whose departure from the United States was occasioned by deportation proceedings, extradition, or other legal process shall be held to be entitled to such exception.

Suppose the United States establishes an inspection center just below its northern border. Alien C, who seeks permanent residence in this country, crosses the Canadian border and presents herself at the INS facility for inspection. Has she "entered" the United States? Or, to ask the question in its most relevant way: if the INS believes C should be sent home, is she entitled to an exclusion hearing or a deportation hearing? A literal reading of the definition would indicate that C had "entered"; she clearly has come into the United States from a foreign place. But this

315

reading cannot be correct. Since inspection centers are usually located on this side of the border, such an interpretation would effectively read exclusion out of the statute. Thus it has been well established that mere physical presence in the United States is not enough to constitute "entry." [1]

Rejecting the test of physical presence may be necessary, but fashioning an acceptable alternative has proven rather difficult. Consider the next two opinions, one from the BIA and the other from a federal district court. Has either developed a coherent, common-sense meaning for "entry?"

MATTER OF LIN

Board of Immigration Appeals, 1982.
Interim Dec. No. 2900.

This case was last before us on October 6, 1981, when we dismissed a Service appeal from the immigration judge's termination of the exclusion proceedings against the applicant. We agreed with his conclusion that the applicant had entered the United States without inspection and was therefore, subject to deportation proceedings instead of exclusion proceedings. The Service has submitted a motion to reconsider our October 6, 1981, decision on this case. The Service motion to reconsider will be granted and the appeal will be sustained.

The applicant is a native and citizen of China who applied for admission to the United States as a nonimmigrant visitor for pleasure on August 22, 1980. At the inspection, he was in possession of a passport which he had purchased in Hong Kong and which bore the name of another person. He was detained by the Service and placed in exclusion proceedings because of alleged excludability under sections 212(a)(19) and 212(a)(20) of the Immigration and Nationality Act, 8 U.S.C. 1182(a)(19) and 1182(a)(20), for attempting entry by fraud or material misrepresentation and lacking a valid immigrant visa. However, prior to the exclusion hearing he absconded from the Service detention facility in St. Paul, Minnesota, until apprehended two days later on September 6, 1980, in New York City. Consequently, the immigration judge terminated the exclusion proceedings, concluding that the applicant had made an "entry" into the United States.

1. The classic case is *Leng May Ma v. Barber*, 357 U.S. 185, 78 S.Ct. 1072, 2 L.Ed.2d 1246 (1958), which concerned a Chinese alien who was detained for over a year after arrival in the United States and then released on parole pending determination of her admissibility. When the government ruled she was not entitled to enter, she applied for withholding of deportation under INA § 243(h) on the ground that she would be persecuted if returned to her native land. At that time, § 243(h) relief was available only if the alien was "within the United States." The court, in a 5 to 4 decision, concluded that the alien's detention and pa-role into the United States did not constitute "entry" and thus she was not "within the United States" within the meaning of the statute. It thus held that she could not invoke § 243(h) relief.

Leng May Ma is still good law as to its conclusion that an alien paroled into the United States has not "entered," as that term is defined by the INA. *See, e.g., Matter of Pierre*, 14 I & N Dec. 467 (BIA 1973). However, the case has been superseded by changes in § 243(h) wrought by the Refugee Act of 1983, which now permits aliens in exclusion hearings to apply for § 243(h) relief. *See* Chapter Eight *infra*.

Our October 6, 1981, decision applied a four element test prescribed in *Matter of Pierre,* 14 I & N Dec. 467 (BIA 1973), for determining when an alien has made an "entry" into the United States and is therefore subject to deportation and not exclusion proceedings. We then stated that the term "entry," is defined in section 101(a)(13) of the Act, 8 U.S.C. 1101(a)(13), as " . . . any coming of an alien into the United States, from a foreign port or place or from an outlying possession. . . . " A survey of the many cases which have treated this subject over the years leads to the following conclusions: An "entry involves (1) a crossing into the territorial limits of the United States, *i.e.* physical presence; plus (2) inspection and admission by an immigration officer, *United States v. Vasilatos,* 209 F.2d 195 (3 Cir.1954); *Lazarescu v. United States,* 199 F.2d 898, 900 (4 Cir.1952); or (3) actual and intentional evasion of inspection at the nearest inspection point, *U.S. ex rel. Giacone v. Corsi,* 64 F.2d 18 (2 Cir.1933); *Morini v. United States,* 21 F.2d 1004 (9 Cir.1927), *cert. denied,* 276 U.S. 623 (1928); *Lew Moy v. United States,* 237 Fed. 50, 52 (8 Cir.1916); *Matter of Estrada-Betancourt,* 12 I & N Dec. 191, 193–4 (BIA 1967); coupled with (4) freedom from restraint, *United States v. Vasilatos, supra; Lazarescu v. United States, supra.*

The applicant physically crossed the United States border at St. Paul where he was detained. He later reached New York City by absconding for two days from a Service detention facility. In *Matter of A–,* 9 I & N Dec. 356 (BIA 1961), and *Matter of A–T–,* 3 I & N Dec. 178 (BIA 1948), we had concluded that escaping from Service detention while awaiting exclusion proceedings constituted an entry which required deportation proceedings instead. We reached the same conclusion in this case applying the *Pierre* test. We concluded that when the applicant absconded, he temporarily achieved freedom from Service restraint, and had made an entry into this country since he was already physically present here. We distinguished two cases cited by the Service in support of its position because there the aliens in question had been paroled into the United States. *See Vitale v. INS,* 463 F.2d 579 (7 Cir.1972); *Klapholz v. Esperdy,* 201 F.Supp. 294 (S.D.N.Y.1961), *aff'd,* 302 F.2d 928 (2 Cir.1962).

However, in its motion to reconsider, the Service has submitted additional arguments which we find convincing. The Service initially contends that the test prescribed in *Matter of Pierre, supra,* is not met here because the applicant did not evade inspection but rather, was inspected and detained pending exclusion proceedings pursuant to section 235 and 236 of the Act, 8 U.S.C. 1225 and 1226. He was served with a Notice to Alien Detained for Hearing by an Immigration Judge (Form I–122) as prescribed by 8 C.F.R. 235.6(a).

The Service also directs our attention to the case of *Luk v. Rosenberg,* 409 F.2d 555 (9 Cir.1969), where an alien had been found excludable, paroled into this country and had absconded for three years. After he was located, his parole was revoked. The court concluded that the alien did not make an "entry" when his parole was revoked, despite his managing to remain for several years after the parole revocation. Congress did not intend to improve such an alien's status, from that of an applicant seeking admission, to that of an alien who has entered the United States and is subject only to deportation proceedings in order to be removed from this country. *Luk v. Rosenberg, supra* at 558.[1]

The Service also points out distinguishing factors in the two cases we previously cited in support of our October 6, 1981, decision, *Matter of A–, supra;* and *Matter of A–T–, supra.* In *Matter of A–T–,* the applicant had been notified of an exclusion hearing when he first applied for entry. He returned later that day, applied again for entry and was admitted. Consequently, there had been two separate applications for entry and his successful second attempt clearly constituted an "entry" since he had been admitted into this country. In *Matter of A–,* the alien had been detained on board a ship as a stowaway pursuant to section 273(d) of the Act, 8 U.S.C. When he escaped and managed to land, his status was similar to that of any alien who surreptitiously crosses our border and enters the United States without inspection.

It is well settled that when an alien is paroled into the United States pursuant to section 212(d)(5) of the Act, 8 U.S.C. 1182(d)(5), and 8 C.F.R. 212.5, pending exclusion proceedings in accordance with sections 235 and 236 of the Act and 8 C.F.R. 235 and 236, he does not gain the additional protections prescribed for deportation proceedings. *Leng May Ma v. Barber,* 357 U.S. 185 (1958).

We reach the same result when, instead of being paroled, the alien is placed in detention within the United States territory, pursuant to 8 C.F.R. 233.1 and 235.3 and manages to abscond from detention while awaiting his exclusion hearing. The service of the Form I–122 after inspection, vests upon the immigration judge the authority to conduct the exclusion proceedings in order to determine the applicant's admissibility. Whether the applicant is then paroled into the United States or instead kept in detention at a Service facility is not determinative. His escaping from Service detention does not place him in the same status as an alien who manages to evade inspection by entering the United States surreptitiously. He has been inspected but not admitted. We therefore, do not choose to extend our decision in *Matter of A–* to aliens physically in this country, who are detained pending exclusion proceedings, and who manage to escape from detention. The motion to reconsider will be granted, the Service appeal will be sustained and the record remanded to the immigration judge for resumption of the exclusion proceedings. It is so ordered.

---

1. An alien in deportation proceedings has avenues of relief from expulsion unavailable in exclusion proceedings, *e.g.* suspension of deportation and voluntary departure pursuant to section 244 of the Act, 8 U.S.C. 1254. He also can request a bond redetermination hearing with a right to appeal to this Board pursuant to 8 C.F.R. 242.-2(b).

IN THE MATTER OF THE APPLICATION OF PHELISNA

United States District Court, Eastern District of New York, 1982.
551 F.Supp. 960.

NICKERSON, DISTRICT JUDGE.

* * *

Petitioner arrived without a visa in the United States on July 5, 1981, in a boat carrying some two hundred Haitians, who disembarked on a Florida beach near Miami. A report of the officers of the Public Safety Department of Dade County, Florida, shows that they apprehended the Haitians on Rickenbaker Causeway one quarter of a mile south of "Sundays Restaurant" and turned them over to the Service.

On July 28, 1981, the Service, claiming that petitioner had made no "entry" into the United States, instituted exclusion proceedings against her pursuant to INA § 236. When the hearing began on September 2, 1981, petitioner's counsel moved to convert it into one for "deportation"—technically, expulsion—on the ground that petitioner had "entered" the United States before being apprehended. Petitioner testified that she had arrived by boat, entered the United States on July 5, 1981, and did not know where she was. The immigration judge, who announced at the inception of the hearing that he would permit only "several questions" of petitioner and would limit "severely" the testimony, refused to subpoena the arresting officer, announced that "[t]he burden is on the applicant" to establish the impropriety of exclusion proceedings, and denied the motion to convert the hearing into one for deportation.

When the exclusion hearing was resumed on December 1, 1981, petitioner's counsel moved for reconsideration of the motion to change the proceeding to one for deportation and offered in evidence "a police report from Miami, Dade County." The immigration judge denied the motion for reconsideration, declined to accept the report in evidence, declined an offer of proof as to what the evidence would be, and found petitioner excludable under INA § 212(a)(20). After the hearing the immigration judge denied asylum and ordered petitioner excluded.

Petitioner appealed to the Board, which dismissed the appeal, holding that (1) petitioner had the burden of showing that she had made an "entry"; (2) intentional evasion of inspection is an element of "entry"; and (3) petitioner had "failed to prove" that element. The present petition followed, asking that petitioner "be restored to a deportation proceeding."

In order to put the issues in context it is useful to note that the immigration laws have long made a distinction between those aliens who have come to the United States seeking admission and those "in" the United States after an "entry," irrespective of its legality. *Leng May Ma v. Barber,* 357 U.S. 185, 187, 78 S.Ct. 1072, 1073, 2 L.Ed.2d 1246 (1958). The Immigration and Nationality Act preserves the distinction. Those seeking admission are subjected to "exclusion proceedings" to determine whether they "shall be allowed to enter or shall be excluded and deported." INA § 236(a). Aliens once they have made an "entry" are subject to "expulsion" if they fall within those categories of aliens who may be "deported" by the Attorney General. INA § 241. Proceedings for expulsion are commonly referred to as "deportation proceedings." As will appear, Congress and the courts have conferred on aliens who have made an "entry" rights in addition to those accorded aliens who have not yet entered.

The government contends that petitioner is "excludable" under INA § 212(a)(20) which provides that among the aliens who "shall be excluded from admission into the United States" are those who when they apply for "admission" do not have a valid visa or other entry document. Petitioner contends that when she landed on the beach she had made an "entry" and should not be "excluded" but is entitled to be deported under INA § 241(a) which provides that an alien shall be "deported" who "at the time of entry" was within a class of aliens "excludable by the law existing at the time of such entry." The term "entry" is defined in INA § 101(a)(13) to encompass, so far as pertinent, "any coming of an alien into the United States, from a foreign port or place, ... whether voluntarily or otherwise."

* * *

Petitioner contends that she made an "entry," by "coming ... into the United States" from a foreign place within the meaning of INA § 101(a)(13). She urges that "entry" occurred when she was present in the United States free from restraint. Quite patently the statute cannot be read to mean that mere presence in the United States is enough to show an entry. The inspection stations at which the United States determines whether aliens are admissible are per force inside the nation's borders. Congress could not have meant that an alien had come "into" the United States when he arrived at one of the usual points where the government is prepared to process applications for admission.

But if the alien crosses the border where there are no inspection facilities, for example, somewhere along the Mexican or Canadian borders or the coast line of the United States, common sense suggests that ordinarily the alien has "entered" the United States. Even under those circumstances the cases have made an exception where the alien has established that he had an intent to be inspected. Thus, in *Thack v. Zurbrick,* 51 F.2d 634 (6th Cir.1931), aliens, long time residents of the United States, returned to Poland for a visit without obtaining certificates entitling them to reentry here within a year. They came back across the Canadian border and headed for the nearest inspection station at Newport, Vermont. On arrival at the station they were arrested and charged with illegal entry. Later they were ordered deported. The court held that an alien who "merely follows the ordinary path from the international line to the nearest inspection point and presents himself for inspection" has not made an "entry" so as to be guilty of "an offense for which Congress intended he should be sent to his former foreign residence and forbidden ever to try to return to this country." 51 F.2d at 635. The court explained that had the aliens "not intended to go to an inspection point" or had they been apprehended "in the effort to evade doing so" the question would be different. *Id.* at 636.

The government and the Board seize on these decisions to argue that petitioner, in order to prove that she had "entered," must demonstrate that when she arrived on the beach she had an intent to "evade" inspection. Aside from the question of burden of proof, this court does not believe that the above cases prescribe as an element of "entry" an intent to evade inspection. It would be enough that the alien had no intention, whether through ignorance or otherwise, to follow the usual path to an inspection station.

But in any event in this court's opinion the Board was not correct in imposing on petitioner more than the burden of proving that she came physically into the United States at some point not in the vicinity of an inspection station. If the government wishes to exclude an alien landing at a point far distant from such a station on the theory that the alien had the particular intent to submit himself to inspection and was on the way to doing so, the government must prove it.

The allocation of the burden of persuasion is, of course, a matter of substantive policy, which Congress may set. But where Congress has not specifically addressed itself to the question and legislative intent is not otherwise apparent, we may assume that the issue has been left to the judiciary for resolution. * * *

The government contends that Congress intended to impose the burden on petitioner and points to language in INA § 291, providing that when a person "makes application for admission, or otherwise attempts to enter the United States, the burden of proof shall be upon such person to establish that he ... is not subject to exclusion." The government asserts that petitioner was "obviously a person 'attempt[ing] to enter the United States.'" But that simply begs the question. The issue is whether "entry" was accomplished. One who is attempting to enter has by hypothesis not yet entered and must show he is entitled to do so. But one who has entered is no longer attempting to do so.

There is thus no express statutory provision allocating the burden of proving "entry," and the court must apply traditional criteria in deciding the question. Plainly what is at stake both for petitioner and for the government is relevant. * * * [U]nder the statutory scheme "entry" is the criterion on which the acquisition of important rights depends. At risk for the alien is the loss of those rights, one of which is regarded by petitioner as literally vital, namely, the right to designate a country to which she is to be sent. At issue for the government is something far less critical, that is, some degree of administrative convenience.

The government argues that the burden of proving petitioner's intent should rest with her since the pertinent evidence on that matter is more accessible to her than to the government. But the significant proof may well be not the self serving declarations of the alien but documentary evidence such as arrest reports and testimony by third persons as to the objective facts from which an inference as to intent may be drawn. The government is ordinarily more likely to have ready access to this evidence than the alien. For example, in this case the government had the resources and the ability to obtain testimony from those who observed the Haitians land on the shore and proceed along the highway and to the local police officers who apprehended them.

Moreover, to impose on petitioner the burden of showing more than the time, place and manner in which she came within the borders of the United States on the beaches of Florida would hardly be the appropriate method of narrowing the issues for decision. If the government contends that an alien had a peculiar intent, not ordinarily inferable from the physical facts, it is not unfair to ask the government to assert that contention and to prove it.

The Board, in addition to imposing on petitioner the burden of proving an intent to evade inspection, also said in its opinion that petitioner "was looking for immigration officials to test her status." There is no evidence in the record to support the supposition that as of the time that petitioner landed on the beach she was seeking out the immigration officials. The only conceivable support for such a finding is the following statement in her later application for asylum: "When we came to the beach in Miami, Florida, we met other Haitians who said that we should see the immigration officials." This language is equally consistent with a lack of intent at the time of landing to seek inspection. Indeed, the statement can scarcely be taken as evidence of the formulation of such an intent even after the landing. It speaks of what others said to her, not what she decided.

* * *

The matter is remanded to the Service for further proceedings consistent with this opinion. So ordered.

Notes

1. The two preceding cases, and the cases described within them, produce the following schematic results.

1. Alien crosses border surreptitiously and is arrested in St. Louis	Entry
2. Alien arrested on causeway shortly after landing on beach and the government cannot prove she was on her way to an inspection station	Entry
3. Alien detained at border escapes into interior of United States and is arrested two days later	No Entry
4. Stowaway alien detained on board ship escapes through porthole and is arrested later in interior of United States	Entry
5. Alien is paroled into country pending determination of admissibility	No Entry

While we might be able to construct a rule that adequately accounts for these results (does the BIA's test in *Lin*?), should we? Is it sensible to have an adjudication system that rewards surreptitious entrants over those who present themselves to border authorities? Can any but the legal mind distinguish between the alien who escapes from an INS detention center and a stowaway detained aboard a ship who escapes through a porthole?

2. Note the curious role that "intent" plays in the *Phelisna* case. In several early cases, it was held that aliens who were apprehended after crossing the border without inspection would not be deemed to have made

an entry if they were on their way to an inspection point (and thus had not intended to evade inspection). *E.g., United States ex rel. Giacone v. Corsi,* 64 F.2d 18 (2d Cir.1933); *Thack v. Zurbrick,* 51 F.2d 634 (6th Cir.1931); *Morini v. United States,* 21 F.2d 1004 (9th Cir.1927), *cert. denied* 276 U.S. 623, 48 S.Ct. 303, 72 L.Ed. 736 (1928). These cases were an obvious attempt to avoid the harshness of a literal reading of the criminal statutes in punishing illegal entry.

In *Phelisna,* the government tried to turn this ameliorative shield into a sword. It asserted that, if under the criminal cases no entry occurs when the alien had intended to present himself for inspection, then an alien should not be deemed to have entered unless he could prove that he had intended to evade inspection. Does the government's position in *Phelisna* necessarily follow from the earlier cases? What does the court hold? Should the intent of the alien matter in deciding whether or not he has entered the United States?

The Difference Between Exclusion and Deportation Proceedings

Usually the fight over what constitutes "entry" is grounded in the alien's desire to be placed in deportation proceedings rather than exclusion proceedings.[2] Some of the reasons why a deportation proceeding might be preferred are: (1) The burden of proof is on the alien in an exclusion proceeding to show she is not subject to exclusion; in a deportation proceeding, the government must prove deportability. INA § 291. (2) Long-term resident aliens may apply for relief from deportation in deportation hearings, INA § 244; such relief is not available to aliens in exclusion hearings. (3) An alien in a deportation hearing may designate the country to which he prefers to be sent, INA § 243(a); an excluded alien must be returned to the country in which he boarded the carrier that brought him here. INA § 237(a)(1).[3] (4) An alien in a deportation proceeding may appeal bond determinations, INA § 242(a); no similar provision exists for aliens in exclusion proceedings. (5) Aliens in deportation hearings may claim the protection of the Fifth Amendment's due process clause (*see* Chapter Five); aliens in exclusion hearings are entitled only to the process Congress affords them (*see* Chapter Three). (6) Aliens detained after an order of deportation generally must be released after six months, INA § 242(c), (d); no similar statutory provisions protect aliens detained following exclusion.

SECTION B. THE RE–ENTRY DOCTRINE

Alien T enters the United States in 1974 and establishes lawful permanent residence. In 1982, without leaving this country, T helps an

---

2. This is not always the case. Since illegal entry is a criminal offense under INA § 275, an alien arrested near the border may prefer to argue that she had not entered the United States at the time of her apprehension. If she prevails, she will receive an exclusion hearing, but avoids a possible criminal charge.

3. If that country will not accept the alien, the statute provides the Attorney General with other options for returning the excluded alien. INA § 237(a)(2).

alien illegally enter the United States and is paid $500. Since entering, T has never left the United States. Although § 241(a)(13) makes such conduct a ground for deportation, the deportation provision is limited to acts committed *within five years* after any entry. Because the conduct occurred eight years after T's first and only entry, he is not deportable under subsection (a)(13).[4]

Now assume that T, having been convicted and served his sentence, takes a two-month trip to the South Pacific in 1983. Upon his return to the United States, he is stopped at the border and told that he will not be able to re-enter because he aided, for gain, the unlawful entry of an alien in 1982. When T wonders out loud how he can be excluded for an act for which he could not be deported, the INS official reads him § 212(a)(31). It requires exclusion of "[a]ny alien who at any time shall have, knowingly and for gain, * * * aided any other alien to enter * * * the United States in violation of law."

Can the INS be correct? Is a permanent resident alien subject to the grounds of exclusion every time he leaves and returns to the United States? May the fact that a permanent resident alien has taken a vacation mean that he will lose his residence in the United States for conduct for which he could not have been deported? The answer to all these questions is yes; and the term used to describe these phenomena is the "re-entry doctrine." Essentially the doctrine holds that the word "entry" in the INA refers to any coming into the United States, not simply the *first* entry of the alien.[5]

In the situation just described, the re-entry doctrine makes possible the *exclusion* of returning residents. As the next case demonstrates, the re-entry doctrine may also trigger the *deportation* of a resident alien where an element of the deportable conduct is that it occur within a certain number of years "after entry."

UNITED STATES ex rel. VOLPE v. SMITH

Supreme Court of the United States, 1933.
289 U.S. 422, 53 S.Ct. 665, 77 L.Ed. 1298.

Mr. Justice McReynolds delivered the opinion of the Court.

In 1906, when sixteen years old, petitioner, Volpe, entered the United States from Italy as an alien. He has resided here continuously since that time, but has remained an alien.

In 1925 he pleaded guilty and was imprisoned under a charge of counterfeiting obligations of the United States—plainly a crime involving moral turpitude.

During June, 1928, without a passport, he made a brief visit to Cuba. Returning, he landed from an airplane at Key West, Florida, and secured admission by Immigrant Inspector Phillips.

---

4. Of course, T may still be prosecuted for the criminal offense.

5. Note that aliens snared by the re-entry doctrine may be able to avail themselves of waivers of excludability provided in INA § 212.

December 15, 1930, Volpe was taken into custody under a warrant issued by the Secretary of Labor which charged him with being unlawfully in this country because "he has been convicted of, or admits the commission of a felony, or other crime or misdemeanor, involving moral turpitude, to-wit: possessing and passing counterfeit U.S. War Savings Stamps, prior to his entry into the United States."

* * *

The only substantial point which we need consider is this:—Was the petitioner subject to deportation because he reëntered the United States from a foreign country after conviction, during permitted residence in the United States, of a crime committed therein which involved moral turpitude? Relevant provisions of the Act of 1917 are in the margin.*

Upon this question federal courts have reached diverse views. The cases are cited in the opinion announced below in the present cause.

We accept the view that the word "entry" in the provision of § 19 which directs that "any alien who was convicted, or who admits the commission, prior to entry, of a felony or other crime or misdemeanor involving moral turpitude; ... shall, upon the warrant of the Secretary of Labor, be taken into custody and deported," includes any coming of an alien from a foreign country into the United States whether such coming be the first or any subsequent one. And this requires affirmance of the challenged judgment.

* * *

An examination of the Immigration Act of 1917, we think, reveals nothing sufficient to indicate that Congress did not intend the word "entry" in § 19 should have its ordinary meaning. Aliens who have committed crimes while permitted to remain here may be decidedly more objectionable than persons who have transgressed laws of another country.

It may be true that if Volpe had remained within the United States, he could not have been expelled because of his conviction of crime in 1925, more than five years after his original entry; but it does not follow that

---

* Sec. 1. That the word "alien" wherever used in this Act shall include any person not a native-born or naturalized citizen of the United States; ...

Sec. 3. That the following classes of aliens shall be excluded from admission into the United States: ... persons who have been convicted of or admit having committed a felony or other crime or misdemeanor involving moral turpitude; ...

Sec. 19. That at any time within five years after entry, any alien who at the time of entry was a member of one or more of the classes excluded by law; any alien who shall have entered or who shall be found in the United States in violation of this Act, or in violation of any other law of the United States; ... except as hereinafter provided, any alien who is hereafter sentenced to imprisonment for a term of one year or more because of conviction in this country of a crime involving moral turpitude, committed within five years after the entry of the alien to the United States, or who is hereafter sentenced more than once to such a term of imprisonment because of conviction in this country of any crime involving moral turpitude, committed at any time after entry; ... any alien who was convicted, or who admits the commission, prior to entry, of a felony or other crime or misdemeanor involving moral turpitude; at any time within three years after entry, any alien ... who enters without inspection, shall, upon the warrant of the Secretary of Labor, be taken into custody and deported: ...

after he voluntarily departed he had the right of reëntry. In sufficiently plain language Congress has declared to the contrary.

The judgment is affirmed.

Discussion

Justice McReynolds attempts to make the result in *Volpe* appear non-controversial. But does not his interpretation of the "sufficiently plain" statutory language make mincemeat of the statutory structure? To see this we must distinguish between two types of deportation grounds: those that help enforce exclusion provisions (*i.e.*, grounds based on conduct prior to entry) and those that concern post-entry conduct following a lawful admission.

Conviction of a crime involving moral turpitude first entered the immigration laws as a ground of exclusion in 1875. In 1903 Congress enacted a general deportation provision that required the deportation, within two years following entry, of aliens who were excludable at time of entry. This provision, accordingly, provided for the deportation of aliens who had committed crimes involving moral turpitude prior to entry but who had not been excluded at time of entry.

The 1917 Act did two things—both of which are reflected in § 19 (reprinted in the footnote to *Volpe*)—in response to demands for tougher laws against alien criminals. First, while it increased the general statute of limitations from two to five years, it eliminated the statute of limitations altogether for crimes involving moral turpitude committed prior to entry. Second, for the first time it provided for the deportation of aliens who committed crimes after a lawful admission to the United States. The new ground required the deportation of an alien who had been "convicted in this country of a crime involving moral turpitude committed within five years after [entry, or two such convictions] committed at any time after entry."

The structure established by the 1917 Act seems plain. Aliens who committed crimes involving moral turpitude prior to their entry into the United States were excludable; and if they managed to evade exclusion at time of entry, they were deportable if caught any time after entry. Aliens convicted of such crimes in this country were treated differently. They were deportable if the conviction occurred within five years of entry; once an alien had lived here more than five years, he would have to be convicted twice before he became deportable. This distinction appears to be an obvious compromise between the view that dangerous criminals should be deported and the recognition that deportation of long-term residents can work serious hardship on the alien and other persons in the United States.

Justice McReynolds' interpretation of the statute undermines this structure. By reading "entry" to mean any entry (not simply the alien's initial entry), he transforms a deportation ground intended to cover aliens excludable for acts committed prior to establishing residence in the United States into a ground that penalizes post-entry conduct. This conflicts with Congress' decision, as reflected in § 19, that aliens who have resided in the United States for more than 5 years should be allowed one wrongful act without triggering deportation. Justice McReynolds may be correct that "[a]liens who have committed crimes while permitted to remain here may be decidedly more objectionable than persons who have transgressed laws of another country." But he has neglected Congress' apparent conclusion that factors other than the simple commission of a crime are relevant in determining whether or not an alien should be deported. In short, the Court's creation of the re-entry doctrine undermines Congress' decision to give some protection to long-term resident aliens.

The tenuousness of the reasoning of *Volpe*, as well as the harsh consequences of the re-entry doctrine, led to calls for legislative repeal of the doctrine. Congress, however, expressly ratified the doctrine [6] when it defined "entry" in the 1952 Act to mean "*any* coming of an alien into the United States." § 101(a)(13) (emphasis supplied). As the next case demonstrates, however, "any" doesn't quite mean "any."

ROSENBERG v. FLEUTI

Supreme Court of the United States, 1963.
374 U.S. 449, 83 S.Ct. 1804, 10 L.Ed.2d 1000.

MR. JUSTICE GOLDBERG delivered the opinion of the Court.

Respondent Fleuti is a Swiss national who was originally admitted to this country for permanent residence on October 9, 1952, and has been here continuously since except for a visit of "about a couple hours" duration to Ensenada, Mexico, in August 1956. The Immigration and Naturalization Service, of which petitioner Rosenberg is the Los Angeles District Director, sought in April 1959 to deport respondent on the ground that at the time of his return in 1956 he "was within one or more of the classes of aliens excludable by the law existing at the time of such entry," Immigration and Nationality Act of 1952, § 241(a)(1). In particular, the Service alleged that respondent had been "convicted of a crime involving moral turpitude," § 212(a)(9), before his 1956 return, and had for that reason been excludable when he came back from his brief trip to Mexico. A deportation order issued on that ground, but it was discovered a few months later that the order was invalid, because the crime was a petty offense not of the magnitude encompassed within the statute. The deportation proceedings were thereupon reopened and a new charge was lodged against respondent: that he had been excludable at the time of his 1956 return as an alien "afflicted with psychopathic personality," § 212(a)(4), by reason of the fact that he was a homosexual. Deportation was ordered on this ground and Fleuti's appeal to the Board of Immigration Appeals was dismissed, whereupon he brought the present action for declaratory judgment and review of the administrative action. It was stipulated that among the issues to be litigated was the question whether § 212(a)(4) is "unconstitutional as being vague and ambiguous." The trial court rejected respondent's contentions in this regard and in general, and granted the Government's motion for summary judgment. On appeal,

6. With two exceptions discussed in the next case.

however, the United States Court of Appeals for the Ninth Circuit set aside the deportation order and enjoined its enforcement, holding that as applied to Fleuti § 212(a)(4) was unconstitutionally vague in that homosexuality was not sufficiently encompassed within the term "psychopathic personality." 302 F.2d 652.

The Government petitioned this Court for certiorari, which we granted in order to consider the constitutionality of § 212(a)(4) as applied to respondent Fleuti. 371 U.S. 859, 83 S.Ct. 117, 9 L.Ed.2d 97. Upon consideration of the case, however, and in accordance with the long-established principle that "we ought not to pass on questions of constitutionality ... unless such adjudication is unavoidable," *Spector Motor Service, Inc. v. McLaughlin,* 323 U.S. 101, 105, 65 S.Ct. 152, 154, 89 L.Ed. 101; we have concluded that there is a threshold issue of statutory interpretation in the case, the existence of which obviates decision here as to whether § 212(a)(4) is constitutional as applied to respondent.

That issue is whether Fleuti's return to the United States from his afternoon trip to Ensenada, Mexico, in August 1956 constituted an "entry" within the meaning of § 101(a)(13) of the Immigration and Nationality Act of 1952, such that Fleuti was excludable for a condition existing at that time even though he had been permanently and continuously resident in this country for nearly four years prior thereto. * * * The question we must consider, more specifically, is whether Fleuti's short visit to Mexico can possibly be regarded as a "departure to a foreign port or place ... [that] was not intended," within the meaning of the exception to the term "entry" created by the statute. Whether the 1956 return was within that exception is crucial, because Fleuti concededly was not excludable as a "psychopathic personality" at the time of his 1952 entry.[2]

The definition of "entry" as applied for various purposes in our immigration laws was evolved judicially, only becoming encased in statutory form with the inclusion of § 101(a)(13) in the 1952 Act. In the early cases there was developed a judicial definition of "entry" which had harsh consequences for aliens. This viewpoint was expressed most restrictively in *United States ex rel. Volpe* v. *Smith* * * *. Although cases in the lower courts applying the strict re-entry doctrine to aliens who had left the country for brief visits to Canada or Mexico or elsewhere were numerous, many courts applied the doctrine in such instances with express reluctance and explicit recognition of its harsh consequences, and there were a few instances in which district judges refused to hold that aliens who had been absent from the country only briefly had made "entries" upon their return.

2. The 1952 Act became effective on December 24, 1952, and Fleuti entered the country for permanent residence on October 9, 1952, a fact which is of significance because § 241(a)(1) of the Act only commands the deportation of aliens "excludable by the law existing at the time of such entry ...." Hence, since respondent's homosexuality did not make him excludable by any law existing at the time of his 1952 entry, it is critical to determine whether his return from a few hours in Mexico in 1956 was an "entry" in the statutory sense. If it was not, the question whether § 212(a)(4) could constitutionally be applied to him need not be resolved.

Reaction to the severe effects produced by adherence to the strict definition of "entry" resulted in a substantial inroad being made upon that definition in 1947 by a decision of the Second Circuit and a decision of this Court. The Second Circuit, in an opinion by Judge Learned Hand, refused to allow a deportation which depended on the alien's being regarded as having re-entered this country after having taken an overnight sleeper from Buffalo to Detroit on a route lying through Canada. *Di Pasquale* v. *Karnuth,* 158 F.2d 878. Judge Hand recognized that the alien "acquiesced in whatever route the railroad might choose to pull the car," *id.,* at 879, but held that it would be too harsh to impute the carrier's intent to the alien, there being no showing that the alien knew he would be entering Canada. "Were it otherwise," Judge Hand went on, "the alien would be subjected without means of protecting himself to the forfeiture of privileges which may be, and often are, of the most grave importance to him." *Ibid.* If there were a duty upon aliens to inquire about a carrier's route, it "would in practice become a trap, whose closing upon them would have no rational relation to anything they could foresee as significant. We cannot believe that Congress meant to subject those who had acquired a residence, to the sport of chance, when the interests at stake may be so momentous." *Ibid.* Concluding, Judge Hand said that if the alien's return were held to be an "entry" under the circumstances, his "vested interest in his residence" would

> "be forfeited because of perfectly lawful conduct which he could not possibly have supposed would result in anything of the sort. Caprice in the incidence of punishment is one of the indicia of tyranny, and nothing can be more disingenuous than to say that deportation in these circumstances is not punishment. It is well that we should be free to rid ourselves of those who abuse our hospitality; but it is more important that the continued enjoyment of that hospitality once granted, shall not be subject to meaningless and irrational hazards." *Ibid.*

Later the same year this Court, because of a conflict between *Di Pasquale* and *Del Guercio* v. *Delgadillo,* 159 F.2d 130 (C.A. 9th Cir.1947), granted certiorari in the latter case and reversed a deportation order affecting an alien who, upon rescue after his intercoastal merchant ship was torpedoed in the Caribbean during World War II, had been taken to Cuba to recuperate for a week before returning to this country. *Delgadillo* v. *Carmichael,* 332 U.S. 388, 68 S.Ct. 10, 92 L.Ed. 17. The Court pointed out that it was "the exigencies of war, not his voluntary act," *id.,* at 391, which put the alien on foreign soil, adding that "[w]e might as well hold that if he had been kidnapped and taken to Cuba, he made a statutory 'entry' on his voluntary return. Respect for law does not thrive on captious interpretations." *Ibid.* Since "[t]he stakes are indeed high and momentous for the alien who has acquired his residence here," *ibid.,* the Court held that

> "[w]e will not attribute to Congress a purpose to make his right to remain here dependent on circumstances so fortuitous and capricious as those upon which the Immigration Service has here seized. The

hazards to which we are now asked to subject the alien are too irrational to square with the statutory scheme." *Ibid.*

* * *

It was in light of all of these developments in the case law that § 101(a)(13) was included in the immigration laws with the 1952 revision. As the House and Senate Committee Reports * * * make clear, the major congressional concern in codifying the definition of "entry" was with "the status of an alien who has previously entered the United States and resided therein . . . ." This concern was in the direction of ameliorating the harsh results visited upon resident aliens by the rule of *United States ex rel. Volpe* v. *Smith, supra,* as is indicated by the recognition that "the courts have departed from the rigidity of . . . [the earlier] rule," and the statement that "[t]he bill . . . [gives] due recognition to the judicial precedents." It must be recognized, of course, that the only liberalizing decisions to which the Reports referred specifically were *Di Pasquale* and *Delgadillo,* and that there is no indication one way or the other in the legislative history of what Congress thought about the problem of resident aliens who leave the country for insignificantly short periods of time. Nevertheless, it requires but brief consideration of the policies underlying § 101(a)(13), and of certain other aspects of the rights of returning resident aliens, to conclude that Congress, in approving the judicial undermining of *Volpe, supra,* and the relief brought about by the *Di Pasquale* and *Delgadillo* decisions, could not have meant to limit the meaning of the exceptions it created in § 101(a)(13) to the facts of those two cases.

The most basic guide to congressional intent as to the reach of the exceptions is the eloquent language of *Di Pasquale* and *Delgadillo* themselves, beginning with the recognition that the "interests at stake" for the resident alien are "momentous," 158 F.2d, at 879, and that "[t]he stakes are indeed high and momentous for the alien who has acquired his residence here," 332 U.S., at 391, 68 S.Ct. at 12. This general premise of the two decisions impelled the more general conclusion that "it is . . . important that the continued enjoyment of . . . [our] hospitality once granted, shall not be subject to meaningless and irrational hazards." 158 F.2d, at 879. See also *Delgadillo, supra,* at 391. Coupling these essential principles of the two decisions explicitly approved by Congress in enacting § 101(a)(13) with the more general observation, appearing in *Delgadillo* as well as elsewhere, that "[d]eportation can be the equivalent of banishment or exile," it is difficult to conceive that Congress meant its approval of the liberalization wrought by *Di Pasquale* and *Delgadillo* to be interpreted mechanistically to apply only to cases presenting factual situations identical to what was involved in those two decisions.

The idea that the exceptions to § 101(a)(13) should be read nonrestrictively is given additional credence by the way in which the immigration laws define what constitutes "continuous residence" for an alien wishing to be naturalized. Section 316 of the 1952 Act, 66 Stat. 242–243, 8 U.S.C. § 1427, which liberalized previous law in some respects, provides that an alien who wishes to seek naturalization does not begin to endanger the five years of "continuous residence" in this country which must precede his application until he remains outside the country for six months, and does not damage his position by cumulative temporary absences unless they total over half of the five years preceding the filing of his petition for naturalization. This enlightened concept of what constitutes a meaningful interruption of the continuous residence which must support a petition for naturalization, reflecting as it does a congressional judgment that an alien's status is not necessarily to be endangered by his absence from the country, strengthens the foundation underlying a belief that the exceptions to § 101(a)(13) should be read to protect resident aliens who are only briefly absent from the country. Of further, although less specific, effect in this regard is this Court's holding in *Kwong Hai Chew* v. *Colding,* 344 U.S. 590, 73 S.Ct. 472, 97 L.Ed. 576, that the returning resident alien is entitled as a matter of due process to a hearing on the charges underlying any attempt to exclude him, a holding which supports the general proposition that a resident alien who leaves this country is to be regarded as retaining certain basic rights.

Given that the congressional protection of returning resident aliens in § 101(a)(13) is not to be woodenly construed, we turn specifically to construction of the exceptions contained in that section as they relate to resident aliens who leave the country briefly. What we face here is another harsh consequence of the strict "entry" doctrine which, while not governed directly by *Delgadillo,* nevertheless calls into play the same considerations which led to the results specifically approved in the Congressional Committee Reports. It would be as "fortuitous and capricious," and as "irrational to square with the statutory scheme," *Delgadillo, supra,* at 391, to hold that an alien may necessarily be deported because he falls into one of the classes enumerated in § 212(a) when he returns from "a couple hours" visit to Mexico as it would have been to uphold the order of deportation in *Delgadillo.* Certainly when an alien like Fleuti who has entered the country lawfully and has acquired a residence here steps across a border and, in effect, steps right back, subjecting him to exclusion for a condition for which he could not have been deported had he remained in the country seems to be placing him at the mercy of the "sport of chance" and the "meaningless and irrational hazards" to which Judge Hand alluded. *Di Pasquale, supra,* at 879. In making such a casual trip the alien would seldom be aware that he was possibly walking into a trap, for the insignificance of a brief trip to Mexico or Canada bears little rational relation to the punitive consequence of subsequent excludability. There are, of course, valid policy reasons for saying that an alien wishing to retain his classification as a permanent resident of this country imperils his status by interrupting his residence too frequently or for an overly long period of time, but we discern no rational policy supporting application of a re-entry limitation in all cases in which a resident alien crosses an international border for a short visit. Certainly if that trip is innocent, casual, and brief, it is consistent with all the discernible signs of congressional purpose to hold that the "departure ... was not intended" within the meaning and ameliorative intent of the exception to § 101(a)(13). Congress unquestionably has the power to exclude all classes of undesirable aliens from this country, and the courts are charged with enforcing such exclusion when Congress has directed it, but we do not think Congress intended to exclude aliens long resident in this country after lawful entry who have merely stepped across an international border and returned in "about a couple of hours." Such a holding would be inconsistent with the general purpose of Congress in enacting § 101(a)(13) to ameliorate the severe effects of the strict "entry" doctrine.

We conclude, then, that it effectuates congressional purpose to construe the intent exception to § 101(a)(13) as meaning an intent to depart in a manner which can be regarded as meaningfully interruptive of the alien's permanent residence. One major factor relevant to whether such intent can be inferred is, of course, the length of time the alien is absent. Another is the purpose of the visit, for if the purpose of leaving the country is to accomplish some object which is itself contrary to some policy reflected in our immigration laws, it would appear that the interruption of residence thereby occurring would properly be regarded as meaningful. Still another is whether the alien has to procure any travel documents in order to make his trip, since the need to obtain such items might well cause the alien to consider more fully the implications involved in his leaving the country. Although the operation of these and other possibly relevant factors remains to be developed "by the gradual process of judicial inclusion and exclusion," *Davidson* v. *New Orleans,* 96 U.S. 97, 104, 24 L.Ed. 616, we declare today simply that an innocent, casual, and brief excursion by a resident alien outside this country's borders may not have been "intended" as a departure disruptive of his resident alien status and therefore may not subject him to the consequences of an "entry" into the country on his return. The more civilized application of our immigration laws given recognition by Congress in § 101(a)(13) and other provisions of the 1952 Act protects the resident alien from unsuspected risks and unintended consequences of such a wholly innocent action. Respondent here, so far as appears from the record, is among those to be protected. However, because attention was not previously focused upon the application of § 101(a)(13) to the case, the record contains no detailed description or characterization of his trip to Mexico in 1956, except for his testimony that he was gone "about a couple hours," and that he was "just visiting; taking a trip." That being the case, we deem it appropriate to remand the case for further consideration of the application of § 101(a)(13) to this case in light of our discussion herein. If it is determined that respondent did not "intend" to depart in the sense contemplated by § 101(a)(13), the deportation order will not stand and adjudication of the constitutional issue reached by the court below will be obviated. The judgment of the Court of Appeals is therefore vacated and the case remanded with directions that the parties be given leave to amend their pleadings to put in issue the question of "entry" in accordance with the foregoing, and for further proceedings consistent herewith.

So ordered.

MR. JUSTICE CLARK, with whom MR. JUSTICE HARLAN, MR. JUSTICE STEWART and MR. JUSTICE WHITE join, dissenting.

I dissent from the Court's judgment and opinion because "statutory construction" means to me that the Court can *construe* statutes but not that it can *construct* them. The latter function is reserved to the Congress, which clearly said what it meant and undoubtedly meant what it said when it defined "entry" for immigration purposes * * *. * * * That this definition of "entry" includes the respondent's entry after his brief trip to Mexico in 1956 is a conclusion which seems to me inescapable. The conclusion is compelled by the plain meaning of the statute, its legislative history, and the consistent interpretation by the federal courts. Indeed, the respondent himself did not even question that his return to the United States was an "entry" within the meaning of § 101(a)(13). Nonetheless, the Court has rewritten the Act *sua sponte,* creating a definition of "entry" which was suggested by many organizations during the hearings prior to its enactment but which was rejected by the Congress. I believe the authorities discussed in the Court's opinion demonstrate that "entry" as defined in § 101(a)(13) cannot mean what the Court says it means, but I will add a few words of explanation.

The word "entry" had acquired a well-defined meaning for immigration purposes at the time the Immigration and Nationality Act was passed in 1952. The leading case was *United States ex rel. Volpe* v. *Smith.* * * *

The federal courts in numerous cases were called upon to apply this definition of "entry" and did so consistently, specifically recognizing that the brevity of one's stay outside the country was immaterial to the question of whether his return was an "entry." A related but obviously distinguishable question did create difficulties for the courts, however, leading to conflicting opinions among the Circuits as to whether a resident alien makes an "entry" when he had no intent to leave the country or did not leave voluntarily. It was decided by this Court in *Delgadillo* v. *Carmichael,* 332 U.S. 388, 68 S.Ct. 10, 92 L.Ed. 17 (1947), which held that an alien whose ship had been torpedoed and sunk, after which he was rescued and taken to Cuba for a week, did not make an "entry" on his return to the United States. The Court discussed the *Volpe* case but distinguished it and others on the ground that "those were cases where the alien plainly expected or planned to enter a foreign port or place. Here he was catapulted into the ocean, rescued, and taken to Cuba. He had no part in selecting the foreign port as his destination." *Id.,* at 390, 68 S.Ct. at 12. The Court specifically relied on *Di Pasquale* v. *Karnuth,* 158 F.2d 878 (C.A. 2d Cir.1947), where an alien who had ridden a sleeping car from Buffalo to Detroit, without knowledge that the train's route was through Canada, was held not to have made an "entry" upon his arrival in Detroit.

These cases and others discussed by the Court establish the setting in which the Immigration and Nationality Act was passed in 1952. The House and Senate reports quoted by the Court show that the Congress recognized the courts' difficulty with the rule that "any coming" of an alien into the United States was an "entry," even when the departure from the country was unintentional or involuntary. The reports discuss the broad rule of the *Volpe* case and the specific limitations of the *Di Pasquale* and *Delgadillo* cases, citing those cases by name. * * *

Thus there is nothing in the legislative history or in the statute itself which would exempt the respondent's return from Mexico from the definition of "entry." Rather, the statute in retaining the definition expressed in *Volpe* seems clearly to cover respondent's entry, which occurred after he knowingly left the United States in order to travel to a city in Mexico. That the trip may have been "innocent, casual, and brief" does not alter the fact that, in the words of the Court in *Delgadillo,* the respondent "plainly expected or planned to enter a foreign port or place." 332 U.S., at 390, 68 S.Ct. at 12.

It is true that this application of the law to a resident alien may be harsh, but harshness is a far cry from the irrationality condemned in *Delgadillo, supra,* at 391, 68 S.Ct. at 12. There and in *Di Pasquale* contrary results would have meant that a resident alien, who was not deportable unless he left the country and reentered, could be deported as a result of circumstances either beyond his control or beyond his knowledge. Here, of course, there is no claim that respondent did not know he was leaving the country to enter Mexico and, since one is presumed to know the law, he knew that his brief trip and reentry would render him deportable. The Congress clearly has chosen so to apply the long-established definition, and this Court cannot alter that legislative determination in the guise of statutory construction. Had the Congress not wished the definition of "entry" to include a return after a brief but voluntary and intentional trip, it could have done so. The Court's discussion of § 316 of the Act shows that the Congress knows well how to temper rigidity when it wishes. Nor can it be said that the Congress was unaware of the breadth of its definition. Even aside from the evidence that it was aware of the judicial precedents, numerous organizations unsuccessfully urged that the definition be narrowed to accomplish what the Court does today. Thus, it was urged that the Act's definition of "entry" "should, we believe, be narrowed so that it will not be applicable to an alien returning from abroad, after a temporary absence, to an unrelinquished domicile here." Other groups complained also that "[t]he term 'entry' is defined to mean any coming of an alien into the United States. It is recommended that this be narrowed to provide that a return, after a temporary absence, to an unrelinquished domicile, shall not constitute a new entry." Despite such urging, however, the Congress made no change in the definition. * * *

All this to the contrary notwithstanding, the Court today decides that one does not really intend to leave the country unless he plans a long trip, or his journey is for an illegal purpose, or he needs travel documents in order to make the trip. This is clearly contrary to the definition in the Act and to any definition of "intent" that I was taught.

What the Court should do is proceed to the only question which either party sought to resolve: whether the deportation order deprived respondent of due process of law in that the term "afflicted with psychopathic personality," as it appears in § 212(a)(4) of the Act, is unconstitutionally vague. Since it fails to do so, I must dissent.

Notes

1. Isn't *Fleuti* an embarrassment to the United States Supreme Court? Isn't the dissent clearly correct that the majority rewrote the statute along the lines of proposals made to, but rejected by, Congress?

What do you make of the fact that Congress has not overturned the Court's interpretation of the statute in *Fleuti?* Does it indicate acquiescence or unconcern? What is the legal effect of a subsequent Congress' "acquiescence" in an incorrect decision by the Court as to a prior Congress' intent? May a subsequent Congress "amend" the statute by not acting?

What do you think motivated the decision of the Court: An appreciation of how Congress, if it had thought about the situation, would have wanted the statute to be interpreted? Concern for the particular alien? Unhappiness with the underlying ground of exclusion?

2. One explanation for the result in *Fleuti* is that the Court read the statute as it did in order to avoid having to rule on the constitutional issue in the case—*i.e.,* whether the exclusion ground was unconstitutionally vague. As Justice Goldberg notes in *Fleuti,* it is a well-established principle that the court will not consider a constitutional issue when the case may be decided on a non-constitutional ground:

> This Court has said repeatedly that it ought not pass on the constitutionality of an act of Congress unless such adjudication is unavoidable. This is true even though the question is properly presented by the record. If two questions are raised, one of non-constitutional and the other of constitutional nature, and a decision of the non-constitutional question would make unnecessary a decision of the constitutional question, the former will be decided.

Alma Motor Co. v. Timken-Detroit Axle Co., 329 U.S. 129, 136, 67 S.Ct. 231, 234, 91 L.Ed. 128 (1946).

Should the Court adopt a preference for non-constitutional grounds of decision? Usually, such a rule is defended on the grounds that constitutional decisions implicate separation of powers concerns and are harder to change. A holding of unconstitutionality may also jeopardize other similar state and federal legislation. Does a rule favoring non-constitutional grounds of decision justify the result in *Fleuti?* Is the process of legislation always better served by a non-constitutional answer (which may well distort congressional intent) than a constitutional one?

Interestingly, the Supreme Court considered the constitutional issue avoided in *Fleuti* four years later in *Boutilier v. INS,* 387 U.S. 118, 87 S.Ct. 1563, 18 L.Ed.2d 661 (1967). It ruled, in a 6 to 3 decision written by Justice Clark, that the statutory provision was not unconstitutionally vague. The membership of the Court in 1967 was the same as in 1963, except Justice Goldberg had been succeeded by Justice Fortas. Does this cast doubt on the *bona fides* of the *Fleuti* majority's use of the canon of construction that constitutional issues are to be avoided? It seems, does it not, that a majority of the Court was not prepared to hold the statute unconstitutional, yet a majority desired to rule in the alien's favor; this led the Court to adopt a dubious interpretation of the statute which it then purported to justify on the ground that it was avoiding a constitutional issue—an issue that really did not exist.

The Ripples of *Fleuti*

While the preceding discussion raises important issues of statutory interpretation, they are largely academic as far as *Fleuti* goes. Whether or not it is possible to defend the decision, its exception to the re-entry doctrine has become firmly imbedded in the law. Indeed, INS Operations Instructions regarding inspection of returning residents have been written to take *Fleuti* into account:

> A returning resident alien suspected of being inadmissible shall be examined to establish whether his absence was meaningfully interruptive of his permanent residence within the purview of *Rosenberg v. Fleuti*, 374 U.S. 449 (June 17, 1963). Interrogation of the alien shall cover, but not be limited to: (1) length of absence and frequency of prior absences, if any; (2) reason for absence; (3) documentation required or obtained; (4) itinerary, and (5) alien's understanding as to his immigration status and admissibility.

> Information developed shall be furnished on Form I–110 to the district director for his determination as to whether the information concerning the absence is sufficient to establish that it was meaningfully interruptive of the alien's permanent residence and referral for hearing before special inquiry officer is warranted.

INS Operations Instruction 235.1k.

Fleuti raised more questions than it answered. How does one decide whether a trip across the border was "meaningfully interruptive of the alien's permanent residence"? Justice Goldberg recommended some guidelines at the end of the opinion, each of which has spawned extensive litigation.

The leading authority describes the developing case law as follows:

> Following the Fleuti decision a brief absence by a lawful permanent resident alien usually has not resulted in an entry for deportation purposes. However, returns to this country have been deemed entries for such purposes when the absence abroad was for a protracted period, or when the alien was absent to engage in an illegal activity, or to face criminal charges, or visited proscribed countries without permission, or left while deportation proceedings were pending against him, or while a final order of deportation was out-standing against him thus executing it, or attempted to smuggle aliens on his return, or when he returned without inspection, or when he reentered the United States as a commuter.

* * *

One court, finding that an alien whose purpose to smuggle aliens was formed while outside the United States did not make an entry upon his return, cautioned on making "a mockery of Fleuti's humanities," the need for "a compassionate interpretation and concomitant administration of the immigration laws," and for the avoidance of "rigoristic rituality." However, a contrary conclusion was adopted in another Circuit, which found it immaterial whether the unlawful purpose was formed before or after the alien's departure from the United States. Moreover, the nature of the absence and return may not be significant when the alien is deportable for activities in this country, *e.g.* narcotics violation, in which deportability does not depend on an entry. G & R § 4.6c.[7]

Where is the *Fleuti* Question Resolved?

The effect of an alien's successful invocation of the *Fleuti* doctrine depends on whether there is a ground of deportation that corresponds to the ground of exclusion which the INS is seeking to enforce against the alien. Where there is no corresponding deportation ground, the alien is permitted to re-enter and remain in the United States. The exclusion ground is not applied because, under the fiction of *Fleuti,* no re-entry has occurred to which the exclusion ground could apply; the alien is in the same situation as if he had never left the United States.

Where, however, there exist identical grounds of deportation and exclusion, answering the *Fleuti* question simply determines whether the alien's right to enter and remain will be determined in an exclusion or deportation hearing. Consider, for example, the exclusion and deportation grounds that apply to narcotics traffickers. INA §§ 212(a)(23) and 241(a)(11). Assume Alien V is stopped at the border and charged with being a narcotics trafficker. V asserts that his short trip to Canada was not meaningfully interruptive of his permanent residence in the United States, and thus, under *Fleuti,* he is not "entering" the United States. Even if the INS agrees, V does not re-enter and live happily ever after. Rather, the INS will simply initiate a deportation proceeding under § 241(a)(11), instead of an exclusion proceeding under § 212(a)(23).

In a situation where the answer to the *Fleuti* question will determine whether the alien receives an exclusion hearing or a deportation hearing, in which kind of hearing should the issue be resolved? The Supreme Court answered this question in *Landon v. Plasencia,* 459 U.S. 21, 103

---

7. Fleuti was a permanent resident alien. Does the *Fleuti* exception apply to non-immigrants as well? The BIA has consistently said no. *Matter of Mundell,* Interim Dec. No. 2950 (BIA 1983); *Matter of Niayesh,* 17 I & N Dec. 231 (BIA 1980); *Matter of Legaspi,* 11 I & N Dec. 819 (BIA 1966).

For a case relying on the spirit of *Fleuti* in the aid of a non-immigrant, *see Joshi v. District Director,* 720 F.2d 799 (4th Cir.1983)

non-immigrant alien applied for adjustment of status; pending adjudication, he sought permission from INS to take brief trip abroad, which INS granted in the form of "advanced parole"; after adjustment of status was denied, Joshi was placed in exclusion proceedings on ground that he was a parolee and applicant for entry; held, Joshi entitled to deportation proceeding).

S.Ct. 321, 74 L.Ed.2d 21 (1982), a case which we have already examined in the consideration of due process in exclusion proceedings.

Recall that Plasencia was a returning resident alien stopped at the border after a brief trip to Mexico. The INS discovered six undocumented aliens in her car, and subsequently sought to exclude her under INA § 212(a)(31) (aiding the illegal entry of an alien for gain). Plasencia asserted that she was entitled to have the issue of whether her trip to Mexico came within the *Fleuti* exception to the re-entry doctrine determined in a deportation proceeding. The Supreme Court disagreed:

> Our analysis of whether [Plasencia] is entitled to a deportation rather than an exclusion hearing begins with the language of the Act. Section 235 of the Act, permits the INS to examine "*[a]ll* aliens" who seek "admission or *readmission* to" the United States and empowers immigration officers to take evidence concerning the privilege of any person suspected of being an alien "to enter, *reenter,* pass through, or reside" in the United States. *Ibid.* (emphasis added). Moreover, "every alien" who does not appear "to be clearly and beyond a doubt entitled to land shall be detained" for further inquiry. *Ibid.* If an alien is so detained, the Act directs the special inquiry officer to determine whether the arriving alien "shall be allowed to enter or shall be excluded and deported." Section 236(a). The proceeding before that officer, the exclusion hearing, is by statute "the sole and exclusive procedure for determining admissibility of a person to the United States ...." *Ibid.*

> The Act's legislative history also emphasizes the singular role of exclusion hearings in determining whether an alien should be admitted. The reports of both the House and Senate state:

> > The special inquiry officer is empowered to determine whether an alien detained for further inquiry shall be excluded and deported or shall be allowed to enter after he has given the alien a hearing. The procedure established in the bill is made the sole and exclusive procedure for determining the admissibility of a person to the United States.

> S.Rep. No. 1137, 82d Cong., 2d Sess., 29 (1952); H.R.Rep. No. 1365, 82d Cong., 2d Sess., 56 (1952).

> The language and history of the Act thus clearly reflect a congressional intent that, whether or not the alien is a permanent resident, admissibility shall be determined in an exclusion hearing. Nothing in the statutory language or the legislative history suggests that the respondent's status as a permanent resident entitles her to a suspension of the exclusion hearing or requires the INS to proceed only through a deportation hearing. Under the terms of the Act, the INS properly proceeded in an exclusion hearing to determine whether respondent was attempting to "enter" the United States and whether she was excludable.

To avoid the impact of the statute, the respondent contends, and the Court of Appeals agreed, that unless she was "entering," she was not subject to exclusion proceedings, and that prior decisions of this Court indicate that she is entitled to have the question of "entry" decided in deportation proceedings.

The parties agree that only "entering" aliens are subject to exclusion. That view accords with the language of the statute, which describes the exclusion hearing as one to determine whether the applicant "shall be allowed to *enter* or shall be excluded and deported." Section 236(a) (emphasis added). But the respondent's contention that the question of entry can be determined only in deportation proceedings reflects a misconception of our decisions.

* * *

The Court of Appeals [below] viewed *Fleuti* as a deportation case rather than an exclusion case and therefore not relevant in deciding whether the question of "entry" could be determined in exclusion proceedings. For guidance on that decision, the Court of Appeals turned to *Kwong Hai Chew v. Colding*, 344 U.S. 590, 73 S.Ct. 472, 97 L.Ed. 576 (1953), which it read to hold that a resident alien returning from a brief trip "could not be excluded without the procedural due process to which he would have been entitled had he never left the country"—*i.e.*, in this case, a deportation proceeding. The court concluded that Plasencia was entitled to litigate her admissibility in deportation proceedings. It would be "circular" and "unfair," thought the court, to allow the INS to litigate the question of "entry" in exclusion proceedings when that question also went to the merits of the respondent's admissibility.

We disagree. The reasoning of *Chew* was only that a resident alien returning from a brief trip has a right to due process just as would a continuously present resident alien. It does not create a right to identical treatment for these two differently situated groups of aliens. As the Ninth Circuit seemed to recognize, if the respondent here was making an "entry," she would be subject to exclusion proceedings. It is no more "circular" to allow the immigration judge in the exclusion proceeding to determine whether the alien is making an entry than it is for any court to decide that it has jurisdiction when the facts relevant to the determination of jurisdiction are also relevant to the merits. Thus, in *United States v. Sing Tuck*, 194 U.S. 161, 24 S.Ct. 621, 48 L.Ed. 917 (1904), this Court held that an immigration inspector could make a determination whether an applicant for admission was an alien or a citizen, although only aliens were subject to exclusion. *Cf. Land v. Dollar*, 330 U.S. 731, 739, 67 S.Ct. 1009, 1013, 91 L.Ed. 1209 (1947) (district court has jurisdiction to determine its jurisdiction by proceeding to a decision on the merits). Nor is it in any way "unfair" to decide the question of

entry in exclusion proceedings as long as those proceedings themselves are fair. Finally, the use of exclusion proceedings violates
neither the "scope" nor the "spirit" of *Fleuti*. As the Court of
Appeals held, that case only defined "entry" and did not designate the forum for deciding questions of entry. The statutory
scheme is clear: Congress intended that the determinations of
both "entry" and the existence of grounds for exclusion could be
made at an exclusion hearing.

Id. at 27–32. Although Justice Marshall dissented from other portions of
the Court's opinion, he concurred in the conclusion that the INA authorized the INS to proceed against Plasencia in an exclusion proceeding.

Proposals to Modify the Re-Entry Doctrine

Although the *Fleuti* decision has blunted much of the criticism of the
re-entry doctrine, it still sparks controversy in debates about immigration
law reform. Witness the most recent discussion of the wisdom of the
doctrine by the Select Commission on Immigration and Refugee Policy.

SCIRP, U.S. IMMIGRATION POLICY AND THE
NATIONAL INTEREST

Final Report 284–86 (1981).

Reentry Doctrine *

*The Select Commission recommends that the reentry doctrine be modified so
that returning lawful permanent resident aliens (those who have departed
from the United States for temporary purposes) can reenter the United States
without being subject to the exclusion laws, except the following:*

- *Criminal grounds for exclusion (criminal convictions while abroad);*
- *Political grounds for exclusion;*
- *Entry into the United States without inspection; and*
- *Engaging in persecution.*

---

* *Commission vote*

Should lawful permanent residents be subject to all of the grounds of exclusion upon
their return from temporary visits abroad?

Option 1: Make no change in current law.

Option 2: (3 votes) Make no change in the
existing law but suggest standards to interpret the Supreme Court's exception to
the reentry doctrine which states that an
"innocent, casual, and brief" trip abroad
does not meaningfully interrupt one's residence in the United States and should not
be regarded as a separate entry in the case
of permanent resident aliens.

Option 3: (2 votes) Eliminate the reentry
doctrine entirely.

Option 4: (8 votes) Modify the reentry doctrine so that returning permanent resident aliens (*i.e.,* those who have departed
from the United States for temporary purposes) could reenter the U.S. without being subject to the exclusion laws except
the following:

a. Criminal grounds for exclusion (criminal convictions while abroad);

b. Political grounds for exclusion;

c. Entry into the U.S. without inspection;
and

d. Engaging in persecution.

Absent (2 votes)

Under existing law, a returning lawful permanent resident alien undergoes an immigration inspection at a port of entry after each trip abroad to determine whether any of the 33 grounds for exclusion should bar his/her reentry into the United States. Witnesses before the Select Commission have criticized the imposition of this reentry doctrine on permanent resident aliens and have cited the harsh consequences which sometimes result when a permanent resident is refused reentry into the United States.

While the Supreme Court has stated that persons who take an innocent, casual and brief trip out of the country should not be considered to be making an entry upon return and that the exclusion laws should not be applied to these aliens, it did not define what was meant by a brief and innocent trip. Therefore, lower courts now decide this on an individual case-by-case basis. The Select Commission has been convinced by the testimony on the need for amendment in this area. It has noted the cases of hardship created by the varying interpretations given to the reentry doctrine. * * *

Several Commissioners believe the problem can be solved with the clarification of the Supreme Court's definition and would amend current law only to include a detailed statutory definition of what constitutes innocent, casual and brief trips abroad. A majority of the Commission's members, however, support the modification of the reentry doctrine itself. Such modification, they find, would eliminate the harsh effects of the reentry doctrine on permanent residents who travel abroad temporarily while retaining the viability of the doctrine where it serves the national interest—exclusion based on criminal or political grounds, entry into the United States without inspection and persecution. In addition, the Commission holds the view that this modification will substantially reduce litigation and appeals and conserve INS resources.

Questions

Had you been a Commissioner, for which option identified in the footnote would you have voted? Why? Before you leap to the conclusion that the doctrine should be discarded in its entirety, consider the following situations:

(1) Alien E is a permanent resident. E takes a two week trip to Costa Rica and commits a crime involving moral turpitude.

(2) Alien N, after attaining lawful permanent resident status, leaves the United States and re-enters without inspection.

(3) Alien T, a non-immigrant student, leaves the United States for spring vacation. The FBI learns that T is making plans to return with arms and plans for terrorist activity in the United States.

(4) Alien R, a permanent resident alien, was a Nazi and is deportable under § 241(a)(19). R leaves the country for a few weeks. If his return is deemed to be an entry, he is excludable under § 212(a)(33).

(5) Alien Y is a lawful permanent resident. During a vacation in the Sahara, Y contracts a deadly contagious disease for which there is no known cure in the United States.

If the re-entry doctrine is abolished, each of these aliens may not be excludable at the border, and some are not even deportable. (Which ones?) Do these hypotheticals affect your opinion of the re-entry doctrine, or are there other ways to deal with the problems they raise?

SECTION C.   A CONCLUDING CONVERSATION

Cynic: The entry cases and the re-entry doctrine represent the worst about legal thinking. The cases draw meaningless distinctions that defy common sense, and the doctrine produces intolerable consequences.

Believer: Nonsense. They represent the beauty of legal thought: the ability to reason from clear and supportable premises to fair results.

Cynic: What "clear and supportable premises" are you referring to?

Believer: First, the United States is entitled to distinguish between aliens seeking entry to this country and aliens who have already entered.

Cynic: O.K.

Believer: Second, entry cannot simply mean physical presence, or the government would be forced to establish all its inspection offices on foreign soil.

Cynic: So far so good.

Believer: Third, it is expensive to detain aliens while determining whether or not they are entitled to enter; thus, the government should be able to allow them to stay in the United States temporarily while their admissibility is being decided. Furthermore, since the alien, *ex hypothesi*, has not yet been lawfully admitted, the government's decision to enlarge her "prison bounds"[1] should not grant her any additional benefits. The alien is "still in theory of law at the boundary line and ha[s] gained no foothold in the United States."[2]

Cynic: I think that sounds all right.

Believer: Fourth, aliens may choose to cross the border far from a designated port of entry. Some, if they are responsible, will try to locate the nearest inspection location. These people should be treated no differently than aliens who arrive at an official border crossing.

Cynic: I agree.

Believer: Well, there you have it.

Cynic: Funny, I don't see it.

Believer: You have just accepted the results in all the above cases.

Cynic: What about *Lin?* I didn't hear anything about aliens escaping detention.

---

1. *Kaplan v. Tod,* 267 U.S. 228, 230, 45   2. *Id.*
S.Ct. 257, 69 L.Ed. 585 (1925).

Believer: Sure you did. The alien in *Lin* who escaped detention originally presented himself to immigration authorities at the border. Surely he should not be treated differently—indeed better—than the alien who waits in detention.

Cynic: True, but why should he be treated worse than an alien who never presented herself to authorities?

Believer: Because she never presented herself to authorities.

Cynic: Is there an echo?

Believer: No. You simply speak more wisdom than you know. I take it that an alien who has surreptitiously landed by boat in Southern Florida and travelled to Chattanooga has "entered" the country within any reasonable meaning of that word.

Cynic: I would have thought so, but common sense does not appear to be of great advantage when interpreting the INA.

Believer: If you grant me that, then how can we distinguish the alien in Chattanooga from the alien in *Phelisna*—so long as there is no proof that Phelisna was on her way to an inspection post?

Cynic: But you're still saying that someone who violates our laws by willfully evading inspection gets benefits that a law abiding alien who presents himself to authorities does not.

Believer: First of all, I'm not so sure all aliens would prefer a deportation hearing. As you know, aliens who are deported may not re-enter the United States for five years without the consent of the Attorney General.[3] Aliens who are excluded need such authorization only for a year.[4]

Secondly, it is not I who am saying this, it is the statute.

Cynic: Then let's change the statute. Even if we can find a set of rules that explains the results, that doesn't make the results right.

Believer: Why would you want to? Just a minute ago you accepted all my initial premises.

Cynic: I'm not so sure, now that I think about it. You said at first that the United States "is entitled" to distinguish between aliens who have entered and those who are arriving at the border. Maybe the government is *entitled to,* but why should it?

Believer: What would you propose instead?

Cynic: I think we should first ask ourselves why we have two different procedures for exclusion and deportation.

Believer: Since 1952, the statute has provided for exclusion and deportation hearings; and it has used the notion of "entry" to determine who gets which. This is how it should be. Congress, under *Knauff* and

3. INA § 212(a)(17).

4. INA § 212(a)(16). [Although this is technically correct, Believer is neglecting to point out that the vast majority of aliens arrested for entry without inspection are permitted to depart voluntarily from the United States without a deportation hearing; thus the five year ban on readmission without permission would not apply.—eds.]

Mezei, is given much more freedom to structure proceedings at the border (*i.e.,* exclusion hearings). This flexibility is needed if we are to maintain control over our borders. Aliens who have already entered and who have established ties to this country are entitled to greater protections before they are sent home.[5] Thus the distinction between exclusion and deportation is perfectly sensible.

Cynic: Doesn't your analysis founder on the re-entry doctrine? Under that doctrine aliens who have established all the ties you mention are subject to the lesser protections you have just defended.

Believer: Maybe so. But that only argues for getting rid of the re-entry doctrine; not for obliterating the distinction between exclusion and deportation.

Cynic: Well, at least we've taken a first step toward sensible reform. Let's go a bit further. To me, the entry cases have produced a set of distinctions that may charitably be described as highly artificial. If we take your reformulation—one that appears to turn on the "stake" of the alien, not "location"—we could of course distinguish between first time entrants and aliens admitted for lawful permanent residence. But what about aliens who have entered without inspection?

Believer: They may have established some ties in the United States, but these were not lawfully acquired. Thus, we need not respect them.

Cynic: Precisely. So under your theory they are entitled only to an exclusion proceeding.[6]

Believer: I suppose so.

Cynic: But that conclusion runs directly counter to the entry cases, which clearly establish that surreptitious entrants are entitled to deportation proceedings. Either your theory or some of the cases it purports to explain must go. My own view is that you are on to something, but it has nothing to do with entry, as that term is defined in the statute.

Believer: What do you recommend?

Cynic: It seems to me that the fundamental (and functional) difference between exclusion and deportation proceedings is that in the former the alien is explaining why he or she has the right to enter and in the latter the government is asserting that the alien has no right to remain. This is what seems to underlie tying the two proceedings to the border/interior distinction.

Believer: So what's wrong with that?

Cynic: The problem is that the border/interior line is not always a useful proxy for the right-to-enter/no-right-to-remain line. An alien who entered surreptitiously, even though inside the United States, has never demonstrated that he is entitled to be here. I think that a

5. *Compare* Martin, *Due Process and Membership in the National Community: Political Asylum and Beyond,* 44 U.Pitt.L. Rev. 165 (1983) *with* Aleinikoff, *Aliens, Due Process and "Community Ties": A Response to Martin, id.* at 237.

6. *See* Martin, *supra,* at 230–34.

different concept would better capture the distinction between exclusion and deportation proceedings: that of *admission after inspection.*

Believer: How would that work?

Cynic: First, it would recognize the obligation of an alien to demonstrate *at least once* her right to enter or reside in the United States. The burden should be on the alien to show this entitlement. Once an alien has been admitted by proper authorities, she should be presumed to be here lawfully until the government demonstrates otherwise.

Believer: How would this apply to aliens who enter without inspection?

Cynic: I think they should be treated as if they were first time entrants. They have never demonstrated to anyone their right to be here. Under this reasoning we avoid the absurd result that aliens who enter by intentionally evading inspection receive benefits not extended to aliens who obey the law and present themselves for inspection at the border.

Believer: And aliens like Lin?

Cynic: Under my theory, *Lin* is an easy case. Lin was never inspected or admitted. He therefore must demonstrate his right to be here.

Believer: And Phelisna?

Cynic: Same result. Notice that this conclusion is reached without tortured reasoning about the intent of the alien or whether the alien or the government has the burden of proof on that issue. Furthermore, it avoids the rather unseemly spectacle created by the current law. In order for an alien like Phelisna to get what she wants (namely, a deportation hearing), she must argue that she had no intention of presenting herself to immigration authorities when she arrived in this country. Why should we reward such an intention?

Believer: Where would this "demonstration" take place? In an exclusion or deportation hearing?

Cynic: Neither. I would establish a new single proceeding. Let's call it an immigration hearing.

In the hearing, once the government presents a *prima facie* case of the person's alienage,[a] the burden would be on the alien to demonstrate either (a) a prior admission after inspection as a permanent resident or (b) a present right to enter as a permanent resident. To establish a right to enter, the alien would have to present proper documentation (*e.g.,* a valid visa) and also show that he is not excludable under § 212(a).

Believer: That's just an exclusion proceeding with a different name.

Cynic: Fair enough. But the crucial point is that it applies to any alien—no matter where located—who has not previously been inspected and admitted.

a. We will discuss this evidentiary burden in the next Chapter. *See* pp. 422–32 *infra.*—eds.

Believer: Like Phelisna and Lin?

Cynic: Exactly. To continue, if an alien can demonstrate that she has been inspected and admitted before as a permanent resident alien, then the burden is on the government to demonstrate (a) that the prior entry was unlawful, or (b) that the alien, following a prior entry after inspection, has committed a deportable act.[7] Note that since we have already agreed (haven't we?) that the re-entry doctrine should be abolished, the "prior entry" I am referring to is the alien's initial admission after inspection.

Believer: But what about an alien who is lawfully admitted, then leaves the country and re-enters without inspection? If the re-entry doctrine is gone, the alien is not deportable.

Cynic: I think you may have a point. I guess I might keep the re-entry doctrine only so far as insuring that aliens submit themselves for inspection each time they cross the border. Even though the other grounds of exclusion would not apply, it would help us to regulate and measure the flow of people across our borders and perhaps stop the unlawful entry of other aliens whom returning residents might help enter surreptitiously.

Believer: I note that so far you have just been talking about aliens admitted for permanent residence. What about nonimmigrant aliens?

Cynic: I'd have to think more about that. My initial reaction is that if we are primarily concerned with the "stake" of the alien, then most nonimmigrants rank fairly low by any measure. Furthermore, applying the proposed procedures to non-immigrants might produce curious results. For example, suppose an alien receives a multiple entry visa as a business visitor and enters the United States for a one week business trip. Then suppose he seeks re-entry for another trip two years later. I don't think the initial admission should immunize him from the grounds of exclusion.

Believer: Then you are keeping the re-entry doctrine for nonimmigrants?

Cynic: It looks that way.

Believer: What else would the merger of exclusion and deportation proceedings accomplish?

Cynic: It could make available to "entering" aliens benefits currently available only in deportation proceedings—such as the right of the alien to designate a country of deportation. It would also, of course, end the embarrassment of the present entry cases and make the

---

7. The government should also be able to show that an alien who had been admitted as a permanent resident and then left the United States for a long period of time has been out of the country so long that she has abandoned resident status. *See* G & R, § 2.19. Such an alien would effectively be a

Supreme Court's decision in *Plasencia* (as to where the *Fleuti* decision should be made) of no import.[b]

Believer: So far you have talked only about a statutory scheme. What happened to the Constitution? Doesn't your proposal destroy the well-established constitutional difference between exclusion and deportation proceedings in terms of the process that Congress may provide?

Cynic: I believe my proposal comports fully with the constitutional requirements of due process under the existing case law. However, I should add that I firmly believe that the border/interior line should be jettisoned in due process analysis. Development of that, however, requires a look at deportation procedures. Let's talk again at the end of Chapter Five.

---

new entrant and would have to demonstrate a right to enter.

    b. One other potential benefit is that putting the burden on the alien to prove an entitlement to enter or a prior admission after inspection would end the game currently played under INA § 291. *See* pp. 430–32 *infra.*—eds.

Chapter Five

DEPORTATION

Deportation, or expulsion, is the removal of an alien who has entered the United States—either legally or illegally. Deportation statutes are nearly as old as the Republic. The Alien and Sedition Acts of 1798 authorized the President to deport (1) resident aliens who were citizens of nations at war with the United States (alien enemies) and (2) aliens whom the President judged "dangerous to the peace and safety of the United States." Act of June 25, 1798, Ch. 58, 1 Stat. 570; Act of July 6, 1798, Ch. 66, 1 Stat. 577. The latter section was apparently never invoked and was allowed to expire two years later by the Jeffersonians. However, the Alien Enemy Act remains on the books today. 50 U.S.C.A. §§ 21–23.

For most of the nineteenth century, the federal government had no general deportation statute.[1] Aliens who entered the country were permitted to remain as long as they wished. Deportation statutes began to flourish with the increased federal involvement in the regulation of immigration in the late 1800's. As the government began to impose restrictions on who could enter, it recognized the need to remove those who had entered in violation of these restrictions. Thus, at first, deportation statutes were viewed primarily as a supplement to the exclusion laws. For example, in 1885 and 1887 Congress passed "contract labor laws," which prohibited the importation of aliens who had pre-existing contracts to perform most kinds of labor or services in the United States. Act of February 26, 1885, Ch. 164, 23 Stat. 332; Act of February 23, 1887, Ch. 220, 24 Stat. 414.[2] These acts were amended in 1888 to authorize the *deportation* of an immigrant who had been "allowed to land contrary to the prohibition" in the earlier laws. Act of Oct. 19, 1888, Ch. 1210, 25 Stat. 566.[3]

The 1891 revision and codification of the immigration laws provided a number of new grounds for exclusion. Concomitantly, it broadened the deportation provision of the 1888 Act to encompass "any alien who shall

---

1. For a brief history of deportation statutes, *see* Maslow, *Recasting Our Deportation Law: Proposals for Reform,* 56 Colum.L.Rev. 309, 311–14 (1956).

2. The statutes did not apply to skilled jobs for which American workers could not be found, domestic servants, professional actors, artists, singers or lecturers.

3. Similarly, the 1892 statute at issue in *Fong Yue Ting v. United States,* p. 20 *supra,* which authorized the deportation of Chinese laborers who failed to obtain certificates of residence, was enacted to help enforce the earlier Chinese exclusion laws.

come into the United States in violation of law." Act of March 3, 1891, Ch. 551, § 11, 24 Stat. 1086.

In 1907, Congress significantly expanded the underlying theory of deportation. It amended the immigration laws to authorize deportation of an alien who was a prostitute "at any time within three years after she shall have entered the United States." Act of February 20, 1907, Ch. 1134, § 3, 34 Stat. 899–900. Thus, for the first time since the Alien and Sedition Acts, Congress authorized the deportation of an alien based on that alien's conduct in the United States *after* he or she had made a lawful entry. Congress has since repeatedly added to the list of post-entry acts that render a lawfully admitted alien deportable. *See* INA § 241.

We have previously considered the constitutional sources of Congress' power to deport aliens as well as the substantive and procedural limits on Congress' power to exclude. As the following cases demonstrate, the Supreme Court has established essentially no limits on Congress' authority to define classes of deportable aliens. This parallels the doctrine developed by the Court in exclusion cases. On procedural matters, however, the Court has drawn a sharp—if difficult to justify—line between due process guarantees in exclusion and deportation proceedings. This chapter is divided into two sections. The first examines Congress' substantive power to deport aliens, and the second considers deportation procedures.

SECTION A. THE DEPORTATION POWER

1. CONSTITUTIONAL PERSPECTIVES

In a case upholding the constitutionality of the deportation of prostitutes under the 1907 Act, as amended in 1910, Justice Holmes wrote:

> It is thoroughly established that Congress has power to order the deportation of aliens whose presence in the country it deems hurtful. The determination by facts that might constitute a crime under local law is not a conviction of crime, nor is the deportation a punishment; it is simply a refusal by the Government to harbor persons whom it does not want.

Bugajewitz v. Adams, 228 U.S. 585, 591, 33 S.Ct. 607, 608, 57 L.Ed. 978 (1913). It is doubtful that Holmes could really have meant that deportation is not punishment, if by "punishment" we mean the imposition of harm or sanctions for misconduct or violation of law. James Madison forcefully made this point long ago in arguing against the Alien and Sedition Acts:

> If the banishment of an alien from a country into which he has been invited as the asylum most auspicious to his happiness,—a country where he may have formed the most tender connections; where he may have invested his entire property, and acquired property of the real and permanent, as well as the movable and temporary kind; where he enjoys, under the laws, a greater share of the blessings of personal security, and personal liberty, than he

can elsewhere hope for; * * *—if a banishment of this sort be not a punishment, and among the severest of punishments, it will be difficult to imagine a doom to which the name can be applied.

4 Elliot's Debates 555 (Philadelphia, J.B. Lippincott & Co., 1881 ed.). Rather, it seems clear that Holmes was making a technical distinction in order to protect congressional exercise of the immigration power from the substantive and procedural limits the Constitution places on criminal proceedings.

The Court's distinction between "deportation" and "punishment" can best be seen in the landmark case of *Wong Wing v. United States*, 163 U.S. 228, 16 S.Ct. 977, 41 L.Ed. 140 (1896), discussed p. 35 *supra*. There, the Court struck down a provision of the 1892 immigration statute that provided for imprisonment, without a judicial trial, of aliens found deportable. In doing so, however, it made clear that the deportation power was subject to virtually no constitutional restraints:

> No limits can be put by the courts upon the power of Congress to protect, by summary methods, the country from the advent of aliens whose race or habits render them undesirable as citizens, or to expel such if they have already found their way into our land and unlawfully remain therein. But to declare unlawful residence within the country to be an infamous crime, punishable by deprivation of liberty and property, would be to pass out of the sphere of constitutional legislation, unless provision were made that the fact of guilt should first be established by a judicial trial. It is not consistent with the theory of our government that the legislature should, after having defined an offence as an infamous crime, find the fact of guilt and adjudge the punishment by one of its own agents.

Id. at 237.

The Supreme Court has gone quite far in immunizing the federal deportation power from substantive constitutional constraints. It has ruled that deportation for past conduct which was legal when undertaken does not violate the Constitution's prohibition against "ex post facto" laws.[4] It has also held inapplicable the constitutional protection against cruel and unusual punishment.[5] Similarly, lower courts have rejected claims that deportation statutes are unconstitutional bills of attainder[6] or

---

4. *See Galvan v. Press*, 347 U.S. 522, 74 S.Ct. 737, 98 L.Ed. 911 (1954); *Flemming v. Nestor*, 363 U.S. 603, 80 S.Ct. 1367, 4 L.Ed.2d 1435 (1960); *Marcello v. Bonds*, 349 U.S. 302, 75 S.Ct. 757, 99 L.Ed. 1107 (1955); *Lehmann v. United States ex rel. Carson*, 353 U.S. 685, 77 S.Ct. 1022, 1 L.Ed.2d 1122 (1957); *Mahler v. Eby*, 264 U.S. 32, 44 S.Ct. 283, 68 L.Ed. 549 (1924).

5. *Fong Yue Ting v. United States*, 149 U.S. 698, 730, 13 S.Ct. 1016, 1028, 37 L.Ed. 905 (1893). *See Santelises v. INS*, 491 F.2d 1254 (2d Cir.1974), *cert. denied* 417 U.S. 968, 94 S.Ct. 3171, 41 L.Ed.2d 1139 (1974).

6. *Ocon v. Guerico*, 237 F.2d 177 (9th Cir. 1956); *Quattrone v. Nicolls*, 210 F.2d 513 (1st Cir.1954), *cert. denied* 347 U.S. 976, 74 S.Ct. 786, 98 L.Ed. 1116 (1954). The Supreme Court has interpreted the bill of attainder clause in Article I, § 9, to prohibit "legislative acts, no matter what their form, that apply either to named individuals or to easily ascertainable members of a group in such a way as to inflict punishment on them without a judicial trial." *United States v. Lovett*, 328 U.S. 303, 315, 66 S.Ct. 1073, 1078, 90 L.Ed. 1252 (1946). *See United States v. Brown*, 381 U.S. 437, 447, 85 S.Ct. 1707,

deny equal protection of the law.[7]

The classic statement of the Supreme Court's reluctance to invalidate congressional deportation decisions is *Harisiades v. Shaughnessy,* which follows. Although the case was decided in 1952, it cannot be dismissed simply as a product of the Cold War and the McCarthy era. The Supreme Court continues to cite *Harisiades* as sound doctrine. *See, e.g., Fiallo v. Bell,* 430 U.S. 787, 792–99, 97 S.Ct. 1473, 1477–81, 52 L.Ed.2d 50 (1977).

A Brief Note on the Deportation of "Subversives"

Harisiades involved the deportation of aliens for their prior membership in the Communist Party. Since 1903, Congress has enacted numerous statutes that mandate exclusion or deportation of aliens deemed to be "subversive" on the basis of their political beliefs and activities. These statutes must be viewed in their historical contexts, coinciding with nativist reaction to Chinese immigration, the growth of a radical labor movement in the late 1880's and earlier 1900's, the assassination of President McKinley in 1901, the Russian Revolution, massive migration of Southern and Eastern Europeans in the first decades of this century, and opposition to American involvement in World War I. Anarchists, Communists, labor organizers, and pacifists all became linked in the public mind with "aliens." "The basic conservatism of the peasant immigrant, with his yearning for tradition, status, and authority," writes William Preston, Jr., "had little influence against nativist fears of foreign extremism. Nor did the alien's overt and steadfast repudiation of various radical movements soften the stereotype." W. Preston, Jr., Aliens and Dissenters: Federal Suppression of Radicals, 1903–1933, at 4 (1963). In short, aliens were often scapegoats for American hysteria over labor and political movements that called into question the basic organization of the American economic and political systems.[8]

1714, 14 L.Ed.2d 484 (1965) (clause intended to prevent "legislative punishment, of any form or severity, of specifically designated persons or groups"). *See generally* L. Tribe, American Constitutional Law §§ 10–4, 10–5 (1978).

7. *See, e.g., Oliver v. United States Department of Justice,* 517 F.2d 426 (2d Cir. 1975), *cert. denied* 423 U.S. 1056, 96 S.Ct. 789, 46 L.Ed.2d 646 (1976). *Cf. Fiallo v. Bell,* p. 125 *supra.*

8. Pinning the blame on foreigners also probably helped deny the legitimacy—or even possibility—of indigenous radical movements. *See, e.g.,* S.Rep. No. 1515, 81st Cong., 2d Sess. 782 (1950):

Communism is, of necessity, an alien force. It is inconceivable that the people of the United States would, of their own volition, organize or become part of a conspiracy to destroy the free institutions to which generations of Americans have devoted themselves. The tremendous political freedom and the corollary standard of living of the United States

have given the people of this country a national entity and heritage far superior to anything which human society has created elsewhere.

* * *

In the light of these facts, it is not strange that the vast majority of those who would establish a Communist dictatorship in this country come from alien lands; and it is easy to see that the forces of world communism must have or find ways and means for getting their minions into this country if they are to maintain the effectiveness of their organization here.

The Comintern realizes that it cannot rely on native Americans because to do so involves the constant risk of having its work impeded or exposed. It is to be expected that the loyalty of a native American or of a citizen of long standing would occasionally reassert itself, despite the most intensive Communist indoctrination.

The view that aliens were the root of civil disorder is evidenced by the 1903 Act which, for the first time, established subversiveness as a ground of exclusion. Passed in the wake of Leon F. Czolgosz' assassination of President McKinley, the Act excluded "anarchists, or persons who believe in or advocate the overthrow by force or violence of the Government of the United States * * * or the assassination of public officials." Act of March 3, 1903, Ch. 1012, § 2, 32 Stat. 1219.[9] (That Czolgosz' heinous act could produce an immigration statute excluding anarchists is somewhat curious; he had only vague ties with the anarchist movement and was a native-born American citizen.)

In 1917, the deportation grounds were extended to include *post-entry* subversive conduct of aliens. Thus "any alien who at any time after entry shall be found advocating or teaching [subversion]" could be deported. Immigration Act of 1917, Ch. 29, § 19, 39 Stat. 889. World War I occasioned further expansions. Aliens who were "members of or affiliated with any organization that entertains a belief in" violent overthrow of the government or anarchism, Anarchist Act of 1918, Ch. 186, § 1, 40 Stat. 1012, as well as aliens who wrote, published, circulated or possessed subversive literature, Act of June 5, 1920, Ch. 251, § 1, 41 Stat. 1008, were made deportable.

The War also brought the Palmer Raids, a repressive campaign directed by the Attorney General of the United States to deport aliens affiliated with allegedly subversive organizations. Thousands of aliens were imprisoned, and over five hundred were eventually deported. What follows is a portion of historian John Higham's account of the Raids.

A new Attorney General, A. Mitchell Palmer, took over * * * in March 1919. Palmer's bulldog jaw belied his simple, placid face. Once the implacable opponent of the political bosses and liquor interests in Pennsylvania, he approached the war against Germany with the same crusading belligerence. * * * He was an ambitious man as well: his eye rested lovingly on the White House. The failure of Palmer's agents to find the perpetrators of several bombing episodes in April must have exasperated him considerably, and when another infernal machine battered the front of his own home in June, Palmer was ready to go with the current. He appealed to Congress for a special appropriation, telling the frightened legislators that he knew exactly when the Reds were planning "to rise up and destroy the Government at one fell swoop." The appropriation became available during the summer, and with it Palmer created a new division of the Bureau of Investigation for the war against radicalism. In anticipation of a peacetime sedition law, the division proceeded to assemble data on all revolutionary activities * * *. * * * [T]he Union of Russian Workers * * * was chosen as the first target.

On November 7, 1919, the second anniversary of the Bolshevik régime in Russia, Palmer's men descended on Russian meet-

9. The Act was upheld against a First Amendment challenge in *United States ex rel. Turner v. Williams,* 194 U.S. 279, 24 S.Ct. 719, 48 L.Ed. 979 (1904).

ing places in eleven cities and seized hundreds of members of the organization. Screening for once was swift. Little more than a month later 249 aliens, most of them netted in the November raids, were on a specially chartered transport en route to Finland. From there they traveled overland to Russia through snows and military lines. Some had to leave behind in America their wives and children, at once destitute and ostracized.

* * *

Basking in the popularity of his anti-Russian raid, Palmer now prepared a mightier blow. On January 2 the Department of Justice, aided by local police forces in thirty-three cities, carried out a vast roundup of alien members of the two communist parties. Officers burst into homes, meeting places and pool rooms, as often as not seizing everyone in sight. The victims were loaded into trucks, or sometimes marched through the streets handcuffed and chained to one another, and massed by the hundreds at concentration points, usually police stations. There officials tried to separate out the alien members of radical organizations, releasing the rest or turning them over to the local police. Many remained in federal custody for a few hours only; some lay in crowded cells for several weeks without a preliminary hearing. For several days in Detroit eight hundred men were held incommunicado in a windowless corridor, sleeping on the bare stone floor, subsisting on food which their families brought in, and limited to the use of a single drinking fountain and a single toilet. Altogether, about three thousand aliens were held for deportation, almost all of them eastern Europeans.

J. Higham, Strangers in the Land: Patterns of American Nativism 1860–1925, at 229–31 (1955).

The January 1920 raids in Boston and other New England towns netted approximately 1000 persons. Twenty aliens who had been arrested and subsequently ordered deported brought suit challenging the legality of the proceedings. The federal district court, in setting aside the deportation of most of the aliens on due process grounds, described the raids and their aftermath:

* * * Pains were taken to give spectacular publicity to the raid, and to make it appear that there was great and imminent public danger, against which these activities of the Department of Justice were directed. The arrested aliens, in most instances perfectly quiet and harmless working people, many of them not long ago Russian peasants, were handcuffed in pairs, and then, for the purposes of transfer on trains and through the streets of Boston, chained together. The Northern New Hampshire contingent were first concentrated in jail at Concord and then brought to Boston in a special car, thus handcuffed and chained together. On detraining at the North Station, the handcuffed and chained aliens were exposed to newspaper photographers and again thus exposed at the wharf where they took the boat for Deer Island.

The Department of Justice agents in charge of the arrested aliens appear to have taken pains to have them thus exposed to public photographing.

Private rooms were searched in omnibus fashion; trunks, bureaus, suit cases, and boxes broken open; books and papers seized. I doubt whether a single search warrant was obtained or applied for. * * *

* * *

At Deer Island the conditions were unfit and chaotic. No adequate preparations had been made to receive and care for so large a number of people. Some of the steam pipes were burst or disconnected. The place was cold; the weather was severe. The cells were not properly equipped with sanitary appliances. There was no adequate number of guards or officials to take a census of and properly care for so many. For several days the arrested aliens were held practically incommunicado. There was dire confusion of authority as between the immigration forces and the Department of Justice forces, and the city officials who had charge of the prison. Most of this confusion and the resultant hardship to the arrested aliens was probably unintentional * * *. Undoubtedly it did have some additional terrorizing effect upon the aliens. Inevitably the atmosphere of lawless disregard of the rights and feelings of these aliens as human beings affected, consciously or unconsciously, the inspectors who shortly began at Deer Island the hearings, the basis of the records involving the determination of their right to remain in this country.

In the early days at Deer Island one alien committed suicide by throwing himself from the fifth floor and dashing his brains out in the corridor below in the presence of other horrified aliens. One was committed as insane; others were driven nearly, if not quite, to the verge of insanity.

After many days of confusion, the aliens themselves, under the leadership of one or two of the most intelligent and most conversant with English, constituted a committee, and represented to Assistant Commissioner Sullivan that, if given an opportunity, they would themselves clean up the quarters and arrange for the orderly service of food and the distribution of mail. This offer was wisely accepted, and thereupon the prisoners created a government of their own, called, ironically, I suppose, "The Soviet Republic of Deer Island." Through the assistance of this so-called Soviet government, conditions orderly, tolerable, not inhumane, were created after perhaps 10 days or 2 weeks of filth, confusion, and unnecessary suffering. It is not without significance that these aliens, thus arrested under charges of conspiracy to overthrow our government by force and violence, were, while under arrest, many of them illegally, found to be capable of organizing amongst themselves, with the consent of and in amicable co-operation with their keepers, an effective and democratic form of local government.

Colyer v. Skeffington, 265 F. 17, 44–45 (D.Mass.1920), reversed in part sub nom. *Skeffington v. Katzeff,* 277 F. 129 (1st Cir.1922).

The Supreme Court played a minor role throughout this period.[10] However, in 1939, it dropped a bombshell on Congress with its decision in *Kessler v. Strecker,* 307 U.S. 22, 59 S.Ct. 694, 83 L.Ed. 1082 (1939). There, by a seven to two vote, it held that an alien who had been a member of the Communist Party after entering the United States but had left the Party prior to his arrest was not deportable under the 1918 Act. Not surprisingly, following *Kessler,* radical organizations "expelled" their alien members in an attempt to immunize them from deportation for subversion.

Congress, upset with the Court's interpretation and the clever action of the proscribed organizations, overruled *Kessler* in the Alien Registration Act of 1940. That statute amended the 1918 Act to provide for deportation of any alien who had been a member of a subversive group "at any time" after entering the United States. The statute specifically applied to aliens "irrespective of the time of their entry into the United States." Alien Registration Act of 1940, Ch. 439, § 23(b), 54 Stat. 673. As stated by the Senate Report on the bill, the amendment was intended to apply to all aliens who were associated with subversive organizations "for no matter how short a time or how far in the past." S.Rep. No. 1796, 76th Cong., 3d Sess. 3 (1940).

The constitutionality of the 1940 amendments to the 1918 Act was challenged in *Harisiades.*

HARISIADES v. SHAUGHNESSY

Supreme Court of the United States, 1952.
342 U.S. 580, 72 S.Ct. 512, 96 L.Ed. 586.

MR. JUSTICE JACKSON delivered the opinion of the Court.

The ultimate question in these three cases is whether the United States constitutionally may deport a legally resident alien because of membership in the Communist Party which terminated before enactment of the Alien Registration Act, 1940.

Harisiades, a Greek national, accompanied his father to the United States in 1916, when thirteen years of age, and has resided here since. He has taken a wife and sired two children, all citizens. He joined the Communist Party in 1925, when it was known as the Workers Party, and served as an organizer, Branch Executive Committeeman, secretary of its Greek Bureau, and editor of its paper "Empros." The party discontinued his membership, along with that of other aliens, in 1939, but he has continued association with members. He was familiar with the principles and philosophy of the Communist Party and says he still believes in them.

---

10. *See, e.g., United States ex rel. Tisi v. Tod,* 264 U.S. 131, 44 S.Ct. 260, 68 L.Ed. 590 (1924) and *United States ex rel. Vajtauer v. Commissioner of Immigration,* 273 U.S. 103, 47 S.Ct. 302, 71 L.Ed. 560 (1927) (upholding deportation of aliens under 1920 statute and rejecting claims of violations of due process).

He disclaims personal belief in use of force and violence and asserts that the party favored their use only in defense. A warrant for his deportation because of his membership was issued in 1930 but was not served until 1946. The delay was due to inability to locate him because of his use of a number of aliases. After hearings, he was ordered deported on the grounds that after entry he had been a member of an organization which advocates overthrow of the Government by force and violence and distributes printed matter so advocating.   * * *

Mascitti, a citizen of Italy, came to this country in 1920, at the age of sixteen. He married a resident alien and has one American-born child. He was a member of the Young Workers Party, the Workers Party and the Communist Party between 1923 and 1929. His testimony was that he knew the party advocated a proletarian dictatorship, to be established by force and violence if the capitalist class resisted. He heard some speakers advocate violence, in which he says he did not personally believe, and he was not clear as to the party policy. He resigned in 1929, apparently because he lost sympathy with or interest in the party. A warrant for his deportation issued and was served in 1946. After the usual administrative hearings he was ordered deported on the same grounds as Harisiades. * * *

Mrs. Coleman, a native of Russia, was admitted to the United States in 1914, when thirteen years of age. She married an American citizen and has three children, citizens by birth. She admits being a member of the Communist Party for about a year, beginning in 1919, and again from 1928 to 1930, and again from 1936 to 1937 or 1938. She held no office and her activities were not significant. She disavowed much knowledge of party principles and program, claiming she joined each time because of some injustice the party was then fighting. The reasons she gives for leaving the party are her health and the party's discontinuance of alien memberships. She has been ordered deported because after entry she became a member of an organization advocating overthrow of the Government by force and violence.   * * *

* * *

I.

These aliens ask us to forbid their expulsion by a departure from the long-accepted application to such cases of the Fifth Amendment provision that no person shall be deprived of life, liberty or property without due process of law. Their basic contention is that admission for permanent residence confers a "vested right" on the alien, equal to that of the citizen, to remain within the country, and that the alien is entitled to constitutional protection in that matter to the same extent as the citizen. Their second line of defense is that if any power to deport domiciled aliens exists it is so dispersed that the judiciary must concur in the grounds for its exercise to the extent of finding them reasonable. The argument goes on to the contention that the grounds prescribed by the Act of 1940 bear no reasonable relation to protection of legitimate interests of the United

States and concludes that the Act should be declared invalid. Admittedly these propositions are not founded in precedents of this Court.

For over thirty years each of these aliens has enjoyed such advantages as accrue from residence here without renouncing his foreign allegiance or formally acknowledging adherence to the Constitution he now invokes. Each was admitted to the United States, upon passing formidable exclusionary hurdles, in the hope that, after what may be called a probationary period, he would desire and be found desirable for citizenship. Each has been offered naturalization, with all of the rights and privileges of citizenship, conditioned only upon open and honest assumption of undivided allegiance to our Government. But acceptance was and is not compulsory. Each has been permitted to prolong his original nationality indefinitely.

So long as one thus perpetuates a dual status as an American inhabitant but foreign citizen, he may derive advantages from two sources of law—American and international. He may claim protection against our Government unavailable to the citizen. As an alien he retains a claim upon the state of his citizenship to diplomatic intervention on his behalf, a patronage often of considerable value. The state of origin of each of these aliens could presently enter diplomatic remonstrance against these deportations if they were inconsistent with international law, the prevailing custom among nations or their own practices.

The alien retains immunities from burdens which the citizen must shoulder. By withholding his allegiance from the United States, he leaves outstanding a foreign call on his loyalties which international law not only permits our Government to recognize but commands it to respect. * * *

Under our law, the alien in several respects stands on an equal footing with citizens,[9] but in others has never been conceded legal parity with the citizen.[10] Most importantly, to protract this ambiguous status within the country is not his right but is a matter of permission and tolerance. The Government's power to terminate its hospitality has been asserted and sustained by this Court since the question first arose.[11]

* * *

9. This Court has held that the Constitution assures him a large measure of equal economic opportunity. *Yick Wo v. Hopkins,* 118 U.S. 356, 6 S.Ct. 1064, 30 L.Ed. 220; *Truax v. Raich,* 239 U.S. 33, 36 S.Ct. 7, 60 L.Ed. 131; he may invoke the writ of habeas corpus to protect his personal liberty, *Nishimura Ekiu v. United States,* 142 U.S. 651, 660, 12 S.Ct. 336, 338, 35 L.Ed. 1146; in criminal proceedings against him he must be accorded the protections of the Fifth and Sixth Amendments, *Wong Wing v. United States,* 163 U.S. 228, 16 S.Ct. 977, 41 L.Ed. 140; and, unless he is an enemy alien, his property cannot be taken without just compensation. *Russian Volunteer Fleet v. United States,* 282 U.S. 481, 51 S.Ct. 229, 75 L.Ed. 473.

10. He cannot stand for election to many public offices. For instance, Art. I, § 2, cl. 2, § 3, cl. 3, of the Constitution respectively require that candidates for election to the House of Representatives and Senate be citizens. See Borchard, Diplomatic Protection of Citizens Abroad, 63. The states, to whom is entrusted the authority to set qualifications of voters, for most purposes require citizenship as a condition precedent to the voting franchise.

11. *Fong Yue Ting v. United States,* 149 U.S. 698, 707, 711–714, 730, 13 S.Ct. 1016, 1019, 1021–1022, 1028, 37 L.Ed. 905.

That aliens remain vulnerable to expulsion after long residence is a practice that bristles with severities. But it is a weapon of defense and reprisal confirmed by international law as a power inherent in every sovereign state. Such is the traditional power of the Nation over the alien and we leave the law on the subject as we find it.

This brings us to the alternative defense under the Due Process Clause—that, granting the power, it is so unreasonably and harshly exercised by this enactment that it should be held unconstitutional.

In historical context the Act before us stands out as an extreme application of the expulsion power. There is no denying that as world convulsions have driven us toward a closed society the expulsion power has been exercised with increasing severity, manifest in multiplication of grounds for deportation, in expanding the subject classes from illegal entrants to legal residents, and in greatly lengthening the period of residence after which one may be expelled. This is said to have reached a point where it is the duty of this Court to call a halt upon the political branches of the Government.

It is pertinent to observe that any policy toward aliens is vitally and intricately interwoven with contemporaneous policies in regard to the conduct of foreign relations, the war power, and the maintenance of a republican form of government. Such matters are so exclusively entrusted to the political branches of government as to be largely immune from judicial inquiry or interference.[16]

These restraints upon the judiciary, occasioned by different events, do not control today's decision but they are pertinent. It is not necessary and probably not possible to delineate a fixed and precise line of separation in these matters between political and judicial power under the Constitution. Certainly, however, nothing in the structure of our Government or the text of our Constitution would warrant judicial review by standards which would require us to equate our political judgment with that of Congress.

Under the conditions which produced this Act, can we declare that congressional alarm about a coalition of Communist power without and Communist conspiracy within the United States is either a fantasy or a pretense? This Act was approved by President Roosevelt June 28, 1940, when a world war was threatening to involve us, as soon it did. Communists in the United States were exerting every effort to defeat and delay our preparations. Certainly no responsible American would say that there were then or are now no possible grounds on which Congress might believe that Communists in our midst are inimical to our security.

Congress received evidence that the Communist movement here has been heavily laden with aliens and that Soviet control of the American Communist Party has been largely through alien Communists. It would be easy for those of us who do not have security responsibility to say that

16. *United States v. Curtiss-Wright Corp.,* 299 U.S. 304, 319–322, 57 S.Ct. 216, 220–222, 81 L.Ed. 255.

those who do are taking Communism too seriously and overestimating its danger. But we have an Act of one Congress which, for a decade, subsequent Congresses have never repealed but have strengthened and extended. We, in our private opinions, need not concur in Congress' policies to hold its enactments constitutional. Judicially we must tolerate what personally we may regard as a legislative mistake.

We are urged, because the policy inflicts severe and undoubted hardship on affected individuals, to find a restraint in the Due Process Clause. But the Due Process Clause does not shield the citizen from conscription and the consequent calamity of being separated from family, friends, home and business while he is transported to foreign lands to stem the tide of Communism. If Communist aggression creates such hardships for loyal citizens, it is hard to find justification for holding that the Constitution requires that its hardships must be spared the Communist alien. When citizens raised the Constitution as a shield against expulsion from their homes and places of business, the Court refused to find hardship a cause for judicial intervention.[17]

We think that, in the present state of the world, it would be rash and irresponsible to reinterpret our fundamental law to deny or qualify the Government's power of deportation. However desirable world-wide amelioration of the lot of aliens, we think it is peculiarly a subject for international diplomacy. It should not be initiated by judicial decision which can only deprive our own Government of a power of defense and reprisal without obtaining for American citizens abroad any reciprocal privileges or immunities. Reform in this field must be entrusted to the branches of the Government in control of our international relations and treaty-making powers.

We hold that the Act is not invalid under the Due Process Clause. These aliens are not entitled to judicial relief unless some other constitutional limitation has been transgressed, to which inquiry we turn.

II.

The First Amendment is invoked as a barrier against this enactment. The claim is that in joining an organization advocating overthrow of government by force and violence the alien has merely exercised freedoms of speech, press and assembly which that Amendment guarantees to him.

The assumption is that the First Amendment allows Congress to make no distinction between advocating change in the existing order by lawful elective processes and advocating change by force and violence, that freedom for the one includes freedom for the other, and that when teaching of violence is denied so is freedom of speech.

Our Constitution sought to leave no excuse for violent attack on the status quo by providing a legal alternative—attack by ballot. To arm all men for orderly change, the Constitution put in their hands a right to

---

17. *Hirabayashi v. United States,* 320 U.S. 81, 63 S.Ct. 1375, 87 L.Ed. 1774 (1943); *Korematsu v. United States,* 323 U.S. 214, 65 S.Ct. 193, 89 L.Ed. 194 (1944). [These cases upheld discriminatory wartime measures taken against American citizens of Japanese descent on the West Coast.—eds.]

influence the electorate by press, speech and assembly. This means freedom to advocate or promote Communism by means of the ballot box, but it does not include the practice or incitement of violence.[18]

True, it often is difficult to determine whether ambiguous speech is advocacy of political methods or subtly shades into a methodical but prudent incitement to violence. Communist governments avoid the inquiry by suppressing everything distasteful. Some would have us avoid the difficulty by going to the opposite extreme of permitting incitement to violent overthrow at least unless it seems certain to succeed immediately. We apprehend that the Constitution enjoins upon us the duty, however difficult, of distinguishing between the two. Different formulae have been applied in different situations and the test applicable to the Communist Party has been stated too recently to make further discussion at this time profitable.[19] We think the First Amendment does not prevent the deportation of these aliens.

III.

The remaining claim is that this Act conflicts with Art. I, § 9, of the Constitution forbidding *ex post facto* enactments. An impression of retroactivity results from reading as a new and isolated enactment what is actually a continuation of prior legislation.

During all the years since 1920 Congress has maintained a standing admonition to aliens, on pain of deportation, not to become members of any organization that advocates overthrow of the United States Government by force and violence, a category repeatedly held to include the Communist Party. These aliens violated that prohibition and incurred liability to deportation. They were not caught unawares by a change of law. There can be no contention that they were not adequately forewarned both that their conduct was prohibited and of its consequences.

In 1939, this Court decided *Kessler v. Strecker*, 307 U.S. 22, 59 S.Ct. 694, 83 L.Ed. 1082, in which it was held that Congress, in the statute as it then stood, had not clearly expressed an intent that Communist Party membership remained cause for deportation after it ceased. The Court concluded that in the absence of such expression only contemporaneous membership would authorize deportation.

The reaction of the Communist Party was to drop aliens from membership, at least in form, in order to immunize them from the consequences of their party membership.

The reaction of Congress was that the Court had misunderstood its legislation. In the Act here before us it supplied unmistakable language that past violators of its prohibitions continued to be deportable in spite of resignation or expulsion from the party. It regarded the fact that an alien defied our laws to join the Communist Party as an indication that he had developed little comprehension of the principles or practice of representative government or else was unwilling to abide by them.

18. *Dennis v. United States,* 341 U.S. 494,   **19.** *Ibid.*
71 S.Ct. 857, 95 L.Ed. 1137.

However, even if the Act were found to be retroactive, to strike it down would require us to overrule the construction of the *ex post facto* provision which has been followed by this Court from earliest times. It always has been considered that that which it forbids is penal legislation which imposes or increases criminal punishment for conduct lawful previous to its enactment. Deportation, however severe its consequences, has been consistently classified as a civil rather than a criminal procedure. Both of these doctrines as original proposals might be debatable, but both have been considered closed for many years and a body of statute and decisional law has been built upon them. *Bugajewitz v. Adams,* 228 U.S. 585, 591, 33 S.Ct. 607, 608, 57 L.Ed. 978 * * *.

* * *

It is contended that this policy allows no escape by reformation. We are urged to apply some doctrine of atonement and redemption. Congress might well have done so, but it is not for the judiciary to usurp the function of granting absolution or pardon. We cannot do so for deportable ex-convicts, even though they have served a term of imprisonment calculated to bring about their reformation.

When the Communist Party as a matter of party strategy formally expelled alien members en masse, it destroyed any significance that discontinued membership might otherwise have as indication of change of heart by the individual. Congress may have believed that the party tactics threw upon the Government an almost impossible burden if it attempted to separate those who sincerely renounced Communist principles of force and violence from those who left the party the better to serve it. Congress, exercising the wide discretion that it alone has in these matters, declined to accept that as the Government's burden.

We find none of the constitutional objections to the Act well founded.
* * *

Mr. Justice Clark took no part in the consideration or decision of these cases.

Mr. Justice Frankfurter, concurring.

It is not for this Court to reshape a world order based on politically sovereign States. In such an international ordering of the world a national State implies a special relationship of one body of people, *i.e.,* citizens of that State, whereby the citizens of each State are aliens in relation to every other State. Ever since national States have come into being, the right of people to enjoy the hospitality of a State of which they are not citizens has been a matter of political determination by each State. (I put to one side the oddities of dual citizenship.) Though as a matter of political outlook and economic need this country has traditionally welcomed aliens to come to its shores, it has done so exclusively as a matter of political outlook and national self-interest. This policy has been a political policy, belonging to the political branch of the Government wholly outside the concern and the competence of the Judiciary.

Accordingly, when this policy changed and the political and law-making branch of this Government, the Congress, decided to restrict the right of immigration about seventy years ago, this Court thereupon and ever since has recognized that the determination of a selective and exclusionary immigration policy was for the Congress and not for the Judiciary. The conditions for entry of every alien, the particular classes of aliens that shall be denied entry altogether, the basis for determining such classification, the right to terminate hospitality to aliens, the grounds on which such determination shall be based, have been recognized as matters solely for the responsibility of the Congress and wholly outside the power of this Court to control.

The Court's acknowledgment of the sole responsibility of Congress for these matters has been made possible by Justices whose cultural outlook, whose breadth of view and robust tolerance were not exceeded by those of Jefferson. In their personal views, libertarians like Mr. Justice Holmes and Mr. Justice Brandeis doubtless disapproved of some of these policies, departures as they were from the best traditions of this country and based as they have been in part on discredited racial theories or manipulation of figures in formulating what is known as the quota system. But whether immigration laws have been crude and cruel, whether they may have reflected xenophobia in general or anti-Semitism or anti-Catholicism, the responsibility belongs to Congress. Courts do enforce the requirements imposed by Congress upon officials in administering immigration laws * * *. But the underlying policies of what classes of aliens shall be allowed to enter and what classes of aliens shall be allowed to stay, are for Congress exclusively to determine even though such determination may be deemed to offend American traditions and may, as has been the case, jeopardize peace.

In recognizing this power and this responsibility of Congress, one does not in the remotest degree align oneself with fears unworthy of the American spirit or with hostility to the bracing air of the free spirit. One merely recognizes that the place to resist unwise or cruel legislation touching aliens is the Congress, not this Court.

I, therefore, join in the Court's opinion in these cases.

MR. JUSTICE DOUGLAS, with whom MR. JUSTICE BLACK concurs, dissenting.

There are two possible bases for sustaining this Act:

(1) A person who was once a Communist is tainted for all time and forever dangerous to our society; or

(2) Punishment through banishment from the country may be placed upon an alien not for what he did, but for what his political views once were.

Each of these is foreign to our philosophy. We repudiate our traditions of tolerance and our articles of faith based upon the Bill of Rights when we bow to them by sustaining an Act of Congress which has them as a foundation.

The view that the power of Congress to deport aliens is absolute and may be exercised for any reason which Congress deems appropriate rests on *Fong Yue Ting v. United States,* 149 U.S. 698, 13 S.Ct. 1016, 37 L.Ed.

905, decided in 1893 by a six-to-three vote. That decision seems to me to be inconsistent with the philosophy of constitutional law which we have developed for the protection of resident aliens. We have long held that a resident alien is a "person" within the meaning of the Fifth and the Fourteenth Amendments. * * * He is entitled to habeas corpus to test the legality of his restraint, to the protection of the Fifth and Sixth Amendments in criminal trials, and to the right of free speech as guaranteed by the First Amendment.

An alien, who is assimilated in our society, is treated as a citizen so far as his property and his liberty are concerned. He can live and work here and raise a family, secure in the personal guarantees every resident has and safe from discriminations that might be leveled against him because he was born abroad. Those guarantees of liberty and livelihood are the essence of the freedom which this country from the beginning has offered the people of all lands. If those rights, great as they are, have constitutional protection, I think the more important one—the right to remain here—has a like dignity.

The power of Congress to exclude, admit, or deport aliens flows from sovereignty itself and from the power "To establish an uniform Rule of Naturalization." U.S. Const., Art. I, § 8, cl. 4. The power of deportation is therefore an *implied* one. The right to life and liberty is an *express* one. Why this *implied* power should be given priority over the *express* guarantee of the Fifth Amendment has never been satisfactorily answered. * * *

The right to be immune from arbitrary decrees of banishment certainly may be more important to "liberty" than the civil rights which all aliens enjoy when they reside here. Unless they are free from arbitrary banishment, the "liberty" they enjoy while they live here is indeed illusory. Banishment is punishment in the practical sense. It may deprive a man and his family of all that makes life worth while. Those who have their roots here have an important stake in this country. Their plans for themselves and their hopes for their children all depend on their right to stay. If they are uprooted and sent to lands no longer known to them, no longer hospitable, they become displaced, homeless people condemned to bitterness and despair.

This drastic step may at times be necessary in order to protect the national interest. There may be occasions when the continued presence of an alien, no matter how long he may have been here, would be hostile to the safety or welfare of the Nation due to the nature of his conduct. But unless such condition is shown, I would stay the hand of the Government and let those to whom we have extended our hospitality and who have become members of our communities remain here and enjoy the life and liberty which the Constitution guarantees.

Congress has not proceeded by that standard. It has ordered these aliens deported not for what they are but for what they once were. Perhaps a hearing would show that they continue to be people dangerous and hostile to us. But the principle of forgiveness and the doctrine of redemption are too deep in our philosophy to admit that there is no return for those who have once erred.

Notes

1. Statutory Developments After *Harisiades*

Subsections (6) and (7) of INA § 241(a) state the current grounds for deportation of subversives.

The Cold War brought a substantial broadening of the statutory grounds. *See, e.g.,* Act of May 25, 1948, Ch. 338, § 1, 62 Stat. 268. Under existing statutes the government was required to demonstrate in the deportation hearing that the organization to which the alien belonged advocated the violent overthrow of the government. The Subversive Activities Control Act (Title I of the Internal Security Act of 1950, Ch. 1024, 64 Stat. 987), sought to overcome this obstacle by identifying the Communist Party by name and making mere membership in, or affiliation with, the Party a ground of deportation. Ch. 1024, § 22, 64 Stat. 1006 (1950).[11] This continues in the law today. INA § 241(a)(6)(C).

The major codification of the immigration laws in 1952 produced the unified list of deportation grounds for subversive activities presently found in the law. The legislation was enacted over President Truman's veto, who objected, among other things, to the breadth and vagueness of the deportation grounds relating to subversion.[12]

Although the Supreme Court has not questioned Congress' authority to pass these laws, it has read them to require proof that the alien's affiliation with a subversive organization entailed a "meaningful association" which included awareness of the "distinct and active political nature of the Communist Party." *See, e.g., Rowoldt v. Perfetto,* 355 U.S. 115, 78 S.Ct. 180, 2 L.Ed.2d 140 (1957); *Gastelum-Quinones v. Kennedy,* 374 U.S. 469, 83 S.Ct. 1819, 10 L.Ed.2d 1013 (1963).[13] These opinions, written in the aftermath of the McCarthy era, have substantially increased the burden of proof on the government.

Despite the numerous and broad grounds of deportation for subversion, these sections are rarely used today. From 1971 to 1981, only 18 aliens were deported for subversive activities.[14]

---

11. In 1951, Congress amended the statute to protect immigrants who had fled Communist regimes in Eastern European countries. It provided that "membership" and "affiliation" did not include involuntary membership occasioned by being under 16 years old, operation of law or the necessity of obtaining a job, food or other essentials of living. Act of March 28, 1951, Ch. 23, § 1, 65 Stat. 28.

12. Veto Statement of President Truman, June 25, 1952, *reprinted in* President's Commission on Immigration and Naturalization,

Whom We Shall Welcome 281–82 (1953). *See generally* Maslow, *supra* note 1, at 333–38.

13. *See also, Bonetti v. Rogers,* 356 U.S. 691, 78 S.Ct. 976, 2 L.Ed.2d 1087 (1958) (technical interpretation of "entry" prevents deportation of alien who had been member of Communist Party between 1932 and 1936).

14. U.S. Dept. of Justice, INS, *1981 Statistical Yearbook of the Immigration and Naturalization Service,* Table 44, p. 104.

2. Constitutionally Protected Liberties and the Deportation Power

The aliens in *Harisiades* claimed that the 1940 Alien Registration Act violated the First Amendment because it subjected them to deportation for the expression of political views. As you can see from the opinion, Justice Jackson gave cursory treatment to the First Amendment issue. He seems to say that the "speech" engaged in by the aliens was not protected and thus deportation based on such speech could not offend the First Amendment.

Jackson's opinion relies heavily upon *Dennis v. United States,* decided the year before *Harisiades. Dennis* upheld the criminal convictions of Communist organizers under the Smith Act.[15] Subsequent case law casts substantial doubt on the continuing vitality of *Dennis.* [16]

If the Supreme Court were to announce that *Dennis* is overruled, would it necessarily overrule *Harisiades?* That is, may Congress deport aliens for engaging in protected speech? Could Congress pass a law today ordering the deportation of any alien who marches in a parade supporting a nuclear freeze or who joins the Ku Klux Klan?

The Supreme Court has never directly confronted these issues, although it has made clear that aliens in the United States are protected by the Bill of Rights.[17] Consider the following comments of Justice Murphy:

> The Bill of Rights is a futile authority for the alien seeking admission for the first time to these shores. But once an alien lawfully enters and resides in this country he becomes invested with the rights guaranteed by the Constitution to all people within our borders. Such rights include those protected by the First and the Fifth Amendments and by the due process clause of the Fourteenth Amendment. None of these provisions acknowledges any distinction between citizens and resident aliens. They extend their inalienable privileges to all "persons" and guard against any encroachment on those rights by federal or state authority. * * *
>
> Since resident aliens have constitutional rights, it follows that Congress may not ignore them in the exercise of its "plenary" power of deportation. * * * [T]he First Amendment and other portions of the Bill of Rights make no exception in favor of deportation laws or laws enacted pursuant to a "plenary" power of the Government. Hence the very provisions of the Constitution negative the proposition that Congress, in the exercise of a

15. The Smith Act was passed as a rider to the Alien Registration Act of 1940 (the statute at issue in *Harisiades*). *See generally* T. Emerson, *The System of Freedom of Expression* 110–29 (1970).

16. *See Hess v. Indiana,* 414 U.S. 105, 94 S.Ct. 326, 38 L.Ed.2d 303 (1973) *(per curiam); Brandenburg v. Ohio,* 395 U.S. 444, 89 S.Ct. 1827, 23 L.Ed.2d 430 (1969) *(per curiam);* Linde, *Clear and Present Danger, Reexamined,* 22 Stan.L.Rev. 1163, (1970); Greena-

walt, *Speech and Crime,* 1980 Am.Bar Found.Res.J. 645, 716–29 (1981).

17. *See, e.g., Yamataya v. Fisher,* 189 U.S. 86, 23 S.Ct. 611, 47 L.Ed. 721 (1903) (Fifth Amendment's guarantee of due process applies in deportation hearing); *Wong Wing v. United States,* 163 U.S. 228, 16 S.Ct. 977, 41 L.Ed. 140 (1896) (alien in criminal proceeding entitled to Fifth and Sixth Amendment protections).

"plenary" power, may override the rights of those who are numbered among the beneficiaries of the Bill of Rights.

Any other conclusion would make our constitutional safeguards transitory and discriminatory in nature. Thus the Government would be precluded from enjoining or imprisoning an alien for exercising his freedom of speech. But the Government at the same time would be free, from a constitutional standpoint, to deport him for exercising that very same freedom. The alien would be fully clothed with his constitutional rights when defending himself in a court of law, but he would be stripped of those rights when deportation officials encircle him. I cannot agree that the framers of the Constitution meant to make such an empty mockery of human freedom.

Bridges v. Wixon, 326 U.S. 135, 161–62, 65 S.Ct. 1443, 1455–56, 89 L.Ed. 2103 (1945) (Murphy, J., concurring).

Do you agree with Justice Murphy that if the First Amendment prohibits the government from imprisoning an alien for protected speech, it also must prohibit the government from deporting the alien? The answer to this question would seem to depend in part upon one's view of the source and nature of the deportation power. Furthermore, if immigration decisions are intimately linked to the process of national self-definition, why should the nation not be able to deny aliens membership on political grounds even if it is unable to control the conduct of present members? Finally, cannot one distinguish imprisonment from deportation on the grounds that the latter is not "punishment," but simply the withdrawal of a privilege to remain in the United States?[18]

3. Congress' Power to Discriminate

Recall Justice Frankfurter's remarks in his concurring opinion in *Harisiades:* "[T]he underlying policies of what classes of aliens shall be allowed to enter and what classes of aliens shall be allowed to stay, are for Congress exclusively to determine even though such determination may be deemed to offend American traditions and may, as has been the case, jeopardize peace." Can this be correct? Could Congress order the deportation of all black aliens or Jewish aliens? Did the cases upholding the

---

18. *Cf. United States v. Robel,* 389 U.S. 258, 88 S.Ct. 419, 19 L.Ed.2d 508 (1967) (invalidating as overbroad a section of the Subversive Activities Control Act of 1950 which prohibited any member of the Communist Party from working "in any defense facility").

Assuming that admission of an alien is a "privilege," may Congress attach *any* condition it wants to a privilege it creates? Although this was once the prevailing view, it is now commonplace to say that the "rights/privilege distinction" is dead. *See, e.g., Sherbert v. Verner,* 374 U.S. 398, 404, 83 S.Ct. 1790, 1794, 10 L.Ed.2d 965 (1963); *Keyishian v. Board of Regents,* 385 U.S. 589,

605–06, 87 S.Ct. 675, 684–85, 17 L.Ed.2d 629 (1967); *Graham v. Richardson,* 403 U.S. 365, 374–75, 91 S.Ct. 1848, 1853, 29 L.Ed.2d 534 (1971). *See generally,* Van Alstyne, *The Demise of the Right-Privilege Distinction in Constitutional Law,* 81 Harv.L.Rev. 1439 (1968). The funeral services, however, may have been premature; and the distinction continues to be viewed as useful and inescapable in some settings. *See Landon v. Plasencia,* 459 U.S. 21, 32, 103 S.Ct. 321, 329, 74 L.Ed.2d 21 (1982); Smolla, *The Reemergence of the Right-Privilege Distinction in Constitutional Law: The Price of Protesting Too Much,* 35 Stan.L.Rev. 69 (1982).

Chinese exclusion laws answer this question? Does *Fiallo v. Bell? See* pp. 125–135 *supra.*

4. Deportation Statutes and the "Ex Post Facto" Clause

The case law makes clear that an alien may be deported for conduct that did not render the alien deportable at the time the act was committed. In constitutional law terms, the cases say that the prohibition against "ex post facto" laws does not apply to deportation statutes. For example, in *Galvan v. Press,* 347 U.S. 522, 74 S.Ct. 737, 98 L.Ed.2d 911 (1954), the Supreme Court considered the constitutionality of retroactive application of the Subversive Activity Control Act, Ch. 1024, 64 Stat. 1006 (1950), which ordered the deportation of any alien who at any time after entry had been a member of the Communist Party. Galvan, an alien of Mexican birth, had entered the United States in 1918. At Galvan's deportation hearing in 1950, the INS Hearing Officer found that he had been a member of the Communist Party between 1944 and 1946. Thus Galvan was ordered deported even though, as pointed out by the dissent of Justice Black (joined by Justice Douglas), at the time of his membership "[Communist] Party candidates appeared on California election ballots, and no federal law then frowned on Communist Party political activities." *Id.* at 532, 74 S.Ct. at 743.

Justice Frankfurter, writing for the Court, rejected Galvan's constitutional claims:

> In light of the expansion of the concept of substantive due process as a limitation upon all powers of Congress, * * * much could be said for the view, were we writing on a clean slate, that the Due Process Clause qualifies the scope of political discretion heretofore recognized as belonging to Congress in regulating the entry and deportation of aliens. And since the intrinsic consequences of deportation are so close to punishment for crime, it might fairly be said also that the *ex post facto* Clause, even though applicable only to punitive legislation, should be applied to deportation.

> But the slate is not clean. As to the extent of the power of Congress under review, there is not merely "a page of history," *New York Trust Co. v. Eisner,* 256 U.S. 345, 349, 41 S.Ct. 506, 507, 65 L.Ed. 943, but a whole volume. Policies pertaining to the entry of aliens and their right to remain here are peculiarly concerned with the political conduct of government. * * * [T]hat the formulation of these policies is entrusted exclusively to Congress has become about as firmly imbedded in the legislative and judicial tissues of our body politic as any aspect of our government. And whatever might have been said at an earlier date for applying the *ex post facto* Clause, it has been the unbroken rule of this Court that it has no application to deportation.

Id. at 530–31, 74 S.Ct. at 742.[19]

19. Justices Black and Douglas dissented: "For joining a lawful political group years ago—an act which he had no possible reason to believe would subject him to the slightest

Are the statutes in *Harisiades* and in *Galvan* truly *ex post facto* laws? Or do they simply restate other grounds of deportation that existed at the time the aliens undertook the conduct which subsequently resulted in their deportation? Recall Justice Jackson's comment in *Harisiades* that "[d]uring all the years since 1920 Congress has maintained a standing admonition to aliens, on pain of deportation, not to become members of any organization that advocates overthrow of the United States Government by force and violence, a category repeatedly held to include the Communist Party." Is the *ex post facto* claim stronger in *Galvan*, where the Subversive Activity Control Act dispensed with proof of the violent purposes of the Communist Party (proof that was required under the 1918 and subsequent statutes)?

Perhaps a clearer example of an *ex post facto* law appears in *Mahler v. Eby,* 264 U.S. 32, 44 S.Ct. 283, 68 L.Ed. 549 (1924). In 1920, Congress added as a ground of deportation violation of the Selective Draft Act or the Espionage Act, both of which were enacted in 1917. Act of May 10, Ch. 174, § 1, 41 Stat. 593. Herbert Mahler was convicted of violating both Acts in 1918 and sentenced to five years in the federal penitentiary at Leavenworth. Mahler was ordered deported in 1921 under the 1920 statute, even though at the time of his conviction in 1918 violations of the Acts were not grounds for deportation. (Furthermore, the criminal statutes had been repealed prior to the deportation proceeding.) The Court, through Chief Justice Taft, rejected the *ex post facto* claim: "Congress by the Act of 1920 was not increasing the punishment for the crimes of which [Mahler] had been convicted, by requiring [his] deportation if found [an] undesirable [resident]. It was, in the exercise of its unquestioned right, only seeking to rid the country of persons who had shown by their career that their continued presence here would not make for the safety or welfare of society." *Id.* at 39, 44 S.Ct. at 286.[20] Is it sensible to limit application of the *ex post facto* clause to criminal legislation, or do the values underlying the clause support scrutiny of non-criminal statutes that impose substantial burdens on individuals for past conduct? *See* Note, *Ex Post Facto Limitations on Legislative Power,* 73 Mich.L.Rev. 1491 (1975).

Even were we to conclude that a deportation statute is not punishment and therefore not condemned by the *ex post facto* clause, our inquiry would not be ended. The Supreme Court has made clear that it will scrutinize, under the due process clause, legislation that imposes new civil duties or liabilities based on past acts. *See, e.g., Usery v. Turner Elkhorn*

penalty—[Galvan] now loses his job, his friends, his home, and maybe even his children, who must choose between their father and their native country." *Id.* at 533, 74 S.Ct. at 744 (Black, J., dissenting).

20. *See also Marcello v. Bonds,* 349 U.S. 302, 75 S.Ct. 757, 99 L.Ed. 1107 (1955). Carlos Marcello, an alien famous in the annals of immigration history for having successfully contested deportation for almost half a century (*see United States ex rel. Marcello v.*

District Director, 634 F.2d 964, 973–79 (5th Cir.1981), *cert. denied* 452 U.S. 917, 101 S.Ct. 3052, 69 L.Ed.2d 421 (1981)), was convicted in 1938 of violating the Marijuana Tax Act. The Immigration and Nationality Act of 1952 made past violations of the 1938 Act a ground of deportation. The Supreme Court rejected Marcello's *ex post facto* law claim. 349 U.S. at 314, 75 S.Ct. at 764.

Mining Co., 428 U.S. 1, 17, 96 S.Ct. 2882, 2893, 49 L.Ed.2d 752 (1976). Since the New Deal, however, the Court has been quite hesitant to strike down retroactive impositions of burdens on industry. *Id.* (upholding sections of Federal Coal Mine Health and Safety Act of 1969 that require mine operators to provide compensation for former employee's death or disability due to black lung disease, even if employee had terminated employment before Act was passed).

Should this judicial deference apply with equal force in the deportation context? If we swallow the fiction that deportation is not punishment, what interests does the government serve by sending someone home for committing an act for which she could not have been deported at the time of the act's commission? Consider Justice Taft's observation in *Mahler v. Eby, supra,* that deportation for past bad acts seems no different from a law prohibiting persons convicted of a felony from practicing medicine. 264 U.S. at 39, 44 S.Ct. at 286. *Cf. De Veau v. Braisted,* 363 U.S. 144, 80 S.Ct. 1146, 4 L.Ed.2d 1109 (1960) (upholding New York State statute that prohibited felon from holding office in any waterfront labor organization).

There are two distinct issues that might concern us about the retroactive application of deportation statutes. The first is the obvious point that it is unfair to impose harsh sanctions upon a person for conduct which was lawful when undertaken. The second issue, which seems to be more at stake in *Harisiades,* is the justness of deporting a person who made a mistake long ago but since has lived a peaceful and productive life in the United States. Justice Douglas has described this problem as "the absence of a rational connection between the imposition of the penalty of deportation and the *present* desirability of the alien as a resident in this country." *Marcello v. Bonds,* 349 U.S. 302, 321, 75 S.Ct. 757, 767, 99 L.Ed. 1107 (1955) (Douglas, J., dissenting) (emphasis in original). Do you agree?

5. Deportation Statutes and "Statutes of Limitations"

Harisiades joined the Communist Party nine years after entering the United States. Mascitti had terminated his membership in the subversive organizations 17 years before deportation proceedings were initiated against him. In neither case was the length of time between entry and commission of the act or between commission of the act and initiation of deportation proceedings relevant to the alien's deportation. Both these issues are often loosely discussed under the name of "statutes of limitations" in immigration law, but you should be clear that they raise distinct issues of law and policy.

a. *Time between entry and the commission of a deportable act*

INA § 241(a)(4) makes deportable an alien who "is convicted of a crime involving moral turpitude *within five years after entry* and either sentenced to confinement or confined therefor in a prison or corrective institution, for a year or more." (Emphasis supplied.) Several other grounds of deportation are limited to a specific number of years following entry. INA § 241(a)(3) (institutionalized at public expense due to mental disease within five years after entry); (a)(15) (convicted of violating Alien Registration Act within five years of entry).

Should there be a statute of limitations for deportation based on acts committed after entry? For some grounds of deportation (*e.g.*, becoming a public charge), but not others (*e.g.*, committing crime of moral turpitude)? At some point, is it fair to say that an alien who has resided for a long period of time in the United States has become a product of American society? What about children who enter at a very young age and commit a crime in their twenties? [21] One response to these slightly slanted questions is that long-term residents have an easy way to avoid deportation: become citizens. Is this a good answer to the aliens in *Harisiades*? Justice Jackson seems to suggest that it is; but note that the Nationality Act of 1940, Ch. 876, 54 Stat. 1137, precluded the naturalization of aliens who belonged to organizations advocating the violent overthrow of the United States government, and the Subversive Activity Control Act of 1950, Ch. 1024, 64 Stat. 687, specifically barred naturalization of members of the Communist Party. *See* G & R § 15.16.

The Select Commission on Immigration and Refugee Policy considered this "statute of limitations" question but reached no agreement:

> The Commission has * * * considered but could not reach a consensus on whether long-term, lawful permanent residence should be a bar to deportation. Some Commissioners believe that the present policy, under which the grounds for deportation are generally applied to all aliens regardless of status and length of stay, should be retained. These Commission members argue that long-term permanent resident aliens can become U.S. citizens through naturalization and by that action remove any threat of deportation. They view the status of permanent resident alien as a privilege, and find suspension of deportation [a] a more appropriate way to deal with long-term permanent residents facing deportation * * *. Other Commission members, however, would bar the institution of deportation proceedings against long-term (perhaps seven to ten years) permanent resident aliens who have committed deportable offenses or crimes, except in cases of heinous crimes. Further, they would bar the institution of deportation proceedings against permanent resident aliens who are under the age of 18 and have committed deportable offenses (except in cases where heinous crimes have been committed), regardless of the length of residence in the United States. These Commis-

21. *See* Hesse, *The Constitutional Status of the Lawfully Admitted Permanent Resident Alien: The Inherent Limits of the Power to Expel*, 69 Yale L.J. 262, 290–95 (1959); President's Commission on Immigration and Naturalization, Whom We Shall Welcome 201–02 (1953) (recommending that no alien be subject to deportation if he was under 16 years old at time of admission for permanent residence or has been lawful permanent resident for 20 years).

a. We will consider suspension of deportation in Chapter Six, *infra.* Essentially, under INA § 244, the Attorney General has the authority to cancel the deportation of long-term residents who otherwise demonstrate good moral character and whose deportation would cause severe hardship to the alien or the alien's immediate relatives in the United States.

sion members believe that permanent residents under 18 years of age who are generally ineligible for naturalization and may not be in a position to derive U.S. citizenship from their parents (if their parents do not wish or cannot qualify for naturalization) should not be penalized because they are unable to avoid deportation on the basis of U.S. citizenship. Commissioners holding this point of view argue that permanent resident aliens and their families suffer undue hardship as a result of deportation when other penalties would be more appropriate to the crime committed. They believe the suspension of deportation process, even if less stringent, will still be cumbersome and expensive.

SCIRP, Final Report 279–81.

Senator Simpson, in his separate comments on the report of the Commission, wrote:

[M]y view is that the policy of the statute of limitations does not apply to deportation. In the criminal law, a statute of limitations prevents prosecution and punishment after a certain period of time following the past act which constitutes the offense. Deportation is not a penalty, which is intended to punish for past offense. Deportation represents a judgment that certain persons are unacceptable for presence in the U.S., because they *currently* represent a threat or because they are otherwise regarded as *currently* undesirable by the American people. Past behavior may well be relevant to both of these reasons for such a judgment.

SCIRP, Final Report 418.

b.   Time between commission of act and initiation of proceedings

So far we have been considering a "statute of limitations" as a bar to deportation of long-time residents who commit acts a number of years *after entry.* This is not the usual way people think about a "statute of limitations." In the criminal law, a statute of limitations normally begins running at the time a crime has been committed. One could envisage adopting a similar rule in immigration law that would prohibit initiation of deportation proceedings a certain number of years *after commission of the act constituting the ground for deportation.* [22]

If you were a member of Congress, would you support this kind of statute of limitations for all grounds of deportation? Some grounds and not others?

---

22. Early immigration laws applied a statute of limitations to the deportation ground of excludable at entry. The 1903 Act provided that: "any alien who shall come into the United States in violation of law * * * shall be deported * * * at any time within two years after arrival." Act of March 3, 1903, Ch. 1012, § 20, 32 Stat. 1218. Subsequent acts extended the limitation period to three years, Act of February 20, 1907, Ch.

1134, § 20, 34 Stat. 904, and then five years. Immigration Act of 1917, Ch. 29, § 19, 39 Stat. 889. The 1952 Act eliminated the limitation. The Senate Judiciary Committee explained the change as follows: "If the cause for exclusion existed at the time of entry, it is believed that such aliens are just as undesirable at any subsequent time as they are within the five years after entry." S.Rep. No. 1515, 81st Cong., 2d Sess. 389 (1950).

Several rationales are generally cited as underlying the use of statutes of limitations in criminal law: (1) the desirability that prosecutions be based on fresh evidence; (2) the likelihood that a person who has refrained from further criminal activity for a period of time has reformed; (3) the decline of the retributive impulse over time; and (4) the desirability of lessening the possibility of blackmail based on a threat to prosecute or disclose evidence to law enforcement officials. Model Penal Code, Comment § 1.07 (Tent.Draft No. 5, 1956). Do these justifications equally support a statute of limitations in immigration law?

On the Construction of Immigration Statutes

Although (or perhaps, because) the Supreme Court has supplied no constitutional check on Congress' power to designate deportable classes of aliens, the Court has generally read deportation statutes quite narrowly. Justice Douglas penned the classic statement of this canon of interpretation:

> We resolve the doubts in favor of that construction [urged by the alien] because deportation is a drastic measure and at times the equivalent of banishment or exile * * *. It is the forfeiture for misconduct of a residence in this country. Such a forfeiture is a penalty. To construe this statutory provision less generously to the alien might find support in logic. But since the stakes are considerable for the individual, we will not assume that Congress meant to trench on his freedom beyond that which is required by the narrowest of several possible meanings of the words used.

Fong Haw Tan v. Phelan, 333 U.S. 6, 10, 68 S.Ct. 374, 376, 92 L.Ed. 433 (1948).[23]

Does the Court's reading of the Constitution appear contradictory to its reading of immigration statutes? Or, does it demonstrate the Court's appreciation of the separation of powers that underlies our form of government? That is, the Supreme Court recognizes broad congressional authority but, because of the harsh consequences of deportation, will insist that Congress state with clarity what conduct shall render the alien deportable. This "clear statement" rule of statutory construction serves at least two purposes: imposition of a duty on Congress to consider carefully the scope of the grounds of deportation, and notice to aliens as to the specific acts that are condemned.

2. GROUNDS OF DEPORTATION

Section 241 of the INA lists the grounds of deportation. Like the exclusion grounds, the deportation provisions betray no coherent theory of organization or purpose. Rather, they are an historical collection of traits and acts that various United States Congresses over the past century have deemed undesirable. Old grounds of deportation never die; they do not even fade away.

---

23. In *Fong Haw Tan,* the government sought to deport a permanent resident alien. Is that case's rule of statutory interpretation appropriate for non-immigrant aliens?

	Ground	First adopted
1.	Excludable at time of entry	1891
2.	Entered without inspection; in the U.S. in violation of law	1891
3.	Institutionalization for mental disease	1952
4.	Crime involving moral turpitude	1917
5.	Failure to register; use of false visa	1938, 1940
6.	Subversive activities	1917, 1950
7.	Engage in activities prejudicial to the U.S.	1952
8.	Public charge	1891
9.	Failure to maintain non-immigrant status	1924
10.	Unlawful entry from contiguous territory	1952
11.	Drug addicts, users or dealers	1922, 1960
12.	Prostitution	1907
13.	Aiding illegal entry	1940
14.	Conviction for possession of particular firearms	1940
15.	Violation of Smith Act within five years of entry	1940
16.	Violation of Smith Act more than once	1940
17.	Undesirable aliens due to convictions for certain crimes	1920
18.	Conviction for importation of persons for immoral purposes	1917
19.	Perpetrator of Nazi persecution between 1933 and 1945	1978

This almost random list of "bad acts" may be divided into three rough (and sometimes overlapping) categories: (1) violation of immigration laws—grounds 1, 2, 5, 9, 10, 13; (2) criminal and subversive activities—grounds 4, 6, 7, 11 (dealers), 12, 14, 15, 16, 17, 18; and (3) immoral conduct or undesirable traits—grounds 3, 8, 11 (addicts), 12, 18, 19.

The following chart indicates the frequency with which these grounds have resulted in the deportation of aliens over the last 75 years.

ALIENS DEPORTED BY CAUSE YEARS ENDED JUNE 30, 1908–1976, JULY–SEPTEMBER 1976, AND YEARS ENDED SEPTEMBER 30, 1977–1981

(Deportation statistics by cause not available
prior to fiscal year 1908.)

C A U S E S

Period	Total	Subversive or anarchistic	Criminal	Immoral	Violation of Narcotic Laws	Mental or Physical Defect	Previously Excluded or Deported	Failed To Maintain or Comply With Conditions of Nonimmigrant Status	Entered Without Proper Documents	Entered Without Inspection or By False Statements	Public Charge	Unable to Read (Over 16 Years of Age)	Miscellaneous
1908–1981	829,432	1,528	48,513	16,586	8,494	27,305	41,142	126,378	155,364	348,548	22,558	16,762	16,254
1908–1910	6,888	–	236	784	–	3,228	–	–	–	1,106	474	–	1,060
1911–1920	27,912	353	1,209	4,324	–	6,364	178	–	–	4,128	9,086	704	1,566
1921–1930	92,157	642	8,383	4,238	374	8,936	1,842	5,556	31,704	5,265	10,703	5,977	8,537
1931–1940	117,086	253	16,597	4,838	1,108	6,301	9,729	14,669	45,480	5,159	1,886	8,329	2,737
1941–1950	110,849	17	8,945	759	822	1,560	17,642	13,906	14,288	50,209	143	1,746	812
1951–1960	129,887	230	6,742	1,175	947	642	4,002	25,260	35,090	54,407	225	5	1,112
1961–1970	96,374	15	3,694	397	1,462	236	3,601	31,334	11,831	43,561	8	–	235
1961	7,438	4	498	73	106	54	357	3,020	400	2,916	2	–	8
1962	7,637	2	493	58	131	53	353	2,967	378	3,185	–	–	17
1963	7,454	4	452	61	158	29	368	2,302	417	3,642	1	–	20
1964	8,746	–	417	40	146	22	373	2,473	688	4,580	–	–	7
1965	10,143	–	385	53	143	23	355	3,241	1,036	4,881	2	–	24
1966	9,168	1	323	30	130	13	336	3,668	984	3,615	–	–	68
1967	9,260	–	320	29	154	14	360	3,126	1,272	3,947	2	–	36
1968	9,130	–	266	21	137	8	345	3,200	1,356	3,777	1	–	19
1969	10,505	3	272	14	155	12	361	2,901	1,789	4,983	–	–	15
1970	16,893	1	268	18	202	8	393	4,436	3,511	8,035	–	–	21
1971–1980	231,683	18	2,515	67	3,622	38	4,028	33,725	16,501	170,955	31	1	182
1971	17,639	2	286	9	232	7	476	4,140	2,979	9,483	4	–	21
1972	16,266	2	266	7	307	3	487	3,966	2,710	8,486	6	–	26
1973	16,842	7	226	7	395	7	594	3,989	2,247	9,342	4	–	24
1974	18,824	3	191	7	396	7	440	3,839	2,086	11,839	2	–	14
1975	23,438	–	225	4	583	6	526	3,649	1,896	16,529	1	–	19
1976	27,998	1	272	8	464	2	481	3,782	1,185	21,777	1	1	24
1976 TO	8,927	–	83	2	110	–	141	1,007	271	7,304	3	–	6
1977	30,228	3	285	6	372	3	315	3,150	1,066	25,012	1	–	15
1978	28,371	–	220	4	314	1	236	2,543	871	24,165	5	–	12
1979	25,888	–	264	9	265	2	202	1,901	707	22,525	3	–	10
1980	17,262	–	197	4	184	–	130	1,759	483	14,493	1	–	11
1981	16,596	–	192	4	159	–	120	1,928	470	13,708	2	–	13

Source: U.S. Department of Justice, Immigration and Naturalization Service, 1981 Statistical Yearbook of the Immigration and Naturalization Service, Table 44, p. 104.

Assume you are a member of Congress considering a major revision of the INA. Which of the present grounds of deportation would you vote to maintain or delete? What underlying principles and values guide your choices? Would you deport an alien for conduct (or a trait) which is not unlawful if done (or possessed) by an American citizen—*e.g.,* mental illness, drug addiction or poverty? To state this question more abstractly, should we insist that those who have joined the American community by immigrating have fewer faults or be less of a burden on society than persons who are born here? Is Congress using the immigration laws, in part, to protect its image of ideal members of our community—an ideal that citizens sometimes fail to fulfill?

Take another look at the list of deportation grounds. What grounds would you *add*? Aliens who are child-abusers? Who do not learn English within a certain number of years? Who violate civil rights laws?

Note that some of the grounds apply to conduct before entry (*e.g.,* 19 (Nazis)); before or after entry (*e.g.,* 13 (aiding illegal entry)); any time after entry (*e.g.,* 6 (subversives)); or within a certain number of years after entry (*e.g.,* 8 (public charge within 5 years of entry from causes not arising after entry)).[24] What accounts for these differences? Is it simply historical happenstance, or is there an underlying set of principles that explains the differences?

a. *Excludable at Time of Entry*

Section 241(a)(1), a direct descendant of an early deportation provision,[25] subjects an alien to deportation if he or she was excludable at time of entry. The obvious purpose of the paragraph is to enable the government to expel aliens who had no right to enter the country. It is, as the leading authorities describe it, "delayed exclusion." G & R, § 4.7a. There is no statute of limitations attached to this provision. Nor does the fact that the alien passed through inspection at the border prevent the government from subsequently deporting her.[26]

Because of the "re-entry doctrine," an alien who was not deportable when he left the United States may be deportable under § 241(a)(1) after his re-entry where his conduct prior to leaving is a ground of exclusion. Recall *United States ex rel. Volpe v. Smith,* and the discussion in Chapter Four, *supra.*

Recognizing the potential harshness of § 241(a)(1), Congress has provided a waiver for aliens, excludable for fraud or misrepresentation in obtaining an immigrant visa or entry, who have close relatives in the United States. INA § 241(f).[27] This provision, added in 1957 and amended in 1961,[28] was the source of a surprising amount of confusion and litigation regarding the kinds of acts and grounds of exclusion it covered. After two interpretations by the Supreme Court, *INS v. Errico,* 385 U.S. 214, 87 S.Ct. 473, 17 L.Ed.2d 318 (1966), and *Reid v. INS,* 420 U.S. 619, 95 S.Ct. 1164, 43 L.Ed.2d 501 (1975), Congress amended the provision in 1981 in an attempt to clarify matters. Act of Dec. 29, 1981, § 8, 95 Stat. 1611. For a thorough discussion of the waiver, *see* G & R, § 4.7c.

---

24. Recall that "entry" refers to every entry of the alien into the United States (except for exceptions following *Rosenberg v. Fleuti*), not simply the initial entry. *See* Chapter Four *supra.* Consider the results this may produce. Assume an alien entered the United States in 1950 and has lived here since as a permanent resident alien. In 1982, he takes a month long vacation in Italy. In 1983 he commits a crime involving moral turpitude and is sentenced to a year in prison. He is now deportable under § 241(a)(4), because the crime was committed within 5 years of his entry following his vacation. If the alien had taken his vacation in Montana, he would not be deportable. Can this result be defended? The harshness of this section can be ameliorated by the sentencing judge, who, under INA § 241(b),

may make a binding recommendation to the Attorney General that the alien not be deported, and by INA § 244, which grants, under certain circumstances, suspension of deportation to long-term residents.

25. Act of March 3, 1891, § 11, 26 Stat. 1086.

26. *See Pearson v. Williams,* 202 U.S. 281, 26 S.Ct. 608, 50 L.Ed. 1029 (1906); C. Gordon, *Finality of Immigration and Nationality Determinations,* 31 U.Chi.L.Rev. 433, 439 (1964).

27. The subsection parallels a similar waiver of exclusion. INA § 212(i).

28. Act of Sept. 11, 1957, § 7, 71 Stat. 640; Act of Sept. 26, 1961, § 16, 75 Stat. 655.

b. Entry Without Inspection or Presence in the United States in Violation of Law

By far the most frequently invoked ground of deportation is INA § 241(a)(2): "entered the United States without inspection * * * or * * * is in the United States in violation of this Act." This provision embraces most of the aliens we commonly think of as "illegal aliens"—that is, those who enter the United States surreptitiously by evading inspection [29] and those who enter lawfully with nonimmigrant visas (as students or visitors, for example) and then stay beyond the time authorized.[30] This ground of deportation has also been deemed applicable to aliens who present themselves at the border and falsely claim American citizenship. The Supreme Court has held that such conduct "so significantly frustrate[s] the process for inspecting incoming aliens" that it renders the alien deportable under § 241(a)(2) as having evaded inspection. *Reid v. INS,* 420 U.S. 619, 95 S.Ct. 1164, 43 L.Ed.2d 501 (1975). *See Goon Mee Heung v. INS,* 380 F.2d 236, 237 (1st Cir.1967), *cert. denied* 389 U.S. 975, 88 S.Ct. 479, 19 L.Ed.2d 470 (1967).

To what extent do paragraphs § 241(a)(1) and (a)(2) overlap? Are all aliens who were excludable at time of entry also in the United States in violation of law? For example, suppose P, a permanent resident alien, had been convicted of a crime involving moral turpitude in his home country but did not disclose that fact to consular officials when applying for a visa or to INS officers at the time of his admission. Is he deportable under (a)(1) and (a)(2)?

Is every alien deportable under § 241(a)(2) also deportable under (a)(1)? Is an alien who surreptitiously crosses the border deportable under (a)(1)? Is a nonimmigrant who stays beyond the time authorized at the time of admission?

Does § 241(a)(2) apply to returning residents who enter without inspection or who enter without inspection and subsequently enter properly? Suppose permanent resident R leaves the United States to help alien S enter this country unlawfully. R and S cross the border surreptitiously but are apprehended five days later. R is charged under § 241(a)(2) with entry without inspection. R's deportation hearing is scheduled for some months in the future. While he is waiting, he leaves the United States and re-enters by showing his green card to INS border officials. At the deportation hearing, R claims that his *last* entry was lawful and thus he can no longer be deemed deportable under § 241(a)(2). What result?

---

29. It should be stressed that most aliens who are apprehended under this paragraph do not go through deportation proceedings. For example, in 1980 there were more than 900,000 apprehensions of aliens believed to have entered the country without inspection; yet only 21,840 aliens were ordered deported for illegal entry. The vast majority availed themselves of "voluntary departure"—a procedure that permits the alien to leave the United States at her own expense within a certain period of time. We will discuss voluntary departure in Chapter Six.

Interestingly, aliens stopped at the southwest border are routinely processed as deportation cases, although most probably should be treated as exclusion cases under INA § 212(a)(20).

30. Non-immigrants who violate the conditions of their admission are also deportable under INA § 241(a)(9).

The BIA considered such a claim in *Matter of Ruis,* Interim Dec. No. 2923 (BIA 1982). It held:

> [S]ection 241(a)(2) of the Act relates to any entry made by an alien who fails to submit to inspection. Consequently, we find that the respondent's deportability for entering without inspection is not prevented by the mere fact that he departed and returned with his Form I–151. To hold otherwise would be to thwart the policies underlying the Act and to provide an opportunity for aliens to violate our immigration laws with impunity.

> We need not decide at this time whether an alien who has entered the United States without inspection will be forever subject to deportation in all circumstances.[2]

Accord, *Gunaydin v. INS,* 742 F.2d 776 (3rd Cir.1984)

The *result* in *Ruis* may well strike you as correct, given the particular facts of the case. But what about the conclusion of the BIA that an entry without inspection is not erased by a subsequent lawful entry? Suppose alien B surreptitiously enters the United States to live with a relative, pending approval of a fifth preference visa. When the visa is approved, B returns home, picks up the visa and enters as a permanent resident alien.[31] Does B's prior illegal entry and residence subject him to deportation under § 241(a)(2)? *Cf. Matter of R.G.,* 8 I & N Dec. 128 (BIA 1958) (prior conviction for attempting entry by misrepresenting self as U.S. citizen does not bar subsequent admission as lawful permanent resident and would not subject alien to immediate deportation after lawful entry under § 241(a)(5)). Or suppose that alien Q, a returning resident, was unaware that she was required to undergo inspection and thus neglected to do so. Is Q deportable under § 241(a)(2)? *Cf. Ex Parte Callow,* 240 F. 212 (D.Colo.1916) (alien who had properly entered U.S. several times deportable for entry without inspection even though unaware of requirement of inspection).

Perhaps it is these types of situations which led the BIA expressly to leave open the implications of its decision and to mention the INS Operations Instruction. Can you formulate a rule that would extend coverage of § 241(a)(2) to appropriate situations and not others? What principles underlie your conclusions as to what an "appropriate situation" is?

c. *Crimes Involving Moral Turpitude: A Discussion of the Meaning of Statutes*

Paragraph (4) of INA § 241(a) provides:

> [An alien shall be deported who] is convicted of a crime involving moral turpitude committed within five years after entry and

---

2. We would note in this regard that the Service has prosecutorial discretion to decline to pursue the deportation of an alien who has entered the United States without inspection despite his possession of documents. *See* Operations Instructions 235.9; *see also* section 101(a)(13) of the Act. [Footnote by the BIA.]

31. This situation is hardly fanciful. *See generally* Portes, *The Return of the Wetback,* 11 Society 40, 41 (March-Apr. 1974) ("The vast majority of new male adult Mexican immigrants have already lived in the United States * * *.")

either sentenced to confinement or confined therefor in a prison or corrective institution, for a year or more, or who at any time after entry is convicted of two crimes involving moral turpitude, not arising out of a single scheme of criminal misconduct, regardless of whether confined therefor and regardless of whether the convictions were in a single trial.

Before we continue, make sure you fully understand this provision by answering the following questions.

Is a permanent resident alien deportable under § 241(a)(4) if the alien

(a) entered the United States in 1960, was convicted in 1962 of larceny and given a six-month jail sentence. [Assume larceny and all other crimes mentioned in these questions are crimes of moral turpitude.]

(b) entered in 1970, was convicted in 1976 of forgery and in 1978 of extortion, and received probation both times.

(c) entered in 1976, was convicted in 1977 of blackmail, and was sentenced to three to five years.

(d) entered in 1971 and was convicted in 1979 of four counts of tax fraud in the filing of a 1978 federal tax return.

(e) entered in 1974, travelled abroad for one month in 1980, was convicted of murder upon return to the United States and sentenced to 15 years in jail. *Cf. Munoz-Casarez v. INS,* 511 F.2d 947 (9th Cir.1975).

(f) entered in 1973, travelled abroad in 1976, was convicted in France of bank robbery and served 15 months in jail, re-entered the United States in 1979. [For a surprise answer, *see Matter of Gian,* 11 I & N Dec. 242 (BIA 1965).]

Why might the provision distinguish between crimes committed within five years of entry and those committed thereafter? Is this a sensible distinction? If you were a member of Congress, would you vote to retain or change the provision?

The phrase "moral turpitude" is not included in the definitions section of the statute (INA § 101). It is not surprising that its use in the immigration laws was challenged on the ground that it did not adequately warn aliens what conduct would subject them to deportation. Equally unsurprising is the Supreme Court's unwillingness to invalidate substantive regulations of immigration.

JORDAN v. DE GEORGE

Supreme Court of the United States, 1951.
341 U.S. 223, 71 S.Ct. 703, 95 L.Ed. 886.

Mr. Chief Justice Vinson delivered the opinion of the Court.

This case presents only one question: whether conspiracy to defraud the United States of taxes on distilled spirits is a "crime involving moral turpitude" within the meaning of § 19(a) of the Immigration Act of 1917.

Respondent, a native and citizen of Italy, has lived continuously in the United States since he entered this country in 1921. In 1937, respondent was indicted * * * for conspiring with seven other defendants to violate twelve sections of the Internal Revenue Code. The indictment specifically charged him with possessing whiskey and alcohol "with intent to sell it in fraud of law and evade the tax thereon." He was further accused of removing and concealing liquor "with intent to defraud the United States of the tax thereon." After pleading guilty, respondent was sentenced to imprisonment in a federal penitentiary for a term of one year and one day.

Respondent served his sentence under this conviction, and was released from custody. Less than a year later, he returned to his former activities and in December 1939, he was indicted again with eight other defendants for violating the same federal statutes. He was charged with conspiring to "unlawfully, knowingly, and willfully defraud the United States of tax on distilled spirits." [5] After being tried and found guilty in 1941, he was sentenced to imprisonment for two years.

While serving his sentence under this second conviction, deportation proceedings were commenced against the respondent under § 19(a) of the Immigration Act [of 1917] which provides:

"... any alien ... who is hereafter sentenced more than once to such a term of imprisonment [one year or more] because of conviction in this country of any crime involving moral turpitude, committed at any time after entry ... shall, upon the warrant of the Attorney General, be taken into custody and deported ...."

After continued hearings and consideration of the case by the Commissioner of Immigration and Naturalization and by the Board of Immigration Appeals, respondent was ordered to be deported in January 1946, on the ground that he had twice been convicted and sentenced to terms of one year or more of crimes involving moral turpitude. Deportation was deferred from time to time at respondent's request until 1949, when the District Director of Immigration and Naturalization moved to execute the warrant of deportation.

Respondent then sought habeas corpus in the District Court, claiming that the deportation order was invalid because the crimes of which he had been convicted did not involve moral turpitude. The District Court held a hearing, and dismissed the petition. The Court of Appeals reversed the order of the District Court and ordered that the respondent be discharged. 1950, 183 F.2d 768. The Court of Appeals stated that "crimes involving moral turpitude," as those words were used in the Immigration Act, "were intended to include only crimes of violence, or crimes which are commonly thought of as involving baseness, vileness or depravity. Such a classification does not include the crime of evading the payment of tax on liquor, nor of conspiring to evade that tax." 183 F.2d at 772. We granted

---

5. The record establishes that respondent was a large-scale violator engaged in a sizable business. The second indictment alone charged him with possessing 4,675 gallons of alcohol and an undetermined quantity of distilled spirits. At the rate of $2.25 a gallon then in effect, the tax on the alcohol alone would have been over $10,000.

certiorari to review the decision, 1950, 340 U.S. 890, 71 S.Ct. 207, as conflicting with decisions of the courts of appeals in other circuits.

* * *

The term "moral turpitude" has deep roots in the law. The presence of moral turpitude has been used as a test in a variety of situations, including legislation governing the disbarment of attorneys and the revocation of medical licenses. Moral turpitude also has found judicial employment as a criterion in disqualifying and impeaching witnesses, in determining the measure of contribution between joint tort-feasors, and in deciding whether certain language is slanderous.

In deciding the case before the Court, we look to the manner in which the term "moral turpitude" has been applied by judicial decision. Without exception, federal and state courts have held that a crime in which fraud is an ingredient involves moral turpitude. In the construction of the specific section of the Statute before us, a court of appeals has stated that fraud has ordinarily been the test to determine whether crimes not of the gravest character involve moral turpitude.

In every deportation case where fraud has been proved, federal courts have held that the crime in issue involved moral turpitude. This has been true in a variety of situations involving fraudulent conduct: obtaining goods under fraudulent pretenses, conspiracy to defraud by deceit and falsehood, forgery with intent to defraud, using the mails to defraud, execution of chattel mortgage with intent to defraud, concealing assets in bankruptcy, issuing checks with intent to defraud. In the state courts, crimes involving fraud have universally been held to involve moral turpitude.[13]

* * *

In view of these decisions, it can be concluded that fraud has consistently been regarded as such a contaminating component in any crime that American courts have, without exception, included such crimes within the scope of moral turpitude. It is therefore clear, under an unbroken course of judicial decisions, that the crime of conspiring to defraud the United States is a "crime involving moral turpitude."

But it has been suggested that the phrase "crime involving moral turpitude" lacks sufficiently definite standards to justify this deportation proceeding and that the statute before us is therefore unconstitutional for vagueness. Under this view, no crime, however grave, could be regarded as falling within the meaning of the term "moral turpitude." The question of vagueness was not raised by the parties nor argued before this Court.

---

13. State decisions have held that the following crimes involve moral turpitude: passing a check with intent to defraud, using the mails to defraud, obtaining money and property by false and fraudulent pretenses, possessing counterfeit money with intent to defraud. One state court has specifically held that the wilful evasion of federal income taxes constitutes moral turpitude.

It is significant that the phrase has been part of the immigration laws for more than sixty years.[14] As discussed above, the phrase "crime involving moral turpitude" has also been used for many years as a criterion in a variety of other statutes. No case has been decided holding that the phrase is vague, nor are we able to find any trace of judicial expression which hints that the phrase is so meaningless as to be a deprivation of due process.

* * *

The essential purpose of the "void for vagueness" doctrine is to warn individuals of the criminal consequences of their conduct. This Court has repeatedly stated that criminal statutes which fail to give due notice that an act has been made criminal before it is done are unconstitutional deprivations of due process of law. It should be emphasized that this statute does not declare certain conduct to be criminal. Its function is to apprise aliens of the consequences which follow after conviction and sentence of the requisite two crimes.

Despite the fact that this is not a criminal statute, we shall nevertheless examine the application of the vagueness doctrine to this case. We do this in view of the grave nature of deportation. The Court has stated that "deportation is a drastic measure and at times the equivalent of banishment or exile . . . . It is the forfeiture for misconduct of a residence in this country. Such a forfeiture is a penalty." *Fong Haw Tan v. Phelan,* [333 U.S. 6, 10, 68 S.Ct. 374, 376, 92 L.Ed. 433 (1948)].

We shall, therefore, test this statute under the established criteria of the "void for vagueness" doctrine.

We have several times held that difficulty in determining whether certain marginal offenses are within the meaning of the language under attack as vague does not automatically render a statute unconstitutional for indefiniteness. Impossible standards of specificity are not required. The test is whether the language conveys sufficiently definite warning as to the proscribed conduct when measured by common understanding and practices.

We conclude that this test has been satisfied here. Whatever else the phrase "crime involving moral turpitude" may mean in peripheral cases, the decided cases make it plain that crimes in which fraud was an ingredient have always been regarded as involving moral turpitude. We have recently stated that doubt as to the adequacy of a standard in less obvious cases does not render that standard unconstitutional for vagueness. But there is no such doubt present in this case. Fraud is the touchstone by which this case should be judged. The phrase "crime involving moral turpitude" has without exception been construed to embrace fraudulent conduct. We therefore decide that Congress suffi-

---

14. The term "moral turpitude" first appeared in the Act of March 3, 1891, 26 Stat. 1084, which directed the exclusion of "persons who have been convicted of a felony or other infamous crime or misdemeanor involving moral turpitude." Similar language was reenacted in the Statutes of 1903 and 1907. § 2, Act of March 3, 1903, 32 Stat. 1213; § 2, Act of Feb. 20, 1907, 34 Stat. 898.
* * *

ciently forewarned respondent that the statutory consequence of twice conspiring to defraud the United States is deportation.

Reversed.

MR. JUSTICE JACKSON, dissenting.

Respondent, because he is an alien, and because he has been twice convicted of crimes the Court holds involve "moral turpitude," is punished with a life sentence of banishment in addition to the punishment which a citizen would suffer for the identical acts. MR. JUSTICE BLACK, MR. JUSTICE FRANKFURTER and I cannot agree, because we believe the phrase "crime involving moral turpitude," as found in the Immigration Act, has no sufficiently definite meaning to be a constitutional standard for deportation.

Respondent migrated to this country from his native Italy in 1921 at the age of seventeen. Here he has lived twenty-nine years, is married to an American citizen, and his son, citizen by birth, is now a university student. In May, 1938, he pleaded guilty to a charge of conspiracy to violate the Internal Revenue Code and was sentenced to imprisonment for one year and one day. On June 6, 1941, he was convicted of a second violation and sentenced to imprisonment for two years. During the decade since, he has not been arrested or charged with any law violation. While still in prison, however, deportation proceedings were instituted against him, resulting in 1946, in a warrant for arrest and deportation.

By habeas corpus proceedings, De George challenged the deportation order upon the ground that his is not a crime "involving moral turpitude." The District Court thought it did and dismissed the writ. The Court of Appeals for the Seventh Circuit thought it did not and reversed. There is a conflict among the circuits.

What the Government seeks, and what the Court cannot give, is a basic definition of "moral turpitude" to guide administrators and lower courts.

The uncertainties of this statute do not originate in contrariety of judicial opinion. Congress knowingly conceived it in confusion. During the hearings of the House Committee on Immigration, out of which eventually came the Act of 1917 in controversy, clear warning of its deficiencies was sounded and never denied.

"Mr. Sabath.... [Y]ou know that a crime involving moral turpitude has not been defined. No one can really say what is meant by saying a crime involving moral turpitude. Under some circumstances, larceny is considered a crime involving moral turpitude—that is, stealing. We have laws in some States under which picking out a chunk of coal on a railroad track is considered larceny or stealing. In some States it is considered a felony. Some States hold that every felony is a crime involving moral turpitude. In some places the stealing of a watermelon or a chicken is larceny. In some States the amount is not stated. Of course, if the larceny is of an article, or a thing which is less than $20 in value, it is a misdemeanor in some States, but in other States there is no distinction."

Despite this notice, Congress did not see fit to state what meaning it attributes to the phrase "crime involving moral turpitude." It is not one which has settled significance from being words of art in the profession. If we go to the dictionaries, the last resort of the baffled judge, we learn little except that the expression is redundant, for turpitude alone means moral wickedness or depravity [6] and moral turpitude seems to mean little more than morally immoral.[7] The Government confesses that it is "a term that is not clearly defined," and says: "The various definitions of moral turpitude provide no exact test by which we can classify the specific offenses here involved."

Except for the Court's opinion, there appears to be universal recognition that we have here an undefined and undefinable standard. The parties agree that the phrase is ambiguous and have proposed a variety of tests to reduce the abstract provision of this statute to some concrete meaning.

It is proposed by respondent, with strong support in legislative history, that Congress had in mind only crimes of violence.[8] If the Court should adopt this construction, the statute becomes sufficiently definite, and, of course, would not reach the crimes of the respondent.

The Government suggests seriousness of the crime as a test and says the statute is one by which it is "sought to reach the *confirmed criminal, whose criminality has been revealed in two serious penal offenses.*" (Italics supplied.) But we cannot, and the Court does not, take seriousness as a test of turpitude. All offenses denounced by Congress, prosecuted by the Executive, and convicted by the courts, must be deemed in some degree "serious" or law enforcement would be a frivolous enterprise. However, use of qualifying words must mean that not all statutory offenses are subject to the taint of turpitude. The higher degrees of criminal gravity are commonly classified as felonies, the lower ones as misdemeanors. If the Act contemplated that repetition of any serious crime would be grounds for deportation, it would have been simple and intelligible to have

6. Black's Law Dictionary defines turpitude as: "[I]nherent baseness or vileness of principle or action; shameful wickedness; depravity." An example of its use alone to signify immorality may be taken from Macaulay, whose most bitter critics would admit he was a master of the English word. "[T]he artists corrupted the spectators, and the spectators the artists, till the turpitude of the drama became such as must astonish all who are not aware that extreme relaxation is the natural effect of extreme restraint." History of England, Vol. I (1849 ed.), p. 374.

7. Bouvier's Law Dictionary, Rawles Third Revision, defines "moral turpitude" as "An act of baseness, vileness or depravity in the private and social duties which a man owes to his fellow men or to society in general, contrary to the accepted and customary rule of right and duty between man and man."

8. "Mr. Woods .... I would make provisions to get rid of an alien in this country who comes here and commits felonies and burglaries, holds you up on the streets, and commits crimes against our daughters, because we do not want that kind of alien here, and they have no right to be here .... The rule is that if we get a man in this country who has not become a citizen, who knocks down people in the street, who murders or who attempts to murder people, who burglarizes our houses with blackjack and revolver, who attacks our women in the city, those people should not be here ...." Hearings before House Committee on Immigration and Naturalization on H.R. 10384, 64th Cong., 1st Sess. 14. Mr. Woods was not an ordinary witness. As the then Police Commissioner of New York City, his testimony appears to have been most influential in this provision of the 1917 Act.

mentioned felonies. But the language used indicates that there are felonies which are not included and perhaps that some misdemeanors are. We cannot see that seriousness affords any standard of guidance.

Respondent suggests here, and the Government has on other occasions taken the position, that the traditional distinction between crimes *mala prohibita* and those *mala in se* will afford a key for the inclusions and exclusions of this statute.[9] But we cannot overlook that what crimes belong in which category has been the subject of controversy for years. This classification comes to us from common law, which in its early history freely blended religious conceptions of sin with legal conceptions of crime. This statute seems to revert to that practice.

The Government, however, offers the *mala prohibita, mala in se* doctrine here in slightly different verbiage for determining the nature of these crimes. It says: "Essentially, they must be measured against the moral standards that prevail in contemporary society to determine whether the violations are generally considered essentially immoral."

Can we accept "the moral standards that prevail in contemporary society" as a sufficiently definite standard for the purposes of the Act? This is a large country and acts that are regarded as criminal in some states are lawful in others. We suspect that moral standards which prevail as to possession or sale of liquor that has evaded tax may not be uniform in all parts of the country, nor in all levels of "contemporary society." How should we ascertain the moral sentiments of masses of persons on any better basis than a guess?

The Court seems no more convinced than are we by the Government's attempts to reduce these nebulous abstractions to a concrete working rule, but to sustain this particular deportation it improvises another which fails to convince us. Its thesis is (1) that the statute is sixty years old, (2) that state courts have used the same concept for various purposes, and (3) that fraud imports turpitude into any offense.

1. It is something less than accurate to imply that in any sense relevant to this issue this phrase has been "part of the immigration laws for more than sixty years." [12]

---

9. In Volume II of Administrative Decisions under Immigration and Nationality Laws of the United States, p. 141, there is an administrative interpretation by the Department then having the administration of the Act. In an opinion on a deportation proceeding decided by the Board June 26, 1944, and approved by the Attorney General July 12, 1944, the statement was quoted with approval:

" 'A crime involving moral turpitude may be either a felony or misdemeanor, existing at common law or created by statute, and is an act or omission which is *malum in se* and not merely *malum prohibitum;* which is actuated by malice or committed with knowledge and intention and not done innocently or [without advertence] or reflection; which

is so far contrary to the moral law, as interpreted by the general moral sense of the community, that the offender is brought to public disgrace, is no longer generally respected, or is deprived of social recognition by good living persons; but which is not the outcome merely of natural passion, of animal spirits, of infirmity of temper, of weakness of character, of mistaken principles, *unaccompanied by a vicious motive or a corrupt mind.*' [Italics supplied.]"

12. We are construing the Act of 1917 and not the earlier Immigration Acts, those of March 3, 1891, 26 Stat. 1084; March 3, 1903, 32 Stat. 1213; February 20, 1907, 34 Stat. 898. All of these prior statutes allowed deportation for conviction for *every felony* or crime, which meant for conviction of every

But, in any event, venerability of a vague phrase may be an argument for its validity when the passing years have by administration practice or judicial construction served to make it clear as a word of legal art. To be sure, the phrase in its present context has been on the statute books since 1917. It has never before been in issue before this Court. * * * There have, however, been something like fifty cases in lower courts which applied this phrase. No one can read this body of opinions and feel that its application represents a satisfying, rational process. If any consistent pattern of application or consensus of meaning could be distilled from judicial decision, neither the Government nor the Court spells it out. Irrationality is inherent in the task of translating the religious and ethical connotations of the phrase into legal decisions. The lower court cases seem to rest, as we feel this Court's decision does, upon the moral reactions of particular judges to particular offenses. What is striking about the opinions in these "moral turpitude" cases is the wearisome repetition of clichés attempting to define "moral turpitude," usually a quotation from Bouvier. But the guiding line seems to have no relation to the result reached. The chief impression from the cases is the caprice of the judgments. How many aliens have been deported who would not have been had some other judge heard their cases, and vice versa, we may only guess. That is not government by law.

2. The use of the phrase by state courts for various civil proceedings affords no teaching for federal courts. The Federal Government has no common-law crimes and the judges are not permitted to define crimes by decision, for they rest solely in statute. Nor are we persuaded that the state courts have been able to divest the phrase of its inherent ambiguities and vagueness.

3. The Court concludes that fraud is "a contaminating component in any crime" and imports "moral turpitude." The fraud involved here is nonpayment of a tax. The alien possessed and apparently trafficked in liquor without paying the Government its tax. That, of course, is a fraud on the revenues. But those who deplore the traffic regard it as much an exhibition of moral turpitude for the Government to share its revenues as for respondents to withhold them. Those others who enjoy the traffic are not notable for scruples as to whether liquor has a law-abiding pedigree. So far as this offense is concerned with whiskey, it is not particularly un-American, and we see no reason to strain to make the penalty for the same act so much more severe in the case of an alien "bootlegger" than it is in the case of a native "moonshiner." I have never discovered that disregard of the Nation's liquor taxes excluded a citizen from our best society and I see no reason why it should banish an alien from our worst.

But it is said he has cheated the revenues and the total is computed in high figures. If "moral turpitude" depends on the amount involved,

crime involving a sentence of not less than a year. It then added another deportable category, to wit, misdemeanors involving moral turpitude. In addition to all crimes involving a sentence of a year or more, the earlier Acts carved out a small category of petty offenses, when they were of a kind "involv-ing moral turpitude," *i.e.,* offenses even though carrying a small sentence having a manifestation of intrinsic badness. But that creates a very different problem from requiring us to discriminate among all offenses, felonies and misdemeanors on the basis of intrinsic badness.

respondent is probably entitled to a place in its higher brackets. Whether by popular test the magnitude of the fraud would be an extenuating or an aggravating circumstance, we do not know. We would suppose the basic morality of a fraud on the revenues would be the same for petty as for great cheats. But we are not aware of any keen sentiment of revulsion against one who is a little niggardly on a customs declaration or who evades a sales tax, a local cigarette tax, or fails to keep his account square with a parking meter. But perhaps what shocks is not the offense so much as a conviction.

We should not forget that criminality is one thing—a matter of law—and that morality, ethics and religious teachings are another. Their relations have puzzled the best of men. Assassination, for example, whose criminality no one doubts, has been the subject of serious debate as to its morality.[15] This does not make crime less criminal, but it shows on what treacherous grounds we tread when we undertake to translate ethical concepts into legal ones, case by case. We usually end up by condemning all that we personally disapprove and for no better reason than that we disapprove it. In fact, what better reason is there? Uniformity and equal protection of the law can come only from a statutory definition of fairly stable and confined bounds.

A different question might be before us had Congress indicated that the determination by the Board of Immigration Appeals that a crime involves "moral turpitude" should be given the weight usually attributed to administrative determinations. But that is not the case, nor have the courts so interpreted the statute. In the fifty-odd cases examined, no weight was attached to the decision of that question by the Board, the court in each case making its own independent analysis and conclusion. Apparently, Congress expected the courts to determine the various crimes includable in this vague phrase.[16] We think that not a judicial function.

* * *

We do not disagree with a policy of extreme reluctance to adjudge a congressional Act unconstitutional. But we do not here question the power of Congress to define deportable conduct. We only question the

---

15. John Stuart Mill, referring to the morality of assassination of political usurpers, passed by examination of the subject of Tyrannicide, as follows: "I shall content myself with saying that the subject has been at all times one of the open questions of morals; that the act of a private citizen in striking down a criminal, who, by raising himself above the law, has placed himself beyond the reach of legal punishment or control, has been accounted by whole nations, and by some of the best and wisest of men, not a crime, but an act of exalted virtue; and that, right or wrong, it is not of the nature of assassination, but of civil war." Mill, On Liberty and Considerations on Representative Government, p. 14, n. 1.

The vice of leaving statutes that inflict penalties so vague in definition that they throw the judge in each case back upon his own notions is the unconscious tendency to

"Compound for Sins they are inclin'd to,

By damning those they have no mind to."

Butler, Hudibras, Vol. I (1772 ed.), 28.

16. However, a statement by the Chairman of the Committee on Immigration and Naturalization may suggest another explanation: "My recollection is that the Supreme Court of the United States has determined what crimes are crimes involving moral turpitude under the Federal law, and if so, that would control, I should think." Hearings before House Committee on Immigration and Naturalization on H.R. 10384, 64th Cong., 1st Sess. 8.

power of administrative officers and courts to decree deportation until Congress has given an intelligible definition of deportable conduct.

Notes

1. "Void For Vagueness"

Justice Jackson's rather witty dissent is disarmingly persuasive, is it not? Indeed, does not the fact that there was a split in the circuits over whether the offense in *De George* was a crime involving moral turpitude almost speak for itself on the issue of vagueness?

Under the "void for vagueness" doctrine the Court has struck down statutes whose indefiniteness "runs afoul of due process concepts which require that persons be given fair notice of what to avoid, and that the discretion of law enforcement officials, with the attendant dangers of arbitrary and discriminatory enforcement, be limited by explicit legislative standards." L. Tribe, *American Constitutional Law* § 12–28 (1978). Furthermore, as noted in a classic study, the doctrine "has been used by the Supreme Court almost invariably for the creation of an insulating buffer zone of added protection at the peripheries of several of the Bill of Rights freedoms." A. Amsterdam, *The Void-For-Vagueness Doctrine in the Supreme Court,* 109 U.Pa.L.Rev. 67, 75 (1960). *See, e.g., Baggett v. Bullitt,* 377 U.S. 360, 84 S.Ct. 1316, 12 L.Ed.2d 377 (1964) (striking down state statutes requiring state employees to take loyalty oaths where the vagueness of the oath operated to inhibit Free Speech); *Papachristou v. City of Jacksonville,* 405 U.S. 156, 92 S.Ct. 839, 31 L.Ed.2d 110 (1972) (voiding city vagrancy ordinance which made criminal "activities which by modern standards are normally innocent").

Few would argue that "moral turpitude" is a phrase that adequately advises aliens of the kinds of crimes the commission of which would render them deportable. But is the vagueness issue in *De George* distinct from the issue involving statutes that inhibit protected or generally accepted conduct? Here, after all, the alien has been convicted of a major crime. Is not the criminal statute itself not only adequate warning to the alien that serious consequences will follow from its violation but also an adequate check on administrative arbitrariness? Does Justice Jackson consider these questions? Should he? Or is the degree of punishment imposed by deportation—often more severe than imprisonment for a term of years—substantial enough to warrant invalidation of indefinite deportation statutes?

2. The Statutory History of "Moral Turpitude"

An 1875 statute provided for the exclusion of "persons who are undergoing a sentence for conviction in their own country of felonious crimes." Act of March 3, 1875, Ch. 141, § 5, 18 Stat. 477. The provision was based on the widespread belief that European nations were shipping convicted criminals to America. *See, e.g.,* H.R.Rep. No. 359, 34th Cong., 1st Sess. (1856). "Moral turpitude" first entered the immigration statutes in 1891. The 1891 Act expanded the 1875 exclusion ground to deny entry to aliens convicted of a "felony or * * * crime or misdemeanor involving moral turpitude." Act of March 3, 1891, Ch. 551, § 1, 26 Stat. 1084. Neither the Act nor the accompanying House and Senate reports attempted to define what crimes were deemed to involve moral turpitude. *See* S.Rep. No. 2165, 61st Cong., 2d Sess. (1891); H.R.Rep. No. 3807, 51st Cong., 2d Sess. (1891).

Once the federal government exercised its power to exclude criminals it began to think about deporting aliens in the United States who committed crimes. The Dillingham Commission Report of 1911 stated that a "serious, and * * * inexcusable, defect" in the immigration laws "is the fact that aliens admitted to this country * * * may pursue a criminal career without danger of deportation." The Commission thus recommended the deportation of criminals, although it added that "[I]t is not believed that the practice of deportation should be sufficiently extended to include minor offenses." Reports of the [Dillingham] Immigration Commission, vol. 1, S.Doc. No. 747, 61st Cong., 3d Sess. 34 (1911).[32] The Commission's report was followed by other congressional reports that advocated deportation of aliens who committed serious criminal offenses. *E.g.,* S.Rep. No. 355, 63d Cong., 2d Sess. 11 (1914).

These recommendations reached fruition in the Immigration Act of 1917. Primarily remembered for its adoption of a literacy requirement, the Act also provided for the deportation of any alien who was sentenced to a prison term of a year or more because of conviction in the United States "of a crime involving moral turpitude committed within five years after * * * entry" or sentenced more than once to such a term because of conviction "of any crime involving moral turpitude, committed at any time after entry." Ch. 29, § 19, 39 Stat. 889. Again the legislative history says almost nothing about Congress' understanding of what constituted a crime of moral turpitude.[33]

It is interesting that even though the provision was carefully scrutinized on the floor of the House, no one raised the issue of vagueness or objected to the inclusion of the phrase in the deportation laws. During debate on the bill, members of Congress repeatedly referred to the phrase "crimes involving moral turpitude," and never stated a concern with the coverage of the phrase. Indeed, Representative Sabath himself proposed three amendments to the new deportation provision, none of which concerned the meaning of "moral turpitude." *See* 53 Cong.Rec. 5167–72 (1916).

Our best reading of the legislative history is that "crimes involving moral turpitude" was a term that presented no definitional difficulties for

32. The Commission also recommended that the new deportation ground have a statute of limitations to ensure that the aliens' "tendency to commit crimes cannot be attributed to conditions arising subsequent to their entry into this country." *Id.*

33. Justice Jackson's dissent mentions the two significant references in the 1917 legislative history to the difficulty of defin-ing moral turpitude. Both of these statements were made during a brief hearing of the House Committee on Immigration and Naturalization after the Committee had reported the bill to the House for consideration. *See* "Restriction of Immigration," Hearings on H.R. 10384 before the House Comm. on Immigration and Naturalization, 64th Cong., 1st Sess. 3 (1916).

the members of Congress. They appear to have thought that it had acquired a commonly known meaning over time and were content to let continuing interpretation by immigration officials and judges control.

In 1950, the Senate Judiciary Committee conducted a massive review of the immigration process and made a set of recommendations that formed the basis of the McCarran-Walter Act of 1952. In a discussion of the provision of the 1917 Act that excluded aliens who had committed crimes involving moral turpitude, the Committee observed that "[t]he term 'moral turpitude' has not been definitely and conclusively defined by the courts." S.Rep. No. 1515, 81st Cong., 2d Sess. 351 (1950). The Report went on to describe proposals for reform suggested by officials who enforced the immigration laws:

> The American consul at Marseille, France, stated that while the visa instructions define moral turpitude as an act which in itself is one of baseness, vileness, or depravity, the applicability of the excluding provision often depends on what the individual officer considers to be baseness, vileness, or depravity. He suggested that there be a listing of crimes and circumstances comprehended within the meaning of moral turpitude.

> An immigration inspector voiced similar objections citing instances where the purpose of the law had been ignored by including petty crimes, such as theft of a newspaper. He suggested a statute of limitations on petty crimes as far as immigration considerations are concerned.

Id. at 353. However, the Committee did not recommend a change in the statutory language. Rather, it seemed satisfied with the suggestion of another INS official that, "although it might be desirable to have the crimes specifically set forth, difficulties might be encountered in getting a phrase that would be broad enough to cover the various crimes contemplated within the law and yet easier to comprehend than the present phrase." *Id.*

The 1952 Act adopted the current version of § 241(a)(4). The Senate and House reports accompanying the legislation reveal no discussion of the meaning of "moral turpitude."[34]

The lesson of the legislative history, such as it is, is that Congress quite simply never attempted to define the meaning of "moral turpitude." The phrase had ancient lineage and application outside the immigration laws when it was included in the statute.[35] No doubt Congress assumed

---

34. A related issue involving § 241(a)(4) arose in the Senate. Senator McCarran's original bill would have permitted the Attorney General to deport an alien convicted of *any* criminal offense if he determined that the alien was an "undesirable alien." The Senate Report defended the provision on the ground that "there are many offenses which, while not involving moral turpitude, are of such a character as to render an alien convicted of such offense undesirable as a resi-

dent." S.Rep. No. 1137, 82d Cong., 2d Sess. 21 (1952). After heated objection to this granting of unbridled discretion to the Attorney General, the provision was deleted from the legislation. *See* 98 Cong.Rec. 5420–21; 5757–58 (1952).

35. *See, e.g.* W. Burdick, The Law of Crime § 87 (1946) (identifying concept in Roman Law); Note, *Crimes Involving Moral Turpitude*, 43 Harv.L.Rev. 117 (1929).

that its meaning in other areas would be imported into the 1891 immigration law. By the time the 1917 statute was under consideration, as Justice Jackson notes in his dissent, the Chairman of the House Committee on Immigration and Naturalization could comment: "[T]he Supreme Court has determined what crimes are crimes involving moral turpitude under the federal law, and if so, that would control, I should think."

In short, Congress left to the courts the task of pouring content into the phrase "moral turpitude." How did Congress intend the courts to do this? Did it believe that the judges should look to the meaning of "moral turpitude" prevailing in 1891 or 1917, or did it intend, as asserted by government counsel in *De George,* that the courts apply "the moral standards that prevail in contemporary society"? The latter view seems more likely: if the purpose of the provision is to rid the nation of aliens who commit particularly deplorable acts, one would expect that Congress intended "moral turpitude" to reflect current notions of deplorableness. If this interpretation is correct, Congress has essentially delegated legislative authority to the courts to determine what crimes involve moral turpitude. To give meaning to the phrase moral turpitude, courts must adopt a common law approach to the interpretation of § 241(a)(4).

This understanding of the way courts should interpret § 241(a)(4), although hardly confined to the immigration field,[36] deviates significantly from traditional ways of thinking about statutory construction. Legal theory normally ascribes to the judge the function of carrying out the will of the legislature by applying a statute whose meanings, aims or purposes the legislature has fixed at the time of enactment. In this way, so the usual argument runs, the court recognizes institutional limits on its competence and does not usurp the role of the legislature. Of course the court will apply the statute in situations not considered or imagined by the drafters. But in doing so, its task is generally described as remaining true to the intent of the legislature or the underlying purposes of the statute.[37] Under § 241(a)(4), however, Congress has apparently invited (or commanded), the courts to legislate. Although on some very general level, perhaps, Congress has given the courts direction (*i.e.,* condemn conduct that violates norms of decency), it is clear, is it not, that under the statute the courts may (are free to?) reach decisions contrary to those that would have been reached by the Congress that enacted the provision. The court's task, then, is not one of discovery and application, but rather one of creation.

Is it desirable for Congress to write a statute in this fashion? Are there plausible alternatives? For example, Congress could have created certainty by making deportation turn on a felony conviction. Why might

---

36. A prime example of a common law approach to a statute is judicial interpretation of § 1 of the Sherman Antitrust Act, 15 U.S.C.A. § 1, which prohibits combinations "in restraint of trade."

37. *See, e.g.,* H. Hart & A. Sacks, *The Legal Process,* Chapter VII (tent. ed. 1958);

F. Frankfurter, *Some Reflections on the Reading of Statutes,* 47 Colum.L.Rev. 527 (1947); Landis, *A Note on "Statutory Interpretation,"* 43 Harv.L.Rev. 886 (1930). For the "realist" critique of this position, *see* Radin, *Statutory Interpretation,* 43 Harv.L. Rev. 863 (1930).

Congress *not* have adopted this approach? [38] Suppose the Supreme Court in *De George* had struck down the challenged provision. What do you think Congress would have done? Does Congress have the time or inclination to list what crimes do or do not involve moral turpitude? (Recall that Congress has specifically listed a number of crimes conviction of which renders the alien deportable. INA § 241(a)(11), (14)–(18).) Is this a burden that the courts, or the American people, should place on the national legislature?

3. Administrative and Judicial Interpretation of "Moral Turpitude"

Now that you have read *Jordan v. De George,* complete the following sentence: A crime involving moral turpitude is a crime _____. If you have difficulty completing the sentence you are not alone. As the leading immigration treatise reports, "[a]ttempts to arrive at a workable definition of moral turpitude never have yielded entire satisfaction. * * * [T]his term defies precise definition, since its limits are charted by human experience." G & R, § 4.13a.

Various formulations have become commonplace in the administrative and judicial decisions. Most popular is the definition borrowed from Black's Law Dictionary: "an act of baseness, vileness, or depravity in the private and social duties which a man owes to his fellow men, or to society in general, contrary to the accepted and customary rule of right and duty between man and man." [39] Other definitions include: "an act that was at common law intrinsically and morally wrong;" [40] and "[a]nything done contrary to justice, honesty, principle or good morals." [41]

To what extent can these abstract definitions decide concrete cases? Take a look at the following list of crimes. Mark in the margin whether they do or do not "involve moral turpitude." (The judicial answers are given in note 50 at the end of this section.)

38. *See, Burr v. INS,* 350 F.2d 87, 90 (9th Cir.1965), *cert. denied* 383 U.S. 915, 86 S.Ct. 905, 15 L.Ed.2d 669 (1966) (use of "felony" as touchstone of deportability would have subjected federal law to "niceties and nuances" of state law). *Cf.* Y. Kamisar, *Betts v. Brady Twenty Years Later: The Right to Counsel and Due Process Values,* 61 Mich.L.Rev. 219, 266–67 (1962) (need for federal definition of crimes triggering right to counsel beyond crimes defined as felonies by the States).

39. *See, e.g., United States v. Smith,* 420 F.2d 428, 431 (5th Cir.1970).

Regarding the use of dictionary definitions consider the comments of Professors Hart and Sacks:

A dictionary, it is vital to observe, never says what meaning a word *must* bear in a particular context. Nor does it ever purport to say this. An unabridged dictionary is simply an historical record, not necessarily all-inclusive, of the meanings

which words in fact *have* borne, in the judgment of the editors, in the writings of reputable authors. The editors make up this record by collecting examples of uses of the word to be defined, studying each use *in context,* and then forming a judgment about the meaning in that context. A good dictionary always gives examples of the use of the word *in context* in each of the meanings ascribed to it.

Hart & Sacks, *supra,* at 1220 (emphasis in original).

40. *Tillinghast v. Edmead,* 31 F.2d 81, 83 (1st Cir.1929) (theft of $15 constitutes moral turpitude).

41. *Guarneri v. Kessler,* 98 F.2d 580, 581 (5th Cir.1938), cert. denied 305 U.S. 648, 59 S.Ct. 229, 83 L.Ed. 419 (1938) (conspiracy to smuggle alcohol is crime of moral turpitude).

1. voluntary manslaughter

2. involuntary manslaughter

3. breaking and entering

4. failure to report for induction

5. tax evasion

6. escape from prison

7. carrying a concealed weapon

8. possessing stolen property

9. sale and possession of LSD

10. aiding alien to enter unlawfully

How should an immigration official or judge go about deciding whether a particular crime involves moral turpitude? What sources should she examine? How does she determine prevailing social views on the depravity of an offense? Should she look to national moral standards or regional or local ones? Consider the following decision of the BIA in thinking about these questions.

MATTER OF R.

Board of Immigration Appeals, 1954.
6 I & N Dec. 444.

* * *

The respondent is a 57-year-old single male, a native and citizen of Italy who has resided in the United States since his lawful admission for permanent residence on June 4, 1914.

* * *

* * * [T]he Service relies upon respondent's conviction in 1942 for violation of the Mann Act as the second of the two crimes involving moral turpitude which must be found to exist to render respondent subject to deportation. If it be found, as was found by the special inquiry officer, that the conviction does not involve moral turpitude, then it must be concluded that this record establishes the conviction of only one crime involving moral turpitude and the charge based on the criminal grounds must necessarily fail.

[The count of the indictment upon which the alien was convicted charged him with] aiding and assisting in obtaining transportation and in transporting from New Jersey to Florida, one L— A—, "with intent and purpose * * * to induce, entice and compel * * * (her) to engage in an immoral practice, to wit, the practice of illicit sexual intercourse with him * * *." We must determine whether this conviction involves moral turpitude. * * *

The special inquiry officer held that moral turpitude was not involved in the conviction. He found that the fundamental crime charged was the practice of illicit sexual intercourse between parties whom there was nothing to show were married and that the offense in essence amounted to the commission of fornication, a crime not involving moral turpitude. * * *

* * *

Counsel argues that the statute, by its inherent nature, does not define a crime necessarily involving moral turpitude; that respondent was not convicted for transporting a woman for purposes of prostitution or commercial vices; and that the specific act of which he was convicted amounts to no more than a conviction for inducing a woman to commit an act or acts of fornication, a crime not involving moral turpitude. Furthermore, counsel urges that the offense is less blameworthy than simple fornication since the gist of the offense was assisting the woman to obtain transportation and it was unnecessary to establish that there had actually been sexual relations.

In view of the Commissioner's urgent representations that * * * the crime in question involves moral turpitude, we shall deal fully with the problem.

In determining whether a crime involves moral turpitude, the courts have given us certain standards which we *must* follow.

The test requires us to first determine what law or specific portion thereof has been violated, and then, without regard to the act committed by the alien, to decide whether that *law inherently* involves moral turpitude; that is, whether violation of the law "under any and all circumstances," would involve moral turpitude. If we find that violation of the law under any and all circumstances involves moral turpitude, then we *must* conclude that *all* convictions under that law involved moral turpitude although the "particular acts evidence no immorality". If, on the other hand, we find that the law punishes acts which do not involve moral turpitude as well as those which do involve moral turpitude, then we *must* rule that *no* conviction under that law involves moral turpitude, although in the particular instance conduct was immoral.[2]

* * *

Does the crime * * * in this case inherently involve moral turpitude? If we find that situations not involving moral turpitude are punishable by the phrases with which we are concerned, then it becomes our duty to find that the crime defined does not involve moral turpitude.

* * *

* * * A consideration of [many] cases makes it quite clear that the crime defined by the language with which we are concerned can be transportation with the intent to induce the commission of a simple act of fornication—an "isolated noncommercial venture based on impulse and reciprocating passion." [United States v. Jamerson, 60 F.Supp. 281, 284

2. The rule set forth exists because a standard must be supplied to administrative agencies; it eliminates the burden of going into the evidence in a case; it eliminates the situation where a nonjudicial agency retries a judicial matter; and it prevents the situation occurring where two people convicted under the same specific law are given different treatment because one indictment may contain a fuller or different description of the same act than the other indictment; and makes for uniform administration of law.

(N.D. Iowa, 1944).] The cases cited by the Service which would indicate that more than an act of fornication is required are not authoritative on the issue.

Not every violation of law involves moral turpitude. Moral turpitude is found in those acts or omissions which are so far "contrary to the moral law, as interpreted by the general moral sense of the community, that the offender is brought to public disgrace, is no longer generally respected, or is deprived of social recognition by good living persons". [*Matter of D—*, 1 I & N Dec. 190, 194 (BIA 1942).] Ordinarily, moral turpitude is not found in conduct, which before it was made punishable as a crime, was not generally regarded as morally wrong, or as offensive to the moral sense of the community.

Does fornication involve moral turpitude? It is necessary to determine this because if fornication, a crime which may be punished under the language of the indictment with which we are concerned, does not involve moral turpitude, then it becomes our duty to rule that the conviction herein was not a crime inherently involving moral turpitude. Fornication is defined as illicit sexual intercourse (37 C.J.S. 117). Administratively, it has uniformly been held that fornication does not involve moral turpitude. The Solicitor of Labor, in a memorandum dated April 29, 1926, stated, "It can scarcely be maintained logically that simple fornication manifests on the part of its perpetrators such personal depravity or baseness as warrants the holding that it is a crime which involves moral turpitude." We have been unable to discover any departure from this view.

Fornication—unlawful or illicit sexual intercourse—was not punishable at common law unless it was accompanied by public acts of indecency (37 C.J.S. 117; L.R.A., 1916, C. 653). Today, fornication is not a criminal offense in the absence of statutory change (37 C.J.S. 119). Some states have not made the statutory change and "occasional illicit intercourse" is not a crime in such states (*Warner v. State of Indiana*, 202 Ind. 479, 175 N.E. 661, 74 A.L.R. 1357; *United States ex rel. Huber v. Sibray*, 178 Fed. 144 (C.C., Pa., 1910), reversed on other grounds 185 Fed. 401 (C.A. 3); *Ex parte Rocha*, 30 F.(2d) 823 (S.D.Tex., 1929)). In some states there have been enacted statutes which punish fornication only if it be committed by parties dwelling together in the same place in the manner of husband and wife for some period of time (37 C.J.S. 121; *Warner v. State of Indiana, supra*); *Ex parte Rocha, supra*). Elsewhere, it may be a crime only if committed between relatives so that it amounts to incest (*State v. Manley*, 74 A. 231, 82 Vt. 556).

The Service request that we find fornication is a crime involving moral turpitude, is based upon the inability to find court cases holding that fornication does not involve moral turpitude.

No court in recent years has directly ruled upon whether fornication is a crime involving moral turpitude; * * * however, the courts have in many instances where fornication was involved, taken action which is consistent only with a finding that fornication did not involve moral turpitude.

This conclusion follows from the fact that one who has committed an act involving moral turpitude is ordinarily denied naturalization on the ground that good moral character has not been established. Both in determining what constitutes good moral character and whether a crime involves moral turpitude, judgment is based upon the court's determination as to what is the generally accepted moral convention current at the time. Courts have found to be persons of good moral character, individuals who have committed illicit sexual acts despite the occurrence of these acts in the periods during which good moral character was required to be established. * * *

Furthermore, it is of some importance to note that under the Immigration and Nationality Act, Congress for the first time set up standards of good moral character. The commission of adultery was listed as requiring a finding that good moral character was lacking. No mention was made of fornication. As pointed out by counsel, it would be most incongruous for an act of illicit sexual intercourse on the part of an unmarried alien to be regarded as a crime involving moral turpitude and the basis for deportation when one who committed such an act could be granted the priceless gift of United States citizenship.

It thus appears that the mores of the community do not to this day require punishment of furtive illicit intercourse or private immoral indulgence of the individual. It would seem that moral turpitude should not be attached to the commission of an act which though immoral is not even regarded as a crime in some communities, and is one which the courts have held would not cause the "common conscience" to strip its perpetrator of good moral character.

We conclude therefore that under the language of the law which resulted in respondent's indictment and conviction, convictions for simple fornication are possible; that simple fornication does not involve moral turpitude; and that the language therefore does not inherently define a crime involving moral turpitude.

* * *

* * * The crime for which respondent was convicted does not involve moral turpitude. The Service has failed to establish that he has been convicted of two crimes involving moral turpitude. The charge must therefore fall.

* * *

Order: It is ordered that the decision of the special inquiry officer terminating proceedings be affirmed.

Notes

1. Are the following decisions of the federal courts consistent with *Matter of R*?

(1) *Velez-Lozano v. INS*, 463 F.2d 1305 (4th Cir.1972) (per curiam): consensual heterosexual anal sodomy is a crime involving moral turpitude;

(2) *Castle v. INS,* 541 F.2d 1064 (4th Cir.1976) (per curiam): carnal knowledge of a 15 year old female by a male not her husband "is so basically offensive to American ethics and accepted moral standards as to constitute moral turpitude *per se.*" (Should it matter in *Castle* that the male was 18 years old? Suppose he were 15? 55?);

(3) *Marciano v. INS,* 450 F.2d 1022 (8th Cir.1971): statutory rape constitutes moral turpitude, even though knowledge of age of minor is not an element of the offense.

2. As pointed out in *De George,* "moral turpitude" is a phrase that provides a standard of conduct in other areas of law. These include disbarment of attorneys,[42] revocation of licenses,[43] impeachment of witnesses,[44] and termination of municipal employment.[45] What relevance should the term's use in these contexts have in immigration law?[46]

3. In *Matter of R,* the BIA refers to the statutory requirement that persons seeking naturalization be of "good moral character." INA § 316(a). The Board notes that the act of fornication is generally not deemed to establish lack of good moral character in the naturalization context. *See* G & R § 15.15b.[47] What should be the relationship between

42. *See, e.g., In re Giddens,* 30 Cal.3d 110, 177 Cal.Rptr. 673, 635 P.2d 166 (1981).

43. *See, e.g., Yurick v. Commonwealth,* 43 Pa.Cmwlth. 248, 402 A.2d 290 (1979) (revocation of osteopathy license).

44. *See, e.g., United States v. Gloria,* 494 F.2d 477, 481 (5th Cir.1974).

45. *See, e.g., Fortman v. Aurora Civil Service Commission,* 37 Ill.App.3d 548, 346 N.E.2d 20 (1976) (discharge of sanitation worker).

46. *See, e.g., Gonzales v. Barber,* 207 F.2d 398 (9th Cir.1953), affirmed on other grounds 347 U.S. 637, 74 S.Ct. 822, 98 L.Ed. 1009 (1954) (assault with a deadly weapon is crime involving moral turpitude for purposes of federal immigration law, irrespective of California Supreme Court opinion that crime did not involve moral turpitude for purposes of attorney disbarment); *Matter of R,* 4 I & N Dec. 644, 647 (BIA 1952) (unlawful disposal of narcotic drug is not a crime involving moral turpitude in immigration cases since narcotic law does not require presence of intent, motive or knowledge, even though it is a crime involving moral turpitude in non-immigration cases).

47. What constitutes "good moral character" is no more clear than what conduct involves "moral turpitude." INA § 101(f) only gives particular examples of what is *not* good moral character. Consider the following remarkably candid observations of Judge Learned Hand in a case raising the issue of whether fornication is a bar to a finding of good moral character in a naturalization proceeding:

[T]he law upon the subject is not free from doubt. We do not see how we can get any help from outside. It would not be practicable—even if the parties had asked for it, which they did not—to conduct an inquiry as to what is the common conscience on the point. Even though we could take a poll, it would not be enough merely to count heads, without any appraisal of the voters. A majority of the votes of those in prisons and brothels, for instance, ought scarcely to outweigh the votes of accredited churchgoers. Nor can we see any reason to suppose that the opinion of clergymen would be a more reliable estimate than our own. The situation is one in which to proceed by any available method would not be more likely to satisfy the impalpable standard, deliberately chosen, than that we adopted in [earlier] cases: that is, to resort to our own conjecture, fallible as we recognize it to be. It is true that recent investigations have attempted to throw light upon the actual habits of men in the petitioner's position, and they have disclosed—what few people would have doubted in any event—that his practice is far from uncommon; but it does not follow that on this point common practice may not have diverged as much from precept as it often does. We have [in other cases] answered in the negative the question whether an unmarried man must live completely celibate, or forfeit his claim to a "good moral character"; but * * * those were cases of continuous, though adulterous, union. We have now to say whether it makes a critical difference that the

crimes of moral turpitude and good moral character? Note that, although INA § 101(f) states that any person whose income comes primarily from illegal gambling or who has been convicted of two or more gambling offenses shall not be deemed to have established "good moral character," the BIA has held that violation of gambling statutes does not constitute an act involving moral turpitude. *E.g., Matter of Gaglioti,* 10 I & N Dec. 719 (BIA 1964) (conspiring to establish gambling games); *Matter of S,* 9 I & N Dec. 688 (BIA 1962) (gambling and owning and operating a gambling establishment).

A Final Word on Moral Turpitude

So as not to leave a misimpression, we wish to stress that for most crimes there is broad agreement as to whether they "involve moral turpitude." The common law method has developed a number of rules that are regularly applied; [48] and authorities publish long lists which place crimes into "involving" and "not involving" moral turpitude categories. *E.g.,* G & R, § 4.14; Annot. 23 A.L.R.Fed. 480–594 (1975). Indeed, a member of the BIA wrote in 1944 that the phrase moral turpitude "has evolved into a definitive workable guide." Wasserman, *Crimes Involving Moral Turpitude,* 1 INS Monthly Rev. 2, 8 (March 1944).

Does this mean that the Supreme Court's decision in *De George* has been vindicated—that is, that the term "moral turpitude" has been rendered acceptably definite through administrative and judicial adjudications? The answer to this question depends upon the reasons for the constitutional principle that vague statutes violate due process. As we mentioned earlier, there are at least three values that are served by clear, definitive statutory commands: notice to regulated parties, control of non-uniform or arbitrary enforcement, and protection of liberty. We believe it is doubtful that the case law concretizing the meaning of "moral turpitude" has contributed much to either the first or third values. It is unlikely that aliens are aware of which crimes have been deemed to involve moral turpitude. Consider *Velez-Lozano v. INS,* 463 F.2d 1305, 1306 (D.C.Cir.1972) (per curiam) (alien not aware that conviction for act of consensual sodomy would render him deportable). Furthermore, the underlying criminal laws themselves circumscribe freedom of action; adjudications limiting the application of the deportation laws are not likely to have much effect on decisions to undertake the forbidden conduct.

alien's lapses are casual, concupiscent and promiscuous, but not adulterous. We do not believe that discussion will make our conclusion more persuasive; but, so far as we can divine anything so tenebrous and impalpable as the common conscience, these added features do not make a critical difference.

Schmidt v. United States, 177 F.2d 450, 451–52 (2d Cir.1949).

48. For example: (1) Following *De George,* crimes with an element of fraud are deemed to involve moral turpitude. *E.g., McNaughton v. INS,* 612 F.2d 457 (9th Cir. 1980) (securities fraud); *Matter of Khalik,* 17 I & N Dec. 518 (BIA 1980) (issuing check with insufficient funds); (2) It is established that it is the "inherent nature" of the offense committed, not the circumstances surrounding the conduct of the alien convicted, which determines whether or not the crime involves moral turpitude. *Hirsch v. INS,* 308 F.2d 562 (9th Cir.1962).

One hundred years of interpretation, however, has probably substantially achieved the second goal—restraining arbitrariness in enforcement.[49] Not only is there general recognition of which crimes involve moral turpitude and which do not (even if the reasons for inclusion and exclusion are not always clear), but the adjudicating bodies have also adopted rules that further attempt to cabin discretion. (Recall footnote 2 in *Matter of R*, explaining why the court should look to the law, and not the conduct of the alien, in determining whether the offense involves moral turpitude.)

If you were unhappy about the result in *De George*, has any of the preceding discussion placated your concern? Consider the conclusion of a student note in the 1929 Harvard Law Review:

> [It] seems inevitable that in the classification of crimes it is perilous and idle to expect an indefinite statutory term to acquire precision by the judicial process of exclusion and inclusion. The legislature can ordinarily better accomplish its purpose by enumerating the proscribed offenses, or by dividing them on the basis of penalty imposed. Either method would replace with a uniform standard the apocalyptic criteria of individual judges.

Note, *Crimes Involving Moral Turpitude*, 43 Harv.L.Rev. 117, 121 (1929). If you were a member of Congress, would you support legislation that sought to amend § 241(a)(4) in either of the ways suggested by the Note? [50]

---

49. Perhaps recognizing that few people are fully aware of legal rules and prohibitions, the Supreme Court has recently stated: "The more important aspect of vagueness doctrine 'is not actual notice, but the other principal element of the doctrine—the requirement that a legislature establish minimal guidelines to govern law enforcement.'" *Kolender v. Lawson*, 461 U.S. 352, 358, 103 S.Ct. 1855, 1858, 75 L.Ed.2d 903 (1983), *quoting Smith v. Goguen*, 415 U.S. 566, 574, 94 S.Ct. 1242, 1247, 39 L.Ed.2d 605 (1974).

50. Answers to the questions on pp. 391–92 *supra*.

(1) Yes. *E.g., Matter of Rosario*, 15 I & N Dec. 416 (BIA 1975) (intentional killing even without malice).

(2) No. *E.g., Vidal Y Planas v. Landon*, 104 F.Supp. 384 (S.D.Cal.1952).

(3) Trick question. Depends upon object of unlawful entry. *Compare Matter of M*, 2 I & N Dec. 721 (A.G.1946) (no moral turpitude where evidence does not disclose that alien intended to permanently deny owner possession of property) *with Matter of Moore*, 13 I & N Dec. 711 (BIA 1971) (intent to commit larceny involves moral turpitude).

(4) No. *E.g., Matter of S*, 5 I & N Dec. 425 (BIA 1953) (conviction does not require "depraved mind or purpose" or fraud).

(5) Yes. *Tseung Chu v. Cornell*, 247 F.2d 929 (9th Cir.1957), *cert. denied* 355 U.S. 892, 78 S.Ct. 265, 2 L.Ed.2d 190 (1957). Note, however, *Matter of S*, 9 I & N Dec. 688 (BIA 1962) (no moral turpitude in failure to file tax return in absence of fraud or evil intent).

(6) No. *Manzella v. Zimmerman*, 71 F.Supp. 534 (E.D.Pa.1947) (statute comprehends escapes in which moral turpitude does not inhere in that an escape may involve the "least imaginable force" and "spring from the basic desire of the human being for liberty of action and freedom from restraint").

(7) No. *Andreacchi v. Curran*, 38 F.2d 498 (D.C.N.Y.1926).

(8) Yes. *Okoroha v. INS*, 715 F.2d 380 (8th Cir.1983); *Wadman v. INS*, 329 F.2d 812 (9th Cir.1964).

(9) No. *Matter of Abreu-Semino*, 12 I & N Dec. 775 (BIA 1968) (violation of regulatory legislation, where evil intent is not an element, does not involve moral turpitude).

(10) Probably yes. *Compare United States v. Raghunandian*, 587 F.Supp. 423 (W.D.N. Y.1984) (conviction for smuggling aliens in violation of INA § 274, constitutes a crime of moral turpitude for the purposes of INA § 241(b); *with United States v. Gloria*, 494 F.2d 477 (5th Cir.), *cert. denied*, 419 U.S. 995 (1974) (misdemeanor conviction under INA

d. The Problem of "Sham" Marriages

You will recall that aliens outside the country who marry United States citizens accrue substantial advantages under the immigration laws. They are admitted as immediate relatives outside the worldwide numerical limitation of 270,000 immigrants. They are also eligible for waivers of certain grounds of exclusion. Furthermore, since nonpreference aliens have not received visas since 1978, marriage to a United States citizen has become a primary route for aliens to gain permanent residence.[51] These factors have created a long-standing enforcement problem for the immigration authorities: "sham" marriages between aliens and United States citizens that last only long enough to enable the alien to enter and establish residence in the United States.[52]

Fraudulent marriages are specifically dealt with by subsection (c) of INA § 241, which provides:

> (c) An alien shall be deported as having procured a visa or other documentation by fraud within the meaning of paragraph (19) of section 212(a), and to be in the United States in violation of this Act within the meaning of subsection (a)(2) of this section, if (1) hereafter he or she obtains any entry into the United States with an immigrant visa or other documentation procured on the basis of a marriage entered into less than two years prior to such entry of the alien and which, within two years subsequent to any entry of the alien into the United States, shall be judicially annulled or terminated, unless such alien shall establish to the satisfaction of the Attorney General that such marriage was not contracted for the purpose of evading any provisions of the immigration laws; or (2) it appears to the satisfaction of the Attorney General that he or she has failed or refused to fulfill his or her marital agreement which in the opinion of the Attorney General was hereafter made for the purpose of procuring his or her entry as an immigrant.

This subsection states that aliens who undertake sham marriages are deportable under INA § 241(a)(2). How might such an alien also be deportable under § 241(a)(1)?

e. Failure to Maintain Nonimmigrant Status

INA § 241(a)(9) provides for the deportation of nonimmigrants who fail to maintain their status or violate the conditions of their entry. This ground is primarily applied to nonimmigrants who stay beyond the time authorized at their admission. It would also cover, for example, nonimmigrants who work without authorization, students who leave school, and

§ 275, does not constitute crime of moral turpitude for purposes of impeachment).

51. Of course, an alien who becomes a spouse of a permanent resident may be eligible for a second preference visa under § 203(a)(2). But he or she would also be subject to the preference and per country quotas.

52. An additional problem confronting the INS is the legitimacy of the asserted marriage (or divorce of an earlier spouse) under the law of the home country and the United States. *See generally* G & R § 2.18(a).

temporary workers who abandon their employment. G & R § 4.9. (Non-immigrants who are out of status or violate conditions on their stay are also deportable under INA § 241(a)(2) because they are deemed to be in this country in violation of law.)

In the midst of the Iranian hostage crisis, Attorney General Civiletti ordered all Iranians admitted as nonimmigrant students to report to INS district offices to demonstrate that they were in a lawful status (*e.g.*, still in the school they were authorized to attend). 44 Fed.Reg. 65,728 (Nov. 14, 1979), *amended* 44 Fed.Reg. 75,165 (Dec. 19, 1979), *rescinded,* 46 Fed.Reg. 25,599 (Apr. 24, 1981). This unprecedented regulation of nonimmigrants was challenged as beyond the Attorney General's authority and a violation of equal protection. A panel of the Court of Appeals for the District of Columbia rejected the claims. *Narenji v. Civiletti,* 617 F.2d 745 (D.C.Cir.1979), *cert. denied* 446 U.S. 957, 100 S.Ct. 2928, 64 L.Ed.2d 815 (1980). Although the vast majority of the more than 50,000 Iranian students who reported to INS offices were found to be lawfully in the United States, those nonimmigrants who were out of status were ordered deported under INA § 241(a)(9). *E.g., Shoaee v. INS,* 704 F.2d 1079 (9th Cir.1983).

Even the American Pastime is not immune to the reaches of INA § 241(a)(9). When Los Angeles Dodgers star pitcher Fernando Valenzuela balked at renewing his contract without a hefty salary increase in early 1982, the INS announced that it was closely watching negotiations between Valenzuela, a Mexican national, and the Dodgers. An INS deputy director stated at the time:

> It's a situation involving a non-resident alien who finds himself without work. * * *

> In this situation we have a petition filed by the Dodger ballclub for Mr. Valenzuela to play baseball for them. This petition was approved last month and will be valid during and until the end of the baseball season. The petition as we view it right now is still valid. But there's a potential problem in the future should he not go and play baseball with them.

> Then he's in violation of his status and then it's a different situation. If he sits out the season then I suspect he'd be required to return home.

L.A. Times, March 4, 1982, III:2. (All worked well for Valenzuela. In February 1983 he became the first player in baseball history to win a $1 million salary in arbitration.)

3. DE FACTO DEPORTATION OF AMERICAN CITIZENS

Would a statute providing for the deportation of American citizens be constitutional?[53] Congress has never passed such a law. However, the

---

53. Deportation of a citizen is often referred to as "banishment" or "exile," a practice common throughout human history, from the banishment of Adam and Eve from the Garden of Eden, Genesis 3:22-24, through the banishment of Alexander Solzhenitsyn from the Soviet Union.

deportation of an alien may often produce the "de facto deportation" of U.S. citizen children born to the alien. As the following case indicates, "de facto deportation" has not been successfully challenged.

ACOSTA v. GAFFNEY

United States Court of Appeals, Third Circuit, 1977.
558 F.2d 1153.

MARIS, CIRCUIT JUDGE.

The United States Immigration and Naturalization Service (herein "INS") acting through its district director, the nominal defendant, appeals from the district court's May 12, 1976 order reversing the INS' orders of deportation and denial of stay of deportation of the alien plaintiffs. The facts of the case are not in dispute and will be briefly stated.

Carlos Acosta, a native and citizen of the Republic of Colombia, was admitted to the United States October 21, 1972 as a nonimmigrant visitor authorized to remain in the United States until October 31, 1972. Maria Dolores Beatriz Velaquez, now Beatriz Acosta, also a Colombian, was admitted on a nonimmigrant basis November 23, 1974 and was authorized to remain until December 5, 1974. The two aliens overstayed the period of their authorized visits and were married in Jackson, New Jersey on December 25, 1974.

The INS instituted deportation proceedings against the Acostas and scheduled a hearing to be held in Newark, New Jersey on September 9, 1975. Upon receipt of a physician's statement that Beatriz, who was then pregnant, was unable to travel, the deportation hearing was rescheduled to take place shortly after the birth, on September 23rd, of the Acostas' daughter, Lina. The Acostas were found to be deportable by the immigration judge on the basis of their own admissions.

* * *

We turn then to consider Lina's claim for relief. Basically it is that she is entitled to a stay of her parents' deportation order because that order, although admittedly valid as against them, will operate, if executed, to deny to her the right which she has as an American citizen to continue to reside in the United States. On her behalf it is argued that she will be deprived of this constitutional right of a citizen because as an infant she must remain with her parents and go with them wherever they go. In the district court Lina also asserted that her constitutional right to equal protection of the laws had been violated by the INS orders. This claim was rejected by the district court and it has not been pressed on appeal. We, accordingly, do not consider it.

The constitutional right upon which Lina relies is somewhat broader than she describes it. It is the fundamental right of an American citizen to reside wherever he wishes, whether in the United States or abroad, and to engage in the consequent travel. *See Schneider v. Rusk*, 377 U.S. 163, 168, 84 S.Ct. 1187, 12 L.Ed.2d 218 (1964); *Kent v. Dulles*, 357 U.S. 116, 125, 78 S.Ct. 1113, 2 L.Ed.2d 1204 (1958). It is the right to exercise a choice of residence, not an obligation to remain in one's native country whether one so desires or not, as is required in some totalitarian countries. In the case of an infant below the age of discretion the right is purely theoretical, however, since the infant is incapable of exercising it. As the Court of Appeals for the Fifth Circuit pointed out in *Perdido v. Immigration and Naturalization Service*, 420 F.2d 1179, 1181 (5th Cir. 1969), "... a minor child who is fortuitously born here due to his parents' decision to reside in this country, has not exercised a deliberate decision to make this country his home, and Congress did not give such a child the ability to confer immigration benefits on his parents. ... It gave this privilege to those of our citizens who had themselves chosen to make this country their home and did not give the privilege to those minor children whose noncitizen parents make the real choice of family residence." [4]

Obviously, as pointed out in the *Perdido* case, an infant of Lina's tender years cannot make a conscious choice of residence, whether in the United States or elsewhere, and merely desires, if she can be thought to have any choice, to be with her parents. It is true, of course, that Carlos and Beatriz could, as Lina's parents and natural guardians, decide that it would be best for her to remain in the United States with foster parents, if such arrangements could be made. But this would be their decision involving the custody and care of their child, taken in their capacity as her parents, not an election by Lina herself to remain in the United States.

The right of an American citizen to fix and change his residence is a continuing one which he enjoys throughout his life. Thus while today Lina Acosta, as an infant twenty-two months of age, doubtless desires merely to be where she can enjoy the care and affection of her parents, whether in the United States or Colombia, she will as she grows older and reaches years of discretion be entitled to decide for herself where she wants to live and as an American citizen she may then, if she so chooses, return to the United States to live. Thus, her return to Colombia with her parents, if they decide to take her with them as doubtless they will, will merely postpone, but not bar, her residence in the United States if she should ultimately choose to live here.

We conclude that the district court was in error in holding that the INS erred in denying a stay of the deportation order in view of its effect upon Lina Acosta. In so holding we are in accord with the decided cases in other courts of appeals. *Mendez v. Major*, 340 F.2d 128, 131 (8th Cir.1965); *Enciso-Cardozo v. Immigration & Naturalization Service*, 504 F.2d 1252, 1253 (2d Cir.1974); *Cervantes v. Immigration and Naturalization Service*, 510 F.2d 89 (10th Cir.1975); *Gonzalez-Cuevas v. Immigration and Naturalization Service*, 515 F.2d 1222 (5th Cir.1975). No contrary

4. In the *Perdido* case section 201(b) of the Immigration and Nationality Act was involved. It provides that United States citizens over 21 years of age can procure the admission of their alien parents as non-quota immigrants. The *Perdidos* sought to secure this status for themselves on the basis of their two minor children who were United States citizens, claiming that their children were denied the equal protection of the laws. The court denied the claim, holding that the statutory distinction between adult children who had made a conscious choice of residence in the United States and minor children who had not was reasonable and contained no constitutional infirmity.

cases have been cited to us and we have found none.[5]   Indeed a contrary holding would open a loophole in the immigration laws for the benefit of those deportable aliens who have had a child born while they were here.

* * *

The order of the district court will be reversed.[a]

SECTION B.   DEPORTATION PROCEDURES

1. INITIATION OF PROCEEDINGS

Until 1956, proceedings to deport an alien began with the arrest of the alien. Today, deportation proceedings begin with the issuance of an order to show cause issued by a district director, deputy district director, assistant district director for investigations or (in certain districts) an officer in charge. The order to show cause—so called because it requires the alien to "show cause" why she should not be deported—informs the alien of the nature of the proceedings, the factual allegations underlying the charge of deportability and the statutory provisions alleged to have been violated. The order requires the alien to appear before an immigration judge for a hearing at a designated time and place.

The order to show cause may be served by mail or by personal service. When an immigration officer serves the order, he is required by regulation to explain the order and advise the alien that anything the alien says may be used against him. The officer must also inform the alien that he has a right to be represented by an attorney (at no expense to the government); if the alien cannot afford an attorney, the officer must advise the alien of free legal services available in the district. 8 C.F.R. § 242.1.

Under INA § 287(a) immigration officials have the authority to arrest an alien whom the officer believes is in the country in violation of the law and is likely to escape before a warrant can be obtained.[54]   An alien arrested under this section must be brought before an immigration officer for an examination. If the examining officer is satisfied that a *prima*

---

5. The Supreme Court has not spoken directly on the issue, although in *Hintopoulos v. Shaughnessy*, 353 U.S. 72, 77 S.Ct. 618, 1 L.Ed.2d 652 (1957), the alien parents urged that their deportation would result in a "serious economic detriment" to their United States citizen child. The Court affirmed the judgment denying suspension of deportation, finding no abuse of discretion.

a. *Accord, Newton v. INS,* 736 F.2d 336 (6th Cir.1984).

Irrespective of the constitutional issues, the immigration laws provide discretionary waivers of exclusion and relief from deportation for certain aliens with close family relatives who are United States citizens. *See, e.g.,* INA §§ 212(h), (i); 244—eds.

54. The arrest powers of immigration officers are subject to the requirements and

restrictions of the Fourth Amendment. *See, e.g., United States v. Martinez-Fuerte,* 428 U.S. 543, 96 S.Ct. 3074, 49 L.Ed.2d 1116 (1976); *United States v. Ortiz,* 422 U.S. 891, 95 S.Ct. 2585, 45 L.Ed.2d 623 (1975); *United States v. Brignoni-Ponce,* 422 U.S. 873, 95 S.Ct. 2574, 45 L.Ed.2d 607 (1975); *Almeida-Sanchez v. United States,* 413 U.S. 266, 93 S.Ct. 2535, 37 L.Ed.2d 596 (1973). However, the Court has increasingly applied a rather relaxed standard of review, *see, e.g., INS v. Delgado,* ___ U.S. ___, 104 S.Ct. 1758, 80 L.Ed.2d 247 (1984), probably based on concerns regarding the number of undocumented aliens entering and residing in the United States and the difficulties of effective enforcement of the INA.

facie case exists that the alien is illegally in the United States, formal deportation proceedings are initiated (unless the alien is permitted to depart the country voluntarily). By regulation, the decision to begin deportation proceedings must be made within 24 hours of the arrest. It is not until the initiation of proceedings that an alien arrested without a warrant is given the warnings mentioned above. 8 C.F.R. § 287.3.

Aliens who are served with an order to show cause may be taken into custody. An immigration officer entitled to issue an order to show cause is authorized to issue the arrest warrant. 8 C.F.R. § 242.2(a). The INS may detain an arrested alien, release her under specific conditions, or set bond.[55] Aliens have the right to apply to an immigration judge for release from custody, change in the conditions of release, or reduction in bond. In many parts of the United States, bond redetermination hearings are conducted over the telephone. 3 Immig. Law Rep. 23 (March 1984). Both the alien and the INS are entitled to appeal the judge's decision to the BIA. 8 C.F.R. § 242.2(b). The BIA has made clear that an alien arrested pending determination of deportability should "be detained or required to post bond [only] * * * upon a finding that he is a threat to the national security * * * or that he is a poor bail risk." *Matter of Patel,* 15 I & N Dec. 666 (BIA 1976). Section 242(a) of the INA also gives the alien the right to file a habeas corpus action in a federal district court challenging the government's detention or bond decision.[56]

The vast majority of aliens served with an order to show cause or arrested for illegal presence in the United States do not go through a deportation hearing. In 1982, over 1,000,000 aliens were apprehended, yet only 54,000 hearings were held. Most aliens who are apprehended avoid a deportation hearing by agreeing to leave the United States voluntarily. (This form of relief from deportation, known as "voluntary departure," is discussed in Chapter Six *infra.*) The INS may also choose to defer deportation proceedings if the alien has applied for an immigration benefit that will regularize his status (such as adjustment of status), if the alien has applied for asylum, or if the Service deems the violation of law trivial or the enforcement of the statute inhumane under the particular circumstances. (Cases in this latter category are sometimes given "deferred action status," also discussed in Chapter Six.)

55. In 1983, INS adopted a regulation that required all bonds in deportation cases to include a rider barring the alien from working unless the District Director determined that employment was appropriate. 8 C.F.R. § 103.6(a)(2)(ii). The regulation was challenged as beyond the authority of the Service and as an unconstitutional deprivation of an alien's constitutionally protected liberty interest in working. The district court granted a preliminary injunction barring enforcement of the regulation on the ground that plaintiffs had a fair chance of succeeding on both of their claims. *National Center for Immigrants Rights, Inc. v. INS,* Civ. No. 83–7927 Kn (JRx) (C.D.Cal., Dec. 16,

1983), *excerpted in* 60 Interp.Rel. 977 (1983), affirmed in relevant part 743 F.2d 1365 (9th Cir.1984).

56. Courts will set aside bail determinations only for abuse of discretion or errors of law. For rare cases reversing the administrative determination, *see Caporali v. Whelan,* 582 F.Supp. 217 (D.Mass.1984); *In re Maringolo,* 303 F.Supp. 1389 (S.D.N.Y.1969). *Cf. Carlson v. Landon,* 342 U.S. 524, 72 S.Ct. 525, 96 L.Ed. 547 (1952) (upholding, against Fifth and Eight Amendment challenges, detention of alleged members of the Communist Party under 1950 Internal Security Act).

2. THE DEPORTATION HEARING

a. *The Constitutional Requirement of Due Process*

We have previously discussed the general unwillingness of the Supreme Court to scrutinize the procedures Congress establishes for the *exclusion* of aliens. "Whatever the procedure authorized by Congress is," the Court stated in *Knauff* and *Mezei*, "it is due process as far as the alien *denied entry* is concerned." *See* pp. 236–48 *supra.*

Perhaps it will strike you as odd that the Court has read the Constitution quite differently when examining the deportation process. The "constitutionalization" of deportation procedures has not occurred through constitutional provisions normally invoked to guarantee criminal defendants full and fair judicial proceedings (such as the Sixth Amendment). This is because the courts have steadfastly stuck to their description of deportation proceedings as "civil" in nature. *E.g., Argiz v. INS,* 704 F.2d 384, 387 (7th Cir.1983) *(per curiam)* (speedy trial guarantee of Sixth Amendment not applicable). Rather, the Constitution has been brought to the deportation setting through the due process clause of the Fifth Amendment. The landmark case that began this process follows.

THE JAPANESE IMMIGRANT CASE

(YAMATAYA v. FISHER)

Supreme Court of the United States, 1903.
189 U.S. 86, 23 S.Ct. 611, 47 L.Ed. 721.

[Kaoru Yamataya, a citizen of Japan, landed at Seattle on July 11, 1901. Four days later an immigration inspector, after investigation, decided that she was deportable because she had been excludable at time of entry as a pauper and a person likely to become a public charge. Yamataya asserted that the investigation had been inadequate because she did not understand English, did not realize that the investigation involved her deportability, was not assisted by counsel, and had not had an opportunity to show she was not deportable.]

MR. JUSTICE HARLAN * * * delivered the opinion of the court.

* * *

The constitutionality of the legislation in question, in its general aspects, is no longer open to discussion in this court. That Congress may exclude aliens of a particular race from the United States; prescribe the terms and conditions upon which certain classes of aliens may come to this country; establish regulations for sending out of the country such aliens as come here in violation of law; and commit the enforcement of such provisions, conditions and regulations exclusively to executive officers, without judicial intervention, are principles firmly established by the decisions of this court. *Nishimura Ekiu v. United States,* 142 U.S. 651, 35 L.Ed. 1146, 12 Sup.Ct.Rep. 336; *Fong Yue Ting v. United States,* 149 U.S. 698, 37 L.Ed. 905, 13 Sup.Ct.Rep. 1016.

* * *

What was the extent of the authority of the executive officers of the Government over the petitioner after she landed? * * * [T]he Secretary of the Treasury, under the * * * act of October 19, 1888, c. 1210, was authorized, within one year after an alien of the excluded class entered the country, to cause him to be taken into custody and returned to the country whence he came. Substantially the same power was conferred by the act of March 3, 1891, c. 551, by the eleventh section of which it is provided that the alien immigrant may be sent out of the country, "as provided by law," at any time within the year after his illegally coming into the United States. Taking all its enactments together, it is clear that Congress did not intend that the mere admission of an alien, or his mere entering the country, should place him at all times thereafter entirely beyond the control or authority of the executive officers of the Government. On the contrary, if the Secretary of the Treasury became satisfied that the immigrant had been allowed to land contrary to the prohibition of that law, then he could at any time within a year after the landing cause the immigrant to be taken into custody and deported. The immigrant must be taken to have entered subject to the condition that he might be sent out of the country by order of the proper executive officer if within a year he was found to have been wrongfully admitted into or had illegally entered the United States. * * *

It is contended, however, that in respect of an alien who has already landed it is consistent with the acts of Congress that he may be deported without previous notice of any purpose to deport him, and without any opportunity on his part to show by competent evidence before the executive officers charged with the execution of the acts of Congress, that he is not here in violation of law; that the deportation of an alien without provision for such a notice and for an opportunity to be heard was inconsistent with the due process of law required by the Fifth Amendment of the Constitution.

Leaving on one side the question whether an alien can rightfully invoke the due process clause of the Constitution who has entered the country clandestinely, and who has been here for too brief a period to have become, in any real sense, a part of our population, before his right to remain is disputed, we have to say that the rigid construction of the acts of Congress suggested by the appellant are not justified. Those acts do not necessarily exclude opportunity to the immigrant to be heard, when such opportunity is of right. It was held in *Murray's Lessee v. Hoboken Land & Improvement Co.*, 18 How. 272, 280, 281, 283, 15 L.Ed. 372, 376, 377, that "though 'due process of law' generally implies and includes *actor, reus, judex*, regular allegations, opportunity to answer and a trial according to some course of judicial proceedings, yet this is not universally true;" and that "though, generally, both public and private wrong are redressed through judicial action, there are more summary extra-judicial remedies for both." Hence, it was decided in that case to be consistent with due process of law for Congress to provide summary means to compel revenue officers—and in case of default, their sureties— to pay such balances of the public money as might be in their hands. Now, it has been settled that the power to exclude or expel aliens belonged to the political department of the Government, and that the order of an executive officer, invested with the power to determine finally the facts upon which an alien's right to enter this country, or remain in it, depended, was "due process of law, and no other tribunal, unless expressly authorized by law to do so, was at liberty to reexamine the evidence on which he acted, or to controvert its sufficiency." *Fong Yue Ting v. United States,* 149 U.S. 698, 713, 37 L.Ed. 905, 913, 13 Sup.Ct.Rep. 1016. But this court has never held, nor must we now be understood as holding, that administrative officers, when executing the provisions of a statute involving the liberty of persons, may disregard the fundamental principles that inhere in "due process of law" as understood at the time of the adoption of the Constitution. One of these principles is that no person shall be deprived of his liberty without opportunity, at some time, to be heard, before such officers, in respect of the matters upon which that liberty depends—not necessarily an opportunity upon a regular, set occasion, and according to the forms of judicial procedure, but one that will secure the prompt, vigorous action contemplated by Congress, and at the same time be appropriate to the nature of the case upon which such officers are required to act. Therefore, it is not competent for the Secretary of the Treasury or any executive officer, at any time within the year limited by the statute, arbitrarily to cause an alien, who has entered the country, and has become subject in all respects to its jurisdiction, and a part of its population, although alleged to be illegally here, to be taken into custody and deported without giving him all opportunity to be heard upon the questions involving his right to be and remain in the United States. No such arbitrary power can exist where the principles involved in due process of law are recognized.

This is the reasonable construction of the acts of Congress here in question, and they need not be otherwise interpreted. In the case of all acts of Congress, such interpretation ought to be adopted as, without doing violence to the import of the words used, will bring them into harmony with the Constitution. An act of Congress must be taken to be constitutional unless the contrary plainly and palpably appears. The words here used do not require an interpretation that would invest executive or administrative officers with the absolute, arbitrary power implied in the contention of the appellant. Besides, the record now before us shows that the appellant had notice, although not a formal one, of the investigation instituted for the purpose of ascertaining whether she was illegally in this country. The traverse to the return made by the Immigration Inspector shows upon its face that she was before that officer pending the investigation of her right to be in the United States, and made answers to questions propounded to her. It is true that she pleads a want of knowledge of our language; that she did not understand the nature and import of the questions propounded to her; that the investigation made was a "pretended" one; and that she did not, at the time, know that the investigation had reference to her being deported from the country. These considerations cannot justify the intervention of the courts. They could have been presented to the officer having primary control of such a case, as well as upon an appeal to the Secretary of the Treasury, who had power to order another investigation if that course was demanded by law or by the ends of justice. It is not to be assumed that either would have refused a second or fuller investigation, if a proper application and showing for one had been made by or for the appellant. Whether further investigation should have been ordered was for the officers, charged with the execution of the statutes, to determine. Their action in that regard is not subject to judicial review. Suffice it to say, it does not appear that appellant was denied an opportunity to be heard. And as no appeal was taken to the Secretary from the decision of the Immigration Inspector, that decision was final and conclusive. If the appellant's want of knowledge of the English language put her at some disadvantage in the investigation conducted by that officer, that was her misfortune, and constitutes no reason, under the acts of Congress, or under any rule of law, for the intervention of the court by *habeas corpus.* We perceive no ground for such intervention—none for the contention that due process of law was denied to appellant.

The judgment is

Affirmed.

MR. JUSTICE BREWER and MR. JUSTICE PECKHAM dissented.

Notes

1. Can you construct a coherent interpretation of the Constitution that accounts for the results in the exclusion due process cases, *Knauff* and *Mezei* (pp. 236–248 *supra*), and *The Japanese Immigrant Case?* Does your theory also answer the question reserved by Justice Harlan—whether an alien who entered without inspection and had been in the United States only a short time can invoke the due process clause in challenging deportation procedures?

We suggest you think about these difficult, but crucial, questions throughout the remainder of this Section. We will spell out our views on these issues at the close of the Chapter.

2. *The Japanese Immigrant Case* stands for the proposition that deportation procedures must conform to the dictates of the due process clause of the Constitution. But note that Yamataya's deportation was *upheld* in that case even though she had had no formal hearing, alleged that she could neither speak nor understand English, and claimed that she was unaware of the reason for her being questioned. Could such a "proceeding" be considered "due process of law" today? Under current judicial interpretations of the constitutional mandate, aliens must be informed of the nature of the proceeding and the grounds of deportation at issue [57] and must be provided with an interpreter when they cannot understand English.[58]

---

57. *See, e.g., Hirsch v. INS,* 308 F.2d 562, 566–67 (9th Cir.1962); *Matter of Rios-Carrillo,* 10 I & N Dec. 291 (BIA 1963).

58. *See, e.g., Tejeda-Mata v. INS,* 626 F.2d 721, 726 (9th Cir.1980), *cert. denied* 456 U.S. 994, 102 S.Ct. 2280, 73 L.Ed.2d 1291 (1982).

b. *The Conduct of a Deportation Hearing*

The history of deportation proceedings has been the increasing "legalization" of the process. The earliest statutes included no specific deportation procedures; they simply stated that aliens unlawfully in the United States were subject to deportation. By regulation, the executive branch provided an informal hearing with an administrative appeal.[59]

It was not until 1952 that deportation procedures were written into a statute.[60] They currently are spelled out in INA § 242.

Approximately 50,000 deportation hearings a year are conducted by immigration judges. The following selection, written by a former member of the BIA and past president of the Association of Immigration and Nationality Lawyers, describes the mechanics of a deportation proceeding.

JACK WASSERMAN, PRACTICAL ASPECTS OF REPRESENTING AN ALIEN AT A DEPORTATION HEARING

14 San Diego L.Rev. 111, 115–20, 127–28 (1976).

GOVERNMENT OFFICIALS PRESENT

The presiding officer at the deportation hearing is the special inquiry officer. He is often referred to as an immigration judge, even though he is not subject to the Administrative Procedure Act. Although the immigration judge wears judicial robes and sits at a desk on a raised platform, the other aspects of the deportation hearing are less formal than are those of judicial proceedings. Witnesses, interpreters, and counsel sit around a conference table equipped with microphones. A recording device rather than a stenographer is used to preserve testimony adduced at the hearing.

The major functions of the immigration judge are to determine deportability, to grant certain forms of discretionary relief, to determine the country of the alien's deportation, and to certify a decision that involves an unusually complex or novel question of law or fact to the Board of Immigration Appeals. As the presiding officer, the immigration judge controls the conduct of the hearing, authorizes deposition testimony, grants continuances, and places both the interpreter and all witnesses under oath. He is required to advise the unrepresented alien of his right to counsel and to ask the alien to state his preference regarding such

---

59. *See generally,* C. Bouvé, *A Treatise on the Laws Governing the Exclusion and Expulsion of Aliens in the United States* 614–681 (1912); S. Kansas, *United States Immigration, Exclusion, and Deportation, and Citizenship of the United States of America* 235–243 (2d ed. 1940) (reprinting regulations relating to deportation). Interestingly, the Chinese exclusion laws provided substantially different procedures, including a hearing before a United States Commissioner or Judge. Bouvé, *supra,* at 628–53.

60. Before and after the enactment of the 1952 statute, Congress and the Supreme Court engaged in a colloquy over the appli-

cability of the Administrative Procedure Act to deportation hearings. In *Wong Yang Sung v. McGrath,* 339 U.S. 33, 70 S.Ct. 445, 94 L.Ed. 616 (1950), the Court construed the APA, enacted in 1946, to apply to deportation proceedings. Congress quickly overturned the decision, passing a statute exempting deportation hearings from the procedural dictates of the APA. Act of Sept. 27, 1950, Ch. 1052, 64 Stat. 1048. Following the specification of procedures in the 1952 Immigration Act, the Court was again asked to find the APA's procedural requirements applicable. It refused. *Marcello v. Bonds,* 349 U.S. 302, 75 S.Ct. 757, 99 L.Ed. 1107 (1955).

representation. The immigration judge is also required to advise the alien that he will have a reasonable opportunity to examine and object to adverse evidence and to cross-examine witnesses. He will have the factual allegations of the order to show cause read to the alien, explained in nontechnical language, and finally entered as an exhibit. The alien is required by the immigration judge to plead to the factual allegations of the order to show cause. After the hearing the judge will render an oral or written decision.

In some districts, a trial attorney is assigned in all deportation cases. Assignment by the District Director is required in all cases in which deportability is an issue, in cases of unrepresented incompetents or children under sixteen, in cases when requested by the immigration judge, or in cases after which nonrecord, confidential information will be submitted to contest the grant of discretionary relief.   * * *

The trial attorney is authorized to present evidence on behalf of the Government and to examine and cross-examine the alien and his witnesses. He is vested with authority to appeal a decision favorable to the alien and may move for reopening and reconsideration of decisions adverse to the Government's contentions. He may also file, in writing, additional charges of deportability. The document evidencing these additional charges will be entered as an exhibit and will serve as a basis for a continuance to allow the alien to meet the additional charges.

Courts have long perceived the importance of utilizing a competent interpreter. Some interpreters are highly skilled and efficient and have great experience and expertise in the art of translation. Others may not have acquired facility in the language. Inexperienced interpreters have problems transposing foreign sentences into English, a difficult task in any event because some languages have no literal counterpart for many English words. Thus, it is important for counsel to ascertain not only whether the interpreter speaks the same language as the alien but also whether the interpreter understands the same dialect.

At deportation hearings, unlike judicial proceedings, the Government furnishes all interpreters at its expense. The interpreter may be an employee of INS, of the State Department, or he may be a nongovernmental individual employed on a contract basis. In appropriate cases, an alien will be permitted to bring his own interpreter into the hearing to monitor the accuracy of the official translation.

PREHEARING CONFERENCES

Neither the statute nor the regulations makes any provisions for prehearing conferences. Informal conferences, however, are frequently desirable * * * in appropriate cases either immediately prior to the deportation hearing or well in advance of the event. Such conferences may result in stipulations shortening the hearing. In some cases they will apprise counsel of adverse information contained in the Service's file. * * *

MOTION PRACTICE

Although there is no formal motion practice in deportation hearings, appropriate motions may be made either orally or in writing. The record of the hearing will reflect all motions. In appropriate cases, the following motions may be utilized: motion for continuance; motion to disqualify the immigration judge; motion for change of venue; motion to exclude spectators; [46] motion for subpoena; [47] motion for deposition; motion to produce favorable evidence; motion to suppress illegally seized evidence; and motion to suppress evidence secured by unlawful electronic surveillance.

PROCEDURE IN THE CONDUCT OF A DEPORTATION HEARING

The immigration judge begins the hearing by turning on his recording machine. He then proceeds to call the case, identify the alien, counsel, the trial attorney, and the interpreter. The alien is asked whether he received the order to show cause which is entered as Exhibit 1. The alien or his attorney then pleads [52] to the allegations of fact set forth in the order to show cause. If the alien has no attorney, he is advised of his rights. If deportability is contested, evidence is adduced on the issue.

Deportability and alienage must be established by substantial evidence—that is, by clear, convincing, and unequivocal evidence. Hearsay

46. Deportation hearings are open to the public. 8 C.F.R. § 242.16(a) (1976). However, the immigration judge may exclude the general public or specific individuals from the hearing. *Id.* This rule will have to be reevaluated in light of recent court decisions. *See* Nebraska Press Ass'n v. Stuart, 96 S.Ct. 2791 (1976); Fitzgerald v. Hampton, 467 F.2d 755 (D.C.Cir.1972). Because the physical facilities for deportation hearings are comparatively small, limitations may be imposed upon the number of spectators in attendance. 8 C.F.R. § 242.16(a) (1976). Generally, neither the press nor the public attends deportation hearings. In those cases in which the alien is well-known, and large numbers of the public or press are present, larger hearing rooms are utilized. [*See also Pechter v. Lyons,* 441 F.Supp. 115 (S.D.N.Y. 1977) (heavy presumption in favor of public attendance)—eds.]

47. District Directors or immigration judges are authorized to issue subpoenas. 8 C.F.R. § 287.4(a)(2) (1976). When the INS requires the attendance of a witness, application is made *ex parte*, frequently without a written application. An alien requesting a subpoena must inform the Service of his request. He is required to state what he expects to prove and that he has made a diligent effort to procure the witness needed. *Id.* The witness who resides more than 100 miles from the place of the hearing is required to appear at the nearest field office, unless he is allowed to appear at the proceeding itself. Anyone over eighteen years of age may serve the subpoena. The alien

must tender one day's attendance and mileage fee at the time of service. *Id.* § 287.4(c).

52. The alien may plead as an affirmative defense to a deportation charge that he is: a United States citizen; that he did not effect an entry (Rosenberg v. Fleuti, 374 U.S. 449 (1963)); that he did not enter illegally or overstay; that an essential allegation supporting deportability is not established by clear, convincing, and unequivocal evidence (Woodby v. INS, 385 U.S. 276 (1966); I. & N. Act § 242(b)(4), 8 U.S.C. § 1252(b)(4) (1970)); that he has a defense under government estoppel (Moser v. United States, 341 U.S. 41 (1951); Corniel-Rodriguez v. INS, 532 F.2d 301 (2d Cir.1976); McLeod v. Peterson, 283 F.2d 180 (3d Cir.1960)); selective deportation based on secret political grounds (Lennon v. INS, 527 F.2d 187 (2d Cir.1975)); adoption of different standard in similar cases (Del Mundo v. Rosenberg, 341 F.Supp. 345 (C.D.Cal. 1972); United States *ex rel.* Partheniades v. Shaughnessy, 146 F.Supp. 772, 774–75 (S.D. N.Y.1956)); res judicata (United States v. Utah Constr. & Mining Co., 384 U.S. 394 (1966); Sunshine Anthracite Coal Co. v. Adkins, 310 U.S. 381 (1940) (The principle of res judicata in deportation proceedings, however, has not been accepted by our Administrators.); or claims of unconstitutionality. *See* Alcala v. Wyoming State Bd. of Barber Examiners, 365 F.Supp. 560 (Wyo.1973) (It is questionable whether it is necessary to raise a constitutional issue administratively.).

is admissible, but uncorroborated hearsay is not substantial evidence. The use of hearsay and guilt by association is considered erroneous. When hearsay is admitted, counsel for the alien should exercise his right to cross-examine by requesting a subpoena or depositions. The prior statements of adverse witnesses may be obtained * * * by making a demand for them. An alien is entitled to equal treatment and nondiscriminatory rulings on evidentiary issues. Failure to accord the alien such treatment results in the hearing being deemed unfair.

Although oral argument is usually not encouraged before an immigration judge, it will be allowed in some cases. Briefs are not usually submitted but should be filed in complicated cases. The alien is called as the first (and sometimes the only) witness. The alien may decline to answer upon grounds of self-incrimination. If deportability is conceded, if it is established, or even when it remains disputed, consideration must be given to applications for discretionary relief. Such applications must be made during the hearing, and the burden of proof is upon the alien to establish that he is entitled to relief.[a]

* * *

DESIGNATING THE PLACE OF DEPORTATION

Prior to the conclusion of the hearing, the alien will be permitted to designate a place of deportation, if he is ordered deported. He may designate only one place of deportation, and this decision must be made in good faith. The alien may not designate contiguous territory or adjacent islands unless he has been a native, citizen, or resident of such places. The immigration judge may designate as an alternative place of deportation the alien's country of citizenship or last residence or any country willing to receive him.

THE IMMIGRATION JUDGE'S DECISION

The immigration judge's decision may be oral or written. If deportability is contested, the decision contains a discussion of the evidence and findings concerning deportability. The decision also contains a discussion of evidence pertinent to discretionary relief and is concluded with an order granting or denying relief. The decision orders termination, grants permanent residence, orders voluntary departure with an alternate order of deportation, or deportation.

If deportability is determined on the pleadings and no discretionary relief other than voluntary departure is requested, the immigration judge enters an order of voluntary departure with an alternate order of deportation to a named country on form I–39 or an order of deportation on form I–38.[b] These forms are served on the alien and his attorney at the conclusion of the hearing, and unless appeal is waived, service of the appeal form (I–290A) is required with advice about the appeal procedure.

a. We will consider various avenues of relief from deportation in Chapter Six.—eds.

b. The issuance of the alternate order of deportation allows the INA to deport the alien without returning to an immigration judge if the alien has not departed within the time granted by the order of voluntary departure.—eds.

When an oral decision is rendered, it is done in the presence of the alien, his counsel, and the trial attorney. Unless an appeal is waived, the appeal form and advice about appeal must be given. Upon request, the decision and a transcript will be provided without cost to enable the alien to pursue his appeal. If no appeal is taken, the immigration judge's decision is final. If the decision is favorable to the alien, the trial attorney has the right to appeal, and in appropriate cases, the case may be certified to the Board of Immigration Appeals for review by the immigration judge, by the Service, or by the Board.

c. Constitutional and Statutory Rights in Deportation Hearings

(i) An Independent Decisionmaker

For most of this century, federal officials who conducted deportation hearings were employees of the immigration service. The Select Commission on Immigration and Refugee Policy, reporting in 1981, found that

> INS does not provide adequate support service to immigration judges, contributing to long delays in the administrative adjudication process; [and]

> [i]mmigration judges are administratively dependent upon officials (INS district directors) who are involved in an adversary capacity in proceedings before the judges[.]

SCIRP, Final Report 246.

A constitutional challenge to the dependence of the adjudicator on the INS was summarily rejected by the Supreme Court shortly after the passage of the McCarran-Walter Act of 1952:

> [T]he only complaint which petitioner can urge concerning the hearing procedures in this case is the objection that the special inquiry officer was subject to the supervision and control of officials in the Immigration Service charged with investigative and prosecuting functions. Petitioner would have us hold that the presence of this relationship so strips the hearing of fairness and impartiality as to make the procedure violative of due process. The contention is without substance when considered against the long-standing practice in deportation proceedings, judicially approved in numerous decisions in the federal courts, and against the special considerations applicable to deportation which the Congress may take into account in exercising its particularly broad discretion in immigration matters.

Marcello v. Bonds, 349 U.S. 302, 311, 75 S.Ct. 757, 762, 99 L.Ed. 1107 (1955).

This arrangement, which was subject to years of criticism,[61] was finally altered in 1983, with the creation of the Executive Office for Immigration Review (EOIR). *See* pp. 89–90 *supra.* Under the new organiza-

---

61. *See, e.g.,* Rosenfield, *Necessary Administrative Reforms in the Immigration* *and Nationality Act of 1952,* 27 Fordham L.Rev. 145 (1958).

tion, immigration judges are under the general supervision of the Director of the EOIR and expressly excepted from the control of the INS Commissioner. 8 C.F.R. §§ 2.1, 3.0.

Another objection often lodged against the deportation procedure provided by the INA is the combination of prosecutive and adjudicative functions in the immigration judge. Section 242(b) provides that an immigration judge "shall administer oaths, present and receive evidence, interrogate, examine, and cross-examine the alien or witnesses, and ... shall make determinations, including orders of deportation." [62] This too has been ameliorated by regulation. In any hearing in which the alien does not admit deportability the judge must request the assignment of a trial attorney to present the government's case. 8 C.F.R. § 242.16(c). *See also* 8 C.F.R. § 242.9. Does this adoption of an inquisitorial model—conferring both prosecuting and judging functions on an immigration judge—violate due process? [63]

(ii) Counsel

The INA, in two separate sections, provides that an alien in a deportation proceeding "shall have the privilege of being represented (at no expense to the Government) by such counsel, authorized to practice in such proceedings, as he shall choose." INA §§ 242(b), 292. (By regulation, law students directly supervised by a faculty member or attorney may represent an alien in a deportation hearing. 8 C.F.R. § 292.1(a)(2).)

Aliens who cannot afford a lawyer must be informed of the free legal service programs available in the district. 8 C.F.R. § 242.16(a). However, for fiscal year 1983 Congress imposed restrictions on the representation of aliens with funds appropriated for the Legal Service Corporation (LSC). Pub.L. No. 97–377, 96 Stat. 1830, 1874–75 (1982). Pursuant to the statute, the LSC promulgated regulations that permit recipients of LSC funds to represent only permanent resident aliens, immediate relatives of U.S. citizens who have applied for adjustment of status, refugees and asylees, and aliens granted withholding of deportation under INA § 243(h). 45 C.F.R. § 1626.4. Thus, under the regulations, most undocumented aliens, aliens applying for asylum, nonimmigrants and parolees may not be

---

62. Note that this subsection prohibits an immigration judge from conducting a hearing "in any case * * * in which he shall have participated in investigative functions or in which he shall have participated (except as provided in this subsection) in prosecuting functions." INA § 242(b).

63. The Supreme Court appeared to give an affirmative answer to this question in *Wong Yang Sung v. McGrath,* 339 U.S. 33, 46, 70 S.Ct. 445, 452, 94 L.Ed. 616 (1950), where, in order to avoid a difficult constitutional issue, it interpreted the APA hearing requirements to apply to deportation proceedings. Yet, when Congress reversed the Court's holding by exempting the INA from the APA, the Court, somewhat surprisingly,

upheld the procedures it had so seriously questioned five years earlier. *Marcello v. Bonds,* 349 U.S. 302, 75 S.Ct. 757, 99 L.Ed. 1107 (1955). *Cf. Richardson v. Perales,* 402 U.S. 389, 408–10, 91 S.Ct. 1420, 1430–31, 28 L.Ed.2d 842 (1971), where the Supreme Court rejected such a due process challenge to social security disability hearings: "[We are not] persuaded by the advocate-judge-multiple-hat suggestion. It assumes too much and would bring down too many procedures designed, and working well, for a governmental structure of great and growing complexity." *See also Winthrow v. Larkin,* 421 U.S. 35, 46–55, 95 S.Ct. 1456, 1463–68, 43 L.Ed.2d 712 (1975).

represented. Congress continued these limitations for fiscal year 1984. Pub.L. No. 98–166, 97 Stat. 1071, 1090–91 (1983).

Does the Constitution require the government to provide counsel to indigent aliens? Recall that the Sixth Amendment's guarantee of appointed counsel is not available to aliens in deportation hearings since the Supreme Court is unwilling to view them as criminal proceedings. Thus, a right to government-provided counsel, if it exists, must be found in the due process clause of the Fifth Amendment.

AGUILERA–ENRIQUEZ v. INS

United States Court of Appeals, Sixth Circuit, 1975.
516 F.2d 565, cert. denied 423 U.S. 1050, 96 S.Ct. 776, 46 L.Ed.2d 638 (1976).

CELEBREZZE, CIRCUIT JUDGE.

Petitioner, Jesus Aguilera-Enriquez, seeks reversal of a deportation order on the ground that he was constitutionally entitled to but was not afforded the assistance of counsel during his deportation hearing. * * *

A thirty-nine-year-old native and citizen of Mexico, Petitioner has resided in the United States since December 18, 1967, when he was admitted for permanent residence. He is a married farm worker, living with his wife and three daughters in Saginaw, Michigan.

In December 1971, Petitioner traveled to Mexico for a vacation. An officer of the Saginaw, Michigan Police Department notified federal customs officers at the Mexican border that he had reason to believe that Petitioner would be returning with a quantity of heroin. When Petitioner crossed the border on his return, he was subjected to a search which produced no heroin but did reveal two grams of cocaine.

On April 12, 1972, Petitioner pleaded guilty in the United States District Court for the Western District of Texas, on one count of knowingly possessing a quantity of cocaine, a Schedule II controlled substance, in violation of 21 U.S.C. § 844(a) (1970). Petitioner received a suspended one-year sentence, was placed on probation for five years, and was fined $3,000, to be paid in fifty-dollar monthly installments over the five-year probationary period. Neither Petitioner's appointed counsel nor the District Court informed him that a narcotics conviction would almost certainly lead to his deportation.

On December 7, 1972, the Immigration and Naturalization Service issued an Order to Show Cause and Notice of Hearing, charging that because of his narcotics conviction, Petitioner should be deported under section 241(a)(11) of the Immigration and Nationality Act.

On February 6, 1973 Petitioner appeared before the Immigration Judge and requested appointed counsel. The Immigration Judge refused this request. After a hearing Petitioner was ordered deported and was not afforded the option of voluntary departure.

Shortly after the Immigration Judge's ruling, Petitioner engaged as counsel a Michigan legal assistance attorney, who in turn secured the services of a Texas attorney.

On February 14, 1973, Petitioner filed an appeal to the Board of Immigration Appeals, stating that the validity of the Texas conviction was being challenged.

On May 23, 1973, Petitioner's Texas counsel filed a motion to withdraw his guilty plea under Rule 32(d), F.R.Crim.P. The motion asserted that the District Court had not followed Rule 11 in accepting the plea because it had not properly determined that there was a factual basis for the plea and that the plea was made with a full understanding of the probable consequences.

On February 1, 1974, after full briefing and oral argument by counsel for Petitioner and the Government, the Board of Immigration Appeals dismissed Petitioner's appeal. A petition for review was timely filed in this Court.

The issue Petitioner raises here is whether an indigent alien has the right to appointed counsel in a deportation proceeding. He attacks the constitutional validity of INA § 242(b)(2), which gives an alien facing deportation proceedings "the privilege of being represented (at no expense to the Government) by such counsel, authorized to practice in such proceedings, as he shall choose."[1] The Immigration Judge held that this section prevented appointment of counsel at Government expense. Since he could not afford to hire a lawyer, he did not have one before the Immigration Judge.

The courts have been vigilant to ensure that aliens receive the protections Congress has given them before they may be banished from our shores. As this Circuit noted in United States ex rel. Brancato v. Lehmann, 239 F.2d 663, 666 (6th Cir.1956),

> Although it is not penal in character, * * * deportation is a drastic measure, at times the equivalent of banishment or exile, for which reason deportation statutes should be given the narrowest of the several possible meanings.

The Supreme Court has held that once an alien has been admitted to lawful residence, "not even Congress may expel him without allowing him a fair opportunity to be heard." Kwong Hai Chew v. Colding, 344 U.S. 590, 598, 73 S.Ct. 472, 478, 97 L.Ed. 576 (1953). Thus, if procedures mandated by Congress do not provide an alien with procedural due process, they must yield, and the constitutional guarantee of due process must provide adequate protection during the deportation process. Yamataya v. Fisher (The Japanese Immigrant Case), 189 U.S. 86, 100, 23 S.Ct. 611, 47 L.Ed. 721 (1903).

The test for whether due process requires the appointment of counsel for an indigent alien is whether, in a given case, the assistance of counsel would be necessary to provide "fundamental fairness—the touchstone of due process." Gagnon v. Scarpelli, 411 U.S. 778, 790, 93 S.Ct. 1756, 1763, 36 L.Ed.2d 656 (1973).[3]

---

1. *See also* INA § 292; 8 C.F.R. § 242.16.

3. The Supreme Court's holdings in Gagnon, Morrissey v. Brewer, 408 U.S. 471, 92

In Petitioner's case the absence of counsel at his hearing before the Immigration Judge did not deprive his deportation proceeding of fundamental fairness.

Petitioner was held to be deportable under section 241(a)(11) of the Immigration and Nationality Act, which states in relevant part:

(a) Any alien in the United States ... shall, upon the order of the Attorney General, be deported who—

. . . . .

(11) ... at any time has been convicted of a violation of ... any law or regulation relating to the illicit possession of or traffic in narcotic drugs ....

Before the Immigration Judge, Petitioner raised no defense to the charge that he had been convicted in April 1972 of a violation of 21 U.S.C. § 844(a). Thus, he was clearly within the purview of section 241(a)(11) of the Act, and no defense for which a lawyer would have helped the argument was presented to the Immigration Judge for consideration. After the decision of the Immigration Judge, Petitioner moved to withdraw his guilty plea in the Texas District Court under Rule 32(d), F.R.Crim.P. He then urged before the Board of Immigration Appeals that this motion took him outside the reach of section 241(a)(11), because the likelihood of success on that motion meant that he had not been "convicted" of a narcotics offense. He was effectively represented by counsel before the Board, and his argument was considered upon briefing and oral argument. The lack of counsel before the Immigration Judge did not prevent full administrative consideration of his argument. Counsel could have obtained no different administrative result. "Fundamental fairness," therefore, was not abridged during the administrative proceedings, and the order of deportation is not subject to constitutional attack for a lack of due process.

* * *

The petition for review is denied.

DeMascio, District Judge (dissenting).[a]

A deportation proceeding so jeopardizes a resident alien's basic and fundamental right to personal liberty that I cannot agree due process is guaranteed by a "fundamental fairness" analysis on a case-by-case basis.

S.Ct. 2593, 33 L.Ed.2d 484 (1972), and In re Gault, 387 U.S. 1, 87 S.Ct. 1428, 18 L.Ed.2d 527 (1967), have undermined the position that counsel must be provided to indigents only in criminal proceedings. Decisions such as Tupacyupanqui-Marin v. Immigration and Naturalization Service, 447 F.2d 603 (7th Cir.1971), and Murgia-Melendrez v. Immigration and Naturalization Service, 407 F.2d 207 (9th Cir.1969), which contain dictum appearing to set forth a *per se* rule against providing counsel to indigent aliens facing deportation, rested largely on the outmoded distinction between criminal cases (where the Sixth Amendment guarantees indigents appointed counsel) and civil proceedings (where the Fifth Amendment applies). Where an unrepresented indigent alien would require counsel to present his position adequately to an immigration judge, he must be provided with a lawyer at the Government's expense. Otherwise, "fundamental fairness" would be violated.

a. [Hon. Robert E. DeMascio, U.S. District Judge for the Eastern District of Michigan, sitting by designation.]

Gagnon v. Scarpelli, 411 U.S. 778, 93 S.Ct. 1756, 36 L.Ed.2d 656 (1973). I think a resident alien has an unqualified right to the appointment of counsel. In re Gault, 387 U.S. 1, 87 S.Ct. 1428, 18 L.Ed.2d 527 (1967). When the government, with plenary power to exclude, agrees to allow an alien lawful residence, it is unconscionable for the government to unilaterally terminate that agreement without affording an indigent resident alien assistance of appointed counsel. Expulsion is such lasting punishment that meaningful due process can require no less. Assuredly, it inflicts punishment as grave as the institutionalization which may follow an In re Gault finding of delinquency. A resident alien's right to due process should not be tempered by a classification of the deportation proceeding as "civil", "criminal", or "administrative." No matter the classification, deportation is punishment, pure and simple.

In *Gagnon,* the Supreme Court acknowledged that it was affording parolees and probationers less due process than it afforded juveniles in In re Gault. It reached this result because a parolee or probationer is in that position solely because he was previously convicted of a crime. The court reasoned that parolees and probationers should be required to demonstrate that an attorney would serve a useful purpose prior to compelling the government to provide counsel at government expense. But, in a deportation proceeding, the respondent need not necessarily be before the immigration judge because of a prior conviction.[2] The fact of conviction is only one of numerous grounds for deportation outlined in the statute. Similar to the juvenile, an alien may only stand accused of an offense.

As noted in *Gagnon,* the function of the probation or parole officer is not to "compel conformance to a strict code of behavior" but to "supervise a course of rehabilitation." 411 U.S. 784, 93 S.Ct. 1760. Insertion of counsel into such a "predictive and discretionary" proceeding could inadvertently circumscribe the officer's flexibility. However, no such justification for the exclusion of counsel exists in deportation proceedings where the sole duty of the immigration law judge is to determine whether a deportable offense has occurred. INA § 241(a).

Further, a probation revocation hearing is a non-adversary proceeding. The government is not represented by a prosecutor. There are no procedural rights which may be lost as in a criminal trial. A deportation hearing on the other hand is always an adversary proceeding.[3] *Gagnon*

2. If the court wishes to extend *Gagnon,* perhaps a better approach is to limit the case-by-case appointment of counsel to proceedings where respondent is being deported because he has a previous conviction and is, therefore, entitled to less due process. In all other instances, counsel should be appointed as a matter of right under the due process clause. The court suggests an indigent alien is entitled to appointed counsel only when it is necessary ". . . to present his position adequately to an immigration judge. . . ." (*See* fn. 3, *supra.*)

3. A reading of INA § 242(b) makes it apparent that the special inquiry officer [now an immigration judge by regulation] functions as a prosecutor, defense lawyer, finder of facts, and judge. While the statute does not provide for the appointment of a government trial attorney, a regulation does. 8 CFR § 242.16(c) provides that if an alien does not admit he is deportable the immigration judge shall appoint a government trial attorney to establish the facts justifying deportation. At the hearing, the rules of evidence do not apply. Hearsay evidence is admissible. During such an adversary hearing, the indigent resident alien stands alone. He does not have a lawyer to meaningfully participate in making a record, a record

does not go so far as to hold that in adversary proceedings due process may be afforded on a case-by-case basis by retrospective determination that the hearing was characterized by "fundamental fairness."

The court today has fashioned a test to resolve whether a resident alien's due-process right requires appointment of counsel. That test is whether "... in a given case, the assistance of counsel would be necessary to provide 'fundamental fairness—the touchstone of due process.' " *Gagnon, supra*. The majority concludes that lack of counsel before the immigration judge did not prevent full consideration of petitioner's sole argument and no different result would have been obtained had counsel been appointed. Accordingly, the court holds the hearing was fundamentally fair.[4] These conclusions are reached by second guessing the record—a record made without petitioner's meaningful participation.

In my view, the absence of counsel at respondent's hearing before the immigration judge inherently denied him fundamental fairness. Moreover, I do not believe that we should make the initial determination that counsel is unnecessary; or that lack of counsel did not prevent full administrative consideration of petitioner's argument; or that counsel could not have obtained a different administrative result. We should not speculate at this stage what contentions appointed counsel could have raised before the immigration judge. For example, a lawyer may well have contended that § 241(a)(11) is an unconstitutional deprivation of the equal protection of the laws by arguing that alienage was the sole basis for the infliction of punishment, additional to that imposed by criminal law; that since the government elected to rely upon the criminal law sanctions, it may not now additionally exile petitioner without demonstrating a compelling governmental interest.

I do not intend to imply such a contention has validity. I cite this only to emphasize the danger of attempting to speculate at this stage whether counsel could have obtained a different result and to show that it is possible that the immigration judge did not fully consider all of petitioner's arguments.

Because the consequences of a deportation proceeding parallels punishment for crime, only a per se rule requiring appointment of counsel will assure a resident alien due process of law. In this case, the respondent, a resident alien for seven years, committed a criminal offense. Our laws require that he be punished and he was. Now, he must face additional punishment in the form of banishment. He will be deprived of the life, liberty, and pursuit of happiness he enjoyed by governmental consent.[6] It may be proper that he be compelled to face the consequences

upon which the Appeals Board and this court will determine whether the order of deportation was supported by evidence that is clear and convincing.

4. The Second Circuit has similarly held that where the respondent admits the allegations in the order to show cause and it does not appear that an attorney would affect the outcome, lack of appointed counsel does not violate due process. Henriques v. Immigra-

tion & Naturalization Service, 465 F.2d 119, 121 (2nd Cir.1972), cert. denied, 410 U.S. 968, 93 S.Ct. 1452, 35 L.Ed.2d 703.

6. Of course, what I have said applies only to a resident alien. I readily agree that an alien who enters illegally is entitled to less due process, if any at all. It is interesting to note that the Immigration Act seems to treat all aliens alike.

of such a proceeding. But, when he does, he should have a lawyer at his side and one at government expense, if necessary. When the government consents to grant an alien residency, it cannot constitutionally expel unless and until it affords that alien due process. Our country's constitutional dedication to freedom is thwarted by a watered-down version of due process on a case-by-case basis.

I would reverse and remand for the appointment of counsel before the immigration judge.

Notes

1. In *Lassiter v. Department of Social Services,* 452 U.S. 18, 101 S.Ct. 2153, 68 L.Ed.2d 640 (1981), the Supreme Court, in a five to four decision, rejected the claim that indigent defendants in a proceeding to terminate their parental status have a right to appointed counsel. Recognizing that due process applies to such proceedings, the Court adopted the approach of *Gagnon v. Scarpelli,* 411 U.S. 778, 93 S.Ct. 1756, 36 L.Ed.2d 656 (1973): the right to appointed counsel should be decided on a case-by-case basis depending upon the particular facts and circumstances and the dictates of "fundamental fairness."

Explaining its decision, the Court summarized its prior decisions on the right to counsel as follows:

> The pre-eminent generalization that emerges from this Court's precedents on an indigent's right to appointed counsel is that such a right has been recognized to exist only where the litigant may lose his physical liberty if he loses the litigation.

Lassiter, 452 U.S. at 25, 101 S.Ct. at 2158. Is deportation a loss of physical liberty, or is it simply an order that aliens pursue their liberty in their home countries?

Earlier cases indicate that the Court has not considered the potential loss of physical liberty enough, by itself, to trigger automatic appointment of counsel. *See Morrissey v. Brewer,* 408 U.S. 471, 92 S.Ct. 2593, 33 L.Ed.2d 484 (1972) (parole revocation); *Gagnon v. Scarpelli,* 411 U.S. 778, 93 S.Ct. 1756, 36 L.Ed.2d 656 (1973) (probation revocation); *Parham v. J.R.,* 442 U.S. 584, 99 S.Ct. 2493, 61 L.Ed.2d 101 (1979) (parent-initiated civil commitment of minors). Which of the following factors might also be considered in determining whether a right to appointed counsel obtains: the adversarial nature of the proceedings, the formality of the hearing, the complexities of the legal standards and issues involved, the fact that the government is usually represented in such proceedings? Do these factors distinguish deportation proceedings from parole and probation revocations or voluntary commitment of minors? *See* Black, *Due Process and Deportation—Is There a Right to Assigned Counsel?,* 8 U.C. Davis L.Rev. 289, 295–96 (1975).

In *Lassiter,* once the Court concluded that a loss of physical liberty was not at issue, it resorted to a due process balancing test enunciated in *Mathews v. Eldridge,* 424 U.S. 319, 96 S.Ct. 893, 47 L.Ed.2d 18 (1976), to decide whether a right to appointed counsel should be found. Under *Eldridge,* the level of procedural protections due depends upon evaluation of the private interests at stake, the government's interest, and the risk that the procedures used will lead to erroneous decisions. The Court stated that the "new balance" of the *Eldridge* calculus must then be weighed against "the presumption that there is a right to appointed counsel only where the indigent, if he is unsuccessful, may lose his personal freedom." *Lassiter,* 452 U.S. at 27, 101 S.Ct. at 2159.

Assume that you are representing an alien appealing an order of deportation entered after a deportation hearing at which counsel was not present. How would you use *Lassiter* and *Eldridge* to argue that your client was denied due process, irrespective of the facts of the particular case?

Assume you are a judge on a federal court of appeals hearing the appeal. How would you rule? If you do not believe that *Lassiter* answers the question, how would you (can you) evaluate and balance the factors identified by the court in *Eldridge?*

Assume you are a member of Congress rewriting the immigration code. Would you provide for appointed counsel for all indigent aliens? Is there additional information you would like (need) to know before reaching a decision?

2. The statute guarantees an alien the privilege to have an attorney at a deportation hearing. Thus, all aliens who can afford to do so have the right to be represented. Does an indigent alien have a good claim that the statutory structure denies her equal protection? *Compare Douglas v. California,* 372 U.S. 353, 83 S.Ct. 814, 9 L.Ed.2d 811 (1963) (State must provide attorney for indigent defendant for first appeal after a criminal conviction) *and Boddie v. Connecticut,* 401 U.S. 371, 91 S.Ct. 780, 28 L.Ed.2d 113 (1971) (State cannot require court fees and costs in order to sue for divorce) *with United States v. Kras,* 409 U.S. 434, 93 S.Ct. 631, 34 L.Ed.2d 626 (1973) (upholding $50 fee for discharge in bankruptcy) *and Ortwein v. Schwab,* 410 U.S. 656, 93 S.Ct. 1172, 35 L.Ed.2d 572 (1973) (*per curiam*) (upholding $25 filing fee for indigent seeking judicial review of reduction in welfare payments). *See The Supreme Court, 1980 Term,* 95 Harv.L.Rev. 91, 139–42 (1981).

3. Can a court exercise reasonable review of the immigration judge's case-by-case determination of whether counsel was needed at the hearing? How can a court rely on the record established at a hearing *without a lawyer* to answer the question of whether a lawyer was needed at that hearing?

Consider the remarks of Professor Yale Kamisar on *Lassiter:*

I cringe a bit when a court says, as the *Lassiter* Court did—on the basis of a record made *without* the assistance of counsel—that "the case presented no especially troublesome points of law, either procedural or substantive." * * * [A] record made *without* the assistance of counsel cannot establish that. It can only *fail* to establish *on its face* that the defendant was not seriously disadvantaged. What does it prove that the record reads well? How would it have read if the defendant had had counsel? What facts might have been uncovered if competent investigations had been made? What defenses might have been advanced if competent legal research had been done? We do not know—at least we cannot be sure.[64]

4. Note Judge DeMascio's statement in footnote 6 of his dissent that "an alien who enters illegally is entitled to less due process [than a resident alien], if any at all." (You will recall that Justice Harlan in *The Japanese Immigrant Case* makes a similar suggestion.) What do these dicta mean?

5. Is it possible to identify particular types of deportation cases in which counsel should automatically be appointed—*e.g.*, claims of U.S. citizenship, permanent residence, or asylum? *See* Appleman, *Right To Counsel in Deportation Proceedings*, 14 San Diego L.Rev. 130 (1976); Black, *Due Process and Deportation—Is There a Right to Assigned Counsel?, supra;* Haney, *Deportation and the Right to Counsel*, 11 Harv.Int'l. L.J. 177 (1970) (arguing for unqualified right to counsel in deportation hearings).

(iii) Evidence: Quality

As with most administrative proceedings, the formal rules of evidence do not apply in deportation hearings. Hearsay and unauthenticated documents may be admitted if they are deemed probative and reliable by the immigration judge.[65] However, courts will occasionally order the exclusion of evidence they find to be untrustworthy or set aside a deportation order based on unauthenticated documents.[66] Why do you think that deportation hearings are not run according to the Federal Rules of Evidence? Should they be?

(iv) Evidence: Standard of Proof

What is the burden of proof at a deportation hearing and who must carry it? Section 242(b) of the INA provides, in part:

---

64. 3 J. Choper, Y. Kamisar & L. Tribe, The Supreme Court: Trends and Developments, 1980–1981, at 174–75 (1982) (emphasis in original). *See generally* Kamisar, *The Right to Counsel and the Fourteenth Amendment: A Dialogue on "The Most Pervasive Right" of an Accused*, 30 U.Chi.L.Rev. 1 (1962).

65. *See, e.g.,* Guzman-Guzman v. INS, 559 F.2d 1149, 1150 (9th Cir.1977) (written statements of aliens admissible at deportation of another alien; statements not "so infirm as to be unable to clear" the "modest" standard of fundamental fairness and probativeness); *Trias-Hernandez v. INS*, 528 F.2d 366 (9th Cir.1975) (holding admissible form written by INS official recording statements of alien). The regulations establish authentica-

tion procedures for official records. 8 C.F.R. § 287.6. However, one court has held the rules to be "permissive," not mandatory. *Hoonsilapa v. INS*, 575 F.2d 735, 738 (9th Cir.1978), *amended* 586 F.2d 755.

66. *See, e.g., Baliza v. INS*, 709 F.2d 1231 (9th Cir.1983) (ruling inadmissible affidavit of alien's ex-wife where INS neither authenticated the document nor attempted to locate witness prior to deportation hearing); *Iran v. INS*, 656 F.2d 469 (9th Cir.1981) (ruling inadmissible unauthenticated INS form and letter from consulate); *McNeil v. Kennedy*, 298 F.2d 323 (D.C.Cir.1962) (per curiam) (setting aside deportation based solely on "unverified and unauthenticated" documents relating to birthplace of alien).

Proceedings before a special inquiry officer [immigration judge] acting under the provisions of this section shall be in accordance with such regulations, not inconsistent with this [Act], as the Attorney General shall prescribe. Such regulations shall include requirements that—

* * *

(4) no decision of deportability shall be valid unless it is based upon reasonable, substantial and probative evidence.

Does this provision establish the standard of proof that an immigration judge must apply in a deportation proceeding or the standard for judicial review of a deportation decision?

The Supreme Court answered this question in the following opinion.

WOODBY v. IMMIGRATION AND NATURALIZATION SERVICE

Supreme Court of the United States, 1966.
385 U.S. 276, 87 S.Ct. 483, 17 L.Ed.2d 362.

MR. JUSTICE STEWART delivered the opinion of the Court.

The question presented by these cases is what burden of proof the Government must sustain in deportation proceedings. We have concluded that it is incumbent upon the Government in such proceedings to establish the facts supporting deportability by clear, unequivocal, and convincing evidence.

* * *

* * * [T]he petitioner is a resident alien who was born in Hungary and entered the United States from Germany in 1956 as the wife of an American soldier. Deportation proceedings were instituted against her on the ground that she had engaged in prostitution after entry. A special inquiry officer and the Board of Immigration Appeals found that she was deportable upon the ground charged.

At the administrative hearing the petitioner admitted that she had engaged in prostitution for a brief period in 1957, some months after her husband had deserted her, but claimed that her conduct was the product of circumstances amounting to duress. Without reaching the validity of the duress defense, the special inquiry officer and the Board of Immigration Appeals concluded that the petitioner had continued to engage in prostitution after the alleged duress had terminated. The hearing officer and the Board did not discuss what burden of proof the Government was required to bear in establishing deportability, nor did either of them indicate the degree of certainty with which their factual conclusions were reached. The special inquiry officer merely asserted that the evidence demonstrated that the petitioner was deportable. The Board stated that the evidence made it "apparent" that the petitioner had engaged in prostitution after the alleged duress had ended, and announced that "it is concluded that the evidence establishes deportability ...."

In denying a petition for review, the Court of Appeals for the Sixth Circuit did not explicitly deal with the issue of what burden of persuasion was imposed upon the Government at the administrative level, finding only that "the Board's underlying order is 'supported by reasonable, substantial, and probative evidence on the record considered as a whole ....'" We granted certiorari, 384 U.S. 904.

In the prevailing opinion in [a companion case, *Sherman v. INS,* 350 F.2d 894 (2d Cir.1965)], the Court of Appeals for the Second Circuit stated that "[i]f the slate were clean," it "might well agree that the standard of persuasion for deportation should be similar to that in denaturalization, where the Supreme Court has insisted that the evidence must be 'clear, unequivocal, and convincing' and that the Government needs 'more than a bare preponderance of the evidence' to prevail. ... But here," the court thought, "Congress has spoken ...." 350 F.2d at 900. This view was based upon two provisions of the Immigration and Nationality Act which use the language "reasonable, substantial, and probative evidence" in connection with deportation orders. The provisions in question are § 106(a)(4) of the Act which states that a deportation order, "if supported by reasonable, substantial, and probative evidence on the record considered as a whole, shall be conclusive," and § 242(b)(4) of the Act which provides *inter alia* that "no decision of deportability shall be valid unless it is based upon reasonable, substantial, and probative evidence."

It seems clear, however, that these two statutory provisions are addressed not to the degree of proof required at the administrative level in deportation proceedings, but to quite a different subject—the scope of judicial review. The elementary but crucial difference between burden of proof and scope of review is, of course, a commonplace in the law. The difference is most graphically illustrated in a criminal case. There the prosecution is generally required to prove the elements of the offense beyond a reasonable doubt. But if the correct burden of proof was imposed at the trial, judicial review is generally limited to ascertaining whether the evidence relied upon by the trier of fact was of sufficient quality and substantiality to support the rationality of the judgment. In other words, an appellate court in a criminal case ordinarily does not ask itself whether it believes that the evidence at the trial established guilt beyond a reasonable doubt, but whether the judgment is supported by substantial evidence.

That § 106(a)(4) relates exclusively to judicial review is made abundantly clear by its language, its context, and its legislative history. Section 106 was added to the Act in 1961 in order "to create a single, separate, statutory form of judicial review of administrative orders for the deportation and exclusion of aliens from the United States." The section is entitled "Judicial Review of Orders of Deportation and Exclusion," and by its terms provides "the sole and exclusive procedure for" the "judicial review of all final orders of deportation." Subsection 106(a)(4) is a specific directive to the courts in which petitions for review are filed.

It is hardly less clear that the other provision upon which the Court of Appeals for the Second Circuit relied, § 242(b)(4) of the Act, is also addressed to reviewing courts, and, insofar as it represents a yardstick for the administrative factfinder, goes, not to the burden of proof, but rather to the quality and nature of the evidence upon which a deportation order must be based. The provision declares that "reasonable, substantial, and probative evidence" shall be the measure of whether a deportability decision is "valid"—a word that implies scrutiny by a reviewing tribunal of a decision already reached by the trier of the facts. The location of this provision in a section containing provisions dealing with procedures before the special inquiry officer has little significance when it is remembered that the original 1952 Act did not itself contain a framework for judicial review—although such review was, of course, available by habeas corpus or otherwise. And whatever ambiguity might be thought to lie in the location of this section is resolved by its legislative history. The Senate Report explained § 242(b)(4) as follows: "The requirement that the decision of the special inquiry officer shall be based on reasonable, substantial and probative evidence means that, where the decision rests upon evidence of such a nature that it cannot be said that a reasonable person might not have reached the conclusion which was reached, the case may not be reversed because the judgment of the appellate body differs from that of the administrative body."

We conclude, therefore, that Congress has not addressed itself to the question of what degree of proof is required in deportation proceedings. It is the kind of question which has traditionally been left to the judiciary to resolve, and its resolution is necessary in the interest of the evenhanded administration of the Immigration and Nationality Act.

The petitioners urge that the appropriate burden of proof in deportation proceedings should be that which the law imposes in criminal cases—the duty of proving the essential facts beyond a reasonable doubt. The Government, on the other hand, points out that a deportation proceeding is not a criminal case, and that the appropriate burden of proof should consequently be the one generally imposed in civil cases and administrative proceedings—the duty of prevailing by a mere preponderance of the evidence.

To be sure, a deportation proceeding is not a criminal prosecution. *Harisiades v. Shaughnessy,* 342 U.S. 580, 72 S.Ct. 512, 96 L.Ed. 586. But it does not syllogistically follow that a person may be banished from this country upon no higher degree of proof than applies in a negligence case. This Court has not closed its eyes to the drastic deprivations that may follow when a resident of this country is compelled by our Government to forsake all the bonds formed here and go to a foreign land where he often has no contemporary identification. * * *

In denaturalization cases the Court has required the Government to establish its allegations by clear, unequivocal, and convincing evidence. The same burden has been imposed in expatriation cases. That standard of proof is no stranger to the civil law.[18]

---

18. This standard, or an even higher one, has traditionally been imposed in cases involving allegations of civil fraud, and in a variety of other kinds of civil cases involving such issues as adultery, illegitimacy of a child born in wedlock, lost wills, oral con-

No less a burden of proof is appropriate in deportation proceedings. The immediate hardship of deportation is often greater than that inflicted by denaturalization, which does not, immediately at least, result in expulsion from our shores. And many resident aliens have lived in this country longer and established stronger family, social, and economic ties here than some who have become naturalized citizens.

We hold that no deportation order may be entered unless it is found by clear, unequivocal, and convincing evidence that the facts alleged as grounds for deportation are true.[19] Accordingly, in each of the cases before us, the judgment of the Court of Appeals is set aside, and the case is remanded with directions to remand to the Immigration and Naturalization Service for such further proceedings as, consistent with this opinion, may be deemed appropriate.

It is so ordered.

MR. JUSTICE CLARK, whom MR. JUSTICE HARLAN joins, dissenting.

The Court, by placing a higher standard of proof on the Government, in deportation cases, has usurped the legislative function of the Congress and has in one fell swoop repealed the long-established "reasonable, substantial, and probative" burden of proof placed on the Government by specific Act of the Congress, and substituted its own "clear, unequivocal, and convincing" standard. This is but another case in a long line in which the Court has tightened the noose around the Government's neck in immigration cases.

I.

I agree that § 106(a)(4), the 1961 amendment to the Immigration and Nationality Act of 1952, relates to judicial review of administrative orders of the Immigration Service but, with due deference, I cannot see how "It is hardly less clear" that § 242(b)(4) of the Act, as the Court says, likewise applies exclusively to judicial review. Indeed, on the contrary, the latter section was specifically enacted as the only standard of proof to be applied in deportation cases.

Before § 242(b) was enacted the immigration laws contained no detailed provision concerning the burden of proof in deportation cases. In *Wong Yang Sung v. McGrath*, 339 U.S. 33, 70 S.Ct. 445, 94 L.Ed. 616 (1950), this Court extended the provisions of the Administrative Procedure Act to deportation proceedings. Congress immediately exempted such proceedings from the Administrative Procedure Act and in 1952 established in § 242(b) an exclusive procedural system for deportation proceedings.

In essence that section, § 242(b), provides for notice and a hearing before a "special inquiry officer" of the Immigration Service; sets the

tracts to make bequests, and the like. See 9 Wigmore, Evidence § 2498 (3d ed. 1940).

19. This standard of proof applies to all deportation cases, regardless of the length of time the alien has resided in this country. It is perhaps worth pointing out, however, that, as a practical matter, the more recent the alleged events supporting deportability, the more readily the Government will generally be able to prove its allegations by clear, unequivocal, and convincing evidence.

standard of proof in such cases as "reasonable, substantial, and probative evidence"; and authorizes the Attorney General to issue regulations. In issuing those regulations the Attorney General established a Board of Immigration Appeals. The Board's relationship to the orders of the special inquiry officer is similar to the relationship an agency has to the orders of a hearing examiner under the Administrative Procedure Act. The section also specifically provides that the regulations shall include requirements that "no decision of deportability shall be valid unless it is based upon reasonable, substantial, and probative evidence" and that this standard shall be the "sole and exclusive procedure for determining the deportability of an alien under this section." This was the first time in our history that Congress had expressly placed a specific standard of proof on the Government in deportation cases. And the language Congress used made it clear that this standard related to the "burden of proof" as well as "the quality and nature of the evidence." The requirement of "reasonable" evidence cannot be meant merely to exclude "unreasonable" or "irrational" evidence but carries the obvious connotation from history and tradition of sufficiency to sustain a conclusion by a preponderance of the evidence.[1] Congress in overruling *Wong Yang Sung, supra,* carved deportation proceedings from the judicial overtones of the Administrative Procedure Act and established a *built-in* administrative procedure.

This is made crystal clear by the reports of both Houses of Congress on § 242(b). The Committee Reports, S.Rep. No. 1137, 82d Cong., 2d Sess., 30; H.R.Rep. No. 1365, 82d Cong., 2d Sess., 57, state in simple, understandable language that:

> "The requirement that the decision of the special inquiry officer shall be based on reasonable, substantial, and probative evidence means that, where the decision rests upon evidence of such a nature that it cannot be said that a reasonable person might not have reached the conclusion which was reached, the case may not be reversed because the judgment of the appellate body differs from that below."

The courts consistently applied the standard of "reasonable, substantial and probative" evidence after the adoption of § 242(b).

The Court, however, in *Shaughnessy v. Pedreiro,* 349 U.S. 48, 75 S.Ct. 591, 99 L.Ed. 868 (1955), once again extended the Administrative Procedure Act's provision respecting judicial review to deportation cases. The reaction of the Congress was identical to that of 1952 when it overruled *Wong Yang Sung, supra.* It enacted, in 1961, § 106(a)(4) of the Act. Just as § 242(b) was the first statutory standard of proof, § 106(a)(4) was the first express statutory standard of judicial review. It provided:

> "... the petition [for review] shall be determined solely upon the administrative record upon which the deportation order is based and

---

1. Thus the judicial review provision of the Administrative Procedure Act, 5 U.S.C. § 1009(e)(5), limits the scope of review to a determination of support by "substantial evidence," and 5 U.S.C. § 1006 limits the agen- cies to acting on "reliable, probative, and substantial evidence." This pattern has traditionally been held satisfied when the agency decides on the preponderance of the evidence.

the Attorney General's findings of fact, if supported by reasonable, substantial, and probative evidence on the record considered as a whole, shall be conclusive."

Why Congress passed § 106(a)(4) if judicial review, as the Court holds, was already exclusively covered by § 242(b) is beyond my comprehension—unless it was engaged in shadow boxing. I cannot believe that it was.

The Court says that both the special inquiry officer and the Board of Immigration Appeals failed to state what the burden of proof was in these cases. Fault is found in the officer's use of the phrase "solidarity" of proof "far greater than required." This language was apparently patterned after this Court's opinion in *Rowoldt* [*v. Perfetto*, 355 U.S. 115, 78 S.Ct. 180, 2 L.Ed.2d 140 (1957)], where the phrase "solidity of proof" was used. The findings of both the officers and the Board in these cases show specifically that the burden of proof followed in each case was that required of the Government in § 242(b) and the Regulations of the Attorney General, *i.e.,* by "reasonable, substantial, and probative evidence." This standard has been administratively followed by the Immigration Service in a long and unbroken line of cases.

The Court now extends the standard of *Schneiderman v. United States,* 320 U.S. 118, 63 S.Ct. 1333, 87 L.Ed. 1796 (1943), in denaturalization cases, *i.e.,* "clear, unequivocal, and convincing evidence," to deportation cases. But denaturalization and expatriation are much more oppressive cases than deportation. They deprive one of citizenship which the United States had previously conferred. The *Schneiderman* rule only follows the principle that vested rights can be canceled only upon clear, unequivocal, and convincing proof; it gives stability and finality to a most precious right—citizenship. An alien, however, does not enjoy citizenship but only a conditional privilege extended to him by the Congress as a matter of grace. Both petitioners, the record shows, knew this, yet they remained in this country for years. * * * Still, neither made any effort to obtain citizenship.

* * *

I regret that my powers of persuasion with my Brethren are not sufficient to prevent this encroachment upon the function of the Congress which will place an undue and unintended burden upon the Government in deportation cases. I dissent.

Notes

1. Is *Woodby* a constitutional decision, or may Congress establish a lower standard of proof in deportation proceedings—*e.g.,* "preponderance of the evidence"?[67] *Compare Vance v. Terrazas,* 444 U.S. 252, 100 S.Ct. 540, 62 L.Ed.2d 461 (1980) (upholding preponderance of the evidence standard in expatriation proceeding; Court states *Woodby* did not purport to be constitutional holding) *with Santosky v. Kramer,* 455 U.S. 745, 102

---

67. The Senate version of the Simpson-Mazzoli bill would have adopted this lower standard. *See* S. 529, § 122(d).

S.Ct. 1388, 71 L.Ed.2d 599 (1982) (due process clause of Fourteenth Amendment requires clear and convincing evidence standard in proceeding to terminate parental rights; *Woodby* seemingly characterized as case based on constitutional notions of fundamental fairness).

2. Where does the majority's standard come from? Precedent? A cost/benefit analysis of the standard of proof in deportation proceedings? John Rawls?

3. Assuming that Congress is free to choose the standard of proof it desires and that you are a member of Congress, what standard would you support?

In thinking about this question, it is important to recognize that opting for a heightened standard of proof does more than simply ensure that fewer aliens are wrongfully deported. It also means that more aliens who should be deported will not be deported because the government will not be able to meet the higher level of proof. Justice Harlan has explained this trade-off as follows:

> In a lawsuit between two parties, a factual error can make a difference in one of two ways. First, it can result in a judgment in favor of the plaintiff when the true facts warrant a judgment for the defendant. The analogue in a criminal case would be the conviction of an innocent man. On the other hand, an erroneous factual determination can result in a judgment for the defendant when the true facts justify a judgment in plaintiff's favor. The criminal analogue would be the acquittal of a guilty man.
>
> The standard of proof influences the relative frequency of these two types of erroneous outcomes. If, for example, the standard of proof for a criminal trial were a preponderance of the evidence rather than proof beyond a reasonable doubt, there would be a smaller risk of factual errors that result in freeing guilty persons, but a far greater risk of factual errors that result in convicting the innocent. Because the standard of proof affects the comparative frequency of these two types of erroneous outcomes, the choice of the standard to be applied in a particular kind of litigation should, in a rational world, reflect an assessment of the comparative social disutility of each.

In re Winship, 397 U.S. 358, 370–71, 90 S.Ct. 1068, 1075–76, 25 L.Ed.2d 368 (1970) (Harlan, J., concurring).

How would you allocate the risk of error in the deportation context? Making a reasonable decision requires consideration of a number of issues, including: (1) by how much will wrongful non-deportations increase and proper non-deportations decrease by imposition of a higher standard of proof?; (2) how do we value a wrongful deportation as compared to a wrongful non-deportation?; and (3) how might other procedural protections—such as provision of counsel—affect the error rate?

The *Woodby* Standard in Action

A major distinction between exclusion and deportation proceedings, it is often said, is that the alien has the burden of proof in the former while the government has the burden of proof in the latter. INA § 291. This difference, while important, oversimplifies. As *Woodby* makes clear, the government must meet a high burden of proof in a deportation proceeding. But the statute specifically places upon the alien in the hearing the burden of showing "the time, place and manner of his entry into the United States." If this burden is not sustained, the alien "shall be presumed to be in the United States in violation of law." *Id.* Generally the courts have required the government first to present a *prima facie* case of alienage, such as a foreign birth certificate or statement by the alien made at time of arrest. Once that is established, the burden is shifted to the alien to present evidence of time, place and manner of entry.

The burden shift and presumption in § 291 are particularly important in proving entry without inspection. Without these devices, the government would have to show that the alien had entered unlawfully—a task made difficult if the alien refuses to answer questions at the deportation hearing.

The effect of § 291 can be seen in the following case describing a deportation hearing where the charge was entry without inspection.

> At their deportation hearings, the petitioners admitted their true names and stipulated that the orders to show cause related to them; however, when confronted with questions regarding their nationality, places of birth and dates of birth, they claimed Fifth Amendment privileges and remained silent. At that point in both hearings, the Government offered and the Immigration Judge accepted into evidence properly authenticated Mexican birth certificates recording the births of individuals with names identical to the petitioners. The petitioners continued their silence in response to questions concerning whether the birth certificates related to them. The Government presented no further evidence.

Corona-Palomera v. INS, 661 F.2d 814, 815 (9th Cir.1981). You be the judge. Has the government met its burden of establishing deportability by clear, unequivocal and convincing evidence? (Note that there is no evidence, other than the aliens' names, linking the aliens before the judge to the particular birth certificates; nor is there any evidence about how the aliens entered the country.)

The immigration judge found the aliens deportable and the court of appeals affirmed. The court held that "identity of names [in the birth certificates and as stated at the hearing by the aliens] is sufficient to prove identity of persons where no effort is made to rebut such proof," and "[e]vidence of foreign birth gives rise to a presumption that the person so born is an alien." Therefore it was

* * * proper for the Immigration Judge to have shifted the burden to petitioners for them to demonstrate the time, place, and manner of their entry into the United States per [INA § 291]. At that point, the additional presumption of illegal entry was in existence by virtue of [§ 291] and it remained unrebutted.

* * *

Based upon the foregoing, it is our view that the record contains reasonable, substantial, and probative evidence to support the Immigration Judge's determination of deportability.

Id. at 816, 818.[68]

Are you persuaded? Has the government proved *anything* here? Are the various presumptions applied by the court consistent with the letter or spirit of *Woodby*? Does this case demonstrate a better appreciation of the reality of the immigration process than the Supreme Court demonstrates in *Woodby*?

Suppose the aliens in the above case had refused to state their names? What result?

Silence and Adverse Inferences

May an immigration judge draw an "adverse inference" from the refusal of an alien to respond to questions? Justice Brandeis, writing for the Court in *United States ex rel. Bilokumsky v. Tod*, 263 U.S. 149, 153–54, 44 S.Ct. 54, 55–56, 68 L.Ed. 221 (1923), gave the classic answer: "Conduct which forms a basis for inference is evidence. Silence is often evidence of the most persuasive character. * * * [T]here is no rule of law which prohibits officers charged with the administration of the immigration law from drawing an inference from the silence of one who is called upon to speak." *See Vajtauer v. Commissioner*, 273 U.S. 103, 111–12, 47 S.Ct. 302, 305–306, 71 L.Ed. 560 (1927).

Aliens have the right to refuse to answer questions based upon a claim of Fifth Amendment privilege.[69] (Note that unlawful entry is a criminal offense as well as ground for deportation. INA § 275.) Can an adverse inference be drawn from an assertion of Fifth Amendment rights? In *Cabral-Avila v. INS*, 589 F.2d 957, 959 (9th Cir.1968), *cert. denied* 440 U.S. 920, 99 S.Ct. 1245, 59 L.Ed.2d 472 (1979), the court held:

---

68. The Ninth Circuit has limited the presumption of § 291 to deportation proceedings involving a charge of illegal entry. Thus, it was held not applicable to proceedings charging a nonimmigrant alien with staying beyond the time period authorized for his visit. *Iran v. INS*, 656 F.2d 469 (9th Cir.1981). The BIA has rejected the Ninth Circuit's reading of the statute, concluding that "the burden and presumption of Section 291 of the Act are applicable with respect to any charge of deportability which draws into question the time, place, or manner of the alien's entry into the United States." The

Board has therefore refused to apply *Iran* outside the circuit in which it was decided. *Matter of Benitez*, Interim Dec. No. 2979 (BIA 1984) (deportation under INA § 241(a)(1) of stowaway).

69. Statements made by aliens who have been ordered to respond after asserting a Fifth Amendment privilege in a deportation hearing may not be used to establish the alien's deportability. *Tashnizi v. INS*, 585 F.2d 781, 782 (5th Cir.1978) (per curiam); *Valeros v. INS*, 387 F.2d 921, 922 (7th Cir. 1967).

Petitioners' decision to remain mute during the deportability phase of the hearing was an appropriate exercise of their Fifth Amendment privilege, but by doing so they do not shield themselves from the drawing of adverse inferences that they are not legally in this country and their silence cannot be relied upon to carry forward their duty to rebut the Government's *prima facie* case.

This conclusion has been criticized. *See, e.g.,* G & R § 5.10c; *Developments,* 96 Harv.L.Rev., at 1388–89. Yet the commentators appeared not to be aware of *Baxter v. Palmigiano,* 425 U.S. 308, 316–20, 96 S.Ct. 1551, 1557–59, 47 L.Ed.2d 810 (1976), which allowed the drawing of an adverse inference from a prisoner's silence after invocation of the Fifth Amendment in a prison disciplinary proceeding. *See generally* R. Heidt, *The Conjurer's Circle: The Fifth Amendment Privilege in Civil Cases,* 91 Yale L.J. 1062, 1109–14 (1982).

(v) Evidence: Fifth and Fourth Amendment Exclusionary Rules

Fifth Amendment: "Miranda Warnings"

In three situations during the deportation process, aliens must be informed of the nature of the deportation charges and told that anything they say may be used against them: (1) when served with an order to show cause, 8 C.F.R. § 242.1(c); (2) when arrested after the initiation of a deportation proceeding, 8 C.F.R. § 242.2(a); and (3) after arrest and a determination by an immigration officer to initiate deportation proceedings. 8 C.F.R. § 287.3.

A careful look at these regulations reveals a gap in coverage. If an alien is arrested without a warrant and brought to an INS district office for questioning before an order to show cause is issued, he will not be immediately advised of his rights. This is not the way things always were.

In 1967, INS amended its regulations to require that aliens arrested without a warrant be given advice of their rights. 32 Fed.Reg. 6260 (April 21, 1967). In 1979, the regulations were amended to push back the time for advice of rights until "[a]fter the examining officer has determined that formal [exclusion or deportation hearings] will be instituted." 44 Fed.Reg. 4654 (Jan. 23, 1979). The gain to law enforcement occasioned by this change should be obvious. Aliens interrogated by INS officials without being told that they may be represented by a lawyer or that anything they say may be used against them often admit alienage, unlawful entry, unauthorized employment or other facts which provide the basis for a deportation charge. Such admissions may also serve as crucial (if not the only) evidence in the deportation proceeding, particularly when an alien refuses to answer questions in that setting.[70] The position of the INS is that valuable, reliable evidence would be lost if an

---

70. *See, e.g., Trias-Hernandez v. INS,* 528 F.2d 366, 368 (9th Cir.1975) (under facts of the case, impossible to prove deportability for illegal entry without statements made by alien following arrest).

alien were given warnings or if a lawyer were present during the initial interrogation.

The 1979 change in the regulations brought vociferous objections from immigration attorneys. The INS responded:

> There is no statutory or constitutional mandate that advice be given to an alien during his interrogation. To safeguard the alien's procedural due process right, the advice concerning his right to counsel, including free legal services will be given to the alien at that stage in the interrogation when the immigration officer has determined that formal proceedings will be instituted.

44 Fed.Reg. 4652 (Jan. 23, 1979). Are you satisfied with this response? Do you support the present regulation? If not, what rule would you propose that adequately balances the alien's interest in a fair proceeding and the government's interest in efficient and effective law enforcement?

Under the famous *Miranda* case,[71] failure to inform the individual of her rights renders any statements she makes during a custodial interrogation inadmissible in her criminal trial. The courts have not read the Constitution to require such warnings in the deportation context, and failure to give warnings will not produce automatic exclusion of the alien's admissions. *E.g., United States v. Alderete-Deras,* 743 F.2d 645 (9th Cir.1984); *Chavez-Raya v. INS,* 519 F.2d 397 (7th Cir.1975); *Matter of Baltazar,* 16 I & N Dec. 108 (BIA 1977).[72] Important to this conclusion is the description of deportation proceedings as "civil," as well as the following considerations:

> A principal purpose of the *Miranda* warnings is to permit the suspect to make an intelligent decision as to whether to answer the government agent's questions. In deportation proceedings, however—in light of the alien's burden of proof, the requirement that the alien answer non-incriminating questions, the potential adverse consequences to the alien of remaining silent, and the fact that an alien's statement is admissible in the deportation hearing despite his lack of counsel at the preliminary interrogation—*Miranda* warnings would be not only inappropriate but could also serve to mislead the alien.

Chavez-Raya v. INS, 519 F.2d at 402. Do you find this explanation satisfactory? Can you fashion "warnings" that would inform the alien of his rights *and* obligations without confusing him? Does it not seem that the court, in guise of protecting the alien, is actually adopting a rule precisely to ensure more deportations?

Although the bright-line test of *Miranda* does not apply, the courts and the BIA will occasionally order the exclusion of prior statements on due process ground where they conclude that the circumstances surrounding the alien interrogation rendered the statements "involuntary." *See,*

---

71. *Miranda v. Arizona,* 384 U.S. 436, 86 S.Ct. 1602, 16 L.Ed.2d 694 (1966).

72. Of course, such statements could be excluded from subsequent criminal proceed-

ings. *See, e.g., United States v. Segovia-Melgar,* 595 F.Supp. 753 (D.D.C.1984).

e.g., Matter of Garcia, 17 I & N Dec. 319 (BIA 1980). The following excerpt describes one such situation where evidence was ordered excluded.

[I]t appears that early in the evening of January 13, 1974, two of the appellant's [Ms. Navia-Duran's] housemates were detained by INS agents at a Boston restaurant, questioned about their alien status, and taken to their residence to get their identification papers. Ms. Navia-Duran's roommate, who was at home when the group arrived, was also questioned. The agents searched the apartment, including the appellant's bedroom, without warrant or consent, and allegedly seized some papers. Two of the three aliens were taken to INS offices, served with orders to show cause why they should not be deported, and held overnight in jail.

Later that same night, at approximately 10 p.m., Ms. Navia-Duran was approached from behind as she was about to enter her apartment. Without addressing her by name, a man identified himself as an INS agent and asked if she spoke English. Ms. Navia-Duran responded that she spoke Spanish. The agent requested identification, which she said was inside the apartment. Extremely frightened by this late-night approach and convinced that she had no choice but to cooperate, Ms. Navia-Duran opened her door and was followed in by this agent and by a second man who identified himself as Mr. Constance. Ms. Navia-Duran produced numerous documents, all of which were confiscated. The agents questioned her in Spanish for approximately one hour concerning her presence in the United States. During this period, Agent Constance told Ms. Navia-Duran that she must return to her native Chile immediately.

At approximately 11:30 p.m., the agents took Ms. Navia-Duran to the INS office and continued questioning her until 2 a.m. Constance showed her a calendar and told her that she must leave the country in two weeks. When the appellant protested that she needed more time, the agent reiterated that she must leave in two weeks; he characterized his offer as a fair deal for her. Throughout the early morning session, Constance insisted that she had no choice but to accept the two-week departure deadline. Fearing that she would not be permitted to go home until she cooperated, Ms. Navia-Duran signed a statement which admitted that she had entered this country on a three-month visitor's visa in 1974 and had never received an extension of time.

Navia-Duran v. INS, 568 F.2d 803, 805 (1st Cir.1977).

Does the "due process" test, by being more flexible, provide a better accommodation between law enforcement needs and the rights of aliens than application of a strict *Miranda* rule?

Fourth Amendment

Should evidence seized in violation of the Fourth Amendment be admissible in deportation hearings?

INS v. LOPEZ–MENDOZA

Supreme Court of the United States, 1984.
—— U.S. ——, 104 S.Ct. 3479, 82 L.Ed.2d 778.

JUSTICE O'CONNOR delivered the opinion of the Court.[†]

This litigation requires us to decide whether an admission of unlawful presence in this country made subsequent to an allegedly unlawful arrest must be excluded as evidence in a civil deportation hearing. We hold that the exclusionary rule need not be applied in such a proceeding.

I

Respondents Adan Lopez-Mendoza and Elias Sandoval-Sanchez, both citizens of Mexico, were summoned to separate deportation proceedings in California and Washington, and both were ordered deported. They challenged the regularity of those proceedings on grounds related to the lawfulness of their respective arrests by officials of the Immigration and Naturalization Service (INS). On administrative appeal the Board of Immigration Appeals (BIA), an agency of the Department of Justice, affirmed the deportation orders.

The Court of Appeals for the Ninth Circuit, sitting en banc, reversed Sandoval's deportation order and vacated and remanded Lopez-Mendoza's deportation order. 705 F.2d 1059 (1983). It ruled that Sandoval's admission of his illegal presence in this country was the fruit of an unlawful arrest, and that the exclusionary rule applied in a deportation proceeding. Lopez-Mendoza's deportation order was vacated and his case remanded to the BIA to determine whether the Fourth Amendment had been violated in the course of his arrest. We granted certiorari, 464 U.S. ——, 104 S.Ct. 697, 79 L.Ed.2d 163 (1984).

A

Respondent Lopez-Mendoza was arrested in 1976 by INS agents at his place of employment, a transmission repair shop in San Mateo, Cal. Responding to a tip, INS investigators arrived at the shop shortly before 8 a.m. The agents had not sought a warrant to search the premises or to arrest any of its occupants. The proprietor of the shop firmly refused to allow the agents to interview his employees during working hours. Nevertheless, while one agent engaged the proprietor in conversation another entered the shop and approached Lopez-Mendoza. In response to the agent's questioning, Lopez-Mendoza gave his name and indicated that he was from Mexico with no close family ties in the United States. The agent then placed him under arrest. Lopez-Mendoza underwent further questioning at INS offices, where he admitted he was born in Mexico, was still a citizen of Mexico, and had entered this country without inspection by immigration authorities. Based on his answers, the agents prepared a "Record of Deportable Alien" (Form I–213), and an affidavit which Lopez-

[†] THE CHIEF JUSTICE joins all but Part V of this opinion.

Mendoza executed, admitting his Mexican nationality and his illegal entry into this country.

* * *

B

Respondent Sandoval-Sanchez * * * was arrested in 1977 at his place of employment, a potato processing plant in Pasco, Wash. INS Agent Bower and other officers went to the plant, with the permission of its personnel manager, to check for illegal aliens. During a change in shift, officers stationed themselves at the exits while Bower and a uniformed Border Patrol agent entered the plant. They went to the lunchroom and identified themselves as immigration officers. Many people in the room rose and headed for the exits or milled around; others in the plant left their equipment and started running; still others who were entering the plant turned around and started walking back out. The two officers eventually stationed themselves at the main entrance to the plant and looked for passing employees who averted their heads, avoided eye contact, or tried to hide themselves in a group. Those individuals were addressed with innocuous questions in English. Any who could not respond in English and who otherwise aroused Agent Bower's suspicions were questioned in Spanish as to their right to be in the United States.

Respondent Sandoval-Sanchez was in a line of workers entering the plant. Sandoval-Sanchez testified that he did not realize that immigration officers were checking people entering the plant, but that he did see standing at the plant entrance a man in uniform who appeared to be a police officer. Agent Bower testified that it was probable that he, not his partner, had questioned Sandoval-Sanchez at the plant, but that he could not be absolutely positive. The employee he thought he remembered as Sandoval-Sanchez had been "very evasive," had averted his head, turned around, and walked away when he saw Agent Bower. Bower was certain that no one was questioned about his status unless his actions had given the agents reason to believe that he was an undocumented alien.

Thirty-seven employees, including Sandoval-Sanchez, were briefly detained at the plant and then taken to the county jail. About one-third immediately availed themselves of the option of voluntary departure and were put on a bus to Mexico. Sandoval-Sanchez exercised his right to a deportation hearing. Sandoval-Sanchez was then questioned further, and Agent Bower recorded Sandoval-Sanchez's admission of unlawful entry.
* * *

* * *

II

A deportation proceeding is a purely civil action to determine eligibility to remain in this country, not to punish an unlawful entry, though entering or remaining unlawfully in this country is itself a crime. INA §§ 262, 266, 275. The deportation hearing looks prospectively, to the respondent's right to remain in this country in the future. Past conduct is relevant only insofar as it may shed light on the respondent's right to remain.

A deportation hearing is held before an immigration judge. The judge's sole power is to order deportation; the judge cannot adjudicate guilt or punish the respondent for any crime related to unlawful entry into or presence in this country. Consistent with the civil nature of the proceeding, various protections that apply in the context of a criminal trial do not apply in a deportation hearing. * * * [A] deportation hearing is intended to provide a streamlined determination of eligibility to remain in this country, nothing more. The purpose of deportation is not to punish past transgressions but rather to put an end to a continuing violation of the immigration laws.

III

The "body" or identity of a defendant or respondent in a criminal or civil proceeding is never itself suppressible as a fruit of an unlawful arrest, even if it is conceded that an unlawful arrest, search, or interrogation occurred. * * *

On this basis alone the Court of Appeals' decision as to respondent Lopez must be reversed. At his deportation hearing Lopez objected only to the fact that he had been summoned to a deportation hearing following an unlawful arrest; he entered no objection to the evidence offered against him. The BIA correctly ruled that "[t]he mere fact of an illegal arrest has no bearing on a subsequent deportation proceeding."

IV

Respondent Sandoval has a more substantial claim. He objected not to his compelled presence at a deportation proceeding, but to evidence offered at that proceeding. The general rule in a criminal proceeding is that statements and other evidence obtained as a result of an unlawful, warrantless arrest are suppressible if the link between the evidence and the unlawful conduct is not too attenuated. *Wong Sun* v. *United States,* 371 U.S. 471, 83 S.Ct. 407, 9 L.Ed.2d 441 (1963). The reach of the exclusionary rule beyond the context of a criminal prosecution, however, is less clear. Although this Court has once stated in dictum that "[i]t may be assumed that evidence obtained by the [Labor] Department through an illegal search and seizure cannot be made the basis of a finding in deportation proceedings," *United States ex rel. Bilokumsky* v. *Tod, supra,* 263 U.S., at 155, 44 S.Ct., at 56, the Court has never squarely addressed the question before. Lower court decisions dealing with this question are sparse.

In *United States* v. *Janis,* 428 U.S. 433, 96 S.Ct. 3021, 49 L.Ed.2d 1046 (1976), this Court set forth a framework for deciding in what types of proceeding application of the exclusionary rule is appropriate. Imprecise as the exercise may be, the Court recognized in *Janis* that there is no choice but to weigh the likely social benefits of excluding unlawfully seized evidence against the likely costs. On the benefit side of the balance "the 'prime purpose' of the [exclusionary] rule, if not the sole one, 'is to deter future unlawful police conduct.'" *Id.,* at 446, 96 S.Ct., at 3028, citing *United States* v. *Calandra,* 414 U.S. 338, 347, 94 S.Ct. 613, 619, 38 L.Ed.2d 561 (1974). On the cost side there is the loss of often probative evidence and all of the secondary costs that flow from the less accurate or more cumbersome adjudication that therefore occurs.

* * *

The likely deterrence value of the exclusionary rule in deportation proceedings is difficult to assess. On the one hand, a civil deportation proceeding is a civil complement to a possible criminal prosecution * * *. The INS does not suggest that the exclusionary rule should not continue to apply in criminal proceedings against an alien who unlawfully enters or remains in this country, and the prospect of losing evidence that might otherwise be used in a criminal prosecution undoubtedly supplies some residual deterrent to unlawful conduct by INS officials. But it must be acknowledged that only a very small percentage of arrests of aliens are intended or expected to lead to criminal prosecutions. Thus the arresting officer's primary objective, in practice, will be to use evidence in the civil deportation proceeding. Moreover, * * * the agency officials who effect the unlawful arrest are the same officials who subsequently bring the deportation action. As recognized in *Janis,* the exclusionary rule is likely to be most effective when applied to such "intrasovereign" violations.

Nonetheless, several other factors significantly reduce the likely deterrent value of the exclusionary rule in a civil deportation proceeding. First, regardless of how the arrest is effected, deportation will still be possible when evidence not derived directly from the arrest is sufficient to support deportation. As the BIA has recognized, in many deportation proceedings "the sole matters necessary for the Government to establish are the respondent's identity and alienage—at which point the burden shifts to the respondent to prove the time, place and manner of entry." *Matter of Sandoval,* 17 I. & N. Dec., at 79. Since the person and identity of the respondent are not themselves suppressible, the INS must prove only alienage, and that will sometimes be possible using evidence gathered independently of, or sufficiently attenuated from, the original arrest. The INS's task is simplified in this regard by the civil nature of the proceeding. As Justice Brandeis stated: "Silence is often evidence of the most persuasive character.... [T]here is no rule of law which prohibits officers charged with the administration of the immigration law from drawing an inference from the silence of one who is called upon to speak.... A person arrested on the preliminary warrant is not protected by a presumption of citizenship comparable to the presumption of innocence in a criminal case. There is no provision which forbids drawing an adverse inference from the fact of standing mute." *United States ex rel. Bilokumsky* v. *Tod,* 263 U.S., at 153–154, 44 S.Ct., at 55–56.

The second factor is a practical one. In the course of a year the average INS agent arrests almost 500 illegal aliens. Over 97.5% apparently agree to voluntary deportation without a formal hearing. Among the remainder who do request a formal hearing (apparently a dozen or so in all, per officer, per year) very few challenge the circumstances of their

arrests. * * * Every INS agent knows, therefore, that it is highly
unlikely that any particular arrestee will end up challenging the lawfulness of his arrest in a formal deportation proceeding. When an occasional
challenge is brought, the consequences from the point of view of the
officer's overall arrest and deportation record will be trivial. In these
circumstances, the arresting officer is most unlikely to shape his conduct
in anticipation of the exclusion of evidence at a formal deportation
hearing.

Third, and perhaps most important, the INS has its own comprehensive scheme for deterring Fourth Amendment violations by its officers.
Most arrests of illegal aliens away from the border occur during farm,
factory, or other workplace surveys. Large numbers of illegal aliens are
often arrested at one time, and conditions are understandably chaotic. To
safeguard the rights of those who are lawfully present at inspected
workplaces the INS has developed rules restricting stop, interrogation,
and arrest practices. These regulations require that no one be detained
without reasonable suspicion of illegal alienage, and that no one be
arrested unless there is an admission of illegal alienage or other strong
evidence thereof. New immigration officers receive instruction and examination in Fourth Amendment law, and others receive periodic refresher
courses in law. Evidence seized through intentionally unlawful conduct is
excluded by Department of Justice policy from the proceeding for which it
was obtained. See Memorandum from Benjamin R. Civiletti to Heads of
Offices, Boards, Bureaus and Divisions, Violations of Search and Seizure
Law (Jan. 16, 1981).[a] The INS also has in place a procedure for investigating and punishing immigration officers who commit Fourth Amendment
violations. See Office of General Counsel, INS, U.S. Dept. of Justice, The
Law of Arrest, Search, and Seizure for Immigration Officers 35 (Jan.
1983). The INS's attention to Fourth Amendment interests cannot guarantee that constitutional violations will not occur, but it does reduce the
likely deterrent value of the exclusionary rule. Deterrence must be
measured at the margin.

Finally, the deterrent value of the exclusionary rule in deportation
proceedings is undermined by the availability of alternative remedies for
institutional practices by the INS that might violate Fourth Amendment
rights. The INS is a single agency, under central federal control, and
engaged in operations of broad scope but highly repetitive character. The
possibility of declaratory relief against the agency thus offers a means for
challenging the validity of INS practices, when standing requirements for
bringing such an action can be met.

Respondents [assert] that retention of the exclusionary rule is necessary to safeguard the Fourth Amendment rights of ethnic Americans,

---

a. Under the Attorney General's policy,
(1) evidence seized through an *intentional*
violation of the Fourth Amendment will be
excluded from the proceeding and the offending officer will be subject to "the highest
administrative penalties available"; (2) evidence seized by a *reckless* violation of law
will be excluded and the official will be
subject to "administrative discipline" less
stringent than that applied to intentional
violators; and (3) officials who violate the
Fourth Amendment through a negligent act
or omission will ordinarily not be subject to
administrative discipline. The policy is reprinted in 58 Interp.Rel. 18 (1981).—eds.

particularly the Hispanic-Americans lawfully in this country. We recognize that respondents raise here legitimate and important concerns. But application of the exclusionary rule to civil deportation proceedings can be justified only if the rule is likely to add significant protection to these Fourth Amendment rights. The exclusionary rule provides no remedy for completed wrongs; those lawfully in this country can be interested in its application only insofar as it may serve as an effective deterrent to future INS misconduct. For the reasons we have discussed we conclude that application of the rule in INS civil deportation proceedings, as in the circumstances discussed in *Janis,* "is unlikely to provide significant, much less substantial, additional deterrence." 428 U.S., at 458, 96 S.Ct., at 3034. Important as it is to protect the Fourth Amendment rights of all persons, there is no convincing indication that application of the exclusionary rule in civil deportation proceedings will contribute materially to that end.

On the other side of the scale, the social costs of applying the exclusionary rule in deportation proceedings are both unusual and significant. The first cost is one that is unique to continuing violations of the law. Applying the exclusionary rule in proceedings that are intended not to punish past transgressions but to prevent their continuance or renewal would require the courts to close their eyes to ongoing violations of the law. This Court has never before accepted costs of this character in applying the exclusionary rule.

* * * Sandoval is a person whose unregistered presence in this country, without more, constitutes a crime.[3] His release within our borders would immediately subject him to criminal penalties. His release would clearly frustrate the express public policy against an alien's unregistered presence in this country. Even the objective of deterring Fourth Amendment violations should not require such a result. The constable's blunder may allow the criminal to go free, but we have never suggested that it allows the criminal to continue in the commission of an ongoing crime. When the crime in question involves unlawful presence in this country, the criminal may go free, but he should not go free within our borders.

Other factors also weigh against applying the exclusionary rule in deportation proceedings. The INS currently operates a deliberately simple deportation hearing system, streamlined to permit the quick resolution of very large numbers of deportation actions, and it is against this

---

3. Sandoval was arrested on June 23, 1977. His deportation hearing was held on October 7, 1977. By that time he was under a duty to apply for registration as an alien. A failure to do so plainly constituted a continuing crime. INA §§ 262, 266. Sandoval was not, of course, prosecuted for this crime, and we do not know whether or not he did make the required application. But it is safe to assume that the exclusionary rule would never be at issue in a deportation proceeding brought against an alien who entered the country unlawfully and then voluntarily admitted to his unlawful presence in an application for registration.

Sandoval was also not prosecuted for his initial illegal entry into this country, an independent crime under INA § 275. We need not decide whether or not remaining in this country following an illegal entry is a continuing or a completed crime under § 275. The question is academic, of course, since in either event the unlawful entry remains both punishable and continuing grounds for deportation. *See* INA § 241(a)(2).

backdrop that the costs of the exclusionary must be assessed. The costs of applying the exclusionary rule, like the benefits, must be measured at the margin.

The average immigration judge handles about six deportation hearings per day. Neither the hearing officers nor the attorneys participating in those hearings are likely to be well versed in the intricacies of Fourth Amendment law. The prospect of even occasional invocation of the exclusionary rule might significantly change and complicate the character of these proceedings. The BIA has described the practical problems as follows:

> "Absent the applicability of the exclusionary rule, questions relating to deportability routinely involve simple factual allegations and matters of proof. When Fourth Amendment issues are raised at deportation hearings, the result is a diversion of attention from the main issues which those proceedings were created to resolve, both in terms of the expertise of the administrative decision makers and of the structure of the forum to accommodate inquiries into search and seizure questions. The result frequently seems to be a long, confused record in which the issues are not clearly defined and in which there is voluminous testimony.... The ensuing delays and inordinate amount of time spent on such cases at all levels has an adverse impact on the effective administration of the immigration laws.... This is particularly true in a proceeding where delay may be the only 'defense' available and where problems already exist with the use of dilatory tactics." *Matter of Sandoval,* 17 I. & N., at 80 (footnote omitted).

This sober assessment of the exclusionary rule's likely costs, by the agency that would have to administer the rule in at least the administrative tiers of its application, cannot be brushed off lightly.

The BIA's concerns are reinforced by the staggering dimension of the problem that the INS confronts. Immigration officers apprehend over one million deportable aliens in this country every year. A single agent may arrest many illegal aliens every day. Although the investigatory burden does not justify the commission of constitutional violations, the officers cannot be expected to compile elaborate, contemporaneous, written reports detailing the circumstances of every arrest. At present an officer simply completes a "Record of Deportable Alien" that is introduced to prove the INS's case at the deportation hearing; the officer rarely must attend the hearing. Fourth Amendment suppression hearings would undoubtedly require considerably more, and the likely burden on the administration of the immigration laws would be correspondingly severe.

Finally, the INS advances the credible argument that applying the exclusionary rule to deportation proceedings might well result in the suppression of large amounts of information that had been obtained entirely lawfully. INS arrests occur in crowded and confused circumstances. Though the INS agents are instructed to follow procedures that adequately protect Fourth Amendment interests, agents will usually be able to testify only to the fact that they followed INS rules. The demand for a precise account of exactly what happened in each particular arrest would plainly preclude mass arrests, even when the INS is confronted, as it often is, with massed numbers of ascertainably illegal aliens, and even when the arrests can be and are conducted in full compliance with all Fourth Amendment requirements.

In these circumstances we are persuaded that the *Janis* balance between costs and benefits comes out against applying the exclusionary rule in civil deportation hearings held by the INS. By all appearances the INS has already taken sensible and reasonable steps to deter Fourth Amendment violations by its officers, and this makes the likely additional deterrent value of the exclusionary rule small. The costs of applying the exclusionary rule in the context of civil deportation hearings are high. In particular, application of the exclusionary rule in cases such as Sandoval's, would compel the courts to release from custody persons who would then immediately resume their commission of a crime through their continuing, unlawful presence in this country. "There comes a point at which courts, consistent with their duty to administer the law, cannot continue to create barriers to law enforcement in the pursuit of a supervisory role that is properly the duty of the Executive and Legislative Branches." *United States* v. *Janis,* 428 U.S., at 459, 96 S.Ct., at 3034. That point has been reached here.

V

We do not condone any violations of the Fourth Amendment that may have occurred in the arrests of respondents Lopez or Sandoval. Moreover, no challenge is raised here to the INS's own internal regulations. Our conclusions concerning the exclusionary rule's value might change, if there developed good reason to believe that Fourth Amendment violations by INS officers were widespread. Finally, we do not deal here with egregious violations of Fourth Amendment or other liberties that might transgress notions of fundamental fairness and undermine the probative value of the evidence obtained.[5] Cf. *Rochin* v. *California,* 342 U.S. 165, 72 S.Ct. 205, 96 L.Ed. 183 (1952). At issue here is the exclusion of credible evidence gathered in connection with peaceful arrests by INS officers. We hold that evidence derived from such arrests need not be suppressed in an INS civil deportation hearing.

The judgment of the Court of Appeals is therefore

Reversed.

JUSTICE BRENNAN, dissenting.

---

5. We note that subsequent to its decision in *Matter of Sandoval,* 17 I. & N. Dec. 70 (1979), the BIA held that evidence will be excluded if the circumstances surrounding a particular arrest and interrogation would render use of the evidence obtained thereby "fundamentally unfair" and in violation of due process requirements of the fifth amendment. *Matter of Toro,* 17 I. & N. Dec. 340, 343 (BIA 1980). *See also Matter of Garcia,* 17 I. & N. Dec. 319, 321 (BIA 1980) (suppression of admission of alienage obtained after request for counsel had been repeatedly refused); *Matter of Ramira-Cordova,* No. A21 095 659 (BIA Feb. 21, 1980) (suppression of evidence obtained as a result of a night-time warrantless entry into the aliens' residence).

I fully agree with JUSTICE WHITE that under the analysis developed by the Court in such cases as *United States* v. *Janis,* 428 U.S. 433, 96 S.Ct. 3021, 49 L.Ed.2d 1046 (1976), and *United States* v. *Calandra,* 414 U.S. 338, 94 S.Ct. 613, 38 L.Ed.2d 561 (1974), the exclusionary rule must apply in civil deportation proceedings. However, * * * I believe the basis for the exclusionary rule does not derive from its effectiveness as a deterrent, but is instead found in the requirements of the Fourth Amendment itself. The Government of the United States bears an obligation to obey the Fourth Amendment; that obligation is not lifted simply because the law enforcement officers were agents of the Immigration and Naturalization Service, nor because the evidence obtained by those officers was to be used in civil deportation proceedings.

JUSTICE WHITE, dissenting.

The Court today holds that the exclusionary rule does not apply in civil deportation proceedings. Because I believe that the conclusion of the majority is based upon an incorrect assessment of the costs and benefits of applying the rule in such proceedings, I respectfully dissent.

* * *

The exclusionary rule rests on the Court's belief that exclusion has a sufficient deterrent effect to justify its imposition, and the Court has not abandoned the rule. As long as that is the case, there is no principled basis for distinguishing between the deterrent effect of the rule in criminal cases and in civil deportation proceedings. The majority attempts to justify the distinction by asserting that deportation will still be possible when evidence not derived from the illegal search or seizure is independently sufficient. However, that is no less true in criminal cases. The suppression of some evidence does not bar prosecution for the crime, and in many cases even though some evidence is suppressed a conviction will nonetheless be obtained.

The majority also suggests that the fact that most aliens elect voluntary departure dilutes the deterrent effect of the exclusionary rule, because the infrequency of challenges to admission of evidence will mean that "the consequences from the point of view of the officer's overall arrest and deportation record will be trivial." It is true that a majority of apprehended aliens elect voluntary departure, while a lesser number go through civil deportation proceedings and a still smaller number are criminally prosecuted. However, that fact no more diminishes the importance of the exclusionary sanction than the fact that many criminal defendants plead guilty dilutes the rule's deterrent effect in criminal cases. The possibility of exclusion of evidence quite obviously plays a part in the decision whether to contest either civil deportation or criminal prosecution. Moreover, in concentrating on the incentives under which the individual agent operates to the exclusion of the incentives under which the agency as a whole operates neglects the "systemic" deterrent effect that may lead the agency to adopt policies and procedures that conform to Fourth Amendment standards.

The majority believes "perhaps most important" the fact that the INS has a "comprehensive scheme" in place for deterring Fourth Amendment violations by punishing agents who commit such violations, but it points to not a single instance in which that scheme has been invoked.[2] Also, immigration officers are instructed and examined in Fourth Amendment law, and it is suggested that this education is another reason why the exclusionary rule is unnecessary. A contrary lesson could be discerned from the existence of these programs, however, when it is recalled that they were instituted during "a legal regime in which the cases and commentators uniformly sanctioned the invocation of the rule in deportation proceedings." *Lopez-Mendoza* v. *INS,* 705 F.2d 1059, 1071 (CA9 1983). Thus, rather than supporting a conclusion that the exclusionary rule is unnecessary, the existence of these programs instead suggests that the exclusionary rule has created incentives for the agency to ensure that its officers follow the dictates of the Constitution. Since the deterrent function of the rule is furthered if it alters either "the behavior of individual law enforcement officers or the policies of their departments," *United States* v. *Leon,* ___ U.S., at ___, 104 S.Ct., at ___, 82 L.Ed.2d 677, 695 (1984), it seems likely that it was the rule's deterrent effect that led to the programs to which the Court now points for its assertion that the rule would have no deterrent effect.

The suggestion that alternative remedies, such as civil suits, provide adequate protection is unrealistic. Contrary to the situation in criminal cases, once the Government has improperly obtained evidence against an illegal alien, he is removed from the country and is therefore in no position to file civil actions in federal courts. Moreover, those who are legally in the country but are nonetheless subjected to illegal searches and seizures are likely to be poor, uneducated, and many will not speak English. It is doubtful that the threat of civil suits by these persons will strike fear into the hearts of those who enforce the Nation's immigration laws.

It is also my belief that the majority exaggerates the costs associated with applying the exclusionary rule in this context. Evidence obtained through violation of the Fourth Amendment is not automatically suppressed, and any inquiry into the burdens associated with application of the exclusionary rule must take that fact into account. In *United States* v. *Leon, supra,* we have held that the exclusionary rule is not applicable when officers are acting in objective good faith. Thus, if the agents neither knew nor should have known that they were acting contrary to the dictates of the Fourth Amendment, evidence will not be suppressed even if it is held that their conduct was illegal.

As the majority notes, the BIA has already held that evidence will be suppressed if it results from egregious violations of constitutional standards. Thus, the mechanism for dealing with suppression motions exists and is utilized, significantly decreasing the force of the majority's predictions of dire consequences flowing from "even occasional invocation of the

---

2. The Government suggests that INS disciplinary rules are "not mere paper procedures" and that over a period of four years 20 officers were suspended or terminated for misconduct toward aliens. The Government does not assert, however, that any of these officers were disciplined for Fourth Amendment violations, and it appears that the 11 officers who were terminated were terminated for rape or assault.

exclusionary rule." Although the standard currently utilized by the BIA may not be precisely coextensive with the good-faith exception, any incremental increase in the amount of evidence that is suppressed through application of *Leon* is unlikely to be significant. Likewise, any difference that may exist between the two standards is unlikely to increase significantly the number of suppression motions filed.

Contrary to the view of the majority, it is not the case that Sandoval's "unregistered presence in this country, without more, constitutes a crime." Section 275 of the Immigration and Nationality Act makes it a crime to enter the United States illegally. The first offense constitutes a misdemeanor, and subsequent offenses constitute felonies. Those few cases that have construed this statute have held that a violation takes place at the time of entry and that the statute does not describe a continuing offense. *Gonzales* v. *City of Peoria,* 722 F.2d 468, 473–474 (CA9 1983); *United States* v. *Rincon-Jiminez,* 595 F.2d 1192, 1194 (CA9 1979). Although this Court has not construed the statute, it has suggested in dictum that this interpretation is correct, *United States* v. *Cores,* 356 U.S. 405, 408, n. 6, 78 S.Ct. 875, 878, n. 6, 2 L.Ed.2d 873, and it is relatively clear that such an interpretation is most consistent with the statutory language. Therefore, it is simply not the case that suppressing evidence in deportation proceedings will "allo[w] the criminal to continue in the commission of an ongoing crime." It is true that some courts have construed § 276 of the Act which applies to aliens previously deported who enter or are found in the United States, to describe a continuing offense. *United States* v. *Bruno,* 328 F.Supp. 815 (W.D.Mo.1971); *United States* v. *Alvarado-Soto,* 120 F.Supp. 848 (S.D.Cal.1954); *United States* v. *Rincon-Jiminez, supra* (dictum). But see *United States* v. *DiSantillo,* 615 F.2d 128 (CA3 1980). In such cases, however, the Government will have a record of the prior deportation and will have little need for any evidence that might be suppressed through application of the exclusionary rule.

Although the majority relies on the registration provisions of INA §§ 262, 266 for its "continuing crime" argument, those provisions provide little support for the general rule laid down that the exclusionary rule does not apply in civil deportation proceedings. First, § 262 requires that aliens register within 30 days of entry into the country. Thus, for the first 30 days failure to register is not a crime. Second, § 266 provides that only *willful* failure to register is a misdemeanor. Therefore, "unregistered presence in this country, without more," does not constitute a crime; rather, unregistered presence plus willfulness must be shown. There is no finding that Sandoval willfully failed to register, which is a necessary predicate to the conclusion that he is engaged in a continuing crime. Third, only aliens fourteen years of age or older are required to register; those under fourteen years of age are to be registered by their parents or guardian. By the majority's reasoning, therefore, perhaps the exclusionary rule should apply in proceedings to deport children under fourteen, since their failure to register does not constitute a crime.

Application of the rule, we are told, will also seriously interfere with the "streamlined" nature of deportation hearings because "[n]either the hearing officers nor the attorneys participating in those hearings are likely to be well-versed in the intricacies of Fourth Amendment law." Yet the majority deprecates the deterrent benefit of the exclusionary rule in part on the ground that immigration officers receive a thorough education in Fourth Amendment law. The implication that hearing officers should defer to law enforcement officers' superior understanding of constitutional principles is startling indeed.

Prior to the decision of the Board of Immigration Appeals in *Matter of Sandoval*, 17 I. & N. Dec. 70 (1979), neither the Board nor any court had held that the exclusionary rule did not apply in civil deportation proceedings. *Lopez-Mendoza v. INS*, 705 F.2d, at 1071. The Board in *Sandoval* noted that there were "fewer than fifty" BIA proceedings since 1952 in which motions had been made to suppress evidence on Fourth Amendment grounds. This is so despite the fact that "immigration law practitioners have been informed by the major treatise in their field that the exclusionary rule was available to clients facing deportation. *See* 1A C. Gordon and H. Rosenfield, Immigration Law and Procedure § 5.2c at 5–31 (rev. ed. 1980)." *Lopez-Mendoza v. INS, supra,* at 1071. The suggestion that "[t]he prospect of even occasional invocation of the exclusionary rule might significantly change and complicate the character of these proceedings," is thus difficult to credit. The simple fact is that prior to 1979 the exclusionary rule was available in civil deportation proceedings and there is no indication that it significantly interfered with the ability of the INS to function.

Finally, the majority suggests that application of the exclusionary rule might well result in the suppression of large amounts of information legally obtained because of the "crowded and confused circumstances" surrounding mass arrests. The result would be that INS agents would have to keep a "precise account of exactly what happened in each particular arrest," which would be impractical considering the "massed numbers of ascertainably illegal aliens." Rather than constituting a rejection of the application of the exclusionary rule in civil deportation proceedings, however, this argument amounts to a rejection of the application of the Fourth Amendment to the activities of INS agents. If the pandemonium attending immigration arrests is so great that violations of the Fourth Amendment cannot be ascertained for the purpose of applying the exclusionary rule, there is no reason to think that such violations can be ascertained for purposes of civil suits or internal disciplinary proceedings, both of which are proceedings that the majority suggests provide adequate deterrence against Fourth Amendment violations. The Court may be willing to throw up its hands in dismay because it is administratively inconvenient to determine whether constitutional rights have been violated, but we neglect our duty when we subordinate constitutional rights to expediency in such a manner. Particularly is this so when, as here, there is but a weak showing that administrative efficiency will be seriously compromised.

In sum, I believe that the costs and benefits of applying the exclusionary rule in civil deportation proceedings do not differ in any significant way from the costs and benefits of applying the rule in ordinary criminal proceedings. Unless the exclusionary rule is to be wholly done away with and the Court's belief that it has deterrent effects abandoned, it should be applied in deportation proceedings when evidence has been obtained by deliberate violations of the Fourth Amendment or by conduct a reasonably competent officer would know is contrary to the Constitution. Accordingly, I dissent.

JUSTICE MARSHALL, dissenting.

I agree with JUSTICE WHITE that application to this case of the mode of analysis embodied in the decisions of the Court in *United States v. Janis,* 428 U.S. 433, 96 S.Ct. 3021, 49 L.Ed.2d 1046 (1976), and *United States v. Calandra,* 414 U.S. 338, 94 S.Ct. 613, 38 L.Ed.2d 561 (1974), compels the conclusion that the exclusionary rule should apply in civil deportation proceedings. However, I continue to believe that that mode of analysis fails to reflect the constitutionally mandated character of the exclusionary rule. In my view, a sufficient reason for excluding from civil deportation proceedings evidence obtained in violation of the Fourth Amendment is that there is no other way to achieve "the twin goals of enabling the judiciary to avoid the taint of partnership in official lawlessness and of assuring the people—all potential victims of unlawful government conduct—that the government would not profit from its lawless behavior, thus minimizing the risk of seriously undermining popular trust in government." *United States v. Calandra,* 414 U.S., at 357, 94 S.Ct., at 624 (BRENNAN, J., joined by MARSHALL, J., dissenting).

JUSTICE STEVENS, dissenting.

[Omitted.]

Notes

1. Are you satisfied with the empirical assumptions in the majority and dissenting opinions regarding the costs and benefits of the exclusionary rule? Even if hard data on the issues were available, how does one assign values to the costs and benefits? *See generally* Kamisar, *Does (Did) (Should) the Exclusionary Rule Rest on a "Principled Basis" Rather than an "Empirical Proposition,"* 16 Creighton L.Rev. 565, 645–67 (1983).

In discussing the "costs" that would be associated with application of an exclusionary rule in deportation proceedings, the Court mentions "the staggering dimension of the problem that the INS confronts" and concludes that "the likely burden on the administration of the immigration laws would be * * * severe." Is the majority saying that our immigration laws simply cannot be effectively enforced if INS officers are held to the dictates of the Fourth Amendment? Consider the remarks of BIA Member Ralph Farb, concurring in *Matter of Sandoval,* 17 I & N Dec. 70, 85 (BIA 1979):

> For Fiscal Year 1977, the Immigration and Naturalization Service reported that it had located 1,042,000 deportable aliens. Of these, 939,000, or 90%, were listed as having entered without inspection. That means that for the vast majority there was no reason to expect that the Immigration and Naturalization Service records contained prior evidence of their identity as aliens. I am

not condoning or encouraging violation of Fourth Amendment rights in the immigration investigator's search for solid proof of identity. If it were done deliberately, discharge from Government service would be appropriate. I simply don't see how we can reasonably bar the use of illegally obtained convincing proof that a person is an alien with no right of presence, when that may be all that will ever be available to identify him. It would be inconsistent with the manifest intention of Congress that the Immigration and Naturalization Service know the location of every alien in the country.

2. Note that Justices Brennan and Marshall dissent, in part, on the ground that the exclusionary rule is not based on notions of deterrence, but rather on the principle that the government should not benefit from its wrongdoing. While this debate goes beyond the scope of an immigration law casebook, it has been the subject of lively scholarly debate. *See, e.g.,* Kamisar, *supra;* Schrock & Welsh, *Up From Calandra: The Exclusionary Rule as a Constitutional Requirement,* 59 Minn.L.Rev. 251 (1974); White, *Forgotten Points in the 'Exclusionary Rule' Debate,* 81 Mich.L.Rev. 1273 (1983).

d. Special Deportation Procedures

The statute provides special deportation procedures for two classes of aliens: (1) alien crewmen who jump ship or overstay their shore leave, INA § 252(b); *see INS v. Stanisic,* 395 U.S. 62, 89 S.Ct. 1519, 23 L.Ed.2d 101 (1969); and (2) certain aliens who unlawfully re-enter following deportation, INA § 242(f). Under what circumstances do these provisions apply? How do they modify the general deportation procedures of INA § 242(b)?

3. THE CONSEQUENCES OF DEPORTATION

What disabilities (other than departure from the United States) does deportation impose on an alien who seeks to re-enter the United States or does re-enter? Take a careful look at the statute; there are at least five. *See* G & R § 4.6d.

The Supreme Court has upheld the constitutionality of a statute that terminates the payment of social security benefits to aliens deported as subversives. *Flemming v. Nestor,* 363 U.S. 603, 80 S.Ct. 1367, 4 L.Ed.2d 1435 (1960).

4. DEPORTATION PROCEDURES: CRIMINAL DUE PROCESS AND CIVIL REGULATORY MODELS

Every part of the preceding discussion of deportation procedures has exposed a fundamental underlying tension between the needs of law enforcement and the rights of aliens threatened with expulsion. This tension represents a conflict among goals and among values. All would agree that accuracy is a primary goal. That is, only those aliens who have in fact violated the law should be deported. But the quest for accuracy may conflict with other values. From the government's perspective, accuracy has a price in terms of time and resources. From the alien's perspective, focussing simply on accuracy may sacrifice other goals, such as deterring unlawful law enforcement activities through adoption of an exclusionary rule.

Even if accuracy were our only goal, we would still be confronted with the difficult questions of deciding what an acceptable degree of accuracy is and what procedures are necessary to get us there. As we have seen in the consideration of the *Woodby* standard, accuracy is not necessarily furthered simply through imposition of procedural protections for the alien; some measures aimed at decreasing the likelihood that aliens are wrongfully deported may increase the likelihood that aliens are wrongfully not deported.

In the sphere of criminal justice, our legal system has opted for an adversarial model with a set of procedures primarily directed at ensuring that innocent persons are not convicted. Thus, for example, criminal defendants are guaranteed counsel at government expense and a high standard of proof (beyond a reasonable doubt). Aliens and their advocates, stressing the drastic consequences of deportation, have urged Congress and the courts to adopt similar protections in deportation proceedings.

We will label the alien's preferred system the "Criminal Due Process Model," and we will contrast it with a system we will call the "Civil Regulatory Model." [73] The fundamental claim of the Criminal Due Process Model might be stated in familiar language: it is better that five illegal aliens remain in the United States than one alien be wrongfully deported. In contrast, the Civil Regulatory Model is essentially concerned with fair and efficient administration of the immigration laws. It recognizes the potential harshness of deportation and therefore seeks to ensure that aliens are given a fair opportunity to contest deportation; but it views minimization of the number of wrongful deportations as simply one goal that must be balanced against the costs of providing criminal-type procedures in deportation hearings.

It seems clear, does it not, that Congress and the Supreme Court have primarily adopted the Civil Regulatory Model for deportation proceedings. Recall the Court's statement in *INS v. Lopez-Mendoza:* "[A] deportation hearing is intended to provide a streamlined determination of eligibility to remain in this country, nothing more. The purpose of deportation is not to punish past transgressions but rather to put an end to a continuing violation of the immigration laws."

The following chart demonstrates how the Civil Regulatory Model diverges from the Criminal Due Process Model in areas we have considered in this Chapter.

73. *Cf.* Packer, *Two Models of the Criminal Process*, 113 U.Pa.L.Rev. 1 (1964) (identifying and contrasting "Crime Control" and "Due Process" models in criminal procedure).

	Civil Regulatory	Criminal Due Process
Counsel	provide on case-by-case basis	provide at government expense to all indigent
Fifth Amendment	exclude only involuntary statements	adopt *Miranda* rule
Advice of rights	after decision to charge	before interrogation
Burden of proof	alien must show time and place of entry (§ 291)	entirely on government
Standard of proof	clear, convincing evidence (or preponderance?)	beyond a reasonable doubt
Fourth Amendment	no exclusionary rule	exclusionary rule
Role of adjudicator	inquisitorial	independent umpire
Evidentiary rules	Federal Rules inapplicable	Federal Rules applicable
Silence of alien	adverse inference permissible	adverse inference impermissible

To say that deportation proceedings are not run under the Criminal Due Process Model is not to say that they are trials by ordeal. Aliens who choose to contest deportability have substantial rights under the due process clause and the INA. An alien in a deportation proceeding may call witnesses and cross-examine adverse witnesses, is entitled to have a lawyer present and the aid of an interpreter, is informed of the availability of free legal assistance, enjoys a standard of proof higher than that applied in most civil contexts and is guaranteed several levels of administrative and judicial review. No country in the world provides greater protections to aliens in deportation proceedings. Indeed, most provide far less.[74]

74. Consider the description of the mass deportation of aliens from Nigeria that occurred in 1983.

Nigeria's President Shehu Shagari accused illegal immigrant workers of ruining his country's economy by taking needed jobs and draining the nation's wealth. He gave the foreign workers two weeks to clear out. The order sent immigrants rushing for the borders in panic. Several hundred thousand made for Chad. Up to 150,000 returned to Niger. And tens of thousands more headed back toward Togo, Benin, Upper Volta, Cameroon and Mali. Ghana was the hardest hit of all—forced to absorb at least a million returnees. The exiles increased the country's population by 10% almost overnight, depleting food stocks and leaving Ghana pleading for emergency supplies.

As the chaos spread, casualties mounted. Thirty people collapsed and died of hunger and exhaustion after walking for several days to the Benin-Togo border. An additional eight drowned when they

fell into the sea in the rush onto freighters in Lagos harbor. One woman was crushed between a ship and the dock. Several other people died in truck and car crashes as convoys 10 miles long pushed along the coconut-fringed coastal highway. In Ghana, six people died and 140 were injured when a truck filled with refugees plunged into a ravine. Many deportees walked for days without eating, too poor even to buy the local bananas.

* * *

In the golden days of Nigeria's oil boom, the foreigners were welcomed as electricians, laborers, nurses, farmers and street peddlers. But when oil prices fell last year, the economy crashed, forcing Shagari to scrap grandiose plans to carve a new capital out of the jungle. Growing unemployment added to Shagari's problems. With presidential elections due in August, he turned on the foreign workers residing in Nigeria as a ready and popular target. Interior Minister Ali Baba or-

If you were a member of Congress rewriting INA § 242, which model, if either, would you adopt? What additional information would you seek in making a judgment? Would you distinguish among classes of aliens? Would other substantial changes in the law—such as imposition of a statute of limitations—make fewer protections acceptable?

Consider the comments of Paul Schmidt, Deputy General Counsel of the INS, who read an earlier version of this Chapter:

> What proof is there that we deport large numbers of * * * lawful permanent residents not subject to deportation? What proof is there that we deport any? If there is no proof, why guarantee rights to those that don't belong here? Why make it harder for already overburdened law enforcement officials to do their jobs?

How would you respond?

5. BEYOND THE ADVERSARY SYSTEM

Calls for reform of immigration adjudications over the years have urged two separate lines of development: (1) they have urged independent adjudicators insulated from enforcement responsibilities, and (2) they have called for more and more of the trappings of the adversarial model to be imported into such proceedings. Today, deportation proceedings have moved a long way toward both objectives. But consider whether *both* such changes are necessary or desirable. In particular, if true independence and neutrality are someday established on the part of the adjudicators, might it make sense to reverse some of the tendency toward adversarial proceedings?

dered police sweeps of hotels and factories. And Radio Lagos declared: "We cannot afford to watch these illegal aliens pollute our much-cherished traditional values."

The first deportees escaped by air and sea. Thousands of Ghanaians crowded into the ramshackle port of Apapa in Lagos, refusing to budge despite threats from Nigerian officials. Entire families camped on the docks. When a rusting freighter of Ghana's Black Star line finally steamed in, a small riot broke out. People fought to get aboard and young men clambered up mooring lines. In the end more than 6,000 people jammed shoulder to shoulder on every available space from the deck to the bridge. Many burst into song as the ship, deep in the water and already listing, limped out of port on the 15-hour voyage to Ghana. Conditions were little better at the airport, where a stuttering shuttle service eventually ferried out 1,000 people a day.

Most departing workers tried to leave by road, but were forced to wait for days to get across the frontier. The main reason: Ghana's revolutionary leader, Flight Lt. Jerry Rawlings, had closed his country's border last September to deter smuggling

and guerrilla attacks. As Ghanaian nationals crowded together in a huge bottleneck at Nigeria's western border, Rawlings refused to reopen his frontier. Fearing the surge of Ghanaian refugees, Benin and Togo also kept their borders tightly sealed to all but their own citizens. With Shagari's deadline approaching and panic growing, Rawlings finally gave in and traffic flooded the coastal highway. Nigerian truck drivers charged premium rates— then crammed up to 100 passengers onto vehicles piled high with battered suitcases and boxes.

"Nigeria's Outcasts: The Cruel Exodus," *Newsweek*, Feb. 14, 1983, at 32–34. Copyright 1983, by Newsweek, Inc. All Rights Reserved, Reprinted by Permission.

Of course, in earlier days aliens in the United States have been subjected to mass deportation programs. *See* pp. 352–355 *supra*, describing the Palmer raids of the World War I era. Far more significant have been enforcement programs directed against Mexican aliens in the United States during the Great Depression in the 1930's and in 1954. *See generally* J.R. Garcia, Operation Wetback: The Mass Deportation of Mexican Undocumented Workers in 1954 (1980).

In some settings, the adversarial model carries one significant draw-back. It presupposes that both sides will be (or will be represented by) skilled advocates. Often this specification simply is not fulfilled—either in the immigration field or in other "mass justice" administrative proceedings—because the individuals involved cannot afford a lawyer. One might remedy this problem, of course, by requiring the government to pay for counsel for the indigent. But such a step would be expensive, and courts have been reluctant to require appointed counsel outside the realm of criminal trials. *See, e.g., Goldberg v. Kelly,* 397 U.S. 254, 270, 90 S.Ct. 1011, 1021, 25 L.Ed.2d 287 (1970); O'Neil, *Of Justice Delayed and Justice Denied: The Welfare Prior Hearing Cases,* 1970 Sup.Ct.Rev. 161, 178. In light of this shortcoming, perhaps alternative hearing models deserve more careful attention, especially if other developments make us more confident about the neutrality and professionalism of the adjudicators. Supreme Court cases have occasionally upheld nonadversary adjudicative procedures against due process objection, in the presence of other factors helping to assure fairness. *See Richardson v. Perales,* 402 U.S. 389, 91 S.Ct. 1420, 28 L.Ed.2d 842 (1971); *Richardson v. Wright,* 405 U.S. 208, 92 S.Ct. 788, 31 L.Ed.2d 151 (1972) (per curiam).

The investigatory or "inquisitorial" model is often condemned because the alleged mixture of roles of prosecutor and judge is said to bias the adjudicator toward an outcome favorable to the prosecution. The fear is that the adjudicator will ask only those questions that develop the prosecutor's side of the case. But is this inevitable? Might it not depend more on the background, training, and orientation of the adjudicating staff?

Assume you found yourself as an immigration adjudicator, charged with the application of the immigration laws in deportation cases brought before you. Assume also that the government rarely assigned a trial attorney to present its case. Most of the time, all you have to start with is the case file, including the charging papers containing the government's allegations and supporting documentation, as developed by the enforcement branch. You also find waiting in your rather lonely courtroom an unrepresented alien respondent, accompanied by a few friends who have offered to serve as witnesses. Do you think you could fairly question the respondent and his witnesses both to explore the government's allegations and also, via questions, to flesh out the elements of any defense the alien seems to have, however inarticulate he may be in stating that defense directly? Could you then, having asked such questions from a variety of perspectives, issue a fair ruling?

European countries often use such nonadversarial proceedings, with minimal involvement by lawyers representing the parties, even at times in criminal proceedings. The results are regarded, at least in those cultures, as reasonably fair. *See, e.g.,* Langbein, *The Criminal Trial Before the Lawyers,* 45 U.Chi.L.Rev. 263 (1978); Friendly, *Some Kind of Hearing,* 123 U.Pa.L.Rev. 1267, 1289–91 (1975). Should such a model be applied to immigration proceedings, if adequate independence and professionalism of the adjudicators can be assured? Might the need for alternative models become more pressing as the number of aliens in such proceedings increases? *See generally* Martin, *Due Process and Member-ship in the National Community: Political Asylum and Beyond,* 44 U.Pitt. L.Rev. 165, 219–21 (1983).

SECTION C. DUE PROCESS, EXCLUSION AND DEPOR-TATION: TOWARDS A NEW APPROACH

As we explored in Chapter Three, the Supreme Court has been unwilling to subject statutory exclusion procedures to serious constitution-al scrutiny. "Whatever the procedure authorized by Congress is," go the famous words of *Knauff* and *Mezei,* "it is due process as far as an alien denied entry is concerned." 338 U.S. 537, 544, 70 S.Ct. 309, 313, 94 L.Ed. 317 (1950); 345 U.S. 206, 212, 73 S.Ct. 625, 629, 97 L.Ed. 956 (1953). This abdication of judicial review at the border is in sharp contrast to the scrutiny that the Supreme Court is willing to apply in the deportation context. The decision in *The Japanese Immigrant Case* in the early years of this century made clear that, as to aliens who have entered the country, "administrative officers, when executing the provisions of a statute involv-ing the liberty of persons, may [not] disregard the fundamental principles that inhere in 'due process of law.'" 189 U.S. 86, 100, 23 S.Ct. 611, 614, 47 L.Ed. 721 (1903).

You should now be quite familiar with the curious results occasioned by a constitutional test that turns on the location of the alien. For example, an alien who arrives at the border with an immigrant visa and a job or family awaiting him in the United States is essentially unprotected by the Constitution's due process clause. However, an alien who is apprehended a few hours after making a surreptitious entry is afforded, as a matter of constitutional right, a hearing, an opportunity to present evidence and cross-examine witnesses, an unbiased decision-maker and, sometimes, counsel.

It would be easy to write off *Knauff* and *Mezei* as Cold War cases that are no longer entitled to our respect. They misread the cases they cited and cannot be squared with several earlier cases they did not cite. *See* Martin, *Due Process and Membership in the National Community: Politi-cal Asylum and Beyond,* 44 U.Pitt.L.Rev. 165, 173–75 (1983); Hart, *The Power of Congress to Limit the Jurisdiction of Federal Courts: An Exercise in Dialectic,* 66 Harv.L.Rev. 1362, 1386–96 (1953). Moreover, they are manifestly out of step with modern developments in constitutional law. But, at least as to first-time entrants, they continue to be viewed as the foundation of settled doctrine. *See, e.g., Landon v. Pasencia,* 459 U.S. 21, 103 S.Ct. 321, 74 L.Ed.2d 21 (1982); *Jean v. Nelson,* 727 F.2d 957 (11th Cir.1984) (*en banc*), *cert. granted,* ___ U.S. ___, 105 S.Ct. 563, 83 L.Ed.2d 504 (1984).

Several rationales could conceivably justify the border/interior dis-tinction. Indeed, two dissenting Justices in the first case to rule on the constitutionality of a deportation statute, *Fong Yue Ting v. United States,* 149 U.S. 698, 13 S.Ct. 1016, 37 L.Ed. 905 (1893), offered different theories as to why constitutional limits should apply to exercises of the deportation power but not the exclusion power. *See* pp. 20–34 *supra*.

Justice Brewer offered a *territorial* justification: the Constitution has no extraterritorial effect and thus aliens who are at the border but have not entered cannot claim its protection. Consider David Martin's critique of this theory:

> [The territorial] approach * * * requires an almost willful shutting of one's eyes to physical realities. In modern exclusion cases * * * the aliens involved will have been physically well inside the border for a significant period of time, either residing in detention facilities managed by the INS or else "paroled" into the United States * * *. More importantly, aliens in exclusion proceedings of whatever kind (as distinguished from those overseas in our consulates applying for permission to travel here) have always been at least within the territorial waters, even if they are detained on board ship while awaiting the admission decision. Such aliens plainly come within the territorial jurisdiction of the United States in the significant sense that this country's sovereign will (no matter which branch of government directs that will) can be applied to them immediately, uncomplicated by any direct contest with another sovereign nation.

Martin, *supra*, at 179. *See also Developments*, 96 Harv.L.Rev., at 1320–22.

A second possible justification for the border/interior distinction was offered in *Fong Yue Ting* by Chief Justice Fuller. He argued that deportation, unlike exclusion, entailed the "deprivation of that which has been lawfully acquired." 149 U.S. at 762, 13 S.Ct. at 1041. In modern constitutional terms, one can interpret this statement in at least two ways. First, this rationale might be seen as an appeal to the "right-privilege" distinction. Second, we might read Fuller's statement as calling attention to the material and social *stake* that a resident alien has established in this country.

Neither interpretation, however, seems to sustain the current doctrine. First, it is unclear how we can distinguish an alien at the border from a resident alien in terms of rights or privileges. If we view a resident alien as having gained an entitlement to remain in the United States, at what point was such an entitlement acquired? One *could* choose the point of admission, but it is hardly obvious that this is a better point than, say, the time an immigrant visa is granted. Taking the earlier time, of course, would give us no cause for distinguishing some first-time entrants (that is, aliens who appear at the border with duly-issued visas) from permanent resident aliens. (Although it may give us good reason for distinguishing lawfully admitted aliens from surreptitious entrants—something that the current border/interior line does not.)

Alternatively, if we start by viewing the initial entrant as having only a privilege to enter this country, again it is not clear how we can distinguish the permanent resident alien. If entry is a privilege extended by a beneficent sovereign, what transmutes that act of grace into a right merely because an alien has accepted it? That is, is not the continued stay of an admitted alien also an act of grace that can be revoked at the sovereign's pleasure? *See Harisiades v. Shaughnessy,* 342 U.S. 580, 586–87, 72 S.Ct. 512, 517, 96 L.Ed. 586 (1952) (alien's stay in the United States "is not his right but is a matter of permission and tolerance").

If the "right-privilege distinction" is inadequate in explaining the current doctrine, perhaps the notion of "stake" can help us: in deciding what process is "due" an alien, it is permissible to take into account that alien's identification with, or ties to, the American community. This justification would recognize that permanent resident aliens have penetrated near to the core of American society; they have jobs, friends, and associations that often make them nearly indistinguishable from citizens. These substantial ties, so the argument might run, justify affording permanent resident aliens substantial process before we take that which has been "lawfully acquired" from them. Such reasoning also supports lesser protections for initial entrants—that is, those aliens who have not yet acquired a substantial stake in this society.

Although the "stake" theory may have a great deal of plausibility, it unfortunately cannot explain the way the Court has developed the border/interior distinction. Recall that under the current doctrine, an undocumented surreptitious entrant is granted greater protections than an alien who arrives at the border holding an immigrant visa. Furthermore it cannot explain *Mezei:* Mezei was a returning lawful resident who had a wife and family in this country.

These considerations lead us to suggest that the border/interior distinction be discarded. It is a nineteenth century doctrine searching in vain for a twentieth century justification. A call for abandonment, however, should be coupled with an alternative proposal. We believe that a reasonable alternative could be based on the "stake" theory described above. The following is David Martin's development of such a theory:

> [T]he basic intuition * * * might be [stated] as follows: * * * we, as a national community, somehow *owe less* in the coin of procedural assurances to the first-time applicant for admission than we do to our fellow citizens or to permanent resident aliens, or even to regular nonimmigrants who have been among us for awhile. This is not necessarily to say that we owe nothing; that would be to repeat the mistakes of *Knauff* and *Mezei.* Instead it is simply to assert that established community ties, which exist to varying degrees with respect to different categories of aliens, ought to count in deciding what process is due. Or perhaps the intuition is more accurately stated the other way around. We *owe more* procedural guarantees—a greater assurance of scrupulous factual accuracy—to citizens and permanent resident aliens than we do to aliens at the threshold of entry into the national community.

* * *

* * * [I]t is not novel to suggest that special, heightened obligations may grow up as a result of particular relationships. Families furnish the central examples, but other relationships,

A. & M.–Immigration Law ACB—18

such as residence in the same neighborhood or town, or membership in the same organization, may also give rise to special
obligations. We might, for example, justly criticize a neighbor for
failing to join in a Saturday work session called to clean up litter
along an adjoining highway. Even though he may never have
agreed to be available for such efforts, we might consider that he
has failed to meet an obligation that attaches simply because of
our relation as neighbors. That obligation might, of course, be
excused, and in this context, a far weaker reason than what is
required to relieve some duty in the context of the family might
suffice. Nevertheless, it is meaningful to consider that, absent
valid excuse, he owes it to the neighbors to take part. Above all,
we feel confident that he would not incur the same criticism if he
failed to join a similar clean-up effort in the next county, even if
he happened to learn of it well in advance. In those circumstances, no relevant relationship exists giving rise to an equivalent
obligation.

* * *

To a significant degree, these relational obligations are
linked to the concept of community. That concept is not a simple
one, and there is a continuing dispute in the philosophical and
sociological literature as to whether communities are mainly
purposive or organic, whether they spring from common purposes
and devotion to the same principles or instead derive from a
shared history or a coincidence of sentiment fostered by organic
historical development. We need not choose among these contending positions, but instead need only note the possible relevance of both principle and sentiment in the creation and maintenance of a community, including a national community. In
either case, a large part of what we mean by "community" is that
relational obligations exist and are to be honored. We may use
the language of community instrumentally, for example as part
of our appeal to a recalcitrant neighbor to join a clean-up crew:
"This is a community effort" or "This is going to benefit the
whole community." More to the point, if we describe a neighborhood as a community, rather than simply as a geographical
location, we probably mean that this kind of interaction and
sharing—this recognition and fulfillment of reciprocal obligations—takes place here.

We have long applied to the nation exactly this language of
community. For example, in 1875, in *Minor v. Happersett*, [88
U.S. (21 Wall.) 162 (1875),] the Supreme Court was called upon to
construe the meaning of the term "citizen" as used in the Constitution. In the course of concluding that the word conveys "the
idea of membership of a nation, and nothing more," the Court
wrote: "There cannot be a nation without a people. The very
idea of a political community, such as a nation is, implies an
association of persons for the promotion of their general welfare."
The hallmark of this community, the Court recognized, is the

concept of reciprocal obligations: "Each one of the persons associ-ated becomes a member of the nation formed by the association. He *owes* it allegiance and is *entitled* to its protection."

* * *

* * * [O]ur notions of membership in the national communi-ty are more complex and multi-layered than can be captured in the concept of citizenship alone. The innermost members may be the only ones entitled to vote and hold office. But permanent resident aliens, members in the next wider circle of concentric communities that make up the nation—if one may indulge that image—are entitled by virtue of that membership alone to enter fully into virtually all other aspects of community life. * * *

Beyond the circle of permanent resident aliens, the mere fact of common residence, even illegal residence, establishes a certain measure of community membership. Undocumented aliens may of course be denied many benefits required to be extended to lawful permanent residents, but as to other advantages of life in this political community, denial is not allowed. * * *

In sum, it is common to recognize different levels of commu-nity membership, and to affirm that "the class of aliens is itself a heterogeneous multitude of persons with a wide-ranging variety of ties to this country." [*Mathews v. Diaz*, 426 U.S. 67, 78–79 (1976).] Or as the Court wrote in *Johnson v. Eisentrager* [, 339 U.S. 763, 770 (1950)]: "The alien, to whom the United States has been traditionally hospitable, has been accorded a generous and as-cending scale of rights as he increases his identity with our society." * * * Levels of membership, then, may properly play a role in assessing what process is due, at least for purposes of decisions on the transcendent question of membership itself—which is what exclusion or deportation cases * * * constitute.

Martin, *supra*, at 191–95, 201–04.[75]

75. Consider Alex Aleinikoff's response to Martin:

[W]hat exactly is the "national communi-ty," and how is it that anyone—citizen or alien—indicates his or her attachment to it? Professor Martin's notion of communi-ty begins with personal relationships and a neighborhood street-cleaning effort and quickly moves to a national community of persons united in a common commitment to the general welfare. I am not con-vinced that this shift can be made so easi-ly. The idea of a political community sharing similar ideas of the meaning of membership and the scope of the common enterprise does not aptly describe a nation as diverse, as pluralistic as the United States. To say that there are serious po-litical and social differences among groups of Americans is to state the obvious. No one ideology, religion or culture unites us.

Ethnic and racial lines continue to sepa-rate Americans into distinct, self-identify-ing groups. The myth of the "melting pot" has given way to more complex de-scriptions that attempt to explain the non-assimilation of groups into one national culture or polity. Perhaps at some very abstract level, we can define a set of prin-ciples that most members of American so-ciety share, such as representative govern-ment or a rule of law. But is it not likely that aliens present in this country, or seeking entry, also share these values?

Furthermore, how do we measure com-mitment to the "national community?" Can one make reasonable assumptions about the level of commitment that vari-ous classes of aliens and citizens have to the American community? It is hardly clear that citizens, by the simple fact of

Interestingly, the reasonableness of this line of analysis is supported, in part, by the case law itself. For, while the Supreme Court has continued to pay verbal homage to the border/interior distinction, in fact, the results of its cases approximate the doctrinal reorientation we propose.

As to permanent resident aliens, *The Japanese Immigrant Case* and its progeny make clear that they are entitled to substantial protections under the due process clause. This accords with our approach, which recognizes the substantial ties to American society that permanent resident aliens are likely to develop. What about returning resident aliens? In our view, the fact that an alien has travelled abroad (so long as he or she has not abandoned residence here) does not generally affect the ties he

birth in the United States, are any more committed, more loyal, to a "national community" than are aliens, most of whom have had to overcome substantial burdens to come to the United States. That aliens are required to pay taxes and are eligible for service in the armed forces seems to indicate as much commitment as we demand from citizens.

* * *

These considerations lead me to question the usefulness of the concept of "membership in a national community" in determining the procedures due aliens before they may be excluded or deported. The idea of a "national community" appears to be too ineffable to be of service; and the model of concentric circles of membership, as Henry Shue has written, raises the difficult-to-answer question: "What exactly is it of which the people at the center share more and people farther from the center share less?" [H. Shue, *Basic Rights: Subsistence, Affluence, and U.S. Foreign Policy* 135 (1980).] How do we measure commitment or loyalty; and why should we assume that the circles of membership are adequate indicators for differing levels of these indicia of membership?

It seems that the problem is not so much in accepting Professor Martin's intuition that we "owe less in the coin of procedural assurances to the first-time applicant for admission than we do to our fellow citizens or to permanent resident aliens." Rather, it is trying to elaborate on that intuition in terms of membership in a national community. It is my belief that our intuition does not depend upon inchoate notions of membership. I think it is more easily explained as a generalization about the stake that certain groups of aliens have in entering in or not being returned to their country of origin. In short, whereas Professor Martin would examine the no-

tion of *community,* I would look at *community ties.* Under this view, what we "owe" persons in terms of process is better understood as a function of what we are taking from them (community ties) than our relationship to them (membership in a national community).

* * * The notion of "community ties," to me, indicates the actual relationships the individual has developed with a society: a family, friends, a job, association memberships, professional acquaintances, opportunities. "Community" is a more amorphous concept. It connotes a sense of identification with others as a group, a sense of common enterprise, a belief in the value of shared experiences and a shared future. Community ties are almost tangible; we can see interactions among people and membership in complex social and financial arrangements. But to see "community," we must catch a glimpse of the *Zeitgeist,* we must peer into people's hearts.

* * * [T]he "community ties" approach is consistent with our intuitional model of a description of aliens and citizens as falling within concentric circles. Although I have argued that viewing the circles as levels of "membership" is not sound, I believe that one can appropriately view the circles as proxies for the different kinds and degrees of community ties that persons in each circle are likely to have developed. Thus, citizens, in the innermost circle, are likely to have the greatest stake in remaining in the United States. Permanent resident aliens occupy the next circle, since they have had opportunities to find employment, make friends, and join community groups. An alien seeking entry for the first time is likely to be able to demonstrate far fewer existing ties to the community.

Aleinikoff, *supra,* at 240–45. *See also, Developments, supra,* at 1324–33 (proposing a "contacts" theory of due process).

or she has with this country. Accordingly, we believe that *Mezei* was wrongly reasoned and should be overruled. Although the Court has stopped short of overruling *Mezei,* not much of it appears to be left: *Plasencia* expressly states that returning residents "can invoke the Due Process Clause on returning to this country." 459 U.S. 21, 32, 103 S.Ct. 321, 329, 74 L.Ed.2d 21 (1982).[76]

Nor do we disagree with the Court's conclusion that lesser constitutional protections apply for initial entrants than resident aliens. Such a result is consistent with our analysis. We do take issue, however, with the statement for which *Knauff* is famous: that due process at the border is whatever Congress decides to give the alien. As a matter of common sense, one cannot take these words at face value. "[T]he Court really could not have meant *carte blanche* for Congress in the treatment of excludable aliens. Surely, had Congress revived trial by ordeal, or the ducking stool, or gladiatorial contests as the procedures for deciding who could enter, the Court—even the Court of the early 1950's—would have found a way to strike down such a practice." Martin, *supra,* at 173. Furthermore, we can see no reason why the United States government should be entirely free from core principles of fair play when acting on persons clearly within the borders of this country and subject to its jurisdiction. It is difficult to find an analogy to this hands-off approach in modern constitutional law,[77] and we see nothing in the nature of the immigration process that demands a complete exception to general norms of due process.

Accordingly, while our theory may give the government substantial flexibility at the border when deciding whether aliens should be permitted to make an initial entry, we see no justification for the *Knauff* principle that Congress is free to do as it wishes. *Plasencia* goes a long way towards blunting the harshness of *Mezei,* but it unfortunately reaffirms the holding of *Knauff* that "an alien seeking initial admission to the United States requests a privilege and has no constitutional rights regarding his application, for the power to admit or exclude aliens is a sovereign

76. The Court in *Plasencia* stated that it "need not now decide the scope of *Mezei;* it does not govern this case, for Plasencia was absent from the country only a few days, and the United States has conceded that she has a right to due process." 459 U.S. at 34, 103 S.Ct. at 330.

77. Over the past two decades, the Supreme Court has brought the due process clause to bear on a wide variety of State proceedings. *See, e.g., In re Gault,* 387 U.S. 1, 87 S.Ct. 1428, 18 L.Ed.2d 527 (1967) (juvenile delinquency proceedings); *Goldberg v. Kelly,* 397 U.S. 254, 90 S.Ct. 1011, 25 L.Ed.2d 287 (1970) (termination of welfare benefits); *Gagnon v. Scarpelli,* 411 U.S. 778, 93 S.Ct. 1756, 36 L.Ed.2d 656 (1973) (revocation of probation); *Goss v. Lopez,* 419 U.S. 565, 95 S.Ct. 729, 42 L.Ed.2d 725 (1975) (suspension of student from school); *Vitek v. Jones,* 445 U.S. 480, 100 S.Ct. 1254, 63 L.Ed.2d 552 (1980) (transfer of prisoner to mental hospital); *Santosky v. Kramer,* 455 U.S. 745, 102 S.Ct. 1388, 71 L Ed.2d 599 (1982) (termination of parental rights). *See generally* L. Tribe, American Constitutional Law 501–63 (1978). Of course, there are numerous cases that have upheld procedures provided by the State as affording due process. *See, e.g., Lassiter v. Department of Social Services,* 452 U.S. 18, 101 S.Ct. 2153, 68 L.Ed.2d 640 (1981) (no automatic right to appointed counsel in parental termination hearings); *Parratt v. Taylor,* 451 U.S. 527, 101 S.Ct. 1908, 68 L.Ed.2d 420 (1981) (negligent loss of prisoner's property does not violate due process clause where adequate state remedy exists). But rarely has the Court exempted from scrutiny under the due process clause such a large area of government conduct as has occurred under the regime of *Knauff.*

prerogative." 459 U.S. at 32, 103 S.Ct. at 329. No persuasive rationale supports even this formulation of the border/interior distinction, and it is time to be rid of it.[78]

Of course, to say that the due process clause applies at the border is not to say what process is due an initial entrant. That issue is usually considered within the framework established by *Mathews v. Eldridge,* 424 U.S. 319, 335, 96 S.Ct. 893, 903, 47 L.Ed.2d 18 (1976), where the Court identified three factors as relevant to the inquiry: the interest at stake for the individual, the risk of an erroneous deprivation of the interest through the procedures used and the likely value of additional procedural safeguards, and the interest of the government (including fiscal and administrative burdens). In applying his analysis to initial entrants, David Martin has concluded:

> [E]xcludable aliens enjoy some measure of shared membership in a relevant community, simply by virtue of their common humanity and physical presence in our territorial jurisdiction. In short, they are not strangers to the Constitution. As human beings, they deserve fulfillment of the promise held out by *Yick Wo* [*v. Hopkins;* see pp. 18–19 *supra*] and by the due process clause itself, which applies, in terms, to "persons." * * * [But while the] excludable alien is not a constitutional stranger, * * * he is not quite intimate family, either. The *Yick Wo* tradition is not offended by appropriately limited recognition of this distinction, so long as it affects only the gradation of due process protection and does not serve to cut off protection altogether. * * *

> * * *

> What is the minimum, then, that fairness should allow as to first-time applicants for admission? It is always hazardous to lay down a procedural code that purports to describe the content of due process in a particular context, because, as Judge Friendly has remarked, a legislative decision to improve one out of a list of safeguards might justify a reduction in other safeguards without transgressing basic fairness. Nevertheless, in most circumstances, aliens at the threshold of entry probably may insist upon the following: an unbiased decision-maker, notice of the proceedings and of the general grounds asserted by the government for denial of admission; a meaningful opportunity to dispute or overcome those grounds, orally or in writing; and a statement of reasons, even if oral and summary, for any adverse decision. Above all, courts should remain open to the legitimacy of highly informal adjudication of claims lodged by first-time applicants for admission. Assuming that the alien has had a real opportunity, however informal, to be heard on the crucial determinations—an opportunity missing in both *Knauff* and *Mezei*—courts should not

---

78. Discarding the border/interior distinction would fatally undermine the Eleventh Circuit's unfortunate extension of *Knauff. Jean v. Nelson,* 727 F.2d 957 (11th Cir.1984) (en banc), *cert. granted,* ___ U.S. ___, 105 S.Ct. 563, 83 L.Ed.2d 504 (1984), discussed pp. 306–314 *supra.*

generally import trial-type procedures or require heavily adversarial proceedings.

Martin, *supra,* at 216, 218–19.

Consider Alex Aleinikoff's response:

The problem [with Martin's analysis] is that no distinction is made among immigrant, non-immigrant and undocumented aliens at the border. All are lumped together apparently because they have not yet lived in the national community; we "owe" them less because they have not been among us, we have not gotten to know or care about them. To me, however, these classes of aliens present distinct issues. To be granted an immigrant visa an alien must normally demonstrate that he or she has a close family relative in this country or is coming to perform a needed job. Generally, someone in the United States—a relative or employer—must have filed a petition on the alien's behalf. Aliens arriving with immigrant visas are entitled to stay as long as they wish (subject to deportation for misconduct). In short, they usually come to this country with a pre-existing stake awaiting them and with an intention to make the United States their permanent home. Most aliens entering the country with non-immigrant visas, on the other hand, come here as temporary visitors with a fixed time limit on their stays. Many must demonstrate that they have "no intention of abandoning" their residence in a foreign country. To be sure, non-immigrants may come with important business to conduct or studies to pursue; but generally the harm imposed upon a non-immigrant wrongfully denied entry is likely to be far less than an immigrant wrongfully excluded.

Since undocumented aliens do not generally reveal their intentions when stopped at the border (unless they claim asylum), it is unclear what stake they may have in entry. They may have family here with whom they seek to live or may simply be seeking a short-term job. But another of the *Mathews* factors applies here: the likelihood that alternative procedures will produce fewer errors. Absence of a visa and a valid unexpired passport are grounds of exclusion. Thus it is unlikely that an undocumented alien—unless he or she claims asylum—will be able to establish eligibility to enter the United States no matter how many procedural rights are provided.

Whether these differences in "personal stake" demand different procedures at the border as a constitutional matter requires careful analysis of the other elements of the *Mathews v. Eldridge* test: the increased accuracy of alternative procedures and the government's interest (including fiscal and administrative burdens). But these factors must be evaluated under Professor Martin's analysis as well. My only purpose here is to suggest that Martin's test of "membership in a national community" does not seem to capture adequately relevant differences among classes of aliens seeking first-time entry.

Aleinikoff, *supra,* at 246–47.[79]

In sum, while the authors may disagree on particular applications of the general theory, we are in firm agreement that procedural due process analysis in immigration law should be fundamentally reoriented. The border/interior distinction, which has held sway since the 1950's, is based on no plausible rationale and is out of step with modern notions of due process. Happily, our approach, which focuses on the relationship of the alien to the community of which he is a part or which he seeks to join, requires more of a shift in judicial explanation than in result: the Court has moved away from the distinction without admitting it. It is time for the Court to go the final step and overrule *Knauff* and *Mezei.*

Are you convinced? What does our theory say about the due process rights of undocumented aliens residing in the United States? *See* Martin, *supra,* at 230–34 (treating them, for constitutional due process purposes, the same as first-time applicants at the border).

A Concluding Dialogue

Believer: You said we should talk again at the end of the deportation chapter and here we are.

Cynic: Yes. Have you read the essay just above?

Believer: Yes.

Cynic: Then you understand that my proposal for a unified immigration proceeding raises no serious constitutional issues.

Believer: It doesn't appear to. But are you suggesting that Congress ought to give all aliens the same hearing procedures?

Cynic: Not at all. I don't think that an alien who can make no colorable claim to be here should receive legal counsel at government expense or other extensive protections to help him contest deportability. There are real costs to guaranteeing a perfect process for all aliens. I would save limited resources for those who need them most—those who have acquired a substantial stake by their presence here.

---

79. Martin responded to Aleinikoff as follows:

There may well be other criteria that should be used to subdivide still further the levels of membership employed in the due process calculus. Professor Hart suggested such an approach in his dialogue, [66 Harv.L.Rev.] at 1392–93 n. 92. He indicated, for example, that applicants bearing duly issued immigrant visas might claim greater protections than other first-time applicants for admission.

Such an approach plainly has conceptual merit; membership, as described here, is largely a continuum, not necessarily a series of sharply defined states. But whether this conceptual sophistication should be employed full-force in judicial decisions is more problematic. At some point, conceptual fidelity must yield to practical limits on implementation, since the doctrine is to be enforced not by a single committee of philosophers but by a far-flung array of disparate judges. In these circumstances a cruder set of categories may be required. But they need not be as crude and ill-fitting as those derived from *Knauff* and *Mezei.*

44 U.Pitt.L.Rev. at 234 n. 238.

Believer: What about resident undocumented aliens? Many have lived here for years and have substantial ties to our community. Would you take away from them what the law now guarantees?

Cynic: Due process applies, of course. But nothing in the due process clause prohibits putting the initial burden on the alien to show a prima facie right to be here. This would require the alien to proffer a valid visa, an I–94, a green card, some other form of documentation, or some reasonable explanation why such documents do not exist. It's not clear to me how a lawyer would help much here.

Believer: I'm not so sure. A lawyer could inform the alien of various avenues of relief available and could also warn the alien about the consequences of making certain statements.

Cynic: True. But, under current regulations, the immigration judge must notify an alien of appropriate forms of relief from deportation.[81] And aliens are presently warned after the issuance of an order to show cause that anything they say may be used against them.[82] If after notification, an undocumented (and, hence, deportable) alien requests a form of relief and makes some showing of a reasonable probability of prevailing, then the alien should receive representation where the immigration judge determines counsel could be helpful in presenting the alien's claim. Certainly this would seem to satisfy *Mathews v. Eldridge.*

Believer: Sounds reasonable. You've made a believer out of me.

Questions

Did Believer give in too easily? Should he have been more cynical?

81. 8 C.F.R. § 242.17(a).   82. 8 C.F.R. § 287.3.

Chapter Six

RELIEF FROM DEPORTATION

From 1976 to 1981 (the last years for which official data are available) the INS averaged over one million apprehensions a year of aliens believed to be deportable. Of these, only about 23,000 per year were actually deported (less than 3% of those apprehended). What happened to the other 97%? In some of the cases the INS decided not to initiate proceedings; in others the immigration judge determined that the government did not prove deportability; and in others the alien disappeared before or after the entry of an order of deportation. But these factors account for only a small part of the difference between apprehensions and deportations. The most significant factor is that the vast majority of deportable aliens are given the opportunity to leave the country *before* the issuance of a deportation order. For the years 1976 to 1979, an average of over 900,000 aliens per year chose this option, known as "voluntary departure." Furthermore, each year hundreds of aliens avoid deportation by taking advantage of one of a number of provisions in the INA that permit aliens, under specified conditions, to regularize their status.

This Chapter will examine the various provisions in the INA that provide relief from deportation. In the majority of deportation hearings, the eligibility for such relief is the only issue: the alien will concede deportability at the outset of the hearing and then request some form of relief from deportation. In examining these sometimes overlapping and highly discretionary forms of relief, ask yourself whether a more coherent process could be created to limit arbitrariness of implementation without sacrificing the flexibility needed to respond to humanitarian concerns.

SECTION A. VOLUNTARY DEPARTURE

1. WHY VOLUNTARY DEPARTURE?

If voluntary departure didn't exist we would have to invent it. The willingness of hundreds of thousands of aliens to waive a deportation hearing and leave the United States before a date certain saves the government untold enforcement resources. Indeed, it is a virtual certainty that the immigration system in this country would break down if all aliens who were apprehended as deportable were to request the deportation hearing the INA provides them. *See generally* E. Harwood, *Can*

Immigration Laws Be Enforced?, The Public Interest, Summer 1983, p. 107.

This may explain why the government would desire a mechanism like voluntary departure.[1] But why would an alien voluntarily choose to leave instead of forcing the government to prove its case in a deportation hearing under the *Woodby* standard of clear, convincing and unequivocal evidence?

It is usual to answer this question by pointing to several provisions in the INA that create a legal incentive for the alien to choose voluntary departure. First and foremost is the fact that aliens who leave the country under an order of deportation and want to re-enter within five years after deportation must obtain the Attorney General's permission to re-apply for admission. An alien who returns without such permission is excludable (INA § 212(a)(17)[2]), may be deported under summary procedures (INA § 242(f)), and is subject to a felony prosecution (INA § 276). None of these provisions applies to an alien who voluntarily departs at his own expense before the entry of an order of deportation. Second, voluntary departure permits an alien to depart to a country of his choice. Furthermore, it saves him the expense, delay, and embarrassment of a deportation hearing.

While these statutorily based reasons no doubt account for many decisions to opt for voluntary departure, it is widely believed that a very different kind of factor plays the dominant role: the inability (or unwillingness) of the United States government to stop the surreptitious entry of aliens over the border. The vast majority of aliens granted voluntary departure are arrested for entering without inspection, and most have no colorable claim of lawful residence. Many of these aliens would rather accept the government's offer of a ride over the border than to stay and fight deportation; their chances of effecting another surreptitious entry are far greater than successfully contesting deportability in a hearing.[3]

1. Voluntary departure may have a darker side as well: one court found that INS officials had coerced aliens into accepting voluntary departure to prevent them from applying for some other benefit—such as political asylum—for which they might be eligible. *Orantes-Hernandez v. Smith,* 541 F.Supp. 351 (C.D.Cal.1982).

2. Until 1981, this provision had considerably more bite to it. Under the pre-1981 provision, a previously deported alien needed the consent of the Attorney General to apply for re-admission, no matter how many years later she applied. The 1981 amendment established a five year "statute of limitations." The amendment, adopted as part of the Immigration and Nationality Act Amendments of 1981, Pub.L. No. 97–116, § 4(1), 95 Stat. 1612, was proposed by INS to relieve the agency of the burden of applications, most of which were granted. *See* H.R. Rep. No. 264, 97th Cong., 1st Sess. 20 (1981).

3. Apparently, even some aliens who have colorable claims for political asylum will accept voluntary departure if the alternative is extended detention in the United States pending determination of their asylum claims.

Consider the finding of a report by the Office of the United Nations High Commissioner for Refugees, which examined treatment of undocumented Salvadorans apprehended by the INS:

[M]any Salvadorans who we spoke to and who had opted for voluntary departure said they preferred to return home, rather than sit in detention indefinitely while their asylum applications were being considered. As one of them put it, "we would rather go back home and die", or in the words of another, "go back and try entering the U.S. again and with luck make it next time." Our impression is that another reason for voluntary return is that many Salvadoran asylum seekers cannot

The availability of voluntary departure, coupled with the realities of law enforcement and the rational decisions of aliens, creates a sequence at the border that is repeated over and over again: unlawful entry, apprehension, detention, return, and another unlawful entry. Consider the following description of the border game at Chula Vista, California.

PAUL EHRLICH, LOY BILDERBACK & ANNE EHRLICH, THE GOLDEN DOOR: INTERNATIONAL MIGRATION, MEXICO, AND THE UNITED STATES

302–04 (1979)

Although it is against Mexican law to leave that country and against United States law to enter this one without proper clearance, nothing much happens to most of those who try. When a *mojado*[a] is apprehended, the agent fills out an INS Form I–213 on him, usually in the field, and calls for a van to pick him up. The illegal is then taken to the Staging Area (formerly called the Detention Facility) at the station, where he is held. In the overwhelming bulk of cases, the illegal is voluntarily repatriated—"VR'ed"—to Mexico within a few hours. In this event a statement is stamped onto the Form I–213 in which the *mojado* admits that he sought to enter the United States illegally, and the *mojado* signs it.

As many as possible are VR'ed to Mexicali, about 100 miles away, simply to put them that much farther from the border at San Ysidro. There are not enough buses to send them all, so most are VR'ed to Tijuana, about a mile and a quarter away. The bus stops at a gate leading from the United States to Mexico, and the people are let through. They are interrogated by a Mexican immigration official who turns back those whom he feels are not Mexican, and the rest are free to try to cross into the United States again that evening.

Record-keeping on the illegals is very skimpy because of the lack of clerical assistance at the station. The I–213 is a manifold form with three copies of the full report and two more copies of basic data on the illegal. The original is simply filed chronologically under the date of apprehension at the station. Another copy is sent to Sector Headquarters, and the third is thrown away. One copy of the smaller, basic-data form is sent to Washington, D.C., and the other is supposed to be filed alphabetically at the station. When the station found itself one and a half years behind in its alphabetical filing, it gave up and now maintains alphabetical files only on smugglers.

* * *

raise the required bond money to secure their release from detention—especially in view of the new INS policy not to grant work authorization to "illegals."

United Nations High Commissioner for Refugees Mission to Monitor INS Asylum Processing of Salvadoran Illegal Entrants—September 13–18, 1981, *reprinted in* 128 Cong. Rec. S827–31 (daily ed. Feb. 11, 1982).

a. Undocumented worker, from the Spanish word for "wet" (hence, the derogatory expression "wetback")—eds.

With 10 percent of the Border Patrol, 5 aircraft, and 43 electronic sensors out to get them, why do more *mojados* pick this 17-mile strip of border than any other? There are three reasons. First, even with this formidable array of men and machines, the border is by no means sealed. Second, nowhere else on the border does a major Mexican city abut a major U.S. city with easy access to the interior. El Paso/Juárez abut one another, but El Paso is still a long way from anything else. Moreover, like almost everyone else, Mexicans want to come to California. Now it is incredibly easy to cross from Tijuana to San Diego, and as urbanization fills in the empty places between the two cities it will become even easier. There is still open country between Tijuana and the towns on the United States side, but it varies from a half-mile to two or three miles. Finally, the volume of persons trying to come in is simply too great for the Patrol agents to stop—a case of safety in numbers.

The Border Patrol at Chula Vista and every other station is proud of the low level of force they use in accomplishing their mission. They are aware that this low level of force is in everyone's interest, including that of the Patrol agents. They do not get tough, and in turn the *mojados* do not resist when apprehended. Occasionally one will run * * * but only rarely does he strike an agent. The *mojados* understand that they will not be beaten up or robbed. At Chula Vista they will merely be locked up for the night and repatriated in the morning. There is little to run from and less to fight over. An illegal does not pay his *coyote*[b] unless the crossing is successful, and most have little chance of making it if separated from the smuggler. It is these attitudes on the part of the *mojados* that make it possible for less than 250 Patrol agents to apprehend 33,000 illegals in a single month.

In addition to offering no resistance, a captured *mojado* ordinarily does not take legal action, and consequently the legal niceties are often overlooked. [A Form] is filled out, a rubberstamp admission of guilt is pressed into the appropriate box, the illegal signs it, and waits in the detention facility for the bus that will take him or her back to Mexico. * * *

2. THE MECHANICS OF VOLUNTARY DEPARTURE

Two distinct sections of the statute authorize the Attorney General to grant voluntary departure. Study the two provisions:

INA § 242(b):

> In the discretion of the Attorney General, and under such regulations as he may prescribe, deportation proceedings, including issuance of a warrant of arrest, and a finding of deportability under this section need not be required in the case of any alien who admits to belonging to a class of aliens who are deportable under section 241 if such alien voluntarily departs from the United States at his own expense, or is removed at Government expense as hereinafter authorized, unless the Attorney General

---

b. A smuggler who helps undocumented workers enter the United States—eds.

has reason to believe that such alien is deportable under paragraph (4), (5), (6), (7), (11), (12), (14), (15), (16), (17), or (18) of section 241(a). If any alien who is authorized to depart voluntarily under the preceding sentence is financially unable to depart at his own expense and the Attorney General deems his removal to be in the best interest of the United States, the expense of such removal may be paid from the appropriation for the enforcement of this Act.

INA § 244(e):

The Attorney General may, in his discretion, permit any alien under deportation proceedings, other than an alien within the provisions of paragraph (4), (5), (6), (7), (11), (12), (14), (15), (16), (17), (18), or (19) of section 241(a) (and also any alien within the purview of such paragraphs if he is also within the provisions of paragraph (2) of subsection (a) of this section), to depart voluntarily from the United States at his own expense in lieu of deportation if such alien shall establish to the satisfaction of the Attorney General that he is, and has been, a person of good moral character for at least five years immediately preceding his application for voluntary departure under this subsection.

What is the difference between these provisions? Is there an explanation for why the statute might include both?

By regulation, the Attorney General has delegated his authority under the two provisions to different classes of immigration officials. Under INA § 242(b), aliens not yet in deportation hearings may be granted relief by district directors, district officers who are in charge of investigations, officers in charge, and chief patrol agents. 8 C.F.R. § 242.5(a)(1). Relief under § 244(e), available after the beginning of a deportation hearing, is granted by an immigration judge. 8 C.F.R. § 242.17(b).

While the overwhelming number of grants of voluntary departure are made to effect the return of undocumented aliens who entered without inspection,[4] voluntary departure is also used to permit some aliens to *stay* in the United States for a period of time without being subject to deportation proceedings. Thus, by regulation, an alien who is an immediate relative of a United States citizen or who has applied for an immigrant visa and has "a priority date for an immigrant visa not more than 60 days later than the date show [sic] in the latest Visa Office Bulletin," may be granted voluntary departure (*i.e.*, permission to remain here) "until the American consul is ready to issue an immigrant visa." 8 C.F.R. § 242.5(a)(2)(vi)(C), (3). When the visa becomes available the alien may leave the United States not subject to an order of deportation, pick up the visa overseas and return as a lawful immigrant.

---

4. *See* 8 C.F.R. § 242.5(a)(2)(i) (voluntary departure may be granted to a statutorily eligible alien who "is a native of a foreign contiguous territory" [read: Mexico] and who is not eligible for an immigrant visa).

Perhaps the most startling, and controversial, form of voluntary departure is "extended voluntary departure" (EVD). This inelegant bit of Newspeak really means extended voluntary non-departure: INS grants EVD primarily to classes of aliens who would otherwise be returned to countries undergoing civil war or other breakdowns in public order. In the past, EVD has been granted to aliens from Cuba, Chile, Vietnam, Lebanon, Ethiopia, Uganda, Nicaragua, Iran, Afghanistan and Poland. The policies underlying the granting of EVD have come under increasing scrutiny because of charges that such relief is granted or denied for improper political and foreign policy reasons. Thus critics of the Reagan Administration have noted that EVD has been granted to Poles but denied to Salvadorans. *See Hotel & Restaurant Employees Union, Local 25 v. Smith*, 594 F.Supp. 502 (D.D.C.1984) (granting government's motion to dismiss Union's challenge to government's practice of denying EVD to Salvadorans). The controversy surrounding EVD is considered in detail in Chapter Eight *infra*.

In our examination of the various forms of relief from deportation, we will notice that the granting of relief usually involves two aspects: the meeting of statutory prerequisites for the relief and a favorable exercise of discretion by the Attorney General. Note that both of these elements are present in INA §§ 242(b) and 244(e).

HIBBERT v. INS

United States Court of Appeals, Second Circuit, 1977.
554 F.2d 17.

MESKILL, CIRCUIT JUDGE:

With some regularity, this Court notes the incredible complexity of the Immigration and Nationality Acts. Chief Judge Kaufman, for example, has aptly compared them to the labyrinth of ancient Crete. *Tim Lok v. INS*, 548 F.2d 37 (2d Cir.1977). Frequently, we are called upon to extricate a hapless immigrant from the maze of statutory and regulatory language in which he finds himself enmeshed. This case, however, provides a graphic illustration of the opposite problem. It demonstrates how a resourceful litigant can exploit the procedural complexities of the immigration laws to render justice anything but "just, speedy and inexpensive." This petitioner has illegally been in the United States for nearly seven years. First ordered to leave the country in 1971, he has put off the day of reckoning time and again by astute legal maneuvers. * * *

FACTS.

Roy Hibbert is a native and citizen of Jamaica. In November, 1970, he illegally entered the United States by paying someone to drive him across the Canadian border into New York. Shortly thereafter, in May 1971, Hibbert "married" Mattie Martin, an American citizen. At this point, the immigration authorities were still unaware of Hibbert's presence in the United States. The following month, a visa petition was filed by Martin on his behalf. * * * Both Hibbert and Martin testified under oath to the *bona fides* of their marriage. In September, 1971, the District

Director approved the visa petition. Accordingly, Hibbert was granted the privilege of voluntary departure until October, 1971. Had all gone according to plan, he could have then legally re-entered the country. He failed, however, to leave the United States at that time.

In June, 1973, Hibbert's wife withdrew her sponsorship of the visa petition. In its place, she gave a sworn statement denying that she and Hibbert had ever been actually married. She stated that she had been paid to enter into a sham marriage, solely to establish Hibbert's immigration status. Armed with this new information, the District Director revoked his approval of the visa petition in October, 1973, pursuant to 8 C.F.R. § 205.1(a). The same day, the INS began deportation proceedings against Hibbert.

At the hearing, Hibbert conceded his deportability, but requested the privilege of voluntary departure, which he had been afforded once before. The immigration judge who heard the case rendered his decision in March, 1974. He found that Hibbert's statements about the fraudulent marriage constituted false testimony under INA § 101(f)(6), and thus that Hibbert was ineligible for the privilege of voluntary departure because of his bad moral character. INA § 244(e). The immigration judge further stated that even in the absence of a statutory bar, he would not exercise his discretion favorably, in view of Hibbert's immigration history of illegal entry and false statements. On review, the Board of Immigration Appeals held, in November, 1974, that the immigration judge was correct in refusing to grant voluntary departure in view of Hibbert's immigration history, whether or not he was eligible under the statute.

Hibbert appealed to this Court in February, 1975, and thus was granted an automatic stay of deportation. INA § 106(a)(3). In April, 1976, Hibbert withdrew this appeal with prejudice.[1] Meanwhile, in March, he had petitioned the Board of Immigration Appeals to reopen the deportation proceedings pursuant to 8 C.F.R. §§ 3.2, 3.8. The grounds alleged for relief were that Hibbert was now married to a resident alien about to become a citizen; he also stated that his new wife was pregnant. The Board, exercising its administrative discretion, denied this petition in May, 1975.

Undaunted, Hibbert then filed a motion to reconsider the Board's refusal to reopen the deportation proceedings, seven days after the withdrawal of his first appeal. Again, he claimed that there was new evidence meriting reconsideration of his case. The grounds alleged were that Hibbert's wife was now a citizen and he was the father of a citizen child.

---

1. The government characterizes that proceeding as a dilatory tactic. The record strongly suggests that this is correct, and that Hibbert never intended to perfect that appeal. We wish to caution the Bar against abusing the process of this Court solely to gain delays in deportation. Such conduct is a serious violation of professional ethics; moreover, it can only create additional equities against the alien. See In re Bithoney, 486 F.2d 319 (1st Cir.1973).

There is an additional danger in such appeals. Hibbert could have attacked the deportation order at that time. By invoking the power of the Court, and then withdrawing the appeal with prejudice, he precluded himself from raising any issue which could have been the subject of that appeal. Thus, the deportation order is now *res judicata,* and petitioner may appeal only from the refusal to reopen.

He further claimed that his bad moral character was no longer a bar to relief because the five-year period set out in INA § 244(e) would expire on August 4, 1976, and thus he was now eligible for voluntary departure. This motion, too, was denied, in June, 1976. In July, just before Hibbert was to report for deportation, he appealed to this Court for the second time.

DISCUSSION.

Hibbert carries a double burden in this case. First, he must establish that he meets the statutory requirements for the discretionary privilege of voluntary departure. Next, he must demonstrate that the Board failed to exercise its discretion, and that there was some likelihood that a remand to the Board of Immigration Appeals would result in a favorable decision.

* * *

As the immigration judge found, Hibbert failed to meet the requirements of § 244(e). The five-year period is not a statute of limitations; it is merely a threshold requirement for relief.[2]

Deportation is a drastic sanction, and we have repeatedly construed the immigration laws to avoid harsh results. At the same time, there is no reason to strain for hypertechnical readings of these involved statutes in order to grant relief to those never intended for the law's benefits. This is such a case.

Hibbert has remained in the United States as long as he has only because of his repeated flouting of lawful orders and frivolous, but well timed, applications for relief. One who fits within the statutory definition of bad moral character does not transform himself into a paragon of virtue by five years of artful dodging. We will not allow the immigration laws to be manipulated in this way, using the courts to create the equities they are meant to discover.

On the final application to the Board to reconsider its decision not to reopen, there was no new evidence. Mrs. Hibbert's citizenship and the birth of Hibbert's child were the natural consequences of her earlier virtual completion of the naturalization process and her pregnancy, all of which was known to the Board at the time of the first motion to reopen.

Marriage to a citizen and the birth of a citizen child is a factor of significance to the INS, even if these events take place after deportation proceedings have begun. Hibbert argues that these factors conceivably support a favorable exercise of discretion by the Board of Immigration Appeals, and thus the case should be remanded for a formal determination of his eligibility. This contention is without merit.

In reviewing a refusal to reopen a deportation proceeding, we are limited to the administrative record and can reverse only for abuse of

2. Petitioner has misconceived the import of the five-year period. It is necessary but not sufficient for a finding of good moral character. INA § 244(e) requires such proof for "at least" five years. Thus, petitioner's argument that the INS *must* find him to be eligible for the exercise of discretion is without foundation. *See also* INA § 101(f) (final clause). Moreover, the burden of proof is not upon the INS, but upon the petitioner.

discretion. Hibbert's unfortunate immigration history amply supports the discretionary refusal to waive deportation. As we noted above, it is clear that the Board possessed all the favorable, as well as unfavorable, facts in Hibbert's case. However, he argues that the Board failed to reach the question of eligibility under INA §§ 101(f) and 244(e) as he claims it was required to do.

It is clear from numerous, unequivocal statements by the immigration judge and the Board that they would not grant Hibbert the discretionary privilege of voluntary departure. In view of this, there is no reason to remand the case to the Board for a pointless determination of his technical eligibility, since the end result will be deportation.

The Supreme Court recently dealt with a closely analogous situation in *INS v. Bagamasbad*, 429 U.S. 24, 97 S.Ct. 200, 50 L.Ed.2d 190 (1976). In a *per curiam* opinion, the Court held that the INS may pretermit threshold questions of eligibility if the result is foregone:

> The District Director of the Immigration and Naturalization Service (INS) denied respondent's application as a matter of discretion because she had made serious misrepresentations to the United States Consul who had issued her visa. For the same reasons, the immigration judge presiding at a later deportation hearing also declined to exercise his discretion in her favor. Neither the District Director nor the immigration judge addressed himself to whether respondent satisfied the specific statutory requirements for permanent residence. The Board of Immigration Appeals affirmed, finding that the circumstances fully supported the discretionary denial of relief and concluding that "the immigration judge could properly pretermit the question of statutory eligibility and deny the application ... as an exercise of discretion."

> A divided Court of Appeals sitting en banc held that although the immigration judge had properly exercised his discretion to deny respondent's application, the statute required the judge to make findings and reach conclusions with respect to respondent's eligibility for admission into this country as a permanent resident. Disagreeing as we do with the Court of Appeals, we grant the petition for certiorari filed by the INS and the motion by respondents to proceed in forma pauperis and reverse the judgment of the Court of Appeals.

> As a general rule courts and agencies are not required to make findings on issues the decision of which is unnecessary to the results they reach. Here it is conceded that respondent's application would have been properly denied whether or not she satisfied the statutory eligibility requirements. In these circumstances, absent express statutory requirement, we see no reason to depart from the general rule and require the immigration judge to arrive at purely advisory findings and conclusions as to statutory eligibility.

Id. at 24–26, 97 S.Ct. at 200–201. (Citations omitted). This case is indistinguishable on this issue from *Bagamasbad*. Regardless of whether the deportation order rested upon a finding of statutory ineligibility or an unfavorable exercise of discretion, it is amply supported by the record, and no contrary result could be expected upon a remand.

The order of the Board of Immigration Appeals is affirmed.

A Note on Motions to Reopen and Motions to Reconsider

In order to forestall deportation, Hibbert filed before the BIA both a motion to reopen his deportation proceeding and a motion asking the BIA to reconsider its decision. A motion to reopen is filed in order to permit the moving party to submit new evidence (such as marriage to a U.S. citizen) that may affect an alien's deportability or to permit an alien to apply for relief from deportation. (An alien may have been unable to apply for relief during the deportation proceeding because he may not then have satisfied one of the prerequisites for relief—such as residence in this country for a certain number of years.) Motions to reopen may be filed before immigration officers, immigration judges or the BIA, as appropriate. 8 C.F.R. §§ 3.2, 103.5, 242.22. The motion must be supported by affidavits or other evidentiary material and may not be granted unless the evidence sought to be offered is deemed material and was not available and could not have been discovered or presented at the former hearing. 8 C.F.R. §§ 3.2, 242.22. If the BIA grants a motion to reopen, the record is returned "to the officer of the Service having administrative jurisdiction over the place where the reopened proceedings are to be conducted." 8 C.F.R. § 3.8(d).

The filing of a motion to reopen does not result in an automatic stay of the execution of an outstanding order of deportation; but the BIA and immigration judges are authorized to stay deportation pending determination of the motion. 8 C.F.R. §§ 3.8(a), 242.22.

A motion to reconsider asks the decision-maker to review claimed errors in her earlier appraisal of the law or the facts. Like motions to reopen, motions to reconsider may be filed before immigration officers, immigration judges or the BIA. 8 C.F.R. §§ 3.2, 103.5, 242.22. Motions to reconsider must state the reasons upon which the motion is based and "shall be supported by such precedent decisions as are pertinent." 8 C.F.R. §§ 3.8(a), 103.5. If a motion to reconsider is granted, the decision-maker may affirm, modify or reverse the original decision made in the case.

See generally G & R §§ 1.10g, 1.9d(6), 3.22a, 5.13a; Hurwitz, *Motion Practice Before the Board of Immigration Appeals,* 20 San Diego L.Rev. 79 (1982).

SECTION B. PROSECUTORIAL DISCRETION

An alien who is deportable will not be deported if the government decides not to initiate proceedings against the alien. Decisions not to prosecute, which typically are said to fall under the heading of "prosecutorial discretion," may be based on a number of factors, such as lack of enforcement resources, compelling humanitarian concerns, or the imminent issuance of documentation that would regularize the alien's status. *See generally* Roberts, *The Exercise of Administrative Discretion Under the Immigration Laws,* 13 San Diego L.Rev. 144, 149–52 (1975).

The exercise of prosecutorial discretion raises difficult issues, several of which are reflected in the following materials. These include: How does the agency establish uniformity of practice among several dozen district offices? Should an alien's ability to remain in the United States turn on the city in which he happens to reside? If the agency seeks to ameliorate potential arbitrariness by promulgating internal guidelines for the exercise of discretion, should those guidelines be enforceable by the courts?

1. DEFERRED ACTION STATUS

For a number of years, INS operated under an internal policy not to proceed against aliens presenting compelling humanitarian reasons to stay in the United States. INS placed such aliens in a "nonpriority" enforcement status—now generally known as "deferred action." Although the existence of the program was known, the actual guidelines used by INS to grant deferred action status did not come to light until the mid-1970's. The attorney for the alien responsible for the disclosure of the guidelines tells the story.

LEON WILDES, THE NONPRIORITY PROGRAM OF THE IMMIGRATION AND NATURALIZATION SERVICE GOES PUBLIC: THE LITIGATIVE USE OF THE FREEDOM OF INFORMATION ACT

14 San Diego L.Rev. 42, 42–49 (1976).

Had it not been for a certain rock musician and former *Beatle* named John Lennon, an article on the nonpriority program might never have been written. The research required a plaintiff willing to patiently await the outcome of numerous administrative requests for information and then to pursue a suit under the Freedom of Information Act (FOIA).[1] The entire program was so shrouded in secrecy that a former District Director of the Immigration and Naturalization Service (INS) actually denied the existence of the program. The *Operations Instruction*[2] embodying the procedure was buried in the *Blue Sheets,* the INS internal regulations never made available to the public. The situation was a classic example of secret law.

* * *

Lennon came to the United States as a visitor in August 1971, and was permitted to remain until late February 1972. At that time the INS instituted deportation proceedings against him as an alleged overstay. Lennon claimed that the proceedings were instituted for political reasons. Among other things, he requested a grant of *nonpriority* status.

1. 5 U.S.C.A. § 552 (1974).   2. [O.I. 103.1(a)(1)(ii).]

Nonpriority status is a euphemism for an administrative stay of deportation which effectively places an otherwise deportable alien in a position where he is not removed simply because his case has the lowest possible priority for INS action. Traditionally, the status was accorded to aliens whose departure from the United States would result in extreme hardship. Lennon and artist Yoko Ono, his wife, had come to this country to fight contested custody proceedings concerning Kyoko, Ono's daughter by a prior marriage. Lennon and Ono were completely successful on the law, with courts in several jurisdictions awarding them custody of Kyoko. However the father absconded with the child and could not be found. In the midst of the frantic search for the child, Lennon and Ono were subjected to expulsion proceedings. They felt, accordingly, that the equities involved in their continued search for the child justified the application for nonpriority status. Hardship notwithstanding, nonpriority status was never even given consideration, and the deportation proceedings relentlessly advanced.

Commencing on May 1, 1972, through extensive correspondence with the INS, Lennon made every conceivable effort to obtain the records relevant to nonpriority procedures before instituting suit in federal court. However, after more than a year's correspondence, the records were not forthcoming. In fact, the Service stated that the data about nonpriority cases were "not compiled" although at no time did it deny the existence of either a nonpriority program or relevant records. Lennon's demands, made pursuant to the FOIA, continued until August 1973, with no response from the Service.

In his deportation proceedings, Lennon moved to depose a Government witness with knowledge of the program. His motion was rejected, however, because the immigration judge thought it irrelevant to any issue over which he could rule. Finally, when attempts to obtain the records through regular administrative channels failed, an action was instituted in district court, requesting injunctive relief pursuant to section (a)(3) of the FOIA. The suit was filed within a short time after filing a companion action against certain Government officials. The companion suit sought a hearing to determine whether such officials had conspired to prejudge an immigration case, to prejudge various applications for discretionary relief and the premature commencement of deportation proceedings against the plaintiff. Among the wrongs alleged was the Government's unexplained failure to consider Lennon's request for nonpriority classification.

* * *

When Lennon's FOIA action was instituted, the rules on nonpriority classification were contained in an INS *Operations Instruction* which was not available to the public. Subsequent to the action and as a direct result of it, this *Instruction* was transferred from the unpublished *Blue Sheets* to the published *White Sheets.*[17] The publication of this *Operations*

17. The INS has available to the public in various district offices, including New York, and in the Central Office in Washington a volume containing the *Operations Instructions* of the INS for its employees. However, not all instructions are made available. Where a deletion has been made, Blue Sheets are inserted in the volume. * *

Instruction was significant, for it was a formal, public acknowledgement by the INS that such a program existed. Even so, of much greater value to the litigant are the records of those cases in which nonpriority status was granted or denied. The records requested at the time of the action consisted of periodic reports by district directors. Each time a nonpriority decision was made the director had to record his reasons, forward his recommendation or decision to his regional commissioner, who then forwarded it to the Central Office in Washington, D.C., where an officer or a committee of officers acted on the decision and kept records.[18]

* * *

[In light of counsel's arguments for release of the records under the FOIA,] the Government decided that its most appropriate course would be to provide the plaintiff with the case histories of all extant approved nonpriority cases—1843 in number. Thus, for the first time, both the procedures and the records of all known approved cases were made available to the public.[a]

———

The release of the INS Operations Instructions on deferred action status predictably led to claims by aliens not granted the status that INS had violated its own regulations in denying their applications. Thus courts were forced to consider whether INS decisions taken pursuant to the Operations Instruction are reviewable; and, if so, what standard they should apply in reviewing agency refusals to confer the status. One court's answer follows.

NICHOLAS v. INS

United States Court of Appeals, Ninth Circuit, 1979.
590 F.2d 802.

TAKASUGI, DISTRICT JUDGE.*

George Bernard Nicholas, the petitioner herein, is a forty-three year old native and citizen of the Bahamas. He has remained in this country at all times since his last entry in 1967, having since married a United States citizen. They have two children, both United States citizens.

---

18. * * * [T]he *Operations Instruction* has recently been revised so that nonpriority applications are handled at the regional level rather than by a Central Office committee. This change was instituted on April 30, 1975, as a result of the litigation described herein.

a. Lennon's immigration difficulties did not end with release of the information on deferred action cases. Both Lennon and Ono sought to adjust their status in the deportation hearing, and the INS concluded that each was eligible for third preference status. However, Lennon was denied adjustment based on a prior conviction in England for possession of cannabis resin. The Second Circuit ultimately reversed, concluding that the prior offense made guilty knowledge irrelevant and thus did not come within § 212(a)(23) (conviction of a law relating to illicit possession of marijuana). *Lennon v. INS*, 527 F.2d 187 (2d Cir.1976).—eds.

* The Honorable Robert M. Takasugi, United States District Judge for the Central District of California, sitting by designation.

On June 26, 1974, the United States Immigration and Naturalization Service served an order to show cause and notice of hearing upon petitioner, charging him with deportability arising from a series of events commencing in the early 1950's.[2] The order was based upon his alleged violation of * * * the Immigration and Nationality Act, in that he was excludable as an alien who had been arrested and deported at the time of his entry in 1967, and that he had not been granted consent to apply for readmission by the proper authority. [INA § 212(a)(17).] During the deportation hearing, petitioner was further charged with deportability as an alien who had been convicted of a crime relating to drugs or narcotics, arising from a 1975 conviction of conspiracy to possess a controlled substance with the intent to distribute * * *.

Prior to the hearing on the order to show cause, petitioner, through counsel, orally requested the District Director of the San Diego office of the INS to grant petitioner non-priority status, deferring action upon the deportation indefinitely. Immigration and Naturalization Service Operations Instruction 103.1(a)(1)(ii). The request was verbally denied at that time.

* * * The Immigration Judge found petitioner deportable on both grounds charged * * *. [The BIA dismissed petitioner's appeal.]

* * *

Petitioner first asks us to overrule the District Director's decision denying nonpriority status [8] under O.I. 103.1(a)(1)(ii).[9] It is first necessary to determine the standard of review which this court must apply to the denial before the propriety of the District Director's decision may be examined. To do this, we analyze the Instruction's purpose and effect, taking into account its language and its prior treatment by the courts.

In urging us to adopt a standard with a wider scope of discretion, the INS points out that O.I. 103.1(a)(1)(ii) is an intra-agency administrative guideline rather than a Statute [sic], passed by Congress. The INS feels that the granting of a non-priority status, therefore, should be viewed as comparable to a prosecutor's discretion in deciding whether to initiate a

---

2. Petitioner was forced to leave the United States in 1954, after the issuance of an order for his deportation.

8. "Non-priority status" is also known as "deferred action category." The two terms are used interchangeably.

9. "(ii) *Deferred action.* In every case where the district director determines that adverse action would be unconscionable because of the existence of appealing humanitarian factors, he shall recommend consideration for deferred action category. His recommendation shall be made to the regional commissioner concerned on Form G–312, which shall be signed personally by the district director. Interim or biennial reviews should be conducted to determine whether approved cases be continued or removed from deferred action category.

"When determining whether a case should be recommended for deferred action category, consideration should include the following: (1) advanced or tender age; (2) many years' presence in the United States; (3) physical or mental condition requiring care or treatment in the United States; (4) family situation in the United States—effect of expulsion; (5) criminal, immoral or subversive activities or affiliations—recent conduct. If the district director's recommendation is approved by the regional commissioner the alien shall be notified that no action will be taken by the Service to disturb his immigration status, or that his departure from the United States has been deferred indefinitely, whichever is appropriate." O.I. 103.-1(a)(1)(ii), p. 371 (12/31/75).

criminal prosecution. As such, it is argued, for reversal, a showing must be made not only that an established pattern of treatment of others similarly situated was departed from without reason, but also that the decision was based upon impermissible considerations, such as race or religion. No such impermissible considerations have been alleged.

A stricter standard is advocated by petitioner * * *. [His standard] would require us to find only that the decision of the District Director was arbitrary or capricious, so as to constitute an abuse of discretion.

Resolution of this divergence of opinion lies in the nature of the Operations Instruction involved. We must determine whether its purpose and effect are more like those of an internal administrative convenience or those of a procedure conferring a substantive right. Our sister circuits appear to be divided in their interpretations.

The Fifth Circuit, expanding upon a footnote appearing in a Second Circuit decision, is clearly of the opinion that the Operations Instruction under scrutiny here is for the administrative convenience of the INS:

"The Second Circuit has described non-priority status as an 'informal administrative stay of deportation' during which the deportation order remains suspended and may be executed at any time, and there is no effect on the substantive ruling by the INS. *Lennon v. Immigration & Naturalization Service*, 527 F.2d 187, 191 n. 5 (2nd Cir.1975). An examination of the *Lennon* opinion suggests that unlike the other forms of relief enumerated in [8 C.F.R.] § 242.17, for which a respondent may apply, non-priority status is in the nature of a voluntary stay of the agency's mandate *pendente lite*, issued in large part for the convenience of the INS. Such a suspension is ... inappropriate where, as here, deportability is conceded and only delay is desired ... The decision to grant or withhold non-priority status therefore lies within the particular discretion of the INS, and we decline to hold that the agency has no power to create and employ such a category for its own administrative convenience without standardizing the category and allowing applications for inclusion in it." *Soon Bok Yoon v. INS*, 538 F.2d 1211, 1213 (5th Cir.1976).

Two recent Eighth Circuit cases, however, have taken an approach to the employment of non-priority status which appears directly at odds with the function attributed to the Operations Instruction by the Fifth Circuit. In *Vergel v. INS*, 536 F.2d 755 (8th Cir.1976), and *David v. INS*, 548 F.2d 219 (8th Cir.1977), the court upheld deportation orders, denying the petitioners relief, but stayed their mandate ninety days *to allow the aliens to apply to their District Directors* for "deferred action category," or non-priority status, under O.I. 103.1(a)(1)(ii). The Eighth Circuit felt the Operations Instruction to be appropriate and advisable *for the very purpose of delay*, in the form of an indefinite stay of deportation. *Vergel, supra*, 536 F.2d at 757–58; *David, supra*, 548 F.2d at 223. These recommendations were based upon the existence of compelling humanitarian factors and not upon administrative convenience.

Seeing such direct conflict between the two circuits which have considered the granting of non-priority status, we turn to the Instruction's language. Three points become readily apparent upon examination: (1) The *sole* basis for granting relief is the presence of humanitarian factors; (2) The Instruction is directive in nature; and (3) The effect of such relief upon a deportation order is *to defer it indefinitely.*

Humanitarian factors, including five express criteria, are set forth as the only basis upon which the District Director is to weigh the propriety of non-priority status (deferred action category):

"(ii) *Deferred action.* In every case where the district director determines that adverse action would be *unconscionable because of the existence of humanitarian factors,* he shall recommend consideration for deferred action category . . . .

"When determining whether a case should be recommended for deferred action category, consideration should include the following: (1) advanced or tender age; (2) many years' presence in the United States; (3) physical or mental condition requiring care or treatment in the United States; (4) family situation in the United States—effect of expulsion; (5) criminal, immoral, or subversive activities or affiliations—recent conduct." O.I. 103.1(a)(1)(ii), *supra.* (Emphasis added).

It is obvious that this procedure exists out of consideration for the convenience of the petitioner, and not that of the INS. In this aspect, it far more closely resembles a substantive provision for relief than an internal procedural guideline.

The Instruction provides that, "In *every* case" where relief is appropriate, the District Director "*shall* recommend" deferred action category. O.I. 103.1(a)(1)(ii), *supra.* The directive nature of the language implies that the District Director is to consider each case which is brought to his attention fully, to satisfy the mandate that all cases for which relief is appropriate receive a recommendation for such relief. This does not ring of the almost limitless discretion of a prosecutor deciding whether to press charges. It sounds more in the nature of an administrative judge's duty to preserve a substantive right, by fully and fairly weighing all matters before him. As such, the scope of review should be more stringent.

Finally, the effect of granting non-priority status is to provide an *indefinite delay* in deportation:

"If the district director's recommendation is approved by the regional commissioner the alien should be notified that no action will be taken by the Service to disturb his immigration status, or that his departure from the United States has been deferred indefinitely, whichever is appropriate." O.I. 103.1(a)(1)(ii), *supra.*

Delay in deportation is expressly the remedy provided by the Instruction. It is the precise advantage to be gained by seeking non-priority status. Clearly, the Instruction, in this way, confers a substantive benefit upon the alien, rather than setting up an administrative convenience.

By further providing for periodic review of non-priority status,[11] the Instruction plainly contemplates a scheme where the status would pre-

11. "Interim or biennial reviews should be conducted to determine whether approved cases be continued or removed from deferred action category." O.I. 103.1(a)(1)(ii), *supra.*

clude any deportation as long as the relevant humanitarian factors are still compelling, rather than being subject to termination at the convenience of the INS. We take a view of the granting of non-priority status which is more closely in accord with that of the Eighth Circuit.

Although it is true that, in the main, operations instructions are nothing more than intra-agency guidelines which create no substantive rights, O.I. 103.1(a)(1)(ii) differs from the norm in that its effect can be final and permanent, with the same force as that of a Congressional statute. It clearly and directly affects substantive rights—the ability of an individual subject to its provisions to continue residence in the United States.   * * *

This court feels that the wide discretion allowed by the Instruction, even if not explicitly created by Statute, should be consistent with the Congressionally approved scheme for review of the status of aliens in this country. It deserves a similar review. Accordingly, we hold that the decision of an INS District Director upon an application for non-priority status will stand unless it so departs from an established pattern of treatment of others similarly situated without reason, as to be arbitrary and capricious, and an abuse of discretion.

The burden upon one who endeavors to establish arbitrary or capricious action is quite heavy. As the traditional standard of review for discretionary decisions, it leaves the District Director with ample flexibility in exercising his judgment. In this instance, although petitioner has prevailed on the question of which standard of review to apply to his appeal, he nevertheless has failed to meet the great burden imposed by this standard.

In order to demonstrate that the decision upon petitioner's application for non-priority status deviated from an established pattern without reason, petitioner must first show what the norm is which allegedly has been violated. He has failed to do so. His evidence consists solely of statistics and conclusions from Wildes, *The Non-priority Program of the Immigration and Naturalization Service Goes Public,* 14 San Diego L.Rev. 42 (1976). Unfortunately, this article digested only the cases in which non-priority status was *approved*. Of course, this makes impossible any effort to glean criteria which are determinative of approval. We are merely able to draw the conclusion that the presence of certain factors, in themselves, are not determinative of denial.

Petitioner notes the limitations of his data in his brief, citing his limited finances as a barrier to presentation of more salient information. The INS has presented no figures of its own. Despite our appreciation for petitioner's predicament, we cannot escape the conclusion that he has failed to lay the groundwork for his challenge. Regardless of the presence of humanitarian factors which, taken alone, could build a compelling case for petitioner, his appeal on this ground must be denied.

* * *

* * * [P]etitioner's appeal is * * * Denied.

Notes

1. Other circuits rejected the holding in *Nicholas*. *See, e.g., Velasco-Gutierrez v. Crossland,* 732 F.2d 792 (10th Cir.1984); *Pasquini v. Morris,* 700 F.2d 658 (11th Cir.1983).

2. The court states that the deferred action Instruction "resembles a substantive provision of relief" and that it "differs from [usual intra-agency guidelines] in that its effect can be final and permanent, with the same force as that of a Congressional statute." Assuming this characterization is correct, does INS have the authority to issue such an Instruction? If so, should not the Instruction have been promulgated according to the procedures established for rule-making by the Administrative Procedure Act (5 U.S.C.A. § 553)? Does the Instruction, in effect, add a ground of relief from deportation not enacted by Congress? Or, is this situation not significantly different from guidelines adopted by federal prosecutors regarding prosecution of trivial violations of criminal statutes? *See* U.S. Dept. of Justice, Principles of Federal Prosecution 7–11 (1980).

3. What is the probable reaction of an agency told by a court that its internal guidelines create rights enforceable by third parties? The Supreme Court considered this issue in *United States v. Caceres,* 440 U.S. 741, 99 S.Ct. 1465, 59 L.Ed.2d 733 (1979) (decided two months after *Nicholas*). In *Caceres,* the Court held that electronic surveillance undertaken in violation of Internal Revenue Service regulations (although not in violation of the Constitution or federal law) need not be suppressed in a criminal prosecution of the taxpayer. The Court noted:

> Regulations governing the conduct of criminal investigations are generally considered desirable, and may well provide more valuable protection to the public at large than the deterrence flowing from the occasional exclusion of items of evidence in criminal trials. Although we do not suggest that a suppression order in this case would cause the IRS to abandon or modify its electronic surveillance regulations, we cannot ignore the possibility that a rigid application of an exclusionary rule to every regulatory violation could have a serious deterrent impact on the formulation of additional standards to govern prosecutorial and police procedures. Here, the Executive itself has provided for internal sanctions in cases of knowing violations of the electronic-surveillance regulations. To go beyond that, and require exclusion in every case, would take away from the Executive Department the primary responsibility for fashioning the appropriate remedy for the violation of its regulations. But since the content, and indeed the existence, of the regulations would remain within the Executive's sole authority, the result might well be fewer and less protective regulations. In the long run, it is far better to have rules like those contained in the IRS Manual, and to tolerate occasional erroneous administration of the kind displayed by this record, than either to have no rules except those

mandated by statute, or to have them framed in a mere precatory form.

Id. at 755–56, 99 S.Ct. at 1473.

Are these concerns relevant here? Is INS likely to scrap deferred action status if it will have to defend itself in court every time it refuses to grant the status?

The Aftermath of *Nicholas*

INS did not revoke the deferred action Operations Instruction following *Nicholas,* but it did amend the Instruction. It now reads as follows:

> The district director may, in his discretion, recommend consideration of deferred action, an act of administrative choice to give some cases lower priority and in no way an entitlement, in appropriate cases.

> The deferred action category recognizes that the Service has limited enforcement resources and that every attempt should be made administratively to utilize these resources in a manner which will achieve the greatest impact under the immigration laws. In making deferred action determinations, the following factors, among others, should be considered:

> (A) the likelihood of ultimately removing the alien, including:

>> (1) likelihood that the alien will depart without formal proceedings (e.g., minor child who will accompany deportable parents);

>> (2) age or physical condition affecting ability to travel;

>> (3) likelihood that another country will accept the alien;

>> (4) the likelihood that the alien will be able to qualify for some form of relief which would prevent or indefinitely delay deportation;

> (B) the presence of sympathetic factors which, while not legally precluding deportation, could lead to unduly protracted deportation proceedings, and which, because of a desire on the part of the administrative authorities or the courts to reach a favorable result, could result in a distortion of the law with unfavorable implications for future cases;

> (C) the likelihood that because of the sympathetic factors in the case, a large amount of adverse publicity will be generated which will result in a disproportionate amount of Service time being spent in responding to such publicity or justifying actions;

(D) whether or not the individual is a member of a class of deportable aliens whose removal has given a high enforcement priority (e.g., dangerous criminals, large-scale alien smugglers, narcotic drug traffickers, terrorists, war criminals, habitual immigration violators).

If the district director determines that a recommendation for deferred action should be made, it shall be made to the regional commissioner concerned on Form G–312, which shall be signed personally by the district director, and the basis for his recommendation shall be set forth therein specifically. Interim or biennial reviews should be conducted to determine whether approved cases should be continued or removed from deferred action category.

Each regional commissioner shall maintain statistics on deferred action cases on a current basis, maintained so that data can be readily extracted upon request. The statistics should be maintained in the following categories: (1) number of cases in deferred action category at the beginning of the fiscal year; (2) number of recommendations received fiscal year to date; (3) number of recommendations approved; (4) number of recommendations denied; (5) number of cases removed from deferred action category; (6) number of deferred action cases pending at the end of the fiscal year.

O.I. 103.1a(1)(ii).

Compare the amended Instruction with the pre-*Nicholas* Instruction, reprinted in footnote 9 of the court's opinion. How was the Instruction changed? Has not the Service attempted to transform the Instruction from a mechanism intended to aid aliens with a compelling need to remain in this country to a guideline for setting law enforcement priorities? Do the changes undercut (or necessitate the overruling of) *Nicholas*? *See, e.g., Wan Chung Wen v. Ferro,* 543 F.Supp. 1016 (W.D.N.Y.1982) (*Nicholas* "severely undermined" by amendment to O.I.). If the *Nicholas* court is correct that the old Operations Instruction created a substantive ground for relief, may INS issue the new Instruction without following the requirements of the Administrative Procedure Act?

Does the issue of whether or not the Instruction creates a benefit affect the reviewability of the agency's decision? Does it affect the standard of review to be applied?

2. OTHER EXERCISES OF PROSECUTORIAL DISCRETION

a. Possession of Marijuana

INS Operations Instruction § 242.1a(26) provides:

Unless prior approval has been received from the regional commissioner, no order to show cause shall be issued in the case of an alien who is a lawful permanent resident of the United

States and whose deportability is based on section 241(a)(11) as one having been convicted of possession, importation or distribution of marijuana for no remuneration: Provided the amount of marijuana involved does not exceed 100 grams:

> Provided further, that in the case of a conviction for distribution without remuneration, the alien has been convicted of only one such offense.

In 1981, Congress amended the statute to permit waiver of deportability based on simple possession of *30 grams* or less of marijuana. INS § 241(f)(2). Now that Congress has spoken, may the INS still exercise the discretion asserted in this Operations Instruction?

b. Stay of Deportation

By regulation, the district director is granted discretion to stay the deportation of an alien under an order of deportation "for such time and under such conditions as he may deem appropriate." 8 C.F.R. § 243.4. This authority is generally used to give the alien a reasonable amount of time to make arrangements prior to deportation; or to forestall deportation pending the outcome of a motion to reopen deportation proceedings. *See, e.g., Bazrafshan v. Pomeroy,* 587 F.Supp. 498 (D.N.J.1984).

SECTION C. REGULARIZATION OF STATUS

Neither voluntary departure nor deferred action status is likely to be the alien's preferred form of relief from deportation. Most aliens who are deportable would like to remain in the United States in a lawful status. The INA provides a number of avenues of relief that authorize the Attorney General to confer upon a deportable alien lawful permanent resident status. For aliens who entered without inspection or as nonimmigrants, such relief makes them permanent resident aliens for the first time. For aliens who entered as immigrants, the Attorney General's action restores their prior lawful status. For all aliens, these forms of relief effectively wipe out the underlying basis for deportation.[5]

1. ADJUSTMENT OF STATUS: INA § 245

In Chapter Three, we noted that aliens who enter the country as nonimmigrants may, under certain conditions, adjust their status to that of lawful permanent residents under INA § 245. The prerequisites for adjustment are (1) inspection and admission or parole into the United States, (2) eligibility for a visa, (3) admissibility (*i.e.,* not excludable), (4) immediate availability of an immigrant visa, and (5) a favorable exercise

---

5. However, it should be noted that the deportation ground can become re-activated. Under § 246 of the INA, the adjustment of a deportable alien's status to that of lawful permanent resident may be rescinded if within five years "it shall appear to the satisfaction of the Attorney General that the person was not in fact eligible for such adjustment of status." Upon rescission, the alien is "subject to all provisions of [the INA] to the same extent as if the adjustment of status had not been made." *Id.* On rescission of adjustment of status, *see* pp. 291– 292 *supra.*

of discretion by the Attorney General. Essentially, the alien applying for adjustment of status stands in the shoes of an alien seeking initial entry as an immigrant.

Section 245 does not include a requirement that an alien seeking adjustment be in a lawful status.[6] Thus, while adjustment is usually granted to aliens who are in a lawful nonimmigrant status, it is also available to aliens who, although deportable, can meet the statutory requirements. The availability of adjustment in the deportation context benefits both the government and the applicant. The government avoids paper work overseas for an alien who can establish he or she is eligible for immediate entry as an immigrant, and an alien avoids a trip home. An alien is also able to seek judicial review of a denial of an adjustment petition; visa decisions by State Department officers abroad are not subject to judicial review.

Note that not all deportable aliens may seek adjustment of status. Surreptitious entrants are not eligible because they have neither been inspected and admitted nor paroled into the country. Furthermore, if the ground of deportation is also a ground of exclusion (and not waivable), adjustment will be denied. *See, e.g., Pasquini v. INS,* 557 F.2d 536 (5th Cir.1977) (alien deportable for marijuana conviction and overstay not eligible for adjustment since conviction is ground of exclusion). Section 245(c) also explicitly denies adjustment to alien crewmen, to most aliens who engage in unauthorized employment, and to aliens who were admitted in transit without visas. Finally, a deportable alien who meets all the statutory prerequisites may still be denied adjustment if the Attorney General refuses to exercise his discretion favorably. *See, e.g., INS v. Bagamasbad,* 429 U.S. 24, 97 S.Ct. 200, 50 L.Ed.2d 190 (1976) *(per curiam); Patel v. INS,* 738 F.2d 239 (7th Cir.1984).

Professional Responsibility Problem *

Alien T was admitted on a nonimmigrant visa in 1982. At time of entry, she was authorized to stay for six months. A year ago she married a permanent resident alien. Last week T was served with an order to show cause asking her to appear at a deportation hearing next month. She has come to you for help.

After consulting the relevant State Department charts, you determine that a visa would be available to her shortly. In conversation with T, nothing you learn leads you to believe that she would be excludable. Accordingly, you believe that she could avoid deportation by requesting adjustment of status. However, later she mentions that she has been supporting herself for several years by providing child-care services to

---

6. The McCarran-Walter Act of 1952 included such a requirement, Act of June 27, 1952, Ch. 477, § 245, 66 Stat. 217 (1952). It was deleted in 1958. Act of August 21, 1958, Pub.L. No. 85-700, § 1, 72 Stat. 699. The Senate's 1983 version of the Simpson-Mazzoli legislation would have returned to the earlier version by amending § 245 to prohib-it adjustment for aliens who had "failed to maintain continuously a legal status since entry into the United States." S. 529, § 131.

* Based on D. Weissbrodt, Immigration Law and Procedure in a Nutshell § 10–2 (1984).

families in the neighborhood. This work, which averaged between 20 and 30 hours a week, earned her just enough money to pay rent and provide other necessities of life. She has never sought, or received, permission from the INS to undertake employment.

This information troubles you because INA § 245(c) prohibits the adjustment of status of an alien who "accepts unauthorized employment prior to filing an application for adjustment of status"; and the relevant form (I–485) specifically states that an alien who has "continued in or accepted unauthorized employment" is not eligible for adjustment. Furthermore, unauthorized employment constitutes an additional ground of deportation under INA § 241(a)(9) and may affect discretionary decisions by the INS or an immigration judge.

(1) Should you help T prepare and file Form I–485 for adjustment of status?

(2) Assume you have informed T of the consequences of her unauthorized employment and, nevertheless, she asks you to represent her in her request for relief at the deportation hearing. Should you do so?

(3) Must you report T's unauthorized employment to the INS?

What bearing do the following Model Rules of Professional Conduct have on these questions?

1. *Rule 1.6.*

(a) A lawyer shall not reveal information relating to representation of a client unless the client consents after consultation, except for disclosures that are impliedly authorized in order to carry out the representation, and except as stated in paragraph (b).

(b) A lawyer may reveal such information to the extent the lawyer reasonably believes necessary:

(1) to prevent the client from committing a criminal act that the lawyer believes is likely to result in imminent death or substantial bodily harm; or

(2) to establish a claim or defense on behalf of the lawyer in a controversy between the lawyer and the client, to establish a defense to a criminal charge or civil claim against the lawyer based upon conduct in which the client was involved, or to respond to allegations in any proceeding concerning the lawyer's representation of the client.

2. *Rule 4.1.*

In the course of representing a client a lawyer shall not knowingly:

(a) make a false statement of material fact or law to a third person; or

(b) fail to disclose material fact to a third person when disclosure is necessary to avoid assisting a criminal or fraudulent act by a client, unless disclosure is prohibited by Rule 1.6.

2. SUSPENSION OF DEPORTATION: INA § 244

Many deportation cases pit the needs of law enforcement against compelling human needs of an alien. Obviously, the longer an alien has lived in the United States—legally or illegally—the greater the ties he or she is likely to have established and the greater the hardship deportation will entail. The costs do not fall solely on the alien: employers may lose productive employees, neighborhoods may lose valued residents, family and friends may be deprived of significant personal relationships. Because of the harshness that deportation may visit upon long-term residents, there have always existed avenues of relief for deportable aliens who have lived in the United States for a substantial period of time. In earlier days, these included statutes of limitations[7] and private bills.[8] Today, the primary form of relief for long-time resident aliens is "suspension of deportation" under INA § 244. From 1977 to 1980, an average of 120 aliens a year were granted § 244 relief.

Subsection (a) of INA § 244 provides:

> As hereinafter prescribed in this section, the Attorney General may, in his discretion, suspend deportation and adjust the status to that of an alien lawfully admitted for permanent residence, in the case of an alien who applies to the Attorney General for suspension of deportation and—

> (1) is deportable under any law of the United States except the provisions specified in paragraph (2) of this subsection; has been physically present in the United States for a continuous period of not less than seven years immediately preceding the date of such application, and proves that during all of such period he was and is a person of good moral character; and is a person whose deportation would, in the opinion of the Attorney General, result in extreme hardship to the alien or to his spouse, parent, or child, who is a citizen of the United States or an alien lawfully admitted for permanent residence; or

> (2) is deportable under paragraphs (4), (5), (6), (7), (11), (12), (14), (15), (16), (17), or (18) of section 241(a); has been physically present in the United States for a continuous period of not less than 10 years immediately following the commission of an act, or the assumption of a status, constituting a ground for deportation, and proves that during all of such period he has been and is a person of good moral character; and is a person whose deportation would, in the opinion of the Attorney General, result in exceptional and extremely unusual hardship to the alien or to his spouse, parent, or child, who is a citizen of the United States or an alien lawfully admitted for permanent residence.

Let us draw your attention to several important aspects of the provision. First, "suspension of deportation" does not simply permit a

---

7. *See* pp. 369–372 *supra.*   8. *See* pp. 547–552 *infra.*

deportable alien to remain in the United States. The granting of the relief adjusts the status of the alien to that of lawful permanent resident. Second, an alien who has entered the country without inspection may be eligible for suspension.[9] (Recall that eligibility for adjustment of status under INA § 245 requires "inspection and admission or parole.") Third, notice the differences between both the classes of deportation grounds and the time periods specified in paragraphs (a)(1) and (a)(2). (Why should the statute so differentiate?) Finally, the Attorney General may, in his discretion, deny suspension even if an alien meets all the statutory prerequisites for relief.

In addition to this express grant of discretion, the explicit statutory guideposts in § 244 are themselves awash in a sea of discretion. Phrases like "good moral character," [10] "extreme hardship," and "exceptional and extremely unusual hardship" are vague formulations, although they have gained some meaning through administrative and judicial opinions. In the following sections, we will consider the roles of Congress, the Department of Justice and the courts in giving content to these terms.

a. "Continuous" Physical Presence

Under paragraphs (a)(1) and (a)(2), an alien applying for suspension must have been "physically present in the United States for a continuous period" of seven and ten years, respectively. Does this mean that an alien who takes a one-week trip to Canada in the middle of an eight year period is ineligible for relief under (a)(1)?

This question should immediately bring to mind the *Fleuti* doctrine. *Rosenberg v. Fleuti,* 374 U.S. 449, 83 S.Ct. 1804, 10 L.Ed.2d 1000 (1963). In *Fleuti,* you will recall, the Supreme Court ameliorated the harshness of the "re-entry doctrine" by holding that a permanent resident alien's brief and casual trip abroad did not meaningfully interrupt his permanent residence in this country; thus his return to the United States did not constitute an "entry" under INA § 101(a)(13). *See* pp. 327–334 *supra.*

Should *Fleuti* apply in the "suspension of deportation" context? Some lower courts so concluded. *See, e.g., Kamheangpatiyooth v. INS,* 597 F.2d 1253 (9th Cir.1979); *Wadman v. INS,* 329 F.2d 812 (9th Cir.1964). *But see Fidalgo-Velez v. INS,* 697 F.2d 1026 (11th Cir.1983). More importantly, should the statutory prerequisite of "continuous" presence be read literally, or, does the BIA have discretion to adopt a flexible interpretation to avoid hardship? The Supreme Court answered these questions in the following case.

---

9. However, abuse of the immigration laws may be a factor considered by the Attorney General in exercising the discretion to suspend deportation granted by § 244. *See, e.g., Ramirez-Gonzalez v. INS,* 695 F.2d 1208 (9th Cir.1983); *Pelupo de Toledo v. Kiley,* 436 F.Supp. 1090 (E.D.N.Y.1977).

10. INA § 101(f) defines what shall not constitute good moral character, but it doesn't give much of a clue as to what shall.

INS v. PHINPATHYA

Supreme Court of the United States, 1984.
464 U.S. 183, 104 S.Ct. 584, 78 L.Ed.2d 401.

JUSTICE O'CONNOR delivered the opinion of the Court.

* * * In this case we must decide the meaning of § 244(a)(1)'s "continuous physical presence" requirement.

I

Respondent, a native and citizen of Thailand, first entered the United States as a nonimmigrant student in October, 1969. Respondent's husband, also a native and citizen of Thailand, entered the country in August, 1968. Respondent and her husband were authorized to remain in the United States until July, 1971. However, when their visas expired, they chose to stay without securing permission from the immigration authorities.

In January, 1977, petitioner, the Immigration and Naturalization Service (INS), commenced deportation proceedings against respondent and her husband pursuant to § 241(a)(2) of the Act. Respondent and her husband conceded deportability and applied for suspension pursuant to § 244(a)(1). An immigration judge found that respondent's husband had satisfied § 244(a)(1)'s eligibility requirements and suspended his deportation. But respondent's own testimony showed that she had left the country during January, 1974, and that she had improperly obtained a nonimmigrant visa from the United States consular officer in Thailand to aid her reentry three months later.[2] On the basis of this evidence, the immigration judge concluded that respondent had failed to meet the seven year "continuous physical presence" requirement of the Act:

> "[Respondent's] absence was not brief, innocent, or casual. The absence would have been longer than three months if she had not obtained the spouse of a student visa as fast as she did obtain it. It was not casual because she had to obtain a new Tha[i] passport, as well as a nonimmigrant visa from the American Consul, to return to the United States. It was not innocent because she failed to inform the American Consul that she was the wife of a student who had been out of status for three years (and therefore not entitled to the nonimmigrant visa she received)."

Accordingly, he denied respondent's application for suspension.

The Board of Immigration Appeals (BIA) affirmed the immigration judge's decision on the "continuous physical presence" issue. BIA ob-

2. About one month prior to her departure, respondent obtained a new Thai passport. However, when she departed for Thailand, respondent did not have a nonimmigrant visa allowing her to reenter this country. After her arrival in Thailand, respondent went to the United States Consul and obtained a nonimmigrant visa as the wife of a foreign student. Although respondent was aware that her husband's student visa had expired more than two years earlier, she failed to inform the consular officer of that fact.

served that respondent was illegally in the United States at the time she left for Thailand and that she was able to return only by misrepresenting her status as the wife of a foreign student. Based on these observations, BIA concluded that respondent's absence was meaningfully interruptive of her continuous physical presence in the United States.

The Court of Appeals reversed. It noted that, although respondent traveled to Thailand for three months, "she intended, at all times, to return to the United States." *Phinpathya v. INS,* 673 F.2d 1013, 1017 (CA 1982). The Court held that BIA had placed too much emphasis on respondent's illegal presence prior to her departure and on the increased risk of deportation that her departure had engendered. Finding BIA's approach legally erroneous, it concluded that:

> "an absence cannot be 'meaningfully interruptive' if two factors are present: (1) the hardships would be as severe if the absence had not occurred, and (2) there would not be an increase in the risk of deportation as a result of the absence." *Id.,* at 1018, and n. 6 (citing *Kamheangpatiyooth v. INS,* 597 F.2d 1253, 1257 (CA9 1979)).

Since BIA "failed to view the circumstances in their totality and [analyze those circumstances] in light of the underlying Congressional purpose," *id.,* at 1017, the Court remanded for further proceedings on the "continuous physical presence" issue.

We granted certiorari, to review the meaning of § 244(a)(1)'s requirement that an otherwise deportable alien have been "physically present in the United States for a continuous period of not less than seven years . . . ." We find that the Court of Appeals' interpretation of this statutory requirement departs from the plain meaning of the Act.

II

This Court has noted on numerous occasions that "in all cases involving statutory construction, 'our starting point must be the language employed by Congress,' . . . and we assume 'that the legislative purpose is expressed by the ordinary meaning of the words used.'" *American Tobacco Co. v. Patterson,* 456 U.S. 63, 68, 102 S.Ct. 1534, 1537, 71 L.Ed.2d 748 (1982), quoting *Reiter v. Sonotone Corp.,* 442 U.S. 330, 337, 99 S.Ct. 2326, 2330, 60 L.Ed.2d 931 (1979), and *Richards v. United States,* 369 U.S. 1, 9, 82 S.Ct. 585, 591, 7 L.Ed.2d 492 (1962). The language of § 244(a) requires certain threshold criteria to be met before the Attorney General or his delegates, in their discretion, may suspend proceedings against an otherwise deportable alien. This language plainly narrows the class of aliens who may obtain suspension by requiring each applicant for such extraordinary relief to prove that he:

> "has been physically present in the United States for a continuous period of not less than seven years immediately preceding the date of such application, . . . that during all such period he was and is a person of good moral character; and is a person whose deportation would, in the opinion of the Attorney General, result in extreme hardship to the alien or to his spouse, parent, or child, who is a citizen of the United States or an alien lawfully admitted for permanent residence . . . ."

The ordinary meaning of these words does not readily admit any "exception[s] to the requirement of seven years of 'continuous physical presence' in the United States to be eligible for suspension of deportation." *McColvin v. INS,* 648 F.2d 935, 937 (CA4 1981).

By contrast, when Congress in the past has intended for a "continuous physical presence" requirement to be flexibly administered, it has provided the authority for doing so. For example, former § 301(b) of the Act, which required two years of "continuou[s] physical presen[ce]" for maintenance of status as a United States national or citizen, provided that "absence from the United States of less than sixty days in the aggregate during the period for which continuous physical presence in the United States is required shall not break the continuity of such physical presence." 86 Stat. 1289, repealing 71 Stat. 644 (12-month aggregate absence does not break continuity of physical presence). The deliberate omission of a similar moderating provision in § 244(a)(1) compels the conclusion that Congress meant this "continuous physical presence" requirement to be administered as written.

Indeed, the evolution of the deportation provision itself shows that Congress knew how to distinguish between actual "continuous physical presence" and some irreducible minimum of "non-intermittent" presence. Prior to 1940, the Attorney General had no discretion in ordering deportation, and an alien's sole remedy was to obtain a private bill from Congress. In 1940, Congress authorized the Attorney General to suspend deportation of aliens of good moral character whose deportation "would result in serious economic detriment" to the aliens or their families. See 54 Stat. 672. Then, in 1948, Congress amended the statute again to make the suspension process available to aliens who "resided continuously in the United States for seven years or more" and who could show good moral character for the preceding five years, regardless of family ties. 62 Stat. 1206. Finally, in 1952, "in an attempt to discontinue lax practices and discourage abuses," Congress replaced the seven year "continuous residence" requirement with the current seven year "continuous physical presence" requirement. H.R.Rep. No. 1365, 82d Cong., 2d Sess., 31 (1952), U.S.Code Cong. & Admin.News 1952, p. 1653. It made the criteria for suspension of deportation more stringent both to restrict the opportunity for discretionary action, see *id.,* and to exclude:

> "aliens [who] are deliberately flouting our immigration laws by the processes of gaining admission into the United States illegally or ostensibly as nonimmigrants but with the intention of establishing themselves in a situation in which they may subsequently have access to some administrative remedy to adjust their status to that of permanent residents." S.Rep. No. 1137, 82d Cong., 2d Sess., pt. 1, 25 (1952).

Had Congress been concerned only with "non-intermittent" presence or with the mere maintenance of a domicile or general abode, it could have retained the "continuous residence" requirement. Instead, Congress expressly opted for the seven year "continuous physical presence" requirement.

The statutory switch from "continuous residence" to "continuous physical presence" was no simple accident of draftsmanship. Congress broadened the class of aliens eligible for admission to citizenship by requiring only five years "continuous residence" and "physical presence" for at least half the period of residency. Concomitantly, it made § 244(a)(1) more restrictive; suspensions of deportations are "grossly unfair to aliens who await abroad their turn on quota waiting lists," and Congress wanted to limit the number of aliens allowed to remain through discretionary action.[9] The citizenship and suspension of deportation provisions are interrelated parts of Congress' comprehensive scheme for admitting aliens into this country. We do justice to this scheme only by applying the "plain meaning of [Section 244(a)], however severe the consequences." *Jay v. Boyd,* 351 U.S. 345, 357, 76 S.Ct. 919, 926, 100 L.Ed. 1242 (1956). The Court of Appeals' inquiry into whether the hardship to be suffered upon deportation has been diminished by the alien's absence fails to do so.

III

Respondent contends that we should approve the Court of Appeals' "generous" and "liberal" construction of the "continuous physical presence" requirement notwithstanding the statute's plain language and history. She argues that the Court of Appeals' construction is in keeping both with our decision in *Rosenberg v. Fleuti,* 374 U.S. 449, 83 S.Ct. 1804, 10 L.Ed.2d 1000 (1963), and with the equitable and ameliorative nature of the suspension remedy. We disagree.

A

* * *

Fleuti is essentially irrelevant to the adjudication of respondent's § 244(a)(1) suspension application. *Fleuti* dealt with a statutory exception enacted precisely to ameliorate the harsh effects of prior judicial construction of the "entry" doctrine. By contrast, this case deals with a threshold requirement added to the statute specifically to limit the discretionary availability of the suspension remedy. Thus, whereas a flexible approach

---

9. The 1952 Act also required an alien to show "exceptional and extremely unusual hardship" to qualify for suspension of deportation. 66 Stat. 214. In 1962, Congress amended § 244(a)(1) to require that the alien show deportation would result in "extreme hardship." 76 Stat. 1248. It retained the literal "continuous physical presence" requirement word-for-word, although it added an express exception in § 244(b) for aliens who had served at least 24 months active service in the armed forces.

JUSTICE BRENNAN cites various statements, especially those of Senator Keating, in the legislative history of the 1962 amendments to support his belief that the Act should not be literally interpreted. These statements, of course, relate not to the "continuous phys-

ical presence" requirement, which Congress retained as a strict condition precedent to deportation suspension, but to the "extreme hardship" requirement. As Senator Keating himself explained: "Section 244 as amended would permit aliens who have been physically present in the United States for 7 years, or, in more serious cases, for 10 years, to apply to the Attorney General for a suspension of deportation as under present section 244. The alien would have to show a specified degree of hardship .... The conference version of section 244 ... has continuing future applicability to any alien who can satisfy either the 7- or the 10-year physical presence requirement in addition to the other criteria for suspension of deportation." 108 Cong.Rec. 23448–23449 (1962).

to statutory construction was consistent with the congressional purpose underlying § 101(a)(13), such an approach would not be consistent with the congressional purpose underlying the "continuous physical presence" requirement.

In *Fleuti,* the Court believed that Congress had not considered the "meaningless and irrational hazards" that a strict application of the "entry" provision could create. Thus, it inferred that Congress would not have approved of the otherwise harsh consequences that would have resulted to Fleuti. Here, by contrast, we have every reason to believe that Congress considered the harsh consequences of its actions. Congress expressly provided a mechanism for factoring "extreme hardship" into suspension of deportation decisions. We would have to ignore the clear Congressional mandate and the plain meaning of the statute to find that *Fleuti* is applicable to the determination whether an otherwise deportable alien has been "physically present in the United States for a continuous period of not less than seven years . . . ." [11] We refuse to do so.

* * *

B

Respondent further suggests that we approve the Court of Appeals' articulation of the "continuous physical presence" standard—that an absence is "meaningfully interruptive" only when it increases the risk and reduces the hardship of deportation—as consistent with the ameliorative purpose of, and the discretion of the Attorney General to grant the suspension remedy. Respondent's suggestion is without merit.

Although § 244(a)(1) serves a remedial purpose, the liberal interpretation respondent suggests would collapse § 244(a)(1)'s "continuous physical presence" requirement into its "extreme hardship" requirement and read the former out of the Act. The language and history of that section suggest that "continuous physical presence" and "extreme hardship" are separate preconditions for a suspension of deportation. It strains the statutory language to construe the "continuous physical presence" requirement as requiring yet a further assessment of hardship.

It is also clear that Congress intended strict threshold criteria to be met before the Attorney General could exercise his discretion to suspend deportation proceedings. Congress drafted § 244(a)(1)'s provisions specifically to restrict the opportunity for discretionary administrative action. Respondent's suggestion that we construe the Act to broaden the Attorney General's discretion is fundamentally inconsistent with this intent. * * * Respondent's suggestion that we construe the Act to broaden the Attorney General's discretion * * * would shift authority to relax the "continuous physical presence" requirement from Congress to INS and, eventually, as is evident from the experience in this case, to the courts. We must

---

11. In *INS v. Wang,* this Court observed that a narrow interpretation of the term "extreme hardship" was "consistent with the 'extreme hardship' language, which itself indicates the exceptional nature of the suspension remedy." 450 U.S. 139, 145, 101 S.Ct. 1027, 1031, 67 L.Ed.2d 123 (1981). Similarly, we find only the plain meaning of the "continuous physical presence" requirement to be consistent with the exceptional nature of the suspension remedy.

therefore reject respondent's suggestion as impermissible in our tripartite scheme of government.[13] Congress designs the immigration laws, and it is up to Congress to temper the laws' rigidity if it so desires.

IV

The Court of Appeals' approach ignores the plain meaning of § 244(a)(1) and extends eligibility to aliens whom Congress clearly did not intend to be eligible for suspension of deportation. Congress meant what it said: otherwise deportable aliens must show that they have been physically present in the United States for a continuous period of seven years before they are eligible for suspension of deportation. The judgment of the Court of Appeals therefore is

Reversed.

JUSTICE BRENNAN, with whom JUSTICE MARSHALL and JUSTICE STEVENS join, concurring in the judgment.

The Court today holds that an unexplained three-month absence from the United States disqualifies an alien from eligibility for relief from deportation under § 244(a)(1) and further, that our decision in *Rosenberg v. Fleuti*, 374 U.S. 449, 83 S.Ct. 1804, 10 L.Ed.2d 1000 (1963), is essentially irrelevant in the § 244 context. I agree with both of these conclusions. In the process of reaching them, however, the court seems to imply that Congress intended the term "continuous" in the phrase "physically present ... for a continuous period" to be interpreted literally. If that is what the Court implies, the status of temporary absences far different from the one at issue in this case—for example, a short vacation in Mexico, an inadvertent train ride through Canada while en route from Buffalo to Detroit, a trip to one's native country to tend to an ailing parent, or some other type of temporary absence that has no meaningful bearing on the attachment or commitment an alien has to this country— would presumably be treated no differently from the absence at issue today. Because such absences need not be addressed to decide this case, and, in any event, because I believe that Congress did not intend the continuous-physical-presence requirement to be read literally, I part company with the Court insofar as a contrary interpretation may be implied.

I

In this case, the Immigration and Naturalization Service (INS) argues that the Court of Appeals has taken too liberal a view of the continuous-physical-presence requirement. It does not argue, however, that the requirement should be interpreted literally; nor does it brief the question

---

13. The Solicitor General admits that prior to "the Ninth Circuit's decision in 1964 in *Wadman v. INS*, 329 F.2d 812, the lower courts and the Board of Immigration Appeals generally applied a strict, literal interpretation of the "continuous physical presence" language in Section 244(a)(1) and held ineligible for suspension of deportation any alien who was absent from the United States during the seven year period, without regard to the circumstances of the absence." Brief of the United States 11–12 (citing cases). Our decision today frees INS from the strictures of *Wadman* and interprets the language as Congress has written it. Contrary to JUSTICE BRENNAN's suggestion, see *post,* at 593, neither we nor INS have authority to create " 'room for flexibility in applying' " § 244 when the language chosen by Congress and its purpose are otherwise.

whether literally continuous, physical presence should be a prerequisite to suspension of deportation. Indeed, at oral argument, counsel for the Government stated that "the [INS] believes that there is room for flexibility in applying [§ 244]." In light of this express position of the INS, the agency charged with responsibility for administering the immigration laws, as well as the fact that petitioner's unexplained three-month absence from the United States plainly disqualifies her for relief under any reasonable interpretation of § 244, I would not address, by implication or otherwise, the question whether the continuous-physical-presence requirement was meant to be interpreted literally.

II

Moreover, if we are to understand that the Court implicitly approves of a literal interpretation of the statute, the error of its analysis is patent. It is a hornbook proposition that "[a]ll laws should receive a sensible construction. General terms should be limited in their application as not to lead to injustice, oppression, or an absurd consequence. It will always, therefore, be presumed that the legislature intended exceptions to its language, which would avoid results of this character. The reason of law in such cases should prevail over its letter." *United States v. Kirby,* 7 Wall. 482, 486–87, 19 L.Ed. 278 (1868). In a case such as this, in which a literal interpretation of a statutory provision may indeed lead to absurd consequences, we must look beyond the terms of the provision to the underlying congressional intent. And in this case, the legislative history of § 244, far from compelling a wooden interpretation of the statutory language, in fact indicates that Congress intended the continuous-physical-presence requirement to be interpreted flexibly.

The Court suggests a contrary conclusion based on two factors: First, the fact that Congress enacted the continuous-physical-presence requirement in 1952 in response to abuses of the more lenient "residence" requirement, which had been in effect since 1948; and second, the fact that former § 301(b) of the Act, which imposed a two-year continuous-physical-presence requirement upon foreign-born citizens seeking to avoid the loss of their citizenship, explicitly provided that "absence from the United States of less than sixty days ... shall not break the continuity of such physical presence." But plainly, neither of these aspects of the Act's legislative history sheds meaningful light on the issue of whether the term "continuous" should be interpreted literally. It is true, of course, that Congress replaced the "residence" requirement with the continuous-physical-presence requirement in order to prevent abuses, as the Court states, but the abuses identified by Congress are hardly in the nature of a vacation in Mexico, a train ride through Canada, or other similar absences that would defeat eligibility for relief under a literal reading of § 244. Instead, Congress sought to prevent much more substantial abuses, such as a situation described in the Senate Report on the Act, in which an alien "has a total of 7 years residence in the United States [but] the alien has been out of the United States for as long as 2 years during the last 7 years." S.Rept. No. 1515, 81st Cong., 2d Sess. 602 (1950). Furthermore, although it is true that the sixty day leeway allowed under § 301(b) for foreign-born citizens has no counterpart in § 244, this only indicates that Congress was unwilling to provide such generous and unrestricted leeway to aliens seeking suspension of deportation. It surely does not indicate that Congress intended *every* type of absence—however innocent or brief—to defeat an alien's eligibility for relief. Finally, as the Court implicitly acknowledges, there is no direct statement in the legislative history of the 1952 Act to indicate that Congress intended to have the term "continuous" interpreted literally. It follows, then, that there is simply no support for giving § 244(a)(1) a literal interpretation.

Indeed, there is direct support for precisely the opposite conclusion in the legislative history of the 1962 amendments to the Act, in which Congress rewrote § 244. The current version of § 244, which barely resembles the original 1952 provision but which retains the continuous-physical-presence requirement, was enacted as part of those amendments. It is the congressional intent underlying the 1962 amendment, therefore, that is central to the question whether Congress meant to have the continuous-physical-presence requirement applied literally. And the legislative history of that amendment, whether viewed as reflecting the 1952 congressional understanding of the continuous-physical-presence requirement, or as establishing a new understanding in the 1962 revision, reveals an express congressional intent to have the term "continuous" interpreted more flexibly than a literal definition of the term would imply. Moreover, prior to the 1962 amendment, the only Court of Appeals that had occasion to interpret the continuous-physical-presence requirement held that the term "continuous" was not intended to be interpreted literally. *McLeod v. Peterson*, 283 F.2d 180 (CA 3 1960). In that case, the court reversed a decision of the INS, holding that an 8-month absence from the United States "does not interrupt the continuity of ... presence in the United States within the meaning of [§ 244]," under circumstances in which the INS had induced the alien to leave the country without the authority to do so. *Id.*, at 187. In explaining its decision, the court stated that § 244 had "sufficient flexibility to permit a rational effecting of the congressional intent." *Ibid.* Of course, when Congress enacts a new law that incorporates language of a pre-existing law, Congress may be presumed to have knowledge of prior judicial interpretations of the language and to have adopted that interpretation for purposes of the new law. Therefore, even in the absence of explicit indications of legislative intent, we would be justified in concluding that Congress intended to have the continuous-physical-presence requirement interpreted flexibly.

In any event, there are explicit indications in the legislative history of the 1962 amendments that Congress did not intend to enact a literal continuous-physical-presence requirement. The 1962 amendments originated as S. 3361. As introduced, the bill contained a provision that would have amended § 249 of the Immigration and Nationality Act. Section 249, which originated in 1929, allows the Attorney General to confer permanent-residence status upon an alien who meets certain qualifications, such as "good moral character," and establishes that he or she has *resided* in the United States since a statutorily provided date.[a] At the time of the 1962 amendment, the operative date was June 28, 1940, and S. 3361, as introduced, would have moved that date up to December 24, 1952. Under the Senate bill, therefore, relief from deportation would have been available to an alien who simply established "residence" since 1952, without regard to whether his or her physical presence in this country was literally continuous. The House, however, declined to amend § 249. Instead, the House sent to the Conference Committee a bill that differed from the Senate bill in that it left June 28, 1940 as the operative date of entry for relief under that section. 108 Cong.Rec. 22608 (1962). The Conference Committee, however, compromised between the House and Senate versions of the bill by adopting an amendment to § 244, instead of an amendment to § 249. And it is that compromise that became the current version of § 244.

Basically, the new § 244 differed from the 1952 version in two respects. First, it compressed a complicated system, in which eligible aliens had to meet one of five different sets of requirements for relief, depending on the cause of their deportability, into a simple two-category system based essentially on the severity of the reason giving rise to deportability. For example, under the 1962 provision, aliens who are deportable for less severe offenses have to meet a seven-year continuous-physical-presence requirement, and those who are deportable for more severe offenses have to meet a ten-year continuous-physical-presence requirement. Second, the new § 244 modified the hardship requirement for aliens who committed less severe offenses from one of "exceptional and extremely unusual hardship" to one of "extreme hardship."

In explaining the intent of the conferees, the Conference Report stated that "[t]he now proposed language is designed to achieve the purpose envisaged by the Senate in a modified manner." H.Rept. No. 2552, 87th Cong., 2d Sess. 4 (1962). That is to say, § 244, as revised, was intended to extend relief from deportation to aliens residing in the United States since 1952, at the earliest. The Report then went on to explain that by revising § 244, rather than § 249, this liberalization of relief would be constrained by two factors that were already built into the first, but not the second, provision. Those factors were, first, a requirement that the Attorney General find that deportation would result in personal hardship before granting relief, and second, a requirement that all grants of relief be subject to congressional review.

When the Conference Committee's compromise was reported on the House floor, one manager stated that "we largely restore title 3 of the Smith Act of 1940 . . . as the guide for the purpose of making a determination of eligibility and obtaining the approval of the Congress for the ruling of the Attorney General," 108 Cong.Rec. 23421 (1962) (statement of Rep. Walter), and another simply restated the Conference Report's emphasis on the congressional-review and personal-hardship provisions of the Conference bill, 108 Cong.Rec. 23423 (1962) (statement of Rep. Feighan). The reference to the Smith Act, formally titled the Alien Registration Act of

---

a. INA § 249—a form of relief known as "registry"—is discussed pp. 552–554 *infra.*— eds.

498 RELIEF FROM DEPORTATION Ch. 6

1940, is particularly significant because that statute, which contained the original suspension-of-deportation remedy, did not impose a continuous-physical-presence requirement. 54 Stat. 672 (1940).[6] Under the Smith Act, residence in the United States provided a sufficient basis for the Attorney General to grant suspension of deportation. It is difficult to see, therefore, how this history suggests that the House intended to impose a literal continuous-physical-presence requirement.

Similarly, various statements made by Senators debating the Conference Committee's version of the bill belie the presence of any intent to impose a strict continuous-physical-presence requirement as a prerequisite to relief. For instance, one of the managers of the bill on the Senate floor, Senator Keating, stated that "[n]o person who would have been eligible for administrative relief under section 249 as the Senate proposed and amended it, would be excluded from consideration for relief under section 244 as the conference report now proposes to amend it." 108 Cong.Rec. 23448 (1962). As pointed out above, under the Senate's original proposal, § 249 would have covered aliens who *resided* in the United States since December 24, 1952, regardless of whether their residence amounted to a "continuous physical presence." Senator Keating, therefore, was clearly stating that such aliens would be eligible for suspension of deportation under § 244 as rewritten by the Conference Committee, even though some of them undoubtedly had left the country temporarily during their period of residency here. Accordingly, unless we are willing to decide that the explanation of the statute provided by one of its principal sponsors was, for some reason, flatly wrong, we cannot conclude that the continuous-physical-presence requirement, as enacted in 1962, was intended to be interpreted literally.[7]

To be sure, we gain only limited insight into congressional intent from statements made during floor debate and from conference reports, but we have always relied heavily upon authoritative statements by proponents of bills in our search for the meaning of legislation. Of necessity, this is particularly true where, as here, a provision was introduced into a bill by a conference committee. The remarks of Senator Keating and the House managers, therefore, plainly illuminate Congress' intent to achieve largely what an updating of § 249 would have achieved, except that the Attorney General was to be constrained by a personal-hardship requirement and congressional review.

---

6. Actually, it was Title 2, not Title 3, of that Act that authorized the suspension of deportation. Title 3 had nothing to do with relief from deportation of any kind. I must assume, therefore, that the reference to "Title 3" was a misstatement.

7. In light of the language that Congress enacted in 1962 and the historical development of that language, we would have to conclude that Senator Keating's rhetoric was somewhat inaccurate to the extent that it implies that continuous physical presence means residence. This inaccuracy, however, does not detract from the basic point that Congress was not thinking in literal terms

when it enacted § 244. If Congress did intend the term "continuous" to be interpreted literally, surely Senator Keating would not have been able to make the statement he made in support of the bill, at least not without some rejoinder.

In support of its interpretation, the Court inexplicably points to another sentence of Senator Keating's remarks in which he used the term "physically present." In that statement, the Senator did not, of course, define the meaning of those words—the issue in this case—or even employ the entire phrase with which we are concerned.

It seems inescapable, therefore, that Congress did not intend to have the continuous-physical-presence requirement interpreted literally. Instead, under a proper construction of § 244, the INS should remain free to apply the requirement flexibly, unconstrained by any limitation *Rosenberg v. Fleuti, supra,* may have imposed. Indeed, in substance, this interpretation conforms with the position of the INS since at least 1967, *see Matter of Wong,* 12 I & N 271 (1967), and is apparently the position to which the agency continues to adhere.

III

Because the Court's opinion seems to interpret the Immigration and Nationality Act in a way that is not briefed by the parties, is unnecessary to decide this case, is contrary to the view of the agency with principal responsibility for administering the Act, is unsupported by the statute's legislative history, and would certainly produce unreasonable results never envisioned by Congress, I cannot join the Court's opinion, but concur only in the judgment.[b]

Issues in Statutory Construction and *Phinpathya*

Note the range of sources and methods of statutory interpretation used by Justices O'Connor and Brennan in their opinions in *Phinpathya.* These include: the historical development of § 244, the legislative history of various amendments to the section, comparison with other sections in the INA, identification of the purposes of § 244, and reliance upon canons of statutory construction.

1. Legislative Intent and the Use of Legislative History

What does it mean to speak of "congressional intent"? How can a multi-member body be said to have a certain "intent," and how can a court identify it?[13] Consider the following critique and defense of the notion of legislative intent.

> It has frequently been declared that the most approved method [of interpreting a statute] is to discover the intent of the legislator. Did the legislator in establishing this determinable have a series of pictures in mind, one of which was this particular determinate? On this transparent and absurd fiction it ought not to be necessary to dwell. * * * A legislature certainly has no intention whatever in connection with words which some two or three men drafted, which a considerable number rejected, and in

---

b. The BIA's interpretation of the continuous physical presence requirement has varied over the years. After initially applying a strict interpretation, the Board adopted the more flexible approach of the Ninth Circuit in 1967. *Matter of Wong,* 12 I & N Dec. 271. Following *Phinpathya,* the Board announced that it would revert to its earlier literal interpretation. *Matter of Dilla,* Interim Dec. No. 2962 (BIA 1984).—eds.

13. Practice in other countries demonstrates that resort to legislative history is not a necessary element of a rational method of statutory construction. For example, "[t]he traditional rule of the English courts, and of the courts of former British dominions, forbids counsel and court alike even to refer to material drawn from internal legislative history." H. Hart & A. Sacks, The Legal Process 1264 (tent. ed. 1958).

regard to which many of the approving majority might have had, and often demonstrably did have, different ideas and beliefs.

That the intention of the legislature is undiscoverable in any real sense is almost an immediate inference from a statement of the proposition. The chances that of several hundred men each will have exactly the same determinate situations in mind as possible reductions of a given determinable, are infinitesimally small. The chance is still smaller that a given * * * litigated issue * * * will not only be within the minds of all these men but will be certain to be selected by all of them as the present limit to which the determinable should be narrowed. In an extreme case, it might be that we could learn all that was in the mind of the draftsman, or of a committee of half a dozen men who completely approved of every word. But when this draft is submitted to the legislature and at once accepted without a dissentient voice and without debate, what have we then learned of the intentions of the four or five hundred approvers? Even if the contents of the minds of the legislature were uniform, we have no means of knowing that content except by the external utterances or behavior of these hundreds of men, and in almost every case the only external act is the extremely ambiguous one of acquiescence, which may be motivated in literally hundreds of ways, and which by itself indicates little or nothing of the pictures which the statutory descriptions imply. It is not impossible that this knowledge could be obtained. But how probable it is, even venturesome mathematicians will scarcely undertake to compute.

Radin. *Statutory Interpretation,* 43 Harv.L.Rev. 863, 869–71 (1930).

The assumption that the meaning of [sic] a representative assembly attached to the words used in a particular statute is rarely discoverable, has little foundation in fact. The records of legislative assemblies once opened and read with a knowledge of legislative procedure often reveal the richest kind of evidence. To insist that each individual legislator besides his aye vote must also have expressed the meaning he attaches to the bill as a condition precedent to predicating an intent on the part of the legislature, is to disregard the realities of legislative procedure. Through the committee report, the explanation of the committee chairman, and otherwise, a mere expression of assent becomes in reality a concurrence in the expressed views of another. A particular determinate thus becomes the common possession of the majority of the legislature, and as such a real discoverable intent.

Legislative history similarly affords in many instances accurate and compelling guides to legislative meaning. Successive drafts of the same act do not simply succeed each other as isolated phenomena, but the substitution of one for another necessarily involves an element of choice often leaving little doubt as to the reasons governing such a choice. The voting down of an amendment or its acceptance upon the statement of its proponent again may disclose real evidence of intent. Changes made in the light of earlier statutes and their enforcement, acquiescence in a known administrative interpretation, the use of interpreted language borrowed from other sources, all give evidence of a real and not a fictitious intent, and should be deemed to govern questions of construction.   * * *

Landis. *A Note on 'Statutory Interpretation,'* 43 Harv.L.Rev. 886, 888–890 (1930).

In *Phinpathya,* both Justices O'Connor and Brennan appear to believe that "congressional intent" is a meaningful concept.   Yet they reach opposite conclusions regarding the intent behind § 244's requirement of continuous physical presence.   Justice O'Connor finds that a flexible reading of § 244 would extend eligibility "to aliens whom Congress clearly did not intend to be eligible for suspension of deportation."   Justice Brennan states that "[i]t seems inescapable * * * that Congress did not intend to have the continuous-physical-presence requirement interpreted literally."

How do both Justices go about discovering congressional "intent"? Are you persuaded that either is correct?   Or do the materials they refer to seem to demonstrate that the issue in *Phinpathya* was simply not considered by Congress and that therefore to speak of "intent" either way is erroneous?

2. The Purposes of a Statutory Provision

Given the difficulty of discovering congressional intent regarding a particular (and usually unanticipated) question of statutory interpretation, interpreters often seek to identify the "purpose" of the provision or the purposes of the statute of which it is a part.   Although the purpose (or purposes) of a statutory provision may not provide a definitive answer, it may provide direction and guidance in choosing among alternative interpretations.   Professors Henry Hart and Albert Sacks, in a classic discussion of statutory construction, describe the task of interpretation as follows:

> 1.   Decide what purpose ought to be attributed to the statute and to any subordinate provision of it which may be involved; and then

> 2.   Interpret the words of the statute immediately in question so as to carry out the purpose as best it can, making sure, however, that it does not give the words either—

> (a) a meaning they will not bear, or

> (b) a meaning which would violate any established policy of clear statement.

Hart & Sacks, *supra,* at 1411.

Does focusing on the purpose of § 244 help resolve the issue in *Phinpathya?*   What *is* the purpose of the suspension provision (or the continuous physical presence requirement, for that matter)? The section, in fact, seems to reflect at least two purposes: ameliorating the hardship of deportation for long-term residents of the United States; and ensuring that deportation of illegal aliens be cancelled only in situations of compelling human need. Together these purposes create the remedy provided in § 244—suspension of deportation for long-term aliens who meet stringent and particular requirements.

Does examination of the purposes of the statute help us in *Phinpathya?* How do Justices O'Connor and Brennan characterize, and rely upon, statutory purpose?

3. The Canons of Construction

Both Justices O'Connor and Brennan rely on "canons" of statutory construction—that is, rules that guide interpretation. Thus, Justice O'Connor states: " 'in all cases involving statutory construction, "our starting point must be the language employed by Congress," ... and we assume "that the legislative purpose is expressed by the ordinary meaning of the words used." ' " And Justice Brennan quotes with equal authority the canon that "[a]ll laws should receive a sensible construction. * * * It will always * * * be presumed that the legislature intended exceptions to its language, which would avoid [unjust, oppressive or absurd] results * * *."

The canons of construction, as Justice Frankfurter has written, "are not in any true sense rules of law. So far as valid, they are what Mr. Justice Holmes called them, axioms of experience. [*Boston Sand & Gravel Co. v. United States,* 278 U.S. 41, 48, 49 S.Ct. 52, 53, 73 L.Ed. 170 (1928).] In many instances, these canons originated as observations in specific cases from which they were abstracted, taken out of the context of actuality, and, as it were, codified in treatises." Frankfurter, *Some Reflections on the Reading of Statutes,* 47 Colum.L.Rev. 527, 544 (1947). If the canons "represent at best only probabilities based on past experience," R. Dickerson, *The Interpretation and Application of Statutes* 228 (1975), how can they decide cases? Can they even substantially help? Do you think that either Justice O'Connor or Justice Brennan would disagree with the reasonableness of the canon cited by the other? We doubt it. Rather, they are far more likely to disagree about the appropriateness of its application to the particular situation. Thus Justice Brennan might agree with Justice O'Connor that the Court should *begin* with the language used by Congress, but he would probably add that a literal reading should not always control. Similarly, Justice O'Connor might have no trouble agreeing that absurd results should be avoided in statutory interpretation, but she might disagree that the results occasioned by a literal reading of § 244(a)(1) are absurd in light of Congress' purposes. It seems that we must first decide the case to decide whether a particular canon should be invoked to decide the case!

Not only do the canons "give an air of abstract intellectual compulsion to what is in fact a delicate judgment," Frankfurter, *supra,* at 544, they also come in matched pairs. In a classic article, Professor Karl

Llewellyn compiled a lengthy list that demonstrated that "there are two opposing canons on almost every point." Llewellyn, *Remarks on the Theory of Appellate Decision and the Rules or Canons About How Statutes Are to be Construed,* 3 Vand.L.Rev. 395, 401 (1950). Llewellyn's twelfth pair of canons should look familiar:

> Thrust: If language is plain and unambiguous it must be given effect.

> Parry: Not when literal interpretation would lead to absurd or mischievous consequences or thwart manifest purpose.

Id. at 403.

4. Congressional Reenactment

Justice Brennan states that "when Congress enacts a new law that incorporates language of a pre-existing law, Congress may be presumed to have knowledge of prior judicial interpretations of the language and to have adopted that interpretation for purposes of the new law." Does this strike you as a reasonable presumption? Consider the rhetorical question of Professors Hart and Sacks: "Would public policy be well served by a doctrine that told the legislature that it cannot exercise the power to amend at all except at the cost of being considered to have committed itself upon every question which has arisen under the provision being amended?" Hart & Sacks, *supra,* at 1403. Before applying such a presumption, would you not want, at the least, some indication in the legislative history that Congress was aware of the judicial interpretations deemed to have been ratified? *See generally* 2A Sutherland's *Statutes and Statutory Construction* § 49.09 (Sands 4th ed., 1973).

5. Administrative Interpretation

It is commonly stated that "the interpretation of an agency charged with administration of a statute is entitled to substantial deference." *Blum v. Bacon,* 457 U.S. 132, 141, 102 S.Ct. 2355, 2361, 72 L.Ed.2d 728 (1982). *See generally* 2 K.C. Davis, *Administrative Law Treatise* § 7:14 (2d ed. 1979). Why might courts adopt this principle of statutory construction?

In *Phinpathya,* Justice Brennan notes that the government, while disagreeing with the liberal reading of § 244(a)(1) adopted by the court of appeals below, did assert before the Supreme Court that "[INS] believes that there is room for flexibility in applying [§ 244]." Furthermore, the BIA had adopted the Ninth Circuit's non-literal reading of "continuous physical presence" in *Matter of Wong,* 12 I & N Dec. 271 (B1A 1967).

What relevance should the agency interpretation have here? What relevance does Justice O'Connor accord it (*see* n. 13 of the majority opinion)?

6. Literalism

We are so used to hearing about the ambiguity of legal language and seeing extended discussions of legislative history in statutory cases that it may be difficult for us to conceive of an adequate defense of a theory of interpretation that relies on the "literal" meaning of statutes. Yet there is evidence—with *Phinpathya* serving as a good example—that the Supreme Court is finding such an approach appropriate with increasing regularity. *See* Note, *Intent, Clear Statements, and the Common Law: Statutory Interpretation in the Supreme Court,* 95 Harv.L.Rev. 892 (1982) (hereinafter cited as *Clear Statements*).

The primary justification for literalism in statutory construction is made in separation of powers terms: Congress, like Horton the Elephant, meant what it said and said what it meant. To read exceptions into clear language is to usurp the role of the legislature. Justice O'Connor makes an explicit appeal to this argument in *Phinpathya*. "We must," she wrote, "* * * reject respondent's suggestion [to read § 244 liberally] as impermissible in our tripartite scheme of government. Congress designs the immigration laws, and it is up to Congress to temper the laws' rigidity if it so desires."

Judicial literalness may also be defended on "process" grounds. If Congress knows that courts will read statutes to mean precisely what they say, it may be more likely to write statutes more carefully. Greater specificity may better focus congressional attention on exactly who will be helped or hurt by the legislation. It will also not permit Congress to leave statutory terms vague with the hope that the courts will resolve tough policy issues later. These process gains may also reinforce representative democracy to the extent that the relevant publics recognize that battles must be fought in legislative, not judicial, forums.

Finally, one might defend literalism as a solution to the troubling problem of discovering legislative intent. "[A] literalist reading of statutory terms" can act "as a surrogate for actual legislative intent. * * * [W]hat Congress enacts is precisely what Congress intends." Note, *Clear Statements, supra,* at 894–95.

Do you find these justifications persuasive? As to the separation of powers argument, it seems reasonable to assume that Congress does not (and cannot) consider every possible application of a statute prior to enactment. Where an unanticipated situation arises, might not a literalist approach actually diminish congressional power if the court refuses to adopt an interpretation that clearly comports with the purposes behind the statute and most likely would have been chosen had Congress considered the question? Such an application of literalist interpretation has regularly been rejected by the Supreme Court precisely in the name of carrying out the will of Congress:

> It is a familiar rule, that a thing may be within the letter of the statute and yet not within the statute, because not within its spirit, nor within the intention of its makers. * * * This is not the substitution of the will of the judge nor that of the legislator; for frequently words of general meaning are used in a statute, words broad enough to include an act in question, and yet a consideration of the whole legislation, or of the circumstances surrounding its enactment, or of the absurd results which follow from giving such broad meaning to the words, makes it unreason-

able to believe that the legislator intended to include the particular act.

Holy Trinity Church v. United States, 143 U.S. 457, 459, 12 S.Ct. 511, 512, 36 L.Ed. 226 (1892).

If literalism, to be true to its own purposes, must include a way to avoid absurd results, does not a judgment about whether a particular result is absurd require examination of the purposes behind the statutory provision? For example, in the *Holy Trinity Church* case quoted above, the Supreme Court held that the 1885 contract labor law (Ch. 164, 23 Stat. 332), which prohibited the importation of alien workers under contract, did not apply to a contract between a church and its English minister. In so concluding, the Court looked to the purpose of the law—to stem the influx of "cheap unskilled labor," *id.* at 464, 12 S.Ct. at 513—and reasoned that Congress could not have intended to cover the Church's actions. If *Holy Trinity Church* is properly decided, is not the separation of powers defense of literalism seriously undermined?

As to the "process" argument, what are the costs of judicial insistence that legislatures establish social policy only through specific, unambiguous commands? Arguably, such a demand places an unreasonable burden on congressional resources in the drafting of legislation. Furthermore, a literalist decision that effectively "remands" the statute for a clearer statement of purpose may unduly intrude upon congressional agenda-setting priorities:

> [O]ne price * * * [of a literalist approach would be] an inordinate amount of delay in correcting what might not have actually been intended—granted the present complicated machinery of the legislative process. It would involve the introduction of bills to correct and adjust, committee hearings, debates, reports, parliamentary maneuvers, log-rolling and, finally, executive surveillance. Another price to pay would be the diversion of a scarce commodity—legislative time—away from high-level study and high-level policy making. In a stable society, the legislative body could better afford the time to deal with particulars, but in a society on the move, change and an accommodating flexibility, rather than constancy and certainty would be more the order of the day. Absorption in the details of policy would paralyze efforts needed for charting the main course. Clearly, then, a certain amount of flexibility in policy detail is needed, and it can be achieved by empowering the court, in the interest of eliminating absurdities, or inequalities, or other obvious policy oversights, to look at a statute not narrowly and exclusively as a rule, but as a principle from which to reason.

Cohen, *Judicial "Legisputation" and the Dimensions of Legislative Meaning,* 36 Ind.L.J. 414, 420 (1961).

Finally, does a literalist answer necessarily do justice to a litigant harmed by a statute where Congress never thought about whether its policy should impose costs on such a litigant? Consider:

A Court using [a literal approach] model lacks the power to test statutory outcomes against Congress' expressed purposes, and thus relinquishes the power to review congressional actions critically. Critical review would not require the Court to reconsider the substantive wisdom of congressional choices, nor would it require the Court to disapprove every inequity resulting from a statute's enforcement. A critical judicial role does demand, however, that the Court approve only those harsh results inevitably attendant on specifically chosen policies. Arbitrary harm unnecessarily imposed on individuals cannot be legitimated.

Yet the limits on Congress' vision mean that the application of general policies may often produce inequitable results in particular cases. Thus, when alternative readings of sovereign commands are plausible * * * an interpreter fails to legitimate those commands when it chooses a reading that produces recognizably unfair results. * * * [L]iteralism * * * makes precisely such a choice by presuming that Congress intends to wield its power to produce unfair results, even when Congress has not expressly considered the unfairnesses its broad command might yield in particular cases.

Note, *Clear Statements, supra,* at 906–07.

7. Who's Right in *Phinpathya*?: The Role of the Interpreting Court

Do you agree with Justice O'Connor's or Justice Brennan's construction of § 244? If—after reviewing the legislative history and purpose, other provisions in the statute, precedent and other guides to interpretation—you are still in doubt, how would you reach a judgment?

Consider these options:

(1) The court should adopt the rule that the original legislature probably would have adopted had it dealt with the problem at the time it enacted the statute. This would include consideration of relevant and reliable evidences of legislative intent even if they lay outside legislative context. It might include occasional items of legislative history.

(2) The court should adopt the rule that a reasonable legislature would probably have adopted. This would presumably, but not necessarily, be the rule that best fits with the statute and other related elements in the legal order, determined as of the time the statute was enacted.

(3) The court should adopt the rule that the present legislature would probably adopt if it were now dealing with the problem.

(4) The court should adopt the rule that a reasonable current legislature would probably adopt. This would presumably, but not necessarily, be the rule that best fits with the statute and

other related elements in the legal order, determined as of the present time.

(5) The court should adopt what the court considers the preferable rule for the kind of situation before it, as determined without regard to legislative intent or the related elements of the legal order, including the statute under consideration.

(6) If none of these approaches succeeds, the court should apply an arbitrary rule of law.

R. Dickerson, *supra,* at 242–43. What are the strengths and weaknesses of each approach? How would each decide *Phinpathya?*

Assuming, in the name of separation of powers, that the primary task of a court is to adopt the interpretation that most comports with congressional will, *which* Congress should we look to: the Congress that passed the statute, the present Congress, or a future Congress? Do you agree with the following position?

As soon as a statute is enacted, it joins the rest of the law, and together with all the rest it speaks to the judge at the moment he decides a case. When it was enacted, to be sure, it was a command, uttered at a certain time in certain circumstances, but it became more than that. It became a part of the law which is now telling the judge, with the case before him and a decision confronting him, what he should now do. And isn't this just what the legislature wanted? The legislature had fashioned the statute, not for any immediate occasion, but for an indefinite number of occasions to arise in an indefinite future, until it was repealed or amended. It was to be used and applied to any such occasion, not only to the variety which might arise out of the particular situation out of which the statute itself had arisen and which had stimulated the legislature to pass it. If that were all the legislature had wanted, or if you please, intended, to do, it could have and should have used more specific terms.

The legislature which passed the statute has adjourned and its members gone home to their constituents or to a long rest from all lawmaking. So why bother about what they intended or what they would have done? Better be prophetic than archaeological, better deal with the future than with the past, better pay a decent respect for a future legislature than stand in awe of one that has folded up its papers and joined its friends at the country club or in the cemetery. Better that the courts should set their decisions up against the possibility of correction than make them under the shadow of a fiction which amounts to denial of any responsibility for the result.

There are lawyers who will call this a crude alternative, my suggestion that the courts would do better to try to anticipate the wishes of their present and future masters than divine their past intentions. It seems crude, partly because lawyers prefer the past to the future, partly because it is candid, and candor is more formidable than any let's pretend. What the courts do, or at any rate say now they do, is not crude. It's rococo. Let the courts deliberate on what the present or a future legislature would do after it had read the court's opinion, after the situation has been explained, after the court has exhibited the whole fabric of the law into which the particular bit of legislation had to be adjusted. The legislature would then be acting, if it did act, in the light of the tradition of the whole of law, which is what the courts expound and still stand for.

Curtis, *A Better Theory of Legal Interpretation,* 3 Vand.L.Rev. 407, 415–16 (1950).

Congressional Response to *Phinpathya*

Five months after the Supreme Court decided *Phinpathya,* Congressman Roybal introduced an amendment during debate on the Simpson-Mazzoli bill to add the following paragraph to § 244:

An alien shall not be considered to have failed to maintain continuous physical presence in the United States * * * if the absence from the United States did not meaningfully interrupt the continuous physical presence.

We reprint excerpts from the congressional debate that ensued.

Mr. ROYBAL. Mr. Chairman, this amendment amends the provisions of the Immigration and Nationalization Act [sic] dealing with suspensions of deportation. To be eligible for suspension of deportation an individual most prove continuous physical presence in the United States for a period of 7 years. This amendment would clarify that the requirements allow brief absences during this 7-year period; that is, absences that do not meaningfully interrupt the continuous physical presence.

Now, the reason for that is to express the intent of Congress that the requirement not be literally or strictly construed in light of the recent Supreme Court opinion that did so. The practical result of the Supreme Court's opinion is to nullify the suspension of deportation provision, a result that the Congress could not have intended.

The more personal result is that the long-time residents of this country are being denied legal status unfairly on the grounds that they may have only briefly made an innocent trip to outside the borders.

Now, this, Mr. Chairman, very frequently happens. There are people in the United States who cross the borders either into Mexico or into Canada only perhaps for a night out. Well, under the Supreme Court's decision that would have to be considered, as an interruption in the person's continuous physical presence.

Now, in that case, the Court stated in effect that if an individual stepped outside the U.S. boundary at any time during the 7-year period for however brief or unintentioned absence from this country, that individual could not be said to have met the requirements of continuous physical presence.

This was not the intent of Congress when the legislation was passed. The administration does not agree with the Supreme Court, and what we are doing with this amendment is simply clarifying the matter and making it quite clear that it is the intent of Congress to make it possible for an individual to be able to physically leave the country in a temporary way and that absence not be a meaningful interruption of his continuous physical presence.

I believe, Mr. Chairman, that this amendment is noncontroversial.

* * *

Mr. FRANK. So the members will understand what happened, the Supreme Court issued an opinion giving very strict construction to this language, which was in fact stricter than the Immigration Service itself wanted to take and we have discussed this with the Immigration Service. While I could not say they have signed off on the exact language of the gentleman from California, the Immigration Service told us in a subcommittee meeting that they are convinced of the need to make some change.

* * *

What we want to say is that if you had no intention of breaking your residence, but if you left on a brief vacation or a family problem, that should not make you start from scratch from the present. That had always been the way it had been interpreted sort of by the INS and others and we really mean to be able through this amendment to work with the Senate and the INS to get the law back to where we thought it was before the Supreme Court decision.

* * *

Mr. RODINO. Mr. Chairman, I merely want to reiterate what the gentleman from Massachusetts [Mr. Frank] has stated. I think it was never the intent of the Congress when it adopted this kind of legislation that a brief visit that could not have been avoided should have been prejudicial to that individual.

As a matter of fact, we have sometimes taken action in the committee, through private legislation, to cure that problem.

So I thank the gentleman and I applaud him for his amendment.

130 Cong.Rec. H5808–09 (daily ed. June 14, 1984). The amendment was adopted by a vote of 411 to 4.

At first blush, the vote by the House appears to be a repudiation of Justice O'Connor's opinion. After all, the House by an overwhelming majority adopted an interpretation consistent with Justice Brennan's approach—an interpretation, in the view of the amendment's sponsor, that was intended by the Congress that enacted § 244.

But why is this Congress' conclusion about what a 1952 or 1962 Congress intended necessarily more accurate than the Supreme Court's finding? Indeed, it seems probable that a present Congress would be likely to interpret the past through its current views of proper policy. If you were a legislator unhappy with the result in *Phinpathya*, wouldn't you couch your arguments in terms of restoring the "original intent" rather than creating a new exception to the deportation laws?

Even assuming that this Congress got it right and Justice O'Connor got it wrong, it is arguable that her opinion is still defensible in "process" terms. That is, by holding Congress to the "plain meaning" of the statute, the Court forced Congress to focus on the problem and provide explicit language to resolve an ambiguity in the statute. There are several responses to this view. First, is not this judicial strategy an interference with Congress' power to set its agenda? Second, how successful was the strategy, given that the Simpson-Mazzoli legislation was not enacted and thus today § 244(a)(1) stands unamended? (Even if the House amendment had become law, how much explicit legislative guidance does it really provide? Do the quoted Congressmen share the same conception of the absences permitted by the bill?) Third, how often will such a judicial strategy be successful? Is not the (limited) congressional action here due simply to the happy coincidence that Congress happened to be considering immigration legislation at the time?

b. "Extreme hardship" under § 244(a)(1)

What constitutes "extreme hardship"? The courts have repeatedly quoted Justice Brandeis' words that deportation may deprive a person "of all that makes life worth living." *Ng Fung Ho v. White,* 259 U.S. 276, 284, 42 S.Ct. 492, 495, 66 L.Ed. 938 (1922). Would not deportation of most resident aliens inflict "extreme hardship"—not only because of what an alien gives up here but also because of the different economic opportunities and standard of living he or she faces in returning to most of the countries of the world?[14] Yet, to grant this argument would effectively read the phrase out of statute, would it not?

How, then, can we arrive at an understanding of what circumstances constitute "extreme hardship?" The BIA and the courts have adopted some rules of thumb. For example, "a long line of authorities * * * state that while economic detriment is a factor for consideration, by itself it does not constitute extreme hardship." *Bueno-Carrillo v. Landon,* 682 F.2d 143, 146 (7th Cir.1982). Such "rules," however, are rarely determinative. Whether the alien has established "extreme hardship" is generally decided on a case-by-case basis, looking at the particular circumstances of

---

14. *See* Park & Busniak, *Redefining Hardship in Mexican Suspension Cases,* 6 Immig. J. 4 (April-June 1983) (arguing that "brutal economic hardship and its derivative effects" occasioned by deportation to Mexico should occupy "central place" in suspension cases of Mexican nationals).

the applicant and the applicant's family—such as length of residence in the United States, family ties, age, medical needs of the alien or his dependents, and economic and educational opportunities in the alien's home country. G & R § 7.9(d)(5). How can an adjudicator value (or balance) these and other factors? Could we create a "point system" assigning particular values to various factors and requiring an alien to achieve a certain point total to establish "extreme hardship"? Would such a system be desirable?

Because of the ultimate subjectivity of a judgment regarding the "hardship" that deportation would impose on an alien, the crucial question may be who makes the judgment: the immigration authorities or the courts? Before we examine the Supreme Court's answer, a few words on "motions to reopen" in suspension cases are in order.

Claims for § 244 relief may end up in a federal court through two different routes. If an alien has been denied suspension of deportation during a deportation proceeding, he may appeal the denial to a federal court of appeals. Alternatively, an alien may move to reopen a deportation proceeding for the purpose of filing a petition for § 244 relief or submitting additional factual material in support of a § 244 claim that had been denied in the deportation proceeding. If the BIA denies an alien's motion to reopen, that denial is then reviewable in federal court.

Motions to reopen are common in suspension cases for at least two reasons. First, suspension under § 244(a)(1) requires seven years presence in the United States. An alien may not have lived here seven years prior to her deportation hearing, yet she may meet the time requirement while her case is on appeal or before the execution of the order of deportation. *See, e.g., Moore v. INS,* 715 F.2d 13 (1st Cir.1983) (per curiam). In such circumstances, the alien may file a motion to reopen the deportation proceeding in order to be able to assert a § 244 claim. Second, a suspension claim often turns on the issue of whether or not the alien has established the requisite degree of hardship, and the degree of hardship is likely to increase the longer the alien remains in the United States. Thus it is often possible to allege new grounds of hardship that arise after the initial denial of the application but before appeals have been completed and deportation has occurred.

Obviously, if the BIA granted all motions to reopen, deportable aliens would have great incentives to file such motions irrespective of the underlying merits of their claims for relief. Accordingly, the BIA has established standards that require, *inter alia,* that aliens establish a *prima facie* case of extreme hardship before the motion to reopen will be granted and the § 244 claim will be considered.

In the following case the Supreme Court considered both the question of who has primary responsibility in defining "extreme hardship" and what standard the federal courts should apply in reviewing BIA denials of motions to reopen deportation proceedings.

INS v. JONG HA WANG

Supreme Court of the United States, 1981.
450 U.S. 139, 101 S.Ct. 1027, 67 L.Ed.2d 123.

PER CURIAM.

Section 244 of the Immigration and Nationality Act (Act), provides that the Attorney General in his discretion may suspend deportation and adjust the status of an otherwise deportable alien who (1) has been physically present in the United States for not less than seven years; (2) is a person of good moral character; and (3) is "a person whose deportation would, in the opinion of the Attorney General, result in extreme hardship to the alien or to his spouse, parent, or child, who is a citizen of the United States or an alien lawfully admitted for permanent residence."   * * *

The § 244 issue usually arises in an alien's deportation hearing. It can arise, however, as it did in this case, on a motion to reopen after deportation has been duly ordered. The Act itself does not expressly provide for a motion to reopen, but regulations promulgated under the Act allow such a procedure.[3] The regulations also provide that the motion to reopen shall "state the new fact to be proved at the reopened hearing and shall be supported by affidavits or other evidentiary material." 8 CFR § 3.8(a) (1979). Motions to reopen are thus permitted in those cases in which the events or circumstances occurring after the order of deportation would satisfy the extreme-hardship standard of § 244. Such motions will not be granted "when a *prima facie* case of eligibility for the relief sought has not been established." *Matter of Lam,* 14 I. & N. Dec. 98 (BIA 1972).

Respondents, husband and wife, are natives and citizens of Korea who first entered the United States in January 1970 as nonimmigrant treaty traders. They were authorized to remain until January 10, 1972, but they remained beyond that date without permission and were found deportable after a hearing in November 1974. They were granted the privilege of voluntarily departing by February 1, 1975. They did not do so. Instead, they applied for adjustment of status under § 245 of the Act, but were found ineligible for this relief after a hearing on July 15, 1975.[4] Their appeal from this ruling was dismissed by the Board of Immigration Appeals in October 1977. Respondents then filed a second motion to reopen their deportation proceedings in December 1977, this time claiming suspension under § 244 of the Act. Respondents by then had satisfied

3. Title 8 CFR § 3.2 (1979) provides in pertinent part:

"Motions to reopen in deportation proceedings shall not be granted unless it appears to the Board that evidence sought to be offered is material and was not available and could not have been discovered or presented at the former hearing; nor shall any motion to reopen for the purpose of affording the alien an opportunity to apply for any form of discretionary relief be granted ... unless the relief is sought on the basis of circumstances which have arisen subsequent to the hearing."

4. Relief was denied because the immigration judge determined that visa numbers for nonpreference Korean immigrants were not available, thus rendering respondents ineligible for the requested relief. The immigration judge also stated that he would have denied the application given respondents' failure to move to Salt Lake City where Mr. Wang's sponsoring employer was located, thus causing doubt whether his services were in fact needed.

the 7-year-continuous-physical-presence requirement of that section. The motion alleged that deportation would result in extreme hardship to respondents' two American-born children because neither child spoke Korean and would thus lose "educational opportunities" if forced to leave this country. Respondents also claimed economic hardship to themselves and their children resulting from the forced liquidation of their assets at a possible loss. None of the allegations was sworn or otherwise supported by evidentiary materials, but it appeared that all of respondents' close relatives, aside from their children, resided in Korea and that respondents had purchased a dry-cleaning business in August 1977, some three years after they had been found deportable. The business was valued at $75,000 and provided an income of $650 per week. Respondents also owned a home purchased in 1974 and valued at $60,000. They had $24,000 in a savings account and some $20,000 in miscellaneous assets. Liabilities were approximately $81,000.

The Board of Immigration Appeals denied respondents' motion to reopen without a hearing, concluding that they had failed to demonstrate a prima facie case that deportation would result in extreme hardship to either themselves or their children so as to entitle them to discretionary relief under the Act. The Board noted that a mere showing of economic detriment is not sufficient to establish extreme hardship under the Act. This was particularly true since respondents had "significant financial resources and there [was] nothing to suggest that the college-educated male respondent could not find suitable employment in Korea." With respect to the claims involving the children, the Board ruled that the alleged loss of educational opportunities to the young children of relatively affluent, educated Korean parents did not constitute extreme hardship within the meaning of § 244.

The Court of Appeals for the Ninth Circuit, sitting en banc, reversed. 622 F.2d 1341 (1980). Contrary to the Board's holding, the Court of Appeals found that respondents had alleged a sufficient prima facie case of extreme hardship to entitle them to a hearing. The court reasoned that the statute should be liberally construed to effectuate its ameliorative purpose. The combined effect of the allegation of harm to the minor children, which the court thought was hard to discern without a hearing, and the impact on respondents' economic interests was sufficient to constitute a prima facie case requiring a hearing where the Board would "consider the total potential effect of deportation on the alien and his family." *Id.*, at 1349.

The Court of Appeals erred in two respects. First, the court ignored the regulation which requires the alien seeking suspension to allege and support by affidavit or other evidentiary material the particular facts claimed to constitute extreme hardship. Here, the allegations of hardship were in the main conclusory and unsupported by affidavit. By requiring a hearing on such a motion, the Court of Appeals circumvented this aspect of the regulation, which was obviously designed to permit the Board to select for hearing only those motions reliably indicating the specific recent events that would render deportation a matter of extreme hardship for the alien or his children.[5]

Secondly, and more fundamentally, the Court of Appeals improvidently encroached on the authority which the Act confers on the Attorney General and his delegates. The crucial question in this case is what constitutes "extreme hardship." These words are not self-explanatory, and reasonable men could easily differ as to their construction. But the Act commits their definition in the first instance to the Attorney General and his delegates, and their construction and application of this standard should not be overturned by a reviewing court simply because it may prefer another interpretation of the statute. Here, the Board considered the facts alleged and found that neither respondents nor their children would suffer extreme hardship. The Board considered it well settled that a mere showing of economic detriment was insufficient to satisfy the requirements of § 244 and in any event noted that respondents had significant financial resources while finding nothing to suggest that Mr. Wang could not find suitable employment in Korea. It also followed that respondents' two children would not suffer serious economic deprivation if they returned to Korea. Finally, the Board could not believe that the two "young children of affluent, educated parents" would be subject to such educational deprivations in Korea as to amount to extreme hardship. In making these determinations, the Board was acting within its authority. As we see it, nothing in the allegations indicated that this is a particularly unusual case requiring the Board to reopen the deportation proceedings.

The Court of Appeals nevertheless ruled that the hardship requirement of § 244 is satisfied if an alien produces sufficient evidence to suggest that the "hardship from deportation would be different and more severe than that suffered by the ordinary alien who is deported." 622 F.2d, at 1346. Also, as Judge Goodwin observed in dissent, the majority of the Court of Appeals also strongly indicated that respondents should prevail under such an understanding of the statute. *Id.*, at 1352. In taking this course, the Court of Appeals extended its "writ beyond its proper scope and deprived the Attorney General of a substantial portion

5. Other Courts of Appeals have enforced the evidentiary requirement stated in 8 CFR § 3.8 (1979). *See, e.g., Oum v. INS,* 613 F.2d 51, 54 (CA4 1980); *Acevedo v. INS,* 538 F.2d 918, 920 (CA2 1976). *See also Tupacyupanqui-Marin v. INS,* 447 F.2d 603, 607 (CA7 1971); *Luna-Benalcazar v. INS,* 414 F.2d 254, 256 (CA6 1969).

Prior to the present procedures, the grant or denial of a motion to reopen was solely within the discretion of the Board. *See Arakas v. Zimmerman,* 200 F.2d 322, 323–324, and n. 2 (CA3 1952). The present regulation is framed negatively; it directs the Board not to reopen unless certain showings are made. It does not affirmatively require the Board to reopen the proceedings under any particular condition. Thus, the regulations may be construed to provide the Board with discretion in determining under what circumstances proceedings should be reopened. *See Villena v. INS,* 622 F.2d 1352 (CA9 1980) (en banc) (Wallace, J., dissenting). In his dissent, Judge Wallace stated that INS had discretion beyond requiring proof of a prima facie case:

"If INS discretion is to mean anything, it must be that the INS has some latitude in deciding when to reopen a case. The INS should have the right to be restrictive. Granting such motions too freely will permit endless delay of deportation by aliens creative and fertile enough to continuously produce new and material facts sufficient to establish a prima facie case. It will also waste the time and efforts of immigration judges called upon to preside at hearings automatically required by the prima facie allegations." *Id.,* at 1362.

of the discretion which § 244(a) vests in him." *Id.,* at 1351 (Sneed, J., dissenting from opinion).

The Attorney General and his delegates have the authority to construe "extreme hardship" narrowly should they deem it wise to do so. Such a narrow interpretation is consistent with the "extreme hardship" language, which itself indicates the exceptional nature of the suspension remedy. Moreover, the Government has a legitimate interest in creating official procedures for handling motions to reopen deportation proceedings so as readily to identify those cases raising new and meritorious considerations. Under the standard applied by the court below, many aliens could obtain a hearing based upon quite minimal showings. As stated in dissent below, "by using the majority opinion as a blueprint, any foreign visitor who has fertility, money, and the ability to stay out of trouble with the police for seven years can change his status from that of tourist or student to that of permanent resident without the inconvenience of immigration quotas. This strategy is not fair to those waiting for a quota." *Id.,* at 1352 (Goodwin, J., dissenting). Judge Goodwin further observed that the relaxed standard of the majority opinion "is likely to shift the administration of hardship deportation cases from the Immigration and Naturalization Service to this court." *Id.,* at 1351.

We are convinced that the Board did not exceed its authority and that the Court of Appeals erred in ordering that the case be reopened. Accordingly, the petition for certiorari is granted, and the judgment of the Court of Appeals is reversed.

So ordered.

JUSTICES BRENNAN, MARSHALL, and BLACKMUN would grant the petition for certiorari and give the case plenary consideration.

Notes

1. In *Wang,* there appear to be two interconnected issues: (a) whether the BIA was required to hold a hearing prior to denying the particular aliens § 244 relief, and (b) whether the aliens had demonstrated extreme hardship. *Wang* has thus been interpreted to speak on both procedural and substantive aspects of judicial review in suspension cases. For example, *Wang* is routinely cited for the proposition that courts should exercise restraint in ordering the BIA to reopen deportation proceedings. *See, e.g., Mesa v. INS,* 726 F.2d 39 (1st Cir.1984) (Board's decision not to reopen must be accepted by court unless arbitrary, capricious or an abuse of power). It is also regularly read to mean that the agency "has considerable discretion to decide what constitutes 'extreme hardship'." *See, e.g., Luna v. INS,* 709 F.2d 126 (1st Cir.1983). Thus *Wang* broadly controls not only cases involving motions to reopen but also direct appeals from denials of suspension.

2. Deference to administrative agencies in the interpretation of statutory language may be defended on several grounds. First, the agency works with the statute on a day-to-day basis and is likely to have a better understanding of the implications of a narrow or broad construc-

tion of a statute. Second, the agency may have aided in the drafting of the statute and, therefore, may have greater insight than the courts in the intent of the language and the purposes of the statutory provision. Third, Congress may have intended—as the Court finds in *Wang*—that the agency be the primary interpreter. Fourth, deference to agency interpretation may create greater uniformity in application of the statute than would be achieved under different opinions among courts of appeals.

Judicial deference may have a major substantive impact on implementation of a statute if the agency and the courts are likely to view the legislation from different perspectives. Such a difference in perspective seems to underlie the issues in *Wang*: the INS and BIA, acting primarily as law enforcement agencies, had adopted a strict standard of "extreme hardship" that the Ninth Circuit, looking at the provision through the eyes of the aliens, found too harsh. In effect, the Supreme Court held that Congress intended the agency's more hard-nosed approach to prevail.

Is it obvious that Congress thought that the law enforcement side of § 244 should outweigh its humanitarian aspects? If not, perhaps we would want to construct an adjudication structure that gives play to both concerns of § 244 by preserving a role for the courts to evaluate the evidence of a suspension claim. This is not to say that a reviewing court should substitute its judgment for that of the agency. That would be an overcorrection, tipping the balance too far in the direction of the alien just as the deference model may tip it too far toward enforcement objectives. Rather, the authority of a court to remand a case may ensure that a dialogue occurs between the agency and the court—a conversation that considers both law enforcement and humanitarian concerns. Is not such a dialogic process silenced by *Wang*?

Suspension of Deportation in the Post-*Wang* Era

Alexander Bickel has written that the "future will not be ruled; it can only possibly be persuaded." A. Bickel, *The Least Dangerous Branch* 98 (1962). Although Bickel was writing of important constitutional cases, his words are equally applicable to the reception of *Wang* in the lower federal courts. The Supreme Court's desire that the courts of appeals be far less intrusive in § 244 cases has not stopped the filing of appeals nor ended the remand of cases by appellate courts to the BIA. Faced with what they deem to be compelling humanitarian concerns, the courts have distinguished, explained, and misunderstood *Wang*. "Notwithstanding *Wang*," say the editors of the Harvard Law Review,

> the courts of appeals have developed standards of review that constrain the agency's discretion to deny suspension of deportation. The primary tools employed by the courts are the requirements that the Board of Immigration Appeals consider all evidence presented by the alien regarding the hardship she will face if deported, that the Board consider that evidence cumulatively, and that the Board "give reasons for its decisions showing that it has properly considered the circumstances." In addition, courts have held that the Board must reopen deportation proceedings to

allow reconsideration of the hardship question whenever the alien comes forward with previously unavailable evidence that, considered cumulatively with the evidence already introduced, could conceivably support a finding of extreme hardship.

Developments, 96 Harv.L.Rev., at 1396.

Consider the following attempt of a Third Circuit panel to avoid *Wang*.

RAVANCHO v. INS

United States Court of Appeals, Third Circuit, 1981.
658 F.2d 169.

SLOVITER, CIRCUIT JUDGE.

This case is before us on rehearing before the original panel following our exercise of our discretionary authority to recall the certified judgment issued in lieu of mandate, an action which we take only in "unusual circumstances." We followed that practice in this case so that we could consider the contention of respondent Immigration and Naturalization Service that our original decision is contrary to the subsequent decision of the Supreme Court in *INS v. Wang*, 450 U.S. 139, 101 S.Ct. 1027, 67 L.Ed.2d 123 (1981). On consideration of the parties' additional briefs and oral arguments, we believe that the primary basis for our original decision, that the Board abused its discretion in refusing to reopen the record to consider psychiatric data not available during previous hearings, is not foreclosed or undermined by the *Wang* decision, and we once again conclude a remand to the Board of Immigration Appeals is appropriate.

Zenaida Ravancho and her husband, Alejandro Ravancho, are both citizens of the Philippines who entered the United States on November 7, 1968 and December 19, 1968 respectively. On December 10, 1969, their daughter Patricia was born in the United States. Zenaida and Alejandro Ravancho were authorized to remain in the United States until February 7, 1974, but remained beyond their authorized stay and were charged with being deportable under INA § 241(a)(2). At the hearings before the immigration judge on February 1, 1978 and on March 15, 1978, the Ravanchos conceded deportability and sought to establish that deportation should be suspended on the ground of "extreme hardship" as provided for in INA § 244(a)(2).

The Ravanchos proved, inter alia, that they are both presently employed; that they have had stable employment records, Mr. Ravancho having been employed as an engineering aide by the Wallace & Tiernan Company of Belleville, New Jersey, since December 1969, and Mrs. Ravancho having been employed by the New Jersey Bell Telephone Company as a keypunch operator since 1970; and that they have purchased a house in New Jersey. They sought to show economic hardship to them which would ensue if they were deported. They also sought to establish hardship to their child (then 8 years old) by their testimony at the hearing on March 15, 1978 that she knows no other life than that in the United States, is unable to speak the Philippine language, was a straight A student in school, and that her "life would be dramatically upset by being uprooted from her home, friends, and the only life she knows."

On October 24, 1978, the immigration judge denied the Ravanchos' applications for suspension of deportation. The judge concluded that the Ravanchos met the physical presence and good moral character requirements for relief under that statute, but had failed to satisfy their statutory burden of showing that extreme hardship would result. He stated:

> A careful review of all the facts as presented including the difficulties the respondents would have in attempting to obtain employment in their native Philippines, their family situation, the loss of the income that they have now in the United States and *the possible transfer of their United States citizen child to relocate in the Philippines* does not appear to satisfy the burden placed upon them to show that they would suffer extreme hardship under this Section of the law. *Such economic disadvantage* does not constitute the required statutory hardship. (emphasis added).

The Ravanchos' appeal to the Board of Immigration Appeals was dismissed on June 14, 1979. The Board held that the immigration judge properly found that the economic detriment the Ravanchos might suffer if deported to the Philippines would not amount to extreme hardship within the purview of the statute. The Board further stated in affirming the decision of the immigration judge: "We also find that their United States citizen child, born less than one year after her mother's arrival in this country as a nonimmigrant visitor, would not suffer extreme hardship." [2] The Ravanchos filed a Motion to Stay Deportation and to Reopen Proceedings on July 31, 1979. They attached to that motion a psychiatric evaluation of Patricia dated July 17, 1979, which had been made to evaluate the effect on Patricia's mental, physical and emotional stability of a return to the Philippines. They also filed an affidavit where they averred, as they had previously testified, that Mrs. Ravancho had a brother and sister who are both lawful permanent residents of the United States and that Mr. Ravancho has a sister who is also a lawful permanent resident of the United States.

[The BIA denied the motion.]

In our original decision, we held that a remand to the Board was appropriate because the Board

> appears to have considered the proffered psychiatrist's report in isolation, only in terms of whether, on its own, that report sufficed to demonstrate extreme hardship within the statutory terms. This is contrary to the requirement that the decision whether to suspend deportation must be made on a consideration of *all* relevant factors. The psychiatrist's report may well have been the increment which would have tipped the balance toward

---

2. According to the record before us, the Ravanchos' daughter was born more than a year after her mother's arrival in the United States. Furthermore, the date of the child's birth more than ten years ago is patently unrelated to her current hardship.

suspension. There is no indication in the Board's opinion that it evaluated the proffered evidence on this basis.

We also stated that the Board appeared to give too little weight to the psychological burden on Patricia, a factor that the immigration judge had erroneously subsumed in his discussion of "economic disadvantage". We concluded our observations with the statements:

> We recognize that the determination of whether petitioners have shown extreme hardship to warrant suspension of deportation is entrusted to the discretion of the immigration judge and Board, in the first instance. However, we hold that petitioners have produced evidence which, on its face, is relevant to that determination and which must be considered by the agency in the exercise of its discretion. (footnote omitted).

The thrust of the respondent's position on rehearing is that "[t]he decision in this case is incorrect because this court substituted its own judgment for that of the Board of Immigration Appeals in determining what will constitute extreme hardship warranting suspension of deportation," Respondent's Brief on Rehearing, p. 7, and thus is contrary to *I.N.S. v. Wang,* 450 U.S. 139, 101 S.Ct. 1027, 67 L.Ed.2d 123 (1981), decided after this court's original decision. Therefore our inquiry must focus upon the Supreme Court's *Wang* decision to determine whether it requires us to reverse our previous disposition remanding this matter to the Board.

* * *

We perceive substantial differences between the *Wang* case and that at issue here. In the first place, this case does not suffer from the first factor stressed by the Supreme Court, the failure of the Wangs to allege and support by affidavit or other evidentiary material "the particular facts claimed to constitute extreme hardship." On the contrary, in this case the Ravanchos filed the necessary affidavit and proffered as evidentiary material the psychiatric evaluation which related to "the particular facts claimed to constitute extreme hardship." Unlike the Wangs who apparently proffered merely a conclusory allegation about a general loss of educational opportunities for their children in Korea, the Ravanchos proffered specific evidence relating to a particular child.

We turn then to the more fundamental question of whether a decision by this court to remand constitutes an encroachment on the authority conferred by the Act on the Attorney General. The respondent views our original decision to remand as based on our observations with respect to the Board's construction of "extreme hardship". As shown by the previously quoted excerpts from our prior opinion, however, the primary basis for our original decision to remand was the failure of the Board to consider the newly proffered evidence in conjunction with that previously submitted in order to determine whether the circumstances justified exercise of the Board's discretion. It is not necessary to speculate whether our previous observations about the Board's narrow construction of "extreme hardship", which appeared to us to be inconsistent with Congressional intent,[6] would withstand scrutiny following the *Wang* decision, since our order granting rehearing withdrew the original opinion. In any event, as petitioners correctly note, those comments were not the ground on which we determined remand was appropriate. Instead, our decision then and now turns on the Board's action, when presented with material evidence previously unavailable, in considering such evidence in isolation in determining whether a prima facie case for reopening was established.

In this respect, this case differs markedly from *Wang* where there was no contention that the Board failed to consider the totality of all of the evidence presented before it. There, the only issue was the substantive evaluation to be given such evidence. The opinion of the Board in this case expressly indicates that reconsideration was denied only on the basis of an analysis of the newly proffered evidence. We express no view on the procedure to be followed by the Board where the petition merely seeks reconsideration based on rearguments with regard to evidence previously submitted. But where, as in this case, petitioners seek to reopen proceedings based on evidence which on its face showed it was not previously available,[7] then we believe the Board abused its discretion in failing to consider the cumulative effect of that evidence. In fact, at the oral argument before us, counsel for the respondent stated that it was the Board's position that in deciding whether there is a prima facie basis for reopening, the Board must consider all of the evidence, not merely the newly proffered evidence. Although counsel also suggested that we should conclude that the Board in fact followed that procedure, it is conceded that there is nothing in the Board's short statement that indicates that anything other than the newly proffered evidence was considered. The Board, after referring to the psychiatric report, stated *"This* is not the type of extreme hardship necessary for a grant of suspension of deportation and, accordingly, we will deny the respondents' request for reconsideration." (emphasis added). We must make our decision based on the Board's own articulation of its actions, rather than on the assumption of or reconstruction by its counsel.

Although respondent argues that the psychiatric evaluation does not demonstrate "severe hardship", we do not understand it to dispute the general proposition that psychological trauma may be a relevant factor in determining whether a United States citizen child will suffer "extreme hardship" within the statute. Thus, had this or any other relevant factor been disregarded by the immigration judge or the Board when the original

---

6. A 1957 House Report refers to the Congressional intent "to provide for liberal treatment of children." *See* H.R.Rep.No. 1199, 85th Cong., 1st Sess. 7, *reprinted in* [1957] U.S.Code Cong. & Ad.News, 2016, 2020. In view of the grounds of our disposition of this case, we need not decide whether the effect of the *Wang* decision is to preclude all appellate consideration of the Board's determination whether a particular petitioner has demonstrated the requisite "extreme hardship." *See generally Brathwaite v. INS*, 633 F.2d 657, 659–60 (2d Cir.1980). We note that the statute does not explicitly so pro-vide, in contrast to other statutes where Congress has expressly committed certain determinations to unreviewable agency discretion. *See, e.g.,* 38 U.S.C. § 211(a) (1976) (decisions regarding veteran's benefits).

7. The psychiatric evaluation was made July 17, 1979 and referred to the drop in Patricia's grades during the school year which had just ended. This occurred substantially after the original hearing conducted by the immigration judge on March 15, 1978.

determination was made, such action would constitute an abuse of discretion. Similarly, if petitioners present a petition to reopen with evidence which is material and was previously unavailable, and the substantive determination is one which must be made on the basis of a consideration of all of the relevant factors, a refusal to reopen would be justified only if the Board found that the cumulative effect of the new evidence could not have affected the decision. No such finding was made in this case.

Decisions as to what circumstances constitute "extreme hardship" require delicate balancing, and are rarely made by the Board on the basis of a single factor alone. * * * Indeed in this case, the Ravanchos may have been somewhat disadvantaged because the immigration judge inexplicably erroneously mischaracterized the state of the record by his statement that the Ravanchos have no close relatives in the United States.[8] As the respondent now concedes in its brief, "Mrs. Ravancho has a brother and sister who are lawful permanent residents of the United States, and Mr. Ravancho has a brother [sic] who is a lawful permanent resident." Mr. Ravancho's sister lives in New Jersey, as do the Ravanchos. In fact the record indicates they lived in adjoining towns at the time of the 1978 hearing. Respondent concedes that "close family ties and the interest in keeping families together are considerations in granting or denying applications for suspension," but argues that the facts do not suggest that deportation in this case will adversely affect close family relationships. Whether that is so is not a determination to be made either by this court or the Board's counsel. It is one to which the immigration judge patently did not give any weight, in light of his mistaken statement that there were no such relatives in the United States, and it is one which the Board did not address because it limited its consideration to the psychiatric evaluation alone.

The Board has expressed the concern that a requirement that it review all prior evidence with each succeeding motion, no matter how insubstantial, would impose an unnecessary burden on the Board. We are not unaware of nor unsympathetic to the Board's problems in processing the substantial caseload before it. However, since the regulations themselves limit petitions to reopen to cases where there is material new

---

8. The immigration judge stated:

The issue to be resolved is whether the deportation of the respondents *who have no close relatives in the United States* would constitute extreme hardship within the contemplation of the statute. (emphasis added)

The immigration judge's statement is particularly inexplicable in light of the fact that the relevant facts were presented not only in a document which might have been overlooked but by petitioners' testimony before that very judge that Mrs. Ravancho has a permanent resident brother in active service in the United States Navy, that she has a sister who is resident in the United States, and that Mr. Ravancho has a sister who is a lawful permanent resident of the United

States. In fact, the immigration judge's erroneous statement that the Ravanchos had no close relatives permanently resident in the United States was twice corrected by the petitioners at the hearing. Nonetheless, the report of the immigration judge again repeated the erroneous statement. The correct facts were again stated in the Ravanchos' affidavit on reopening, which set forth the following status of the family as of that date: Zenaida Ravancho's brother continues as a lawful permanent resident in military service, and has two children born in the United States. Her sister is a lawful permanent resident married to a United States citizen. Alejandro Ravancho's sister is a lawful permanent resident.

evidence previously unavailable, 8 C.F.R. § 3.2, the Board itself has limited its reopening to preclude insubstantial motions.

We read the Supreme Court's *Wang* decision as reiterating the basic precept, which our prior opinion had also referred to, that Congress entrusted to the Attorney General, and not to the courts, discretion to determine whether a petitioner has shown extreme hardship to warrant suspension of deportation. We do not read that decision as foreclosing all judicial review regarding such matters, since such review is expressly provided in the statute. INA § 106.

While the scope of such review may be narrow, it extends at least to a determination as to whether the procedure followed by the Board in a particular case constitutes an improper exercise of that discretion. This court has previously held that where the record contains uncontradicted affidavits showing grounds for a suspension of deportation and yet lacks any reasoned evaluation by the INS of these grounds, an order to reopen is proper. *Martinez de Mendoza v. INS,* 567 F.2d 1222, 1224 (3d Cir.1977). We view this case in the same light.

Accordingly, we will grant review of the order of the Board and remand so that the Board can determine whether, taking into consideration all of the relevant factors on this record, the facts set forth in the psychiatric evaluation could not have affected the substantive decision on the petition for suspension of deportation, and whether reopening would be appropriate.

ALDISERT, CIRCUIT JUDGE, dissenting

* * *

I.

Unlike the majority, I am unable to perform the court's reviewing function by selectively abstracting a few portions from the entire record before the Board. I am unable to do this because I recognize that the concept of discretion is founded on equitable considerations; a court that reviews for abuse of discretion, like the agency charged with its exercise, must view the totality of circumstances in reaching a decision. It cannot remove the question for decision from the larger context in which it is presented.

In their review of the record, the majority have glossed over a number of facts that I find quite revealing. For example, they ignore the deception of Mrs. Ravancho when she applied to the American consulate for a visa on September 26, 1968. At that time she claimed to be single and to be employed as a sales manager. In fact, she was married and had worked as an accounting clerk for the United States Navy. She repeated these falsehoods on January 21, 1969, when she applied for an extension of her visa.

The majority also ignore the record of the husband which parallels that of his wife. He first applied for a visa at the American consulate in the Philippines. After he was turned down he arranged for a "travel agency" to obtain a visa for him. He did not disclose the first rejection and, like his wife, he claimed before the authorities that he was single. Mr. Ravancho received a visa for business travel, but at the deportation hearing, he denied having any business in the United States. At the hearing, Mr. Ravancho at first denied seeking a visa from the embassy, but finally admitted that he had. Moreover, the evidence disclosed that the visa attached to his passport had been made out in the name of "Avan." The letters "r" and "cho" had been added in a different ink to change the name to "Ravancho." [1] When questioned about the alteration, Mr. Ravancho was evasive and denied knowing about it. After his arrival on December 19, 1968, he, too, applied for and received an extension of his stay, again representing that he was single. He claimed on the application for an extension of his visa that he wished to continue touring the country. The evidence disclosed that at the latest, he began working about six months later. Less than one year after this extension was granted, the Ravanchos' child, Patricia, was born. The immigration service thereafter granted another extension of their visas until February 7, 1974. Deportation proceedings for overstay were begun on December 5, 1977. These facts present a serious question about whether the petitioners are sincere in their application for reopening for the sake of their daughter, or whether they are stalling for an additional extension of an illegal stay *now amounting to over seven years.*

The majority have confused the question of statutory *eligibility* under INA § 244 and the question of whether the Board can consider the totality of the circumstances in exercising its *discretion.*   * * *

II.

Turning now to the narrow focus of the majority's analysis and assuming the validity of that focus, I am unable to agree with their result. The Ravanchos have shifted emphasis in their petition to reopen, but their allegations remain substantially the same. They claim that they meet the statutory requirements, that they have relatives in this country, that they have behaved themselves while residents here, and that deportation would have a traumatic effect on their child. Their argument now, however, centers on the child and the excuse for their petition to reopen is a psychiatric evaluation of the effect of deportation on her.

In my view, the psychiatric evidence does not require the case to be reopened. Motions to reopen are governed by INS regulations, not by statute. They permit, but do not require, the service to re-examine a case previously decided when *significant* developments have occurred since the case was first heard.

This court has observed that the regulations bar consideration of evidence or contentions which could have been presented at the original proceeding. In the present case the record is barren of evidence suggesting that the adjustments Patricia would need to make in moving to the Philippines could not have been presented at that time. The utterly

---

1. Evidently this visa was one of many originating in the Philippines that had been altered in a similar manner.

innocuous psychiatric report, set forth in pertinent part in the margin,[3] had significance only insofar as it confirmed the obvious: "the child will miss her friends in the United States and will have to adjust to life in the Philippines." I submit that the symptoms described in this report would parallel those of most ten year olds facing a move to a new neighborhood or to another part of the United States, let alone to a foreign country. In this regard, it should be kept in mind that the Ravanchos are natives of the Philippines with relatives and friends there who undoubtedly could ease the strain of adjustment for their daughter. To hold that this de minimis showing requires the Board to reopen a deportation hearing is to invite every deportable alien to challenge endlessly the Board's procedures. My views on this have not changed since the time the petition for review was originally presented. The Board implicitly found that the new evidence failed to meet the threshold requirement of materiality and, therefore, in my view, properly dismissed the motion.

The majority also consider significant the immigration judge's error in stating that the Ravanchos have no close relatives in the United States. The history of § 244 discloses that it was intended to deal with hardships to family relationships which would result from deportation. C. Gordon & H. Rosenfield, Immigration Law and Procedure § 7.9a (1980). The Ravanchos never attempted to demonstrate that they had any relationship with these family members, let alone that they would suffer from moving back to the country where their parents and other relatives live. Because there was no evidence of hardship either to the family members in the United States or to the Ravanchos, the error of the immigration judge was immaterial.[4]

---

3. The relevant portions of the report follow:

Psychiatric Evaluation of Patricia Ravancho
This 10 year old, fifth grade student was referred for psychiatric evaluation to determine [the] effect on her physical, mental and emotional stability if she is forced to return to the Philippines. Patricia was born in the United States and does not [speak] Tugallah.

. . . .

Interview with Patricia:

This clean, neat, well developed and well nourished, quiet, inhibited 10 year old sat anxiously awaiting her turn to be interviewed. She wrote her name very neatly in script, gave her age, grade, date of birth, address and school. Anxiety was revealed in her voice.

She was able to talk about her friends and her interests.

School has been all right for her except "arithmetic", "fractions", and "measurement".

This year her grades have gone down.

Fears are of "being frightened by other people", "heights", "bugs", "beetles", "wild animals", and "dying".

Ambition is to be a doctor.

When asked about her 3 wishes, she was able to state only one "Not have to go to the Philippines". When asked why she would not want to go there, she replied, "I would have to leave all of my friends whom I have known since kindergarten." She also mentioned the language problem, climate, and food.

Health: Health has been good. Sometimes she has trouble sleeping when weather is hot. Her insecurities were revealed in her HTP drawings. It took her a while to do the person, and she was so fearful of making a mistake that she traced the figure in the air first. When she called it "finished" there was no face or hands.

The house and tree showed isolation and inaccessibility.

Impression: Insecure child who relies on known friends and relatives for guidance and security.

4. The majority conclude that the Board did not consider the residence of these family members in its decision to reopen "because it limited its consideration to the psychiatric evaluation alone." I read the

III.

My principal disagreement with the majority, however, is their cavalier treatment of the Supreme Court's decision in *I.N.S. v. Wang,* 450 U.S. 139, 101 S.Ct. 1027, 67 L.Ed.2d 123 (1981) (per curiam). While not identical with the *facts* presented here, *Wang* addresses the specific *problem* before us in this case: the appropriate scope of judicial review of INS discretion. Unlike the majority, I read that decision broadly because I believe that the Court was deciding more than the issue presented by the precise facts before it. The Court was signalling to the courts of appeals the proper degree of deference to be accorded the Board's decisions on reopening. This reading is mandated because the Court did not stop with identifying the ninth circuit's error in ignoring the INS regulation requiring a petition to reopen to be supported by affidavits. That error alone would have justified the decision. Instead, the Court identified what it described as the circuit court's "fundamental" error of improvidently encroaching on the discretionary authority of the Attorney General and his designees. My reading of *Wang* convinces me that the majority here commit the same fundamental error as did the ninth circuit.[5]

Of particular relevance to the case before us is the language quoted by the Court in *Wang* from Judge Wallace's dissent in *Villena v. INS,* 622 F.2d 1352, 1362 (9th Cir.1980) (in banc), decided by the ninth circuit with *Wang:*

> If INS discretion is to mean anything, it must be that the INS has some latitude in deciding when to reopen a case. The INS should have the right to be restrictive. Granting such motions too freely will permit endless delays of deportation by aliens creative and fertile enough to continuously produce new and material facts sufficient to establish a prima facie case. It will also waste the time and efforts of immigration judges called upon to preside at hearings automatically required by the prima facie allegations.

record differently. The residential status of the Ravanchos' relatives was set forth in the affidavit appended to their motion to reopen. The Board then considered both the affidavit and the psychiatric evaluation.

5. The majority attempt to distinguish *Wang* on the ground that there the Board undertook a cumulative review of the evidence presented, whereas here the Board reviewed only the new evidence. The majority indicates the Board's reference to the psychiatric report and its statement that "[t]his is not the type of extreme hardship necessary for a grant of suspension of deportation ...."

A reading of the entire paragraph reveals that this was not the case. The Board considered *both* the Ravanchos' affidavit which set forth the facts on which they based their initial petition for relief, *and* the psychiatric report:

The only evidence submitted in support of the respondents' motion is *their own affidavit and a psychiatric evaluation of their ten-year-old United States citizen child.* This evidence does not establish the necessary hardship to the respondents or to their daughter for the purposes of relief from deportation under section 244 of the Immigration and Nationality Act, 8 U.S.C. 1254. Although the respondents have placed great reliance on the report of Dr. Prystowsky on their daughter, we find that it indicates no more than that the child will miss her friends in the United States and will have to adjust to life in the Philippines. This is not the type of extreme hardship necessary for a grant of suspension of deportation and, accordingly, we will deny the respondents' request for reconsideration.

Quoted 450 U.S. at 143 fn. 5, 101 S.Ct. at 1031 fn. 5. The Court quoted this language in connection with its recognition that the regulation providing for a procedure to reopen is framed negatively; it directs that the Board may not reopen absent a showing of specified conditions: "Thus the regulations may be construed to provide the Board with discretion in determining under what circumstances a proceeding should be reopened." *Id.* The Court then explained the legitimate government interest in limiting conditions on which reopening would be granted. The majority here, like the discredited ninth circuit *Wang* court, would require a reopening upon a minimal showing. *See* 450 U.S. at 144, 101 S.Ct. at 1031. This deprives the Board of its discretionary authority to determine under what circumstances reopening should be granted.

The majority pay only lip service to the legitimate interest of the government "in creating official procedures for handling motions to re-open deportation proceedings so as readily to identify those cases raising new and meritorious considerations." *Wang,* 450 U.S. at 145, 101 S.Ct. at 1031. The reason for according such procedures deference is clear: it is unfair to allow those aliens who have deliberately flouted the immigration laws to find shelter in those same laws, absent extraordinary circumstances, while requiring patient, law-abiding citizens of foreign states to follow the letter and spirit of the laws while awaiting a quota. The minimal showing that satisfies the majority will inevitably bring about further delays in this case, and worse, the decision invites any similarly situated alien to begin anew a groundless course of agency and judicial proceedings.

* * *

* * * What the majority have done is, in Karl Llewellyn's words, to treat the Supreme Court's decision in *Wang* as an "unwelcome precedent." Their grudging use of that decision seems to say that "[t]he rule holds only of redheaded Walpoles in pale magenta Buick cars."[6] I am confident that the majority's singular treatment of the Supreme Court's direction will have little precedential or institutional value in this or in other courts.

Notes

Numerous other § 244 cases have been remanded to the BIA, notwithstanding the holding (and implications) of *Wang.* *See, e.g., Zavala-Bonilla v. INS,* 730 F.2d 562 (9th Cir.1984) (reversing denial of suspension for failure of BIA "to consider all relevant factors"); *Rios-Pineda v. INS,* 720 F.2d 529 (8th Cir.1983) (reversing denial of motion to reopen on ground that BIA based decision on "improper and irrelevant factors"), *reversed* __ U.S. __, 105 S.Ct. 2098, 85 L.Ed.2d 452 (1985); *Luna v. INS,* 709 F.2d 126 (1st Cir.1983) (alien established *prima facie* case of hardship warranting reopening and full consideration of § 244 claim); *Batoon v. INS,* 707 F.2d 399 (9th Cir.1983) (denial of motion to reopen reversed on ground that Board's opinion did not indicate consideration of important

6. K. Llewellyn, *The Bramble Bush* 66–67 (1960).

evidence); *Reyes v. INS,* 673 F.2d 1087 (9th Cir.1982) ("manifestly unfair" for BIA to disbelieve facts stated in affidavit submitted in support of motion to reopen). Are these cases consistent with the letter and spirit of *Wang?*

Of course, not all the cases have gone this way. *See, e.g., LeBlanc v. INS,* 715 F.2d 685 (1st Cir.1983) (holding that BIA may deny motion to reopen as matter of discretion without determining whether alien has established prima facie case for relief); *Bueno-Carrillo v. Landon,* 682 F.2d 143 (7th Cir.1982) (upholding BIA finding of no extreme hardship); *Hee Yung Ahn v. INS,* 651 F.2d 1285 (9th Cir.1981) (rejecting hardship claim and commenting that while decisions of different panels of the same court "indicate that this court will strain to find reasons to reverse the Board despite *Wang,* that is not the sort of precedent we are bound to follow"); *Barrera-Leyva v. INS,* 653 F.2d 379 (9th Cir.1981) (vacating pre-*Wang* decision that had remanded case).

Can the attempts by some lower courts to supervise suspension decisions succeed? Consider the following answer.

> In the long run * * * the techniques employed by the courts to control the Board's exercise of discretion may prove ineffective. The abuse-of-discretion standard devised by the courts of appeals does not significantly restrain the Board of Immigration Appeals: the Board may evade the teeth of the standard simply by taking care to include language in its opinions suggesting that the cumulative effect of all the evidence presented by the alien was insufficient to establish hardship. Unless one is confident that simply forcing the Board to articulate the factors it considered in reaching its decision will necessarily lead it to reach fairer and more humane results, the assertion that the post-*Wang* standard of review developed by the courts of appeals will serve as a real check on agency discretion seems unconvincing.

> Although the full consideration of all relevant facts is essential to proper exercise of administrative discretion, the manner in which that discretion is exercised is not determined solely by the deliberative process. The disagreement between the courts of appeals and the Board may ultimately be substantive rather than procedural: the cases strongly suggest that the courts have taken a more generous view of the extent to which relief should be available to deportable aliens than has the Board. But because *Wang* seems to preclude the courts from enforcing their own substantive notions about the appropriateness of granting discretionary relief from deportation, the courts may be unable to affect anything more than the language in which the Board couches its conclusions. Thus, effective judicial control of agency discretion to deny relief from deportation may be a short-lived phenomenon.

Developments, supra, at 1397–98.

c. The Discretionary Aspect of § 244 Relief

(i) Administrative Limits on Discretion

As the Supreme Court has noted, "[s]uspension of deportation is a matter of discretion and of administrative grace, not mere eligibility; discretion must be exercised even though statutory prerequisites have been met." *United States ex rel. Hintopoulos v. Shaughnessy,* 353 U.S. 72, 77, 77 S.Ct. 618, 621, 1 L.Ed.2d 652 (1957). Here we run into the same problems we faced in trying to pour content in the phrase "extreme hardship." What factors should the adjudicators consider in exercising the discretion the statute grants them? The cases indicate a number of factors that may be relevant. These include the alien's prior history of violations of the immigration laws, subversive activities, reliance on public assistance, and the absence of substantial ties in this country. *See, e.g., Vaughn v. INS,* 643 F.2d 35 (1st Cir.1981); G & R § 7.9e. What additional factors do you think could or should be considered?

Would it be advisable to promulgate regulations that would guide the exercise of discretion? Interestingly, in 1979 the INS issued proposed regulations that sought to identify factors to be considered in the exercise of discretion under INA § 245 (adjustment of status) and other provisions of the statute. 44 Fed.Reg. 36187 –93 (1979). A year and a half later the project was abandoned. INS explained its decision not to publish a final rule as follows:

> There is an inherent failure in any attempt to list those factors which should be considered in the exercise of discretion. It is impossible to list or foresee all of the adverse or favorable factors which may be present in a given set of circumstances. Listing some, even with the caveat that such list is not all inclusive, still poses a danger that the use of the guidelines may become so rigid as to amount to an abuse of discretion.

> In the exercise of discretion, all relevant factors are considered. The adverse factors are weighed against the favorable factors in the judgment and conscience of the responsible officials. Service officials are required to prepare a record justifying their actions when they deny a benefit in the exercise of administrative discretion. Summary and stereotyped denials are not acceptable.

> To avoid the possibility of hampering the free exercise of discretionary authority, the proposed rule is cancelled and a final rule will not be published.

46 Fed.Reg. 9119 (1981).

Maurice Roberts, former Chairman of the BIA, has argued that regulations to guide the exercise of discretion are both desirable and possible:

> [Discretion] is exercised by impressionable and fallible human beings at all levels of the administrative hierarchy. While the Act commits enforcement responsibility to the Attorney General and, upon his delegation, to the Commissioner of Immigration

and Naturalization, in practice decision making has been delegated to and is exercised by a host of lesser officials. * * * In actual practice, most of the Service's decisions, which go out over the facsimile signatures of the various District Directors, are not made by the District Directors themselves, but are made in their name by adjudicators at various levels, who are not required to be lawyers or otherwise formally trained in the appraisal of evidence.

In the absence of carefully considered and clearly articulated standards for the exercise of the various types of discretionary powers, the resulting decisions must necessarily vary with the personal attitudes and biases of the individual decision makers. Adjudicators with hard-nosed outlooks are likely to be more conservative in the evidentiary appraisals and in their dispensation of discretionary bounties than their counterparts with more permissive philosophies. It must be recognized as a fact of life that Service officers and Board members are no more immune than other persons to the influences that result in individual bias and predilection. To set up as a standard that a case must be "meritorious" before discretion is favorably exercised in behalf of an eligible applicant is therefore illusory. Too many subjective elements go into the making of such a value judgment.

* * *

It should be possible to achieve greater uniformity of decision, while at the same time minimizing the opportunities for result-oriented adjudication based on an adjudicator's subjective feelings, by defining with greater precision not only the policies to be served but also the elements to be considered. It does not matter whether the guiding principles are laid down in published regulations or in the Board's published precedent decisions, which are binding on the Service. Certainly, greater care should be taken in thinking through and then defining those elements which should be considered "adverse" and those which can be properly juxtaposed in mitigation. Great precisiveness need not completely strait-jacket the adjudicator or limit the range of elements which may properly be considered.

Of course, even with more precise definition of the relevant factors, the adjudicator must still determine how much weight to assign to each of the competing elements and in this appraisal his subjective notions can still come into play. It is at this point that clear policy statements become of overriding importance as a guide to action.

Uniformity of decision with mathematical precision is, of course, possible. Specific point values could be prescribed for each element deemed relevant, e.g., so many minus points for a preconceived intent, so many for a wife abroad, so many for each minor child abroad, so many for being responsible for the break-up of the foreign marriage, so many for each intentional misstatement to the Service, etc. Plus points could be assigned for an American citizen or permanent resident wife, for each American child, for each year of the alien's residence here, and the like. An appropriate plus score could be fixed as a prerequisite to the favorable exercise of discretion. * * *

Any notion of such mechanical jurisprudence would, of course, be summarily rejected if seriously suggested. Yet, unless more realistic and specific guidelines are laid down, the opposite extreme becomes possible if it is left to each individual adjudicator to determine for himself, on the basis of his own subjective experiences and beliefs, just what factors in the alien's life should be determinative in exercising discretion and how much weight should be accorded each factor. An intolerant adjudicator could deny relief to aliens whose cultural patterns, political views, moral standards or life styles differed from his own. Worse still, a hostile or xenophobic adjudicator could vent his spleen on aliens he personally considered offensive without articulating the actual basis for his decision.

Unless standards are laid down which are not illusory and can be uniformly applied in the real world, we depart from even-handed justice and the rule of law. * * *

Roberts, *The Exercise of Administrative Discretion Under the Immigration Laws,* 13 San Diego L.Rev. 144, 147–48, 164–65 (1975).[15]

Do you agree with former Chairman Roberts? What are the costs and benefits of establishing guidelines for the exercise of discretion?

(ii) Judicial Review of Administrative Discretion in § 244 Cases

How should a court review the exercise of discretion in a § 244 case? If the statute itself provides no standards, on what basis may a court determine that the adjudicators erred? Should we simply conclude, fortified by § 701 of the Administrative Procedure Act, *see* 5 U.S.C.A. § 701 (no judicial review where "agency action is committed to agency discretion by law"), that such decisions are not subject to judicial review? The (perhaps unsurprising) answer is no. Although § 701 of the APA excludes from judicial review actions committed by law to agency discretion, § 706 of the APA authorizes a court to set aside an agency action for "abuse of discretion." In the tussle that has ensued between these apparently conflicting provisions, reviewability has nearly always won out. *Citizens to Preserve Overton Park v. Volpe,* 401 U.S. 402, 410, 91 S.Ct. 814, 820, 28 L.Ed.2d 136 (1971) (Section 701 "is a very narrow exception * * * [and] is applicable in those rare instances where 'statutes are drawn in such broad terms that in a given case there is no law to apply.' ") *See generally* K.C. Davis, *Administrative Law Treatise* § 28.16 (Supp.1982).

15. *See also* Diver, *The Optimal Precision of Administrative Rules,* 93 Yale L.J. 65, 92–97 (1983) (concluding that "most of the reasons for discretionary grant or denial [by the INS] could be subjected to greater anterior specification without offending an applicant's humanity").

Judge Henry Friendly has written the definitive opinion on the reviewability of the discretionary aspect of the suspension of deportation decision.

WONG WING HANG v. INS

United States Court of Appeals, Second Circuit, 1966.
360 F.2d 715.

FRIENDLY, CIRCUIT JUDGE:

Wong Wing Hang asks us to set aside a final order of the Board of Immigration Appeals insofar as this denied, as a matter of discretion, his application under the Immigration and Nationality Act § 244, for suspension of a concededly valid order directing his deportation to Formosa.

The petitioner, a 37-year old native and citizen of China, entered the United States in 1951 on a false claim that he was the son of a United States citizen. Two years later he fraudulently applied for a certificate of citizenship, and in December 1955, when questioned by a United States attorney, gave false information as to his identity and that of other Chinese immigrants. Shortly thereafter he furnished the correct information when called before a grand jury, and subsequently revealed his identity to the INS and surrendered his certificate. In 1956 he was indicted as a member of a conspiracy to perpetrate passport frauds for other Chinese, the last overt act being the giving of false testimony in court on December 12, 1955; he was convicted on a plea of guilty in 1961, and, receiving a suspended sentence, was placed on probation for a year.

In September 1963, the INS held proceedings to determine whether Wong should be deported for having entered the United States without inspection, § 241(a)(2). Not disputing deportability, Wong applied for suspension. A hearing before a Special Inquiry Officer revealed that during the course of his probation Wong told his probation officer that his wife was in China and afterwards, in August 1962, when asked by an investigator of the INS where his wife and children were and whether they had ever entered the United States, stated under oath that they had never entered this country and were living in Kowloon; in fact, as Wong well knew, the wife and children had fraudulently entered Canada in 1958 as the spouse and children of a Canadian citizen and at the time of the statement to the investigator were visiting Wong in New York. The Special Inquiry Officer, after questioning Wong closely as to the extent of his wife's visits and whether she was spending most of the time here, reserved decision pending report of a character investigation being conducted by the Government. The following December, in the course of the investigation, the wife was found in Wong's apartment, having entered the United States two months before as a Canadian citizen saying she wanted to remain for three weeks or a month.

* * *

* * * Wong's application for suspension was denied not for ineligibility but because, in the language of the Special Inquiry Officer, "far from acting as a person who regretted his previous actions and was attempting to act in a law abiding fashion," Wong had "deliberately concealed the whereabouts and status of his wife and children" and had permitted his wife to enter the United States repeatedly with documents known to him to be fraudulent and to remain beyond the period of her admission. Wong complains that he is being penalized for protecting his wife and children as any husband and father would.

* * *

* * * [W]e turn for illumination to * * * the Administrative Procedure Act * * *. Here we encounter the familiar conflict between the preamble of [5 U.S.C.A. § 701] "Except so far as * * * agency action is by law committed to to agency discretion," and the command of [5 U.S.C.A. § 706] that the reviewing court shall "set aside agency action * * * found to be * * * arbitrary, capricious, an abuse of discretion, or otherwise not in accordance with law."

Some help in resolving the seeming contradiction may be afforded by the distinction drawn by Professors Hart and Sacks between a discretion that "is not subject to the restraint of the obligation of reasoned decision and hence of reasoned elaboration of a fabric of doctrine governing successive decisions" and discretion of the contrary and more usual sort, see The Legal Process 172, 175–177 (Tent. ed. 1958); only in the rare— some say non-existent—case where discretion of the former type has been vested, may review for "abuse" be precluded. An argument could be made that the change from the earlier versions of the suspension provision, "the Attorney General may suspend if he finds," 54 Stat. 672 (1940), 62 Stat. 1206 (1948), to its present form affords an indication that Congress meant to accord the Attorney General or his delegate *ad hoc* discretion of that sort. But the Attorney General himself has not thought so; applications for suspension of deportation, whether under § 244 or § 243(h) of the Immigration and Nationality Act, have long been subjected to various administrative hearing and appeal procedures, see the history recounted in Jay v. Boyd, 351 U.S. 345, 351–352, 76 S.Ct. 919, 100 L.Ed. 1242 (1956), with their concomitants of "the obligation of reasoned decision." Despite language in Jay v. Boyd, supra at 353–356, 76 S.Ct. 919, that could be read as supporting unreviewability of the ultimate exercise of discretion, the contrary view is implicit in United States ex rel. Hintopoulos v. Shaughnessy, 353 U.S. 72, 77, 77 S.Ct. 618, 1 L.Ed.2d 652 (1957), where the Court reviewed the discretionary denial of suspension and affirmed the agency decision because it did not represent an abuse of discretion and the reasons on which it was based were neither "capricious nor arbitrary." * * * This court has long held discretionary denials of suspension to be reviewable for "abuse."

What is not so clear is precisely what this means. In the absence of standards in the statute itself, proper administration would be advanced and reviewing courts would be assisted if the Attorney General or his delegate, without attempting to be exhaustive in an area inherently insusceptible of such treatment, were to outline certain bases deemed to warrant the affirmative exercise of discretion and other grounds generally militating against it. When we turn to the books, we find that "abuse of discretion" has been given two rather different meanings. In one version it appears as a sort of "clearly erroneous" concept, perhaps best expressed in Judge Magruder's formulation that "when judicial action is taken in a discretionary matter, such action cannot be set aside by a reviewing court unless it has a definite and firm conviction that the court below committed a clear error of judgment in the conclusion it reached upon a weighing of the relevant factors." In re Josephson, 218 F.2d 174, 182 (1 Cir.1954). *See* Pearson v. Dennison, 353 F.2d 24, 28 & n. 6 (9 Cir.1965). Under a more limited notion discretion is held to be abused only when the action "is arbitrary, fanciful or unreasonable, which is another way of saying that discretion is abused only where no reasonable man would take the view" under discussion. *See* Delno v. Market St. Ry. Co., 124 F.2d 965, 967 (9 Cir.1942). A narrower meaning seems more appropriate when a court is reviewing the exercise of discretion by an administrative agency or an executive officer as distinguished from hearing an appeal from a decision of a judge—particularly so when the relevant statute expressly confides "discretion" to the agency or officer; this assists in reconciling what conflict there is in * * * the APA. Without essaying comprehensive definition, we think the denial of suspension to an eligible alien would be an abuse of discretion if it were made without a rational explanation, inexplicably departed from established policies, or rested on an impermissible basis such as an invidious discrimination against a particular race or group, or, in Judge Learned Hand's words, on other "considerations that Congress could not have intended to make relevant." [United States ex rel. Kaloudis v. Shaughnessy, 180 F.2d 489, 491 (2d Cir.1950).]

Wong contends that the determination here comes under the first rubric since it is internally inconsistent—he was found to have possessed "good moral character" during the several years prior to his application for discretionary relief, yet was faulted for prevarication and concealment during that same period. But the answer lies in the very point so strongly pressed by him, that his falsehoods were prompted by the natural human motive to protect his wife and children and keep his family together. To say that such conduct does not demonstrate lack of good moral character but nevertheless may not demand a favorable exercise of discretion by the Immigration Service is by no means a self-contradiction. If the immigration authorities choose to say that a man who has gained entry by a false claim of United States citizenship and has cooperated with others in similar efforts, can win their favor only by a spotless record in later dealings with them, and apply this standard with an even hand, we cannot hold their decision to be so wanting in rationality as to be an abuse of the discretion which Congress vested in them.

The petition to review must therefore be denied.

Notes

How can an alien prove that a discretion-based denial of § 244 relief—or any equivalent discretionary relief under the INA—departed from established policies or rested on a hidden impermissible basis? Would he be entitled to extensive discovery of INS internal documents (perhaps to be gathered nationwide, if the issue is departure from established policy), or to depositions of numerous INS officers? What threshold showing should be required before INS is subjected to these kinds of discovery burdens? A request for discovery in these circumstances can pose thorny problems for a court, because it is often hard to see how an alien could establish even a prima facie case of administrative flaws of this type without *first* obtaining highly burdensome discovery. For one court's efforts to balance the relevant concerns, *see Munoz-Santana v. INS*, 742 F.2d 561 (9th Cir. 1984).

d. § 244 in Action

What follows are fact situations drawn from two cases in which an alien applied for suspension of deportation. Put yourself in the role of the immigration judge and decide whether or not you would grant the benefit. Have the statutory prerequisites for relief been met? How would you exercise your discretion? How do you view your mission? To "do justice"? Protect American borders? Help dependents of aliens who are United States citizens? How does your perspective on the purposes of § 244 affect your judgment as to which factors are pertinent to your decision?

(1) Mr. and Mrs. J and M R., citizens of the Phillipines, entered the United States in July, 1961, as nonimmigrant visitors for pleasure. They obtained permission to stay until April, 1962. In February, 1962, J was hired by an advertising company in Chicago. M got a job as a medical technologist at a Chicago hospital. M gave birth to children in Chicago in 1968 and 1970. In 1974, J was transferred to Dallas, and the family moved there. M got another job as a medical technologist. J's parents, who are lawful permanent residents living in Chicago, partially depend upon J and M for financial support.

At the deportation hearing in 1977, J and M claim extreme hardship based on the following facts: 1) their children, now aged 6 and 8, are "in all respects culturally American;" they do not speak the language of the Phillipines, nor do they have any ties to the Phillipines; 2) their oldest son had been traumatized by the move from Chicago to Dallas, and a move to the Phillipines could cause a more severe trauma. A psychiatrist's report submitted at the hearing stated that after the move to Dallas, the son "would not talk in school for several months. His father had to attend school with him. He has already shown symptoms of school phobia and transient elective mutism. He would be particularly vulnerable to exacerbation of these symptoms especially if he were forced to move outside of the country."; 3) J's parents would be deprived of emotional and financial support; and 4) J and M would face difficulty in getting similar employment for similar pay in the Phillipines.

How do you rule? *Cf. Ramos v. INS*, 695 F.2d 181 (5th Cir.1983).

(2) M, a citizen of Pakistan, entered the United States in September 1970 on a nonimmigrant student visa. He was authorized to remain for four years. He received a college degree in electrical engineering and South Asian studies. M failed to leave the country at the end of his authorized stay and was apprehended in 1980 and placed in deportation

proceedings. At the hearing he conceded deportability and applied for § 244 relief.

In support of his "extreme hardship" claim he submitted the following evidence: 1) he had resided in the United States for ten years and thus had become culturally acclimated; 2) he had family ties in the United States (a cousin), although his immediate family lived in Pakistan; 3) the quota for Pakistani immigrants was oversubscribed; 4) it would be a financial burden to leave the United States only to return later; 5) he had always cooperated with the immigration authorities; 6) he was of good moral character and an accomplished student; 7) he was scheduled to begin law school that fall; and 8) he would suffer psychological trauma in Pakistan on account of his religion. In support of the last claim M testified that he was a member of the Zoroastrian faith—a religion that claimed five thousand adherents among a total population of seventy million. Zoroastrians had been persecuted by the Moslems in the 1970 civil war. In 1977 a military dictator overthrew the democratically elected president and established an Islamic order. The Zoroastrians are being systematically removed from government jobs. Furthermore, Zoroastrians have been harassed because of their involvement in businesses not sanctioned by the Islamic order, such as liquor shops, and because they have been financially successful. Furthermore, all citizens were required to apply for a national identity card that identifies the applicant's religion. M asserted that because he had not applied for such a card he would be subject to criminal prosecution. Finally, he stated that he will be deprived of his livelihood because he has not worked as an electrical engineer for eight years and he cannot practice Western law in Pakistan.

How do you rule? *Cf. Minwalla v. INS*, 706 F.2d 831 (8th Cir.1983).

e. An Aside on Congressional Review of Executive Branch Decisions to Suspend Deportation

Section 244 not only reflects a tension between the conflicting desires to deport aliens who violate the law and to avoid imposing substantial harms on human beings; it also reflects a tension over who should make the decision to resolve the first tension. Congress, in enacting § 244 in 1952, recognized the necessity of administrative decisions, but it was unwilling to grant the Attorney General unreviewable authority to exempt aliens from the operation of the deportation statutes. Thus it provided in § 244(c) for congressional review of executive branch decisions to suspend deportation. The Supreme Court has recently traced the history of the provision:

> The Immigration Act of 1924, Pub.L. No. 139, § 14, 43 Stat. 153, 162, required the Secretary of Labor to deport any alien who entered or remained in the United States unlawfully. The only means by which a deportable alien could lawfully remain in the United States was to have his status altered by a private bill enacted by both Houses and presented to the President pursuant to the procedures set out in Art. I, § 7 of the Constitution. These

private bills were found intolerable by Congress. In the debate on a 1937 bill introduced by Representative Dies to authorize the Secretary to grant permanent residence in "meritorious" cases, Dies stated:

"It was my original thought that the way to handle all these meritorious cases was through special bills. I am absolutely convinced as a result of what has occurred in this House that it is impossible to deal with the situation through special bills. We had a demonstration of that fact not long ago when 15 special bills were before the House. The House consumed 5½ hours considering four bills and made no disposition of any of these bills." 81 Cong.Rec. 5542 (1937).

Representative Dies' bill passed the House, id., at 5574, but did not come to a vote in the Senate. 83 Cong.Rec. 8992–8996 (1938).

Congress first authorized the Attorney General to suspend the deportation of certain aliens in the Alien Registration Act of 1940, ch. 439, § 20, 54 Stat. 671. That Act provided that an alien was to be deported, despite the Attorney General's decision to the contrary, if both Houses, by concurrent resolution, disapproved the suspension.

In 1948, Congress amended the Act to broaden the category of aliens eligible for suspension of deportation. In addition, however, Congress limited the authority of the Attorney General to suspend deportations by providing that the Attorney General could not cancel a deportation unless both Houses affirmatively voted by concurrent resolution to *approve* the Attorney General's action. Act of July 1, 1948, ch. 783, 62 Stat. 1206. The provision for approval by concurrent resolution in the 1948 Act proved almost as burdensome as private bills. Just four years later, the House Judiciary Committee, in support of the predecessor to § 244(c)(2), stated in a report:

"In the light of experience of the last several months, the committee came to the conclusion that the requirements of affirmative action by both Houses of the Congress in many thousands of individual cases which are submitted by the Attorney General every year, is not workable and places upon the Congress and particularly on the Committee on the Judiciary responsibilities which it cannot assume. The new responsibilities placed upon the Committee on the Judiciary [by the concurrent resolution mechanism] are of purely administrative nature and they seriously interfere with the legislative work of the Committee on the Judiciary and would, in time, interfere with the legislative work of the House." H.R.Rep. No. 362, 81st Cong., 1st Sess. 2 (1949).

The proposal to permit one House of Congress to veto the Attorney General's suspension of an alien's deportation was incorporated in the Immigration and Nationality Act of 1952, Pub.L. No. 414, 66 Stat. 163, 214.

INS v. Chadha, 462 U.S. 919, 103 S.Ct. 2764, 2774–75, 77 L.Ed.2d 317 (1983).

In 1983, the Supreme Court wrote the last chapter on congressional review of suspension decisions. In a landmark case that apparently invalidates over 200 federal statutes, the Court held the congressional veto provision [16] unconstitutional. *INS v. Chadha, supra.* The Court reached this conclusion by determining that the veto provision was "legislative" in character and effect. Accordingly, it was subject to the strictures of Art. I, § 7 of the Constitution, which require that legislation be approved by both Houses of Congress and presented to the President for approval or disapproval. These were not met by the mechanism provided in § 244(c), since it purported to authorize invalidation of the decision of the Attorney General to suspend deportation by a vote of a single House and without submission to the President.

Although the Court invalidated the legislative veto in § 244, it further held that the provision was severable from the remainder of the section. Accordingly, suspension of deportation under § 244 is still available. Decisions to suspend must still be reported to Congress, however, and permanent resident status cannot be granted until two sessions of Congress have elapsed following the report. *See Lewis v. Sava,* 602 F.Supp. 571 (S.D.N.Y.1984). Whether Congress could validly disapprove suspension and order deportation of a named alien by means of regular legislation remains questionable, in light of the constitutional ban on bills of attainder. *See INS v. Chadha, supra,* 103 S.Ct. at 2776 n.8, 2785 n.17.

How might Congress constitutionally amend the statute if it is still interested in maintaining some control over the Attorney General's decisions? What other sources of influence, short of legislation, are at Congress' disposal? *See generally* Elliott, *INS v. Chadha: The Administrative Constitution, The Constitution, and the Legislative Veto,* 1983 S.Ct.Rev. 125, 156–60; Kaiser, *Congressional Action to Overturn Agency Rules: Alternatives to the "Legislative Veto,"* 32 Ad.L.Rev. 667 (1980).

3. WAIVER OF EXCLUSION GROUNDS IN DEPORTATION HEARINGS OF LONG–TERM PERMANENT RESIDENT ALIENS: § 212(c)

Section 212(c) of the INA provides:

> (c) Aliens lawfully admitted for permanent residence who temporarily proceeded abroad voluntarily and not under an order of deportation, and who are returning to a lawful unrelinquished domicile of seven consecutive years, may be admitted in the discretion of the Attorney General without regard to the provisions of paragraphs (1) through (25) and paragraphs (30) and (31) of subsection (a). * * *

You may wonder why we are discussing a waiver of exclusion grounds in a chapter dealing with relief from deportation. The answer is *Francis v.*

---

16. For a fuller description of such provisions, *see* Martin, *The Legislative Veto and* *the Responsible Exercise of Congressional Power,* 68 Va.L.Rev. 253 (1982).

INS, 532 F.2d 268 (2d Cir.1976), a case which held that the equal protection component of the Fifth Amendment's due process clause requires extension of the exclusion waiver to similarly situated aliens in deportation hearings. To fully understand the case, we must examine a series of earlier administrative and judicial interpretations of § 212(c).

Section 212(c) is the descendant of the Seventh Proviso of § 3 of the 1917 Immigration Act, which authorized the waiver of grounds of exclusion for "aliens returning after a temporary absence to an unrelinquished United States domicile of seven consecutive years." This Proviso, which on its face only applies to re-entries, made its way into the deportation context in *Matter of L.,* 1 I & N Dec. 1 (BIA & A.G. 1940). There the alien had been admitted in 1909 and was convicted of stealing a watch in 1924. At that time the deportation ground for crimes of moral turpitude was limited to crimes committed within 5 years of entry. Thus L was not deportable in 1924. In 1939 L left the United States to visit a seriously ill sister in Yugoslavia for two months. He was readmitted upon his return. Several months later he was arrested and placed in deportation proceedings. Why? Because § 19 of the 1917 Act included as a ground of deportation conviction of a crime involving moral turpitude "prior to entry." Thus, L, who would not have been deportable had he remained in the United States, was now deportable because he had been convicted of a crime prior to his re-entry in 1939. The re-entry doctrine had struck again. *See United States ex rel. Volpe v. Smith,* 289 U.S. 422, 53 S.Ct. 665, 77 L.Ed. 1298 (1933); pp. 323–327 *supra.*

L invoked the Seventh Proviso, asserting that the ground of exclusion was waivable at time of entry. He therefore asked the Attorney General to apply the waiver provision in the deportation case. The Attorney General consented. Although the Attorney General recognized that the Act made no provision for such waivers outside of an exclusion proceeding, he concluded that "Congress [could not have] intended the immigration laws to operate in so capricious and whimsical a fashion":

> Granted that respondent's departure in 1939 exposed him on return to the peril of a fresh judgment as to whether he should be permitted to reside in the United States, such judgment ought not to depend upon the technical form of the proceedings. No policy of Congress could possibly be served by such irrational result. Had respondent obtained his readmission in 1939 by deceptive concealment of his prior conviction, the case would have been different. But the record throws no doubt upon his good faith. This being so, he should be permitted to make the same appeal to discretion that he could have made if denied admission in 1939, or that he could make in some future application for admission if he now left the country. To require him to go to Canada and reenter will make him no better resident of this country. To require him to wait a year before reentry [following deportation], while his resources are exhausted and his shoe-shining business * * * is destroyed, will make him a worse one.

Accordingly the Attorney General exercised the authority granted by the Seventh Proviso *nunc pro tunc,* stating that such action under the circumstances of the case "amounts to little more than a correction of a record of entry." 1 I & N Dec. at 5–6.

In the 1952 Act, the Seventh Proviso was amended slightly and renumbered as § 212(c). In an early interpretation of the new section, the BIA concluded that the use of the Proviso in a deportation case survived the revision of the statute. *Matter of S.,* 6 I & N Dec. 392 (BIA 1954), affirmed by the Attorney General, *id.* at 397 (1955).

The next expansion of the form of relief came in *Matter of G.A.,* 7 I & N Dec. 274 (BIA 1956). There the alien had been admitted in 1913 and convicted of importation of 142 grains of marijuana in 1947. He had last re-entered the United States in 1952. Several years later, G.A. was placed in deportation proceedings on the ground that the 1947 conviction rendered him deportable under § 241(a)(11). G.A. requested a § 212(c) waiver in the deportation hearing, and the BIA found him eligible for such relief. It reasoned that the § 212(c) waiver would have been exercised at the time of the alien's re-entry in 1952; and that that waiver would have prevented initiation of a deportation proceeding based on the same charge waived at time of entry. The BIA therefore analogized G.A.'s situation to that of the earlier cases: the waiver should be available in the deportation proceeding when it could have been exercised at time of re-entry and would have wiped out the deportation ground.

While there is some surface plausibility to the BIA's reasoning in *Matter of G.A.,* the case is materially different from *Matter of L.* In the latter case, the alien was rendered deportable solely by operation of the re-entry doctrine. He was not deportable at the time he left the United States, nor did he commit an act while outside the United States which would have made him deportable upon return. Section 212(c) seems clearly drafted to ameliorate the capricious effects of the re-entry doctrine; and the situation in *Matter of L.* can reasonably be placed among them.

In *Matter of G.A.,* however, the alien's re-entry appears to work capriciously *in his favor.* He was deportable under § 241(a)(11) irrespective of his re-entry. Yet the BIA concluded that once he had left, the ground could have been waived at readmission; thus it should also be waivable in a deportation proceeding after re-entry. Rather than triggering the ground of deportation, the re-entry triggered the waiver.

Now consider the alien who is a long-time resident and has never left the United States. Assume he commits a crime for which he is deportable—one that would also cause him to be excluded should he leave the country and try to re-enter. In his deportation hearing he invokes § 212(c), startling the immigration judge. When the judge states that § 212(c) only applies to returning residents, the alien claims that such an interpretation draws an arbitrary line between him and the alien in *Matter of G.A.* "Why should G.A. get the benefit of § 212(c)," asks the alien, "simply because he happened to leave the country? Both of us are deportable whether or not we leave and return. Can the immigration laws really mean that, although I am not eligible for relief from deportation now, I could become so by taking a month's vacation in Europe?" The immigration judge recognizes the seeming arbitrariness, but nonetheless denies the relief. "Section 212(c)," she states, "applies to returning residents in exclusion proceedings. I simply cannot read the section as authorizing relief in deportation proceedings to aliens who have never left the country." The alien responds, "I think your position violates standards of equal protection. You admit that, but for a fortuity, I am in the same position as G.A. No one made you read the section to apply to him. But once you do, you must now apply it on my behalf as well."

Who's correct? Read *Francis.*

FRANCIS v. INS

United States Court of Appeals, Second Circuit, 1976.
532 F.2d 268.

LUMBARD, CIRCUIT JUDGE:

* * *

Ernest Francis was admitted to this country as a permanent resident on September 8, 1961. Mr. Francis, a citizen and native of Jamaica, West Indies, is 55 years old, married and the father of a nine year old daughter. He is presently employed as a handyman and resides with his family in the Bronx. Petitioner's wife and daughter are citizens of the United States. His three brothers and one sister are also citizens. Petitioner's father, Joseph Francis, was, at the time of his death, a citizen of this country.

On October 20, 1971, following a plea of guilty, petitioner was convicted of criminal possession of dangerous drugs (marijuana). He was sentenced to a term of probation by the Supreme Court, Bronx County on December 14, 1971. Apart from this conviction and a twenty-five dollar fine for gambling in September, 1973, petitioner has no criminal record.

The Immigration and Naturalization Service ("INS") instituted a deportation proceeding against petitioner on December 6, 1972 by issuing an order to show cause and notice of hearing. The INS charged him with being deportable under Section 241(a)(11) of the INA, by reason of the marijuana conviction. * * *

Francis did not, and does not now, dispute his deportability under Section 241(a)(11). Rather, he argues that he was eligible for discretionary relief under Section 212(c) of the INA, a provision which is primarily applicable to exclusion proceedings.[2] * * *

---

2. Section 212(a)(23) provides for the exclusion of:

Any alien who has been convicted of a violation of, or a conspiracy to violate, any law or regulation relating to the illicit possession of or traffic in narcotic drugs or marihuana, or who has been convicted of a violation of, or a conspiracy to violate, any

law or regulation governing or controlling the taxing, manufacture, production, compounding, transportation, sale, exchange, dispensing, giving away, importation, exportation, or the possession for the purpose of the manufacture, production, compounding, transportation, or exportation of opium, coca leaves, heroin, marihuana,

On February 20, 1974, in an oral decision, the Immigration judge held that Section 212(c) consideration was not available and ordered petitioner deported. Petitioner appealed that decision to the Board on February 28, 1974. On August 15, 1974, the Board dismissed the appeal holding that petitioner was ineligible "for any form of discretionary relief from deportation."

Petitioner seeks a declaration from this court that he is eligible to apply to the Attorney General for discretionary relief under Section 212(c).

[The court then discusses administrative precedents including *Matter of L.* and *Matter of G.A.*]

The statutory interpretation which this petitioner complains of derives from the decision in *Matter of Arias-Uribe,* 13 I. & N.Dec. 696 (1971). There the Board declined to extend Section 212(c) to an otherwise eligible alien who had not departed the country since his narcotics conviction.

* * * In denying Section 212(c) treatment to the alien, the Board seized upon the change in language between the Seventh Proviso, which required that the alien be "returning [to the United States] after a temporary absence", and Section 212(c), which requires that the alien have "temporarily proceeded abroad voluntarily and not under an order of deportation." The Board viewed this as meaning that Congress intended by this clause to require an actual departure and return to this country.[4] In a brief per curiam opinion, the Ninth Circuit affirmed this construction of the statute. *Arias-Uribe v. INS,* 466 F.2d 1198 (1972). Although there is nothing in the legislative history of the 1952 Act which indicates that Congress intended to change prior case law in this respect, we agree with the Ninth Circuit that the Board's interpretation is consistent with the language of Section 212(c). See S.Rep.No. 1137, 82nd Cong., 2d Sess. (1952); H.R.No. 1365, 82nd Cong., 2d Sess. (1952); U.S.Code Cong. & Admin.News 1952, p. 1653.

It is the petitioner's contention that if this statutory construction is applied to his case, then he is deprived of the equal protection of the laws as guaranteed by the fifth amendment.[5] He argues that the statute as so applied creates two classes of aliens identical in every respect except for the fact that members of one class have departed and returned to this

---

or any salt derivative or preparation of opium or coca leaves, or isonipecaine or any addiction-forming or addiction-sustaining opiate; or any alien who the consular officer or immigration officers know or have reason to believe is or has been an illicit trafficker in any of the aforementioned drugs:

The Section parallels Section 241(a)(11), which applies to deportation proceedings.

4. The Board felt its position did not conflict with its interpretation in *Matter of Smith,* 11 I. & N. Dec. 325 (1965) which allowed Section 212(c) discretion to be applied in conjunction with a Section 245 adjustment of status without a physical depar-

ture. 13 I. & N. Dec. at 698–99. [Francis was not eligible for adjustment of status, and thus the benefits of *Matter of Smith,* because at the time § 245 relief was not available to natives of the Western Hemisphere.—eds.]

5. "[I]f a classification would be invalid under the Equal Protection Clause of the Fourteenth Amendment, it is also inconsistent with the due process requirement of the Fifth Amendment." *Johnson v. Robison,* 415 U.S. 361, 364 n. 4, 94 S.Ct. 1160, 1164, 39 L.Ed.2d 389, 396 (1974); *Bolling v. Sharpe,* 347 U.S. 497, 74 S.Ct. 693, 98 L.Ed. 884 (1954).

country at some point after they became deportable. Thus the distinction is not rationally related to any legitimate purpose of the statute.

The authority of Congress and the executive branch to regulate the admission and retention of aliens is virtually unrestricted. Enforcement of the immigration laws is often related to considerations both of foreign policy and the domestic economy. Nevertheless "[i]n the enforcement of these policies, the Executive Branch of the Government must respect the procedural safeguards of due process. . . ." *Galvan v. Press,* 347 U.S. 522, 74 S.Ct. 737, 98 L.Ed. 911 (1954).

It has long been held that the constitutional promise of equal protection of the laws applies to aliens as well as citizens, *Yick Wo v. Hopkins,* 118 U.S. 356, 6 S.Ct. 1064, 30 L.Ed. 220 (1886). * * * Although the right of a permanent resident alien to remain in this country has never been held to be the type of "fundamental right" which would subject classifications touching on it to strict judicial scrutiny, the Supreme Court has observed that "deportation can be the equivalent of banishment or exile. . . ." *Delgadillo v. Carmichael,* 332 U.S. 388, 391, 68 S.Ct. 10, 12, 92 L.Ed. 17, 19 (1947).

Under the minimal scrutiny test, which we consider applicable in this case, distinctions between different classes of persons "must be reasonable, not arbitrary, and must rest upon some ground of difference having a fair and substantial relation to the object of the legislation, so that all persons similarly circumstanced shall be treated alike." *Stanton v. Stanton,* 421 U.S. 7, 14, 95 S.Ct. 1373, 1377, 43 L.Ed.2d 688, 694 (1975).

In determining whether the Board's policy survives minimal scrutiny, the purpose of Section 212(c) must be examined. As the government notes in its brief, Congress was concerned that there be some degree of flexibility to permit worthy returning aliens to continue their relationships with family members in the United States despite a ground for exclusion. Realizing that these considerations apply with equal force to an alien who has already reentered, perhaps illegally, the Board chose to expand eligibility to that group. *Matter of G.A.,* 7 I. & N. Dec. 274 (1956). Thus an alien who had been convicted of two crimes involving moral turpitude and, therefore, was deportable under Section 241(a)(4), was eligible for Section 212(c) discretion because he was able to demonstrate that several months after his last conviction he left the country for a few hours to attend a funeral in Canada. *Matter of Edwards,* 1C I. & N. Dec. 506 (1963). The government has failed to suggest any reason why this petitioner's failure to travel abroad following his conviction should be a crucial factor in determining whether he may be permitted to remain in this country. Reason and fairness would suggest that an alien whose ties with this country are so strong that he has never departed after his initial entry should receive at least as much consideration as an individual who may leave and return from time to time.

It is the government's position that Congress has chosen to treat these two classes of aliens somewhat differently by providing a separate but analogous scheme of discretionary relief to the non-departing alien. Section 244(a)(2), allows the Attorney General to exercise discretion regarding certain deportable aliens who have been in the country for ten years following the act which was the ground for deportation.[7] This argument overlooks the fact that a deportable resident alien who briefly sojourns in Bermuda and then returns is eligible for discretionary consideration under Section 244(a)(2) as a non-departing alien.[a] In addition, if otherwise qualified, he is eligible for Section 212(c) relief. *See Matter of G.A., supra.*

Fundamental fairness dictates that permanent resident aliens who are in like circumstances, but for irrelevant and fortuitous factors, be treated in a like manner. We do not dispute the power of the Congress to create different standards of admission and deportation for different groups of aliens. However, once those choices are made, individuals within a particular group may not be subjected to disparate treatment on criteria wholly unrelated to any legitimate governmental interest. We find that the Board's interpretation of Section 212(c) is unconstitutional as applied to this petitioner.

Accordingly, the petition is granted. The case is remanded to the Board so that the Attorney General's discretion under Section 212(c) may be exercised.[b]

Notes

1. *Francis* does not hold Section 212(c) of the INS unconstitutional; rather, it holds that the agency's interpretation of the section violates equal protection. (*Francis* almost says, does it not, that if the BIA is going to redraft or misinterpret the section, it must do so in an even-handed fashion?) Even if the BIA had not issued the decisions discussed in *Francis,* would the statute still have created two classes of aliens—one eligible for relief and the other not—that seem indistinguishable in terms of the purposes of the statute? Consider the remarks of Board Member Appleman, concurring in *Matter of Silva,* 16 I & N Dec. 26, 32 (BIA 1976):

> [A]s the court pointed out in *Francis v. INS,* in section 212(c) the Congress created, perhaps inadvertently, an avenue of relief under the statute for the permanent resident alien who took a temporary trip abroad after a ground of deportability arose, whereas the same alien could not get that relief if he remained here. Two classes of aliens thus existed, identical in every respect, except for the fact that members of one class got relief, and the others did not—a distinction, in the words of the court, not rationally related to any legitimate purpose of the statute.
>
> * * * [O]ne cannot help but be puzzled by that portion on the *Francis* decision which lays this deficiency in the statute at the feet of the Board of Immigration Appeals. The fact is that if there had been no Board interpretations whatsoever, the lack of

---

7. Less than five years have elapsed since petitioner's conviction. Thus he is ineligible for this discretionary provision.

a. Does *INS v. Phinpathya,* 464 U.S. 183, 104 S.Ct. 584, 78 L.Ed.2d 401 (1984), undermine the court's reasoning here?—eds.

b. *Accord, Tapia-Acuna v. INS,* 640 F.2d 223 (9th Cir.1981).

"equal treatment," noted in *Francis,* would still have existed. The long-term resident who left the United States, and who received section 212(c) relief when applying for readmission, was thereafter not deportable on the waived ground. To hold otherwise would seem to render the waiver meaningless. Yet the same alien, if unable to leave the United States for a visit abroad, could be deportable. If this discrimination is irrational and unconstitutional, it is so, not because of a Board interpretation, but because of the language of the statute itself. The *Francis* opinion notes the "facial" limitations of section 212(c) and agrees that the reading given the statute in *Arias-Uribe* [13 I & N Dec. 696 (BIA 1971), *affirmed per curiam* 466 F.2d 1198 (9th Cir. 1972)], was consistent with the language of section 212(c). While the court did not attempt to find the statute unconstitutional, there is at least a possibility that this is the underlying, if unexpressed, basis for the *Francis* decision.[4]

Under what (reasonable) interpretation of § 212(c) might the BIA and the courts conclude that the section applies to *neither* of the classes described by Board Member Appleman's opinion? Would not such an interpretation eliminate the equal protection problem that Board Member Appleman finds inherent in the statute?

2. Although it seems clear that § 212(c) was intended to mitigate the harshness of the re-entry doctrine, *Francis* goes far beyond this purpose. It, in effect, provides a general power in the Attorney General to waive any ground of deportation analogous to an exclusion ground for long-time resident aliens. While this may seem like a sensible policy—a matter we will explore at the end of the Chapter—has not Congress already provided such a form of relief in § 244? Indeed, given the careful consideration in § 244 of the grounds that may be waived, the time period required for eligibility and the like, does not *Francis* create a new form of relief for deportable aliens quite at odds with the congressional scheme?

One answer to this is that *Francis* does not create a new avenue for relief; it simply demands equal treatment of similarly situated aliens. The Second Circuit essentially said to the agency: *if* you allow aliens like G.A. to apply for § 212(c) relief, then you must also allow aliens like Francis to do the same. The BIA, thus, could avoid *Francis* by simply overruling its decision in *Matter of G.A.* For example, it could conclude that § 212(c) relief should be available only to aliens who are rendered deportable *because* of a brief absence abroad and re-entry. The BIA,

4. Challenges to substantive due process under the immigration laws (including those going to the categories of aliens to whom relief may be granted) have been uniformly rejected by the courts. The power to control immigration is inherent in national sovereignty and hence vested in the legislature not the judiciary. See *Harisiades v. Shaughnessy,* 342 U.S. 580 (1952); *Fong Yue Ting v. United States,* 149 U.S. 698 (1893). *Francis* purports to rest on a violation of *procedural* due process. [Does it?—eds.] Here the courts readily exercise authority since the challenge is to the manner in which the law is applied rather than to the law itself. Accordingly, the *Francis* decision, by invalidating a Board "interpretation" of the statute, on its face does not offend the precedents. It is, of course, entirely speculative whether a possible limitation on the courts authority to invalidate the statute played any part in the direction taken by the decision. [Footnote by Board Member Appleman.]

however, has not chosen to adopt this reformulation. Rather, in *Matter of Silva,* 16 I & N Dec. 26 (BIA 1976), it announced that it would abide by *Francis* and apply § 212(c) to aliens who had never left the United States. The BIA stated: "In light of the constitutional requirements of due process and equal protection of the law, it is our position that no distinction shall be made between permanent resident aliens who temporarily proceed abroad and non-departing permanent resident aliens." *Id.* at 30.

With the BIA's acquiescence in *Francis,* have not an administrative agency and a federal court effectively amended the INA without Congress' participation?

3. Note that *Francis* only "works" if the ground of deportation charged is also a ground of exclusion waivable under § 212(c). *See Matter of Wadud,* Interim Dec. No. 2980 (BIA 1984) (§ 212(c) not available where deportation ground is § 241(a)(14) (possession of a sawed-off shotgun) since no corresponding exclusion ground exists). Accordingly, aliens deportable for entry without inspection are not eligible for § 212(c) relief because § 241(a)(2) has no cognate in § 212(a).[17] And aliens deportable under § 241(a)(19) (Nazis) may not receive the benefits of § 212(c) even though such conduct is a ground of exclusion (§ 212(a)(33)), because the exclusion ground is not waivable under § 212(c).

The BIA has not required absolute congruence between the exclusion and deportation grounds. For example, in *Matter of Salmon,* 16 I & N Dec. 734 (BIA 1978), § 212(c) relief was deemed available to an alien deportable for having been convicted of a crime involving moral turpitude, even though the exclusion provision (§ 212(a)(9)) is not precisely the same as the deportation provision (§ 241(a)(4)).

4. Section 212(c) requires that an alien be returning "to a lawful unrelinquished domicile of seven consecutive years" in order to be eligible for relief. Contrast this phraseology with § 244(a)'s requirement that an alien be "physically present in the United States for a continuous period of not less than seven years immediately preceding the date of * * * application." "Domicile" connotes something more than mere physical presence: "[i]n general, the domicile of an individual is his true, fixed and permanent home and place of habitation. It is the place to which, whenever he is absent, he has the intention of returning." *Martinez v. Bynum,* 461 U.S. 321, 103 S.Ct. 1838, 1844, 75 L.Ed.2d 879 (1983), *quoting Vlandis v. Kline,* 412 U.S. 441, 454, 93 S.Ct. 2230, 2237, 37 L.Ed.2d 63 (1973). *See Matter of Sanchez,* 17 I & N Dec. 218, 221 (BIA 1980) (domicile under § 212(c) requires intention of making United States one's home for the indefinite future).

How could an alien (1) satisfy § 212(c)'s requirement without satisfying § 244(a)'s, or (2) satisfy § 244(a)'s requirement without satisfying § 212(c)'s? Is there an underlying logic that explains why § 212(c) adopts "unrelinquished domicile" and § 244(a) "continuous physical presence"?

17. Such aliens also fail § 212(c)'s requirement of "lawful * * * domicile." *See Lok v. INS,* 681 F.2d 107, 110 (2d Cir.1982).

5. Does § 212(c)'s requirement of "*lawful* unrelinquished domicile" mean that all seven years must have been preceded by a *lawful admission for permanent residence?* This issue can arise under the following circumstances. First, an alien may reside here unlawfully for three years and then attain lawful permanent residence. Would she be eligible for § 212(c) relief after her fourth year as a lawful permanent resident? Second, some classes of nonimmigrant aliens (such as foreign government officials) as well as parolees and aliens admitted as refugees under INA §§ 207 and 208 are able to maintain lawful domicile in the United States.[18] If such aliens become lawful permanent residents, may they count their earlier time in the United States towards the seven years required by § 212(c)?

As to the first situation, it is established that all seven years of an alien's residence must be lawful for the alien to qualify for § 212(c) relief. *See Lok v. INS (Lok II)*, 681 F.2d 107 (2d Cir.1982). However, courts of appeals have split over the second question—whether time spent lawfully in the United States prior to attainment of permanent resident status can count for purposes of § 212(c). *Compare Lok v. INS*, 548 F.2d 37 (2d Cir.1977) *(Lok I)* (yes) *with Chiravacharadhikul v. INS*, 645 F.2d 248 (4th Cir.1981), *cert. denied* 454 U.S. 893, 102 S.Ct. 389, 70 L.Ed.2d 207 (1981) *and Castillo-Felix v. INS*, 601 F.2d 459 (9th Cir.1979) (no). *Lok I* has not been followed by the BIA outside the Second Circuit. *Matter of Anwo*, 16 I & N Dec. 293 (BIA 1977), *affirmed per curiam*, 607 F.2d 435 (D.C.Cir. 1979). *See generally* Griffith, *Exclusion and Deportation—Waivers Under Section 212(c) and Section 244(a)(1) of the Immigration and Nationality Act*, 32 DePaul L.Rev. 523, 528–42 (1983); Steel, *Lawful Domicile and Permanent Residence Under Section 212(c): Lok and Luck*, 7 Immig.J. 28 (Jan.-June, 1984).

6. In determining whether the alien has established seven years lawful continuous physical presence, when does "lawful domicile" end:

(a) when the deportable conduct occurs (considered, but rejected, in *Marti-Xiques v. INS*, 741 F.2d 350 (11th Cir.1984))?

(b) when deportation proceedings begin (adopted by the Court in *Marti-Xiques v. INS, supra*)?

(c) when the deportation order is administratively final (*Lok v. INS*, 681 F.2d 107 (2d Cir.1982))?

(d) when judicial review of the BIA decision is final (*Wall v. INS*, 722 F.2d 1442 (9th Cir.1984))?

7. The BIA has held that § 212(h) (authorizing waiver of exclusion grounds § 212(a)(9), (10) and (12)), may, like § 212(c), be granted "nunc pro tunc in deportation proceedings in order to cure a ground of inadmissibility at the time of entry." *Matter of Sanchez*, 17 I & N Dec. 218, 222 (BIA 1980). This is consistent with the BIA's pre-*Francis* interpretation of

---

18. The vast majority of nonimmigrants cannot establish *lawful* domicile in this country because, to be eligible for visas, most classes of nonimmigrants must have resi- dences in foreign countries which they have no intention of abandoning. INA § 101 (a)(15).

§ 212(c). Under *Matter of G.A.* and *Francis,* may an alien who enters lawfully and then becomes deportable under § 241(a)(4)—which is roughly analogous to exclusion grounds § 212(a)(9) and (10)—be eligible for § 212(h) relief in a deportation proceeding? *See Osuchukwu v. INS,* 744 F.2d 1136 (5th Cir.1984) (apparently assuming the availability of § 212(h) waiver in such circumstances).

SECTION D.   PRIVATE BILLS

1. In the winter of 1980, a massive FBI undercover investigation of corruption in Congress hit the newspapers.   The so-called "Abscam" operation involved FBI agents posing as representatives of an Arab sheik willing to pay for congressional favors.   Videotapes, which appeared in courtrooms and on television, showed public officials accepting large amounts of cash—a token of the "sheik's" appreciation for the legislators' help in attaining, among other things, immigration benefits.

The New York Times reported the details:

> The FBI agents reportedly talked to [Congressman] Lederer about the sheik's immigration problems.   According to authorities, Representative Lederer spoke of introducing a private bill in Congress to gain residency status for the Arabs, but said that his action would appear less unusual if the Arab agreed to invest in the Philadelphia area.
>
> At a later videotaped meeting at the Kennedy Airport hotel, Mr. Lederer accepted $50,000 in a paper bag, according to law enforcement officials.
>
> * * *
>
> Investigators said that Representative Myers also accepted $50,000, in an envelope, after agreeing to help the sheik gain residency in this country.   * * * Mr. Myers boasted of having connections in the State Department who could aid his efforts.
>
> * * *
>
> * * * [Representative] Jenrette was reportedly assured of getting $50,000 as a down payment and another $50,000 after introducing a bill to keep one of the sheiks in the United States. According to authorities, Mr. Jenrette later acknowledged to the agents posing as associates of the sheik that he received the $50,000 picked up for him by an associate.

New York Times, Feb. 3, 1980, pp. 1, 26.

Despite these recent events, the use of private bills in the immigration context has a perfectly honorable pedigree.   Indeed, in the early years of our immigration laws, private bills were the primary form of relief from deportation.   Such bills have often been used to create humanitarian flexibility in a law that, if applied as written, would produce harsh results. Furthermore, "private bills have frequently been the forerunners of significant amendments to existing general immigration laws":

> Before the Immigration and Nationality Act accorded "nonquota" status to spouses of American citizens irrespective of their ancestry, Asian spouses of American citizens were subject to quota restrictions. The stationing of American servicemen in the Far East and the resulting marriages between American citizens and alien spouses of Asian ancestry led to the introduction and passage of a considerable number of private bills according the individual Asian spouse "nonquota" status. The increasing volume of this type of private bills led eventually to public legislation giving "nonquota" status to the spouses of American servicemen irrespective of their ancestry and later led to the provision in the Immigration and Nationality Act which placed alien spouses of all American citizens on equal footing irrespective of race. Similarly, the provision of the Act of September 3, 1954 exempting petty offenders from the excluding provisions of the general law was preceded by a series of private bills seeking relief in cases of individual aliens, mostly alien wives of American servicemen who, during the post-war period, had been convicted for minor offenses.

> General legislation of recent years was preceded by an increasing volume of private acts which pointed out the desirability of amendments to the existing general laws. The following statement of the House Judiciary Committee recommending the passage of legislation which vested the Attorney General with discretionary authority to admit aliens who had been convicted of crimes involving moral turpitude or who had a past record of prostitution and who are close relatives of American citizens or permanent resident aliens, serves as an illustration:

> "The Committees on the Judiciary of the House and the Senate have a considerable number of private bills before them under which the conduct of such aliens, considering their family situation, would be condoned. A great number of such private bills passed the Congress and were enacted into law during the last few years. It appears to the committee that it is unfair and improper to extend the benefit of legislative relief solely to a few selected individuals who are in a position to reach the Congress for redress of their grievances. It is felt that humanitarian approach should be extended to an entire defined class of aliens rather than to selected individuals." [14]

E. Harper, Jr. & R. Chase, *Immigration Laws of the United States* 657–59 (1975).[19] *See also* Immigration and Nationality Act Amendments of 1981,

---

14. House Report No. 1199, 85th Congress, First Session, p. 11. This and similar ameliorative legislation was incorporated in the Immigration and Nationality Act by the Act of September 26, 1961. [This waiver was codified as INA § 212(h).—eds.]

19. Another example is provided by Sidney B. Rawitz, former General Counsel of the Senate Judiciary Committee:

Pub.L. No. 97–116, §§ 2(b), (c), 95 Stat. 1611 (amending INA §§ 101(b)(1)(E) and 212(h) to deal with problems that were often the subject of private bills).

2. The following table indicates the number of private bills introduced and enacted over the last forty years.

YEAR	CONGRESS	INTRODUCED	ENACTED
1979–1980	96th Congress	902	83
1977–1978	95th Congress	1,024	138
1975–1976	94th Congress	1,023	99
1973–1974	93rd Congress	1,085	63
1971–1972	92nd Congress	2,866	62
1969–1970	91st Congress	6,266	113
1967–1968	90th Congress	7,293	218
1965–1966	89th Congress	5,285	279
1963–1964	88th Congress	3,647	196
1961–1962	87th Congress	3,592	544
1959–1960	86th Congress	3,069	488
1957–1958	85th Congress	4,364	927
1955–1956	84th Congress	4,474	1,227
1953–1954	83rd Congress	4,797	755
1951–1952	82nd Congress	3,669	729
1949–1950	81st Congress	2,811	505
1947–1948	80th Congress	1,141	121
1945–1946	79th Congress	429	14
1943–1944	78th Congress	163	12
1941–1942	77th Congress	430	22
1939–1940	76th Congress	601	65
1937–1938	75th Congress	293	30

United States Department of Justice, INS, 1980 *Statistical Yearbook of the Immigration and Naturalization Service,* Table 66, at 130.

3. Although one might think that the huge gap between the number of bills introduced and the number enacted make private bills a high-risk form of relief, such is not necessarily the case. After introduction of a private bill, the House or Senate Judiciary Committee may issue a request for a report from the INS on the alien who is the beneficiary of the bill. Under Operations Instruction 107.1c, "a stay of deportation will generally be authorized" by INS following receipt of a committee's request for a report. Accordingly, the alien may be able to forestall deportation for a

A private bill can be transformed into a public law. The metamorphosis begins when it is amended on the floor of either House to take on the substance of a public bill. A perfect example is P.L. 95–579 of November 2, 1978. In embryonic form as S. 2247, it was a private bill to exempt an elderly female alien from the English literacy requirements in Section 312. After passing the Senate, it was amended by the House to provide a general statutory waiver of the literacy requirements for all naturalization applicants over 50 years of age with 20 or more years of lawful residence on the date of filing the petition. The Senate concurred in the House amendment, the President signed, and it became a law. [*See* INA § 312(1).]

Rawitz, *In the Hands of Congress: Suspension of Deportation and Private Bills,* 57 Interp.Rel. 76, 80 (1980).

considerable period of time through the introduction of a private bill, irrespective of its ultimate chance for passage.

In earlier days, mere introduction of a private bill automatically guaranteed a stay of deportation. *See United States ex rel. Knauff v. McGrath,* 181 F.2d 839 (2d Cir.1950), *vacated as moot per curiam* 340 U.S. 940, 71 S.Ct. 504, 95 L.Ed. 678 (1957). Today, rules of the relevant House and Senate Subcommittees limit the circumstances under which requests for INS reports will be made. The House Subcommittee's rules are as follows:

RULES OF PROCEDURE

1. The introduction of a private bill does not stay the deportation of aliens illegally in the United States or who have overstayed the terms of their visa. The Committee shall not intervene in any such deportation proceedings and it will not address any communications to the Attorney General to request stays of deportation on behalf of beneficiaries of private bills, except as indicated in Rule 4.

2. No bill shall be scheduled until all administrative remedies are exhausted, including suspension of deportation, asylum, and labor certification.

3. The Subcommittee shall not take any further action on legislation which has been tabled by the full Committee.

4. The Subcommittee shall entertain consideration of a request for a departmental report upon receipt of a letter from the author of the bill. In the case of beneficiaries who are in the United States, a determination on the request shall be subject to debate at a formal meeting of the Subcommittee and only those cases designed to prevent extreme hardship to the beneficiary or a U.S. citizen will merit a request for a report. The Immigration and Naturalization Service may honor a request for a report by staying deportation until final action is taken on the legislation.

5. A quorum of the Subcommittee shall consist of two Members for the purpose of holding hearings on private bills.

6. Testimony at private bill hearings shall not be received from any person other than the author of the private bill. All requests to testify shall be addressed in writing to the Chairman of the Subcommittee.

7. No private bill shall be considered where court proceedings are pending.

8. Action on legislation shall not be deferred on more than one occasion due to nonappearance of the author.

9. The Subcommittee shall await receipt of departmental reports before taking final action on any legislation.

10. All requests for consideration of a private bill shall commence with a letter directed to the Chairman of the Subcom-

mittee outlining relevant facts of the case and attaching thereto all pertinent data. The following shall be submitted in triplicate:

(a) Date and place of birth of all beneficiaries. Address and telephone number in the United States.

(b) Dates of all entries (legal and illegal) and departures from the United States and type of visas for admission. Consulate where the beneficiary obtained a visa for entry to the U.S.; or where the beneficiary shall seek a visa.

(c) Status of any proceedings with the INS and whether any nonimmigrant or immigrant petitions have been filed on the beneficiary's behalf.

(d) Name, address, and telephone number of interested parties in the U.S.

(e) Names, address, dates and places of birth of all close relatives in the U.S. and abroad.

(f) Occupations, recent employment record and salary of beneficiaries.

(g) Copies of all communications to and from INS or the State Department.

The information above represents the minimum requirements for Subcommittee consideration. Pertinent data about the case and an explanation of the extreme hardship to the beneficiary or U.S. citizen must also accompany a request for processing of the private bill.

11. Requests for consideration of a bill shall be accompanied by a statement by the beneficiary that he or she desires the relief sought by the bill and waiving the Freedom of Information Act and Privacy Act.

12. A notice of meeting date shall be sent to the authors of all legislation which is scheduled.

129 Cong.Rec. E730 (daily ed. March 2, 1983). The Senate Rules, which do not differ from the House Rules in material respects, are reprinted in 60 Interp.Rel. 455–56 (1983).

4. On the politics of private bills, consider the following:

Examining the process of handling private bills affords a glimpse of a few members of Congress dispensing valuable favors and funds to private individuals or groups under circumstances far removed from public consciousness, scrutiny, participation, or concern. And that combination always spells trouble.

* * *

When considering private bills, Congress acts as a court of last resort. Persons seeking relief by private bill are required to have already exhausted their efforts and failed to secure relief from government agencies or from the courts. Such persons are in effect petitioning Congress to make an exception for them by means of direct legislation. Private bills, then, seek to accommodate the rigor and inflexibility of general, impersonal legal rules with the ethical demands for justice and equity in the individual case.

Senators and representatives tend to feel somewhat ambivalent about private bills. On the one hand, these bills are unique political assets; the legislator can directly serve his constituent with a knotty problem about which the constituent feels very intensely. If the legislator does no more than introduce the bill, not only the constituent, but his or her family and friends are likely to regard the legislator in heroic dimensions. If the bill passes, the legislator can probably count on undying loyalty from members of the constituent's circle. Best of all, the legislator can do so without using up any of his political "chips," for such bills are rarely controversial, have no ideological overtones, invoke no alliances, and breach no principles. Private bills, in the jargon of the social scientist, confer divisible benefits on small, intensely affected groups of constituents without alienating anyone else. From the politician's point of view, such bills are "pure gravy." They are also excellent logrolling material. By supporting private bills introduced by other politicians, the legislator can also build up a stock of favors which he can then trade for these politicians' support on public laws in which he is deeply interested or which are more visible to his larger constituency. And the politician can obtain all these benefits at essentially no personal cost, for he need only introduce the private bill, a meaningless gesture requiring little of the legislator's own time.

The Ralph Nader Congress Project (P. Schuck, Dir.), A Study of the House and Senate Judiciary Committees 243–45 (1975).

SECTION E.   OTHER FORMS OF RELIEF FROM DEPORTATION

1. REGISTRY: § 249

Section 249 of the INA establishes a form of relief for deportable aliens, generally referred to as "registry." It provides:

A record of lawful admission for permanent residence may, in the discretion of the Attorney General and under such regulations as he may prescribe, be made in the case of any alien, as of the date of the approval of his application or, if entry occurred prior to July 1, 1924, as of the date of such entry, if no such record is otherwise available and such alien shall satisfy the Attorney General that he is not inadmissible under section 212(a) insofar as it relates to criminals, procurers and other immoral persons, subversives, violators of the narcotic laws or smugglers of aliens, and he establishes that he—

(a) entered the United States prior to June 30, 1948;

(b) has had his residence in the United States continuously since such entry;

(c) is a person of good moral character; and

(d) is not ineligible to citizenship.

Gordon and Rosenfield describe the purpose and history of the registry provision as follows:

> Registry originated with the Act of March 2, 1929. Originally it related to aliens who had arrived before the temporary quota law of May 19, 1921, and permitted creation of a record of lawful entry for permanent residence on behalf of those who could meet certain prescribed conditions. The purpose was to legalize the residence of aliens who had entered improperly before that date, or whose entry record could not be located, but whose deportation was precluded by the statute of limitations then in effect. The registry statute was codified in the Nationality Act of 1940. The only significant change was to advance the controlling date to July 1, 1924, the effective date of the basic quota law.
>
> In its studies that preceded the 1952 Act, the Senate Judiciary Committee expressed approval of the registry procedure and recommended that it be retained. This recommendation was followed, and the registry requirements and procedure were continued without any significant change. A major revision in 1958 advanced the cutoff date to June 28, 1940 and eliminated the complete disqualification of those subject to deportation. Instead the 1958 amendment disqualified only those inadmissible for certain aggravated grounds. Elimination of the disqualification of deportables has made this procedure for administrative adjustment of status available to many who previously were deportable as overstayed nonimmigrants or as illegal entrants. In 1965 the cutoff date was again advanced to June 30, 1948.
>
> Although the principal purpose of registry originally was to aid persons who wished to be naturalized, the record of lawful entry established in such proceedings is recognized as valid for all purposes under the immigration and naturalization laws. In effect it has become a form of statute of limitations for illegal entrants, based on affirmative grant of discretion to applicants who satisfy specified eligibility requirements.
>
> In the light of the statute's fixed cutoff date, registry has become a remedy of constantly decreasing utility. Proposals to advance the cutoff date have frequently been urged, thus far unsuccessfully. The latest such proposal appeared in the so-called amnesty program submitted by President Carter in 1977, which suggested advancing the cutoff date to January 1, 1977. The need for periodic adjustments of the cutoff date seems pointless, and it would be preferable for the statute to fix a specific

qualifying period, similar to that prescribed for suspension of deportation.

G & R § 7.6a.*

For the years 1978, 1979 and 1980, 423, 262 and 236 aliens, respectively, were granted § 249 relief.

The Simpson-Mazzoli "legalization" (or "amnesty") provisions for long-term undocumented aliens were similar in form and purpose to § 249. We will examine them in Chapter Nine.

2. ESTOPPEL

Suppose the conduct of the government is a contributing cause of the alien's deportability—for example, because the alien has relied upon bad advice from the government or because the government has taken so long to adjudicate a matter that the alien's condition has changed. Or suppose the government has misled an excludable alien into believing that his entry and residence in the United States are lawful. Should the government be estopped from deporting the alien? The traditional answer, consistent with basic principles of administrative law, is usually not: "When the Government is unable to enforce the law because the conduct of its agents has given rise to an estoppel, the interest of the citizenry as a whole in obedience to the rule of law is undermined. It is for this reason that it is well-settled that the Government may not be estopped on the same terms as any other litigant." *Heckler v. Community Health Services of Crawford County, Inc.,* ___ U.S. ___, 104 S.Ct. 2218, 2224, 81 L.Ed.2d 42, 52 (1984). *See generally* K.C. Davis, Administrative Law Text Ch. 17 (1972); W. Gellhorn, C. Byse & P. Strauss, Administrative Law: Cases and Comments 410–19 (1979). This notion is clearly evident in § 241(a)(1) of the INA, which renders deportable aliens who were excludable at time of entry; notions of estoppel are not deemed to prevent the government from correcting a prior incorrect admission of the alien. *See, e.g., Santiago v. INS,* 526 F.2d 488 (9th Cir.1975) (*en banc*), *cert. denied* 425 U.S. 971, 96 S.Ct. 2167, 48 L.Ed.2d 794 (1976).

The general principle that there is no estoppel against the government has not come tumbling down, but chinks have appeared in the wall in recent years. *See generally* Comment, *Emergence of an Equitable Doctrine of Estoppel Against the Government—The Oil Shale Cases,* 46 U.Col.L.Rev. 433 (1975). As the next case demonstrates, the Supreme Court has left open the question of whether INS could be estopped if an alien demonstrates the traditional elements required for estoppel as well as "affirmative misconduct" on the part of the agency.[20]

---

* Copyright © 1984 by Matthew Bender & Co., Inc. and reprinted with permission from C. Gordon and H. Rosenfield, Immigration Law and Procedure.

20. *Cf. Heckler v. Community Health Services of Crawford County, Inc., supra,* ___ U.S. at ___, 104 S.Ct. at 2224, 81 L.Ed.2d at 52:

[W]e are hesitant * * * to say that there are *no cases* in which the public interest in ensuring that the Government can enforce the law free from estoppel might be outweighed by the countervailing interest of citizens in some minimum standard of decency, honor, and reliability in their dealings with their Government.

INS v. MIRANDA

Supreme Court of the United States, 1982.
459 U.S. 14, 103 S.Ct. 281, 74 L.Ed.2d 12.

PER CURIAM.

Respondent Horacio Miranda, a citizen of the Philippines, entered the United States in 1971 on a temporary visitor's visa. After his visa expired, he sayed in this country, eventually marrying Linda Milligan, a citizen of the United States, on May 26, 1976. Shortly thereafter, Milligan filed a visa petition with the Immigration and Naturalization Service (INS) on respondent's behalf. She requested that he be granted an immigrant visa as her spouse. Respondent simultaneously filed an application requesting the INS to adjust his status to that of a permanent resident alien. Section 245(a) of the Immigration and Nationality Act of 1952 conditions the granting of permanent resident status to an alien on the immediate availability of an immigrant visa. Milligan's petition, if approved, would have satisfied this condition.

The INS did not act on either Milligan's petition or respondent's application for 18 months. Following the breakup of her marriage with respondent, Milligan withdrew her petition in December 1977. At that point, the INS denied respondent's application for permanent residence because he had not shown that an immigrant visa was immediately available to him. The INS also issued an order to show cause why he should not be deported.

At a deportation hearing, respondent conceded his deportability but renewed his application for permanent resident status because of his marriage to Milligan. Although the marriage had ended, he claimed that a previous marriage was sufficient to support his application. The immigration judge rejected this claim, concluding that the immediate availability of an immigrant visa was a necessary condition to respondent's application. Since Milligan had withdrawn her petition for an immigrant visa before the INS had acted on it, respondent was ineligible for permanent resident status.

Respondent appealed the decision to the Board of Immigration Appeals. For the first time, he raised the claim that the INS was estopped from denying his application because of its "unreasonable delay." He argued that the "failure to act was not only unreasonable, unfair and unjust but also an abuse of governmental process if the delay was deliberate." The Board rejected respondent's claim. It found "no evidence of any 'affirmative misconduct'" and no basis for an equitable estoppel.

Respondent sought review of the Board's decision in the Court of Appeals for the Ninth Circuit. The Court of Appeals reversed, holding that "[t]he unexplained failure of the INS to act on the visa petition for an eighteen-month period prior to the petitioner's withdrawal ... was affirmative misconduct by the INS." *Miranda v. INS*, 638 F.2d 83, 84 (1980). We granted certiorari, vacated the judgment of the Court of Appeals, and remanded the case for further consideration in light of *Schweiker v. Hansen,* 450 U.S. 785, 101 S.Ct. 1468, 67 L.Ed.2d 685 (1981). 454 U.S. 808, 102 S.Ct. 81, 70 L.Ed.2d 77 (1981).

On remand, the Court of Appeals adhered to its earlier decision. 673 F.2d 1105 (1982) *(per curiam).* It found *Hansen* inapplicable for three reasons. First, the Government's conduct in *Hansen* had not risen to the level of affirmative misconduct. In this case, however, affirmative misconduct was established by the INS's unexplained delay in processing respondent's application. Second, although the private party in *Hansen* subsequently had been able to correct the Government's error, the INS's error here inflicted irrevocable harm on respondent. Finally, unlike the private party in *Hansen* who sought to recover from the public treasury, respondent was seeking only to become a permanent resident—a result that would entail no burden on the public fisc. The Court of Appeals determined "that the Supreme Court's conclusion that the government was not estopped in *Hansen* neither compels nor suggests the same conclusion here." 673 F.2d, at 1106.

In *Hansen,* we did not consider whether estoppel will lie against the Government when there is evidence of affirmative misconduct. We found that a Government official's misstatement to an applicant for federal insurance benefits, conceded to be less that affirmative misconduct, did not justify allowing the applicant to collect retroactive benefits from the public treasury. See 450 U.S., at 788–789, 101 S.Ct., at 1470–1471. Although *Hansen* involved estoppel in the context of a claim against the public treasury, we observed that "[i]n two cases involving denial of citizenship, the Court has declined to decide whether even 'affirmative misconduct' would estop the Government from denying citizenship, for in neither case was 'affirmative misconduct' involved." *Id.,* at 788, 101 S.Ct., at 1470.

The Court of Appeals thus correctly considered whether, as an initial matter, there was a showing of affirmative misconduct. *See INS v. Hibi,* 414 U.S. 5, 8–9, 94 S.Ct. 19, 21–22, 38 L.Ed.2d 7 (1973) *(per curiam); Montana v. Kennedy,* 366 U.S. 308, 314–315, 81 S.Ct. 1336, 1340–1341, 6 L.Ed.2d 313 (1961). *Hibi* and *Montana* indicate, however, that the Court of Appeals erred in determining that the evidence in this case established affirmative misconduct. In *Montana,* a Government official had incorrectly informed the petitioner's mother that she was unable to return to the United States because she was pregnant. The Court found that the official's misstatement "falls far short of misconduct such as might prevent the United States from relying on petitioner's foreign birth" as a basis for denying him citizenship. 366 U.S., at 314–315, 81 S.Ct., at 1340–1341. In *Hibi,* Congress had exempted aliens serving in the United States Armed Forces from certain requirements normally imposed on persons seeking naturalization. We found that neither the Government's failure to publicize fully the rights accorded by Congress nor its failure to make an authorized naturalization representative available to aliens serving outside of the United States estopped the Government from rejecting respondent's untimely application for naturalization. *See* 414 U.S., at 8–9, 94 S.Ct., at 21–22.

Unlike *Montana* and *Hibi,* where the Government's error was clear, the evidence that the Government failed to fulfill its duty in this case is at best questionable. The only indication of negligence is the length of time that the INS took to process respondent's application. Although the time was indeed long, we cannot say in the absence of evidence to the contrary that the delay was unwarranted.[3] Both the number of the applications received by the INS and the need to investigate their validity may make it difficult for the agency to process an application as promptly as may be desirable.[4] Even if the INS arguably was negligent in not acting more expeditiously, its conduct was not significantly different from that in *Montana* and *Hibi*. Nor is the harm to respondent different. *Montana* and *Hibi* make clear that neither the Government's conduct nor the harm to the respondent is sufficient to estop the Government from enforcing the conditions imposed by Congress for residency in this country.

The final distinction drawn by the Court of Appeals between this case and *Hansen* is unpersuasive. It is true that *Hansen* relied on a line of cases involving claims against the public treasury. But there was no indication that the Government would be estopped in the absence of the potential burden on the fisc. An increasingly important interest, implicating matters of broad public concern, is involved in cases of this kind. Enforcing the immigration laws, and the conditions for residency in this country, is becoming more difficult. *See* n. 4, *supra*. Moreover, the INS is the agency primarily charged by Congress to implement the public policy underlying these laws. *See, e.g., INS v. Jong Ha Wang*, 450 U.S. 139, 144–145, 101 S.Ct. 1027, 1031, 67 L.Ed.2d 123 (1981) *(per curiam)*; *Hibi, supra*, at 8. Appropriate deference must be accorded its decisions.

This case does not require us to reach the question we reserved in *Hibi*, whether affirmative misconduct in a particular case would estop the Government from enforcing the immigration laws. Proof only that the Government failed to process promptly an application falls far short of establishing such conduct. Accordingly, we grant the petition for certiorari and reverse the judgment of the Court of Appeals.

It is so ordered.

JUSTICE MARSHALL, dissenting.

I dissent from the Court's summary reversal of the Court of Appeals. The Court concedes that the INS's 18-month delay in processing respondent's application "was indeed long," but concludes that it "cannot say in the absence of evidence to the contrary that the delay was unwarranted." The Court relies on a presumption of regularity which it says attends the official acts of public officers. In view of the unusual delay in the processing of respondent's application, I do not agree that this case should be summarily disposed of on the basis of this convenient presumption. If

---

3. The INS has maintained consistently that the 18-month delay was reasonable because of the need to investigate the validity of respondent's marriage. Because the issue of estoppel was raised initially on appeal, the parties were unable to develop any factual record on the issue.

4. In 1976, the year in which Milligan filed her petition on behalf of respondent, some 206,319 immediate-relative petitions were filed. *See* INS Ann.Rep. 11 (1976).

The Service has noted: "In dealing with these petitions, an inordinate amount of fraud, particularly in relation to claimed marriages, has been uncovered.... For a fee, partners are provided and marriages contracted to establish eligibility under the statutes for visa issuance benefits." *Ibid.* We cannot discount the need for careful investigation by the INS that these petitions demand.

the Court believes, as I do not, that this case raises an issue of sufficient importance to justify the exercise of our certiorari jurisdiction, and if the Court also believes that oral argument should be dispensed with, I would at least notify the parties that the Court is considering a summary disposition, so that they may have an opportunity to submit briefs on the merits.[a]

3. ADDITIONAL FORMS OF RELIEF

INA § 208 (asylum) and § 243(h) (withholding of deportation) allow otherwise deportable aliens to remain in the United States if they can demonstrate that they are likely to be persecuted upon return to their home countries. We will consider these sections in detail when we explore all of the INA's refugee provisions together in Chapter Eight.

A Concluding Question

Does it make sense for the INA to have so many different and overlapping forms of relief from deportation? Viewed together, they display no obvious underlying theory of which aliens merit relief from what kinds of deportation grounds: the list of waivable grounds varies from section to section (*compare* § 244(e) *with* § 212(c) and § 244(a)); the period of residence required for each is not the same (*compare* § 212(c) *with* § 244(a)(2) and § 249); and even the description of that residence is not uniform. *See, e.g.*, § 212(c) (unrelinquished domicile); § 244(a) (continuous physical presence); § 249 (continuous residence). Do these differences represent legislative fine-tuning or historical happenstance?

Consider the following hypothetical legislative proposal.

Section 1. Except as provided in Section 2, all provisions for relief from deportation are hereby repealed.

Section 2. The Attorney General may waive any ground of deportation and adjust the status of an alien on whose behalf the ground is waived to that of lawful permanent resident if the Attorney General determines that such waiver and adjustment are justified by humanitarian concerns or are otherwise in the national interest.

Section 3. A determination by the Attorney General under Section 2 shall not be set aside by a court unless it is arbitrary or capricious.

If you were a member of Congress, would you support the proposal? If not, what additional legislative guidelines would you add? Would you distinguish between (1) immigrants and nonimmigrants; (2) aliens who were admitted and aliens who entered without inspection; and (3) aliens

a. For a review of Supreme Court and lower court decisions, *see Equitable Estoppel in Immigration Cases*, 3 Imm.L.Rep. 33 (May 1984); Asimow, *Estoppel Against the Government: The Immigration and Naturalization Service*, 2 Chicano L.Rev. 4 (1975); Hing, *Estoppel in Immigration Proceedings—New Life from* Akharin *and* Miranda, 20 San Diego L.Rev. 11 (1982).

who have resided here for a short while and those who are long-time residents? [21]

How would you resolve the tension that we have traced throughout this Chapter: the conflict between the twin goals of establishing clear rules to limit executive branch discretion and creating avenues of relief flexible enough to respond to the particular facts of each alien's case? [22]

---

21. An alternate route would be to eliminate discretionary relief altogether and enact a "statute of limitations" on deportation instead. Do you find this proposal satisfactory?

22. For a discussion of the tradeoffs of formulating legal principles as clear determinable rules or policies and standards, *see* Kennedy, *Form and Substance in Private Law Adjudication*, 89 Harv.L.Rev. 1685, 1687–89, 1694–1701 (1976).

Chapter Seven

JUDICIAL REVIEW

Decisions under the immigration laws can carry the most telling personal consequences known to the federal administrative process. To be sure, a ratemaking order or a broadcast licensing proceeding might mean millions of dollars in profit or loss to the contending parties—sums far beyond what one encounters in the immigration field. But those on the losing side, even in such titanic administrative battles, can go home and relieve their disappointment among family and friends. Immigration decisions, in contrast, often bear directly on just where home will be, and on which family members and friends will share daily in life's triumphs and losses.

In light of the potential stakes, both the alien and ultimately the government have the strongest reasons for wanting to be sure that such decisions are done correctly. To serve this end, complex mechanisms for administrative review have evolved, varying considerably depending on the precise application or decision at issue. The basic structure of administrative review is sketched in Chapter Two.[1]

1. You may wish to review that Chapter at this point, as the materials to follow presuppose a basic familiarity with the scheme of administrative review. In essence, practice within the Justice Department involves two main avenues for such review. The Board of Immigration Appeals hears appeals from the most potent administrative decisions—orders of exclusion and deportation, which are handed down initially by immigration judges—and also reviews a handful of other categories of decisions. Many of the latter never go before an immigration judge. For example, INS district directors decide on visa petitions. If they deny a petition founded on alleged family relationships, the petitioner may ask the BIA to review the denial. Many other decisions reached by district directors are appealable, not to the Board, but to the Associate Commissioner for Examinations in the Central Office (for example, visa petitions based on occupational preferences). Some decisions of the district director (e.g., denial of an extension of stay sought by a nonimmigrant) are not appealable. Others are not strictly appealable but may be filed de novo with the immigration judge once

deportation proceedings begin (e.g., applications for adjustment of status). And at virtually every stage there are ways to petition for a reopening or reconsideration by whatever organ issued the latest decision. For a panoramic judicial summary of these matters, see Johns v. Department of Justice, 653 F.2d 884, 889–92 (5th Cir.1981).

Outside of the Justice Department, other agencies have their own review systems. For example, the Department of Labor subjects initial decisions on labor certification to review by administrative law judges who are employees of the Department, but maintain a measure of independence, under statutes creating their positions.

The cases in this Chapter will generally set forth clearly enough the administrative review mechanism applicable to the particular determination at issue. But it will be worthwhile each time to reflect on how those mechanisms fit into the overall scheme, to consider whether other administrative mechanisms would work better, and to ponder how any such administrative changes would or should affect judicial review.

But Americans have probably always harbored a measure of distrust for bureaucrats, even those who serve in purely corrective or appellate roles. Perhaps as a result, the federal courts, staffed with life-tenured judges, have come to be seen as the ultimate guarantors of administrative reliability. *See generally* S. Breyer & R. Stewart, *Administrative Law and Regulatory Policy* 38 (1979). Whether or not this great faith in the bench's capacity is always well-placed, *see* Schuck, *The Transformation of Immigration Law,* 84 Colum.L.Rev. 1, 62 and *passim* (1984), nonetheless this judicial role is a well-entrenched feature of modern life. Under doctrines worked out over the last thirty years or so, federal agency actions are now presumptively subject to review in the courts. *Abbott Laboratories v. Gardner,* 387 U.S. 136, 140–41, 87 S.Ct. 1507, 1510, 1511, 18 L.Ed.2d 681 (1967); *Barlow v. Collins,* 397 U.S. 159, 166, 90 S.Ct. 832, 837, 25 L.Ed.2d 192 (1970).

The Administrative Procedure Act (APA), enacted in 1946 (Pub.L. No. 404, 60 Stat. 237), provides the fundamental foundation for such review. The APA framework is highly flexible, at least so long as the statutes establishing the administrative project do not expressly eliminate or channel the judicial role. The APA states that in the absence *or inadequacy* of specialized provisions for judicial review set forth in the statutes governing a particular agency, a person adversely affected by agency action may seek review using "any applicable form of legal action, including actions for declaratory judgments or writs of prohibitory or mandatory injunction or habeas corpus, in a court of competent jurisdiction." 5 U.S.C.A. § 703. Litigants in immigration cases at various times have attempted to make use of all these possibilities for review of various decisions under the immigration laws.

But the interest in accuracy of administration—an interest shared, in the end, by the alien and the government (whether or not this is always remembered and observed by particular officials cloaked with governmental authority)—is not the only force that impels the people involved to go into court. Even aliens with no colorable claim to the benefit at issue may have a strong interest in stringing out the procedures as long as possible. For in nearly every case, the alien remains in the United States as long as the process of review—both administrative and judicial—continues. And even when a particular chain of review seems to have come to an end, it remains possible to ask some decisionmaker along the way to reopen or reconsider the earlier decision, based on a claim of new information or new legal arguments. Reconsideration might be erroneously denied; it is impossible to design an adjudication system so perfect as to exclude that contingency. And so the theoretical foundation is laid for a new chain of review, testing whether or not such an error has occurred.

Here, then, as in other areas of immigration law, we encounter a familiar tension. We do not want to stint on measures meant to assure accurate and humane application of the system. At the same time we do not want to foster manipulation by well-counseled aliens seeking only to prolong a stay to which they are not entitled. How can the appropriate balance be achieved? At different stages in our history, Congress, the courts, and the agencies have provided different answers to this underlying riddle. It suggests several subsidiary questions. At what stage in the administrative proceedings should review take place? What form of action is appropriate? Which judicial forum should hear the case? What if the same or similar issues have been heard before? What should be the standard for judicial review? The materials in this Chapter touch on these questions.[2]

SECTION A. BACKGROUND

From the beginning, federal immigration statutes have regularly provided that orders of executive branch officers in deportation and exclusion cases are to be "final." [3] Some early Supreme Court decisions seemed to read that specification in its harshest literal sense, as though it precluded any possible judicial role.[4] But that phase did not last long.

2. This Chapter is selective; it gives detailed consideration to only a few issues of major significance that appear from the cases considering judicial review of immigration decisions. Most of the opinions excerpted at length, however, evince some attention to the whole list of questions set forth in the text.

Also, you may find a few of those questions familiar ones, especially those dealing with the standard or scope of review of administrative action. Should the courts reverse an administrative decision when they determine that the findings are not supported by "substantial evidence" on the record? (And just what does "substantial evidence" mean anyway?) Or should courts reverse only when there has been an "abuse of discretion" or administrative action deemed "arbitrary and capricious" (formulations usually considered more deferential to the administrators)? *See generally Citizens to Preserve Overton Park v. Volpe,* 401 U.S. 402, 413–16, 91 S.Ct. 814, 822, 823, 28 L.Ed.2d 136 (1971).

The answer may vary depending on the precise statutory provision at issue. Moreover, each of these formulations may carry its own specific connotations and implications, again depending on the precise nature of the substantive scheme. Consequently, we have found it more logical to consider some issues of this sort in other Chapters, because the questions can be so closely linked to an understanding of the substantive provisions of the INA. *See, e.g., Wong Wing Hang v. INS,* 360 F.2d 715 (2d Cir.

1966), at page 531, *supra* (a leading decision both on the meaning of suspension of deportation under § 244 and also on standards for review of administrative decisions under statutes explicitly vesting an administrator with discretion). More detailed consideration of the intricate disputes over scope of review is standard fare in general administrative law courses; we will not try to cover the same ground. *See generally, e.g.,* K.C. Davis, *Administrative Law of the Seventies* chs. 29, 30 (1976); L. Jaffe, *Judicial Control of Administrative Action* 586–98 (1965); G. Robinson, E. Gellhorn & H. Bruff, *The Administrative Process* 38–42 (2d ed. 1981); B. Schwartz, *Administrative Law* 591–616 (1976).

3. For a summary, *see Heikkila v. Barber,* 345 U.S. 229, 233–35, 73 S.Ct. 603, 605, 606, 97 L.Ed. 972 (1953). The INA still contains such language. *See* §§ 236(c), 242(b). Interestingly, the only significant provisions establishing a different structure appeared in the Chinese exclusion laws, which envisioned a judicial determination of deportability. Once general deportation provisions were applied to Chinese aliens, however, the judicial procedure fell into disuse. *See* G & R § 8.2 n. 1; *Ng Fung Ho v. White,* 259 U.S. 276, 279–81, 42 S.Ct. 492, 493–94, 66 L.Ed. 938 (1922).

4. *See, e.g., Nishimura Ekiu v. United States,* 142 U.S. 651, 660, 664, 12 S.Ct. 336, 340, 35 L.Ed. 1146 (1892); *Lem Moon Sing v. United States,* 158 U.S. 538, 549, 15 S.Ct. 967, 971, 39 L.Ed. 1082 (1895); *Fok Yung Yo*

Soon the courts began to entertain cases challenging the decisions of the administrators in exclusion and deportation cases. Often the substantive standard for review was extraordinarily deferential to the administrators, when viewed from a modern perspective, but the immigration authorities did not always prevail. Above all, though, the mere fact of judicial consideration was significant, in the face of the statute's command of finality.[5]

These cases allowing judicial review present an apparent puzzle. Federal courts are courts of limited jurisdiction, and they must ordinarily trace their power to hear a case to a specific congressional authorization. The early immigration statutes merely set forth the administrative arrangements and purported to make the resulting orders final. Clearly *they* bestowed no review authority on the courts. Indeed, it was not until 1961 that any general provisions for judicial review appeared in our immigration laws. Just how did the courts manage to assume jurisdiction?

The answer derives from the brute requirements of the process of deportation and exclusion. An unwilling alien could not (and obviously still cannot) be removed without being physically restrained at some point. Classically, such physical restraint—custody—is the foundation for issuance of the Great Writ, the writ of habeas corpus, a remedy guaranteed in the text of the Constitution.[6] The early review cases were all habeas corpus cases, and for decades, the writ of habeas corpus provided the only avenue for court review of exclusion and deportation orders.

The exclusiveness of habeas review answered many of the questions we posed earlier, often by drawing on the common law doctrines relating to habeas corpus. The scope of review in such cases was relatively narrow, frequently expressed as follows: the courts would inquire whether the hearing conformed to minimum due process requirements, whether there was any evidence to support the conclusion, and whether the

---

v. United States, 185 U.S. 296, 305, 22 S.Ct. 686, 689, 46 L.Ed. 917 (1902).

5. *See, e.g., Yamataya v. Fisher (The Japanese Immigrant Case)*, 189 U.S. 86, 100–02, 23 S.Ct. 611, 614, 615, 47 L.Ed. 721 (1903); *Chin Yow v. United States*, 208 U.S. 8, 12, 28 S.Ct. 201, 202, 52 L.Ed. 369 (1908); *Gegiow v. Uhl*, 239 U.S. 3, 9, 36 S.Ct. 2, 60 L.Ed. 114 (1915). For a general summary of these developments, *see* Hart, *The Power of Congress to Limit the Jurisdiction of the Federal Courts: An Exercise in Dialectic*, 66 Harv.L.Rev. 1362, 1389–96 (1953).

6. Article I, section 9, clause 2 states: "The privilege of the Writ of Habeas Corpus shall not be suspended, unless when in Cases of Rebellion or Invasion the public Safety may require it." It can be quite difficult to decide just what restrictions on the writ will constitute an invalid "suspension," especially when restrictions are accompanied by the opening of other procedural avenues for a prisoner to test the confinement. *See gen-*

erally Swain v. Pressley, 430 U.S. 372, 97 S.Ct. 1224, 51 L.Ed.2d 411 (1977).

The habeas corpus remedy was also the subject of federal statutes well before the first immigration acts were passed, and sometimes it is not clear whether particular features of habeas practice as we have come to know them derive from constitutional command or from statutory refinement. *See* Saltzburg, *Habeas Corpus: The Supreme Court and the Congress*, 44 Ohio St.L.J. 367 (1983). Most of the time it has not been important to make such distinctions; habeas practice in immigration cases has conformed in general to the outlines established in the general federal habeas provisions. 28 U.S. C.A. §§ 2241 et seq. But some recent proposals for immigration reform, including bills that passed the Senate in 1982 and 1983, would have limited the writ in deportation and exclusion cases to its minimum content "under the Constitution." Specifying that content would not be easy.

statutory requirements had been properly construed.[7] Furthermore, the exclusivity of the habeas corpus remedy minimized the chances of interrupting the administrative process with premature review or burdening it with repetitious litigation. Custody often began only at the end of the process; and a familiar prerequisite to issuance of the writ was the petitioner's exhaustion of other available remedies.

But litigants still sought other avenues into the courts, for a simple reason. The very foundation of the high regard Anglo-American jurisprudence has maintained for the habeas corpus remedy—its availability at the moment when a person was restrained of his or her liberty—also resulted in its major disadvantage. As habeas was ordinarily understood until recent years, the alien could not petition for the writ until he was actually in physical custody. By then he may have had to sell his belongings, bid farewell to family and friends, and wait from his jail cell for the court's decision.

In 1934, Congress passed the Declaratory Judgment Act, 28 U.S.C.A. § 2201, allowing litigants in certain circumstances to seize the initiative for securing a judicial hearing in a federal court earlier than was otherwise possible, provided the plaintiff presented "a case of actual controversy within [the court's] jurisdiction." At one point it appeared that aliens might use that procedure to contest immigration rulings without having to undergo physical custody. *See McGrath v. Kristensen*, 340 U.S. 162, 168–71, 71 S.Ct. 224, 228–30, 95 L.Ed. 173 (1950). But a few years later, when the issue was squarely presented, the Supreme Court disavowed such a conclusion. In *Heikkila v. Barber*, 345 U.S. 229, 73 S.Ct. 603, 97 L.Ed. 972 (1953), the Court staunchly reaffirmed the exclusiveness of the habeas remedy (except in extremely narrow circumstances):

> Congress may well have thought that habeas corpus, despite its apparent inconvenience to the alien, should be the exclusive remedy in these cases in order to minimize opportunities for repetitious litigation and consequent delays as well as to avoid possible venue difficulties connected with any other type of action.

Id. at 237, 73 S.Ct. at 607. *See also Shung v. Brownell,* 346 U.S. 906, 74 S.Ct. 237, 98 L.Ed. 405 (1953).

But it turned out that the *Heikkila* doctrine was quite short-lived. The case arose in 1950, before passage of the INA but after the APA had been enacted, and Heikkila tried to claim declaratory review not only under the Declaratory Judgment Act, but also under the APA. *See* 5 U.S.C.A. §§ 701–706. The Court ruled against him on both grounds. But crucially, its holding applied only to the immigration laws extant in 1950 (the most important being the Immigration Act of 1917). The Court did not decide the effect of the 1952 INA, even though that law was already on the books by the time the decision issued.

---

7. *See, e.g., Kwock Jan Fat v. White,* 253 U.S. 454, 457–58, 40 S.Ct. 566, 567, 64 L.Ed. 1010 (1920); *United States ex rel. Rongetti v. Neelly,* 207 F.2d 281, 284 (7th Cir.1953).

In 1955 the Court decided that the new INA made a profound difference. *Shaughnessy v. Pedreiro,* 349 U.S. 48, 75 S.Ct. 591, 99 L.Ed. 868 (1955). The 1952 Congress had not specifically exempted future immigration decisions from the judicial review provisions of the 1946 APA. Because the APA itself established a presumption that later-enacted administrative statutes would be subject to APA requirements, the congressional silence was considered determinative.[8] From that moment on, declaratory and injunctive relief were to be available under the APA to test deportation orders under the INA. In 1956 the Court reached the same conclusion with respect to exclusion cases. *Brownell v. Shung,* 352 U.S. 180, 77 S.Ct. 252, 1 L.Ed.2d 225 (1956).

For immigration litigants, these were wonderful developments. Aliens could at last clearly contest exclusion and deportation orders without having to go to jail. Congress, however, was less pleased with the results. Although many members were prepared to afford some mechanism for court review of deportation orders in advance of custody, the key committees feared that the procedures made available under *Pedreiro* would be abused to string out court review beyond all reasonable bounds. *See, e.g.,* H.R.Rep. 1086, 87th Cong., 1st Sess., 28–32 (1961). Several tales of delay and manipulation were presented in the congressional testimony. But one case stands out—that of Carlos Marcello, a reputed racketeer who had been brought to the United States from Italy at the age of one but had never become a citizen. INS had been trying to deport him since virtually the moment in 1952 when the INA became effective. A deportation order became administratively final in 1953, but court orders had prevented its execution. One committee report reprinted the text of a letter detailing Marcello's use of the courts to impede deportation:

March 25, 1959

Hon. Sam J. Ervin, Jr.,

U.S. Senate.

Dear Senator Ervin: It has been called to my attention that yesterday at the hearing of the Senate Select Committee on Improper Activities in the Labor and Management Field you

---

8. *Pedreiro* did not decide that all provisions of the APA applied to all aspects of implementation under the 1952 INA. In fact, the same year the Court reached the opposite conclusion regarding the application of the rather stringent separation-of-function requirements the APA establishes for agency adjudicators. These were held inapplicable to special inquiry officers, because INA § 242(b) contains its own (watered-down) set of requirements on this subject. *See Marcello v. Bonds,* 349 U.S. 302, 75 S.Ct. 757, 99 L.Ed. 1107 (1955). As a result, although the INA postdates the APA, the APA applies only in patchwork fashion to decisions under the INA. Indeed, this patchwork quality was augmented in 1961 when Congress enacted special

judicial review provisions as § 106 of the INA. That section, which will claim most of our attention throughout this Chapter, exempts exclusion and deportation orders from the procedural specifications of the APA governing judicial review. Specifically, it forbids review of such orders in declaratory actions brought in accordance with the APA. But observe that § 106 provides special and exclusive judicial review channels only for exclusion and deportation orders; it leaves APA procedures applicable to judicial review of other decisions under the immigration laws. (The APA's requirements for public notice and opportunity for comment in advance of rulemaking also apply to the promulgation of regulations under the INA.)

made inquiries concerning the deportation proceedings against Carlos Marcello. I thought you would be interested in knowing the steps the Department of Justice has taken to rid the country of this undesirable alien. Attached herewith is a summary of the chronology of the litigation involved in these proceedings.

You will notice that on six separate occasions Marcello has instituted various suits in the district courts of the United States raising issues incident to the deportation order. Each case has been contested vigorously. On several occasions, he has sought review in the court of appeals, and on three occasions has been to the Supreme Court of the United States. Although the deportation order has been successfully defended on all occasions, and the Government has been successful on most of the other issues raised, it has been under court-imposed restraint from deporting Marcello during much of this time.

During periods when there was no court imposed restraint, deportation has not been possible because of the lack of an Italian passport, without which deportation was not possible. In August 1955 when travel documentation was available and Marcello had been directed to surrender for deportation, the Italian consul at New Orleans revoked the passport on the day he was to be deported. Thereafter, further litigation was instituted and was decided favorably to the Government. After continuous negotiations, the Italian authorities on October 31, 1956, issued another passport which was limited in time. However, on the day before its issuance, Marcello filed a new suit and obtained a temporary restraining order preventing deportation.

Another suit was instituted by Marcello to delay deportation and, in addition, he started proceedings in the Italian courts for a judgment declaring him not to be a citizen of Italy, as a result of which the Italian Foreign Office was enjoined from issuing any travel documents until that suit is terminated. Nevertheless, the Government has continued to exert every effort for the issuance of an Italian passport and I have personally participated in this effort.

At the present time the deportation order against Marcello is still outstanding. In his last effort to delay deportation, he applied for an administrative stay on the ground that he would suffer physical persecution if deported to Italy. When this was denied and the Government's position upheld in the U.S. District Court for the District of Columbia, he sought review in the court of appeals. The latter court held that the Immigration Service had not given him adequate time to collect and present evidence in support of his claim that he would be subject to persecution. He was given such an opportunity and on February 20, 1959, the Service denied the requested relief.

Although presently there is no pending litigation, deportation cannot be effected because no passport is available. If this obstacle is overcome there is no guarantee that deportation can be expeditiously effected. On the basis of past experience it is expected that Marcello will attempt other delaying tactics in the courts.

In connection with the delays often encountered in effecting deportation, I would like to call your attention to the fact that the administration for the past 5 years has sought legislation which would strengthen our immigration laws by limiting judicial review of deportation orders within reasonable bounds so as to avoid its repeated use solely as a delaying tactic.

* * *

I urge the Congress to enact this much needed legislation at the earliest possible moment.

Sincerely,

William P. Rogers,

Attorney General

H.R.Rep. No. 565, 87th Cong., 1st Sess. 6–7 (1961). The committee reprinted the Attorney General's chronology, updating it with references to later events, including the three new federal actions Marcello had filed between 1959 and mid-1961. The committee also noted "that Marcello's repetitious court proceedings are principally begun (with their accompanying requests for interim stays) just when the Government manages to obtain a travel document and is about to enforce departure—many years after the order of deportation was entered." *Id.* at 11.[9]

After considering all these developments, Congress ultimately added section 106 to the INA in order to restructure the judicial review arrangements. Act of Sept. 26, 1961, Pub.L. No. 87–301, § 5, 75 Stat. 651. This enactment constituted the first specific statutory provision governing the judicial review of exclusion and deportation orders. You may wish at this point to consult the text of § 106.

Consider first the changes Congress wrought for exclusion cases. Section 106(b) restores habeas corpus as the exclusive means for review of exclusion orders. Early declaratory review, as authorized by the 1956 *Shung* decision, *supra,* under the authority of the APA, was thus foreclosed. Congress evidently accepted that aliens in the excludable category would have to submit to custody before gaining access to the courts. Interestingly, however, Congress viewed the changes implemented by this

---

9. The chronology also reveals some questionable government behavior in INS's ceaseless efforts to remove Marcello. *See United States ex rel. Marcello v. District Director,* 634 F.2d 964, 966 (5th Cir.1981), *cert. denied* 452 U.S. 917, 101 S.Ct. 3052, 69 L.Ed.2d 421 (1981) ("arguably Marcello was shanghaied to Guatemala" by INS in 1961, although he soon reentered without inspection). That 1981 Fifth Circuit decision, which is excerpted later in this Chapter, reprints the committee's chronology as an appendix to the opinion and also reveals some of the later developments in the Marcello saga. *See also Marcello v. INS,* 449 F.2d 349 (5th Cir.1971). As of this writing, Marcello is still in the United States.

subsection primarily in procedural terms. It apparently did not intend that the return to exclusive habeas review should drastically limit the range of issues or narrow the standard of review to be applied when the courts finally did take jurisdiction of the case.[10] Petitions for the writ of habeas corpus in exclusion cases are almost invariably filed in the federal district courts, and the action proceeds according to the usual rules applicable to habeas actions. *See generally* 28 U.S.C.A. §§ 2241 et seq.; G & R § 8.7. The losing party at the district court level may appeal that determination to the court of appeals and, if unsuccessful at that stage, may petition for certiorari in the Supreme Court.

As for review of deportation orders, § 106(a) takes a wholly new approach and does not relegate deportable aliens to the old habeas procedure.[11] Section 106(a) provides that the procedure prescribed by the Hobbs Act (now codified at 28 U.S.C.A. Chapter 158) "shall apply to, and shall be the sole and exclusive procedure for, the judicial review of all final orders of deportation * * * pursuant to administrative proceedings under Section 242(b) of this Act or comparable provisions of any prior Act * * *." The Hobbs Act, which also governs review for several other administrative agencies, including the Federal Communications Commission, the Federal Maritime Commission, the Interstate Commerce Commission, and others, takes the reviewing role out of the district courts and places it in the courts of appeals. Review is initiated by a petition for review filed in the appropriate circuit; such petitions must be filed no later than six months after the entry of the deportation order. § 106(a)(1). Service of the petition on the INS automatically stays deportation of the alien, although the court has authority to vacate the stay if INS moves for such relief. For the details of practice under this subsection, *see* G & R § 8.9A.

Although this enactment, like the APA-based declaratory review it replaced, allows aliens to secure judicial review without submitting to the rigors of physical custody, Congress believed that three other central features of INA § 106 would limit the opportunities for delay and manipulation. First, there is a strict requirement that all administrative remedies be exhausted before review is available (a prescription that applies with equal force to exclusion cases). INA § 106(c). Second, the law specifically requires that every petition for review or for habeas corpus must state whether the validity of the challenged order has been previously determined in any judicial action. If so, further review is forbidden, unless certain narrow conditions are met. *See* § 106(c) (second and third

---

10. As one treatise explains, under the 1961 provisions for exclusion, "the court's authority for review is not limited to the procedural aspects of the administrative proceedings, but extends also to the substantive ground on which the exclusion order was based. Thus the alien is afforded a test not only of whether he received a fair hearing, but also whether his exclusion had been ordered on a ground specified by statute." E. Harper, Immigration Laws of the United States 500 (3d ed. 1975), citing H.R.Rep. No.

1086, 87th Cong., 1st Sess., 30–32 (1961). *See also* G & R § 8.13.

11. INA § 106(a)(9) does, however, preserve the availability of habeas for "any alien held in custody." Just how this provision is to fit with the "sole and exclusive procedure" established in the earlier parts of the subsection has posed some knotty issues, which we will consider in connection with the *Marcello* and *Daneshvar* cases in Section E below.

sentences). And finally, § 106(a) eliminates one layer of court review—the district courts, which had been the initial forum for judicial involvement both before and after *Pedreiro*. The courts of appeals are directed to carry out their reviewing functions strictly on the basis of the administrative record, *see* § 106(a)(4), and there can be no new factfinding at this stage.[12] As a result, there is only one further layer of direct review for an alien who is unsuccessful in the court of appeals: a petition for certiorari to the U.S. Supreme Court.

The rest of this Chapter considers the modern review provisions in greater detail.

SECTION B.   PETITIONS TO REVIEW ORDERS OF DEPORTATION

Despite its length and detail, INA § 106(a) leaves many questions unanswered. Once the court of appeals receives a petition for review, exactly what issues are within its reviewing reach? The determination of deportability alone? Decisions to deny discretionary relief? All decisions on potential relief, or only those passed on by an immigration judge? Or should the court take jurisdiction and try to resolve all complaints the deportable alien might have about decisions under the immigration laws that at any time have gone against him?

The Supreme Court struggled with these questions in an important triad of cases that reached it within a few years after the enactment of the 1961 INA amendments. We reprint here the third decision of the group, for it adequately recounts the outcome of the other two cases.

---

12. The statute provides a special exception to these requirements when the petitioner makes a nonfrivolous claim to U.S. nationality. If the issue cannot be resolved strictly as a matter of law, the case is transferred to a district court for de novo judicial factfinding on this question. INA § 106(a)(5). *See Agosto v. INS*, 436 U.S. 748, 98 S.Ct. 2081, 56 L.Ed.2d 677 (1978). This provision in effect implements the Supreme Court's ruling in *Ng Fung Ho v. White*, 259 U.S. 276, 42 S.Ct. 492, 66 L.Ed. 938 (1922). There the Court held that persons *within* the United States who make supported claims to U.S. citizenship may not be deported strictly on the basis of an administrative finding against their claims. There must be a de novo judicial decision on the citizenship allegation. The ruling rested on the Fifth Amendment's due process clause, and the Court adverted to the "difference in security of judicial over administrative action." *Id.* at 285. But if such claimants are not within the country—and specifically if they are in exclusion proceedings—final administrative determination of the citizenship claim is permissible, under *United States v. Ju Toy*, 198 U.S. 253 (1905). Section 360 of the INA seems generally to follow the contours of the *Ju Toy/Ng Fung Ho* doctrine. It permits claimants within the United States full judicial determination of a citizenship claim when it has been denied by a governmental official or agency. INA § 360(a). But claimants outside the United States are granted by the INA only a procedure permitting them to travel to this country to have the citizenship issue tried in the relatively disadvantageous setting of an exclusion proceeding. *Id.* § 360(b), (c). Nevertheless, later court decisions have opened far wider avenues to judicial determination of a citizenship claim, even if the claimant is outside the United States, by means of ordinary declaratory judgment proceedings. *See Rusk v. Cort*, 369 U.S. 367 (1962); G & R § 8.29.

CHENG FAN KWOK v. INS

Supreme Court of the United States, 1968.
392 U.S. 206, 88 S.Ct. 1970, 20 L.Ed.2d 1037.

Mr. Justice Harlan delivered the opinion of the Court.

The narrow question presented by this case is whether jurisdiction to review the denial of a stay of deportation, if the pertinent order has not been entered in the course of a proceeding conducted under § 242(b) of the Immigration and Nationality Act, is, under § 106(a) of the Act, vested exclusively in the courts of appeals. The question arises from the following circumstances.

Petitioner, a native and citizen of China, evidently entered the United States in 1965 as a seaman. The terms of his entry permitted him to remain in this country for the period during which his vessel was in port, provided that this did not exceed 29 days. See INA § 252(a). He deserted his vessel, and remained unlawfully in the United States. After petitioner's eventual apprehension, deportation proceedings were conducted by a special inquiry officer under the authority of § 242(b). Petitioner conceded his deportability, but sought and obtained permission to depart the United States voluntarily.[4] Despite his protestations of good faith, petitioner did not voluntarily depart, and was ultimately ordered to surrender for deportation. He then requested a stay of deportation from a district director of immigration, pending the submission and disposition of an application for adjustment of status under 8 U.S.C. § 1153(a)(7) (1964 ed., Supp. II).[a] The district director concluded that petitioner is ineligible for such an adjustment of status, and denied a stay of deportation.

Petitioner thereupon commenced these proceedings in the Court of Appeals for the Third Circuit, petitioning for review of the denial of a stay. The Court of Appeals held that the provisions of § 106(a), under which it would otherwise have exclusive jurisdiction to review the district director's order, are inapplicable to orders denying ancillary relief unless those orders either are entered in the course of a proceeding conducted under § 242(b), or are denials of motions to reopen such proceedings. The court dismissed the petition for want of jurisdiction. We granted certiorari because the courts of appeals have disagreed as to the proper construction of the pertinent statutory provisions. For reasons that follow, we affirm.

I.

It is useful first to summarize the relevant provisions of the Immigration and Nationality Act and of the regulations promulgated under the Act's authority. Section 242(b) provides a detailed administrative proce-

---

4. We note, as we did in Foti v. Immigration and Naturalization Service, 375 U.S. 217, 84 S.Ct. 306, 11 L.Ed.2d 281, that the "granting of voluntary departure relief does not result in the alien's not being subject to an outstanding final order of deportation."

a. Formerly INA § 203(a)(7)—the old seventh preference—which then permitted the adjustment of status of certain persons, *inter*

alia, those who demonstrated that they feared persecution in "any Communist or Communist-dominated country." The seventh preference was repealed by the Refugee Act of 1980, which fashioned a completely different structure for the admission of refugees. We will consider these matters in more detail in Chapter Eight.—eds.

dure for determining whether an alien may be deported. It permits the entry of an order of deportation only upon the basis of a record made in a proceeding before a special inquiry officer, at which the alien is assured rights to counsel, to a reasonable opportunity to examine the evidence against him, to cross-examine witnesses, and to present evidence in his own behalf. By regulation, various forms of discretionary relief may also be sought from the special inquiry officer in the course of the deportation proceeding; an alien may, for example, request that his deportation be temporarily withheld, on the ground that he might, in the country to which he is to be deported, "be subject to persecution * * *." *See* 8 U.S.C. § 1253(h) (1964 ed., Supp. II).[b]

Other forms of discretionary relief may be requested after termination of the deportation proceeding. The regulations thus provide that an alien "under a final administrative order of deportation" may apply to the district director "having jurisdiction over the place where the alien is at the time of filing" for a stay of deportation. 8 CFR § 243.4. The stay may be granted by the district director "in his discretion." Ibid. If the stay is denied, the denial "is not appealable" to the Board of Immigration Appeals. Ibid.

Section 106(a) provides that the procedures for judicial review prescribed by the Hobbs Act, 64 Stat. 1129, 68 Stat. 961, "shall apply to, and shall be the sole and exclusive procedure for, the judicial review of all final orders of deportation heretofore or hereafter made against aliens * * * pursuant to administrative proceedings under section 242(b) of this Act * * *." These procedures vest in the courts of appeals exclusive jurisdiction to review final orders issued by specified federal agencies. In situations to which the provisions of § 106(a) are inapplicable, the alien's remedies would, of course, ordinarily lie first in an action brought in an appropriate district court.

The positions of the various parties may be summarized as follows. We are urged by both petitioner and the Immigration Service to hold that the provisions of § 106(a) are applicable to the circumstances presented by this case, and that judicial review thus is available only in the courts of appeals. The Immigration Service contends that § 106(a) should be understood to embrace all determinations "directly affecting the execution of the basic deportation order," whether those determinations have been reached prior to, during, or subsequent to the deportation proceeding. In contrast, amicus [9] urges, as the Court of Appeals held, that § 106(a) encompasses only those orders made in the course of a proceeding conducted under § 242(b) or issued upon motions to reopen such proceedings.

II.

This is the third case in which we have had occasion to examine the effect of § 106(a). In the first, Foti v. Immigration and Naturalization Service, 375 U.S. 217, 84 S.Ct. 306, 11 L.Ed.2d 281 [1963], the petitioner, in

---

b. INA § 243(h) still permits withholding of deportation in these circumstances, but the wording has been altered somewhat. *See* Chapter Eight.—eds.

9. Since the Immigration Service had aligned itself with petitioner on this ques-

tion, the Court invited William H. Dempsey, Jr., Esquire, a member of the Bar of this Court, to appear and present oral argument as *amicus curiae* in support of the judgment below.

the course of a proceeding conducted under § 242(b), conceded his deportability but requested a suspension of deportation under § 244(a)(5). The special inquiry officer denied such a suspension, and petitioner's appeal from the denial was dismissed by the Board of Immigration Appeals. Petitioner commenced an action in the district court, but the action was dismissed on the ground that, under § 106(a), his exclusive remedy lay in the courts of appeals. He then petitioned for review to the Court of Appeals for the Second Circuit, but it dismissed for want of jurisdiction. A divided court held *en banc* that the procedures of § 106(a) were inapplicable to denials of discretionary relief under § 244(a)(5). * * * On certiorari, we reversed, holding that "all determinations made during and incident to the administrative proceeding conducted by a special inquiry officer, and reviewable together by the Board of Immigration Appeals * * * are * * * included within the ambit of the exclusive jurisdiction of the Court of Appeals under § 106(a)."

In the second case, Giova v. Rosenberg, 379 U.S. 18, 85 S.Ct. 156, 13 L.Ed.2d 90, petitioner moved before the Board of Immigration Appeals to reopen proceedings, previously conducted under § 242(b), that had terminated in an order for his deportation. The Board denied relief. The Court of Appeals for the Ninth Circuit concluded that the Board's denial was not embraced by § 106(a), and dismissed the petition for want of jurisdiction. On certiorari, this Court held, in a brief *per curiam* opinion, that such orders were within the exclusive jurisdiction of the courts of appeals.

Although *Foti* strongly suggests the result that we reach today, neither it nor *Giova* can properly be regarded as controlling in this situation. Unlike the order in *Foti*, the order in this case was not entered in the course of a proceeding conducted by a special inquiry officer under § 242(b); unlike the order in *Giova* the order here did not deny a motion to reopen such a proceeding. We regard the issue of statutory construction involved here as markedly closer than the questions presented in those cases; at the least, it is plainly an issue upon which differing views may readily be entertained. In these circumstances, it is imperative, if we are accurately to implement Congress' purposes, to "seiz[e] everything from which aid can be derived." Fisher v. Blight, 2 Cranch 358, 386, 2 L.Ed. 304.

It is important, first, to emphasize the character of the statute with which we are concerned. Section 106(a) is intended exclusively to prescribe and regulate a portion of the jurisdiction of the federal courts. As a jurisdictional statute, it must be construed both with precision and with fidelity to the terms by which Congress has expressed its wishes. Utah Junk Co. v. Porter, 328 U.S. 39, 44, 66 S.Ct. 889, 892, 90 L.Ed. 1071. Further, as a statute addressed entirely to "specialists," it must, as Mr. Justice Frankfurter observed, "be read by judges with the minds of * * * specialists."

We cannot, upon close reading, easily reconcile the position urged by the Immigration Service with the terms of § 106(a). A denial by a district director of a stay of deportation is not literally a "final order of deportation," nor is it, as was the order in *Foti*, entered in the course of administrative proceedings conducted under § 242(b).[11]   Thus, the order in this case was issued more than three months after the entry of the final order of deportation, in proceedings entirely distinct from those conducted under § 242(b), by an officer other than the special inquiry officer who, as required by § 242(b), presided over the deportation proceeding.   The order here did not involve the denial of a motion to reopen proceedings conducted under § 242(b), or to reconsider any final order of deportation.   Concededly, the application for a stay assumed the prior existence of an order of deportation, but petitioner did not "attack the deportation order itself but instead [sought] relief not inconsistent with it."   Mui v. Esperdy, 371 F.2d 772, 777 (C.A.2nd cir.).   If, as the Immigration Service urges, § 106(a) embraces all determinations "directly affecting the execution of" a final deportation order, Congress has selected language remarkably inapposite for its purpose.   As Judge Friendly observed in a similar case, if "Congress had wanted to go that far, presumably it would have known how to say so."   Ibid.

The legislative history of § 106(a) does not strengthen the position of the Immigration Service.   The "basic purpose" of the procedural portions of the 1961 legislation was, as we stated in *Foti*, evidently "to expedite the deportation of undesirable aliens by preventing successive dilatory appeals to various federal courts * * *."   Congress prescribed for this purpose several procedural innovations, among them the device of direct petitions for review to the courts of appeals.   Although, as the Immigration Service has emphasized, the broad purposes of the legislation might have been expected to encompass orders denying discretionary relief entered outside § 242(b) proceedings, there is evidence that Congress deliberately restricted the application of § 106(a) to orders made in the course of proceedings conducted under § 242(b).

Thus, during a colloquy on the floor of the House of Representatives, to which we referred in *Foti*, Representative Moore, co-sponsor of the bill then under discussion, suggested that any difficulties resulting from the separate consideration of deportability and of discretionary relief could be overcome by "a change in the present administrative practice of considering the issues * * * piecemeal.   There is no reason why the Immigration

---

11. We find the emphasis placed in dissent upon the word "pursuant" in § 106(a) unpersuasive.   First, § 106(a) was evidently limited to those final orders of deportation made "pursuant to administrative proceedings under section 242(b)" simply because Congress preferred to exclude from it those deportation orders entered without a § 242(b) proceeding.   This would, for example, place orders issued under INA § 252(b) by which the Immigration Service may revoke a seaman's conditional permit to land and deport him, outside the judicial review procedures of § 106(a).   Perhaps this suggests, as *amicus* urges, that § 106(a) was intended to be limited to situations in which quasi-judicial proceedings, such as those under § 242(b), have been conducted.   It certainly indicates that the reference in § 106(a) to § 242(b) proceedings was intended to limit, and not to broaden, the classes of orders to which § 106(a) may be applied.   Second, it must be reiterated that § 106(a) does not, as the dissenting opinion suggests, encompass "all orders" entered pursuant to § 242(b) proceedings: it is limited to "final orders of deportation."   The textual difficulty, with which the dissenting opinion does not deal, is that the order in question here neither is a final order of deportation, nor is it, as was the order in *Foti*, "made during the same proceedings" in which a final order of deportation has been issued.   This cannot be overcome merely by examination of the meaning of the word "pursuant."

Service could not change its regulations to permit contemporaneous court consideration of deportability and administrative application for relief." In the same colloquy, Representative Walter, the chairman of the subcommittee that conducted the pertinent hearings, recognized that certain forms of discretionary relief may be requested in the course of a deportation proceeding, and stated that § 106(a) would apply to the disposition of such requests, "just as it would apply to any other issue *brought up in deportation proceedings*." Similarly, Representative Walter, in a subsequent debate, responded to a charge that judicial review under § 106(a) would prove inadequate because of the absence of a suitable record, by inviting "the gentleman's attention to the law in section 242, in which the procedure for the examiner is set forth in detail."

We believe that, in combination with the terms of § 106(a) itself, these statements lead to the inference that Congress quite deliberately restricted the application of § 106(a) to orders entered during proceedings conducted under § 242(b), or directly challenging deportation orders themselves. This is concededly "a choice between uncertainties," but we are "content to choose the lesser." Burnet v. Guggenheim, 288 U.S. 280, 288, 53 S.Ct. 369, 371, 77 L.Ed. 748.

We need not speculate as to Congress' purposes. Quite possibly, as Judge Browning has persuasively suggested, "Congress visualized a single administrative proceeding in which all questions relating to an alien's deportation would be raised and resolved, followed by a single petition in a court of appeals for judicial review * * *." Yamada v. Immigration & Naturalization Service, 384 F.2d 214, 218. It may therefore be that Congress expected the Immigration Service to include within the § 242(b) proceeding "all issues which might affect deportation." Ibid. Possibly, as *amicus* cogently urges, Congress wished to limit petitions to the courts of appeals to situations in which quasi-judicial hearings had been conducted. It is enough to emphasize that neither of these purposes would be in any fashion impeded by the result we reach today. We hold that the judicial review provisions of § 106(a) embrace only those determinations made during a proceeding conducted under § 242(b), including those determinations made incident to a motion to reopen such proceedings.[16]

This result is entirely consistent with our opinion in *Foti*. There, it was repeatedly stated in the opinion of THE CHIEF JUSTICE that the order held reviewable under § 106(a) had, as the regulations required, been entered in the course of a proceeding conducted under § 242(b). * * * It was emphasized that "the administrative discretion to grant a suspension of deportation," the determination involved in *Foti*, "has historically been consistently exercised as an integral part of the proceedings which have led to the issuance of a final deportation order." * * * A suspension of deportation "must be requested prior to or during the deportation hearing." Moreover, it was explicitly recognized that, although modification of the pertinent regulations might "effectively broaden or narrow the

---

16. We intimate no views on the possibility that a court of appeals might have "pendent jurisdiction" over denials of discretionary relief, where it already has before it a petition for review from a proceeding conducted under § 242(b).

scope of review available in the Courts of Appeals," this was "nothing anomalous." [17]   An essential premise of *Foti* was thus that the application of § 106(a) had been limited to orders "made during the same proceedings in which deportability is determined   * * *."

The *per curiam* opinion in *Giova* did not take a wider view of § 106(a). The denial of an application to reopen a deportation proceeding is readily distinguishable from a denial of a stay of deportation, in which there is no attack upon the deportation order or upon the proceeding in which it was entered. Petitions to reopen, like motions for rehearing or reconsideration, are, as the Immigration Service urged in *Foti*, "intimately and immediately associated" with the final orders they seek to challenge. Thus, petitions to reopen deportation proceedings are governed by the regulations applicable to the deportation proceeding itself, and, indeed, are ordinarily presented for disposition to the special inquiry officer who entered the deportation order.[19]   The result in *Giova* was thus a logical concomitant of the construction of § 106(a) reached in *Foti;* it did not, explicitly or by implication, broaden that construction in any fashion that encompasses this situation.

The result we reach today will doubtless mean that, on occasion, the review of denials of discretionary relief will be conducted separately from the review of an order of deportation involving the same alien. Nonetheless, this does not seem an onerous burden, nor is it one that cannot be avoided, at least in large part, by appropriate action of the Immigration Service itself. More important, although "there is no table of logarithms for statutory construction," it is the result that we believe most consistent both with Congress' intentions and with the terms by which it has chosen to express those intentions.

Affirmed.

Mr. Justice White, dissenting.

If the special inquiry officer had possessed jurisdiction to issue a stay order pending petitioner's efforts to obtain discretionary relief from the District Director, I take it that his denial of the stay, like a refusal to re-open, would have been appealable to the Court of Appeals. But, as I understand it, no stay could have been granted by the hearing officer and it was sought from the District Director as an immediate consequence of there being outstanding a final order of deportation, which, if executed, might moot the underlying request for relief from the District Director. Section 106 does not limit judicial review in the Court of Appeals to orders entered "in the course of" § 242(b) proceedings, but extends it to all orders against aliens entered "pursuant" to such proceedings, that is, at least as

---

17. The opinion of the Court emphasized, in addition, that "[c]learly, changes in administrative procedures may affect the scope and content of various types of agency orders and thus the subject matter embraced in a judicial proceeding to review such orders."

19. See 8 CFR § 242.22. If, however, the order of the special inquiry officer is appealed to the Board of Immigration Appeals, a subsequent motion to reopen or reconsider is presented to the Board for disposition. The motion in *Giova* was presented to the Board and decided by it.

Webster would have it,* "acting or done in consequence" of the § 242(b) proceedings. Except for the order of deportation, there would have been no occasion or need to seek a stay. It hardly strains congressional intention to give the word "pursuant" its ordinary meaning in the English language. If there are reasons based on policy for the court's contrary conclusion, they are not stated. I would reverse the judgment.

Notes

1. The majority acknowledges a substantial congressional policy that is somewhat undercut, at the very least, by the Court's interpretation of § 106(a): the broad legislative purpose "to expedite the deportation of undesirable aliens by preventing successive dilatory appeals to various federal courts." Justice White, in dissent, suggests that the majority could locate no countervailing policy reasons that would justify its conclusion. But the majority does not rest solely on linguistic analysis. It at least hints at certain policies that are served by its holding. What are those policies? Are they weighty enough to justify the outcome, especially when the Court agrees that it was faced with "a choice between uncertainties." If you were redrafting the statute, how would you choose to provide for review in these situations?

2. The Court extends a none too subtle invitation to the Justice Department to change its regulations if it is really so intensely interested in assuring that deportable aliens have only one avenue of appeal to the courts. Nevertheless, the regulations still essentially reserve to the district directors the authority to issue post-order stays of deportation. 8 C.F.R. § 243.4. Why do you suppose the Department has maintained this structure for decisionmaking? (Consider the usual scenarios in which such a stay may be needed and the probable logistics involved in securing such an order. *See generally Matter of Santos*, Interim Dec. No. 2969 (BIA 1984).) Should it now change?

Cheng Fan Kwok clearly prevents a court of appeals from reviewing a *post*-deportation-order decision by the immigration authorities when it is considering a petition under § 106(a) (unless that decision happens to arise on a motion to reopen or to reconsider). But what about *pre*-order determinations under the immigration laws, if they were made outside the § 242(b) hearing? Sometimes such decisions are intimately linked with the issues in the deportation proceedings, and to that extent, the case may be stronger for allowing judicial review as part of the review of the order itself. Under § 106(a), can the court of appeals review the propriety of the earlier determination? The next case considers this question.

---

* Merriam-Webster, Webster's New International Dictionary, Second Edition, unabridged (1957), defines "pursuant" as:

"1. Acting or done in consequence or in prosecution (of anything); hence, agreeable; conformable; following; according * * *

"2. That is in pursuit or pursuing * * *."

KAVASJI v. INS

United States Court of Appeals, Seventh Circuit, 1982.
675 F.2d 236.

PER CURIAM.

Petitioner Ardesheer P. Kavasji seeks review of a final order of deportation issued against him by the Board of Immigration Appeals on September 3, 1980. The Board of Immigration Appeals affirmed the decision of an Immigration Law Judge [sic] which held that the petitioner was deportable under § 241(a)(2) of the Immigration and Nationality Act, since Kavasji had remained in the United States beyond the period authorized by the terms of his admission as a nonimmigrant student.

Ardesheer P. Kavasji is a twenty-five year old citizen and national of Pakistan who entered the United States on September 4, 1970 to study engineering at the Indiana Institute of Technology at Fort Wayne, Indiana. Kavasji was authorized as a nonimmigrant student to remain in the United States until July 30, 1979. In the early part of 1979, Kavasji sought to transfer from the Indiana Institute of Technology to Huntington College in Huntington, Indiana. To that end Kavasji requested permission from the Immigration and Naturalization Service ("INS") to transfer schools and to extend his stay in this country. In February 1979, Kavasji and his attorney prepared and mailed to the INS office in Huntington, Indiana a Form I–538 petition to transfer and a Form I–20 from Huntington College as required by INS regulation. According to Kavasji's counsel, the application for a transfer and extension were either lost in the mail or lost by the INS. Consequently, Kavasji never received authorization from the INS to transfer schools or to remain beyond July 30, 1979.

Kavasji nonetheless attended Huntington College without an application being filed. About August 10, 1979, Kavasji submitted another application for an extension of stay and a transfer of schools with the assistance of the Dean of Students of Huntington College. That application was denied on November 1, 1979 by the INS for the express reason that Kavasji violated his nonimmigration status by remaining in the United States beyond his authorized stay. Accordingly, the INS district director ordered Kavasji to depart by December 1, 1979.[a]

When Kavasji failed to leave the country by December 1, 1979, the INS commenced deportation proceedings against him. To that end the INS issued an Order to Show Cause dated January 7, 1980 charging that Kavasji was subject to deportation pursuant to § 241(a)(2) of the Immigration and Nationality Act for having remained in the United States for a longer time than permitted.

At the deportation hearing before an Immigration Law Judge on March 5, 1980, Kavasji admitted all of the allegations in the Order to Show Cause, including the fact that he had received a Form I–541 notification that his application for an extension was denied on November 1, 1979 because he was deemed an overstay. Kavasji's counsel argued that the district director's decision to deny an extension of a temporary

---

a. District directors can't issue deportation orders. What do you suppose the court—rather inartfully—is describing here? —eds.

stay was arbitrary and capricious in light of the fact that Kavasji had attempted in February of 1979 to obtain permission to transfer and to extend his stay. The hearing was adjourned in order to give Kavasji an opportunity to present his case to the district director for reconsideration of the earlier denial of his request for a temporary stay.

Upon the resumption of the deportation hearing proceedings Kavasji's attorney stated that the district director refused to reconsider Kavasji's case. His attorney again contended that the district director acted arbitrarily and capriciously and moved to terminate the proceedings. The Immigration Law Judge held that he had no jurisdiction to review the district director's denial of a temporary stay because the matter was strictly within the discretion of the district director. Accordingly, the Immigration Law Judge refused to admit evidence and argument concerning an alleged abuse of discretion by the district director.

In the Decision of the Immigration Law Judge dated May 15, 1980, the motion to terminate the proceedings submitted by Kavasji's counsel was denied on the ground that under relevant regulations of the Immigration and Naturalization Service there is no jurisdiction for the Immigration Law Judge to review the denial by the district director of an application for transfer of schools or extension of stay, citing 8 C.F.R. 103.1(n); 8 C.F.R. 214.1(c). It was further noted that under relevant regulation no appeal lies from the decision of the district director. 8 C.F.R. 214.2(f)(7). The Immigration Law Judge held that a nonimmigrant alien becomes deportable as an "overstay" when the period of his admission expires, unless he receives a grant of an extension of stay from the district director. Accordingly, Kavasji was found deportable by clear, convincing, and unequivocal evidence.

On appeal the Board of Immigration Appeals upheld the Immigration Law Judge's findings and conclusions and granted Kavasji until October 30, 1980 to depart voluntarily. On October 6, 1980 Kavasji filed this petition for review.

In this petition for review Kavasji claims that the action taken by the district director was a manifest abuse of discretion. Also Kavasji claims that it was error for the Immigration Law Judge to refuse to permit evidence pertinent to certain lost documents or concerning the alleged arbitrary and capricious action of the district director. Thus petitioner contends that the denial of the request to terminate the proceedings was improper and that deportability was not proven by clear, convincing, and unequivocal evidence.

The respondent INS on the other hand contends that this court does not have jurisdiction to review the district director's denial of the request for a transfer and extension of stay. The respondent is correct in this contention. Under § 106(a) of the Immigration and Nationality Act, this court's jurisdiction extends to "final orders of deportation ... made against aliens within the United States pursuant to administrative proceedings under § 242(b)." The Supreme Court in *Cheng Fan Kwok v. INS* held that the discretionary denial by a district director of a stay of deportation is not reviewable as a final order of deportation because

Congress restricted the application of § 106(a) to orders entered during deportation proceedings conducted under § 242(b), or directly challenging deportation orders themselves.

Since the applications to the district director for an extension of a temporary stay and to transfer were not submitted pursuant to a proceeding under § 242(b), nor were they incident to a motion to reopen such a proceeding, this court is without jurisdiction to review the district director's denial of the applications in question.

Although petitioner attempts to distinguish *Cheng* on the basis that the present case does not involve a denial of a stay of deportation as in *Cheng* but rather a denial of an extension of a temporary stay, petitioner does not show how that distinction is significant for the purpose of demonstrating that the discretionary determination by the district director in this case was made during the course of deportation proceedings. In short, Kavasji's challenge to the actions of the district director properly belongs in the district court. *See, e.g., Richards v. INS,* 554 F.2d 1173 (D.C.Cir.1977).

Finally, the regulations make clear that the Immigration Law Judge had no jurisdiction to review the district director's discretionary actions taken in this case. Therefore it was not error for the Immigration Law Judge to refuse to consider the evidence pertinent to Kavasji's claim that the district director abused its discretion.

The petitioner does not otherwise challenge the basis of the decision of the Immigration Law Judge. In any event, it is clear that the deportability of Kavasji was established by clear, convincing, and unequivocal evidence. Therefore the order of the Immigration and Naturalization Service requiring petitioner to depart voluntarily is affirmed.

Notes

1. Would it be possible for INS to avoid the prospect of piecemeal reviews in these circumstances by changing its regulations? What kinds of changes would bring the issues Kavasji wants to raise within the reach of the court of appeals? What might be the disadvantages of such changes? Should the regulations be modified in such a fashion?

2. *Kavasji* reflects the predominant view among the courts on the question of jurisdiction to review immigration determinations made outside the forum of a § 242(b) proceeding—even if those determinations were handed down earlier and form a crucial link in the chain of events that ultimately led to the finding of deportability. But there are a few exceptions. For example, in *Bachelier v. INS,* 625 F.2d 902 (9th Cir.1980), the court considered, as part of a review proceeding under § 106, the propriety of an earlier decision, under INA § 246, to rescind an adjustment of status previously granted under § 245. Under the regulations, rescission is adjudicated by an immigration judge, but the rescission proceedings are wholly separate from the deportation proceedings (which may or may not be instituted once permanent resident status is rescinded). To be sure, in *Bachelier,* if the earlier rescission order was valid,

there was no real dispute over the alien's deportability—but the same was true of *Kavasji*, with reference to the propriety of the district director's denial of his transfer application. The *Bachelier* court provides only a rather cryptic statement of reasons for extending its jurisdiction in this fashion (and in any event it found against the alien on the merits). Are *Bachelier* and *Kavasji* inconsistent? Are there any pertinent reasons for distinguishing the two situations? *See generally* Note, *Jurisdiction to Review Prior Orders and Underlying Statutes in Deportation Appeals,* 65 Va.L.Rev. 403 (1979).

Jurisdiction Under *Chadha*

The majority rule, as applied in *Kavasji*, marks out a bright line that is usually quite easy to apply. Jurisdiction extends to "orders entered during deportation proceedings conducted under § 242(b)." If the matter was not decided during such proceedings, review must be had elsewhere; the issue cannot come up as part of proceedings in the courts of appeals under § 106(a).

But that bright-line rule poses a problem when the alien levels a constitutional challenge at her deportation proceedings, and particularly when she claims that the underlying statute is itself unconstitutional. Under longstanding practice (similar to the practice of other administrative agencies, *see Califano v. Sanders,* 430 U.S. 99, 109, 97 S.Ct. 980, 986, 51 L.Ed.2d 192 (1977)), immigration judges and the BIA consider themselves to be without authority to hear constitutional challenges to the statutes they administer. Thus no matter how forcefully the alien protests that the provision is unconstitutional, and no matter how persuasive her position, there will be no determination on the matter as part of the proceedings under § 242(b). Is she then foreclosed from raising her constitutional claim in the court of appeals?

This jurisdictional issue reached the Supreme Court in the well-known case of *INS v. Chadha,* 462 U.S. 919, 103 S.Ct. 2764, 77 L.Ed.2d 317 (1983). See pp. 535–537 *supra.* There the alien petitioner, Chadha, initially had been granted suspension of deportation by an immigration judge under INA § 244, but the House of Representatives voted a resolution disapproving suspension, exercising its purported one-house veto authority under § 244(c)(2). Chadha contended that this legislative veto was unconstitutional. The Justice Department clearly agreed with Chadha on the merits of the constitutional issue; it had been arguing the point for years on behalf of Presidents of both political parties, both in the courts and before Congress. Nevertheless the Department decided that it had to go ahead and proceed with routine deportation of Chadha until directed otherwise by a court. Thus when the deportation order was entered following the purported House veto, Chadha petitioned for review under § 106(a). The Supreme Court ultimately used this case for its landmark ruling that legislative vetoes are unconstitutional, but first it had to deal with the tricky jurisdictional question posed by *Cheng Fan Kwok.*

Consider as you read the following passage from *Chadha* (the entirety of the Court's discussion of this jurisdictional issue) whether Kavasji could now insist, under *Chadha's* holding, that the court of appeals reach the merits of his challenge to the district director's denial of his transfer petition. We will then take up one court's post-*Chadha* attempt to determine what the Supreme Court meant in a case whose facts are much like *Kavasji*.

It is contended that the Court of Appeals lacked jurisdiction under § 106(a) of the Act. That section provides that a petition for review in the Court of Appeals "shall be the sole and exclusive procedure for the judicial review of all final orders of deportation ... made against aliens within the United States pursuant to administrative proceedings under section 242(b) of this Act." Congress argues that the one-House veto authorized by § 244(c)(2) takes place outside the administrative proceedings conducted under § 242(b), and that the jurisdictional grant contained in § 106(a) does not encompass Chadha's constitutional challenge.

In *Cheng Fan Kwok v. INS*, this Court held that "§ 106(a) embrace[s] only those determinations made during a proceeding conducted under § 242(b), including those determinations made incident to a motion to reopen such proceedings." It is true that one court has read *Cheng Fan Kwok* to preclude appeals similar to Chadha's. See *Dastmalchi v. INS*, 660 F.2d 880 (CA3 1981).[11] However, we agree with the Court of Appeals in this case that the term "final orders" in § 106(a) "includes all matters on which the validity of the final order is contingent, rather than only those determinations actually made at the hearing." 634 F.2d, at 412. Here, Chadha's deportation stands or falls on the validity of the challenged veto; the final order of deportation was entered against Chadha only to implement the action of the House of Representatives. Although the Attorney General was satisfied that the House action was invalid and that it should not have any effect on his decision to suspend deportation, he appropriately let the controversy take its course through the courts.

This Court's decision in *Cheng Fan Kwok, supra,* does not bar Chadha's appeal. There, after an order of deportation had been entered, the affected alien requested the INS to stay the execution of that order. When that request was denied, the alien sought review in the Court of Appeals under § 106(a). This Court's holding that the Court of Appeals lacked jurisdiction was

---

11. Under the Third Circuit's reasoning, judicial review under § 106(a) would not extend to the constitutionality of § 244(c)(2) because that issue could not have been tested during the administrative deportation proceedings conducted under § 242(b). *Dastmalchi v. INS*, 660 F.2d 880 (CA3 1981). The facts in *Dastmalchi* are distinguishable, however. In *Dastmalchi*, Iranian aliens who had entered the United States on nonimmi- grant student visas challenged a regulation that required them to report to the District Director of the INS during the Iranian hostage crisis. The aliens reported and were ordered deported after a § 242(b) proceeding. The aliens in *Dastmalchi* could have been deported irrespective of the challenged regulation. Here, in contrast, Chadha's deportation would have been *cancelled* but for § 244(c)(2).

based on the fact that the alien "did not 'attack the deportation order itself but instead [sought] relief not inconsistent with it.' " Here, in contrast, Chadha directly attacks the deportation order itself and the relief he seeks—cancellation of deportation—is plainly inconsistent with the deportation order. Accordingly, the Court of Appeals had jurisdiction under § 106(a) to decide this case.

103 S.Ct. at 2777–78.

MOHAMMADI–MOTLAGH v. INS

United States Court of Appeals, Ninth Circuit, 1984.
727 F.2d 1450.

HUG, CIRCUIT JUDGE:

Majid Mohammadi-Motlagh petitions for review of an order of deportation. He was found deportable because he violated the conditions of his nonimmigrant visa by transferring schools without obtaining prior permission. Mohammadi-Motlagh claims the District Director erred in refusing his transfer request. Because we are without jurisdiction to review that claim, we affirm the decision of the Board of Immigration Appeals.

Mohammadi-Motlagh, a native and citizen of Iran, entered the United States in January 1979 as a nonimmigrant student. He was authorized to study at the American Language and Cultural Institute in New York and later given permission to transfer to Wagner College, also in New York. In January 1980 Mohammadi-Motlagh transferred to the College of Great Falls in Montana. He neither sought nor received INS permission to make the transfer prior to enrolling at the college. In August 1980, after attending the college for several months, Mohammadi-Motlagh filed an application for permission to transfer. The District Director denied the request, noting that Mohammadi-Motlagh had been "in unauthorized attendance at the College of Great Falls for some seven months prior to submitting the instant request."

The INS then issued an order to show cause, charging that Mohammadi-Motlagh was subject to deportation for failure to comply with the conditions of his nonimmigrant status. In a hearing before an immigration judge, Mohammadi-Motlagh attempted to argue the merits of his transfer request. He claimed that transferring without prior permission was justified and that the delay in filing the transfer request occurred despite his best efforts to comply with the application requirement. The immigration judge did not consider these contentions because he concluded he had no jurisdiction to review the District Director's denial of Mohammadi-Motlagh's request. He found Mohammadi-Motlagh deportable and granted him voluntary departure. The BIA also refused to review the District Director's decision, citing 8 C.F.R. § 214.2(f)(7) (1982). It dismissed Mohammadi-Motlagh's appeal and ordered his voluntary departure within fifteen days.

Mohammadi-Motlagh's petition for review first challenges the refusals of the immigration judge and the BIA to review the decision of the District Director. The refusals were based on an interpretation of 8

C.F.R. § 214.2(f)(7), which provides that "[n]o appeal shall lie from the decision" of the District Director denying permission to transfer to another school. This interpretation is entitled to deference. *Tooloee v. INS*, 722 F.2d 1434, 1436 (9th Cir.1983); *Ghorbani v. INS*, 686 F.2d 784, 791 (9th Cir.1982). We have held the conclusion that the denial of an appeal right deprives the immigration judge and BIA of jurisdiction is not unreasonable. *Id.* We therefore reject Mohammadi-Motlagh's claim.

Mohammadi-Motlagh next contends we have jurisdiction to review the District Director's decision. In *Ghorbani*, we were presented with an almost identical factual situation. We held the District Director's decision was not a final order reviewable under INA § 106(a). *Id.* Following our decision in *Ghorbani*, the Supreme Court decided *INS v. Chadha*, 462 U.S. 919, 103 S.Ct. 2764, 77 L.Ed.2d 317 (1983), *aff'g* 634 F.2d 408 (9th Cir.1980). We must consider how *Chadha* affected our jurisdictional analysis in *Ghorbani*.

In *Ghorbani* our analysis began with section 106(a), which confers on the courts of appeals exclusive jurisdiction to review final orders of deportation made pursuant to administrative proceedings under § 242(b). We noted the Supreme Court had narrowly construed the instances in which courts of appeals could assume pendent jurisdiction over discretionary decisions made incident to the final deportation order. Two circumstances in which the use of pendent jurisdiction was justified were identified in *Ghorbani*: (1) when there has been a factual hearing on the issue of discretionary relief or (2) when such a hearing is unnecessary.

In *Chadha*, we held pendent jurisdiction permitted review of the House of Representatives' veto of the suspension of Chadha's deportation. 634 F.2d at 413. We defined pendent jurisdiction as encompassing certain determinations "on which the final order of deportation is contingent." *Id.* We then reviewed a purely legal question: the constitutionality of the one-house veto. Our review was made without the benefit of a prior administrative record. The immigration judge and the BIA had not considered this question since they lack authority to determine constitutional issues. However, review was possible without an administrative record since only a question of law was presented. *Ghorbani*, 686 F.2d at 790.

The Supreme Court's decision in *Chadha* approved our assumption of pendent jurisdiction. The Court emphasized that Chadha would not have been deported but for the veto. 462 U.S. at ___ & n. 11, 103 S.Ct. at 2777 & n. 11, 77 L.Ed.2d at 336 & n. 11. It thus sanctioned our definition of the class of cases encompassed by the grant of pendent jurisdiction. The Court did not consider, as we were required to in *Ghorbani*, the instances in which utilization of pendent jurisdiction is justified. Because it was presented with a purely legal question, the application of pendent jurisdiction to factual questions was not before the Court. *Chadha* therefore does not signify that the Court has retreated from the narrow construction of section 106(a) adopted in *Cheng Fan Kwok v. INS*, 392 U.S. 206, 216, 88 S.Ct. 1970, 1976, 20 L.Ed.2d 1037 (1968). Our jurisdictional analysis in

Ghorbani is consistent with each of these Supreme Court cases and thus remains viable.

As in *Ghorbani*, Mohammadi-Motlagh asserts challenges to the District Director's decision that raise factual questions as to whether discretion was properly exercised. The BIA lacked authority to hear and determine these factual issues and did not do so. We are therefore without jurisdiction to consider these claims. They must be raised in the first instance in the district court. * * *

The decision of the BIA is Affirmed.

Notes

1. The doctrine of pendent jurisdiction is usually associated with questions of federal court jurisdiction to consider state law claims for which there is otherwise no jurisdictional basis. The Supreme Court has held that federal courts may exercise pendent jurisdiction to hear such claims, despite the absence of an independent jurisdictional foundation, when the state claim shares "a common nucleus of operative fact" with a federal law claim over which the court clearly has cognizance. *See United Mine Workers v. Gibbs*, 383 U.S. 715, 725, 86 S.Ct. 1130, 1138, 16 L.Ed.2d 218 (1966). But exercise of such jurisdiction is discretionary, and the pendent cause of action is considered "a separate but parallel ground for relief." *Id.* at 722, 726, 86 S.Ct. at 1136, 1139. *Cf. Hagans v. Lavine*, 415 U.S. 528, 548, 94 S.Ct. 1372, 1385, 39 L.Ed.2d 577 (1974) (jurisdiction under 28 U.S.C.A. § 1343 to hear constitutional claim also authorizes exercise of pendent jurisdiction to hear related federal statutory claim; the opinion suggests that courts should more readily exercise pendent jurisdiction to hear other federal claims than they would to consider state law claims, owing to considerations of comity in a federal system).

Is the pendent jurisdiction rubric a helpful framework for making sense of the Supreme Court's unelaborated notion of "contingency"? Isn't a pendent claim the antithesis of what actually happened in the *Chadha* case? (Chadha's constitutional argument wasn't parallel and separate; it was fundamental to the deportation order itself.) The Ninth Circuit's decision in *Chadha*, moreover, which is quoted in the key passage of the Supreme Court's jurisdictional holding, never makes use of the "pendent jurisdiction" notion. *Cf. Ghorbani v. INS, supra*, 686 F.2d at 792 (Poole, J., concurring specially) (agreeing with the decision that the court lacked jurisdiction under § 106(a) to consider the district director's earlier ruling, but protesting application of the "pendent jurisdiction" terminology).[13]

Whether one uses this terminology or not, are the tests employed in *Mohammadi-Motlagh* sound means for deciding the reach of jurisdiction in the courts of appeals under the "contingency" rule? Would the courts

13. *See also Martinez de Mendoza v. INS*, 567 F.2d 1222, 1224–25 & n. 5 (3d Cir.1977), where the court of appeals took jurisdiction to consider a post-order denial of a stay of deportation by the district director. The case seems to fit more comfortably into customary notions of pendent jurisdiction, as the court notes, although it ultimately does not rely on the pendent jurisdiction theory as the basis for its power to decide the particular substantive issue.

be better advised to hold straightforwardly that § 106 reaches outside the issues determined in the § 242(b) hearing only when the alien challenges the constitutionality of the statutes? Or would they do better to use *Chadha* as the excuse for reaching nearly all pre-deportation-order disputes and thus undoing much of the unfortunate fragmentation of judicial review that came in the wake of *Cheng Fan Kwok* ?

2. Other courts wrestling with the meaning of the jurisdictional holding in *Chadha* have come up with different tests for implementation. But they have seemed just as reluctant as the Ninth Circuit in *Mohammadi-Motlagh* to find that *Chadha* opens wide the circuit court's doors to review of pre-deportation-order decisions. For example, in *Ghaelian v. INS*, 717 F.2d 950 (6th Cir.1983), the court rejected the attempt of a student in a situation similar to Mohammadi-Motlagh (he had overstayed his visa and sought a belated extension) to expand the range of review and have the court of appeals pass on certain earlier decisions of the district director. After quoting the key language from *Chadha*, the court went on (*id.* at 952):

> There remains, however, the difficulty of determining when an issue renders a final order "contingent" and is thus within the ambit of this court's jurisdiction. The Supreme Court's decision in *Chadha* indirectly offers two tests of "contingency": (1) does the deportation "stand or fall[ ] on the validity of the challenged [issue]"; (2) is the relief sought "plainly inconsistent with the deportation order".

How should Kavasji's claim be handled under these tests? How should Bachelier's? Are these criteria better or worse than the criteria employed in *Mohammadi-Motlagh* for deciding which matters not directly considered in a § 242(b) proceeding ought to be reviewed by court of appeals on a petition to review?

3. Given all the intricacies of practice under § 106(a), the judicial resources expended in resolving issues that arise, and the possible consequences for aliens should they guess wrong on the court where review is to be sought, should the petition-to-review procedure be retained? Recall the reasons underlying Congress's choice of this device. Are they still being served? If not, what should be done to overcome the problems?

Judge Friendly, after reviewing the jurisdictional confusion and the attendant delays caused by § 106(a), voiced strong views about the needed medicine: "The clear answer to this problem is to place appeals from all final deportation orders back in the district courts, and expect the courts of appeals to give expeditious treatment to those orders of the district courts that are appealed." H. Friendly, Federal Jurisdiction: A General View 175–76 (1973). Testifying before Congress ten years later, Maurice Roberts, editor of *Interpreter Releases* and former chairman of the BIA, suggested a different cure:

> INA § 106(a) [should be amended] to make it clear that in reviewing a final order of deportation the court shall review every challenged INS determination relevant to the alien's status, regardless of whether the determination was made as part of the

deportation proceedings or preceded or followed it. Under the present provision, as construed in *Cheng Fan Kwok,* only those issues raised and determined in the deportation hearing before the immigration judge and considered on appeal by the BIA are reviewable in the Court of Appeals. This makes for bifurcation of review, which § 106(a) was designed to eliminate. A one-package review of all related issues in the Court of Appeals under § 106(a) would make more sense.

The Immigration Reform and Control Act of 1983, Hearings Before the Subcomm. on Immigration, Refugees, and International Law of the House Comm. on the Judiciary, 98th Cong., 1st Sess. 955 (1983).[14]

We will consider in the final section of this Chapter the approach Congress came close to enacting as part of the unsuccessful Simpson-Mazzoli reform bills—an approach that differs from both of the above proposals. Be thinking about which changes you would make, if any, in the current judicial review scheme. *See also* Currie & Goodman, *Judicial Review of Federal Administrative Action: Quest for the Optimum Forum,* 75 Colum.L.Rev. 1, 35–36 (1975) (basically endorsing the current scheme because judicial review of immigration decisions made outside the § 242(b) hearing often requires further factual development (best done in a district court) owing to the inadequacies of the informal agency record).

SECTION C. REVIEW IN THE DISTRICT COURT

Both *Cheng Fan Kwok* and *Kavasji* state that the aliens involved should have gone into the district court to secure judicial review of their particular complaints. But exactly how does one get there? Federal courts remain courts of limited jurisdiction, and a plaintiff must plead and prove his jurisdictional basis.

The Administrative Procedure Act, as we have noted, establishes a broad presumption that administrative actions are reviewable. But the Supreme Court held, after years of controversy in the lower courts, that the APA did not itself constitute an independent grant of jurisdiction. *Califano v. Sanders,* 430 U.S. 99, 103, 97 S.Ct. 980, 983, 51 L.Ed.2d 192 (1977). A litigant seeking district court review must anchor his claim elsewhere, although, once he does so, he can usually take advantage of the other general provisions of the APA governing judicial review.

One important potential jurisdictional foundation is 28 U.S.C.A. § 1331, which vests in the district courts general federal question jurisdiction. Until 1976, § 1331 imposed a jurisdictional amount requirement:

---

14. Roberts has also been a leading advocate for the creation of a separate Article I court system (with both "trial" and "appellate" levels) as the exclusive forum for review of decisions under the immigration laws—save for ultimate review authority in the Supreme Court on petition for certiorari. *See* Roberts, *Proposed: A Specialized Statutory Immigration Court,* 18 San Diego L.Rev. 1 (1980). The Select Commission on Immigration and Refugee Policy endorsed this basic idea, *see* SCIRP, Final Report, 248–50 but Congress has not chosen to pursue it in its recent consideration of immigration reform legislation.

district court jurisdiction attached only if the amount in controversy exceeded $10,000. Since immigration disputes usually involve personal stakes not easily translated into dollar figures, this could have been a difficult barrier. But in 1976, Congress amended the section to eliminate the monetary requirement where suit was brought against the United States, a federal agency, or an official or employee sued in official capacity. Pub.L. No. 94–574, § 2, 90 Stat. 2721 (1976). (Section 1 of the same statute amended the APA to make clear that sovereign immunity should not bar otherwise proper suits brought to secure judicial review of agency action. *See* 5 U.S.C.A. § 702, as amended.) Then in 1980 Congress determined that "arising under" jurisdiction should no longer depend on the monetary stakes, no matter who the defendant might be. Pub.L. No. 96–486, § 2(a), 94 Stat. 2369 (1980). That amendment changed § 1331 to a simple and direct grant of power. It now reads in full: "The district courts shall have original jurisdiction of all civil actions arising under the Constitution, laws, or treaties of the United States."

One might expect that this change would greatly simplify litigation of immigration disputes in the district courts, and for the most part it has. But there are some remaining complications. Most importantly, § 1331 does not override other specialized arrangements for review of agency determinations; § 1331 jurisdiction is still subject to preclusion-of-review statutes enacted by Congress. *See Califano v. Sanders,* 430 U.S. at 105, 97 S.Ct. at 984. This means, for example, that an alien who wants to lodge a direct challenge to an order directing his deportation must still adhere to the requirements of § 106(a) (the "sole and exclusive procedure" for such review); he must file a petition for review in the court of appeals.[15]

But that may not be the only obstacle to the use of § 1331, for the INA contains another jurisdictional provision deriving from the original enactment in 1952. Section 279 reads:

> The district courts of the United States shall have jurisdiction of all causes, civil and criminal, arising under any of the provisions of this title. It shall be the duty of the United States attorney of the proper district to prosecute every such suit when brought by the United States. Notwithstanding any other law, such prosecutions or suits may be instituted at any place in the United States at which the violation may occur or at which the person charged with a violation under section 275 or 276 may be apprehended. No suit or proceeding for a violation of any of the provisions of this title shall be settled, compromised, or discontinued without the consent of the court in which it is pending and any such settlement, compromise, or discontinuance shall be entered of record with the reasons therefor.

The last three sentences suggest that Congress was preoccupied with granting jurisdiction in cases where the government would be the plaintiff

15. This subordination to preclusion-of-review provisions apparently also accounts for the continued refusal of most courts to review the denial of a visa by a United States consul. *See generally Pena v. Kissinger,* 409 F.Supp. 1182 (S.D.N.Y.1976), considered in Chapter Three, *supra.*

(such as in proceedings to collect on a bond forfeiture). Indeed, it might even have been possible at one time to read the statute as a grant of judicial authority *only* when the United States was a plaintiff. But the courts have not moved in this direction at all; § 279 has been read as a grant of district court jurisdiction in a wide variety of settings.

Perhaps the most perplexing questions derive from the limitation in § 279 to "causes arising under any of the provisions *of this title.*" The reference is to title II ("Immigration") of the INA, which includes §§ 201 through 293. Thus excluded from the jurisdictional grant are sections 101 through 106 (which are part of title I, General), all of title III, Nationality and Naturalization, and title IV, Miscellaneous and Refugee Assistance.

This restriction proved fatal to the plaintiffs' attempt in *Chen Chaun-Fa v. Kiley,* 459 F.Supp. 762 (S.D.N.Y.1978), to secure early judicial review in the district court. The plaintiffs had unsuccessfully petitioned the district director for political asylum. At the time, prior to passage of the Refugee Act of 1980, there was no specific statutory provision for political asylum,[16] and the petition had been filed under what was then 8 C.F.R. Part 108. The district court determined that it had no jurisdiction. After quoting the language of the first sentence of § 279, the court stated:

> Because this section appears in [title] II of the Act, the jurisdiction of the district courts is limited to causes arising under [title] II.
>
> Plaintiffs' request that this Court review the decision of the INS District Director denying political asylum does not present a claim arising under [title] II. Plaintiff's asylum claims were submitted pursuant to the regulations set out in 8 C.F.R. Part 108. The statutory basis for these regulations is section 103 of the Act [the general grant of authority to the Attorney General to administer and enforce the immigration laws], a provision contained in the *first* [title] of the Act. Thus, section 279 fails on its face to confer jurisdiction on this Court.

459 F.Supp. at 764. This holding on the application of § 279 also worked to foreclose relief under 28 U.S.C.A. § 1331:

> The only jurisdictional basis alleged by plaintiffs in their complaint is 28 U.S.C. section 1331. This section confers jurisdiction on federal courts to review agency action, subject, however, to preclusion of review statutes created by Congress. *See Califano v. Sanders.* This exception to judicial review of agency decisions clearly applies here.
>
> We find that Congress intended to limit judicial review to those claims arising under [title] II of the Immigration and Nationality Act. This conclusion is based on the legislative

---

16. There was a closely related provision in § 243(h), however, which authorized the withholding of deportation of aliens who would be subject to persecution in their homelands. But the court evidently treated this as a wholly separate form of relief, or at least as a provision unavailable as a title II hook for jurisdiction under § 279. On the complex interrelationships between political asylum and withholding of deportation under § 243(h), *see* Chapter Eight, *infra.*

history of section 279 which evidences a deliberate attempt to narrow the jurisdiction of the district court.

Id. at 765. A footnote contained the court's entire discussion of that legislative history (*id.* at 764 n. 6):

Congress' intent to limit jurisdiction to causes arising under the second [title of the INA] appears to have been deliberate. In 1917, the Act vested the district courts with jurisdiction of all causes arising under any of the provisions of the *Act.* In 1940, this was amended to causes arising under any of the provisions of the *Chapter.* Jurisdiction was further restricted in 1952 when the jurisdictional section was amended to include only causes arising under the second [title] of the Act.

Do you find this holding persuasive? [17] Does § 279 read like a preclusion-of-review statute? (It is, at the very least, worded quite differently from § 106(a) and (b), which are unambiguously intended to preclude review of deportation and exclusion orders in any other manner than the course specified therein.) If the court's ruling is correct, then any immigration decisions based solely on title I of the INA—including any decisions based on regulations adopted solely under the Attorney General's general authority bestowed by § 103—will escape judicial review. Does the legislative history the court recites demonstrate a deliberate congressional decision to foreclose district court review altogether in these circumstances? What would be Congress's reason for limiting review in this fashion?

Cf. Martinez v. Bell, 468 F.Supp. 719, 726 & n. 6 (S.D.N.Y.1979) (similarly suggesting that the limitations on review under § 279 would restrict review under § 1331); *Karmali v. INS,* 707 F.2d 408 (9th Cir.1983) (approving jurisdiction in the district court to review denial of intra-company transferee visa application under INA § 101(a)(15)(L), because denial also implicated § 214(c), which is within title II).

Whatever complications holdings like *Chen Chaun-Fa* may introduce upon occasion, most immigration disputes do arise under title II of the INA. Thus, most of the time a plaintiff seeking relief in the district court will have little difficulty invoking jurisdiction under either § 279 or 28 U.S.C.A. § 1331—or both—provided only that she is not directly challenging an exclusion or deportation order, for which § 106 unambiguously provides exclusive review channels. (She will also have to be sure she has standing to bring the suit—that is, that she is a proper party with a sufficient personal stake to initiate the action. *See* G & R § 8.3.) The Gordon and Rosenfield treatise lists the following matters which have been held reviewable in the district courts (with comprehensive citations for each category, omitted here):

denials of visa petitions, registry, benefits under the agricultural workers program, waivers for exchange visitors, denial of parole

---

17. The court also based its dismissal on a more solidly grounded ruling that the plaintiffs had not adequately exhausted administrative remedies, since they could essentially renew their asylum claim before the immigration judge and then, if unsuccessful, secure judicial review in the court of appeals. 459 F.Supp. at 765.

to entry applicant, of approval for a school qualified to accept nonimmigrant students, or withdrawal of such approval, change from one nonimmigrant status to another, denial of a labor certification, improper seizure or retention of the alien's passport, denial of extension of temporary stay, of asylum claim, claim of arbitrary, discriminatory, and unconstitutional action in bringing deportation proceeding when prosecutive discretion usually exercised to withhold deportation proceedings in similar cases, exclusion from a list of companies authorized to conduct immigration medical examinations, breach of immigration bond, denial of advance parole, and adjustment of status.

G & R § 8.23.   The list probably does not exhaust the possibilities.

But if all these matters are subject to review in the district courts, when should or must review be sought? Congress thought it important to confine the period for bringing a petition to review under § 106(a) to six months after entry of the deportation order (actually a rather generous length of time compared to the periods afforded elsewhere in the American administrative and judicial system for seeking further review of initial orders).   Does any comparable statute of limitations restrict actions under § 279?   Could Kavasji go back even today and demand district court review of the denial of his transfer application?   As a matter of policy, should he be allowed to?   Congress paid heed to this difficulty in its deliberations on the Simpson-Mazzoli reform bills, as we shall see in Section F below.

SECTION D.   OTHER RESTRICTIONS ON JUDICIAL REVIEW

1. EXHAUSTION OF REMEDIES

A fundamental principle of administrative law ordinarily requires a party to exhaust available administrative remedies before invoking a court's authority to review the decision. *See, e.g., Myers v. Bethlehem Shipbuilding Co.,* 303 U.S. 41, 50–52, 58 S.Ct. 459, 463–64, 82 L.Ed. 638 (1938); *McKart v. United States,* 395 U.S. 185, 193–94, 89 S.Ct. 1657, 1662–63, 23 L.Ed.2d 194 (1969); *McGee v. United States,* 402 U.S. 479, 483–86, 91 S.Ct. 1565, 1568–70, 29 L.Ed.2d 47 (1971). The exhaustion rule "is based on the need to allow agencies to develop the facts, to apply the law in which they are particularly expert, and to correct their own errors. The rule ensures that whatever judicial review is available will be informed and narrowed by the agencies' own decisions. It also avoids duplicative proceedings, and often the agency's ultimate decision will obviate the need for judicial intervention." *Schlesinger v. Councilman,* 420 U.S. 738, 756–57, 95 S.Ct. 1300, 1312–13, 43 L.Ed.2d 591 (1975). Occasionally this principle blocks premature district court review of immigration decisions when an alien seeks the court's aid under general grants of jurisdiction set forth in INA § 279 and 28 U.S.C.A. § 1331, even though neither of those sections specifically mentions the exhaustion requirement. *See, e.g., Chen Chaun-Fa v. Kiley,* 459 F.Supp. 762, 765 (S.D.N.Y.1979) (alternative ground for dismissal); G & R § 8.4.

But when a petitioner seeks judicial review of an exclusion or deportation order under INA § 106, he must contend not just with the general principle, but also with a specific statutory requirement set forth in § 106(c): "An order of deportation or exclusion shall not be reviewed by any court if the alien has not exhausted the administrative remedies available to him as of right under the immigration laws and regulations * * *." The following case depicts the usual implementation of this provision.

BAK v. INS

United States Court of Appeals, Third Circuit, 1982.
682 F.2d 441.

PER CURIAM:

Petitioners arrived in this country as visitors for pleasure from Poland, Josef Bak in November 1979 and Teresa Dworniczak in March 1980. Both overstayed the times appointed for their departure, and the Immigration and Naturalization Service (INS) instituted deportation proceedings. On September 8, 1980, both were found deportable for overstays under INA § 241(a)(2) and were granted the right to depart voluntarily prior to January 8, 1981. Petitioners did not appeal these decisions by the immigration judge to the Board of Immigration Appeals; in fact, they both specifically waived this right.

Petitioners subsequently requested that the immigration judge reopen their deportation proceedings so that they could apply for political asylum in the United States. On March 20, 1981, the immigration judge denied these motions to reopen, on the ground that "no new facts are available, which were not available at the original deportation hearing." Petitioners did not appeal this decision to the Board of Immigration Appeals either; instead, they filed petitions for review with this Court pursuant to INA § 106.

The INS has moved to dismiss these consolidated appeals, claiming that the Court is without jurisdiction to entertain the petitions. We agree.

At the outset, we note that we have no jurisdiction to review the immigration judge's original deportation orders. Section 106(a)(1) clearly provides that "a petition for review may be filed not later than six months from the date of the final deportation order." Petitioners here are out of time: they received their orders to deport on September 8, 1980, but delayed filing this appeal until July 14, 1981, more than six months later. *See Chudshevid v. Immigration and Naturalization Service,* 641 F.2d 780, 783 (9th Cir.1981); *Oum v. Immigration and Naturalization Service,* 613 F.2d 51 (4th Cir.1980).

The fact that we have no jurisdiction to review the underlying deportation orders does not end our inquiry, however, for petitioners moved before the immigration judge to reopen their deportation proceedings. These motions were denied on March 20, 1981, and the present petitions were filed within six months of this latter date. The general rule is that a motion to reopen deportation proceedings is a new, independently reviewable order within the jurisdiction of the court of appeals pursuant to section 106. *Giova v. Rosenberg,* 379 U.S. 18, 85 S.Ct. 156, 13 L.Ed.2d 90 (1964), *reversing* 308 F.2d 347 (9th Cir.1962); *see Bufalino v. Immigration and Naturalization Service,* 473 F.2d 728, 737 (3d Cir.1973) (Adams, J., concurring) (while ordinarily "the right to appeal from an order of deportation is extinguished when the six-month period expires," a court of appeals "may review judgments on motions to reopen"; therefore, limited jurisdiction was present to consider whether the INS abused its discretion in denying petitioner's motion to reopen); *see also Jacobe v. Immigration and Naturalization Service,* 578 F.2d 42 (3d Cir.1978) (Service's refusal to reopen proceedings was subject to review for abuse of discretion).

Despite this general rule, we have no jurisdiction to review petitioners' motions to reopen in the matter *sub judice,* because petitioners failed to exhaust their administrative remedies—that is, they did not appeal the immigration judge's refusal to reopen their proceedings to the Board of Immigration Appeals. Section 106(c) of the Act explicitly proscribes judicial review of an order of deportation if the alien "has not exhausted the administrative remedies available to him as of right under the immigration laws and regulations." Because petitioners never sought review by the Board of the immigration judge's denial of their motions to reopen, we have no jurisdiction to entertain these appeals. *See Jacobe, supra,* 578 F.2d at 44 ("Failure to exhaust administrative remedies results in a lack of jurisdiction in the Court of Appeals").

Anticipating this outcome, petitioners argue that they should not be obligated to exhaust, because to do so would be "futile." Petitioners contend that exhaustion is not necessary if an order is challenged solely on an issue of law. They claim that the immigration judge, in refusing to reopen their proceedings, did so because he was absolutely bound by Service regulations (specifically, 8 C.F.R. §§ 103.5 & 242.22), and that the Board, had it confronted their appeals, would have arrived at precisely the same result because of these regulations. Thus petitioners seek protection under the rule of *Beltre v. Kiley,* 470 F.Supp. 87, 89 (S.D.N.Y.1979). In that case, the court deemed exhaustion unnecessary because the INS district director reached a decision mandated by an INS definitional regulation; the court found, therefore, that if the matter had been presented to the Board, it could not help but have rendered the same decision. *Beltre* is inapplicable here, however. The regulations about which petitioners complain merely provide for the possibility of reopening a deportation proceeding, and direct the immigration judge to reopen only if evidence that is "material and was not available and could not have been discovered or presented" at the original hearing is proffered. These regulations did not in any sense "dictate" the outcome of petitioners' motions. The Board, had an appeal been brought to it, quite conceivably could have determined that the immigration judge erred in not opening the proceedings anew, in view of the showing made to him by petitioners.

This case, then, is unlike *Beltre,* in which the decision of the Board was foreordained because of explicit regulatory mandates. Here, the Board could have reversed the immigration judge, and thus exhaustion is necessary under section 106(c) and *Jacobe.*[1]

We conclude that we have no jurisdiction to review any of petitioners' claims having to do with the validity of their underlying deportation orders. With respect to the motions to reopen, we dismiss these petitions because petitioners failed to exhaust their administrative remedies.

Notes

1. This case reflects many of the salient rules that apply when an alien seeks reopening or reconsideration of exclusion or deportation proceedings. First, there is no time limit on filing such a motion. Protection against abuse of this device ostensibly derives from the relatively stringent substantive standards observed before the motion will be granted. *See generally INS v. Wang,* 450 U.S. 139, 101 S.Ct. 1027, 67 L.Ed.2d 123 (1981), reprinted in Chapter Six, *supra.* Second, the motion is filed with whichever authority, BIA or immigration judge, last considered the matter. *See* 8 C.F.R. §§ 3.2, 103.5, 242.22 (1984). Bak here, for example, properly filed his motion to reopen with the immigration judge, because he had waived his rights to take the initial deportation order up to the BIA. Finally, in deportation cases, the alien has a new six-month period after the denial of a motion to reopen or reconsider during which to seek review in the court of appeals under § 106(a). But, under the prevailing doctrine, that denial does not then give the court of appeals authority to reach the merits of the original deportation order. The court considers only whether the BIA abused its discretion in denying the motion (or approving the immigration judge's denial of the motion). *See* G & R § 8.9Ab.[18]

2. The *Bak* case refers to two judge-made exceptions to the exhaustion requirement: when pursuit of the additional remedies would be "futile," and when there is a convincing showing of "fundamental errors." Are these exceptions consistent with the statute? Aren't errors that are convincingly fundamental the kind most likely to be corrected in the administrative review process without having to draw on judicial resources?

In *Haitian Refugee Center v. Smith,* 676 F.2d 1023 (5th Cir.1982), the court carved out what may be an even larger potential exception to the

1. We note that this is not a situation in which the exhaustion requirement might be waived as the result of a convincing showing that "fundamental errors" were committed in the administrative proceedings, *see McLeod v. Peterson,* 283 F.2d 180 (3d Cir. 1960).

18. If the motion to reopen or reconsider is filed within the six-month period, however, and the alien then prosecutes a timely petition after the motion is denied, the court of appeals may have jurisdiction to consider both that denial and the original deportation order. *Chudshevid v. INS,* 641 F.2d 780, 784 (9th Cir.1981).

exhaustion requirement. The plaintiffs there, a class of over 4000 deportable Haitians who had sought political asylum in the United States, claimed that they were denied due process and equal protection in the course of accelerated processing carried out by INS. As the district court had summarized the issues, "the gravamen of the plaintiffs' complaint is that INS [including immigration judges] instituted a program 'to achieve expedited mass deportation of Haitian nationals' irrespective of the merits of an individual Haitian's asylum application and without regard to the constitutional, treaty, statutory, and administrative rights of the plaintiff class."

Since regular deportation processing, including review by the BIA, had not been concluded in most of the cases by the time the district court ruled, the complaint obviously presented significant questions under exhaustion-of-remedies doctrine and specifically under § 106(c). The Fifth Circuit nonetheless ruled that the district court had jurisdiction. We set forth here that portion of the opinion (676 F.2d at 1032–35) dealing with the three counts, out of a much lengthier complaint, which specifically focused on asserted procedural defaults by the immigration judges as part of the proceedings conducted under § 242(b).

HAITIAN REFUGEE CENTER v. SMITH

United States Court of Appeals, Fifth Circuit, 1982.
676 F.2d 1023.

We proceed now to examine the jurisdictional issues raised by the government's appeal. With respect to the first three counts of the plaintiffs' complaint, the government presents two arguments: (1) the district court lacked subject matter jurisdiction because these matters lie within the exclusive jurisdiction conferred upon the courts of appeals in § 106(a), and (2) even if the district court properly had jurisdiction, it should have declined to exercise that jurisdiction because the plaintiffs have failed to exhaust their administrative remedies. * * *

A

Under section 106(a) of the Immigration and Nationality Act, the courts of appeals are vested with exclusive jurisdiction to review "all final orders of deportation ... made against aliens within the United States pursuant to administrative proceedings under section 242(b) [deportation hearings] ...." According to the government, the Supreme Court has construed the scope of a court of appeals' jurisdiction under this statute to encompass all determinations made by an immigration judge during and incident to a deportation hearing and reviewable by the Board of Immigration Appeals (BIA). *Foti v. INS,* 375 U.S. 217, 229, 84 S.Ct. 306, 313, 11 L.Ed.2d 281 (1963). The first three counts in the complaint attack aspects of the deportation proceedings—the failure to suspend proceedings when an asylum claim was raised, the setting of ten-day limits for filing asylum claims, and the mass scheduling of hearings.

The government's point is not without merit. * * * [T]he Court in *Cheng Fan Kwok v. INS,* 392 U.S. 206, 88 S.Ct. 1970, 20 L.Ed.2d 1037

(1968), held that a district director's denial of a stay of deportation was not reviewable in the first instance in the court of appeals. The Court's analysis broadly suggested, however, that any attack *upon the proceeding* in which a deportation order was entered or upon any matter " 'intimately and immediately associated' " with the final order or *"governed by the regulations applicable to the deportation proceeding* itself, and ... ordinarily presented to the special inquiry officer who entered the deportation order" would fall within the court of appeals' exclusive jurisdiction under section 106(a).

Under the principles of these cases, it is arguable that count one (failure to suspend the deportation hearing) is reviewable only in the court of appeals. The ruling at issue was made by the immigration judge during the course of the deportation hearing, was a matter governed by INS Operations Instructions, and presumably would be reviewable by the BIA upon appeal of the deportation order itself. Whether counts two and three allege actions within section 106(a) jurisdiction is even more ambiguous.

Notwithstanding any surface appeal to the government's argument, we are convinced that insofar as the first three counts set forth matters alleged to be part of a pattern and practice by immigration officials to violate the constitutional rights of a class of aliens they constitute wrongs which are independently cognizable in the district court under its federal question jurisdiction.[22] Although a court of appeals may have sole jurisdiction to review alleged procedural irregularities in an individual deportation hearing *to the extent these irregularities may provide a basis for reversing an individual deportation order,* that is not to say that a program, pattern or scheme by immigration officials to violate the constitutional rights of aliens is not a separate matter subject to examination by a district court and to the entry of at least declaratory and injunctive relief. The distinction we draw is one between the authority of a court of appeals to pass upon the merits of an individual deportation order and any action in the deportation proceeding to the extent it may affect the merits determination, on the one hand, and, on the other, the authority of a district court to wield its equitable powers when a wholesale, carefully orchestrated, program of constitutional violations is alleged.

In concluding that the district court had jurisdiction over the first three counts, we wish to emphasize the factual uniqueness of this case. Our holding is not to be construed as permitting a constitutional challenge in the district court based on a procedural ruling in a deportation proceeding with which an alien is dissatisfied. We refuse to condone any such end-run around the administrative process. Casting as a constitutional violation an interlocutory procedural ruling by an immigration judge will not confer jurisdiction on the district court. Such a result would indeed defeat the congressional purpose behind the enactment of section 106(a)—the elimination of dilatory tactics by aliens challenging deportation orders in piecemeal fashion. Congress resolved this problem

---

22. 28 U.S.C. § 1331(a). The district court is also given jurisdiction over claims arising under the immigration statutes. INA § 279.

by consolidating jurisdiction over challenges to final orders of deportation in one court, the court of appeals. We do not intend by our holding today to emasculate that solution, and given the narrowness of our holding, we do not expect such a result.

B

The government also contends that the procedural errors challenged in counts one through three and in counts four through sixteen are subject to internal agency review and, therefore, are not subject to judicial review prior to exhaustion of available administrative remedies.[24] As a general rule parties are required to pursue administrative remedies before resorting to the courts to challenge agency action. We agree with the district court, however, that the exhaustion requirement is not a jurisdictional prerequisite but a matter committed to the sound discretion of the trial court. *NLRB v. Industrial Union of Marine and Shipbuilding Workers,* 391 U.S. 418, 419, 426 n. 8, 88 S.Ct. 1717, 1719, 1723 n. 8, 20 L.Ed.2d 706 (1968); *see Ecology Center of Louisiana, Inc. v. Coleman,* 515 F.2d 860, 865–66 (5th Cir.1975). For a number of reasons, we conclude that the district court did not abuse its discretion in exercising jurisdiction notwithstanding any failure of the plaintiffs to exhaust administrative remedies.

The policies advanced by allowing the administrative process to run its full course are not thwarted by judicial intervention in this case. Among those policies are (1) allowing the agency to develop a more complete factual record; (2) permitting the exercise of agency discretion and expertise on issues requiring this; (3) preventing deliberate disregard and circumvention of established agency procedures; and (4) enhancing judicial efficiency and eliminating the need for judicial vindication of legal rights by giving the agency the first opportunity to correct any error. *McKart v. United States,* 395 U.S. 185, 193–95, 89 S.Ct. 1657, 1662–63, 23 L.Ed.2d 194 (1969); *see Ecology Center of Louisiana, Inc.,* 515 F.2d at 866.

With respect to the plaintiffs' attack on actions taken by immigration judges (counts 1–3), further development of the factual record via completion of deportation hearings and subsequent appeal to the BIA would not significantly aid judicial review; to the extent these procedural irregularities are alleged to constitute part of a scheme denying the due process and equal protection rights of the Haitians, they raise legal and not factual issues. Moreover, they present the kind of issues on which the INS possesses no particular expertise. In addition, there is no danger that the exercise of jurisdiction will promote disregard of agency procedures since we have indicated above that it is the rare case in which jurisdiction to review procedural rulings made in a deportation hearing properly lies in the district court.

Finally, the judicial efficiency argument fails to convince us that the trial court should have insisted on exhaustion. As did the district court,

---

24. The members of the plaintiff class are at varying stages in the administrative process.

we find the rationale of *Mathews v. Eldridge,* 424 U.S. 319, 96 S.Ct. 893, 47 L.Ed.2d 18 (1976), more persuasive. Faced with a procedural due process attack on the adequacy of an agency's proceedings and an exhaustion of remedies argument, the Supreme Court deemed it insignificant that the agency in that case possessed the power to change the content of its procedures and thus could have pretermitted the necessity for judicial intervention. The Court commented: "It is unrealistic to expect that the Secretary would consider substantial changes in the current administrative review system at the behest of a single aid recipient raising a constitutional challenge in an adjudicatory context." The assumption that the INS or the BIA would have substantially revised the procedures established for the Haitian program is equally naive. In addition, in concluding that review of the plaintiff's constitutional challenge was appropriate in *Mathews* despite a conceded failure to exhaust internal agency review measures, the Court deemed it significant that the plaintiff's "constitutional challenge is entirely collateral to his substantive claim of entitlement" to the benefit denied him by the agency. Similarly here the plaintiffs mount a constitutional attack on the procedures devised for the processing of their asylum claims and do not seek a reversal of the district director's denial of their claims for asylum.

In sum, we believe that judicial economy was enhanced by the district judge's consideration of counts 1–3 in light of the role the immigration judges were alleged to play in the single scheme to deny the Haitians' constitutional rights.[26] The doctrine of exhaustion of administrative remedies erected no bar to the district court's jurisdiction, and the trial judge acted within his discretion in considering these claims.

Notes

1. The court concludes that the exhaustion of remedies requirement "is not a jurisdictional prerequisite but a matter committed to the sound discretion of the trial court," citing a labor law case and an environmental law case. But the court here was not simply adapting a common-law doctrine to make it work in a particular setting. It had before it a specific statutory requirement. In *Cheng Fan Kwok,* the court stated that jurisdictional statutes "must be construed both with precision and with fidelity to the terms by which Congress has expressed its wishes." Does the court's interpretation here meet that standard?

2. The court stresses that the exception to § 106 exclusivity recognized here should be taken as a narrow one. More than once it emphasizes that it will not countenance end-runs around the procedural framework established by the statute. But isn't this brave assertion a bit naive in light of the standards the court establishes for invoking the exception? The district court appears to have jurisdiction—and the exhaustion requirement appears waivable—whenever "a wholesale, carefully orchestrated, program of constitutional violations *is alleged"* (emphasis added).

---

26. The district court found that the immigration judges worked hand in hand with the district director to expedite the processing of Haitians at all costs and thus were an integral part of the accelerated program which the plaintiffs attack.

What is to prevent any deportation respondent with a colorable complaint about his treatment from alleging that his plight is a common one affecting a whole class of similarly situated aliens? Of course, INS may deny that such a pattern exists, but INS likewise denied in this case that any unconstitutional conspiracy was underway. Wouldn't those denials go to the merits rather than the court's jurisdiction? *Cf. Jean v. Nelson,* 727 F.2d 957, 979–81 (11th Cir.1984), *cert. granted,* ___ U.S. ___, 105 S.Ct. 563, 83 L.Ed.2d 504 (1984), where the court relied on the *HRC v. Smith* doctrine to hold that the district court had jurisdiction to consider a particular facet of the plaintiffs' claim despite their failure to exhaust administrative remedies, but then went ahead to rule on the merits that INS's challenged practice violated no constitutional or statutory rights.

3. Take a close look at the court's detailed reasons for excusing the plaintiffs' failure to exhaust administrative remedies, beginning with the third-to-last paragraph of the excerpt above. Why is it that counts 1–3 are seen to raise legal rather than factual issues? Is this a fair characterization? The BIA was not specifically named as a party to the claimed conspiracy to deny constitutional, statutory, and administrative rights. Why does the court assume that no relief would be forthcoming if plaintiffs had to pursue appeals to the Board before coming into court?

2. DEPARTURE FROM THE COUNTRY WHILE REVIEW IS PENDING

Section 106(c) not only denies review rights when an alien fails to exhaust remedies. It also states: "An order of deportation or exclusion shall not be reviewed by any court if the alien * * * has departed from the United States after issuance of the order." [19] What does this requirement mean, and why did Congress include it? What if the alien's departure is forced upon him by pressing business, by illness in the family, by a need for indispensable personal medical treatment, or by alleged government misbehavior?

In *Mendez v. INS,* 563 F.2d 956 (9th Cir.1977), INS executed a deportation order about one month after it had become final. This was permissible, for § 106 grants no automatic stay during the six months an alien is allowed to petition for review to the courts of appeals. A stay takes effect automatically (subject to being vacated by the court of appeals) only when the petition is served on INS. But here INS provided no notice of the impending removal to the alien's counsel of record, as it was required to do under the regulations. Violation of the regulation was uncontested. INS nevertheless contended that the court lacked jurisdiction to consider the case because of the departure preclusion in § 106(c). The court responded (*id.* at 958–59):

> We are of the opinion that "departure" in the context of § 106 cannot mean "departure in contravention of procedural due process." We hold that "departure" means "legally executed" departure when effected by the government. We base our

19. In parallel fashion, the regulations bar BIA consideration of a motion to reopen or reconsider if the alien has departed from the country. 8 C.F.R. § 3.2 (1984).

holding on the Supreme Court's decision in *Delgadillo v. Carmichael,* 332 U.S. 388, 68 S.Ct. 10, 92 L.Ed. 17 (1947). In that case the Court held that an alien does not make an "entry" into the United States when he had no intent to "depart," or left involuntarily. * * *

Appellee's contention that its decisions are immune from judicial review when the alien is physically out of the country— without regard to the manner in which this "departure" was accomplished—is just such a "captious interpretation" [of the kind condemned in *Delgadillo*]. Appellee's argument would serve to thwart the jurisdiction of this court in a case where the alien has been "kidnapped" and removed as easily as it would apply to this case involving deportation in derogation of procedural due process.

* * *

Nor is it necessary to invoke constitutional grounds in order to dispose of this appeal. Courts have looked with disfavor upon actions taken by federal agencies which have violated their own regulations. * * *

Here, failure to notify appellant's counsel amounted not only to a violation of 8 C.F.R. 292.5(a), but also to appellant's right to counsel as provided in INA § 242(b). We order the Immigration and Naturalization Service to admit appellant into the United States, granting appellant the same status he held prior to the May 15, 1975 deportation. This will permit appellant to pursue any administrative and judicial remedies to which he is lawfully entitled.

For a somewhat unusual application of the holding of *Mendez, see Juarez v. INS,* 732 F.2d 58 (6th Cir.1984) (dismissing petition to review filed under § 106(a) for failure to exhaust administrative remedies; court suggests that administrative appeals pursued from abroad after an allegedly wrongful deportation may constitute a type of remedy which must be exhausted).

SECTION E. HABEAS CORPUS IN DEPORTATION CASES

Most of this Chapter has considered the complexities that arose because of Congress' attempt to force all judicial review of deportation orders (and at least some related matters) into the courts of appeals under § 106(a). But a rather obscure provision buried at the end of that subsection seems to leave open a significant path for review in the district court. Section 106(a)(9) states simply that "any alien held in custody pursuant to an order of deportation may obtain judicial review thereof by habeas corpus proceedings." Just how wide a path into the district courts does this import? The next two cases consider that question and reach sharply different conclusions. The first case, incidentally, features Carlos Marcello—the same Carlos Marcello so much on the mind of Congress in 1961 when it passed § 106. In 1981 he was still making creative use of the possibilities for judicial review.

UNITED STATES ex rel. MARCELLO v. DISTRICT DIRECTOR

United States Court of Appeals, Fifth Circuit, 1981.
634 F.2d 964, cert. denied, 452 U.S. 917.

GEE, CIRCUIT JUDGE:

Carlos Marcello, a foreign national permanently resident in the United States, was first ordered deported in 1953, almost thirty years ago, on the basis of a 1938 marijuana conviction. The order was not executed until 1961, however, when it was apparently executed illegally: arguably Marcello was shanghaied to Guatemala without prior notice to him or his attorney by means of a Guatemalan birth certificate that the Immigration and Naturalization Service (INS) may have known was a forgery. About a month later, Marcello reentered the United States without permission and, later in 1961, was the subject of another deportation order, this one based both on the 1938 conviction and the illegal entry after the apparently irregular 1961 deportation. The validity of neither the 1953 order nor of the 1961 order, insofar as it rests on the 1938 conviction, is contested here.

In 1972, Marcello filed an application for suspension of deportation, and in 1976 the Board of Immigration Appeals (Board) denied the application on two independent grounds: that Marcello had not shown the good moral character required for suspension by INA § 244(a) and that the Board did not choose to exercise its discretion to suspend deportation. The Board relied primarily on a 1968 conviction for assault and expressly stated that it did not consider Marcello's reentry after the 1961 deportation.

Marcello then filed this habeas action in federal district court. The court, after concluding that it had habeas jurisdiction, found that the Board both erred in finding that Marcello lacked good moral character and abused its discretion in denying suspension of deportation. The court vacated the Board's decision and remanded the cause for a determination of the validity of the 1961 deportation and a reassessment of Marcello's character. 472 F.Supp. 1199. We reverse.

Although the facts of Marcello's case are relatively straightforward, we find the legal issues posed by astute counsel on both sides both doubtful and difficult. We treat them in what seems to us their logical order.

IS HABEAS AVAILABLE AS A REMEDY?

Commendably, as a matter of advocacy, the government's first contention goes for the jugular. It urges us to hold that the district court lacked jurisdiction to pass on this matter at all. The contention is not without force, and the reasons why we must reject it require some explication.

In 1961, concerned by the lengthy delays in deportations occasioned by developing judicial precedent, the Congress attempted to streamline these arrangements. It did so by enacting § 106, which provides that the courts of appeals are to be the "sole" organs of review for final deportation orders and thus restricts resort to the district courts in such cases. The legislative purpose and background of this statute are extensively reviewed in *Foti v. Immigration Service,* 375 U.S. 217, 84 S.Ct. 306, 11 L.Ed.2d 281 (1963), and need not be further discussed here except in the one respect that is material.

The sweep of section 106 could not be a clean one because of Article I, section 9 of the Constitution, providing, among other things, that the Great Writ should not be suspended unless rebellion or invasion was in progress. This Congress recognized in section 106(a)(9) of the statute, which provides that an "alien held in custody pursuant to an order of deportation" can seek judicial relief via habeas corpus. The government urges upon us that since Marcello is not presently "held in custody," but merely subjected to reporting requirements and travel restrictions, habeas relief is not available to him.

It is true that in 1961, when the amending act was passed, "custody" for habeas purposes meant primarily physical detention by the government. Since most aliens subject to deportation orders are not physically detained, the habeas exception to exclusive review in the courts of appeals was then a minor one. Since 1961, however, the Supreme Court has expanded the concept of custody for habeas proceedings after conviction to encompass any significant restraint on liberty, including parole, *Jones v. Cunningham,* 371 U.S. 236, 83 S.Ct. 373, 9 L.Ed.2d 285 (1963), and release on one's own recognizance, *Hensley v. Municipal Court,* 411 U.S. 345, 93 S.Ct. 1571, 36 L.Ed.2d 294 (1973). If this broader notion of custody applies generally to habeas under section 106(a)(9), then the court below had jurisdiction, habeas commencing in the district court remains an alternative vehicle of review in most deportation proceedings, and the judicial reform that Congress attempted to bring about by enacting section 106— elimination of the district court step in review of deportation orders—is in great part stultified.

* * *

The legislative history of section 106 leaves little doubt that by enacting it Congress meant to establish two mutually exclusive modes for reviewing deportation orders: a general scheme of statutory review for cases where the alien was not "held in custody" and a provision for habeas review where he was. The Report of the House Committee provides on its first page that:

> The bill provides that with certain specified exceptions (made necessary by the unique subject matter of the bill), all the provisions of the act of December 29, 1950 (64 Stat. 1129, 68 Stat. 961; 5 U.S.C. 1031 et seq.), shall apply to and be the sole and exclusive procedure for judicial review of orders of deportation. In substance, an alien aggrieved by such an order may seek judicial review by filing a petition in the U.S. circuit court of

appeals. The writ of habeas corpus is specifically reserved to an alien held in custody pursuant to an order of deportation.

Also included in the report is the text of a letter from then Deputy Attorney General, now Justice, Byron R. White to the chairman of the committee explaining, in response to his request, the Justice Department's view of the legislation and providing in pertinent part:

Aliens seeking review of administrative orders should be given full and fair opportunity to do so, but the present possibilities of review pose undesirable obstacles to deportation of aliens who have been ordered deported and have had their day in court. An alien subject to a deportation order, having lost his case in a declaratory judgment or injunction proceeding may thereafter sue out of a writ of habeas corpus when taken into custody. Moreover, as the law now stands, it is possible to seek relief by habeas corpus repeatedly.

The bill proposes to meet this problem by providing an exclusive method of review of deportation orders for aliens not in custody. This would be by petition for review in the appropriate court of appeals. The procedure is generally as prescribed by the act of December 29, 1950 (64 Stat. 1129; 68 Stat. 961; 5 U.S.C. 1031), relating to judicial review of orders of Federal agencies. The bill also provides "any alien held in custody pursuant to an order of deportation may obtain judicial review thereof by habeas corpus proceedings." In order to meet the problem of repeated proceedings, no petition for review by the court of appeals or for habeas corpus may be entertained if the validity of the deportation order has been previously determined in any civil or criminal proceeding unless (1) the petition presents grounds which the court finds could not have been presented in the prior proceeding, or (2) the court finds that the remedy provided by the prior proceeding was inadequate or ineffective to test the validity of the order. Administrative findings of fact in deportation cases are made conclusive if supported by reasonable, substantial, and probative evidence.

Also in order to speed up the judicial review, the special statutory review proceeding provided in the bill must be instituted not later than 6 months from the date of the final order of deportation. At the present time there is no time limitation applicable to judicial review.

Finally, in the portion of the report entitled "Analysis of the Bill" it is asserted that "[t]he bill carefully preserves the writ of habeas corpus to an alien detained in custody pursuant to a deportation order."

It is apparent, therefore, that Congress meant by enacting section 106 to provide for two modes of review, one for those "held in custody" and one for those not so held. It remains for us to inquire what was intended by the phrase "held in custody." We think the statutory pattern and structure make plain that what was meant is actual, physical custody in a place of detention. Until that had occurred, we do not think the remedy of review by habeas corpus proceedings was meant to apply but rather that of review by direct appeal.

Examining the pattern of the statute, as well as legislative material such as the Justice Department letter quoted in part above, leaves little room for doubt that Congress attempted to severely limit the availability of habeas review. The basic pattern of review is meant to be by petition to the appellate court, not by resort to habeas in the district court.

Section (a)(7) of § 106, separated from section (a)(9), which preserves the habeas remedy to those "held in custody" only by a housekeeping provision, provides:

> (7) nothing in this section shall be construed to require the Attorney General to defer deportation of an alien after the issuance of a deportation order because of the right of judicial review of the order granted by this section, or to relieve any alien from compliance with subsections (d) and (e) of section 242. Nothing contained in this section shall be construed to preclude the Attorney General from detaining or continuing to detain an alien or from taking him into custody pursuant to subsection (c) of section 242 at any time after the issuance of a deportation order[.]

Subsections (c), (d), and (e) of section 242, referred to above, provide respectively for a six-month period following the order of deportation or of the reviewing court for deportation of the alien, with authorization to the Attorney General to provide places of detention for those taken into custody; for mandatory supervision of aliens against whom final orders of deportation have been outstanding for so much as six months; and for criminal penalties for those seeking to evade deportation.

* * *

Thus, we view a congressional pattern for deportation proceedings that contemplates:

> First, a final administrative deportation order;

> Second, a six-month period thereafter during which review in the court of appeals may be sought and during which the Attorney General may seek to deport the alien, with or without taking him into physical custody;

> Third, mandatory and restrictive supervision of those aliens remaining here after the six-month period; and

> Fourth, judicial review by means of habeas corpus proceedings for aliens held in custody.

Viewing this plan, it is at once plain that the Congress, when enacting section 106, did not see the mere existence of an outstanding deportation order against an alien as placing him in the status of "held in custody." Had it done so, a main procedural innovation of the enactment—eliminating resort to the district courts in the majority of cases—would have been an entire futility from its outset, since habeas in the district court would have been immediately available to all persons ordered deported, without any further assertion of "custody" over them, and resort to the district court routinely had, doubtless, by the delay-minded.

The Government Contention Here

Reasoning from the above premises, the government contends that habeas is not available to Marcello here, since at the time his petition was filed he was not in physical custody. As we noted at the outset, the argument has force, a force derived from its congruence with apparent congressional intent in crafting and enacting the statutory plan.

At the time this petition was filed, when Marcello was subject only to the deportation order, we do not doubt that resort to the court of appeals was available to him as a remedy. Nor do we doubt that, having once so appealed, his right to obtain review in that mode would not have been disturbed by his being taken into "custody." If it were in the Attorney General's power to destroy the appellate remedy by moving under section 106(a)(7), quoted above, to seize an appellant, it would be of little value indeed. Nor, once such an appeal has been lodged, would the alien be well advised to dismiss it upon coming into custody and institute habeas proceedings in its stead. Such a course—indeed a mere failure to appeal at all within the six-month period provided—would raise immediate questions of deliberate bypass of statutory remedies, and should the occurrence of such a bypass be determined, habeas relief would likely be held unavailable as well—except perhaps for matters excepted by section 106(c).[10]

Here, however, the converse has occurred; Marcello filed his habeas petition at a time when, arguably, he was merely subject to a deportation order and not "held in custody." Perhaps a timely motion to dismiss, timely acted upon, might have forestalled this present cause before "custody" attached. This did not take place, however; and if the Supreme Court's expanded concepts of custody apply here, then Marcello presently is and for a long time has been in that condition.[11] We can discern little,

---

10. Those "which the court finds could not have been presented in such prior proceeding, or the court finds that the remedy provided by such prior proceeding was inadequate or ineffective to test the validity of the order."

In the analogous context of 28 U.S.C. § 2255, we have often observed that a deliberate bypass of the provided remedy of a federal appeal generally forecloses raising by the extraordinary means of habeas issues that could have been asserted in the foregone appeal. We have specifically held under § 2255, moreover, that "habeas will not be permitted to substitute for an appeal when the choice to seek habeas relief is made to seize some legal or tactical advantage." The quest for such a tactical advantage—an added stage of review with its resulting delays—will doubtless usually be apparent in such cases as this.

11. We recognize that in *Cunningham* and *Hensley,* the parole and release cases discussed above in text, the release from (or absence of) physical custody occurred during the habeas proceeding, so that a holding that these events terminated custody would have aborted the ongoing habeas proceedings. The Court lays no special stress on this circumstance, however, and in *Hensley* the petitioner had in fact never been in physical custody at any time after the conviction as to which he sought the writ. The conditions of his custody, moreover, appear less stringent than those applied here to Marcello. *See* 411 U.S. at 348, 93 S.Ct. at 1573. Marcello is under supervised parole, which requires him to report quarterly to the INS and notify it whenever he intends to leave Louisiana for more than 48 hours. Hensley seems to have been subject to no reporting requirements except to appear when ordered to do so. *Id.*

if any, practical difference between the condition of Marcello and that of Hensley, who was held by the Court to have been in custody for habeas purposes. *Hensley v. Municipal Court*, 411 U.S. 345, 93 S.Ct. 1571, 36 L.Ed.2d 294 (1973). We conclude that since Marcello is presently in custody, though perhaps he was not for section 106 purposes when this habeas petition was filed, we have jurisdiction of his appeal.

Next, the government urges us to discern and apply to Marcello's attempt to obtain relief in this case, pursuant to 28 U.S.C. § 2241, the exhaustion requirements that are applied in actions brought pursuant to sections 2254 (state criminal convictions) and 2255 (federal ones). Only when the alien has availed himself of the normal mode of appeal provided him by section 106, it is said, should the courts entertain a plea for the extraordinary relief of habeas corpus. There is force and reason in this contention as well; however, to apply it now would be to bar Marcello from any review whatever, the six-month period for an appeal having long passed. Absent a finding of deliberate bypass of the direct appeal,[12] we do not believe such an outcome just or appropriate.

Finally, the government argues persuasively that Congress intended by section 106 to restrict habeas review to the constitutional minima, both as to availability and as to scope of review. There can be no doubt that there exists a constitutional core of habeas corpus authority, derived from the Common Law, guarded by Article I, section 9, and proof against congressional or executive tampering save in the event of invasion or rebellion. The statutory enactments overlaying the Great Writ—28 U.S.C. §§ 2241, 2254, and 2255—are, the argument runs, congressional additions to its scope that may be limited or withdrawn at the pleasure of the Congress so long as the constitutional core is not disturbed. This, according to the government, is what was done by section 106: a more than adequate statutory appellate remedy was provided, together with a highly restricted version of habeas—one embodying only the constitutional core, added solely to render the enactment constitutionally viable.

We agree with the government that such a plan and purpose would be a rational and probably desirable one. The difficulty here is that there is little or no indication, either in the statute or the legislative history, that it was the *congressional* plan and purpose in enacting section 106. To the contrary, as we have noted above, these materials seem to indicate that the Congress contemplated alternative methods of obtaining review, one available to aliens not "held in custody" and the other to those who were. We see little logic and less fairness in laying it down that the scope of review available to an alien may be narrowed by the occurrence of an event quite beyond his control, the action of the Attorney General in taking him into custody. Rather than such an effect, what Congress intended, we think, was to abolish in as many cases as possible the district court step in direct appeals and the employment by the alien of *both* modes of review successively. Our conclusion in this line is reinforced by the simple language of section 106(a)(9), providing that "judicial *review*" of

---

12. The court below did not make such a finding. In the circumstances of this case, and in view of Marcello's long experience with the laws governing deportation and his demonstrated ability in evading them, we might almost do so as a matter of law.

the deportation order may be had in habeas corpus proceedings by an alien in custody.

Thus, it appears that the government's attacks on jurisdiction and propriety of review here must, perhaps unfortunately, fail.

THE MERITS

Our standard of review of the order of the Board denying suspension of deportation, then, is the same as that on direct appeal of a final order of deportation. It is whether "reasonable, substantial, and probative evidence on the record considered as a whole" supports the order. § 106(a)(4). That question is one of law as to which we review the district court's decision free of the trammels of the clearly erroneous standard. The district court concluded that substantial evidence did not support the order. We disagree.

In a majority opinion, the Board dismissed Marcello's application for suspension of deportation, both for failure to establish statutory eligibility and in the exercise of its discretion. It did so on the basis of numerous facts detailed therein, all of which are supported by substantial evidence in the record and most of which are not seriously disputed. Among these are a 1938 drug conviction, a 1930 state conviction for assault and robbery, and a 1968 felony conviction for assault on a federal officer. In view of these matters, we cannot say that the Board's decision that Marcello failed to establish good moral character for the requisite ten-year period is unsupported by substantial evidence. Nor can we conclude that the Board's discretion to deny suspension was abused, a ground independent of the statutory prerequisites. *United States ex rel. Hintopoulous v. Shaughnessy,* 353 U.S. 72, 77 S.Ct. 618, 1 L.Ed.2d 652 (1957).

* * *

The judgment of the district court is Reversed and that of the Board is Affirmed.

DANESHVAR v. CHAUVIN

United States Court of Appeals, Eighth Circuit, 1981.
644 F.2d 1248.

ARNOLD, CIRCUIT JUDGE.

Bizhan Daneshvar appeals the dismissal by the district court of that portion of his petition for writ of habeas corpus in which he sought judicial review of an order of the United States Immigration and Naturalization Service (INS) which required his deportation from the United States. The district court concluded that it lacked jurisdiction to review final deportation orders of the INS in a habeas corpus proceeding. We affirm.

Appellant Daneshvar is an Iranian citizen who entered this country as a nonimmigrant student, eventually enrolling at the University of Arkansas at Little Rock in June of 1978. His student status gave him a right to remain in the United States until June 29, 1979. On November 29, 1979, the INS issued a show cause order, pursuant to 8 C.F.R. § 242.1, alleging that Daneshvar had failed to maintain his nonimmigrant student status and was therefore subject to deportation. At a hearing held on January 9, 1980, Daneshvar appeared with an attorney and admitted that he was deportable. The immigration judge subsequently ordered his deportation but permitted Daneshvar to leave the United States voluntarily. Daneshvar did not appeal the judge's order.

Daneshvar, however, did not leave the United States within the time allowed. He instead filed a motion to reopen or reconsider the deportation order. On September 12, 1980, while the motion to reopen was still pending, Daneshvar was arrested by the United States Border Patrol, acting pursuant to the deportation order,[2] and placed in jail. On September 14, 1980, Daneshvar petitioned the district court for a writ of habeas corpus. He claimed that the order of deportation in his case threatened to deprive him of liberty without due process of law because, among other reasons, he did not understand English well enough to appreciate the nature of the proceedings against him. The district court moved with appropriate solicitude for the right of personal liberty. The court admitted Daneshvar to bail, perhaps feeling that his motion to reopen, which had been pending for some four months, was not being treated with reasonable expedition. In addition, the district court ordered the INS not to deport Daneshvar until further order of the district court or of a court of appeals having jurisdiction. In all other respects, however, the petition was dismissed for want of jurisdiction. The district court held that its habeas jurisdiction was limited to review of ancillary or preliminary actions of the INS (for example, its taking Daneshvar into custody while delaying a ruling on his motion to reopen), and that the courts of appeals had exclusive jurisdiction to review the final order of deportation itself. A partial final judgment was entered under Fed.R.Civ.P. 54(b), and Daneshvar then appealed.[4]

Daneshvar argues that the district court had jurisdiction to consider the validity of the deportation order itself. He relies on two provisions of law. First, Section 279 of the Immigration and Nationality Act of 1952, provides:

> The district courts of the United States shall have jurisdiction of all causes, civil and criminal, arising under any of the provisions of this subchapter.

The reference to "this subchapter" denotes Subchapter II of Chapter 12 of Title 8 of the United States Code, and includes 8 U.S.C. §§ 1151–1362 [INA §§ 201–293]. In addition, we are cited to Section 106(a)(9):

> (9) any alien held in custody pursuant to an order of deportation may obtain judicial review thereof by habeas corpus proceedings.

2. The filing of a motion to reopen or for reconsideration does not stay the execution of a deportation order. 8 C.F.R. § 242.22.

4. In addition to appealing to this Court, the appellant has filed with the United States Court of Appeals for the Sixth Circuit an appeal from the denial by the INS of his motion to reopen or reconsider the deportation order, which was denied on September 16, 1980. This case was pending in the Sixth Circuit at the time of the oral argument in the instant appeal before this Court.

The government, on the other hand, relies on another portion of Section 106(a), * * * under which petitions for review in a court of appeals are

> the sole and exclusive procedure for, the judicial review of all final orders of deportation. . . .

The question presented here is whether the district courts have jurisdiction to review final orders of deportation when the plaintiff's form of action is habeas corpus. The answer is not immediately clear from the language of the three statutes involved, pertinent parts of which we have quoted. These provisions present, to say the least, a question of interpretation. We have no great difficulty with the suggestion that § 279, a general grant of jurisdiction to the district courts of cases arising under the immigration title of the 1952 Act, is applicable here. *Foti v. Immigration & Naturalization Serv.*, 375 U.S. 217, 84 S.Ct. 306, 11 L.Ed.2d 281 (1963), suffices to dispose of this contention. There, the Supreme Court explained that Section 106(a) of the Act, as added by the 1961 amendment, was intended to make a definite change in pre-existing law, including § 279. "The key feature of the congressional plan . . . was the elimination of the previous initial step in obtaining judicial review—a suit in a District Court—and the resulting restriction of review to Courts of Appeals, subject only to the certiorari jurisdiction of this Court." * * * "[T]he declared purpose of § 106(a) [is] to eliminate the District Court stage of the judicial review process in an effort to prevent dilatory tactics." * * * *Foti* holds that discretionary determinations of the Attorney General, relating to the suspension of deportation under § 244(a)(5) of the Act, are, like final orders of deportation themselves, reviewable exclusively in the courts of appeals.

Later cases elaborate the line between final orders of deportation reviewable only in courts of appeals, and certain other kinds of orders reviewable in district courts. See *Immigration & Naturalization Serv. v. Stanisic*, 395 U.S. 62, 68 n. 6, 89 S.Ct. 1519, 1523 n. 6, 23 L.Ed.2d 101 (1969) (denial by the Attorney General of an application to withhold deportation, under Section 243(h) of the Act, to a country where the alien would be subject to persecution, is reviewable in the district courts, "[b]ecause the . . . determination [to deny the application] was not pursuant to § 242(b)," the provision specifically referred to in the 1961 amendment); [a] *Cheng Fan Kwok v. Immigration & Naturalization Serv.*, 392 U.S. 206, 215, 88 S.Ct. 1970, 1975, 20 L.Ed.2d 1037 (1968) (". . . Congress quite deliberately restricted the application of § 106(a) to orders entered during proceedings conducted under § 242(b), or directly challenging deportation orders themselves" (footnote omitted)); *Giova v. Rosenberg*, 379 U.S. 18, 85 S.Ct. 156, 13 L.Ed.2d 90 (1964) (per curiam) (courts of appeals have exclusive jurisdiction to review denials of motions to reopen § 242(b) deportation proceedings); *Mendez v. Major*, 340 F.2d 128 (8th Cir.1965); *Chadha v. Immigration & Naturalization Serv.*, 634 F.2d 408 (9th Cir. 1980) (review of final deportation orders includes review of matters upon

---

a. Under regulations adopted after *Stanisic* was decided, applications for relief under § 243(h) are now adjudicated, in most circumstances, as part of the deportation hearing before the immigration judge. *See* Chapter Eight—eds.

which the final order is contingent); *Reyes v. Immigration & Naturalization Serv.,* 571 F.2d 505 (9th Cir.1978).

Some of the distinctions drawn by these cases among different types of orders relating to deportation are hard to follow, at least for us. But the common thread running through all the cases is that judicial review of final orders of deportation, when the question of deportability is in question, is exclusively in the courts of appeals. This is so even when deportability under the statute is conceded, but the alien plaintiff claims that the statute itself is unconstitutional. *Shodeke v. Attorney General,* 391 F.Supp. 219 (D.D.C.1975). In the instant case deportation proceedings were commenced under Section 242(b) of the Act, and the final order of deportation was entered in those proceedings. Attempts by Daneshvar to contest the validity of this order fall squarely within Section 106(a), and that specific, later-enacted provision must prevail, as the Supreme Court held in *Foti,* over the earlier-enacted general grant of jurisdiction to the district courts.

It remains to consider the habeas corpus provision, Section 106(a)(9), which is on its face an exception to the general rule of exclusivity set out in Section 106(a). Daneshvar argues that the habeas corpus paragraph must be given the effect of creating district-court jurisdiction, even to review final orders of deportation, when the affected person is in custody. Although that construction of the statute is unquestionably one that the words will bear, we decline to accept it. The proper solution to this problem, we think, is explained by Judge Becker in *United States ex rel. Parco v. Morris,* 426 F.Supp. 976, 978 n. 4 (E.D.Pa.1977). There, habeas corpus jurisdiction in the district courts was upheld where plaintiff was not seeking review of the merits of the deportation order itself, but only to contest the denial of a stay of deportation. "Habeas corpus is an appropriate proceeding to review the denial of discretionary relief from deportation where deportability itself is not in issue." "Custody," in the present context, refers not only to confinement in jail, as in Daneshvar's case, but also that restriction of movement resulting from any final order of deportation. *United States ex rel. Parco v. Morris, supra,* 426 F.Supp. at 978 n. 4. The suggestion that Section 106(a)(9) be construed to create district-court habeas jurisdiction whenever the petitioner is in custody, while the general language of Section 106(a) would confer jurisdiction on courts of appeals to review final orders of deportation at the suit of petitioners who are not in custody, does not, therefore, make a great deal of sense. Under this interpretation, the exception would swallow the rule. Since the issuance of a final order of deportation itself subjects the affected person to "custody" for habeas purposes, it is hard to see what, if anything, would be left of the courts of appeals' exclusive jurisdiction. It makes more sense, and furthers the congressional purpose to avoid delay, explained in *Foti,* to construe Section 106(a) to confer exclusive jurisdiction on courts of appeals in all cases where the validity of a final order of deportation is drawn in question, and to limit Section 106(a)(9) to review of the denial of discretionary relief where deportability itself is not an issue.

The district court's memorandum and order, accompanying the judgment from which this appeal is taken, dismissed for want of jurisdiction "the petitioner's request for review of the administrative determinations regarding his deportation." This decision was based on what we hold to be a correct construction of the jurisdictional statutes, and the judgment is

Affirmed.[6]

Notes

1. Both courts note that concepts of "custody" have expanded in habeas corpus cases handed down since Congress enacted § 106 in 1961. The key decisions were *Jones v. Cunningham,* 371 U.S. 236, 83 S.Ct. 373, 9 L.Ed.2d 285 (1963), which held that a former prisoner on parole was sufficiently in custody to claim federal jurisdiction in habeas, and *Hensley v. Municipal Court,* 411 U.S. 345, 93 S.Ct. 1571, 36 L.Ed.2d 294 (1973), which reached the same conclusion as to a person at large on his own recognizance in advance of the commencement of his sentence. But those cases are not immigration cases. The first paragraph of each opinion states that the Supreme Court was called upon there to construe the meaning of "custody" in a specific federal statute, 28 U.S.C.A. § 2241. Although that statute is obviously closely related to the habeas provisions in INA § 106, must we assume that Congress intended to base the reach of the immigration provision on the changing boundaries of the other remedy?

At the very least the fundamental setting is quite different. Section 2241 governs when state prisoners may have access to the federal courts by means of habeas corpus. Had the parolee in *Jones* been found not to be in custody, for example, he might never have had an opportunity to raise his constitutional claims in a federal forum. The aliens in the two cases here clearly have, or had, opportunities for federal court review, by means of the regular petition for review envisioned by § 106(a). Would this difference support a distinction in the way that "custody" is understood in the two settings?

Daneshvar does not seem aware of the possible distinctions. In this respect, it is in the company of several other courts, which have rather hastily assumed that the Supreme Court's expanded custody notions applied with equal vigor under § 106(a)(9). *See, e.g., Flores v. INS,* 524 F.2d 627 (9th Cir.1975); *Sotelo-Mondragon v. Ilchert,* 653 F.2d 1254 (9th Cir.1980); *United States ex rel. Parco v. Morris,* 426 F.Supp. 976, 978 n. 4

---

6. Appellant, we assume, remains at large on the bond fixed by the district court, and is protected by that court's order of October 6, 1980, enjoining appellees from deporting him. In view of the fact that Daneshvar has a petition for review of the order denying his motion to reopen pending in the Sixth Circuit, pursuant to which his deportation has been stayed by that court, he may no longer need the protection of the injunction entered by the district court in this case. It is entirely possible that the stay of deportation entered by the district court should be dissolved, and, if it is, we know of no reason why Daneshvar's case should remain pending on that court's docket. We leave these issues to the district court. It is better able than we to assess the parties' present status, including anything that may have occurred in the Sixth Circuit since the oral argument before us, and take whatever action is equitable.

(E.D.Pa.1977). But *see Smith v. Morris,* 442 F.Supp. 712, 713 (E.D.Pa. 1977), suggesting that "actual physical custody" may be required before jurisdiction attaches under § 106(a)(9).

The *Marcello* court, in contrast, is apparently aware of the potential distinctions. Moreover, it devotes several paragraphs to showing why the 1961 Congress unmistakably intended that habeas be available to deportation respondents only when they are actually taken into physical custody. Just why then does the court end up finding Marcello sufficiently in custody to invoke the habeas remedy? The third paragraph of the section of the court's opinion headed "The Government Contention Here" contains the crucial passages, but there the court's musings sound a bit like "The Love Song of J. Alfred Prufrock." The shift from "if" to "since" (referring to the application of the *Hensley* standards) is so subtle as to elude recognition. But the question remains: should the *Hensley* standards govern here? [20] Wouldn't a rather strict physical custody requirement narrow the otherwise formidable loophole that § 106(a)(9) represents in a more useful and constructive manner than the *Daneshvar* approach, which focuses instead on narrowing the scope of issues to be raised?[21]

SECTION F. CONTINUING PROBLEMS: THE CONGRESSIONAL RESPONSE

In the early 1980's, as part of its immigration reform efforts, Congress hoped to overcome the jurisdictional problems it perceived. Though other controversies have so far prevented passage of the reform bills, there was fairly clear congressional consensus on most of the jurisdictional amendments believed necessary. The bill that passed the Senate in 1983 (S. 529) would have made the following changes in the judicial review provisions of the INA. (The House bill was identical in most respects, but did differ significantly over the habeas corpus provisions; the House would not have attempted to cut the cognizable issues back as severely as the Senate.) Language in the current statute that would have been deleted by the Senate bill appears in braces; language that would have been added is italicized.

Work your way carefully through the changes.[22] As to each one, consider what the Senate was evidently trying to accomplish—what it

---

20. The same poetic talents are displayed when the court discusses the exhaustion of remedies and "deliberate bypass" doctrines. Just why is it, again, that Marcello is not precluded from habeas corpus review on these grounds?

21. For decisions reaching a similar result to *Daneshvar,* concluding that only a limited range of issues is open to review on habeas corpus under INA § 106(a)(9), *see Salehi v. District Director,* 575 F.Supp. 1237 (D.Colo.1983); *In re Meljarajo,* 552 F.Supp. 573 (N.D.Ill.1982). For sharp criticism of *Daneshvar, see* Gordon, *Habeas Corpus: New*

Limits for an Ancient Remedy?, 4 Imm.J. 7 (1981).

22. Some additional information about other sections of the Senate bill may be helpful in evaluating the Senate's work. The bill would have created a United States Immigration Board within the Department of Justice. That Board would perform many of the same functions as the current BIA, but it would be statutorily created and would enjoy a few additional guarantees of independence. Immigration judges would also be directly under the new Board, and hence more fully dissociated from INS. Fi-

must have considered problematic about current arrangements. Consider also what effect these amendments would have had on the outcome of each of the principal cases in this chapter. What, for example, would happen to Cheng Fan Kwok? To Kavasji? To Marcello and Daneshvar? Is the Senate provision for each such fact pattern superior to current law? If not, are there other alternatives that might ameliorate each of the apparent problems? (You may wish to refer back to the Friendly and Roberts proposals in Section B above.) Which of the alternatives do you prefer?

JUDICIAL REVIEW OF ORDERS OF DEPORTATION, {AND} EXCLUSION, *AND ASYLUM*

Sec. 106. (a) {The procedure prescribed by, and all the provisions of the [Hobbs Act] shall apply to, and shall be the sole and exclusive procedure for, the judicial review of all final orders of deportation heretofore or hereafter made against aliens within the United States pursuant to administrative proceedings under section 242(b) of this Act or comparable provisions of any prior Act} *Notwithstanding section 279 of this Act, section 1331 of title 28, United States Code, or any other provision of law (except as provided under subsection (b)), the procedures prescribed by and all the provisions of chapter 158 of title 28, United States Code [successor to the Hobbs Act], shall apply to, and shall be the sole and exclusive procedure for, the judicial review of all final orders of exclusion or deportation (including determinations respecting asylum encompassed within such orders and regardless of whether or not the alien is in custody and not including exclusion effected without a hearing pursuant to section 235(b)(1)(B)) made against aliens within (or seeking entry into) the United States*, except that—

(1) a petition for review may be filed {not later than six months from the date of the final deportation order or from the effective date of this section, whichever is the later} *by the alien involved or the Service not later than 45 days from the date of the final order*;

(2) the venue of any petition for review under this section shall be in the judicial circuit in which the administrative proceedings before {a special inquiry officer} *an immigration judge* were conducted in whole or in part, or, *in the case of review sought by an individual petitioner*, in the judicial circuit wherein is the residence, as defined in this Act, of the petitioner, but not in more than one circuit;

(3) *in the case of review sought by an individual petitioner*, the action shall be brought against the Immigration and Naturalization Service, as respondent. Service of the petition to review shall be made upon the Attorney General of the United States and upon the official of the Immigration and Naturalization Service in charge of the Service district in which the office of the clerk of the court is

nally, a new § 235(b)(1) would have provided for summary exclusion, without a hearing before an immigration judge, of un- documented aliens who do not claim asylum or U.S. citizenship.

located. {The service} *In the case of judicial review of an order of deportation, the service* of the petition for review upon such official of the Service shall stay the deportation of the alien pending determination of the petition by the court, unless the court otherwise directs;

{(4) except as provided in} *(4)(A) except as provided in subparagraph (B) and in* clause (B) of paragraph (5) of this subsection, the petition shall be determined solely upon the administrative record upon which the *exclusion or* deportation order is based and the {Attorney General's findings of fact} *findings of fact in the order*, if supported by {reasonable, substantial, and probative} *substantial* evidence on the record considered as a whole, shall be conclusive; *(B) to the extent that an order relates to a determination on an application for asylum, the court shall only have jurisdiction to review (i) whether the jurisdiction of the immigration judge or the United States Immigration Board was properly exercised; (ii) whether the asylum determination was made in accordance with applicable laws and regulations, (iii) the constitutionality of the laws and regulations pursuant to which the determination was made, and (iv) whether the decision was arbitrary and capricious;*

* * *

{(9) any alien held in custody pursuant to an order of deportation may obtain judicial review thereof by habeas corpus proceedings.}

{(b) Notwithstanding the provisions of any other law, any alien against whom a final order of exclusion has been made heretofore or hereafter under the provisions of section 236 of this Act or comparable provisions of any prior Act may obtain judicial review of such order by habeas corpus proceedings and not otherwise.}

(b)(1) Nothing in this section shall be construed as limiting the right of habeas corpus under the Constitution of the United States.

(2) Notwithstanding any other provision of law, no court of the United States shall have jurisdiction to review determinations of immigration judges or of the United States Immigration Board respecting the reopening or reconsideration of exclusion or deportation proceedings or asylum determinations outside of such proceedings, the reopening of an application for asylum because of changed circumstances, the Attorney General's denial of a stay of execution of an exclusion or deportation order, or the exclusion of an alien from the United States under section 235(b)(1).

(c) An order of {deportation or of exclusion} *an immigration judge* shall not be reviewed by any court if the alien has not exhausted the administrative remedies available to him as of right under the immigration laws and regulations or if he has departed from the United States after the issuance of the order. Every petition for review or for habeas corpus shall state whether the validity of the order has been upheld in any prior judicial proceeding, and, if so, the nature and date thereof, and the court in which such proceeding took place. No petition for review or for habeas corpus shall be entertained if the validity of the order has been previously determined in any civil or criminal proceeding, unless the petition presents grounds which the court finds could not have been presented in such prior proceeding, or the court finds that the remedy provided by such prior proceeding was inadequate or ineffective to test the validity of the order.

JURISDICTION OF DISTRICT COURTS

Sec. 279. {The district courts} *(a) Except as otherwise provided under Section 106, the district courts* of the United States shall have jurisdiction of all causes, civil and criminal, arising under any of the provisions of this title. It shall be the duty of the United States attorney of the proper district to prosecute every such suit when brought by the United States. Notwithstanding any other law, such prosecutions or suits may be instituted at any place in the United States at which the violation may occur or at which the person charged with a violation under section 275 or 276 may be apprehended. No suit or proceeding for a violation of any of the provisions of this title shall be settled, compromised, or discontinued without the consent of the court in which it is pending and any such settlement, compromise, or discontinuance shall be entered of record with the reasons therefor.

(b) An action for judicial review of any administrative action arising under this Act, or regulations issued pursuant to this Act, may not be filed later than thirty days after the date of the final administrative action or from the effective date of this section, whichever is later.

Chapter Eight

REFUGEES AND POLITICAL ASYLUM

A refugee, in the usual conception, is among the world's most unfortunate people. Besides being a victim—of persecution, war, or natural disaster—a refugee has also been uprooted, forced to leave familiar territory because of that same oppression or destruction. But paradoxically, under modern international law, to be a refugee—a recognized refugee—is also to assume a position of privilege. Refugees, unlike millions of other deprived people throughout the globe, benefit from distinctive programs for relief and assistance, and often from arrangements for distant resettlement. A specialized office of the United Nations, the UN High Commissioner for Refugees (UNHCR), with an annual budget running to several hundred million dollars and a large staff that includes dozens of lawyers known as protection officers, watches over their treatment and seeks to find durable solutions.

Nearly a hundred nations, moreover, have become parties to treaties [1] that set forth specific, and sometimes quite extensive, legal protections for refugees. Domestic legal provisions in many nations augment these requirements, spelling out the circumstances under which refugees who have reached their territory may claim political asylum—which usually entails indefinite rights to resettle and establish a new life in the receiving nation, even if the refugee violated the regular provisions of the immigration laws in the course of arriving there. In spite of these paradoxical advantages, however—or more likely, because of them—the legal conception of refugee is narrower than the usual popular conception. The most common legal definitions of "refugee" focus only on persecution. They do not recognize economic deprivation or natural disasters, or even the outbreak of military hostilities in the homeland, as the source of refugee status.[2]

---

1. The two most important treaties are the Convention relating to the Status of Refugees, *done* July 28, 1951, 189 U.N.T.S. 137 [hereinafter cited as UN Convention]; and the Protocol relating to the Status of Refugees, *done* Jan. 31, 1967, 19 U.S.T. 6223, T.I.A.S. No. 6577, 606 U.N.T.S. 267 [hereinafter cited as UN Protocol]. For useful general treatments of the international law relating to refugees, *see* G. Goodwin-Gill, *The Refugee in International Law* (1983), and A.

Grahl-Madsen, *The Status of Refugees in International Law* (2 vols. 1966, 1972).

2. Some treaties and other legal provisions do use a more expansive definition. For example, the Organization of African Unity Convention Governing the Specific Aspects of Refugee Problems in Africa, *entered into force,* June 20, 1974, 691 U.N.T.S. 14, defines "refugee" to include those having a well-founded fear of persecution (the central

Thus there is an inherent tension that runs through all political and legal decisionmaking on refugee and asylum questions in the United States. The notion of refugee evokes sympathy. The possibility of resulting privileges, especially a potential right to resettle indefinitely, evokes suspicion that the unworthy are trying to claim that status.

Compounding the difficulty is the inherent vagueness of the governing legal standard for deciding just who is a "refugee." Under the usual legal definitions, a "refugee" is someone who demonstrates "a well-founded fear of persecution" in his or her homeland. But when is a fear well-founded? What is persecution? What kind of evidence is necessary to prove the needed facts? When the standard is this vague, there remains plenty of room for manipulation, by those who favor a less generous policy as well as by those who favor a more generous one.

As more and more asylum-seekers from nearby nations like Haiti, Cuba, Nicaragua, and El Salvador have reached the United States, this built-in tension in American immigration law has become more glaringly apparent. As a result, the controversy over U.S. treatment of asylum-seekers has become more acrimonious, especially after INS changed policy in 1981 and began incarcerating nearly all of the newly arriving asylum-seekers. This Chapter therefore treats subjects that are probably the most controversial in the whole immigration field.[3] Some of the harshness of the debate, as well as some flavor of the genuinely difficult dilemmas involved, comes through in the following selection of charges and countercharges:

> As far as many of the detained Haitians are concerned, the main difference is * * * between black refugees and white ones. "I think they're holding me because I'm black," says Francesca Dorgille, who left an infant son behind in her search for prosperity, only to wind up at Fort Allen [a detention center in Puerto Rico]. "If I were white, they would let me free." Many of the Haitians' American supporters agree that race is a prime factor; this, they suggest, was the "shock" that led to last summer's new policies [mandating detention for nearly all excludable aliens, even those who have applied for asylum]. * * *

> [T]he suspicion lingers that if 15,000 white Poles fleeing the crackdown showed up in New York Harbor, they would not be shipped off to * * * Fort Allen—a comparison the Haitians themselves make over and over again.

—*Refugees or Prisoners?,* Newsweek, February 1, 1982, at 28–29.*

component of the definition set forth in the UN treaties), but it goes on to embrace as well those who are outside the home country "owing to external aggression, occupation, foreign domination or events seriously disturbing public order * * *." The laws of the United States, however, like those of most other western countries, employ only the narrower definition derived from the UN Convention and Protocol.

3. Nor is this uniquely an American phenomenon. Serious controversies persist in Western Europe over the treatment of asy-

lum-seekers and decisions to grant or deny asylum to particular groups or individuals. *See generally, e.g.,* Aleinikoff, *Political Asylum in the Federal Republic of Germany and the Republic of France: Lessons for the United States,* 17 U.Mich.J.L.Ref. 183 (1984); Avery, *Refugee Status Decision-Making: The Systems of Ten Countries,* 19 Stan.L.Rev. 235 (1983).

[Writing of "asylum as a growth industry":] The "asylum strategy" has become well-known in countries of out-migration, and increasing numbers of persons ineligible for refugee or immigrant admission are choosing to enter the country illegally (or on temporary visitors' visas) in order to claim asylum.

—Teitelbaum, *Political Asylum in Theory and Practice,* 76 The Public Interest 74, 77–78 (1984).

The Haitians' advocates, however, argue that a great many of the refugees are victims of repression. Even those who had no trouble before they left Haiti could be viewed as traitors for seeking asylum here, claims Kurzban [one of the lawyers for the Haitians]. Thus, he asserts, they have as much right to stay as Cubans who fled Castro or Nicaraguans who fled the Sandinists. The government's efforts to expel the Haitians, he says, come from a blend of racism and loyalty to Duvalier's regime.

* * *

Inman [General Counsel of INS] dismisses these statements with an angry wave. "This is *war,*" he declares. "The war is to in effect eliminate the definition of refugee and to open our borders to anybody that wants to come in and have a worldwide equalization of wealth and property." Kurzban and the [other lawyers for the Haitians], he says, "are orchestrating some massive program to open our doors for all immigration."

—Bruck, *Springing the Haitians,* The American Lawyer, September 1982, at 36, 39.

I think that frustrated would-be immigrants have come to see the asylum system as a loophole or a back door in our immigration policy. And, to be frank again, I think that some activist and some human rights groups, and some immigration lawyers, bear a great deal of responsibility for this development. When large groups of aliens file asylum claims in what is really a political gesture or a protest against U.S. foreign policy and without reference to the factors of individual cases, this action threatens the integrity of the entire asylum system and damages the position of those applicants whose claims are meritorious. And when so-called public interest lawyer's groups or human rights groups urge whole categories of migrants to file asylum claims en masse, despite the lack of any persuasive evidence that they are all refugees rather than migrants, once again the system is threatened and its ability to protect refugees is diminished.

—from a speech by a State Department official, quoted in *Asylum Adjudications: An Evolving Concept and Responsibility for the Immigration and Naturalization Service* (INS Staff Study, mimeo, June 1982).

Dessine asked a question he had asked before, one that comes in a perpetual refrain from incarcerated Haitians: "Why are we in jail? We are not criminals. Can you explain it?"

"I said that this administration doesn't want you here but that I don't agree, and I'm doing everything I can," says Levine [Dessine's pro bono lawyer].

He shakes his head. "You can't really answer that. As far as I'm concerned they're in a concentration camp. You can call them detainees, but you can call black white. It makes me ashamed to be an American."

—Bruck, *supra*, at 36.

Recently, the INS decided to fight back against the lawyers' principal weapon—delay, which attorneys use to buy time so that their clients can obtain spouses, good jobs or anything else that might win them better preference categories. The major stratagem for winning delay in recent years has been to apply for political asylum. Applications for asylum have spiked from 3,800 in 1979 to 178,000 today—clear evidence of a new lawyerly device at work.

—*Games Illegals Play*, Newsweek, June 25, 1984, at 26.*

SECTION A. OVERVIEW

We consider in this Chapter all the important legal provisions relating to refugees. You should keep in mind, however, that an alien's successful claim that she is a refugee may lead to permanent residence in the United States through two quite different paths. Although courts and commentators often fail to make the distinction when speaking of U.S. refugee programs, this failure only compounds a confusion that is already too widespread. Each path has its own distinctive set of procedures, constraints, and legal and policy dilemmas. We will usually refer to the first (and less controversial) path as "overseas refugee programs" and to the second as "political asylum."

Overseas refugee programs are analytically akin to the material we covered in Chapter Three relating to admissions. We focused in that Chapter on two broad characteristics that serve as the basis for permission to migrate permanently to the United States: family ties and labor needs. Refugee status constitutes a third and completely independent characteristic that may be the basis for an alien's securing, while she remains in a foreign country, permission to immigrate to the United States. Unlike a preference immigrant or an immediate relative, she will not receive an immigrant visa, *see* INA §§ 207(c), 211(c), but this is merely a minor paperwork detail. The effect is basically the same: with the demise of nonpreference immigration to the United States, refugee status constitutes the only significant basis for possible immigration open to those who lack family ties here and who would meet no demonstrated employment needs. Typically those who gain admission through the overseas refugee programs are located in a refugee camp in a foreign country at the time of their selection, but occasionally they may be within their countries of origin.[4]

The statutory provisions governing such admissions have changed rather frequently since World War II, as Congress and the executive branch have struggled to find a framework that would provide a reasonable degree of control and predictability, while at the same time retaining adequate flexibility to respond to new crises. With the Refugee Act of 1980,[5] the United States seems to have achieved a relatively stable statutory framework for accommodating these contradictory ends, and thereby establishing, year by year, the number of refugee admissions and the allocation of those admission spaces among refugee groups.

The second path to permanent residence based on refugee status comes through filing a claim for political asylum, and as indicated, this remains a highly controversial subject. We are still far from having a statutory framework and administrative apparatus regarded as adequate and reliable for coping with political asylum applications. The controversy derives from the very nature of the process. Unlike beneficiaries of the overseas refugee programs, who do not reach U.S. soil until they have been processed, screened, selected, and plied with documents in some other country, applicants for asylum reach the territorial United States on their own and only then claim protection against involuntary return. Some applicants enter on nonimmigrant visas and overstay. Others enter without inspection before filing their claims somewhere in the interior. Still others lodge an asylum claim at a border post or even on the beach where they first encounter the border patrol. And a handful are nonimmigrants still in status who file, for example, because a sudden political change at home makes it risky for them to return.

Because of this characteristic, there is no reasonable way to screen asylum applications in advance nor to impose strict limits on the overall number of applicants. (Beginning in 1981, however, the Reagan Administration has tried, with some success, to reduce the number of applications by means of several deterrent measures we will consider later in this Chapter.) Of course, not all applicants will manage to prove their entitlement to asylum. In fact, the percentage of successful applications historically has been rather low. But in nearly all circumstances the applicants will remain in the United States while their claims are adjudicated.

4. See INA § 101(a)(42)(B). In this respect, U.S. law applies a broader definition of refugee than does the leading international treaty, the UN Convention, *supra* note 1, which considers no one a refugee unless he or she is outside the home country. The difference is of minor importance, however, since the refugees will obviously be outside the home country before they are actually admitted to the United States. Moreover, in practice, a program to bring refugees direct-

ly from their country of origin can be established only in rather unusual circumstances. *See* Martin, *The Refugee Act of 1980: Its Past and Future,* in Transnational Legal Problems of Refugees, 1982 Mich.Y.B. Int'l L.Stud. 91, 101–04.

5. Pub.L. No. 96–212, 94 Stat. 102 (1980) (codified at various sections of 8, 22 U.S.C. A.).

Adjudication has proved to be a lengthy and tangled process, owing both to inadequacies in administration and to a complex interaction between the courts and the political branches. The result has been a series of significant problems in deciding what arrangements should be made for the care and maintenance of the applicants, over the months or years that may pass while the adjudication proceeds. Should they be detained? If not, should they be allowed to work? What kinds of public assistance should be provided? Moreover, as noted before, because the governing standards are vague and difficult to apply, there is ample room for controversy about whether political considerations have intruded on the decisions.

Political asylum is analytically akin to the provisions for relief from deportation that we examined in Chapter Six, but it is potentially more potent than any of the provisions reviewed there. For one thing, a political asylum claim can provide relief from exclusion as well as deportation; its protection extends to parolees and to persons apprehended before they ever make a formal entry. Beyond this, there is no waiting period before one qualifies (unlike the seven years required for suspension of deportation under INA § 244), and a grant of asylum may lead rather directly to permanent residence rights (thus distinguishing, for example, voluntary departure and the exercise of prosecutorial discretion). Moreover, if the alien establishes entitlement to protection by demonstrating that his life or freedom would be threatened in his home country, both statutory law and treaty requirements forbid the application of nearly all other exclusion criteria or eligibility qualifications.

All these features—the difficulty of imposing control over numbers, the delays in the adjudication process, the potency of a successful asylum claim, and charges of political manipulation of the system—give rise to the divisive legal and policy issues concerning political asylum.

We begin our more detailed consideration of the legal provisions relating to refugees with the overseas refugee programs.[6]

SECTION B. OVERSEAS REFUGEE PROGRAMS

Only with the end of World War II was there much systematic attention in the United States to admission programs for refugees.[7] By

6. Besides the sections we will consider in detail here, there are at least two other legal provisions whose implementation may require an assessment of the threat of persecution faced by the applicant in her home country. INA § 212(e) bars many exchange visitors—beneficiaries of "J" visas—from returning to the United States as permanent residents until they have spent two years back in the home country, but a proviso permits the waiver of this requirement for aliens who show "exceptional hardship" or demonstrate that they would be "subject to persecution on account of race, religion, or political opinion." Secondly § 13 of the Act of September 11, 1957, 8 U.S.C.A. § 1255b, allows the adjustment of status of certain diplomats (beneficiaries of "A" and "G" visas) to lawful permanent resident status if "the alien has shown compelling reasons demonstrating * * * that the alien is unable to return to the [home] country," and meets certain other criteria.

7. Much of the impetus for new American and international efforts after the war derived from a recognition that pre-war efforts, especially on behalf of Jewish refugees,

directive in 1945, President Truman ordered priority use of regular immigration quota numbers for the admission of some of the millions of displaced persons left stranded by World War II. In 1948, Congress passed the first significant refugee legislation in American history in order to meet the same problem. The Displaced Persons Act [8] of that year provided a temporary program for the admission of 400,000 people in the categories specified in the legislation. Throughout the next decade, Congress enacted other statutes providing specific numbers of admission spaces for designated groups of refugees. Each measure was conceived as a one-time response to known problems and did not set up an ongoing statutory mechanism to treat future episodes.[9]

When the Soviet Union put down the Hungarian revolution in 1956, its action sent hundreds of thousands of Hungarians across the borders, mainly to Austria, and created strong pressure for a quick United States response. But adequate admission provisions were unavailable to offer resettlement and thereby assist the overburdened first-asylum countries. The Eisenhower Administration finally decided to act anyway, and it chose to bring over 30,000 Hungarian refugees here using the Attorney General's parole power. The same approach was employed after Fidel Castro came to power in Cuba. Beginning in the early 1960's, parole was used increasingly for the thousands of Cubans who sought refuge in the United States.

From the executive branch's standpoint, the parole power was outstandingly convenient. It allowed for flexible response to developing crises without the need for new legislation. But its use carried certain disadvantages. Parole, as you recall from our discussion in Chapter Three, is technically not an admission of the alien. A parolee remains constructively at the border and is subject to exclusion rather than deportation proceedings if the government later chooses to remove the individual—even years later. Moreover, when the Hungarian and Cuban programs began, there was no direct way to adjust the status of a parolee to permanent resident status, even though both programs clearly were intended to bring the refugees here for a permanent stay and the beginning of a new life in a new country. Congress eventually cured the latter problem by special statutes authorizing adjustment of status for Hungarians and Cubans.[10] But more and more members of Congress asserted that

were shamefully inadequate. *See generally* J. Simpson, The Refugee Problem (1939); D. Wyman, Paper Walls: America and the Refugee Crisis, 1938–1941 (1968); H. Feingold, The Politics of Rescue: The Roosevelt Administration and The Holocaust, 1938–1945 (1970).

8. Displaced Persons Act of 1948, Ch. 647, 62 Stat. 1009.

9. *See, e.g.,* Refugee Relief Act of 1953, Ch. 336, 67 Stat. 400; Act of Sept. 11, 1957, Pub.L. No. 85–316, § 15, 71 Stat. 639, 643–44; Refugee Fair Share Law, Pub.L. No. 86–648, 74 Stat. 504 (1960). *See generally* Congressional Research Service, 96th Cong.,

2d Sess., Review of U.S. Refugee Resettlement Programs and Policies (Comm.Print, Senate Comm. on the Judiciary, 1980).

10. Act of July 25, 1958, Pub.L. No. 85–559, 72 Stat. 419 (providing for adjustment of status of Hungarians who had been in the United States at least two years); Act of Nov. 2, 1966, Pub.L. No. 89–732, 80 Stat. 1161 (providing similar adjustment opportunity for Cubans). Both provisions granted the Attorney General discretionary authority over such adjustment. Recent litigation challenged the Attorney General's refusal, for nearly four years, to use the Cuban statute to regularize the status of Cubans who

the parole power was being misused to bring in large groups of refugees without direct legislative approval.

The Hungarian and Cuban programs also taught an additional lesson. These two episodes disabused Americans of any notion that refugee problems would disappear once World War II's displaced persons had all found new homes. Some permanent provision for refugee programs, available to meet new crises, would have to be made.

The landmark 1965 immigration amendments provided the occasion for major changes. In addition to the six regular preference categories which that Act established for deciding admission priorities in place of the old national origins quotas, Congress adopted a new seventh preference designed to be a permanent provision for overseas refugee resettlement programs. It made available for refugees up to six percent of the annual numerically limited immigration numbers, but the provision applied only to refugees as precisely defined therein. A person could qualify for this program only by establishing that he had "fled" persecution in a "Communist or Communist-dominated country" or a "country within the general area of the Middle East." [11] This seventh preference provision was often called "conditional entry," because its beneficiaries did not come in on immigrant visas. They entered in a somewhat more tenuous status known as "conditional entrant," which in most respects, save the name, was identical to parole. But importantly, the 1965 law provided for fairly routine adjustment out of conditional entrant status to permanent resident status two years after initial arrival, barring the discovery of new disqualifying conditions.

Congressional committee reports accompanying the 1965 amendments stated that parole was not to be used in the future for large groups of refugees, now that permanent provision for such admissions had been made through the seventh preference. This legislative history, however, had stunningly little effect. President Johnson announced a major new parole program for Cubans during the very ceremony, held at the base of the Statue of Liberty, in which he signed the 1965 Act into law. That program came to be known as the Freedom Flights, because the Administration negotiated arrangements with the Cuban government allowing direct air travel from Havana to Florida. By the time Cuba halted the program in 1973, over 700,000 Cubans had immigrated to the United States since Fidel Castro's rise to power. When the Freedom Flights ended, the controversy over the use of parole for refugees diminished for awhile. But in 1975 the Administration used its parole power to bring in over 100,000 Vietnamese who fled when Saigon fell. After a lull in 1976 and 1977, the exodus from Indochina picked up again and reached

were part of the 1980 Mariel boatlift. After initially contesting the suit, the Administration eventually came to agree with the plaintiffs and commenced adjustments. *See* 61 Interp. Rel. 294, 847–50 (1984).

11. Immigration and Nationality Act Amendments of 1965, Pub.L. No. 89–236, § 3, 79 Stat. 911, 913, amending § 203(a)(7) of the INA. This section also authorized

admission of "persons uprooted by catastrophic natural calamity", but that provision was never used. *See generally* Parker, *Victims of Natural Disasters in United States Refugee Law and Policy,* in Transnational Legal Problems of Refugees, *supra* note 4, at 137.

enormous proportions in the late 1970's. The United States responded with large new refugee paroles.

The permanent seventh preference provision (which by 1978 allowed the admission of 17,400 people a year) was plainly not adequate to meet the high numerical demand experienced in times of refugee emergencies. Moreover, by this time the United States had established other, but much smaller, refugee resettlement programs for persons not from Communist countries or from the Middle East—such as modest programs for former political prisoners from Argentina and Chile. The evident inadequacy of the seventh preference, coupled with lingering doubts about the legitimacy of using the parole power for refugees, convinced Congress and the executive branch of the need for new legislation. Their combined efforts led to the Refugee Act of 1980, which establishes the current framework for admissions.

The Refugee Act repealed the old, numerically limited, seventh preference in its entirety. It had become apparent that a single fixed ceiling, applicable every year, simply would not fit the variable needs created by the rise and fall of refugee flows. At the same time, congressional drafters of the Refugee Act were unwilling to leave refugee admissions totally ungoverned by numerical limits fixed in some systematic fashion. That is, although they wanted to avoid a single numerical ceiling applicable year in and year out, they did not want to treat refugee admissions in the same fashion as immediate relatives and special immigrants, admission categories that are governed only by qualitative and not numerical criteria. (*See* Chapter Three.) The Refugee Act therefore established a third broad admission structure governed by a decisionmaking system quite different from quota immigration and the numerically unlimited system for immediate relatives. Before we explore its operation, you may wish to review the current provisions that govern overseas refugee programs, INA §§ 101(a)(42), 207 and 209, in the Appendix.

Annually, before the beginning of the fiscal year, the President is required to consult with the Judiciary Committees of the Congress on the executive branch's plans for refugee admissions. The Act lays out in some detail the procedures to be observed in this consultation process, and it specifies a variety of reports and data to be presented to Congress. Following consultation, the President issues a Determination that sets a total numerical ceiling applicable for the next fiscal year. That Presidential Determination also allocates this total among various refugee groups, formally based on a determination as to which refugees are of "special humanitarian concern." As a result of the allocations, not all who might meet the statutory definition of "refugee" in INA § 101(a)(42) are to be considered equally eligible to migrate to the United States. Some groups, though clearly meeting the definition, might be refused an allocation of numbers altogether—based on a judgment, for example, that conditions may soon settle down in the home country allowing voluntary repatriation, or that local settlement in the first asylum country is preferable to distant resettlement, or that this group has sufficient opportunities to resettle in distant lands other than the United States. The formal Presidential Determinations, however, have tended to use very broad allocation categories. More precise criteria for selection and priorities are included in the annual consultation documents submitted to Congress, and in guidelines issued to field officers.

The Presidential Determination for fiscal year 1984 follows:

PRESIDENTIAL DETERMINATION NO. 83–11

MEMORANDUM for the Honorable H. Eugene Douglas, United States Coordinator for Refugee Affairs

SUBJECT: FY 1984 Refugee Ceilings

In accordance with the relevant statutes and after appropriate consultations with the Congress, I have determined that:

● The admission of up to 72,000 refugees to the United States during FY 1984 is justified by humanitarian concerns or is otherwise in the national interest;

● The 72,000 worldwide refugee admission ceiling shall be allocated among the regions of the world as follows: 50,000 for East Asia; 12,000 for the Soviet Union/Eastern Europe; 6,000 for the Near East/South Asia; 3,000 for Africa; and 1,000 for Latin America/Caribbean; and

● An additional 5,000 refugee admissions numbers shall be made available for the adjustment to permanent residence status of aliens who have been granted asylum in the United States, as this is justified by humanitarian concerns or is otherwise in the national interest.

In accordance with provisions of the Immigration and Nationality Act and after appropriate consultations with the Congress, I specify that special circumstances exist such that, for the purposes of admission under the limits established above, the following persons, if they otherwise qualify for admission, may be considered refugees of special humanitarian concern to the United States even though they are still within their countries of nationality or habitual residence:

● Persons in Vietnam with past or present ties to the United States; and

● Present and former political prisoners, and persons in imminent danger of loss of life, and their family members, in countries of Latin America and the Caribbean.

You will inform the appropriate committees of the Congress of these determinations.

This memorandum shall be published in the *Federal Register*.

Ronald Reagan

Work through this Presidential Determination and satisfy yourself as to the significance of each provision. Consider especially the paragraph relating to persons "still within their countries of nationality or habitual residence." Review INA § 101(a)(42)(A) and the definitional provision of the UN Convention Relating to the Status of Refugees, from which this part of the statutory definition was derived. Why do you suppose the UN provision is limited to persons outside their country of nationality or habitual residence? Would it be a good idea to change the international definition so as to include all people who have a well-founded fear of persecution, even if they have not managed to cross their own national boundaries? Why does INA § 101(a)(42)(B) broaden the definition only "in such circumstances as the President after appropriate consultation * * may specify"? On these and other questions concerning the operation of the provisions governing overseas refugee programs, *see* Martin, *supra* note 4, at 101–104.

Refugee emergencies, of course, might also spring up anew in the middle of a fiscal year. The Refugee Act makes provision for "unforeseen emergency refugee situations" by authorizing a new round of consultations followed by a new Presidential Determination in such circumstances. That new Determination may add further admission numbers, but in the succeeding fiscal year (which begins the following October), admission spaces to meet that particular crisis must be worked into the regular consultation process and the standard Presidential Determination issued at the beginning of that new admissions period.

Once the numbers and allocations are established, the Attorney General has authority under INA § 207(c) to admit persons who meet the relevant allocation criteria. Unlike most other forms of immigration, there is no requirement that the process be initiated by a petition in the United States (from a family member or potential employer). Usually the alien can initiate the process herself, but only at U.S. overseas facilities designated as refugee processing posts. Some of the exclusion provisions from § 212(a) are waived for all refugees, and the Attorney General has the authority, in individual cases, to waive most of the others. INA § 207(c)(3).

A beneficiary of the overseas refugee program, once selected and given the necessary documents for travel to the United States, enters in a new immigration status, created by the Refugee Act of 1980 and known, sensibly enough, as "refugee." In some respects this status resembles parole for the first year after entry, because such a "refugee" can be removed through exclusion rather than deportation proceedings if a ground for expulsion is discovered.[12] But virtually all who are in this "refugee" status will adjust routinely to lawful permanent resident status

---

12. Congress accomplished this through some easily missed subtleties in § 209(a). That section provides that aliens "admitted to the United States under Section 207"— that is, in refugee status—return after a year of physical presence in the United States "to the custody of the Service for inspection and examination for admission to the United States as an immigrant *in accordance with the provisions of sections 235, 236, and 237*" (emphasis added). Any who do not pass this second round of screening are thus held for exclusion proceedings, because the referenced sections govern exclusion, not deportation. (Incidentally, the custody prescribed is constructive only; refugees have never been physically seized at this stage, to our knowledge.)

The phrasing of these sections raises some interesting questions under the usual doctrines for applying due process to aliens. As we indicated in Chapters Three and Five, due process entitlements may turn on whether or not one has accomplished an entry—which is usually the same as asking whether one is in exclusion or deportation proceedings. Here the statute says that refugees have been "admitted," and yet it puts them in exclusion proceedings. Which level of due process entitlement do they enjoy? The issue has never arisen in any reported case. Perhaps if it did, it would present an occasion for realizing, and thus eliminating, the arbitrariness of the basic due process doctrines under which we currently operate.

after one year. INA § 209(a). This adjustment of status is also retroactive in effect, so that the clock starts running toward qualification for citizenship from the initial date of arrival in the United States. § 209(a)(2). Persons who enter as part of our overseas refugee programs also are entitled to a broad range of federal assistance and retraining programs provided under INA §§ 411–414 (added by the Refugee Act). *See generally Chu Drua Cha v. Noot,* 696 F.2d 594 (8th Cir.1982); *Nguyen v. U.S. Catholic Conference,* 548 F.Supp. 1333 (W.D.Pa.1982), affirmed 719 F.2d 52 (3d Cir.1983).

There are two other threshold requirements for admission as a "refugee," however, that must claim our attention here. These are *individual* qualifications, and an applicant for inclusion in the refugee program must satisfy an immigration officer that they are met, even if she clearly falls within one of the geographical allocation groups and admission numbers are available.

First, she is ineligible if she is "firmly resettled" in a third country. This requirement simply serves to reserve U.S. refugee program spaces for those who have not already received and pursued resettlement offers elsewhere. In 1971 the Supreme Court approved INS's application of such a requirement even though the statutes at the time did not explicitly disqualify firmly resettled refugees. The "central theme of U.S. refugee legislation," the Court held, has been "the creation of a haven for the world's *homeless* people," not simply the maintenance of a preference for people who at one time had to flee persecution. *Rosenberg v. Yee Chien Woo,* 402 U.S. 49, 55, 91 S.Ct. 1312, 1315, 28 L.Ed.2d 592 (1971) (emphasis added). Congress restored the "firmly resettled" language to the text of the INA when it passed the Refugee Act, *see* INA § 207(c)(1), and regulations have clarified the application of the concept. 8 C.F.R. §§ 207.1(b) (overseas refugee programs); 208.8(f)(1)(ii) and 208.14 (asylum) (1984). *See generally Matter of Lam,* 18 I & N Dec. 15 (BIA 1981); *Matter of Portales,* Interim Dec. No. 2905 (BIA 1982).

Second, and more importantly, the officer must find that the applicant is a "refugee" within the statutory definition. Section 101(a)(42) of the INA defines "refugee" as:

> (A) any person who is outside any country of such person's nationality or, in the case of a person having no nationality, is outside any country in which such person last habitually resided, and who is unable or unwilling to return to, and is unable or unwilling to avail himself or herself of the protection of, that country because of persecution or a well-founded fear of persecution on account of race, religion, nationality, membership in a particular social group, or political opinion, or (B) in such circumstances as the President after appropriate consultation (as defined in section 207(e) of this Act) may specify, any person who is within the country of such person's nationality or, in the case of a person having no nationality, within the country in which such person is habitually residing, and who is persecuted or who has a well-founded fear of persecution on account of race, religion,

nationality, membership in a particular social group, or political opinion. The term "refugee" does not include any person who ordered, incited, assisted, or otherwise participated in the persecution of any person on account of race, religion, nationality, membership in a particular social group, or political opinion.

The definition is derived from the UN Convention and Protocol relating to the Status of Refugees. (You may wish to review the first article of each treaty, reprinted in the Appendix.) The key element of the definition is the requirement of a "well-founded fear of persecution on account of race, religion, nationality, membership in a particular social group, or political opinion." There was wide support in Congress for this more universal definition at the time when the Refugee Act was under consideration—especially in comparison to the old limitations that applied to the seventh preference. The former provisions limiting overseas refugee programs to persons who fled Communist countries or countries in the Middle East were widely denounced as "geographic and ideological discrimination."

Nevertheless, several questions can be raised regarding the wisdom of limiting overseas refugee programs by requiring that all beneficiaries meet this UN definition. For one thing, although the United States became a party to the Protocol in 1968 (and hence became derivatively bound to all the important provisions of the Convention), nothing in the Convention or Protocol obligates a country to use this definition in its *admission* decisions. The Convention, as its name suggests, is largely devoted to resolving questions about the status of persons *already physically present* in the territory of a contracting state who are determined to be "refugees," and most of its articles address matters like rights to education, public assistance, or employment.

Therefore, properly understood, the UN treaties create important obligations for the United States, but virtually all of those obligations relate to the *asylum* program rather than to the overseas refugee program. The Convention and Protocol, by their terms, do not require states parties to admit anyone. On the other hand, they clearly were not meant to narrow the discretion of states to choose to admit persons based on other humanitarian considerations. A few other industrialized nations that are parties to the Convention and Protocol have statutory provisions expressly allowing the admission, as part of overseas refugee programs, of needy people who may not technically meet the UN definition of refugee. *See, e.g.,* Canadian Immigration Act, 1976, 25–26 Eliz. II, Ch. 52, § 6(2) (providing for admission, without regard to other regulations under the Act, of Convention refugees and also of groups "designated by the Governor in Council as a class, the admission of members of which would be in accordance with Canada's humanitarian tradition with respect to the displaced and the persecuted").

Against this background, is it sound for the United States to employ the same definition to govern overseas programs as the one used in the political asylum context? Further, should the definition used in the overseas program (and possibly the definition used for political asylum

purposes as well) be expanded in light of significant changes the world has
experienced since the UN definition was drafted in 1951? The following
readings explore these issues, primarily in the context of overseas programs. But definitional questions are crucial to all aspects of refugee law.
One might almost say that all the controversies over current policy reduce
to definitional arguments—sometimes between those who urge a broader
conception and those who urge a narrower one, sometimes between those
who favor an application of the definition that reflects the politics of the
refugees or the regime they flee, and those who strive for, and believe
possible, a more neutral application. *See generally* Helton, *Political
Asylum under the 1980 Refugee Act: An Unfulfilled Promise,* 17 U.Mich.J.
L.Ref. 243, 260–62 and *passim* (1984). Keep the points raised here in
mind, therefore, as you read on into the later sections of the Chapter.

ASTRI SUHRKE, GLOBAL REFUGEE MOVEMENTS AND STRATEGIES OF RESPONSE

U.S. Immigration and Refugee Policy: Global and
Domestic Issues 157–162
(M. Kritz ed. 1983)

The definitional question is crucial because persons identified as
refugees typically have special protection and benefits that are not accorded those identified as migrants. This preferential status is recognized in
international law on the grounds that the refugee is a person in need who
cannot turn to his government for protection. The international community consequently is obliged to render assistance, even if this means
limiting the customary rights of states to decide the terms of entry and
sojourn of individuals. The principal international definitions at present
are the U.N. concepts that were formulated in the immediate post-World
War II period, largely in response to European refugee flows. Contemporary movements, by contrast, originate primarily in the Third World.
This has raised questions about the relevance of conventional concepts to
current realities.

Concern over definitions is closely related to the notion that refugee
flows have increased at a rapid pace in recent years, and will probably
continue to do so in the future. Increased demand for assistance generates pressures to adjust the definition of beneficiaries, particularly in view
of the resource restraints evident in many industrialized countries today.
Fears that huge international flows of destitute persons will be a permanent feature of the future partly stem from the appearance of large flows
at present—including the Indochinese, the Somalis, the Cubans, the
Haitians, and the Afghans. However, it may be rash to conclude that
these flows constitute a pattern and a trend, rather than a coincidence
causing a temporary peak.

* * *

A refugee can be defined in three ways: legally (as stipulated in national
or international law); politically (as interpreted to meet political exigencies); and sociologically (as reflecting an empirical reality). A legal
definition must limit the numbers demanding assistance, otherwise the
very existence of a refugee program may be jeopardized. On the other

hand, it should also be sufficiently broad to accommodate people requiring international protection. Historically, this has been the concept of a refugee in international law; the current concern is to what extent new situations have arisen that are not adequately recognized by legal norms. A brief review of the types of legal norms now in existence indicates the trade-offs associated with each.

The principal international definition is that of the United Nations, which has been adopted by many nations. The U.N. definition limits the numbers in many ways. Only persons who are outside their country of origin qualify. The key criterion determining refugee status is persecution, which usually means an act of government against individuals, thereby excluding those fleeing from generalized conditions of insecurity and oppression, as well as victims of nature-made disasters. Persecution, moreover, is generally interpreted to mean loss of certain rights, as opposed to exploitation, which implies failure to enjoy those rights in the first place. Masses of poverty-stricken and powerless people in the Third World therefore are excluded. * * *

Nor does the U.N. definition specifically cite economic factors as a reason for persecution. This omission has reinforced conventional notions to the effect that persons who leave their country for political reasons are refugees, while those who move for economic reasons are migrants. International lawyers maintain, however, that, if membership in a particular economic class is the main reason for persecution, the person in question would qualify as a refugee. This interpretation opens the way for a potentially very large number of applicants, including the poverty-stricken masses. The main corrective lies in arguing, as is customarily done, that systematic economic deprivation does not constitute persecution.

The limitations in the U.N. definition also reflect the political climate at the time it was adopted (1951). The concept of rights parallels that put forth in the 1948 Universal Declaration of Human Rights; political, civic, and legal rights are stressed, while economic rights are much less prominent. Refugees from European colonialism—that is, majority victims of minority rule—are not accounted for explicitly. The emphasis on loss of existing rights implied in the term persecution tends to favor disposed elites, while persons who normally possess few, if any, rights would not as readily qualify.

The U.N. definition is vulnerable to attack from two directions. First, as a product of Western liberal thinking and Western political supremacy in the early 1950s, it reflects particularist notions of needs and rights. Can this be the basis for a definition that aspires to universality? Second, contemporary population outflows from many Third World countries consist of persons who flee generalized conditions of insecurity and oppression, as well as the economic refugees who seek to escape severe economic deprivation. These people typically cannot count on the protection of their government to provide basic physical, economic, or political security. Their need may be equal to those who are persecuted in the sense of the U.N. definition.

Slightly broader definitions have been adopted to accommodate some of these categories of need. The most important is the 1969 Convention of the Organization of African Unity (OAU) which stipulates that persons fleeing generalized conditions of insecurity and oppression due to colonial rule, or for other reasons, should be viewed as refugees. A similar provision has not been adopted by any country outside Africa, even though these types of outflows are a common result of instability in many Third World nations. However, the UNHCR has for some time included such flows under its mandate, as a matter of administrative practice.

The reasons behind the OAU innovation may help to explain why other states have been reluctant to follow suit. African states were prepared to accept the additional obligations resulting from a broadened definition partly because wars of independence were a major cause of mass outflows. African solidarity and mutual assistance in the name of independence was a moral imperative. Ethnic groups frequently cut across state boundaries and made it easy to accept new arrivals. Repatriation, moreover was—and is—a frequent solution. Many conflicts were solved in a way that enabled the displaced persons to return home (that is, the end of colonial rule), and refugee movements did not typically flow from very poor to very rich states. The refugees, consequently, had no strong incentives to remain in the country of first asylum once the conflict at home had subsided.

A few European countries have experimented with a definition that is broader than that of the United Nations. The criteria for refugees is relaxed to include persons who require assistance on humanitarian grounds generally, but those who qualify are usually given benefits equivalent to a second-class status, or B-status. The concept remains controversial, but it does reflect the needs of many Third World groups that flee generalized conditions of insecurity and oppression. Giving limited benefits to such groups could help to protect the integrity of a more generous policy designed for those who are most victimized. On the other hand, is it feasible and desirable to have first- and second-class refugees, any more than it is to have first- and second-class citizens? It is further objected that even B-status programs will attract hordes of destitute Third World nationals that the rich countries cannot reasonably accommodate. While humanitarian reasons could be interpreted narrowly to keep the numbers down, considerations of equity will likely generate pressures in the other direction.

There are two kinds of more narrow definitions: a highly politicized one that requires that the applicant must only meet certain political criteria, and one that limits asylum or refugee status to the political activist.

The first category is exemplified by U.S. law prior to 1980 and current legislation in most communist countries. The principal criterion in the U.S. definition was that a person leaving a communist country *ipso facto* was a refugee. Need was inferred to apply categorically to all such persons. In communist countries, asylum provisions typically stipulate that the beneficiary must have struggled on behalf of the working class or a similar cause. One presumed advantage of a politicized definition is that the numbers and kinds of beneficiaries can be regulated with relative ease, because there is no pretense in the first place that refugee policy should be equitable and relative to need. However, if one category of established beneficiaries suddenly swells, this can create problems and force a reevaluation of terms: should these be treated as refugees or as migrants? Another problem is that politicized definitions usually reflect hostile relations between the sending and the receiving countries, hence there is little alternative but to accept all outflows as refugees, since a return process cannot easily be arranged. U.S. problems with Indochinese and Cuban arrivals are cases in point.

Another way of limiting the definition is to include only political activists. This concept is contained in most Latin American treaties, which limit asylum to persons who have committed a political crime. Past refugee movements in the region mainly consisted of political activists, and generous asylum provisions involved few obligations. The typical exile was educated and had independent means, his asylum frequently was temporary, and the total number was low. At present, however, a new pattern is emerging in Latin America, similar to that in Africa. Mass flows of common people spill across national boundaries due to internal strife. This is a challenge to the traditional Latin American concept of asylum, and to the kinds of legal, socioeconomic and political rights that have been associated with refugee status in the region. So far, Latin American scholars and policymakers are only beginning to explore ways of meeting that challenge.

* * *

Existing legal norms define need primarily with respect to the causes that led the person to flee. The numbers are then limited partly by stipulating types of causes, for instance, political activism, political dissidence, and ethnic minority status. Some critics argue that it is more meaningful to build a definition around the concept of need, regardless of causes. This means discarding the distinction between those who are actively persecuted and those who flee generalized conditions of insecurity, between persecuted minorities and majorities, between "refugees-in-place," who have been unable to leave and those who have left, between economic and political reasons for leaving, and so on. People in all these categories would be potentially eligible for refugee status, and the final determination would be based on an assessment of relative need. Such a concept would be relevant to contemporary realities, indeed, to any reality. The numbers could be limited according to the degree of need, it is argued. A refugee program may not be the most appropriate response for all these situations, but the important point is that some groups of very vulnerable persons would not *a priori* be excluded from consideration.

DAVID A. MARTIN, THE REFUGEE ACT OF 1980: ITS PAST AND FUTURE

1982 Mich.Y.B.Int'l L.Stud. 91, 101, 111–114.

[The Refugee] Act limits resettlement [as part of U.S. overseas refugee programs] to those who meet the United Nations definition of "refugee," derived from the 1951 Convention relating to the Status of Refugees: a person outside his or her homeland, unable or unwilling to return or otherwise claim its protection because of persecution or a well-founded fear of persecution based on race, religion, nationality, membership in a particular social group, or political opinion. This definition forms the basis for a growing body of international law which, in the view of the bill's proponents, deserved to be strengthened and built upon. There was little controversy over the definition's adoption. Indeed, because its use eliminated the geographic restrictions that marred the conditional entry provisions, it was widely welcomed.

In some respects, however, this definition serves to narrow eligibility for U.S. programs, because it excludes certain people who had been eligible under earlier refugee legislation and, indeed, who are popularly thought of as "refugees." The UN definition does not embrace those who flee natural disasters, nor, in most cases, those displaced by military operations or civil strife. (People who stream away from a battlefront generally are not fleeing persecution targeted at them, but rather are seeking personal safety.) The theory behind this technical limitation on the refugee category is apparently that the bombs will cease falling, the floods will recede, but persecution is implacable. Obviously such a generalization has sharp limits, but, as an exceedingly general rule of thumb, the theory is useful. It distinguishes those uprooted persons who are more likely to be able to pick up the pieces of their lives again in the place where they originated, and who therefore have less need of resettlement in a distant land. The drafters of the Refugee Act sought ways to contain the claims on inevitably limited U.S. resettlement opportunities, and this restriction provided one such method.

Little thought was given during consideration of the Refugee Act, however, to the difficulty inherent in making the individualized and fine-grained determination of likely persecution which the UN definition seems to require.

* * *

[T]he Refugee Act expressly links the grant of asylum to the applicant's satisfying Part A of the statute's refugee definition. There is nothing surprising in this linkage, since Part A essentially restates the Convention definition, which by treaty already governed asylum determinations. A problem arises, however, because this is exactly the definition that sets the threshold qualifications for the U.S. overseas refugee programs. Critics have charged vociferously that the *de facto* standard applied overseas is far more relaxed than that applied to asylum applicants. Vietnamese boat people, they claim, benefit from a presumption that all who risked their lives at sea faced persecution at home and therefore meet the refugee definition. Yet Haitians, who also crossed the seas in flimsy boats but happened to land directly in the United States, enjoy no similar presumption. To claim asylum, they must show more than the simple fact of flight or the existence of human rights abuses in Haiti. They must provide evidence that they themselves are likely to be singled out for persecution on return, and their stories will be minutely scrutinized.

These critics are right. There is, *de facto*, a difference in the application of the "well-founded fear of persecution" standard. Administration pronouncements often try to dodge the issue by pointing to the formal (but routine) INS finding that the UN refugee definition is met by each beneficiary of overseas programs. As the provisions are actually administered, however, the UN definition poses a significantly higher hurdle for asylum applicants. Overseas refugee staffs devote very little attention to the question of likely persecution; INS and State Department officials involved in passing on asylum claims examine that issue in great detail.

The interesting question, however, is what conclusions to draw from this revelation of a dual standard. In quest of consistency, one might relax the scrutiny of asylum claims, thereby reducing the showing of likely persecution required of an applicant. A demonstration that the home government often abuses human rights, for example, might be sufficient without any demonstration that the individual is a likely target. But the practical consequences of such a change in asylum scrutiny could easily be enormous.

Asylum constitutes a wild card in the immigration deck. No other provision of the INA opens such a broad potential prospect of U.S. residency to aliens without the inconvenience of prescreening or selection. An alien may enter in flagrant disregard of U.S. immigration laws, but if he meets the asylum test, he is entitled to stay in the United States indefinitely and to advance toward permanent residence here. By the very nature of the UN Protocol commitment, the United States is not entitled to apply other criteria in deciding whether to extend this protection—criteria such as family ties, other U.S. connections, or employment skills, routinely applied to other intending immigrants. If the alien proves a well-founded fear of persecution, then, by law, he or she cannot be returned to the home country.

This system need not be alarming, if wisely administered. Asylum became an immigration law loophole for good reasons. Returning people to situations where they are almost sure to face persecution, no matter how they reached U.S. shores, would flatly contradict American tradition. But if it becomes too easy to establish entitlement to asylum, if the United States does not stringently require the applicant to show solid reasons why he or she is likely to be singled out for persecution on return, then great numbers of illegal aliens would probably be happy to surface and claim the benefits of asylum. The United States is also accessible to thousands more in the Caribbean, Central America, and conceivably, in South America, who would leave countries with poor enough human rights records to make any claim to asylum at least initially plausible.

Because the "well-founded fear of persecution" standard is the only criterion the Protocol permits parties to apply (assuming that the applicant is neither a spy nor a criminal), there are strong incentives to administer that standard with scrupulous care and to insist on more than a showing of general abuses by the home government. The UNHCR handbook on determination of refugee status generally indicates such a circumscribed and individualized standard, and American judicial decisions support that approach. A relaxation of asylum scrutiny is thus unlikely.

The second option for bringing consistency to U.S. application of the UN refugee definition is to tighten scrutiny overseas. In fact, large populations in temporary asylum areas probably do contain many who could not prove entitlement if subjected to asylum-type scrutiny. Particularly as it becomes known that the United States and other attractive countries are resettling large numbers from the first-asylum camps, migrants are surely drawn there for reasons other than fear of persecution.

Any tightening in overseas scrutiny, however, would require a much greater commitment of staff and resources. As asylum processing demonstrates, establishing with reasonable confidence that an applicant fears persecution and that the fear is well-founded requires careful interviewing, steps to verify the events claimed as the basis of the fear, and ultimately a difficult assessment of the applicant's credibility. American field staff is already stretched thin in applying the other, more accessible, screening criteria currently employed. Devoting additional resources to a more finely-tuned application of the refugee definition is not worthwhile, for a simple reason. Finding a Vietnamese national in Malaysia or an Eastern European in Frankfort to be a refugee within the UN definition furnishes only the first step in a process that may or may not lead to resettlement in the United States. Physical distance virtually assures that that person will not come to the United States unless selected for the resettlement program, and the Refugee Act's allocation provisions clearly authorize the use of other screening criteria. The practical imperative for stringent application of the refugee definition is therefore minor. Screening can be done, and in its most important respects will continue to be done, on the basis of other criteria.

The availability of other screening criteria overseas, coupled with the inevitable difficulty and expense entailed in scrupulous application of the refugee definition in any context, amply justifies the *de facto* difference in application of the "refugee" definition. And justified or not, the divergence is quite likely to continue.

As long as the statute, however, formally applies the same definitional test to asylum and refugee determinations, this inconsistency will remain a powerful fulcrum for complaints about denials of asylum. The only adequate remedy for the problem would be an amendment to the Act to separate the two standards, recognizing forthrightly the different imperatives that govern review of the respective applicants' compliance with the refugee definition.

Notes

1. Martin suggests that the differential application of the definition—stringently in asylum processing but generously in overseas pro-

grams—is justified because of the contrasting arrangements that can be made to control the overall numbers of people admitted in either fashion. But is this disparity really justifiable? Should it make so much difference whether a putative refugee happens to land in Thailand, rather than the United States, as a first-asylum country? Is the claimed justification just a pleasant way of disguising ideological discrimination in the application of a standard Congress meant to apply impartially to all people seeking haven?

Before the Refugee Act was passed, the parole power was used predominantly to bring in refugees from Marxist countries (even though parole, unlike conditional entry, was not formally limited to refugees from Communist countries and the Middle East). From 1968 (the date of U.S. accession to the UN Protocol) through 1980, parole was used to admit 7,150 people from non-Communist countries and 608,365 from Communist countries. Helton, *Political Asylum under the 1980 Refugee Act, supra,* 17 U.Mich.J.L.Ref. at 248. A glance at the Presidential Determination reprinted above reveals that refugees from Communism still claim the overwhelming majority of refugee admission spaces. Indeed, the proportions are even more heavily weighted in that direction than may immediately appear; most of the spaces for the Near East/South Asia will be used for Afghan refugees, and in recent years most of the African admissions slots have been claimed by Ethiopians. Both Ethiopia and Afghanistan are currently ruled by Marxist governments. Is this allocation justified? Helton argues that standards Congress meant to be "uniform and neutral" have been rendered "subservient to foreign and domestic policy considerations." *Id.* at 243.

2. On the other hand, is there really anything wrong with an "ideological" refugee policy? Perhaps the statute ought to be more candid about the de facto requirements, but if it were, would such an approach, favoring the enemies of our clearest international adversaries, be undesirable? Morally wrong? Might these questions depend on the overall numbers seeking refuge? On the severity of the treatment that the various groups of refugees can expect in their home countries if returned, or on their treatment in the country of first asylum, if they are forced to remain there?

The philosopher Michael Walzer—who is clearly not a Cold Warrior himself—has treated these questions at length in his book *Spheres of Justice* (1983), portions of which were reprinted in Chapter One, *supra.* His conclusions are surprisingly favorable to an "ideological" refugee admission policy. Many of the dilemmas have no satisfactory answers, he acknowledges, but he offers in part the reflections that follow (the entire section of his book is well worth consulting):

> Toward some refugees, we may well have obligations of the same sort that we have toward fellow nationals. This is obviously the case with regard to any group of people whom we have helped turn into refugees. The injury we have done them makes for an affinity between us: thus Vietnamese refugees had, in a moral sense, been effectively Americanized even before they

arrived on these shores. But we can also be bound to help men and women persecuted or oppressed by someone else—if they are persecuted or oppressed because they are like us. Ideological as well as ethnic affinity can generate bonds across political lines, especially, for example, when we claim to embody certain principles in our communal life and encourage men and women elsewhere to defend those principles. * * * [C]onsider the thousands of men and women who fled Hungary after the failed revolution of 1956. It is hard to deny them a similar recognition [as a kind of kin], given the structure of the Cold War, the character of Western propaganda, the sympathy already expressed with East European "freedom fighters." These refugees probably had to be taken in by countries like Britain and the United States. The repression of political comrades, like the persecution of co-religionists, seems to generate an obligation to help, at least to provide a refuge for the most exposed and endangered people. Perhaps every victim of authoritarianism and bigotry is the moral comrade of a liberal citizen: that is an argument I would like to make. But that would press affinity too hard, and it is in any case unnecessary. So long as the number of victims is small, [the principle of] mutual aid will generate similar practical results; and when the number increases, and we are forced to choose among the victims, we will look, rightfully, for some more direct connection with our own way of life. * * * Once again, communities must have boundaries; and however these are determined with regard to territory and resources, they depend with regard to population on a sense of relatedness and mutuality. Refugees must appeal to that sense. One wishes them success; but in particular cases, with reference to a particular state, they may well have no right to be successful.

Id. at 49–50.

3. Although the Martin article assumed that the differential application of the definition as between asylum processing and refugee processing would persist quietly, INS actually seemed to be trying, at one stage, to apply the definition with the same skepticism and toughness in both settings—and the result was a highly public controversy over the issue. In 1981, when a new district director, Joseph Sureck, arrived in the Hong Kong district office, the office with authority over the overseas refugee program for Indochinese, he ordered that immigration officers tighten up their review of this question, in order to render it consistent with the application of the definition in asylum cases. Apparently neither the State Department nor the higher levels of the Justice Department had been consulted before the change ensued; it was simply a matter of applying the statute, and the statute used the same definition of "refugee" in both settings.

Suddenly thousands of Indochinese boat people and land escapees found their applications for refugee status provisionally denied, on the ground that they could not individually document reasons to fear persecution. This result slowed resettlements out of the camps, complicated diplomatic relations with countries of first asylum, as well as with other resettlement countries, and outraged the voluntary organizations who had been closely involved in the resettlement and sponsorship process. In consequence, the shift promptly attracted the personal attention of both the Attorney General and the Secretary of State, and the involvement of the congressional committees with jurisdiction over immigration matters.

After months of review and deliberation, new guidelines were implemented that generally restored, in practice, the status quo ante. Most of the Indochinese in the camps would again be adjudged to satisfy the refugee definition (although they might well still be denied a space in the U.S. resettlement program because of a failure to meet other selection criteria). Although the guidelines place some emphasis on "case by case" determinations, they also establish certain categories of applicants determined "to share common characteristics that identify them as targets of persecution in their particular countries." Indochinese who fit into such a category do not need to offer further proof of individualized persecution. No similar presumptions are available to asylum applicants. *See generally* House Comm. on the Judiciary, 97th Cong., 2d Sess., Refugee Issues in Southeast Asia and Europe (Comm.Print 1982); *INS Guidelines for Overseas Processing of Refugees Evaluated, Problems Identified,* Refugee Reports, September 7, 1984, at 1–3.

Is the restored policy appropriate? Are group presumptions consistent with the Refugee Act?

4. Suhrke describes proposals to create a new refugee definition built upon the concept of need. Can you construct such a definition, in a form suitable for *legal* application? Should such a concept focus on individual need, or is it more likely to be workable if applied to groups? Under either alternative, can the governing definition be particularized in ways that will minimize the discretion of the government officials who apply it? The obstacles in the way of translating the concept of need into legally workable provisions are obviously substantial. But the main question is this: would such a definition be any more prone to erratic application or political distortion than is the current formula?

5. As Suhrke suggests, one of the major controversies concerns the definition's application to so-called economic migrants. Some people question the significance of the attempted distinction between refugees and economic migrants. Others concede its potential applicability to some migration flows, but urge that refugee status be recognized when economic deprivation results from deliberate political decisions by those in power—for example, political decisions made in order to enrich the ruling elite.

> At the heart of the matter is a dispute about whether the Haitians are fleeing oppression or poverty: are they in danger from the regime of Jean-Claude (Baby Doc) Duvalier, or are they, as the U.S. government argues, simply people who want to better their lot in life? For many Haitians, the victims of swindles, extortion and abuse at the hands of the Tontons Macoutes, the distinction is an artificial one. Their poverty, they say, is due to

a system in which agents of the state exploit the people economically. One 48-year-old Haitian accountant in Miami * * * concedes [that the] refugees are fleeing poverty, * * * but "it is the way [Haiti] is policed that pushed them into that situation. . . . No one can tell me they ought to separate the economic situation from the political situation."

Refugees or Prisoners?, Newsweek, February 1, 1982, at 26.*

Can the economic be distinguished from the political in these settings? If pure economic deprivation can be the foundation for refugee status whenever political decisions have contributed to the population's economic suffering, how severe must the deprivation be? How close must be the linkage to political decisions? Are there any impoverished countries where the population's deprivation is not linked in some fashion to earlier political decisions or corruption by the ruling elite? Should deprivation of this kind qualify the victims for resettlement as refugees in industrialized nations?

SECTION C.   POLITICAL ASYLUM

1.   INTRODUCTION

From the very beginning of federal immigration laws, Congress has recognized that special exemptions may be necessary for otherwise deportable or excludable aliens who have become political enemies of the nation to which they would be sent. In 1875, when Congress provided that convicts would be excludable, it exempted persons who had been convicted of political offenses. Similar exemptions appeared with regularity in later laws.[13]

In 1950, Congress adopted the first clearcut political asylum provision exempting aliens from deportation "to any country in which the Attorney

---

* Copyright 1982, by Newsweek, Inc. All Rights Reserved. Reprinted by Permission.

13. *See, e.g.,* Act of March 3, 1875, Ch. 141, § 5, 18 Stat. 477; Act of August 3, 1882, Ch. 376, § 4, 22 Stat. 214; Act of March 3, 1891, Ch. 551, § 1, 26 Stat. 1084; Act of Feb. 20, 1907, Ch. 1134, § 2, 34 Stat. 898, 899; Immigration Act of 1917, Ch. 29, § 3, 39 Stat. 874, 877.

This exemption is similar to provisions in most extradition treaties banning the return of those who are sought by the requesting state in order to be tried for "political offenses." But both the judicial and the executive branches have found it difficult to apply this concept consistently in extradition cases, especially to so-called "relative political offenses," acts that would be common crimes (murder, theft, property destruction), but which are allegedly committed for political ends. *See* Note, *Extradition Reform and the Statutory Definition of Political Offenses,*

24 Va.J.Int'l L. 419, 429–32 (1984); *Eain v. Wilkes,* 641 F.2d 504, 519 (7th Cir.), *cert. denied,* 454 U.S. 894 (1981). Moreover, the political offense exception to extradition is not coextensive with the shelter provided by the political asylum provisions of the immigration laws. Occasionally, an alien fugitive has escaped extradition because of a political offense ruling, only to be adjudged deportable nonetheless, sometimes after the denial of a political asylum application. *See, e.g., Matter of McMullen,* 17 I. & N. Dec. 542 (BIA 1980), *rev'd,* 658 F.2d 1312 (9th Cir. 1981); O'Higgins, *Disguised Extradition: The Soblen Case,* 27 Mod.L.Rev. 521 (1964). Is there any reason to have the same basic commodity—protection against return to a state where the individual fears severe consequences—thus governed by discontinuous standards? *See generally* G. Goodwin-Gill, *supra* note 1, at 78–81.

General shall find that such alien would be subjected to physical persecution." Internal Security Act of 1950, Ch. 1024, § 23, 64 Stat. 987, 1010. Early court decisions ostensibly imposed onerous factfinding responsibilities on the Attorney General under this provision. *See, e.g., Sang Ryup Park v. Barber,* 107 F.Supp. 605 (N.D.Cal.1952); *Harisiades v. Shaughnessy,* 187 F.2d 137, 142 (2d Cir.1951), affirmed on other grounds, 342 U.S. 580, 72 S.Ct. 512, 96 L.Ed. 586 (1951). As a result, Congress rewrote the provision when it drafted the Immigration and Nationality Act in 1952. Section 243(h) of that Act authorized the Attorney General, *in his discretion,* to withhold deportation of an alien within the United States who was subject to physical persecution in his country of nationality. In 1958, the Supreme Court construed this provision rather rigidly, holding that it covered only aliens in deportation proceedings and afforded no protection for a parolee even if she were equivalently jeopardized. *Leng May Ma v. Barber,* 357 U.S. 185, 78 S.Ct. 1072, 2 L.Ed.2d 1246 (1958). But eventually INS found ways to afford parallel protection to people in exclusion proceedings, through special use of the parole power when it deemed that the persecution claim was valid.

You will recall that the old seventh preference provision, added by the 1965 immigration act amendments, as well as some of its predecessor provisions for overseas programs, treated as refugees only people who fled Communist countries or countries in the general area of the Middle East. Arrangements for the withholding of deportation or for equivalent protections through the parole power were never formally subject to the same limitations. It remains clear, nevertheless, that these asylum-type provisions were administered for many years under the strong influence of Cold War assumptions. Successful asylum claimants were, in overwhelming proportions, refugees from Communist countries.

In 1968, the United States became a party to the United Nations Protocol relating to the Status of Refugees, and so became derivatively bound by all of the important substantive provisions of the UN Convention relating to the Status of Refugees.[14] Congress enacted no changes in the statutory provisions relating to asylum at that time, because the Departments of State and Justice had assured the Senate, while it was considering ratification, that the Protocol could be implemented without requiring any changes in the immigration laws. It is questionable, however, whether the Senators fully appreciated the consequences of our accepting the treaty. What had previously been purely discretionary provisions permitting, but not requiring, the Attorney General to withhold deportation were transformed into firm legal obligations. The treaty recognizes no discretion to return an alien if he proves he is a refugee and comes within Article 33's protection against *refoulement* (the French term commonly used to refer to the return of refugees in such circumstances). *See* Note, *The Right of Asylum under United States Law,* 80 Colum.L.Rev. 1125 (1980).

Moreover, the executive branch's testimony had merely stated that the treaty could be implemented under existing *statutes.* It did not

---

14. *See* note 1 *supra.* Portions of both treaties are reprinted in the Appendix.

promise that former administrative criteria for the exercise of discretion could remain unchanged once the treaty became law. (Nor did it promise the opposite; it was simply silent on this crucial question.) The BIA had ruled many years before ratification that an alien would be accorded discretionary relief under § 243(h) only if he demonstrated "a clear probability of persecution." Soon after ratification of the Protocol, litigants began to argue that this standard was too severe, and that the touchstone should be "a well-founded fear of persecution," as set forth in Article 1 of the UN Convention—presumably a standard somewhat easier to satisfy. The Board ultimately decided that no change was warranted, despite the new treaty obligation. *Matter of Dunar,* 14 I. & N. Dec. 310 (1973). The Board's ruling is discussed at greater length in connection with the Supreme Court's *Stevic* ruling, which we will consider later in this section.

More significant changes in the actual implementation of political asylum protections came in the wake of the Kudirka incident in 1970. A Lithuanian seaman named Simas Kudirka managed to escape in U.S. territorial waters from a Russian vessel to a Coast Guard cutter, the *Vigilant,* tied alongside for a discussion of fishing rights. After a series of miscalculations and missed communications, and with stunning blindness to the likely political fallout, the Coast Guard permitted Soviet crewmen to come aboard, forcibly seize Kudirka, and return him to the Russian ship.[15] As a result of the ensuing outcry, the Nixon Administration launched a major review of all U.S. arrangements for political asylum. This process eventually resulted in formal regulations and guidelines issued by several agencies, including the State Department and INS.[16] The INS regulations, issued in 1974, were the first to spell out in detail the procedures to be followed when applying for political asylum. 39 Fed.Reg. 41,832 (1974). In ensuing years, INS made several changes in

---

15. *See* Mann, *Asylum Denied: The Vigilant Incident,* 62 U.S. Naval War College Int'l L.Stud. 598 (1980); Goldie, *Legal Aspects of the Refusal of Asylum by U.S. Coast Guard on 23 November 1970, id.,* at 626.

16. The policy of the State Department is still in force in essentially the same form adopted in 1972. *See* Public Notice 351, 37 Fed.Reg. 3447 (1972); modified, Public Notice 728, 45 Fed.Reg. 70,621 (1980). One feature deserves special mention: the specific disavowal of the custom of diplomatic asylum. Diplomatic asylum is a practice, rejected by most countries around the world but accepted by many Latin American states, whereby certain threatened persons (usually members of a political elite endangered by a sudden change of government) are offered initial shelter in a diplomatic mission, and, ordinarily, are then provided a safe-conduct pass that will permit their removal to the territory of the asylum country. *See generally* The Asylum Case, 1950 I.C.J. 266. Official U.S. policy, however, does allow for short-term harborage in diplomatic facilities under some circumstances—for example, to protect persons pursued by an angry mob. *See* 2 A. Grahl-Madsen, The Status of Refugees in International Law 6 (1972) (commenting on this practice of "temporary refuge" in diplomatic facilities).

The stated policy often presents very difficult practical problems in implementation, once asylum-seekers (seeking haven against the host government rather than mob violence) have managed to enter U.S. diplomatic facilities. Though there is no legal requirement for sheltering them, at times the likely domestic political consequence of ejection have prompted the Department to allow a lengthy stay in an embassy. For example, a family of Pentecostals remained in the American embassy in Moscow for several years before arrangements were finally concluded to move them to the United States. *See generally* Nash, *Contemporary Practice of the United States Relating to International Law: Diplomatic Asylum,* 75 Am.J.Int'l L. 142 (1981).

these regulations, many of them in response to the pressure of litigation. *See, e.g.,* 40 Fed.Reg. 3407–08 (1975), 44 Fed.Reg. 21,258–59 (1979); *Sannon v. United States,* 631 F.2d 1247 (5th Cir.1980) (recounting the history of some of the important litigation).

Although by 1980 the controversy over the provisions for political asylum and their implementation was mounting, Congress did not use the occasion of the Refugee Act to undertake a thorough review of these issues. Congressional attention was preoccupied with the overseas refugee programs. Nevertheless, the Act made a few important improvements respecting political asylum. For example, the word "asylum" had never before appeared in the immigration laws of the United States. To be sure, successful applicants who proved the required degree of threatened persecution in the homeland were protected against involuntary return, but there was no immigration status clearly available to reflect that decision and clarify the beneficiary's right to stay indefinitely.

The Refugee Act added a new § 208 to the INA, specifically curing the earlier omission and establishing what amounts to a new immigration status—"asylum" status. This status can be provided, in the discretion of the Attorney General, to applicants in the United States who show that they meet the UN definition of refugee—that is, who have a "well-founded fear of persecution" if returned to their home countries. Persons in "asylum" status are entitled to the same types of federal assistance that beneficiaries of the overseas refugee programs receive. But in other respects, "asylees" differ importantly from "refugees"—meaning those who have entered as part of the overseas programs. For example, the asylum provisions of the INA (§§ 208 and 209(b)) place greater emphasis on continuing review of conditions in the asylee's home country. "Asylum" status is to be terminated if circumstances change abroad so that the threat of persecution is ended. "Refugee" status carries no equivalent vulnerability. *See* INA §§ 207(c)(4), 209(a). Moreover, although asylees are provided a mechanism for adjusting their status to lawful permanent resident status after one year in the United States, the Refugee Act expressly limits the number of adjustments to a maximum of 5,000 per year, and the executive branch need not make the full 5,000 available in any given year. (Look again at the Presidential Determination reprinted above at page 624. What provision was made in fiscal year 1984 for asylum adjustments?) In contrast, there is no ceiling on the adjustments of persons who are in "refugee" status. (*Compare* INA § 209(a)(2) with § 209(b).) Finally, under the regulations, "asylum" status is provided in one year increments, assuring periodic INS review of the alien's continuing qualification for such status. *See* 8 C.F.R. § 208.8(e).

Perhaps the most fundamental change effectuated by the Refugee Act was the amendment to § 243(h) of the INA, the provision that had since 1952 given the Attorney General discretion to withhold the deportation of aliens subject to persecution. First, this provision was expressly expanded so as to include aliens in exclusion proceedings. Second, it was changed from a discretionary to a mandatory provision. Return now must be withheld if the alien shows that his "life or freedom would be threatened * * * on account of race, religion, nationality, membership in a particular social group, or political opinion." This language is taken directly from Article 33 of the UN Convention. Certain exceptions to this mandatory obligation appear in § 243(h)(2), serving generally to disqualify spies, dangerous criminals, and persons who themselves participated in the persecution of others. Do these exceptions place us in violation of the treaty? Congress intended to avoid any such result, and the legislative history states explicitly that the exceptions are to be construed consistently with exceptions to the Protocol's protections. *See* Articles 1(F) and 33(2) of the UN Convention. But the wording of § 243(h)(2)(A), disqualifying those who have "ordered, incited, assisted or otherwise participated in" persecution of others, is extraordinarily broad.[17] To what provisions in the Convention does it correspond?

Applications for asylum protections under either § 208 or § 243(h) are initiated by the filing of a Form I–589. *See* 8 C.F.R. Part 208. In addition to asking the ultimate question—why the person believes he or she will be persecuted if returned home—that Form poses additional queries that may throw light on the claim. It asks about past activities and organizational affiliations, current whereabouts and condition of family members, circumstances of departure, and the like. Once the I–589 has been received, the regulations require that in every case the views of the State Department be sought before proceeding to a decision. (We will consider certain problems raised by this role for the State Department later in the Chapter.)

If no exclusion or deportation proceedings have been initiated, the request for asylum will be heard initially by an officer in the district office, who will interview the applicant before sending the file on to the State Department for its views. These officers are specifically instructed to carry out the interview in a "nonadversarial manner." *See* 61 Interp. Rel. 522, 523 (1984) (policy memorandum with detailed guidance on all aspects of asylum adjudications and documentation in the district office). After that advice is received, the officer will proceed to reach a decision,

---

17. The apparent breadth of this exception reflects its provenance, for the language mirrors the language of § 241(a)(19), a particularly strict provision directed at Nazi persecutors. During the 1970's, several former Nazi collaborators were discovered in the United States, many of them having entered in the late 1940's under the Displaced Persons program, usually by concealing their true identities. Because of the passage of time, there had been difficulties in securing their deportation under the regular provisions of the immigration laws. Congresswoman Elizabeth Holtzman took the lead in pushing for their removal, and § 241(a)(19) was adopted in 1978 under legislation known as the Holtzman Amendment. Persons deportable under this provision are explicitly declared ineligible for most forms of relief from deportation, including withholding under § 243(h) and suspension under § 244.

As § 241(a)(19) has been interpreted by the BIA, it provides for the removal of those who assisted the Nazis in persecution, even if they did so involuntarily and under duress. *See Matter of Fedorenko,* Interim Dec. No. 2963 (BIA 1984); *Matter of Laipenieks,* Interim Dec. No. 2949 (BIA 1983), *reversed, Laipenieks v. INS,* 750 F.2d 1427 (9th Cir. 1985) (holding that "active personal involvement in persecutorial acts needs to be demonstrated" for a finding of deportability under this provision). It is not yet clear whether the BIA would interpret the parallel language in § 243(h)(2) in such a draconian fashion, *see Matter of McMullen,* Interim Dec. No. 2967, at 9–10 (BIA 1984), reprinted later in this Chapter. But it is doubtful whether such a harsh construction, however appropriate it might be for Nazi collaborators, would be consistent with Article 1(F) of the UN Convention.

issued in the name of the district director. A negative decision is not appealable, but the asylum request may be renewed before the immigration judge once exclusion or deportation proceedings begin, and the judge then decides the matter de novo. The applicant may put on additional evidence concerning the claim at the formal—"adversarial"—deportation or exclusion hearing. Alternatively, if such proceedings are already underway before an asylum application is filed, the asylum claim is heard exclusively by the immigration judge.[18] And if the applicant applies for asylum only after exclusion or deportation has been ordered, the claim must be raised by means of a motion to reopen, which "must reasonably explain the failure to request asylum prior to the completion of the exclusion or deportation proceeding." 8 C.F.R. § 208.11.

The immigration judge's decision is appealable to the Board of Immigration Appeals. Most of the time, any judicial review of the decision comes at this stage, after the Board has ruled, but there have been exceptions when judicial review was deemed proper at an earlier stage because of the nature of the issues raised—particularly when it was alleged that there had been major procedural defaults in the early stages of the asylum proceedings. See, e.g., Haitian Refugee Center v. Smith, 676 F.2d 1023, 1033–36 (5th Cir.1982) reprinted in relevant part in Chapter Seven, supra. Judicial review takes place initially either in the district court or the court of appeals, depending on whether the applicant is in exclusion or deportation proceedings.

Information about asylum applications is supposed to remain confidential, both to protect family members and friends still in the home country, and to make sure that the mere fact of filing for asylum will not add in any measure to the risks that might be faced by the applicant. Although this policy of confidentiality had been implemented unevenly in the past, both INS and the State Department have taken added steps recently to safeguard such information. See, e.g., 60 Interp.Rel. 917–18 (1983).

The regulations provide that an application for asylum under § 208 shall also be treated by the immigration judge as an application for § 243(h) relief. 8 C.F.R. § 208.3(b) (1984). Why then have two separate provisions pointing generally toward the same kinds of protection for the same class of persons? Try to think of possible explanations on your own, before examining the BIA's approach to these issues in the following case.

---

18. Asylum claims at this stage are automatically treated as requests for withholding of exclusion or deportation under § 243(h). 8 C.F.R. § 208.3(b). For technical reasons, they are not so considered when they are before the district director. Relief under § 243(h) is predicated on a finding that the alien is excludable or deportable, and only immigration judges make such findings. Hence only immigration judges are authorized to consider requests for § 243(h) relief. District directors may simply proceed to grant asylum without formally deciding whether the alien is excludable or deportable. Granting asylum, of course, achieves the same end as § 243(h) (as well as bringing additional benefits); ordinarily an alien would not be deported or excluded while he remains in asylum status.

MATTER OF SALIM

Board of Immigration Appeals, 1982.
Interim Decision No. 2292.

The applicant appeals from the March 24, 1982, decision of the immigration judge denying his applications for asylum pursuant to section 208 of the Immigration and Nationality Act, and temporary withholding of deportation pursuant to section 243(h). The appeal will be sustained in part and dismissed in part. The immigration judge's decision will be modified so as to deny the application for political asylum as a matter of discretion but grant the application for temporary withholding of deportation to Afghanistan.

The applicant's excludability under section 212(a)(19) and 212(a)(20) is not at issue and was conceded at the exclusion hearing on March 24, 1982. The applicant arrived in the United States from Pakistan on February 18, 1982, with someone else's passport which he had fraudulently purchased in order to obtain a visa as a nonimmigrant visitor for business. He appeals from the immigration judge's conclusion that he had not established the requisite well-founded fear of persecution in his native Afghanistan and therefore was ineligible for asylum and temporary withholding of deportation. The immigration judge reached that conclusion despite a State Department Bureau of Human Rights and Humanitarian Affairs (BHRHA) advisory opinion dated March 12, 1982, that the applicant had established a well-founded fear of persecution in his native country.

We agree with the applicant that he has established the requisite probability of persecution in Afghanistan. The applicant contended that he had been a member of the Mujahidin rebels in Kandahar and that two of his brothers have been arrested by the Soviet controlled Babrak regime for similar membership. Another brother was taken by Russian troops at Kandahar, and the applicant does not know his whereabouts or whether he is still alive. The immediate reason for his fleeing Afghanistan was that he refused to join the Soviet controlled Afghan army in its war against Afghan rebels presently fighting against the Soviet invasion.

The State Department BHRHA conclusion that the applicant would be persecuted is consistent with its report on Afghanistan in the 1981 Country Reports on Human Rights Practices at 929, 931, Joint Committees of the Senate and House of Representatives, 97th Congress, 1st Session (1981). The report emphasizes that due to mass desertion by Afghan soldiers who refuse to fight under Soviet command against their compatriots, the army resorts to dragooning and forcibly impressing into its forces men and boys as replacements. This clearly differs from persecution claims by aliens who merely seek to avoid military service in their country. *See Kovac v. INS*, 407 F.2d 102 (9 Cir.1969). Under the facts of this case, we attach significant weight to the State Department's conclusion that this applicant would be persecuted if returned to Afghanistan. Consequently, we conclude that the applicant has established a well-founded fear of persecution despite the immigration judge's conclusion to the contrary. The immigration judge's specific finding that the applicant left Afghanistan for mere economic reasons apparently stemmed from a misunderstanding of the applicant's testimony that he came to the United States seeking employment. That statement was a repetition of his immediately preceding testimony that he left Pakistan because he could not support his family left behind in Afghanistan, while unemployed in Pakistan. It was not an explanation of why he left Afghanistan.

Having concluded that the applicant established the requisite likelihood of persecution, a grant of temporary withholding of deportation to Afghanistan is required in this case pursuant to section 243(h) of the Act as amended by the Refugee Act of 1980, Pub.L. No. 96–212, 94 Stat. 102 (March 17, 1980). That section now specifies that "the Attorney General shall not deport or return any alien ... to a country if the Attorney General determines that such alien's life or freedom would be threatened on account of ... political opinion." Under section 243(h) as drafted prior to the 1980 Amendment such relief was discretionary.[4]

We next address the question of asylum which section 208(a) of the Act provides is discretionary in nature. It specifically states that an alien applicant "*may* be granted asylum in the discretion of the Attorney General if the Attorney General determines that such alien is a refugee within the meaning of section 101(a)(42)(A)." (Emphasis supplied). Once it is determined that the requisite probability of persecution has been established for section 243(h) relief, such a conclusion is also binding on the issue of persecution for purposes of asylum under section 208 of the Act. *Matter of Lam,* Interim Decision 2857 (BIA 1981). Therefore, the applicant's statutory eligibility for asylum has been established. However, the Service contends that the application for political asylum in the United States should be denied as a matter of discretion due to the circumstances of his arrival in the United States with a fraudulently purchased passport bearing someone else's name. Similarly, the State Department BHRHA recommended in its advisory letter that the asylum application be denied for policy considerations since the applicant misused our immigration laws to gain an advantage over all other similarly situated Afghan refugees in Pakistan who are following the established procedures for legally immigrating to the United States.

This Board has not previously considered the exercise of discretion in asylum cases where it was found that the alien would be persecuted if returned to his native country. Until May 1979 neither immigration judges nor this Board addressed asylum claims, as jurisdiction to adjudicate asylum applications then lay exclusively with the District Directors. The immigration judges and this Board only had jurisdiction to consider applications for withholding of deportation under section 243(h). Effective May 19, 1979, however, the regulations gave authority to immigration judges and this Board to consider asylum applications made after the commencement or completion of deportation proceedings. *See* 8 C.F.R. 108.3. Interim regulations promulgated pursuant to the Refugee Act of 1980 similarly provide that asylum applications made after the institution of exclusion or deportation proceedings shall be considered by immigration judges. *See* 8 C.F.R. 208.3(b) (effective June 1, 1980). In view of this

4. The previous language of section 243(h) read: "the Attorney General is authorized to withhold deportation." The case before us does not involve any issue of ineligibility for relief under the grounds set forth in section 243(h)(2). Moreover, this applicant is not deportable under the provision of section 241(a)(19) of the Act.

Board's recent acquisition of jurisdiction over asylum claims and the revision of the laws in this area in 1980, many issues raised before the Board relating to asylum are issues of first impression.

The language in section 208(a) specifying the discretionary nature of asylum relief is clear, and since that section was enacted subsequent to the 1967 protocol it controls over any conflicting language in the protocol under the applicable rules of statutory interpretation. Consequently, under the present statute an otherwise eligible alien whom [sic] the Attorney General determines that his life or freedom would be threatened in his native country on account of race, religion, nationality, membership in a particular social group, or political opinion is entitled to 243(h) relief and may also be granted asylum relief, but only as a matter of discretion.

Section 243(h) relief is "country specific" and accordingly, the applicant here would be presently protected from deportation to Afghanistan pursuant to section 243(h). But that section would not prevent his exclusion and deportation to Pakistan or any other hospitable country under section 237(a) if that country will accept him. In contrast, asylum is a greater form of relief. When granted asylum the alien may be eligible to apply for adjustment of status to that of a lawful permanent resident pursuant to section 209 of the Act, after residing here one year, subject to numerical limitations and the applicable regulations. *See* 8 C.F.R. 209. Considering this relationship between asylum and 243(h) relief, we now examine the discretionary factors in this case.

As stated above, the Board had never before considered a discretionary denial of asylum relief. However, the lack of direct precedents does not mean that useful guidelines are unavailable. For example, 8 C.F.R. 208.8(f)(1) precludes the District Director from granting asylum relief to specific classes of applicants, and 8 C.F.R. 208.8(f)(2) states that the District Director shall consider all relevant factors such as whether an outstanding offer of resettlement is available to the applicant in a third country and the public interest involved in the specific case. The regulations, in essence, summarize the specific preclusions in the Act against aliens who persecuted others abroad with this Board's and the judicially developed principles for the exercise of discretionary relief from deportation. *See Rosenberg v. Woo,* 402 U.S. 49 (1971). Although those regulations are addressed to the District Director and are not binding on this Board, we consider them as useful guidelines in the exercise of discretion over asylum requests.

Attempting entry into the United States by way of fraudulently obtained documentation has consistently been considered a strong negative discretionary factor. *See Balami v. INS,* 669 F.2d 1157 (6 Cir.1982). This applicant is excludable under section 212(a)(19) of the Act. We note that section 212(a)(19) excludability would require a waiver pursuant to section 209(c), for refugee adjustment of status cases.[7] Finally, as the

7. Under the terms of section 209(c), the provisions of sections 212(a)(14), (15), (20), (21), (25), and (32), do not apply to an alien seeking adjustment of status under section

209. The Attorney General "*may* waive any other provision of such section (other than paragraphs (27), (29), or (33) and other than so much of paragraph (23) as relates to traf-

Service and the State Department letter suggested, the public interest requires that we do not condone this applicant's attempt to circumvent the orderly procedures that our government has provided for refugees to immigrate lawfully. The fraudulent passport was obtained after the applicant had escaped from Afghanistan, with the sole purpose of reaching this country ahead of all the other refugees awaiting their turn abroad. This is not the case where an alien was forced to resort to fraudulently obtained documentation in order to escape or prevent being returned to the country in which he fears persecution. *See Matter of Ng,* 17 I & N Dec. 536 (BIA 1980). This Board finds that the fraudulent avoidance of the orderly refugee procedures that this country has established is an extremely adverse factor which can only be overcome with the most unusual showing of countervailing equities. This case before us does not present such equities. Consequently, the application for asylum relief will be denied as a matter of discretion.

* * *

ORDER: The appeal from the denial of asylum relief will be dismissed, the appeal from the denial of 243(h) relief to Afghanistan will be sustained and the motion to remand denied.

FURTHER ORDER: The applicant is excluded and deported to Pakistan.

FURTHER ORDER: The applicant's deportation to Afghanistan pursuant to sections 237(a)(2)(A) and (B) if the government of Pakistan refuses to accept his deportation to that country pursuant to section 237(a)(1), will be temporarily withheld as provided by section 243(h) of the Act.

[An opinion concurring in part and dissenting in part is omitted.]

Notes

1. The chief reason for the Board's unfavorable exercise of discretion with respect to asylum under § 208 is Salim's "fraudulent avoidance of the orderly refugee procedures this country has established." This statement implies that Salim's default consists of jumping the queue—that if he had simply waited his turn he could have immigrated as part of our overseas refugee programs for Afghans. But there were over two million Afghan refugees in Pakistan at the time of Salim's departure. Only a few thousand U.S. resettlement spaces were being provided each year for this population, governed by specific screening criteria and selection priorities. It is quite possible that Salim would never have qualified, no matter how patient he might have been.

Virtually every alien who applies for asylum, moreover, will be out of compliance with the regular provisions of our laws—thus will have "misused our immigration laws to gain an advantage over all other similarly situated" persons. Can this factor then serve as a justifiable basis for an unfavorable exercise of discretion under § 208?

ficking in narcotics) with respect to such an alien for humanitarian purposes, to assure family unity, or when it is otherwise in the public interest." (Emphasis added).

Most other asylum applicants, however, will not have even a remote prospect of going to a third country if their applications for asylum are denied. In the overwhelming majority of cases, the only options consist of indefinite stay in the United States or else return to the country of nationality. Is the possible availability of a return to Pakistan here a justifiable ground for denying Salim asylum under § 208, even though relief under § 243(h) is granted? What should happen to Salim if Pakistan refuses to accept his return and no other country, other than Afghanistan, will take him in? May he be held in detention in the United States indefinitely? Check Article 31 of the UN Convention. Does it provide much assistance in answering this question?

2. The Board suggests that the discretionary nature of asylum relief might not be in compliance with the nation's obligations under the UN Protocol, but it holds that it must nevertheless adhere to the later-enacted provisions of the Refugee Act. To begin with, this is a questionable application of governing doctrine. Abrogation of a treaty by mere implication from a later-enacted statute is not favored, and it is well-established that new statutes are to be construed and implemented consistently with old treaties if at all possible. *See Cook v. United States,* 288 U.S. 102, 120, 53 S.Ct. 305, 311, 77 L.Ed. 641 (1932). Here the discretion granted by the Act *could* be implemented in such a way as not to contravene any mandatory treaty requirements.

But in fact the Act is probably not inconsistent with the treaty. A review of Articles 12 through 24 of the UN Convention, which deal with juridical status, gainful employment, and welfare—the same general benefits that come with a grant of "asylum" status under U.S. law—will reveal that most of these protections are required only for refugees "lawfully in" or "lawfully staying in" the country of refuge. The drafters of the treaty explained:

> The expression "lawfully within their territory" throughout this draft Convention would exclude a refugee who while lawfully admitted has overstayed the period for which he was admitted or was authorized to stay or who has violated any other condition attached to his admission or stay.

UN Economic and Social Council, Report of the Ad Hoc Committee on Statelessness and Related Problems, at 47 (Mar. 2, 1950) (UN Doc. E/1618/Corr.1; E/AC.32/5/Corr.1). The mere recognition of refugee status—that is, acceptance of the claimant's assertion that he has a well-founded fear of persecution—does not by itself render the person's presence lawful.

Unlike the situation in the aftermath of World War II, which claimed the major attention of the Convention's drafters, today most asylum-seekers are not lawfully in the country of refuge. Hence there is, strictly speaking, no obligation to accord them most of the rights spelled out in such detail in the Convention. The Convention leaves to the discretion of the states parties the decision whether to accord those rights to refugees who are not "lawfully in" the country—mirroring the discretion enjoyed under § 208. But a few of the rights under the Convention do apply irrespective of unlawful entry or sojourn. The most important of these, of course, is the protection against refoulement guaranteed by Article 33. *See generally* UNHCR, *Handbook on Procedures and Criteria for Determining Refugee Status* 7 (1979); G. Goodwin-Gill, *The Refugee in International Law* 115–23 (1983) (explaining the differences, in international usage, between asylum and nonrefoulement).

The extent of a refugee's entitlements under the treaty (assuming he is lawfully in the country of refuge—either because he applied while in status or because his status has been regularized, *e.g.,* by a grant of "asylum" status) varies depending on the precise benefit at issue. Sometimes he is entitled to treatment equivalent to that afforded nationals (*e.g.,* Art. 23, public relief); sometimes most-favored-nation treatment (*e.g.,* Art. 15, right of association); sometimes treatment equivalent to aliens generally (*e.g.,* Art. 18, self-employment). For a comprehensive description see Weis, *The International Protection of Refugees,* 48 Am.J.Int'l L. 193 (1954). The fine distinctions established to regulate the treatment of refugees with respect to all these different aspects of life have not been very important in American practice. In most cases, a person granted asylum is entitled to treatment equivalent to that received by lawful permanent residents—which in most respects amounts to treatment on a par with nationals.

3. Cases like *Salim* have been relatively rare. Nearly all who have proved their entitlement to relief under § 243(h) have also been given asylum status under § 208. Perhaps for this reason, most people who speak of "asylum" do not use the term in its technical sense to refer only to the benefits of § 208. They refer instead to one or all of the elements of the protection normally available to a person who proves the required degree of threat in the homeland.[19] The most important of these elements, of course, is nonrefoulement—the guarantee against return to the country that threatens persecution—which is mandated under § 243(h) and Article 33 of the UN Convention. *Cf. Matter of Castellon,* 17 I & N Dec. 616, 620–21 (BIA 1981). Under this nontechnical usage, § 243(h) (the "withholding" provision) is one of the political asylum provisions of the U.S. immigration laws. Most of the time we will use the term "asylum" in this looser way, to encompass the protections established under both § 208 and § 243(h).

2. STANDARDS FOR PROVING ENTITLEMENT TO ASYLUM AND NONREFOULEMENT

Adjudication of asylum claims presents some formidable difficulties.

19. There are signs that this practice may change in the future, particularly after the Supreme Court's decision in the *Stevic* case, reprinted below, which seemed to place heavy emphasis on the distinctions between the two sections. The Board apparently has also begun to use discretion more frequently to deny asylum to persons who have established entitlement to § 243(h) protection. *See Matter of Shirdel,* Interim Dec. No. 2958 (BIA 1984).

In international circles, as well, the term "asylum" bears many shades of meaning, some of which differ from its usages in the American legal system. Often this imprecision has led to confusion. *See generally* G. Goodwin-Gill, *supra* note 1, at 101–23. Our treatment here focuses on the American usage.

[T]he asylum determination rests on uniquely elusive grounds. It will usually turn on facts which are strikingly inaccessible by U.S. courts and agencies. Applicants typically base their claims on events in a distant land, about which the U.S. Government may otherwise have no information—matters such as their own past political activities, or abuses visited on them or their families and friends. Bona fide applicants are unlikely to have left their homelands with corroborating documentation in hand or with supporting witnesses. On the other hand, fraudulent applicants can probably count on the government's inability to produce evidence disproving their stories. Asylum determinations therefore revolve critically around a determination of the applicant's credibility. Moreover, even if past events can be established with some certainty, the crucial determination does not stem directly from these factual findings of the classical sort. Instead, one must venture into the realm of prediction to decide whether a given showing of the prevalence of persecution in the home country makes a particular applicant's fear well-founded. Applications present a continuum, running from clearly legitimate claims, through borderline cases from countries where all residents are exposed to some risk of persecution, to fanciful fears and bogus applications. The process, however, demands a flat yes or no answer in each case. Because of the large gray area, political considerations—the U.S. Government's hostility or friendship for the allegedly persecuting regime—might easily affect the results. And even where the government is committed to avoiding that practice, it will be hard-pressed to prove that political considerations did not intrude.

Martin, *supra* note 4, at 115.

Beyond problems in establishing the facts and predicting future governmental behavior, the legal standards themselves are not easy to translate into specific adjudicative guidelines. Take the key phrase from the refugee definition: "a well-founded fear of persecution on account of race, religion, nationality, membership in a particular social group, or political opinion." INA § 101(a)(42)(A). When is a fear of persecution well-founded? Or, to use the terminology from § 243(h), when is life or freedom sufficiently threatened? How close a link to the five enumerated factors must be established for a threat to be recognized as the type that justifies asylum? A proper understanding is essential, for the relative breadth or narrowness of the standards of proof will determine the scope of protection available to potentially oppressed people who reach our shores. These standards also provide the only reliable doctrinal control on the numbers of people the United States will wind up sheltering under these numerically open-ended guarantees.

a. Basic Legal Standards

In asylum cases the Board has usually required the applicant to demonstrate some *individualized* threat he would face on return. In *Matter of Sibrun,* Interim Dec. No. 2932, at 7–8 (BIA 1983), the Board detailed its approach, with extensive citation to those judicial and administrative precedents that support each part of the holding—citations we have omitted here:

> The alien bears the burden of proof to establish a well-founded fear of persecution. The alien must demonstrate a likelihood that he individually will be singled out and subjected to persecution. The showing of a "well-founded fear of persecution" requires that the alien present some objective evidence which establishes a realistic likelihood of persecution in his homeland; an alien's own speculations and conclusional statements, unsupported by corroborative evidence, will not suffice. Otherwise stated, the test is whether objective evidence of record is significantly probative of the likelihood of persecution to this alien, sufficient to establish a well-founded fear * * *.

> * * *

> The type of persecution upon which asylum eligibility may be predicated is not merely that which threatens life or freedom generally; the Act requires that this qualifying persecution derive solely on account of one of the five prescribed grounds in the statute. Generalized oppression by a government of virtually the entire populace does not come within those specified grounds.

Singling out. When there is clear proof that a particular government does engage in persecution (and this is probably the case with a majority of the world's nations), any applicant from that country has, in a sense, a well-founded fear of persecution. Her claimed fear is not fanciful. It is founded on the reality of the home government's practices, even if she had never been politically active before and even if the government had never mistreated her before her departure. But it is clear that neither the UN Protocol nor the Refugee Act was meant to authorize wide-scale relocation just because some people at home are persecuted. The "singled out for persecution" criterion is manifestly designed to limit the exposure of the United States to resettlement obligations in situations of this sort. A generalized risk is insufficient; some showing of targeted persecution must be presented.[20] *See Carvajal-Munoz v. INS,* 743 F.2d 562, 573–74 (7th Cir.1984); *Martinez-Romero v. INS,* 692 F.2d 595 (9th Cir.1982); *Fleurinor v. INS,* 585 F.2d 129, 133–34 (5th Cir.1978). This "singling out" requirement remains controversial, however, because it may erect a high barrier to asylum for people who have not been prominent dissidents or members of a political elite, but who may nonetheless be in real jeopardy.

Beyond this, the Board has sometimes been extremely demanding in its implementation of this standard. In *Zavala-Bonilla v. INS,* 730 F.2d 562 (9th Cir.1984), the Board had affirmed an immigration judge's denial of asylum to a former union activist from El Salvador, despite extensive evidence of the risks faced there by union activists (in the form of letters from friends in El Salvador, a letter from her union, and numerous press

---

20. The Board has ruled, however, that it is error for an immigration judge to exclude background evidence, even if voluminous, touching upon general human rights conditions in the alien's country of origin. *Matter of Exame,* Interim Dec. No. 2920 (BIA 1982).

accounts and international organization reports of conditions in that country). Even the State Department had provided an advisory letter provisionally favoring the grant of asylum. The Board nonetheless discounted her evidence and concluded that despite the proof of her own past confrontations with authorities in her role with the union, "the record simply presents nothing to indicate a continuing and contemporaneous cognizance of the respondent and her past activities." The court of appeals reversed. It held that the Board improperly discounted the evidence presented by the applicant. But it also held that the Board's standard was too demanding. Proof of a "continuing and contemporaneous cognizance" by the home government is simply not required to demonstrate the necessary likelihood of persecution. *Id.* at 565. *See also Bolanos-Hernandez v. INS*, 749 F.2d 1316, 1323 (9th Cir.1984) (rejecting BIA's theory that a specific threat to a Salvadoran's life was insufficient simply because it was "representative of the general level of violence in El Salvador"; if anything, that made the threat even more credible).

Even if the Board now ceases to use the continuing cognizance test, is "singling out" required by the statute and the treaties? What about someone who fears persecution founded on group characteristics, such as race, or religion, or ethnic background? Should such a person have to show that he personally had trouble with the authorities before he left, in an effort to show that they are likely to single him out if he returns? Even in the political sphere, is singling out always relevant? What if the rulers are indiscriminately vicious whenever they believe that political opposition has been voiced, and the sanctions fall unpredictably on whole villages?

Objective evidence. The Board's *Sibrun* decision requires the alien to present "objective evidence," and it contrasts such evidence with "the alien's own speculations and conclusional statements." At times, the Board has applied this notion with severity, seeming to insist that asylum claims cannot be granted solely on the basis of the applicant's testimony (which is sometimes denigrated as "subjective" evidence). There must be additional corroboration in the form of documents or testimony from disinterested witnesses. *See also Dally v. INS,* 744 F.2d 1191, 1195–96 (6th Cir.1984).

But at other times the Board has been more sympathetic to the dilemma applicants face in making their cases. In *Matter of Maroquin,* 61 Interp.Rel. 78 (1984) (nonprecedent decision, October 28, 1983), the Board reversed a denial of asylum and remanded the case to the immigration judge. It held that the judge's hypertechnical rulings sustaining numerous objections to evidence or lines of questioning had denied the applicant a fair chance: "[I]t is also the duty of the immigration judge to ensure that the respondent has the opportunity to present what may be the only evidence he has, his own testimony," citing *Matter of Dunar,* 14 I. & N.Dec. 310 (BIA 1973). *See also Matter of Sihasale,* 11 I. & N.Dec. 531, 532–33 (BIA 1966); *Matter of Acosta,* Interim Dec. No. ___, slip op. at 6–7 (BIA, March 1, 1985); *Bolanos-Hernandez, supra,* at 1323–24. Which approach better fulfills the statutory mandate? Should asylum ever be granted based solely on subjective evidence in this sense—that is, based solely on the applicant's own uncorroborated testimony?

The debate over objective and subjective elements of an asylum claim also takes another form, and it is important not to confuse it with the previous evidentiary controversy. For example, the *Handbook on Procedures and Criteria for Determining Refugee Status,* published by the UNHCR, places a relatively strong emphasis on the subjective component of the definition in its advice on how to determine refugee status. The Handbook states:

> The term "well-founded fear" * * * contains a subjective and an objective element, and in determining whether well-founded fear exists, both elements must be taken into consideration. * * *
> The subjective character of fear of persecution requires an evaluation of the opinions and feelings of the person concerned. It is also in the light of such opinions and feelings that any actual or anticipated measures against him must necessarily be viewed. Due to variations in the psychological make-up of individuals and in the circumstances of each case, interpretations of what amounts to persecution are bound to vary.[21]

Is this a sound way to administer the asylum provisions of the immigration laws? Did Congress intend immigration judges to expend adjudication resources on close inquiry into the psychological makeup of individual applicants? Should equivalent showings of objective risk lead to equal results, whatever the varying states of mind of the claimants? Assume, that A and B show the same degree of threat in their home country. They were both local leaders of an opposition political party, for example, and there is now substantial evidence that the government is suppressing that party. Suppose A puts on proof about his subjective fears and what impact the threat has been having on him (nightmares, interference with work, other physical symptoms). B, for whatever reason, provides no equivalent evidence. Should A be regarded as having made a stronger case for asylum?

21. Office of the United Nations High Commissioner for Refugees, Handbook on Procedures and Criteria for Determining Refugee Status 12, 14 (1979). This Handbook has played an important role in U.S. asylum practice, having been cited on various occasions by the Board and the courts as an authoritative guide to relevant standards under the UN treaties and hence under U.S. law. *See, e.g., Matter of Rodriguez-Palma,* 17 I. & N.Dec. 465, 468 (BIA 1980); *Stevic v. Sava,* 678 F.2d 401, 406, 409 (2d Cir.1982), reversed on other grounds, ___ U.S. ___, 104 S.Ct. 2489, 81 L.Ed.2d 321 (1984). Nevertheless the preface to the Handbook states that the work "has been conceived as a practical guide and not as a treatise on refugee law," *id.* at 1, and some of the guidelines as they emerged from the UN drafting process are so painstakingly balanced as to be of little utility. For example, in discussing the so-called objective element of the definition, the Handbook states: "authorities that are called upon to determine refugee status are not required to pass judgment on conditions in the applicant's country of origin. The applicant's statements cannot, however, be considered in the abstract, and must be viewed in the context of the relevant background situation. A knowledge of the conditions in the applicant's country of origin—while not a primary objective—is an important element in assessing the applicant's credibility. In general, the applicant's fear should be considered well-founded if he can establish, to a reasonable degree, that his continued stay in his country of origin has become intolerable to him for the reasons stated in the definition, or would for the same reasons be intolerable if he returned there." *Id.* at 12–13.

b. Stevic

In addition to the legal standards examined in the preceding section, since the 1950's the Board has required applicants to demonstrate a "clear probability of persecution" before awarding asylum-type relief under any of the statutory provisions. This standard was initially established as a criterion governing the exercise of the discretion given to the Attorney General by the original wording of § 243(h). When asylum-type protection became, in effect, mandatory after U.S. accession to the UN Protocol in 1968—for persons meeting the treaty standards—litigants claimed that the Board was required to relax that criterion. The Board disagreed. In *Matter of Dunar,* 14 I. & N.Dec. 310 (BIA 1973), it determined that the treaty worked no change in the governing standards, and it determined to continue employing the "clear probability" test.

Not long after the Refugee Act was passed in 1980, litigants renewed the argument. The Court of Appeals for the Second Circuit ruled that Congress, by amending the asylum provisions and conforming their language more closely to the wording of the treaty, intended to ease the requirements for proving entitlement to asylum in this country. *Stevic v. Sava,* 678 F.2d 401 (2d Cir.1982). Although it declined to specify in detail the new criteria, it indicated that "asylum may be granted, and under Section 243(h), deportation must be withheld, upon a showing far short of a 'clear probability' that an individual will be singled out for persecution." The court reached this conclusion after a lengthy review of the history of the legal provisions, both domestic and international, governing political asylum:

> The Protocol adopted, with certain changes not relevant here, the definition of "refugee" used in the 1951 Convention * * *. Under the Protocol, a "refugee" is a person who,
>
>> owing to a *well-founded fear of being persecuted* for reasons of race, religion, nationality, membership of a particular social group, or political opinion, is outside the country of his nationality....
>
> (Emphasis supplied). No party to the Protocol may, under Article 33 of the Convention,
>
>> return ... a refugee ... to ... territories where his life or freedom would be threatened on account of race, religion, nationality, membership of a particular social group or political opinion....
>
> The language of the Protocol seems considerably more generous than the "clear probability" test applied under Section 243(h). * * * Moreover, the history of the Convention's definition of "refugee" demonstrates that the drafters believed a showing of "good reason" to fear persecution was sufficient to prove one's status as a "refugee." United Nations Economic and Social Council, *Report of the Ad Hoc Committee on Statelessness and Related Problems* 39 (1950) (E/1618; E/AC.32/5). * * *

Interpretation is also informed by the United Nations High Commissioner for Refugees' *Handbook on Procedures and Criteria for Determining Refugee Status* (Geneva, 1979). The *Handbook* is a response to requests for guidance as to the Protocol's requirements and is based on the High Commissioner's 25 years of experience, the practices of governments acceding to the Protocol and literature on the subject. It, too, supports the view that the Protocol embodies a more generous standard than the "clear probability" test.

Briefly summarized, it states that a "well-founded fear" has subjective as well as objective elements. The applicant's state of mind is thus relevant, as are conditions in the country of origin, its laws, and experiences of others. The applicant must show "good reason why he individually fears persecution," but a desire "to avoid a situation entailing the risk of persecution" may be enough. Persecution means a threat to life or freedom.

Our examination of the Protocol, its language, history and subsequent usage as derived from the *Handbook* leads us to conclude that it is somewhat more generous than the BIA's administrative practice in applying Section 243(h), which has required an applicant to show a "clear probability" that he or she will be singled out for persecution. The "clear probability" test had been initially articulated by the BIA as its preferred way of implementing what had been the wholly discretionary authority of Section 243(h). *Matter of Joseph,* 13 I. & N.Dec. 70 (1968); *see Cheng Kai Fu v. INS,* [386 F.2d 750, 753 (2d Cir.1967), cert. denied 390 U.S. 1003, 88 S.Ct. 1247, 20 L.Ed.2d 104 (1968)]; *Lena v. INS,* [379 F.2d 536, 538 (7th Cir.1967)]. Since Article 33 of the Convention imposes an absolute obligation upon the United States, standards developed in an era of discretionary authority require some adjustment.

678 F.2d, at 405–06. Although this reasoning would seem to suggest that the Board's practice had been in error ever since 1968, when the United States became a party to the Protocol, the court's actual holding was more limited. It ruled only that, in passing the Refugee Act in 1980, Congress intended to require that the BIA end its former administrative practice and adopt a more generous standard for asylum determinations.

Shortly thereafter the Court of Appeals for the Third Circuit announced its disagreement with the Second Circuit's *Stevic* decision. In *Rejaie v. INS,* 691 F.2d 139 (3d Cir.1982), the court held that Congress mandated no change in the governing standard when it adopted the Refugee Act: "We read 'well-founded fear' within the circumstances of its use and hold that it equates with 'clear probability.'" Moreover, the Third Circuit thought that the Second Circuit had "attributed a stringency to the phrase 'clear probability'" that was not justified. In reality, said the court, that criterion simply requires aliens to "'show some evidence that they would be subject to persecution,' [quoting *Cheng Kai Fu v. INS, supra,* 386 F.2d, at 753,] a formulation that closely approximates the *Dunar* definition of 'well-founded fear' as 'realistic likelihood of persecution.'" *Id.* at 146.

The Supreme Court then granted certiorari in the *Stevic* case to resolve the conflict in the circuits. Observers hoped that the decision would resolve the long-running battle over whether "well-founded fear" equates with "clear probability," (or "realistic likelihood," or some other phrase), under the Protocol and the statutes. Perhaps the court's judgment would also clarify whether the singling-out concept was appropriate, and the extent to which both objective and subjective factors should play a role in the determination. What the court actually did was a surprise—and in many respects a disappointment.

INS v. STEVIC

Supreme Court of the United States, 1984.
___ U.S. ___, 104 S.Ct. 2489, 81 L.Ed.2d 321.

JUSTICE STEVENS delivered the opinion of the Court.

For over 30 years the Attorney General has possessed statutory authority to withhold the deportation of an alien upon a finding that the alien would be subject to persecution in the country to which he would be deported. The question presented by this case is whether a deportable alien must demonstrate a clear probability of persecution in order to obtain such relief under § 243(h) of the Immigration and Nationality Act of 1952, as amended by § 203(e) of the Refugee Act of 1980, Pub.L. No. 96–212, 94 Stat. 107.

I

[Predrag Stevic, a Yugoslavian national who had overstayed a visitor's visa, initially sought asylum by means of a motion to reopen his deportation proceedings, filed with the immigration judge in 1977. The BIA upheld the denial of that motion to reopen, ruling in 1979 that Stevic had not presented "prima facie evidence that there is a clear probability of persecution to be directed at the individual respondent." Stevic did not then seek judicial review, but when he received notice to surrender for deportation in 1981, he filed a second motion to reopen. Again he sought relief under § 243(h), but by then that section had been amended by the Refugee Act. The second motion met the same fate as the first; the Board again applied the "clear probability" test.]

The United States Court of Appeals for the Second Circuit reversed and remanded for a plenary hearing under a different standard of proof. *Stevic v. Sava,* 678 F.2d 401 (1982). Specifically, it held that respondent no longer had the burden of showing "a clear probability of persecution," but instead could avoid deportation by demonstrating a "well founded fear of persecution." The latter language is contained in a definition of the term "refugee" adopted by a United Nations Protocol to which the United States has adhered since 1968. The Court of Appeals held that the Refugee Act of 1980 changed the standard of proof that an alien must satisfy to obtain relief under § 243(h), concluding that Congress intended to abandon the "clear probability of persecution" standard and substitute the "well-founded fear of persecution" language of the Protocol as the standard. Other than stating that the Protocol language was "considerably more generous" or "somewhat more generous" to the alien than the former standard, *id.*, at 405, 406, the court did not detail the differences between them and stated that it "would be unwise to attempt a more detailed elaboration of the applicable legal test under the Protocol," *id.*, at 409. The court concluded that respondent's showing entitled him to a hearing under the new standard.

Because of the importance of the question presented, and because of the conflict in the Circuits on the question, we granted certiorari, 460 U.S. 1010, 103 S.Ct. 1249, 75 L.Ed.2d 479 (1983). We now reverse and hold that an alien must establish a clear probability of persecution to avoid deportation under § 243(h).

II

The basic contentions of the parties in this case may be summarized briefly. Petitioner contends that the words "clear probability of persecution" and "well-founded fear of persecution" are not self-explanatory and when read in the light of their usage by courts prior to adoption of the Refugee Act of 1980, it is obvious that there is no "significant" difference between them. If there is a "significant" difference between them, however, petitioner argues that Congress' clear intent in enacting the Refugee Act of 1980 was to maintain the status quo, which petitioner argues would mean continued application of the clear-probability-of-persecution standard to withholding of deportation claims. In this regard, petitioner maintains that our accession to the United Nations Protocol in 1968 was based on the express "understanding" that it would not alter the "substance" of our immigration laws.

Respondent argues that the standards are not coterminous and that the well-founded-fear-of-persecution standard turns almost entirely on the alien's state of mind. Respondent points out that the well-founded fear language was adopted in the definition of a refugee contained in the United Nations Protocol adhered to by the United States since 1968. Respondent basically contends that ever since 1968, the well-founded-fear standard should have applied to withholding of deportation claims, but Congress simply failed to honor the Protocol by failing to enact implementing legislation until adoption of the Refugee Act of 1980, which contains the Protocol definition of refugee.

Each party is plainly correct in one regard: in 1980 Congress intended to adopt a standard for withholding of deportation claims by reference to pre-existing sources of law. We begin our analysis of this case by examining those sources of law.

III

UNITED STATES REFUGEE LAW PRIOR TO 1968

Legislation enacted by the Congress in 1950, 1952, and 1965 authorized the Attorney General to withhold deportation of an otherwise deportable alien if the alien would be subject to persecution upon deportation.   At least before 1968, it was clear that an alien was required to demonstrate a "clear probability of persecution" or a "likelihood of persecution" in order to be eligible for withholding of deportation under § 243(h) of the Immigration and Nationality Act of 1952.   With certain exceptions, this relief was available to any alien who was already "within the United States," albeit unlawfully and subject to deportation.

* * *

[In addition,] the Attorney General was authorized under § 203(a)(7) of the Immigration and Nationality Act of 1952, to permit "conditional entry" as immigrants for a number of refugees fleeing from a Communist-dominated area or the Middle East "because of persecution or fear of persecution on account of race, religion, or political opinion."   See also § 212(d)(5) (granting Attorney General discretion to "parole" aliens into the United States temporarily for emergency reasons).   An alien seeking admission under § 203(a)(7) was required to establish a good reason to fear persecution.   *Compare In re Tan,* 12 I. & N.Dec. 564, 569–570 (BIA 1967) with *In re Ugricic,* 14 I. & N.Dec. 384, 385–386 (Dist.Dir.1972).

THE UNITED NATIONS PROTOCOL

In 1968 the United States acceded to the United Nations Protocol Relating to the Status of Refugees, Jan. 31, 1967, [1968] 19 U.S.T. 6223, T.I.A.S. No. 6577.   The Protocol bound parties to comply with the substantive provisions of Articles 2 through 34 of the United Nations Convention Relating to the Status of Refugees, 189 U.N.T.S. 150 (July 28, 1951) with respect to "refugees" as defined in Article 1.2 of the Protocol.

Article 1.2 of the Protocol defines a "refugee" as an individual who

"owing to a well-founded fear of being persecuted for reasons of race, religion, nationality, membership of a particular social group or political opinion, is outside the country of his nationality and is unable or, owing to such fear, is unwilling to avail himself of the protection of that country; or who, not having a nationality and being outside the country of his former habitual residence, is unable or, owing to such fear, is unwilling to return to it."

Two of the substantive provisions of the Convention are germane to the issue before us.   Article 33.1 of the Convention provides: "No Contracting State shall expel or return ('refouler') a refugee in any manner whatsoever to the frontiers of territories where his life or freedom would be threatened on account of his race, religion, nationality, membership of a particular social group or political opinion."   19 U.S.T. 6276 (1968). Article 34 provides in pertinent part: "The Contracting States shall as far as possible facilitate the assimilation and naturalization of refugees...." *Ibid.*[10]

10.   Article 32.1 of the Convention provides: "The Contracting States shall not expel a refugee lawfully in their territory save on grounds of national security or public order."   19 U.S.T. at 6275.   It seems plain that respondent could not invoke Art. 32, since he was not lawfully in the country when he overstayed his visa.   United Na-

The President and the Senate believed that the Protocol was largely consistent with existing law.   * * * It was also believed that apparent differences between the Protocol and existing statutory law could be reconciled by the Attorney General in administration and did not require any modification of statutory language. *See, e.g.,* S. Exec. K, 90th Cong., 2d Sess., VIII (1968).

UNITED STATES REFUGEE LAW: 1968–1980

Five years after our accession to the Protocol, the Board of Immigration Appeals was confronted with the same basic issue confronting us today in the case of *In re Dunar,* 14 I. & N.Dec. 310 (1973). The deportee argued that he was entitled to withholding of deportation upon a showing of a well-founded fear of persecution, and essentially maintained that a conjectural possibility of persecution would suffice to make the fear "well founded." The Board rejected that interpretation of "well founded," and stated that a likelihood of persecution was required for the fear to be "well founded." *Id.,* at 319. It observed that neither § 243(h) nor Art. 33 used the term "well founded fear," and stated:

"Article 33 speaks in terms of threat to life or freedom on account of any of the five enumerated reasons. Such threats would also constitute subjection to persecution within the purview of section 243(h). The latter has also been construed to encompass economic sanctions sufficiently harsh to constitute a threat to life or freedom, *Dunat v. Hurney,* 297 F.2d 744 (3 Cir., 1962); *cf. Kovac v. INS,* 407 F.2d 102 (9 Cir., 1969). In our estimation, there is no substantial difference in coverage of section 243(h) and Article 33. We are satisfied that distinctions in terminology can be reconciled on a case-by-case consideration as they arise." *Id.,* at 320.

The Board concluded that "Article 33 has effected no substantial changes in the application of section 243(h), either by way of burden of proof, coverage, or manner of arriving at decisions."   * * *.

Although before *In re Dunar,* the Board and the courts had consistently used a clear probability or likelihood standard under § 243(h), after that case the phrase "well founded fear" was employed in some cases. The Court of Appeals for the Seventh Circuit, which had construed § 243(h) as applying only to "cases of clear probability of persecution" in a frequently cited case decided before 1968, *Lena v. INS,* 379 F.2d 536, 538 (1967), reached the same conclusion in a case decided after our adherence to the Protocol. *Kashani v. INS,* 547 F.2d 376 (1977). In that opinion Judge Swygert reasoned that the "well founded fear of persecution" language could "only be satisfied by objective evidence," and that it would

tions Economic and Social Council, Report of Ad Hoc Committee on Statelessless and Related Problems, at 47 (Mar. 2, 1950) (U.N. Doc. E/1618/Corr.1;   E/AC.32/5/Corr.1). ("The expression 'lawfully within their territory' throughout this draft Convention would exclude a refugee who while lawfully admitted has overstayed the period for which he was admitted or was authorized to stay or who has violated any other condition attached to his admission or stay"); see also United Nations Economic and Social Council, Report of the Ad Hoc Committee on Statelessless and Related Problems, Second Session 11, ¶ 20 (Aug. 25, 1950) (U.N. Doc. E/1850; E/AC.32/8). Accord, *In re Dunar,* 14 I. & N.Dec. 310, 315–318 (BIA 1973) (citing additional authority).

"in practice converge" with the "clear probability" standard that the Seventh Circuit had previously "engrafted onto [§] 243(h)." *Id.,* at 379. Other Courts of Appeals appeared to reach essentially the same conclusion. See *e.g., Fleurinor v. INS,* 585 F.2d 129, 132, 134 (CA5 1978); *Pereira-Diaz v. INS,* 551 F.2d 1149, 1154 (CA9 1977); *Zamora v. INS,* 534 F.2d 1055, 1058, 1063 (CA2 1976).

While the Protocol was the source of some controversy with respect to the standard for § 243(h) claims for withholding of deportation, our accession did not appear to raise any questions concerning the standard to be applied for § 203(a)(7) requests for admission. The "good reason to fear persecution" language was employed in such cases. *See, e.g., In re Ugricic,* 14 I. & N.Dec., at 385–386.

IV

Section 203(e) of the Refugee Act of 1980 amended the language of § 243(h), basically conforming it to the language of Art. 33 of the United Nations Protocol. The amendment made three changes in the text of § 243(h), but none of these three changes expressly governs the standard of proof an applicant must satisfy or implicitly changes that standard. The amended § 243(h), like Art. 33, makes no mention of a probability of persecution or a well-founded fear of persecution. In short, the text of the statute simply does not specify how great a possibility of persecution must exist to qualify the alien for withholding of deportation. To the extent such a standard can be inferred from the bare language of the provision, it appears that a likelihood of persecution is required. The section literally provides for withholding of deportation only if the alien's life or freedom "would" be threatened in the country to which he would be deported; it does not require withholding if the alien "might" or "could" be subject to persecution. Finally, § 243(h), both prior to and after amendment, makes no mention of the term "refugee;" rather, any alien within the United States is entitled to withholding if he meets the standard set forth.

Respondent understandably does not rely upon the specific textual changes in § 243(h) in support of his position that a well-founded fear of persecution entitles him to withholding of deportation. Instead, respondent points to the provision of the Refugee Act which eliminated the ideological and geographical restrictions on admission of refugees under § 203(a)(7) and adopted an expanded version of the United Nations Protocol definition of refugee. This definition contains the well-founded-fear language and now appears under § 101(a)(42)(A) of the Immigration and Nationality Act. Other provisions of the Immigration and Nationality Act, as amended, now provide preferential immigration status, within numerical limits, to those qualifying as refugees under the modified Protocol definition and renders a more limited class of refugees, though still a class broader than the Protocol definition,[a] eligible for a discretion-

---

a. What does the Court mean here? How is the class eligible for asylum broader than the class defined by the Protocol definition? (Subparagraph B of § 101(a)(42) clear-

ly goes beyond the Protocol definition, but only subparagraph A is relevant for asylum determinations.) Unless the Court is referring obliquely to the rarely invoked provi-

ary grant of asylum.[18]

Respondent, however, is not seeking discretionary relief under these provisions, which explicitly employ the well-founded-fear standard now appearing in § 101(a)(42)(A). Rather, he claims he is entitled to withholding of deportation under § 243(h) upon establishing a well-founded fear of persecution. Section 243(h), however, does *not* refer to § 101(a)(42)(A). Hence, there is no textual basis in the statute for concluding that the well-founded-fear-of persecution standard is relevant to a withholding of deportation claim under § 243(h).

Before examining the legislative history of the Refugee Act of 1980 in order to ascertain whether Congress nevertheless intended a well-founded-fear standard to be employed under § 243(h), we observe that the Refugee Act itself does not contain any definition of the "well-founded fear of persecution" language contained in § 101(a)(42)(a). The parties vigorously contest whether the well-founded-fear standard is coterminous with the clear-probability-of-persecution standard.

Initially, we do not think there is any serious dispute regarding the meaning of the clear-probability standard under the § 243(h) case law.[19] The question under that standard is whether it is more likely than not that the alien would be subject to persecution. The argument of the parties on this point is whether the well-founded-fear standard is the same as the clear-probability standard as just defined, or whether it is more generous to the alien.

Petitioner argues that persecution must be more likely than not for a fear of persecution to be considered "well founded." The positions of respondent and several *amici curiae* are somewhat amorphous. Respondent seems to maintain that a fear of persecution is "well founded" if the evidence establishes some objective basis in reality for the fear. This would appear to mean that so long as the fear is not imaginary—*i.e.,* if it

sions of Article 1.D of the treaty, we are not able to locate the difference.—eds.

18. A new § 208(a) directed the Attorney General to establish procedures permitting aliens either in the United States or at our borders to apply for "asylum." Under § 208(a), in order to be eligible for asylum, an alien must meet the definition of refugee contained in § 101(a)(42)(A), a standard that also would qualify an alien seeking to immigrate under § 207. Meeting the definition of refugee, however, does *not* entitle the alien to asylum—the decision to grant a particular application rests in the discretion of the Attorney General under § 208(a).

After passage of the Refugee Act, regulations relating to asylum previously contained in 8 CFR Pt. 108 were repealed, and regulations were promulgated under the new § 208 of the Act. Those regulations, like the statute, expressly provide that a "well founded fear of persecution" renders an alien eligible for a discretionary grant of asylum under § 208. 8 CFR § 208.5 (1983).

We note that when such asylum requests are made after the institution of deportation proceedings, they "shall *also* be considered as requests" under § 243(h). 8 CFR § 208.-3(b) (1983) (emphasis supplied). This does not mean that the well founded fear standard is applicable to § 243(h) claims. Section 208.3(b) simply does not speak to the burden of proof issue; rather, it merely eliminates the need for filing a separate request for § 243(h) relief if a § 208 claim has been made. We further note that a § 243(h) request is not automatically also considered as a § 208 request under the regulations. Indeed, the alien may be barred from asserting a § 208 claim while still allowed to invoke § 243(h). *See* 8 CFR § 208.11 (1983).

19. The term "clear probability" was used interchangably with "likelihood"; the use of the word "clear" appears to have been surplusage. We think there is no merit to the suggestion that the Board was applying a "clear and convincing" standard to the persecution issue. * * *

is founded in reality at all—it is "well founded." A more moderate position is that so long as an objective situation is established by the evidence, it need not be shown that the situation will probably result in persecution, but it is enough that persecution is a reasonable possibility.

Petitioner and respondent seem to agree that prior to passage of the Refugee Act, the Board and the Courts actually used a clear-probability standard for § 243(h) claims. That is, prior to the amendment, § 243(h) relief would be granted if the evidence established that it was more likely than not that the alien would be persecuted in the country to which he was being deported; relief would not be granted merely upon a showing of some basis in reality for the fear, or if there was only a reasonable possibility of persecution falling short of a probability. Petitioner argues that some of the prior case law using the term "well-founded fear" simply used that term interchangably with the phrase "clear probability." Respondent agrees in substance, but argues that although prior cases employed the term "well-founded fear," they misconstrued the meaning of the phrase under the United Nations Protocol.

For purposes of our analysis, we may assume, as the Court of Appeals concluded, that the well-founded-fear standard is more generous than the clear-probability-of-persecution standard because we can identify no basis in the legislative history for applying that standard in § 243(h) proceedings or any legislative intent to alter the pre-existing practice.

The principal motivation for the enactment of the Refugee Act of 1980 was a desire to revise and regularize the procedures governing the admission of refugees into the United States. The primary substantive change Congress intended to make under the Refugee Act, and indeed in our view the only substantive change even relevant to this case, was to eliminate the piecemeal approach to *admission* of refugees previously existing under § 203(a)(7) and § 212(d)(5) of the Immigration and Nationality Act, and § 108 of the regulations, and to establish a systematic scheme for admission and resettlement of refugees. S.Rep. No. 96–256, p. 9.1 (1979); H.Rep. No. 96–608, pp. 1–5 (1979). The Act adopted, and indeed, expanded upon, the Protocol definition of refugee, S.Rep., at 19; H.Rep., at 9–10, and intended that the definition would be construed consistently with the Protocol, S.Rep., at 9, 20. It was plainly recognized, however, that "merely because an individual or group of refugees comes within the definition will not guarantee resettlement in the United States. The Committee is of the opinion that the new definition does not create a new and expanded means of entry, but instead regularizes and formalizes the policies and practices that have been followed in recent years." H.Rep., at 10. The Congress distinguished between discretionary grants of refugee admission or asylum and the entitlement to a withholding of deportation if the § 243(h) standard was met. *See id.,* at 17–18.

Elimination of the geographic and ideological restrictions under the former § 203(a)(7) was thought to bring our scheme into conformity with our obligations under the Protocol, see S.Rep., at 4, 15–16, and in our view these references are to our obligations under Art. 34 to facilitate the naturalization of refugees within the definition of the Protocol. There is, as always, some ambiguity in the legislative history—the term "asylum," in particular, seems to be used in various ways, see, *e.g.,* S.Rep., at 9, 16—but that is understandable given that the same problem with nomenclature has been evident in case law as well. *See In re Lam,* Interim Dec. No. 2857, p. 5 (BIA, Mar. 24, 1981). Going to the substance of the matter, however, it seems clear that Congress understood that refugee status alone did not require withholding of deportation, but rather, the alien had to satisfy the standard under § 243(h), S.Rep., at 16. The amendment of § 243(h) was explicitly recognized to be a mere conforming amendment, added "for the sake of clarity," and was plainly not intended to change the standard. H.Rep., at 17–18.

The Court of Appeals' decision rests on the mistaken premise that every alien who qualifies as a "refugee" under the statutory definition is also entitled to a withholding of deportation under § 243(h). We find no support for this conclusion in either the language of § 243(h), the structure of the amended Act, or the legislative history.[22]

22. Nor is there any merit to respondent's argument that this construction is inconsistent with the Protocol. Existing domestic statutory law in 1968 was largely consistent with the Protocol. Under the Protocol, however, attaining the status of "refugee" was essential in order for an alien to assert his right under Art. 33 to avoid deportation, and then he was protected only against deportation to a territory where his "life or freedom" would be threatened. Under our statutory scheme, on the other hand, no alien in the United States would be deported to a country where he was likely to be "persecuted," a seemingly broader concept than threats to "life or freedom." In addition, the alien would qualify for withholding even if he might not be a "refugee" under the Protocol because, for example, he was not outside his country of nationality owing to a fear of persecution. *Cf. Rosenberg v. Yee Chien Woo,* 402 U.S. 49, 57, 91 S.Ct. 1312, 1316, 28 L.Ed.2d 592 (1971). [What can this mean? An alien applying for withholding must be in the United States—and thus clearly outside the country of nationality.—eds.] Moreover, the domestic statute and regulations provided many additional procedural safeguards as well, including a right to be represented by counsel and a right to judicial review.

While refugee status was not essential to avoid withholding of deportation, it was essential under domestic law to qualify for preferential immigration status. Our definition of a refugee under § 203(a)(7) was of course consistent with the Protocol. Indeed, the relevant statutory language virtually mirrored the Protocol definition. [One will search in vain in the old section 203(a)(7) for any such mirroring. See Pub.L. No. 89–236, § 3, 79 Stat. 913 (1965). The word "refugee" is never even used, much less defined. The

section simply makes conditional entries available to "aliens" who meet the requirements, including the geographic and ideological limitations.—eds.] The geographic and ideological limitations were limits on admission. That was not inconsistent with the Protocol—the Protocol did not require admission at all, nor did it preclude a signatory from exercising judgment among classes of refugees within the Protocol definition in determining whom to admit. Article 34 merely called on nations to facilitate the admission of refugees *to the extent possible;* the language of Article 34 was precatory and not self-executing. [Article 34, by its terms, deals with "assimilation and naturalization." We can find nothing there about admission.—eds.] The point is not, however, that the Senate was merely led to *believe* accession would work no substantial change in the law; the point is that it did not work a substantial change in the law.

There were of course differences between the Protocol and the text of domestic law. The most significant difference was that Art. 33 gave the refugee an entitlement to avoid deportation to a country in which his life or freedom would be threatened, whereas domestic law merely provided the Attorney General with discretion to grant withholding of deportation on grounds of persecution. The Attorney General, however, could naturally accommodate the Protocol simply by exercising his discretion to grant such relief in each case in which the required showing was made, and hence no amendment of the existing statutory language was necessary. * * *

Finally, the Protocol required a showing that the "refugee's life or freedom would be threatened" while § 243(h) required that the alien would be subject to "persecution." Al-

We have deliberately avoided any attempt to state the governing standard beyond noting that it requires that an application be supported by evidence establishing that it is more likely than not that the alien would be subject to persecution on one of the specified grounds. This standard is a familiar one to immigration authorities and reviewing courts, and Congress did not intend to alter it in 1980. We observe that shortly after adoption of the Refugee Act, the Board explained: "As we have only quite recently acquired jurisdiction over asylum claims, we are only just now beginning to resolve some of the problems caused by this addition to our jurisdiction, including the problem of determining exactly how withholding of deportation and asylum are to fit together." *In re Lam,* Interim Dec. No. 2857, p. 6, n. 4 (BIA, Mar. 24, 1981). Today we resolve one of those problems by deciding that the "clear probability of persecution" standard remains applicable to § 243(h) withholding of deportation claims. We do not decide the meaning of the phrase "well-founded fear of persecution" which is applicable by the terms of the Act and regulations to requests for discretionary asylum. That issue is not presented by this case.

The Court of Appeals granted respondent relief based on its understanding of a standard which, even if properly understood, does not entitle an alien to withholding of deportation under § 243(h). Our holding does, of course, require the Court of Appeals to reexamine this record to determine whether the evidence submitted by respondent entitles him to a plenary hearing under the proper standard.

The judgment of the Court of Appeals is reversed, and the cause is remanded for further proceedings consistent with this opinion.

It is so ordered.

Notes

1. The Court recognizes that Congress intended the Refugee Act to bring U.S. asylum practices into harmony with the nation's obligations under the UN Protocol, and it believes that there are no conflicts between its construction and the treaty. We need some perspective to evaluate this belief. What the Court has said, relying heavily on the mere fact of differences in wording between Article 1 and Article 33 of the UN Convention (and the equivalent differences between § 101(a)(42)(A) and § 243(h)), is that there is a discontinuity between the notion of a "refugee" who shows a well-founded fear of persecution and a person whose life or freedom would be threatened. The first category is probably broader than

though one might argue that the concept of "persecution" is broad enough to encompass matters other than threats to "life or freedom"—deprivations of property, for example—and therefore that the Protocol was narrower than the coverage of the section, we perceive no basis for concluding that the particular mention of the alien's interest in "life or freedom" made the Protocol any more generous than domestic law.

In summary, then, to the extent that domestic law was more generous than the Protocol, the Attorney General would not alter existing practice; to the extent that the Protocol was more generous than the bare text of § 243(h) would necessarily require, the Attorney General would honor the requirements of the Protocol and hence there was no need for modifying the language of § 243(h) itself. * * *

the second; it probably takes more to show a threat to life or freedom, the Court's dicta suggest, than to show a well-founded fear of persecution. Someone could be a refugee, in other words, and yet it would be lawful under the treaty for a signatory state to return him to the very country whose practices undergirded his successful claim to refugee status. That is, he would qualify for all the treaty benefits except the protection accorded by Article 33, because that article alone is controlled by the higher standard of proof.

In your view, would the drafters of the treaty have intended such a result? What would be their reason for such a distinction? Isn't Article 33's protection against refoulement the central *raison d'être* for an international scheme of refugee protection? Should the Court's linguistic analysis give way in light of the evident purposes of both the framers of the treaty and the legislators who passed the Refugee Act? In any event, isn't it possible to construe the words of Article 33 in such a way as to find them coextensive with the definition in Article 1, without doing violence to the language of either provision?

2. The sharp distinction the Court draws between asylum under § 208 and withholding under § 243(h) came as a surprise. Nothing in the Board's practice foreshadows or furnishes much support for the notion. Instead, the Board seemed to be moving in the opposite direction, using the same basic standard as a threshold for either form of relief. This trend is evident from the *Salim* decision, reprinted earlier in these materials. It may be even clearer in *Matter of Lam,* 18 I & N Dec. 15 (BIA 1981), where the Board pointed out that the same application form, Form I–589, is used for both types of benefit, and that under the regulations, an application for asylum is also considered automatically an application for withholding. Further, it stated:

> Although section 243(h) was amended by the Refugee Act to substitute "life or freedom would be threatened" for "persecution," we have, after examining the legislative history of the new Act, held that this broader choice of words in the Refugee Act was not intended to change the prior law requiring persecution by the government in the country to which the alien is returnable (or persecution at the hands of an organization or person from which the government cannot or will not protect the alien). * * *. Similarly, we do not believe that the use of the word "persecution" in section 101(a)(42)(A), instead of "life or freedom would be threatened," as in section 243(h), is a significant distinction between withholding of deportation and asylum.

Id. at 17 n. 3. *See also Matter of Martinez-Romero,* 18 I & N Dec. 73, 77 n. 5 (BIA 1981).[22]

22. Courts and commentators had also generally come to treat the two types of relief as identical, or at least as governed by the same basic standards. For example, in *Zavala-Bonilla v. INS,* 730 F.2d 562, 563 n.1 (9th Cir.1984), writing before the Supreme Court's decision, the court stated:

An application for political asylum filed, as here, during deportation proceedings is considered as an application for "withholding of deportation" under [INA § 243(h)]. 8 C.F.R. § 208.3(b) (1983). Although technically called requests for "withholding of deportation," such requests are considered, and actually are, requests for asylum.

In some settings, we have seen, the Supreme Court has been extraordinarily deferential to the Board's construction of the statutes it administers. *See, e.g., INS v. Wang,* 450 U.S. 139, 101 S.Ct. 1027, 67 L.Ed.2d 123 (1981), reprinted at page 512 *supra.* Here the Court cites and discusses *Lam;* why doesn't it show the same deference to the Board's views? Are there other policy reasons for the Court's conclusions?

In *Matter of Salim,* the BIA explained that "asylum is a greater form of relief" than withholding, and it outlined the various additional entitlements which are entailed in a grant of asylum and which are denied to someone merely given § 243(h) protection—most importantly, the likely acquisition of permanent resident status after a year's wait. *Salim* suggests further that asylum will be *more* difficult to claim than withholding. In other words, some people like Salim may merit the lesser, country-specific remedy, but not be held to qualify for the greater remedy—for example, when there are good reasons to insist that the alien settle in a third country that is willing to receive him, or possibly when the alien has committed other flagrant misbehavior, not quite serious enough to disqualify him from protection under § 243(h)(2) or the Protocol.

The Supreme Court in *Stevic* seems to contemplate exactly the opposite: that the threshold for asylum will be more generous, although still subject to discretionary limitations. This amounts to saying that Congress intended to qualify a wider group of threatened people for the more potent form of immigration relief, but then delegated to the Service and the Board authority to decide, in their discretion (not channeled by further statutory standards), which of these aliens will be selected.

3. Suppose the Board were to agree that a uniform threshold for relief under either § 208 or § 243(h) is desirable. Does it have authority to announce in a post-*Stevic* case that, in the exercise of discretion, no one will receive asylum henceforth unless they have established a clear probability of persecution? Or must the discretion under the asylum provision be exercised case-by-case according to other, more traditional standards (as happened in *Salim,* where the BIA followed its usual practice and regarded fraud as a strongly negative factor cutting against a favorable exercise of discretion)? *See generally Fook Hong Mak v. INS,* 435 F.2d 728 (2d Cir.1970) (rejecting, in a somewhat different setting, the claim that discretion granted by INA § 245 must always be exercised case-by-case, and allowing INS to adopt regulations excluding whole categories from the favorable exercise of discretion). Alternatively, is the Board in a position to hold fast to what it had ruled in *Dunar* —namely that "well-founded fear" and "clear probability" are the same thing—and argue that the Court's language to the contrary in *Stevic* is simply dictum?

4. The Court has much to say in Part IV of the opinion about the possible meaning of various standards for determining risks of persecu-

tion, including some rather striking commentary on the positions of the respondents and the various amici. This extended dictum—particularly the description of the views the Court regards as "a more moderate position"—may well structure the predictable forthcoming debates over the meaning of "well-founded fear of persecution" for purposes of § 208.

Nevertheless, for all the Court's words about the various formulations, it still has not helped much to clarify the precise standards that will govern under § 243(h) in the future. Although we know that the Board may continue to require a clear probability of persecution, we are told that "clear" is probably surplusage, and that the Board's formulation simply requires proof that "it is more likely than not that the alien would be subject to persecution." *See* the text at the Court's footnote 19. But does "would be subject to persecution" mean the same thing as "would be persecuted"? Two paragraphs later the Court speaks as though they are the same: under pre-Refugee Act practice, which the Court now perpetuates, the opinion states that an applicant for withholding had to show that "it was more likely than not that the alien *would be persecuted* in the country to which he was being deported." (Emphasis added.) Yet in the first paragraph of Part IV, the Court sometimes seems to equate "subject to persecution" with the notion of being "threatened."

In any event, the wording of § 243(h) is "life or freedom *would be threatened*," not "would be taken away" or "would be impaired." Suppose, to take a fanciful case, that the alien could show with mathematical certainty that, should he return, there is one chance in three that he would be hanged by his thumbs in a dungeon for his religious beliefs. Is it more likely than not that he would be *persecuted* on return? Is it more likely than not that he would be *subject to persecution* on return? Is it fair to say that his life or freedom would be *threatened* if he returns?

5. The *Stevic* decision departed rather sharply from the understanding and expectations of most people knowledgeable about refugee law, and contains several assumptions that, at best, sound odd to practitioners in the field (as you may have guessed from the editors comments in the notes to the opinion). *See* Helton, *Stevic: The Decision and its Implications,* 3 Imm.L.Rep. 49, 54 (1984) (lamenting the "complications" that the decision "reintroduces"). The decision poses a real challenge to INS, the State Department, the Board, and the Solicitor General (who must decide about future appellate litigation), in deciding where to go from here.

Of course, if the Court had maintained a unified standard for purposes of both §§ 243(h) and 208, the difficult questions would remain: what should that standard be? What kinds of threats should be recognized? How serious and imminent must they be? How sharply focused on the particular petitioner? Of all the different possibilities sketched out in Part IV of the opinion, which one seems the soundest to you?

6. Several courts have attempted to define the evidentiary standards for asylum and withholding in the wake of *Stevic,* but their conclusions are quite diverse. Some have determined that the two sections require different standards, with "well-founded fear" being more generous to the

alien. *See Bolanos-Hernandez v. INS*, 749 F.2d 1316, 1321 (9th Cir. 1984). Others adhere to the view that the two standards are identical. *See Sotto v. INS*, 748 F.2d 832, 836 (3d Cir. 1984). And still others appear to have difficulty deciding, finding the two "very similar," but "not identical." *See Carvajal-Munoz v. INS*, 743 F.2d 562, 574–76 (7th Cir. 1984); *Youkhanna v. INS*, 749 F.2d 360, 362 (6th Cir. 1984).

The Board surveyed these precedents in *Matter of Acosta*, Interim Dec. No. ___ (BIA, March 1, 1985), a lengthy opinion evidently intended as a comprehensive statement of the Board's views on this and a host of other questions that arise in applying §§ 208 and 243(h). It held (slip op. at 19–20):

> One might conclude that "a well-founded fear of persecution," which requires a showing that persecution is likely to occur, refers to a standard that is different from "a clear probability of persecution," which requires a showing that persecution is "more likely than not" to occur. As a practical matter, however, the facts in asylum and withholding cases do not produce clear-cut instances in which such fine distinctions can be meaningfully made. Our inquiry in these cases, after all, is not quantitative, *i.e.*, we do not examine a variety of statistics to discern to some theoretical degree the likelihood of persecution. Rather, our inquiry is qualitative: we examine the alien's experiences and other external events to determine if they are of a kind that enable us to conclude the alien is likely to become the victim of persecution. In this context, we find no meaningful distinction between a standard requiring a showing that persecution is likely to occur and a standard requiring a showing that persecution is more likely than not to occur. As we construe them, both the well-founded-fear standard for asylum and the clear-probability standard for withholding of deportation require an alien's facts to show that the alien possesses a characteristic a persecutor seeks to overcome by punishing the individuals who possess it, that a persecutor is aware or could easily become aware the alien possesses this characteristic, that a persecutor has the capability of punishing the alien, and that a persecutor has the inclination to punish the alien. Accordingly, we conclude that the standards for asylum and withholding of deportation are not meaningfully different and, in practical application, converge.

c. *Bootstrap Refugees*

The beneficiaries of the old seventh preference for refugees (repealed by the Refugee Act of 1980) had to show that they "fled" because of a fear of persecution. The current statutory definition of "refugee" (in INA § 101(a)(42)(A)), like the UN definition from which it is derived, contains no equivalent requirement. The claimant need only show that he is now outside the country where the threat exists and is unwilling to return or otherwise claim the protection of that country, based on a well-founded fear of persecution.

Clearly the new language makes better provision for one type of potential asylum claim. Sometimes prominent political figures, travelling outside the country after a routine departure at a time when they faced no threats, find themselves jeopardized by a coup d'etat or other drastic political change that occurred at home during their absence. If the threat is genuine, it would be hypertechnical to deny asylum because of the timing of their journey abroad. The UNHCR Handbook, *supra* note 21, at 22, refers to such persons as refugees *"sur place."*

But suppose that the asylum applicant does not assert that there have been any dramatic changes in the political scene at home. Suppose he admits he was in no danger before he left, but does claim that he would now be persecuted because (a) he left without permission or deviated from the prescribed terms of his exit visa, and that the home government imposes severe sanctions for such violations of its travel laws, or (b) he is now at risk either because of political activities that began only after arrival in the United States or simply because the home government will regard the mere fact that he has applied for political asylum as punishable political opposition.

Does such an applicant merit asylum, if he can prove his allegations? If so, he will in a sense have picked himself up by his own bootstraps, since he created the conditions that validate the claim at a time when he was otherwise in no danger. The prospect of rewarding manipulative behavior by applicants has prompted concern about bootstrapping, and in any event such claims pose real dilemmas for those who must decide on individual applications.

Consider first the situation based on application of the home country's travel laws (category (a) above). The general consensus seems to be that mere application of such sanctions would not support a claim to asylum. Other nations are entitled to have exit laws more severe than we would find acceptable, and the populace must comply, just as it must with other police regulations. But various aggravating factors might change this outcome. For example, if the law is applied with excessive severity, and particularly if it seems to be applied discriminatorily, this fact may validate the asylum claim. *See Sovich v. Esperdy,* 319 F.2d 21, 29 (2d Cir.1963); UNHCR Handbook, *supra* note 21, at 16. *Cf. Coriolan v. INS,* 559 F.2d 993, 1000 (5th Cir.1977). Whether a particular country's laws fit this description can be a very tough call. Some decisions also suggest that prosecution under the illegal departure laws may constitute persecution if the applicant's motive in leaving was political, although this theory has been somewhat submerged in recent years. *See Matter of Janus and Janek,* 12 I. & N. Dec. 866, 876 (BIA 1968); *Kovac v. INS,* 407 F.2d 102, 104–05 (9th Cir.1969); *Berdo v. INS,* 432 F.2d 824, 845–47 (6th Cir.1970).

Assertions under category (b) above are probably more vexing. The connection to political persecution is more direct, but the bootstrapping seems more blatant in such a case—or at least the potential for manipulation is more troublesome. Why didn't the person simply keep quiet here or abstain from claiming asylum, since he was otherwise in no difficulty at home?

Professor Grahl-Madsen, in his treatise on international refugee law, suggests that a distinction can be drawn between actions which are taken out of genuine political motives or which inadvertently result in some political danger, on the one hand, and similar acts committed "for the sole purpose of creating a pretext for invoking a fear of persecution," on the other. In his view, a consensus exists that applicants in the latter case may be denied refugee status, under the general legal principle requiring good faith. 1 A. Grahl-Madsen, *supra* note 1, at 247–52 (1966).

To our knowledge, this principle has not been used, as such, in American practice. Should it be? How would such bona fides be determined? Is it any comfort, if the person is persecuted on return, to know that he brought it on himself by committing a political act that he need not have committed? Isn't the threat equally avoidable for virtually anyone persecuted because of political opinion—even those who escape only after their political activities have put them in danger and hence would unquestionably merit refugee status? After all, in most circumstances, they *could* simply have kept their political opinions to themselves.[23]

The UNHCR Handbook makes clear that persons may become refugees *sur place* based on their own actions abroad, even if there are no changes in the political scene at home. It goes on to say, however, that in such cases there should be "careful examination of the circumstances. Regard should be had in particular to whether such actions may have come to the notice of the authorities of the person's country of origin and how they are likely to be viewed by those authorities." Handbook, *supra* note 21, at 22.

The Board has often seemed more doctrinaire: "For the most part [we have] not considered that joining protest groups or making public statements after entering the United States supports a withholding of deportation under section 243(h)." *Matter of Nghiem*, 11 I. & N.Dec. 541, 544 (1966). In any event, most of the time, the courts and the Board have looked closely at the available evidence to determine whether the applicant was politically active, or was in some way viewed as a known opponent of the government, *before* departing from the home country. *See, e.g., Matter of Williams*, 16 I. & N.Dec. 697, 701 (BIA 1979); *Paul v. INS*, 521 F.2d 194, 196 (5th Cir.1975); *Gena v. INS*, 424 F.2d 227, 233 (5th Cir.1970). *See also Cisternas-Estay v. INS*, 531 F.2d 155 (3d Cir.1976), cert. denied 429 U.S. 853, 97 S.Ct. 145, 50 L.Ed.2d 127 (1977) (asylum denied to Chilean who had held a press conference in the United States to denounce the Pinochet regime shortly after initial denial of his asylum claim; application had previously rested on a fear of persecution at the hands of the Allende government, which Pinochet overthrew). Is this approach too severe? Other authorities suggest greater receptivity to such claims. *See Haitian Refugee Center v. Civiletti*, 503 F.Supp. 442, 477, 480–81 (S.D.Fla. 1980), *modified sub nom. Haitian Refugee Center v. Smith*, 676 F.2d 1023

---

23. The situation is different with asylum applications based on "involuntary" grounds of persecution like race or nationality—and possibly religion as well.

(5th Cir.1982); Note, *Basing Asylum Claims on a Fear of Persecution Arising from a Prior Asylum Claim,* 56 Notre Dame Law. 719 (1981).

In 1981, several senators introduced a bill proposing changes in the law in order to reduce the possibilities for abuse or manipulation by bootstrap asylum claimants. The sponsors evidently were concerned because a large proportion of Haitian asylum claims then pending asserted no danger before departure but only a fear based on the fact of the time spent in the United States. The bill would have amended § 208 to authorize a grant of asylum only if the Attorney General determined that the applicant "is a refugee within the meaning of section 101(a)(42)(A) and if such alien establishes the acquisition of such refugee status which is based on facts existing before his departure from his [home] country." S. 776, 97th Cong., 1st Sess. (1981).

This bill never reached the Senate floor, but in your opinion, should such a measure be adopted? Would it be consistent with the UN Convention and Protocol? Should similar restrictions be imposed on § 243(h)? How would the bill have affected each of the various scenarios described here involving applicants who were not in danger at the time of departure from the home country?

d. Exceptions

Even those who prove a well-founded fear of persecution or a threat to life or freedom may be denied the benefits of asylum under some circumstances. For example, if the threat to the alien's freedom derives from a legitimate prosecution for bank robbery, his claim will probably fail on two grounds. First, he is not facing a threat "on account of" race, religion, nationality, membership in a particular social group, or political opinion. Second, he would be barred from the benefits of the withholding provision by INA § 243(h)(2)(C), because there are reasons to believe that he committed a serious nonpolitical crime in the home country. In fact, all of § 243(h)(2) consists of exceptions to the withholding requirement, which are meant to parallel the exception provisions of the UN treaties. See Articles 1(F) and 33(2) of the UN Convention. The same exceptions have been made applicable by regulation to applications for asylum under § 208. 8 C.F.R. § 208.8(f). *See also* the second sentence of the statutory definition of "refugee," INA § 101(a)(42). The following case explores the meaning of some of these provisions.

MATTER OF McMULLEN

Board of Immigration Appeals, 1984.
Interim Decision No. 2967.

On October 1, 1980, this Board sustained the Immigration and Naturalization Service's appeal from a decision of an immigration judge finding the respondent deportable but granting his applications for asylum and withholding of deportation pursuant to sections 208(a) and 243(h) of the Immigration and Nationality Act. *Matter of McMullen,* 17 I & N Dec. 542 (BIA 1980). On October 13, 1981, the United States Court of Appeals for the Ninth Circuit granted the respondent's petition for review and reversed this Board's finding that the respondent had not established the likelihood of persecution at the hands of the Provisional Irish Republican Army (hereinafter "the PIRA") and that the government in Ireland was unable or unwilling to protect him. *McMullen v. INS,* 658 F.2d 1312 (9th Cir.1981). In its order, the Ninth Circuit did not grant the respondent asylum or withholding of deportation; nor did it resolve all of the issues presented. Although the court did not specifically remand the case for further consideration, the parties agree that the case is properly before the Board. We will, therefore, reconsider our decision of October 1, 1980, under the provisions of 8 C.F.R. 3.2. Upon reconsideration, the Service's appeal is again sustained.

The respondent is a 36-year-old native and citizen of the Republic of Ireland and the United Kingdom. He last entered the United States on April 29, 1978, as a nonimmigrant visitor, using a fraudulent passport bearing the name of Kevin O'Shaughnessy. * * * His deportability is not at issue.

The facts of this case have previously been discussed in both the Ninth Circuit's decision and our prior order. Respondent claims that he would be subject to persecution by the PIRA if deported to the Republic of Ireland. The record overwhelmingly establishes that the PIRA is a clandestine, terrorist organization committed to the use of violence to achieve its objectives. During the course of these proceedings the respondent has submitted 37 exhibits, containing more than 300 pages, consisting of newspaper and magazine articles, scholarly reports, and other publications, documenting PIRA terrorist activities between 1968 and 1979. The statement of Dr. Jeffrey Prager, submitted on appeal as Exhibit A to the respondent's May 5, 1982 supplemental brief, indicates that the PIRA, formally established in 1969, grew out of the increased political agitation in Northern Ireland in the late 1960's. He states that it represented a break with the controlling faction of the Irish Republican Army (hereinafter "the IRA") committed to the use of parliamentary, nonviolent means of achieving a unified Ireland. The PIRA's commitment to physical force is characterized by attacks on both government civilian institutions and military installations, random violence against innocent civilian populations through indiscriminate bombing campaigns, the murder or maiming of targeted individuals for political reasons based on their public opposition to the PIRA, and the use of violence to maintain order and discipline within the PIRA's membership. Its operations have been funded, in part, through the commission of thousands of armed robberies.

* * *

The respondent testified that the PIRA's use of violence and bombing campaigns rapidly escalated following the Government's institution of its internment (detention without trial) policy in August 1971. He also claimed responsibility for the bombing of the British Army's Palace Barracks outside of Belfast, Northern Ireland, in January 1972. The respondent testified that the PIRA engages in beatings, kneecappings (crippling by shooting into or crushing the victim's knees), and murder to maintain discipline within its membership. He contended that the PIRA commits its violent crimes in the context that it is acting as a government, that it recognizes no other courts or government, and that it is the only source of law and order in the country.

In January 1972, the respondent deserted his British Army unit and joined the PIRA. The respondent's duties with the PIRA included providing military training to its members and conducting special operations which involved intelligence collection and execution of operations. In 1972 he was sent to the United States by the PIRA's General Headquarters in Dublin to coordinate arms purchases and shipments. He stated that he was responsible for coordinating a considerable number of arms shipments back to Northern Ireland. The respondent testified that he had no fear of reprisals in 1974 after his initial resignation from the PIRA, as he had been on excellent terms with the organization between 1972 and 1974, and that until his refusal in 1977 to participate in a PIRA operation to kidnap an American citizen for ransom, he was highly respected as an effective member. The record reflects that the respondent refused to carry out the kidnapping for reasons of personal security based on his belief that the operation would not be successful.

On review, the Ninth Circuit found that the respondent's evidence established that the PIRA is a clandestine, terrorist organization, that the government of the Republic of Ireland is unable to control the PIRA, and that the respondent was likely to suffer persecution by the PIRA if returned to the Republic of Ireland. The Ninth Circuit did not reach the question of whether the persecution the respondent was likely to suffer would be the result of his political opinions within the meaning of the Act. In reaching this question now, we note at the outset that the burden is on the respondent to show that the persecution he fears by the PIRA is based on his race, religion, nationality, membership in a particular social group, or political opinion. 8 C.F.R. 208.5; *Matter of McMullen, supra.* We conclude that the respondent has failed to establish that the persecution he fears is based on his political opinion or any of the other enumerated grounds within the Act for which asylum and withholding of deportation may be granted.

The respondent argues that his resignation from the PIRA in 1974 and his subsequent refusal in 1977 to participate in the kidnapping of a United States citizen for ransom represents political opinion for which the PIRA now seeks his persecution. He argues that his refusal to carry out the kidnapping assignment and the subsequent PIRA Court of Inquiry in 1978 charging him with the "military violation" of failing to carry out an order was the culmination of 4 years of conflict and differences between the respondent and the PIRA. The record does not support this argument. By his own admissions he was on excellent terms with the PIRA in 1974 and did not fear any reprisals by the organization as a result of his resignation at that time. Nor does the record contain any evidence of ill will by the PIRA towards the respondent because of the resignation. Following his release from prison in 1977 the PIRA approached the respondent and requested his assistance. Despite his claim that he agreed to work for the PIRA because of threats, he subsequently testified that the reason he began working with the PIRA in 1977 was because "[t]hey were low on manpower and money and the organization was trying to get back on its feet." The only evidence in the record suggesting a basis for the PIRA's persecution of the respondent is his refusal to carry out the kidnapping assignment. With regard to this refusal, the respondent testified that his reasons were primarily for his personal security based on his belief that too many people knew about the operation and that as a result it more than likely would have failed.

We are satisfied from a review of the record that the respondent has not established that the persecution he fears by the PIRA is based on political opinion or any other designated ground within the Act. His refusal to commit the crime of kidnapping for reasons of personal safety does not constitute political opinion. Nor does it represent conduct which Congress intended to protect by its adoption of the asylum and withholding provisions contained in sections 208(a) and 243(h) of the Act. The record clearly shows that the PIRA uses violence and threats of violence internally to maintain discipline and order within the rank and file of its membership. As such, the PIRA's use of violence against its members is essentially apolitical, representing an indifference to the personal views and opinions of those members who are subject to sanctions. We conclude that this internal use of violence by the PIRA does not constitute persecution within the meaning of the Act. *See Matter of Pierre,* 15 I & N Dec. 461 (BIA 1975). Moreover, its use of internal violence existed at the time the respondent joined the PIRA and continued throughout his active membership. Having elected to participate in the PIRA, with knowledge of its internal disciplinary policies, the respondent is not now in a position to complain.

We further conclude that the respondent, by his membership in the PIRA, participated in the persecution of others and may not, therefore, be considered a refugee. He is, accordingly, statutorily ineligible for both asylum and withholding of deportation. Section 208(a) of the Act authorizes the Attorney General, in his discretion, to grant asylum to an alien who is determined to be a refugee within the meaning of section 101(a)(42) of the Act. * * * Section 101(a)(42) specifically excludes from the definition of "refugee" "any person who ordered, incited, assisted, or otherwise participated in the persecution of any person on account of race, religion, nationality, membership in a particular social group, or political opinion." The identical limitation regarding the scope of coverage also prohibits granting withholding of deportation pursuant to section 243(h)(2)(A). *See* 8 C.F.R. 208.8(f)(1)(iii).

While there is no universally accepted definition of "persecution," "a threat to life or freedom on account of race, religion, nationality, political opinion or membership of a particular social group is always persecution." *Matter of Laipenieks,* Interim Decision 2949 (BIA 1983). We recognize that the persecution contemplated under the Act is not limited to the conduct of organized governments, but may, under certain circumstances, be committed by individuals or nongovernmental organizations. *Rosa v. INS,* 440 F.2d 100 (1st Cir.1971); *Matter of McMullen, supra; Matter of Pierre, supra; Matter of Tan,* 12 I & N Dec. 564 (BIA 1967).

The record demonstrates that the PIRA engages in the persecution of targeted individuals based on their public opposition to the organization and its terrorist activities. These political assassinations are exemplified by the murder of Ross McWhirter [who had campaigned for IRA terrorists to be charged with treason and thus receive the death penalty] and the suspected responsibility for the murder of Sir Richard Sykes [British ambassador to the Netherlands] and Lord Mountbatten. This persecution by the PIRA is distinguished from its use of violence to maintain discipline and order within the rank and file of its membership and its indiscriminate bombing campaigns, neither of which involve persecution based on political opinion.

We find that the respondent, by his active and effective membership in the PIRA, participated in the persecution of others. Our finding is supported by the London Agreement of 8 August 1945 and Charter of the International Military Tribunal which includes in the definition of "crimes against humanity," "persecutions on political, racial or religious grounds" and states with regard to any such crimes that "[l]eaders, organizers, instigators and accomplices participating in the formulation or execution of a common plan or conspiracy to commit any of the foregoing crimes are responsible for all acts performed by any persons in execution of such plan." The record reflects that at the time the respondent joined the PIRA its use of violence was escalating. The respondent testified that he was respected as an effective member of the PIRA until 1977 and that his duties included training other PIRA members and conducting special operations. We find it significant that the respondent was personally responsible for coordinating a considerable number of illegal arms shipments from the United States to Northern Ireland. Through those arms shipments the respondent directly provided, in part, the instrumentalities with which the PIRA perpetrated its acts of persecution and violence. We have no difficulty in concluding that these arms were directly involved in the murder, torture, and maiming of innocent civilians who publicly opposed the PIRA, and are unwilling to isolate these arm shipments from their ultimate use by the PIRA in conducting its campaign of terror. Thus, we find clear evidence that the respondent aided and assisted in the persecution of others within the meaning of the Act. *See Fedorenko v. United States*, 449 U.S. 490, 101 S.Ct. 737, 66 L.Ed.2d 686 (1981); *Matter of Laipenieks, supra; see also United States v. Kowalchuk*, 571 F.Supp. 72 (E.D.Pa.1983); *United States v. Osidach*, 513 F.Supp. 51 (E.D.Pa.1981).

The provisions of sections 101(a)(42) and 243(h)(2)(A), by excluding from the definition of "refugee" persons who have participated in the persecution of others, parallel and are consistent with the fundamental principles embodied in the United Nations 1951 Convention and 1967 Protocol Relating to the Status of Refugees. This exclusion from refugee status under the Act represents the view that those who have participated in the persecution of others are unworthy and not deserving of international protection. The persecution which forms the basis of the exclusion is not limited to acts committed in an official capacity but is equally applicable to persons who have committed such persecution within the framework of various nongovernmental groupings, whether officially rec-

676 REFUGEES AND POLITICAL ASYLUM Ch. 8

ognized, clandestine, or self-styled. This restriction on the scope of refugee status applies even though the person so excluded may, in fact, be the subject of persecution and notwithstanding that his persecution of others was politically motivated. The prohibited conduct is deemed so repugnant to civilized society and the community of nations that its justification will not be heard.

We are also satisfied from a review of the record that "there are serious reasons for considering" that the respondent by his activities as a member of the PIRA has committed "serious nonpolitical crimes," making him statutorily ineligible for asylum and withholding of deportation. 8 C.F.R. 208.8(f)(1)(v); section 243(h)(2)(C) of the Act; *see Matter of Rodriguez-Palma*, 17 I & N Dec. 465 (BIA 1980); *cf. Matter of Frentescu*, Interim Decision 2906 (BIA 1982). Whether crimes are of a political character is primarily a question of fact. *Ornelas v. Ruiz*, 161 U.S. 502, 16 S.Ct. 689, 40 L.Ed. 787 (1896). In evaluating the political nature of a crime, we consider it important that the political aspect of the offense outweigh its common-law character. This would not be the case if the crime is grossly out of proportion to the political objective or if it involves acts of an atrocious nature.

The record before us reflects that during the period of the respondent's active membership in the PIRA, that organization's use of random bombings of civilian targets increased. An example of this random bombing, depicted in the respondent's exhibits, was the detonation of 500 pounds of explosives contained in a van parked on a Belfast street, half a block from the Europa, the city's principal hotel. The exhibits further reflect the common practice of using vehicles parked in residential streets containing 100–300 pounds of explosives. These bombings are not generally directed at specific targets, but rather are designed to randomly terrorize the public. We note that such terrorist bombings have been universally condemned as atrocious in nature. The record further reflects that the respondent's duties as a member of the PIRA included the training of other PIRA members and the conduct of special operations. One such operation was the coordination of a considerable number of arms shipments to Northern Ireland for use by the PIRA. The actions and policies of the PIRA of which the respondent was fully cognizant and participated in while a member provide serious reasons to believe that he is responsible for committing "serious non-political crimes."

We find that the respondent's involvement in the terrorist use of explosives and his participation in the PIRA's campaign of violence randomly directed against civilians represent acts of an atrocious nature out of proportion to the political goal of achieving a unified Ireland and are not, therefore, within the political offense exception. *See Ornelas v. Ruiz, supra; Eain v. Wilkes*, 641 F.2d 504, 519–24 (7th Cir.1981), cert. denied, 454 U.S. 894, 102 S.Ct. 390, 70 L.Ed.2d 208 (1981). *Ornelas* involved extradition proceedings related to a raid on a Mexican village and its military garrison by more than a hundred men, resulting in murder, arson, robbery, assault, and kidnapping of both Mexican soldiers and private citizens. The Court there refused to apply the political offense exception, "in view of the character of the foray, the mode of attack, the persons killed or captured, and the kind of property taken or destroyed" notwithstanding the political intentions and objectives of those who committed the violent crimes. *Ornelas v. Ruiz, supra,* at 510–12. It is apparent that the Court viewed the civilian status of the victims as significant in evaluating the applicability of the political offense exception and considered the raid a form of political activity not encompassed within the exception.

In *Eain,* also involving extradition proceedings, the Seventh Circuit refused to apply the political offense exception to the bombing of a West Bank marketplace, crowded with civilians, by a Palestinian Liberation Organization terrorist. The court distinguished between acts directed at civilians, "terrorist activity," and those directed at a government, with only the latter type possibly being within the political offense exception. Characterizing this distinction as the difference between "isolated acts of social violence" such as the killing of civilians, and a more concerted effort to topple the existing government in a country, the court stated:

> The definition of "political disturbance," with its focus on organized forms of aggression such as war, rebellion and revolution, is aimed at acts that disrupt the political structure of a State, and not the social structure that established the government. The exception does not make a random bombing intended to result in the cold-blooded murder of civilians incidental to a purpose of toppling a government, absent a direct link between the perpetrator, a political organization's political goals, and the specific act. Rather, the indiscriminate bombing of a civilian populace is not recognized as a protected political act even when the larger "political" objective of the person who sets off the bomb may be to eliminate the civilian population of a country....

Eain v. Wilkes, supra, at 520–21. Comparing terrorist activities directed at the civilian population with those of the anarchist, the court concluded:

> As recent commentators have stated, "an offense having its impact upon the citizenry, but not directly upon the government, does not fall within the political offense exception." Lubet & Czaczkes at 202. *See* Costello, *International Terrorism and the Development of the Principle Aut Dedere Aut Judicare,* 10 J.Int'l Law & Econ. 475, 501 (1975) quoting U.N. Secretariat study: "[T]he legitimacy of a cause does not in itself legitimize the use of certain forms of violence especially against the innocent[.]"

Eain v. Wilkes, supra, at 521. In view of the respondent's effective participation in the PIRA and the nature of the offenses perpetrated against innocent civilians, we conclude that he has committed "serious non-political crimes" and is ineligible for the requested relief.

Moreover, considering the record in its entirety, we find that the respondent is not deserving of asylum and specifically deny this relief in the exercise of discretion. *Matter of Salim,* Interim Decision 2922 (BIA 1982). In *Salim,* asylum was denied in the exercise of discretion based on the alien's avoidance of this country's orderly refugee procedures through the use of fraudulently obtained documentation. Although present in the instant case, the respondent's use of fraudulently obtained documentation is clearly overshadowed by the serious adverse factor of his involvement in the PIRA's random violence directed against innocent civilians. He may not separate the active and effective role he played in the PIRA's operations from responsibility for that organization's indiscriminate bombing campaigns or its murder, torture, and maiming of innocent civilians who disagreed with the PIRA's objectives or methods. The record contains no countervailing equities to overcome the extremely negative discretionary factors present.

Accordingly, we will again sustain the appeal.

Order: On reconsideration, the appeal is sustained, and the respondent shall be deported to the Republic of Ireland.

Notes

1. This is a somewhat curious asylum case, since the underlying issue here is not persecution by the government if McMullen is deported to Ireland, but persecution by a terrorist organization that considers itself a government. Nevertheless, it is well established that "persecution within the meaning of § 243(h) includes persecution by non-governmental groups * * *, where it is shown that the government of the proposed country of deportation is unwilling or unable to control that group." *McMullen v. INS*, 658 F.2d 1312, 1315 n. 2 (9th Cir.1981). Here the BIA treats the case under this rubric, in light of the earlier remand by the court of appeals (although a close reading of the opinion in that case, *id.*, reveals precious little attention to the issue of whether the government of Ireland is unwilling or unable to control the PIRA on its soil).

2. Note how readily the Board finds that the PIRA's activities directed at civilians involved persecution *on account of* political opinion—resulting in McMullen's disqualification from asylum as one who, before his disaffection, assisted in such persecution. But when it turns to analyze the threat to McMullen himself, the Board rather easily concludes that his risk has nothing to do with political opinion, being instead solely a matter of internal discipline. Is this a fair characterization? Remember that the Board would find McMullen disqualified from all protection on this ground alone, even if he had never participated in the persecution of others or committed serious crimes himself. In this light, should the Board be so finicky about the underlying reasons for the danger when it accepts that persecution is clearly probable?

Some courts have been skeptical of the validity of such a narrow approach. For example, in *Sarkis v. Nelson*, 585 F.Supp. 235 (E.D.N.Y. 1984), the Board had denied the asylum and withholding applications of two Iraqi Christians who testified that they left Iraq after suffering detention and beatings for declining to join the ruling Ba'ath Party. The court reversed and remanded the case for further consideration:

> The Board held that petitioners had not shown that their refusal to join the Ba'ath Party was based on their "religious" beliefs. That may be. But both [§ 208(a) and § 243(h)] encompass persecution based upon "political opinion" as well as reli-

gious beliefs. Thus, the Board should have determined whether petitioners' refusal to join the Ba'ath Party constituted a statement of political opinion for which petitioners could legitimately fear reprisal if returned to Iraq.

Equally disturbing is the Board's finding that petitioners failed to show any characteristics in common with those who may have been persecuted for political activity in opposition to the Iraqi government. Petitioner Sarkis's brother, Doman Sarkis, testified at the exclusion hearing that a third Sarkis brother * * was tortured to death by the Iraqi Army during his military service.

Although the Board does advert to this testimony, it makes no attempt, in its opinion, to reconcile this dramatic testimony with its finding that petitioners have failed to demonstrate characteristics in common with individuals who have suffered persecution in Iraq. Rather, the Board concludes that petitioners have not shown that a decision by the Iraqi Government to inflict the death penalty upon them for draft evasion would be influenced by petitioners' religion or political opinions.

Accepting the Board's *sangfroid* premise that uniform application of admittedly harsh penal laws constitutes prosecution and not persecution, I am, nevertheless, unable on this record to find substantial evidence supporting the Board's finding that possible infliction of the death penalty upon these petitioners for draft evasion would not be religiously or politically motivated.

Id. at 238–39. (Upon remand, the Board gave more careful consideration to the elements of the asylum claim that had troubled the court, but persisted in denying relief under either § 208 or § 243(h). The district court then accepted this decision. *Sarkis v. Sava*, 599 F.Supp. 724 (E.D.N.Y. 1984).)

3. In *Matter of Acosta*, Interim Dec. No. __ (BIA, March 1, 1985), the Board restated its strict approach to determining whether threatened persecution is based on "political opinion." The deportation respondent, a former taxi driver in San Salvador, had received death threats from the guerrillas in that country because he refused to take part in work stoppages they were sponsoring. The Board wrote (slip op. at 25–26):

* * * The fact that the respondent was threatened by the guerrillas as part of a campaign to destabilize the government demonstrates that the guerrillas' actions were undertaken to further their political goals in the civil controversy in El Salvador. However, conduct undertaken to further the goals of one faction in a political controversy does not necessarily constitute persecution "on account of political opinion" so as to qualify an alien as a "refugee" within the meaning of the Act.

As we have previously discussed, the term "persecution" means the infliction of suffering or harm in order to punish an individual for possessing a particular belief or characteristic the persecutor seeks to overcome. It follows, therefore, that the requirement of "persecution on account of political opinion" means that the particular belief or characteristic a persecutor seeks to overcome in an individual must be his political opinion. Thus, the requirement of "persecution on account of political opinion" refers not to the ultimate political end that may be served by persecution, but to the belief held by an individual that causes him to be the object of the persecution. * * *

In the respondent's case there are no facts showing that the guerrillas were aware of or sought to punish the respondent for his political opinion; nor was there any showing that the respondent's refusal to participate in the work-stoppages was motivated by his political opinion. Absent such a showing the respondent failed to demonstrate that the particular belief the guerrillas sought to overcome in him was his political opinion. Therefore he does not come within this ground of persecution.

One court has taken a far different approach. It reversed the Board's decision in a somewhat similar case involving another Salvadoran asylum applicant and ordered the Board both to grant withholding of deportation and to consider the applicant eligible for asylum. *Bolanos-Hernandez v. INS*, 749 F.2d 1316 (9th Cir. 1984). On the question whether the threatened harm was based on "political opinion," the court wrote (*id.* at 1324–26):

The government concedes that Bolanos has consciously chosen not to join either of the contending forces in El Salvador because he wishes to remain neutral, yet it argues that any persecution Bolanos might suffer would not be because of his political opinion. We find it somewhat difficult to follow the government's argument. The government contends that Bolanos' decision to remain politically neutral is not a political choice. There is nothing in the record to support this contention. Presumably the government is suggesting either that neutrality is always apolitical or that an individual who chooses neutrality must establish that the choice was made for political reasons. We disagree with both of these contentions.

Choosing to remain neutral is no less a political decision than is choosing to affiliate with a particular political faction. * * * When a person is aware of contending political forces and affirmatively chooses not to join any faction, that choice is a political one. A rule that one must identify with one of two dominant warring political factions in order to possess a political opinion, when many persons may, in fact, be opposed to the views and policies of both, would frustrate one of the basic objectives of the Refugee Act of 1980—to provide protection to all victims of persecution regardless of ideology. Moreover, construing "political opinion" in so short-sighted and grudging a manner could result in limiting the benefits under the ameliorative provisions of our immigration laws to those who join one political extreme or another; moderates who choose to sit out a battle would not qualify.

The government's second suggestion is equally unconvincing. The motive underlying any political choice may, if examined closely, prove to be, in whole or in part, non-political. Certainly a political affiliation may be undertaken for non-political, as well as political, reasons. A decision to join a particular political party may, for example, be made to curry favor, gain social acceptability, advance one's career, or obtain access to money or positions of power. Similarly, a decision to remain neutral may be made, in whole or in part, for non-political reasons. However, the reasons underlying an individual's political choice are of no significance for purposes of sections 243(h) and 208(a) and the government may not inquire into them. Whatever the motivation, an individual's choice, once made, constitutes, for better or for worse, a manifestation of political opinion.

* * * It does not matter to the persecutors what the individual's motivation is. The guerrillas in El Salvador do not inquire into the reasoning process of those who insist on remaining neutral and refuse to join their cause. They are concerned only with an act that constitutes an overt manifestation of a political opinion. Persecution because of that overt manifestation is persecution because of a political opinion.

4. The respondent in *Acosta, supra,* also claimed he would be persecuted based on "membership in a particular social group," namely, taxi drivers in San Salvador. What standards should be used in deciding what constitutes a social group for these purposes? *Compare id.,* slip op. at 23–25 (rejecting claim because "the common characteristic that defines the group * * * must be one that the members of the group cannot change, or should not be required to change because it is fundamental to their individual identities or consciences") *with Fernandez-Roque v. Smith,* 599 F.Supp. 1103 (N.D.Ga.1984) (remanding to BIA for reopening because the plaintiffs had made a prima facie showing that Cubans who arrived in the United States as part of the Mariel boatlift would face persecution in Cuba; Marielitos constitute a "particular social group").

5. The Board's summary of the record in *Matter of McMullen, supra,* does not tie McMullen directly to any violent acts except the bombing of a British military barracks. And it is not established that any of the arms he acquired were used in the PIRA's activities directed at civilians. Was the Board entitled to find, on such a record, that McMullen "assisted [or] participated in the persecution of any person on account of race, religion, nationality, membership in a particular social group, or political opinion"?

Furthermore, was the Board entitled to find that his crimes were nonpolitical, since there is no direct link to violence directed at anyone other than military forces? Or should violent attacks even on military forces always be considered common crimes—punishable terrorist actions—at least if the government involved is a democratic one? Note that the Board determines what crimes are nonpolitical by reference to precedents construing similar concepts in the context of extradition proceedings. But cases such as *Eain v. Wilkes,* 641 F.2d 504 (7th Cir.1981), *cert. denied* 454 U.S. 894, 102 S.Ct. 390, 70 L.Ed.2d 208 (1981), on which the Board relied heavily, involved an individual who personally planted the bomb that caused the civilian injuries. This has not been shown as to McMullen. *Eain* also suggests that a violent crime *would* be considered a political offense if the bombing were directed solely at military targets in the course of a violent uprising. *Id.* at 522–23. Does that doctrine make sense?

For other decisions considering the exceptions to asylum when the alien has committed a "serious nonpolitical crime" or a "particularly serious crime," see *Matter of Rodriguez*, Interim Dec. No. 2985 (BIA 1985); *Matter of Frentescu*, 18 I & N Dec. 244 (BIA 1982); *Matter of Rodriguez-Palma*, 17 I & N Dec. 465 (BIA 1980); *discussed in* 62 Interp.Rel. 218–19 (1985).

3. THE STANDARDS IN ACTION: TRANSCRIPT OF AN ASYLUM HEARING

Now that we have considered several features of the refugee definition, the standard of proof required under §§ 208 and 243(h), and the exceptions to these protections, it is time to examine actual implementation. Reproduced below are portions of the transcript of an actual asylum hearing before an immigration judge, although some names and places have been altered. It involves the claim of a Haitian applicant; Haitian cases have presented, and continue to present, some of the most difficult and divisive issues in the American controversy over asylum. We do not suggest that this case is necessarily representative of all claims filed by Haitians—indeed, the tendered proof is probably more detailed and specific than the norm. Rather, we offer it because it reflects the difficulty of the decisions faced by adjudicators of asylum cases, and the weight of responsibility they may bear.

Some background information about Haiti may prove useful. Haiti was the second state in the Western Hemisphere to become an independent republic, in 1804. But unlike the experience of its predecessor and northern neighbor, no tradition of enlightened or generous leadership took root. Haiti suffered almost from the beginning from autocratic, selfish, and occasionally extraordinarily vicious rulers.[24] Decades of misrule, combined with poor agricultural practices, environmental degradation, and overpopulation, turned what had been France's most prosperous colony into the Hemisphere's poorest nation. The per capita annual

---

24. The U.S. Agency for International Development once described the role of government there in these words:

Throughout much of Haiti's history, government has been a prize to capture, with the victor gaining the spoils in terms of appointing friends and relatives to the payroll and using government positions for private profit. * * * Haiti does not have a tradition of government as a servant of the people.

Quoted in R. Roberts, *Impediments to Economic and Social Development in Haiti* 8 (Congressional Research Service, June 19, 1978).

income is now less than $235 per year—an average figure that obscures the sharply skewed distribution of national wealth. Eighty percent of the people are estimated to live on less than $100 per capita annually. Lawyers Committee for International Human Rights, Violations of Human Rights in Haiti, June 1981—September 1982: A Report to the Organization of American States 7–8 (1982).

Not surprisingly, in light of conditions at home, Haitians have developed a tradition of migrating to other Caribbean nations in search of work, often taking the hardest, least desirable jobs, which are spurned by the local population. For example, Haitians cut much of the sugar cane harvested throughout the region. When a tourist boom began in the Bahamas in the 1950's, Haitians migrated there to provide the cheap labor that was suddenly in great demand. At one time, before a Bahamian government crackdown on illegal migrants in 1978, Haitians were estimated to constitute as much as a fifth of the population of those islands. *See* M. Lundahl, Peasants and Poverty: A Study of Haiti 623–28 (1979).

But Haitian adversity is not solely economic; the political scene is at least equally bleak. As indicated, the nineteenth century established a rarely broken pattern of government misrule. Shortly after the turn of the twentieth century, conditions deteriorated even further. A period of great disorder and bloodshed culminated in 1915 with the gruesome murder of President Vilbrun Guillaume Sam. At that point the United States intervened and imposed a military occupation. That was the era of American gunboat diplomacy, and the United States acted out of an apparent mix of humanitarian and financial motives. *See* Logan & Needler, *Haiti,* in Political Systems of Latin America 153–59 (M. Needler, ed., 1964). Although rule from the North introduced numerous physical improvements in the country, continued local resentment and occasional violent resistance eventually brought about U.S. withdrawal, in 1934.

Thereafter Haiti was ruled by a series of presidents, most of whom were forced from office before the end of their stated terms. In 1957 Dr. Francois Duvalier became president. With a combination of voodoo-based demagoguery and determined manipulation, he consolidated his hold on the country and in 1964 declared himself President-for-Life. One of the main props to his power was a corps of secret police who became known as the Tonton Macoutes (literally Uncle Knapsack—the Creole term for bogeyman). Created as a counterweight to the regular military, which had often been responsible for the ouster of Haitian presidents who became unpopular, the Tonton Macoutes under Papa Doc compiled a record of extortion, bullying, and atrocities. Duvalier opponents were tortured and killed; sometimes whole villages were massacred. Much of Haiti's elite, including perhaps 80 percent of physicians, lawyers, engineers and other professionals, emigrated in the early Duvalier years. *See* R. Rotberg, Haiti: The Politics of Squalor 243–49 (1971). A large proportion moved to the United States, concentrating in the New York area.

Papa Doc died in 1971, and his 19-year-old son, Jean Claude, succeeded him as President-for-Life. Baby Doc, as he is known, promised to bring in a new era of democracy, economic progress and social peace. While most observers would credit him with an end to the reign of systematic government terror under Papa Doc, the country remains in poor condition, both politically and economically. The Macoutes were reorganized as a militia known as the Volunteers for National Security (VSN) and brought under some greater control, but they still wield fairly extensive governmental powers. Mildly independent journals appeared, as did politicians who openly styled themselves as opposition party leaders. But periods of tolerance for these activities have alternated with periods of crude repression (although still short of Papa Doc's brutality). Human rights meetings have been broken up by thugs (probably VSN in civilian garb), and leading political and journalistic figures have been imprisoned off and on, often suffering severe beatings while in detention. The highs and lows of these cycles of repression have often seemed to correspond with developments in U.S. human rights diplomacy. One of the strongest recent crackdowns, for example, occurred in November 1980, a few weeks after the American Presidential election. *See generally* Lawyers Committee, *supra;* Paley, *Haiti's Dynastic Despotism: From Father to Son to ...,* 13 Caribbean Rev. 13 (1984); Stepick, *Haitian Boat People: A Study in the Conflicting Forces Shaping U.S. Immigration Policy,* 45 Law & Contemp. Probs. 175 (Spring 1982); State Department, *Country Reports on Human Rights Practices* for 1983, 98th Cong., 2d Sess. 600–06 (Jt. Comm. Print 1984).

Non-elite Haitians began coming in noticeable numbers to the United States, usually by boat, in the early 1970's. Many of the early applications for asylum were adjudicated solely by the district directors under the old regulations. This practice was attacked in the first of many cases brought to challenge an array of INS practices affecting Haitians, with much of the litigation supported by a variety of church, civic, and lawyers' groups that rallied to support the asylum-seekers. These multifarious lawsuits, some still being litigated, as well as the executive branch responses, are summarized in P. Weiss Fagen, Applying for Political Asylum in New York: Law, Policy and Administrative Practice 21–29 (Occasional Paper No. 41, New York Research Program in Inter-American Affairs, 1984), and General Accounting Office, Detention Policies Affecting Haitians 7–14 (Report GAO/GGD–83–68, 1983). As more of the challenges succeeded, the adjudication backlog grew, and, in an unfortunate cycle of polarization, INS adopted new hasty or severe measures to catch up. Often this only led to new court challenges and new judicial orders to go back and redo the adjudications.[25]

---

25. The polarization is reflected in some of the quotes that opened this Chapter. It also prompted one immigration judge to remark that "he thinks that the only way these [Haitian] cases will be fairly heard is with new judges and new lawyers—the old cast is too battle-scarred." Bruck, *Springing the Haitians, The American Lawyer,* Sept. 1982, at 35, 39. And the Senate, evidently responding to its perception of this phenomenon, added an unusual feature to the version of the Simpson-Mazzoli bill it passed in 1982.

Section 124 of the bill provided that a specialized corps of immigration judges would henceforth hear all asylum claims, but it further stated that no former immigration judge could become one of these specialists. S. 2222, 97th Cong., 2d Sess. (1982). The 1983 version softened this provision so that it simply required special training for former IJ's before they could become asylum adjudicators under the new scheme. S. 529, § 124.

Pressure was mounting for a new policy in 1980, but before those proposals were acted upon, the Mariel boatlift began, bringing 125,000 Cubans to Florida in the spring and summer of that year. The Carter administration ultimately decided to treat all Haitians with pending cases in the same fashion as the Cubans, giving them a special "Cuban-Haitian entrant" status—a form of parole—and seeking special legislation ultimately to regularize their status. No such legislation has yet passed, but those in the "entrant" class still benefit from their status and may remain and work in the United States. (On the Reagan administration's decision to adjust the status of the Cubans under the 1966 Cuban Adjustment Act, and on the continuing legislative efforts to provide equivalent opportunities to the Haitian "entrants," see 61 Interp.Rel. 847–50 (1984); 62 *id.* 36 (1985).)

One of the premises of this special Cuban-Haitian program was a commitment that it would be a one-time special measure to cope with a unique crisis. Caribbean asylum seekers arriving after 1980 have been required to go through the regular process of individual adjudications of their claims to political asylum. It should be noted, however, that virtually no Cubans have arrived since the end of the boatlift. Haitians continued to come. Eventually the Reagan administration responded with a variety of deterrent measures, which we will consider more closely later in this chapter.

Against this background, the debate over Haitian asylum applicants continues. Advocates for the Haitians point to the long history of repression in Haiti, the continued determination of the Duvalier government to strike at its political opponents, and the essentially lawless discretion that the VSN and other security forces in Haiti can wield. They also argue that the economic deprivation in Haiti is the result of deliberate political decisions by the ruling powers, and so should be regarded as a political condition that might validly support an asylum claim. *See, e.g., Haitian Refugee Center v. Civiletti,* 503 F.Supp. 442, 509 (S.D.Fla.1980), *modified sub nom. Haitian Refugee Center v. Smith,* 676 F.2d 1023 (5th Cir.1982). And they point to evidence that those who departed and filed for asylum will be regarded as traitors upon return—thus risking persecution even if they had not been active politically before they left. *Id.* at 477–82. *See generally* P. Weiss Fagen, *supra,* at 30.

In response, U.S. government officials argue that most of the Haitians are simply departing, understandably, to escape economic deprivation, and that few of the current applicants were politically active before they left. U.S. government efforts to monitor the treatment of returnees have rarely discovered any political difficulties after return. (These monitoring efforts, however, have come in for severe criticism from the supporters of the Haitians.) Officials point as well to the tradition of Haitian labor migration throughout the Caribbean, and suggest that Florida is simply the latest Caribbean destination. Most Haitians state in their first encounters with INS that they simply came to seek a job, and it is only after a period of time spent with lawyers that they come forward with asylum claims. Many of the basic claims conform, officials contend, to what they call "the five basic Tonton Macoute stories," which are believed to be false or at least exaggerated. *See* P. Weiss Fagen, *supra,* at 31.

Court litigation continues, and the vast majority of Haitian asylum claims are still denied. The 1983 GAO study reported a 91 percent denial rate for Haitians from October 1, 1980 through May 31, 1982, compared with an overall denial rate of 72 percent. This latter is an average, however. The pattern of grants and denials varies widely among nationalities, and some experience a higher denial rate than the Haitians. *See* General Accounting Office, *supra,* at 2, 32.

As you read the transcript that follows, assume that you are the immigration judge. How would you decide the case? How do the materials in previous sections help in that endeavor? Has the applicant met his burden of proof? Does the persecution he alleges come within the purview of §§ 208 and 243(h)?

MATTER of X.Y.

May 10, 1984.

[All questions to X.Y. translated into Creole.]

[All answers by X.Y. translated into English.]

THE COURT: Sir, is your name X.Y.?

INTERPRETER: Yes.

THE COURT: And what language do you speak and understand best?

INTERPRETER: Creole.

THE COURT: All right. And sir, the interpreter who is present will translate from English to Creole and Creole to English to you for your benefit. Do you understand?

INTERPRETER: Yes.

THE COURT: And sir, the Form I–122, the Notice of Hearing is already in evidence and marked as Exhibit 1. Is this your attorney sitting near you?

INTERPRETER: Yes.

* * *

THE COURT: * * * Has [the asylum application, Form I–589] been completed and filed?

* * *

TRIAL ATTORNEY: Yes, it has, your Honor.

* * *

THE COURT: I see. If it's offered, then it will be marked into evidence and assigned Exhibit Number 2. Was there any request for a State Department advise?

TRIAL ATTORNEY: Yes, there was. We have a letter dated from the State * * * by Lawrence Arthur[a] and I call that it be placed into evidence.

THE COURT: All right. And let the record show that [Counsel] is looking at the letter at this point.

COUNSEL: I have an objection to that being received into evidence.

THE COURT: I see. * * * Do you wish to be heard on your objection or not?

COUNSEL: Yes, I do.

THE COURT: Okay, you may proceed.

COUNSEL: I am objecting to the admission into evidence of the State Department's reply in this case * * * on the grounds that absent the allowance of deposition and subpoenas to propose or to present as a witness and have testify Mr. Lawrence Arthur that it should not be received into evidence * * *. * * * [The State Department reply] makes no particular [or] individual references [to the] quite specific matters set forth in the I–589 and indeed is a form of response similar to the responses received in our other cases. The only distinguishing factor is the substitution of Mr. X.Y.'s name instead of those of other aliens. In view of its uniform character and non-particular character, * * * we ask that absent the allowance of the deposition of Mr. Arthur * * * that [the document] not be received into evidence at all if you are going to afford any weight at all to it.

THE COURT: Now, does the Government wish to answer to that statement?

TRIAL ATTORNEY: Yes. The Government would oppose the motion based on the fact, first of all, that the counsel for the applicant has not shown in fact whether or not the State Department Official would be available to be deposed. It would cause an extreme hardship to the Government as a burden to produce Mr. Arthur at this time. He has not made an offer of proof that his testimony is, in fact, essential and this is nothing more than a fishing expedition and dilatory tactics by counsel, but more importantly, whether Mr. Arthur or any other State Department Official actually possesses knowledge on any particular political conditions in Haiti, is not the problem. The problem is the likelihood of this particular issue, that this particular applicant be subject to persecution if he is returned to Haiti. I believe that that motion should be denied.

* * *

THE COURT: All right. The objection to the entry of the State Department Reply into evidence will be overruled as it is required by regulation. It is not binding upon the Immigration Judge, but it's some evidence to be taken into consideration. The alternate motion to depose Mr. Arthur will be denied because the Court is able to adopt

---

a. At the time of the hearing, Lawrence Arthur was Director of the Asylum Office in   the State Department's Bureau of Human Rights and Humanitarian Affairs.—eds.

the Government's arguments that it will be extremely cumbersome and intolerably cumbersome to ask Mr. Arthur to be deposed in this one of many cases in which he looks at items on asylum. And it's really a question of what might be found out or not. It has the possible breedings of a fishing expedition. Therefore, the Department of State Reply will be entered into evidence [and] assigned Exhibit Number 3. * * *

* * *

THE COURT: All right. Mr. X.Y., if you will raise your right hand and swear that the testimony that you will give in this proceeding to be the truth, the whole truth and nothing but the truth, so help you God?

INTERPRETER: Yes.

THE COURT: You may put your hand down. All right. Now, [Counsel], you may question.

* * *

COUNSEL: When were you born?

INTERPRETER: September 19, 1942.

COUNSEL: And where were you born?

* * *

INTERPRETER: Haiti.

* * *

COUNSEL: Did you live there all your life?

INTERPRETER: All my life.

COUNSEL: And what was your occupation?

INTERPRETER: Cultivator.

COUNSEL: Now, Mr. X.Y., I'd like now to ask you about various problems that your family and you have had with the Government of Haiti.

INTERPRETER: Yes.

COUNSEL: For lack of a better methodology, I'll begin first with what happened to your Uncle in 1967. If you could describe what happened, to the Immigration Judge.

INTERPRETER: My Uncle was a cultivator and had a lot of land to work with. He used to make a lot of money; and the Tonton Macoutes, when they told us that they killed him, they dissected his heart.

THE COURT: All right. You may proceed.

INTERPRETER: When my family and I went to get the coffin to bury him, they said * * * he could not have a proper burial [—that we would] have to bury him in a hole like a dog where he died.

* * *

COUNSEL: Did the Tonton Macoute do anything else after he was killed?

INTERPRETER: After he was killed they set him in the bushes and burned him up as a pig. When we went to touch the dead body, the skin stuck to our hands.

COUNSEL: Now, Mr. X.Y., I would like to ask you about what happened [to another uncle] in 1972 or 1973 if you could describe what happened to him to the Immigration Judge.

INTERPRETER: Because he owed the Tonton Macoutes ten dollars, they locked him up in jail for one month.

* * *

COUNSEL: Does Mr. X.Y. know who that Tonton Macoute was?

INTERPRETER: Yes.

COUNSEL: Does he know the name?

INTERPRETER: Yes. * * *

COUNSEL: Now. Mr. X.Y., I would like to now * * * talk about what happened to you.

INTERPRETER: Yes.

COUNSEL: In particular, I would like to go back to early March of 1982 and I would like you to describe to the Immigration Judge what happened at that time.

INTERPRETER: After they killed my Uncle, my family and I, we went fleeing from the Government and they wanted the same thing to happen to the whole family that happened to the Uncle. I woke up March [1st] and I found three men.

* * *

COUNSEL: Can you describe to the Immigration Judge what happened to you on that day, starting with you going to work, etc.

* * *

INTERPRETER: When I was going to work, I saw three men. I ignored them because they were not my friends, since they killed my Uncle. When I ignored them, they walked towards me. When they reached me they asked me for my identification card. And the reason they asked me that is because they wanted to attack me and have the same thing happen to me. I told them I didn't have an identification card because my wife doesn't have any kind of business and I am recently in the country. And they said the reason I'm not working is because I'm talking badly about the President. And they took me and they hit me. I can even show the Judge the bruises and markings on my body.

COUNSEL: And I would ask permission for that examination.

THE COURT: Government's position?

TRIAL ATTORNEY: I have no objection.

* * *

THE COURT: * * * [W]here are the bruises?

COUNSEL: On the back.

THE COURT: There is no way of telling where he got them and when he got them. There is no way of telling anything. All that could be surmised was that he perhaps had some bruises on his body which he might have gotten in 1950 or 1981 or 1980 or 1975. I don't know the—

COUNSEL: I am not resting my entire case on the [recitation] of facts he made. My point is that [there is] objective [evidence] * * * consistent with his testimony [in] that they are not bruises but massive scarrings in connection with the beatings that he has sustained that he has been testifying to. I have as well a copy [of] an affidavit of a doctor that examined Mr. X.Y. * * * that contains a report that finds that the scarring observed is consistent [with] the report that he gave to the doctor of the beatings that he sustained at that time. I would ask you to view the physical abused scarring as well to receive the report into evidence, as objective [indicia] * * * supporting the asylum [claim].

THE COURT: You've brought the report with you, then? Show the copies of the report to the Government. What is the Government's position on the affidavit?

TRIAL ATTORNEY: No objection.

THE COURT: Marked into evidence as Exhibit 4. * * * I don't see how my viewing of the scars could add particularly. Not only would I [not] be able to * * * know what period of time the scars had occurred and in what connection, but I am not a medical expert either [or] anything close to a medical expert, so I will decline to view the scars, but the affidavit * * * has been entered into evidence as Exhibit 4. * * *

* * *

COUNSEL: I would like to ask you, X.Y., if you could describe the dispute that you had with the Tonton Macoute as you were before? Just continue.

INTERPRETER: When they asked me for my identification card, I told them I don't need one because I was not working and my wife was not working. And the reason that I am not working is not that I am talking bad about the Government, but that the President doesn't supply enough jobs. They arrested me for being a politician.

* * *

COUNSEL: Could you just state to the Immigration Judge, Mr. X.Y. who, if anyone, accused you of criticizing the President?

INTERPRETER: * * * [They] [c]alled me *camoquin*. They put me in jail. I stayed in jail for seven months in a small stockade.

COUNSEL: Let me refer particularly to the dispute with the three Tonton Macoute. Did they accuse you of criticizing the President?

INTERPRETER: Yes.

COUNSEL: What happened after that?

INTERPRETER: They accused me of criticizing the President and also [there] were five other men who were also criticizing the government. They all escaped to [the Dominican Republic] and I stayed in Haiti.

* * *

COUNSEL: What does *camoquin* mean?

INTERPRETER: *Camoquin* means President's enemy.

COUNSEL: Now, after you had the dispute with the three Tonton Macoutes on your way to work, particularly what happened right after that?

INTERPRETER: They beat me up.

COUNSEL: And what happened after that?

INTERPRETER: They sent me to prison. I spent seven months in prison.

COUNSEL: Now, can you tell the Immigration Judge about the situation? Under what conditions were you in prison?

INTERPRETER: I spent seven months in prison and they beat me up until one day they took me where there was a lot of people and finally I was set free. They took me and seven others to repair a bridge somewhere.

* * *

COUNSEL: Were formal charges ever brought against you?

INTERPRETER: That was the only charge.

COUNSEL: Were formal proceedings ever brought against you by the Haitian Government at this time? Did you go before a Judge prior to this imprisonment or during this imprisonment or any time in Haiti?

INTERPRETER: No, I did not see a Judge at all, [nor] an attorney.

COUNSEL: Now, can you tell the Immigration Judge about the cell in which you were imprisoned in for those seven months?

INTERPRETER: Yes, I could.

COUNSEL: Well, please?

INTERPRETER: Where I was, they gave me a bucket like this. That's where I do everything. Wash my face, take a bath, go to the bathroom. The only time I see the outside is when they come and pick me up in the morning to go and clean the bucket out. Often they come to pick you up, there is always some job to do. When it is feeding time, they bring you corn meal.

COUNSEL: Did you see anyone there?

INTERPRETER: No.

COUNSEL: Did you see a doctor when you were in prison?

INTERPRETER: No. Never. When I was in Miami, I had this bruise and in Miami, they took care of it.

COUNSEL: Mr. X.Y., could you explain to the Immigration Judge how it is that you got out of prison?

INTERPRETER: It was a rainy day and they came to get me and five other prisoners to go clean up a broken bridge. While we were cleaning, I asked permission of one of the guards if I could go to the bathroom and then I escaped.

* * *

COUNSEL: And the record should show this as indicated in the I–589. Now, can you explain to the Immigration Judge what happened after that?

INTERPRETER: After I escaped, I stayed away from the street. I went to * * * a forest place and I went until I reached a place North. I went to this person and I explained my problem, and this person understood my problem and he knew that I would not have any kind of life if I stayed there. There were others and we put our heads together. We stole the boat and escaped. We took food from people's gardens. When we escaped we did [not] know where we were going.

COUNSEL: And particularly, how did you escape and what happened?

INTERPRETER: * * * There was bad weather. There was a lot of wind and we spent three days in the ocean. And there was this big container where we were cooking in. And the wind blew everything. The food, the fire. One day, at 6:00 o'clock, we decided that we were going to die and we saw a flag and soon we saw another ship and it was a boat from Haiti * * *. When we saw them, we signaled them and they came to us. We climbed into their boat, then left the little that we had to their boat * * *. Most of the boat broke and they took us to a city * * * in Cuba.

COUNSEL: How long did you stop in Cuba?

INTERPRETER: Eleven days. The reason we spent eleven days was because the boat [broke]. We need[ed] directions to get here. They look[ed] for another sail and they put us back to sea. They gave us directions.

COUNSEL: Mr. X.Y., can you tell the Immigration Judge the reason you left Haiti?

INTERPRETER: Yes.

COUNSEL: Well, could you please tell him now?

INTERPRETER: Because I can't live in Haiti. Because if I stay in Haiti I will die. * * *

COUNSEL: Now, after the repairs in Cuba, where did you go?

INTERPRETER: The boat came to Miami.

COUNSEL: What happened then?

INTERPRETER: We left from Miami waters and a guard from Miami came and got us. Since we were picked up, we were put in jail.

* * *

COUNSEL: Where [were you] taken after that?

INTERPRETER: They took [me] to prison.

* * *

COUNSEL: And what happened after that?

INTERPRETER: They transferred us to New York here.

COUNSEL: Mr. X.Y., what do you believe would happen to you if you were to return to Haiti now?

INTERPRETER: I am here. I don't even know how my family is, what would happen to them.

COUNSEL: What do you believe would happen to you if you returned?

INTERPRETER: They would kill me at the airport and my family would not even know I was sent home.

THE COURT: All right. Now, 212(a)(20) [b] is conceded. I take it?

COUNSEL: Yes, it is, * * *.

THE COURT: All right. 212(a)(20) is conceded. And do you wish to cross-examine, [Trial Attorney]?

TRIAL ATTORNEY: Yes, sir.

* * *

THE COURT: Okay. Go ahead.

TRIAL ATTORNEY: Mr. X.Y., you earlier testified that your Uncle * * had been killed in 1967. You told us how he had been killed. Were you present during that or did someone tell you about that?

INTERPRETER: I was there.

TRIAL ATTORNEY: Where were you?

INTERPRETER: In Haiti.

TRIAL ATTORNEY: Were you in the same area where it happened or were you in the same town that it happened?

INTERPRETER: I was in the same place.

TRIAL ATTORNEY: Where did it happen?

INTERPRETER: I don't understand.

TRIAL ATTORNEY: Did it happen in a house, out in the street, in the woods?

INTERPRETER: In the garden, in the woods.

TRIAL ATTORNEY: Apart from the two uncles that you have told us about and yourself, have any other members of your family ever been

b. Entry without proper documents.—
eds.

arrested while living in Haiti because of their race, religion or political beliefs or opinions?

INTERPRETER: Yes. They would have arrested more people in my family if four of my cousins [had] not escape[d].

TRIAL ATTORNEY: You escaped with four cousins?

INTERPRETER: They escaped to the Dominican Republic.

TRIAL ATTORNEY: Earlier, you testified that * * * your family and you weren't friendly with the Government after your Uncle was killed. Were you friendly prior to when your Uncle was killed with the Government?

INTERPRETER: I was never friendly with them because they were always abusing people.

TRIAL ATTORNEY: Apart from this one occasion that you were arrested in 1982, have you ever been arrested prior to that while living in Haiti?

INTERPRETER: They never arrested me but they arrested other people. When I see that, I stood aside since I am human.

TRIAL ATTORNEY: Earlier, you testified that you left Haiti because of the conditions in Haiti. Did you mean by this the fact that you had been imprisoned?

INTERPRETER: Yes. Because the reason I left Haiti was because I can't live with the Government.

TRIAL ATTORNEY: Is it also true that * * * one of the conditions was that you didn't have work in Haiti?

INTERPRETER: If it was for work, I would stay in Haiti because I am a married man and have three children to take care of.

TRIAL ATTORNEY: Have you, apart from the occasion which you were arrested by the three Tonton Macoute, did you ever express your political opinions while living in Haiti?

COUNSEL: Excuse me. Before and afterwards?

TRIAL ATTORNEY: Yes, while, prior to, before that occasion.

INTERPRETER: If you live in Haiti, you cannot talk badly of the Government because of what is happening there.

TRIAL ATTORNEY: I have no further questions.

THE COURT: Any further questions, [Counsel]?

COUNSEL: No, I have nothing further.

THE COURT: Now, do you have any further evidence to present?

COUNSEL: Yes, I do. I have an expert witness that I would like to present in this case and I would like to make a documentary [submission] in that connection as well * * *. I am prepared to make an offer of proof orally, on the record, in respect to the expert, at this point, and I would like to set a date when I can submit a written offer of proof.

THE COURT: All right.

COUNSEL: I can tell you that the expert that I plan to present is Michael Posner. He is the Executive Director of the Lawyer's Committee for International Human Rights. He is qualified as an expert in the case of *Haitian Refugee Center v. Civiletti* in the Southern District of Florida [503 F.Supp. 442 (S.D.Fla.1980), *modified sub nom. Haitian Refugee Center v. Smith*, 676 F.2d 1023 (5th Cir. 1982)]. * * * He is presently in Uganda, but will be available as of May 25. I would hope to present him after an offer of proof shortly after that in connection with his testimony. He would testify and his opinion would be on information that Mr. X.Y. does have a well-founded fear of persecution in his political opinion. Or, to put it another way, his life and freedom would be threatened on account of political opinion if he were returned to Haiti and he would state that opinion with a reasonable professional certainty. The basis of that opinion would be the materials set forth in the Form I–589, as amplified by X.Y.'s testimony in these proceedings, and in particular, reference to the cruel persecution of his family in Haiti and their imprisonment and torture which resulted in his escape from Haiti and his flight to the United States.

THE COURT: What's the Government's position? Does the Government seek a written offer of proof?

TRIAL ATTORNEY: Yes.

* * *

THE COURT: All right. Written offer of proof by June 1. Okay. Hearing adjourned until that time.

Hearing is Adjourned Until June 1, 1984.

[Hearing of June 1, 1984]

* * *

THE COURT: All right. At the last hearing, the case was adjourned for an offer o[f] proof regarding a possible witness. I have been given an affidavit of Michael H. Posner. I believe he was the potential witness. Is that correct * * *?

COUNSEL: That is correct.

THE COURT: And do you wish to be heard on the offer of proof or to rest on the affidavit?

COUNSEL: I would want to speak for that connection.

THE COURT: All right. You may proceed.

COUNSEL: In particular, I would note for the record that Mr. Posner is the Executive Director of the [Lawyers Committee for] International Human Rights in New York, that he has demonstrated in his affidavit not only familiarity with the conditions in Haiti and leadership of the organization that is responsible for mostly monitoring conditions in Haiti, but, as noted in the affidavit, he was accepted by the Court as an expert on conditions in Haiti in the case of Haitian Refugee Center against Benjamin Civiletti * * *. [T]his is reflected in the findings of fact in that decision. The offer goes on to show that * * * in Mr. Posner's opinion, Mr. X.Y. has a well-founded fear of persecution because of political opinion. I'll put it another way. Mr. X.Y.'s life and freedom would be threatened by political opinion should he be returned to Haiti. And he states that opinion with reasonable professional certainty. * * * Mr. Posner notes in his affidavit that he would elaborate in his testimony regarding his knowledge and current conditions in Haiti that confirm his opinion in that connection. For that reason, I ask that this proceeding be continued and that Mr. Posner be presented with testimony from that connection.

* * *

THE COURT: All right. And does the Government have any objection to the offer of proof being entered into evidence?

TRIAL ATTORNEY: No, your Honor, the Government has no objection.

THE COURT: All right. That will be marked Exhibit 5. Does the Government wish to be heard on the offer of proof?

TRIAL ATTORNEY: Yes, your Honor. The Government objects to the testimony of Mr. Posner. Basically, the Government believes the best testimony has already been heard in this case and that would be the testimony of the applicant. The Government feels that the applicant has not made out a well-founded fear of persecution based on race, religion, nationality, political opinion or membership in a particular social group, that this testimony of Mr. Posner would be general in nature. He was not present at the time[ ] [t]hat Mr. X.Y. or his family had alleged problems with the Haitian authorities. He would be testifying to general conditions in Haiti which would burden the record and I believe that the best testimony has been Mr. X.Y.'s testimony. This would not add anything to that testimony at this point in time, your Honor, and that this testimony should be denied.

* * *

THE COURT: All right. The Court is able to adopt essentially the arguments of the Government and finds it particularly convincing. The Government's arguments that the best evidence is that of the testimony of the applicant and that the testimony of Mr. Posner would appear to be essentially general in nature. And I will deny the request for Mr. Posner to be a witness. However, I have marked the affidavit, the offer of proof into evidence and assigned it Exhibit 5. Now, anything further from either party?

COUNSEL: Yes, your Honor. I have a letter from the United Nations High Commissioner [for Refugees] concerning Mr. X.Y. It's a letter dated May 22, 1984 from the Regional Legal Advisor, noting that[,] assuming the information presented to us [is true], * * * [we] find[ ] this refugee's claim to be valid under the provisions of the United Nations Convention and/or Protocol on the Status of Refugees. For that reason, I would ask that this letter be marked into evidence as an evidence of the validity of Mr. X.Y.'s well-founded fear of persecution and refugee status.

THE COURT: Has the Government had an opportunity to see this?

TRIAL ATTORNEY: No, your Honor, if I may briefly read it.

THE COURT: Yes.

TRIAL ATTORNEY: The Government would object to this letter being introduced into evidence at this time. The U.N. High Commissioner [is] not binding on this Court or the U.S. Government and in fact, the letter states that they emphasize the decision to grant asylum status rests with the U.S. authorities. * * * There was no hearing given by the U.N. High Commissioner. It was done on the political asylum application then and this has no weight whatsoever on this Court and it should not be allowed to be introduced into evidence at this point in time, your Honor.

* * *

THE COURT: I'm going to allow it into evidence and I'm going to mark it Exhibit 6. And the weight will be attached to it as whatever weight I feel appropriate. I mark it into evidence. Is there anything further?

COUNSEL: Yes, your Honor. I have an index documentary exhibit which I would like to submit to assist you in your determination of the asylum claim in this matter. They include significant court decisions including the decision of the Haitian Refugee Center against Benjamin Civiletti, * * * as well as a State Department Report on Human Rights Practices and various reports from the Lawyer's Committee for International Human Rights, a report of Amnesty International, a statement by Shirley Chisolm and I believe [these] will be of assistance in appreciating the context of Mr. X.Y.'s asylum application and determining the validity of that application.

THE COURT: All right. Does the Government wish to be heard on these exhibits?

* * *

TRIAL ATTORNEY: Your Honor, the Government objects to the following documents in this packet. The Government would object to Exhibit Number A which is *Haitian Refugee Center vs. Civiletti* and the findings of fact in that case. That case is presently on appeal. It is from the Southern District of Florida which has no jurisdiction over this Court. It is not binding on this Court and states that the document or that Exhibit should be kept out of evidence at this point in time. The Government has no objections to Exhibit B, C, D, E, F, G, H, I, J, but does object to Number K, the last exhibit, which [is] * * various newspaper articles gathered by counsel and basically states that they are general in nature. They do not mention Mr. X.Y. anywhere in these articles and they should not be allowed into evidence at this point in time.

* * *

THE COURT: All right. I find that it would be objectionable for me to consider the findings of fact of the *Haitian Refugee Center v. Civiletti*. That would, in my mind, promote Judge King to an expert on Haitian items and affairs. It would promote, certainly, witnesses in that case to the stature of persons who had knowledge and expertise of first hand in the life of Mr. X.Y. and it would bind this jurisdiction where it need not and should not be bound. * * * Therefore, I will reject these findings of fact. Do you wish to be heard on the newspaper articles further?

COUNSEL: * * * I think [the articles] should be received in order to appreciate the context of Mr. X.Y.'s asylum request and his request for relief under Section 243(h) in this proceeding.

* * *

THE COURT: All right. I would find that essentially the newspaper articles would deal with general items, probably not Mr. X.Y., and maybe I could be stretching a point a little if I said * * * it would be more likely to find something about me in the newspaper articles than about Mr. X.Y. These newspaper articles are rejected. Is there anything further in this case?

[Various motions by Counsel for the applicant are renewed and rejected.]

* * *

COUNSEL: I have no further applications. I do have a very brief argument to make in connection with the substance of the asylum claim.

THE COURT: I am not going to allow argument. That would be, in effect, to allow the attorney to testify. Therefore, I do not believe that it is appropriate unless the Government feels that an argument by counsel would be productive.

TRIAL ATTORNEY: No, your Honor. The Government does not wish to have any arguments in this case. I believe your Honor has heard all the facts and seen all the evidence in this case. And all the ones that are necessary to reach a decision.

THE COURT: I do not believe, as I've stated before, that oral argument would be in order in this case. This is * * * not a jury case, and normally, oral argument is not part of the deportation hearings. What the counsel for the applicant may have wished to bring out would have been and should have been brought out [in] testimony of Mr. X.Y. Therefore, I will deny an oral argument. Is there anything further?

COUNSEL: I have nothing further.

THE COURT: All right. This is my decision * * *.

Assume you are the immigration judge. Before reading further, determine how you would decide X.Y.'s claim.

UNITED STATES DEPARTMENT OF JUSTICE

IMMIGRATION COURT

New York, New York 10278.

File: [deleted]   Date: June 1, 1984

In the Matter of: IN EXCLUSION PROCEEDINGS
X.Y.
—Applicant

Charge: I. & N. Act—Section 212(a)(20)—Immigrant
without valid visa.

APPLICATION: Termination; in alternative, asylum proceeding.

Oral Decision of the Immigration Judge

The applicant is a forty-one year old male alien, a native and citizen of Haiti, who last arrived in the United States at or about Miami, Florida on or about November 1, 1982, at which time he was detained for hearing [on] excludability. The Government has charged that the applicant is excludable from the United States under Section 212(a)(20) of the Immigration and Nationality Act. The truth and substance of the Government's charge under Section 212(a)(20) of this Act has been conceded and the applicant is found excludable under Section 212(a)(20) of said Act.

The applicant has made a request for asylum in the United States. In order to merit a grant of asylum, he must establish a clear probability of particularized persecution of him by the present Government of Haiti should he return or be returned there. *See Matter of Dunar*, 14 I. & N. Decision 310 (BIA 1973). The burden is upon the applicant to establish that he would be subject to persecution should he return or be returned to Haiti. 8 CFR, Section 108.3(a). The claim of the applicant of possible persecution should he be returned to Haiti has been considered by the Department of State of the United States and its office of Human Rights and Humanitarian Affairs has concluded that the applicant has not made out a valid claim for asylum (Exhibit 3). I must reach a decision independently of that conclusion.

The applicant has testified that an uncle of his was killed by the Tonton Macoute in 1967. This was seventeen years ago. He has also testified that another uncle was in jail for one month. This was in 1972 or 1973. That is, it occurred eleven or twelve years ago. This applicant, himself, has stated that the Tonton Macoute detained him and mistreated him on or about March 1, 1982 in Haiti because he was talking against Duvalier.

The applicant has stated that he spent seven months in prison, but escaped when he was taken on a work detail to clean a bridge. He has stated that he escaped into the forest at that time. He has stated he believes if he stayed in Haiti he would die. Although, if his testimony is credible, previously he was detained and obviously not killed. This is the sum, in essence, of the applicant's testimony.

The attorney for the applicant has presented many motions in this case * * *. These motions were all denied, essentially upon the good and cogent arguments of the Government. * * * Certain other applications to place newspaper articles and other documents in evidence were rejected as not considered worthy of acceptance into evidence. An offer of proof for a witness to testify was permitted into evidence but the witness, it was considered, would add nothing substantial to the direct testimony of Mr. X.Y. In sum, the burden being upon the applicant to establish that he would be subject to persecution should he return or be returned to Haiti and the evidence of record reflecting essentially conjecture that he would be subject to persecution should he return to Haiti, I must find that his claim is not sufficient to merit a grant of asylum. *See Matter of Vardjan,* 10 I & N Decision 567 (BIA 1964). The arrests of two uncles were some years ago and if there was indeed a detention of the applicant, one must believe that the guards of the applicant—after detaining him for some seven months—were improvident enough to allow him to escape after that time. The totality of the record does not amount to a case in which asylum should be granted.

Order: It is Ordered that the applicant be excluded and deported from the United States pursuant to Law.

IT IS FURTHER ORDERED that the request for the applicant's asylum in [the] United States be denied.

John K. Speer
Immigration Judge

Questions

Why exactly is the application for asylum and withholding denied? Is X.Y.'s story simply disbelieved? How did INS counsel and the judge go about testing the veracity of the claim? How should they have done so? Or is X.Y.'s story credited but his persecution deemed not the kind that validly supports asylum?

The judge employs what is essentially the *Dunar* standard, requiring that the applicant show "a clear probability of particularized persecution." Is this the key to denial of the claim? Was that standard properly applied here? Would it have made a difference if X.Y. had only to show a "reasonable likelihood" of persecution, or merely "good reason" to fear persecution? In other words, if the Second Circuit's position in the *Stevic* case above had prevailed, would this case have come out differently? In any event, should it?

Judicial review

Before enactment of the Refugee Act in 1980, courts traditionally reviewed asylum denials using an "abuse of discretion" test—theoretically the review standard most deferential to the administrative agency whose action is under scrutiny. After the Refugee Act changed § 243(h) from a discretionary to a mandatory provision, however, several courts have decided that they should employ the somewhat more demanding "substantial evidence" test in reviewing denials of withholding under that section. *See, e.g., McMullen v. INS,* 658 F.2d 1312, 1316–17 (9th Cir.1981); *Chavarria v. Department of Justice,* 722 F.2d 666 (11th Cir.1984). Some courts have also ruled that the substantial evidence standard applies in reviewing the factual determinations that underlie the discretionary decision whether or not to grant asylum under § 208. *Bolanos-Hernandez v. INS,* 749 F.2d 1316, 1321 n. 9 (9th Cir. 1984); *Carvajal-Munoz v. INS,* 743 F.2d 562, 567 (7th Cir. 1984); *Sarkis v. Nelson,* 585 F.Supp. 235, 237–38 (E.D.N.Y.1984). If the BIA were to affirm the outcome in X.Y.'s case and the decision reached you as a district judge for judicial review, how would you go about deciding whether this review standard is met? What does it mean to have substantial evidence supporting a negative determination in a case where the applicant bears the burden of proof? If the immigration judge had squarely rested his denial on a credibility judgment, would there be substantial evidence to sustain that determination? *Compare Saballo-Cortez v. INS,* 749 F.2d 1354, 1359–61 & n. 4 (9th Cir. 1984) *with id.* at 1361–65 (Pregerson, J., dissenting).

One court has suggested that the abuse of discretion test should still be used. *Marroquin-Manriquez v. INS,* 699 F.2d 129 (3d Cir.1983), *cert. denied* __ U.S. __, 104 S.Ct. 3553, 82 L.Ed.2d 855 (1984). In dictum, the court rejected the substantial evidence test "because it ignores the necessary application of expertise in the determination that a fear of persecution is well-founded." *Id.* at 133 n. 5. In what respect is expertise employed in the *X.Y.* case above? Which judicial review standard is more appropriate? Which did Congress intend for courts to employ? *See also Sotto v. INS,* 748 F.2d 832 (3d Cir. 1984) (applying abuse of discretion standard to denial of relief under both §§ 208 and 243(h), in accordance with *Marroquin-Manriquez,* but finding such abuse in BIA's failure to consider a key affidavit).

4. THE ROLE OF THE STATE DEPARTMENT

Neither immigration judges nor district directors (nor any of their delegates who actually adjudicate asylum claims) are likely to have any special expertise regarding conditions in foreign countries. Probably for this reason, the regulations implementing the Refugee Act continue the longstanding practice of seeking advisory opinions from the State Department's Bureau of Human Rights and Humanitarian Affairs. 8 C.F.R. §§ 208.7, 208.10. That Bureau typically "clears" its advice letters with other offices in the State Department, including the desk officer responsible for the country whose practices are at issue, before sending the letters on to the district office or the immigration judge.

ZAMORA v. INS

United States Court of Appeals, Second Circuit, 1976.
534 F.2d 1055.

FRIENDLY, CIRCUIT JUDGE:

These petitions to review decisions of the Board of Immigration Appeals which dismissed appeals from orders of Immigration Judges (IJ) denying requests, under § 243(h) of the Immigration and Nationality Act for stays of deportation on the ground that "the alien would be subject to persecution on account of race, religion, or political opinion," are typical of an unusually large number of such petitions that have recently reached us.

* * *

The prime subject of complaint by the petitioners in both cases is the admission of the letters from the Department of State in response to the District Director's requests for recommendations concerning their applications for asylum. Although we could dispose of these cases on the basis of lack of objection before the IJ or the Board of Immigration Appeals, the problem is a recurring one, and we think a statement of our views may be useful.

* * *

The admissibility of ORM recommendations [a] in a § 243(h) proceeding has been considered in a series of cases in the Ninth Circuit. Admissibility was sustained in *Asghari v. INS*, 396 F.2d 391 (1968), on the basis that the "advice came from a knowledgeable and competent source," citing *Hosseinmardi v. INS*, 391 F.2d 914 (9 Cir.1968). However, the panel opinion in *Hosseinmardi* was withdrawn and did not resurface in the bound volume of the Federal 2d reports until the denial of rehearing on January 29, 1969, 405 F.2d 25. Meanwhile the Ninth Circuit had decided *Kasravi v. INS*, 400 F.2d 675 (July 23, 1968), where, although denying the petition, apparently on the ground that orders denying withholding of deportation under § 243(h) could be reviewed only for an abuse of discretion, the court said of an ORM letter:

> Not only does this letter lack persuasiveness, but the competency of State Department letters in matters of this kind is highly questionable.... Such letters from the State Department do not carry the guarantees of reliability which the law demands of admissible evidence. A frank, but official, discussion of the political shortcomings of a friendly nation is not always compatible with the high duty to maintain advantageous diplomatic relations with nations throughout the world. The traditional foundation required of expert testimony is lacking; nor can official position be said to supply an acceptable substitute. No hearing officer or court has the means to know the diplomatic

a. The State Department letters, so called because they then originated from the Office of Refugee and Migration Affairs (ORM).—eds.

necessities of the moment, in the light of which the statements must be weighed.

In the decision on rehearing in *Hosseinmardi,* 405 F.2d 25, 28, the majority said, after taking note of the statement in *Kasravi* just quoted:

> The generalities regarding conditions in [the foreign state] which appear in the letter were severely challenged by petitioner's expert witnesses. It might well have been improper had the Board given substantial weight to those generalities without corroboration or further inquiry.

The judge who had authored the original opinion reiterated his belief in the admissibility of the letter, citing the Ninth Circuit's earlier decision in *Namkung v. Boyd,* 226 F.2d 385 (1955), which had upheld the admissibility of a letter from a foreign Consul General, indeed a diplomat from the very country to which the alien was resisting deportation.

Recently the Fifth Circuit has been confronted with the same problem—with the added fillip that the ORM letter was shown to be in error in its statement of petitioners' claims and consequently to have been unresponsive to them. *Paul v. INS,* 5 Cir., 521 F.2d 194 (1975). In affirming the denial of withholding of deportation, the majority said that petitioners' arguments regarding the ORM communication "might be persuasive if it appeared from the record that the telegram influenced the decision of the Immigration Judge and the Board of Immigration Appeals, but such is not the case," 521 F.2d at 200. Judge Godbold, dissenting, disagreed with the latter conclusion, 521 F.2d at 204–05.

We think solution of the problem lies in Professor Kenneth Culp Davis' famous distinction between adjudicative and legislative facts. The attitude of the country of prospective deportation toward various types of former residents is a question of legislative fact, on which the safeguards of confrontation and cross-examination are not required and on which the IJ needs all the help he can get. He cannot expect much from the applicants who, as Judge Waterman wrote in *Sovich v. Esperdy,* 319 F.2d 21, 29 (2 Cir.1963), are often "unlettered persons who have been away from their native countries for many years" and "typically have available to them no better methods for ascertaining current political conditions abroad than does the average citizen." The worse complexion the alien puts on his previous conduct or the character of the present regime, the greater will be the likelihood that he may indeed be persecuted if his § 243(h) application fails; hence he might logically be under some compulsion to understate his case—although perusal of these and other petitions scarcely indicates such a tendency. Also, the greater the likelihood of persecution in the foreign country, the less will be the possibility of obtaining information from relatives or friends who are still there. Only rarely will an applicant be able to locate and enlist the services of an expert on conditions in the foreign country, as was done in *Berdo v. INS,* 432 F.2d 824 (6 Cir.1970). Counsel for the INS may not be much better off. The obvious source of information on general conditions in the foreign country is the Department of State which has diplomatic and consular representatives throughout the world. While there is undoubted truth in the observation in *Kasravi, supra,* 400 F.2d at 677 n. 1, as to there being some likelihood of the Department's tempering the wind in comments concerning internal affairs of a foreign nation, it is usually the best available source of information and the difficulty could be mitigated by not spreading its views on the record, as [8] C.F.R. § 242.17(c) permits. We therefore see no bar to the admissibility of statements of the Department of State or its officials abroad which inform the IJ and the Board of Immigration Appeals of the extent to which the nation of prospective deportation engages in "persecution on account of race, religion, or political opinion" of the class of persons to whom an applicant under § 243(h) claims to belong, and reveal, so far as feasible, the basis for the views expressed, but do not attempt to apply this knowledge to the particular case, as the ORM does in making recommendations with respect to requests for political asylum.

The difficulty with introducing ORM letters into hearings under § 243(h) is that they do both too little and too much. The ones in these cases and in others that we have seen give little or nothing in the way of useful information about conditions in the foreign country. What they do is to recommend how the district director should decide the particular petitioner's request for asylum. When these letters are introduced into the § 243(h) inquiry, they present ORM's conclusion as to an adjudicative fact, based, in the present examples, solely on the alien's own statements and phrased in the very language of the § 243(h) standard. Adjudication in the withholding process is, however, the task of the IJ and the Board of Immigration Appeals. Particularly in light of the difficulties confronting the alien in proving his case, there is a risk that such communications will carry a weight they do not deserve. It should not be difficult for the INS and the Department of State to conform their practices in the future to the views here expressed.

On the other hand we are unwilling to announce a rule that would call for reversal of all denials of § 243(h) applications where an ORM recommendation has been received at the hearing. Before we would reverse because of the receipt of ORM recommendations, a petitioner must show some likelihood that it influenced the result.

* * *

[The Court went on to hold that introduction of the State Department letters constituted harmless error in the cases under review, because the IJ had reached an independent conclusion regarding the likelihood of persecution.]

Notes

Despite Judge Friendly's optimism about the ready conformance of INS and State Department practices to the guidelines *Zamora* lays down, the opinion seems to have had little impact in this regard. State Department letters still typically take a position on the merits of the individual application under review (although they are often form letters which provide little detailed information explaining why the Department reached its conclusions). *See Asylum Adjudications: An Evolving Concept and Responsibility for the Immigration and Naturalization Service* 58 (INS Staff Study, mimeo, June 1982). *See also Hotel and Restaurant Employees Union, Local 25 v. Smith*, 594 F.Supp. 502, 510–14 (D.D.C. 1984) (partially distinguishing *Zamora*, the court approves use of individual advisory opinions in Salvadoran cases; the court's opinion provides considerable information on how the advisory opinions are prepared). In another respect, however, *Zamora* has affected the practices of immigration judges; they are now probably more careful to recite in opinions denying asylum that they were not influenced by a negative advisory opinion from State, and have reached their own conclusions. And occasionally there are cases where a decision runs counter to the State Department recommendation. *See, e.g.,* 60 Interp.Rel. 26, 106 (1983) (reporting on IJ decisions granting asylum to a Nicaraguan and an Afghan applicant, respectively, despite negative letters from the State Department); *Zavala-Bonilla v. INS,* 730 F.2d 562 (9th Cir.1984) (reversing IJ denial of asylum in case of a Salvadoran as to whom State had issued an advisory opinion favoring asylum).[26] (A cynic might suggest, however, that if these cases are representative, the independence of the IJ's on such matters has its own decided political bent.)

Nevertheless, evidence suggests that the impact of a negative letter is still considerable. For example, the *Asylum Adjudications* study, *supra,* at 62, quotes various INS officials on this subject. Some of the unnamed interviewees found the letters of little use, but the collection includes these remarks: "I would never, never overrule the State Department." "I don't believe our people are capable of making independent decisions without input from the State Department." [27] *See also,* Avery, *supra* note 3, at 333.

The State Department has taken other steps, however, that come closer to meeting Judge Friendly's prescriptions. Under a statutory mandate (adopted to promote human rights diplomacy and not with a view to providing information in immigration proceedings), the Department now prepares annual reports on the human rights practices of governments around the world. These are submitted to Congress and

---

26. *Zavala-Bonilla* states several times that the State Department letter should have been regarded "with deference." 730 F.2d, at 566–67. The court also considered that letter especially significant "in light of the fact, acknowledged by the Government at oral argument, that Salvadorans rarely receive a State Department opinion supportive of a political asylum application." *Id.* at 567. *Zamora* is never discussed. Are the two cases inconsistent?

27. In light of the letters' potential impact, does due process require that the applicant be able to cross-examine the author of the State Department letter as to the reasoning and sources that underlie the negative conclusion? The BIA considered the issue in a case where the applicant had requested only the opportunity to pose written interrogatories to the author of the letter. It

decided that there was no error in the IJ's denial of the request in this particular case and that as a general rule such interrogatories would not be permitted. Although it acknowledged that the opinion letters were "ex parte declarations which are submitted without the traditional safeguards required of admissible evidence in judicial proceedings," the Board considered this drawback outweighed by other factors: the nonbinding nature of the advice, the applicant's opportunity to rebut it by presenting his own evidence in response, and the heavy workload that would be created, to the further delay of asylum adjudications, if interrogatories were often permitted. *Matter of Exilus,* 18 I & N Dec. 2 (1982). *See also Edmond v. Nelson,* 575 F.Supp. 532, 536–37 (E.D.La. 1983) (generally approving *Exilus* approach).

published each February as Committee Prints. Copies are disseminated to INS district offices, immigration courts, and libraries; they are widely available. *See, e.g.,* State Department Country Reports on Human Rights Practices for 1983, 98th Cong., 2d Sess. (Jt.Comm. Print 1984). These reports contain the Department's judgments about the observance of human rights, country by country. The discussion is broken down by topic to consider, for example, torture and other cruel treatment, arbitrary arrests and detentions, civil and political rights, economic conditions, etc.

Presumably these reports set forth "legislative facts," but it turns out that the reports are often of little precise help in deciding whether the particular asylum application before the immigration judge or the INS adjudicator should be granted. As to a great many countries, the report confirms that the home government has been known to persecute. But the question remains whether such a fate would befall the applicant based on what he has claimed about his activities and his past or expected encounters with the government.

Given these various inadequacies, are there ways to redesign our adjudication system to make better use of current and detailed information about conditions in foreign countries? Consider the following suggestions for U.S. asylum processing, reached after a study of practices in Germany and France.[28]

T. ALEXANDER ALEINIKOFF, POLITICAL ASYLUM IN THE FEDERAL REPUBLIC OF GERMANY AND THE REPUBLIC OF FRANCE: LESSONS FOR THE UNITED STATES

17 U.Mich.J.L.Ref. 183, 234–36 (1984).

1. The need for an independent federal agency to adjudicate asylum claims —Foremost is the need for the United States to create an independent federal agency to adjudicate asylum claims. [Under current regulations] an alien may apply for asylum to an INS official or an immigration judge. Adjudicating asylum claims may be a small portion of these officials' duties. Moreover, few have specialized training in international law or refugee matters; they therefore almost universally rely upon "advice" received from the State Department. The involvement of the State Department creates opportunities for political considerations to

---

28. The Select Commission on Immigration and Refugee Policy reached somewhat similar conclusions. It recommended the creation of asylum adjudications officers in INS whose full-time job would be the adjudication of asylum claims, who would receive special training in interviewing techniques and legal principles concerned with refugee determinations, and who could call upon area experts (the Commission did not further specify who these should be) to obtain information on conditions in the source countries. SCIRP, Final Report, at 173–74. An internal INS staff study of asylum adjudications also offered many parallel suggestions, after an extremely revealing discussion of the inadequacies in training and staffing that had previously hampered asylum adjudications. *See Asylum Adjudications: An Evolving Concept and Responsibility for the Immigration and Naturalization Service* 16–36 (INS Staff Study, mimeo, 1982). And the various versions of the Simpson-Mazzoli bill all would have created a specialized corps of asylum adjudicators, although with slightly differing arrangements for their independence and their use of foreign affairs information. *See, e.g.,* H.R. 1510, §§ 122, 124; S. 529, §§ 122, 124.

affect decisions on the merits of the claim and adds another layer to the process.

The adjudication systems in West Germany and France suggest an alternative for the United States. Both countries have a centralized federal agency whose only mission is to adjudicate asylum claims. The existence of such an institution fosters the development of expertise and knowledge, the evenhanded application of rules and policies, and far less reliance upon the foreign ministries for information and advice. In both countries, decision makers can concentrate on particular countries and become thoroughly familiar with conditions, events, political parties, and social groups in those countries. This kind of expertise significantly improves the ability of the decision makers to judge the credibility of the applicant.

Adoption of this model in the United States could help ensure a similar expertise in decision making. Furthermore, the centralization of asylum adjudications would also end the present maldistribution of asylum claims among INS districts. It would also facilitate the creation of a library and documentation center which could be available to both decision makers and lawyers. Obviously some logistical problems would occur. But both Germany and France have recently opened up a few suboffices in other cities. That model could be adopted here, or adjudicators could conceivably "ride circuit."

The establishment of an independent agency to adjudicate asylum claims would have the additional salutary effect of decreasing the likelihood of court intervention in the processing of claims. Under the current system, courts have ordered intrusive injunctive relief when faced with evidence of massive violations of due process. The adjudication of Haitian asylum claims, for example, has been tied up by courts for nearly a decade. Independent agency adjudication of asylum claims would help alleviate this problem; courts would have increased confidence in the fairness and accuracy of decisions reached by an agency operating with a corps of professional, well-trained adjudicators who are removed from the enforcement side of the immigration system.

2. *The independence of the federal agency and the removal of the advisory role of the State Department* —A serious problem with the present American asylum system is the widely shared perception that it is politically biased. The German and French experiences demonstrate that no governmental agency is fully immune from political pressures. But the general perception in both countries is that the federal asylum agencies are *largely* free from political influence. No such perception exists in the United States. The relative ease with which Eastern Europeans and Cubans have been granted asylum as opposed to the extremely low recognition rates for Haitians and Salvadorans casts a long shadow on the proclaimed neutrality of the system. A major purpose of the Refugee Act of 1980 was to remove the political and ideological aspects of American refugee law, but many persons involved in the process are not convinced that this has occurred. Establishment of an agency outside the Department of Justice and not dependent upon the

State Department would help eliminate the appearance of, and potential for, political influence in the asylum process. The agency could be run by a Board of Directors appointed for lengthy, staggered terms by the President with advice and consent from the Senate. The Board would be responsible for selecting an Executive Director who would hire qualified adjudicators and other staff. The agency's independence could be further demonstrated by following Germany's example of permitting the UNHCR to have a permanent observer at the agency.

Crucial to the independence of the agency would be the termination of the State Department's "advisory" role. Presently, the asylum section of the State Department's Bureau on Human Rights and Humanitarian Affairs is asked to issue an opinion on each asylum claim, and such opinions generally must be "cleared" with the relevant country desk in the Department. Officials in both the French and West Germany agencies openly talked about the problems of crediting information and advice from foreign service officers and ambassadors who have diplomatic roles to perform. The centralized, single-mission nature of both agencies has permitted each to develop sufficient expertise to make reliance upon the respective foreign ministry unnecessary.

Obviously, it would be a mistake to deny the State Department any role in the asylum process. It is perhaps the best source of information on conditions in other countries, and both the French and German agencies often seek information from their foreign ministries. But the independent asylum agency should use information from other sources as well, such as newspapers, Amnesty International, academics, and expert witnesses. In no case should the State Department be asked to render an opinion on whether or not the individual is entitled to refugee status; rather, the State Department should be seen as precisely what it is: one very good source of information, but not the decision maker.

This limited role for the State Department is bound to benefit the government as much as the alien. It will help deflect charges of political interference, and it will clearly separate the legal issue of "refugeeship" from the political issues of foreign policy.

5. DUE PROCESS IN ASYLUM CASES AND THE CONTROVERSY OVER ADVICE OF THE RIGHT TO APPLY FOR ASYLUM

Asylum adjudications of course constitute a type of immigration proceeding, and they are therefore subject to the same broad due process rules developed in other immigration settings. The starting point, then, is the traditional doctrine, examined in Chapters Three and Five, providing that deportable aliens may claim significant procedural due process rights, and excludable aliens far less—conceivably no constitutional rights of this sort, depending upon the continued vitality of *Knauff v. Shaughnessy*, 338 U.S. 537, 70 S.Ct. 309, 94 L.Ed. 317 (1950), and *Shaughnessy v. Mezei*, 345 U.S. 206, 73 S.Ct. 625, 97 L.Ed. 956 (1953).

Excludable aliens do retain, however, "such statutory rights as Congress grants," as well as rights under duly promulgated regulations. *Augustin v. Sava*, 735 F.2d 32, 36 (2d Cir.1984). And the courts often assume a significant role in making sure that such rights, though they are of less than constitutional stature, are actually honored in particular cases. In *Augustin*, for example, the court reversed and remanded a denial of asylum to an excludable Haitian, primarily because the translation by the INS interpreter was so bad as to be "nonsensical" and thus violated "procedural rights protected by statute and INS regulations". *Id.* at 38.

But on the constitutional questions, the traditional doctrines furnish only starting points. As indicated at greater length in Chapter Three (see pages 261–263, *supra*), the Supreme Court has insisted that someone claiming constitutional due process protections identify an interest fairly characterized as "life, liberty, or property" at stake in the government action, before the courts will assume an independent role in evaluating the adequacy of the procedures.

This requirement poses trickier issues than might be expected in the asylum setting. It is not enough for the claimant merely to assert that on return he will be persecuted (which obviously involves, in an elemental way, interests in life and liberty). There must also be particular kinds of entitlements established in the governing legal standards. "[W]hen dispensation of a statutory benefit is clearly at the discretion of an agency, or when a statute only provides that certain procedural guidelines be followed in arriving at a decision, then there is no creation of a substantive interest protected by the Constitution." *Jean v. Nelson,* 727 F.2d 957, 981 (11th Cir.1984) (en banc), *cert. granted* ___ U.S. ___, 105 S.Ct. 563, 83 L.Ed.2d 504 (1984), citing *Hewitt v. Helms,* 459 U.S. 460, 103 S.Ct. 864, 74 L.Ed.2d 675 (1983). The *Jean* court concluded that the "grant of asylum does not, therefore, create an interest protected by the due process clause." 727 F.2d, at 981–82.

But *Jean* focused on the benefits of § 208, and apparently was not intending to pronounce on entitlements under § 243(h). *See id.* at 981 n. 33. When the Refugee Act changed the latter section from a discretionary to a mandatory provision, did it alter the constitutional consequences? *Augustin*, although resting its reversal of the BIA primarily on a finding of statutory and regulatory violations, also considered the constitutional dimension (735 F.2d at 37):

> Moreover, these elemental procedural protections may well be required not only by the pertinent statutes and regulations but also by the due process clause of the Fifth Amendment. In the absence of protected interests which originate in the Constitution itself, constitutionally protected liberty or property interests may have their source in positive rules of law creating a substantive entitlement to a particular government benefit. In such a case, limited due process rights attach. [INA § 243(h)] prohibits the Attorney General from deporting or returning an alien to a country in which his life or freedom would be jeopardized. This statute creates a substantive entitlement to relief from deportation or return to such a country. Thus, despite the unavailability of due process protections in most exclusion proceedings, *see*

Landon v. Plasencia, [459 U.S. 21, 103 S.Ct. 321, 329, 74 L.Ed.2d 21 (1982)], and whether or not due process protections apply to an application for a discretionary grant of asylum, *compare Jean v. Nelson, supra* (no due process rights) *with id.* at 989–90 (Kravitch, J., dissenting) (some due process rights), it appears likely that some due process protection surrounds the determination of whether an alien has sufficiently shown that return to a particular country will jeopardize his life or freedom so as to invoke the mandatory prohibition against his return to that country. As we recently observed, an alien's "interest in not being returned [to a country where he fears persecution] may well enjoy some due process protection not available to an alien claiming only admission." *Chun v. Sava,* 708 F.2d 869, 877 (2 Cir.1983).

Suppose Congress grows tired of due process review by the courts in asylum cases. Could it block such judicial intervention in the future simply by reverting to the old language, and leaving § 243(h) relief again to the discretion of the Attorney General? Or does the last sentence of the excerpt from *Augustin* suggest some more potent due process entitlement for asylum applicants, based on the nature of the risks they assert, whatever the precise statutory language used in the asylum provisions? Whatever that court meant to suggest, should asylum applicants have more extensive procedural due process protections than other excludable aliens, because of the consequences they allege if returned home? Which protections? A right to appointed counsel? A right to take discovery of State Department experts? Are mere allegations of dire consequences upon return a solid enough foundation for such heightened protections? What about a citizen of Switzerland resisting deportation on several grounds, one of which happens to be a claim to political asylum? Should that person receive greater procedural protections than other Swiss respondents, simply because he chose to include in his defense a claim of threatened persecution? *See generally* Martin, *Due Process and Membership in the National Community: Political Asylum and Beyond,* 44 U.Pitt. L.Rev. 165, 221–24 (1983); Aleinikoff, *Aliens, Due Process, and "Community Ties": A Response to Martin, id.* at 237, 247–53.

These questions bring us a good way into the debates over due process protections in asylum cases, and they reach both levels of the usual due process inquiry: (1) Is a cognizable "life, liberty, or property" interest at stake? (2) If so, what process is due? The following case explores both questions in the context of a long-running debate over whether excludable and deportable aliens should be affirmatively advised of the right to apply for asylum before being returned to the home country.

NUNEZ v. BOLDIN

United States District Court, Southern District of Texas, 1982.
537 F.Supp. 578.

VELA, DISTRICT JUDGE.

This cause was filed as a class action by four citizens of El Salvador and one citizen of Guatemala against the Immigration and Naturalization

Service (INS) and officers thereof, asking for certain injunctive and declaratory relief from various practices and procedures of the INS relating to the detention of citizens of El Salvador and Guatemala at the INS detention facility at Los Fresnos, Texas.

* * *

FINDINGS OF FACT

1. Plaintiffs are detainees at the INS detention facility at Los Fresnos, Texas. Petitioners filed this cause as a class action, seeking to represent all citizens and nationals of El Salvador and Guatemala detained at the facility.

2. The Los Fresnos facility is located approximately 20 miles from Brownsville, Texas and 30 miles from Harlingen, Texas.

The facility houses about 250 detainees for processing for deportation, a large number of which are citizens and nationals of El Salvador and Guatemala. While all detainees have the right to a deportation hearing before an immigration judge, a majority of the detainees are returned to their country of origin through voluntary departure. The alien admits to being in the country illegally, chooses the country he wishes to return to, and is returned without a hearing. He is, however, informed of his right to have a hearing.

* * *

9. Defendants do not advise detained aliens prior to voluntary departure nor prior to the issuance of an Order To Show Cause of their right to apply for political asylum. Citizens and nationals of El Salvador detained at the INS facility are predominantly uneducated as to the U.S. legal system, and are not familiar with the rights and procedures established by the Refugee Act of 1980.

CONCLUSIONS OF LAW

* * *

The real issue of controversy for this Court's determination is whether plaintiffs are entitled to temporary injunctive relief requiring defendants to notify members of the alleged class that they have the right to apply for political asylum in the United States. The Court is of the opinion that there is a substantial likelihood of plaintiffs prevailing on the merits as to this claim.

In March of 1980 Congress enacted The Refugee Act of 1980, setting forth a comprehensive system for the admission of refugees into this country. Congress in that Act declared that "it is the historic policy of the United States to respond to the urgent needs of persons subject to persecution in their homelands." Pub.L. 96–212, 94 Stat. 102 (March 17, 1980).

Indeed, this policy had been recognized by Congress in 1952 when it granted the Attorney General the authority to withhold the deportation of aliens who would be subjected to "physical persecution" if they were deported. Immigration and Nationality Act, Ch. 477, § 243(h), 66 Stat. 212 (1952). The Refugee Act of 1980 amended this section, which now *prohibits* the deportation of aliens to countries where they would face "persecution on account of race, religion, or political opinion." INA § 243(h).

In 1968 the United States became a signatory to the 1967 United Nations Protocol Relating To The Status of Refugees. The Protocol incorporates Article 33 of the 1951 Convention Relating to the Status of Refugees, which *prohibits* the deportation of a refugee "to the frontiers of territories where his life or freedom would be threatened on account of his race, religion, nationality, membership of a particular social group or political opinion." *Id.*

Section 208 of the Immigration and Nationality Act was added by the Refugee Act of 1980, and directs the Attorney General to "establish a procedure for an alien physically present in the United States ... to apply for asylum ..." and gives to the Attorney General the authority to grant asylum to qualified refugees. The regulations establishing the procedure for applying for asylum are codified in the Code of Federal Regulations, at 8 C.F.R. Pt. 208 (1981).

What is obvious to the Court at this point is that the United States has, by treaty, statute, and regulations, manifested its intention of hearing the pleas of aliens who come to this country claiming a fear of being persecuted in their homelands. The intention is not necessarily stated as granting the privilege of asylum to all who come to this country but of hearing those pleas.

As submitted by plaintiffs, the failure of the Immigration Service to notify detainees of the right to apply for asylum may effectively render the treaties and statutes discussed above, as well as the intentions behind them, virtually non-existent for the majority of persons who might claim their benefits. The defendants' argument that, since no regulation specifically requires the INS to inform detainees of their right to apply, they therefore do not have to, is not persuasive. While the Court acknowledges that traditionally it has a more limited scope of review when it comes to immigration matters, *Fiallo v. Bell,* 430 U.S. 787, 792, 97 S.Ct. 1473, 1477, 52 L.Ed.2d 50 (1977), it is always within the Court's province to act when an agency decision or practice frustrates the congressional policy underlying a statute.

Plaintiffs also submit that the failure of defendants to inform detainees that they have the right to apply for political asylum is violative of the Fifth Amendment's due process guarantee.

The guarantees of procedural due process apply only to governmental decisions which deprive individuals of "liberty" or "property" interests within the meaning of the Due Process Clause of the Fifth or Fourteenth Amendment. *Mathews v. Eldridge,* 424 U.S. 319, 332, 96 S.Ct. 893, 901, 47 L.Ed.2d 18 (1976). *Board of Regents v. Roth,* 408 U.S. 564, 569, 92 S.Ct. 2701, 2705, 33 L.Ed.2d 548 (1971). Defendants herein do not dispute that aliens within the borders of the United States, whether legally or illegally, are protected by the requirements of due process. *Mathews v. Diaz,* 426

U.S. 67, 77, 96 S.Ct. 1883, 1890, 48 L.Ed.2d 478 (1977). Defendants argue, however, that the right of aliens to apply for political asylum or withholding of deportation is not an interest protected by constitutional due process guarantees.

A determination of whether due process is required in a given case must be made by first examining the nature of the interest at stake. *See, Morrissey v. Brewer,* 408 U.S. 471, 92 S.Ct. 2593, 33 L.Ed.2d 484 (1972). As stated in regards to the due process required in the processing of an application for asylum:

> "In a very graphic sense, the political asylum applicant who fears to return to his homeland because of persecution has raised the specter of truly severe deprivations of life, liberty, and property; in this case, harassment, imprisonment, beatings, torture, and death."

Haitian Refugee Center v. Civiletti, 503 F.Supp. 442, 455 (S.D.Fla.1980). The interest of an alien with the same fear is no less simply because, not knowing he has the right, he has not filed an application for asylum. It is not necessary to discuss in depth the conditions existing in El Salvador and Guatemala. The daily news reports from these countries sufficiently detail the foundation for the fears many refugees have. Certainly the interests here are life and liberty.

Although the grant or denial of asylum is within the discretion of the Attorney General, the Refugee Act of 1980 must be held to at least require that a claim for asylum be heard. Furthermore, the withholding of deportation or return to a country where "such alien's life or freedom would be threatened in such country on account of race, religion, nationality, membership in a particular social group, or political opinion" is statutorily prohibited. INA § 243(h)(1). Benefits prescribed by statute often come within the protection of procedural due process. *See e.g., Goldberg v. Kelly,* 397 U.S. 254, 90 S.Ct. 1011, 25 L.Ed.2d 287 (1969).

Defendants further assert that, assuming the opportunity to apply for asylum is a protectable interest, procedures currently in effect satisfy due process. This claim necessitates a review of those procedures.

Aliens present in the United States illegally may be caused to leave basically in one of two ways—either directly deported, or through what is known as "voluntary departure." Formal deportation proceedings are initiated by an Order to Show Cause, which order informs the alien of the nature of the proceeding, the legal authority for such proceeding, and the time and place for the deportation hearing. The alien is also told that he has the right to remain silent and the right to be represented by counsel of his choice at no expense to the United States. 8 C.F.R. § 242.1.

The Attorney General is authorized to allow certain classes of deportable aliens to voluntarily depart from the United States. An alien in this instance admits to being in this country illegally, and no hearing is had in his case. He is informed that he has the right to consult a lawyer and the right to ask for a hearing.

The provisions for voluntary departure can be beneficial to both the INS and the alien. The INS benefits because for the great number of aliens voluntarily departing prior to the commencement of deportation proceedings, the Service is spared the time and expense of providing those proceedings. The alien can benefit in two ways; first, voluntarily departing can save him from spending weeks or months in detention pending the outcome of his case. Secondly, the alien will not have a deportation order on his record and thus may be eligible to enter the country legally at a later date.

* * *

Except in one instance, the present regulations do not require the INS to notify aliens of their right to apply for political asylum or for withholding of deportation. The exception applies to cases wherein deportation proceedings have already commenced.

In this case the alien must be told by the Immigration Judge that if he is finally ordered deported, he may designate the country to which he wishes to be deported. The Immigration Judge then designates one or more alternative countries to which the alien will be deported in the event the country designated by the alien fails to accept him, or if he fails to designate a country of his choice. 8 C.F.R. § 242.17(c). He must then be advised that he may apply for temporary withholding of deportation to the country or countries designated by the Immigration Judge. *Id.* If the alien designates a country and is in fact ordered deported to that country, he is not notified that he may apply for asylum.

Due process is a flexible concept that requires such procedural protections as the particular situation demands. *Greenholz v. Inmates of Nebraska Penal and Correctional Complex,* 442 U.S. 1, 99 S.Ct. 2100, 60 L.Ed.2d 668 (1979); *Morrissey v. Brewer,* 408 U.S. 471, 92 S.Ct. 2593, 33 L.Ed.2d 484 (1972). The fundamental requirement of due process is the opportunity to be heard "at a meaningful time and in a meaningful manner." *Armstrong v. Manzo,* 380 U.S. 545, 552, 85 S.Ct. 1187, 1191, 14 L.Ed.2d 62 (1965). The Supreme Court has provided the following framework for determining the "specific dictates of due process" in a particular case.

> "[O]ur prior decisions indicate that identification of the specific dictates of due process generally requires consideration of three distinct factors: First, the private interest that will be affected by the official action; second, the risk of an erroneous deprivation of such interest through the procedures used, and the probable value, if any, of additional or substitute procedural safeguards; and finally, the Government's interest, including the function involved and the fiscal and administrative burdens that the additional or substitute procedural requirement would entail."

Mathews v. Eldridge, 424 U.S. 319, 334–335, 96 S.Ct. 893, 902–903, 47 L.Ed.2d 18 (1976).

The Plaintiff's interest herein, as stated, is obvious. Deportation or voluntary return to a country where the detainee fears persecution could result in injury or even death. The present procedures do not sufficiently assure that genuine asylum claims will be heard, nor do they assure that an alien subject to persecution will not be returned to the country of his persecutors. It is important to realize the circumstances present. The majority of detainees are completely uneducated as to INS procedures. They do not speak the English language, nor can they read the English language asylum application required for consideration. The detention center is not located in an area where detainees can easily find legal representation, nor are they entitled to appointed counsel under the law.

The Immigration Service argues that the cornerstone of American jurisprudence is the adversary system, and that notifying detainees of their right to apply for asylum goes against the grain of that system. Our system of jurisprudence, however, is designed for determining the truth, with the premise that the truth is best arrived at by full development of all the issues involved. Full development of the claims of asylum of these fleeing people, however, must start with notice of that issue, lest they never have their day.

Notice to persons of their rights or remedies has been required by the Courts in other situations. For example, notice to housing project tenants of their right to receive retroactive housing benefits was required by the court in *Holbrook v. Pitt,* 643 F.2d 1261, 1281 (7th Cir.1981), and notice to a debtor not only of an attempt to garnish an account, but also notice of the legal exemptions to which she might be entitled, was required in *Finberg v. Sullivan,* 634 F.2d 50, 62 (3rd Cir.1980).

The burden on the Government as a result of this requirement is not the giving of the notice, but the likelihood of persons without valid claims of asylum applying for that relief, thereby causing the time and expense of needless hearings, and causing those persons to remain in detention much longer than necessary, especially where they might instead be returned voluntarily after only a short period of detention. It is true that giving such notice may result in unworthy claims being filed and in a longer than necessary detention for some aliens. The Court is of the opinion, however, that this possibility does not override the need for those with worthy claims to have them heard.

While plaintiffs claim that this notice must be given before voluntary departure, before a deportation hearing, and during a deportation hearing, the Court finds that the notice will be sufficient if given before the alien is caused to depart, whether voluntarily or by deportation, and if given at such time that allows those aliens wishing to apply for asylum to do so meaningfully.

Besides showing a likelihood of prevailing on the merits, plaintiffs have also met their burden of showing that they may suffer irreparable injury if this injunction does not issue. Deportation to a country where one's life would be threatened obviously would result in irreparable injury. Furthermore, once deported or returned, an alien loses any chance he may have had to have his deportation reviewed. INA § 106(c).

The Court further finds that the injury threatened to plaintiffs outweighs the possible harm of the injunction to defendants, and that granting this injunctive relief is in the public interest. This Court fully appreciates the burden that may result to defendants due to the requirements of this Order. Providing refuge to those facing persecution in their homeland, however, goes to the very heart of the principles and moral precepts upon which this country and its Constitution were founded. It is unavoidable that some burdens result from the protection of these principles. To let these same principles go unprotected would amount to nothing less than a sacrilege.

For the reasons set forth above, this Court is of the opinion that the temporary injunctive relief prayed for by plaintiffs should be and is hereby GRANTED, and it is hereby;

Ordered that the Preliminary Injunction issued by this Court on January 5, 1982, remain in force and effect, and further

Ordered that Defendants are enjoined from failing to give notice to detainees who are citizens and nationals of El Salvador or Guatemala, prior to their deportation or voluntary return, of their right to apply for political asylum in the United States.

Notes

1. Judge Vela's order requires notice of the right to apply for asylum to all citizens of El Salvador and Guatemala before they are returned to their home countries. Suppose a citizen of Panama were to intervene in the case and claim equivalent rights for himself and all other Panamanian nationals. Should the order be expanded? How about a Bolivian? A Costa Rican? A Canadian? How should one decide? Are "daily news reports from these countries," as referred to in the decision, an adequate foundation for broad orders of this sort? Or should such warnings be provided routinely to all aliens before they are returned, either by means of exclusion and deportation, or by means of a voluntary departure agreement?

2. The court in *Jean v. Nelson, supra,* took a very different view of the notice requirement. First, as indicated above, it held that no constitutional due process rights could be asserted in this context. But it also determined that Congress did not want such warnings to be given, and it suggested certain policy problems if notice became routine:

> [P]laintiffs must ultimately fall back on the assertion that a right to notice derives *a fortiori* from the establishment of an asylum procedure. The weakness with this argument is that Congress provides many opportunities to the people of this country without requiring the government to publicize their availability or to take affirmative action to notify possible beneficiaries. It has never been held, for example, that the government must inform individuals that they have the right to sue the government for tort claims, or the right to seek educational loans or public assistance. In addition, requiring mandatory notice of the opportunity to seek asylum may actually serve to frustrate Congress' intention of preserving aliens with a well-founded fear of persecution in their home countries from repatriation. As one commentator notes:

[B]lanket notice will also tempt even those without any fear of persecution to latch on to asylum as their last hope. ...

[T]oo many asylum applications may only bury the truth by straining INS resources and preventing careful assessment of individual claims. If the volume of asylum claims rises significantly, the INS may feel compelled to rely more and more on group profiles and less on individual evidence and credibility.

Note, *Protecting Aliens from Persecution Without Overloading the INS: Should Illegal Aliens Receive Notice of the Right to Apply for Asylum?,* 69 Va.L.Rev. 901, 922, 924 (1983).

We therefore conclude that although aliens have a protected statutory and regulatory right to petition for asylum, neither the Constitution nor the Refugee Act and its accompanying regulations require the INS to inform all potential applicants of their right to seek asylum.

727 F.2d at 982–83. *See also Ramirez-Osorio v. INS,* 745 F.2d 937 (5th Cir. 1984) (after lengthy consideration of factors to be balanced—and, unlike *Jean,* considering both §§ 208 and 243(h)—court concludes that blanket warnings are not required, relying in part on statement of former Acting Commissioner that INS policy calls for notice of asylum rights if initial questioning suggests that alien may fear persecution on return); *Villegas v. INS,* 745 F.2d 950 (5th Cir. 1984) (court remands to immigration judge for hearing on allegation that INS did not comply with notice procedures stated by Acting Commissioner and relied on in *Ramirez-Osorio;* "Here we make plain that those procedures must be abided.")

3. Congress considered the issue of notice of asylum rights in its deliberations on the Simpson-Mazzoli bill. The bill the Senate passed in 1982, S. 2222, 97th Cong., 2d Sess., contained the following provision:

Sec. 121. Section 235(b) is amended—

(1) by striking out the first sentence and inserting in lieu thereof the following:

"(b)(1) If an examining immigration officer at the port of arrival determines that an alien does not have the documentation required to obtain entry into the United States, does not have any reasonable basis for entry into the United States, and has not applied for asylum under section 208, such alien shall not be admissible and shall be excluded from entry into the United States without further inquiry or hearing.

* * *

"(4) The Attorney General shall establish procedures, after consultation with the Judiciary Committees of the Congress, which assure that aliens are not excluded under paragraph (1) without an inquiry into the reasons for unlawfully seeking entry into the United States.

718   REFUGEES AND POLITICAL ASYLUM   Ch. 8

"(5) In the case of an alien who would be excluded from entry under paragraph (1) but for an application for asylum under section 208, the exclusion hearing with respect to such entry shall be limited to the issues raised by the asylum application."

The Committee Report explained (S.Rep. No. 485, 97th Cong., 2d Sess., at 34):

Section 121—Inspection and exclusion

Section 121 amends the INA to provide that if an immigration officer at the port of entry determines that an alien does not have the documentation required for entry, does not have any reasonable basis for legal entry, and has not applied for asylum, such alien must be summarily excluded from entry into the United States, without any hearing or further inquiry. If the alien claims asylum, the exclusion hearing is limited to the asylum issue.

This section also requires the Attorney General to establish a procedure to assure that this summary exclusion procedure is not used with respect to an alien unless some inquiry has been made into such alien's reason for unlawfully seeking entry into the United States. It is the intention of the Committee that this be a general inquiry and should not include advice of any right to claim asylum or leading questions with respect to persecution. Only if the alien's answers to such general inquiry provide evidence that the alien may have a well-founded fear of persecution on account of race, religion, nationality, membership in a particular social group, or political opinion should the immigration officer specifically inquire about persecution and the alien's desire to claim asylum.

Provisions virtually identical to those quoted above appeared in the bills passed by the Senate and the House in the 98th Congress, but other disagreements prevented the chambers from reconciling their respective bills, and the Simpson-Mazzoli bill did not pass. Had it passed, would the summary exclusion provisions set forth above, including their arrangements respecting political asylum claims, have been constitutional? Would they have been good policy? Consider the following commentary, from Hearings on Immigration Reform Legislation, Subcomm. on Immigration and Refugee Policy, Sen. Comm. on the Judiciary, 98th Cong., 1st Sess. (Feb. 25, 1983) (statement of Prof. David A. Martin):

I believe the court decisions requiring blanket advance warnings misunderstood Congress's intentions in passing the Refugee Act. Although that Act strengthened the asylum provisions in important ways, asylum is still to be viewed as an extraordinary form of relief for those who can prove that they are likely to be targeted for persecution *and* who take steps to make that risk known to the Immigration Service. Obviously this does not mean that they have to be well schooled in the intricacies of our immigration law nor that they have to cite the precise sections of the statutes that give them this protection. But it is not unreasonable to expect a person who believes himself a likely target for persecution upon return to his home country to manifest that fear in some fashion on his own initiative. Asylum, in other words, remains an extraordinary protection to be *invoked* by the alien, not a right presumed applicable unless expressly *waived* after extensive advice of rights by immigration officials.

This stand against advance warnings of asylum rights may seem harsh. One can ask, "What do we lose if we advise the alien fully of the law and then proceed to flesh out and adjudicate any possible claims he may have?" It is a fair question. But the reasons for resisting a blanket warning requirement derive from the inherent nature of the difficult asylum adjudication process. Once asylum applications are filed, it is very hard to weed out frivolous or ill-founded claims without going through the whole painstaking adjudication process, at least if the person comes from a country with any significant level of human rights abuses. We simply have no second line of defense reasonably available to assure that ill-founded applications do not consume large quantities of available asylum adjudication resources. Thus the risk of overburdening the system is significant if all aliens are, in effect, invited to apply for asylum. On the other hand, an alien's lack of initiative to express significant apprehension about return provides a relatively good indication that he or she has no substantial claim to asylum. Those people who are really meant to be protected by the asylum provisions generally are those so likely to face a threat that we can expect them to resist return in some way.

Plainly, we must be concerned that even shy and unschooled people with legitimate fears of persecution can have their claims heard—yet without overwhelming the system with ill-founded claims. I believe the current bill carefully balances these competing concerns. It mandates some INS inquiry into an alien's reasons for entry or attempted entry into the United States before summary exclusion, but the legislative history makes clear that leading questions and explicit references to political asylum are not to be employed at this stage. Only if the alien, under this general questioning initiated by INS, then expresses some fear of return, however inarticulate, is the asylum application process to be initiated. Of course, continuing congressional oversight will be helpful to make sure that the agents doing this preliminary questioning remain responsive to any significant expression of fear about return, but the basic system is well-designed.

Would legislative oversight be adequate to the task of assuring that INS undertakes a genuine, noncoercive inquiry into the reasons why undocumented aliens captured at the border are seeking entry? Past experience has raised doubts in the minds of some that INS would respond adequately to inarticulate but genuine manifestations of an alien's fear to return. For example, the court in *Orantes-Hernandez v. Smith*, 541 F.Supp. 351 (C.D.Cal.1982) imposed a blanket warning requirement for

Salvadorans only in part because of broad conclusions about the statutory and constitutional requirements. The court's holding rested primarily on its findings about past INS misbehavior that may have interfered with the full development of asylum claims.

Is there some middle ground between complete reliance on INS (subject only to legislative oversight) and a blanket requirement that all aliens be advised of the right to apply for asylum? The law review note cited in *Jean v. Nelson, supra,* supports the basic framework set forth in the Simpson-Mazzoli bill, but suggests that the UNHCR be asked to undertake an extensive monitoring role to assure that officials at the border are actually responsive to any showing of resistance to return. Note, *supra,* 69 Va.L.Rev., at 927–29.

Could a court legitimately order INS or the Justice Department to develop innovative monitoring arrangements, or other such systemic changes—assuming that the plaintiffs in the case had proven a record of questionable behavior like that established in *Orantes-Hernandez, supra?* Or are courts limited to more traditional procedural remedies, like the blanket notice approach, to deal with such problems. *See generally* Mashaw, *The Management Side of Due Process,* 59 Cornell L.Rev. 772 (1974) (arguing that courts should be more innovative in ordering managerial remedies rather than resorting too readily to ill-fitting procedural fixes drawn from the standard judicial models).

6. DETERRENCE OF ASYLUM SEEKERS

The Cuban boatlift from the port of Mariel started many people thinking about how to avoid such "mass asylum" situations in the future. The Select Commission on Immigration and Refugee Policy was deeply affected by this event, which occurred in the midst of its two-year investigations. Ultimately, it offered several suggestions on the subject:

SCIRP, U.S. IMMIGRATION POLICY AND THE NATIONAL INTEREST
Final Report 165–68 (1981)

V.B. MASS FIRST ASYLUM ADMISSIONS

Until 1980, the U.S. experience with asylum consisted of infrequent requests from individuals or small groups, which generally met with favorable public reaction. Then, last year, the sudden, mass arrival of Cubans seeking asylum, added to the continuing arrival of Haitian boats, resulted in national dismay, consternation and confusion. Considering the possible recurrence of mass first asylum situations and the exponential growth in new asylum applicants other than Cubans and Haitians, the Select Commission has made a series of recommendations as to how the United States should attempt to manage such emergencies. These recommendations stem from the view of most Commissioners that:

- The United States, in keeping with the Refugee Act of 1980, will remain a country of asylum for those fleeing oppression.

- The United States should adopt policies and procedures which will deter the illegal migration of those who are not likely to meet the criteria for acceptance as asylees. Therefore, asylee policy and programs must be formulated to prevent the use of asylum petitions for "backdoor immigration."

● The United States must process asylum claims on an individual basis as expeditiously as possible and not hesitate to deport those persons who come to U.S. shores—even when they come in large numbers—who do not meet the established criteria for asylees.

V.B.1. PLANNING FOR ASYLUM EMERGENCIES

THE SELECT COMMISSION RECOMMENDS THAT AN INTER-AGENCY BODY BE ESTABLISHED TO DEVELOP PROCEDURES, INCLUDING CONTINGENCY PLANS FOR OPENING AND MANAGING FEDERAL PROCESSING CENTERS, FOR HANDLING POSSIBLE MASS ASYLUM EMERGENCIES.

Recent experience has highlighted the importance of advanced planning in dealing with mass first asylum emergencies. Situations comparable to the Haitian migration and the Cuban push-out may arise in the future. To deal with these situations the United States needs a clear federal strategy to provide care for potential asylees while their individual cases are being determined.

Among the many problems experienced in 1980 were the lengthy delays in processing Haitian claims, the perception on the part of many persons that Haitians were being discriminated against because of race, the vacillating policy of the federal government with respect to work authorization for Haitians, the haphazard placement of Cubans in processing centers, the strong, negative public reaction in communities with processing centers and the difficulty in finding persons skilled in delivering the kinds of services required by the centers. Most of these problems could have been avoided with proper planning and the coordination of the efforts of the various public and private agencies involved in the processing of asylum claims and the care and housing of the applicants.

The Commission recommends that an interagency body be established to develop procedures for handling possible mass asylum emergencies in the future. A variety of agencies needs to be involved, including the White House, the U.S. Coordinator for Refugee Affairs, INS, the Departments of State, Justice, Health and Human Services and Education, the Department of the Army and the Federal Bureau of Investigation. In addition, voluntary agencies and local government representatives from communities located near potential processing centers must also be involved if tensions are to be minimized. Planning will facilitate the rapid and fair processing of asylum petitions, and allow the establishment of clear lines of authority and responsibility for asylum emergencies.

The Select Commission further recommends that this planning body develop contingency plans for opening and managing federal asylum processing centers, where asylum applicants would stay while their applications were processed quickly and uniformly. Although some Commissioners who voted against this proposal believe that the existence of such centers could act as an incentive to those using asylum claims as a means of gaining entry to the United States, the Commission majority holds that these centers could provide a number of important benefits:

- Large numbers of asylum applications could be processed quickly. No delays would result because addresses were unknown or because of the time required to travel to an examination site;

- Staff whose training and experience make them uniquely qualified to deal with mass asylum situations could be provided;

- Applicants could be centrally housed, fed and given medical aid;

- Law enforcement problems, which might arise as a result of a sudden influx of potential asylees, could be minimized;

- Resettlement of those applicants who, for a variety of reasons, were not accepted by the United States would be facilitated by providing a setting for the involvement of the U.N. High Commissioner for Refugees and the regional mechanism the Commission has proposed to deal with migration issues.

- Ineligible asylum applicants would not be released into communities where they might later evade U.S. efforts to deport them or create costs for local governments; and

- A deterrent would be provided for those who might see an asylum claim as a means of circumventing U.S. immigration law. Applicants would not be able to join their families or obtain work while at the processing center.

Detention of Asylum Seekers

The Select Commission calls for developing new facilities called "asylum processing centers," in part for the purpose of deterring marginal or abusive claims. Despite the polite label, wouldn't such facilities in reality be detention centers (or even concentration camps, as attorney Levine called them at the beginning of this Chapter)? Is such detention consistent with international law, especially as reflected in the UN Convention and Protocol? Check the Convention, with special attention to Articles 9, 26, and 31.

The Commission assumes that an applicant's stay in the centers will be relatively short, and that confinement can end as soon as a decision is reached on the application. But experience has shown that final, enforceable decisions on asylum applications often require months or years. How long could or should applicants be held in such centers if the Commission's hopes about quick processing do not become reality? How long if asylum is denied and return or distant resettlement arrangements cannot be made because other governments fail to cooperate?

We explored some of these questions in Chapter Three, pages 293– 314 *supra,* with particular attention to the constitutional issues. The judicial response has been mixed. But that is only the beginning of the inquiry. Is detention a good idea as a matter of policy?

Early in its tenure, the Reagan administration made detention a key element in its overall approach to the problem of illegal migration. The new policy was announced in Attorney General Smith's initial congressional testimony presenting the administration's proposed immigration reform legislation. Stating that we, as a nation, "have lost control of our borders," Smith emphasized: "We must more effectively deter illegal immigration to the United States—whether across our expansive borders or by sea." *Administration's Proposals on Immigration and Refugee Policy, Joint Hearing before the House Subcomm. on Immigration, Refugees, and Int'l Law and the Sen. Subcomm. on Immigration and Refugee Policy,* 97th Cong., 1st Sess. 6 (1981). He outlined the components of the legislative package, and laid special stress on two of them, "the reform of exclusion proceedings, and the necessity of detaining illegal aliens pending exclusion." *Id.* at 11. He explained:

> As recently as fiscal year 1978 fewer than 3,800 asylum applications were received. But in fiscal year 1980, 19,485 applications for asylum were received, and the number of pending applications will reach 60,000 during the current fiscal year, not including the approximately 140,000 applications filed by Cubans and Haitians.

> In the face of these circumstances, our policies and procedures for dealing with asylum applicants, which have been generous and deliberate, have crumbled under the burden of overwhelming[a] numbers. Our [streamlined] procedures should be adequate to secure the national interest. The procedural reforms we propose are fair. Moreover, they are the only rational and workable way to preserve the framework that Congress has established to govern the inspection and admission of persons seeking asylum.

> Second, the administration will seek additional resources for the construction of permanent facilities in which to house undocumented aliens temporarily until their eligibility for admission can be determined. By treating those who arrive by sea in the same way we have long treated those who arrive over our land borders, our policy will be evenhanded, and we can avoid the severe community disruptions that result from large-scale migrations.

Id. at 12.

Many of the components of the administration's reform package—especially the employer sanctions meant to penalize employers who hire aliens not authorized to work in the United States—required congressional action before they could be effectuated. But the administration began implementing its detention plans right away, simply by ending the custom

---

a. Are the numbers "overwhelming"? Do the figures provided here make a persuasive case for new deterrence measures? Current estimates place the total undocumented population at between 3.5 and 6 million. Even with 60,000 pending asylum applications, isn't this an insignificant portion of the illegal immigration problem? (Another portion of the Administration package would have permitted nearly all the 140,000 Cubans and Haitians to stay.) Or are there features of the asylum concept and adjudication process that make this problem more significant than the raw numbers suggest?—eds.

of paroling most aliens in exclusion proceedings—a custom which had prevailed since Ellis Island closed in 1954. Eventually a court ruled that the new practice was invalid because the administration had not conformed to the notice-and-comment rulemaking requirements of the Administrative Procedure Act. *Louis v. Nelson,* 544 F.Supp. 973 (S.D.Fla. 1982). *See also Bertrand v. Sava,* 684 F.2d 204 (2d Cir.1982) (sustaining the new detention practices as applied to a class of Haitian asylum applicants held in New York). But INS thereupon immediately promulgated new detention regulations in conformance with the APA procedures. *See* 47 Fed.Reg. 30,044 (1982) (interim rule); 47 Fed.Reg. 46,493 (1982) (final rule), codified at 8 C.F.R. §§ 212.5, 235.3 (1984). And in light of this change (and a distinctive view of the governing constitutional and statutory requirements), the Eleventh Circuit eventually vacated and remanded the district court's decision in the *Louis* case. *Jean v. Nelson,* 727 F.2d 957 (11th Cir.1984) (en banc), *cert. granted* ___ U.S. ___, 105 S.Ct. 563, 83 L.Ed.2d 504 (1984), discussed in Chapter Three, *supra.*

The 1982 regulations currently govern, and they establish a strong presumption that undocumented aliens in exclusion proceedings will be incarcerated throughout the course of those proceedings (usually including judicial review). Overwhelmingly, the impact of this detention policy falls on asylum applicants. Moreover, especially in the early days of its implementation, it resulted disproportionately in the detention of Haitian asylum applicants. General Accounting Office, Detention Policies affecting Haitian Nationals 5–7 (Report GAO/GGD–83–68, 1983).

Detaining nearly all excludable aliens while adjudication proceeds certainly may deter marginal asylum applicants. Is this a valid goal of public policy? If so, when should detention be employed to serve such an end? Does detention overdeter—that is, close down the prospect of asylum for people the United States should be trying to protect? What other changes in the overall system for treatment and processing of asylum claimants might better serve the same basic ends?

Interdiction

In addition to its new detention policies, in October 1981 the Reagan administration also adopted a program of Coast Guard interdiction of boats in the waters between Haiti and the United States, clearly meant to cut down on the number of asylum-seekers. (Supporters of interdiction also base such a policy on the need to end the exploitation—and occasionally the extreme abuse—of migrants by smugglers and boat captains. *See generally United States v. Saintil,* 753 F.2d 984 (11th Cir. 1985) (evidence of atrocities on ship carrying Haitians to U.S. was admissible in prosecution for smuggling).) The documents establishing the program carefully stated that no genuine refugees were to be returned to Haiti, *see* Proclamation 4865, 46 Fed.Reg. 48107 (1981); Executive Order 12324, 46 Fed. Reg. 48109 (1981), and INS agents were stationed aboard the Coast Guard cutter in order to interview the passengers of any interdicted boats. As of mid-1984, the Coast Guard had stopped and returned 56 vessels and 1367 Haitians. The INS interviewers had not found a single Haitian with a claim deemed strong enough to merit moving him or her to the United States, even for purposes of further inquiry.

Critics have voiced strong objections to the interdiction program:

Interdiction represents a radical departure from normal inspection and inquiry procedures which afford an alien the opportunity to present his or her case, through counsel, to an immigration judge. As to refugees, interdiction runs afoul of the obligations under the domestic withholding provision and its international law correlative—Article 33 of the Protocol relating to the Status of Refugees—to refrain from refoulement. * * *

A refugee who would otherwise undergo persecution might be returned upon interdiction without any recourse simply because of an inability to articulate the reasons feared, or to persuade an on-ship inspector that the fear is well-founded, or simply because he or she is afraid to speak to authorities. This is particularly so since there would be no access to counsel under these circumstances.

A refugee fleeing persecution after a stressful and surreptitious journey often lacks the documentary resources, the psychological reserve, and even perhaps the willingness to persuade someone of the integrity of his or her asylum claim. Indeed, the *Handbook on Procedures and Criteria for Determining Refugee Status* of the United Nations High Commissioner for Refugees, used by the United States in the analysis of asylum claims, emphasizes the difficulties experienced by aliens in pursuing asylum at a national border: "[The applicant for refugee status] finds himself in an alien environment and may experience serious difficulties, technical and psychological, in submitting his case to the authorities of a foreign country, often in language not his own." The *Handbook* recommends taking special care in processing such applications.

Helton, *Political Asylum Under the 1980 Refugee Act: An Unfulfilled Promise,* 17 U.Mich.J.L.Ref. 243, 255–56 (1984).

There are two issues here. First, to what extent are true asylum candidates returned to Haiti because of inhibitions that prevent them from voicing their claims? This raises subsidiary questions. Is the role of counsel at this stage as significant as Helton suggests? Should we be as solicitous of potential claimants as the UNHCR Handbook seems to call for, or may we assume that those with legitimate fears will resist return in some way that will signal their fears and thus prompt further processing? In a somewhat similar setting, you recall, Simas Kudirka, the Lithuanian sailor who bolted from a Soviet ship in 1970 (mentioned earlier in this Chapter), fought vigorously before he was finally overcome and physically bound and gagged by the Soviet seamen sent to retrieve him. There was no mistaking that he feared return. *See* Mann, *supra* note 15.

But Kudirka's experience raises the second set of questions. Even if we can envision an interdiction system fairly run with appropriate inquiries made before anyone is returned, how sure can we be that any particular program operates fairly? Interdiction, after all, is carried out on the high seas, away from the scrutiny of the press and the public—and perhaps out of the reach of the federal courts. *See Haitian Refugee Center, Inc. v. Gracey*, 600 F.Supp. 1396 (D.D.C. 1985) (holding that plaintiffs had standing to challenge the interdiction program, but finding no cognizable violations of statutes, treaties, or the constitution). Are there other administrative checks that might provide assurances of fair implementation? Or is this objection so basic that interdiction should be abandoned—at least short of true emergencies?

Whatever the answers to all these questions, it is clear that the deterrence program implemented in 1981, embracing both detention and interdiction, has had an impact in reducing the flow of asylum seekers.[29] The effect is most clearly reflected in the statistics concerning Haitians. From a peak of 15,093 in 1980, the number of known Haitian arrivals declined to 8,069 the following year, and to a mere 99 during the first nine months of 1982, according to the General Accounting Office study, *supra*, at 2. In fiscal year 1983, only 154 Haitian asylum claims were filed, and from October 1983 through March 1984, an additional 317 were filed.

SECTION D.   SAFE HAVEN (INCLUDING "EXTENDED VOLUNTARY DEPARTURE")

To establish an asylum claim, an applicant must show some likelihood that he or she would be targeted for persecution. (The strength of the showing required, and the degree to which the alien must establish that he or she would be "singled out," remain matters of dispute, which the Supreme Court's *Stevic* decision, reprinted earlier, did not resolve.) Consequently, those who flee war zones or civil strife often cannot begin to establish the necessary proof, even though they are usually referred to, in common parlance, as "refugees." They have not been targeted; they simply got in the way of the fighting. In *Martinez-Romero v. INS*, 692 F.2d 595 (9th Cir.1982), the court sustained a BIA ruling denying asylum to a national of El Salvador. The court's judgment reads in its entirety:

> The orders of the Immigration and Naturalization Service before us for review are affirmed.

> If we were to agree with the petitioner's contention that no person should be returned to El Salvador because of the reported

---

29. Over the last several years, other western countries have experienced similar increases in asylum applications and have also adopted various deterrence measures in response. The best known example is the Federal Republic of Germany, which cut benefits available to applicants awaiting a decision, restricted work authorizations, and instituted communal housing arrangements—austere locations where most applicants are required to live while awaiting a final decision. The application rate dropped sharply, but the German practices, like the American, have sparked intense debate. *See* Aleinikoff, *supra* note 3, at 196–213, 230–33 (1984).

anarchy present there now, it would permit the whole population, if they could enter this country some way, to stay here indefinitely. There must be some special circumstances present before relief can be granted.

This may be an understandable approach for implementing the fixed and open-ended legal obligation the United States undertook when it became a party to the UN Protocol. But shouldn't there be a way to provide at least a minimal level of protection—some type of safe haven—in a broader range of circumstances? Persons who flee anarchy, war, or civil strife present strong humanitarian claims, at least to receive temporary permission to remain within the confines of U.S. borders for as long as the fighting continues. And their claims are of course stronger whenever some risk of targeted persecution also underlies their resistance to return, even if the proof is insufficient to win protection under § 208, § 243(h), or the UN Convention and Protocol.

Is there, or should there be, room within our immigration laws for some such temporary protection? If so, what factors should be considered before deciding which groups or individuals are to benefit? Who should make such a decision? Should such persons be allowed free movement in the society—with work authorizations and perhaps certain claims on public assistance? Or should they be confined in federal centers or camps? (Such detention would, after all, provide the physical safety that is the main rationale for such protection, while at the same time assuring that these arrangements do not become a vehicle for "backdoor immigration." But at what cost in terms of the impact on the individuals thus detained?)

Some groups have in fact received a form of ad hoc protection along these lines under the label of "extended voluntary departure" (EVD), which is essentially an exercise of prosecutorial discretion.[30] When INS decides, usually on the advice of the State Department, to grant blanket EVD to nationals of a certain country, this action means that INS will take no action to force departure for as long as the policy remains in effect. But EVD also often means that INS takes note of the probable illegality of the alien's presence. (If the alien could qualify for other, less tenuous, categories—for example through marriage to an American citi-

30. For persons new to immigration lingo, this terminology is extremely confusing. Indeed, it can be confusing to INS staff themselves, as a recent internal study discovered. *Asylum Adjudications, supra* note 28, at 66–71. As a result, there is some movement afoot to rename this and related forms of tolerance (such as parole for the same basic reasons of disturbed conditions in the home country), and to call them all "safe haven." *See id.* at 69, 72. As a serious student of immigration law now into your eighth chapter of these materials, however, you should be in a position to understand why the "voluntary departure" category is employed. *See generally* 61 Interp.Rel. 103 (1984) (INS policy memorandum explaining the differences between extended voluntary departure of the safe-haven variety and other uses of voluntary departure); 62 Interp. Rel. 256–58 (1985) (sample letter notifying certain "EVD eligibles" of their status). EVD "status" is largely equivalent to parole—a discretionary arrangement meant to cut through other technical requirements and meant to be granted and terminated with relative ease. Because of the intricacies associated with the entry doctrine, however, parole cannot be given to people who have already entered the country. And most of the people for whom safe haven has been a significant issue have already made an entry, either as nonimmigrants or as surreptitious entrants.

zen—he would have every incentive to claim the conventional immigration status.)

It remains unclear what other rights and benefits flow from EVD "status," although INS has usually issued work authorizations. Certainly there is no special program for federal assistance like that available to refugees under INA §§ 411–414, but it may be that EVD beneficiaries qualify for other general public assistance programs otherwise closed to "illegal aliens." *Cf. Holley v. Lavine,* 553 F.2d 845 (2d Cir.1977), *cert. denied* 435 U.S. 947, 98 S.Ct. 1532, 55 L.Ed.2d 545 (1978); *Rubio v. Employment Division,* Fed.Imm.L.Rep. para. 18,177 (Ore.Ct.App., Jan. 18, 1984); *Berger v. Sec'y of Health and Human Services, id.,* para. 18,202 (E.D.N.Y., May 23, 1984). In any event, no routine mechanism exists for eventual adjustment from EVD to lawful permanent resident status.

A recent INS staff study located 15 occasions since 1960 in which extended voluntary departure had been granted to aliens because of disturbed conditions in the home country. *Asylum Adjudications, supra* note 28, at 66–68. The terms varied widely, as did the decisionmaking background. A description of several recent uses of EVD, derived from *id.* and from a 1981 letter from the Acting Commissioner to Senator Edward Kennedy, reprinted in 128 Cong.Rec. S831–32 (daily ed. Feb. 11, 1982), may usefully introduce the subject.

● In July 1977, the State Department recommended blanket EVD for Ethiopian nationals then in the United States. Many of the beneficiaries had been in the country since before the 1974 overthrow of the Emperor, Haile Selassie, and in any event the country was then in the midst of a bloody series of purges known as the Red Terror. EVD was granted in one-year increments, and was continually extended until 1981. In 1981 the Deputy Secretary of State sent a letter to INS indicating that conditions had stabilized in Ethiopia and that the blanket policy should be ended. INS sent out a policy wire conforming to the recommendation. *See* 58 Interp.Rel. 482–83 (1981). This change touched off widespread criticism, led by several members of Congress, arguing that conditions were still extremely dangerous because of both the continued civil war and the regime's unabated human rights abuses. In an embarrassing reversal, INS and State reinstated EVD for Ethiopians six months after the initial cancellation, but only for Ethiopians who had arrived before June 1980. The reinstatement letter indicated that the tight exit controls in effect in Ethiopia as of that date justified such a policy; people who left thereafter would almost surely have the blessing of the government and so would not merit special protection. *See* 59 Interp.Rel. 456 (1982).

● In April 1978, the Department of State recommended EVD for Ugandans in the United States, because of the savagery of the Idi Amin regime then ruling the country, and because of the spreading violence in opposition. Amin was overthrown in 1979, but conditions remained unsettled thereafter, and State declined on several occasions to change its recommendation. *See, e.g.,* 61 Interp.Rel. 899 (1984).

● In March 1979, the State Department recommended blanket EVD for nationals of Iran, then experiencing the turmoil associated with the ouster of the Shah and the eventual return of the Ayatollah Khomeini. When the U.S. embassy in Teheran was seized and American diplomats were taken hostage in November 1979, however, EVD status was abruptly cancelled as part of the overall U.S. response to the crisis. *See Yassini v. Crosland,* 618 F.2d 1356 (9th Cir.1980). (Asylum claims of course could still be lodged, and the State Department ultimately decided not to process advisory letters on Iranians for so long as the hostage situation continued. This practice achieved functionally the same result as EVD for those Iranians who filed a Form I–589; they would not be removed until those claims were adjudicated, and no claims were processed until after the hostages were released in January 1981.)

● In June 1979 the State Department recommended EVD for nationals of Nicaragua. A civil war had been underway in that country for several months by the time this recommendation was issued, and the dictator, Anastasio Somoza, was overthrown about a month after the policy went into effect. With extensions, EVD status lasted until September 1980, at which time State advised that conditions had stabilized to the point that further extensions were unnecessary.

● In December 1981, the Polish government declared martial law and seized many of the labor union activists whose Solidarity union movement had previously won important concessions from the Polish government. Many Poles departed for other European countries, and the State Department moved promptly to recommend to INS a grant of blanket EVD to Polish nationals within the United States who resisted return (with exceptions for those with a third-country residence or a criminal conviction in the United States). The INS agreed, and this policy was continued even after martial law ended in Poland. At first the policy applied only to persons who arrived before December 24, 1981, but in 1984 its reach was expanded to include those who arrived no later than July 21, 1984. *See* 61 Interp.Rel. 899–900, 1070 (1984).

● Since December 1980, EVD has been provided to all Afghan nationals. As of this writing it remains in effect, owing to the continuing war between the Afghan government—supported primarily by Soviet troops— and various Afghan resistance movements. See 62 Interp.Rel. 106 (1985).

The Salvadoran Controversy

Much of the current debate over EVD focuses on the situation faced by nationals of El Salvador. The government has staunchly resisted calls for extending that status to Salvadorans, for a variety of reasons that appear from the following materials. The controversy has taken place on two levels—first, a debate over the facts concerning the level of danger in El Salvador, and second, a debate over the standards that should be employed in deciding which groups merit EVD. Advocates for granting such status argue that the general level of fighting and human rights abuses in the home country parallels that experienced in Nicaragua, for example, when EVD was granted in 1979. They also argue that the real risks faced by most of the Salvadorans exceed those faced by others now protected by EVD, especially Polish nationals.

In late 1981, at the time when EVD was being implemented for Poles, Congress gave consideration to proposals for blanket EVD for Salvadorans. The following compromise measure eventually passed, as part of the International Security and Development Cooperation Act of 1981, Pub.L. No. 97–113, 95 Stat. 1519.

> Sec. 731. It is the sense of the Congress that the administration should continue to review, on a case-by-case basis, petitions for extended voluntary departure made by citizens of El Salvador who claim that they are subject to persecution in their homeland, and should take full account of the civil strife in El Salvador in making decisions on such petitions.

Sense-of-the-Congress resolutions, as the name suggests, do not constitute binding law. But suppose the administration decided to accede to sentiment expressed here. You are the INS officer assigned to implement this policy. What exactly does it mean? What instructions would you issue to field offices? (The State Department had recommended similar policies in the past, for example, in 1976 with respect to Lebanese nationals, see 128 Cong.Rec. at S831, but INS has apparently always been puzzled over the exact meaning of such a recommendation. See *Asylum Adjudications, supra* note 28, at 71.)

Following this enactment, pressure for a changed EVD policy did not abate. Congressional committees held hearings, and a labor union filed, on behalf of its Salvadoran members, an equal protection lawsuit against the administration's denial of EVD. To the surprise of many, this lawsuit survived the government's first motion for summary judgment. *Hotel and Restaurant Employees Union, Local 25 v. Smith,* 563 F.Supp. 157 (D.D.C.1983). (For incisive commentary on the opinion, *see* Schuck, *The Transformation of Immigration Law,* 84 Colum.L.Rev. 1, 58–62 (1984).) Seventeen months later, after discovery had taken place, the district court changed its approach significantly and granted the government's renewed motion for summary judgment. The court apparently concluded that judicial review of EVD decisions is precluded because of the exclusive authority granted to the executive branch to judge foreign policy interests and to exercise prosecutorial discretion. 594 F.Supp. 502 (D.D.C.1984). The opinion comments further:

> For a Court to order EVD in this case would set a far-reaching precedent, wholly within the prerogatives of Congress, and might then apply to all situations of widespread fighting, destruction and the breakdown of public services and order throughout the world. Also, such situations as famine, drought, or other natural disasters might at any time also raise "humanitarian" concerns, wherever they might occur. To require the Attorney General to grant blanket EVD status to all such nationals would be to open up irresponsibly the floodgates to illegal aliens, without regard to foreign policy and internal immigration concerns, or, of equal importance, to the concerns of American working men and women in the United States and our taxpayers generally.

Id. at 508.

When a group of 89 members of Congress wrote to the Attorney General and the Secretary of State in April 1983 asking that EVD be provided for Salvadorans, the Administration responded with the following letter. It was carefully drafted with an eye toward both the current political controversy and the pending *Employees Union* litigation (mindful, at the time, of the court's *first* ruling, 563 F.Supp. 157, which had held that the standards for EVD decisions were readily ascertainable and presented no "political questions" of a kind that rendered the dispute nonjusticiable).

July 19, 1983

Dear Congressman:

This is in response to your letter of April 28, 1983, concerning El Salvador and requesting the Salvadoran nationals be provided temporary sanctuary in the United States. The delay in this response has been due to our taking a close look at the situation. I share your concern about the disturbances in areas of El Salvador, and the unfortunate plight of the Salvadoran nationals who have been displaced from their homeland. However, after careful consideration and review, I have concluded that the present circumstances do not warrant a granting of "extended voluntary departure" to El Salvadorans presently in the United States illegally.

As your letter points out, there have been occasions when the Attorney General, in consultation with the Secretary of State, has determined to delay temporarily expulsion of aliens of particular nationalities. Although somewhat of a misnomer, this form of discretionary relief from enforcement of our immigration laws most often has been referred to as "extended voluntary departure." Because of the serious foreign and domestic policy ramifications of withholding the expulsion of illegal aliens on nationality-based classifications, grants of such relief have been rare and limited to those cases where, in the judgment of the senior Executive Branch officials responsible for such policy, the best interests of the United States are served by such extraordinary measures.

It is true, as you further point out, that "extended voluntary departure" has been granted to nationals of Ethiopia, Nicaragua, Poland, and Uganda, at times when such countries were experiencing significant civil disturbances. It is inaccurate, however, to assume that there exists any specific criterion or criteria, such as the occurrence of violence or political instability, by which grants of "extended voluntary departure" are determined. As reflected in our immigration laws, it is an unfortunate reality that our country cannot provide sanctuary to all foreign nationals whose homelands are experiencing political or economic misfortune. The decisions made as to "extended voluntary departure" are reached on a situation by situation basis and are not readily susceptible to comparison or generalization. Each determination is based on examination of a variety of factors unique to each country's situation.

Because of our shared concern regarding the citizens of El Salvador, I requested new and additional advice of the Secretary of State on this matter. By recent letter, Secretary Shultz has responded that in his judgment our present U.S. efforts to assist the Salvadoran people constitute the most constructive course of action in light of our foreign policy interests, and that the Department of State does not recommend that "extended voluntary departure" be granted to Salvadoran nationals in the United States.

In addition to the counsel provided by Secretary Shultz, I have carefully considered a number of other factors. As you know, it is estimated that there are hundreds of thousands of illegal Salvadoran aliens already in the United States. This is but one facet of the current crisis in which our country is experiencing a floodtide of illegal immigrants. A grant of "extended voluntary departure" to the Salvadorans undoubtedly would encourage the migration of many more such aliens. Because of the present and potential political and economic instability in other countries in close geographic proximity to the United States, any grants of conditional immigration benefits must be considered in light of its potential inducement to further influxes of illegal immigrants. Our recent experiences with the mass migrations of Cuban and Haitian nationals to the United States have underscored the need for proper concern in such matters for the finite capacity of our country's law enforcement and social support systems. It is also clear that, notwithstanding our improving economy, the continuing problems of unemployment and budget deficits can only be exacerbated by any action which would increase substantially the number of people competing for employment and social services.

I have also considered the fact that there are adequate alternatives by which the Salvadoran nationals may seek relief. For example, as you know, our immigration laws provide various specific procedures whereby aliens may lawfully secure the right to enter and remain in the United States, including application for asylum where there is a properly demonstrated claim of fear of individual persecution in the alien's homeland. This is not to suggest that grants of "extended voluntary departure" and asylum are based upon the same considerations and criteria; however, I do view it as significant that the provisions of the Immigration and Nationality Act contain numerous forms of relief for which aliens may apply to remain in the United States. Both the number of Salvadoran aliens and past experience suggest the possibility that many such aliens may seek to remain in the United States for economic improvement as well as the fact that many such aliens passed through third countries which would afford sanctuary were that the sole objective of the migrants.

Thus, I believe it appropriate to address the Salvadorans' request for relief on an individual by individual basis, as is the normal course under our immigration laws.

Finally, as you know, the Department of State has made periodic reports on the conditions in El Salvador and has concluded that, while serious problems remain, the risk to the general citizenry from civil disturbance is not prevalent throughout the country and, in some areas, the risk has diminished.

Although it is my judgment under the present circumstances not to institute a discretionary grant of relief from enforcement of our immigration laws to all Salvadoran nationals now in the United States, I have attempted to convey the serious attention that has been given to the matters raised in your letter. Please be assured that we shall continue to monitor the situation carefully, and will make every effort to ensure the fair and humane administration of our immigration laws and policies with respect to the many Salvadoran and other aliens now in our country.

> Sincerely,
> William French Smith
> Attorney General

Though the letter tries to downplay the notion that there are any specific criteria for EVD decisions, what rough standards are implicit from the letter? Are they valid? What would you add to the list? What would you subtract? Compare the following proposal, from the testimony of Congressman Mike Lowry presented in House hearings held in April 1984.

Although the context of violence is indisputable, it is difficult to obtain full documentation of the degree of risk that our current policy presents to deported Salvadoran refugees. However, the Center for Immigration Rights has studied a list of 2500 deportees. The preliminary results indicate that 50 appeared on death lists compiled by independent Salvadoran human rights organizations. That is to say, about 2% of the deportees studied were killed. Because the records are not always reliable, the total number of victims in this group could be higher.

It seems to me that there is only one responsible and humane way of reacting to this finding. That is to recognize that 2% is far too high a figure to be acceptable to us, as Americans whose government deported these individuals as a matter of policy. I do not mean to suggest that those 50 individuals were killed because they had been refugees. I do mean to suggest that their chances of dying violent deaths were far greater because we sent them back to El Salvador than if they had been allowed to stay in the United States, temporarily, until conditions in their country improve.

It was reported in one of the Seattle newspapers that a spokesman for the Immigration and Naturalization Service responded to this study with this statement: "Just because those people were returned and may have become innocent victims of some level of random violence in El Salvador does not mean the judgment on their asylum claims was inaccurate."

That is exactly the point. Asylum is appropriate for people who face threats of individual persecution. It may well have not been appropriate for those 50 Salvadorans. Yet they lost their lives in acts of violence. That is why we should grant extended voluntary departure status to those Salvadorans who remain in the United States, rather than processing them on a case-by-case basis for an asylum status designed to help a category of people with different problems.

Simply put, if we have reason to believe that a policy of deporting refugees from the United States may lead to death for 2% of them, it seems to me that a study of this policy is not too much to ask, and that while the study is going on, the policy should be suspended. That is what H.R. 4447 [the bill that was the subject of the House hearings] would do: It would suspend the deportation of Salvadorans from the U.S. pending a study of the conditions they face.

Temporary Suspension of Deportation of Certain Aliens, Hearing before the Subcomm. on Immigration, Refugees, and International Law, House Comm. on the Judiciary, 98th Cong., 2d Sess., at 44 (April 12, 1984). What are Congressman Lowry's standards for granting EVD? What other groups could be expected to meet them? Don't his standards ethically require an affirmative *admissions* policy for large numbers of Salvadorans, rather than simply a policy of non-return? What is the proposed study supposed to discover?

Several months after receipt of the Attorney General's letter, reprinted above, Congress again spoke to the issue, this time in somewhat more specific terms. It adopted the following provision as part of the Department of State Authorization Act, Pub.L. No. 98–164, 97 Stat. 1062 (Nov. 22, 1983):

Sec. 1012. (a) The Congress finds that—

(1) ongoing fighting between the military forces of the Government of El Salvador and opposition forces is creating potentially life-threatening situations for innocent nationals of El Salvador;

(2) thousands of El Salvadoran nationals have fled from El Salvador and entered the United States since January 1980;

(3) currently the United States Government is detaining these nationals of El Salvador for the purpose of deporting or otherwise returning them to El Salvador, thereby irreparably harming the foreign policy image of the United States;

(4) deportation of these nationals could be temporarily suspended, until it became safe to return to El Salvador, if they are provided with extended voluntary departure status; and

(5) such extended voluntary departure status has been granted in recent history in cases of nationals who fled from Vietnam, Laos, Iran, and Nicaragua.

(b) Therefore, it is the sense of the Congress that—

(1) the Secretary of State should recommend that extended voluntary departure status be granted to aliens—

(A) who are nationals of El Salvador,

(B) who have been in the United States since before January 1, 1983,

(C) who otherwise qualify for voluntary departure (in lieu of deportation) under section 242(b) or 244(e) of the Immigration and Nationality Act, and

(D) who were not excludable from the United States at the time of their entry on any ground specified in section 212(a) of the Immigration and Nationality Act other than the grounds described in paragraphs (14), (15), (20), (21), and (25); and

(2) such status should be granted to those aliens until the situation in El Salvador has changed sufficiently to permit their safely residing in that country.

What is the significance of the January 1, 1983 dateline in subsection (b)(1)(B), and why do you suppose it was adopted? Is such a dateline sound policy? What standards for deciding when to provide EVD (and later, to end it) are implicit in this enactment? Why would Congress take the nonbinding sense-of-the-Congress approach rather than use its plenary power over immigration to require EVD for Salvadorans under the conditions set forth?

The debate continues, as the following exchange suggests. Again, be alert to the standards each writer implicitly employs in deciding when EVD is appropriate. How concerned should the United States be about conditions in other possible countries of asylum, such as Mexico or Honduras? Do the crudeness of the camps there or the existence of local antipathy furnish sufficient reason for adopting an EVD policy in the United States? Should U.S. policy be geared toward assuring not only some safe haven somewhere, but safe haven that is as secure and comfortable as what could be provided in this country? For more on the factual disputes only sketched here, see Temporary Suspension Hearings, supra; National Immigration and Alien Rights Project [ACLU], Salvadorans in the United States: The Case for Extended Voluntary Departure (1983); S. Masanz, U.S. Policy Towards Undocumented Salvadorans (Cong. Research Service 1983); Staff of the Sen. Subcomm. on Immigration and Refugee Policy of the Comm. on the Judiciary, 98th Cong., 1st Sess., Refugee Problems in Central America (Comm. Print 1984).

ALAN K. SIMPSON, * WE CAN'T ALLOW ALL SALVADORANS TO STAY

Washington Post, July 10, 1984, at A13.

According to current estimates, nearly 500,000 Salvadorans are living in the United States as illegal immigrants. As the conflict in El Salvador continues, there have been urgent calls for suspending the deportation of this entire group of people.

While these requests have been based on compassion and charity, they have also been founded on mistaken assumptions and undertaken without consideration for the full consequences. There are reasonable, humanitarian alternatives to sending Salvadorans back to contested areas in their homeland, but allowing *all* of them—refugees or economic migrants—to stay in the United States until the conflict subsides is not one of them.

It is therefore most important to place the issue of undocumented Salvadoran "refugees" in perspective. El Salvador has traditionally generated the second-largest flow of illegal aliens, exceeded only by Mexico. Since long before the conflict in that country heated up in 1979, hundreds of thousands of Salvadorans have migrated illegally to the United States in search of economic opportunity.

These "pre-conflict" Salvadorans are estimated to constitute 350,000 of the approximately 500,000 undocumented Salvadorans here today. The Spanish International Network (SIN) conducted an exit poll of Salvadoran voters during that country's recent presidential elections. Seventy percent of Salvadorans polled said they would like to emigrate to work in the United States.

Almost all Salvadorans come to the United States by land routes. In doing so, they must cross at least two countries to reach our border. All of them must pass through Mexico and Guatemala, and some also travel through Honduras. Both Mexico and Honduras have allowed "safe haven" for Salvadorans, and the U.N.'s High Commission for Refugees has established a presence in each country. In a legal sense, then, it is these nations that are the country of safe "first asylum," not the United States.

While it may be true that many Salvadorans left their homeland because they perceived their lives to be in danger, they did not travel 2,000 miles through the friendly and accepting country of Mexico because of a continuing threat of personal violence.

Their reasons for traveling on through Mexico are reasonable—to find better employment opportunities or to live with friends or family in the United States—but this is the motivation of most legal and illegal immigrants around the world, not of the true refugees. The United States and the United Nations define such a refugee as having a "well-founded fear of persecution based on race, religion, nationality, membership in a particular social group, or political opinion."

* * *

* Chairman of the Senate Subcommittee on Immigration and Refugee Policy.

Undeniably, [this] is a difficult test to pass, but that is because the U.N. and U.S. definition of a refugee is very specific, and the manner in which that definition should be interpreted—according to the U.N. Handbook on Criteria and Procedures for Determining Refugee Status—is very strict. The low approval rates for political asylum worldwide are caused not by "political prejudice," or "covering up our involvement in Central America," but by the exacting international standards on who may be considered to be a "refugee." Of the 500,000 or so Salvadorans in this nation today, only 20,000 to 30,000 have applied for political asylum.

The suspension of deportation of *all* Salvadorans illegally present in the United States would be a most curious policy. It would require simply that the United States *not* deport those people who clearly are not refugees according to the U.N. definition, who clearly are economic migrants, and who could return home without any significant risk. It would also send a quite explicit message to the people of El Salvador: all you have to do is get here; once you do, we will allow you to stay regardless of your circumstances. Given the tattered disarray of current U.S. immigration laws, this would be an absurd precedent.

Some strident and often partisan critics of current policy would have us believe that the violence in El Salvador prevents anyone from living there with any reasonable expectation of personal safety. This is most assuredly untrue. There is relatively little violence in the western provinces of El Salvador. There are displaced-person camps throughout the country that are rarely, if ever, in danger and that are receiving increased amounts of assistance from the U.S. government and the international community. Honduras provides safe refugee camps open to *all* Salvadorans seeking haven. It is beyond dispute that internally displaced Salvadorans experience poor living conditions, but this should be addressed through increased humanitarian assistance, not by relaxing further our strained immigration laws.

What should the United States do with deportable Salvadorans? First, we should return those who would choose to go voluntarily or who express no significant apprehension over returning. When the State Department began conducting a recent random survey of 500 returned Salvadorans in El Salvador, it learned that not only had not one person been found killed or abused because of political violence, but no relatives or neighbors of those sought had even heard rumors about any of the returnees disappearing or being abused.

Second, the United States should remove those Salvadorans who express significant fears of returning and place them in refugee camps in Honduras, or in secure displaced-person camps in El Salvador. Correspondingly, the United States should provide sufficient aid to these present facilities so that an additional number of people could be handled and adequate living conditions be assured.

Finally, we should develop guidelines that would identify certain classes of people who might well be subject to particular risk if returned to El Salvador. There is evidence that this may be true of teachers and medical personnel. In such instances, a "case-by-case" review of the need for extended voluntary departure would certainly be in order.

We must not distort our laws concerning political asylum. Serious risks are taken by those who would grant "sanctuary" to those who are not refugees. Such an indiscriminate selection process would only further the "compassion fatigue," which will lessen our nation's willingness to respond to the millions of truly persecuted humans all over the planet.

SHARON KIRMEYER, THERE'S NO 'SAFE HAVEN' IN EL SALVADOR

Washington Post, July 14, 1984, at A17.

I appreciate Sen. Alan Simpson's concern that the United States needs to be wary of increasing our "compassion fatigue" as we attempt to respond to the needs of persecuted and oppressed persons by being wise in our allocation of assistance and refuge. However, the information on which he bases his argument against suspending deportations of Salvadorans is greatly at odds with the firsthand information I have worked with in the past eight years as a demographer concentrating on Central American affairs.

Fundamental to Simpson's argument are the estimates that 500,000 undocumented Salvadorans live in the United States today and that the majority of them (350,000) came in pre-conflict days (prior to 1980). All would agree that reliable figures do not exist, but one basis for estimation follows from the 94,000 Salvadorans enumerated by the U.S. Census, 51,000 of whom were estimated to be here illegally. It is highly unlikely that the ratio of unenumerated to enumerated undocumented persons would be 7:1. A 1984 report by the Bureau of the Census reflects the assessment of most professionals monitoring the refugee flows: "Salvadorans began fleeing their country en masse in April 1980."

Bordering countries do not now offer a place of refuge for Salvadorans. Impoverished Honduras' capacity to give refuge became saturated in the first year of the conflict. Guatemala continues to experience much violence and thus does not constitute a safe haven. Mexico, while on record as welcoming Salvadoran refugees, has had an economy that deteriorated greatly since first offering that haven. Mexican newspapers repeatedly editorialize against the acceptance of Salvadoran refugees. The experience of Salvadorans passing through Mexico in the past few years has been one of hostility, robbery and sometimes violence. One social fact stands out: there exists a regional antipathy against Salvadorans, a population known for its enterprising character.

Contrary to Simpson's suggestion, safe haven does not realistically exist within El Salvador either. The internal refugee camps neither provide safety (they are viewed by the violent right as being "bases of subversion") nor offer decent living conditions. While the western area of the country is relatively less violent at this time, persons without family ties to the west really have no means to become established in that area, whereas having a family member in the United States provides a more concrete anchor (despite the risks in passage north).

If U.S. citizens are concerned that suspending deportations of Salvadorans during the conflict would lead to a large permanent population, the case of Nicaragua provides a good parallel. The vast majority of Nicaraguans who left during the civil war in the late 1970s returned at its termination in July 1979 (which was followed by a smaller outflow of a separate group of Nicaraguans).

At the heart of debate on giving Salvadorans "extended stay" is the designation of Salvadorans as either economic or political refugees. All the Salvadoran families that I have interviewed in the United States have reported recent deaths of family members of close co-workers. The risk of another death is seen to be too large, and thus they take what seems to be the only viable option: to travel north.

Finally, the efforts of churches and families in the United States giving "sanctuary" should not be criticized, but applauded and supported. While they do not offer a total solution for the accommodation of the large members of refugees, they provide a model for economic and psychological assistance that leads to a self-sufficient, if temporary, stay.

Notes

Both authors refer to the granting of "sanctuary" to Salvadorans by churches and families in the United States. Such sheltering, despite the Salvadorans' undocumented status, draws on the religious tradition of civil disobedience against governmental policies seen as immoral, and on the medieval custom of inviolable sanctuary within churches for offenders against secular authority. In the early stages of the movement, the Justice Department generally took a hands-off approach, based on its judgment of enforcement priorities. More recently, however, as the movement expanded, the Department began a concerted effort to prosecute those involved. *See generally United States v. Elder*, 601 F.Supp. 1574 (S.D.Tex.1985) (denying motions to dismiss indictment against a prominent figure in the sanctuary movement); 62 Interp.Rel. 364, 382–85 (1985) (resolution of city council declaring Cambridge, Mass., a "sanctuary city").

Finally, consider a recent proposal for a thorough restructuring of our arrangements for temporary protection of threatened populations.

STATEMENT OF T. ALEXANDER ALEINIKOFF, REFUGEE ASSISTANCE

Hearings on H.R. 3195 Before the Subcomm. on Immigration, Refugees and International
Law of the House Comm. on the Judiciary.
98th Cong., 1st Sess. 102–04 (1983)

It seems to me that much of the disagreement over refugee matters actually involves aliens who do not satisfy the relatively narrow definition of "refugee" under the INA and the 1951 Geneva Convention. The reasons that these people—be they Salvadorans, Haitians, Cubans or Vietnamese—trigger debate is because they generally have reasonable and legitimate fears about returning home; thus they warrant our humanitarian concern. Yet they are often unable to demonstrate that their claims of persecution distinguish them from all other members of their society. I will call these aliens "de facto refugees"—a phrase I borrow from a 1975 draft recommendation of a committee of the Council of Europe.[1]

I would include among de facto refugees the following groups of aliens:

(1) Persons from a country experiencing civil war, a general breakdown of public order, or occupation by a foreign power;

(2) Persons likely to suffer substantial infringement of human rights if returned home, where such treatment cannot be considered persecution based on political or religious belief, race, nationality or membership in a social group;

(3) Persons fleeing severe economic deprivation due to natural causes (e.g., drought) or social conditions; and

(4) Persons in this country who do not choose to apply for asylum—even though they might be granted refugee status—because they would like to return to their home countries once conditions change or are fearful that their applications will not be fairly adjudicated here.

I would also include in the category of de facto refugees persons whom the United States government permits to remain here, whether or not they are true refugees, under a blanket grant of extended voluntary departure. This list is used for illustrative purposes and is not exhaustive.

The failure to recognize the category of "de facto refugee" has created a serious distortion in our refugee law. We have no intermediate statutory stage between "asylee" and "illegal alien." Thus the government and advocates for asylum applicants attempt to place groups of aliens in one category or the other, although the reality of the situation is obviously far more complex than the two extreme labels reveal. Clearly all Salvadoran entrants are not entitled to asylum, yet neither are they all economic migrants. Most are best described as persons who merit humanitarian concern because they are fleeing a country involved in a brutal civil war that threatens the lives of all Salvadorans.

Curiously, even though our law does not recognize the category of de facto refugees, our administrative practices do. Despite constant efforts by Congress, sometimes joined by the Executive Branch, to limit the use of parole, time and again we have seen the need to allow persons who do not technically fit the definition of refugee to enter and reside in the United States. The most recent legislative attempt to curb the parole power—the 1980 Refugee Act's amendment of § 212(d)(5) of the INA—did not prevent the parole of 125,000 Cubans a few months later. Another administrative technique used to protect persons who do not qualify for refugee status in "extended voluntary departure"—an inelegant phrase used to describe a

---

1. *See also* Paul Weis, *Convention Refugees and De Facto Refugees* in Melander and Nobel, eds., "African Refugees and the Law" 15–22 (1978).

practice with questionable statutory authorization. Although extended voluntary departure has received much attention lately, there have been 15 extended voluntary departure programs over the past two decades. Using both parole and extended voluntary departure, the administrative agencies have created de facto refugees for years.

My proposal is to establish some middle ground in the debate, a statutory mechanism for the recognition of some classes of de facto refugees on a temporary basis when compelling humanitarian concerns are present. The phrase "safe haven" has been suggested by others before, and I will adopt it here.

Safe haven would be granted on a group basis by a Presidential proclamation in consultation with Congress.[2] The statute authorizing the granting of safe haven should spell out certain classes of de facto refugees who might merit particular concern (such as those I have mentioned earlier), but it should also leave the President flexibility in designating groups of aliens. The statute should make clear that it creates no entitlement to safe haven and that the granting of safe haven would be a political act, unreviewable in court. Safe haven would be a temporary status, permitting the designated group to remain until the conditions which warranted the status have ended. Persons granted safe haven should be authorized to work but should not be eligible for federal benefits or for aid available to refugees.

At first glance this proposal may sound like a return to a broad parole power under another name. I do not think it is. The controversy surrounding the use of the parole power to admit refugees before the Refugee Act of 1980 largely concerned the fact that the granting of parole by the Executive Branch effectively conferred permanent resident status on the refugees. In contrast, safe haven would be a temporary status that would endow the alien with no right to become a permanent resident.

The establishment of statutory authority to grant safe haven would bring extended voluntary departure out of the shadows. The conferring of extended voluntary departure is a mysterious process, which appears to be a joint decision of the Justice and State Departments. These are the same two Departments that are involved with the adjudication of asylum claims. Both decisions—asylum and extended voluntary departure—are linked in the public mind as emanating from the same institutions for the same policy reasons. If the granting or denial of extended voluntary departure to a particular group is viewed as essentially a political decision, it is almost inevitable that asylum decisions concerning that group will also be seen as driven by political considerations.

To restore faith in the asylum process, we must create structures that help separate political decisions from asylum decisions. I believe that the establishment of authority to grant safe haven would move us in this direction. It would allow the United States to extend temporary protection to persons of humanitarian concern without either distorting the

---

2. The INA currently grants the President the power to suspend entry of any aliens or class of aliens whose entry "would be detrimental to the interests of the United States." INA § 212(f), 8 U.S.C. § 1182(f).

definition of "refugee" in our laws or increasing the number of aliens who seek permanent residence here. It would provide a statutory basis for administrative practices that have developed without careful thought or congressional oversight. It would foster public debate on issues that have previously been handled out of the public eye. And it would provide a channel for political decisions separate from the asylum process.

This proposal raises at least two problems which should be addressed. First, can any temporary status really be temporary, or is it likely that persons granted safe haven will never return home? I think the answer to this is that it depends. The original granting of "safe haven" can be analogized to the issuance of a non-immigrant visa, valid for as long as the troubling situation in the home country continues. While we know that there are many non-immigrant visa abusers, we also know that most non-immigrant aliens leave the United States once they have accomplished the purpose of their visit. Perhaps I am being somewhat naive here; perhaps history demonstrates that once certain groups are permitted to stay in this country for a few years—no matter how temporary their initial admission—political pressure mounts to adjust their status to permanent residency. I concede that this is a risk, but it is one I think the United States should be willing to take. By definition, aliens granted safe haven will have compelling humanitarian reasons for staying in the United States, even if they do not satisfy a strict interpretation of "refugee" under the INA. Furthermore, I think we tend to overestimate the percentage of persons who will want to remain permanently in this country. The best evidence we have regarding undocumented Mexican workers shows that the majority desire only a temporary stay in this country. Finally, creation of the authority to bestow safe haven will not entitle any group of aliens to receive it. If the President, in consultation with Congress, believes that certain groups are unlikely to return home, safe haven need not be granted.

A second problem concerns the magnetic effect safe haven might have. Suppose, for example, safe haven were granted to Salvadorans. Would this encourage other Salvadorans to enter the United States in order to come under the safe haven umbrella? I cannot deny that it might, but I am not sure that such a possibility should prevent the granting of safe haven. First, our porous borders apparently do not presently do a very effective job of keeping out undocumented Salvadorans. Thus it is not clear how great an incentive safe haven would add. Second, we should be greatly concerned about the return of any Salvadoran to El Salvador. In the past we have granted extended voluntary departure to Nicaraguans, Chileans, Ethiopians and Iranians during times of civil war in their countries of origin. On what humanitarian basis can we distinguish the Salvadorans?

It seems that there are six possible options for dealing with undocumented Salvadorans in the United States: (1) deport them to El Salvador; (2) deport them to Mexico; (3) place them in refugee camps pending resolution of the civil war; (4) grant them temporary safe haven; (5) grant them asylum; or (6) continue our present laissez-faire policy of deporting those we happen to find. I think the first option (deportation to El

Salvador) is immoral given the present conditions of civil strife. Deportation to Mexico may simply be the first step toward deportation to El Salvador, depending upon the actions of the Mexican government. Long-term detention of the Salvadorans is inhumane and probably the most expensive option. Granting all Salvadorans blanket refugee status would seriously distort the case-by-case adjudication of asylum claims called for by § 208 of the INA. The sixth option (continuance of our present "policy") is not acceptable because the policy is arbitrary and hypocritical. Publicly we seek to deter illegal Salvadoran immigration by returning illegal entrants we discover; but, in reality, due to inadequate enforcement and long delays in asylum adjudications, we tolerate the presence of thousands of undocumented Salvadorans in this country. In short, we have a de facto safe haven policy. It seems to me much more sensible to make this an explicit policy carried out under appropriate statutory authorization. Although a safe haven program may not be ideal, it is the best option available to us.

Chapter Nine

UNDOCUMENTED ALIENS

In previous chapters, we have been primarily concerned with lawful immigration to the United States. We have explored the visa process, numerical limitations, grounds of exclusion and the process of admission for permanent resident aliens. We have also examined other lawful avenues of entry, such as admission as a refugee, asylee, or parolee. In doing so, we may well be accused of exalting legal procedures over the true picture of immigration. For we have only barely touched upon illegal immigration to the United States.

The entry and presence of undocumented workers and their families in the United States provide perhaps the most pressing, and certainly the most controversial, aspect of immigration policy facing this nation. As we examine the issues in this Chapter, we will be confronted at every point by a dismaying lack of information and a confusing array of contradictory theories, explanations and projections. There is no scholarly agreement concerning the number of undocumented aliens presently in the United States, the effect of such workers on the employment of legal residents and U.S. citizens, the burdens that illegal aliens place on public services and programs, or the benefits that illegal workers provide to the American economy. Since there is no consensus on the scope or nature of the problem (or even if a problem exists), it should hardly surprise you that there are widely divergent views on what should be done about illegal migration.

The purpose of this Chapter is to familiarize you with the terms of the debate and the range of scholarly opinion. We suggest that you approach these materials as if you were a member of Congress considering immigration reform legislation. You should ask yourself what the goals of American immigration policy should be, how far the present deviates from the ideal, and what proposals for change are likely to be both effective and politically feasible in dealing with the problems you identify.

SECTION A. UNDOCUMENTED ALIENS IN THE UNITED STATES

1. HISTORICAL PERSPECTIVE

The current controversy regarding illegal migration cannot be understood without appreciation of the historical flow of labor across the borders of the United States. Illegal migration is but one part of the migration of labor. That flow of labor is responsive to the supply of and demand for labor here and abroad, government policies and enforcement practices, events in foreign countries, and past labor migrations. While we have chosen to label some of the migration legal and some of it illegal, to focus simply on the legal rules is to lose sight of the larger phenomenon. Moreover, some even argue that the label "illegal" is misleading because enforcement policies have, in effect, tolerated the entry of undocumented aliens.[1]

The next readings are intended to provide an historical and social picture of Mexican migration to the United States, the largest (and most studied) category of undocumented workers in this country.

SCIRP, U.S. IMMIGRATION POLICY AND THE NATIONAL INTEREST
Staff Report 465–68 (1981).

With the annexation of Texas in 1845, the Treaty of Guadalupe Hildalgo in 1848 and the Gadsen Purchase in 1854, the United States established its sovereignty over a vast territory with an existing Hispanic population.* The Mexicans who decided to remain after acquisition had the choice of retaining Mexican citizenship or becoming U.S. citizens without forfeiting the rights to their property or the freedom to practice their religion. This Mexican community remained relatively small throughout the nineteenth century, growing mainly as a result of natural increases in population rather than immigration. The lands near the Mexican border, mostly desert and plain with the exception of parts of California and Texas, were themselves inhospitable to settlement, while the terrain of the routes from Mexico to these territories made any type of travel difficult. By the end of the century, however, technological innovations had conquered many of the obstacles to migration. Railroads made travel easier, and agricultural irrigation made many more jobs available in the Southwest.

At the same time, a growing differential in wages between Mexico and the United States and a high level of inflation in Mexico, made migration all the more attractive. In addition, a growing amount of internal migration in Mexico paved the way for movement across the border. The first serious student of Mexican migration, Victor S. Clark, writing in 1908, suggested that Mexicans migrating to Texas "come largely from the migratory labor class of their own country." The development of mining and industry in northern Mexico was attracting settlers from the southern part of the country; these internal migrants often gained skills that they could later convert into higher wages in the

1. *See* Fogel, *Illegal Alien Workers in the United States,* 16 Indus.Rel. 243, 246 (1977): "[I]llegal immigration from Mexico has been an integral part of a *de facto* U.S. policy with respect to use of Mexican labor. Bluntly stated, the *de facto* policy has been—bring them in when they are needed, send them back when they aren't."

* Under the Treaty of Guadalupe Hildago, following the war with Mexico, the United States came into possession of about one-third of Mexico's territory, including California, and not including Texas. The Gadsen Purchase annexed another 30,000 square miles in what is now Arizona and New Mexico.

United States. Some worked for U.S.-owned mines in Mexico, and there became familiar with opportunities and customs that prevailed north of the border.

Between 1900 and 1930 over 700,000 Mexican immigrants were legally admitted to the United States. Many thousands more entered without inspection or the permission of U.S. authorities. Two historians estimate that more than one million undocumented Mexicans may have settled in the United States during this period. Some came into the country illegally because they were unfamiliar with U.S. regulations; others wished to avoid the expense of a visa and head tax. Many were recruited by labor contractors, some of whom openly advertised in border towns despite the restrictions on recruitment in the Alien Contract Labor Law of 1885. Since it was not illegal to sign contracts with workers on the U.S. side of the border, most recruiters waited until the aliens crossed the border before hiring them. The Mexicans, for their part, became familiar with and adapted themselves to these practices. According to Clark's 1908 study, Mexican migrants "appear at the border in sombrero, serape, and sandals, which, before crossing the river, they usually exchange for a suit of 'American' clothing, shoes, and a less conspicuous hat. In fact, at Juarez and at El Paso a thriving trade of old clothes has sprung up to meet this demand."

During the financial-boom days of the 1920s, most U.S. citizens were indifferent to the immigration of Mexicans, whatever their legal status. Some official steps were taken, though, during this period to control illegal entry. In 1924 the Border Patrol was formed in the Immigration and Naturalization Service to police both the Mexican and Canadian borders. During the next several years, funding and personnel increases for the Border Patrol were matched by increases in the numbers of aliens apprehended trying to enter the country. In 1925, 4,641 smuggled aliens were apprehended, while in 1929, over 29,000 were captured. During the same decade, the numbers of deportations also increased, from 2,762 in 1920 to 12,908 in 1929.

CONGRESSIONAL RESEARCH SERVICE, ILLEGAL ALIENS: ANALYSIS AND BACKGROUND

House Committee on the Judiciary, 95th Cong., 1st Sess., 50–55, 48–49 (Comm.Print 1977).

Mexicans were first made an exception to the general rule of U.S. immigration policy under an administrative Departmental Order of 1918 issued by the Commissioner General of Immigration, with approval of the Secretary of Labor. This order waived the head tax, contract labor laws, and literacy requirements for Mexican laborers, under the authority of the ninth proviso to Section 3 of the Immigration Act of 1917.[52] The Departmental Order was a wartime measure as was, approximately 25 years later, the Bracero program. Both continued in effect well after the end of the immediate manpower shortages they had been created to meet.

In 1929, in action apparently inspired more by a desire to head off restrictionist efforts to place a statutory ceiling on Mexican immigration

52. Act of Feb. 5, 1917, 39 Stat. 878.

than by an awareness of the impending economic depression, administrative control of the Mexican border was significantly tightened.   * * *
[T]he State Department believed that such a ceiling would have a harmful effect on our relations with Mexico.   During the lengthy debate on the subject at the end of the 1920s, the State Department combined an appeal to Pan-Americanism with more stringent enforcement of the provisions of existing immigration law in a successful attempt to decrease immigration levels in the opening years of the depression.   According to a State Department press release in June 1930,

> ... proper enforcement of existing immigration laws can and will
> be maintained in the future, in Mexico as in other countries, so as
> to prevent effectively the recurrence of conditions existing a few
> years ago, when the recorded admissions of Mexican laborers
> were very high.

The public view of alien workers in the early 1930s, during the opening years of the Great Depression, is described by one commentator as follows: "In the manner of a crusade, the idea was promulgated that aliens were holding down high-paying jobs and that by giving those jobs to Americans, the depression could be cured."[54]   The Los Angeles *Times* quoted the Los Angeles County Supervisor as saying, "If we were rid of the aliens who have entered this country illegally since 1931 ... our present unemployment would probably shrink to the proportions of a relatively flat spot in business."

During the 1930s, Mexican out-migration far exceeded immigration— more than 89,000 legally admitted Mexicans left the United States, compared to 27,900 who immigrated on a permanent visa.   The factors involved were many, including both the dismal employment prospects here, and wide-scale "repatriation."   According to one author, "the outstanding feature of this troubled era, in the Southwest as well as elsewhere, was the repatriation of numerous people of Mexican descent—of legal and illegal immigrants, temporary workers and permanent residents, U.S. citizens and aliens."[57]   Of those leaving, some were deported illegal aliens, and others were legally admitted Mexicans returning voluntarily or involuntarily, some with the assistance of the Mexican government.   The withholding of U.S. welfare payments to which the "Mexicans" were legally entitled was among the means used to induce them to leave.   The Mexican born population in this country declined from 639,-000 in 1930 to 377,000 in 1940.

In 1942, in response to the U.S. manpower shortage arising from World War II, the United States and Mexico negotiated a treaty permitting the entry of Mexican farm workers on a temporary basis under contract to U.S. employers.   This emergency wartime measure was the beginning of the Bracero program, which continued under various legal

54. Vilma S. Martinez, "Illegal Immigration and the Labor Force: An Historical and Legal View," American Behavioral Scientist, Vol. 19, Jan./Feb. 1976, p. 340.

57. Leo Grebler, Mexican Immigration to the United States: the Record and its Implications. Mexican-American Study Project, Advance Report 2, Dec. 1965, p. 25.

authorizations for 22 years and involved approximately 4.8 million Mexican workers.

The program operated on the basis of international treaty until 1951. On July 12, 1951, Congress enacted Public Law 78 (65 Stat. 119) authorizing the importation of temporary Mexican agricultural workers under the Agricultural Act of 1949, as amended. This authorization originally had an expiration date of Dec. 31, 1951. It was extended by successive amendments until Dec. 31, 1964, when it was allowed to expire.

The Bracero program's lengthy history is both complex and controversial. One of the more intriguing controversies is whether it was a cause or a cure of the illegal alien problem of the time. It appears to have been both. Without question, both its existence and its termination are causes of the current illegal alien problem.

The Bracero program is credited with "the dramatic reduction, if not the total elimination, of the Wetback traffic" by Ernesto Galarza in his otherwise highly critical examination of the program:

> Between 1920 and 1954 commercial agriculture in the border states, operating by its own admission above the law and beneath morals, had organized a freely flowing labor market that brought together rich lands and poor men. It was an arrangement that did not commend itself to many. Its beneficiaries were a small group of employers in a comparatively narrow belt of borderlands whose easy access to illegals gave them an advantage over their northern competitors. The incidents of the Wetback way of life made the governments of two great republics blush, the Mexican with indignation, the American with shame. The traffic was suppressed only when it became possible to assure farm employers, substantially on their terms, that they could have as many contract laborers as they might demand.[60]

Average annual apprehensions of illegal aliens were less than 80,000 during the ten-year period, 1956–1965, following Operation Wetback, the full-scale roundup of Mexican illegal aliens led by the Border Patrol in 1954–1955. Commenting on the success of the INS Operation Wetback in dealing with the illegal alien problem in the mid-1950s, Galarza indicates that a key factor was

> ... the change in attitude of farm employers, hundreds of whom had come to accept the legal *braceros* as a practical and safe alternative [to Wetbacks] and had joined associations to procure them. By the time the operation was launched the bracero system had shown its economic and political feasibility.[61]

On the other hand, Julian Samora, among others, argues that the Bracero program actually stimulated illegal migration to the United States, in part because more Mexicans wished to come than were legally permitted, and partly because it was often easier to enter illegally than

60. Ernest Galarza. Merchants of Labor.   **61.** Ibid., p. 70.
McNally and Loftin, 1964, p. 255.

legally.[62] Samora notes that during the 22-year life of the Bracero program, over 5 million wetbacks were apprehended, a figure exceeding the 4.8 million braceros contracted.[63]

Regarding other aspects of the Bracero program, the 1951 President's Commission on Migratory Labor was among the many critics of what it saw to be the program's adverse impact on U.S. farm labor:

> It is our conclusion that the evidence demonstrates that the agencies of Government responsible for importing and contracting foreign labor have not been successful in protecting domestic farm labor from detrimental effects of imported contract alien labor. We find alien labor has depressed farm wages and, therefore, has been detrimental to domestic labor.

Considering the program in the context of national immigration policy, the Commission was equally critical:

> Thus, temporary foreign laborers passing in and out of this country with little restriction have come to substitute for a supply subject to stringent numerical restrictions, thereby furnishing the very competition to American labor that it is the purpose of the immigration law to prevent.

> This undermining of national policy stands out more clearly in that it has been the negotiators for foreign governments, notably of Mexico, rather than our own representatives, who have secured reasonable limitation of numbers and some protection to labor standards. While their motive is primarily to protect the standards of their own nationals working in the United States, the effect of their concern, fortunately, is also to help sustain the tenets of American policy. The contrast in this curious difference of attitudes is heightened by the fact that through the negotiations of their governments, foreign laborers have actually achieved, in most instances, better living and working conditions than domestic workers whose protection is a main concern of American immigration law.

It will be noted that the responsible U.S. administrative agencies, rather than U.S. employers or the braceros themselves, are the primary objects of the Commission's criticism. Thus, the passage quoted above is preceded by the following:

> ... official vigilance for the protection of living and working standards of alien farm laborers was largely abandoned in the postwar phase. Responsible United States administrative agencies practically ceased to exert effective effort to preserve the requirements of national immigration policy. The same ineffectiveness or laxity that undermined protective standards in the contract spread also to the official scrutiny of the number of foreign laborers that employers claimed they needed.

62. [J. Samora, *Los Mojados: The Wet-*   **63.** *Ibid.,* p. 19.
back Story (1971),] pp. 44–45.

Similar observations are carefully documented by Galarza, who implicitly—and sometimes explicitly—charges collusion between the U.S. Department of Labor and U.S. employers involved in agribusiness in the administration of the Bracero program.

Apprehensions of illegal aliens began mounting steadily with the termination of the Bracero program in mid-sixties. Quoting from the INS 1970 *Annual Report,*

> Since expiration of the Mexican Agriculture Act on December 31, 1964, the number of deportable aliens located has continued an upward climb. For the 6-year period, fiscal years 1965–70, 71 percent of the 1,251,466 total deportable aliens located were of Mexican nationality. Year by year, the annual percentage of this nationality group has risen, from 50 percent in 1965 to 80 percent this year.

The patterns of employment which grew up during the Bracero period, as well as the elimination of legal channels for temporary employment provided by the program, are viewed by many as significant causal factors in the current illegal alien problem. The case is well stated as follows:

> Another significant "pull" factor is a clear result of former American policy. Many Mexicans who were employed as braceros brought their families with them to the border areas and relied on American employment as their sole source of income. When the bracero program was terminated, the only work available to the ex-bracero was illegal employment in the United States. In short, the present influx of illegals reflects the operation of socioeconomic forces set in motion by the United States over two decades ago.[68]

This analysis is borne out by research cited by the Domestic Council Committee on Illegal Aliens:

> Several studies have also pointed out that the areas [in Mexico] from which many illegal aliens come are precisely those areas which provided the bulk of the "braceros" during the life of that program (1942–1964). One researcher [Wayne Cornelius] has suggested that the "bracero" program in a sense never stopped, but merely went underground.[69]

From the point of view of the U.S. employers who hire them, the illegal alien has replaced the legal bracero worker. Writing in 1960, Galarza noted:

> In considering alternatives to Public Law 78 [authority for the Bracero program], the return of the Wetback could not be ruled out. This did not seem probable, especially in the light of

68. Note, *Commuters, Illegals and American Farmworkers: the Need for a Broader Approach to Domestic Farm Labor Problems,* New York University Law Review, vol. 48, June 1973, p. 482.

69. [U.S.] Domestic Council Committee on Illegal Aliens, [Preliminary Report] (Dec. 1976), p. 135.

public reaction in the middle 1950's. The indignation of high federal officials, influential citizens, religious organizations and even farm employers over the evils of labor bootlegging might be aroused again. But the door was not entirely closed. When the immigration code was revised in 1952 it was carefully provided that employers could not be prosecuted for harboring illegals. . . . Senator Hayden once warned his colleagues that the demand for laborers north of the border and their abundance south of it would be brought together legally if possible, and outside the law if it could not be done otherwise. Congressman Poage of Texas urged the House of Representatives in June 1960 to extend Public Law 78 on the ground that otherwise "there is going to be a stream of wetbacks to fill all of the area close to the border." Braceros on their terms or Wetbacks remained a feasible choice, in the opinion of many employers.[70]

From the point of view of the aliens themselves, the 22-year program, in the words of the North-Houstoun report, "created patterns of explicitly work-related movements of aliens, from South to North." Continuing:

> . . . it created the braceros' expectations of higher wages than were possible within the Mexican economy; it provided them with U.S. job contacts and job skills; it exposed them to the Anglo demand for their labor; language and Anglo customs—including the work habits of INS. For many rural Mexican males, the bracero program was an eye-opener; they learned about American jobs and American wages; many responded to their U.S. employers' interest in bypassing the federally regulated program during its existence; and many kept traveling north after the program ended, despite the fact those trips were illegal ones.[71]

It can be argued that the bracero program reinforced rather than created these patterns which, in fact, originated not with the labor shortage of World War II, but of World War I. Thus, Cardenas describes the Departmental Order of 1918 as, "in terms of the United States immigration policy toward Mexico, . . . the first Bracero Program."[72]

The Mexican component of the current illegal alien problem can be viewed as an unregulated and illegal continuation of the Bracero program, with all the evils this suggests, including the exploitation of alien workers, and the lack of protection of domestic workers from adverse competition.
* * *

* * *

It is argued that the underlying rationale governing our immigration policy toward Mexico is the ebb and flow of the U.S. need for Mexican labor. The pattern has been a cyclical one, in which periods of a high demand for Mexican workers have been followed—coincidentally, at 20

---

70. Galarza (1964), pp. 251–252.

71. [D. North & M. Houstoun, *The Characteristics and Role of Illegal Aliens in the U.S. Labor Market: An Exploratory Study* (March 1976)], p. 12.

72. [G. Cardenas, *United States Immigration Policy toward Mexico: An Historical Perspective,* 2 Chicano L. Rev. 66, 68 (1975).]

year intervals—by periods when Mexican workers are more or less officially viewed as a threat to American labor generally because of disturbances in the U.S. economy. According to this argument, the "illegal alien problem" of the 1970s is the result less of a sudden upsurge in the number of illegals, but of a downturn in U.S. economic conditions.

A similar observation was made in general terms, without specific reference to Mexico, by the Domestic Council Committee on Illegal Aliens: "illegal migration in times of prosperity tends to be viewed as a handmaiden of economic growth but it becomes transformed into a threat in times of economic downturn." [44] North and Houstoun spell out the implications of this interpretation, again in general terms, as follows:

> Increasingly adverse public opinion should not, however be simply attributed to increasing adverse effects of this underground and therefore obviously unknown phenomenon. The public outcry against illegal aliens too closely resembles the 1930s, when similar ascriptions of their adverse economic role, under all too similar conditions, led to the "repatriation" of tens of thousands of Mexicans, with little regard for their real legal status, or their legal relatives. Public concern with the economic adversities brought about by illegals today likewise coincides with a time of scarcity, both real and perceived, when the interests of all groups seem threatened. [45]

With specific reference to Mexico, far from blaming the illegal aliens for the present problem, Cardenas assigns much of the responsibility for illegal immigration to the past practices of the United States:

> ... Mexican aliens in the United States have entered at the behest and through the active solicitation and encouragement of many of the same economic interests that today proselytize for their expulsion and exclusion through the rigorous application or change in immigration laws. For example, serving as open invitations to Mexican migration have been bracero type programs throughout this century, allowing commuter status, and utilization of illegals. In these forms Mexican aliens have been told that their labor is welcomed in the United States, and they have responded accordingly.

> The "illegal alien" problem is therefore one whose seed has been planted time and again by the United States when it has been in need of Mexican labor. When expediency better serves, however, immigration laws have been administered and changed in response to a problem perceived as having been created by illegal aliens, when in fact it is largely of the United States' own making. [46]

44. Domestic Council Committee on Illegal Aliens report (Dec.1976), p. 2.

45. North/Houstoun study (March 1976), p. 29.

46. Cardenas (1975), pp. 88–89.

Without question, the statistical pattern of Mexican entries to this country is unique, in terms of the heavy dominance of temporary workers and illegals. According to North and Houstoun, "Almost ten times as many Mexican nonimmigrant workers and apprehended illegals were reported to have crossed its 1,945-mile land border, as compared to the number of Mexican immigrants between the years 1870–1970." [47]

Julian Samora describes the problem in more detail:

> The number of illegal Mexicans reportedly located is particularly significant when compared to legal Mexican immigration. In the last 100 years, no more than 1,525,928 Mexicans were admitted into the United States as legal immigrants. In the twenty-six year period from 1942 to 1968, 5,050,093 Mexican nationals were imported into the United States as temporary contract laborers (braceros). Yet, in the forty-five year period from 1924 to 1969, 5,628,712 illegal Mexican aliens were reportedly located (apprehended) by the United States Immigration and Naturalization Service. [48]

Samora interprets these statistics as reflecting "the evolution of an immigration policy that may best be understood as an extensive farm labor program," and continues "This policy stands out as a legitimized and profitable means of acquiring needed labor without incurring the price that characterized the immigration, utilization, and the eventual settlement of European and Oriental immigrants." [49]

A related interpretation of the causes underlying the early development of the apparently symbiotic relationship between Mexican workers and certain U.S. employers is presented, in terms more favorable to the U.S., by North and Houstoun in their recent Labor Department-financed study, as follows:

> Given the developing labor-intensive economy in the north and the pool of unskilled labor in the south, a historic precedent of northbound migration, the Spanish-speaking culture which bridged the border, and the political insignificance (for so many years) of the border itself, workers moved easily from their homes in Mexico to jobs in the States, as those jobs came into being. [50]

WAYNE A. CORNELIUS, MEXICAN MIGRATION TO THE UNITED STATES: THE LIMITS OF GOVERNMENT INTERVENTION

2–4 (Working Papers in U.S.–Mexican Studies, 5) (1981).

It is important to recognize that Mexican migration to the United States represents a deeply institutionalized, multigenerational social process. Ever since United States railroads and agricultural employers began recruiting workers in Mexico in the mid-1880s, there has been a

---

47. North/Houstoun study (March 1976), p. 9.

48. Samora (1971), p. 57.

49. *Ibid.*

50. North/Houstoun study (March 1976), p. 11.

continuous flow of migrants to the United States Southwest and the Midwest industrial corridor (cities like Chicago, Detroit, and Gary). While there have been several major waves of Mexican migration to the United States (the latest dating from the late 1960s) the movement of Mexican workers back and forth across the border has never ceased during the last hundred years, even during the Great Depression.

This migratory process often spans three or more generations within the same families, particularly in the villages and towns of Mexico's central plateau region and several of the northern states bordering the United States. These areas have supplied the majority of Mexican migrants for at least the last sixty years. The most recent data, from a nationwide sample survey of 62,500 households in Mexico completed in January 1979, confirm that the eleven central plateau states continue to provide nearly 70 percent of the migrants, and the northern border counties contribute another 11 percent. Taken together, these states and counties, which contain only about a third of Mexico's total population, supply more than 80 percent of all migrants to the United States.[3]

This high concentration of migratory activity in certain regions and localities of Mexico makes it more likely that local attitudes, expectations, and traditions supportive of migration will develop. Numerous field studies conducted during the past five years have demonstrated the existence of communities and regions where residents seem to "specialize" in migrating to the United States in search of employment opportunities. Among nine rural communities in northeastern Jalisco studied by the author in 1975–76, the proportion of adult residents who had worked in the United States varied from 22 percent in one community to 74 percent in another. It is common to find communities in central plateau states like Michoacan, Zacatecas, and Guanajuato where more than half of all working residents have been employed at some time in the United States.

Over a period of several decades, these areas have become increasingly dependent on cash income earned in the United States, both by residents working temporarily in the United States and sending part of their earnings to dependents at home and by former residents who have moved permanently to the United States but still send money from time to time to relatives in Mexico. For people in these areas, migration to the United States has indeed become a way of life. They grow up viewing employment in the United States as one of the few options available to them for subsisting and for accumulating the capital needed to achieve some long-term economic mobility for themselves or their children.

A century of migration from these places has led to the development of many thousands of binational kinship-employer networks that directly link potential migrants in Mexico to their United States-based relatives and United States employers. These networks play a fundamental role in making migration an attractive and economically feasible option for many

3. Carlos H. Zazueta and Fernando Mercado, "*El Mercado de Trabajo Norteamericano y los Trabajadores Mexicanos*" (Paper presented at the Mexico-United States Seminar on Undocumented Migration, Centro de Estudios Economicos y Sociales del Tercer Mundo, Mexico, D.F., September 4–6, 1980), p. 19.

Mexicans. The migrant's choice of destination is influenced primarily by the location of job opportunities, which in turn is influenced mainly by the presence of relatives and friends in those places.

The United States-based portion of the kinship network serves as an informal employment agency for newly arriving migrants. It communicates information about job opportunities in the United States to the migrants even before they leave their hometowns. After the migrants arrive in the United States, their relatives introduce them to potential employers, often the same ones employing the relatives. The relatives become aware of job openings in their workplaces as soon as they occur, sometimes even before the employer knows that a given employee intends to leave, and assist the employer in filling the vacancies. Thus the United States-based relatives serve as labor recruiters for their American employers. In particular businesses this results in large clusters of workers who come from the same town in Mexico and even from the same extended family.

Among Mexican workers now migrating to the United States, the vast majority have relatives and friends who preceded them to the United States. This is particularly true of those who migrate with the intention of remaining in the United States as permanent residents, contrasted with those who migrate only for short-term employment. Among 822 Mexican immigrants interviewed in one recent study, all of whom had sought and obtained permanent legal resident status in the United States, less than 3 percent had no familial or friendship ties in the United States at the time of their entry as permanent resident aliens.[4] Among 185 Mexican immigrants (both legal and undocumented) the author interviewed in 1978 in California and Illinois, most of whom were permanently resettled in the United States, 82 percent had fathers and 53 percent had grandfathers who had migrated at least once to the United States. Thus the settlement of this third generation in the United States represents the continuation of an extensive family history of migration over a sixty to seventy year period. Many of the interviewees also had Mexico-based relatives who continued to migrate for temporary employment.

This is the complex social reality to which United States immigration policy must respond. Regardless of what policy is adopted, it is quite impossible at this time to legislate these binational kinship-employer networks out of existence. The United States cannot turn the clock back to the mid-1880s, when many of these networks began to form, or to the early 1940s, when labor recruitment in Mexico under the bracero program brought of thousands of new communities into the migratory stream. The existence of family and community traditions of migration actively supported by relatives and employers makes it more likely that each succeeding generation will participate in the movement, at a level that is not determined by public policies.

4. Marta Tienda, "Familism and Structural Assimilation of Mexican Immigrants in the United States," *International Migration Review* 14 (Fall 1980): 395.

2. CHARACTERISTICS OF UNDOCUMENTED ALIENS

It is commonly assumed that nearly all illegal aliens in the United States are citizens of Mexico, that they all cross the southwest border of the United States by swimming the Rio Grande or traversing the desert, that most do "stoop labor" in Texas or California, that most earn below the minimum wage, and that many come to the United States to gain access to generous public assistance programs. While there is much we do not know about undocumented workers, it is fairly well established that this "conventional wisdom" is wrong.[3]

It is true that the vast majority of illegal aliens *apprehended* in the United States are from Mexico. Over the past several years, more than 90% of the one million aliens arrested each year for illegal border crossing were Mexican. But these numbers reflect INS enforcement priorities more than the composition of the undocumented alien population in the United States. By most estimates, Mexicans constitute no more than 50 to 60% of the illegal aliens in the United States.[4] Who are the others, why do they come and how do they arrive? The following materials offer some answers.

a. How Many Undocumented Aliens Reside in the United States?

JOHN CREWDSON, THE TARNISHED DOOR: THE NEW
IMMIGRANTS AND THE TRANSFORMATION OF
AMERICA 98–106 (1983)

[A]t the bottom of every debate over immigration policy there is a fundamental question: How many foreigners are living in the United States without permission? One might as well ask an astronomer how many stars are in the universe. The answer is not only that no one knows but that no one can ever know. Because illegal aliens are in the country illegally and because they take some pains to keep themselves invisible, no record exists of who or where they are. If they could be counted, after all, they could also be deported. Estimates proliferate; but they are only estimates, and the confusion that has resulted from claims by competing interests has contributed neither to understanding the new immigration nor to mapping realistic policies to control and shape it.

A few authorities recognize the dangers inherent in the numbers game. Among them is Lawrence Fuchs, the distinguished Brandeis historian picked to head the Select Commission on Immigration and Refugee Policy, who dismisses the existing research on the number of illegal immigrants with the admonition that "Gossip about gossip is still gossip." Such cautions, however, have done little to prevent a number of responsible officials, academies, and institutions from using such figures as exist to try to quantify illegal immigration. Douglas Massey, the Princeton

---

3. For a summary of current public perceptions of illegal migration, *see* W. Cornelius, *America in the Era of Limits: Nativist Reactions to the 'New' Immigration* (Work-

ing Papers in U.S.—Mexican Studies, 3) (1982).

4. *See* SCIRP, Staff Report 454.

demographer, puts the number of illegal aliens in the United States at around 4 million. So does the CIA. The State Department says it is 7 million. *The Washington Post* estimates that between 250,000 and 500,-000 are coming here each year. Maxwell Taylor, the retired chairman of the Joint Chiefs of Staff, thinks the number is a cool 1 million. The Environmental Fund assures subscribers to its newsletter that "The Border Patrol knows that for every illegal alien who is apprehended, perhaps four go uncaught" and that "those who are caught eventually get in." Zero Population Growth warns that "one-fourth to one-half" of the nation's population growth is attributable to immigration. The Federation for American Immigration Reform (FAIR) declares that the number of illegal aliens who have come here over the past decade totals more than 4 million.

All these assertions share two things in common: there is no evidence that any of them is true. There is also no evidence that any of them is not true. There is no evidence, period. Not that those who debate the immigration issue can be blamed for tossing such numbers around. So many of the questions that surround illegal immigration depend for answers on how many illegal aliens there are. And the government, after all, has been playing the immigration numbers game ever since 1972, when the INS first put the number of illegal aliens in the country at an even million. Three years later, Leonard F. Chapman, the commissioner of immigration, touched off an alien "scare" when he spoke of "a vast army" of 4 to 12 million Mexicans. The INS refused to make the basis for either of the estimates public—for the simple reason, officials conceded later, that neither had any basis in fact. But it hurriedly reduced its "official" estimate to between 5 and 8 million, a figure it obtained by the highly unscientific method of asking its regional directors for their best guesses about the number of illegal aliens living and working in their jurisdictions. Then, in 1978, the INS lowered the number further still, to somewhere between 3 and 6 million.

The only certainty in all this was that while the government's estimates of the number of illegal aliens were decreasing, the number of aliens was increasing; no one suggests that there were fewer illegals in the country in 1978 than in 1975. Leonel Castillo, Jimmy Carter's immigration commissioner, himself called the 1978 estimate "soft," and it may have been no accident that it came in the midst of an economic recession, at a time when the Carter administration might have wished to play down the potential impact of illegal aliens on the job market. Nor was it a coincidence that when the Mexican government, acutely sensitive to the rising antialien sentiment in this country, released its own estimate in 1980, it was the lowest of all, a mere 488,000 to 1.22 million.

The U.S. Census Bureau countered with a figure of 3 to 5 million that, though much higher, was still well below the Chapman era estimates. Although both the Census Bureau and Mexican government estimates received considerable publicity at the time, like those that had come before, neither had any foundation in fact. The INS and the Census Bureau both have since acknowledged the obvious—that you cannot count what you cannot see, that there is simply no way of knowing how many illegal aliens are entering the United States or how many are already here.

* * *

Wayne Cornelius, the noted University of California researcher who has interviewed hundreds of Mexicans returning home from the United States about their experiences here, believes that for every illegal Mexican alien who settles in this country, as many as eight others "commute" between their homes in Mexico and their jobs in the United States. Largely for that reason, Cornelius argues, the number of illegal aliens living permanently in the States is relatively small, somewhere between 1 million and 3 million. Other experts dispute his estimate as too low, suggesting that while he does have some good data, they do not support all his conclusions; even Cornelius agrees that "no one can estimate with any precision what the total numbers of illegals of all nationalities are."

* * *

The apprehension statistics, which have fluctuated greatly over the years, did not begin their geometric increase until the mid-1960's. Despite the high unemployment rates that prevailed during the Great Depression, for example, only 14,000 illegal aliens were caught, on the average, in each of the depression years. During most of World War II, when thousands of Mexican farmworkers were imported under the Bracero Program to offset the agricultural labor shortage caused by the drafting of domestic workers, the number of apprehensions was even lower. It began to rise again following the war, averaging around 500,000 a year until 1954, when the notorious Operation Wetback raids netted just over 1 million illegals, most of them Mexican workers in California and the Southwest. Over the next decade the number of apprehensions dropped again, to around 100,000 a year. But after the Bracero Program was ended in 1964, many of the Mexicans who had worked in this country under its auspices began returning to the United States illegally. As a result, between 1965 and 1969 apprehensions of illegal aliens averaged 200,000 a year, reaching 345,000 in 1970. Two years later apprehensions passed 500,000, and in 1976 they numbered 866,000. The million mark was reached in 1977, and the total has hovered near there ever since: 1,057,977 in 1978; 1,076,418 in 1979; 910,000 in 1980.

Like visa approvals and denials, the apprehension statistics are a good crude indicator of the order of magnitude of illegal immigration, but they contain some gaping holes. One * * * is that because the bulk of the INS's resources are concentrated along the Mexican border, it is there that most of the apprehensions occur. Meantime, the far more sparsely guarded Canadian border remains wide open to illegal alien traffic, and the relatively small number of apprehensions made there each year is probably no longer indicative of the true scope of the cross-Canada border traffic. A far more important statistical problem, however, is that many of those arrested along either border are repeat offenders. Because the Border Patrol lacks the resources to detain, deport, or prosecute all but the tiniest fraction, when it catches an illegal alien, he is almost always permitted to return home, usually within a few hours, free to try his luck again. (Fewer than 5 percent of the illegal aliens apprehended in this country are ever formally deported.) When the same alien is caught crossing the border a second time, or a third, or a fourth, he becomes a separate statistic. Because of the INS's chaotic record-keeping system, and because many aliens never give the Border Patrol the same name twice, there is no way to separate repeat offenders from first-time border crossers. One INS inspector says, "I've got one friend from Mexico who's been arrested thirty times over the years, and each time he's recorded as a completely different guy. The records don't ever cross." The inspector's point, frequently lost in the debate over illegal immigration, is that the number of apprehensions of illegal aliens in a given year—a statistic that has become a favorite of everyone on both sides of the debate—is probably larger, and perhaps considerably larger, than the number of living, breathing human beings who tried to cross the border in that year.

The problem is that no one knows how much larger. On the average, 1 apprehended alien in 3 admits during questioning that he has been arrested before. But how many times before and in which years are not recorded, and even if they were, there would be no reason to accept such answers as truthful. Nor is there any reason to believe that the 7 aliens in every 10 who deny prior arrests are telling the truth. The result, a most unfortunate one from the standpoint of the policymakers, is that the number of aliens apprehended trying to enter the country each year tells us nothing. A million apprehensions might mean anything: It could represent 500,000 aliens, each of whom was arrested twice; or 250,000 aliens, each arrested four times; or only 100,000 aliens, each arrested ten times. And even if the answer to *that* question was known, there is no way of knowing what happened to those aliens in the end. Did all of them finally succeed in evading arrest and enter the United States successfully, or did only half succeed and the other half give up and go home, or what?

Because the Border Patrol's manpower has not increased by anything even remotely matching the increase in apprehensions, however, it is safe to assume that the ever-increasing number of illegal aliens caught over the past decade probably means that more of them are coming than before. But despite the appeal of apprehension statistics to headline writers (ILLEGAL IMMIGRATION UP 34%), despite the INS's use of them to back its pleas for more funds, despite the temptation for academicians to use them as a basis for suggesting improvements in immigration policy, even knowing exactly how many illegal aliens were caught in any year would be of no use whatever in determining how many were not caught. And that, of course, is what we need to know. One might, for example, interpret the drop in 1980 apprehensions as representing a lessening of the cross-border flow when, in fact, that flow was probably greater than ever; central Mexico was hit by a severe drought that year, ruining crops and forcing many small farmers, who in other years would have stayed home, across the border in search of work. The drop in apprehensions occurred because of gasoline and manpower shortages that resulted when hundreds of Border Patrol agents were pulled off the Mexican border and sent to Key West to handle the Mariel crisis.

Even INS agents cannot agree on how many illegal aliens there are. Some veterans are convinced that they catch only 1 illegal alien in every 10. Others put the figure at 1 in 5, the most cautious at 1 out of every 2. Not knowing how many aliens are caught to begin with makes such impressionistic estimates worthless, but some scholars have nonetheless relied on them in trying to "count" the illegal alien traffic, an enterprise that is even more futile when one considers that illegal border crossers are by no means the only illegal aliens.

Hundreds of thousands of inadmissible aliens enter the country each year with bogus passports and other documents, not to mention the visa abusers, who come as tourists or students and overstay their visas. As with the border crossers, no one knows how many visa abusers there are, and only by making a number of impossible assumptions do the available data lend themselves to the formulation of "upper" and "lower" estimates.

Assume, for example, that every illegal alien apprehended last year by the INS was caught nine other times that same year and decided to go home following his tenth arrest. Assume, further, that the INS catches 1 alien out of every 2 who come here and that of those who escape detection, only 1 in 8 settles permanently in the United States. Assume, finally, that of the 1.2 million foreign visitors last year who were never recorded as leaving the United States, 9 out of 10 are nothing more than record-keeping errors and that of the remaining 10 percent half eventually leave on their own. In that case, the number of illegal aliens taking up permanent residence in the United States last year was a mere 72,500. Assume, on the other hand, that every alien apprehended is a first-time offender, that the immigration service catches only 1 alien in 10, and that 1 out of every 2 aliens who get by the INS remains here permanently. Assume, also, that all of the 1.2 million foreign travelers unaccounted for are still here and plan on staying. In that case, the country gained 5.7 million new illegal alien residents last year.

It can therefore be stated with near-absolute certainty that the number of illegal aliens who entered the United States in 1980 is somewhere between 72,500 and 5.7 million. As with the number of stars in the universe, any other number is just a guess. For whatever they are worth, however, most guesses by what are commonly referred to as responsible observers suggest that there were between 1 million and 3 million illegal aliens living in the United States in 1975 and that there have been half a million new arrivals each year since then. Such an assumption would put the current number of illegal aliens at between 4 million and 6 million, or about 3 percent of the nation's current population of 226 million, not a very large number. But as should now be clear, even that estimate is not worth very much. None of this is meant to suggest, by the way, that the current concern over illegal immigration and its effects on the American economy is unfounded, only that those who play the numbers game are at risk. Clearly a good many people from other countries now wish to live and work in this country. Just as clearly many more of them are coming here now than ever before. Almost certainly the new arrivals number at least a couple of hundred thousand a year, and there are probably several million people now living in this country without official permission.[a]

b.   What Are the Characteristics of the Undocumented Worker Population?

The path-breaking study on the demographic make-up of the undocumented alien population in the United States was conducted by David S. North and Marion F. Houstoun in 1976.   The study was based on interviews with 793 apprehended illegal aliens (of whom 481 were from Mexico) who had worked for wages for at least two weeks in the United States.   Obviously, it is impossible to conduct scientific random sampling of the undocumented population.   Thus, the authors recognize that "[e]xtrapolation of the quantitative survey results to the universe from which the sample was drawn * * * requires judgment, and the reader must remain aware that generalizations reached by such a procedure may be in error."   Furthermore, the authors were particularly careful to point out that (1) the reported high rate of tax payment and the relatively low rate of welfare usage are what might be expected from a study group such as this one of healthy working-age males, and (2) that the extent to which the undocumented make use of income-transfer programs can best be obtained by research conducted within those programs.   Nonetheless, the North and Houstoun study remains the best guess we have of the characteristics of illegal migrants in the United States.

DAVID NORTH & MARION HOUSTOUN, THE CHARACTERISTICS AND ROLE OF ILLEGAL ALIENS IN THE U.S. LABOR MARKET: AN EXPLORATORY STUDY

S-4 to S-14 (March 1976).

SURVEY FINDINGS

1. *Motivation in Coming to the U.S.*   Almost three-quarters (74.2%) of the 793 respondents reported they came to the U.S. to get a job.   The 481 Mexican illegals were more likely to have come to the U.S. for economic reasons than were the 237 illegals from other nations in the Western Hemisphere (WH respondents) or the 75 illegals from the Eastern Hemisphere (EH respondents): 88.9% of the Mexican, 60.4% of the WH, and 23.0% of the EH respondents reported that they came to the United States in order to get a job.   Other reasons reported by the respondents were "to see U.S." (8.9% of the study group), "to study" (7.5%), "to visit relatives" (4.4%), and "other" (4.8%).   In addition, though all respondents were required by INS to return to their country of origin, a majority (414 respondents) said they planned to come back to the United States, primarily 283 reported, to get (or, in a few instances, to keep) a job here.

2. *Entry Technique.*   A substantial majority (70.7%) of the 785 respondents to a question concerning their status at entry were EWI

---

a. *See also,* Corwin, *The Numbers Game: Estimates of Illegal Aliens in the United* States, 1970–1981, 45 Law & Cont.Probs. 223 (Spring 1982); SCIRP, Staff Report 480–83.

[entry without inspection]. In addition, 21.3% had entered the U.S. with a tourist visa; 4.5%, with a student visa; and 1.7% had been crewmen. The remaining 1.9% had entered with other kinds of visas. Thus, most respondents (555) were EWIs, though a substantial minority (238) were visa abusers. As predictable, virtually all (95.4%) of the Mexican respondents reported that they had been EWIs. The majority (55.5%) of the WH respondents had entered as tourists; an unexpected 37.6% of all respondents from this region were EWIs. Only 17.3% of the EH respondents had been EWIs, as compared with 34.7% who had entered with student visas, 26.7% who had been tourists, and 13.3% who had been crewmen.

3. *Duration in the U.S.* Respondents in the study group had been in the U.S. for an average of 2.5 years. The majority (53.4%) had been here two or more years; those 423 respondents had been in the U.S. for an average of 4.2 years. The 370 respondents who had been here less than two years had been in the U.S. for an average of .5 years. EH respondents had been in the nation an average of 3.1 years, as compared with 2.5 and 2.4 years for the WH and Mexican respondents, respectively.[a]

4. *Age.* Most respondents were young adults. The average age of the study group was 28.5 years, as compared with 39.0 years, the average age of males in the U.S. labor force. More precisely, 40.1% of the respondents were 16–24 years of age; 38.0% were 25–34, and 21.9% were 35 or older.

5. *Education.* The study group had about half the education of the U.S. civilian labor force 18 years or older: an average of 6.7 as compared with 12.4 years of schooling. Respondents from Mexico had substantially less education (4.9 years of schooling) than WH respondents, and WH respondents had significantly less (8.7 years) than EH respondents (11.9), who came close to the U.S. norm.

6. *Sex and Marital Status.* The respondents, like apprehended illegals generally, were predominantly male (90.8%), and were less likely to be married than U.S. men of the same age. For example, 36.9% of the 318 respondents who were 25–34 years old were single, as compared with 15.9% of U.S. males the same age. Less than half (47.4%) of all respondents were married at the time of the interview.

7. *Dependents in Country of Origin.* Despite the relatively low incidence of marriages in the study group, respondents reported substantial family responsibilities in their country of origin. Almost 80% of all respondents reported that they supported or helped to support at least one relative in their country of origin. As a group, respondents supported or helped support an average of 4.6 persons in their homeland. The Mexican respondents were more likely than WH or EH respondents to report country of origin dependents, and they were more likely to report more dependents.

* * *

a. *Cf.* J. Reichert & D. Massey, *Patterns of Migration from a Rural Mexican Town to the U.S.: A Comparison of Legal and Illegal Migrants* (1979) (81.4% stayed one year or less)—eds.

9. *Relatives in U.S.* Seventeen percent of the study group (135 respondents) reported that their spouse lived in the U.S.; 12.7% reported they had one or more children here. Respondents here two or more years were five times as likely to have a spouse in the U.S. as those here less than two years (27.4% and 5.1%, respectively). WH respondents were more likely to report spouses in the U.S. than either EH or Mexican respondents (27.8% as compared with 21.3% and 11.0%, respectively). More generally, 33.8% of the study group reported the presence of at least one relative (spouse, child, parent, or sibling), whose legal residence here may permit respondents to legalize their status. WH respondents were the most likely to have one or more such relatives here (38.4%), followed by EH respondents (33.3%), and Mexican respondents (31.6%).

* * *

11. *Apprehensions by INS.* All respondents in the study group were in the custody of INS at the time of the interview. Mexican respondents were, however, eight times more likely to report a previous apprehension than non-Mexican respondents, though respondents in the latter group had been in the U.S. for a slightly longer period of time than the former group (2.4 years for the Mexicans; 2.6 years for the non-Mexicans).

* * *

14. *Work Experience in Home Country.* Despite their relative youth, few respondents were new entrants to the labor market when they entered the U.S. Less than 10% of the study group had worked for wages less than one year. As a group, respondents had worked for wages in their home country an average of 9.4 years. WH respondents had been employed in their homeland for an average of 10.7 years, as compared with 9.4 years for the Mexican and 5.8 for the EH respondents.

* * *

17. *Occupation in Country of Origin.* Respondents were substantially more likely to have been low-skilled than skilled workers in their homeland. The 628 respondents who had been employed in their country of origin since 1970 were twice as likely to have been farmworkers (35.7%) as white-collar workers (17.6%), and they were even more likely to have been blue-collar workers (41.5%). Few, however, had been service workers (5.2%). Respondents' occupation in their country of origin since 1970 was highly correlated with their region of origin and education. For example, the 407 Mexican respondents (4.9 years of schooling) were the most likely to have been farmworkers in their homeland (49.3%) and the least likely to have been white-collar workers (6.8%). The 48 EH respondents (11.9 years of schooling) were the most likely to have been white-collar workers (47.9%) and the least likely to have been farmworkers (2.1%). The 173 WH respondents (8.7 years of schooling) were less likely than EH respondents to have been white-collar workers in their homeland (34.1%) and were more likely to have been farmworkers (12.7%).

18. *Comparison of Country of Origin and U.S. Occupations.* Almost half the respondents who had been farmworkers in their home country moved into nonagricultural work in the U.S., and two-thirds of the

respondents who had been white-collar workers in their country of origin became blue-collar or service workers. Thus, * * * though the U.S. labor market tended to homogenize the occupational status of these 628 respondents, its net effect was a depressive one. Their occupational distribution in their most recent U.S. job was significantly less like that of U.S. employed persons than it had been when they were employed in their homeland.

19. *Occupation in U.S.* Since the 1965 Amendments to the Immigration & Nationality Act went into effect, aliens can become immigrants only if they are qualified relatives of U.S. legal residents, political refugees, or needed workers. Aliens applying for immigrant status as needed workers are automatically denied labor certification by the Department of Labor if they are seeking U.S. jobs in "Schedule B" occupations, e.g., assemblers, cleaners, clerks, kitchen helpers. Three-quarters (575) of the 788 respondents who reported their most recent U.S. occupation were employed in a Schedule B job; 8 had been self-employed, and 205 did not have Schedule B jobs, though a number were employed in low-skilled jobs, e.g., were working as waiters or drycleaning operatives. The occupational distribution of these 788 respondents was as follows: professional, technical and kindred (1.8%); owners, managers, and administrators, except farm (1.5%); sales workers (1.5%); clerical and kindred (1.6%); craft and kindred (16.0%); operatives (27.5%); nonfarm laborers (13.7%); farm laborers (15.6%); service workers (20.7%).

20. *Wages.* The average hourly wage of the 793 respondents in their most recent U.S. job was $2.71. Average hourly wages differed substantially according to respondents' region of origin and the location of their U.S. job. The Mexican respondents earned an average hourly wage of $2.34, as compared with average hourly wages of $3.05 for WH and $4.08 for EH respondents. The 223 respondents employed in the Southwest earned an average hourly wage of $1.98, as compared with $2.60, the average hourly wage of the 231 California respondents; $3.18, the average hourly wage of the 104 respondents employed in the Mid- and Northwest; and $3.29, the average hourly wage of the 235 respondents employed on the East Coast. In addition, the 136 respondents employed in U.S. agriculture earned a lower average hourly wage than the 657 respondents employed in nonagricultural work: $2.11, as compared with $2.83.

* * *

21. *Average Hourly and Weekly Earnings and Hours.* Respondents (excluding those in agriculture and private households) earned substantially less than U.S. production and nonsupervisory workers: an average hourly wage of $2.66 as compared with $4.47. * * * [R]espondents worked longer hours but consistently earned significantly less per week than U.S. workers.

22. *The Question of Exploitation.* Four sets of factors were regarded as indicators of exploitation of respondents in their most recent U.S. job:

- minimum wage violations;
- respondents' perceptions of their working conditions;

- respondents' reports of the presence of other illegals in their workplace; and

- payment of wages in cash.

Minimum Wage Violations. More than a fifth (23.8%) of the 766 respondents who were wage workers and for whom complete data on their most recent U.S. job were available appear to have been paid less than the minimum hourly wage, which was roughly defined for this study as $1.80 for respondents employed in farms, forestry, and fisheries; $2.00 an hour for those employed in sales, services, or private households; and $2.10 for those employed in other industries.

Respondents employed as domestics or farmworkers were more likely to be paid illegal wages than respondents employed in other industries (almost two-thirds of the 23 respondents employed as domestics and one-third of those employed as farmworkers (136 respondents) appear to have been paid less than the minimum wage). In addition, respondents employed in the Southwest, but particularly respondents employed in the 23 counties bordering Mexico, were significantly more likely to be paid less than the minimum wage than respondents employed in other regions in the U.S.

Respondents' Perceptions of Their Working Conditions. Although approximately one-sixth of all respondents were unwilling to make judgments about the practices of their former U.S. employers,

- 17.9% of the entire study group (142 respondents) reported that they had been hired because they were illegal. Respondents employed in the Southwest were two to three times more likely to report they had been hired because they were illegal than respondents employed in California, the Mid- and Northwest, or the East Coast;

- 16.0% (127 respondents) reported that they had been paid less than legal coworkers;

- 11.7% (93 respondents) reported that they had been paid less than the minimum wage; and

- only 3.5% (28 respondents) reported that they had been "badly treated" by their employer.

Other Illegals in the Workplace. Although almost 30% of the study group refused to answer questions relating to other illegals or claimed ignorance concerning the matter, a slight majority of the respondents to this question (306 illegals or 38.6% of all respondents) reported that there was at least one other illegal in their workplace. As a group, respondents had worked with an average of 8 other illegals. The Mexican respondents were three times more likely to report the presence of illegal coworkers as WH or EH respondents. Respondents employed in California, the Southwest, and the Mid- and Northwest were roughly twice as likely as illegals in the East Coast to report illegal coworkers.

Cash Wage Payments. More than one-fifth (22.1%) of all respondents reported that their wages had usually been paid in cash, an obvious means of avoiding the documentation of wages that payment by check would entail, and hence an indicator of possible exploitation. The 68 illegals employed in the counties bordering Mexico were most likely to report payment of wages in cash (63.3%) of any subgroup considered, and respondents employed in the Southwest were more likely to report cash wages (36.0%) than respondents employed in the East (21.0%), in California (14.8%), or the Mid- and Northwest (10.7%).

23. *Union Membership.* Only 10.2% of the study group reported that they had belonged to a labor union in their country of origin, but 130 respondents (16.4% of the study group) had joined a union in the U.S., and almost half (62 respondents) had belonged for two or more years. Membership in a U.S. union tended to be negatively correlated with low wages as well as the indicators of exploitation described above, *e.g.,* the extremely low-paid respondents employed in the counties bordering Mexico were the least likely to belong to a union in the U.S.—though they were most likely to have belonged in their country of origin (1.5% belonged to a U.S. union as compared with 17.7% who had belonged to a union in Mexico). Further, only 1.4% of the low-paid respondents employed in the Southwest reported membership in a U.S. union, as compared with 15.6% of those employed in California, 23.8% of those employed in the Mid- and Northwest, and 29.0% of those in the East Coast.

24. *Participation in Tax-Paying and Tax-Using Programs.* The respondents were more likely to have participated in tax-paying systems (many of which are automatic) than to have used tax-supported programs.

*Extent of Participation of Apprehended Illegal Alien Respondents In
Tax-Paying and Tax-Supported Programs*

Program Activity	Percentage of Respondent Participation
Input	
Social Security taxes withheld	77.3
Federal income taxes withheld	73.2
Hospitalization payments withheld	44.0
Filed U.S. income tax returns	31.5
Output	
Used hospitals or clinics	27.4
Collected one or more weeks of unemployment insurance	3.9
Have children in U.S. schools	3.7
Participated in U.S.-funded job training programs	1.4
Secured food stamps	1.3
Secured welfare payments	0.5

c. Why Do Undocumented Aliens Enter the United States?

Aliens enter the United States unlawfully for a number of reasons. Some come to join family members, some to flee persecution in their homeland, some to go to school. These motivations are normally referred to as "push" and "pull" factors. "Push" factors are those considerations that lead an alien to want to leave his or her home country; "pull" factors are those considerations that lead an alien to choose the United States as the country to move to.

Virtually all scholars agree that the most frequent motivation for illegal entry and residence is economic.[5] America offers jobs to unemployed or underemployed laborers from less developed nations and wages that are generally substantially above prevailing wages in the aliens' countries of origin (even if the wages the aliens receive here are below wages normally paid to U.S. citizens or legal immigrants). One study, conducted in 1976, found that "the average landless agricultural worker * * * in northeastern Jalisco [a Mexican state] was earning about 35 pesos (U.S. $1.35) per day * * *. By comparison, the average illegal migrant * * * working in the U.S. in 1976 was earning (U.S.) $2.50 per *hour* * * *."[6] This wage differential, of course, has been greatly exacerbated by the devaluation of the Mexican peso.[7]

It is doubtful that these factors alone can explain the massive amount of unlawful migration that the United States has witnessed throughout this century. As Gerald Lopez points out, "There have been numerous instances * * * where economic disparity between nations—even adjoining nations—exists but mass migration is absent. In other words, economic disparity is necessary but not sufficient for migration.   * * * [E]conomic disparity [does not] account for the pattern of Mexican migration. Primary Mexican source regions for today's undocumented migration are areas that provided labor earlier in this century. Yet the economic disparity between these source regions and the United States is no greater than that existing between numerous other regions in Mexico and this country."[8]

Accordingly, Lopez offers the following hypothesis as an alternative to the conventional "push-pull" explanation: "Where there is substantial economic disparity between two adjoining countries and the potential destination country promotes *de jure* or *de facto* access to its substantially superior minimal wage, that promotion encourages migrants reasonably to rely on the continuing possibility of migration, employment, and

5. *See* SCIRP, Staff Report 490–99.

6. W. Cornelius, *Mexican and Caribbean Migration to the U.S.: The State of Current Knowledge and Priorities for Future Research* (1978) (prepared for the Ford Foundation), *quoted in* SCIRP, Staff Report 494.

7. *See also* Jenkins, *Push/Pull in Recent Mexican Migration to the U.S.,* 11 Int'l Migration Rev. 178 (1977) (arguing that push factors such as rapid population growth, scarcity of land, and farm mechanization, are stronger incentives for Mexican migration than pull factors in United States).

8. Lopez, *Undocumented Mexican Migration: In Search of a Just Immigration Law and Policy,* 28 UCLA L.Rev. 615, 640 (1981).

residence, until a competitive economic alternative is made available in the source country." [9]

Lopez' hypothesis is useful because it forces us to consider the role that public and private actors in this country have played in encouraging, or at least tolerating, unlawful immigration. Examination of history, federal statutes and regulations, and enforcement practices reveals a complex set of federal policies toward undocumented labor—policies that may promote illegal migration much more than is commonly acknowledged by federal decision-makers.

To see this one need look no further than section 274(a) of the INA, which includes the so-called "Texas Proviso." This provision, which dates from 1952,[10] states that employment of an illegal alien shall not constitute unlawful harboring. The Texas Proviso did not create illegal migration. It simply recognized the existence of an international flow of labor that began late in the last century and continues today.

Government policy regarding unlawful migration may also be discovered through observation of enforcement practices and priorities. Clearly, entries without inspection could be reduced were the United States to build a wall or station an army division on its southern border. Similarly, visa abusers could be caught if the federal government kept extensive computer files detailing aliens' places of employment, friends and relatives, travel plans and the like. These kinds of enforcement procedures may be ruled out on many grounds, such as cost, other priorities, invasion of privacy, or "big brotherness."

Underenforcement may, however, also be a function of official ambivalence regarding the underlying substantive law. History discloses numerous instances of collusion between immigration authorities and employers of undocumented workers.[11] As noted in the Staff Report of the Select Commission on Immigration and Refugee Policy, "[o]ver the years, the U.S. government has failed to enforce the laws barring illegal entry effectively and evenly and has in effect perpetuated a 'half-open door' policy—officially forbidding illegal entry while essentially condoning it through lax enforcement." [12] Furthermore, border patrol operations have been notoriously underfunded for years. Currently, the number of Border Patrol agents controlling the borders of the United States is no larger than the police force that guards the Capitol in Washington, D.C.[13] Given the repeated recommendations by the INS, study commissions, and scholars to increase border enforcement, it is difficult to believe that the lack of resources is an unintentional or unconscious decision of Congress.

9. *Id.* at 640–41.

10. Act of March 20, 1952, Ch. 108, 66 Stat. 26.

11. *See* J. Samora, *Los Mojados: The Wetback Story,* Chapter II (1971); M. Garcia y Griego, *The Importation of Mexican Contract Laborers to the United States, 1942–1964: Antecedents, Operation and Legacy* (Working Papers in U.S.-Mexican Studies, 11) (1981); E. Galarza, *Merchants of Labor: The Mexican Bracero Story* 63 (1964) (report-

ing the following statement of a chief INS enforcement official before Congress: "We do feel we have the authority to permit to remain in the United States aliens who are here as agricultural workers whether they are here legally or not.")

12. SCIRP, Staff Report 560.

13. S. Hewlett, *Coping with Illegal Immigrants,* 60 For.Aff. 358, 375 (1981/82). *See* SCIRP, Final Report 46–49.

Congressional recognition of the usefulness of undocumented workers to the American economy is amply demonstrated in its consideration of the Simpson-Mazzoli bill. Although the legislation, as will be discussed below, would have imposed sanctions on employers, both the House and Senate bills included measures to aid current employers of illegal aliens. The House version adopted an amendment proposed by Congressman Panetta of California that would have permitted growers to bring in large numbers of temporary alien workers to pick crops if American labor were not available to do the job. *See* H.R. 1510, § 214. The program was based on the recognition that currently such jobs are performed by undocumented aliens. In short, the House program would simply have legalized part of the present illegal flow.

The Senate, while not authorizing a special temporary worker program, accepted an amendment proposed by Senator DeConcini of Arizona that would have permitted employers to phase out their use of illegal workers over a three year period. S. 529, § 214. Senator Kennedy, speaking in support of the amendment, stated:

> I believe the DeConcini amendment * * * will provide a transition period that is necessary to allow growers a reasonable opportunity to adjust to the new requirements of this legislation * * *.

> There has been an understandable concern on the part of many agricultural employers that it will take them some period of time to adjust to [the employer sanctions] provisions—since under existing law they have tacitly been encouraged to hire undocumented aliens.

129 Cong.Rec. S6659 (daily ed. May 12, 1983).

In sum, the migration of undocumented labor to the United States is a complex social process influenced by conditions in the aliens' home countries, the demand for labor and better living conditions in the United States, and the policies and practices of the United States government. It is important to see the interconnectedness of these variables in assessing the likely efficacy of proposals for dealing with the problem of illegal migration.

d. How Do Undocumented Aliens Enter the United States?

JOHN CREWDSON, THE TARNISHED DOOR: THE NEW IMMI-
GRANTS AND THE TRANSFORMATION OF AMERICA
21–25, 30–33, 37–40, 42–43 (1983).

[ENTRY WITHOUT INSPECTION AND SMUGGLING]

[T]he romantic notion of a small band of men on a solitary passage through the desert is fast becoming an anachronism, a throwback to a simpler age. For as the number of foreigners desperate to live and work in the United States increases exponentially, the organized smuggling of illegal aliens into this country is becoming a big business—so big, officials say, that it is now one of the two predominant money-making industries along the Mexican border, rivaling in profitability even the smuggling of narcotics. Arrests in alien-smuggling cases have more than tripled in the last five years, and INS officials estimate that half of all illegal aliens who cross the Mexican and Canadian borders now do so with the assistance of a smuggler. Every day, they say, countless thousands seeking better lives, the majority of them from Mexico and the rest from virtually every country in the world, are infiltrated across this country's borders by the sophisticated, highly organized rings that traffic in human contraband.

Many of the smuggled aliens are neophytes, first-time visitors unfamiliar with the culture, customs, language, and geography of the United States, strangers in a strange land who are willing to pay those who know America well to guide them across its borders. But the smugglers also provide a relatively safe journey into the American interior, and even seasoned aliens willing to risk walking across the border on their own are now turning to the professionals for help with their travel plans. The professionals are good, but they are not cheap: Fees run $400 for delivery from the Mexican border to Denver, $600 to Chicago, $850 or more to Detroit or New York City. It is a great deal of money—half the annual income of some Mexican workers—but a small investment compared to what those workers can earn in the United States.

So competitive has the smuggling business become that some of the smugglers even give guarantees—a second crossing for free if the first one does not succeed—and the more sophisticated rings attract clients by offering packages of false documents as part of their service: birth certificates, Social Security cards, driver's licenses, whatever pieces of paper are needed for them to live and work in the United States. Others specialize, smuggling only prostitutes to big-city vice rings or Mexican babies to black-market adoption mills, where a fair-skinned infant can bring up to $10,000. Still others fill telephone orders from "labor contractors" or business people, supplying truckloads of workers on demand to apple ranches in Washington, feedlots in Colorado, citrus groves in Florida, garment sweatshops in Los Angeles, and factories in Chicago. Sometimes the companies at the other end of the pipeline are nationally known; several big construction outfits and at least one nationwide hotel and restaurant chain have alien smugglers on their corporate payrolls to ensure their operations a continuous supply of cheap labor.

* * *

The smuggling process begins at the public "staging areas" that can be found in big cities and small towns all along the Mexican side of the border. Almost any day a visitor to Juárez can see the smugglers gathering at the Plaza Monumental, their gold Rolex wristwatches glinting in the bright sunshine. "They're like peddlers going around," says Bob Barber, who runs the Border Patrol's antismuggling unit across the Rio Grande in El Paso. "You can see negotiations being made all over the place." While the "coyotes," as the smugglers call themselves, trade prospective passengers back and forth like commodities on an exchange, each trying to assemble a full load for his particular destination, their *pollos,* or chickens, wait in shabby hotels along the Calle Mariscal that specialize in the rough trade. Once a group, or "load," is assembled, it is led on foot by the coyote across the border at a safe distance from town—because the Border Patrol tends to concentrate its resources closer to population centers, such crossings are usually successful—and when they are safely in the United States, the aliens are hidden again, in one of the "wetback motels" that are a feature of every American border city or in private houses or apartments rented by the smugglers. When the coast seems clear, the *pollos* are loaded, usually with little food or water to sustain them (the smugglers are low-overhead operators), into vehicles so crowded that there is often no room to lie down or even to sit. Then, preceded by spotters in radio-equipped scout cars, the vehicles—beer trucks, motor homes, moving vans, school buses, even horse trailers—set out from the border on their northward journeys.

So profitable has the people-smuggling business become—an average-sized ring moving 500 aliens a week across the border can easily gross $12 million a year—that it is now attracting criminal syndicates that once handled only marijuana and cocaine. "The big alien-smuggling operators make just as much as the drug smugglers," says Bert Moreno, who heads the INS's antismuggling operations in Washington. "There are hundreds of rings making money off this, and there are scores of them making big, big money." Bill Selzer, the deputy Border Patrol chief in Chula Vista, California, just across the border from Tijuana, estimates that at least a quarter of the narcotics-smuggling rings in the San Diego area are now "comingling their loads," bringing both aliens and narcotics across the border at the same time. The field is also crowded with thousands of smaller part-time operations, known to the Border Patrol as Mom and Pop shops, some headed by rather improbable amateurs like the wives of some naval officers stationed at Camp Pendleton, California, who were found to be hauling illegal aliens from Tijuana to Los Angeles in their station wagons. Others recently charged with alien smuggling include a U.S. Customs officer, a San Diego air traffic controller, and a Roman Catholic priest in Texas. The priest, one INS official said, "was looking at it as a humanitarian thing."

* * *

The great majority of the aliens smuggled into this country comes in across the 2,000-mile Mexico-U.S. border. But some of the rings are now beginning to recognize the advantages of using the even less well-guarded Canadian northern border, first flying their charges from Latin America and Asia to Canada, which, unlike the United States, does not require most visitors to have visas, then smuggling them south into New York and California. A favored crossing place for Chinese, Haitians, and other Caribbean islanders headed for the East Coast is the 800-mile stretch of heavily forested, sparsely patrolled border between Canada and New England, where many of the ports of entry on the American side are closed between midnight and morning for lack of money and manpower. On some roads running south from Canada, like those that snake across the border near the tiny village of Derby Line, Vermont, there are no border stations at all. Latin Americans who can afford the air fare to Toronto are taking advantage of the Canadian connection. So are Hong

Kong Chinese and Taiwanese bound for San Francisco and Los Angeles, who fly first to Vancouver and are then smuggled across the border to Seattle to begin their trip south. Toronto police recently broke up a particularly aggressive smuggling ring that, not content to wait for aliens to come to it, was actually recruiting Caribbean islanders in their home-lands, flying them to Montreal aboard Air Canada and Air France, then taking them south into the United States.

* * *

The antismuggling effort is aimed at only one species of illegal alien: the clandestine border crosser. But not all illegal aliens, perhaps not even the majority, come to the United States by slipping across its borders. The others enter the country openly—posing as students who never go to school and tourists who never take a tour, walking boldly through immigration inspection stations with counterfeit documents and credentials, even paying Americans to become their wives and husbands. In all of these ways and more, they take advantage of this country's tradition of welcome for foreign visitors, its fundamentally humane immi-gration laws, its heterogeneous, melting-pot society, which makes it easy for a stranger to seem to belong; its repugnance for any attempt to number and catalogue its citizens.

[VISA ABUSERS]

The ease with which a foreigner can gain official permission to enter the United States can be clearly seen in the line of visa seekers that, on most days, extends out the back gate of the cubelike American embassy in Mexico City and all the way around the block to the broad Paseo de la Reforma. Like the throngs standing patiently outside American embas-sies in dozens of other countries around the world, those who begin lining up in Mexico City before dawn hope to leave with one of the most sought-after pieces of paper in the world: a temporary visa allowing them to visit the United States as tourists or students, or on business. Some of those in line on any given morning are clearly what they seem to be: corporation executives with business in the United States or well-to-do families on their way to spend the weekend at Disneyland, skiing in Colorado, or lying on the beach in Miami. The others are hoping to get lucky, hoping that the visa officer will be in an expansive mood and not question them too closely about their plans, for unless they are caught, they have no intention of ever returning to Mexico, and more than likely they will never be caught.

The INS spends most of its time and money looking for illegal border crossers, not "visa abusers," as such bogus visitors are known. In 1980 it found only 64,000 foreigners who had overstayed their visas. Nobody knows how many it did not find, but indications are that their numbers were enormous; the same year 12 million foreigners entered the United States with nonimmigrant visas, but only 10.5 million were recorded as ever having left. Some of the 1.5 million shortfall is doubtless due to careless record keeping by the INS and the airlines that bring the visitors here and take them home—but not all of it. Daniel Vining of the

University of Pennsylvania, who has calculated net migration to this country by air, estimates the number of overstayers at around 200,000 a year, and others think it may be twice that.

Either way, the contribution of visa abusers to illegal immigration is both significant and growing, and the inclination of the American government to encourage foreign visitors by not looking too closely at who the tourists are makes such abuses easier still. So does the active promotion of tourism by Mexicans to the United States, a particular priority because it off-sets the balance-of-payments deficit created by the millions of American tourists who visit Mexico each year. "We've got a third of a million people a year who want to travel to the U.S.," says one consular officer in Mexico City. "They're spending a considerable amount of money there. Let's say we investigated all these cases. What would happen? We'd end up not being able to issue visas to people in a day's time the way we do now. We'd have to have a staff of investigators, and it would cost the taxpayers a lot of money."

Like their counterparts in nearly every country in the world, the American vice-consuls who hand out the visas in Mexico City—most of them young Foreign Service officers on their first tours of duty abroad— know that some of those standing in the hazy sunshine or sitting on the backless green benches in the embassy's courtyard are planning not merely to visit the United States but to live here. The problem is that they do not know which ones, and they have almost no way of finding out. Whether those on line are legitimate visitors or not, most of them have brought with them documents they hope will convince the visa officers that they have good reason to return home: a bank statement showing a solid record of deposits, for example, or a letter from a longtime employer attesting to their reliability. Such documents are easily obtainable on the black market, and even those that were genuine yesterday need not be so today: Employees can quit their jobs, and savings accounts can be converted into travelers' checks.

With 1,200 visa applicants to process in an average seven-hour day, quick decisions are the rule, and the visa officers are forced to rely mainly on their instincts. "If the documents seem reasonable and reasonably current, what else can you do?" asks Allan Otto, who heads the Mexico City consulate. "It would take a tremendous effort and tremendous resources to check these things out." Adds Jim Kerr, the chief of the consular section, "We just don't have the people." The consuls are frankly guessing, and because of the press of time, they often guess wrong. "We tend to be a bit more generous than we should be sometimes," admits one young consul on her first overseas assignment, "because we need to make quick decisions." In the next five minutes she decides whether or not to grant or deny visas to a Mexico City woman who says she wants to take a trip to Puerto Rico, a German exchange student on a Mexican vacation from his studies in the United States, a well-dressed young man who wants to visit his brother in Texas, and a slight, shy young woman who says she has worked for a local doctor for four years and has always wanted to see Los Angeles. Granted, granted, denied, denied. The odds are better than even that at least one of the four is not telling the truth, but in a sense it does not matter. Anyone whose visa application is denied can always hop a bus to the border and find a coyote to take him across. "That's one factor we have to take into consideration," says Ruth McLendon, a former American consul general in Mexico City. "To refuse them a visa doesn't really stop them if they want to enter the U.S. If they're bad applicants, they can always walk."

So tempting a target for abuse has the visa process become that some alien smugglers are now actually securing visas for their clients and bringing them into the United States as members of "tour groups" rather than sneaking them across the border at night. Ted Giorgetti, the chief INS investigator in Chicago, says that "only God knows the number" of illegal Polish aliens living in that city who came there to visit relatives and never left, and an INS official in Detroit believes that at least half of that city's sizable Arab community came into the country the same way. In 1981 the INS uncovered a foreign-based ring that was smuggling Armenian "tourists" from Beirut to California, and earlier this year it broke up an organization in Los Angeles that was funneling Indonesian domestics to Beverly Hills housewives, providing them with passports, airline tickets, and enough "spending money" to convince the American consuls in Jakarta who issued them tourist visas that they were coming here for a vacation.

* * *

[SHAM MARRIAGES]

Fraudulent marriages are only one of a multitude of lesser-known but equally effective ways to gain entry to the United States, all of which only complicate further the nation's already losing battle to enforce its immigration laws. In keeping with the government's conviction that Americans should not be separated from their loved ones by international boundaries, marrying an American citizen entitles an alien to an immediate permanent resident visa, the so-called green card. (There are no visa number quotas for spouses, parents, and children of adult U.S. citizens as there are for all other categories of immigrant.) Although humanitarian in its intent, this law has spawned a false marriage racket of such proportions that "marriages of convenience" are now one of the most popular means of emigration for aliens who are otherwise inadmissible. In nearly every big city on the East and West coasts there are dozens of thriving marriage fraud rings, some run by shady immigration lawyers or alien-smuggling organizations as part of a package service, often using prostitutes as "wives" and seeking clients through ads in men's magazines ("Nice Mexican, Oriental ladies seek friendship and marriage ...").

In 1980 the INS received 115,000 applications for permanent residence status from aliens who had married American citizens. It interviewed 36,000 of them and charged more than 4,600—a record number—with having entered fraudulent marriages for immigration purposes. * *

* * *

[FRAUDULENT ENTRY]

Many illegal aliens * * * come here in the boldest possible manner, flashing bogus passports and green cards at harried immigration inspectors as they stream through the turnstiles along the borders and at the nation's airports. David North, a highly respected immigration researcher, estimates that half a million aliens bearing fraudulent documents of one kind or another enter the United States each year, perhaps as many people as cross the Mexican border illegally in the same period of time. The immigration inspectors have some success at spotting counterfeits but, considering the vast numbers of entrants they must deal with, not nearly enough. The problem is now compounded by the INS's new "citizen by-pass" procedure, under which an American—or an alien with a forged U.S. passport—can circumvent the immigration inspectors and go directly to Customs, whose officers are far less expert in detecting bogus documents than the INS. In 1978, 163 million people, aliens and citizens alike, entered the United States at official inspection stations from Mexico alone, and another 87 million came in from Canada. At airports, seaports, and along the border it is up to the person requesting admission to establish his citizenship or legal residency. But inside the country the burden of proof is shifted, and the proliferation of false documents makes the job of the INS even tougher than it is already. Under existing law, a U.S. immigration officer may, within certain broad limits, stop and question anyone believed to be in this country illegally. But because citizens are not required to carry any verifying credentials, the responsibility for proving illegality is on the officer, not on the suspected alien. An illegal alien, especially one who is newly arrived and has not yet learned the rules of the game, will frequently admit his or her illegal status after a couple of perfunctory questions. But if the alien asserts citizenship and backs up the assertion with documents, the officer has little choice but to extract a confession or to let him or her go.

* * *

The INS has files on more than 6,000 suspected sellers of fake birth certificates and other false identity documents, and there are at least 150 known sources of counterfeit immigration documents, like green cards and border crossing cards. But the magnitude of the traffic in false documentation was never really apparent until one afternoon in 1973, when agents stumbled upon the unheard-of quantity of 60,000 counterfeit green cards left in a locker at the Greyhound bus station in Los Angeles. The cards—such good copies that they even contained the secret identifying marks known only to immigration inspectors—could easily have commanded $500 apiece. Such a price is unusually high. All along the Mexican side of the border, buying a birth certificate or green card is almost as easy as buying a Coca-Cola, and almost as cheap. The document vendors, who tend to carry their inventories in their pockets and do business from back booths in bars and restaurants, can, in their favorite phrase, "get you everything for fifty bucks," not just the heavyweight credentials but the lesser ones that lend credence to the former: library cards; student identification cards; business and membership

A. & M.–Immigration Law ACB—28

cards of all kinds. As a consequence, a well-documented illegal alien often has more "proof" of his identity than do most American citizens.

* * *

[BORDER CROSSING CARDS]

For years Americans have associated Mexico with bargains. Americans cross the border to drink 50-cent beer and dine on $5 filet mignon, fill their cars with cheap gas, mail letters back to the United States for 9 cents apiece, visit cut-rate doctors and dentists, and stock up on staples— sugar, milk, coffee, fruits, and vegetables at a fraction of their U.S. prices. But Mexicans also come to the United States to buy, both because the quality of some products made here is better than those produced in Mexico and because items marked "Made in U.S.A." confer status on their owners in Mexico. Stores like those along Convent Street in Laredo, Texas, where $3 of every $4 are spent by Mexicans, sell more merchandise per square foot of floor space than anywhere else in America, even Beverly Hills' Rodeo Drive or New York's Fifth Avenue. For years a single Laredo grocery store has sold more Tide, Pet milk, and Kool-Aid than any in America.

Such cross-border commerce is encouraged by the United States, enhancing as it does the U.S. balance of payments with Mexico, which is now this country's most important source of foreign exchange. In 1981 more than 3 million Mexicans spent $2.5 billion here. Mexicans are now spending more money in the United States than Americans are leaving behind in Mexico. Americans need no special permission to walk across the border and shop in Mexican stores; no one assumes that they are likely to take up residence there. The same does not, however, apply to Mexicans, who must have a border crossing card, a pass that permits the holder to remain in the United States for up to seventy-two hours to shop or visit friends, for any reason except to work. As might be expected, the demand for such cards among Mexicans is fierce, and those seeking them often begin lining up outside INS offices at the border the day before they make their applications.

In theory, to get a crossing card, a Mexican must show convincing evidence that he or she is a "stable" resident of Mexico: a house, a bank account, a good job, or other viable reason to believe that he or she will not use the visiting privileges to move to the United States. As with everything else, however, the INS lacks the manpower to check an applicant's bona fides, and the cards are handed out almost as fast as they can be printed, an average of one every eight minutes in El Paso. There are perhaps 2 million such cards now outstanding, but the INS also has no way to monitor what the cardholders do after they enter the United States, to ensure that they observe the seventy-two-hour limit or the prohibition against working. So lax is the system, in fact, that the border crossing card has become one of the favored ways for Mexican workers to enter the United States illegally. Mexican women from cities like Tijuana and Juárez have used their cards for years to commute to their jobs as domestics on the American side of the border, but Mexicans headed for big cities in the north are also using such cards to cross the border, then mailing them back to their homes in Mexico before proceeding north to look for work. If they are captured, the aliens tell the INS that they slipped across the border illegally, and when they return home, their crossing cards are there waiting, ready to be used to make another trip.

3. IMPACT OF ILLEGAL MIGRATION IN THE UNITED STATES

The existence of undocumented workers in the United States may have a number of impacts on American society. Most obviously, a supply of undocumented labor may affect the employment opportunities and wages of U.S. citizens and legal aliens. Additionally, illegal aliens may affect state and local finances—contributing tax dollars, using public services and participating in social programs. The presence of undocumented workers may also implicate federal foreign policy concerns.

You will not be surprised to learn that gathering reliable data on any of these issues presents monumental problems for social scientists and that substantial disagreements exist. Some scholars believe that undocumented workers take jobs from American citizens (primarily from the least well off members of American society) and hinder the development of productivity-increasing technology. Others assert that illegal labor fills jobs that Americans won't take, and that to stop the flow would put some U.S. businesses (and their citizen employees) out of work. Similar lack of agreement exists regarding the impact of undocumented aliens on public services and welfare programs. The following excerpt from the Staff Report of the Select Commission on Immigration and Refugee Policy summarizes the literature on these issues.

SCIRP, U.S. IMMIGRATION POLICY AND THE NATIONAL INTEREST
Staff Report 506–16, 519–30 (1981).

IMPACT ON THE LABOR MARKET

The impact of undocumented/illegal migration on the labor market is generally believed to be its major consequence. Of primary concern in evaluating this impact are the issues of displacement of U.S. workers and the depression of wages and working standards.

North and Houstoun, in their work on the characteristics and impact of undocumented/illegal migration, summarized what they believed were the adverse impacts of such migration:

- it will depress the educational and skill level of the labor force
- it will depress labor standards in the secondary sector, which in some cases will create an underground market of illegal wages, hours, and workers;
- it will cause a displacement of low-skill legal resident workers;
- it will create a new class of disadvantaged workers, one which inextricably conjoins national origins and illegal status in the U.S.; and

- it will inhibit efforts to improve job satisfaction in the secondary sector.[56]

Their basic assumption is that undocumented/illegal aliens take jobs that might otherwise go to legal U.S. residents and/or make otherwise acceptable jobs unacceptable to U.S. workers. This assumption further leads to the conclusion that these adverse effects outweigh any possible benefit—increased productivity, for example—that might accrue from the presence of undocumented/illegal aliens in the work force.[57]

This perspective is shared by others. Donald Elisburg, then Assistant Secretary of Labor for Employment Standards, testified at the Select Commission's New York hearing that "in taking jobs in the United States, [undocumented/illegal aliens] depress working conditions and adversely affect employment opportunities, particularly among the most vulnerable people in our economy—minority teenagers and women who head households, among others." [58] Vernon Briggs argues similarly that undocumented/illegal aliens, especially in border areas, displace Mexican Americans from jobs and depress sectors of the economy.[59]

Michael Wachter examined the "distribution of benefits and costs of illegal aliens" in a recent essay, "The Labor Market and Illegal Immigration: The Outlook for the 1980s." Wachter's approach is to treat the flow of undocumented/illegal aliens as an increase in the supply of unskilled labor. While he admits that this view omits consideration of some of the outcomes of illegal status, he argues that the demographic characteristics of the aliens are more important than their legal status. Wachter concludes:

> Given this framework, the impact of illegal aliens, at least in today's labor market, seems indisputable. Although the magnitude of the effect would vary depending upon the actual number of illegal aliens in this country who are working, the direction of the impact is known. First, illegal aliens depress the wages of the lower skilled native American work force. Second, given existing levels of minimum wages and welfare, for which the Americans but not the aliens are eligible, the wage reduction resulting from illegal immigration may also cause higher unemployment rates for lower skilled native workers.[60]

Wachter's conclusions stem from a theoretical perspective that defines workers as either complements of or substitutes for each other. Those who are substitutes are in greater competition with each other than those who are complements. Under this theory, the smaller the divergence is between workers' skill levels, the greater the competition for jobs.

56. [D. North & M. Houstoun, *The Characteristics and Role of Illegal Aliens in the U.S. Labor Market*, S–19 (March 1976).]

57. *Ibid.*, p. S–20.

58. Donald Elisburg, unpublished testimony, public hearing before the Select Commission on Immigration and Refugee Policy, New York City, January 21, 1980.

59. Vernon Briggs, "*Mexican Workers in the U.S. Labor Market: A Contemporary Dilemma*" *International Labour Review* 112 (November 1975): p. 351–368, *en passim.*

60. Michael L. Wachter, "*The Labor Market and Illegal Immigration: The Outlook for the 1980s*" *Industrial and Labor Relations Review* 33 (April 1980): 350.

In an advanced economy with relatively few unskilled jobs, increasing the number of workers without industrial skills increases the competition for what is in any case a scarcity.[61]

Such competition is also believed to have an adverse effect on wages in areas with high concentrations of undocumented/illegal aliens. Barton A. Smith and Robert J. Newman, in one of the few empirical studies on this issue, found that in metropolitan areas near the Texas-Mexico border, annual real income is $684 lower than in metropolitan areas further from the border. The wage differential in this study was found to be slightly higher for Mexican Americans and for unskilled workers. The authors of the study believe that these wage differentials may be caused in part by undocumented/illegal migration, but conclude that "if migration from Mexico is having a negative impact on wages along the border it is not as severe as many have contended." They argue that the less-than-expected real differential in wages may be explained by two factors. First, they suggest, Mexican aliens may be taking jobs unwanted by U.S. laborers, and, second, both Anglo American and Mexican American laborers, may be so highly mobile that large-scale internal migration may prevent wage disparities from becoming too large.[62]

Other researchers also believe that undocumented/illegal aliens may not represent a source of competition that displaces U.S. workers and depresses wages. Gilbert Cardenas argues, for example, that undocumented/illegal aliens usually represent an additional, not substitute, supply of labor.[63] And, in a hearing held by the Select Commission, Edwin Reubens—discussing, as does Wachter, skill level rather than legal status—suggested that "when we break it down by occupations and types of activities, we find that the degree of real competition of these aliens with Americans seeking jobs to be of a much smaller magnitude.[64]

These scholars base much of their argument on the unavailability of U.S. workers for many of the jobs held by undocumented/illegal aliens. Wayne Cornelius wrote in a study of undocumented/illegal Mexican migration:

> Workers cannot be displaced if they are not there, and there is no evidence that disadvantaged native Americans have ever held, at least in recent decades, a significant proportion of the kinds of jobs for which illegals are usually hired, especially in the agricultural sector.[65]

61. *Ibid.*

62. Barton A. Smith and Robert J. Newman, *"Depressed Wages Along the U.S.-Mexico Border: An Empirical Analysis" Economic Inquiry* 15 (January 1977): 51–66.

63. Gilbert Cardenas, "Illegal Aliens in the Southwest: A Case Study" in National Council on Employment Policy, *Illegal Aliens: An Assessment of the Issues* (Washington, D.C.: 1976). Cited in Wayne Cornelius, *Illegal Mexican Migration to the United States: Recent Research Findings and Policy Implications,* cited in *Cong.Rec.* July 13,

1977: H7063. See also Gilbert Cardenas, "Manpower Impact and Problems of Mexican Illegal Aliens in an Urban Labor Market." Ph.D. dissertation, University of Illinois at Champaign-Urbana: 1977.

64. Edwin Reubens, unpublished testimony, public hearing before the Select Commission on Immigration and Refugee Policy, Baltimore, October 29, 1979.

65. Cornelius, *"Research Findings," Congressional Record* July 13, 1977: H7063.

Cornelius acknowledges that undocumented/illegal workers are also taking industrial jobs in urban centers, but suggests that for Mexicans, at least, the trend toward such employment is gradual. Further, even in the industrial sector, he argues, undocumented/illegal aliens take jobs U.S. workers will not accept. To substantiate this assertion, he points to the failures of two programs—in Los Angeles and San Diego—that were explicitly designed to attract U.S. workers to jobs vacated by apprehended aliens. In both cases, U.S. workers refused the jobs; in San Diego they were eventually filled by legal commuter workers from Mexico.[66]

Michael Piore provides an explanation of the unavailability of U.S. workers for these jobs, and argues:

> Industrial societies seem systematically to generate a variety of jobs that full-time, native-born workers either reject out of hand or accept only when times are especially hard. Farm labor, low-level service positions like dishwasher or hospital orderly, and heavy, dirty unskilled industrial work all fit into this category. Jobs like these—referred to by manpower analysts as jobs in the "secondary labor market"—offer little security, opportunity for advancement, or prestige. Often they are seen as degrading. Finding people to fill them poses a continual problem for any industrial system.[67]

What is undesirable to a U.S. citizen, though, may be highly valued by an undocumented/illegal alien. As Piore suggests, such workers may see their employment as temporary, and they may therefore be more willing or able to tolerate difficult conditions. In addition, the wage differentials between U.S. jobs and those of the home country may make even secondary labor market jobs desirable. Piore summarizes his arguments by calling the belief that undocumented/illegal aliens replace U.S. workers a misconception. He says that the jobs held by these aliens fall into two categories, both of which complement or aid U.S. workers. Some of the secondary labor market jobs that undocumented/illegal aliens take are in industries that would close or relocate outside the United States if there were no alien work force. Since these industries also often have jobs desired by U.S. workers, undocumented/illegal aliens actually provide opportunities rather than displace citizens. In the other group are jobs which contribute to the standard of living of many U.S. citizens, for example, domestic and restaurant work.

Wachter suggests that the argument that is based on unavailability of U.S. workers is more complicated than it appears, and that it does not rebut his argument about the displacement effects of undocumented/illegal migration. Even though the direct displacement effects may be reduced in the situations described by Piore and others, the indirect effects may still adversely affect U.S. workers. Wachter constructs an hypothetical situation in which undocumented/illegal aliens are forced to return to their home countries immediately.

66. *Ibid.*

67. Michael Piore, *"The 'Illegal Aliens' Debate Misses the Boat" Working Papers for a New Society* (March–April 1978): 60.

Under such a circumstance, he says, pressure to improve wages at the bottom of the job ladder would be increased substantially. Although some jobs would be lost because employers could not afford the higher wages, other jobs would see an increase. With undocumented/illegal workers out of the job market and an increase in wages, many domestic workers would be interested in formerly undesirable jobs. Wachter estimates that of a possible 6 million jobs filled by undocumented/illegal aliens, 2.5 million would be available to U.S. workers at higher wages.[68]

Wachter's position is speculative and rests on his assumption, that "there is a built-in mechanism that prevents serious disruption: For any job that is 'vital,' real wages will be bid up in the absence of illegal aliens to ensure the availability of domestic workers." [69] What he does not take into account is Piore's point that certain industries might as easily go abroad in search of labor as raise their wages, although he does say that skilled workers in firms that hire undocumented/illegal aliens could suffer a decline in income.

Although there is great disagreement regarding job displacement and the overall wage effects created by undocumented/illegal migration, there is less dissension over its impact on the wages and working conditions of the secondary labor market. Certainly not all undocumented/illegal aliens experience abuse, but most experts agree that serious problems do exist in some quarters. An undocumented/illegal alien who testified at a Select Commission hearing described his experience:

> They say that because we do not have U.S. papers we are not entitled to protection by the U.S. Constitution. Because of this we are often paid low wages and are forced to live and work in subhuman conditions. In Florida we work carrying 100 pound bags up ladders that are sometimes 20 feet high. If we fall from a ladder or are otherwise injured on the job we rarely receive workmen's compensation. Many undocumented workers in Florida live in small house trailers that accommodate more than 20 workers, and often pay high rent for such living space.[70]

Difficult conditions, however, are also found in many urban settings. A labor leader at another Commission hearing described conditions in the New York garment industry:

> During the last year our organizers have located over 500 small, nonunion garment shops in the Bronx, the second smallest borough of New York City. Additionally, they found over 200 small shops in Manhattan, and they estimate that there are several hundred more in Brooklyn and Queens. Conditions in these shops vary somewhat, but in virtually all of them workers are paid poorly, and the work environment is far from humane. Minimum hourly wages are nonexistent.... Homework, the scourge of our industry 70 to 80 years ago, has returned with a

---

68. Wachter, "*Outlook*", p. 352.

69. *Ibid.*

70. Anonymous undocumented/illegal alien, unpublished testimony, public hearing before the Select Commission on Immigration and Refugee Policy, Miami, December 4, 1979.

vengeance.... Basic health and safety standards are completely neglected in the new sweatshops.[71]

The differential in wages between the home countries of most undocumented/illegal aliens and the United States may make these aliens less concerned than their citizen counterparts about the actual level of their U.S. wages. The potential threat of apprehension and deportation may also make undocumented/illegal workers more willing to work for lower wages. At the Select Commission hearing in Los Angeles, a representative of the International Ladies Garment Workers Union (ILGWU) told of instances where employers, whom he cited specifically, used the Immigration Service to intimidate workers:

> *Daisy of California:* A supervisor spreads a rumor of a possible INS raid. Out of a work force of 130, only six remain working. Several days later, company announces a pay reduction and erosion of benefits.

> *High Tide:* A strike occurs. INS arrives and 17 pickets are apprehended, detained and, by evening, deported.

> *California Sample:* One hour before another federal agency, the National Labor Relations Board, is to conduct an election, INS van parks near dock within full view of employees as company spokesman speaks of impending INS raid.

> *Hollander Manufacturing:* Three days after an election in which the company lost, INS raids the plant picking up all union supporters. Retaliation or coincidence? When questioned, INS produces a letter on company stationery requesting the raid.[a]

Although it should again be noted that not all employers of undocumented/illegal aliens are guilty of such practices, abuses of working conditions and wages do exist. Further, undocumented/illegal aliens, to some extent, are valued by employers because of their vulnerability.

* * *

IMPACT ON SOCIAL SERVICES

Measuring the overall impact of undocumented/illegal aliens on U.S. social services—cash assistance, medical assistance and educational services in particular—is as difficult as measuring their impact on the labor market and overall economy. Again, few reliable facts are known, although theoretical and emotional responses abound. In order to gauge the effect of these undocumented aliens, several factors must be taken into account: their contributions through taxes to social services, their

---

71. Jay Masur, unpublished testimony, public hearing before the Select Commission on Immigration and Refugee Policy, New York, New York, January 21, 1980.

a. Many of these reported employer actions might render the employer liable for backpay and other sanctions under the National Labor Relations Act. In *Sure-Tan,* *Inc. v. NLRB,* ___ U.S. ___, 104 S.Ct. 2803, 81 L.Ed.2d 732 (1984), the Supreme Court ruled, "[c]ounterintuitive though it may be," that an employer's action to report apparently illegal alien employees to INS would constitute an unfair labor practice if done with intent to retaliate for protected union-related activities.—eds.

own utilization of programs, and the effects that labor market displacement and wage depression may have on the use of services by U.S. citizens and permanent resident aliens.

The argument often heard about undocumented/illegal migrants is that they use social services, for which they do not pay and are therefore a burden on U.S. taxpayers. The Select Commission heard testimony from many state and local officials about the financial burdens imposed on them by undocumented/illegal aliens. Of particular concern was the burden placed on medical services. According to Richard A. Berman, Director of the New York State Office of Health Systems Management, "a review of the $100 million total deficit shared by New York State hospitals, exclusive of the Health and Hospitals Corporation facilities, suggests that a substantial portion of that deficit is the result of providing free care to undocumented, medically indigent aliens." [75] Peter F. Schabarum, Supervisor, First District, County of Los Angeles, testified similarly as to the financial burden on localities: "We conservatively estimate that local property taxpayers will spend $75 million this year to cover the cost of nonreimbursed health care provided to illegal aliens by our Department of Health Services, and that cost is escalating dramatically." [76]

The hearing testimony makes it apparent that, although many are concerned about costs, few hospital administrators or local officials question the responsibility of local hospitals to provide emergency treatment to all patients, regardless of legal status. According to a study made by the Department of Health, Education and Welfare in 1979, the type of services that undocumented/illegal aliens receive from hospitals varies by city. Emergency room treatment is rarely denied, and maternity services are generally given when the patient can demonstrate an ability to pay at least a portion of the expenses. Traumatic injuries appear to be routinely treated, although the Select Commission did hear evidence to the contrary. In Texas, for example, a representative of the Camino Real Health Systems Agency reported during a Commission site visit that undocumented/illegal aliens reporting injuries and emergency medical conditions were turned down by hospitals in the area. [77]

The issue here is the question of payment—who has the financial responsibility for the payment of medical care given to undocumented/illegal aliens. The localities often claim that these aliens are a federal responsibility, The federal government has the duty to enforce immigration laws, according to this argument, and therefore the federal government should bear whatever burden comes from ineffective enforcement.

---

75. Richard A. Berman, unpublished testimony, public hearing before the Select Commission on Immigration and Refugee Policy, New York, January 21, 1980.

76. Peter F. Schabarum, unpublished testimony, public hearing before the Select Commission on Immigration and Refugee Policy, Los Angeles, February 5, 1980; *see also* Los Angeles, County Department of Health Services, *Non-Resident Cost Study:* *Impact on Los Angeles County's Health Care Systems* (Los Angeles: July 1977).

77. Office of Special Concerns, Office of the Assistant Secretary for Planning and Evaluation, U.S. Department of Health, Education and Welfare, *Unpaid Medical Costs and Undocumented Workers,* Executive Summary; San Antonio Site Visit of the Select Commission (Jose Contreras of Camino Real Health Systems Agency).

The Los Angeles County Board of Supervisors has submitted several claims to the federal government through the Immigration Service and the Department of Health and Human Services (formerly HEW) requesting reimbursement for services provided to undocumented/illegal aliens.[78] Legislation has also been introduced repeatedly to place responsibility for undocumented aliens clearly with the federal government.

Critics of this point of view question the accuracy of the data used and the interpretations made by those claiming financial burden. The estimates used in some studies, for example, have been criticized because of the methods used to identify undocumented/illegal aliens. Untrained in immigration matters, hospital personnel often are unable to make an accurate judgment about legal status. In some cases, members of ethnic minorities who are unable to pay their bills and who are not covered by some type of third-party reimbursement plan are automatically judged to be undocumented/illegal aliens.[79] Further, hospitals and local government officials, according to Fred Arnold, formerly Research Director of the Select Committee on Population, U.S. House of Representatives, have a vested interest in supporting the highest possible estimate of costs, particularly if they are arguing for reimbursement.[80]

A number of studies that have examined the use of medical services from the perspective of the undocumented/illegal alien also raise questions regarding the accuracy of the local estimates of financial burden. Most of these studies do show that a significant proportion of undocumented/illegal aliens in the samples examined use hospitals or clinics. The North-Houston study shows that 27.4 percent used such services; the Orange County Taskforce study shows 28 percent usage; and the Keely, et al. study of Haitian[s] and Dominicans points to 44.5 percent and 76.5 percent, respectively. These statistics present only a part of the picture. A much lower proportion of the samples' undocumented/illegal aliens used free medical care: 4.6 percent in the North-Houstoun study, less than 9 percent in the Orange County Task Force project, 8 percent in the Jorge Bustamante study, and 15.4 percent in Cornelius's. The cost of medical care is often paid by the undocumented/illegal migrants themselves or by insurance plans in which they participate. A third or more of those questioned by North and Houstoun, Keely, and Orange County stated that hospitalization insurance had been deducted from their pay. In the North-Houstoun study, 83 percent of those who said they had used medical services had insurance coverage.

Evidence about other services points to even less use. The North-Houstoun study of apprehended aliens shows that 0.5 percent received welfare funds, 1.3 percent food stamps, 3.9 percent unemployment compensation and 3.7 percent used public schools. The Keely study of Haitians and Dominicans revealed that none of the former and 5.9

78. Jane Reister Conrad, *"Health care for indigent illegal aliens: whose responsibility?" University of California, Davis Law Review* 8 (1975): 119.

79. See Office of Special Concerns, HEW, *Unpaid Medical Costs.*

80. Fred Arnold, *"Providing medical services to undocumented immigrants: costs and public policy" International Migration Review* 13 (winter 1979): 711.

percent of the latter received welfare funds. One exception to this pattern was found in a study of undocumented/illegal aliens who visited a counseling center in Los Angeles. At the time of the interviews, 8.1 percent of the respondents reported that they currently received welfare support. Women were the most frequent users of public assistance programs with 15.6 percent receiving some kind of financial assistance. Since that time, however, Los Angeles has instituted a new program that has significantly reduced the number of undocumented/illegal migrants applying for Aid to Families with Dependent Children.

The generally low use of social services by undocumented/illegal aliens can be explained by several factors. First, undocumented/illegal migrants are ineligible to receive most forms of financial assistance, and many communities require documentation of citizenship or legal permanent residence before payments are made. Second, the majority of these migrants come to this country to work, and if they cannot find employment, they return to their home countries. Third, many are temporary visitors—whatever the reason for their entry into the United States. They often do not bring their families with them and, therefore, do not need many of the services (for example, public schools) that permanent residents use. Fourth, many undocumented/illegal aliens fear detection if they apply for these programs.

Even if undocumented/illegal aliens were to make use of social services, it is by no means established that they are an economic burden to U.S. citizens. To determine the net cost of service usage by undocumented/illegal aliens, it would be necessary to determine:

- Their contributions to the public coffers through tax payments;

- Their contributions to overall economic growth; and

- The extent to which prices are restrained because of available undocumented labor.

There is no research on the last two factors, but recent research studies show a wide range in the proportion of undocumented/illegal aliens who pay federal and/or state taxes. It appears from samples taken of temporary agricultural workers in border areas that these aliens are less likely than those in other samples to have taxes withheld. Avante Systems' report, "A Survey of the Undocumented Population in Two Texas Border Areas, 1978," shows that in El Paso and McAllen/Edinburgh, only 17 percent of a sample of less than 600 paid taxes.[82] On the other hand, North-Houston found that 73.2 percent of their sample of apprehended aliens had paid income taxes. In Bustamante's study, 61.8 percent paid taxes, and in Cornelius's sample, 64 percent paid. The evidence overall points to a significant level of tax payment among undocumented/illegal aliens. This evidence is persuasive enough to prompt some researchers to conclude, as does Fred Arnold, that there are some indications "that these tax payments may more than offset the cost

82. [H. Cross & J. Sandos, *The Impact of Undocumented Mexican Workers* (Battelle PDP Working Paper No. 15, Nov. 1979), p. 30.]

of providing health care and other social services to undocumented aliens." [83]

Before any definitive conclusions can be reached, however, one more factor should be taken into account in measuring the impact of undocumented/illegal migration on social services—the effect of U.S. worker displacement on the use of services by legal residents. If U.S. workers are being displaced by undocumented/illegal aliens and are therefore unemployed, they may be making increased use of cash and medical assistance programs as well as unemployment insurance benefits. Estimates by the Congressional Budget Office indicate that "a one point increase in the unemployment rate automatically increases transfer payment outlays by about $7 billion. With a total labor force of about 100,000,000 a single point increase in the unemployment rate equals about 1,000,000 persons, and the cost of a single unemployed worker would thus be $7,000 (7 billion divided by 1 million)." [84]

Such allegations rest on unproven assumptions, though. Until the debate on the displacement effects of undocumented/illegal migration is resolved, it is impossible to measure the effect of this phenomenon.

Despite the lack of consensus about the degree to which undocumented/illegal aliens impose on U.S. taxpayers, there is agreement that failure to use some services—particularly health ones—could have serious ramifications for U.S. society. Undocumented/illegal aliens are generally fearful of approaching those in authority and, therefore, often avoid using hospital services, even when such services are greatly needed. Moreover, those who do seek care often fail to return for follow-up treatment or give false information because of their fear of detection. As Suzanne Dandoy, Director of the Arizona Department of Health Services stated at the Phoenix hearing of the Commission:

> Continuity of care is limited by incorrect information supplied by Mexican nationals who fear for their own legal status or that of others close to them. The potential danger from this practice of giving incorrect addresses and information is awesome in the area of communicable diseases or life-threatening conditions.[85]

Richard Berman, Director of the New York State Office of Health Systems Management also commented upon the public health hazards of undocumented/illegal migration. He testified that these migrants have been found to be carriers of hepatitis, tuberculosis, salmonellosis, shigellosis, amebiases and parasitic diseases. He also suggested that "as a further complication, many aliens are employed as food processors, dishwashers, hospital aides, and in other occupations involved in the delivery or handling of food," and concluded that "without question, lack of access to

---

83. Arnold, *"Providing medical services"*, p. 711.

84. David S. North, *Enforcing the Immigration Law: A Review of the Options* (Washington, D.C.: Center for Labor and Migration Studies, September 1980), p. 17–18.

85. Suzanne Dandoy, unpublished testimony, public hearing before the Select Commission on Immigration and Refugee Policy, Phoenix, February 4, 1980.

appropriate care for these persons creates a clear public health problem which requires both state and federal attention." [86]

The public health hazard is not the only serious ramification of an underground population. Psychological problems are reported to be particularly troublesome. Marta Timbres, a psychiatric social worker, testified that "[the undocumented/illegal] population tends to be withdrawn and the children learn to isolate themselves and be guarded in their peer relationships . . . . The fear of being discovered contributes to the under-utilization of social agencies and mental health centers that would alleviate some of the stresses." [87] * * *

SECTION B. PROPOSALS FOR CONTROLLING, REGULATING AND LEGALIZING THE FLOW OF UNDOCUMENTED WORKERS

Professor Niles Hansen writes:

The informal undocumented migration system continues to operate largely because it benefits all parties concerned, at least so long as each party looks only at its own situation and what it would be if undocumented migration were strictly curtailed. A key factor in the system is that most undocumented Mexicans are in the United States on a temporary basis. The United States gains relatively cheap labor willing to perform tasks that citizen workers are reluctant to undertake. The available evidence shows that undocumented Mexican workers do not use social services to any significant extent, though they do pay numerous taxes. For demographic reasons, in the near future fewer Americans will be available to take low-wage, entry-level jobs, so the issue of the displacement of American workers by undocumented Mexicans is likely to decline in importance. Mexico exports some of its unemployment and gains foreign exchange that workers send or bring home as well as some technical skills when workers return home. The migrants gain higher incomes and, frequently, better working conditions than in Mexico. These phenomena explain why undocumented Mexican workers have long been a "normal, functioning ingredient" of the southwest borderlands, where they have been encouraged and utilized "with the approval and support of social and cultural institutions of the region with the tacit cooperation of border control agencies and legal authorities." [14]

86. Richard A. Berman, unpublished testimony, public hearing before the Select Commission on Immigration and Refugee Policy, New York, January 21, 1980.

87. Marta Timbres, unpublished testimony, public hearing before the Select Commission on Immigration and Refugee Policy, Phoenix, February 4, 1980.

14. N. Hansen, The Border Economy: Regional Development in the Southwest 158–59 (1981) (quoting, E. Stoddard, *Illegal Mexican Labor in the Borderlands: Institutionalized Support of an Unlawful Practice,* 19 Pac.Soc.Rev. 175 (1976).)

If Hansen has correctly described undocumented migration, is there a problem at all? Need we consider proposals to eliminate, regulate, control, regularize, or legalize the flow of illegal workers? Has not the market reached a solution (with a little help from political institutions) that is beneficial to all parties involved?

Most scholars would answer these questions in the negative, although the reasons for their responses diverge dramatically. Those who view undocumented labor as harmful to American workers are likely to support restrictive policies that attempt to cut down the amount of unlawful migration. Those who believe that illegal migration is beneficial to the American economy, that it is difficult to stop without causing serious economic disruptions, or that undocumented workers are exploited are likely to favor reforms that legalize the status of illegal aliens and regularize the flow of labor.

Even if one concludes that undocumented aliens do not do serious economic harm to the United States, it is still possible to support measures that seek to curtail the flow. According to the Staff Report of the Select Commission on Immigration and Refugee Policy:

> One can see undocumented/illegal migration presenting no serious economic problem negatively and still view it as a serious social problem which requires attention before it becomes worse.
> * * *
>
> The long-term social consequences of a growing undocumented/illegal alien population seem clear:
>
> - Expansion of an underground population with negative consequences for public health, education and the U.S. criminal justice system;
>
> - Promotion of the idea that certain kinds of labor are fit only for foreigners and a growing U.S. dependence on foreign labor for the performance of those jobs;
>
> - Institutionalization of a double standard of legal due process and equal protection for a growing alien population, with concomitant litigation growing out of that ambiguity; and
>
> - Growing disrespect for the law generally and a specific lack of regard for an immigration law which penalizes those who obey it and wait their turn to enter the United States legally.

SCIRP, Staff Report 532–33.[15]

---

15. See Morganthau, *Closing the Door?*, Newsweek, June 25, 1984, at 18, 21:

[W]hy crack down at all? [Senator] Alan Simpson has one answer—a display of forged identification cards and papers seized several years ago by the INS, all of which had been used by one ingenious illegal alien. "Here's my whole pitch," Simpson says. "[The illegal] got an Illinois driver's license, he enrolled in college, got tuition [aid], picked up food stamps, got a social security card, got an AFL–CIO card, got a supplemental food card, got Medicare and Medicaid, got another driver's license. And he got unemployment ... If we allow this to continue, our systems will be gimmicked to death and will break down ... I just think it's kind of foolish to have a law on the books that allows people to laugh at it."

Copyright © 1984, by Newsweek, Inc. All Rights Reserved. Reprinted by Permission.

The Simpson-Mazzoli bill represents the most recent attempt of the federal government to deal with illegal immigration. The legislation would have provided a multi-part program. Both the House and Senate bills would have (1) imposed sanctions on employers who hired undocumented aliens, (2) provided for the legalization of undocumented aliens who had lived in the United States for a certain period of time, (3) increased resources for enforcement, and (4) raised the numerical limitation for Mexico. As mentioned above, the House bill would also have authorized a special temporary worker program.

This package of proposals was crafted to deal with the (often conflicting) concerns of the major groups interested in immigration reform. The strategy succeeded in the Senate, which passed the bill by an overwhelming majority in 1983. In the House, the attempt to include something for everyone had less success: every provision added to satisfy one group seemed to antagonize another. While the bill managed to squeak through the House in 1984, it died in the House-Senate Conference called to resolve differences between the two chambers' bills.

The following materials describe the several proposals and the spirited debate they engendered.[16] As you read through, ask yourself whether or not you would have voted for or against the provisions or how you would have modified them.

1. EMPLOYER SANCTIONS

As noted above, under current federal law there is no penalty for employers who hire aliens unlawfully in the country. Proposals to impose "employer sanctions" have been numerous over the past decade. *See, e.g.,* H.R. 16188, 92d Cong., 2d Sess. (1972); H.R. 982, 93d Cong., 1st Sess. (1973); Domestic Council Comm. on Illegal Aliens, Preliminary Report (Dec. 1976). The straightforward reasoning behind these proposals is that (1) imposing penalties on employers of illegal aliens will deter the hiring of such aliens; (2) deterring the hiring of illegal aliens will reduce the incentives for illegal entry, since most undocumented aliens come to the United States primarily to find jobs; and (3) enlisting the aid of private employers in deterring illegal migration will help overburdened INS enforcement personnel. The Senate Report on the Simpson-Mazzoli bill made the case for employer sanctions as follows:

> There are only two types of solutions available to the problem of illegal immigration.

> The first is direct enforcement: (A) to physically prevent illegal entry into the United States, for example through border control, fences, and interdiction, and (B) to find and deport those who are successful in entering illegally, as well as those who enter legally and then violate the terms of their visa.

> The second type of solution involves reducing the incentives to enter.

---

16. The provisions which would have authorized higher appropriations for enforcement activities, § 114 of S. 529 and § 111 of H.R. 1510, will not be discussed. The proposal to raise the numerical limitation for Mexico is described at pp. 111–112 *supra*.

Reliance on direct enforcement alone would require massive increases in enforcement in the interior—in both neighborhoods and work places—as well as at the border. This would be more costly and intrusive, as well as less effective, than a program which combines direct enforcement at reasonable levels with a reduction in the incentives to enter the United States.

At the present time there is a substantial disparity in job opportunity between the United States and Third World countries—a disparity which may well continue or even widen as a result of political and social conditions in those countries. Such disparity exists not only in rates of unemployment, but in wages and working conditions. Even if the unemployment rates were reduced, a difficult task in light of the high birth rates in these countries, the disparity in wages and working conditions would remain.

As long as greater job opportunities are available to foreign nationals who succeed in physically entering this country, intense illegal immigration pressure on the United States will continue. This pressure will decline only if the availability of United States employment is eliminated, or the disparity in wages and working conditions is reduced, through improvement in the Third World or deterioration in the United States.

The United States should, of course, assist Third World development, but the achievement of substantially higher living standards there is a prospect only for the long run, and in the short run Third World development may actually increase migration to the United States. Since deterioration in the United States is certainly not an attractive resolution, only one approach remains: To prohibit the knowing employment of illegal aliens.

All objective, comprehensive studies of the problem of illegal immigration, including those by the Ford, Carter and Reagan Administrations, as well as the Select Commission on Immigration and Refugee Policy, have concluded that adequate enforcement of U.S. Immigration laws cannot be achieved by direct enforcement alone. The Committee agrees.

S.Rep. No. 62, 98th Cong., 1st Sess. 7–8 (1983). *See also* H.R.Rep. No. 115, pt. 1, 98th Cong., 1st Sess. 32–34 (1983); SCIRP, Final Report 61–69.

The logic and implications of employer sanctions have been seriously questioned:

B. STRICKLAND, IMMIGRATION REFORM AND LEGAL RIGHTS: A CRITICAL ANALYSIS OF THE SIMPSON–MAZZOLI BILL

America's New Immigration Law: Origins, Rationales, and Potential Consequences
103, 109–12 (W. Cornelius & R. Montoya, eds.) (Center for U.S.-Mexican
Studies Monograph Series, 11, 1983).

Effectiveness

No evidence, historical or theoretical, has ever demonstrated that employers and industries which depend on the undocumented can or will recruit domestic workers. Nor have employer sanctions had any demonstrable effect on the employment of undocumented aliens in those states and countries which have enacted such laws. Since the enforcement of employer sanctions laws will necessarily be selective, some employers will undoubtedly find their present practices of recruiting the undocumented more economical than increasing wages and improving working conditions to the point that jobs become attractive to domestic workers.

The schemes by which an employer could attempt to avoid the sanctions are practically endless. They could pay employees on a cash-only basis and upon inquiry deny the existence of such employees. They could have several employees work under a single set of legal documents. Or they could simply show the employee's date of hiring to be a date prior to the enactment of the bill, since the sanctions do not apply to present employees.

Costs of Enforcement

Recent research has shown that the majority of the undocumented work for small businesses with few employees. The INS does not have the personnel or resources to investigate these thousands of businesses and prosecute violations at this level. They would be forced to concentrate resources in sporadic and largely ineffective "raids," in much the same way that they now attempt to detect the undocumented. The amount spent per enforcement effort will necessarily be high and the cost in social divisiveness incalculable. The proposal for a national employment identity card, moreover, will create incredible costs. The costs of simply upgrading the Social Security card by including the sex and birthdate of the holder and printing the card on "security" paper has been estimated at $850 million and would require 62,000 staff-years. Since no evidence suggests that undocumented aliens adversely impact our society at anywhere near this level, one wonders whether the cure is worse than the perceived illness.

Exploitation of Aliens

Although it cannot achieve its announced objectives, an employer sanctions law, even if only sporadically enforced, will have an adverse impact on the undocumented. Many of these workers are already exploited by employers who fail to pay minimum wages or force employees to work in unsafe conditions. The risk involved in hiring the undocumented after the enactment of employer sanctions will tempt employers to increase these abuses. They will pay their employees in cash rather than by check, thus making minimum wage violations easier to perpetrate and more difficult to verify. Since they will be keeping no formal payroll records, employers could also deny that they employed individuals who suffered injuries on the job. The increased vulnerability of undocumented workers to their employers' whims will make them even more reluctant to report minimum-wage and health and safety violations, and they will become even less likely to engage in organizational activities and could more easily be used as strikebreakers.

DISCRIMINATION AGAINST CITIZENS

Several factors will contribute to a tendency for employer sanctions to increase discrimination against ethnic Americans. First, since the necessity of selective enforcement and a shortage of resources will force the INS to concentrate its enforcement efforts, an employer who hires large numbers of ethnic workers will run a much greater risk of undergoing investigation. Since such investigations will cost the employers time and money, many of them may attempt to avoid even the possibility of an investigation by reducing the number of ethnic workers that they employ. Since employers are seldom in a position to evaluate the authenticity of documents presented by an employee, many will presume ethnic workers to be illegal and therefore to represent a risk. After the passage of California's employer sanctions law, for example, employers laid off large numbers of Hispanic workers.

Employer sanctions will also contribute to discrimination against ethnic Americans by creating a climate of hostility against certain ethnic groups, especially Latinos and Asians. Since INS enforcement priorities overwhelmingly emphasize the Latino and Asian immigrant, they have already created, to a certain extent, the perception that most members of these ethnic groups are "illegal." One sees this hostility demonstrated when people worry about a Hispanic "Quebec" in the United States. The perception that the Latino immigrant is somehow linguistically and culturally unassimilable has already gained wide acceptance, despite studies which show that almost no third-generation Hispanics still use Spanish as their dominant language. By singling out Latinos and Asians as potential problems in the workplace, employer sanctions will in practice increase popular hostility towards all members of these groups.

DANGER FOR CIVIL LIBERTIES

Finally, employer sanctions and the provision for a national employment identification system create a tremendous potential for the abuse of civil liberties. The existence of such a system will create the temptation to use the identification document for purposes other than determining eligibility for employment, a tendency already manifest in the amendment permitting local police to inquire into immigration status. In recent years, the FBI, IRS, and CIA have abused their powers, and we have no assurance that government agencies will not similarly abuse the employment eligibility card, which would make available an incredible amount of information on any given individual. This response to a perceived problem itself implies much greater risks than does the "problem" which it purports to solve.

———

The employer sanctions provisions had two parts: (1) a requirement that an employer verify the status of an applicant for a job, and (2) a prohibition against hiring "an alien knowing the alien is an unauthorized alien * * * with respect to such employment." S. 529, § 101(a)(1); H.R. 1510, § 101(a)(1). An "unauthorized alien" was defined as an alien who was not either lawfully admitted for permanent residence or authorized to be employed by the Act or by the Attorney General. *Id.*[17]

The legislation was expected to work in the following way. A prospective employee would approach an employer in search of a job. Before hiring the individual, the employer would ask the applicant to present some form of identification that would establish that the person was not unlawfully in the country. If the individual presented appropriate documentation, the employer would make a record of it and then could proceed to hire the individual. The verification requirement was justified on two grounds: it made illegal hires less likely and provided the employer with an affirmative defense if it later turned out that the individual hired was in fact an illegal alien.

This overall scheme presented several difficult problems for the legislators. First, it was generally believed that a widespread underground market in false identity papers existed. Thus, to be effective, the identification required would have to be made counterfeit-proof. Several proposals were suggested, including a counterfeit-proof social security card; a national identity card; and a computerized phone-in system (similar to that used for verifying credit card charges). Second, objections were raised that the verification and record-keeping requirements were too burdensome on small businesses and individual employers. Third, it was argued that the new provisions would foster discrimination against foreign-looking persons, particularly Mexican-Americans: employers would demand identification more often from persons who appeared to be Hispanic, and employers bent on denying employment on the basis of race or national origin could do so and then claim that they thought the applicants were illegal aliens. (Supporters of the bill responded to the

17. The Senate version contained stiffer penalties: employers who failed to verify the status of employees would be subject to a civil penalty of $500 for each violation; employers found to have knowingly hired illegal aliens would be fined $1,000 for the first violation and $2,000 for each subsequent offense. The Senate bill also established criminal penalties (a maximum fine of $1000 and six months in prison) for persons who engaged in a "pattern or practice" of violations. Under the House version, first-time violators of both the verification and hiring requirements would simply receive citations. Employers who thereafter failed to verify the status of employees would be fined $500 for each violation; and those who violated the hiring prohibition would receive a $1,000 fine for the second offense and a $2,000 fine for each subsequent offense. Furthermore, the House bill provided for no criminal penalties: the Attorney General was limited to seeking injunctive relief against "pattern or practice" violators.

last argument by pointing to the mechanics of the verification system. Covered employers would have to demand identification from *all* job applicants, not only those who appeared foreign, and an applicant's provision of the specified documents would furnish an affirmative defense to the employer in all cases.)

One of the most hotly debated issues was whether or not some kind of national identification system should be established to prevent the use of fraudulent papers and to relieve employers of concerns about whether the documents presented to them were valid. Both bills permitted usual forms of identification (such as U.S. passports, Social Security cards, birth certificates, driver's licenses) to suffice in the short run. The Senate bill also would have required the President, within three years of enactment, to "implement such changes in [the documentation requirements] * * * as may be necessary to establish a secure system to determine employment eligibility." S. 529, § 101(a)(1). The House, after a bitter and emotional debate, deleted a provision calling for a presidential study. Indeed, an amendment was adopted in the House which stated:

> [N]othing in this section shall be construed to authorize, directly or indirectly, the issuance or use of national identification cards or the establishment or administration of a national identification card or system.

H.R.1510, § 101(a)(1).

The objection raised most vociferously against the employer sanctions provisions was that they would encourage discrimination on the basis of national origin and race. The following excerpts from the House debate provide a glimpse of the differing positions.

Mr. DE LA GARZA.

* * *

* * * I have a basic human right as a creature of God, and I have a basic right assured me by our Constitution that many of us have fought for and many of our people have died for, that I do not have to identify myself beyond the norm to ask for a job. And this is what the Simpson-Mazzoli bill is going to do, I do not care how you slice it, I do not care how you explain it. If someone looks like me, I have got to show them social security or some document, a passport or driver's license.

* * *

Mr. MAZZOLI. Mr. Chairman, if the gentleman would yield, I just want to be sure that the implication was not left that somehow we are asking a certain class of people to go beyond what another class of people would have to do. We are asking everyone to do the same thing. The gentleman objected, we are asking everyone to do the same thing.

* * *

Mr. GARCIA. But those people will not be asked. It will be us that will be asked. That is the point we have been trying to make.

* * *

Mrs. BOXER.

* * *

It is important to note that this kind of discrimination has already taken place, and I would cite to you Time magazine in 1982 which did a story on "Project Jobs" that happened in California, when the Immigration Service went in and raided to find illegal aliens.

I think it is important to note that we have a track record on what happens when these kinds of raids take place. Time stated that "Employers admitted reluctance even to rehire workers who managed to prove their legal status to arresting officers." You can imagine how that feels; not only are you subjected to this unbelievable discrimination, to this kind of rough treatment, because you look different and you sound different, but once you have proven that you are not different, that you are a citizen or that you are here legally, you cannot even get your job back. I think that is a major problem that this bill poses for us.

* * *

So sanctions will not only create new forms of discrimination; they will serve to perpetuate existing job discrimination. So how anyone who proposes this bill can say it will not occur, we know discrimination is occurring right now, and the passage of Simpson-Mazzoli will make it worse.

* * *

Mr. LUNGREN. * * *

Mr. Chairman, the gentlewoman mentioned an article that appeared in Time magazine which described a situation that exists under present law in which an INS raid takes place at a particular area of employment, and after that the people may discriminate because they are fearful of hiring someone who is here illegally unknowingly. That is what the current law is.

The Simpson-Mazzoli bill sets up a procedure whereby a simple verification done with respect to everybody, whether they speak with an accent, whether they have blond hair, blue eyes, or whatever, just as a very simple thing, and then the results of that slight imposition of a paperwork burden act as a protection. So where is there the incentive to discriminate as a result of Simpson-Mazzoli versus the discrimination that the gentlewoman describes that takes place now because of the uncertainty of the present law.

* * *

Mrs. SCHROEDER:

* * * In my part of the country it is the moderate and small businessman who is the major employer, and they never quite have the money to have the fancy personnel departments or the fancy lawyers who can go to all the fancy seminars to learn what the law is today.

And as a consequence, what happens is that somebody tells them, "Hey, guess what? The Congress just passed employer sanctions."

So that guy says, "Well, the last thing I want is the Feds sticking their nose in here, and what do I have to do to keep them out?" And if his image is that Hispanics will trigger the Feds coming in to stick their nose in his business and look at the records, and so forth, and so on, he has always got 25 reasons why he can hire someone else, and he is going to tend to go in that direction.

130 Cong.Rec. H5572, H5574 (daily ed. June 11, 1984); *id.* at H5628–30 (daily ed. June 12, 1984).

The arguments of those opposing employer sanctions produced some concessions. The House accepted an amendment proposed by Congressman Frank that would have defined as an "unfair immigration-related employment practice" discrimination against any person with respect to employment "because of such individual's national origin or alienage."[18] This prohibition would have been enforced by a "Special Counsel" to the U.S. Immigration Board (which would have replaced the BIA), who was authorized to investigate and prosecute complaints of an unfair employment practice. Persons found to have violated the anti-discrimination provision could have been subject to civil penalties and orders for back pay. (If the fear was that employer sanctions would lead to discrimination against "foreign-looking" U.S. citizens, what policies support the far broader scope of the Frank Amendment?)

2. LEGALIZATION

The "legalization" provisions of the Simpson-Mazzoli legislation would have permitted aliens who had resided unlawfully in the United States for a certain number of years to regularize their status. The Senate bill provided for a two-tier program. An alien who could establish unlawful residency prior to January 1, 1977 could apply for adjustment of status to permanent resident alien. An alien who could establish unlawful residency beginning between January 1, 1977 and December 31, 1979 would be eligible for temporary resident status; after three years as a temporary

---

18. While Title VII of the 1964 Civil Rights Act, 42 U.S.C. § 2000e–2(a), prohibits discrimination in employment based on race or national origin, the Supreme Court has held that the Act does not reach discrimination based on alienage. *See Espinoza v. Far-* *ah Manufacturing Co., Inc.,* 414 U.S. 86, 94 S.Ct. 334, 38 L.Ed.2d 287 (1973). Furthermore, Title VII only applies to employers with 15 or more employees. 42 U.S.C. § 2000e(b).

resident, the alien could apply for permanent resident status. S. 529, § 301(a). The House bill adopted a different approach. It would have allowed an alien who had been present illegally in the United States before January 1, 1982 to acquire the status of "lawfully admitted for temporary residence." After a year in that status, an alien could apply for adjustment to permanent resident status. Under both bills, aliens granted temporary resident status could be adjusted to permanent resident status only upon a showing that they (1) could meet the naturalization requirements of knowledge of English and American history (INA § 312), or (2) were "satisfactorily pursuing a course of study" to achieve such knowledge.[19]

Why legalize the status of aliens who are residing here in direct and continuing violation of the law? The House Report explained the reasons for the program as follows.

> The United States has a large undocumented alien population living and working within its borders. Many of these people have been here for a number of years and have become a part of their communities. Many have strong family ties here which include U.S. citizens and lawful residents. They have built social networks in this country. They have contributed to the United States in myriad ways, including providing their labor and tax dollars. However, because of the undocumented status, these people live in fear, afraid to seek help when their rights are violated or they become ill. Moreover, their presence, in violation of our immigration law, bears witness to our past failure to maintain the integrity of our borders.

> Continuing to ignore this situation is harmful to both the United States and the aliens. However, the alternative of attempting mass deportations would be both costly and ineffective.

> The Committee believes that the solution lies in legalizing the status of aliens who have been present in the United States for several years, recognizing that past failures to enforce the immigration laws have allowed them to enter and to settle here. The Administration and scholars have testified in support of such a program. This step would enable INS to target its enforcement efforts on new flows of undocumented aliens and, in conjunction with the proposed employer sanctions programs, help stem the flow of undocumented people to the United States. It would allow qualified aliens to contribute more to society and it would help to prevent the exploitation of this vulnerable population in the workplace. It would also provide for the first time reliable data on the source and characteristics of undocumented aliens to further facilitate enforcement efforts to curtail future flows. As the Administration testified, "... a one-time legalization program is a necessary part of an effective enforcement program...."

H.R.Rep. No. 115, pt. 1, 98th Cong., 1st Sess. 37 (1983).

19. The bills would have also provided a lawful status for Cubans and Haitians granted temporary "entrant status" at the time of the Mariel boatlift. *See* p. 685 *supra.*

How would you evaluate the following arguments against legalization?

(1) legalization creates an incentive for future illegal migration;

(2) legalization will produce increased burdens on taxpayers as aliens who attain lawful status become eligible for state and federal social programs;

(3) legalization rewards lawbreakers and is unfair to aliens who have obeyed the law by patiently waiting in their home countries for a visa to become available;

(4) legalization will substantially increase lawful migration as the legalized aliens become citizens and are thereafter entitled to bring to the United States immediate relatives; and

(5) legalization will not accomplish its objectives because many undocumented aliens in the country will be unwilling to present themselves to government authorities.

In light of some of these considerations, various restrictions were written into the legalization provisions. For example, under the House bill, aliens granted lawful temporary residence were made ineligible for most federal financial and medical assistance programs for five years. Would you have supported such a limitation?

3. TEMPORARY WORKER PROGRAMS

The inclusion of employer sanctions in the Simpson-Mazzoli legislation was an attempt to stop the flow of undocumented workers to the United States. But, making the big assumption that such sanctions would be effective, what would be the result? To whom would current employers of thousands—if not millions—of illegal aliens turn? Could citizens and legal resident aliens be persuaded to fill the jobs? At what cost?

Those who believe that American labor cannot replace illegal migrant labor have often recommended that some augmented temporary worker programs accompany employer sanctions. In short, the suggestion is to legalize part of the present illegal flow.

As described in Chapter Three, pp. 175–181 *supra*, the INA presently permits the entry of workers on non-immigrant visas to perform (1) "services of an exceptional nature" requiring "distinguished merit and ability" (INA § 101(a)(15)(H)(i)), or (2) temporary services or labor, if unemployed persons capable of performing such service or labor cannot be found in this country (INA § 101(a)(15)(H)(ii)). Why, one might be led to ask, are not these current statutory provisions adequate to meet the demands of American employers? Why is there discussion of a new temporary worker program?

The answer must begin with appreciation of the fact that most employers who hire aliens to perform temporary labor do not do so through the H–2 program. They hire undocumented aliens who have entered illegally or non-immigrant aliens who have entered for a purpose other than working (*e.g.*, visitors or students). Since it is not presently illegal to hire aliens not authorized to work in the United States, the employer saves time and money hiring whomever he can find rather than going through the process required by the Justice and Labor Departments under the H–2 program. Furthermore, southwestern agriculture has generally needed a large mobile work force for a short period of time to harvest perishable crops. For many growers, the cumbersome procedures of the H–2 program are not viewed as providing the requisite flexibility. *See* Lungren & Holsclaw, *An Analysis of the H–2 Program: the Admission of Temporary Foreign Agricultural Workers into the United States,* 1 Yale L. & Policy Rev. 240, 243 (1983). These circumstances have led to the curious situation in which approximately 20–30,000 aliens per year enter under the H–2 program to cut sugar cane in Florida or pick apples in New York while hundreds of thousands of aliens illegally cross the southwest border to take jobs around the country.

What should be done to control the flow of temporary labor into the United States? The Senate and House versions of Simpson-Mazzoli adopted different strategies. The Senate would have tinkered with the H–2 program in an attempt to streamline its administration. S. 529, § 211. *See* S.Rep. No. 62, *supra,* at 18–19. The House adopted a controversial amendment that would have established a new temporary agricultural worker program ("H–2P") to aid producers of perishable goods. H.R. 1510, § 211. Representative Panetta, sponsor of the amendment, defended his proposal as follows:

> [If we are going to restrict undocumented workers from coming into this country], then it seems to me the legislation has to recognize some basic realities.
>
> One of those realities is the nature of the perishable crop industry in this country. Those crops are extremely sensitive to changing weather conditions. You cannot pin down at what exact moment a perishable crop is ready for harvesting. It must be picked within a short period of time at that point and it sometimes can be only a few hours that a grower has in order to salvage that crop.
>
> The second point is that the perishable crop industry in this country happens to be a substantial industry. Production today is valued at almost $23 billion in the perishable crop area, and that area hires over 1 million workers at the present time. It pays about $4 billion in wages. It is an important industry to the people that are part of it and to the consumers of America that are part of that industry as well.
>
> * * *
>
> The third reality is that this is an area that is labor intensive. Some mechanization has developed for the purpose of picking these crops but, very frankly, it is basically labor intensive. In order to pick these crops you need workers.
>
> The fourth reality is that this very diversified industry has had to rely largely on foreign workers to harvest the crops. You

may not like it and it may not be a good idea, but that is the reality we deal with. That industry has relied to a large extent on foreign workers and it is a history that goes back for many years in this country, back to before World War I.

In World War I there was a program that was initiated for that purpose. In World War II as well as the H–2 Program, a work force was built in for the perishable crop industry that began with Italians, Filipinos, with Asians and Mexicans and Hispanics all working in the field.

My father, when he first came to this country, worked in the field with his brothers because that was the nature of the jobs that were required in the perishable crop area.

It has not been the kind of work, unfortunately, that has attracted large numbers of domestic workers. There are all kinds of reasons: wages, the kind of work that is involved here. It is not pleasant work. Believe me, I have done it. It is not pleasant work. It is tough work.

So for all those reasons there is this reliance on foreign workers. Even when there was an effort to shut down use of foreign workers it continued. When the Bracero Program was brought to a close, did that stop the use of foreign workers? Absolutely not. We went into the massive illegal immigration problem that continues to supply the workers in the fields.

Today 50 to 80 percent of many of the crews are illegal. That is a reality that we have to deal with.

Thus, if this bill works, and it terminates or substantially reduces the number of undocumented workers who enter this country, then those who are involved in the perishable crop industry face a choice: Hire domestic workers if they are available, if they are qualified, if they are there. If not, perhaps hire illegals, undocumented workers, or lose the crop. Those are the choices that are going to face farmers in this area.

The point, it seems to me, is to construct a bill that will not force that kind of choice between hiring illegals or losing your crop. That is not what we should be about in developing this legislation.

The choice ought to be this: Hire domestic workers or hire legalized foreign workers in a program that provides safeguards, that provides protections, that provides the kind of security that is not available to the undocumented workers who now work in the field.

130 Cong.Rec. H5839 (daily ed. June 14, 1984).[20]

---

20. The amendment was unsuccessfully opposed on a number of grounds:

Mr. RICHARDSON. * * *

The program reduces Government involvement and limits protections for foreign and domestic workers. Specifically—

The following materials provide a number of different perspectives on temporary worker programs. As you read them, notice what factual and theoretical assumptions underlie each viewpoint.

RICHARD N. SINKIN, SIDNEY WEINTRAUB & STANLEY R. ROSS, A PHASED OUT GUEST WORKER PROPOSAL

SCIRP, Staff Report, Appendix F, 344, 346–59 (1981).

The current system does provide needed labor, usually at modest cost, and thereby provides a general subsidy in the form of cheaper goods and services. It also provides sending countries with a safety valve for economic and political discontent and enables them to acquire a substantial number of dollars through remittances. The major cost is that the current system of half-hearted enforcement of our immigration laws, of some exploitation of vulnerable and tractable foreign workers, of possible

First, the Panetta amendment provides even fewer protections than the bracero program of the forties, fifties, and sixties, which was highly criticized for its adverse effect on domestic and foreign workers.

Second, past guestworker programs of this kind both here—bracero—and in Europe have been found to spur undocumented immigration on the part of foreign workers who simply don't return home.

Third, in an effort to encourage foreign workers to return home, the amendment would require contributions to a trust fund that could not be given back to an alien until he returned to his home country. However, these contributions may not be sufficient to induce aliens to leave the United States.

Fourth, foreign workers could be admitted for up to 11 months at a time. This is another reason why it is foolish to believe that they will return home and seek legal reentry to the United States next year.

Fifth, there is no ceiling on the number of foreign workers to be admitted. The numbers could range from 150,000 to 500,000 yearly, which would cause severe competition with domestic workers.

Sixth, domestic workers wouldn't have to be recruited until after an employer's application for foreign workers had been approved. Even then, there is no means set out in the amendment for enforcing the recruiting requirement.

Seventh, recruitment of domestic workers would only have to be done locally. Thus, domestic workers available outside a local area of recruitment might not be made aware of job opportunities.

Eighth, domestic workers displaced by temporary workers will be disproportionately Hispanic. Additionally Hispanics in urban areas will be vulnerable to the competition of the displaced rural workers who move to cities seeking employment.

Ninth, since the Panetta amendment doesn't guarantee foreign workers a minimum period of employment, a large pool of foreign workers in the United States will begin to compete with one another and with domestic workers. This will ultimately depress farm wages and working conditions.

Tenth, although Panetta provides that wages and working conditions for foreign workers should not adversely affect the wages and conditions for domestic labor, there is no standard established to measure such adverse effect.

Eleventh, foreign workers would enter the country without guaranteed employment or a contract with any particular employer. Consequently, they could spend a considerable amount of money to get here and find no jobs once they arrive.

Twelfth, there is no standard for determining whether housing that an employer provides a foreign worker is adequate.

Thirteenth, although employers could be penalized for violations of the program, [no] mechanism is set out in the Panetta amendment to carry out this enforcement provision.

Fourteenth, foreign workers would be ineligible for Federal legal services.

130 Cong.Rec. H5868 (daily ed. June 14, 1984).

damage to those U.S. citizens who compete with illegal entrants, and the establishment of a dual society violates fundamental U.S. principles of justice and equity. The benefit of the system for the majority may come at the expense of the most disadvantaged minority (the unemployed and the lowest income groups) in our society. Our own view is that preference should be given to improving the lot of the most disadvantaged U.S. citizens, including the reduction of the potential or actual negative impact of illegal migrants on those most likely to be hurt. One final consideration argues for altering current practices in the near future. As the populations of major sending countries, particularly Mexico, increase substantially, the pressures may reach such a level that bilateral agreements may not be possible.

* * *

What follows is a proposal to reduce the negative impact of large numbers of undocumented workers now present in the U.S. This could be accomplished by negotiating with major sending countries, especially Mexico, a guest worker program of limited duration with a declining number of guest worker visas each year, ideally reaching zero at the end of the period. The critical element of this proposal is that it is a limited program, to be phased down and out over a clearly defined period of time, that regularizes and legalizes what is now clandestine and illegal.

* * *

A. BILATERAL NEGOTIATIONS

One of the central premises of this proposal is that in order to minimize the negative foreign policy consequences of any change from the current situation, cooperation between the United States and the major sending countries, particularly Mexico, is desirable. Therefore, we believe that the United States should indicate its willingness to negotiate a series of bilateral intergovernmental agreements for the establishment of the phased out guest worker program. Since Mexico is the largest single sending country, the United States should begin the program with Mexico. The terms of the agreement negotiated with Mexico could then become a model for a series of intergovernmental agreements with sending countries in the Caribbean and Central America. The relative numbers of visas would be tailored to estimates of the migration patterns already existing. This means that Mexico would receive the largest number with the smaller countries receiving correspondingly smaller quotas of visas. It is important to remember that while the number of undocumented workers coming from the Caribbean and Central America may be smaller than the number of Mexicans, the impact [on] these sending societies may be just as significant.

B. THE NUMBERS

Because large numbers of undocumented workers are already residents in the U.S., the beginning number of guest worker visas should be substantial—in the hundreds of thousands rather than the tens of thousands of the H–2 program. The final number could be determined by an assessment, carried out by the Department of Labor, of current U.S. needs for temporary foreign labor with minimal damage to the domestic labor force. In addition, the needs of the sending countries should be taken into consideration during the bilateral negotiations. In the final analysis, the number chosen must be a political decision.

The phased out guest worker program assumes that the U.S. government will issue a general amnesty for those who have established roots in this society. It would not be equitable to provide work permits for foreigners not in the United States while making it impossible for persons already here to regularize their status. In our proposal, those who do not qualify for such an amnesty but can demonstrate that they have been working in the U.S. would have the highest preference for a temporary work permit. Clearly, the cut-off date will play a major role in determining the beginning number of the guest worker program. A generous amnesty will concomitantly reduce the size of the initial number of visas; a restrictive amnesty will necessarily force adoption of a larger number.

A second critical factor in determining the beginning number is the method used to determine the areas where guest workers can work. We propose that the Department of Labor, as part of its general assessment of labor need, certify certain sectors of the economy like agricultural sectors now using large numbers of undocumented workers, certain service sectors like hotels and restaurants, and construction, where it would be legal to employ guest workers. Again, the more sectors that are certified, the larger the beginning number will have to be.

The certification of sectors rather than specific jobs as is now done under the H–2 program has several advantages. The first is that it reduces the cumbersome and often slow certification process. Moreover, it would be impractical to certify hundreds of thousands of individual jobs. The most obvious disadvantage is it may be difficult to define precisely [what] "sector" means.

C. METHOD OF DECLINE

We propose that the guest worker program last no more than five years. Any shorter period would not allow sufficient time for the parties concerned to make the necessary adjustments to the future absence of undocumented workers. A sudden stoppage of our current system could cause severe disruptions in both the U.S. economy and in Mexico and the Caribbean, and it would surely produce further tension in the relations between the two countries. A longer period would make the transition easier but less certain, and it would also allow the affected parties to postpone making the difficult decisions required by an end to the current system.

The size of the program should be reduced by a fixed amount each year until ideally it reaches zero at the end of five years. For example, should the beginning number be established at 500,000 guest worker visas for the first year (a figure used only for illustrative purposes), then the decline would take place at a rate of 100,000 per year.

* * *

Because in all probability some H–2 type program will continue, the zero figure in the sixth year is a goal that may have to have some flexibility. Nevertheless, we believe that the number of foreign temporary workers should be minimal, and that even the current H–2 program should be phased down or out along with the new guest worker program.

D. PATTERN OF WORK

To make the phased out program work, five crucial areas of actual working conditions must be included. These are: (1) where within the certified sectors will the guest worker be entitled to work: for a single employer or wherever employment can be found; (2) how long will the guest worker be permitted to remain legally in the U.S.; (3) how will the holder of a temporary work permit be paid; (4) how will the guest worker be recruited; and (5) how will the guest workers be protected?

1. For Whom Will Guest Workers Work?

There are basically two options: (a) bind the guest worker to a single employer for a specific period of time, or (b) allow the guest worker the freedom to seek work in any of the sectors certified by the Department of Labor. Each of these has advantages and disadvantages.

The single employer option would allow the U.S. to control more effectively the presence of foreign workers in the labor market. Its principal drawback is that, like the *bracero* program of 1942–1964, it raises the issue of indentured workers bound to a single employer without the alternative to seek better working conditions. This has been the experience of the earlier *bracero* program and the current H–2 program.

The freedom to seek work in the certified sectors option removes the objection of indentured workers and the lack of freedom associated with the single employer option. On the other hand, there are several problems with the free market option. The first is that allowing guest workers such freedom raises the possibility that because there would be reduced controls many might overstay their visas. In addition, there will surely be more difficulties in guaranteeing that workers remain in the certified sectors. And, third, allowing temporary foreign workers such mobility to compete in the labor market could raise serious political opposition to the entire phased out guest worker program.

There are some compelling reasons for the worker to have the freedom to seek work in any of the certified sectors, particularly in light of the many abuses that occurred under the *bracero* program. Many of the objections against the freedom of mobility option could be removed if the U.S. implemented an effective employer sanctions program (which would be necessary in any event to control illegal immigration) and strengthen enforcement of our immigration laws. Moreover, it seems reasonable to require employers to report the hiring of guest workers and to notify the agency in charge of departures of workers holding temporary work permits. Through a reporting system the movement of temporary workers could be monitored. And, finally, the freedom of the guest worker to move puts pressures on employers to comply with minimum wage and working condition laws, which is one of the principal purposes of our proposal. Indeed, both the current undocumented system and the bracero program essentially removed incentives for employers to upgrade jobs so that they would be attractive to the domestic work force.

2. How Long a Temporary Work Permit?

The central concept guiding this proposal is that there should not be a permanent work force made up of nonimmigrant laborers. For that reason, we believe that nonimmigrant labor should be concentrated in temporary jobs, those lasting less than one year. Although the temporary work permit could last anywhere from three months to one year, our preference is for nine months. This is sufficient time to meet the demands for agricultural workers (three months would not be enough time) while at the same time satisfying the temporary qualities of the overall program. The choice of the duration of the temporary work permit should be based on the demonstrated needs of the employers even though it is clearly recognized that the final length of time will be an arbitrary decision that will not satisfy all interested parties.

A related issue concerns the eligibility of previous guest workers to receive another temporary work permit in a succeeding year. Our preference here is to allow those who have experience and have established networks within the U.S. to be eligible for as long as possible under the phased out system. There is no reason to exclude past guest workers from participating again and indeed, there may be many reasons for desiring repeaters. One is to limit the number of new persons entering into the migratory flow who might, at the end of the program, make demands for permanent entry or increase the level of demands within the sending countries. On the other hand, the sending countries may have strong desires to allow new migrants exposure to our economy, and these goals should be considered during the negotiations.

3. How Will Guest Workers Be Recruited?

The issue of how temporary workers will be recruited breaks down into two subsidiary concerns: where and by whom? Basically, there are two places where the recruiting contracts could be negotiated: in the sending country or in the U.S. Should recruiting take place within the border of the U.S., it would be an invitation for many to cross the border illegally in the search for a job that would then give them a temporary work permit. Such a recruiting system has the advantage that it would require little in the way of a recruitment mechanism. Also it would not involve foreign governments directly in the recruiting process. Nevertheless, even though a recruiting procedure on foreign soil has many more complications, it seems preferable to us for several reasons. First, it would not encourage illegal crossings of the border, and a major thrust of this proposal is to reduce the U.S. demand that induces illegal crossings. Second, recruitment abroad would allow more effective control over the numbers of temporary workers who come into the country. Third, the already established H–2 recruiting mechanism might provide an administrative vehicle for guest worker recruiting on a larger scale. And, fourth, contracting abroad assures the cooperation of the sending countries.

Another critical aspect of this problem is who does the recruiting. Basically, there are two options: the U.S. government can recruit and then allocate to those applying for guest workers; or the private sector can do its own recruiting. Traditionally, Mexico has insisted on U.S. government participation to ensure proper treatment of its citizens. Since our preference is for the simplest possible execution of the program, it seems preferable for the private sector to be responsible for the recruiting of temporary workers. This would remove the U.S. government as an intermediary in the recruitment process, but we anticipate government oversight.

A central issue of the terms of recruitment is whether families will be allowed to join the guest worker. It can be argued that for humanitarian reasons families should be allowed to enter with the temporary worker. We believe, however, that families should be excluded, principally because the jobs will be of short-term duration. Also, the presence of families will substantially increase the social costs of the program and reduce the incentives for return.

4. How Will Guest Workers Be Paid?

Under our program, all workers whether temporary or permanent would be paid the legally established minimum or prevailing wage and would have all the payroll taxes withheld. In addition, guest workers would be eligible for whatever benefits regular employees receive. There would, however, be special provision made so that the payroll deductions—social security, unemployment, workman's compensation, retirement—paid by the guest worker would be returned to him upon his return to his native country. Generally these are deductions undocumented workers can never hope to recover and are frequently withheld by the employer but not paid to the government. This aspect of the proposal has several merits. First, the prospect of a nest egg (often the principal motive for migrating in the first place) should serve as an incentive for return. Returning withheld taxes also meets one of the central criticisms of the current system that undocumented workers pay more into the system than they take out. And the return of payroll taxes after the guest worker returns home will cushion the transitional impact of the return.

5. How Will Guest Workers Be Protected?

Under the current system, undocumented workers are vulnerable to abuses of various kinds: low wages, poor working conditions, excessive hours, and other forms of exploitation. Under the *bracero* program there were many cases of abuses. Above all, a phased out guest worker program must have built-in safeguards for the temporary workers. We propose that the program have a grievance procedure, perhaps administered by the Department of Labor or the Department of Justice. However the procedure is constructed, there is little doubt that foreign consuls must be included in some way. In the bilateral negotiations that will precede the establishment of the phased out guest worker program, one of the central elements will have to include the role of foreign consuls in the complaint procedures.

Also essential to the successful operation of a guest worker program is the right of temporary workers to join unions and share in the benefits of the union. Indeed, much evidence exists already to suggest that undocumented workers frequently join labor unions. This right should be a fundamental part of the U.S. negotiating position.

* * *

E.   SOME IMPLICATIONS OF A PHASED OUT GUEST WORKER PROGRAM

* * *

2.   Impact on the United States Economy

The loss of a major source of labor will inevitably cause some significant changes in the U.S. economy, not all of them favorable. It would be impossible to list all the possible consequences of a successful phased out guest worker program, but several are worth mentioning here. Undoubtedly, many jobs would be mechanized, as apparently is the case with tomato harvesting in Florida, and ultimately jobs would be lost. Since these are jobs primarily held by nonimmigrant laborers, the impact of this loss would be minimal to U.S. labor. In other cases, wages and working conditions would have to be improved to attract national workers, and this might raise the costs and thus the price for most of us. We find it hard to imagine that there is no price sufficient to attract nationals to what are now undesirable jobs at the terms and conditions offered. Clearly, then, a reduction in the employment of cheap foreign labor will have the impact of raising the price of some goods and services.

A second possible economic impact is that many functions would have to be upgraded—productivity would have to be increased by the addition of capital—and these jobs would no longer be suitable for unskilled labor. This might require an expanded job training program targeted on the affected industries.

Or it is conceivable that some productive functions would have to be exported. This would be the reverse of the pattern of bringing labor to capital; instead, we would be bringing capital to labor. This is one of the ways to promote economic development and employment creation in the developing sending countries.

Thus the major economic adaptations will in all likelihood involve raising the price for domestic labor, training for upgraded jobs, eliminating some jobs to raise productivity, and the export of some industries. All of these adaptations are likely to occur. It is doubtful that there would be a one-for-one substitution of domestic for foreign labor, but there might be a one-half-for-one shift. At a time of high minority youth unemployment in most urban areas, it would be an attractive incentive to force employers to seek out domestic sources of labor. In rural areas, the struggle for unionization undoubtedly would take a different turn if growers could not rely on cheap and docile foreign labor.

A. & M.–Immigration Law ACB—29

MICHAEL J. PIORE, ILLEGAL IMMIGRATION IN THE UNITED
STATES: SOME OBSERVATIONS AND POLICY SUGGESTIONS

Illegal Aliens: An Assessment of the Issues
25–27, 29–34 (The National Council on Employment Policy, Oct. 1976).

The growth of clandestine migration into the United States appears to
be a manifestation of a general process through which industrial societies
fill the bottom positions in their occupational hierarchy. Industrial
societies seem to generate a series of jobs, at the bottom of the social
structure, which their own labor force is reluctant to fill. Such jobs are
generally viewed as menial and demeaning; their chief economic characteristic appears to be a lack of job security and career opportunity. They
are rejected in favor of higher level employment opportunities whenever
the latter become available and, sometimes, even in periods of unemployment when there are no alternatives. The rejection of these jobs by
native workers leads industrialists to recruit migrants from underdeveloped rural areas.

Such migrants tend to view their stay in the industrial society as
temporary; they see themselves as permanently attached to the communities from which they came and the jobs an instrumental to their roles at
home. Because they see themselves as outsiders and their stay as temporary, they are undeterred by the inferior social status which the jobs carry
in the society where they are located nor by the relative insecurity and
lack of advancements.

Temporary migrants who are utilized in this way can be drawn either
from domestic or foreign areas. European economic development appears
historically to have drawn upon domestic migrants from underdeveloped
areas within national boundaries and to have moved toward massive
reliance upon foreign workers only in the post-World War II period. In
the United States we relied initially upon foreign workers and turned to
our domestic labor reserves only when foreign immigration was cut off by
World War I and the postwar legislative restrictions. Heavy internal
migration of blacks and Spanish-speaking citizens was then delayed by the
Depression and thus concentrated in the 1940s and 1950s. It is the
exhaustion of the domestic labor reserves in the middle sixties which has,
this suggests, led to a resumption of massive foreign immigration in the
last decade.

This line of argument implies that the heavy emphasis in public
policy discussions upon the competition between native and foreign workers is misplaced. Foreign workers are coming essentially to fill jobs which
native workers have rejected. To the extent that these jobs are critical to
the functioning of an industrial society—and, while there are exceptions,
the jobs taken as a group do seem to be critical—the aliens are complementary to native workers and to domestic consumption patterns. Any
wholesale attempt to end the migration is, therefore, likely to be exceedingly disruptive to the operation of the society and to the welfare of
various interest groups within it, and to meet, for this reason, with
widespread resistance. The gap between the *de jure* policy, which is one

of virtual exclusion of unskilled migrants, and the *de facto* presence of large numbers of such workers is no doubt a result of this fact.

This argument can be restated and directed more explicitly at the current policy debate. A part of that debate centers around the questions of, first, whether or not the current immigration is the result more of push than pull forces and, second, whether it is technically feasible to stop that immigration. My argument is that there is a process involved in which there are jobs in the United States which are vacant for want of labor and that there are workers abroad who want these jobs. *If* the workers were not coming on their own—indeed when the workers *do not* come on their own—the employers who need them look for them, find them, and directly and indirectly encourage their immigration. It is probably technically possible to stop this immigration but the political and social processes in Western industrial societies do not appear conducive to such policies. The attempt to stop the process *de jure* seems invariably to lead to an underground *de facto* immigration system in which the movement of labor continues. In this respect, current U.S. history with respect to the problem mirrors the separate experiences of half a dozen Western European countries. The reason why it is so difficult to effectuate an exclusionary policy, I believe, is because immigrants are basically complementary to native workers and supportive of entrenched patterns of work and consumption. But, even if this were not true, or the truth were very limited, history suggests that the attempt to *stop* immigration is unrealistic and diverts attention from the possibilities for controlling it, channelling its impact and limiting its detrimental effects.

* * *

The thrust of the preceding is that *de jure* policy tends to cut across the grain of the social and economic processes which are motivating the migration. It argues for a policy which tries instead to work within the constraints of these processes and mold them in a direction more conducive to the society's goals.

The main characteristic of the process from this point of view is that the migration is basically temporary; the migrant himself desires only temporary employment, and so long as his employment is temporary, his role in the United States is complementary to that of native workers. It is only when the migrant remains in this country that he begins to move into higher level positions, to develop roots, and to form a family whose members will constitute a second generation with aspiration for social mobility that brings them into competition with native Americans.

On the other hand, it seems exceedingly important not to attempt to *force* the migration into a temporary mold by measures which penalize, either directly or indirectly, the second generation, once that generation begins to emerge. That generation, if it [has] grown up within an industrial society, is likely to share that society's values. Indeed, to the extent that what differentiates the migrant from the native is simply his temporary status and the fact that he sees himself as a stranger, and not any underlying difference in basic values, the second generation is, for all intents and purposes, native. Its members are unlikely to passively accept their parents' jobs and will be unwilling, possibly even unable, to return to their parent's homes. If they cannot move up into jobs they find, they will come to constitute an alienated, hostile underclass, like the black youth who rioted in the urban ghettos of the 1960s. In order to avoid this and to maximize their ability to meet their aspirations, they must have legitimate legal status and access to educational and other institutions which promote advancement in the society.

Thus, in sum, the ideal immigration policy would be one which met four goals:

a. The maximization of the temporary nature of the process, i.e. the probability that the individual migrant will remain in the U.S. for a short period of time and return home.

b. The maximization of the chances for upward mobility in the second generation.

c. The minimization of the development of an illegal labor market with substandard wages and working conditions.

d. The provision of controls over the labor market in which aliens are working which would minimize the amount of competition with native workers and instill among natives a sense of order and control.

In designing a policy, it is useful to distinguish between the basic institutional arrangement within which immigration occurs, and the strategy pursued given that institutional structure. This may be a useful distinction in any area of public policy, but it is a particularly important factor in immigration where one is trying to mold, directly and indirectly, an evolving social process.

The goals outlined above appear to imply an institutional structure with the following characteristics:

a. A system of visas, permitting temporary migration to the United States to work with the right to return frequently. The visa itself would be relatively permanent but to maintain a valid visa the worker would be required to leave the country for several months a year.

b. The number of such visas would be linked in the long term to some estimate of the numbers of the kinds of low status, low wage jobs for which migrants appear to be currently recruited. But in the immediate short term, they would have to take account of existing migration streams because it is desirable to bring these within the law. The number of visas could also be adjusted cyclically, to provide expanded opportunities for natives in periods of high unemployment. *However,* all adjustments would take place in new visas issued, since experience suggests that efforts cutting off existing immigrants acts perversely to force them to go underground and, by delaying returns home, to encourage permanent settlement.

c. The temporary visas would be convertible to permanent resident alien status upon application, after some period of years (e.g.

seven) in order to permit the second generation access to the institutions required for upward mobility.

   d. It would be possible to make a temporary visa conditional upon working outside certain geographic regions where competition with the existing labor force is intense; for example, the Southwest. It seems unwise to link the visa to a required residency or occupation since the economic function of migrants is as a geographically and industrially mobile work force. The natural tendencies of the economy to utilize the immigrants in this way seems to have undermined European visa systems with tight geographic and industry occupation specifications.

The institution of a system of this kind would involve substantial changes in our *de jure* immigration policy, but it is not so very far from the *de facto* policy as one might think. On the west coast, for Mexican workers, *de facto* policy is very close to one of open temporary immigration with rather wide opportunity for the [regularization] of status for those who acquire permanent attachments. Existing Immigration and Naturalization Service activity does not appear to constitute a very strong deterrent to entry or reentry. The North-Houstoun study found that although the average Mexican alien in their sample lived in the U.S. a total of two and one-half years, he returned home an average of every six months, a finding which would not be possible if entry were difficult. The system of equity which permits certain relatives of U.S. citizens and resident aliens to enter outside [the numerical limits] provides a system of regularizing the status of permanent migrants, since people who become permanent tend to acquire precisely such relationships. It is quite common for Mexicans to work illegally in the United States while waiting for the papers which will legitimize their status to be processed in Mexico, and even common for the relationships on the basis of which legal status is acquired to have been developed while illegally in the U.S. as well. The practice whereby most illegal aliens are allowed to depart voluntarily works to protect this process since deportation acts as a bar to subsequent legitimization. The immigration courts go to extraordinary lengths to grant voluntary departure to apprehended aliens who have already acquired "equity" in the United States.

* * *

The enforcement policies of the INS are also fairly consonant with the goal of minimizing competition between natives and aliens. The severe limitations upon the budget of the INS gives it a great deal of discretion in deciding which aspects of the law to enforce and, by and large, discretion has been used to minimize the competition between native and alien workers. The concentration of resources in the rural Southwest, where such competition is by all reports most intense, has this effect. Elsewhere, resources tend to be allocated in response to complaints by native workers, which also works to the same end. To this extent, the real problem is that the budget is nowhere near sufficient to handle all such complaints. The policy of allocating resources in response to complaints also has certain very grave disadvantages in terms of the goals we have outlined.   It tends to make the INS an instrument in the hands of employers seeking to abuse their labor forces.   Occasionally, the INS has become an instrument in family quarrels.   These abuses, however, could be curtailed by administrative policy of the INS within the existing system, and an increase in the budgetary resources allocated in accord with existing budgetary priorities, amended to screen out employer complaints and personal quarrels, would have much the same impact upon the labor market as the institutional structure I have advocated.   Again, however, it would remain inequitable.

In any case, the argument is not that the present system is ideal or even desirable.   Simply, that it is not as bad as it looks, and could be made better by apparently minor changes of existing legislation and administrative regulations.   * * *

For the kind of policy I am advocating, however, it is probably a mistake to concentrate too heavily upon institutional arrangements.   It is here that the distinction between those arrangements and the strategy of policy becomes important.   It is difficult to make this point in a general way, but perhaps it can be illustrated by examples of strategies, which can be pursued within a number of institutional structures and which may be more important than the structures themselves in the pursuit of any policy.

What we know about the migration process suggests that once it gets going it is very difficult to halt.   The economy of the home village becomes dependent upon immigrant remittances, creating great pressure for people to participate in the migration process.   Members of the home community have relatives and friends in a number of U.S. cities who can provide job contacts, residences, and resources to finance the immigration. These contacts and those who return home also provide information on multiple, sophisticated border crossing techniques.   For migrations already in process, the push factors, the pull factors, and the techniques of response are at their maximum.   New migration streams should, by contrast, be relatively easy to forestall; and the pay-off to doing so lies not only in those who are actually apprehended but in the prevention of the development of a long-term migration stream.   This implies that enforcement resources should be concentrated on locating and halting the new. In the current institutional structure, this implies, the INS should devote less resources toward halting flows from areas of Mexico which are major contributors and focus instead in investigating aliens coming through Mexico from the rest of Latin America and Mexicans from previously isolated states.   Similarly the State Department ought to worry less about policing visas from areas where abuse is already known to be large and concentrate on screening visa applicants from areas where traffic is generally slight but which might constitute the opening wedge in a new migration flow.   In the institutional structure I have proposed, such a policy would imply that temporary visas should be restricted on the basis of existing flows.

Considerations similar to those in policing aliens apply to the policing of employers.   Once an industry has become adjusted to the use of immigrants, it will be very difficult to weed them out. The techniques of production and management will be accommodated to a supply of alien labor; the cost structure of the industry will be adjusted to this supply of alien labor as well. Techniques of entry and recruitment will be carefully worked out so that apprehended aliens are readily replaced. In the case of new industries, however, where the flow is just developing, the industry may be more willing to meet its labor shortages in other ways. This implies that the INS will be more effective, concentrating, for example, on northern New England where aliens are just beginning to penetrate manufacturing than on New York or Los Angeles where whole industries have already become dependent upon them. To effectively forestall immigration, however, it appears that more than enforcement is required. The industry must be helped to meet its labor shortages in other ways.

One of the major motivations of immigrant workers appears to be the accumulation of funds to finance social advancement at home. The number of plans for return migration which are actually realized, however, depends very much upon the opportunity structure of the home country. In most of these countries that structure is rapidly changing and the changes are responsive to governmental policies. It should be possible to mold these opportunities, through policy, so as to encourage return. Since the immigrants have resources in the form of capital and skills, which are attractive to their home country and important in the development process, this would seem to fit readily with the existing policy goals of the countries of origin. The possibility of capturing these resources through a process which at the same time fosters the temporary character of migration would seem, in other words, to provide the fulcrum around which a community of interest between the donor and receiving countries could be developed. Such cooperation must be based upon an appreciation of the nature of the social processes underlying the migration. The migrants see the process as one which involves the accumulation of capital to finance enterprises which give them a modicum of economic independence. A strategy based upon small enterprises which migrants can finance out of their earnings abroad and manage themselves appears to be called for.

WAYNE A. CORNELIUS, MEXICAN MIGRATION TO THE UNITED STATES: THE LIMITS OF GOVERNMENT INTERVENTION

4–6, 8–11 (Working Papers in U.S.-Mexican Studies, 5) (1981).

The level of migration from Mexico that can be expected during the next twenty years will be determined by such factors as the magnitude of the real wage differential between the United States and Mexico (which now averages 7-to-1 for unskilled jobs but can reach 13-to-1 for agricultural work); the rate of inflation in Mexico (which reached an annual rate of 30 percent in 1980); the rate of labor-force growth in Mexico (700,000 to 800,000 new job seekers entering the Mexican labor market each year in the early 1980s, rising to 1,200,000 new entrants per year by the early 1990s, then falling); the rate of new job creation in the Mexican economy (about 700,000 per year in 1979–80); and the size of the backlog of already unemployed or underemployed workers in Mexico (an estimated 10 million workers in 1980). If the Mexican economy as measured by its GNP continues to grow at its 1979–80 rate of 8 percent or more a year, it may generate enough new jobs to absorb a portion of this backlog. But many of those who cannot be accommodated, particularly unskilled workers in rural areas and small cities, will continue to seek at least short-term employment in the United States.

The number of Mexicans in the United States labor market will also depend to a large extent on the level of United States employer demand for Mexican labor. The United States public and many of its political leaders tend to view workers from Mexico as superfluous to United States economic needs. Mexican migrants are not seen as necessary for the functioning and growth of the United States economy, and their presence in low-wage, low-skill labor markets is believed to affect adversely the economic interests of large numbers of American citizens. The presence of Mexicans (and most other foreign workers) in United States labor markets is treated like a cancer—a pathological phenomenon—that can and should be cut out of the economy and society. In this view, the United States has not become structurally dependent on Mexican and other immigrant labor. Such labor is just a subsidy to greedy employers intent on protecting their profit margins and to middle-class consumers who do not want to pay more for their restaurant meals, clothing, agricultural produce, and maid service. This subsidy can and should be ended by purging the labor market of these "unnecessary" workers. This can be accomplished through government action designed to make it far more difficult for undocumented migrants to enter the United States and find jobs. Such a policy may produce some short-term disruptions and unpleasant side effects: Consumer prices for some items now produced with Mexican labor would go up; a few declining, economically marginal businesses would be forced to close; and the United States might have to accept a slightly lower rate of overall economic growth. But these are all prices worth paying, according to proponents of this view, who say "good riddance to the Mexican work force."

This view of the role of Mexican labor in the United States economy is contradicted by the analyses and projections of other social scientists, who foresee an increasingly important—and essential—place for Mexican workers in the United States economy into the next century. Proponents of this view see labor migration not as an artificial or pathological phenomenon, but rather as one of several processes that are inexorably promoting—for good or ill—the integration of the United States and Mexican economies. Moreover, the formation of a truly binational labor market will continue to occur, regardless of what the United States or Mexican government tries to do about it. The Mexican presence in the United States labor market is too large and too deeply institutionalized to be "cut out." To assume that government action can restructure the low-skill, low-wage labor markets in the United States in order to purge them of foreign workers is an exercise in fantasy and wishful thinking.

* * *

* * * [T]he view that the United States does not need Mexican laborers stems from an anachronistic, romanticized image of the United States labor market, where disadvantaged young Americans will take any job if only it pays well and offers humane working conditions, regardless of how socially undesirable the work may be, regardless of how dirty, boring, or repetitious the task and regardless of how limited the prospects are for advancement. Clearly, low wage scales are not the only disincentive to taking the jobs now performed by Mexicans and other foreign workers, and the United States government's capacity to eliminate these other disincentives is quite limited. Even in terms of wage scales, the government cannot force private employers to pay more than the legal minimum wage, which they are already paying for the overwhelming majority of jobs now held by Mexican workers, particularly outside of agriculture.

Under these circumstances, it serves little purpose to speculate about ways of phasing out the use of Mexican labor to fill low-skilled, manual-labor jobs. It is not simply a matter of capitalism seeking to protect its profits. The demand for Mexican labor in the United States economy is selective; not all United States capitalists need Mexican labor, and those who do usually need Mexicans to fill only a few categories of jobs in their enterprises. The selectivity of the United States demand is a direct reflection of certain structural features of the political economy that cannot be easily manipulated through government action.

* * * All available evidence indicates that there will continue to be a substantial number of Mexican workers in the United States labor market, whether or not the general public or United States officials like it. Indeed, there is no evidence that any step taken by the United States government in the last one hundred years to restrict immigration from Mexico has had any appreciable effect on the underlying, structural demand for Mexican labor in the United States economy. The burden of proof remains on those who argue that the present level of United States employer demand for Mexican workers can be altered dramatically in the short-to-medium run, at least at a cost that would be economically, politically, and morally acceptable.

Purging United States labor markets of Mexican workers in the next two decades would require the kinds of government controls on individual movement, hiring practices, and other aspects of daily life that would be intolerable in the United States. It would involve a massive intrusion of the federal government into the lives of citizens and the decisions of private businesses at a time when public opinion in the United States favors a reduction in the role and cost of the federal government.

Such an approach would increase social tensions, rather than reduce them. It would increase racial discrimination in hiring, rather than provide more job opportunities for Hispanic citizens. It would create an anti-immigrant backlash so strong that it would become politically necessary for local and state government agencies to exclude or discriminate against undocumented immigrants and their children in the provision of basic human services like health care and education. This exclusionary treatment would create a permanent underclass of immigrant settlers and their offspring, some of whom may become public charges, thus increasing the long-term burden on United States taxpayers. Finally, this approach would accelerate the flight of United States manufacturers to other countries, while driving many small businesses into bankruptcy, resulting in increased concentration of ownership in agriculture, construction, and urban service sectors.

An alternative approach—more responsive to social, economic, and political realities—would be to concentrate less on trying to reduce the migratory flow, and more on improving the status and bargaining power of Mexicans and other foreign migrants working in the United States. This approach would require the United States to accept the existence of a permanent scarcity of domestic labor to fill low-skill, manual, entry-level jobs, at least in the United States Southwest and other regions with highly expansive economies. Attention would then focus on reducing the vulnerability of foreign workers to exploitation and abuse. Some of the ways to accomplish this would be to increase the opportunities for these workers to enter the United States legally, on both a permanent and temporary basis; stringently enforce existing antidiscrimination laws, the minimum wage, and fair labor standards laws; and vigorously promote the unionization of workers in sectors of the economy where Mexicans and other foreign migrants cluster.

Promoting unionization of the Mexican work force in the United States would require a permanent ban on immigration law enforcement activities in workplaces (the so-called factory raids on businesses suspected of hiring undocumented workers). It would also require United States labor unions to end their long-standing ambivalence or open hostility toward foreign workers in the United States labor market and to recognize these workers as targets for unionization rather than threats to hard-won labor standards. The myth that Mexican workers are unorganizable is gradually being eroded by the successes of local unions in states like California, Arizona, Texas, and Illinois. In several of the Western European countries that imported large numbers of foreign "guest-workers" in the 1960s and early 1970s, unions vigorously recruited these workers as members. Union leaders also insisted that the wages of the lowest-skilled workers rise at a faster rate than those for upper-status workers. As a result, wage scales in the low-skill job categories have not been severely depressed, and the wage gap between low-skill and high-skill workers has narrowed, despite the huge influx of foreign workers, many of whom remained as permanent residents.

Finally, it must be recognized that the current wave of Mexican migration to the United States is the result of literally millions of uncoordinated decisions by individuals, kinship groups, and employers on both sides of the border. The large number of decisions makes this phenomenon less susceptible to government control. Even more important, however, are the high stakes involved in these decisions. Basic human needs motivate most Mexican workers who seek employment in the United States. The income they earn in the United States may make the difference between adequate medical care or death from lack of it;

between enabling children to complete school or going to work; between having enough capital to get married and build a house or living with parents in an already overcrowded home. Such elemental human needs and desires will continue to drive Mexican workers across the border, no matter how harshly United States immigration laws are enforced and no matter what hardships they have to endure to get here.

VERNON M. BRIGGS, JR., FOREIGN LABOR PROGRAMS AS AN ALTERNATIVE TO ILLEGAL IMMIGRATION: A DISSENTING VIEW

The Border that Joins; Mexican Migrants and U.S. Responsibility
223, 235–43 (P. Brown & H. Shue, eds. 1983).

CRITICISMS OF NEW FOREIGN WORKER PROPOSALS

By common agreement of all of the literature, the effect of the presence of illegal immigrants is disproportionately felt in the low-wage labor markets of the United States. Most of the illegal immigrants—especially those from Mexico and the Caribbean area—are themselves poorly skilled, poorly educated, and have language limitations. Even those persons without these characteristics are often downgraded into the same labor market due to their fear of exposure or their inability to produce proper credentials.

It is not necessary to nitpick the deficiencies of proposals for a new foreign labor program. Obviously all of them are simply conceptual sketches. None has scratched the surface of such critical issues as how the workers are recruited, what are their job entitlements, what are the limitations to be placed on employer prerogatives to limit exploitation, what means are to be used to test for job certification, and what protections are to be included for citizen workers and for unions to assure that prevailing standards are not undermined. Moreover, none of them even considers the fact that the INS is in a current state of total administrative chaos. The INS cannot handle the paperwork associated with the legal immigration system, let alone the illegal immigrants. It is inconceivable that INS could administer a new foreign worker program. All of these matters must, of course, be settled before such a foreign worker program is initiated. But anyone familiar with the history of regulatory efforts associated with the H–2 programs, the bracero programs, and the various border commuter systems knows that the task will be—to put it mildly—formidable.

Aside from these administrative matters, the major criticisms of foreign worker programs are their conceptual design, their impact, and their magnitude. All of these considerations are sufficiently serious to counter any alleged merits they might have.

The rationale for proposals for new foreign worker programs is the existence of illegal entry on a massive scale. It is not based on the existence of a demonstrated need in the labor market. Unemployment rates in the United States are among the highest of any of the Western industrialized nations. Moreover, the unemployment rates among Hispanics, blacks, women, and youth far exceed the national aggregate unemployment rates. All of the proposals (as well as the existing foreign worker programs) are designed exclusively for recruiting more workers for the unskilled and semiskilled occupations in primarily low-wage industries. These are precisely the same secondary labor-market jobs in which those citizen workers with the highest unemployment rates are already found. No one is suggesting that there be a foreign worker program to supply more doctors, professors, lawyers, or business executives. Not only would such proposals lead to charges of a "brain drain" from emerging nations, but also the domestic opposition of these privileged and protected workers in the primary labor market could be counted upon to kill any such idea at the moment of its conception. Rather, it is because it is a program that may benefit the privileged but will adversely affect opportunities for the less fortunate and the least politically organized groups in American society that such proposals are put forth. The proposal for a foreign worker program is clearly class-biased.

There is no evidence at all that citizen workers will not do the work illegal immigrants now do. This fundamental point is asserted—without one shred of empirical evidence to support it—in the works of Piore, Cornelius, and Böhning, to mention only a few. But none of these works cites a single occupation or industry in which they can deny that the vast majority of workers are U.S. citizens. Hence, it cannot be the type of work that makes illegal immigrants attractive. Rather, it is the prevailing wage rates and working conditions that determine worker availability. Each year thousands of persons apply for the privilege of collecting garbage in San Francisco and New York City, but they do not do so in many other communities. Why? Because garbage collectors in these two cities are very highly paid, they are unionized, and they enjoy liberal fringe benefit packages. The same can be said of applicants for apprenticeship positions in the building, machinist, and printing trades, where supply always exceeds demand, although the jobs are often dirty, dangerous, and physically demanding. Again, it is not the type of job, but rather the fact that the associated economic benefits are good that explains why applicants seek such jobs in such great numbers. For the contentions of Piore, Cornelius, and Böhning to be valid they must be willing to argue that, no matter what the wages or benefits associated with certain occupations in the American economy, there will be few people who will want to do the work. Certainly no one can seriously argue this point when it is regularly refuted by everyday practice.

Some studies can show selected labor markets in which illegal immigrants have made a collective impact on certain occupations and certain industries. They can find employers who hire illegal immigrants and who contend that U.S. citizens are increasingly difficult to find. But it is just as valid as a counter-argument to say that it is precisely because of the presence of sizable numbers of illegal immigrants that citizen workers are more difficult to recruit. In other words, these employer arguments are a self-fulfilling prophecy. It is because illegal immigrants crowd into certain industries that many low-income citizen workers are forced to withdraw. Few citizen workers can satisfactorily compete with illegal immigrants when the ground rules favor whoever will work for the least pay and under the most arbitrary terms. Yet it is for exactly these same low-wage occupations and industries that foreign worker programs would be designed to supply additional workers.

* * *

As every economist knows, it is impossible to separate the employment effects from the wage effects whenever there is a change in the supply of labor. Hence, the presence of foreign workers would not only affect job opportunities but also affect wage levels in any given labor market. The wage effects are part of the attractiveness of illegal immigrants to American employers. These employers are able to obtain workers at less cost than would be the case in their absence. This does not mean that most employers exploit these workers by paying wages below the federal minimum wage. Obviously, some malevolent employers do pay lower than legal wages, but this is clearly the exception in the present era. Available research shows that most illegal immigrants do receive at least the federal minimum wage, and many receive much more. A foreign worker program, therefore, would not serve as a means of raising wages to the established federal wage floor, since most illegal immigrants are already at that level or beyond. Rather, its presence would modulate against pressures for wages to increase in the low-wage labor market over time.

Most of the wage exploitation that occurs at present is simply the result of the fact that illegal immigrants are available at wage rates that are lower than they would be if the same employers had to hire only citizen workers. This situation, of course, can only be exacerbated by the additional supply of foreign workers. This is exactly the impact that the braceros had in the past. The thorough report on the bracero program by the President's Commission on Migratory Labor found, with respect to wage levels for agricultural workers, "that wages by states were inversely related to the supply of alien labor." Likewise, North's comprehensive study of the commuters found that the minimum wage was essentially the prevailing wage for most commuters. From the fact that the border region contains the three poorest standard metropolitan statistical areas in the country (Brownsville, McAllen, and El Paso), plus the facts that the unemployment rates all along the border are consistently above national rates (frequently they are in double digits) and the labor force participation rates (especially among women) are among the lowest in the nation, it is obvious what the employment and wage effects of a foreign worker program will be upon citizen workers in the secondary labor market.

But the real cause for exploitation is that foreign workers can be expected to be docile workers. Citizen workers know that they have job entitlements, which include minimum wage protection and also extend into a number of other areas, such as overtime pay provisions, safety requirements, equal employment opportunity protection, and collective bargaining rights. It is these additional employee entitlements that an employer can often escape if foreign workers are available. For even though foreign workers (and illegal immigrants too, for that matter) may technically be covered by these work standards, their presence creates a situation in which these safeguards cannot be guaranteed in practice; since enforcement mechanisms for most of these laws are based largely upon employee complaints or actions. It is highly unlikely that foreign workers will know their rights. Even if they are so knowledgeable, they will probably be reluctant to do anything about abuses for fear of losing their jobs. In fact, given the job alternatives available in their native lands, they may not even perceive the violations are being exploitative.

As for unionization, the occupations in which illegal immigrants and commuters are concentrated are rarely unionized at present. The availability of foreign workers will virtually guarantee that unionization will not occur in these labor markets. Hence, a foreign worker program would definitely function as an antiunion device.

Even if the wage rates that an employer must pay are identical for foreign workers and for citizen workers, the foreign workers will be preferred. The probability that foreign workers will be less likely to make demands for job rights or to join unions will make them highly prized. Thus, these will be the critical considerations that will provide, as they now do, the crucial advantages for employers in hiring illegal immigrants.

Another flaw in these proposals is their intended magnitude. A foreign worker program cannot do anything to reduce illegal immigration unless the program is significant in size (at least in the 500,000- to 750,000-person range). But the larger the program, the greater the certainty of adverse impact on citizens. On the other hand, if the scale of the program is small, where will be the deterrence to illegal entry? There must be some limitation on the size of the program and, if there is, what will prevent others, who are not selected, from coming, or others, whose period of work has expired but who wish to remain, from staying? All of the unresolved features of the present system (i.e., employer sanctions, the identification question, amnesty, the use of the voluntary departure system, and the budget and personnel deficiencies of the INS) would remain. A foreign worker program does not resolve any of the current policy problems, but it certainly adds a host of new ones. Certainly, no move should be made even to consider a foreign worker program until all of the ancillary questions are settled.

Moreover, most of the discussions of the foreign worker option assume, implicitly or explicitly, that the program would be a bilateral arrangement with Mexico. This has certainly been true of past experience. But times have changed in both Mexico and the United States. Indeed, it is no accident that the momentum for immigration reform began in the 1960s and 1970s when there was heightened domestic interest in civil rights and the eradication of poverty. The point is that illegal immigrants are streaming into the United States from almost every country in the world. President Carter's message accompanying his immigration proposals stated that 60 countries are "regular" sources of illegal immigration. Fifteen countries have been identified as the major source countries of illegal immigrants. Although about 90 percent of the illegal immigrants apprehended annually are from Mexico, this is merely the result of the concentration of INS apprehension techniques on undocumented entrants in the Southwest. It is doubtful if Mexicans compose as much as 60 percent of the total stock of illegal immigrants in the United States. There are millions of other illegal immigrants who are not Mexicans. Generally, they enter the country with proper documents but overstay their visas. Many face situations of economic deprivation and political persecution at home that are worse than those conditions confronting Mexicans. In fact, compared to many other countries in the Caribbean, Central America, and South America, economic life in Mexico is considerably better. Many of these other countries in the Caribbean—such as Haiti, the Dominican Republic, Jamaica, Barbados, and Trinidad—have large black populations; all of them (and others) are regular sources of "visa abusers." In many instances, the question is not why so many of them seek entry into the United States but, rather, why any of them stay behind, given the bleak futures that confront them. The same can be said of many Asians from Hong Kong, Korea, the Philippines, and Singapore, which are also major sources of illegal immigration. Hence, it is very unlikely that any foreign worker program could be or should be restricted to workers from Mexico. If it were, it would be a racist proposal and it would have nothing to offer as a solution to illegal entry from other nations of the world.

In addition, the proposals for a foreign worker program completely neglect all of the experience that the United States has had (as well as many cases in Europe) with foreign worker programs. Specifically, when workers come from economically less-developed countries to a country such as the United States, they are made aware of opportunities often beyond their wildest imagination. The relatively higher wages and the broader array of job opportunities will create, as they have in the past, a tendency for many to remain. A situation is also set up in which children are born and marriages occur. Both of these actions involve potential claims for citizenship. In the United States, with its multiracial and multiethnic groups, it is far more likely that these pressures will occur than would ever be the case in Europe. Rather than reduce the costs of uncontrolled immigration to American society, a foreign worker program will only add to the problem.

* * *

H.L. Mencken once quipped that "For every complex problem there is always a simple answer—and it is always wrong." A foreign worker program is no answer to the complex problem of illegal immigration. To be effective, it would have to be substantial in size; but if it were substantial in size, it would clearly have an adverse impact on certain segments of the domestic labor force. Furthermore, even if it were conceptually feasible, the INS, as now staffed and budgeted, is totally incapable of administering such a program without its becoming a fiasco. Likewise, it is also very doubtful that the Department of Labor could handle such a program.

A foreign worker program would certainly increase illegal immigration by exposing more foreign workers to the economic attractions of the

American labor market. It would also adversely affect job and income opportunities for many of the persons in the American economy who are the least able to defend themselves from competition. It is not surprising, therefore, that a 1979 conference on "Jobs for Hispanics"—sponsored by the Labor Council for Latin American Advancement and attended by both Hispanic trade unionist[s] and many nonunionists from Hispanic community groups across the country—took a strong and unanimous stand against a foreign worker program. In their conference manifesto, called the "Declaration of Albuquerque," they called for a number of policy changes that would be beneficial for and protective of illegal immigrants. But with respect to the idea of a "guestworker" program, they emphatically stated: "The federal government should *not* include any type of 'Bracero' program or foreign labor importation, as a solution to the current problem of undocumented workers."

Foreign worker programs are of interest to employers only as a means of reducing their costs of production or enhancing their control over their workers, who are completely dependent upon their employers. Citizen workers who compete with foreign workers will find, as in the past, that their existing work conditions usually become frozen or decline. Under few circumstances will they improve. Efforts to establish unions are thwarted or, at a minimum, made more difficult. These callous motivations should not be rewarded.

A foreign worker program will in no way diminish the need to reform the existing immigration system of the United States. Until the system is made capable of accomplishing its stated goals of effectively regulating the flow of immigrants into the United States, illegal immigration will flourish regardless of the existence of a foreign worker program. But if such a program were enacted, it might deceive some people into thinking that an answer had been provided. Indeed, a foreign worker program has great political attractiveness *because* it gives the appearance of being a remedy while avoiding the necessity of taking the actions that are mandatory for the achievement of an end to illegal immigration.

In 1980, the United States admitted over 808,000 legal immigrants and refugees. This is a commendable attribute of American society, for not only did the number exceed the total legal immigrants admitted by all the remaining nations of the world combined, but the admissions were essentially on a nondiscriminatory basis. This accomplishment should not be allowed to be tarnished by the continued flow of millions of others who have flouted the legal system by illegal entry. The proposals for a foreign worker program must be recognized as being simply a placebo: they offer an imaginary remedy to a real problem. Such an idea is not neutral in its long-term effects, since it can only make an already bad situation much worse. What is offered as a tonic is actually toxic.

PHILIP L. MARTIN, LABOR–INTENSIVE AGRICULTURE
249 Scientific Am. 54, 57–59 (Oct. 1983).

The basic administrative question in the H–2 program is simple: Where does the duty of the farmer to hire an American work force stop and the obligation of the Federal Government to open the border start? Clearly if farmers have to scour the U.S. looking for workers and must offer high wages, transportation, adequate housing, inexpensive food and other amenities, they will find more American workers and will need fewer foreign ones. They will also have a greater incentive to mechanize. On the other hand, if farmers have few obligations in recruitment, wages and housing, they will find it easier and cheaper to simply hire aliens. The H–2 program is controversial because it is trying to strike a balance between conflicting goals: protecting American farm workers and ensuring a plentiful supply of low-cost farm labor.

The debate over the need for alien workers in fruit and vegetable farming diverts attention from an unsettling shadow on the horizon: competition from other nations. The automobile industry faced a similar juncture in the late 1960's. In an affluent and health-conscious society the demand for fruits and vegetables is expanding, and farmers envision continued expansion and profits if the Federal Government does not enact costly new labor regulations. Just as the automobile industry waged largely successful battles against air bags and environmental controls that diverted attention from increasing foreign competition, so fruit and vegetable farmers are fighting to continue using seasonal alien farm workers in order to compete with the fruits and vegetables other nations are beginning to export in quantity. Cheap labor benefits agriculture in the short run, but it also helps to blind farmers to the technological changes they will have to make in order to compete with foreign producers who have access to even cheaper labor.

Products such as citrus fruits, strawberries and tomatoes require relatively little land but a great deal of labor. The cost of hand harvesting is 20 percent of the price the farmer gets for oranges and lemons and up to 40 percent of the price for lettuce, strawberries and tomatoes. The wages of farm workers in the U.S., however, are five times higher than they are in Greece and 10 times higher than they are in Mexico. As other nations expand their labor-intensive agriculture, the already loud complaints by American farmers about Brazilian oranges, Greek raisins, Mexican tomatoes and Italian wine will intensify.

The increasing dependence of American fruit and vegetable farmers on alien workers confronts policymakers with two options: (1) preserve the status quo by approving an open-ended temporary-worker program or (2) encourage the fruit and vegetable industry to mechanize in order to limit its need for alien farm workers. If the U.S. gradually reduced the supply of alien farm workers, the production of labor-intensive commodities that cannot easily be mechanized could be shifted abroad by removing import barriers, thereby increasing employment in Mexico and the Caribbean basin and decreasing incentives to migrate illegally to the U.S.

Debates on farm labor often fail to recognize these linkages of immigration, trade and technology. Instead many fruit and vegetable farmers believe the optimal strategy is to preserve the status quo with an open-ended temporary-worker program. They recognize that mechanization is inevitable, but they want to decide when and how machinery will replace workers instead of being confronted with the sudden elimination of traditional labor supplies. Organizations of farm workers oppose a temporary-worker program because they believe aliens selected from a huge pool of foreign labor will always be preferred to Americans, who are often the castoffs of other labor markets. These organizations also oppose mechanization that displaces farm workers.

Machines have taken the place of seasonal workers in the fruit and vegetable industry in an uneven pattern since research on this kind of mechanization was begun in the 1940's. Most of the root vegetables such as potatoes are dug mechanically, some of the leafy vegetables such as spinach and processing cabbage are lifted and cut by machine, and a few of the field crops such as pickling cucumbers and processing squash can be machine-harvested. Crops that are intended to be sold fresh, however, still call for hand labor; for example, most carrots and green onions are still pulled and bunched by hand, and iceberg lettuce, broccoli and celery are hand-cut and hand-packed. Strawberries, melons and most fresh-market tomatoes are hand-picked.

Mechanization slowed in the 1970's because workers were readily available. Nevertheless, harvesting machines are still being adopted by some farmers. Grapes that are processed into wine can be mechanically harvested by a machine operating over the row to shake the grapes loose and catch them on conveyor belts. This machine is being modified to harvest the raisin grapes that are now picked by hand. Most nut crops such as almonds, pecans and walnuts are harvested by a hydraulic arm that grasps the tree trunk and shakes the nuts to the ground, where they are swept up by another machine. A tree shaker with a padded catcher can harvest prune plums, cling peaches, apples and tart cherries, but the machine damages the fruit so much that the crop must be processed soon after harvesting.

Several of the crops that are now picked by hand could be harvested mechanically if workers were not available; among them are peaches, lettuce and tomatoes. The mechanization of many others will require the coordinated efforts of plant scientists, engineers, growers and processors. Trees and plants that yield uniformly ripening crops able to withstand machine harvesting could be developed. Growers would have to prune or plant them in such a way as to facilitate mechanical harvesting. Engineers could improve the optical and laser sorting devices that can sort the crop in the field, thereby cutting costs, but processors would have to schedule their work precisely so that the harvested and sorted produce would not deteriorate. Equipment manufacturers and seed companies could work with growers to diffuse new technology on the one hand and new plant varieties on the other.

The most plausible coordinator of this systems approach to mechanization is government, primarily through the established land-grant universities. These nonprofit institutions do the basic plant and engineering research that growers, processors and equipment manufacturers do not undertake. Moreover, the academic people who are engaged in this work have enough influence on both growers and processors to encourage changes in the practices that impede mechanization.

An increased role by the universities will be controversial, particularly in California, where the University of California is defending itself in a lawsuit brought by representatives of farm workers. The suit charges that the university's research on mechanization is biased in the direction of helping the operators of large farms and undermining farm-worker unions. Universities can head off some of the controversy by making clear the importance of mechanization in preserving a profitable fruit and vegetable industry and by taking pains to avoid conflicts of interest in research programs.

Public policy is trying to discourage agriculture from using aliens by enacting laws and making regulations forcing farmers to meet certain standards of recruitment, wages and working conditions. A better way to reduce dependence on alien workers is to link immigration reform to a plan for restructuring the fruit and vegetable industry. One way to forge such a link is with an H–2 trust, which would levy a tax on the wages earned by alien farm workers and would apply the funds to restructure the production of commodities that depend on alien workers.

Such a trust could be established for each commodity whose growers asked for alien workers. The amount of money available to each trust would be determined by the level of the payroll tax and the extent of the commodity's dependence on alien labor. One can arrive at an estimate of what the level of taxation might be by taking into account the fact that farmers do not now have to pay the Social Security tax of 6.7 percent or the Federal unemployment-insurance tax of .8 percent on the wages of H–2 workers. In addition most states exempt those wages from the state unemployment-insurance tax (ranging from 3 to 6 percent) that farmers must pay on the wages earned by most of the farm workers who are U.S. citizens. These various exemptions suggest an H–2 wage tax of at least 10 percent. If a modified H–2 program admitted 300,000 alien farm workers annually and the average worker earned $5,000 during the year, the H–2 trusts would collect 10 percent of $1.5 billion, or $150 million per year.

Farmers are familiar with the concept of assessments to support commodity-related research and promotion. Since H–2 trusts could be established on a commodity-by-commodity basis, administrators familiar with the problems associated with the particular commodity could fine-tune the programs for reducing dependence on alien labor, choosing from a variety of options including research on mechanization, the training of workers and changes in processing. A commodity-specific H–2 trust would create both a direct link between a commodity's dependence on alien workers and the means to end that dependence.

The U.S. Select Commission on Immigration and Refugee Policy, which studied the subject from 1979 to 1981, recommended that no industry depend indefinitely on alien workers. The commission argued that such workers constitute a subsidy to employers unable or unwilling to attract American workers, to mechanize or to produce abroad, and it could find no justification for such a subsidy just to maintain a given industry in the U.S. If one accepts this reasoning, H–2 trusts would provide a way of emphasizing the transitional nature of alien farm workers in fruit and vegetable agriculture.

Mechanization is not the only way to reduce agriculture's dependence on alien workers. Intermediate back-saving technologies such as conveyor belts to eliminate heavy field bags and hydraulic lifts to replace ladders and fruit bags would help to encourage women and older workers to harvest crops. Experienced farm workers might prolong their average of from five to 10 years in harvest work if more farmers and employment associations offered a series of jobs that reduced unemployment.

The continued dependence of the $18-billion fruit and vegetable industry in the U.S. on alien farm workers for handwork spells disaster in the long run. The industry has two choices: it can move toward mechanization, meanwhile trying to improve conditions for handworkers by adopting modern personnel policies and installing equipment that facilitates handwork, or it can obtain access to a rotating pool of alien farm workers with another program of the bracero type. The second option would imply an indefinite dependence on an alien work force.

Few U.S. citizens will become seasonal hand-harvest workers at the prevailing wages or even at higher wages because workers with options reject the uncertainties of the seasonal farm-labor market. The U.S. will have an American work force in fruit and vegetable agriculture when that industry is mechanized. The farmers who grow wheat, corn and soybeans can find Americans to operate their machinery, and the fruit and vegetable farmers who have mechanized are having the same experience.

Mechanization is one answer to the problems of productivity, labor and immigration in fruit and vegetable agriculture. Without mechanization the U.S. must both accept an isolated, alien-dominated labor force for seasonal handwork and erect trade barriers to keep out produce grown abroad at even lower wages. If farmers successfully oppose the immigration reforms that could begin to alter this picture, they may win the short-run battle over labor but will lose the long-run war for survival in the increasingly competitive international fruit and vegetable economy.

GERALD P. LOPEZ, UNDOCUMENTED MEXICAN MIGRATION: IN SEARCH OF A JUST IMMIGRATION LAW AND POLICY

28 UCLA L.Rev. 615, 695–707 (1981).

Our moral obligation to undocumented Mexican workers will be developed in two arguments. The first general argument does not depend on past injustice; prior wrong is irrelevant. The argument assumes that one owes moral obligations to members of one's own community and questions why they should end at the border. The moral question is particularly troubling when one thinks of people with whom one has established a significant, longstanding social and economic nexus: Can one comfortably treat them with the same indifference that one might feel toward a total stranger?

The second general argument depends upon past injustice. It aims to repair past wrongs and requires nothing of the destination country unless the present condition of undocumented Mexicans is attributable to a history of injustice.

a. *The first argument.* Under the Constitution and notions of sovereignty, entry into the United States can be conditioned on an express denial of any long-term obligation. Even legal exercise of sovereign power can, however, raise serious moral issues. If people who entered really understood our express denial of long-term obligation and did not inevitably develop a different set of expectations, our moral posture toward termination of access might be respectable. It is not possible, however, to have persons live, work, and participate in a community over many years without creating in them a sense of entitlement to some benefits of community membership and a moral obligation based on their reasonable expectations. No matter how strongly our formal laws deny it, our conduct creates the obligation.

The widely accepted, though largely unarticulated, view of sovereignty assumes that access to the benefits of national community membership must be granted as a moral matter only to documented members: "documented members take priority." This view presupposes the answer to one, if not the, central question in moral and political philosophy: What is the relevant moral community for purposes of non-selfish moral obligations? In other words, what constitutes membership in the morally relevant community?

To conclude that documented members take priority assumes that existing documented membership in the national community, "shared citizenship," is either intrinsically what morally matters or is a presumptively reliable proxy for, an indicator of, what morally matters. Either view might be defensible. If citizenship alone is so significant as to justify greater obligation to documented than to non-documented persons, then status becomes the ground for a superior moral tie. To command moral authority, any such claim would have to identify and justify attributes always and exclusively shared among citizens.

Alternatively, certain attributes or facts, more often than not shared among citizens, might justify greater obligation. In this case, the attributes or facts, and not the status itself, are the grounds for a superior moral bond. The legitimacy of using shared citizenship as a proxy in this way depends on the justification for the chosen attributes and on the reliability of citizenship as an indicator of those attributes.

The inchoate justification allowing or mandating priority to fellow documented members is probably to be found in notions of intimacy and ideology. For some, kinship may matter most in ordering priorities; for others, shared political or religious beliefs are most important. For most, it seems fair to assume, some combination of intimacy and ideology allows the conclusion that, while some documented members may take priority over others (friends over non-friends, Mormon conservatives over non-Mormon liberals), all documented members sharing citizenship take priority over non-documented persons. But any adequate justification of the conclusion must demonstrate either that shared citizenship, intrinsically or as a proxy, is coextensive with membership in the moral community relevant to the priority in question or that the underinclusiveness is necessary and unavoidable.

Shared citizenship "seems" both relevant and appropriate to shared access partly because of unexamined assumptions. National governments do not normally explain why only citizens deserve access, and citizens seldom examine what sharing citizenship with others means.

Exclusionary policies likely proceed from the premise that individuals have the moral right to form distinct and stable communities. If these communities are to retain their distinctiveness and stability, they must be able to regulate access, particularly since physical access can lead to documented membership in the community. Thus the "right of closure," the right to admit and exclude through an immigration law, is thought to be a necessary corollary to the right to form communities. Nations asserting an absolute sovereign right to decide whom to admit or exclude can thus be seen as asserting the right to form communities and the right to keep them distinctive and stable.

One can accept this general moral scheme as plausible, even forceful, without necessarily accepting that, at any time, community membership for purposes of sharing access is justifiably defined by a set of attributes that all and only citizens have in common. Yet this claim is implicit in the position that there is no moral impediment to the termination of access for undocumented Mexicans.

Perhaps the legitimacy of this specific claim is best measured initially by posing the following hypothetical question: Assuming that the United States has determined that a certain number of jobs in the secondary market are available to foreign workers, then (disregarding problems of transportation and know-how) should they go first to Mexicans or to poorer Pakistanis? While the answer to this question is not easy, it is revealing because, I take it, more Americans than not, perhaps a majority, would embrace a moral scheme that would render Mexican claims superior to Pakistani claims.

At least three separable though admittedly overlapping intuitions about the ties of history, shared effort, and propinquity underlie both the presupposed national consensus and an answer to the broader moral question of how to distribute access to benefits. First, there is a sense of a special historical claim based on the fact that Mexicans have helped us to fill our domestic needs. True, they were paid; they may have gotten what they wanted, what they bargained for. But partners in a bargain do tend to have special feelings of obligation to one another.

Second, undocumented Mexicans, despite the formal illegality of their entrance and presence, are the people who hold the jobs and share in our efforts; they are "here." It would be callous to upset expectations by shifting benefits from one needy person to another, even if the claims of both were the same. Justice sometimes requires "grandfather" clauses.

Finally, propinquity evokes analogies to family members and neighbors. As a society, we place some value on the present and the near. Our sense of community extends more willingly to those whose lives touch ours. That proposition may seem irrational or unfair to some, but most of us do feel that those close by must first be satisfied.

These intuitions reveal two important propositions. First, involvement (past contribution and present connection) and neighborhood (presence and proximity) are attributes or facts that, in some combination with need, society finds relevant in ordering claims to jobs. That is why we would distribute access through immigration law to Mexicans before Pakistanis, even if Pakistanis are needier in some absolute sense.

Second, the nature of the relationship defines the nature of the claim on community benefits. While we would grant undocumented Mexicans access to jobs, we might not grant them access to welfare, even though each might help satisfy their needs.

These propositions, in turn, suggest why immigration law must now, as matter of simple justice, serve the needs of undocumented Mexicans. So long as our community was self-contained and accurately defined by national boundaries, the needs of other than the sovereign, documented people could generally be disregarded. Under those circumstances, community membership was shared among all and only those sharing citizenship for purposes of sharing access to jobs, and for purposes of virtually all other priorities. Only citizens shared a presumably justifiable, even if unarticulated, set of attributes. If that set of attributes is now shared by people without citizenship, the interests of that group must be acknowledged and considered; any moral theory of community status that fails to take account of these interests will lose its purpose for being. One who meets, in part, the requirements of community membership merits a superior claim vis-à-vis other non-members and the right to demand of *de jure* members many of the non-selfish moral obligations implicit in the concept of community.

This departure from the view that those sharing citizenship take priority may seem unruly and threatening. A conception of non-selfish moral obligations that might result in "misshapen" moral communities not coterminous with political boundaries is perhaps too difficult for the *de jure* system to administer. Moreover, a conception of non-selfish moral obligation that even occasionally accords citizenship, either intrinsically or as a proxy, less weight than other attributes or facts might undermine the security implicit in existing views. Presupposing that citizens take priority reflects and is a source of a state of mind thought by some to be necessary to a national community, to "the common perceptions of a number of individuals that for some purposes they properly think of themselves as 'we.' " Any conception that jeopardizes that state of mind and expectations about the behavior of fellow citizens threatens the trust that begets the very sense of non-selfish moral obligation to members of one's community.

These are not trivial problems, but they can be exaggerated. Our national community presently accepts, both *de facto* and *de jure*, a matrix of sharing principles that is both unruly and threatening in the abstract. It is commonly understood, for example, that though we live in a national community, "neither individuals nor groups can exist without some measure of a life of their own." [480]   Independence implies sharing principles inconsistent with the broad mandate that non-selfish moral obligations extend first to citizens. As a result, national community is not a perfect unity, but "rather a unity in diversity, ... some things are shared while others are not." [481]

Nor is less than perfect sharing confined to *de facto* situations or to small intimate groups like family and friends. Our constitution allows a state to favor, to some degree, its own residents in the sharing, dividing and distribution of public resources within the state. This favoritism is presumptively valid even when it conflicts with nonresident claims (claims by those sharing national but not state citizenship) to equal shares of the opportunities available throughout the Union. If a national community can accommodate less than perfect sharing among national citizens, should it not recognize in proper cases that some things must be shared with non-citizens? Or even that some things should be shared first with some non-citizens even to the exclusion of citizens?

Sharing that sometimes disregards or straddles national political boundaries stretches perhaps the concept of "unity in diversity," and creates new "we's" to be sure. If "we" have in fact changed, and coincidentally the border has been disregarded, is it not consistent with our sense of trust, with the feelings that beget non-selfish moral obligations, to acknowledge the living community? Our *de facto* adjustment, individual and institutional, to the continuing presence of millions of undocumented Mexicans may reflect, in part, an implicit recognition of the relevant moral community.

The legal and philosophical problems presented by such a conception of sharing are varied and perplexing; the same has been said of the problems presented by any theory that seeks to explain our present *de jure* system of communities within communities. The point is not that the problems raised by every system of competing and overlapping communities are identical, but that they are both tractable and more alike than not. These problems reflect the difficulty in advancing sharing principles that fairly accommodate our need for smaller communities and our evolution toward social, economic, and political interdependency.

b. *The second argument: past injustice.* The second argument for moral obligation is based on the proposition that undocumented Mexican workers have been reduced to their present condition by a history of injustice. Fired by righteous indignation, writers from Marx to Nozick have already advanced the arguments that past injustice creates moral obligations that require corrective injustice or reparations. The following argument is more modest: it is aimed at establishing the past injustice.

* * *

From nearly the time of the Treaty of Guadalupe Hidalgo, the national community derived, in part through the subtle manipulation of

---

480. Friedrich, *The Concept of Community in the History of Political and Legal Philosophy, in* NOMOS II: Community 5 (1959).

481. *Id.*

immigration law, extraordinary economic advantages from Mexican laborers, while employing familiar chauvinistic propaganda and affirming the inferior status of yet another minority group. As each technique for the sanctioned use of migrant Mexican labor faded into the "irreparable past," a new and related technique would mysteriously, almost imperceptibly, arise, replace the old, yet evade critical assault until so firmly entrenched as to be nearly immovable.

The events that comprise the process since the Chinese Exclusion Act of 1882 reveal a dramatic mismatch of bargaining power with the national community totally insensitive to intentional and negligent wrongs to the Mexican worker. Perhaps the use of temporary Mexican labor was accepted as another device for ensuring freedom of the human will and benefits of an unregulated economic system. It may have been thought legitimate to use cheap foreign labor, willing to work, for mutual economic advantage, especially to fill the serious manpower shortages resulting from involvement in World War I. One might, for example, interpret the 1918 Departmental Order waiving the application of immigration restrictions to Mexican labor as a device for permitting a bargaining process between two apparently willing and anxious parties. Yet in other areas of American society, effort was expended to control the excesses of the market bargaining process. For example, working conditions in factories were scrutinized and regulated by the national community. By contrast, virtually no effort was expended to discover whether there was misuse of the instrumentalities provided by the national community to employers of Mexican migrants.

* * *

In the 1930s there was a break in the continuity of our treatment of Mexican migrants. Any claim that this hiatus wiped the slate clean, reducing the period of wrongdoing to the post-depression years, is undercut by the purely self-serving reasons for that hiatus. Importation of Mexican labor stopped in the 1930s only because a depression removed the need for foreign workers. "Okies" and "Arkies" filled the jobs so menial, so low-paying, and so backbreaking, that until then only Mexicans would accept them. When the United States decided to get rid of the Mexicans, it ignored their needs and failed to treat them as human beings. Mexicans were rounded up like cattle and shipped over the border. As soon as conditions in this country changed, and poor whites fled "Mexican" jobs with a kind of shocked triumph, the old ways returned.

The formal beginning of the next era occurred in 1942 with the signing of the treaty with Mexico establishing the Bracero Program. With its controls over the conditions of employment, the Bracero Program provided hope for dignified treatment and conscionable bargains. One hastens to add that the protections incorporated into the treaty to protect Mexican workers were derived largely from Mexican domestic law and were not the product of the American community's conscience. Fatuous as the treaty provisions now sound, they no doubt seemed to promise fair and humane treatment.

But the promises were counterfeit, the reality reminiscent of earlier bargains. Conscious violations of contractual obligations by private employers and grossly inadequate federal law enforcement insured the breach of the promise. Apparently, migrant Mexican workers were seen to lack sufficient dignity to merit the enforcement of promises made by the national community. * * *

Nor could the national community legitimately deny responsibility for acts and practices of private employers in contravention of treaty obligations. Governmental complicity was plainly established by a conscious policy of underenforcement of the law. The treaty was so loosely drafted that it permitted the federal government to give employers virtually all they wanted. For example, Congress exempted agriculture—by this time the primary employing industry, and one with relatively few affected domestic workers—from the National Labor Relations Act and the Fair Labor Standards Act. Run by private entrepreneurs, who neither felt compulsion to honor their promises nor feared sanctions by the national community, the system allowed unbridled discretion to hire even those illegally here, and to set the wage, the living conditions and the terms of discharge and payment.

To make matters worse, Congress, in response to the undocumented phenomena that coincided with the Bracero Program, "unaccountably" cut back dollars available for the services of Border Patrol officers. Even this transparent act produced no significant public reaction. There were some citizens and documented residents whose sense of justice was engaged and whose efforts to generate concern were praiseworthy. The national community, however, was preoccupied with the arrival and impact of *Brown v. Board of Education;* even for those whose sense of justice was at work, that event was tumultuous and all-consuming.

Yet the strongest, continuing evidence of the national government's central role in the injustice is embodied in the federal proviso enacted in 1952, specifically exempting employers from liability for the employment of otherwise illegal aliens. The proviso, from its passage, through the Bracero Program, to the present, has served as legislative license for the employment of Mexican workers. Attacked and assaulted from nearly every angle over the past seventeen years, its survival and importance are attributable to the logrolling that distinguishes the nation's legislative process. Its continued existence now seems secure for just reasons unrelated to its initial economic objective. In any event, the proviso offers ample testimony to federal government complicity in the employment of undocumented workers.[a]

a. For a comparative perspective on foreign worker programs, *see* Martin & Miller, *Guestworkers: Lessons from Western Europe,* 33 Indus. & Lab.Rel.Rev. 315 (1980); Teitelbaum, *Right Versus Right: Immigration and* *Refugee Policy in the United States,* 59 Foreign Affs. 21 (1980); J. Power, Migrant Workers in Western Europe and the United States (1979).—eds.

Chapter Ten

CITIZENSHIP

Congress enacted the first federal nationality and citizenship law in 1790, 85 years before it initiated federal regulation of immigration. This timing reflects the different treatment accorded the two realms of governmental authority in the Constitution itself. Although federal authority to control immigration, as we have seen, must be derived by implication from other portions of the constitutional text or from certain structural features of the nation it created, the Constitution explicitly vests in Congress the power to "establish an uniform Rule of Naturalization." Art. I, Sec. 8, cl. 4.[1]

This venerable field of law presents a host of interesting historical, philosophical, constitutional, administrative and technical issues worthy of a more extended treatment than we can provide here. This Chapter, therefore, will be even more selective than the earlier Chapters on immigration. We shall examine briefly the rules governing acquisition of U.S. citizenship by birth and by naturalization, and we shall look at the modern rules governing loss of nationality.[2] In each setting we consider a

---

1. The requirement of uniformity should not be read as a broad equal protection guarantee—that is, as an authorization to courts to strike down naturalization requirements whenever different conditions are prescribed for various categories of aspiring citizens. In fact, such varying requirements are an established feature of our naturalization laws. The Framers mandated "an uniform Rule" in order to change the confusing practice that had prevailed under the Articles of Confederation, when each state separately enacted its own naturalization rules. *See* The Federalist No. 42 (J. Madison); J. Kettner, The Development of American Citizenship, 1608–1870, at 213–32 (1978). Judicial decisions generally have refused to find that the Constitution requires more of Congress than geographic uniformity in this sense. *See, e.g., Samras v. INS*, 125 F.2d 879 (9th Cir.1942), cert. denied 317 U.S. 634, 63 S.Ct. 34, 87 L.Ed. 511 (1942). Under the prevailing interpretation, moreover, even certain kinds of geographic disparities are allowed. *See Petition of Lee Wee*, 143 F.Supp. 736

(S.D.Cal.1956) (gambling offenses preclude a finding of good moral character necessary for naturalization, even though the same behavior would not have been criminal in a nearby locality).

2. We will generally use "citizenship" and "nationality" as equivalent terms here. There is, however, a potential distinction, worth noting in passing, between a "citizen" of the United States, who ordinarily enjoys full rights of participation in the national polity, and a noncitizen "national" of the United States, who owes allegiance to this country but does not enjoy the full measure of such political rights. *See* INA §§ 101(a)(21), (22) (defining the terms "national" and "national of the United States"). In addition, at times in our national history some noncitizen nationals did not have the right of free movement from the outlying territory to the "metropolitan" United States. See Philippine Independence Act of 1934, Ch. 84, § 8, 48 Stat. 462 (providing that Filipinos, who were at the time U.S.

few of the important cases establishing or explaining the governing standards, or illustrating their implementation. But we begin with a rather impressionistic review of the concept of citizenship itself. What does it mean? What should it mean? Why the intense interest in its acquisition or loss?

SECTION A.   IS CITIZENSHIP IMPORTANT?

American citizenship is the major objective of many aliens who come to the United States—the ultimate culmination of the American immigration process. Naturalization ceremonies tend to be occasions for great joy, the outpouring of emotion, heartfelt expressions of attachment to the new citizens' new land.

On the other hand, large numbers of resident aliens seem quite indifferent to the blandishments of U.S. citizenship. Many never make the change, remaining here indefinitely, as they are entitled to do, in permanent resident status. Others eventually become U.S. citizens, but plainly find little reason to hurry to change their nationality. Although patterns vary considerably by country of origin, over a fifth of the 166,317 people who naturalized in 1981 had come to the United States before 1965. *United States Department of Justice, 1981 Statistical Yearbook of the Immigration and Naturalization Service,* Table 29, pp. 79–81.

Moreover, the Supreme Court sometimes seems to be of two minds on the issue. An important line of equal protection cases, beginning with *Graham v. Richardson,* 403 U.S. 365, 91 S.Ct. 1848, 29 L.Ed.2d 534 (1971), purposely made the difference between citizen and alien count for a good deal less than it traditionally had. In many settings, the very distinction amounts, the Court has said, to a "suspect classification," and States may

nationals, were to be treated as aliens for purposes of the immigration laws).

The distinction between citizen and mere national was far more important around the turn of the century, when the United States acquired numerous outlying territorial possessions, principally as a result of the Spanish-American War. The local populations were held to American allegiance, but were not considered citizens. The Supreme Court struggled, in a series of decisions that came to be known as the Insular Cases, with questions of personal status and constitutional protections in such circumstances, finally accepting a somewhat reduced level of protection in those territories held not to be "incorporated" into the United States. *See, e.g.,* Balzac v. Porto Rico, 258 U.S. 298, 42 S.Ct. 343, 66 L.Ed. 627 (1922); Gonzales v. Williams, 192 U.S. 1, 24 S.Ct. 177, 48 L.Ed. 317 (1904); G & R §§ 11.3b, 12.7; Coudert, *The Evolution of the Doctrine of Territorial Incorporation,* 26 Colum.L.Rev. 823 (1926). The continued vitality of the incorporation doctrine is unclear. See *Reid v. Covert,* 354

U.S. 1, 14, 77 S.Ct. 1222, 1229, 1 L.Ed.2d 1148 (1957) (plurality opinion); *Torres v. Puerto Rico,* 442 U.S. 465, 468–70, 99 S.Ct. 2425, 2428–29, 61 L.Ed.2d 1 (1979); and *id.* at 475–76 (Brennan, J., concurring in the judgment).

In recent decades, however, the nationality questions associated with such territories have become relatively insignificant (even though other associated political issues have remained complex, *see, e.g.,* Time for Decision: The United States and Puerto Rico (J. Heine ed. 1984)). Congress has gradually either granted full citizenship to the local population, as happened, for example, with Puerto Rico, or passed legislation leading to the independence of the territory, as happened with the Philippines. Today only American Samoa and Swains Island constitute outlying possessions of the United States for purposes of the nationality laws, and essentially only the local inhabitants there constitute noncitizen nationals. *See* INA § 101(a)(29).

employ the distinction between aliens and citizens only if they demonstrate compelling reasons for doing so.

Not too many years previous to that, however, the same Court, after a decade of sharp division, concluded that a person could not be involuntarily deprived of U.S. citizenship. *Afroyim v. Rusk,* 387 U.S. 253, 87 S.Ct. 1660, 18 L.Ed.2d 757 (1967). In that case, and in preceding cases that laid the groundwork for such a holding (to be reviewed later in this Chapter), several Justices wrote at length about the preciousness of citizenship status. *See, e.g., Trop v. Dulles,* 356 U.S. 86, 101, 78 S.Ct. 590, 598, 2 L.Ed.2d 630 (1958) (plurality opinion) (deprivation of citizenship "is a form of punishment more primitive than torture, for it destroys for the individual the political existence that was centuries in the development"); *Kennedy v. Mendoza-Martinez,* 372 U.S. 144, 160, 83 S.Ct. 554, 563, 9 L.Ed.2d 644 (1963) ("American citizenship * * * is 'one of the most valuable rights in the world today' ").

Which view is correct? Is citizenship important? Should it be? For what purposes? The debate is an ancient one. The readings that follow reflect some of its main contours.

ALEXANDER M. BICKEL, CITIZEN OR PERSON?: WHAT IS NOT GRANTED CANNOT BE TAKEN AWAY

The Morality of Consent, Ch. 2 (1975).

In the view both of the ancients and of modern liberal political theorists, the relationship between the individual and the state is largely defined by the concept of citizenship. It is by virtue of his citizenship that the individual is a member of the political community, and by virtue of it that he has rights. Remarkably enough—and as I will suggest, happily—the concept of citizenship plays only the most minimal role in the American constitutional scheme.

* * *

There is a great deal to the Hobbesian notion that we are all really subjects held to obedience, if no longer by divine command then by a simple fear of our fellows. To the extent that this explanation does not fit our situation or ought not, to the extent that it is not the true or the good explanation, liberal as well as classic thought has considered us citizens who owe obedience, as we owe allegiance, chiefly because we are self-governing, and as self-governing because we are citizens. When they freed themselves from subjection, the makers of the French Revolution called each other citizen, denoting their participation in the state; so the communists later called each other comrade, denoting their common allegiance to an ideology, a movement.

Both classic and later liberal statements of the duty to obey law thus subsume the concept of citizenship, even though not as a wholly necessary or sufficient condition. Also subsumed are the clarity and economy of the law to be obeyed, and of the process by which that law is formed. The classic among classics is, of course, the statement of Socrates as reported in the *Crito:* "In war as in the court of justice, and everywhere, you must do whatever your state and your country tell you to do, or you must persuade them that their commands are unjust." It is the citizen who has the standing to persuade his fellow citizens that what they are doing is unjust. Our own system does not resemble the one subsumed in the statement of Socrates in clarity or in economy of application, and not in the immediacy with which the citizen can affect the process of law-formation. That makes a difference; so, also, although less directly and certainly, does the striking ambivalence, the great ambiguity that has surrounded the concept of citizenship in our law and in our tradition.

The original Constitution, prior to Reconstruction, contained no definition of citizenship and precious few references to the concept altogether. The subject was not entirely ignored by the Framers. They empowered Congress to make a uniform rule of naturalization. But, wishing to attract immigrants, they rejected nativist suggestions for strict naturalization requirements, such as long residence. They plainly assumed that birth as well as naturalization would confer citizenship but they made nothing depend on it explicitly, aside from a few offices: president, congressman, senator, but notably not judge. State citizenship provided one, but only one of several, means of access to federal courts (under the diversity jurisdiction) and conferred the not unqualified right, under the privileges and immunities clause of article IV, section 2, to be treated generally by each state in the same fashion as its own citizens were treated. Discrimination on the sole ground of not holding citizenship in a given state is forbidden; discrimination on other and reasonable grounds is, however, allowed. Discriminations on the basis of residence, which is different in concept from citizenship, are permitted; and where state citizenship is a reasonable requirement, as for officeholding, discrimination is not prohibited. But if no special reason restricts a privilege sensibly to the state's own citizens, the state must extend it to the citizens of other states as well.

There is no further mention of citizenship in the Constitution before the Civil War amendments, even though there were plenty of occasions for making rights depend on it. The Preamble speaks of "We the people of the United States," not, as it might have, of we the citizens of the United States at the time of the formation of this union. And the Bill of Rights throughout defines rights of people, not of citizens. * * * To be sure, implicitly, the citizen had a right freely to enter the country, whereas the alien did not; and implicitly also the citizen, while abroad, could be held to an obligation of allegiance and might under very specific conditions be found guilty of the crime of treason for violating it, while the alien generally could not. But these were hardly critical points, as the Framers demonstrated by saying nothing explicit about them. It remains true that the original Constitution presented the edifying picture of a government that bestowed rights on people and persons, and held itself out as bound by certain standards of conduct in its relations with people and persons, not with some legal construct called citizen. This idyllic state of affairs was rudely disturbed by the crisis of the 1850s. Like so much else, it foundered on the contradiction of slavery. A majority of the Supreme Court seized on the concept of citizenship in the

Dred Scott case,[4] in a futile and misguided effort, by way of a legalism and an unfounded legalism at that, to resolve the controversy over the spread of slavery.

Dred Scott, the slave of one John Sandford in Missouri, brought suit in the Circuit Court of the United States for his freedom. * * * However, Scott could come into federal court only by claiming to be a citizen of Missouri; Sandford, who held Scott in Missouri, was himself a citizen of New York. Scott could not be a citizen of Missouri, Sandford said, because he was "a negro of African descent, whose ancestors were of pure African blood, and who were brought into this country and sold as slaves." If Scott was not a citizen of Missouri, there could be no federal jurisdiction, and that was an end of the matter. The significance of citizenship was in question. * * *

In the Supreme Court the majority opinion was written by Chief Justice Roger Taney, Marshall's successor, * * * [who was] a political progressive—if that is a correct designation for a Jacksonian populist—an economic liberal, and a racist who persuaded himself by mid-life that slavery was not only a necessary evil, if that, but right as well. Taney combined personal kindness with public ferocity, he freed his own slaves and cared for them afterward, but he was opposed politically to any large-scale manumission. He was an able man, broken on the rack of slavery. Dred Scott, Taney held, could not be a citizen, not because he was a slave but because, even if he were a free man, he was "a negro of African descent, whose ancestors were of pure African blood, and who were brought into this country and sold as slaves." The words "people of the United States" and "citizens" are synonymous terms, he held, used interchangeably in the Constitution: "They both describe the political body who, according to our republican institutions, form the sovereignty, and who hold the power and conduct the government through their representatives. They are what we familiarly call the [single] 'sovereign people' and every citizen is one of this people, and a constituent member of this sovereignty."

At the time of the framing of the Constitution Taney continued, even free Negroes were not viewed as being a portion of "this people," the constituent membership of the sovereignty. They were not viewed as citizens or as entitled to any of the rights and privileges the Constitution held out to citizens. In this Taney was probably wrong, as the dissenters, I think, demonstrated. Taney's Constitution held out rights and privileges to citizens, even though the document itself holds out few to citizens as such, does not bother to define the status of citizenship, and altogether appears to set very little store by it. Taney, by an *ipse dixit,* argued that when the Constitution says "people" it means the same thing as citizens. Yet the Constitution says citizens rarely, and people most of the time, and never the two interchangeably.

When the Constitution was formed, Taney said, Negroes were "considered as a subordinate and inferior class of beings, who had been subjugated by the dominant race, and, whether emancipated or not, yet

4. Scott v. Sandford, 60 U.S. (19 Howard) 393 (1857).

remained subject to their authority, and had no rights or privileges but such as those who held the power and the Government might choose to grant them." Now, this is a perversion of the complex, guilt-ridden, and highly ambivalent attitude of the Framers toward slavery, and of their vague, and possibly evasive and culpably less than candid expectation of some future evolution away from it. It is possible to have some compassion for the Framers in their travail over the contradiction of slavery. It is not possible to have compassion for Taney's hardening of the Framers' position, his stripping it of its original aspirations to decency as well as of its illusions, and his reattribution to the Framers of the position thus altered. * * *

The original Constitution's innocence of the concept of citizenship was thus violated in the *Dred Scott* case, in an encounter with the contradiction of slavery. A rape having occurred, innocence could never be restored. But remarkably enough, after a period of reaction to the trauma, we resumed behaving as if our virginity were intact and with a fair measure of credibility at that. Fewer than four months after the Thirteenth Amendment became law, in December 1865, Congress enacted the Civil Rights Act of 1866. With the express intention of overruling *Dred Scott,* the act declared that "all persons born in the United States and not subject to any foreign power, excluding Indians not taxed, are hereby declared to be citizens of the United States." This was the first authoritative definition of citizenship in American law. It had become necessary to make clear that race and descent from slaves was no ground of exclusion. * * * The *Dred Scott* decision used the concept of citizenship negatively, as exclusionary. It indicated who was not under the umbrella of rights and privileges and status and thus entrenched the subjection of the Negro in the Constitution. The Civil Rights Act of 1866 was equally negative; *Dred Scott* had to be exorcised. In the process, as a matter of syntactic compulsion, of stylistic necessity, as a matter of the flow of the pen, the concept of citizenship was revived.

When the same Congress that passed the 1866 Civil Rights Act wrote the Fourteenth Amendment, it forbade any state to "abridge the privileges or immunities of citizens of the United States." The author of this phrase was John A. Bingham, a Representative from Ohio, a Republican of abolitionist antecedents. He was a type that frequently occurred in our political life, a man of enthusiastic rhetorical bent, on the whole of generous impulse, and of zero analytical inclination or capacity. A Republican colleague in the House recalling quite specifically the privileges and immunities clause, and that it came from Bingham, said: "Its euphony and indefiniteness of meaning were a charm to him." The only explanation of this clause that was attempted in the long course of the congressional debate on the amendment came from Bingham, and it confirms his contemporaries' estimate of him—it was highly confused. As an afterthought, by amendment in the Senate of the text passed in the House, a definition of citizenship modeled on the Civil Rights Act of 1866 was added: "All persons born or naturalized in the United States and subject to the jurisdiction thereof [which may exclude the children of foreign ambassadors, and means little, if anything, more than that], are citizens of the United States and of the state wherein they reside."

The *Dred Scott* decision had to be effectively, which is to say constitutionally, overruled by a definition of citizenship in which race played no part. So, in a fashion no one quite understood but everyone apparently found necessary, *Dred Scott* was exorcised. That having been done, the rest of section 1 of the Fourteenth Amendment made no further reference to citizens. * * *

At this stage of our history we stood at a point where the status of citizenship might have become all-important, not because of a deliberate, reasoned decision, but owing to the particular dialectic of the *Dred Scott* case, which one may view as an accident, and of the natural reaction to it. Actually, the concept of citizenship, once inserted in the Fourteenth Amendment, survived as a drafting technique in three later constitutional amendments which safeguard the right to vote against particular infringements. But on the whole the development was away from this concept— owing to yet another accident.

This other accident was the decision in the *Slaughter-House Cases* [12] of 1873, in which the Supreme Court for the first time construed the newly enacted Fourteenth Amendment. The first reading of the great Reconstruction amendment had nothing to do with Negroes, slavery, civil rights, or in any other way with the aftermath of the Civil War. The case arose instead out of a more than ordinarily corrupt enactment of the Louisiana legislature in 1869, which created a slaughtering monopoly in New Orleans. * * *

The main purpose of the Fourteenth Amendment's definition of citizenship, Justice Samuel F. Miller began for the Court, was to overrule the *Dred Scott* case and "to establish the citizenship of the negro." In addition, the definition clarified what Miller thought was a previously open but hardly world-shaking question: whether a person born not in a state, but in a territory or in the District of Columbia, who was therefore not a citizen of any state, could be a citizen of the United States. He could be. The Fourteenth Amendment made sure there would be no limbo.

But what could be meant by privileges and immunities of citizens of the United States? The sole purpose of the privileges and immunities clause of the original Constitution, article IV, section 2, said Justice Miller, was "to declare to the several States, that whatever those rights, as you grant or establish them to your own citizens, or as you limit or qualify or impose restrictions on their exercise, the same, neither more nor less, shall be the measure of rights of citizens of other States within your jurisdiction." But the rights themselves did not depend on the federal government for their existence or protection. Their definition and their limitation lay within the power of the states.

Was the Fourteenth Amendment, by creating national citizenship, meant to work the radical change * * * of making basic relationships

---

12. Slaughter-House Cases, 83 U.S. (16 Wallace) 36 (1872).

between the individual and the state turn on federal law? * * * Miller answered for the majority with a vigorous negative. The purpose of the privileges and immunities clause was to define, secure, and protect the citizenship of the newly freed slaves, that and no more. It was a close decision; the Court divided 5 to 4.

Was the privileges and immunities clause, then, entirely meaningless? Why did the draftsman put it in? We know why—because John A. Bingham liked the sound of it. But that is not good enough. Statutory and particularly constitutional enactments must be invested with some meaning, which Miller proceeded to do. National citizenship, he said, confers the right to come to the seat of government, a right protected for inanimate things, and for aliens as well, by the commerce clause; the right to seek (though probably not to claim) the protection of the government when outside the United States; the right to use the navigable waters of the United States, which under international law may be forbidden to aliens. That was about it.

* * *

The decision in the *Slaughter-House Cases*, however narrowly reached, has stuck so far as the argument proceeding from the privileges and immunities clause is concerned. And what it did was to bring us back to where we started. It concluded the flurry of the *Dred Scott* case, came around just about full circle, and left matters almost as they were before that episode. While we now have a definition of citizenship in the Constitution we still set very little store by it.

* * *

The consequences of the decision in the *Slaughter-House Cases* with respect to the role played in our polity by the concept of citizenship have followed with inexorable logic. Although the Fifteenth, Nineteenth, and Twenty-sixth Amendments guarantee the right to vote in terms of citizenship, and the right to vote is now generally a function of United States citizenship, it was not always, and in some states not recently, so; and in any case it is not the Constitution that ties even that most symbolically charged act of participation in governance to the status of citizenship. There have been other, aberrant departures from the logic of the *Slaughter-House Cases*. But when challenged they are most often found to be insupportable contradictions, and are eliminated.

[Bickel then reviews several cases in the line that spawned the potent equal protection doctrine of *Graham v. Richardson*, 403 U.S. 365 (1971), which shields aliens from most State law discrimination, unless the State can demonstrate a compelling governmental interest.]

That is not quite an end of the matter. Resident aliens are under the protection of our Constitution substantially no less than citizens, but conditions may be attached to entry permits, and in time of war even resident enemy aliens may be subject to fairly harsh restrictions. But that is a consequence, I suggest, of our perception of the meaning of foreign citizenship and of the obligations it may impose more than it is a consequence of the significance of the status of citizen in our own domestic law. * * * The citizen has a right as against the whole world to be here. The alien does not, although once the alien is permanently resident his right to remain, if qualified, is substantial and covered by constitutional protections. The decision of who may enter and remain as of right must be made by every nation-state in a world of nation-states, else it places its existence at risk. Citizenship can be and is made, though rarely, the basis for the extraterritorial application of domestic law (such as the draft, the tax law, rules requiring appearance in court) and, most significantly, for the extraterritorial reach of the quintessential crime of allegiance, the crime of treason, which is defined by the Constitution closely and narrowly in terms of persons, not citizens.

* * *

* * * Special qualifications for naturalization do exist and are enforced. Good moral character is one. However, qualifications that seek to pour ideological and political meaning into the concept of citizenship meet with judicial resistance. Nor has Congress been permitted to define the allegiance of those already citizens by providing for their involuntary expatriation—the involuntary loss of citizenship—upon commission of acts inconsistent with allegiance. Such acts by citizens and even by noncitizens may be punished, but loss of citizenship cannot be predicated on them. And the irony is that in the decisions that denied a power to impose involuntary expatriation and thus seemed to follow the tradition of denuding the concept of citizenship in our law of any special role and content, the Supreme Court returned to a rhetoric of exalting citizenship which echoes the Taney opinion in *Dred Scott*.

In the early years of the Republic, Hamilton and his followers believed that, like British subjects, Americans should be tied indissolubly to the state; a right of voluntary expatriation would encourage subversion. But voluntary expatriation has long been permitted by our law. Jefferson supported such a right, and in the end his view prevailed. In 1868 Congress, having for the first time defined citizenship, passed a statute still on the books providing, in warm language, that "the right of expatriation is a natural and inherent right of all people, indispensable to the enjoyment of the rights of life, liberty and the pursuit of happiness," and was not to be denied. We had, after all, fought in 1812 against British claims that immigrants from Great Britain who were sailors in our navy could be treated by the British as deserters because they had never lost their British nationality, and in the 1860s we were indignant at British treatment of naturalized Irish-Americans arrested in Ireland for participation in anti-British activities.

Congress listed as expatriating behavior such acts as voting in a foreign political election or deserting from the armed forces in time of war, or, for a naturalized citizen, taking up permanent residence in the country of his or her birth. In the end the Court held them all unconstitutional,[35] although there is some slight evidence that the Court as now constituted might be willing to some extent to rethink the whole ques-

35. *Afroyim v. Rusk,* 387 U.S. 253, 87 S.Ct. 1660, 18 L.Ed.2d 757 (1967); *Schneider* *v. Rusk,* 377 U.S. 163, 84 S.Ct. 1187, 12 L.Ed.2d 218 (1964).

tion.[36] The Court said, in effect, in these cases holding the involuntary expatriation statutes unconstitutional, that Congress may not put that much content into the concept of citizenship. It seemed to reaffirm the traditional minimal content of the concept of citizenship, the minimal definition of allegiance. But its language was at war with its action. "This government was born of its citizens," wrote Chief Justice Earl Warren,

> it maintains itself in a continuing relationship with them, and, in my judgment, it is without power to sever the relationship that gives rise to its existence. I cannot believe that a government conceived in the spirit of ours was established with power to take from the people their most basic right.

> Citizenship *is* man's basic right for it is nothing less than the right to have rights. Remove this priceless possession and there remains a stateless person, disgraced and degraded in the eyes of his countrymen. He has no lawful claim to protection from any nation, and no nation may assert rights on his behalf. His very existence is at the sufferance of the state within whose borders he happens to be. [As if our government were in the habit of beheading people for not being citizens!] In this country the expatriate would presumably enjoy, at most, only the limited rights and privileges of aliens....

> The people who created this government endowed it with broad powers.... But the citizens themselves are sovereign, and their citizenship is not subject to the general powers of their government.[37]

Citizenship, Warren concluded, is "that status, which alone assures the full enjoyment of the precious rights conferred by our Constitution." Ten years later, when these views came to command a majority,[38] Justice Black wrote: "In our country the people are sovereign and the Government cannot sever its relationship to the people by taking away their citizenship." And: "Its citizenry is the country and the country is its citizenry."

All this, as we have seen, is simply not so. It is not so on the face of the Constitution, and it certainly has not been so since the *Slaughter-House Cases* of 1873. The Warren language was a regression to the confusions of Bingham and, what is worse, to the majority opinion in *Dred Scott v. Sandford*, which held that the terms "people of the United States" and "citizens" are synonymous and that they "both describe the political body who according to our republican institutions form the sovereignty." Who said, "They are what we familiarly call the single 'sovereign people,'

36. *See Rogers v. Bellei*, 401 U.S. 815, 91 S.Ct. 1060, 28 L.Ed.2d 499 (1971). [*But see Vance v. Terrazas*, 444 U.S. 252, 100 S.Ct. 540, 62 L.Ed.2d 461 (1980) (to be considered later in this Chapter), decided several years after Bickel's essay was written.—eds.]

37. *Perez v. Brownell*, 356 U.S. 44, 64–65, 78 S.Ct. 568, 579–80, 2 L.Ed.2d 603 (1957) (footnotes omitted) (Warren, Black, and Douglas dissenting). This dissent within the

decade became the prevailing view. The chief justice took his clue from an unguarded comment by Brandeis, made in a quite different context, to the effect that deportation of one who claims to be a citizen may result in the loss of "all that makes life worth living." *Ng Fung Ho v. White*, 259 U.S. 276, 284 (1922).

38. *Afroyim v. Rusk*, 387 U.S. 253, 87 S.Ct. 1660, 18 L.Ed.2d 757 (1967).

and every citizen is one of this people and a constituent member of the sovereignty"? Roger B. Taney did, and Earl Warren and Hugo L. Black echoed it a century later, unwittingly to be sure. Who said that noncitizens "had no rights or privileges but such as those who held the power and the government might choose to grant them"? Roger B. Taney, to the same curious later echo.

No matter to what purpose it is put and by whom, this is regressive. Its thrust is parochial and exclusive. A relationship between government and the governed that turns on citizenship can always be dissolved or denied. Citizenship is a legal construct, an abstraction, a theory. No matter what the safeguards, it is at best something given, and given to some and not to others, and it can be taken away. It has always been easier, it always will be easier, to think of someone as a noncitizen than to decide that he is a nonperson, which is the point of the *Dred Scott* case. Emphasis on citizenship as the tie that binds the individual to government and as the source of his rights leads to metaphysical thinking about politics and law, and more particularly to symmetrical thinking, to a search for reciprocity and symmetry and clarity of uncompromised rights and obligations, rationally ranged one next and against the other. Such thinking bodes ill for the endurance of free, flexible, responsive, and stable institutions and of a balance between order and liberty. It is by such thinking, as in Rousseau's *The Social Contract,* that the claims of liberty may be readily translated into the postulates of oppression. I find it gratifying, therefore, that we live under a Constitution to which the concept of citizenship matters very little, that prescribes decencies and wise modalities of government quite without regard to the concept of citizenship. It subsumes important obligations and functions of the individual which have other sources—moral, political, and traditional— sources more complex than the simple contractarian notion of citizenship. "The simple governments," wrote Burke, "are fundamentally defective, to say no worse of them." Citizenship is at best a simple idea for a simple government.

SUGARMAN v. DOUGALL

Supreme Court of the United States, 1973.
413 U.S. 634, 93 S.Ct. 2842, 37 L.Ed.2d 853.

MR. JUSTICE REHNQUIST, dissenting.

[Justice Rehnquist's dissent applies both to *Sugarman v. Dougall,* 413 U.S. 634, 93 S.Ct. 2842, 37 L.Ed.2d 853 (1973) (wherein the Court invalidated New York's law barring aliens from state civil service jobs) and *In re Griffiths,* 413 U.S. 717, 93 S.Ct. 2851, 37 L.Ed.2d 910 (1973) (holding that Connecticut could not make citizenship a requirement for admission to the bar).]

* * *

The Court, by holding in these cases and in *Graham v. Richardson,* 403 U.S. 365, 91 S.Ct. 1848, 29 L.Ed.2d 534 (1971), that a citizen-alien classification is "suspect" in the eyes of our Constitution, fails to mention, let alone rationalize, the fact that the Constitution itself recognizes a basic difference between citizens and aliens. That distinction is constitutionally important in no less than 11 instances in a political document noted for its brevity. Representatives, U.S. Const. Art. I, § 2, cl. 2, and Senators, Art. I, § 3, cl. 3, must be citizens. Congress has the authority "[t]o establish an uniform Rule of Naturalization" by which aliens can become citizen members of our society, Art. I, § 8, cl. 4; the judicial authority of the federal courts extends to suits involving citizens of the United States "and foreign States, Citizens or Subjects," Art. III, § 2, cl. 1, because somehow the parties are "different," a distinction further made by the Eleventh Amendment; the Fifteenth, Nineteenth, Twenty-Fourth, and Twenty-Sixth Amendments are relevant only to "citizens." The President must not only be a citizen but "a natural born Citizen," Art. II, § 1, cl. 5. One might speculate what meaning Art. IV, § 2, cl. 1, has today.

Not only do the numerous classifications on the basis of citizenship that are set forth in the Constitution cut against both the analysis used and the results reached by the Court in these cases; the very Amendment which the Court reads to prohibit classifications based on citizenship establishes the very distinction which the Court now condemns as "suspect." The first sentence of the Fourteenth Amendment provides:

> "All persons born or naturalized in the United States and subject to the jurisdiction thereof, are citizens of the United States and of the State wherein they reside."

In constitutionally defining who is a citizen of the United States, Congress obviously thought it was doing something, and something important. Citizenship meant something, a status in and relationship with a society which is continuing and more basic than mere presence or residence. The language of that Amendment carefully distinguishes between "persons" who, whether by birth or naturalization, had achieved a certain status, and "persons" in general. That a "citizen" was considered by Congress to be a rationally distinct subclass of all "persons" is obvious from the language of the Amendment.

* * *

HANNAH ARENDT, THE ORIGINS OF TOTALITARIANISM
293–302 (2d ed. 1962).

[After a thorough review of the situation of stateless people in Europe between the two world wars and of "displaced persons" immediately after World War II, the author continues:]

The Rights of Man, supposedly inalienable, proved to be unenforceable—even in countries whose constitutions were based upon them—whenever people appeared who were no longer citizens of any sovereign state.
* * *

The first loss which the rightless suffered was the loss of their homes, and this meant the loss of the entire social texture into which they were born and in which they established for themselves a distinct place in the world. This calamity is far from unprecedented; in the long memory of history, forced migrations of individuals or whole groups of people for political or economic reasons look like everyday occurrences. What is unprecedented is not the loss of a home but the impossibility of finding a new one. Suddenly, there was no place on earth where migrants could go without the severest restrictions, no country where they would be assimilated, no territory where they could found a new community of their own. This, moreover, had next to nothing to do with any material problem of overpopulation; it was a problem not of space but of political organization. Nobody had been aware that mankind, for so long a time considered under the image of a family of nations, had reached the stage where whoever was thrown out of one of these tightly organized closed communities found himself thrown out of the family of nations altogether.

The second loss which the rightless suffered was the loss of government protection, and this did not imply just the loss of legal status in their own, but in all countries. Treaties of reciprocity and international agreements have woven a web around the earth that makes it possible for the citizen of every country to take his legal status with him no matter where he goes (so that, for instance, a German citizen under the Nazi regime might not be able to enter a mixed marriage abroad because of the Nuremberg laws). Yet, whoever is no longer caught in it finds himself out of legality altogether (thus during the last war stateless people were invariably in a worse position than enemy aliens who were still indirectly protected by their governments through international agreements).

* * *

The calamity of the rightless is not that they are deprived of life, liberty, and the pursuit of happiness, or of equality before the law and freedom of opinion—formulas which were designed to solve problems *within* given communities—but that they no longer belong to any community whatsoever. Their plight is not that they are not equal before the law, but that no law exists for them; not that they are oppressed but that nobody wants even to oppress them. Only in the last stage of a rather lengthy process is their right to live threatened; only if they remain perfectly "superfluous," if nobody can be found to "claim" them, may their lives be in danger. Even the Nazis started their extermination of Jews by first depriving them of all legal status (the status of second-class citizenship) and cutting them off from the world of the living by herding them into ghettos and concentration camps; and before they set the gas chambers into motion they had carefully tested the ground and found out to their satisfaction that no country would claim these people. The point is that a condition of complete rightlessness was created before the right to live was challenged.

The same is true even to an ironical extent with regard to the right of freedom which is sometimes considered to be the very essence of human rights. There is no question that those outside the pale of the law may have more freedom of movement than a lawfully imprisoned criminal or that they enjoy more freedom of opinion in the internment camps of democratic countries than they would in any ordinary despotism, not to mention in a totalitarian country. But neither physical safety—being fed by some state or private welfare agency—nor freedom of opinion changes in the least their fundamental situation of rightlessness. The prolongation of their lives is due to charity and not to right, for no law exists which could force the nations to feed them; their freedom of movement, if they have it at all, gives them no right to residence which even the jailed criminal enjoys as a matter of course; and their freedom of opinion is a fool's freedom, for nothing they think matters anyhow.

These last points are crucial. The fundamental deprivation of human rights is manifested first and above all in the deprivation of a place in the world which makes opinions significant and actions effective. Something much more fundamental than freedom and justice, which are rights of citizens, is at stake when belonging to the community into which one is born is no longer a matter of course and not belonging no longer a matter of choice, or when one is placed in a situation where, unless he commits a crime, his treatment by others does not depend on what he does or does not do. This extremity, and nothing else, is the situation of people deprived of human rights. They are deprived, not of the right to freedom, but of the right to action; not of the right to think whatever they please, but of the right to opinion. Privileges in some cases, injustices in most, blessings and doom are meted out to them according to accident and without any relation whatsoever to what they do, did, or may do.

We became aware of the existence of a right to have rights (and that means to live in a framework where one is judged by one's actions and opinions) and a right to belong to some kind of organized community, only when millions of people emerged who had lost and could not regain these rights because of the new global political situation. The trouble is that this calamity arose not from any lack of civilization, backwardness, or mere tyranny, but, on the contrary, that it could not be repaired, because there was no longer any "uncivilized" spot on earth, because whether we like it or not we have really started to live in One World. Only with a completely organized humanity could the loss of home and political status become identical with expulsion from humanity altogether.

Before this, what we must call a "human right" today would have been thought of as a general characteristic of the human condition which no tyrant could take away. Its loss entails the loss of the relevance of speech (and man, since Aristotle, has been defined as a being commanding the power of speech and thought), and the loss of all human relationship (and man, again since Aristotle, has been thought of as the "political animal," that is one who by definition lives in a community), the loss, in other words, of some of the most essential characteristics of human life. This was to a certain extent the plight of slaves, whom Aristotle therefore did not count among human beings. Slavery's fundamental offense against human rights was not that it took liberty away (which can happen in many other situations), but that it excluded a certain category of people even from the possibility of fighting for freedom—a fight possible under tyranny, and even under the desperate conditions of modern terror (but not under any conditions of concentration-camp life). Slavery's crime against humanity did not begin when one people defeated and enslaved its enemies (though of course this was bad enough), but when slavery became an institution in which some men were "born" free and others slave, when it was forgotten that it was man who had deprived his fellow-men of freedom, and when the sanction for the crime was attributed to nature. Yet in the light of recent events it is possible to say that even slaves still belonged to some sort of human community; their labor was needed, used, and exploited, and this kept them within the pale of humanity. To be a slave was after all to have a distinctive character, a place in society— more than the abstract nakedness of being human and nothing but human. Not the loss of specific rights, then, but the loss of a community willing and able to guarantee any rights whatsoever, has been the calamity which has befallen ever-increasing numbers of people. Man, it turns out, can lose all so-called Rights of Man without losing his essential quality as man, his human dignity. Only the loss of a polity itself expels him from humanity.

* * *

These facts and reflections offer what seems an ironical, bitter, and belated confirmation of the famous arguments with which Edmund Burke opposed the French Revolution's Declaration of the Rights of Man. They appear to buttress his assertion that human rights were an "abstraction," that it was much wiser to rely on an "entailed inheritance" of rights which one transmits to one's children like life itself, and to claim one's rights to be the "rights of an Englishman" rather than the inalienable rights of man. According to Burke, the rights which we enjoy spring "from within the nation," so that neither natural law, nor divine command, nor any concept of mankind such as Robespierre's "human race," "the sovereign of the earth," are needed as a source of law.

The pragmatic soundness of Burke's concept seems to be beyond doubt in the light of our manifold experiences. Not only did loss of national rights in all instances entail the loss of human rights; the restoration of human rights, as the recent example of the State of Israel proves, has been achieved so far only through the restoration or the establishment of national rights. The conception of human rights, based upon the assumed existence of a human being as such, broke down at the very moment when those who professed to believe in it were for the first time confronted with people who had indeed lost all other qualities and specific relationships— except that they were still human. The world found nothing sacred in the abstract nakedness of being human. And in view of objective political conditions, it is hard to say how the concepts of man upon which human rights are based—that he is created in the image of God (in the American formula), or that he is the representative of mankind, or that he harbors within himself the sacred demands of natural law (in the French formula) —could have helped to find a solution to the problem.

The survivors of the extermination camps, the inmates of concentration and internment camps, and even the comparatively happy stateless people could see without Burke's arguments that the abstract nakedness of being nothing but human was their greatest danger. Because of it they were regarded as savages and, afraid that they might end by being considered beasts, they insisted on their nationality, the last sign of their former citizenship, as their only remaining and recognized tie with humanity. Their distrust of natural, their preference for national, rights comes precisely from their realization that natural rights are granted even to savages. Burke had already feared that natural "inalienable" rights would confirm only the "right of the naked savage," and therefore reduce civilized nations to the status of savagery. Because only savages have nothing more to fall back upon than the minimum fact of their human origin, people cling to their nationality all the more desperately when they have lost the rights and protection that such nationality once gave them. Only their past with its "entailed inheritance" seems to attest to the fact that they still belong to the civilized world.

* * *

Burke's arguments therefore gain an added significance if we look only at the general human condition of those who have been forced out of all political communities. Regardless of treatment, independent of liberties or oppression, justice or injustice, they have lost all those parts of the world and all those aspects of human existence which are the result of our common labor, the outcome of the human artifice.

* * *

Since the Greeks, we have known that highly developed political life breeds a deep-rooted suspicion of [the] private sphere, a deep resentment against the disturbing miracle contained in the fact that each of us is made as he is—single, unique, unchangeable. This whole sphere of the merely given, relegated to private life in civilized society, is a permanent threat to the public sphere, because the public sphere is as consistently based on the law of equality as the private sphere is based on the law of universal difference and differentiation. Equality, in contrast to all that is involved in mere existence, is not given us, but is the result of human organization insofar as it is guided by the principle of justice. We are not born equal; we become equal as members of a group on the strength of our decision to guarantee ourselves mutually equal rights.

* * *

The great danger arising from the existence of people forced to live outside the common world is that they are thrown back, in the midst of civilization, on their natural givenness, on their mere differentiation. They lack that tremendous equalizing of differences which comes from being citizens of some commonwealth and yet, since they are no longer allowed to partake in the human artifice, they begin to belong to the human race in much the same way as animals belong to a specific animal species. The paradox involved in the loss of human rights is that such loss coincides with the instant when a person becomes a human being in general—without a profession, without a citizenship, without an opinion, without a deed by which to identify and specify himself—*and* different in general, representing nothing but his own absolutely unique individuality which, deprived of expression within and action upon a common world, loses all significance.

* * *

Notes

1. Both Bickel and Rehnquist describe the same set of constitutional references to the citizenship concept, yet they reach radically different conclusions about the Framers' understanding of, and reliance on, that status. Which characterization strikes you as more persuasive? Is the glass half empty or half full?

2. What understandings of citizenship—its meaning, its psychological freight, its burdens and entitlements—underlie the essays by Bickel and Arendt? How do they differ? How are they similar?

3. Other useful discussions of these and related issues may be found in M. Walzer, *Spheres of Justice: A Defense of Pluralism and Equality* 31–63 (1983); and Rosberg, *Aliens and Equal Protection: Why Not the Right to Vote?*, 75 Mich.L.Rev. 1092 (1977).

SECTION B. ACQUISITION OF NATIONALITY BY BIRTH

Two basic principles for the acquisition of nationality at birth are known to international practice: the *jus soli*, literally right of land or ground—conferment of nationality based on birth within the national territory; and the *jus sanguinis*, or right of blood—the conferment of nationality based on descent, irrespective of the place of birth. *See generally* Harvard Research in International Law, *Nationality*, 23 Am.J. Int'l L. 27–29 (Special Supp.1929). Anglo-American nationality law is fundamentally based on the *jus soli*, although both principles have played a role in the transmission of United States citizenship ever since the first nationality statute was passed. Act of March 26, 1790, Ch. 3, 1 Stat. 103.

Jus Soli

We consider here first the *jus soli*. As is evident from Professor Bickel's essay earlier in this chapter, citizenship based on birth in the national territory is rooted in the language of the first sentence of the Fourteenth Amendment. Adopted in 1868, that provision states: "All persons born or naturalized in the United States, and subject to the jurisdiction thereof, are citizens of the United States and of the State wherein they reside." But what does it mean to be born "subject to the jurisdiction thereof"?

The Supreme Court's first holding on the subject suggested that the court would give a restrictive reading to the phrase, potentially disqualifying significant numbers of persons born within the physical boundaries of the nation. In *Elk v. Wilkins*, 112 U.S. 94, 5 S.Ct. 41, 28 L.Ed. 643 (1884), the court ruled that native Indians were not U.S. citizens, even if they later severed their ties with their tribes. The words "subject to the jurisdiction thereof," the Court held, mean "not merely subject in some respect or degree to the jurisdiction of the United States, but completely subject to their political jurisdiction, and owing them direct and immediate allegiance." Most Indians could not meet the test. "Indians born within the territorial limits of the United States, members of, and owing immediate allegiance to, one of the Indian tribes, (an alien though dependent power,) although in a geographical sense born in the United States, are no more 'born in the United States and subject to the jurisdiction thereof,' * * * than the children of subjects of any foreign government born within the domain of that government * * *." *Id.* at 102.

Congress eventually passed legislation overcoming the direct effects of this holding. The Allotment Act of 1887 conferred citizenship on many Indians who resided in the United States, and later statutes expanded the scope of the grant. Since at least 1940 (and possibly since 1924—the application of the statute enacted that year to Indians born thereafter was unclear), all Indians born in the United States are U.S. citizens at birth. *See* G & R § 12.6e, INA § 301(b).

But in the meantime, in the years following *Elk,* the Chinese exclusion laws were being tightened. The question arose whether children born in the United States to Chinese parents would be citizens under *Elk*'s reading of the Fourteenth Amendment. After all, opponents of such citizenship pointed out, Chinese had always been excluded from naturalization,[3] and the Chinese exclusion laws themselves restated that bar. Did the impossibility of their parents' obtaining U.S. citizenship also somehow render such persons not subject to the jurisdiction of the United States, within the meaning of the Fourteenth Amendment, at the time of their birth?

The Supreme Court's answer came in a case involving one Wong Kim Ark, born in San Francisco to Chinese parents who had taken up residence in this country under the original treaties that had encouraged such migration. Excluded from entry in 1895 on returning from a brief visit to China, Wong Kim Ark claimed a right to admission as a citizen, based on the locus of his birth. In a landmark decision, a divided Supreme Court held that the words "born in the United States and subject to the jurisdiction thereof" should be given an expansive reading; hence Wong Kim Ark was indeed a citizen by virtue of the Fourteenth Amendment. Both the majority and dissenters wrote lengthy scholarly opinions examining common law and civil law rules for the acquisition of citizenship at birth. After quoting the key constitutional language, the majority held:

> As appears upon the face of the amendment, as well as from the history of the times, this was not intended to impose any new restrictions upon citizenship, or to prevent any persons from becoming citizens by the fact of birth within the United States, who would thereby have become citizens according to the law

---

3. The original naturalization laws opened citizenship only to "free white persons." In 1870, in the wake of the Civil War, Congress extended naturalization eligibility to "persons of African descent." Western Hemisphere natives were included in 1940. Not until 1943 were Chinese made eligible for naturalization—a somewhat belated token of support extended to a World War II ally. Only in 1952 were all racial and national origin bars eliminated from the naturalization laws. INA § 311. *See generally* G & R §§ 15.2, 15.12.

existing before its adoption. It is declaratory in form, and enabling and extending in effect. Its main purpose doubtless was, as has been often recognized by this court, to establish the citizenship of free negroes, which had been denied in the opinion delivered by Chief Justice Taney in *Dred Scott v. Sandford*, (1857) 19 How. 393; and to put it beyond doubt that all blacks, as well as whites, born or naturalized within the jurisdiction of the United States, are citizens of the United States. But the opening words, "All persons born," are general, not to say universal, restricted only by place and jurisdiction, and not by color or race * * *.

* * *

The decision in *Elk v. Wilkins* concerned only members of the Indian tribes within the United States, and had no tendency to deny citizenship to children born in the United States of foreign parents of Caucasian, African or Mongolian descent, not in the diplomatic service of a foreign country.

The real object of the Fourteenth Amendment of the Constitution, in qualifying the words, "All persons born in the United States," by the addition, "and subject to the jurisdiction thereof," would appear to have been to exclude, by the fewest and fittest words, (besides children of members of the Indian tribes, standing in a peculiar relation to the National Government, unknown to the common law,) the two classes of cases—children born of alien enemies in hostile occupation, and children of diplomatic representatives of a foreign State—both of which, as has already been shown, by the law of England, and by our own law, from the time of the first settlement of the English colonies in America, had been recognized exceptions to the fundamental rule of citizenship by birth within the country.

* * *

This sentence of the Fourteenth Amendment is declaratory of existing rights, and affirmative of existing law, as to each of the qualifications therein expressed—"born in the United States," "naturalized in the United States," and "subject to the jurisdiction thereof"—in short, as to everything relating to the acquisition of citizenship by facts occurring within the limits of the United States. But it has not touched the acquisition of citizenship by being born abroad of American parents; and has left that subject to be regulated, as it had always been, by Congress, in the exercise of the power conferred by the Constitution to establish an uniform rule of naturalization.

United States v. Wong Kim Ark, 169 U.S. 649, 676, 682, 688, 18 S.Ct. 456, 467, 469, 472, 42 L.Ed. 890 (1898).

Some of the language of the majority opinion seemed to leave open the status of children born within the United States to alien parents only temporarily present within the national borders. But in fact the *Wong*

Kim Ark decision has served to establish for the United States a "general rule of universal citizenship" by birth, in the words of the leading immigration treatise, G & R § 12.5.   Birth in the territorial United States, even to parents fresh across the border after an illegal entry, results in U.S. citizenship.   The only exceptions to this *jus soli* rule are exceedingly narrow: birth to foreign sovereigns and accredited diplomatic officials; birth on foreign public vessels—meaning essentially warships, not commercial vessels—even while they are located in U.S. territorial waters (we wonder: does this ever happen?); birth to alien enemies in hostile occupation of a portion of U.S. territory.   *See* G & R § 12.6.

Special considerations may apply, however, in determining the effect of birth in an outlying territory of the United States.   The issue is whether birth there resulted in full citizenship or only in status as a noncitizen national.   *See* note 2, *supra*.   Care must be taken to consult the relevant rules in effect for the particular territory at the time of the birth, and, if full citizenship was not granted, to track later developments affecting the status of the territory and its inhabitants.[4]   Sometimes the governing rules, in light of intervening changes, can be exceedingly complex.   *See* G & R §§ 12.8–12.16.   As of today, however, the regular *jus soli* rules are in effect in all territories except American Samoa and Swains Island—meaning that children now born in any U.S. territorial possessions except those two become full citizens at birth.

Jus Sanguinis

Since 1790 Congress has made special provision for the transmission of U.S. nationality *jure sanguinis* to children born abroad to American parents.   The current *jus sanguinis* rules are set forth in INA §§ 301(c), (d), (e), (g), 308(2), and 309.   The most important relate to children born outside U.S. territory to parents either one or both of whom are U.S. citizens.   If both are citizens, the child acquires citizenship at birth, provided only that one of the parents had a residence in the United States at some time prior thereto.   INA § 301(c).[5]   *See Weedin v. Chin Bow,* 274 U.S. 657, 47 S.Ct. 772, 71 L.Ed. 1284 (1927) (parental residence must precede birth of the child).   If one parent is an alien, however, then the citizen parent must have been physically present in the United States for a total of ten years before the birth, including at least five years after the age of fourteen.   Certain kinds of government and military service abroad count as physical presence in the United States for these purposes. § 301(e).

4. Filipinos, for example, were noncitizen nationals of the United States from 1899 to 1946, but became aliens when independence was granted to the Philippines in the latter year and their allegiance was declared transferred to the new nation. *See Rabang v. Boyd,* 353 U.S. 427, 77 S.Ct. 985, 1 L.Ed.2d 956 (1957).

5. The statute provides that the term "residence" means "the place of general abode; the place of general abode of a person means his principal, actual dwelling place in fact, without regard to intent." INA § 101(a)(33). This strict objective test of residence was adopted in reaction to administrative rulings which had found that even temporary sojourn in the United States, lasting no more than a few days, might fulfill the parental residence requirements of earlier statutes. *See, e.g., Matter of E.,* 1 I&N Dec. 40 (AG 1941); *Matter of V.,* 6 I&N 1 (AG 1954). *See generally* G & R § 13.4c.

These current rules are fairly straightforward, but until 1978 the statute included several other provisos, rendered even more complicated for ready application by the fact that the rules had been modified frequently over the years. *See* G & R §§ 13.4–13.11, and *Rogers v. Bellei,* page 905 below (recounting many of the statutory changes). The complexities result from evolving congressional views about how a fairly consistent aim should be achieved. From the beginning, Congress has sought to avoid the creation of a class of expatriates who may transmit U.S. citizenship to their children indefinitely, even though the family has had no close contact with actual life in the United States for generations. The issue has been what type of contact, on the part of the parents and/or the child, should be required.

Congress has employed two principal means toward this end. First, American citizen parents lacking a specified period of historical residence in the United States have been unable to transmit citizenship to their children. Second, from 1934 until 1978, the child had to establish his or her own residence in the United States for a specified number of years within stated periods, or else lose the citizenship acquired at birth. The length of residence, as well as the ages during which it had to be established, have been altered several times.

The first type of limitation, concerning parental residence before the child's birth, has raised few constitutional issues. The second came under potent attack after *Afroyim v. Rusk,* 387 U.S. 253, 87 S.Ct. 1660, 18 L.Ed.2d 757 (1967), imposed strict constitutional limits on the power of Congress to deprive persons of U.S. citizenship involuntarily. But the Supreme Court, by a vote of five to four, eventually held that Congress retained the power to impose such a residence requirement as a "condition subsequent" on persons who are U.S. citizens by virtue of their birth to U.S. nationals abroad. *Rogers v. Bellei,* 401 U.S. 815, 91 S.Ct. 1060, 28 L.Ed.2d 499 (1971). As indicated, we will consider this holding in detail below, when we review the entire series of nationality-deprivation cases together.

Despite the judicial endorsement of this type of post-acquisition residence requirement, Congress chose in 1978 to remove all such provisions from the immigration laws. Current law therefore relies solely on *parental* residence requirements to avoid the indefinite perpetuation of U.S. citizenship *jure sanguinis* within families that realistically have lost touch with their American roots. Act of Oct. 10, 1978, Pub.L. No. 95–432, 92 Stat. 1046. This change has considerably simplified the operation of current *jus sanguinis* rules, but Congress did not make its amendment retroactive. Persons who had already lost their citizenship under the earlier residency requirements, before the effective date of the 1978 changes, remain denationalized. To determine whether a person born outside the territorial jurisdiction is a United States citizen, therefore, it is not enough to consult the present INA, unless birth occurred after enactment of the 1978 statute. One must check carefully the precise requirements in effect at the time of the birth of the individual in question, and also see whether any requirements for later residence in the

United States have been fulfilled. For a good summary of the relevant rules, broken down by date of birth, *see* G & R §§ 13.6–13.9A.

SECTION C. NATURALIZATION AND DENATURALIZATION

As a country of immigration, the United States from its earliest days has made provision for the relatively easy acquisition of citizenship by persons born with another nationality. A brief review of the history of U.S. naturalization legislation will throw considerable light on the current scheme.

CHARLES GORDON AND HARRY N. ROSENFIELD, IMMIGRATION LAW AND PROCEDURE

Vol. 3, § 14.2 (rev. ed. 1984).*

* * *

In the original statute of March 26, 1790, Congress prescribed that a free white alien who had resided in the United States for 2 years, including residence of 1 year in any State, might be naturalized by any common law court of record, provided he was of good moral character and took an oath to support the Constitution. Five years later the 1790 statute was repealed by the Act of January 29, 1795, which re-enacted most of its provisions, with the following additions: The period of required residence in the United States was increased to 5 years; federal courts were also empowered to grant naturalization; a formal declaration of intention 3 years before admission to citizenship was made a prerequisite; applicants were required to renounce their former allegiance and to swear allegiance to the United States; and it was prescribed that the applicant establish to the satisfaction of the court that he was attached to the Constitution of the United States and well disposed to the good order and happiness of the United States.

The statutory requirements for naturalization formulated at this juncture resembled very closely the substantive requirements now generally prescribed. However, the 1795 law was short lived. The country had entered a period of reaction characterized by outbursts against aliens. One product of this interlude of hysteria was the enactment of the Alien and Sedition acts; another was the Act of June 18, 1798 which repealed the lenient provisions of the 1795 statute, and announced more restrictive naturalization requirements. The period of required residence was increased to 14 years in the United States and 5 years in a State; a declaration of intention at least 5 years old was prescribed; all aliens were required to register; and residence for the purposes of naturalization could be proved only upon production of a certificate of registry. Naturalization of alien enemies was prohibited. Clerks of court were required to transmit to the Secretary of State abstracts of declarations of intention filed in their courts.

Fortunately this interval of reaction soon ended. The Act of April 14, 1802 repealed the 1798 statute and restored the reasonable requirements of the 1795 law, which have remained in effect through almost two centuries. The 1802 law also introduced the requirement of witnesses to support the application for naturalization.

* * *

Although the early laws established acceptable substantive requirements, they were silent concerning the procedure to be followed. There were thousands of naturalization courts throughout the country, most of which were local courts in the various states, and each tribunal determined the procedure it would pursue in applications for naturalization. There was no centralized federal agency charged with the responsibility of enforcing the naturalization statutes.

This situation may have been adequate when there were few courts and a moderate quota of applicants for naturalization. With the expansion of immigration and the consequent augmentation in the number of aliens who sought naturalization, serious shortcomings in the naturalization process became evident. The absence of procedural standards and safeguards bred wide divergences in the practices of different naturalization courts, in the records they maintained, and in the type of evidence of citizenship they issued. The courts had no facilities to investigate the applications presented to them and many of the court officials were not scrupulous in insisting upon compliance with the requirements fixed by law.

As a result of these conditions, widespread frauds developed, which frequently made a mockery of the naturalization process. It was a notorious practice in many courts, for example, regularly to naturalize large groups of aliens on the eve of a political election. In many instances mill owners would load large numbers of alien employees into trucks a day or two before an election and transport them to the local court so that they might be naturalized in time to vote—presumably for the right candidate. Frequently the courts would approve the applications of persons who had no familiarity with American language or traditions, who could not meet the qualifications fixed by law, and who had no conception of the meaning of the naturalization process.

On March 1, 1905 President Theodore Roosevelt appointed a Commission to investigate the abuses in the naturalization process and to recommend appropriate revisions. As the result of the report of this Commission, Congress enacted the basic Naturalization Act of June 29, 1906. Under this statute the courts retained the ultimate authority to grant or deny citizenship, but administrative supervision over naturalization was vested in a federal agency (originally the Bureau of Immigration and Naturalization in the Department of Commerce and Labor). Among the statute's innovations were the following:

(1) Power to naturalize was removed from State courts of inferior jurisdiction.

(2) Every petitioner for naturalization who arrived in the United States after June 29, 1906 had to obtain an official certificate of his lawful admission, and it was required that such certificate be attached to and made part of the petition for naturalization.

(3) Uniform naturalization forms were prescribed.

(4) Uniform naturalization fees were fixed and clerks of court were required to account for such fees.

(5) It was directed that duplicates of all naturalization documents filed in and issued by the courts be transmitted to the Bureau of Immigration and Naturalization.

(6) Every applicant was required to sign the petition in his own handwriting and to speak the English language if physically able to speak.

(7) Each petition was to be supported by two citizen witnesses who would testify to the applicant's general qualifications for citizenship.

(8) Courts were prohibited from hearing or granting any petition until the expiration of 90 days after its filing, and then only on a stated day fixed by rule of court for the hearing of naturalization cases; and hearings on petitions for naturalization were prohibited within 30 days before a general election.

(9) Provision was made for court proceedings to cancel certificates of naturalization that were fraudulently or illegally procured.

* * *

The Nationality Act of 1940 was enacted as a codification and revision of all existing nationality laws, following a comprehensive study and report of a committee appointed by President Franklin D. Roosevelt and consisting of the Secretary of State, the Attorney General, and the Secretary of Labor. The nationality code adopted by Congress on October 14, 1940 followed closely the recommendations of this committee and included the following principal revisions:

(1) Provision was made for appointment of designated naturalization examiners by the Commissioner and for extension of the designated examiner system to the State courts.

(2) The required waiting period after filing the petition for naturalization was reduced from 90 days to 30 days and the period immediately prior to general elections during which naturalization was prohibited was increased from 30 days to 60 days.

(3) Authorization was granted for naturalization of natural children and adopted children on petition of their citizen parent or parents.

(4) The racial restrictions on naturalization were eased by adding descendants of races indigenous to the Western Hemisphere as a new class of eligibles in addition to white persons and persons of African nativity or descent. On December 17, 1943 Chinese

persons or persons of Chinese descent were added as a fourth class of persons eligible for naturalization.

* * *

The last major milestone in the historical pattern was the Immigration and Nationality Act of 1952, which is now the basic statute for immigration and nationality. * * * Among the major changes effected by the 1952 Act were the following:

(1) The racial qualifications for naturalization were completely eliminated, and the statute specifically prohibited denial of naturalization because of race or sex.

(2) The statute, incorporating an enactment of 1950, specifically prohibited the naturalization of certain members of subversive groups.

(3) A specific disqualification was prescribed for aliens who had sought relief and had been relieved from military service on the ground of alienage.

(4) Naturalization was precluded for aliens against whom a deportation proceeding or order was outstanding.

(5) Special provision was made for the naturalization of aliens who had performed military service during certain periods of hostilities.

(6) The declaration of intention and the certificate of arrival were eliminated as requirements for naturalization.

(7) The grounds for expatriation and denaturalization were enlarged.

A key feature of the 1906 Act was the creation of a procedure to take away citizenship if a later judicial proceeding determines that the naturalization was illegally or fraudulently acquired. This procedure has changed little since that time. Denaturalization proceedings may be brought only by United States Attorneys, not by private parties, and only when based on an affidavit of good cause, which is ordinarily prepared by officials of the Immigration Service. *See* G & R §§ 20.5b, 20.5c; *United States v. Zucca*, 351 U.S. 91, 76 S.Ct. 671, 100 L.Ed. 964 (1956). The current statutory provision for denaturalization appears in § 340 of the INA.

For many years, it was also possible for naturalized citizens to lose their citizenship, not for defects in the original grant, but because of certain actions following naturalization—actions which had been declared by Congress to result in such forfeiture. Most of these grounds of expatriation applied equally to naturalized and native-born citizens, but a few imposed more stringent requirements on those who had gained citizenship by naturalization. Occasionally the loss of citizenship in this manner has also been called denaturalization, but we will avoid that terminology here. We will use the term "denaturalization" to mean only the revocation of the citizenship of a naturalized alien based on fraud or illegality in the original naturalization. Any other deprivation of citizenship, whether applied to native-born or naturalized citizens, will be called "expatriation."[6]

The standards and procedures applied in denaturalization proceedings differ from those in the naturalization setting. *See generally* G & R § 20.5. Most importantly, the burden of proof shifts to the government. In a major decision handed down in 1943, *Schneiderman v. United States,* 320 U.S. 118, 63 S.Ct. 1333, 87 L.Ed. 1796, a divided Court established important standards that the government must meet in a denaturalization proceeding. Schneiderman had been naturalized in 1927, and the naturalization court found, as the statutes then and now require, that he was "attached to the principles of the Constitution of the United States and well disposed to the good order and happiness of the United States." Later, Schneiderman became prominent in the leadership of the Communist Party, of which he had been a member since at least 1924. Though he had never been arrested for lawless acts, the government brought a denaturalization proceeding in 1939, claiming that his membership and his advocacy of Marxist doctrine demonstrated that he lacked the necessary attachment at the time of naturalization. The lower courts agreed and ordered denaturalization, but the Supreme Court reversed:

> This is not a naturalization proceeding in which the Government is being asked to confer the privilege of citizenship upon an applicant. Instead the Government seeks to turn the clock back twelve years after full citizenship was conferred upon petitioner by a judicial decree, and to deprive him of the priceless benefits that derive from that status. In its consequences it is more serious than a taking of one's property, or the imposition of a fine or other penalty. For it is safe to assert that nowhere in the world today is the right of citizenship of greater worth to an individual than it is in this country. It would be difficult to exaggerate its value and importance. By many it is regarded as the highest hope of civilized men. This does not mean that once granted to an alien, citizenship cannot be revoked or cancelled on legal grounds under appropriate proof. But such a right once conferred should not be taken away without the clearest sort of justification and proof. So, whatever may be the rule in a naturalization proceeding (see United States v. Manzi, 276 U.S. 463, 467, 48 S.Ct. 328, 329, 72 L.Ed. 654), in an action instituted under § 15 for the purpose of depriving one of the precious right of citizenship previously conferred we believe the facts and the law should be construed as far as is reasonably possible in favor of the citizen. Especially is this so when the attack is made long after the time when the certificate of citizenship was granted and

---

6. As will become clear in Section D, over the last thirty years the Supreme Court has progressively imposed tighter constitutional limitations on Congress's power to expatriate unwilling citizens, whether native-born or naturalized. But none of the decisions in this series has seriously questioned Congress's authority to protect the integrity of the original naturalization process by permitting later deprivation of citizenship that was acquired illegally or through fraud.

the citizen has meanwhile met his obligations and has committed no act of lawlessness.   * * *

* * *

* * * If a finding of attachment can be so reconsidered in a denaturalization suit, our decisions make it plain that the Government needs more than a bare preponderance of the evidence to prevail. The remedy afforded the Government by the denaturalization statute has been said to be a narrower one than that of direct appeal from the granting of a petition. Tutun v. United States, 270 U.S. 568, 579, 46 S.Ct. 425, 427, 70 L.Ed. 738; cf. United States v. Ness, 245 U.S. 319, 325, 38 S.Ct. 118, 121, 62 L.Ed. 321. Johannessen v. United States states that a certificate of citizenship is "an instrument granting political privileges, and open like other public grants to be revoked if and when it shall be found to have been unlawfully or fraudulently procured. It is in this respect closely analogous to a public grant of land * * *." 225 U.S. 227, 238, 32 S.Ct. 613, 615, 56 L.Ed. 1066. To set aside such a grant the evidence must be "clear, unequivocal, and convincing"—"it cannot be done upon a bare preponderance of evidence which leaves the issue in doubt". Maxwell Land-Grant Case (United States v. Maxwell Land-Grant Co.), 121 U.S. 325, 381, 7 S.Ct. 1015, 1029, 30 L.Ed. 949. This is so because rights once conferred should not be lightly revoked. And more especially is this true when the rights are precious and when they are conferred by solemn adjudication, as is the situation when citizenship is granted. The Government's evidence in this case does not measure up to this exacting standard.

320 U.S. at 122–23, 125, 63 S.Ct. at 1335, 1337.

Both naturalization and denaturalization cases have provided occasions for courts to construe the meaning of the substantive naturalization requirements established by the statute. In connection with the following readings, you should review the sections setting forth those substantive requirements, INA §§ 311–331, and 337, with special attention to §§ 312, 313, 316, and 337; and the sections dealing primarily with procedures relating to naturalization, §§ 310, 318, and 332–348, with special attention to §§ 335 and 336.

DAVID WEISSBRODT, IMMIGRATION LAW AND PROCEDURE IN A NUTSHELL

161–64, 165–170, 172–78, 184–90 (1984).

B.   REQUIREMENTS OF NATURALIZATION

(1) Residence and Physical Presence

Section 316(a) of the Immigration and Nationality Act requires that, except as otherwise provided, no person shall become a U.S. citizen by being naturalized unless (1) he or she has resided continuously in the United States for five years as a lawfully admitted permanent resident, (2) during the five years immediately prior to filing the petition for naturalization he or she has been physically present in the United States for at least half of the time, and (3) has resided within the state in which he or she filed the petition for at least six months. The petitioner must also reside continuously within the United States from the date of the petition up to the time of admission to citizenship. 8 U.S.C.A. § 1427 [INA § 316.] The acknowledged purpose of the residency requirements is to create a reasonable period of "probation" that will enable candidates to discard their foreign attachments, to learn the principles of the U.S. system of government, and to develop an identification with the national community.

To comply with the statute a legal residence is necessary and a valid statutory residence prior to naturalization cannot be founded on an illegal entry into the country. Congress has defined "residence" under the 1952 Act to mean "the place of general abode ... [a person's] principal actual dwelling place in fact, without regard to intent." 8 U.S.C.A. § 1101(a)(33) [INA § 101(a)(33).] The question of residence thus turns on a determination of where an applicant has actually lived, not on declarations of where he or she intends to live.

An applicant for citizenship need not show that he or she stayed at the claimed residence each day of the five year statutory period. Temporary absences from the place of abode—even from the United States—does not alone break the continuity of an applicant's residence. Absence from the United States for less than six months during the statutory period does not affect continuous residence, while an absence of more than six months but less than one year presumptively breaks the continuity. 8 U.S.C.A. § 1427(b) [INA § 316(b).] The applicant can overcome the presumption by "establish[ing] to the satisfaction of the court that he did not in fact abandon his residence during such period." An absence from the United States for one year or more will as a matter of law break the continuity of residence, and the applicant will be required to complete a new period of residence after he or she returns to the United States.

As an exception to the physical residency requirement, persons who expect to be away from the United States for a year or more in service of the United States government, an American corporation engaged in foreign trade and commerce, a public international organization of which the United States is a member by treaty or statute, or a religious organization, may apply for permission to be absent without breaking their residence for purposes of naturalization. Before seeking such exception, however, an applicant must have continuously resided in the United States—following lawful admission—for one year or more. 8 U.S.C.A. §§ 1427(b), 1428 [INA §§ 316(b), 317.]

* * *

The exemption to the one year absence requirement concerning continuity of residence, which is provided to certain applicants, 8 U.S.C.A. § 1427(b)(1) [INA § 316(b)(1),] does not relieve such persons from the requirement of physical presence within the United States for one-half of the statutory five year period. 8 U.S.C.A. § 1427(c) [INA § 316(c).] Persons employed by the United States government, however, are exempted completely from the physical presence requirements of section 1427(a) [INA § 316(a).] 8 U.S.C.A. § 1427(c) [INA § 316(c).]

* * *

(2) Age

To file a petition for naturalization an applicant must have attained the age of eighteen years. 8 U.S.C.A. § 1445(b)(1) [INA § 334(b)(1).] A parent or adoptive parent, however, can file an application on behalf of a child under age eighteen, if the parent is a citizen—either by birth or naturalization—at the time the petition is filed.[a] 8 U.S.C.A. [§§ 1431–33, INA §§ 320–22.]

(3) Literacy and Educational Requirements

Unless he or she is physically unable to do so through blindness or deafness, an applicant for naturalization must be able to speak and understand simple English, as well as read and write it. [INA § 312(1).] * * * [The Act now exempts from this requirement] any person who was over the age of fifty years *at the time of filing their petition,* and who had been lawfully admitted for permanent residence for periods totalling twenty years. * * *

The statute further requires "a knowledge and understanding of the fundamentals of history, and of the principles and form of government, of the United States." 8 U.S.C.A. § 1423(2) [INA § 312(2).] Each person applying for naturalization, including the older persons mentioned above, must pass an examination demonstrating the requisite knowledge and understanding of the United States. An interpreter may be used to test the applicant's knowledge of United States history, principles, and form of government, if he or she is exempt from the literacy requirement. 8 C.F.R. § 312.2. The Immigration Service generally applies the educational requirements in a lenient manner with due consideration given to such factors as the extent of petitioner's education, background, age, and length of residence in the United States. Moreover, the regulations provide for second and third opportunities to pass the examinations. 8 C.F.R. § 312.3.

The power of Congress to establish these literacy requirements has withstood constitutional challenge. In *Trujillo-Hernandez v. Farrell* [, 503 F.2d 954] (5th Cir.1974), petitioner brought a class action, attacking the statute on equal protection grounds. The Court of Appeals for the Fifth

---

a. The child must also be permanently residing in the United States with the petitioning parent at the time of the petition, with minor exceptions. In such cases, the child is excused from residency requirements; that is, he or she need not fulfill the usual five-year waiting period. INA § 322. It should also be noted that this petitioning provision is used rather infrequently. In most cases, minor children, if resident in the United States at the appropriate time, acquire U.S. citizenship when their parents are naturalized. This latter acquisition of citizenship happens automatically by operation of law, and there is no need—or provision—for a petition or judicial proceeding relating to the child. The child's new status is known as derivative citizenship. *See* §§ 320, 321, G & R §§ 17.2, 18.3.—eds.

Circuit held that a direct attack on Congress' exercise of its naturalization power was foreclosed and nonjusticiable, as such power was part of the foreign relations responsibilities committed to the Congress.

(4) Good Moral Character

An applicant for naturalization must show that, during the five year statutory period before filing and up until the final hearing of the naturalization petition, he or she "has been and still is a person of good moral character...." 8 U.S.C.A. § 1427(a) [INA § 316(a).] * * * The burden of establishing good moral character falls upon the petitioner, as an applicant must prove his or her eligibility for citizenship in every respect. *Berenyi v. [District Director,* 385 U.S. 630, 87 S.Ct. 666, 17 L.Ed.2d 656 (1967).]

Courts have struggled with the issue of what constitutes good moral character. Judge Learned Hand stated that it is a "test, incapable of exact definition; the best we can do is to improvise the response that the 'ordinary' man or woman would make, if the question were put whether the conduct was consistent with a 'good moral character'." *Posusta v. United States* [, 285 F.2d 533] (2d Cir.1961). Prior to 1952, no attempt had been made to define good moral character by statute. Then in the 1952 Act, Congress chose to define by enumerated exclusions what would *preclude* a finding of good moral character. A person could not be considered of good moral character if he or she was at any time during the five year period:

(1) an habitual drunkard;

(2) one who has committed adultery;

(3) a polygamist, a person illegally connected with prostitution or narcotics, or one convicted of a crime involving moral turpitude;

(4) a convicted gambler or one whose income is derived principally from illegal gambling activities;

(5) one who has given false testimony for the purpose of obtaining any benefits under the Act;

(6) one who has been convicted and jailed for 180 days or more;

(7) one who *at any time* has been convicted of the crime of murder. (emphasis added). 8 U.S.C.A. [§ 1101(f), INA § 101(f).]

The fact that a person is not within the classes enumerated does not preclude a finding for other reasons that he or she lacks the requisite good moral character.

* * *

[A 1981 amendment removed adultery from this list.] Congress stated its rationale for repeal in the report accompanying the legislation:

With respect to adultery, the Committee believes that the Immigration Service should not be required to inquire into the sex lives of applicants for naturalization. Such questions clearly represent an invasion of privacy. Furthermore, in testimony before the 96th Congress witnesses concurred in the view that the adultery bar was merely "window dressing" in the law; INS estimated that "7 out of 10 persons today who would admit to that conduct would fall within one or more of the judicial interpretations which excuse that conduct for purposes of naturalization."

(5) Attachment to Constitutional Principles

An applicant must show that he or she is "attached to the principles of the Constitution of the United States, and well disposed to the good order and happiness of the United States." 8 U.S.C.A. § 1427(a) [INA § 316(a).] The purpose behind this requirement is the admission to citizenship of only those persons who are in general accord with the basic principles of the community. Courts have defined attachment to the Constitution as a belief in representative democracy, a commitment to the ideals embodied in the Bill of Rights, and a willingness to accept the basic social premise that change only be effected in an orderly manner. Similarly, a favorable disposition to the good order and happiness of the United States has been characterized as a belief in the political processes of the United States, a general satisfaction with life in the United States, and a hope for future progress and prosperity. Neither requirement is thought to preclude a belief that change in our form of government within constitutional limits is desirable.

* * *

Although the general requirements of attachment to the Constitution allow judicial discretion in evaluating a case on its own facts, several statutes enacted in 1952 specifically and automatically preclude naturalization of certain persons. Individuals belonging to the Communist Party or other totalitarian groups, * * * and persons who—irrespective of membership in any organization—advocate the overthrow of the United States government by force or violence or other unconstitutional means may not obtain naturalization. 8 U.S.C.A. § 1424 [INA § 313.] An applicant is not disqualified, however, if he or she can show that the membership in the prescribed organization is or was involuntary. 8 U.S.C.A. § 1424(d) [INA § 313(d).] Moreover, if the applicant can establish that such membership or affiliation occurred and terminated prior to the alien's attaining sixteen years of age, or such membership or affiliation was by operation of law or for purposes of obtaining employment, food, or other essentials, he or she may yet qualify for naturalization. In *Grzymala-Siedlecki v. United States* [, 285 F.2d 836] (5th Cir.1961), therefore, petitioner's enrollment in the Polish Naval Academy, which automatically conferred Communist Party membership, did not disqualify him from naturalization where the college education was necessary to the applicant's earning a livelihood in Poland.

A few courts have added another exception to the disqualification for Communist membership. Such membership or affiliation does not disqualify an applicant unless it is or was a "meaningful association." The Supreme Court had held, in the context of deportation proceedings, that a "meaningful association" signifies at minimum "[an] awareness of the Party's political aspect." *Rowoldt v. Perfetto* [, 355 U.S. 115, 78 S.Ct. 180, 2 L.Ed.2d 140] (1957). The federal district court of Puerto Rico applied the same analysis in *In re Pruna* [, 286 F.Supp. 861] (1968) holding that where petitioner's membership in an organization supporting Fidel Castro's revolution in Cuba in 1958 resulted from a belief that the organization's objective was to restore to the Cuban people a representative democracy, and where he was unaware that the organization was connected with the Communist Party, his participation did not constitute a "meaningful association" with a subversive group. His membership thus did not preclude him from naturalization.

An applicant may escape the preclusion statute if more than ten years have passed, between his or her membership in the subversive organization or the act of advocating overthrow of the government, and the filing of the petition for naturalization. 8 U.S.C.A. § 1424(c) [INA § 313(c).]

Section 314 of the 1952 Act permanently precludes the naturalization of anyone who, during the time that the U.S. "has been or shall be at war," deserts the U.S. armed forces or leaves the country with the intent of avoiding the military draft, and is convicted of that offense by a court-martial or a court of competent jurisdiction. * * *

Section 315(a) of the Act provides that an alien who seeks and obtains exemption from service in the armed forces on the ground that he or she is an alien becomes permanently ineligible for citizenship. 8 U.S.C.A. § 1426(a) [INA § 315(a).] Selective Service records are conclusive on the issue of whether an alien secured the exemption because of alienage. 8 U.S.C.A. § 1426(b) [INA § 315(b).]

(6) Oath of Allegiance to the United States

Related to the requirement that an applicant be attached to the Constitution of the United States, he or she must also take an oath of renunciation and allegiance in open court. Section 337(a) of the 1952 Act requires that the petitioner pledge (1) to support and bear true allegiance to the Constitution of the United States; (2) to renounce all allegiance to any foreign state or sovereign; (3) to support and defend the Constitution and laws of the United States against all enemies, foreign and domestic; (4) to bear arms on behalf of the United States when required by law, or to perform noncombatant service in the armed forces; or to perform civilian work of national importance when required by law. 8 U.S.C.A. § 1448 [INA § 337.]

If an applicant can show by clear and convincing evidence, to the naturalization court's satisfaction, that he or she is opposed to the bearing of arms, the applicant may revise the pledge to perform only noncombatant services in the armed forces. Similarly, if the applicant can show by the same standard of proof that he or she opposes any type of service in the armed forces by reason of "religious training and belief," he or she may pledge merely to perform important civilian work. 8 U.S.C.A. § 1448(a) [INA § 337(a).]

The present statute was designed to codify judicial decisions relieving conscientious objectors of naturalization requirements to bear arms. The moral stand taken by conscientious objectors frequently resulted in the denial of their naturalization petitions between the world wars—a result the Supreme Court affirmed in *United States v. Schwimmer* [, 279 U.S. 644, 49 S.Ct. 448, 73 L.Ed. 889] (1929) and *United States v. Macintosh* [, 283 U.S. 605, 51 S.Ct. 570, 75 L.Ed. 1302] (1931). In the 1946 case of *Girouard v. United States,* [328 U.S. 61, 66 S.Ct. 826, 90 L.Ed. 1084] however, the Court overruled these prior cases and held that religious objection to bearing arms was not of itself incompatible with allegiance to the United States. Congress adopted the Supreme Court's holding by enacting the statute currently in effect.

* * *

[The Act also relaxes certain of the usual naturalization requirements for special classes of applicants. The most important are spouses "living in marital union with the citizen spouse," for whom the residency requirement is reduced to three years (§ 319); children of U.S. citizens (several of the usual requirements are relaxed, §§ 322, 337(a), for those infrequent cases where the child did not automatically acquire U.S. citizenship under the *jus soli* or *jus sanguinis* rules nor by derivation at the time when his or her parents were naturalized); and current or former members of the armed forces (§§ 328, 329).]

* * *

D. JUDICIAL NATURALIZATION PROCEDURES

(1) Jurisdiction to Naturalize

Exclusive jurisdiction to naturalize is vested in the federal district courts, state courts of record, and territorial courts of record. 8 U.S.C.A. § 1421(a) [INA § 310(a).] The court ultimately decides whether a petitioner has complied with the strict statutory conditions for citizenship, and if the petitioner has failed to comply with any conditions, the court lacks jurisdiction to naturalize. 8 U.S.C.A. § 1421(d) [INA § 310(d).] State courts are authorized, but not required, to aid in the administration of the naturalization laws through the hearing of petitions, unless state law specifically prohibits them from exercising such jurisdiction. Conversely, states may impose a duty on their state courts to take jurisdiction of naturalization cases, but most naturalization proceedings occur in federal courts.

A court's power to hear petitions for naturalization extends only to persons who reside within its territorial jurisdiction. 8 U.S.C.A. § 1421(a) [INA § 310(a).] Once the petition is filed, jurisdiction remains with the court of filing, even if the petitioner thereafter moves his or her residence to another district.

(2) Preliminary Application

An applicant for naturalization must first file a preliminary application to enable the Immigration and Naturalization Service to conduct an initial assessment of the applicant's qualifications. 8 U.S.C.A. § 1445(b) [INA § 334(b).] The application (form N–400) consists of several pages wherein the applicant must provide background information regarding family history, periods of residence in the United States, and the names of witnesses who will support the petition for naturalization.[b] An applicant may also file a formal declaration of intention to naturalize, but such declaration is no longer mandatory. 8 U.S.C.A. § 1445(f) [INA § 334(f).] Several documents and pieces of information must accompany the application, including three identical photographs of the applicant to be affixed to the naturalization certificates and application form, 8 U.S.C.A. § 1444(a) [INA § 333(a),] a record of the applicant's fingerprints, alien registration number, biographical information, and the date of arrival in the United States.

(3) Preliminary Investigation

Before filing the formal petition for naturalization, the applicant and two citizen witnesses [c] who can testify to the applicant's qualifications for citizenship must appear before a naturalization examiner. 8 C.F.R. § 332.11 requires that witnesses and applicant give their testimony under oath. Each applicant and witness is interrogated separately, during which questioning the applicant's attorney or representative may be present (provided the attorney or representative has filed a notice of appearance) to observe without taking part. Although a stenographic transcript of the proceeding may be ordered by the examiner, the hearing is not formal and the rules of evidence do not apply.

If after completion of the questioning, the examiner determines that the application lacks any necessary qualifications, he or she advises the applicant of that determination. An applicant is not bound, however, by the examiner's findings, and may as a matter of right file the petition for naturalization in a court authorized to take jurisdiction. 8 C.F.R. § 334.1.

(4) The Petition for Naturalization

The applicant next files the petition in person with the clerk of the court having naturalization jurisdiction, unless the applicant demonstrates that s/he is prevented by sickness or other disability from appearing in the clerk's office at the court. In these circumstances the applicant may file the petition at such other place as the clerk of court may designate. 8 C.F.R. § 334.13. The petition must contain a statement that the petitioner intends to reside permanently in the United States; the petitioner must sign the document in the English language (unless excused from English language requirement by being over 50 years old and

b. A 1981 amendment removed all statutory provisions which, since 1802, had required the involvement of two citizen witnesses at various stages of the naturalization proceedings. Pub.L. No. 97–116, § 15, 95 Stat. 1619. The committee report on the bill explained that the witness requirement had become "time-consuming, unnecessary, and unproductive. Any information which may be required on the petitioner's fitness for citizenship can be determined by an INS investigation." H.R.Rep. 97–264, 97th Cong., 1st Sess. 25 (1981). Examiners retain discretion, of course, to require the testimony of any witnesses they deem necessary, as part of their investigation.—eds.

c. See note b, supra.—eds.

having been a resident in the U.S. for 20 years) and pay a twenty-five dollar fee. 8 C.F.R. § 334.13. For indigent persons the fee may be waived.

(5) Preliminary Examination

Prior to the court hearing, a formal examination takes place before an Immigration and Naturalization Service employee known as the "designated examiner." 8 C.F.R. § 335.11(b). The petitioner's attorney may take an active part in this hearing, present evidence, subpoena witnesses, make objections, and conduct cross-examination of the government's witnesses. The examination is under oath and open to the public, a stenographic or mechanical record is created for purposes of judicial review. Upon consideration of the testimony of the applicant, hearing the witnesses, and review of all documents properly submitted in support or opposition, the designated examiner recommends to the court whether the petition for naturalization should be granted or denied. 8 C.F.R. § 335.12.

(6) Final Hearing

If the examiner recommends approval of the petition and the regional commissioner of the Immigration and Naturalization Service concurs (8 C.F.R. § 335.13(b)), the petitioner will be granted citizenship at a hearing in open court after he or she takes the oath of allegiance to the United States. 8 U.S.C.A. § 1447 [INA § 336.] In the case of verified illness or disability of the petitioner, the court may excuse his or her attendance at the final hearing. 8 C.F.R. § 336.15.

The examiner may recommend approval but with the proviso that the facts should be presented to the court, in which case the examiner prepares a memorandum setting forth findings of fact and conclusions of law, together with the recommendation. 8 C.F.R. § 335.12. The court may conduct its own questioning under oath of the applicant at the final hearing. 8 U.S.C.A. § 1447(a) [INA § 336(a).]

If the naturalization examiner recommends denial of the petition, the petitioner or his/her attorney must receive notice of the denial by certified mail. 8 C.F.R. § 335.13(a). The petitioner is entitled to a final court determination regarding eligibility for citizenship (8 C.F.R. § 334.1), unless s/he currently faces a deportation proceeding or order—a condition which precludes naturalization in the first place. 8 U.S.C.A. § 1429 [INA § 318.]

The final hearing arising from a denial is a hearing *de novo* and the court having naturalization jurisdiction must decide the issues upon testimony and facts presented to the court, not upon testimony heard by the examiner, or the examiner's recommendations to the court. The court conducts a full hearing with presentation of evidence and testimony of witnesses, including direct and cross-examination by both parties. 8 C.F.R. § 336.11.

In the event the naturalization court sustains the denial of the petition, a petitioner may appeal the adverse judgment to an appellate court. Conversely, the United States government may appeal a decree granting naturalization, even though the applicant has received a certificate of naturalization. The time limit for appeal in the federal courts is 60 days, with which appellants must comply to preserve a reviewing court's jurisdiction.

As with appeals in federal courts generally, judicial review of naturalization court proceedings is limited. A reviewing tribunal will ordinarily reverse a decision only upon finding it "clearly erroneous," FRCP 52(a), giving due deference to the trier-of-fact's opportunity to examine the demeanor and credibility of both witnesses and the applicant.

(7) Certificate of Naturalization

Upon granting the petition for citizenship, the court issues a certificate of naturalization. 8 U.S.C.A. § 1449 [INA § 338.] The certificate itself does not convey citizenship, but simply serves as evidence that the court has granted citizenship. The statute prescribes the information that the naturalization certificate will contain, including the number of the petition and the certificate, date of naturalization, the name, signature, place of residence, signed photograph, and personal description of the naturalized person (including age, sex, marital status, and country of former nationality), and a statement that the court has found the petition in full compliance with the requirements of the naturalization laws and has ordered the petitioner be admitted to citizenship. 8 U.S.C.A. § 1449 [INA § 338.]

Minor clerical errors do not affect the evidentiary value of the certificate nor do informalities in the certificate—such as the misspelling of names or the misnaming of the applicant.

Generally, an order granting naturalization by a court of competent jurisdiction enjoys the same force and effect as any other judgment and cannot be collaterally attacked if the order is valid on its face, even when the ground for collateral attack is fraudulent procurement or forgery. Nonetheless, a naturalization order is subject to *direct* attack in independent [denaturalization] proceedings as prescribed by the Congress.[d] 8 U.S.C.A. § 1451(a) [INA § 340(a).] * * *

Over the last ten years for which statistics are available, petitions for naturalization ranged from a low of 109,897 in 1971 to a high of 192,230 in

d. Even when the original naturalization order was issued by a State court, the Justice Department always brings the denaturalization suit in federal district court. Despite this unusual setting, such a denaturalization action is still considered a direct rather than a collateral attack on the original order. See generally G & R § 20.5c; *United States v. Ness,* 245 U.S. 319, 38 S.Ct. 118, 62 L.Ed. 321 (1917). In light of this and other peculiarities, the Supreme Court has experienced difficulty in deciding on the exact nature of judicial naturalization and denaturalization proceedings, and in determining how each should be deemed to fit with other statutory and constitutional requirements governing the role of state and federal courts. Highlights of the Court's theoretical and practical meanderings may be traced from *Johannessen v. United States,* 225 U.S. 227, 32 S.Ct. 613, 56 L.Ed. 1066 (1912) (which initially approved the new denaturalization remedy, using a theory that later proved troublesome), through *Ness, supra; Tutun v. United States,* 270 U.S. 568, 46 S.Ct. 425, 70 L.Ed. 738 (1926); and *Bindczyck v. Finucane,* 342 U.S. 76, 72 S.Ct. 130, 96 L.Ed. 100 (1951). —eds.

1980. The denial rate ran between one and two percent in the first part of that decade, but it picked up in 1978, and has been running closer to 2.5 percent since then. U.S. Dept. of Justice, 1981 Statistical Yearbook of the Immigration and Naturalization Service, Table 19, p. 50. The overwhelming majority of the denials were based on two reasons: lack of prosecution, or withdrawal of the petition by the petitioner. *Id.,* Table 30, p. 82. In 1981, the most recent year for which statistics are available, 171,073 petitions for naturalization were filed, 166,317 were granted, and 4,316 were denied. *Id.,* Table 19, p. 50. Of this last group, 2,506 were denied for lack of prosecution, and 1,699 were counted as denied because the petitioner withdrew the petition—leaving only 111 denied on other specified grounds under the INA. *Id.,* Table 30, p. 82.

TIERI v. INS

United States Court of Appeals, Second Circuit, 1972.
457 F.2d 391.

Per Curiam:

Frank Tieri appeals from an order entered on July 22, 1969 in the United States District Court for the Eastern District of New York, John F. Dooling, Jr., Judge, denying his petition for naturalization on the ground that he had "not sustained the burden of establishing good moral character during the five years immediately preceding the filing of the petition for naturalization." We find no error and affirm the judgment.

Born in Italy in 1904, petitioner has resided continuously in the United States since his lawful admission for permanent residence at the age of seven. He has been married to an American citizen since 1929. Deportation proceedings instituted against petitioner by the Immigration and Naturalization Service in 1961 were terminated in 1966, whereupon petitioner applied for naturalization pursuant to INA § 316(a). Petitioner's application listed six arrests between 1922 and 1959, two of which resulted in convictions, for robbery in 1922, and for bookmaking in 1946. The record of the deportation proceeding revealed that prior to 1953 petitioner had maintained an adulterous relationship with one Mrs. Musso, who bore him two children. Armed with the foregoing information, and apparently motivated in part by the firm but unprovable conviction that petitioner was connected with the "Mafia," the Immigration and Naturalization Service conducted an extensive investigation pursuant to INA § 335(a) into petitioner's eligibility for citizenship. Following an order of the district court to complete the investigation and to hold a final hearing, the designated examiner on July 5, 1968 recommended the petition be denied on the ground that petitioner had given false testimony in order to facilitate his naturalization. [INA § 101(f)(6).]

Appellant's principal attack, on the role of the designated examiner, is without substance. The designated examiner conducted herself entirely in accordance with the applicable statute (INA § 335) and its implementing regulation (8 C.F.R. 335.11). Inasmuch as the preliminary examination is not intended to culminate in a determination on the merits at the final hearing,[2] the role of the designated examiner, who is permitted both

2. *Compare* the statute (INA § 242) and regulation (8 C.F.R. 242) governing deporta- tion proceedings in which the presiding officer does make a determination on the mer-

to conduct the examination in a non-adversary context[3] and to make a non-binding recommendation to the district court, is consistent with due process. Moreover, petitioner made no objection to the designated examiner, advanced no argument that his case called for the discretionary appointment of an examining officer to present the government's case (8 C.F.R. 335.11(c)), called no witnesses, and failed to request a trial *de novo* in district court (INA § 336(b))—surely the obvious cure if he believed himself prejudiced before the designated examiner.

At the final hearing in the district court, the government called only one witness, otherwise relying on the record of the preliminary examination and final hearing before the designated examiner, and her recommendation the petition be denied. As we have noted, petitioner did not request a trial *de novo,* nor did he testify or introduce witnesses on his own behalf.

Petitioner's contention that the district court should properly have limited itself to consideration of petitioner's conduct during the statutory period has no merit in the light of INA § 316(e) which specifically provides that "the court shall not be limited to petitioner's conduct during the five years preceding the filing of the petition, but may take into consideration ... the petitioner's conduct and acts at any time prior to that period." Petitioner was not condemned for sins of the distant past, nor was an unreasonable burden placed upon him. But his conduct prior to the statutory period was relevant and a proper subject of inquiry to determine whether he had, in effect, reformed. Petitioner failed to measure up to the standard of § 101(f)(6). That the statutory period for petitioner, married to an American citizen, was three years (INA § 319(a)) rather than five, was plainly irrelevant to petitioner's failure.

The district court analyzed in detail six specific areas of inquiry before the designated examiner in the light of the undisputed principle that the burden to prove his good moral character rested on petitioner, Berenyi v. District Director, 385 U.S. 630, 637, 87 S.Ct. 666, 17 L.Ed.2d 656 (1967), with any doubts to be resolved against him, United States v. Manzi, 276 U.S. 463, 467, 48 S.Ct. 328, 72 L.Ed. 654 (1928), and found a "pattern of untruth and evasion" mandating denial of the petition. Since we are not bound by the evaluation of the credibility of the sole witness before the court below, we have conducted an independent review of the record. We are persuaded that petitioner persistently attempted to obscure any past conduct which he feared might prove suspicious or embarrassing to his cause, and that, accordingly, the district court was not mistaken in discerning a pattern of deception in the whole mosaic of petitioner's testimony.

Judgment affirmed.

its. * * * [P]etitioner had the opportunity to demand a trial of the law and the facts *de novo* in the district court * * *.

3. In controlling the course of the examination, the designated examiner reviews all preliminary investigative material, may introduce evidence, issue subpoenas and interrogate witnesses, and rules on all objections to the introduction of evidence, subject to the review of the naturalization court (8 C.F.R. 335.11).

Notes

1.   May the court validly treat Tieri's failure to demand a de novo trial as an effective waiver of complaints about the procedure before the examiner? In light of the substantial interests at stake for the petitioner in such proceedings, should the courts insist on stronger procedural safeguards at the stage of preliminary investigation or preliminary examination?

2.   Why do you suppose that the current system employs two rounds of administrative involvement: (1) the preliminary investigation, based on the N–400 and taking place before the actual petition is filed, and (2) the preliminary examination, based on the formal petition for naturalization? *See* G & R §§ 16.3—16.5. (Usually the same examiner conducts both stages of the administrative inquiry. *Id.* § 16.5a.) Most other countries employ an administrative process for naturalization, sometimes with a right of judicial appeal in disputed cases. *See* Harvard Research in International Law, *Nationality,* 23 Am.J.Int'l L. 83–87 (Special Supp. 1929); Laws Concerning Nationality, UN Legislative Series, UN Doc. ST/LEG/SER.B/4 (1954 and Supp.1959). What values are served by the American system's decision to maintain judicial involvement in virtually every naturalization? In light of the two-stage administrative process already employed, and of the outcome in cases like *Tieri,* should the United States change to an administrative naturalization system?

CHAUNT v. UNITED STATES

Supreme Court of the United States, 1960.
364 U.S. 350, 81 S.Ct. 147, 5 L.Ed.2d 120.

Opinion of the Court by MR. JUSTICE DOUGLAS, announced by MR. JUSTICE HARLAN.

Petitioner, a native of Hungary, was admitted to citizenship by a decree of the District Court in 1940. Respondent filed a complaint to revoke and set aside that order as authorized by § 340(a) of the Immigration and Nationality Act of 1952, on the ground that it had been procured "by concealment of a material fact or by willful misrepresentation." The complaint stated that petitioner had falsely denied membership in the Communist Party and that by virtue of that membership he lacked the requisite attachment to the Constitution, etc., and the intent to renounce foreign allegiance. It also alleged that petitioner had procured his naturalization by concealing and misrepresenting a record of arrests. The District Court cancelled petitioner's naturalization, finding that he had concealed and misrepresented three matters—his arrests, his membership in the Communist Party, and his allegiance. The Court of Appeals affirmed, reaching only the question of the concealment of the arrests. The case is here on a writ of certiorari.

One question, on a form petitioner filled out in connection with his petition for naturalization, asked if he had ever been "arrested or charged with violation of any law of the United States or State or any city ordinance or traffic regulation" and if so to give full particulars. To this question petitioner answered "no." There was evidence that when he was questioned under oath by an examiner he gave the same answer. There was also evidence that if his answer had been "yes," the investigative unit of the Immigration Service would check with the authorities at the places where the arrests occurred "to ascertain ... whether the full facts were stated."

The District Court found that from 10 to 11 years before petitioner was naturalized he had been arrested three times as follows:

(1) On July 30, 1929, he was arrested for distributing handbills in New Haven, Connecticut, in violation of an ordinance. He pleaded not guilty and was discharged.

(2) On December 21, 1929, he was arrested for violating the park regulations in New Haven, Connecticut, by making "an oration, harangue, or other public demonstration in New Haven Green, outside of the churches." Petitioner pleaded not guilty. Disposition of the charge is not clear, the notation on the court record reading "Found J.S." which respondent suggests may mean "Judgment Suspended" after a finding of guilt.

(3) On March 11, 1930, he was again arrested in New Haven and this time charged with "General Breach of the Peace." He was found guilty by the City Court and fined $25. He took an appeal and the records show "nolled April 7, 1930."

Acquisition of American citizenship is a solemn affair. Full and truthful response to all relevant questions required by the naturalization procedure is, of course, to be exacted, and temporizing with the truth must be vigorously discouraged. Failure to give frank, honest, and unequivocal answers to the court when one seeks naturalization is a serious matter. Complete replies are essential so that the qualifications of the applicant or his lack of them may be ascertained. Suppressed or concealed facts, if known, might in and of themselves justify denial of citizenship. Or disclosure of the true facts might have led to the discovery of other facts which would justify denial of citizenship.

On the other hand, in view of the grave consequences to the citizen, naturalization decrees are not lightly to be set aside—the evidence must indeed be "clear, unequivocal, and convincing" and not leave "the issue ... in doubt." *Schneiderman v. United States,* 320 U.S. 118, 125, 158, 63 S.Ct. 1333, 1336, 1352, 87 L.Ed. 1796; *Baumgartner v. United States,* 322 U.S. 665, 670, 64 S.Ct. 1240, 1243, 88 L.Ed. 1525. The issue in these cases is so important to the liberty of the citizen that the weight normally given concurrent findings of two lower courts does not preclude reconsideration here, for we deal with "judgments lying close to opinion regarding the whole nature of our Government and the duties and immunities of citizenship." *Baumgartner v. United States, supra,* 671, 64 S.Ct. 1243, 1244. And see *Klapprott v. United States,* 335 U.S. 601, 612 and (concurring opinion) 617, 69 S.Ct. 384, 389, 391, 93 L.Ed. 266.

While disclosure of them was properly exacted, the arrests in these cases were not reflections on the character of the man seeking citizenship.

The statute in force at the time of his naturalization required that "he has behaved as a person of good moral character, attached to the principles of the Constitution of the United States, and well disposed to the good order and happiness of the United States" during the previous five years. These arrests were made some years prior to the critical five-year period. They did not, moreover, involve moral turpitude within the meaning of the law. No fraudulent conduct was charged. They involved distributing handbills, making a speech, and a breach of the peace. In one instance he was discharged, in one instance the prosecution was "nolled," and in the other (for making a speech in a park in violation of city regulations) he apparently received a suspended sentence. The totality of the circumstances surrounding the offenses charged makes them of extremely slight consequence. Had they involved moral turpitude or acts directed at the Government, had they involved conduct which even peripherally touched types of activity which might disqualify one from citizenship, a different case would be presented. On this record the nature of these arrests, the crimes charged, and the disposition of the cases do not bring them, inherently, even close to the requirement of "clear, unequivocal, and convincing" evidence that naturalization was illegally procured within the meaning of § 340(a) of the Immigration and Nationality Act.

It is argued, however, that disclosure of the arrests made in New Haven, Connecticut, in the years 1929 and 1930 would have led to a New Haven investigation at which leads to other evidence—more relevant and material than the arrests—might have been obtained. His residence in New Haven was from February 1929 to November 1930. Since that period was more than five years before his petition for naturalization, the name of his employer at that time was not required by the form prepared by the Service. It is now said, however, that if the arrests had been disclosed and investigated, the Service might well have discovered that petitioner in 1929 was "a district organizer" of the Communist Party in Connecticut. One witness in this denaturalization proceeding testified that such was the fact. An arrest, though by no means probative of any guilt or wrongdoing, is sufficiently significant as an episode in a man's life that it may often be material at least to further enquiry. We do not minimize the importance of that disclosure. In this case, however, we are asked to base materiality on the tenuous line of investigation that might have led from the arrests to the alleged communistic affiliations, when as a matter of fact petitioner in this same application disclosed that he was an employee and member of the International Workers' Order, which is said to be controlled by the Communist Party. In connection with petitioner's denial of such affiliations, respondent argues that since it was testified that the IWO was an organization controlled and dominated by the Communist Party, it is reasonable to infer that petitioner had those affiliations at the time of the application. But by the same token it would seem that a much less tenuous and speculative nexus with the Communist Party, if it be such, was thereby disclosed and was available for further investigation if it had been deemed appropriate at the time. It is said that IWO did not become tainted with Communist control until 1941. We read the record differently. If the Government's case is made out, that taint extended back at least as far as 1939. Had that disclosure not been made in the application, failure to report the arrests would have had greater significance. It could then be forcefully argued that failure to disclose the arrests was part and parcel of a project to conceal a Communist Party affiliation. But on this record, the failure to report the three arrests occurring from 10 to 11 years previously is neutral. We do not speculate as to why they were not disclosed. We only conclude that, in the circumstances of this case, the Government has failed to show by "clear, unequivocal, and convincing" evidence either (1) that facts were suppressed which, if known, would have warranted denial of citizenship or (2) that their disclosure might have been useful in an investigation possibly leading to the discovery of other facts warranting denial of citizenship.

There are issues in the case which we do not reach and which were not passed upon by the Court of Appeals. Accordingly the judgment will be reversed and the cause remanded to it so that the other questions raised in the appeal may be considered.

It is so ordered.

MR. JUSTICE CLARK, with whom MR. JUSTICE WHITAKER and MR. JUSTICE STEWART join, dissenting.

Petitioner swore in his application for naturalization that he had never been under arrest when in fact he had been arrested in New Haven, Connecticut, on three separate occasions within an eight-month period. * * * Both the District Court and the Court of Appeals have found that petitioner's falsification "was an intentional concealment of a material fact and a willful misrepresentation which foreclosed the Immigration and Naturalization Service and the district court from making a further investigation as to whether he had all the qualifications for citizenship. . . ." These findings, as such, are not disputed. It is nowhere suggested, for example, that the petitioner's falsehoods were the result of inadvertence or forgetfulness—that they were anything but deliberate lies. This Court, however, brushes these findings aside on the ground [1] that the arrests "were not reflections on the character of the man seeking citizenship." The Swiss philosopher Amiel tells us that "character is an historical fruit and is the result of a man's biography." Petitioner's past, if truthfully told in his application, would have been an odorous one. So bad that he dared not reveal it. For the Court to reward his dishonesty is nothing short of an open invitation to false swearing to all who seek the high privilege of American citizenship.

1. The Court says that "[t]he totality of the circumstances surrounding the offenses charged makes them of extremely slight consequence." However, it overlooks the fact that neither the content of the handbills or of the harangue in the park nor the nature of the conduct leading to the conviction in the city court for a general breach of the peace appears in the record. Time has served petitioner well, for even the disposition of the cases is not too clear. But to extrapolate the character of petitioner's conduct solely from these meager circumstances smacks of the psychic. Moreover, to say that the offenses "did not . . . involve moral turpitude" is gratuitous. This Court has never so held.

The Court first says that arrests of this nature, "the crimes charged, and the disposition of the cases do not bring them, inherently, even close to the requirement of 'clear, unequivocal, and convincing' evidence that naturalization was illegally procured." The Court, of course, knows that this is not the applicable test where one has deliberately falsified his papers and thus foreclosed further investigation. This basis for the reversal, therefore, misses the point involved and should have been of no consequence here.

The test is not whether the truthful answer in itself, or the facts discovered through an investigation prompted by that answer, would have justified a denial of citizenship. It is whether the falsification, by misleading the examining officer, forestalled an investigation which *might have resulted* in the defeat of petitioner's application for naturalization. The Courts of Appeals are without disagreement on this point and it is, of course, a necessary rule in order to prevent the making of misrepresentations for the very purpose of forestalling inquiry as to eligibility. The question as to arrests is highly pertinent to the issue of satisfactory moral character, the *sine qua non* of good citizenship. Petitioner's false answer to the question shut off that line of inquiry and was a fraud on the Government and the naturalization court. The majority makes much of the fact that the arrests occurred prior to the five-year statutory period of good behavior, but that is of no consequence. Concealment at the very time of naturalization is the issue here and that act of deliberate falsification before an officer of the Government clearly relates to the petitioner's general moral character. Indeed, the Congress has long made it a felony punishable by imprisonment for a maximum of five years. Certainly this does not fall within a class of peccadilloes which may be overlooked as being without "reflections on the character of the man seeking citizenship." In fact it strips an offender of all civil rights and leaves a shattered character that only a presidential pardon can mend.

The Court concludes that the false denial of prior arrests was "neutral" because the petitioner revealed in his preliminary application that he was an employee of the International Workers Order, which the Court adds, "is said to be controlled by the Communist Party." What the Court fails to point out is that the sole evidence, in this record, as to the International Workers Order was presented in 1955, 15 years after petitioner's deception of the examiner. * * * The truth of the matter is that in his final naturalization application petitioner said he was employed by the "Fraternal Benefit Society of Internation [sic] Workers Order," a name which would lead one to believe that it was an insurance society.
* * *

As I read the record, it clearly supports the findings of the two courts below. Even if petitioner had told the truth, and the conduct causing the arrests was found not to relate to his present fitness for naturalization, it does not follow that citizenship would have been awarded. It might well have been that in checking on the handbills, the harangue in the public park, and the general breach of the peace the investigator would have been led to discover that petitioner was, in 1940, a leader in the Communist Party. I think it more logical than not that the Government would have discovered petitioner's Communist affiliations through such an investigation, and that the deliberate falsification in 1940 forestalled this revelation for 15 years. But whether or not that be the case, the Government was entitled to an honest answer from one who sought admission to its citizenship. We should exact the highest standards of probity and fitness from all applicants. American citizenship is a valuable right. It is prized highly by us who have it and it is sought eagerly by millions who do not. It is asking little enough of those who would be vested with its privileges to demand that they tell the truth.

I would affirm.

Notes

1. The *Chaunt* majority relies on the doctrine of *Schneiderman,* which requires the government to prove its case in a denaturalization proceeding by "clear, unequivocal, and convincing" evidence. But is that requirement relevant here? From all that appears in the opinions, the government's proof was solid, and apparently Chaunt does not here dispute the fact of his arrests or the willfulness of his misrepresentations when the form asked about them.

2. If this is not a case about inadequate factual showings, then, what exactly is the theory of the majority opinion? Is it based on a decision that the lies were not material? The statute provides for denaturalization when citizenship was procured "by concealment of a material fact or by willful misrepresentation." Has the majority misread the statute when it applies the notion of materiality to a case of misrepresentation, rather than concealment? If the naturalization form had merely asked "Are there any other matters bearing on good moral character that we ought to know about?" instead of asking specifically about arrests, the issue would be concealment and materiality would be relevant. But that is not this case.

3. How would the majority have responded if Chaunt's arrests (and hence his misrepresentations) had come to light 15 days after the naturalization proceedings, rather than approximately 15 years later? Perhaps *Chaunt* amounts to a crude judicial attempt to fashion a de facto statute of limitations, in light of the harsh consequences of denaturalization when a relatively minor flaw in the naturalization proceedings is unearthed after many years of unblemished citizenship. If so, does this approach work? Does such an effort represent a legitimate judicial role?

4. Is the Court serious when it says that "[f]ull and truthful response to all relevant questions required by the naturalization procedure is, of course, to be exacted, and temporizing with the truth must be vigorously discouraged"? Doesn't *Chaunt* encourage applicants to conceal or even lie about troublesome parts of their past, whenever there is doubt whether the hidden information would disqualify them? If their deception is successful, then the relevance of the information will be tested only under the stringent standards that apply in *denaturalization* proceedings, if indeed it is ever unearthed and tested at all. Is this what the Court meant? Is it a sound way to construe the statute?

The Supreme Court has avoided later opportunities to clarify *Chaunt*, and the lower courts have struggled with its meaning and application, as the next two cases reveal.

IN RE PETITION OF HANIATAKIS

United States Court of Appeals, Third Circuit, 1967.
376 F.2d 728.

FREEDMAN, CIRCUIT JUDGE.

This is an appeal by the United States from an order granting a petition for naturalization. The appellee, whose petition was granted by the court below, has presented no argument to us, although we had sought to have her present her views.

Petitioner is a twenty-two year old native of Greece who has been a lawful permanent resident of the United States since June 4, 1956. In 1964, she applied for naturalization in her maiden name in the District Court for the Western District of Pennsylvania. The standard procedure, which she followed, required her first to present a written application to file a petition for naturalization and later to be examined under oath in regard to it, after which she swore to the application as corrected by the hearing examiner, and finally to file the verified petition itself. In her written application of June 9, 1964, again during her oral examination under oath by the hearing examiner on June 17, and also in the petition for naturalization, filed on the same date, petitioner stated that she was unmarried. In fact, however, she had been married on May 18, 1964 to a Greek seaman who had been arrested for illegal entry into the United States on June 10, and had voluntarily returned to Greece on August 3. Petitioner had also falsely stated her prior places of residence, declaring both in her written application and her oral statements under oath that she had been a resident of Pennsylvania continuously since her entry into the United States, although for part of that time she had been a resident both of Indiana, where she had been married, and of Ohio.

After an investigation by the Immigration and Naturalization Service had revealed the fact of her marriage, a further preliminary examination was held at which petitioner acknowledged the falsity of her statement that she was unmarried. She explained that she had concealed her marriage out of fear that her naturalization would be held up for five more years if the fact of her marriage to another alien had been revealed. Her explanation makes her conduct all the more tragic, for the Immigration and Naturalization Service declares that her marriage to another alien would not have affected her application.

As a result of her testimony the hearing examiner concluded that petitioner had testified falsely to obtain benefits under the Immigration and Nationality Act, and that she was consequently ineligible for naturalization, because she lacked the "good moral character" required by the Act for admission to citizenship. The District Court, however, granted the petition for naturalization in petitioner's married name, feeling bound to follow the decision of another judge of the same court in Petition for Naturalization of Sotos, 221 F.Supp. 145 (W.D.Pa.1963). It concluded that petitioner's false testimony did not affirmatively demonstrate the absence of "good moral character," since her misrepresentations were not material and the facts concealed would not themselves have been a barrier to her naturalization. 246 F.Supp. 545 (W.D.Pa.1965). The United States appeals from this ruling.

Section 316(a)(3) of the Immigration and Nationality Act provides that no person shall be naturalized unless, *inter alia,* he "has been and still is a person of good moral character" during the five-year period immediately preceding the date of filing of his petition for naturalization and the period thereafter until admission to citizenship. Section 101(f) of the Act specifies a number of instances in which an applicant shall not be regarded to be of good moral character. Among those is the case of "one who has given false testimony for the purpose of obtaining any benefits under this chapter." This section is mandatory in its terms.

Petitioner's false answers were given both in the written application and in the petition for naturalization. Were this all, we would be required to determine whether false statements in applications or other written documents sworn to before an officer duly authorized to administer oaths would constitute "false testimony," which the statute makes conclusive proof of lack of good moral character. The same false statements, however, were given orally as testimony at the preliminary investigation, and this brings the case clearly within the proscription of the statute. The remaining question, therefore, is whether we should narrow the plain words of the statute and read into it an exception which would distinguish between material and immaterial matters in the giving of false testimony.

The federal courts have consistently refused to draw a distinction between materiality and immateriality of false testimony in cases where such a distinction would have had clear application. See Berenyi v. District Director, 385 U.S. 630, 87 S.Ct. 666, 17 L.Ed.2d 656 (1967); Stevens v. United States, 190 F.2d 880 (7 Cir.1951); Del Guercio v. Pupko, 160 F.2d 799 (9 Cir.1947). The statute is not concerned with the significance or materiality of a particular question, but rather, as the Supreme Court has recently indicated in Berenyi v. District Director, intends that naturalization should be denied to one who gives false testimony to facilitate naturalization.

The reason for denying naturalization whenever false testimony is given in an attempt to gain it goes beyond a judgment that one who gives false testimony to deceive the government is by that fact unworthy of the privileges of citizenship; it is also based on the practical ground that a false answer to a query which on its face appears innocuous may effectively cut off a line of inquiry which might have revealed further facts bearing on the petitioner's eligibility for citizenship. Having asked a question which it deems significant to determine the qualifications of one seeking citizenship, the government is entitled to full disclosure. Berenyi

v. District Director, supra at 638, 87 S.Ct. 666. See also United States v. Montalbano, 236 F.2d 757, 759–760 (3 Cir.1956), cert. denied, sub nom. Genovese v. United States, 352 U.S. 952, 77 S.Ct. 327, 1 L.Ed.2d 244 (1956), involving revocation of citizenship. Indeed, the contention that the misrepresentations made here were immaterial is quite misleading, for the failure to give truthful answers regarding marital status has been deemed a "material fact" under § 340(a) of the Act, which permits the more drastic action of cancellation of naturalization where it has been "procured by concealment of a material fact or by willful misrepresentation." See, e.g., United States v. D'Agostino, 338 F.2d 490, 491 (2 Cir.1964).

Both the court below and the court in Petition for Naturalization of Sotos, 221 F.Supp. 145 (W.D.Pa.1963), relied upon Chaunt v. United States, 364 U.S. 350, 81 S.Ct. 147, 5 L.Ed.2d 120 (1960), in concluding that false testimony given to facilitate naturalization does not bar naturalization unless the concealed matter itself would bar it. There the Supreme Court refused to revoke and set aside the naturalization twenty years before of an American citizen even though he had failed to reveal, as then required by the naturalization form, that he had previously been arrested. Although the Court's decision in *Chaunt* rested upon the immateriality of the false testimony, this does not help the petitioner here. To begin with, the provision of the Act involved in *Chaunt,* § 340(a), specifically required that the fact concealed be "material." Moreover, in *Chaunt* the government attempted to withdraw the privileges of citizenship from one who had already been admitted to their benefits. What is involved here, on the other hand, is the decision whether the petitioner should be admitted to the benefits of that citizenship. Much turns on this distinction, since the immigration law historically has chosen to afford greater protections to those who have been admitted to citizenship. Thus, the Supreme Court recently declared in the *Berenyi* case, *supra,* 385 U.S. at 636–637, 87 S.Ct. at 610:

"When the Government seeks to strip a person of citizenship already acquired, or deport a resident alien and send him from our shores, it carries the heavy burden of proving its case by 'clear, unequivocal, and convincing evidence.' But when an alien seeks to obtain the privileges and benefits of citizenship, the shoe is on the other foot. He is the moving party, affirmatively asking the Government to endow him with all the advantages of citizenship. Because that status, once granted, cannot lightly be taken away, the Government has a strong and legitimate interest in ensuring that only qualified persons are granted citizenship. For these reasons, it has been universally accepted that the burden is on the alien applicant to show his eligibility for citizenship in every respect. This Court has often stated that doubts 'should be resolved in favor of the United States and against the claimant.' E.g., United States v. Macintosh, 283 U.S. 605, 626 [51 S.Ct. 570, 75 L.Ed. 1302]."

Falling as she does within the class of those seeking citizenship, petitioner was obliged to prove her suitability for it. This, unfortunately, she has not done.

The judgment of the district court will be reversed.

UNITED STATES v. SHESHTAWY

United States Court of Appeals, Tenth Circuit, 1983.
714 F.2d 1038.

McKAY, CIRCUIT JUDGE.

Adel Sheshtawy, a naturalized citizen of the United States, appeals a district court decision to revoke his citizenship and cancel his certificate of naturalization.

The appellant initially sought naturalization in 1978; however, his naturalization was delayed because his character witnesses had not known him for the requisite period of time. Approximately three weeks before the appellant's rescheduled naturalization hearing, he was arrested and charged with concealing stolen property. Shortly after the arrest, he received a standard form questionnaire from the Immigration and Naturalization Service, which he was required to fill out in order to update the information on his application for a petition for naturalization. The third question asked whether he had ever been arrested, which he falsely answered "no." As instructed, the appellant took the form with him to his naturalization hearing, where he turned it in to a naturalization examiner and was ultimately naturalized. About six weeks later, the state trial judge, at the end of the preliminary hearing, dismissed the criminal charges against the appellant, finding that no crime had been committed. At some later date, the INS discovered that the appellant had been arrested, and these proceedings were commenced.

In revoking the appellant's citizenship, the trial court held that disclosure of the arrest would have caused a substantial delay in the appellant's naturalization pending investigation, that the appellant willfully answered the arrest question falsely in order to avoid the consequences that a true answer might have had on his naturalization thereby facilitating his acquisition of citizenship, and that the defendant willfully misrepresented and concealed a material fact.

This case is squarely governed by principles established in *Chaunt v. United States,* 364 U.S. 350, 81 S.Ct. 147, 5 L.Ed.2d 120 (1960). There, the Supreme Court held that the government carries a heavy burden when it seeks to revoke citizenship under INA § 340(a) for the willful misrepresentation or concealment of a material fact.[1] For a fact to be "material," the government must "show by 'clear, unequivocal, and convincing' evidence either (1) that facts were suppressed which, if known, would have warranted denial of citizenship or (2) that their disclosure might have been useful in an investigation possibly leading to the discovery of other facts warranting denial of citizenship." *Id.* at 355, 81 S.Ct. at 150.

In this case, the government made no claim that the arrest itself would have resulted in a denial of citizenship. Nor did the government attempt to show that an investigation would have turned up other facts

---

1. * * * The Court has read both the willfulness and materiality requirements as applying to both concealments and misrepresentations. *See, e.g., Fedorenko v. United States,* 449 U.S. 490, 493, 101 S.Ct. 737, 740, 66 L.Ed.2d 686 (1981).

warranting a denial of citizenship. Rather, it argues that *Chaunt* requires only that disclosure might have led to the discovery of disqualifying facts—that is, that an investigation would have been undertaken.[2] Thus, the substance of the government's position, which the trial court accepted, is that the test for materiality

> is not whether the truthful answer in itself, or the facts discovered through an investigation prompted by that answer, would have justified a denial of citizenship. It is whether the falsification, by misleading the examining officer, forestalled an investigation which *might have resulted* in the defeat of petitioner's application for naturalization.

Id. at 357, 81 S.Ct. at 151 (Clark, J., dissenting) (emphasis supplied). This test, however, was the one espoused by the *Chaunt* dissent and rejected by the majority.

In *Fedorenko v. United States,* 449 U.S. 490, 101 S.Ct. 737, 66 L.Ed.2d 686 (1981), the Court avoided reviewing a similar construction of the *Chaunt* test by the Fifth Circuit, by choosing to resolve the case on a different theory. In his concurring opinion, however, Justice Blackmun carefully reviewed the *Chaunt* test and concluded that it requires that the government demonstrate the existence of actual disqualifying facts—facts that themselves would have warranted denial of petitioner's citizenship. *Id.* at 523–26, 101 S.Ct. at 755–57 (Blackmun, J., concurring).[3] While there has been substantial disagreement over the meaning of *Chaunt,*[4] its characterizations by Justice Blackmun appear to us to be correct, and until *Chaunt* as thus interpreted has been rejected or overturned by the Supreme Court, we must follow it.

At issue in these cases is a balance of the importance of securing the stability and security of naturalized citizenship against the risk, arguably posed by *Chaunt,* of encouraging lying in connection with applications for citizenship. Our reading of *Chaunt* is unlikely to provide persons who have in their background a clearly disqualifying experience with additional incentive to lie, since their citizenship would be revoked even under our interpretation of *Chaunt.* Nor does *Chaunt* encourage persons with no doubtful experiences in their lives to lie. The only group possibly affected are those who are uncertain whether a particular event would disqualify

---

2. There is evidence in the record that had the INS known of the appellant's arrest, it would have delayed the naturalization decision and conducted an investigation that would have consisted of a tape-recorded interview with the appellant, an examination of the police reports, and probably a recommendation that the investigative department make a complete check of the appellant's moral character.

3. Justice Stevens' view of the *Chaunt* test substantially coincides with that of Justice Blackmun. He reads *Chaunt* as requiring that disclosure would have led to an investigation, that a disqualifying circumstance actually exist, and that it would have

been discovered in the investigation. *Fedorenko,* 449 U.S. at 537, 101 S.Ct. at 762 (Stevens, J., dissenting). Thus, although the Court declined to follow what is essentially the version of *Chaunt* for which the government argues on this appeal, only two of the justices specifically rejected it; and Justice White was the only one who embraced it, *id.* at 528, 101 S.Ct. at 758 (White, J., dissenting).

4. *Compare La Madrid-Peraza v. INS,* 492 F.2d 1297, 1298 (9th Cir.1974) *with United States v. Oddo,* 314 F.2d 115, 118 (2d Cir.), *cert. denied,* 375 U.S. 833, 84 S.Ct. 50, 11 L.Ed.2d 63 (1963).

them from naturalization. We believe the *Chaunt* Court considered this tension and, in effect, concluded that even though there may be some who are encouraged to lie, the importance of putting naturalized citizenship well beyond the danger of unwarranted revocation justifies the adoption of so severe a test.

Since the government does not claim to have established facts that would have warranted denial of the appellant's citizenship, it has not met *Chaunt*'s rigorous test, and revocation under section 340(a) is not justified.

The government alternatively argues that revocation is justified because the appellant did not meet all of the statutory prerequisites to naturalization. Only "a person of good moral character" is eligible for naturalization, INA § 316(a)(3), and "one who has given false testimony for the purpose of obtaining any benefits under this chapter" cannot be found to be a person of good moral character, § 101(f)(6). Since the appellant lied to gain naturalization benefits, the government argues that he was not of good moral character and therefore ineligible for naturalization.

We believe, however, that in denaturalization proceedings, section 101(f)(6) applies only to false testimony concerning material facts. In *Fedorenko,* the Supreme Court construed a section of the Displaced Persons Act, providing that any person who made a willful misrepresentation in order to gain benefits under that Act—i.e., admission to the United States—should thereafter not be admissible, to apply only to material misrepresentations. The Court simply noted that materiality is required to revoke citizenship for concealments or misrepresentations under section § 340(a) and asserted that "[l]ogically, the same principle should govern the interpretation of this provision of the DPA." The wording of section 101(f)(6) closely tracks that of the statute in *Fedorenko,* and the context within which we are construing the statute—that is, denaturalization of a citizen—and the interests at stake are the same. We therefore conclude that *Fedorenko* compels reading a materiality requirement into section 101(f)(6) when it is invoked for denaturalization purposes.[6]

The remaining question is the legal standard for materiality under section 101(f)(6). Although the Court in *Fedorenko* refrained from deciding whether the *Chaunt* test for materiality applied to misrepresentations on visa applications, it reaffirmed the test's applicability to determine the materiality of misrepresentations on citizenship applications. Thus, *Chaunt* is the controlling authority for materiality decisions under section 101(f)(6), and the government's case under this section must fail for the reasons set out *ante.*

---

6. Both the Second and Third Circuits have refused to read a materiality requirement into § 101(f)(6); however, both of those cases involved naturalization, not denaturalization, proceedings so that the important interest of the naturalized citizen in retaining his or her citizenship was not implicated. *See Kovacs v. United States,* 476 F.2d 843, 845 (2d Cir.1973); *In re Haniatakis,* 376 F.2d 728, 730 (3d Cir.1967). They are therefore inapposite in the denaturalization context.

McWILLIAMS, JUDGE, dissents.

It is incongruous that Sheshtawy should be rewarded for his dishonesty. If Sheshtawy had answered the question truthfully and informed the authorities that he had been recently arrested on a charge of concealing stolen goods, such disclosure *might* have been useful in an investigation *possibly leading* to the discovery of other facts warranting denial of citizenship. Such meets the second test in *Chaunt v. United States*, 364 U.S. 350, 81 S.Ct. 147, 5 L.Ed.2d 120 (1960), as I read that case. I would affirm the trial court.

Questions

Is it possible to construct a theory under which *Haniatakis* and *Sheshtawy* are consistent? If Sheshtawy can get away with a deliberate lie because the matter involved turns out not to have been a disqualifying factor in an application for naturalization, why shouldn't Haniatakis enjoy the same forgiveness? Can the timing of the discovery legitimately make so much difference? If you were a member of Congress, what changes, if any, would you make in the naturalization and denaturalization provisions in light of *Chaunt, Berenyi, Haniatakis, Fedorenko,* and *Sheshtawy?*

SECTION D.   EXPATRIATION

As indicated in Section C, denaturalization proceedings constitute one important way in which U.S. citizenship today may be taken away. In such proceedings, the government must establish, under a fairly stringent standard of proof, that the original naturalization was acquired illegally or through fraud. But through the years, Congress also added to the nationality statutes various provisions to deprive individuals of citizenship status based on specified behavior not related to defects in the acquisition process. Whether the citizen subjectively intended to surrender citizenship when the allegedly expatriating behavior occurred was usually irrelevant.

The Supreme Court wrestled for several decades with the constitutionality of these grounds for involuntary expatriation.[7] The divisions among the Justices were bitter, and for a while, as we shall see, the results in the cases, sometimes sustaining the expatriation provisions, sometimes striking them down, traced an odd pattern. But today the Court has apparently reached unanimity on the basic substantive doctrine, although skirmishing persists regarding some of the procedural details. The materials to follow reveal the historical development of the

7. We use the term "involuntary expatriation" here to mean a loss of citizenship imposed on persons based on certain behavior, such as lengthy residence abroad or marriage to a foreign national, whether or not they subjectively wished to surrender their citizenship thereby. But supporters of the practice have often noted that such expatriation is not involuntary in the strongest sense. That is, American statutes have never tried to deprive persons of citizenship except on the basis of actions (moving overseas, marrying, etc.) that the citizen voluntarily performed—with statutory notice, even if not willing acceptance, of the consequences.

statute and the constitutional rules that have, by now, almost completely replaced the statutory specifications.

DONALD K. DUVALL, EXPATRIATION UNDER UNITED STATES LAW, *PEREZ* TO *AFROYIM:* THE SEARCH FOR A PHILOSOPHY OF AMERICAN CITIZENSHIP

56 Va.L.Rev. 408, 411–17 (1970).

HISTORICAL DEVELOPMENT OF EXPATRIATION LAW

When ratified in 1789, the Constitution contained no definition of citizenship or provision for its loss, but merely authorized Congress "[t]o establish an uniform Rule of Naturalization." Subsequently, the Supreme Court held that while this constitutional provision gave the naturalized citizen the same rights as a native, it did not authorize Congress to enlarge or abridge those rights.

The rule of *jus soli* —citizenship by birth within the country—was first given statutory expression in section 1 of the Civil Rights Act of 1866, the substance of which was adopted as the fourteenth amendment during the same year. Previously, the *jus soli* rule had been generally applied on the basis of the English common law, which had been adopted by the United States as its main body of law after independence. Likewise, the rule of *jus sanguinis* —citizenship by blood relation to citizen parent—was statutorily recognized * * *. Although the United States followed a liberal immigration and naturalization policy based on both the *jus soli* and *jus sanguinis* rules during its formative years, before 1907 there was no general statute governing expatriation. As might be expected in an expanding new nation, the United States until the Civil War was primarily concerned with assimilating its millions of immigrants and establishing the legal primacy of national citizenship over state citizenship.

The scope of US citizenship was further beclouded in the early days because the judiciary felt bound to apply the adopted English common law of indefeasible perpetual allegiance, which precluded renunciation of citizenship without the consent of the sovereign. Great Britain's adherence to this rule in its impressments on the high seas of naturalized American seamen, formerly of British nationality, contributed to the War of 1812. And events of 1868 further aggravated Anglo-American friction, when the British failed to respect the rights of naturalized US citizens involved in criminal activities with the Fenian movement in Ireland. These incidents led to the passage of the Expatriation Act of 1868,[31] which, *inter alia,* declared "the right of expatriation" to be an "inherent right of all people," thus enabling naturalized Americans to cast off, at least under United States law, the claims to allegiance advanced by their states of origin. The Act further extended to naturalized citizens traveling abroad "the same protection of persons and property that is accorded to native-born citizens in like situations," and declared that whenever a US citizen was unjustly deprived of his liberty by or under the authority

31. Ch. 249, 15 Stat. 223.

of any foreign government, the President had the duty to extend protection in appropriate ways short of war.

While the Act of 1868 clarified the right of expatriation and was construed to include the citizen's right to shed his citizenship, it provided no specific method for exercising that right. Furthermore, even though naturalization under the domestic law of the United States required the citizen to "renounce and adjure" all allegiance to his former sovereign, effective protection of US naturalized citizens abroad still depended upon reciprocal recognition by foreign states of the exclusive nature of voluntarily acquired American citizenship. Accordingly, in 1868 the United States began negotiating bilateral treaties [known as the Bancroft Treaties] with various foreign states to protect the status of its naturalized citizens on a reciprocal basis in an effort to reduce or eliminate the conflicting claims of different sovereignties arising out of dual nationality. Some of these treaties, including the current multilateral Rio Treaty of 1906, provided not only for mutual acceptance of the right to abandon one nationality and acquire another but also that two years continuous residence by a naturalized citizen in his former country gave rise to a rebuttable presumption of intention to remain permanently. Prolonged return to the state of origin was therefore grounds for treating the citizen as having renounced his naturalized citizenship.

Pursuant to the report of a Citizenship Board appointed by the Secretary of State in 1906, Congress enacted the Expatriation Act of 1907,[38] the first general statute providing for loss of US nationality. Section 2 of the Act of 1907 provided for the expatriation of any national who obtained naturalization in a foreign state or took an oath of allegiance to a foreign state. Section 3 of the Act provided for the expatriation of an American woman who married a foreigner. These provisions attempted to prevent dual nationality, which had previously led to conflicting national claims upon the allegiance of the US citizen whenever he returned, even temporarily, to his former country, or voluntarily entered the military or civil service of a third state.

The constitutionality of the 1907 Act was first tested in the landmark decision of *Mackenzie v. Hare*,[40] in which the Supreme Court upheld the power of Congress to expatriate, during the period of coverture, a female US citizen who obtained foreign nationality by marriage to a foreign national, because such action was a "necessary and proper" implementation of the "inherent power of sovereignty" in foreign relations, especially under "conditions of national moment." Conceding that expatriation could not be imposed "without the concurrence of the citizen," the Court inferred assent from the fact that the expatriating act had been "voluntarily entered into, with notice of the consequences." In sum, the concept of voluntary renunciation of citizenship proclaimed in the 1868 Expatriation Act was interpreted in *Mackenzie* to include voluntary performance of an expatriating act without regard to whether the citizen actually intended

---

38. Ch. 2534, 34 Stat. 1228.

40. 239 U.S. 299, 36 S.Ct. 106, 60 L.Ed. 297 (1915). Act of Sept. 22, 1922, ch. 411, § 3, 42 Stat. 1022, and Act of March 3, 1931, ch. 442, §§ 4(a), (b), 46 Stat. 1511, eliminated marriage to a foreigner as an expatriating act.

or desired to lose his US nationality.[43] By extending the meaning of "voluntary," the Court apparently sought to reconcile the intent of Congress to minimize international frictions arising out of dual nationality with the statutory guarantee and tradition of voluntary expatriation.

The 1938 Report of the President's Commission on Revision and Codification of the Nationality Laws led to the Nationality Act of 1940.[45] This Act, the first comprehensive codification of the nationality laws, substantially increased the number of actions which, when performed voluntarily, would automatically result in the loss of US nationality.[46] The increased number of statutory provisions relating to loss of nationality may be explained in several ways. First, most of the provisions were codifications of existing statutory or common law which had evolved from established diplomatic and administrative practice. Second, the 1940 Act was drafted and approved at a time of economic stress and increasing security-consciousness caused by the onset of World War II. Third, World War I and its aftermath had produced a complete reversal of America's traditional "open door" immigration policy, thus leading to stricter requirements for acquisition and retention of US nationality.

Following World War II, the stage was again set for retrenchment and consolidation of the nationality laws. The post-war climate and Cold War hyper-security-consciousness produced the Immigration and Nationality Act of 1952, which Congress approved over President Truman's veto. Essentially a reenactment of the pertinent provisions of the 1940 Act, the 1952 law made few significant changes in loss of nationality. The Act added a section permitting expatriation of persons who acquired dual nationality at birth and "voluntarily sought or claimed benefits" of their foreign nationality and resided in the foreign state for three continuous years after age 22. It also created a non-rebuttable presumption of

---

43. For an explicit exposition of this objective standard of voluntary expatriation, see *Savorgnan v. United States,* 338 U.S. 419, 70 S.Ct. 292, 94 L.Ed. 287 (1950).

45. Ch. 876, 54 Stat. 1137.

46. Specifically, the Act provided for loss of United States nationality in the following ways:

For any national, native or naturalized, by

1. Obtaining naturalization in a foreign state.

2. Taking an oath of allegiance to a foreign state.

3. Entering or serving in the armed forces of a foreign state while a national thereof without legal authorization.

4. Holding any office, post or employment in the government of a foreign state or any subdivision thereof.

5. Voting in a political election in a foreign state.

6. Formal renunciation before a US diplomatic or consular officer in a foreign state.

7. Formal renunciation in the United States approved by the Attorney General during wartime.

8. Court martial conviction and discharge from armed forces for desertion during wartime.

9. Court martial or civil court conviction for treason, attempting by force to overthrow, or bearing arms against the United States.

10. Departing from or remaining outside of the United States during wartime for purpose of evading training and service in armed forces.

For nationals born abroad (retention provision), by

11. Failing to take up permanent residence in the United States before attaining 16 years of age, subject to certain exceptions.

For naturalized US nationals, by

12. Fraudulent naturalization.

13. Residing continuously for 3 years in foreign state of birth or for 5 years in any other foreign state, with certain exceptions.

voluntariness for each of the statute's expatriating acts when performed by a national of a foreign state, who had been physically present in such state for at least ten years.

In 1961 Congress added a statutory standard of proof—preponderance of the evidence—necessary to prove performance of an expatriating act or to rebut the usual presumption of voluntariness. This standard was a relaxation of that previously required by the Supreme Court in *Gonzales v. Landon* [53] and *Nishikawa v. Dulles,* [54] where the Court had imposed upon the Government the burden of proving the act and its voluntariness by clear, unequivocal and convincing evidence.

Another substantial change in the construction of the expatriation provisions of the 1952 Act occurred in 1962, when the Attorney General ruled [55] that in the absence of clear and compelling statutory language, he was "unwilling to attribute to Congress an intention that the United States citizenship of an individual should be forfeited by reason of actions taken at a time when he was unaware of his citizenship." Finally, the Expatriation Act of 1954 [57] amended the Immigration and Nationality Act of 1952 by adding, as additional grounds for expatriation, conviction of certain existing crimes, including rebellion and insurrection, seditious conspiracy and advocating the overthrow of the Government in any manner proscribed by law.

———

For many years, the *Mackenzie* decision seemed to have settled the question of Congress's powers over expatriation. But as a leading commentator has remarked, "[t]his apparent consensus was resoundingly shattered in 1958, * * * when the court decided three cases in which reargument had been directed after argument during the previous term had failed to produce decisions." Gordon, *The Citizen and the State: Power of Congress to Expatriate American Citizens,* 53 Geo.L.J. 315, 326–27 (1965). A sharply divided Court sustained one ground of expatriation, held another unconstitutional, and vacated a third expatriation order on procedural grounds. *Perez v. Brownell* was the first of the trilogy.

PEREZ v. BROWNELL

Supreme Court of the United States, 1958.
356 U.S. 44, 78 S.Ct. 568, 2 L.Ed.2d 603.

MR. JUSTICE FRANKFURTER delivered the opinion of the Court.

[Perez, the petitioner, was born in Texas in 1909, and thus became a citizen of the United States at birth. He had lived most of his life, however, in Mexico, where he voted in a political election in 1946. The

53. 350 U.S. 920, 76 S.Ct. 210, 100 L.Ed. 806 (1955) (per curiam) (proof of the act).

54. 356 U.S. 129, 78 S.Ct. 612, 2 L.Ed.2d 659 (1958) (proof of voluntariness).

55. Freddie Norman Chatty-Suarez, 9 I. & N. Dec. 670 (1962).

57. Ch. 1256, § 2, 68 Stat. 1146. * * *

lower courts held that he had lost his U.S. citizenship under, inter alia, § 401(e) of the Nationality Act of 1940, as amended, which provided:

A person who is a national of the United States, whether by birth or naturalization, shall lose his nationality by:

* * *

(e) Voting in a political election in a foreign state or participating in an election or plebiscite to determine the sovereignty over foreign territory * * *.

[Justice Frankfurter begins his opinion with a lengthy review of American expatriation laws and practices, pointing out the usual connection between expatriation grounds and the conduct of foreign affairs. The specific provision at issue here was one of the newer additions to the list, enacted only in 1940. It came in large measure as a response to the participation of numerous American citizens in a 1935 plebiscite on the annexation of the Saar region to Hitler's Germany. The chairman of the House Committee on Immigration and Naturalization remarked at one point during hearings on the proposed law: "I know we had a lot of Nazis, so-called American citizens, go to Europe who have voted in the Saar for the annexation of territory to Germany, and Germany says that they have the right to participate and to vote, and yet they are American citizens." (Quoted in the dissenting opinion of Chief Justice Warren, 356 U.S. at 76.) Later, on the House floor, the chairman explained the intention behind the expatriation provisions included in the bill (there were many others in addition to the voting provision): "this bill would put an end to dual citizenship and relieve this country of the responsibility of those who reside in foreign lands and only claim citizenship when it serves their purposes." (Quoted in Justice Frankfurter's opinion, *id.* at 55.)]

* * *

The first step in our inquiry must be to answer the question: what is the source of power on which Congress must be assumed to have drawn? Although there is in the Constitution no specific grant to Congress of power to enact legislation for the effective regulation of foreign affairs, there can be no doubt of the existence of this power in the law-making organ of the Nation. *See* United States v. Curtiss-Wright Export Corp., 299 U.S. 304, 318, 57 S.Ct. 216, 220, 81 L.Ed. 255; Mackenzie v. Hare, 239 U.S. 299, 311–312, 36 S.Ct. 106, 108, 60 L.Ed. 297. The States that joined together to form a single Nation and to create, through the Constitution, a Federal Government to conduct the affairs of that Nation must be held to have granted that Government the powers indispensable to its functioning effectively in the company of sovereign nations. The Government must be able not only to deal affirmatively with foreign nations, as it does through the maintenance of diplomatic relations with them and the protection of American citizens sojourning within their territories. It must also be able to reduce to a minimum the frictions that are unavoidable in a world of sovereigns sensitive in matters touching their dignity and interests.

The inference is fairly to be drawn from the congressional history of the Nationality Act of 1940, read in light of the historical background of expatriation in this country, that, in making voting in foreign elections (among other behavior) an act of expatriation, Congress was seeking to effectuate its power to regulate foreign affairs. The legislators, counseled by those on whom they rightly relied for advice, were concerned about actions by citizens in foreign countries that create problems of protection and are inconsistent with American allegiance. Moreover, we cannot ignore the fact that embarrassments in the conduct of foreign relations were of primary concern in the consideration of the Act of 1907, of which the loss of nationality provisions of the 1940 Act are a codification and expansion.

Broad as the power in the National Government to regulate foreign affairs must necessarily be, it is not without limitation. The restrictions confining Congress in the exercise of any of the powers expressly delegated to it in the Constitution apply with equal vigor when that body seeks to regulate our relations with other nations. Since Congress may not act arbitrarily, a rational nexus must exist between the content of a specific power in Congress and the action of Congress in carrying that power into execution. More simply stated, the means—in this case, withdrawal of citizenship—must be reasonably related to the end—here, regulation of foreign affairs. The inquiry—and, in the case before us, the sole inquiry—into which this Court must enter is whether or not Congress may have concluded not unreasonably that there is a relevant connection between this fundamental source of power and the ultimate legislative action.

Our starting point is to ascertain whether the power of Congress to deal with foreign relations may reasonably be deemed to include a power to deal generally with the active participation, by way of voting, of American citizens in foreign political elections. Experience amply attests that in this day of extensive international travel, rapid communication and widespread use of propaganda, the activities of the citizens of one nation when in another country can easily cause serious embarrassments to the government of their own country as well as to their fellow citizens. We cannot deny to Congress the reasonable belief that these difficulties might well become acute, to the point of jeopardizing the successful conduct of international relations, when a citizen of one country chooses to participate in the political or governmental affairs of another country. The citizen may by his action unwittingly promote or encourage a course of conduct contrary to the interests of his own government; moreover, the people or government of the foreign country may regard his action to be the action of his government, or at least as a reflection if not an expression of its policy.

It follows that such activity is regulable by Congress under its power to deal with foreign affairs. And it must be regulable on more than an *ad hoc* basis. The subtle influences and repercussions with which the Government must deal make it reasonable for the generalized, although clearly limited, category of "political election" to be used in defining the area of regulation. That description carries with it the scope and meaning of its context and purpose; classes of elections—nonpolitical in the colloquial sense—as to which participation by Americans could not possibly have any effect on the relations of the United States with another country are excluded by any rational construction of the phrase. The classification that Congress has adopted cannot be said to be inappropriate to the difficulties to be dealt with. Specific applications are of course open to judicial challenge, as are other general categories in the law, by a "gradual process of judicial inclusion and exclusion."

The question must finally be faced whether, given the power to attach some sort of consequence to voting in a foreign political election, Congress, acting under the Necessary and Proper Clause, Art. I, § 8, cl. 18, could attach loss of nationality to it. Is the means, withdrawal of citizenship, reasonably calculated to effect the end that is within the power of Congress to achieve, the avoidance of embarrassment in the conduct of our foreign relations attributable to voting by American citizens in foreign political elections? The importance and extreme delicacy of the matters here sought to be regulated demand that Congress be permitted ample scope in selecting appropriate modes for accomplishing its purpose. The critical connection between this conduct and loss of citizenship is the fact that it is the possession of American citizenship by a person committing the act that makes the act potentially embarrassing to the American Government and pregnant with the possibility of embroiling this country in disputes with other nations. The termination of citizenship terminates the problem. Moreover, the fact is not without significance that Congress has interpreted this conduct, not irrationally, as importing not only something less than complete and unswerving allegiance to the United States but also elements of an allegiance to another country in some measure, at least, inconsistent with American citizenship.

Of course, Congress can attach loss of citizenship only as a consequence of conduct engaged in voluntarily. See Mackenzie v. Hare, 239 U.S. 299, 311–312, 36 S.Ct. 106, 108, 60 L.Ed. 297. But it would be a mockery of this Court's decisions to suggest that a person, in order to lose his citizenship, must intend or desire to do so. The Court only a few years ago said of the person held to have lost her citizenship in Mackenzie v. Hare, supra: "The woman had not intended to give up her American citizenship." Savorgnan v. United States, 338 U.S. 491, 501, 70 S.Ct. 292, 298, 94 L.Ed. 287. And the latter case sustained the denationalization of Mrs. Savorgnan although it was not disputed that she "had no intention of endangering her American citizenship or of renouncing her allegiance to the United States." What both women did do voluntarily was to engage in conduct to which Acts of Congress attached the consequence of denationalization irrespective of—and, in those cases, absolutely contrary to—the intentions and desires of the individuals. Those two cases mean nothing—indeed, they are deceptive—if their essential significance is not rejection of the notion that the power of Congress to terminate citizenship depends upon the citizen's assent.

* * *

Judgment affirmed.

Mr. Chief Justice Warren, with whom Mr. Justice Black and Mr. Justice Douglas join, dissenting.

* * *

Generally, when congressional action is challenged, constitutional authority is found in the express and implied powers with which the National Government has been invested or in those inherent powers that are necessary attributes of a sovereign state. The sweep of those powers is surely broad. In appropriate circumstances, they are adequate to take away life itself. The initial question here is whether citizenship is subject to the exercise of these general powers of government.

What is this government, whose power is here being asserted? And what is the source of that power? The answers are the foundation of our Republic. To secure the inalienable rights of the individual, "Governments are instituted among Men, deriving their just powers from the consent of the governed." I do not believe the passage of time has lessened the truth of this proposition. It is basic to our form of government. This Government was born of its citizens, it maintains itself in a continuing relationship with them, and, in my judgment, it is without power to sever the relationship that gives rise to its existence. I cannot believe that a government conceived in the spirit of ours was established with power to take from the people their most basic right.

Citizenship *is* man's basic right for it is nothing less than the right to have rights. Remove this priceless possession and there remains a stateless person, disgraced and degraded in the eyes of his countrymen. He has no lawful claim to protection from any nation, and no nation may assert rights on his behalf. His very existence is at the sufferance of the state within whose borders he happens to be. In this country the expatriate would presumably enjoy, at most, only the limited rights and privileges of aliens, and like the alien he might even be subject to deportation and thereby deprived of the right to assert any rights. This government was not established with power to decree this fate.

The people who created this government endowed it with broad powers. They created a sovereign state with power to function as a sovereignty. But the citizens themselves are sovereign, and their citizenship is not subject to the general powers of their government. Whatever may be the scope of its powers to regulate the conduct and affairs of all persons within its jurisdiction, a government *of* the people cannot take away their citizenship simply because one branch of that government can be said to have a conceivably rational basis for wanting to do so.

The basic constitutional provision crystallizing the right of citizenship is the first sentence of section one of the Fourteenth Amendment. It is there provided that "All persons born or naturalized in the United States, and subject to the jurisdiction thereof, are citizens of the United States and of the State wherein they reside." United States citizenship is thus the constitutional birth-right of every person born in this country. This Court has declared that Congress is without power to alter this effect of birth in the United States, United States v. Wong Kim Ark, 169 U.S. 649, 703, 18 S.Ct. 456, 477, 42 L.Ed. 890. The Constitution also provides that citizenship can be bestowed under a "uniform Rule of Naturalization," but there is no corresponding provision authorizing divestment. Of course, naturalization unlawfully procured can be set aside. But apart from this circumstance, the status of the naturalized citizen is secure. As this Court stated in Osborn v. Bank of United States, 9 Wheat. 738, 827, 6 L.Ed. 204:

> "[The naturalized citizen] becomes a member of the society possessing all the rights of a native citizen, and standing, in the view of the constitution, on the footing of a native. *The constitution does not authorize Congress to enlarge or abridge those rights.* The simple power of the national Legislature, is to prescribe a uniform rule of naturalization, and the exercise of this power exhausts it, so far as respects the individual." (Emphasis added.)

Under our form of government, as established by the Constitution, the citizenship of the lawfully naturalized and the native-born cannot be taken from them.

There is no question that citizenship may be voluntarily relinquished. The right of voluntary expatriation was recognized by Congress in 1868. Congress declared that "the right of expatriation is a natural and inherent right of all people * * *." Although the primary purpose of this declaration was the protection of our naturalized citizens from the claims of their countries of origin, the language was properly regarded as establishing the reciprocal right of American citizens to abjure their allegiance.

* * *

It has long been recognized that citizenship may not only be voluntarily renounced through exercise of the right of expatriation but also by other actions in derogation of undivided allegiance to this country. While the essential qualities of the citizen-state relationship under our Constitution preclude the exercise of governmental power to divest United States citizenship, the establishment of that relationship did not impair the principle that conduct of a citizen showing a voluntary transfer of allegiance is an abandonment of citizenship. Nearly all sovereignties recognize that acquisition of foreign nationality ordinarily shows a renunciation of citizenship. Nor is this the only act by which the citizen may show a voluntary abandonment of his citizenship. Any action by which he manifests allegiance to a foreign state may be so inconsistent with the retention of citizenship as to result in loss of that status. In recognizing the consequence of such action, the Government is not taking away United States citizenship to implement its general regulatory powers, for, as previously indicated, in my judgment citizenship is immune from divestment under these powers. Rather, the Government is simply giving formal recognition to the inevitable consequence of the citizen's own voluntary surrender of his citizenship.

* * *

* * * Mackenzie v. Hare should not be understood to sanction a power to divest citizenship. Rather this case, like Savorgnan, simply

acknowledges that United States citizenship can be abandoned, temporarily or permanently, by conduct showing a voluntary transfer of allegiance to another country.

* * *

The precise issue posed by Section 401(e) is whether the conduct it describes invariably involves a dilution of undivided allegiance sufficient to show a voluntary abandonment of citizenship. Doubtless under some circumstances a vote in a foreign election would have this effect. For example, abandonment of citizenship might result if the person desiring to vote had to become a foreign national or represent himself to be one.

* * *

The fatal defect in the statute before us is that its application is not limited to those situations that may rationally be said to constitute an abandonment of citizenship. In specifying that any act of voting in a foreign political election results in loss of citizenship, Congress has employed a classification so broad that it encompasses conduct that fails to show a voluntary abandonment of American citizenship. "The connection between the fact proved and that presumed is not sufficient." * * * Voting in a foreign election may be a most equivocal act, giving rise to no implication that allegiance has been compromised. Nothing could demonstrate this better than the political history of this country. It was not until 1928 that a presidential election was held in this country in which no alien was eligible to vote. Earlier in our history at least 22 States had extended the franchise to aliens. It cannot be seriously contended that this Nation understood the vote of each alien who previously took advantage of this privilege to be an act of allegiance to this country, jeopardizing the alien's native citizenship. How then can we attach such significance to any vote of a United States citizen in a foreign election? It is also significant that of 84 nations whose nationality laws have been compiled by the United Nations, only this country specifically designates foreign voting as an expatriating act.

My conclusions are as follows. The Government is without power to take citizenship away from a native-born or lawfully naturalized American. The Fourteenth Amendment recognizes that this priceless right is immune from the exercise of governmental powers. If the Government determines that certain conduct by United States citizens should be prohibited because of anticipated injurious consequences to the conduct of foreign affairs or to some other legitimate governmental interest, it may within the limits of the Constitution proscribe such activity and assess appropriate punishment. But every exercise of governmental power must find its source in the Constitution. The power to denationalize is not within the letter or the spirit of the powers with which our Government was endowed. The citizen may elect to renounce his citizenship, and under some circumstances he may be found to have abandoned his status by voluntarily performing acts that compromise his undivided allegiance to his country. The mere act of voting in a foreign election, however, without regard to the circumstances attending the participation, is not sufficient to show a voluntary abandonment of citizenship.

* * *

[Separate dissenting opinions by Justices Douglas and Whittaker are omitted.]

Questions

What is Justice Frankfurter's test for deciding the constitutionality of expatriation provisions? Should this particular provision, apparently not adopted by any other nation in the world, be held to meet that test? How would expatriation of voters in foreign elections avoid national embarrassment or entanglement in disputes? What kinds of disputes are anticipated? With whom? If this statute passes muster, what kinds of statutes would fail?

———

On the same day that *Perez* was decided, the court struck down, also by a vote of five to four, a section of the nationality laws that was meant to strip citizenship from those convicted of desertion from the military during time of war. *Trop v. Dulles*, 356 U.S. 86, 78 S.Ct. 590, 2 L.Ed.2d 630 (1958). Chief Justice Warren wrote the plurality opinion, joined by the other three *Perez* dissenters. He repeated his view that Congress lacked the power to expatriate, but also found the statute invalid on a separate ground. This provision was intended by its framers, he determined, to be a punishment; as such, it was subject to the Eighth Amendment. And because denationalization in these circumstances involves "the total destruction of the individual's status in organized society," it amounted to cruel and unusual punishment that could not stand. Justice Brennan, the crucial swing vote, concurred separately. As his agreement with the majority in *Perez* indicated, he believed that Congress had the power to expatriate. But he found this particular provision wanting because "the requisite rational relation between the statute and the war power does not appear." The other four members of the *Perez* majority dissented.

In the third expatriation case decided that day, *Nishikawa v. Dulles*, 356 U.S. 129, 78 S.Ct. 612, 2 L.Ed.2d 659 (1958), the Court reversed an expatriation ruling without having to reach the constitutional issues. The lower court had ruled that a dual national's service in the Japanese army during World War II resulted in his expatriation, over his claim that his service was involuntary because he was conscripted by his other country of nationality. A majority of the Supreme Court determined that once the issue of duress was raised, the statute required the government to shoulder the burden of proving that the allegedly expatriating behavior had been performed voluntarily. Moreover, the government would have to make its case by clear, unequivocal, and convincing evidence, "[b]ecause the consequences of denationalization are so drastic * * *." Justice Black attached a concurring opinion reiterating the view he and Justice Douglas had favored in both *Perez* and *Trop*: that Congress lacks power to expatriate and that *Mackenzie v. Hare* should be overruled to the extent that it was inconsistent with this position.

The 1958 trilogy thus revealed a badly divided court, and it established no clearly prevailing framework for deciding when involuntary expatriation was permissible. Indeed, the results of the three cases seem intuitively backwards. The rather innocent act of voting in a Mexican election (about which Mexico had made no complaint) resulted in forfeiture of citizenship. Yet a wartime deserter and a citizen who served with an enemy army escaped the same fate.

In 1963, the Court returned to the same arena, but the decision cast little new light on the contours of the doctrine. At issue in *Kennedy v. Mendoza-Martinez*, 372 U.S. 144, 83 S.Ct. 554, 9 L.Ed.2d 644 (1963) was the section of the statute decreeing expatriation for those who left or remained outside the United States during time of war to evade military service. By a vote of five to four, the Court held this provision unconstitutional, following an approach similar to that of the *Trop* plurality. The majority first examined the legislative history and concluded that the statute employed expatriation as a punishment. As such, the sanction could not be employed without prior observance of the procedural safeguards guaranteed by the Fifth and Sixth Amendments, meaning "a prior criminal trial and all its incidents."

The following year, the Court struck down a provision that decreed loss of U.S. citizenship for a naturalized citizen who returned to reside in his native country for three years. *Schneider v. Rusk*, 377 U.S. 163, 84 S.Ct. 1187, 12 L.Ed.2d 218 (1964). The vote was five to three, with Justice Brennan not participating. Justice Douglas's brief majority opinion restated his belief that Congress lacked power to expatriate. Acknowledging that this position "has not yet commanded a majority of the entire Court," however, he ultimately rested the invalidation on a different ground. The statute, he wrote, "proceeds on the impermissible assumption that naturalized citizens as a class are less reliable and bear less allegiance to this country than the native born." (Is this a fair characterization? Are assumptions made about "naturalized citizens as a class"? Or is the assumption instead merely that the small subclass of naturalized citizens who live for a long period in their native countries are more likely to experience conflicting allegiances than others who have no such prior tie—and so should be put to a choice of ending the residence in that country or forfeiting citizenship? Is such an assumption irrational? Is it even unreasonable?)

The majority then applied its understanding of the *Perez* standards under the Fifth Amendment due process clause. It concluded that the statute contravened equal protection principles embraced in that clause: "The discrimination aimed at naturalized citizens drastically limits their rights to live and work abroad in a way that other citizens may. It creates indeed a second-class citizenship." Congress henceforth would not be permitted to distinguish between naturalized and native-born citizens for purposes of expatriation, although it could still provide for denaturalization if the original naturalization was tainted with fraud or other illegality, properly proven.

In 1967, the Court returned to the precise ground of expatriation that had been upheld in *Perez.*

AFROYIM v. RUSK

Supreme Court of the United States, 1967.
387 U.S. 253, 87 S.Ct. 1660, 18 L.Ed.2d 757.

MR. JUSTICE BLACK delivered the opinion of the Court.

Petitioner, born in Poland in 1893, immigrated to this country in 1912 and became a naturalized American citizen in 1926. He went to Israel in 1950, and in 1951 he voluntarily voted in an election for the Israeli Knesset, the legislative body of Israel. In 1960, when he applied for renewal of his United States passport, the Department of State refused to grant it on the sole ground that he had lost his American citizenship by virtue of § 401(e) of the Nationality Act of 1940 which provides that a United States citizen shall "lose" his citizenship if he votes "in a political election in a foreign state." Petitioner then brought this declaratory judgment action in federal district court alleging that § 401(e) violates both the Due Process Clause of the Fifth Amendment and § 1, cl. 1, of the Fourteenth Amendment which grants American citizenship to persons like petitioner. Because neither the Fourteenth Amendment nor any other provision of the Constitution expressly grants Congress the power to take away that citizenship once it has been acquired, petitioner contended that the only way he could lose his citizenship was by his own voluntary renunciation of it. Since the Government took the position that § 401(e) empowers it to terminate citizenship without the citizen's voluntary renunciation, petitioner argued that this section is prohibited by the Constitution. The District Court and the Court of Appeals, rejecting this argument, held that Congress has constitutional authority forcibly to take away citizenship for voting in a foreign country based on its implied power to regulate foreign affairs. Consequently, petitioner was held to have lost his American citizenship regardless of his intention not to give it up. This is precisely what this Court held in *Perez v. Brownell,* 356 U.S. 44, 78 S.Ct. 568, 2 L.Ed.2d 603.

Petitioner, relying on the same contentions about voluntary renunciation of citizenship which this Court rejected in upholding § 401(e) in *Perez,* urges us to reconsider that case, adopt the view of the minority there, and overrule it. That case, decided by a 5–4 vote almost 10 years ago, has been a source of controversy and confusion ever since, as was emphatically recognized in the opinions of all the judges who participated in this case below. Moreover, in the other cases decided with [4] and since [5] *Perez,* this Court has consistently invalidated on a case-by-case basis

4. *Trop v. Dulles,* 356 U.S. 86, 78 S.Ct. 590, 2 L.Ed.2d 630; *Nishikawa v. Dulles,* 356 U.S. 129, 78 S.Ct. 612, 2 L.Ed.2d 659.

5. *Kennedy v. Mendoza-Martinez,* 372 U.S. 144, 83 S.Ct. 554, 9 L.Ed.2d 644; *Schneider v. Rusk,* 377 U.S. 163, 84 S.Ct.

1187, 12 L.Ed.2d 218. In his concurring opinion in *Mendoza-Martinez,* MR. JUSTICE BRENNAN expressed "felt doubts of the correctness of *Perez* . . . ." 372 U.S., at 187, 83 S.Ct., at 577.

various other statutory sections providing for involuntary expatriation. It
has done so on various grounds and has refused to hold that citizens can
be expatriated without their voluntary renunciation of citizenship. These
cases, as well as many commentators, have cast great doubt upon the
soundness of *Perez*. Under these circumstances, we granted certiorari to
reconsider it, 385 U.S. 917, 87 S.Ct. 232, 17 L.Ed.2d 142. In view of the
many recent opinions and dissents comprehensively discussing all the
issues involved, we deem it unnecessary to treat this subject at great
length.

* * *

First we reject the idea expressed in *Perez* that, aside from the
Fourteenth Amendment, Congress has any general power, express or
implied, to take away an American citizen's citizenship without his assent.
This power cannot, as *Perez* indicated, be sustained as an implied attribute
of sovereignty possessed by all nations. Other nations are governed by
their own constitutions, if any, and we can draw no support from theirs.
In our country the people are sovereign and the Government cannot sever
its relationship to the people by taking away their citizenship. Our
Constitution governs us and we must never forget that our Constitution
limits the Government to those powers specifically granted or those that
are necessary and proper to carry out the specifically granted ones. The
Constitution, of course, grants Congress no express power to strip people
of their citizenship, whether in the exercise of the implied power to
regulate foreign affairs or in the exercise of any specifically granted
power. And even before the adoption of the Fourteenth Amendment,
views were expressed in Congress and by this Court that under the
Constitution the Government was granted no power, even under its
express power to pass a uniform rule of naturalization, to determine what
conduct should and should not result in the loss of citizenship. On three
occasions, in 1794, 1797, and 1818, Congress considered and rejected
proposals to enact laws which would describe certain conduct as resulting
in expatriation. * * *

[Justice Black then spends several pages describing these proposals and
reprinting excerpts from the congressional debates.]

* * *

Although these * * * statements may be regarded as inconclusive and
must be considered in the historical context in which they were made, any
doubt as to whether prior to the passage of the Fourteenth Amendment
Congress had the power to deprive a person against his will of citizenship
once obtained should have been removed by the unequivocal terms of the
Amendment itself. It provides its own constitutional rule in language
calculated completely to control the status of citizenship: "All persons
born or naturalized in the United States ... are citizens of the United
States...." There is no indication in these words of a fleeting citizenship,
good at the moment it is acquired but subject to destruction by the
Government at any time. Rather the Amendment can most reasonably
be read as defining a citizenship which a citizen keeps unless he voluntarily relinquishes it. Once acquired, this Fourteenth Amendment citizen-

ship was not to be shifted, canceled, or diluted at the will of the Federal Government, the States, or any other governmental unit.

It is true that the chief interest of the people in giving permanence and security to citizenship in the Fourteenth Amendment was the desire to protect Negroes. The *Dred Scott* decision, 19 How. 393, 15 L.Ed. 691, had shortly before greatly disturbed many people about the status of Negro citizenship. But the Civil Rights Act of 1866 had already attempted to confer citizenship on all persons born or naturalized in the United States. Nevertheless, when the Fourteenth Amendment passed the House without containing any definition of citizenship, the sponsors of the Amendment in the Senate insisted on inserting a constitutional definition and grant of citizenship. They expressed fears that the citizenship so recently conferred on Negroes by the Civil Rights Act could be just as easily taken away from them by subsequent Congresses, and it was to provide an insuperable obstacle against every governmental effort to strip Negroes of their newly acquired citizenship that the first clause was added to the Fourteenth Amendment. Senator Howard, who sponsored the Amendment in the Senate, thus explained the purpose of the clause:

> "It settles the great question of citizenship and removes all doubt as to what persons are or are not citizens of the United States.... We desired to put this question of citizenship and the rights of citizens ... under the civil rights bill beyond the legislative power...." Cong. Globe, 39th Cong., 1st Sess., 2890, 2896 (1866).

This undeniable purpose of the Fourteenth Amendment to make citizenship of Negroes permanent and secure would be frustrated by holding that the Government can rob a citizen of his citizenship without his consent by simply proceeding to act under an implied general power to regulate foreign affairs or some other power generally granted. Though the framers of the Amendment were not particularly concerned with the problem of expatriation, it seems undeniable from the language they used that they wanted to put citizenship beyond the power of any governmental unit to destroy. In 1868, two years after the Fourteenth Amendment had been proposed, Congress specifically considered the subject of expatriation. Several bills were introduced to impose involuntary expatriation on citizens who committed certain acts. With little discussion, these proposals were defeated. Other bills, like the one proposed but defeated in 1818, provided merely a means by which the citizen could himself voluntarily renounce his citizenship. Representative Van Trump of Ohio, who proposed such a bill, vehemently denied in supporting it that his measure would make the Government "a party to the act dissolving the tie between the citizen and his country ... where the statute simply prescribes the manner in which the citizen shall proceed to perpetuate the evidence of his intention, or election, to renounce his citizenship by expatriation." * * But even Van Trump's proposal, which went no further than to provide a means of evidencing a citizen's intent to renounce his citizenship, was defeated. The Act, as finally passed, merely recognized the "right of expatriation" as an inherent right of all people.

The entire legislative history of the 1868 Act makes it abundantly clear that there was a strong feeling in the Congress that the only way the citizenship it conferred could be lost was by the voluntary renunciation or abandonment by the citizen himself. And this was the unequivocal statement of the Court in the case of *United States v. Wong Kim Ark,* 169 U.S. 649, 18 S.Ct. 456, 42 L.Ed. 890. * * * Quoting Chief Justice Marshall's well-considered and oft-repeated dictum in *Osborn* [*v. Bank of the United States,* 22 U.S. (9 Wheat.) 738, 6 L.Ed. 204 (1824),] to the effect that Congress under the power of naturalization has "a power to confer citizenship, not a power to take it away," the Court said:

> "Congress having no power to abridge the rights conferred by the Constitution upon those who have become naturalized citizens by virtue of acts of Congress, *a fortiori* no act ... of Congress ... can affect citizenship acquired as a birthright, by virtue of the Constitution itself.... The Fourteenth Amendment, while it leaves the power, where it was before, in Congress, to regulate naturalization, has conferred no authority upon Congress to restrict the effect of birth, declared by the Constitution to constitute a sufficient and complete right to citizenship." *Id.,* at 703, 18 S.Ct., at 477.

To uphold Congress' power to take away a man's citizenship because he voted in a foreign election in violation of § 401(e) would be equivalent to holding that Congress has the power to "abridge," "affect," "restrict the effect of," and "take ... away" citizenship. Because the Fourteenth Amendment prevents Congress from doing any of these things, we agree with The Chief Justice's dissent in the *Perez* case that the Government is without power to rob a citizen of his citizenship under § 401(e).

Because the legislative history of the Fourteenth Amendment and of the expatriation proposals which preceded and followed it, like most other legislative history, contains many statements from which conflicting inferences can be drawn, our holding might be unwarranted if it rested entirely or principally upon that legislative history. But it does not. Our holding we think is the only one that can stand in view of the language and the purpose of the Fourteenth Amendment, and our construction of that Amendment, we believe, comports more nearly than *Perez* with the principles of liberty and equal justice to all that the entire Fourteenth Amendment was adopted to guarantee. Citizenship is no light trifle to be jeopardized any moment Congress decides to do so under the name of one of its general or implied grants of power. In some instances, loss of citizenship can mean that a man is left without the protection of citizenship in any country in the world—as a man without a country. Citizenship in this Nation is a part of a cooperative affair. Its citizenry is the country and the country is its citizenry. The very nature of our free government makes it completely incongruous to have a rule of law under which a group of citizens temporarily in office can deprive another group of citizens of their citizenship. We hold that the Fourteenth Amendment was designed to, and does, protect every citizen of this Nation against a congressional forcible destruction of his citizenship, whatever his creed, color, or race. Our holding does no more than to give to this citizen that which is his own, a constitutional right to remain a citizen in a free country unless he voluntarily relinquishes that citizenship.

Perez v. Brownell is overruled.   The judgment is

Reversed.

MR. JUSTICE HARLAN, whom MR. JUSTICE CLARK, MR. JUSTICE STEWART, and MR. JUSTICE WHITE join, dissenting.

* * *

The Court today overrules *Perez,* and declares § 401(e) unconstitutional, by a remarkable process of circumlocution.   First, the Court fails almost entirely to dispute the reasoning in *Perez;* it is essentially content with the conclusory and quite unsubstantiated assertion that Congress is without "any general power, express or implied," to expatriate a citizen "without his assent." [1]   Next, the Court embarks upon a lengthy, albeit incomplete, survey of the historical background of the congressional power at stake here, and yet, at the end, concedes that the history is susceptible to "conflicting inferences."   The Court acknowledges that its conclusions might not be warranted by that history alone, and disclaims that the decision today relies, even "principally," upon it.   Finally, the Court declares that its result is bottomed upon the "language and the purpose" of the Citizenship Clause of the Fourteenth Amendment; in explanation, the Court offers only the terms of the clause itself, the contention that any other result would be "completely incongruous," and the essentially arcane observation that the "citizenry is the country and the country is its citizenry."

I can find nothing in this extraordinary series of circumventions which permits, still less compels, the imposition of this constitutional constraint upon the authority of Congress.   I must respectfully dissent.

There is no need here to rehearse Mr. Justice Frankfurter's opinion for the Court in *Perez;* it then proved and still proves to my satisfaction that § 401(e) is within the power of Congress.   It suffices simply to supplement *Perez* with an examination of the historical evidence which the Court in part recites, and which provides the only apparent basis for many of the Court's conclusions.   As will be seen, the available historical evidence is not only inadequate to support the Court's abandonment of

---

1. It is appropriate to note at the outset what appears to be a fundamental ambiguity in the opinion for the Court. The Court at one point intimates, but does not expressly declare, that it adopts the reasoning of the dissent of THE CHIEF JUSTICE in *Perez.* THE CHIEF JUSTICE there acknowledged that "actions in derogation of undivided allegiance to this country" had "long been recognized" to result in expatriation, *id.,* at 68; he argued, however, that the connection between voting in a foreign political election and abandonment of citizenship was logically insufficient to support a presumption that a citizen had renounced his nationality. *Id.,* at 76, 78 S.Ct. at 586. It is difficult to find any semblance of this reasoning, beyond the momen-

tary reference to the opinion of THE CHIEF JUSTICE, in the approach taken by the Court today; it seems instead to adopt a substantially wider view of the restrictions upon Congress' authority in this area. Whatever the Court's position, it has assumed that voluntariness is here a term of fixed meaning; in fact, of course, it has been employed to describe both a specific intent to renounce citizenship, and the uncoerced commission of an act conclusively deemed by law to be a relinquishment of citizenship. Until the Court indicates with greater precision what it means by "assent," today's opinion will surely cause still greater confusion in this area of the law.

Perez, but, with due regard for the restraints that should surround the judicial invalidation of an Act of Congress, even seems to confirm *Perez'* soundness.

I.

Not much evidence is available from the period prior to the adoption of the Fourteenth Amendment through which the then-prevailing attitudes on these constitutional questions can now be determined. The questions pertinent here were only tangentially debated; controversy centered instead upon the wider issues of whether a citizen might under any circumstances *renounce* his citizenship, and, if he might, whether that right should be conditioned upon any formal prerequisites. Even the discussion of these issues was seriously clouded by the widely accepted view that authority to regulate the incidents of citizenship had been retained, at least in part, by the several States. It should therefore be remembered that the evidence which is now available may not necessarily represent any carefully considered, still less prevailing, viewpoint upon the present issues.

Measured even within these limitations, the Court's evidence for this period is remarkably inconclusive; the Court relies simply upon the rejection by Congress of legislation proposed in 1794, 1797, and 1818, and upon an isolated dictum from the opinion of Chief Justice Marshall in *Osborn v. Bank of the United States,* 9 Wheat. 738, 6 L.Ed. 204. This, as will appear, is entirely inadequate to support the Court's conclusion, particularly in light of other and more pertinent evidence which the Court does not notice.

[There follows a brief review of the legislative debates of 1794 and 1797.]

The debates in 1817 and 1818, upon which the Court so heavily relies, are scarcely more revealing. * * * [T]he Court selects portions of statements made by three individual Congressmen, who apparently denied that Congress had authority to enact legislation to deprive unwilling citizens of their citizenship. These brief dicta are, by the most generous standard, inadequate to warrant the Court's broad constitutional conclusion. Moreover, it must be observed that they were in great part deductions from constitutional premises which have subsequently been entirely abandoned. They stemmed principally from the Jeffersonian contention that allegiance is owed by a citizen first to his State, and only through the State to the Federal Government. * * * Surely the Court does not revive this entirely discredited doctrine; and yet so long as it does not, it is difficult to see that any significant support for the ruling made today may be derived from the statements on which the Court relies. To sever the statements from their constitutional premises, as the Court has apparently done, is to transform the meaning these expressions were intended to convey.

Finally, it must be remembered that these were merely the views of three Congressmen; nothing in the debates indicates that their constitutional doubts were shared by any substantial number of the other 67

members who eventually opposed the bill. They were plainly not accepted by the 58 members who voted in the bill's favor. * * *

* * *

The most pertinent evidence from this period upon these questions
has been virtually overlooked by the Court. Twice in the two years
immediately prior to its passage of the Fourteenth Amendment, Congress
exercised the very authority which the Court now suggests that it should
have recognized was entirely lacking. In each case, a bill was debated
and adopted by both Houses which included provisions to expatriate
unwilling citizens.

In the spring and summer of 1864, both Houses debated intensively
the Wade-Davis bill to provide reconstruction governments for the States
which had seceded to form the Confederacy. Among the bill's provisions
was § 14, by which "every person who shall hereafter hold or exercise any
office ... in the rebel service ... is hereby declared not to be a citizen of
the United States." Much of the debate upon the bill did not, of course,
center on the expatriation provision, although it certainly did not escape
critical attention. Nonetheless, I have not found any indication in the
debates in either House that it was supposed that Congress was without
authority to deprive an unwilling citizen of his citizenship. The bill was
not signed by President Lincoln before the adjournment of Congress, and
thus failed to become law, but a subsequent statement issued by Lincoln
makes quite plain that he was not troubled by any doubts of the constitutionality of § 14. Passage of the Wade-Davis bill of itself "suffices to
destroy the notion that the men who drafted the Fourteenth Amendment
felt that citizenship was an 'absolute.' "

Twelve months later, and less than a year before its passage of the
Fourteenth Amendment, Congress adopted a second measure which included provisions that permitted the expatriation of unwilling citizens.
Section 21 of the Enrollment Act of 1865 provided that deserters from the
military service of the United States "shall be deemed and taken to have
voluntarily relinquished and forfeited their rights of citizenship and their
rights to become citizens...." The same section extended these disabilities to persons who departed the United States with intent to avoid "draft
into the military or naval service...." The bitterness of war did not
cause Congress here to neglect the requirements of the Constitution; for it
was urged in both Houses that § 21 as written was *ex post facto,* and thus
was constitutionally impermissible. Significantly, however, it was never
suggested in either debate that expatriation without a citizen's consent
lay beyond Congress' authority. Members of both Houses had apparently
examined intensively the section's constitutional validity, and yet had
been undisturbed by the matters upon which the Court now relies.

* * *

* * * [I]t is surely plain that the Court's conclusion is entirely
unwarranted by the available historical evidence for the period prior to
the passage of the Fourteenth Amendment. The evidence suggests, to the
contrary, that Congress in 1865 understood that it had authority, at least
in some circumstances, to deprive a citizen of his nationality.

II.

The evidence with which the Court supports its thesis that the Citizenship Clause of the Fourteenth Amendment was intended to lay at rest any doubts of Congress' inability to expatriate without the citizen's consent is no more persuasive. The evidence consists almost exclusively of two brief and general quotations from Howard of Michigan, the sponsor of the Citizenship Clause in the Senate, and of a statement made in a debate in the House of Representatives in 1868 by Van Trump of Ohio. Measured most generously, this evidence would be inadequate to support the important constitutional conclusion presumably drawn in large part from it by the Court; but, as will be shown, other relevant evidence indicates that the Court plainly has mistaken the purposes of the clause's draftsmen.

The Amendment as initially approved by the House contained nothing which described or defined citizenship. * * *

In the Senate, however, it was evidently feared that unless citizenship were defined, or some more general classification substituted, freedmen might, on the premise that they were not citizens, be excluded from the Amendment's protection. Senator Stewart thus offered an amendment which would have inserted into § 1 a definition of citizenship, and Senator Wade urged as an alternative the elimination of the term "citizen" from the Amendment's first section.[38] After a caucus of the chief supporters of the Amendment, Senator Howard announced on their behalf that they favored the addition of the present Citizenship Clause.

* * * Nothing in the debates, however, supports the Court's assertion that the clause was intended to deny Congress its authority to expatriate unwilling citizens. The evidence indicates that its draftsmen instead expected the clause only to declare unreservedly to whom citizenship initially adhered, thus overturning the restrictions both of *Dred Scott* and of the doctrine of primary state citizenship, while preserving Congress' authority to prescribe the methods and terms of expatriation.

* * *

There is, however, even more positive evidence that the Court's construction of the clause is not that intended by its draftsmen. Between the two brief statements from Senator Howard relied upon by the Court, Howard, in response to a question, said the following:

> "I take it for granted that after a man becomes a citizen of the United States under the Constitution he cannot cease to be citizen, *except by* expatriation or *the commission of some crime by which his citizenship shall be forfeited.*" (Emphasis added.)

It would be difficult to imagine a more unqualified rejection of the Court's position; Senator Howard, the clause's sponsor, very plainly believed that it would leave unimpaired Congress' power to deprive unwilling citizens of their citizenship.

---

38. Wade would have employed the formula "persons born in the United States or naturalized under the laws thereof" to measure the section's protection. Cong.Globe, 39th Cong., 1st Sess., 2768–2769.

* * *

[Justice Harlan then reviews the legislative history of two contemporary statutes containing provisions bearing on loss of citizenship, the 1867 Act for the Relief of certain Soldiers and Sailors, and the Expatriation Act of 1868. The debates reflect no belief on the part of the members of Congress that the Fourteenth Amendment, recently passed by both houses and then well on the way to ratification by the states, deprived Congress of the power to expatriate.]

There is, moreover, still further evidence, overlooked by the Court, which confirms yet again that the Court's view of the intended purposes of the Citizenship Clause is mistaken. While the debate on the Act of 1868 was still in progress, negotiations were completed on the first of a series of bilateral expatriation treaties, which "initiated this country's policy of automatic divestment of citizenship for specified conduct affecting our foreign relations." *Perez v. Brownell, supra,* at 48, 78 S.Ct., at 571. Seven such treaties were negotiated in 1868 and 1869 alone; each was ratified by the Senate. If, as the Court now suggests, it was "abundantly clear" to Congress in 1868 that the Citizenship Clause had taken from its hands the power of expatriation, it is quite difficult to understand why these conventions were negotiated, or why, once negotiated, they were not immediately repudiated by the Senate.

Further, the executive authorities of the United States repeatedly acted, in the 40 years following 1868, upon the premise that a citizen might automatically be deemed to have expatriated himself by conduct short of a voluntary renunciation of citizenship; individual citizens were, as the Court indicated in *Perez,* regularly held on this basis to have lost their citizenship. * * * [T]he Court today has not ventured to explain why the Citizenship Clause should, so shortly after its adoption, have been, under the Court's construction, so seriously misunderstood.

It seems to me apparent that the historical evidence which the Court in part recites is wholly inconclusive, as indeed the Court recognizes; the evidence, to the contrary, irresistibly suggests that the draftsmen of the Fourteenth Amendment did not intend, and could not have expected, that the Citizenship Clause would deprive Congress of authority which it had, to their knowledge, only recently twice exercised. * * *

The Citizenship Clause thus neither denies nor provides to Congress any power of expatriation; its consequences are, for present purposes, exhausted by its declaration of the classes of individuals to whom citizenship initially attaches. Once obtained, citizenship is of course protected from arbitrary withdrawal by the constraints placed around Congress' powers by the Constitution; it is not proper to create from the Citizenship Clause an additional, and entirely unwarranted, restriction upon legislative authority. The construction now placed on the Citizenship Clause rests, in the last analysis, simply on the Court's *ipse dixit,* evincing little more, it is quite apparent, than the present majority's own distaste for the expatriation power.

I believe that *Perez* was rightly decided, and on its authority would affirm the judgment of the Court of Appeals.

Notes

Justice Black seems almost to concede that the historical materials on which he relies have been rendered suspect by the patient historical research of Justice Harlan (of which only a portion is reprinted here). The last textual paragraph in the majority opinion retreats to an invocation of "the language and the purpose of the Fourteenth Amendment" as the real ground of decision. But does the language by itself support the majority's conclusions? If not, how can we know the purpose apart from inquiry into the historical views of the drafters?

Even those who share, in Justice Harlan's words, "the present majority's distaste for the expatriation power" might wish to have some more solid basis for the conclusion reached by the majority in *Afroyim*. Can you construct such a basis? Reconsider Chief Justice Warren's dissent in *Perez*. How does it differ in reasoning, or at least in emphasis, from Justice Black's majority opinion in *Afroyim*? Does it furnish a more reliable foundation for the conclusions reached? *See generally* C. Black, *Structure and Relationship in Constitutional Law* (1964).

————

The durability of *Afroyim* was called into question by a holding, again reached by a five-four margin, handed down four years later, after two Justices had retired and been replaced by new appointees.

ROGERS v. BELLEI

Supreme Court of the United States, 1971.
401 U.S. 815, 91 S.Ct. 1060, 28 L.Ed.2d 499.

Mr. Justice Blackmun delivered the opinion of the Court.

Under constitutional challenge here, primarily on Fifth Amendment due process grounds, but also on Fourteenth Amendment grounds, is § 301(b) of the Immigration and Nationality Act of June 27, 1952, 66 Stat. 236.

Section 301(a) of the Act defines those persons who "shall be nationals and citizens of the United States at birth." Paragraph (7) of § 301(a) includes in that definition a person born abroad "of parents one of whom is an alien, and the other a citizen of the United States" who has met specified conditions of residence in this country. Section 301(b), however, provides that one who is a citizen at birth under § 301(a)(7) shall lose his citizenship unless, after age 14 and before age 28, he shall come to the United States and be physically present here continuously for at least five years. We quote the statute in the margin.[1]

---

1. "Sec. 301. (a) The following shall be nationals and citizens of the United States at birth:

"(1) a person born in the United States, and subject to the jurisdiction thereof;

. . .

"(7) a person born outside the geographical limits of the United States and its outlying possessions of parents one of whom is an alien, and the other a citizen of the United

The plan thus adopted by Congress with respect to a person of this classification was to bestow citizenship at birth but to take it away upon the person's failure to comply with a post-age-14 and pre-age-28 residential requirement. It is this deprival of citizenship, once bestowed, that is under attack here.

I

The facts are stipulated:

1. The appellee, Aldo Mario Bellei (hereinafter the plaintiff), was born in Italy on December 22, 1939. He is now 31 years of age.

2. The plaintiff's father has always been a citizen of Italy and never has acquired United States citizenship. The plaintiff's mother, however, was born in Philadelphia in 1915 and thus was a native-born United States citizen. She has retained that citizenship. Moreover, she has fulfilled the requirement of § 301(a)(7) for physical presence in the United States for 10 years, more than five of which were after she attained the age of 14 years. The mother and father were married in Philadelphia on the mother's 24th birthday, March 14, 1939. Nine days later, on March 23, the newlyweds departed for Italy. They have resided there ever since.

3. By Italian law the plaintiff acquired Italian citizenship upon his birth in Italy. He retains that citizenship. He also acquired United States citizenship at his birth under Rev.Stat. § 1993, as amended by the Act of May 24, 1934, § 1, 48 Stat. 797, then in effect. That version of the statute, as does the present one, contained a residence condition applicable to a child born abroad with one alien parent.

4. The plaintiff resided in Italy from the time of his birth until recently. He currently resides in England, where he has employment as an electronics engineer with an organization engaged in the NATO defense program.

5. The plaintiff has come to the United States five different times. [No visit lasted longer than five months. His U.S.] passport was first issued on June 27, 1952. His last application approval, in August 1961, contains the notation "Warned abt. 301(b)." The plaintiff's United States passport was periodically approved to and including December 22, 1962, his 23d birthday.

States who, prior to the birth of such person, was physically present in the United States or its outlying possessions for a period or periods totaling not less than ten years, at least five of which were after attaining the age of fourteen years: *Provided....*

"(b) Any person who is a national and citizen of the United States at birth under paragraph (7) of subsection (a), shall lose his nationality and citizenship unless he shall come to the United States prior to attaining the age of twenty-three years and shall immediately following any such coming be continuously physically present in the United

State[s] for at least five years: *Provided,* That such physical presence follows the attainment of the age of fourteen years and precedes the age of twenty-eight years.

"(c) Subsection (b) shall apply to a person born abroad subsequent to May 24, 1934...."

* * * Pub.L. 85–316, § 16, 71 Stat. 644, 8 U.S.C. § 1401b, enacted in September 1957, provides that absences of less than 12 months in the aggregate "shall not be considered to break the continuity of [the] physical presence" required by § 301(b).

6. On his fifth visit to the United States, in 1965, the plaintiff entered with an Italian passport and as an alien visitor. He had just been married and he came with his bride to visit his maternal grandparents.

7. The plaintiff was warned in writing by United States authorities of the impact of § 301(b) when he was in this country in January 1963 and again in November of that year when he was in Italy. Sometime after February 11, 1964, he was orally advised by the American Embassy at Rome that he had lost his United States citizenship pursuant to § 301(b). In November 1966 he was so notified in writing by the American Consul in Rome when the plaintiff requested another American passport.

* * *

Plaintiff thus concededly failed to comply with the conditions imposed by § 301(b) of the Act.

II

The plaintiff instituted the present action against the Secretary of State in the Southern District of New York. He asked that the Secretary be enjoined from carrying out and enforcing § 301(b), and also requested a declaratory judgment that § 301(b) is unconstitutional as violative of the Fifth Amendment's Due Process Clause, the Eighth Amendment's Punishment Clause, and the Ninth Amendment, and that he is and always has been a native-born United States citizen. * * *

[The District Court held § 301(b) unconstitutional.]

III

The two cases primarily relied upon by the three-judge District Court are, of course, of particular significance here. [The Court then describes the facts and opinions in *Schneider v. Rusk* and *Afroyim v. Rusk.*]

* * *

It is to be observed that both Mrs. Schneider and Mr. Afroyim had resided in this country for years. Each had acquired United States citizenship here by the naturalization process (in one case derivative and in the other direct) prescribed by the National Legislature. Each, in short, was covered explicitly by the Fourteenth Amendment's very first sentence: "All persons born or naturalized in the United States and subject to the jurisdiction thereof, are citizens of the United States and of the State wherein they reside." This of course accounts for the Court's emphasis in *Afroyim* upon "Fourteenth Amendment citizenship." 387 U.S., at 262, 87 S.Ct., at 1665.

IV

The statutes culminating in § 301 merit review:

1. The very first Congress, at its Second Session, proceeded to implement its power, under the Constitution's Art. I, § 8, cl. 4, to "establish an uniform Rule of Naturalization" by producing the Act of March 26, 1790, 1 Stat. 103. That statute, among other things, stated, "And the

children of citizens of the United States, that may be born beyond sea, or out of the limits of the United States, shall be considered as natural born citizens: *Provided,* That the right of citizenship shall not descend to persons whose fathers have never been resident in the United States. . . ."

2.   A like provision, with only minor changes in phrasing and with the same emphasis on paternal residence, was continuously in effect through three succeeding naturalization Acts. Act of January 29, 1795, § 3, 1 Stat. 415; Act of April 14, 1802, § 4, 2 Stat. 155; Act of February 10, 1855, c. 71, § 1, 10 Stat. 604. The only significant difference is that the 1790, 1795, and 1802 Acts read retrospectively, while the 1855 Act reads prospectively as well. See *Weedin v. Chin Bow,* 274 U.S. 657, 664, 47 S.Ct. 772, 774, 71 L.Ed. 1284 (1927), and *Montana v. Kennedy,* 366 U.S. 308, 311, 81 S.Ct. 1336, 1338, 6 L.Ed.2d 313 (1961).

3.   Section 1 of the 1855 Act, with changes unimportant here, was embodied as § 1993 of the Revised Statutes of 1874.[3]

4.   The Act of March 2, 1907, § 6, 34 Stat. 1229, provided that all children born abroad who were citizens under Rev.Stat. § 1993 and who continued to reside elsewhere, in order to receive governmental protection, were to record at age 18 their intention to become residents and remain citizens of the United States and were to take the oath of allegiance upon attaining their majority.

5.   The change in § 1993 effected by the Act of May 24, 1934 * * * eliminated the theretofore imposed restriction to the paternal parent and prospectively granted citizenship, subject to a five-year continuous residence requirement [immediately previous to the child's eighteenth birthday] and an oath, to the foreign-born child of either a citizen father or a citizen mother. This was the form of the statute at the time of plaintiff's birth on December 22, 1939.

6.   The Nationality Act of 1940, § 201, 54 Stat. 1138, contained a similar condition directed to a total of five years' residence in the United States between the ages of 13 and 21.

7.   The Immigration and Nationality Act, by its § 407, 66 Stat. 281, became law in December 1952. Its § 301(b) contains a five years' continuous residence condition (alleviated, with the 1957 amendment, see n. 1, by an allowance for absences less than 12 months in the aggregate) directed to the period between 14 and 28 years of age.

* * *

The application of these respective statutes to a person in plaintiff Bellei's position produces the following results:

1.   Not until 1934 would that person have had any conceivable claim to United States citizenship. For more than a century and a half no statute was of assistance. Maternal citizenship afforded no benefit. One

---

3.   "All children heretofore born or hereafter born out of the limits and jurisdiction of the United States, whose fathers were or may be at the time of their birth citizens thereof, are declared to be citizens of the United States; but the rights of citizenship shall not descend to children whose fathers never resided in the United States."

may observe, too, that if Mr. Bellei had been born in 1933, instead of in 1939, he would have no claim even today.

2. Despite the recognition of the maternal root by the 1934 amendment, in effect at the time of plaintiff's birth, and despite the continuing liberalization of the succeeding statutes, the plaintiff still would not be entitled to full citizenship because, although his mother met the condition for her residence in the United States, the plaintiff never did fulfill the residential condition imposed for him by any of the statutes.

3. This is so even though the liberalizing 1940 and 1952 statutes, enacted after the plaintiff's birth, were applicable by their terms to one born abroad subsequent to May 24, 1934, the date of the 1934 Act, and were available to the plaintiff.

Thus, in summary, it may be said fairly that, for the most part, each successive statute, as applied to a foreign-born child of one United States citizen parent, moved in a direction of leniency for the child. For plaintiff Bellei the statute changed from complete disqualification to citizenship upon a condition subsequent, with that condition being expanded and made less onerous, and, after his birth, with the succeeding liberalizing provisions made applicable to him in replacement of the stricter statute in effect when he was born. The plaintiff nevertheless failed to satisfy any form of the condition.

V

It is evident that Congress felt itself possessed of the power to grant citizenship to the foreign born and at the same time to impose qualifications and conditions for that citizenship. Of course, Congress obviously felt that way, too, about the two expatriation provisions invalidated by the decisions in *Schneider* and *Afroyim*.

We look again, then, at the Constitution and further indulge in history's assistance:

Of initial significance, because of its being the foundation stone of the Court's decisional structure in *Afroyim*, and, perhaps by a process of after-the-fact osmosis, of the earlier *Schneider* as well, is the Fourteenth Amendment's opening sentence:

> "All persons born or naturalized in the United States and subject to the jurisdiction thereof, are citizens of the United States and of the State wherein they reside."

The central fact, in our weighing of the plaintiff's claim to continuing and therefore current United States citizenship, is that he was born abroad. He was not born in the United States. He was not naturalized in the United States. And he has not been subject to the jurisdiction of the United States. All this being so, it seems indisputable that the first sentence of the Fourteenth Amendment has no application to plaintiff Bellei. He simply is not a Fourteenth-Amendment-first-sentence citizen. His posture contrasts with that of Mr. Afroyim, who was naturalized in the United States and with that of Mrs. Schneider, whose citizenship was derivative by her presence here and by her mother's naturalization here.

The plaintiff's claim thus must center in the statutory power of Congress and in the appropriate exercise of that power within the restrictions of any pertinent constitutional provisions other than the Fourteenth Amendment's first sentence.

The reach of congressional power in this area is readily apparent:

1. Over 70 years ago the Court, in an opinion by Mr. Justice Gray, reviewed and discussed early English statutes relating to rights of inheritance and of citizenship of persons born abroad of parents who were British subjects. *United States v. Wong Kim Ark,* 169 U.S. 649, 668–671, 18 S.Ct. 456, 464–465, 42 L.Ed. 890 (1898). The Court concluded that "naturalization by descent" was not a common-law concept but was dependent, instead, upon statutory enactment. * * *

* * *

[3.] Mr. Justice Gray * * * observed that the first sentence of the Fourteenth Amendment was "declaratory of existing rights, and affirmative of existing law," so far as the qualifications of being born in the United States, being naturalized in the United States, and being subject to its jurisdiction are concerned. *United States v. Wong Kim Ark,* 169 U.S., at 688, 18 S.Ct., at 472. Then follows a most significant sentence:

> "But it [the first sentence of the Fourteenth Amendment] has not touched the acquisition of citizenship by being born abroad of American parents; and has left that subject to be regulated, as it had always been, by Congress, in the exercise of the power conferred by the Constitution to establish an uniform rule of naturalization."

Thus, at long last, there emerged an express *constitutional* definition of citizenship. But it was one restricted to the combination of three factors, each and all significant: birth in the United States, naturalization in the United States, and subjection to the jurisdiction of the United States. The definition obviously did not apply to any acquisition of citizenship by being born abroad of an American parent. That type, and any other not covered by the Fourteenth Amendment, was necessarily left to proper congressional action.

4. The Court has recognized the existence of this power. It has observed, "No alien has the slightest right to naturalization unless all statutory requirements are complied with...." *United States v. Ginsberg,* 243 U.S. 472, 475, 37 S.Ct. 422, 425, 61 L.Ed. 853 (1917). See *United States v. Ness,* 245 U.S. 319, 38 S.Ct. 118, 62 L.Ed. 321 (1917); *Maney v. United States,* 278 U.S. 17, 49 S.Ct. 15, 73 L.Ed. 156 (1928). And the Court has specifically recognized the power of Congress not to grant a United States citizen the right to transmit citizenship by descent. [*Montana v. Kennedy,* 366 U.S. 308, 81 S.Ct. 1336, 6 L.Ed.2d 313 (1961).] * * *

Further, it is conceded here both that Congress may withhold citizenship from persons like plaintiff Bellei and may prescribe a period of residence in the United States as a condition *precedent* without constitutional question.

Thus we have the presence of congressional power in this area, its exercise, and the Court's specific recognition of that power and of its having been properly withheld or properly used in particular situations.

VI

This takes us, then, to the issue of the constitutionality of the exercise of that congressional power when it is used to impose the condition subsequent that confronted plaintiff Bellei. We conclude that its imposition is not unreasonable, arbitrary, or unlawful, and that it withstands the present constitutional challenge.

1. The Congress has an appropriate concern with problems attendant on dual nationality. *Savorgnan v. United States,* 338 U.S. 491, 500, 70 S.Ct. 292, 297, 94 L.Ed. 287 (1950); N. Bar-Yaacov, Dual Nationality xi and 4 (1961). These problems are particularly acute when it is the father who is the child's alien parent and the father chooses to have his family reside in the country of his own nationality. The child is reared, at best, in an atmosphere of divided loyalty. We cannot say that a concern that the child's own primary allegiance is to the country of his birth and of his father's allegiance is either misplaced or arbitrary.

The duality also creates problems for the governments involved. MR. JUSTICE BRENNAN recognized this when, concurring in *Kennedy v. Mendoza-Martinez,* 372 U.S. 144, 187, 83 S.Ct. 554, 577, 9 L.Ed.2d 644 (1963), a case concerning native-born citizens, he observed: "We have recognized the entanglements which may stem from dual allegiance...." In a famous case MR. JUSTICE DOUGLAS wrote of the problem of dual citizenship. *Kawakita v. United States,* 343 U.S. 717, 723–736, 72 S.Ct. 950, 955–962, 96 L.Ed. 1249 (1952). He noted that "[o]ne who has a dual nationality will be subject to claims from both nations, claims which at times may be competing or conflicting," that one with dual nationality cannot turn that status "into a fair-weather citizenship," and that "[c]ircumstances may compel one who has a dual nationality to do acts which otherwise would not be compatible with the obligations of American citizenship." * * *

* * *

4. The solution to the dual nationality dilemma provided by the Congress by way of required residence surely is not unreasonable. It may not be the best that could be devised, but here, too, we cannot say that it is irrational or arbitrary or unfair. Congress first has imposed a condition precedent in that the citizen parent must have been in the United States or its possessions not less than 10 years, at least five of which are after attaining age 14. It then has imposed, as to the foreign-born child himself, the condition subsequent as to residence here. * * * The same policy is reflected in the required period of residence here for aliens seeking naturalization.

5. We feel that it does not make good constitutional sense, or comport with logic, to say, on the one hand, that Congress may impose a condition precedent, with no constitutional complication, and yet be powerless to impose precisely the same condition subsequent. Any such distinction, of course, must rest, if it has any basis at all, on the asserted

"premise that the rights of citizenship of the native born and of the naturalized person are of the same dignity and are coextensive," *Schneider v. Rusk,* and on the announcement that Congress has no "power, express or implied, to take away an American citizen's citizenship without his assent," *Afroyim v. Rusk.* But, as pointed out above, these were utterances bottomed upon Fourteenth Amendment citizenship and that Amendment's direct reference to "persons born or naturalized in the United States." We do not accept the notion that those utterances are now to be judicially extended to citizenship not based upon the Fourteenth Amendment and to make citizenship an absolute. That it is not an absolute is demonstrated by the fact that even Fourteenth Amendment citizenship by naturalization, when unlawfully procured, may be set aside. *Afroyim v. Rusk,* 387 U.S., at 267 n. 23, 87 S.Ct., at 1667.

6. A contrary holding would convert what is congressional generosity into something unanticipated and obviously undesired by the Congress. Our National Legislature indulged the foreign-born child with presumptive citizenship, subject to subsequent satisfaction of a reasonable residence requirement, rather than to deny him citizenship outright, as concededly it had the power to do, and relegate the child, if he desired American citizenship, to the more arduous requirements of the usual naturalization process. The plaintiff here would force the Congress to choose between unconditional conferment of United States citizenship at birth and deferment of citizenship until a condition precedent is fulfilled. We are not convinced that the Constitution requires so rigid a choice. If it does, the congressional response seems obvious.

7. Neither are we persuaded that a condition subsequent in this area impresses one with "second-class citizenship." That cliché is too handy and too easy, and, like most clichés, can be misleading. That the condition subsequent may be beneficial is apparent in the light of the conceded fact that citizenship to this plaintiff was fully deniable. The proper emphasis is on what the statute permits him to gain from the possible starting point of noncitizenship, not on what he claims to lose from the possible starting point of full citizenship to which he has no constitutional right in the first place. His citizenship, while it lasts, although conditional, is not "second-class."

8. The plaintiff is not stateless. His Italian citizenship remains. He has lived practically all his life in Italy. He has never lived in this country; although he has visited here five times, the stipulated facts contain no indication that he ever will live here. He asserts no claim of ignorance or of mistake or even of hardship. He was warned several times of the provision of the statute and of his need to take up residence in the United States prior to his 23d birthday.

We hold that § 301(b) has no constitutional infirmity in its application to plaintiff Bellei. The judgment of the District Court is reversed.

Judgment reversed.

MR. JUSTICE BLACK, with whom MR. JUSTICE DOUGLAS and MR. JUSTICE MARSHALL join, dissenting.

Less than four years ago this Court held that

"the Fourteenth Amendment was designed to, and does, protect every citizen of this Nation against a congressional forcible destruction of his citizenship, whatever his creed, color, or race. Our holding does no more than to give to this citizen that which is his own, a constitutional right to remain a citizen in a free country unless he voluntarily relinquishes that citizenship." *Afroyim v. Rusk,* 387 U.S. 253, 268, 87 S.Ct. 1660, 1668, 18 L.Ed.2d 757 (1967).

The holding was clear. Congress could not, until today, consistently with the Fourteenth Amendment enact a law stripping an American of his citizenship which he has never voluntarily renounced or given up. Now this Court, by a vote of five to four through a simple change in its composition, overrules that decision.

* * *

The Constitution, written for the ages, cannot rise and fall with this Court's passing notions of what is "fair," or "reasonable," or "arbitrary." The Fourteenth Amendment commands:

"All persons born or naturalized in the United States and subject to the jurisdiction thereof, are citizens of the United States and of the State wherein they reside."

Speaking of this very language, the Court held in *Afroyim* that no American can be deprived of his citizenship without his assent. Today, the Court overrules that holding. This precious Fourteenth Amendment American citizenship should not be blown around by every passing political wind that changes the composition of this Court. I dissent.

* * *

The Court today holds that the Citizenship Clause of the Fourteenth Amendment has no application to Bellei. The Court first notes that *Afroyim* was essentially a case construing the Citizenship Clause of the Fourteenth Amendment. Since the Citizenship Clause declares that: "All persons born or naturalized in the United States ... are citizens of the United States ...," the Court reasons that the protections against involuntary expatriation declared in *Afroyim* do not protect *all* American citizens, but only those "born or naturalized in the United States." Afroyim, the arguments runs, was naturalized in this country so he was protected by the Citizenship Clause, but Bellei, since he acquired his American citizenship at birth in Italy as a foreign-born child of an American citizen, was neither born nor naturalized in the United States and, hence, falls outside the scope of the Fourteenth Amendment guarantees declared in *Afroyim.* One could hardly call this a generous reading of the great purposes the Fourteenth Amendment was adopted to bring about.

* * *

Under the view adopted by the majority today, all children born to Americans while abroad would be excluded from the protections of the Citizenship Clause and would instead be relegated to the permanent status of second-class citizenship, subject to revocation at the will of Congress. The Court rejected such narrow, restrictive, and super-technical interpretations of the Citizenship Clause when it held in *Afroyim* that that Clause "was designed to, and does, protect every citizen of this Nation...."

Afroyim's broad interpretation of the scope of the Citizenship Clause finds ample support in the language and history of the Fourteenth Amendment. Bellei was not "born ... in the United States," but he was, constitutionally speaking, "naturalized in the United States." Although those Americans who acquire their citizenship under statutes conferring citizenship on the foreign-born children of citizens are not popularly thought of as naturalized citizens, the use of the word "naturalize" in this way has a considerable constitutional history. Congress is empowered by the Constitution to "establish an uniform Rule of Naturalization," Art. I, § 8. Anyone acquiring citizenship solely under the exercise of this power is, constitutionally speaking, a naturalized citizen. The first congressional exercise of this power, entitled "An Act to establish an uniform Rule of Naturalization," was passed in 1790 at the Second Session of the First Congress. It provided in part:

> "And the children of citizens of the United States, that may be born beyond sea, or out of the limits of the United States, shall be considered as natural born citizens: *Provided,* That the right of citizenship shall not descend to persons whose fathers have never been resident in the United States." 1 Stat. 103, 104.

This provision is the earliest form of the statute under which Bellei acquired his citizenship. Its enactment as part of a "Rule of Naturalization" shows, I think, that the First Congress conceived of this and most likely all other purely statutory grants of citizenship as forms or varieties of naturalization. However, the clearest expression of the idea that Bellei and others similarly situated should for constitutional purposes be considered as naturalized citizens is to be found in *United States v. Wong Kim Ark.* * * * As shown in *Wong Kim Ark,* naturalization when used in its constitutional sense is a generic term describing and including within its meaning all those modes of acquiring American citizenship other than birth in this country. All means of obtaining American citizenship which are dependent upon a congressional enactment are forms of naturalization. * * * Moreover, this concept of naturalization is the only one permitted by this Court's consistent adoption of the view that the Fourteenth Amendment was intended to supply a comprehensive definition of American citizenship. * * *

The majority opinion appears at times to rely on the argument that Bellei, while he concededly might have been a naturalized citizen, was not naturalized "in the United States." This interpretation obviously imposes a limitation on the scope of the Citizenship Clause which is inconsistent with the conclusion expressed above that the Fourteenth Amendment provides a comprehensive definition of American citizenship, for the majority's view would exclude from the protection of that Clause all those who acquired American citizenship while abroad. I cannot accept the narrow and extraordinarily technical reading of the Fourteenth Amendment employed by the Court today. If, for example, Congress should decide to vest the authority to naturalize aliens in American embassy officials abroad rather than having the ceremony performed in this country, I have no doubt that those so naturalized would be just as fully protected by the Fourteenth Amendment as are those who go through our present naturalization procedures. Rather than the technical reading adopted by the majority, it is my view that the word "in" as it appears in the phrase "in the United States" was surely meant to be understood in two somewhat different senses: one can become a citizen of this country by being born *within* it or by being naturalized *into* it. * * *

* * *

Of course the Court's construction of the Constitution is not a "strict" one. On the contrary, it proceeds on the premise that a majority of this Court can change the Constitution day by day, month by month, and year by year, according to its shifting notions of what is fair, reasonable, and right. There was little need for the founders to draft a written constitution if this Court can say it is only binding when a majority finds it fair, reasonable, and right to make it so. That is the loosest construction that could be employed. It is true that England has moved along very well in the world without a written constitution. But with complete familiarity with the English experience, our ancestors determined to draft a written constitution which the members of this Court are sworn to obey. While I remain on the Court I shall continue to oppose the power of judges, appointed by changing administrations, to change the Constitution from time to time according to their notions of what is "fair" and "reasonable." I would decide this case not by my views of what is "arbitrary," or what is "fair," but rather by what the Constitution commands.

I dissent.

Mr. Justice Brennan, with whom Mr. Justice Douglas joins, dissenting.

* * * Concededly petitioner was a citizen at birth not by constitutional right, but only through operation of a federal statute. In the light of the complete lack of rational basis for distinguishing among citizens whose naturalization was carried out within the physical bounds of the United States, and those, like Bellei, who may be naturalized overseas, the conclusion is compelled that the reference in the Fourteenth Amendment to persons "born or naturalized in the United States" includes those naturalized through operation of an Act of Congress, wherever they may be at the time. Congress was therefore powerless to strip Bellei of his citizenship; he could lose it only if he voluntarily renounced or relinquished it. *Afroyim v. Rusk.* I dissent.

Notes

1. Would Justice Black permit Congress to rewrite the statute so that children born abroad to a single U.S. citizen parent obtained citizenship only *after* satisfying a residency requirement? (Justice Brennan clearly would accept such a congressional determination.) If not, Justice

Black would essentially be holding that some form of immediate *jus sanguinis* transmission of citizenship is mandated by the Constitution. But just what relationships would have to be included in such a constitutional rule? In any event, on what grounds could one base such a conclusion? The language of the Fourteenth Amendment would seem to pose no obstacles to a congressional choice to abolish all *jus sanguinis* rules.

If then Justice Black would be forced to concede that Congress has such power, isn't his position somewhat incongruous? Aren't the offspring who never will fulfill this type of residency requirement in a better position having twenty-three years of U.S. citizenship than having none at all? Is the difference between a condition precedent and a condition subsequent a persuasive basis on which to rest such important constitutional distinctions?

2. Justice Black's position requires acceptance of the notion that those who acquire U.S. citizenship by descent upon birth in a foreign country are "naturalized" citizens. He acknowledges that this characterization is inconsistent with the popular usage of the term; people who acquired U.S. citizenship at birth in this fashion typically do not think of themselves as naturalized.

Popular terminology may not be significant in this respect, but should a deliberate congressional decision on the matter carry more weight? In fact, the INA makes clear that transmission of U.S. citizenship by descent to children born abroad is not to be considered naturalization. The INA sets forth its *jus sanguinis* rules in a section that begins: "The following shall be nationals and citizens of the United States at birth * * *." INA § 301. Meanwhile the definitional section of the Act defines "naturalization" as "the conferring of nationality of a state upon a person *after birth,* by any means whatsoever." INA § 101(a)(23) (emphasis added); *cf.* Harvard Research, *supra,* 23 Am.J.Int'l L. (Special Supp.) at 24 (suggesting that international usage conforms to this definition).[8]

3. In Part VI(6) of his opinion for the Court, Justice Blackmun criticizes the "rigid" choice the dissenters would apparently impose on Congress—between residency requirements imposed as a condition precedent, thus delaying acquisition of U.S. citizenship, and outright conferment of citizenship at birth unconstrained by subsequent residency requirements. He also strongly suggests, although his exact wording is ambiguous, that Congress would choose the former option—the more severe one—if put to the test.

---

8. In light of *Schneider v. Rusk,* whether children born abroad to U.S. citizen parents are considered naturalized or not probably has little practical significance outside the particular debate involved in *Bellei.* But conceivably the characterization might have a bearing in determining whether such citizens qualify for the Presidency; the Constitution—regrettably—opens that office only to "natural born" citizens. Art. II, § 1, cl. 5. *See generally* Gordon, *Who Can Be President of the United States,* 26 Md.L.Rev. 1 (1968). This term has not been authoritatively construed. It seems, however, that Justice Blackmun's approach, recognizing three separate types of citizenship (by birth in the United States, by birth outside the United States, and by naturalization), would be more amenable than Justice Black's to a conclusion that citizens *jure sanguinis* are eligible.

This guess about congressional sentiment proved to be far wide of the mark. Despite *Bellei*'s express endorsement of such residency requirements imposed as a condition subsequent, Congress chose in 1978 to eliminate them altogether—but for prospective application only. Act of October 10, 1978, Pub.L. No. 95–432, 92 Stat. 1046. (*See* the current version of § 301, with particular attention to § 301(g).) Henceforth someone born in Bellei's situation need never establish residence in the United States in order to preserve his citizenship. He may have to do so, however, if he wishes to transmit citizenship to his own children. *See* Section B, *supra*.

Dual Nationality: A Brief Digression

In sustaining the statute, the majority in *Bellei* relies heavily on the problems attendant on dual nationality. A little background may help in evaluating the seriousness of such problems and the appropriateness of the remedy.

It is clear that dual nationality may in some circumstances place the individual involved in the most serious kind of high-stakes dilemma. *Kawakita v. United States*, 343 U.S. 717, 72 S.Ct. 950, 96 L.Ed. 1249 (1952), referred to in Justice Blackmun's opinion, affirmed the treason conviction—and death sentence—imposed on a dual national of Japan and the United States. Finding himself in Japan when war broke out between his two countries in 1941, Kawakita served as an interpreter for a company for which American prisoners of war were forced to work. There was extensive evidence that he engaged in serious mistreatment of the prisoners. He was tried and convicted, however, not for war crimes under general international standards, but for treason against the United States, an offense which by definition can be committed only by someone who owes allegiance to this nation.

In considering his appeal, the Supreme Court, per Mr. Justice Douglas, first rejected his claim that certain of his actions in Japan amounted to an effective renunciation of his U.S. citizenship, relying in large part on the findings of the jury. Then it proceeded to consider the requirements imposed on a dual national, "a status long recognized in law," in time of war (*id.* at 733–36):

> One who has a dual nationality will be subject to claims from both nations, claims which at times may be competing or conflicting. The nature of those claims has recently been stated as follows:
>
>> "A person with dual nationality may be subjected to taxes by both states of which he is a national. He is not entitled to protection by one of the two states of which he is a national while in the territorial jurisdiction of the other. Either state not at war with the other may insist on military service when the person is present within its territory. In time of war if he supports neither belligerent, both may be aggrieved. If he supports one belligerent, the other may be aggrieved. One state may be suspicious of his loyalty to it

and subject him to the disabilities of an enemy alien, including sequestration of his property, while the other holds his conduct treasonable." Orfield, The Legal Effects of Dual Nationality, 17 Geo.Wash.L.Rev. 427, 429.

Dual nationality, however, is the unavoidable consequence of the conflicting laws of different countries. One who becomes a citizen of this country by reason of birth retains it, even though by the law of another country he is also a citizen of it. He can under certain circumstances be deprived of his American citizenship through the operation of a treaty or an act of Congress; he can also lose it by voluntary action. But American citizenship, until lost, carries obligations of allegiance as well as privileges and benefits. For one who has a dual status the obligations of American citizenship may at times be difficult to discharge. An American who has a dual nationality may find himself in a foreign country when it wages war on us. The very fact that he must make a livelihood there may indirectly help the enemy nation. In these days of total war manpower becomes critical and everyone who can be placed in a productive position increases the strength of the enemy to wage war. Of course, a person caught in that predicament can resolve the conflict of duty by openly electing one nationality or the other and becoming either an alien enemy of the country where he resides or a national of it alone. Yet, so far as the existing law of this country is concerned, he need not make that choice but can continue his dual citizenship. It has been stated in an administrative ruling of the State Department that a person with a dual citizenship who lives abroad in the other country claiming him as a national owes an allegiance to it which is paramount to the allegiance he owes the United States. That is a far cry from a ruling that a citizen in that position owes no allegiance to the United States. Of course, an American citizen who is also a Japanese national living in Japan has obligations to Japan necessitated by his residence there. There might conceivably be cases where the mere nonperformance of the acts complained of would be a breach of Japanese law. He may have employment which requires him to perform certain acts. The compulsion may come from the fact that he is drafted for the job or that his conduct is demanded by the laws of Japan. He may be coerced by his employer or supervisor or by the force of circumstances to do things which he has no desire or heart to do. That was one of petitioner's defenses in this case. Such acts—if done voluntarily and willfully—might be treasonable. But if done under the compulsion of the job or the law or some other influence, those acts would not rise to the gravity of that offense. The trial judge recognized the distinction in his charge when he instructed the jury to acquit petitioner if he did not do the acts willingly or voluntarily "but so acted only because performance of the duties of his employment required him to do so or because of other coercion or compulsion." In short, petitioner was held accountable by the jury only for performing acts of hostility toward this country which he was not required by Japan to perform.

If he can retain that freedom and still remain an American citizen, there is not even a minimum of allegiance which he owes to the United States while he resides in the enemy country. That conclusion is hostile to the concept of citizenship as we know it, and it must be rejected. One who wants that freedom can get it by renouncing his American citizenship. He cannot turn it into a fair-weather citizenship, retaining it for possible contingent benefits but meanwhile playing the part of the traitor. An American citizen owes allegiance to the United States wherever he may reside.

Manifestly, dual nationality can impose difficult choices on the persons who hold that status. In time of war, they may have to judge with exquisite care what kind of support to provide to the country in which they are then resident, at risk of death for treason in one nation or the other, should they go too far or not far enough.[9] See generally N. Bar-Yaacov, Dual Nationality 54–62 (1961). But does the existence of those problems justify provisions in U.S. law decreeing *involuntary* expatriation of U.S. citizens, based on certain objective behavior, since even under *Kawakita* they retain the option of voluntary renunciation of citizenship at all times? What difference does it make to the government? Even if Kawakita had never been a U.S. citizen, presumably he could still have committed the same cruelties against American POW's.

Most of the arguments in favor of the expatriating provisions of the original 1952 Act have not rested on scenarios like that involved in *Kawakita*. Instead, they have looked to entanglements that may result from this government's attempts to provide diplomatic protection under circumstances of real or perceived dual nationality—that is, involving U.S. nationals who also have extensive connections with the other nation involved. For example, in *Schneider v. Rusk, supra,* the Court summarized the government's principal arguments in defense of that particular statutory provision: "Other nations, it is said, frequently attempt to treat such persons [former nationals naturalized in the United States] as their own citizens, thus embroiling the United States in conflicts when it attempts to afford them protection. It is argued that expatriation is an alternative to withdrawal of diplomatic protection." 377 U.S. at 165. And Justice Clark's dissent also makes reference to such conflicts. *Id.* at 173–74.

In order to assess the risks and consequences of such conflicts, one must understand just what is meant by "diplomatic protection." The classic work in the field, E. Borchard, *The Diplomatic Protection of Citizens Abroad* (1922), summarizes (*id.* at v–vi):

---

9. As it happened, Kawakita's death sentence was later commuted to life imprisonment by President Eisenhower. He returned to Japan in 1963 upon securing release from prison. D. Weissbrodt, Immigration Law and Procedure in a Nutshell 144 (1984).

The individual abroad finds himself in legal relation to two countries, the country of which he is a citizen, and the country in which he resides or establishes his business. From the point of view of the one, he is a citizen abroad; from the point of view of the other, he is an alien. The common consent of nations has established a certain standard of conduct by which a state must be guided in its treatment of aliens. In the absence of any central authority capable of enforcing this standard, international law has authorized the state of which the individual is a citizen to vindicate his rights by diplomatic and other methods sanctioned by international law. This right of diplomatic protection constitutes, therefore, a limitation upon the territorial jurisdiction of the country in which the alien is settled or is conducting business.

The standard of treatment which an alien is entitled to receive is incapable of exact definition. The common practice of the civilized nations and the adjudication of conflicts between nations, particularly by arbitration, arising out of alleged violations of the rights of citizens abroad, have nevertheless developed certain fundamental principles from which no nation can depart without incurring international responsibility to the national state of the person injured. The right which every state possesses to protect its citizens abroad is correlative to its obligation to accord foreigners a measure of treatment satisfying the requirements of international law and applicable treaties, and to its responsibility for failure to accomplish this duty. Practice has demonstrated that the mere fact that aliens have been granted the rights authorized by local law, and equality of treatment with natives, is not necessarily regarded as a final compliance with international obligations, if the local measure of justice and administration in a given case falls below the requirements of the international standard of civilized justice, although it is always a delicate proceeding, in the absence of extraterritoriality, to charge that a rule of municipal law or administration fails to meet the international standard.

Citizens abroad, therefore, have in the vindication of their rights an extraordinary legal remedy not open to natives. However just it may be to confine the alien to the rights granted by local law, predicating state liability merely upon the state's failure to make its grant effective, practice has shown that nations of the Western European type are unwilling unreservedly to concede the application of this principle to some of the weaker countries of the world. While tacitly undertaking to abide by the local law, a rule supported by principle, international practice has given aliens a reserved power, after the vain exhaustion of local remedies, to call upon the diplomatic protection of their own government, if their rights, as measured not necessarily by the local, but by the international, standard have been violated. The citizen abroad has no legal right to require the diplomatic protection of his national government. Resort to this remedy of diplomatic protection is solely a right of the government, the justification and expediency of its employment being a matter for the government's unrestricted discretion. This protection is subject in its grant to such rules of municipal administrative law as the state may adopt, and in its exercise internationally to certain rules which custom has recognized.

What exactly does a government do when it is engaged in diplomatic protection? The term embraces a wide variety of actions. At its simplest level, protection consists simply of informal diplomatic or consular contacts with local officials to help straighten out a misunderstanding involving a national. If the matter is not resolved, however, protection can escalate to a higher level of diplomatic negotiation, perhaps accompanied or followed by the formal presentation of a claim for redress, which under some circumstances may be submitted to arbitration or trial before an international tribunal.

At the extreme, diplomatic protection may entail the use of armed force or a full-scale declaration of war. The War of 1812, it has often been pointed out, resulted at least in part from dual nationality problems. Great Britain at the time followed the theory of perpetual allegiance, and refused to recognize the claimed American nationality of its subjects who had been naturalized in the United States. The resulting forcible impressment of American sailors into British service inflamed local passions and brought on hostilities. Naturally, diplomatic protection, even when pushed to that extreme, does not invariably secure *actual* protection of the individual's interests. Moreover, at any stage the government involved is considered to have discretion to abstain from pressing the claim any further. *See id.* at 435–56, 590–91.[10]

In light of this brief discussion, how great a problem—for the nation in its conduct of foreign affairs, not the individual—is dual nationality today? How persuasive are the arguments based on dual nationality in support of expatriation provisions in any country's nationality laws? What other solutions to the difficulties are available, short of involuntary expatriation?

---

10. It should also be noted that the concept of diplomatic protection has been in considerable flux since the days when Borchard wrote, producing changes associated in part with the end of colonialism and the increased assertiveness of Third World nations. Controversy is particularly intense over the content of the "international standard" to be applied to the behavior of host governments, especially in connection with matters like the expropriation of foreign-owned property. *See generally* International Law of State Responsibility for Injuries to Aliens (R. Lillich ed. 1983). Also, the former doctrine that a country may not extend diplomatic protection to a dual national against the other country of nationality, *see* E.

Borchard, *supra,* at 575–91, seems to be eroding, in favor of a rule recognizing that the country of "effective" or "dominant" nationality is entitled to pursue a claim. *See* McDougal, Lasswell, and Chen, *Nationality and Human Rights: The Protection of the Individual in External Areas,* 83 Yale L.J. 900, 987–91 (1974). *See generally* P. Weis, Nationality and Statelessness in International Law (2d ed. 1979); D.W. Greig, International Law 369–80 (2d ed. 1976). Nevertheless, whatever the standard to be applied or the precise circumstances in which it can be invoked, the practice of diplomatic protection undeniably remains an important feature of modern international relations.

The principal dissent in *Bellei* charges that the majority had over-ruled *Afroyim* sub silentio, and it concludes with a complaint about "the power of judges, appointed by changing administrations, to change the Constitution from time to time * * *." This dissent is written, however, by the author of *Afroyim,* which overtly overruled, not merely distinguished, a precedent less than ten years old. Is this an instance of the pot calling the kettle Black?

In any event, Justice Black proved to be a poor prophet in his assessment of *Afroyim*'s future after *Bellei.*

VANCE v. TERRAZAS

Supreme Court of the United States, 1980.
444 U.S. 252, 100 S.Ct. 540, 62 L.Ed.2d 461.

MR. JUSTICE WHITE delivered the opinion of the Court.

Section 349(a)(2) of the Immigration and Nationality Act (Act) provides that "a person who is a national of the United States whether by birth or naturalization, shall lose his nationality by . . . taking an oath or making an affirmation or other formal declaration of allegiance to a foreign state or a political subdivision thereof." The Act also provides that the party claiming that such loss of citizenship occurred must "establish such claim by a preponderance of the evidence" and that the voluntariness of the expatriating conduct is rebuttably presumed. § 349(c), as added, 75 Stat. 656. The issues in this case are whether, in establishing loss of citizenship under § 349(a)(2) a party must prove an intent to surrender United States citizenship and whether the United States Constitution permits Congress to legislate with respect to expatriation proceedings by providing the standard of proof and the statutory presumption contained in § 349(c).

I

Appellee, Laurence J. Terrazas, was born in this country, the son of a Mexican citizen. He thus acquired at birth both United States and Mexican citizenship. In the fall of 1970, while a student in Monterrey, Mexico, and at the age of 22, appellee executed an application for a certificate of Mexican nationality, swearing "adherence, obedience, and submission to the laws and authorities of the Mexican Republic" and "expressly renounc[ing] United States citizenship, as well as any submission, obedience, and loyalty to any foreign government, especially to that of the United States of America, . . ." The certificate, which issued upon this application on April 3, 1971, recited that Terrazas had sworn adherence to the United Mexican States and that he "has expressly renounced all rights inherent to any other nationality, as well as all submission, obedience, and loyalty to any foreign government, especially to those which have recognized him as that national." Terrazas read and understood the certificate upon receipt.

A few months later, following a discussion with an officer of the United States Consulate in Monterrey, proceedings were instituted to determine whether appellee had lost his United States citizenship by obtaining the certificate of Mexican nationality. Appellee denied that he had, but in December 1971 the Department of State issued a certificate of loss of nationality. The Board of Appellate Review of the Department of State, after a full hearing, affirmed that appellee had voluntarily renounced his United States citizenship. As permitted by § 360(a) of the Act, appellee then brought this suit against the Secretary of State for a declaration of his United States nationality. Trial was *de novo*.

The District Court recognized that the first sentence of the Fourteenth Amendment, as construed in *Afroyim v. Rusk,* " 'protect[s] every citizen of this Nation against a congressional forcible destruction of his citizenship' " and that every citizen has " 'a constitutional right to remain a citizen ... unless he voluntarily relinquishes that citizenship.' " A person of dual nationality, the District Court said, "will be held to have expatriated himself from the United States when it is shown that he voluntarily committed an act whereby he unequivocally renounced his allegiance to the United States." Specifically, the District Court found that appellee had taken an oath of allegiance to Mexico, that he had "knowingly and understandingly renounced allegiance to the United States in connection with his Application for a Certificate of Mexican Nationality," and that "[t]he taking of an oath of allegiance to Mexico and renunciation of a foreign country [*sic*] citizenship is a condition precedent under Mexican law to the issuance of a Certificate of Mexican Nationality." The District Court concluded that the United States had "proved by a preponderance of the evidence that Laurence J. Terrazas knowingly, understandingly and voluntarily took an oath of allegiance to Mexico, and concurrently renounced allegiance to the United States," and that he had therefore "voluntarily relinquished United States citizenship pursuant to § 349(a)(2) of the ... Act."

In its opinion accompanying its findings and conclusions, the District Court observed that appellee had acted "voluntarily in swearing allegiance to Mexico and renouncing allegiance to the United States," and that appellee "knew he was repudiating allegiance to the United States through his actions." The court also said that "the declaration of allegiance to a foreign state in conjunction with the renunciatory language of United States citizenship 'would leave no room for ambiguity as to the intent of the applicant.' "

The Court of Appeals reversed. As the Court of Appeals understood the law—and there appears to have been no dispute on these basic requirements in the Courts of Appeals—the United States had not only to prove the taking of an oath to a foreign state, but also to demonstrate an intent on appellee's part to renounce his United States citizenship. The District Court had found these basic elements to have been proved by a preponderance of the evidence; and the Court of Appeals observed that, "[a]ssuming that the proper [evidentiary] standards were applied, we are convinced that the record fully supports the court's findings." The Court of Appeals ruled, however, that under *Afroyim v. Rusk,* Congress had no power to legislate the evidentiary standard contained in § 349(c) and that the Constitution required that proof be not merely by a preponderance of the evidence, but by "clear, convincing and unequivocal evidence." The case was remanded to the District Court for further proceedings.

The Secretary took this appeal under 28 U.S.C. § 1252. Because the invalidation of § 349(c) posed a substantial constitutional issue, we noted probable jurisdiction.

II

The Secretary first urges that the Court of Appeals erred in holding that a "specific intent to renounce U.S. citizenship" must be proved "before the mere taking of an oath of allegiance could result in an individual's expatriation." His position is that he need prove only the voluntary commission of an act, such as swearing allegiance to a foreign nation, that "is so inherently inconsistent with the continued retention of American citizenship that Congress may accord to it its natural consequences, *i.e.*, loss of nationality." We disagree.

In *Afroyim v. Rusk*, the Court held that § 401(e) of the Nationality Act of 1940, 54 Stat. 1168–1169, which provided that an American citizen "shall lose his nationality by ... [v]oting in a political election in a foreign state," contravened the Citizenship Clause of the Fourteenth Amendment. Afroyim was a naturalized American citizen who lived in Israel for 10 years. While in that nation, Afroyim voted in a political election. He in consequence was stripped of his United States citizenship. Consistently with *Perez v. Brownell,* 356 U.S. 44, 78 S.Ct. 568, 2 L.Ed.2d 603 (1958), which had sustained § 401(e), the District Court affirmed the power of Congress to expatriate for such conduct regardless of the citizen's intent to renounce his citizenship. This Court, however, in overruling *Perez,* "reject[ed] the idea ... that, aside from the Fourteenth Amendment, Congress has any general power, express or implied, to take away an American citizen's citizenship without his assent." The *Afroyim* opinion continued: § 1 of the Fourteenth Amendment is "most reasonably ... read as defining a citizenship which a citizen keeps unless he voluntarily relinquishes it."

The Secretary argues that *Afroyim* does not stand for the proposition that a specific intent to renounce must be shown before citizenship is relinquished. It is enough, he urges, to establish one of the expatriating acts specified in § 349(a) because Congress has declared each of those acts to be inherently inconsistent with the retention of citizenship. But *Afroyim* emphasized that loss of citizenship requires the individual's "assent," in addition to his voluntary commission of the expatriating act. It is difficult to understand that "assent" to loss of citizenship would mean anything less than an intent to relinquish citizenship, whether the intent is expressed in words or is found as a fair inference from proved conduct. *Perez* had sustained congressional power to expatriate without regard to the intent of the citizen to surrender his citizenship. *Afroyim* overturned this proposition. It may be, as the Secretary maintains, that a requirement of intent to relinquish citizenship poses substantial difficulties for the Government in performance of its essential task of determining who is a citizen. Nevertheless, the intent of the Fourteenth Amendment, among other things, was to define citizenship; and as interpreted in *Afroyim,* that definition cannot coexist with a congressional power to specify acts that work a renunciation of citizenship even absent an intent to renounce. In the last analysis, expatriation depends on the will of the citizen rather than on the will of Congress and its assessment of his conduct.

The Secretary argues that the dissent in *Perez,* which it is said the Court's opinion in *Afroyim* adopted, spoke of conduct so contrary to undivided allegiance to this country that it could result in loss of citizenship without regard to the intent of the actor and that "assent" should not therefore be read as a code word for intent to renounce. But *Afroyim* is a majority opinion, and its reach is neither expressly nor implicitly limited to that of the dissent in *Perez.* Furthermore, in his *Perez* dissent, Mr. Chief Justice Warren, in speaking of those acts that were expatriating because so fundamentally inconsistent with citizenship, concluded by saying that in such instances the "Government is simply giving formal recognition to the inevitable consequence of the citizen's own voluntary surrender of his citizenship." This suggests that the Chief Justice's conception of "actions in derogation of undivided allegiance to this country," in fact would entail an element of assent.

In any event, we are confident that it would be inconsistent with *Afroyim* to treat the expatriating acts specified in § 349(a) as the equivalent of or as conclusive evidence of the indispensable voluntary assent of the citizen. "Of course," any of the specified acts "may be highly persuasive evidence in the particular case of a purpose to abandon citizenship." *Nishikawa v. Dulles,* 356 U.S. 129, 139, 78 S.Ct. 612, 618, 2 L.Ed.2d 659 (1958) (Black, J., concurring). But the trier of fact must in the end conclude that the citizen not only voluntarily committed the expatriating act prescribed in the statute, but also intended to relinquish his citizenship.

This understanding of *Afroyim* is little different from that expressed by the Attorney General in his 1969 opinion explaining the impact of that case. 42 Op.Atty.Gen. 397. An "act which does not reasonably manifest an individual's transfer or abandonment of allegiance to the United States," the Attorney General said, "cannot be made a basis for expatriation." Voluntary relinquishment is "not confined to a written renunciation," but "can also be manifested by other actions declared expatriative under the [A]ct, if such actions are in derogation of allegiance to this country." Even in these cases, however, the issue of intent was deemed by the Attorney General to be open; and, once raised, the burden of proof on the issue was on the party asserting that expatriation had occurred. "In each case," the Attorney General stated, "the administrative authorities must make a judgment, based on all the evidence, whether the individual comes within the terms of an expatriation provision and has in fact voluntarily relinquished his citizenship." It was under this advice, as the Secretary concedes, that the relevant departments of the Government have applied the statute and the Constitution to require an ultimate finding of an intent to expatriate.

* * * Insofar as we are advised, this view remained the official position of the United States until the appeal in this case.

As we have said, *Afroyim* requires that the record support a finding that the expatriating act was accompanied by an intent to terminate United States citizenship. The submission of the United States is inconsistent with this holding, and we are unprepared to reconsider it.

III

With respect to the principal issues before it, the Court of Appeals held that Congress was without constitutional authority to prescribe the standard of proof in expatriation proceedings and that the proof in such cases must be by clear and convincing evidence rather than by the preponderance standard prescribed in § 349(c). We are in fundamental disagreement with these conclusions.

In *Nishikawa v. Dulles,* 356 U.S. 129, 78 S.Ct. 612, 2 L.Ed.2d 659 (1958), an American-born citizen, temporarily in Japan, was drafted into the Japanese Army. The Government later claimed that, under § 401(c) of the Nationality Act of 1940, 54 Stat. 1169, he had expatriated himself by serving in the armed forces of a foreign nation. The Government agreed that expatriation had not occurred if Nishikawa's army service had been involuntary. Nishikawa contended that the Government had to prove that his service was voluntary, while the Government urged that duress was an affirmative defense that Nishikawa had the burden to prove by overcoming the usual presumption of voluntariness. This Court held the presumption unavailable to the Government and required proof of a voluntary expatriating act by clear and convincing evidence.

Section 349(c) soon followed; its evident aim was to supplant the evidentiary standards prescribed by *Nishikawa.* The provision "sets up rules of evidence under which the burden of proof to establish loss of citizenship by preponderance of the evidence would rest upon the Government. The presumption of voluntariness under the proposed rules of evidence, would be rebuttable—similarly—by preponderance of the evidence, ..." H.R.Rep. No. 1086, 87th Cong., 1st Sess., 41, U.S.Code Cong. & Admin.News, p. 2985 (1961).

We see no basis for invalidating the evidentiary prescriptions contained in § 349(c). *Nishikawa* was not rooted in the Constitution. The Court noted, moreover, that it was acting in the absence of legislative guidance. Nor do we agree with the Court of Appeals that, because under *Afroyim* Congress is constitutionally devoid of power to impose expatriation on a citizen, it is also without power to prescribe the evidentiary standards to govern expatriation proceedings. Although § 349(c) had been law since 1961, *Afroyim* did not address or advert to that section; surely the Court would have said so had it intended to construe the Constitution to exclude expatriation proceedings from the traditional powers of Congress to prescribe rules of evidence and standards of proof in the federal courts. This power, rooted in the authority of Congress conferred by Art. 1, § 8, cl. 9, of the Constitution to create inferior federal courts, is undoubted and has been frequently noted and sustained.

We note also that the Court's opinion in *Afroyim* was written by Mr. Justice Black who, in concurring in *Nishikawa,* said that the question whether citizenship has been voluntarily relinquished is to be determined on the facts of each case and that Congress could provide rules of evidence for such proceedings. In this respect, we agree with Mr. Justice Black; and since Congress has the express power to enforce the Fourteenth Amendment, it is untenable to hold that it has no power whatsoever to address itself to the manner or means by which Fourteenth Amendment citizenship may be relinquished.

We are unable to conclude that the specific evidentiary standard provided by Congress in § 349(c) is invalid under either the Citizenship Clause or the Due Process Clause of the Fifth Amendment. It is true that in criminal and involuntary commitment contexts we have held that the Due Process Clause imposes requirements of proof beyond a preponderance of the evidence. *Mullaney v. Wilbur,* 421 U.S. 684, 95 S.Ct. 1881, 44 L.Ed.2d 508 (1975); *Addington v. Texas,* 441 U.S. 418, 99 S.Ct. 1804, 60 L.Ed.2d 323 (1979). This Court has also stressed the importance of citizenship and evinced a decided preference for requiring clear and convincing evidence to prove expatriation. *Nishikawa v. United States, supra.* But expatriation proceedings are civil in nature and do not threaten a loss of liberty. Moreover, as we have noted, *Nishikawa* did not purport to be constitutional ruling, and the same is true of similar rulings in related areas. *Woodby v. INS,* 385 U.S. 276, 285, 87 S.Ct. 483, 487, 17 L.Ed.2d 362 (1966) (deportation); *Schneiderman v. United States,* 320 U.S. 118, 125, 63 S.Ct. 1333, 1336, 87 L.Ed. 1779 (1943) (denaturalization). None of these cases involved a congressional judgment, such as that present here, that the preponderance standard of proof provides sufficient protection for the interest of the individual in retaining his citizenship. Contrary to the Secretary's position, we have held that expatriation requires the ultimate finding that the citizen has committed the expatriating act with the intent to renounce his citizenship. This in itself is a heavy burden, and we cannot hold that Congress has exceeded its powers by requiring proof of an intentional expatriating act by a preponderance of evidence.

IV

* * *

It is important at this juncture to note the scope of the statutory presumption. Section 349(c) provides that any of the statutory expatriating acts, if proved, are presumed to have been committed voluntarily. It does not also direct a presumption that the act has been performed with the intent to relinquish United States citizenship. That matter remains the burden of the party claiming expatriation to prove by a preponderance of the evidence. As so understood, we cannot invalidate the provision.[9]

---

9. The Secretary asserts that the § 349(c) presumption cannot survive constitutional scrutiny if we hold that intent to relinquish citizenship is a necessary element in proving expatriation. The predicate for this assertion seems to be that § 349(c) presumes intent to relinquish as well as voluntariness. We do not so read it. Even if we did, and

The majority opinion in *Nishikawa* referred to the "ordinary rule that duress is a matter of affirmative defense" to be proved by the party claiming the duress. Justices Frankfurter and Burton, concurring in the result, also referred to the "ordinarily controlling principles of evidence [that] would suggest that the individual, who is peculiarly equipped to clarify an ambiguity in the meaning of outward events should have the burden of proving what his state of mind was." And Mr. Justice Harlan, in dissent with Mr. Justice Clark, pointed to the "general rule that consciously performed acts are presumed voluntary" and referred to Federal Rule of Civil Procedure 8(c), which treats duress as a matter of affirmative defense. Yet the Court in *Nishikawa,* because it decided that "the consequences of denationalization are so drastic" and because it found nothing indicating a contrary result in the legislative history of the Nationality Act of 1940, held that the Government must carry the burden of proving that the expatriating act was performed voluntarily.

Section 349(c), which was enacted subsequently, and its legislative history make clear that Congress preferred the ordinary rule that voluntariness is presumed and that duress is an affirmative defense to be proved by the party asserting it. * * * The rationality of the procedural rule with respect to claims of involuntariness in ordinary civil cases cannot be doubted. To invalidate the rule here would be to disagree flatly with Congress on the balance to be struck between the interest in citizenship and the burden the Government must assume in demonstrating expatriating conduct. It would also constitutionalize that disagreement and give the Citizenship Clause of the Fourteenth Amendment far more scope in this context than the relevant circumstances that brought the Amendment into being would suggest appropriate. Thus we conclude that the presumption of voluntariness included in § 349(c) has continuing vitality.

V

In sum, we hold that in proving expatriation, an expatriating act and an intent to relinquish citizenship must be proved by a preponderance of the evidence. We also hold that when one of the statutory expatriating acts is proved, it is constitutional to presume it to have been a voluntary act until and unless proved otherwise by the actor. If he succeeds, there can be no expatriation. If he fails, the question remains whether on all the evidence the Government has satisfied its burden of proof that the expatriating act was performed with the necessary intent to relinquish citizenship.

The judgment of the Court of Appeals is reversed, and the case is remanded for further proceedings consistent with this opinion.

So ordered.

* * *

even if we agreed that presuming the necessary intent is inconsistent with *Afroyim,* it would be unnecessary to invalidate the section insofar as it presumes that the expatriating act itself was performed voluntarily.

Mr. Justice Marshall, concurring in part and dissenting in part.

I agree with the Court's holding that a citizen of the United States may not lose his citizenship in the absence of a finding that he specifically intended to renounce it. I also concur in the adoption of a saving construction of INA § 349(a)(2) to require that the statutorily designated expatriating acts be done with a specific intent to relinquish citizenship.

I cannot, however, accept the majority's conclusion that a person may be found to have relinquished his American citizenship upon a preponderance of the evidence that he intended to do so. The Court's discussion of congressional power to "prescribe rules of evidence and standards of proof in the federal courts," is the beginning, not the end, of the inquiry. It remains the task of this Court to determine when those rules and standards impinge on constitutional rights. As my Brother Stevens indicates, the Court's casual dismissal of the importance of American citizenship cannot withstand scrutiny. * * *

For these reasons I cannot understand, much less accept, the Court's suggestion that "expatriation proceedings ... do not threaten a loss of liberty." Recognizing that a standard of proof ultimately " 'reflects the value society places' " on the interest at stake, *Addington v. Texas,* 441 U.S. 418, 425, 99 S.Ct. 1804, 1809, 60 L.Ed.2d 372 (1979), I would hold that a citizen may not lose his citizenship in the absence of clear and convincing evidence that he intended to do so.

Mr. Justice Stevens, concurring in part and dissenting in part.

The Court today unanimously reiterates the principle set forth in *Afroyim v. Rusk,* that Congress may not deprive an American of his citizenship against his will, but may only effectuate the citizen's own intention to renounce his citizenship. I agree with the Court that Congress may establish certain standards for determining whether such a renunciation has occurred. It may, for example, provide that expatriation can be proved by evidence that a person has performed an act that is normally inconsistent with continued citizenship and that the person thereby specifically intended to relinquish his American citizenship.

I do not agree, however, with the conclusion that Congress has established a permissible standard in § 349(a)(2). Since we accept dual citizenship, taking an oath of allegiance to a foreign government is not necessarily inconsistent with an intent to remain an American citizen. Moreover, as now written, the statute cannot fairly be read to require a finding of specific intent to relinquish citizenship. The statute unambiguously states that

"a national of the United States ... shall lose his nationality by—

. . . . .

"(2) taking an oath or making an affirmation or other formal declaration of allegiance to a foreign state or a political subdivision thereof."

There is no room in this provision to imply a requirement of a specific intent to relinquish citizenship. The Court does not attempt to do so, nor does it explain how any other part of the statute supports its conclusion that Congress required proof of specific intent.[1]

I also disagree with the holding that a person may be deprived of his citizenship upon a showing by a mere preponderance of the evidence that he intended to relinquish it. The Court reasons that because the proceedings in question are civil in nature and do not result in any loss of physical liberty, no greater burden of proof is required than in the ordinary civil case. Such reasoning construes the constitutional concept of "liberty" too narrowly.

The House Report accompanying the 1961 amendment to the Immigration and Naturalization Act of 1952 refers to "the dignity and the priceless value of U.S. citizenship." That characterization is consistent with this Court's repeated appraisal of the quality of the interest at stake in this proceeding. In my judgment a person's interest in retaining his American citizenship is surely an aspect of "liberty" of which he cannot be deprived without due process of law. Because the interest at stake is comparable to that involved in *Addington v. Texas,* 441 U.S. 418, 99 S.Ct. 1804, 60 L.Ed.2d 372 [which dealt with involuntary civil commitment], essentially for the reasons stated in The Chief Justice's opinion for a unanimous Court in that case, I believe that due process requires that a clear and convincing standard of proof be met in this case as well before the deprivation may occur.

MR. JUSTICE BRENNAN, with whom MR. JUSTICE STEWART joins as to Part II, dissenting.

The Court holds that one may lose United States citizenship if the Government can prove by a preponderance of the evidence that certain acts, specified by statute, were done with the specific intent of giving up citizenship. Accordingly, the Court, in reversing the judgment of the Court of Appeals, holds that the District Court applied the correct evidentiary standards in determining that appellee was properly stripped of his citizenship. Because I would hold that one who acquires United States citizenship by virtue of being born in the United States, U.S.Const., Amdt.

---

1. It could perhaps be argued that a specific intent requirement can be derived from INA § 349(c). That subsection creates a rebuttable presumption that any expatriating act set forth in subsection (a) was performed "voluntarily." The term "voluntary" could conceivably be stretched to include the concept of a specific intent to renounce one's citizenship. While the person seeking to retain his citizenship would thus have the burden of showing a lack of specific intent, such a construction would at least provide a statutory basis for bringing the issue of intent into the proceeding. The majority apparently would not be willing to accept such a construction in order to salvage the statute, however, inasmuch as it rejects the Secretary's argument that, if there is a requirement of specific intent, it is also subject to the presumption applicable to voluntariness.

The majority's assumption that the statute can be read to require specific intent to relinquish citizenship as an element of proof is also contradicted by the Court's treatment in *Afroyim* of a different subsection of the same statute. Like the subsection at issue here, subsection (a)(5) provided that an American automatically lost his nationality by performing a specific act: in that case, voting in a foreign election. If the majority's analysis in this case was correct, the Court in *Afroyim* should not have invalidated that provision of the statute; rather, it should merely have remanded for a finding as to whether Afroyim had voted in a foreign election with specific intent to relinquish his American citizenship. That the Court did not do so is strong evidence of its belief that the statute could not be reformed as it is today.

14, § 1, can lose that citizenship only by formally renouncing it, and because I would hold that the act of which appellee is accused in this case cannot be an expatriating act, I dissent.

I

This case is governed by *Afroyim v. Rusk*. *Afroyim*, emphasizing the crucial importance of the right of citizenship, held unequivocally that a citizen has "a constitutional right to remain a citizen ... unless he voluntarily relinquishes that citizenship." "[T]he only way the citizenship ... could be lost was by the voluntary renunciation or abandonment by the citizen himself." The Court held that because Congress could not "abridge," "affect," "restrict the effect of," or "take ... away" citizenship, Congress was "without power to rob a citizen of his citizenship" because he voted in a foreign election.

The same clearly must be true of the Government's attempt to strip appellee of citizenship because he swore an oath of allegiance to Mexico. Congress has provided for a procedure by which one may formally renounce citizenship.[2] In this case the appellant concedes that appellee has not renounced his citizenship under that procedure. Because one can lose citizenship only by voluntarily renouncing it and because appellee has not formally renounced his, I would hold that he remains a citizen. Accordingly, I would remand the case with orders that appellee be given a declaration of United States nationality.

II

I reach the same result by another, independent line of reasoning. Appellee was born a dual national. He is a citizen of the United States because he was born here and a citizen of Mexico because his father was Mexican. The only expatriating act of which appellee stands accused is having sworn an oath of allegiance to Mexico. If dual citizenship, *per se*, can be consistent with United States citizenship, *Perkins v. Elg*, 307 U.S. 325, 329, 59 S.Ct. 884, 887, 83 L.Ed. 1320 (1939),[5] then I cannot see why an oath of allegiance to the other country of which one is already a citizen should create inconsistency. One owes allegiance to any country of which one is a citizen, especially when one is living in that country. *Kawakita v. United States*, 343 U.S. 717, 733–735, 72 S.Ct. 950, 960–961, 96 L.Ed. 1249 (1952). The formal oath adds nothing to the existing foreign citizenship and, therefore, cannot affect his United States citizenship.

2. INA § 349(a)(5) provides that "a national of the United States whether by birth or naturalization, shall lose his nationality by ... making a formal renunciation of nationality before a diplomatic or consular officer of the United States in a foreign state, in such form as may be prescribed by the Secretary of State." The Secretary of State has prescribed such procedures in 22 CFR § 50.-50 (1979). See Department of State, 8 Foreign Affairs Manual § 225.6 (1972). Congress also provided for renunciation by citizens while in the United States [during time of war. § 349(a)(6).] This last provision is not relevant to our case.

5. *Rogers v. Bellei*, 401 U.S. 815, 91 S.Ct. 1060, 28 L.Ed.2d 499 (1971), is not to the contrary. Bellei's citizenship was not based on the Fourteenth Amendment, and the issue before the Court was whether Bellei could lose his statutory citizenship for failure to satisfy a condition subsequent contained in the same statute that accorded him citizenship.

Notes

1. Are the dissenters right concerning the procedural issue? Does the Court's approval of the preponderance standard and the presumption of voluntariness represent a significant retreat from its earlier judgments about the preciousness of U.S. citizenship? Why or why not?

2. How do the views of Justice Marshall and Justice Stevens differ? Which is more persuasive on the question of statutory construction? Consider INA § 356 in connection with your answer.

3. Suppose Terrazas had been able to show that he executed the oath—after reading it—only because a Mexican citizenship certificate was required in order to secure a specific job in Mexico. He asserts that, subjectively, his strongest wish throughout the whole process was to retain his dual nationality. Suppose further that he spoke of this wish to many witnesses at the time; hence there is adequate factual support for his assertion. He was not motivated by a desire to surrender his U.S. affiliation, but instead by his desire to get a job. Could he then, consistently with the Constitution, be considered expatriated? What does it mean to find that an individual had a "specific intent to renounce U.S. citizenship"? *See Richards v. Secretary of State,* 752 F.2d 1413, 1421–22 (9th Cir.1985).

4. In 1976 and 1978, Congress amended the law to remove several expatriation provisions that had been declared unconstitutional by the Supreme Court. Pub.L. No. 94–412, § 501(a), 90 Stat. 1258 (1976); Pub.L. No. 95–432, §§ 1, 2, 4, 92 Stat. 1046 (1978). Those that remain appear in the current version of INA § 349, as qualified by §§ 351, 356, and 357. Look through § 349. Which of these provisions are still valid after *Terrazas?*

5. In 1978, several inmates of a state prison in Lucasville, Ohio, wrote to the State Department renouncing their U.S. citizenship and claiming status as citizens of the Soviet Union. Apparently they believed that they might in this way secure the diplomatic interposition of their alleged new country of nationality to protect the human rights they claimed were violated by their incarceration. These letters were clearly meant to be direct expressions of specific intent to terminate U.S. nationality. Yet the State Department refused to consider the inmates as validly expatriated. *See* INA §§ 349(a)(5), (6), 351(a); 22 C.F.R. § 50.50.

What policies are reflected in the provisions of the statute just cited? *See generally Gillars v. United States,* 182 F.2d 962, 981–83 (D.C.Cir.1950); *Davis v. District Director,* 481 F.Supp. 1178 (D.D.C.1979). Do these policies make sense in the conditions of the modern world? However prudent they may be, are they constitutionally valid? That is, in light of the priority *Terrazas* places on the individual's voluntary decisions about his or her own citizenship status, is it permissible to require the commission of specified objective acts (which some persons may have difficulty performing) in addition to an unambiguous expression of intent to renounce?

6. For fiscal year 1981, INS records showed a total of 1,537 persons expatriated, 1,446 of these on the grounds of naturalization in a foreign state. *U.S. Dept. of Justice, 1981 Statistical Yearbook of the Immigration and Naturalization Service*, Table 35, p. 90. The *Statistical Yearbook* provides no comparable figures for denaturalizations (which, as you recall, are imposed only on the ground of fraud or illegality in the original grant). But judging from the volume of reported cases, denaturalizations have almost surely increased in recent years. The increase results from a systematic effort, carried out by the Special Investigations Unit of the Department of Justice, to locate former Nazis and Nazi collaborators who entered the United States illegally, or by fraud or misrepresentation, in the chaotic period following World War II. *See, e.g., Fedorenko v. United States*, 449 U.S. 490, 101 S.Ct. 737, 66 L.Ed.2d 686 (1981); *United States v. Schellong*, 717 F.2d 329 (7th Cir.1983), *cert. denied*, ___ U.S. ___, 104 S.Ct. 1002, 72 L.Ed.2d 234 (1984); *United States v. Kairys*, 600 F.Supp. 1254 (E.D.Ill.1984).

SECTION E.   A CONCLUDING PROBLEM: CITIZENS, ALIENS, AND THE RIGHT TO VOTE

Should permanent resident aliens be entitled to vote in state and federal elections? This question forces us to consider what we mean by the concept of "citizenship". The preceding Chapters have suggested a number of possible answers: citizens are those people who have the power and authority to write the membership (immigration and naturalization) rules of a society; citizens are those people whom a nation cannot send home (deport); citizens are those people who owe a nation allegiance and are entitled to that nation's protection.

Running through each of these descriptions is the idea of membership in a *political community*—a group of human beings united by, and for, self-governance. The Supreme Court has expressed this view of citizenship as follows:

> The exclusion of aliens from basic governmental processes is not a deficiency in the democratic system but a necessary consequence of the community's process of political self-definition. Self-government, whether direct or through representatives, begins by defining the scope of the community of the governed and thus of the governors as well: aliens are by definition outside of this community.

Cabell v. Chavez-Salido, 454 U.S. 432, 439–40, 102 S.Ct. 735, 740, 70 L.Ed.2d 677 (1982).

If this view accurately captures the essence of citizenship, then it is understandable why we, as a society, have little trouble denying aliens the right (or privilege) of voting in state and federal elections. To guarantee aliens a right to vote, so the argument might run, would destroy one of the few remaining distinctions between aliens and citizens and would fatally undermine our understanding of a nation as a self-governing political community.

Counterarguments, however, are possible. The Supreme Court, at least in the nineteenth century, recognized that the terms "voter" and "citizen" were not coterminous. *Minor v. Happersett*, 88 U.S. (21 Wall.) 162, 22 L.Ed. 627 (1875) (upholding state law denying women the right to vote). Furthermore, throughout the nineteenth century a number of states extended voting rights to aliens. Rosberg, *Aliens and Equal Protection: Why Not the Right to Vote?*, 75 Mich.L.Rev. 1092, 1093–1100 (1977).

Consider the following attempt to unlink the concepts of voting and citizenship.

GERALD M. ROSBERG, ALIENS AND EQUAL PROTECTION: WHY NOT THE RIGHT TO VOTE?

75 Mich.L.Rev. 1092, 1127–1135 (1977).

Immigrants who have arrived recently in the United States may know little about this country's institutions of government or about the issues on which election campaigns are fought. They can certainly learn about these matters, and it would not take very long for many of them to gain this knowledge. But in all likelihood many immigrants are also largely ignorant of this country's values and traditions and therefore cannot have developed an appreciation of or commitment to them. The naturalization requirement for voting could be seen as responsive to this concern in two different ways. First, the durational residence feature gives the immigrant an opportunity to develop a feel for American values and traditions. Second, the act of naturalization itself represents a formal and solemn commitment to the country, its values, and its institutions. The testing of a prospective citizen's loyalty, knowledge, and character is critical, under this view, not so much because it screens out the undeserving candidate but rather because it makes the attainment of naturalization difficult and meaningful. The judicial setting and the oath of renunciation and allegiance (with its grand language about foreign princes and potentates and bearing true faith and allegiance to the United States) drive home to the new citizen the significance of the occasion. It all adds up to a very deliberate and ritualized act of opting into the community and accepting its values and traditions as one's own.

In my view, this argument is the most substantial one that can be made in defense of the citizenship qualification for voting. And yet it is by no means free of difficulty. If everything is going to turn on a sense of commitment to the country's values and traditions, it would seem important to know exactly what values and traditions * * * we have in mind. * * *

The very fact that neither candidate in an election wins all the votes is in itself a good indication that the electorate is already divided on fundamental value questions. Political analysts typically assume that different segments of American society—Catholics, Chicanos, blue-collar workers, Polish-Americans—have their own values and traditions that influence their voting behavior. To which set of values and traditions are the aliens expected to commit themselves? Do we exclude them from the polls until they have narrowed the choice to two—the Democratic tradition and the Republican tradition—and then turn them loose to make a free choice between Alexander Hamilton and Thomas Jefferson? Or is it rather that the central value and tradition of this country is that there is no central value and tradition? Perhaps aliens are entitled to hold whatever views they want, but they cannot be allowed to vote until they have come to understand and cherish the fact that they may hold whatever views they want. One has an intuitive sense that an alien who has not been socialized in the United States will lack certain characteristics or attitudes that are fundamentally American. But given the diversity of socialization experiences available in the United States, this intuition would seem a rather treacherous foundation on which to build an argument of compelling state interest.

Instead of trying to determine the substantive content of the country's values and traditions, one might do better to focus on the act of commitment to the United States that naturalization apparently involves. In terms of values, culture, and language, resident aliens may be indistinguishable from at least some group of American citizens. And their loyalty may be beyond question, at least in the sense that they think well of the country and wish it no harm. But what may be lacking is a willingness on the part of resident aliens to identify themselves with the country and its people and to give up once and for all their attachment to the countries in which they were born. The unnaturalized alien is perhaps holding something back, refusing to join in. * * *

[But] it is simply not correct to say that unnaturalized aliens have made no commitment to the United States. In contrast to native-born citizens, whose commitment, if any, is tacit, resident aliens have committed themselves knowingly and voluntarily. They have all had to make considerable effort to qualify for an immigrant visa, which is ordinarily a good deal harder to obtain than a certificate of naturalization. Even after proving themselves qualified, they have had to wait months and even more often years for a visa to become available. And they have given up their homes in the countries of their birth and resettled in the United States. Moreover, most resident aliens had ties to the United States even before they arrived, for they have tended to follow their countrymen and kinsmen in chains of migration. * * *

* * *

* * * We have come to accept and even cherish the fact that many citizens will retain what Justice Frankfurter called "old cultural loyalty"[125] to another country, and the line between cultural matters and political matters is known to be indistinct. The internment during the Second World War of persons of Japanese ancestry—citizen and alien alike—is a powerful reminder of how far we have been willing to go on the supposition that national origin may be much more accurately predictive of loyalty than is citizenship. In short, it is hard to see what it is about

125. * * * *Baumgartner v. United States,*
322 U.S. 665, 674 (1944).

resident aliens that makes us insist on excluding them from the polls for want of the necessary commitment to the United States.

Yet it may be objected that the net effect of this kind of argument is to deny the existence of any distinction at all between the citizen and the alien. If the alien is indistinguishable from the citizen in terms of knowledge of affairs in the United States, loyalty, and commitment to the people and institutions of the United States, and if for that reason the alien has a constitutional right to vote, then it may appear that the concept of citizenship has been robbed of all its meaning. Plainly, nothing that I have said would jeopardize the distinction between the citizen and the nonresident alien. But one might insist that under the view presented here resident aliens would in effect be naturalized as of the moment they take up residence in the United States. Much of the difficulty arises, however, from the assumed equation of citizenship and voting. My argument is not that resident aliens look like citizens, so therefore they must be citizens. It is rather that in pertinent respects resident aliens are enough like citizens that it may be unconstitutional to distinguish between them in allocating the right to vote.

Citizens have historically enjoyed certain rights and undertaken certain obligations that resident aliens did not share. Every time one of those rights or obligations is passed on to aliens the gap between citizens and aliens narrows. If we are determined to maintain a gap, to preserve a sense of "we" and "they," we could disqualify aliens from owning land or deny them welfare benefits or make them all wear green hats. The imposition of these disabilities on aliens may seem intolerable. But why should it be any more tolerable to make the burden of preserving the distinction between citizens and aliens fall exclusively on the right to vote, the most precious right of all?

Moreover, extending the franchise to aliens would not, in fact, completely close the gap between citizens and aliens, since voting is not the only distinction between the two that survives the Supreme Court's recent decisions on the rights of aliens. By the terms of the Constitution itself aliens are ineligible to hold certain offices in the government of the United States. Aliens do not have the same right as citizens to gain admission to the United States. Citizens born abroad can take up residence in this country whenever they desire. Citizens can abandon their residence in the United States without fear of losing their right to return. Aliens, on the other hand, gain the right to reside in the United States only upon compliance with the stringent terms of the immigration laws. And resident aliens who abandon their domicile in this country will not necessarily be readmitted. When citizens travel outside the United States they carry American passports, and they expect and ordinarily receive the diplomatic protection of the United States when the need for it arises. Aliens, even resident aliens, have no right to call upon the United States for that protection and would not receive it in any case. Citizens are entitled to have the government represent their interests in international tribunals. Aliens have no such right, and under international law the government would be barred from representing them even if it had any interest in doing so. Citizens are generally free from any obligation to register with the government or to inform the government regularly of their whereabouts. Aliens are subject to rather elaborate reporting requirements. Citizens can be held to account in American courts for conduct overseas in some circumstances where aliens apparently cannot. Citizens can confer an immigration preference on their relatives overseas in a considerable number of situations where aliens cannot.

* * * Considering the primacy of the right to vote one could reasonably argue that it is distinctions like these that should bear the burden of differentiating citizens from aliens, and not the distinction between voting and not voting. We could, in other words, grant the right to vote to resident aliens and still leave them readily distinguishable from citizens. Yet that result would remain unacceptable to those who believe that allowing aliens to vote would eviscerate the concept of citizenship. Their assumption must be that political rights are inherently and properly rights of citizenship, whereas civil rights have no necessary connection with citizenship and properly belong to "persons." In the earliest part of the country's history, however, the assumption was precisely the reverse: citizenship "carried with it civil rights but no political privileges." [128] Citizenship, and in particular naturalization, was thought important because it determined whether or not a new settler would be able to own and convey land. Even today, * * * the Supreme Court insists that citizenship as such confers no right to vote. Indeed, it would seem anomalous to equate citizenship with voting so long as we separate the power to make persons citizens from the power to make persons voters. The former power inheres in the national government, the latter in the states.

Yet I cannot deny the existence of a widespread assumption that the right to vote is not only a right of citizenship, but the quintessential right of citizenship. And the conferral of the right to vote on aliens would undermine that assumption. But where does the assumption come from, and why should we insist on preserving it? Intuitively, it seems that there must be some explanation for the assumption. After all, the very fact that it is so widespread may be an indication that it responds to some important inner need of citizens to distinguish themselves from what are perceived to be outsiders, even where the outsiders are their neighbors. But I do not believe that it is possible to articulate an explanation for this assumption without moving the discussion to a level of extremely high abstraction and without putting a great deal of weight on symbolic values. To sustain the disenfranchisement of aliens on the strength of that kind of reasoning would be fundamentally inconsistent, it seems to me, with our ordinary approach in determining which state interests are compelling. I am reluctant to conclude that, because I have so much difficulty articulating the state's interest, it must be less than compelling. But I am confident at least that the validity of laws denying aliens the vote is by no means self-evident. It is surely not enough to tip one's hat at the state interest in having knowledgeable and loyal voters and let it go at that.

---

128. Start, *Naturalization in the English Colonies in North America,* in American Historical Assn., Annual Report for the Year 1893, at 319 (1894).

Questions

Suppose the Supreme Court were to decide that state laws denying permanent resident aliens the right to vote in state elections violate the Equal Protection Clause. Would such a ruling rob citizenship of all its meaning? Is the right to participate in political affairs the only remaining significant difference between U.S. citizens and permanent resident aliens? What *does* it mean to be a *citizen* of the United States?

Appendix A

THE IMMIGRATION AND NATIONALITY ACT

Selected Provisions

Act of June 27, 1952, 66 Stat. 163,

as amended through 1984, 8 U.S.C.A. 1101, et seq.

TITLE I—GENERAL

DEFINITIONS

Sec. 101. [8 U.S.C. 1101] (a) As used in this Act—

* * *

(3) The term "alien" means any person not a citizen or national of the United States.

(4) The term "application for admission" has reference to the application for admission into the United States and not to the application for the issuance of an immigrant or nonimmigrant visa.

* * *

(8) The terms "Commissioner" and "Deputy Commissioner" mean the Commissioner of Immigration and Naturalization and a Deputy Commissioner of Immigration and Naturalization, respectively.

(9) The term "consular officer" means any consular, diplomatic, or other officer of the United States designated under regulations prescribed under authority contained in this Act, for the purpose of issuing immigrant or nonimmigrant visas.

(10) The term "crewman" means a person serving in any capacity on board a vessel or aircraft.

* * *

(13) The term "entry" means any coming of an alien into the United States, from a foreign port or place or from an outlying possession, whether voluntarily or otherwise, except that an alien having a lawful permanent residence in the United States shall not be regarded as making an entry into the United States for the purposes of the immigration laws if the alien proves to the satisfaction of the Attorney General that his departure to a foreign port or place or to an outlying possession was not intended or reasonably to be expected by him or his presence in a foreign

port or place or in an outlying possession was not voluntary: *Provided,* That no person whose departure from the United States was occasioned by deportation proceedings, extradition, or other legal process shall be held to be entitled to such exception.

(14) The term "foreign state" includes outlying possessions of a foreign state, but self-governing dominions and territories under mandate or trusteeship shall be regarded as separate foreign states.

(15) The term "immigrant" means every alien except an alien who is within one of the following classes of nonimmigrant aliens—

(A)(i) an ambassador, public minister, or career diplomatic or consular officer who has been accredited by a foreign government recognized de jure by the United States and who is accepted by the President or by the Secretary of State, and the members of the alien's immediate family;

(ii) upon a basis of reciprocity, other officials and employees who have been accredited by a foreign government recognized de jure by the United States, who are accepted by the Secretary of State, and the members of their immediate families; and

(iii) upon a basis of reciprocity, attendants, servants, personal employees, and members of their immediate families, of the officials and employees who have a nonimmigrant status under (i) and (ii) above;

(B) an alien (other than one coming for the purpose of study or of performing skilled or unskilled labor or as a representative of foreign press, radio, film, or other foreign information media coming to engage in such vocation) having a residence in a foreign country which he has no intention of abandoning and who is visiting the United States temporarily for business or temporarily for pleasure;

(C) an alien in immediate and continuous transit through the United States, or an alien who qualifies as a person entitled to pass in transit to and from the United Nations Headquarters District and foreign countries, under the provisions of paragraphs (3), (4), and (5) of section 11 of the Headquarters Agreement with the United Nations (61 Stat. 758);

(D) an alien crewman serving in good faith as such in any capacity required for normal operation and service on board a vessel (other than a fishing vessel having its home port or an operating base in the United States) or aircraft, who intends to land temporarily and solely in pursuit of his calling as a crewman and to depart from the United States with the vessel or aircraft on which he arrived or some other vessel or aircraft;

(E) an alien entitled to enter the United States under and in pursuance of the provisions of a treaty of commerce and navigation between the United States and the foreign state of which he is a national, and the spouse and children of any such alien if accompanying or following to join him: (i) solely to carry on substantial trade, principally between the United States and the foreign state of which he is a national; or (ii) solely to develop and direct the operations of an enterprise in which he has invested, or of an enterprise in which he is actively in the process of investing, a substantial amount of capital;

(F)(i) an alien having a residence in a foreign country which he has no intention of abandoning, who is a bona fide student qualified to pursue a full course of study and who seeks to enter the United States temporarily and solely for the purpose of pursuing such a course of study at an established college, university, seminary, conservatory, academic high school, elementary school, or other academic institution or in a language training program in the United States, particularly designated by him and approved by the Attorney General after consultation with the Secretary of Education, which institution or place of study shall have agreed to report to the Attorney General the termination of attendance of each nonimmigrant student, and if any such institution of learning or place of study fails to make reports promptly the approval shall be withdrawn, and (ii) the alien spouse or minor children of any such alien if accompanying him or following to join him;

(G)(i) a designated principal resident representative of a foreign government recognized de jure by the United States, which foreign government is a member of an international organization entitled to enjoy privileges, exemptions, and immunities as an international organization under the International Organizations Immunities Act (59 Stat. 669) [22 U.S.C. 288, note], accredited resident members of the staff of such representatives, and members of his or their immediate family;

(ii) other accredited representatives of such a foreign government to such international organizations, and the members of their immediate families;

(iii) an alien able to qualify under (i) or (ii) above except for the fact that the government of which such alien is an accredited representative is not recognized de jure by the United States, or that the government of which he is an accredited representative is not a member of such international organization, and the members of his immediate family;

(iv) officers, or employees of such international organizations, and the members of their immediate families;

(v) attendants, servants, and personal employees of any such representative, officer, or employee, and the members of the immediate families of such attendants, servants, and personal employees;

(H) an alien having a residence in a foreign country which he has no intention of abandoning (i) who is of distinguished merit and ability and who is coming temporarily to the United States to perform services of an exceptional nature requiring such merit and ability, and who, in the case of a graduate of a medical school coming to the United States to perform services as a member of the medical profession, is coming pursuant to an invitation from a public or nonprofit private education or research institution or agency in the United States to teach or conduct research, or both, at or for such institution or agency; or (ii) who is coming temporarily to the United States to perform temporary services or labor, if unemployed persons capable of performing such service or labor cannot be found in this country, but this clause shall not apply to graduates of medical schools coming to the United States to perform services as members of the medical profession; or (iii) who is coming temporarily to the United States as a trainee, other than to receive graduate medical education or training; and the alien spouse and minor children of any such alien specified in this paragraph if accompanying him or following to join him;

(I) upon a basis of reciprocity, an alien who is a bona fide representative of foreign press, radio, film, or other foreign information media, who seeks to enter the United States solely to engage in such vocation, and the spouse and children of such a representative if accompanying or following to join him;

(J) an alien having a residence in a foreign country which he has no intention of abandoning who is a bona fide student, scholar, trainee, teacher, professor, research assistant, specialist, or leader in a field of specialized knowledge or skill, or other person of similar description, who is coming temporarily to the United States as a participant in a program designated by the Director of the United States Information Agency, for the purpose of teaching, instructing or lecturing, studying, observing, conducting research, consulting, demonstrating special skills, or receiving training and who, if he is coming to the United States to participate in a program under which he will receive graduate medical education or training, also meets the requirements of section 212(j), and the alien spouse and minor children of any such alien if accompanying him or following to join him;

(K) an alien who is the fiancée or fiancé of a citizen of the United States and who seeks to enter the United States solely to conclude a valid marriage with the petitioner within ninety days after entry, and the minor children of such fiancée or fiancé accompanying him or following to join him;

(L) an alien who, immediately preceding the time of his application for admission into the United States, has been employed continuously for one year by a firm or corporation or other legal entity or an affiliate or subsidiary thereof and who seeks to enter the United States temporarily in order to continue to render his services to the same employer or a subsidiary or affiliate thereof in a capacity that is managerial, executive, or involves specialized knowledge, and the alien spouse and minor children of any such alien if accompanying him or following to join him.

(M)(i) an alien having a residence in a foreign country which he has no intention of abandoning who seeks to enter the United States temporarily and solely for the purpose of pursuing a full course of study at an established vocational or other recognized nonacademic institution (other than in a language training program) in the United States particularly designated by him and approved by the Attorney General, after consultation with the Secretary of Education, which institution shall have agreed to report to the Attorney General the termination of attendance of each nonimmigrant nonacademic student and if any such institution fails to make reports promptly the approval shall be withdrawn, and (ii) the alien spouse and minor children of any such alien if accompanying him or following to join him.

* * *

(18) The term "immigration officer" means any employee or class of employees of the Service or of the United States designated by the Attorney General, individually or by regulation, to perform the functions of an immigration officer specified by this Act or any section thereof.

(19) The term "ineligible to citizenship," when used in reference to any individual, means, notwithstanding the provisions of any treaty relating to military service, an individual who is, or was at any time, permanently debarred from becoming a citizen of the United States under section 3(a) of the Selective Training and Service Act of 1940, as amended (54 Stat. 885; 55 Stat. 844), or under section 4(a) of the Selective Service Act of 1948, as amended (62 Stat. 605; 65 Stat. 76) [50 U.S.C. App. 454], or under any section of this Act, or any other Act, or under any law amendatory of, supplementary to, or in substitution for, any of such sections or Acts.

(20) The term "lawfully admitted for permanent residence" means the status of having been lawfully accorded the privilege of residing permanently in the United States as an immigrant in accordance with the immigration laws, such status not having changed.

(21) The term "national" means a person owing permanent allegiance to a state.

(22) The term "national of the United States" means (A) a citizen of the United States, or (B) a person who, though not a citizen of the United States, owes permanent allegiance to the United States.

(23) The term "naturalization" means the conferring of nationality of a state upon a person after birth, by any means whatsoever.

* * *

(26) The term "nonimmigrant visa" means a visa properly issued to an alien as an eligible nonimmigrant by a competent officer as provided in this Act.

(27) The term "special immigrant" means—

(A) an immigrant, lawfully admitted for permanent residence, who is returning from a temporary visit abroad;

(B) an immigrant who was a citizen of the United States and may, under section 324(a) or 327 of title III, apply for reacquisition of citizenship;

(C)(i) an immigrant who continuously for at least two years immediately preceding the time of his application for admission to the United States has been, and who seeks to enter the United States solely for the purpose of carrying on the vocation of minister of a religious denomination, and whose services are needed by such religious denomination having a bona fide organization in the United States; and (ii) the spouse or the child of any such immigrant, if accompanying or following to join him;

(D) an immigrant who is an employee, or an honorably retired former employee, of the United States Government abroad, and who has performed faithful service for a total of fifteen years, or more, and his accompanying spouse and children: *Provided,* That the principal officer of a Foreign Service establishment, in his discretion, shall have recommended the granting of special immigrant status to such alien in exceptional circumstances and the Secretary of State approves such recommendation and finds that it is in the national interest to grant such status;

(E) an immigrant, and his accompanying spouse and children, who is or has been an employee of the Panama Canal Company or Canal Zone Government before the date on which the Panama Canal Treaty of 1977 (as described in section 3(a)(1) of the Panama Canal Act of 1979) enters into force, [October 1, 1979] who was resident in the Canal Zone on the effective date of the exchange of instruments of ratification of such Treaty, [April 1, 1979] and who has performed faithful service as such an employee for one year or more;

(F) an immigrant, and his accompanying spouse and children, who is a Panamanian national and (i) who, before the date on which such Panama Canal Treaty of 1977 enters into force, [October 1, 1979] has been honorably retired from United States Government employment in the Canal Zone with a total of 15 years or more of faithful service, or (ii) who on the date on which such Treaty enters into force, has been employed by the United States Government in the Canal Zone with a total of 15 years or more of faithful service and who subsequently is honorably retired from such employment; or

(G) an immigrant, and his accompanying spouse and children, who was an employee of the Panama Canal Company or Canal Zone government on the effective date of the exchange of instruments of ratification of such Panama Canal Treaty of 1977, [April 1, 1979] who has performed faithful service for five years or more as such an employee, and whose personal safety, or the personal safety of whose spouse or children, as a direct result of such Treaty, is reasonably placed in danger because of the special nature of any of that employment; or

(H) an immigrant, and his accompanying spouse and children, who—

(i) has graduated from a medical school or has qualified to practice medicine in a foreign state,

(ii) was fully and permanently licensed to practice medicine in a State on January 9, 1978 and was practicing medicine in a State on that date,

(iii) entered the United States as a nonimmigrant under subsection (a)(15)(H) or (a)(15)(J) of this section before January 10, 1978, and

(iv) has been continuously present in the United States in the practice or study of medicine since the date of such entry.

* * *

(29) The term "outlying possessions of the United States" means American Samoa and Swains Island.

(30) The term "passport" means any travel document issued by competent authority showing the bearer's origin, identity, and nationality if any, which is valid for the entry of the bearer into a foreign country.

(31) The term "permanent" means a relationship of continuing or lasting nature, as distinguished from temporary, but a relationship may be permanent even though it is one that may be dissolved eventually at the instance either of the United States or of the individual, in accordance with law.

(32) the term "profession" shall include but not be limited to architects, engineers, lawyers, physicians, surgeons, and teachers in elementary or secondary schools, colleges, academies, or seminaries.

(33) The term "residence" means the place of general abode; the place of general abode of a person means his principal, actual dwelling place in fact, without regard to intent.

(34) The term "Service" means the Immigration and Naturalization Service of the Department of Justice.

(35) The term "spouse", "wife", or "husband" does not include a spouse, wife, or husband by reason of any marriage ceremony where the contracting parties thereto are not physically present in the presence of each other, unless the marriage shall have been consummated.

* * *

(39) The term "unmarried", when used in reference to any individual as of any time, means an individual who at such time is not married, whether or not previously married.

* * *

(42) The term "refugee" means (A) any person who is outside any country of such person's nationality or, in the case of a person having no nationality, is outside any country in which such person last habitually resided, and who is unable or unwilling to return to, and is unable or unwilling to avail himself or herself of the protection of, that country because of persecution or a well-founded fear of persecution on account of race, religion, nationality, membership in a particular social group, or political opinion, or (B) in such circumstances as the President after appropriate consultation (as defined in section 207(e) of this Act) may

specify, any person who is within the country of such person's nationality or, in the case of a person having no nationality, within the country in which such person is habitually residing, and who is persecuted or who has a well-founded fear of persecution on account of race, religion, nationality, membership in a particular social group, or political opinion. The term "refugee" does not include any person who ordered, incited, assisted, or otherwise participated in the persecution of any person on account of race, religion, nationality, membership in a particular social group, or political opinion.

(b) As used in titles I and II—

(1) The term "child" means an unmarried person under twenty-one years of age who is—

(A) a legitimate child; or

(B) a stepchild, whether or not born out of wedlock, provided the child had not reached the age of eighteen years at the time the marriage creating the status of stepchild occurred; or

(C) a child legitimated under the law of the child's residence or domicile, or under the law of the father's residence or domicile, whether in or outside the United States, if such legitimation takes place before the child reaches the age of eighteen years and the child is in the legal custody of the legitimating parent or parents at the time of such legitimation;

(D) an illegitimate child, by, through whom, or on whose behalf a status, privilege, or benefit is sought by virtue of the relationship of the child to its natural mother;

(E) a child adopted while under the age of sixteen years if the child has thereafter been in the legal custody of, and has resided with, the adopting parent or parents for at least two years: *Provided,* That no natural parent of any such adopted child shall thereafter, by virtue of such parentage, be accorded any right, privilege, or status under this Act; or

(F) a child, under the age of sixteen at the time a petition is filed in his behalf to accord a classification as an immediate relative under section 201(b), who is an orphan because of the death or disappearance of, abandonment or desertion by, or separation or loss from, both parents, or for whom the sole or surviving parent is incapable of providing the proper care and has in writing irrevocably released the child for emigration and adoption; who has been adopted abroad by a United States citizen and spouse jointly, or by an unmarried United States citizen at least twenty-five years of age, who personally saw and observed the child prior to or during the adoption proceedings; or who is coming to the United States for adoption by a United States citizen and spouse jointly, or by an unmarried United States citizen at least twenty-five years of age, who have or has complied with the preadoption requirements, if any, of the child's proposed residence: *Provided,* That the Attorney General is satisfied that proper care will be furnished the child if admitted to the United States: *Provided further,* That no natural parent or prior adoptive parent of any such child shall thereafter, by virtue of such parentage, be accorded any right, privilege, or status under this Act.

(2) The term "parent", "father", or "mother" means a parent, father, or mother only where the relationship exists by reason of any of the circumstances set forth in (1) above.

(3) The term "person" means an individual or an organization.

(4) The term "special inquiry officer" means any immigration officer who the Attorney General deems specially qualified to conduct specified classes of proceedings, in whole or in part, required by this Act to be conducted by or before a special inquiry officer and who is designated and selected by the Attorney General, individually or by regulation, to conduct such proceedings. Such special inquiry officer shall be subject to such supervision and shall perform such duties, not inconsistent with this Act, as the Attorney General shall prescribe.

(5) The term "adjacent islands" includes Saint Pierre, Miquelon, Cuba, the Dominican Republic, Haiti, Bermuda, the Bahamas, Barbados, Jamaica, the Windward and Leeward Islands, Trinidad, Martinique, and other British, French, and Netherlands territory or possessions in or bordering on the Caribbean Sea.

(c) As used in title III—

(1) The term "child" means an unmarried person under twenty-one years of age and includes a child legitimated under the law of the child's residence or domicile, or under the law of the father's residence or domicile, whether in the United States or elsewhere, and, except as otherwise provided in sections 320, 321, 322, and 323 of title III, a child adopted in the United States, if such legitimation or adoption takes place before the child reaches the age of sixteen years, and the child is in the legal custody of the legitimating or adopting parent or parents at the time of such legitimation or adoption.

(2) The terms "parent", "father", and "mother" include in the case of a posthumous child a deceased parent, father, and mother.

* * *

(f) For the purposes of this Act—

No person shall be regarded as, or found to be, a person of good moral character who, during the period for which good moral character is required to be established, is, or was—

(1) a habitual drunkard;

(2) Repealed.

(3) a member of one or more of the classes of persons, whether excludable or not, described in paragraphs (11), (12), and (31) of section 212(a) of this Act; or paragraphs (9), (10), and (23) of section 212(a), if the offense described therein, for which such person was convicted or of which he admits the commission, was committed during such period;

(4) one whose income is derived principally from illegal gambling activities;

(5) one who has been convicted of two or more gambling offenses committed during such period;

(6) one who has given false testimony for the purpose of obtaining any benefits under this Act;

(7) one who during such period has been confined, as a result of conviction, to a penal institution for an aggregate period of one hundred and eighty days or more, regardless of whether the offense, or offenses, for which he has been confined were committed within or without such period;

(8) one who at any time has been convicted of the crime of murder.

The fact that any person is not within any of the foregoing classes shall not preclude a finding that for other reasons such person is or was not of good moral character.

(g) For the purposes of this Act any alien ordered deported (whether before or after the enactment of this Act) who has left the United States, shall be considered to have been deported in pursuance of law, irrespective of the source from which the expenses of his transportation were defrayed or of the place to which he departed.

* * *

POWERS AND DUTIES OF THE ATTORNEY GENERAL AND THE COMMISSIONER

Sec. 103. [8 U.S.C. 1103] (a) The Attorney General shall be charged with the administration and enforcement of this act and all other laws relating to the immigration and naturalization of aliens, except insofar as this Act or such laws relate to the powers, functions, and duties conferred upon the President, the Secretary of State, the officers of the Department of State, or diplomatic or consular officers: *Provided, however,* That determination and ruling by the Attorney General with respect to all questions of law shall be controlling. He shall have control, direction, and supervision of all employees and of all the files and records of the Service. He shall establish such regulations; prescribe such forms of bond, reports, entries, and other papers; issue such instructions; and perform such other acts as he deems necessary for carrying out his authority under the provisions of this Act. He is authorized, in accordance with the civil-service laws and regulations and the Classification Act of 1949, to appoint such employees of the Service as he deems necessary, and to delegate to them or to any officer or employee of the Department of Justice in his discretion any of the duties and powers imposed upon him in this Act; he may require or authorize any employee of the Service or the Department of Justice to perform or exercise any of the powers, privileges, or duties conferred or imposed by this Act or regulations issued thereunder upon any other employee of the Service. He shall have the power and duty to control and guard the boundaries and borders of the United States against the illegal entry of aliens and shall, in his discretion, appoint for that purpose such number of employees of the Service as to him shall appear necessary and proper. He is authorized to confer or impose upon any employee of the United States, with the consent of the head of the Department or other independent establishment under whose jurisdiction the employee is serving, any of the powers, privileges, or duties conferred or imposed by this Act or regulations issued thereunder upon officers or employees of the Service. He may, with the concurrence of the Secretary of State, establish offices of the Service in foreign countries; and, after consultation with the Secretary of State, he may, whenever in his judgment such action may be necessary to accomplish the purposes of this Act, detail employees of the Service for duty in foreign countries.

(b) The Commissioner shall be a citizen of the United States and shall be appointed by the President, by and with the advice and consent of the Senate, and shall receive compensation at the rate of $17,500 per annum. He shall be charged with any and all responsibilities and authority in the administration of the Service and of this Act which are conferred upon the Attorney General as may be delegated to him by the Attorney General or which may be prescribed by the Attorney General.

POWERS AND DUTIES OF THE SECRETARY OF STATE; BUREAU OF SECURITY AND CONSULAR AFFAIRS

Sec. 104. [8 U.S.C. 1104] (a) The Secretary of State shall be charged with the administration and the enforcement of the provisions of this Act and all other immigration and nationality laws relating to (1) the powers, duties and functions of diplomatic and consular officers of the United States, except those powers, duties and functions conferred upon the consular officers relating to the granting or refusal of visas; (2) the powers, duties and functions of the Bureau of Consular Affairs; and (3) the determination of nationality of a person not in the United States. He shall establish such regulations; prescribe such forms of reports, entries and other papers; issue such instructions; and perform such other acts as he deems necessary for carrying out such provisions. He is authorized to confer or impose upon any employee of the United States, with the consent of the head of the department or independent establishment under whose jurisdiction the employee is serving, any of the powers, functions, or duties conferred or imposed by this Act or regulations issued thereunder upon officers or employees of the Department of State or of the American Foreign Service.

(b) There is established in the Department of State a Bureau of Consular Affairs, to be headed by an Assistant Secretary of State for Consular Affairs. The Assistant Secretary of State for Consular Affairs shall be a citizen of the United States, qualified by experience, and shall maintain close liaison with the appropriate committees of Congress in order that they may be advised regarding the administration of this Act by consular officers. He shall be charged with any and all responsibility and authority in the administration of the Bureau and of this Act which are conferred on the Secretary of State as may be delegated to him by the Secretary of State or which may be prescribed by the Secretary of State.

He shall also perform such other duties as the Secretary of State may prescribe.

(c) Within the Bureau there shall be a Passport Office, a Visa Office, and such other offices as the Secretary of State may deem to be appropriate, each office to be headed by a director. The Directors of the Passport Office and the Visa Office shall be experienced in the administration of the nationality and immigration laws.

(d) The functions heretofore performed by the Passport Division and the Visa Division of the Department of State shall hereafter be performed by the Passport Office and the Visa Office, respectively, of the Bureau of Consular Affairs.

(e) There shall be a General Counsel of the Visa Office, who shall be appointed by the Secretary of State and who shall serve under the general direction of the Legal Adviser of the Department of State. The General Counsel shall have authority to maintain liaison with the appropriate officers of the Service with a view to securing uniform interpretations of the provisions of this Act.

* * *

JUDICIAL REVIEW OF ORDERS OF DEPORTATION AND EXCLUSION

Sec. 106. [8 U.S.C. 1105a] (a) The procedure prescribed by, and all the provisions of the Act of December 29, 1950, as amended[1] (64 Stat. 1129; 68 Stat. 961; 5 U.S.C. 1031 et seq.), shall apply to, and shall be the sole and exclusive procedure for, the judicial review of all final orders of deportation heretofore or hereafter made against aliens within the United States pursuant to administrative proceedings under section 242(b) of this Act or comparable provisions of any prior Act, except that—

(1) a petition for review may be filed not later than six months from the date of the final deportation order or from the effective date of this section, whichever is the later;

(2) the venue of any petition for review under this section shall be in the judicial circuit in which the administrative proceedings before a special inquiry officer were conducted in whole or in part, or in the judicial circuit wherein is the residence, as defined in this Act, of the petitioner, but not in more than one circuit;

(3) the action shall be brought against the Immigration and Naturalization Service, as respondent. Service of the petition to review shall be made upon the Attorney General of the United States and upon the official of the Immigration and Naturalization Service in charge of the Service district in which the office of the clerk of the court is located. The service of the petition for review upon such official of the Service shall stay the deportation of the alien pending determination of the petition by the court, unless the court otherwise directs;

1. Act of Dec. 29, 1950, as amended, was repealed by Pub.L. 89–554, Sept. 6, 1966, § 8, 80 Stat. 656, and reenacted by § 4(e) thereof, 80 Stat. 621, as chapter 158 of title 28, United States Code.

(4) except as provided in clause (B) of paragraph (5) of this subsection, the petition shall be determined solely upon the administrative record upon which the deportation order is based and the Attorney General's findings of fact, if supported by reasonable, substantial, and probative evidence on the record considered as a whole, shall be conclusive;

(5) whenever any petitioner, who seeks review of an order under this section, claims to be a national of the United States and makes a showing that his claim is not frivolous, the court shall (A) pass upon the issues presented when it appears from the pleadings and affidavits filed by the parties that no genuine issue of material fact is presented; or (B) where a genuine issue of material fact as to the petitioner's nationality is presented, transfer the proceedings to a United States district court for the district where the petitioner has his residence for hearing de novo of the nationality claim and determination as if such proceedings were originally initiated in the district court under the provisions of section 2201 of title 28, United States Code. Any such petitioner shall not be entitled to have such issue determined under section 360(a) of this Act or otherwise;

(6) if the validity of a deportation order has not been judicially determined, its validity may be challenged in a criminal proceeding against the alien for violation of subsection (d) or (e) of section 242 of this Act only by separate motion for judicial review before trial. Such motion shall be determined by the court without a jury and before the trial of the general issue. Whenever a claim to United States nationality is made in such motion, and in the opinion of the court, a genuine issue of material fact as to the alien's nationality is presented, the court shall accord him a hearing de novo on the nationality claim and determine that issue as if proceedings had been initiated under the provisions of section 2201 of title 28, United States Code. Any such alien shall not be entitled to have such issue determined under section 360(a) of this Act or otherwise. If no such hearing de novo as to nationality is conducted, the determination shall be made solely upon the administrative record upon which the deportation order is based and the Attorney General's findings of fact, if supported by reasonable, substantial and probative evidence on the record considered as a whole, shall be conclusive. If the deportation order is held invalid, the court shall dismiss the indictment and the United States shall have the right to appeal to the court of appeals within thirty days. The procedure on such appeals shall be as provided in the Federal rules of criminal procedure. No petition for review under this section may be filed by any alien during the pendency of a criminal proceeding against such alien for violation of subsection (d) or (e) of section 242 of this Act;

(7) nothing in this section shall be construed to require the Attorney General to defer deportation of an alien after the issuance of a deportation order because of the right of judicial review of the order granted by this section, or to relieve any alien from compliance with subsections (d) and (e) of section 242 of this Act. Nothing contained

in this section shall be construed to preclude the Attorney General
from detaining or continuing to detain an alien or from taking him
into custody pursuant to subsection (c) of section 242 of this Act at
any time after the issuance of a deportation order;

(8) it shall not be necessary to print the record or any part
thereof, or the briefs, and the court shall review the proceedings on a
typewritten record and on typewritten briefs; and

(9) any alien held in custody pursuant to an order of deportation
may obtain judicial review thereof by habeas corpus proceedings.

(b) Notwithstanding the provisions of any other law, any alien
against whom a final order of exclusion has been made heretofore or
hereafter under the provisions of section 236 of this Act or comparable
provisions of any prior Act may obtain judicial review of such order by
habeas corpus proceedings and not otherwise.

(c) An order of deportation or of exclusion shall not be reviewed by
any court if the alien has not exhausted the administrative remedies
available to him as of right under the immigration laws and regulations
or if he has departed from the United States after the issuance of the
order. Every petition for review or for habeas corpus shall state whether
the validity of the order has been upheld in any prior judicial proceeding,
and, if so, the nature and date thereof, and the court in which such
proceeding took place. No petition for review or for habeas corpus shall
be entertained if the validity of the order has been previously determined
in any civil or criminal proceeding, unless the petition presents grounds
which the court finds could not have been presented in such prior
proceeding, or the court finds that the remedy provided by such prior
proceeding was inadequate or ineffective to test the validity of the order.

TITLE II—IMMIGRATION
Chapter 1.   Selection System

NUMERICAL LIMITATIONS

Sec. 201. [8 U.S.C. 1151] (a) Exclusive of special immigrants defined in section 101(a)(27), immediate relatives specified in subsection (b)
of this section, and aliens who are admitted or granted asylum under
section 207 or 208, the number of aliens born in any foreign state or
dependent area who may be issued immigrant visas or who may otherwise
acquire the status of an alien lawfully admitted to the United States for
permanent residence, shall not in any of the first three quarters of any
fiscal year exceed a total of seventy-two thousand and shall not in any
fiscal year exceed two hundred and seventy thousand: *Provided,* That to
the extent that in a particular fiscal year the number of aliens who are
issued immigrant visas or who may otherwise acquire the status of aliens
lawfully admitted for permanent residence, and who are subject to the
numerical limitations of this section, together with the aliens who adjust
their status to aliens lawfully admitted for permanent residence pursuant
to subparagraph (H) of section 101(a)(27) or section 19 of the Immigration
and Nationality Amendments Act of 1981, exceed the annual numerical

limitation in effect pursuant to this section for such year, the Secretary of State shall reduce to such extent the annual numerical limitation in effect pursuant to this section for the following fiscal year.

(b) The "immediate relatives" referred to in subsection (a) of this section shall mean the children, spouses, and parents of a citizen of the United States: *Provided,* That in the case of parents, such citizen must be at least twenty-one years of age. The immediate relatives specified in this subsection who are otherwise qualified for admission as immigrants shall be admitted as such, without regard to the numerical limitations in this Act.

NUMERICAL LIMITATION TO ANY SINGLE FOREIGN STATE

Sec. 202. [8 U.S.C. 1152] (a) No person shall receive any preference or priority or be discriminated against in the issuance of an immigrant visa because of his race, sex, nationality, place of birth, or place of residence, except as specifically provided in sections 101(a)(27), 201(b), and 203: *Provided,* That the total number of immigrant visas made available to natives of any single foreign state under paragraphs (1) through (7) of section 203(a) shall not exceed 20,000 in any fiscal year: *And provided further,* That to the extent that in a particular fiscal year the number of such natives who are issued immigrant visas or who may otherwise acquire the status of aliens lawfully admitted for permanent residence and who are subject to the numerical limitation of this section, together with the aliens from the same foreign state who adjust their status to aliens lawfully admitted for permanent residence pursuant to subparagraph (H) of section 101(a)(27) or section 19 of the Immigration and Nationality Amendments Act of 1981, exceed the numerical limitation in effect for such year pursuant to this section, the Secretary of State shall reduce to such extent the numerical limitation in effect for the natives of the same foreign state pursuant to this section for the following fiscal year.

(b) Each independent country, self-governing dominion, mandated territory, and territory under the international trusteeship system of the United Nations, other than the United States and its outlying possessions shall be treated as a separate foreign state for the purposes of the numerical limitation set forth in the proviso to subsection (a) of this section when approved by the Secretary of State. All other inhabited lands shall be attributed to a foreign state specified by the Secretary of State. For the purposes of this Act the foreign state to which an immigrant is chargeable shall be determined by birth within such foreign state except that (1) an alien child, when accompanied by his alien parent or parents, may be charged to the same foreign state as the accompanying parent or of either accompanying parent if such parent has received or would be qualified for an immigrant visa, if necessary to prevent the separation of the child from the accompanying parent or parents, and if the foreign state to which such parent has been or would be chargeable has not exceeded the numerical limitation set forth in the proviso to subsection (a) of this section for that fiscal year; (2) if an alien is chargeable to a different foreign state from that of his accompanying spouse, the foreign state to which such alien is chargeable may, if necessary to prevent the separation of husband and wife, be determined by the foreign state of the accompanying spouse, if such spouse has received or would be qualified for an immigrant visa and if the foreign state to which such spouse has been or would be chargeable has not exceeded the numerical limitation set forth in the proviso to subsection (a) of this section for that fiscal year; (3) an alien born in the United States shall be considered as having been born in the country of which he is a citizen or subject, or if he is not a citizen or subject of any country then in the last foreign country in which he had his residence as determined by the consular officers; and (4) an alien born within any foreign state in which neither of his parents was born and in which neither of his parents had a residence at the time of such alien's birth may be charged to the foreign state of either parent.

(c) Any immigrant born in a colony or other component or dependent area of a foreign state overseas from the foreign state, other than a special immigrant, as defined in section 101(a)(27), or an immediate relative of a United States citizen, as defined in section 201(b), shall be chargeable for the purpose of the limitation set forth in section 202(a), to the foreign state, and the number of immigrant visas available to each such colony or other component or dependent area shall not exceed six hundred in any one fiscal year.

(d) In the case of any change in the territorial limits of foreign states, the Secretary of State shall, upon recognition of such change, issue appropriate instructions to all diplomatic and consular offices.

(e) Whenever the maximum number of visas have been made available under section 202 to natives of any single foreign state as defined in subsection (b) of this section or any dependent area as defined in subsection (c) of this section in any fiscal year, in the next following fiscal year a number of visas, not to exceed 20,000, in the case of a foreign state or 600 in the case of a dependent area, shall be made available and allocated as follows:

(1) Visas shall first be made available, in a number not to exceed 20 per centum of the number specified in this subsection, to qualified immigrants who are the unmarried sons or daughters of citizens of the United States.

(2) Visas shall next be made available, in a number not to exceed 26 per centum of the number specified in this subsection, plus any visas not required for the classes specified in paragraph (1), to qualified immigrants who are the spouses, unmarried sons, or unmarried daughters of an alien lawfully admitted for permanent residence.

(3) Visas shall next be made available, in a number not to exceed 10 per centum of the number specified in this subsection, to qualified immigrants who are members of the professions, or who because of their exceptional ability in the sciences or the arts will substantially benefit prospectively the national economy, cultural interests, or welfare of the United States, and whose services in the professions, sciences, or arts are sought by an employer in the United States.

(4) Visas shall next be made available, in a number not to exceed 10 per centum of the number specified in this subsection, plus any visas not required for the classes specified in paragraphs (1) through (3), to qualified immigrants who are the married sons or the married daughters of citizens of the United States.

(5) Visas shall next be made available, in a number not to exceed 24 per centum of the number specified in this subsection, plus any visas not required for the classes specified in paragraphs (1) through (4), to qualified immigrants who are the brothers or sisters of citizens of the United States, provided such citizens are at least twenty-one years of age.

(6) Visas shall next be made available, in a number not to exceed 10 per centum of the number specified in this subsection, to qualified immigrants capable of performing specified skilled or unskilled labor, not of a temporary or seasonal nature, for which a shortage of employable and willing persons exists in the United States.

(7) Visas so allocated but not required for the classes specified in paragraphs (1) through (6) shall be made available to other qualified immigrants strictly in the chronological order in which they qualify.

ALLOCATION OF IMMIGRANT VISAS

Sec. 203. [8 U.S.C. 1153] (a) Aliens who are subject to the numerical limitations specified in section 201(a) shall be allotted visas as follows:

(1) Visas shall be first made available, in a number not to exceed 20 per centum of the number specified in section 201(a), to qualified immigrants who are the unmarried sons or daughters of citizens of the United States.

(2) Visas shall next be made available, in a number not to exceed 26 per centum of the number specified in section 201(a), plus any visas not required for the classes specified in paragraph (1), to qualified immigrants who are the spouses, unmarried sons or unmarried daughters of an alien lawfully admitted for permanent residence.

(3) Visas shall next be made available, in a number not to exceed 10 per centum of the number specified in section 201(a), to qualified immigrants who are members of the professions, or who because of their exceptional ability in the sciences or the arts will substantially benefit prospectively the national economy, cultural interests, or welfare of the United States, and whose services in the professions, sciences, or arts are sought by an employer in the United States.

(4) Visas shall next be made available, in a number not to exceed 10 per centum of the number specified in section 201(a), plus any visas not required for the classes specified in paragraphs (1) through (3), to qualified immigrants who are the married sons or the married daughters of citizens of the United States.

(5) Visas shall next be made available, in a number not to exceed 24 per centum of the number specified in section 201(a), plus any visas not required for the classes specified in paragraphs (1) through (4), to qualified

immigrants who are the brothers or sisters of citizens of the United States, provided such citizens are at least twenty-one years of age.

(6) Visas shall next be made available, in a number not to exceed 10 per centum of the number specified in section 201(a), to qualified immigrants who are capable of performing specified skilled or unskilled labor, not of a temporary or seasonal nature, for which a shortage of employable and willing persons exists in the United States.

(7) Visas authorized in any fiscal year, less those required for issuance to the classes specified in paragraphs (1) through (6), shall be made available to other qualified immigrants strictly in the chronological order in which they qualify. Waiting lists of applicants shall be maintained in accordance with regulations prescribed by the Secretary of State. No immigrant visa shall be issued to a nonpreference immigrant under this paragraph, or to an immigrant with a preference under paragraph (3) or (6) of this subsection, until the consular officer is in receipt of a determination made by the Secretary of Labor pursuant to the provisions of section 212(a)(14). No immigrant visa shall be issued under this paragraph to an adopted child or prospective adopted child of a United States citizen or lawfully resident alien unless (A) a valid home-study has been favorably recommended by an agency of the State of the child's proposed residence, or by an agency authorized by that State to conduct such a study, or, in the case of a child adopted abroad, by an appropriate public or private adoption agency which is licensed in the United States; and (B) the child has been irrevocably released for immigration and adoption: *Provided,* That no natural parent or prior adoptive parent of any such child shall thereafter, by virtue of such parentage, be accorded any right, privilege, or status under this Act. No immigrant visa shall otherwise be issued under this paragraph to an unmarried child under the age of sixteen except a child who is accompanying or following to join his natural parent.

(8) A spouse or child as defined in section 101(b)(1)(A), (B), (C), (D), or (E) shall, if not otherwise entitled to an immigrant status and the immediate issuance of a visa under paragraphs (1) through (7), be entitled to the same status, and the same order of consideration provided in subsection (b), if accompanying, or following to join, his spouse or parent.

(b) In considering applications for immigrant visas under subsection (a) consideration shall be given to applicants in the order in which the classes of which they are members are listed in subsection (a).

(c) Immigrant visas issued pursuant to paragraphs (1) through (6) of subsection (a) shall be issued to eligible immigrants in the order in which a petition in behalf of each such immigrant is filed with the Attorney General as provided in section 204.

(d) Every immigrant shall be presumed to be a nonpreference immigrant until he establishes to the satisfaction of the consular officer and the immigration officer that he is entitled to a preference status under paragraphs (1) through (6) of subsection (a), or to a special immigrant status under section 101(a)(27), or that he is an immediate relative of a United States citizen as specified in section 201(b). In the case of any alien claiming in his application for an immigrant visa to be an immediate relative of a United States citizen as specified in section 201(b) or to be entitled to preference immigrant status under paragraphs (1) through (6) of subsection (a), the consular officer shall not grant such status until he has been authorized to do so as provided by section 204.

(e) For the purposes of carrying out his responsibilities in the orderly administration of this section, the Secretary of State is authorized to make reasonable estimates of the anticipated numbers of visas to be issued during any quarter of any fiscal year within each of the categories of subsection (a), and to rely upon such estimates in authorizing the issuance of such visas. The Secretary of State shall terminate the registration of any alien who fails to apply for an immigrant visa within one year following notification to him of the availability of such visa, but the Secretary shall reinstate the registration of any such alien who establishes within two years following notification of the availability of such visa that such failure to apply was due to circumstances beyond his control. Upon such termination the approval of any petition approved pursuant to section 204(b) shall be automatically revoked.

PROCEDURE FOR GRANTING IMMIGRANT STATUS

Sec. 204. [8 U.S.C. 1154] (a) Any citizen of the United States claiming that an alien is entitled to a preference status by reason of a relationship described in paragraph (1), (4), or (5) of section 203(a), or to an immediate relative status under section 201(b), or any alien lawfully admitted for permanent residence claiming that an alien is entitled to a preference status by reason of the relationship described in section 203(a)(2), or any alien desiring to be classified as a preference immigrant under section 203(a)(3) (or any person on behalf of such an alien), or any person desiring and intending to employ within the United States an alien entitled to classification as a preference immigrant under section 203(a)(6), may file a petition with the Attorney General for such classification. The petition shall be in such form as the Attorney General may by regulations prescribe and shall contain such information and be supported by such documentary evidence as the Attorney General may require. The petition shall be made under oath administered by any individual having authority to administer oaths, if executed in the United States, but, if executed outside the United States, administered by a consular officer or an immigration officer.

(b) After an investigation of the facts in each case, and after consultation with the Secretary of Labor with respect to petitions to accord a status under section 203(a)(3) or (6), the Attorney General shall, if he determines that the facts stated in the petition are true and that the alien in behalf of whom the petition is made is an immediate relative specified in section 201(b) or is eligible for a preference status under section 203(a), approve the petition and forward one copy thereof to the Department of State. The Secretary of State shall then authorize the consular officer concerned to grant the preference status.

(c) Notwithstanding the provisions of subsection (b) no petition shall be approved if the alien has previously been accorded a nonquota or preference status as the spouse of a citizen of the United States or the spouse of an alien lawfully admitted for permanent residence, by reason of a marriage determined by the Attorney General to have been entered into for the purpose of evading the immigration laws.

(d) Notwithstanding the provisions of subsections (a) and (b) of this section no petition may be approved on behalf of a child defined in section 101(b)(1)(F) unless a valid home-study has been favorably recommended by an agency of the State of the child's proposed residence, or by an agency authorized by that State to conduct such a study, or, in the case of a child adopted abroad, by an appropriate public or private adoption agency which is licensed in the United States.

(e) Nothing in this section shall be construed to entitle an immigrant, in behalf of whom a petition under this section is approved, to enter the United States as a preference immigrant under section 203(a) or as an immediate relative under section 201(b) if upon his arrival at a port of entry in the United States he is found not to be entitled to such classification.

(f) The provisions of this section shall be applicable to qualified immigrants specified in paragraphs (1) through (6) of section 202(e).

(g) * * *.

* * *

ANNUAL ADMISSION OF REFUGEES AND ADMISSION OF EMERGENCY SITUATION REFUGEES

Sec. 207. [8 U.S.C. 1157] (a)(1) Except as provided in subsection (b), the number of refugees who may be admitted under this section in fiscal year 1980, 1981, or 1982, may not exceed fifty thousand unless the President determines, before the beginning of the fiscal year and after appropriate consultation (as defined in subsection (e)), that admission of a specific number of refugees in excess of such number is justified by humanitarian concerns or is otherwise in the national interest.

(2) Except as provided in subsection (b), the number of refugees who may be admitted under this section in any fiscal year after fiscal year 1982 shall be such number as the President determines, before the beginning of the fiscal year and after appropriate consultation, is justified by humanitarian concerns or is otherwise in the national interest.

(3) Admissions under this subsection shall be allocated among refugees of special humanitarian concern to the United States in accordance with a determination made by the President after appropriate consultation.

(b) If the President determines, after appropriate consultation, that (1) an unforeseen emergency refugee situation exists, (2) the admission of certain refugees in response to the emergency refugee situation is justified by grave humanitarian concerns or is otherwise in the national interest, and (3) the admission to the United States of these refugees cannot be accomplished under subsection (a), the President may fix a number of refugees to be admitted to the United States during the succeeding period (not to exceed twelve months) in response to the emergency refugee situation and such admissions shall be allocated among refugees of special humanitarian concern to the United States in accordance with a determination made by the President after the appropriate consultation provided under this subsection.

(c)(1) Subject to the numerical limitations established pursuant to subsections (a) and (b), the Attorney General may, in the Attorney General's discretion and pursuant to such regulations as the Attorney General may prescribe, admit any refugee who is not firmly resettled in any foreign country, is determined to be of special humanitarian concern to the United States, and is admissible (except as otherwise provided under paragraph (3)) as an immigrant under this Act.

(2) A spouse or child (as defined in section 101(b)(1)(A), (B), (C), (D), or (E)) of any refugee who qualifies for admission under paragraph (1) shall, if not otherwise entitled to admission under paragraph (1) and if not a person described in the second sentence of section 101(a)(42), be entitled to the same admission status as such refugee if accompanying, or following to join, such refugee and if the spouse or child is admissible (except as otherwise provided under paragraph (3)) as an immigrant under this Act. Upon the spouse's or child's admission to the United States, such admission shall be charged against the numerical limitation established in accordance with the appropriate subsection under which the refugee's admission is charged.

(3) The provisions of paragraphs (14), (15), (20), (21), (25), and (32) of section 212(a) shall not be applicable to any alien seeking admission to the United States under this subsection, and the Attorney General may waive any other provision of such section (other than paragraph (27), (29), or (33) and other than so much of paragraph (23) as relates to trafficking in narcotics) with respect to such an alien for humanitarian purposes, to assure family unity, or when it is otherwise in the public interest. Any such waiver by the Attorney General shall be in writing and shall be granted only on an individual basis following an investigation. The Attorney General shall provide for the annual reporting to Congress of the number of waivers granted under this paragraph in the previous fiscal year and a summary of the reasons for granting such waivers.

(4) The refugee status of any alien (and of the spouse or child of the alien) may be terminated by the Attorney General pursuant to such regulations as the Attorney General may prescribe if the Attorney General determines that the alien was not in fact a refugee within the meaning of section 101(a)(42) at the time of the alien's admission.

(d)(1) Before the start of each fiscal year the President shall report to the Committee on the Judiciary of the House of Representatives and of the Senate regarding the foreseeable number of refugees who will be in need of resettlement during the fiscal year and the anticipated allocation of refugee admissions during the fiscal year. The President shall provide for periodic discussions between designated representatives of the President and members of such committees regarding changes in the worldwide refugee situation, the progress of refugee admissions, and the possible need for adjustments in the allocation of admissions among refugees.

(2) As soon as possible after representatives of the President initiate appropriate consultation with respect to the number of refugee admissions under subsection (a) or with respect to the admission of refugees in response to an emergency refugee situation under subsection (b), the Committees on the Judiciary of the House of Representatives and of the Senate shall cause to have printed in the Congressional Record the substance of such consultation.

(3)(A) After the President initiates appropriate consultation prior to making a determination under subsection (a), a hearing to review the proposed determination shall be held unless public disclosure of the details of the proposal would jeopardize the lives or safety of individuals.

(B) After the President initiates appropriate consultation prior to making a determination, under subsection (b), that the number of refugee admissions should be increased because of an unforeseen emergency refugee situation, to the extent that time and the nature of the emergency refugee situation permit, a hearing to review the proposal to increase refugee admissions shall be held unless public disclosure of the details of the proposal would jeopardize the lives or safety of individuals.

(e) For purposes of this section, the term "appropriate consultation" means, with respect to the admission of refugees and allocation of refugee admissions, discussions in person by designated Cabinet-level representatives of the President with members of the Committees on the Judiciary of the Senate and of the House of Representatives to review the refugee situation or emergency refugee situation, to project the extent of possible participation of the United States therein, to discuss the reasons for believing that the proposed admission of refugees is justified by humanitarian concerns or grave humanitarian concerns or is otherwise in the national interest, and to provide such members with the following information:

(1) A description of the nature of the refugee situation.

(2) A description of the number and allocation of the refugees to be admitted and an analysis of conditions within the countries from which they came.

(3) A description of the proposed plans for their movement and resettlement and the estimated cost of their movement and resettlement.

(4) An analysis of the anticipated social, economic, and demographic impact of their admission to the United States.

(5) A description of the extent to which other countries will admit and assist in the resettlement of such refugees.

(6) An analysis of the impact of the participation of the United States in the resettlement of such refugees on the foreign policy interests of the United States.

(7) Such additional information as may be appropriate or requested by such members.

To the extent possible, information described in this subsection shall be provided at least two weeks in advance of discussions in person by designated representatives of the President with such members.

ASYLUM PROCEDURE

Sec. 208. [8 U.S.C. 1158] (a) The Attorney General shall establish a procedure for an alien physically present in the United States or at a land border or port of entry, irrespective of such alien's status, to apply for asylum, and the alien may be granted asylum in the discretion of the Attorney General if the Attorney General determines that such alien is a refugee within the meaning of section 101(a)(42)(A).

(b) Asylum granted under subsection (a) may be terminated if the Attorney General, pursuant to such regulations as the Attorney General may prescribe, determines that the alien is no longer a refugee within the meaning of section 101(a)(42)(A) owing to a change in circumstances in the alien's country of nationality or, in the case of an alien having no nationality, in the country in which the alien last habitually resided.

(c) A spouse or child (as defined in section 101(b)(1)(A), (B), (C), (D), or (E)) of an alien who is granted asylum under subsection (a) may, if not otherwise eligible for asylum under such subsection, be granted the same status as the alien if accompanying, or following to join, such alien.

ADJUSTMENT OF STATUS OF REFUGEES

Sec. 209. [8 U.S.C. 1159] (a)(1) Any alien who has been admitted to the United States under section 207—

(A) whose admission has not been terminated by the Attorney General pursuant to such regulations as the Attorney General may prescribe,

(B) who has been physically present in the United States for at least one year, and

(C) who has not acquired permanent resident status,

shall, at the end of such year period, return or be returned to the custody of the Service for inspection and examination for admission to the United States as an immigrant in accordance with the provisions of sections 235, 236, and 237.

(2) Any alien who is found upon inspection and examination by an immigration officer pursuant to paragraph (1) or after a hearing before a special inquiry officer to be admissible (except as otherwise provided under subsection (c)) as an immigrant under this Act at the time of the alien's inspection and examination shall, notwithstanding any numerical limitation specified in this act, be regarded as lawfully admitted to the United States for permanent residence as of the date of such alien's arrival into the United States.

(b) Not more than five thousand of the refugee admissions authorized under section 207(a) in any fiscal year may be made available by the Attorney General, in the Attorney General's discretion and under such regulations as the Attorney General may prescribe, to adjust to the status of an alien lawfully admitted for permanent residence the status of any alien granted asylum who—

(1) applies for such adjustment,

(2) has been physically present in the United States for at least one year after being granted asylum,

(3) continues to be a refugee within the meaning of section 101(a)(42)(A) or a spouse or child of such a refugee,

(4) is not firmly resettled in any foreign country, and

(5) is admissible (except as otherwise provided under subsection (c)) as an immigrant under this Act at the time of examination for adjustment of such alien.

Upon approval of an application under this subsection, the Attorney General shall establish a record of the alien's admission for lawful permanent residence as of the date one year before the date of the approval of the application.

(c) The provisions of paragraphs (14), (15), (20), (21), (25), and (32) of section 212(a) shall not be applicable to any alien seeking adjustment of status under this section, and the Attorney General may waive any other provision of such section (other than paragraph (27), (29), or (33) and other than so much of paragraph (23) as relates to trafficking in narcotics) with respect to such an alien for humanitarian purposes, to assure family unity, or when it is otherwise in the public interest.

Chapter 2. Qualifications for Admission of Aliens; Travel Control of Citizens and Aliens

DOCUMENTARY REQUIREMENTS

Sec. 211. [8 U.S.C. 1181] (a) Except as provided in subsection (b) and subsection (c) no immigrant shall be admitted into the United States unless at the time of application for admission he (1) has a valid unexpired immigrant visa or was born subsequent to the issuance of such visa of the accompanying parent, and (2) presents a valid unexpired passport or other suitable travel document, or document of identity and nationality, if such document is required under the regulations issued by the Attorney General. With respect to immigrants to be admitted under quotas of quota areas prior to June 30, 1968, no immigrant visa shall be deemed valid unless the immigrant is properly chargeable to the quota area under the quota of which the visa is issued.

(b) Notwithstanding the provisions of section 212(a)(20) of this Act in such cases or in such classes of cases and under such conditions as may be by regulations prescribed, returning resident immigrants, defined in section 101(a)(27)(A), who are otherwise admissible may be readmitted to the United States by the Attorney General in his discretion without being required to obtain a passport, immigrant visa, reentry permit or other documentation.

(c) The provisions of subsection (a) shall not apply to an alien whom the Attorney General admits to the United States under section 207.

GENERAL CLASSES OF ALIENS INELIGIBLE TO RECEIVE VISAS AND EXCLUDED FROM ADMISSION; WAIVERS OF INADMISSIBILITY

Sec. 212. [8 U.S.C. 1182] (a) Except as otherwise provided in this Act, the following classes of aliens shall be ineligible to receive visas and shall be excluded from admission into the United States:

(1) Aliens who are mentally retarded;

(2) Aliens who are insane;

(3) Aliens who have had one or more attacks of insanity;

(4) Aliens afflicted with psychopathic personality, or sexual deviation, or a mental defect;

(5) Aliens who are narcotic drug addicts or chronic alcoholics;

(6) Aliens who are afflicted with any dangerous contagious disease;

(7) Aliens not comprehended within any of the foregoing classes who are certified by the examining surgeon as having a physical defect, disease, or disability, when determined by the consular or immigration officer to be of such a nature that it may affect the ability of the alien to earn a living, unless the alien affirmatively establishes that he will not have to earn a living;

(8) Aliens who are paupers, professional beggars, or vagrants;

(9) Aliens who have been convicted of a crime involving moral turpitude (other than a purely political offense), or aliens who admit having committed such a crime, or aliens who admit committing acts which constitute the essential elements of such a crime; except that aliens who have committed only one such crime while under the age of eighteen years may be granted a visa and admitted if the crime was committed more than five years prior to the date of the application for a visa or other documentation, and more than five years prior to date of application for admission to the United States, unless the crime resulted in confinement in a prison or correctional institution, in which case such alien must have been released from such confinement more than five years prior to the date of the application for a visa or other documentation, and for admission, to the United States. Any alien who would be excludable because of the conviction of a misdemeanor classifiable as a petty offense under the provisions of section 1(3) of title 18, United States Code, by reason of the punishment actually imposed, or who would be excludable as one who admits the commission of an offense that is classifiable as a misdemeanor under the provisions of section 1(2) of title 18, United States Code, by reason of the punishment which might have been imposed upon him, may be granted a visa and admitted to the United States if otherwise admissible: *Provided*, That the alien has committed only one such offense, or

admits the commission of acts which constitute the essential elements of only one such offense.

(10) Aliens who have been convicted of two or more offenses (other than purely political offenses), regardless of whether the conviction was in a single trial or whether the offenses arose from a single scheme of misconduct and regardless of whether the offenses involved moral turpitude, for which the aggregate sentences to confinement actually imposed were five years or more;

(11) Aliens who are polygamists or who practice polygamy or advocate the practice of polygamy;

(12) Aliens who are prostitutes or who have engaged in prostitution, or aliens coming to the United States solely, principally, or incidentally to engage in prostitution; aliens who directly or indirectly procure or attempt to procure, or who have procured or attempted to procure or to import, prostitutes or persons for the purpose of prostitution or for any other immoral purpose; and aliens who are or have been supported by, or receive or have received, in whole or in part, the proceeds of prostitution or aliens coming to the United States to engage in any other unlawful commercialized vice, whether or not related to prostitution;

(13) Aliens coming to the United States to engage in any immoral sexual act;

(14) Aliens seeking to enter the United States, for the purpose of performing skilled or unskilled labor, unless the Secretary of Labor has determined and certified to the Secretary of State and the Attorney General that (A) there are not sufficient workers who are able, willing, qualified (or equally qualified in the case of aliens who are members of the teaching profession or who have exceptional ability in the sciences or the arts), and available at the time of application for a visa and admission to the United States and at the place where the alien is to perform such skilled or unskilled labor, and (B) the employment of such aliens will not adversely affect the wages and working conditions of the workers in the United States similarly employed. The exclusion of aliens under this paragraph shall apply to preference immigrant aliens described in section 203(a)(3) and (6), and to nonpreference immigrant aliens described in section 203(a)(7);

(15) Aliens who, in the opinion of the consular officer at the time of application for a visa, or in the opinion of the Attorney General at the time of application for admission, are likely at any time to become public charges;

(16) Aliens who have been excluded from admission and deported and who again seek admission within one year from the date of such deportation, unless prior to their reembarkation at a place outside the United States or their attempt to be admitted from foreign contiguous territory the Attorney General has consented to their reapplying for admission;

(17) Aliens who have been arrested and deported, or who have fallen into distress and have been removed pursuant to this or any prior act, or who have been removed as alien enemies, or who have been removed at

Government expense in lieu of deportation pursuant to section 242(b), and who seek admission within five years of the date of such deportation or removal, unless prior to their embarkation or reembarkation at a place outside the United States or their attempt to be admitted from foreign contiguous territory the Attorney General has consented to their applying or reapplying for admission;

(18) Aliens who are stowaways;

(19) Any alien who seeks to procure, or has sought to procure, or has procured a visa or other documentation, or seeks to enter the United States, by fraud, or by willfully misrepresenting a material fact;

(20) Except as otherwise specifically provided in this Act, any immigrant who at the time of application for admission is not in possession of a valid unexpired immigrant visa, reentry permit, border crossing identification card, or other valid entry document required by this Act, and a valid unexpired passport, or other suitable travel document, or document of identity and nationality, if such document is required under the regulations issued by the Attorney General pursuant to section 211(a);

(21) Except as otherwise specifically provided in this Act, any immigrant at the time of application for admission whose visa has been issued without compliance with the provisions of section 203;

(22) Aliens who are ineligible to citizenship, except aliens seeking to enter as nonimmigrants; or persons who have departed from or who have remained outside the United States to avoid or evade training or service in the armed forces in time of war or a period declared by the President to be a national emergency, except aliens who were at the time of such departure nonimmigrant aliens and who seek to reenter the United States as nonimmigrants;

(23) Any alien who has been convicted of a violation of, or a conspiracy to violate, any law or regulation relating to the illicit possession of or traffic in narcotic drugs or marihuana, or who has been convicted of a violation of, or a conspiracy to violate, any law or regulation governing or controlling the taxing, manufacture, production, compounding, transportation, sale, exchange, dispensing, giving away, importation, exportation, or the possession for the purpose of the manufacture, production, compounding, transportation, sale, exchange, dispensing, giving away, importation, or exportation of opium, coca leaves, heroin, marihuana, or any salt derivative or preparation of opium or coca leaves, or isonipecaine or any addiction-forming or addiction-sustaining opiate; or any alien who the consular officer or immigration officers know or have reason to believe is or has been an illicit trafficker in any of the aforementioned drugs;

(24) Aliens (other than aliens described in 101(a)(27)(A) and aliens born in the Western Hemisphere) who seek admission from foreign contiguous territory or adjacent islands, having arrived there on a vessel or aircraft of a nonsignatory line, or if signatory, a noncomplying transportation line under section 238(a) and who have not resided for at least two years subsequent to such arrival in such territory or adjacent islands;

(25) Aliens (other than aliens who have been lawfully admitted for permanent residence and who are returning from a temporary visit abroad) over sixteen years of age, physically capable of reading, who cannot read and understand some language or dialect;

(26) Any nonimmigrant who is not in possession of (A) a passport valid for a minimum period of six months from the date of the expiration of the initial period of his admission or contemplated initial period of stay authorizing him to return to the country from which he came or to proceed to and enter some other country during such period; and (B) at the time of application for admission a valid nonimmigrant visa or border crossing identification card;

(27) Aliens who the consular officer or the Attorney General knows or has reason to believe seek to enter the United States solely, principally, or incidentally to engage in activities which would be prejudicial to the public interest, or endanger the welfare, safety, or security of the United States;

(28) Aliens who are, or at any time have been, members of any of the following classes:

(A) Aliens who are anarchists;

(B) Aliens who advocate or teach, or who are members of or affiliated with any organization that advocates or teaches, opposition to all organized government;

(C) Aliens who are members of or affiliated with (i) the Communist Party of the United States, (ii) any other totalitarian party of the United States, (iii) the Communist Political Association, (iv) the Communist or any other totalitarian party of any State of the United States, of any foreign state, or of any political or geographical subdivision of any foreign state, (v) any section, subsidiary, branch, affiliate, or subdivision of any such association or party, or (vi) the direct predecessors or successors of any such association or party, regardless of what name such group or organization may have used, may now bear, or may hereafter adopt: *Provided*, That nothing in this paragraph, or in any other provision of this Act, shall be construed as declaring that the Communist Party does not advocate the overthrow of the Government of the United States by force, violence, or other unconstitutional means;

(D) Aliens not within any of the other provisions of this paragraph who advocate the economic, international, and governmental doctrines of world communism or the establishment in the United States of a totalitarian dictatorship, or who are members of or affiliated with any organization that advocates the economic, international, and governmental doctrines of world communism or the establishment in the United States of a totalitarian dictatorship, either through its won utterances or through any written or printed publications issued or published by or with the permission or consent of or under the authority of such organization or paid for by the funds of, or funds furnished by, such organization;

(E) Aliens not within any of the other provisions of this paragraph, who are members of or affiliated with any organization during the time it is registered or required to be registered under section 7 of the Subversive Activities Control Act of 1950,[2] unless such aliens establish that they did not have knowledge or reason to believe at the time they became members of or affiliated with such an organization (and did not thereafter and prior to the date upon which such organization was so registered or so required to be registered have such knowledge or reason to believe) that such organization was a Communist organization;

(F) Aliens who advocate or teach or who are members of or affiliated with any organization that advocates or teaches (i) the overthrow by force, violence, or other unconstitutional means of the Government of the United States or of all forms of law; or (ii) the duty, necessity, or propriety of the unlawful assaulting or killing of any officer or officers (either of specific individuals or of officers generally) of the Government of the United States or of any other organized government, because of his or their official character; or (iii) the unlawful damage, injury, or destruction of property; or (iv) sabotage;

(G) Aliens who write or publish, or cause to be written or published, or who knowingly circulate, distribute, print, or display, or knowingly cause to be circulated, distributed, printed, published, or displayed, or who knowingly have in their possession for the purpose of circulation, publication, distribution, or display, any written or printed matter, advocating or teaching opposition to all organized government, or advocating or teaching (i) the overthrow by force, violence, or other unconstitutional means of the Government of the United States or of all forms of law; or (ii) the duty, necessity, or propriety of the unlawful assaulting or killing of any officer or officers (either of specific individuals or of officers generally) of the Government of the United States or of any other organized government, because of his or their official character; or (iii) the unlawful damage, injury, or destruction of property; or (iv) sabotage; or (v) the economic, international, and governmental doctrines of world communism or the establishment in the United States of a totalitarian dictatorship;

(H) Aliens who are members of or affiliated with any organization that writes, circulates, distributes, prints, publishes, or displays, or causes to be written, circulated, distributed, printed, published, or displayed, or that has in its possession for the purpose of circulation, distribution, publication, issue, or display, any written or printed matter of the character described in paragraph (G);

(I) Any alien who is within any of the classes described in subparagraphs (B), (C), (D), (E), (F), (G), and (H) of this paragraph because of membership in or affiliation with a party or organization or a section, subsidiary, branch, affiliate, or subdivision thereof, may,

2. Section 7 of the Subversive Activities Control Act of 1950 (50 U.S.C. 786) was repealed by the Act of Jan. 2, 1968 (81 Stat. 766).

A. & M.–Immigration Law ACB—34

if not otherwise ineligible, be issued a visa if such alien establishes to the satisfaction of the consular officer when applying for a visa and the consular officer finds that (i) such membership or affiliation is or was involuntary, or is or was solely when under sixteen years of age, by operation of law, or for purposes of obtaining employment, food rations, or other essentials of living and where necessary for such purposes, or (ii)(a) since the termination of such membership or affiliation, such alien is and has been, for at least five years prior to the date of the application for a visa, actively opposed to the doctrine, program, principles, and ideology of such party or organization or the section, subsidiary, branch, or affiliate or subdivision thereof, and (b) the admission of such alien into the United States would be in the public interest. Any such alien to whom a visa has been issued under the provisions of this subparagraph may, if not otherwise inadmissible, be admitted into the United States if he shall establish to the satisfaction of the Attorney General when applying for admission to the United States and the Attorney General finds that (i) such membership or affiliation is or was involuntary or is or was solely when under sixteen years of age, by operation of law, or for purposes of obtaining employment, food rations, or other essentials of living and when necessary for such purposes, or (ii)(a) since the termination of such membership or affiliation, such alien is and has been, for at least five years prior to the date of the application for admission actively opposed to the doctrine, program, principles, and ideology of such party or organization or the section, subsidiary, branch, or affiliate or subdivision thereof, and (b) the admission of such alien into the United States would be in the public interest. The Attorney General shall promptly make a detailed report to the Congress in the case of each alien who is or shall be admitted into the United States under (ii) of this subparagraph:

(29) Aliens with respect to whom the consular officer or the Attorney General knows or has reasonable ground to believe probably would, after entry, (A) engage in activities which would be prohibited by the laws of the United States relating to espionage, sabotage, public disorder, or in other activity subversive to the national security, (B) engage in any activity a purpose of which is the opposition to, or the control or overthrow of, the Government of the United States, by force, violence, or other unconstitutional means, or (C) join, affiliate with, or participate in the activities of any organization which is registered or required to be registered under section 7 of the Subversive Activities Control Act of 1950;

(30) Any alien accompanying another alien ordered to be excluded and deported and certified to be helpless from sickness or mental or physical disability or infancy pursuant to section 237(e), whose protection or guardianship is required by the alien ordered excluded and deported;

(31) Any alien who at any time shall have, knowingly and for gain, encouraged, induced, assisted, abetted, or aided any other alien to enter or to try to enter the United States in violation of law;

(32) Aliens who are graduates of a medical school not accredited by a body or bodies approved for the purpose by the Secretary of Education (regardless of whether such school of medicine is in the United States) and are coming to the United States principally to perform services as members of the medical profession, except such aliens who have passed parts I and II of the National Board of Medical Examiners Examination (or an equivalent examination as determined by the Secretary of Health and Human Services) and who are competent in oral and written English. The exclusion of aliens under this paragraph shall apply to preference immigrant aliens described in section 203(a)(3) and (6) and to nonpreference immigrant aliens described in section 203(a)(7). For the purposes of this paragraph, an alien who is a graduate of a medical school shall be considered to have passed parts I and II of the National Board of Medical Examiners examination if the alien was fully and permanently licensed to practice medicine in a State on January 9, 1978, and was practicing medicine in a State on that date;

(33) Any alien who during the period beginning on March 23, 1933, and ending on May 8, 1945, under the direction of, or in association with—

(A) the Nazi government in Germany,

(B) any government in any area occupied by the military forces of the Nazi government of Germany,

(C) any government established with the assistance or cooperation of the Nazi government of Germany, or

(D) any government which was an ally of the Nazi government of Germany,

ordered, incited, assisted, or otherwise participated in the persecution of any person because of race, religion, national origin, or political opinion.

(b) The provisions of paragraph (25) of subsection (a) shall not be applicable to any alien who (1) is the parent, grandparent, spouse, daughter, or son of an admissible alien, or any alien lawfully admitted for permanent residence, or any citizen of the United States, if accompanying such admissible alien, or coming to join such citizen or alien lawfully admitted, and if otherwise admissible, or (2) proves that he is seeking admission to the United States to avoid religious persecution in the country of his last permanent residence, whether such persecution be evidenced by overt acts or by laws or governmental regulations that discriminate against such alien or any group to which he belongs because of his religious faith. For the purpose of ascertaining whether an alien can read under paragraph (25) of subsection (a), the consular officers and immigration officers shall be furnished with slips of uniform size, prepared under direction of the Attorney General, each containing not less than thirty nor more than forty words in ordinary use, printed in plainly legible type, in one of the various languages or dialects of immigrants. Each alien may designate the particular language or dialect in which he desires the examination to be made and shall be required to read and understand the words printed on the slip in such language or dialect.

(c) Aliens lawfully admitted for permanent residence who temporarily proceeded abroad voluntarily and not under an order of deportation, and who are returning to a lawful unrelinquished domicile of seven consecutive years, may be admitted in the discretion of the Attorney General without regard to the provisions of paragraph (1) through (25) and paragraphs (30) and (31) of subsection (a). Nothing contained in this subsection shall limit the authority of the Attorney General to exercise the discretion vested in him under section 211(b).

(d)(1) The provisions of paragraphs (11) and (25) of subsection (a) shall not be applicable to any alien who in good faith is seeking to enter the United States as a nonimmigrant.

(2) The provisions of paragraph (28) of subsection (a) of this section shall not be applicable to any alien who is seeking to enter the United States temporarily as a nonimmigrant under paragraph (15)(A)(iii) or (15)(G)(v) of section 101(a).

(3) Except as provided in this subsection, an alien (A) who is applying for a nonimmigrant visa and is known or believed by the consular officer to be ineligible for such visa under one or more of the paragraphs enumerated in subsection (a) (other than paragraphs (27), (29), and (33)), may, after approval by the Attorney General of a recommendation by the Secretary of State or by the consular officer that the alien be admitted temporarily despite his inadmissibility, be granted such a visa and may be admitted into the United States temporarily as a nonimmigrant in the discretion of the Attorney General, or (B) who is inadmissible under one or more of the paragraphs enumerated in subsection (a) (other than paragraphs (27), (29), and (33)), but who is in possession of appropriate documents or is granted a waiver thereof and is seeking admission, may be admitted into the United States temporarily as a nonimmigrant in the discretion of the Attorney General.

(4) Either or both of the requirements of paragraph (26) of subsection (a) may be waived by the Attorney General and the Secretary of State acting jointly (A) on the basis of unforeseen emergency in individual cases, or (B) on the basis of reciprocity with respect to nationals of foreign contiguous territory or of adjacent islands and residents thereof having a common nationality with such nationals, or (C) in the case of aliens proceeding in immediate and continuous transit through the United States under contracts authorized in section 238(d).

(5)(A) The Attorney General may, except as provided in subparagraph (B), in his discretion parole into the United States temporarily under such conditions as he may prescribe for emergent reasons or for reasons deemed strictly in the public interest any alien applying for admission to the United States, but such parole of such alien shall not be regarded as an admission of the alien and when the purposes of such parole shall, in the opinion of the Attorney General, have been served the alien shall forthwith return or be returned to the custody from which he was paroled and thereafter his case shall continue to be dealt with in the same manner as that of any other applicant for admission to the United States.

(B) The Attorney General may not parole into the United States an alien who is a refugee unless the Attorney General determines that compelling reasons in the public interest with respect to that particular alien require that the alien be paroled into the United States rather than be admitted as a refugee under section 207.

(6) The Attorney General shall prescribe conditions, including exaction of such bonds as may be necessary, to control and regulate the admission and return of excludable aliens applying for temporary admission under this subsection.

(7) The provisions of subsection (a) of this section, except paragraphs (20), (21), and (26), shall be applicable to any alien who shall leave Guam, Puerto Rico, or the Virgin Islands of the United States, and who seeks to enter the continental United States or any other place under the jurisdiction of the United States. Any alien described in this paragraph, who is excluded from admission to the United States, shall be immediately deported in the manner provided by section 237(a) of this Act.

(8) Upon a basis of reciprocity accredited officials of foreign governments, their immediate families, attendants, servants, and personal employees may be admitted in immediate and continuous transit through the United States without regard to the provisions of this section except paragraphs (26), (27), and (29) of subsection (a) of this section.

(9) Repealed.

(10) The provisions of paragraph (15) of subsection (a) shall not be applicable to any alien who is seeking to enter the United States as a special immigrant under subparagraph (E), (F), or (G) of section 101(a)(27) and who applies for admission as such a special immigrant not later than March 31, 1982.

(e) No person admitted under section 101(a)(15)(J) or acquiring such status after admission (i) whose participation in the program for which he came to the United States was financed in whole or in part, directly or indirectly, by an agency of the Government of the United States or by the government of the country of his nationality or his last residence, (ii) who at the time of admission or acquisition of status under section 101(a)(15)(J) was a national or resident of a country which the Director of the United States Information Agency, pursuant to regulations prescribed by him, had designated as clearly requiring the services of persons engaged in the field of specialized knowledge or skill in which the alien was engaged, or (iii) who came to the United States or acquired such status in order to receive graduate medical education or training, shall be eligible to apply for an immigrant visa, or for permanent residence, or for a nonimmigrant visa under section 101(a)(15)(H) or section 101(a)(15)(L) until it is established that such person has resided and been physically present in the country of his nationality or his last residence for an aggregate of at least two years following departure from the United States: *Provided,* That upon the favorable recommendation of the Director of the United States Information Agency, pursuant to the request of an interested United States Government agency, or of the Commissioner of Immigration and Naturalization after he has determined that departure from the United

States would impose exceptional hardship upon the alien's spouse or child (if such spouse or child is a citizen of the United States or a lawfully resident alien), or that the alien cannot return to the country of his nationality or last residence because he would be subject to persecution on account of race, religion, or political opinion, the Attorney General may waive the requirement of such two-year foreign residence abroad in the case of any alien whose admission to the United States is found by the Attorney General to be in the public interest: *And provided further,* That, except in the case of an alien described in clause (iii), the Attorney General may, upon the favorable recommendation of the Director of the United States Information Agency, waive such two-year foreign residence requirement in any case in which the foreign country of the alien's nationality or last residence has furnished the Secretary of State a statement in writing that it has no objection to such waiver in the case of such alien.

(f) Whenever the President finds that the entry of any aliens or of any class of aliens into the United States would be detrimental to the interests of the United States, he may by proclamation, and for such period as he shall deem necessary, suspend the entry of all aliens or any class of aliens as immigrants or nonimmigrants, or impose on the entry of aliens any restrictions he may deem to be appropriate.

(g) Any alien who is excludable from the United States under paragraph (1) of subsection (a) of this section, or any alien afflicted with tuberculosis in any form who (A) is the spouse or the unmarried son or daughter, or the minor unmarried lawfully adopted child, of a United States citizen, or of an alien lawfully admitted for permanent residence, or of an alien who has been issued an immigrant visa, or (B) has a son or daughter who is a United States citizen, or an alien lawfully admitted for permanent residence, or an alien who has been issued an immigrant visa, shall, if otherwise admissible, be issued a visa and admitted to the United States for permanent residence in accordance with such terms, conditions, and controls, if any, including the giving of a bond, as the Attorney General, in his discretion after consultation with the Surgeon General of the United States Public Health Service, may by regulations prescribe. Any alien excludable under paragraph (3) of subsection (a) of this section because of past history of mental illness who has one of the same family relationships as are prescribed in this subsection for aliens afflicted with tuberculosis and whom the Surgeon General of the United States Public Health Service finds to have been free of such mental illness for a period of time sufficient in the light of such history to demonstrate recovery shall be eligible for a visa in accordance with the terms of this subsection.

(h) Any alien, who is excludable from the United States under paragraphs (9), (10), or (12) of subsection (a) of this section or paragraph (23) of such subsection as such paragraph relates to a single offense of simple possession of 30 grams or less of marihuana, who (A) is the spouse or child, including a minor unmarried adopted child, of a United States citizen, or of an alien lawfully admitted for permanent residence, or (B) has a son or daughter who is a United States citizen or an alien lawfully admitted for permanent residence, shall, if otherwise admissible, be issued a visa and admitted to the United States for permanent residence (1) if it shall be established to the satisfaction of the Attorney General that (A) the alien's exclusion would result in extreme hardship to the United States citizen or lawfully resident spouse, parent, or son or daughter of such alien, and (B) the admission to the United States of such alien would not be contrary to the national welfare, safety, or security of the United States; and (2) if the Attorney General, in his discretion, and pursuant to such terms, conditions, and procedures as he may by regulations prescribe, has consented to the alien's applying or reapplying for a visa and for admission to the United States.

(i) Any alien who is the spouse, parent, or child of a United States citizen or of an alien lawfully admitted for permanent residence and who is excludable because (1) he seeks, has sought to procure, or has procured, a visa or other documentation, or entry into the United States, by fraud or misrepresentation, or (2) he admits the commission of perjury in connection therewith, may be granted a visa and admitted to the United States for permanent residence, if otherwise admissible, if the Attorney General in his discretion has consented to the alien's applying or reapplying for a visa and for admission to the United States.

* * *

(k) Any alien, excludable from the United States under paragraph (14), (20), or (21) of subsection (a) of this section, who is in possession of an immigrant visa may, if otherwise admissible, be admitted in the discretion of the Attorney General if the Attorney General is satisfied that exclusion was not known to, and could not have been ascertained by the exercise of reasonable diligence by, the immigrant before the time of departure of the vessel or aircraft from the last port outside the United States and outside foreign contiguous territory or, in the case of an immigrant coming from foreign contiguous territory, before the time of the immigrant's application for admission.

* * *

Admission of Nonimmigrants

Sec. 214. **[8 U.S.C. 1184]** (a) The admission to the United States of any alien as a nonimmigrant shall be for such time and under such conditions as the Attorney General may by regulations prescribe, including when he deems necessary the giving of a bond with sufficient surety in such sum and containing such conditions as the Attorney General shall prescribe, to insure that at the expiration of such time or upon failure to maintain the status under which he was admitted, or to maintain any status subsequently acquired under section 248, such alien will depart from the United States. No alien admitted to Guam without a visa pursuant to section 212(1) may be authorized to enter or stay in the United States other than in Guam or to remain in Guam for a period exceeding fifteen days from date of admission to Guam.

(b) Every alien shall be presumed to be an immigrant until he establishes to the satisfaction of the consular officer, at the time of application for a visa, and the immigration officers, at the time of application for admission, that he is entitled to a nonimmigrant status under section 101(a)(15). An alien who is an officer or employee of any foreign government or of any international organization entitled to enjoy privileges, exemptions, and immunities under the International Organizations Immunities Act [22 U.S.C. 288, note], or an alien who is the attendant, servant, employee, or member of the immediate family of any such alien shall not be entitled to apply for or receive an immigrant visa, or to enter the United States as an immigrant unless he executes a written waiver in the same form and substance as is prescribed by section 247(b).

(c) The question of importing any alien as a nonimmigrant under section 101(a)(15)(H) or (L) in any specific case or specific cases shall be determined by the Attorney General, after consultation with appropriate agencies of the Government, upon petition of the importing employer. Such petition shall be made and approved before the visa is granted. The petition shall be in such form and contain such information as the Attorney General shall prescribe. The approval of such a petition shall not, of itself, be construed as establishing that the alien is a nonimmigrant.

(d) A visa shall not be issued under the provisions of section 101(a)(15)(K) until the consular officer has received a petition filed in the United States by the fiancée or fiancé of the applying alien and approved by the Attorney General. The petition shall be in such form and contain such information as the Attorney General shall, by regulation, prescribe. It shall be approved only after satisfactory evidence is submitted by the petitioner to establish that the parties have a bona fide intention to marry and are legally able and actually willing to conclude a valid marriage in the United States within a period of ninety days after the alien's arrival. In the event the marriage with the petitioner does not occur within three months after the entry of the said alien and minor children, they shall be required to depart from the United States and upon failure to do so shall be deported in accordance with sections 242 and 243. In the event the marriage between the said alien and the petitioner shall occur within three months after the entry and they are found otherwise admissible, the Attorney General shall record the lawful admission for permanent residence of the alien and minor children as of the date of the payment of the required visa fees.

TRAVEL DOCUMENTATION OF ALIENS AND CITIZENS

Sec. 215. [8 U.S.C. 1185] (a) Unless otherwise ordered by the President, it shall be unlawful—

(1) for any alien to depart from or enter or attempt to depart from or enter the United States except under such reasonable rules, regulations, and orders, and subject to such limitations and exceptions as the President may prescribe;

(2) for any person to transport or attempt to transport from or into the United States another person with knowledge or reasonable

cause to believe that the departure or entry of such other person is forbidden by this section;

(3) for any person knowingly to make any false statement in an application for permission to depart from or enter the United States with intent to induce or secure the granting of such permission either for himself or for another;

(4) for any person knowingly to furnish or attempt to furnish or assist in furnishing to another a permit or evidence of permission to depart or enter not issued and designed for such other person's use;

(5) for any person knowingly to use or attempt to use any permit or evidence of permission to depart or enter not issued and designed for his use;

(6) for any person to forge, counterfeit, mutilate, or alter, or cause or procure to be forged, counterfeited, mutilated, or altered, any permit or evidence of permission to depart from or enter the United States;

(7) for any person knowingly to use or attempt to use or furnish to another for use any false, forged, counterfeited, mutilated, or altered permit, or evidence of permission, or any permit or evidence of permission which, though originally valid, has become or been made void or invalid.

(b) Except as otherwise provided by the President and subject to such limitations and exceptions as the President may authorize and prescribe it shall be unlawful for any citizen of the United States to depart from or enter, or attempt to depart from or enter, the United States unless he bears a valid passport.

(c) The term "United States" as used in this section includes the Canal Zone, and all territory and waters, continental or insular, subject to the jurisdiction of the United States. The term "person" as used in this section shall be deemed to mean any individual, partnership, association, company, or other incorporated body of individuals, or corporation, or body politic.

(d) Nothing in this section shall be construed to entitle an alien to whom a permit to enter the United States has been issued to enter the United States, if, upon arrival in the United States, he is found to be inadmissible under any of the provisions of this Act, or any other law, relating to the entry of aliens into the United States.

(e) The revocation of any rule, regulation, or order issued in pursuance of this section shall not prevent prosecution for any offense committed, or the imposition of any penalties or forfeitures, liability for which was incurred under this section prior to the revocation of such rule, regulation, or order.

(f) Passports, visas, reentry permits, and other documents required for entry under this Act may be considered as permits to enter for the purposes of this section.

Chapter 3. Issuance of Entry Documents

ISSUANCE OF VISAS

Sec. 221. [8 U.S.C. 1201] (a) Under the conditions hereinafter prescribed and subject to the limitations prescribed in this Act or regulations issued thereunder, a consular officer may issue (1) to an immigrant who has made proper application therefor, an immigrant visa which shall consist of one copy of the application provided for in section 222, visaed by such consular officer, and shall specify the quota, if any, to which the immigrant is charged, the immigrant's particular status under such quota, the preference, nonpreference, immediate relative, or special immigration classification to which the alien is charged, the date on which the validity of the visa shall expire, and such additional information as may be required; and (2) to a nonimmigrant who has made proper application therefor, a nonimmigrant visa, which shall specify the classification under section 101(a)(15) of the nonimmigrant, the period during which the nonimmigrant visa shall be valid, and such additional information as may be required.

(b) Each alien who applies for a visa shall be registered and fingerprinted in connection with his application, and shall furnish copies of his photograph signed by him for such use as may be by regulations required. The requirements of this subsection may be waived in the discretion of the Secretary of State in the case of any alien who is within that class of nonimmigrants enumerated in sections 101(a)(15)(A), and 101(a)(15)(G), or in the case of any alien who is granted a diplomatic visa on a diplomatic passport or on the equivalent thereof.

(c) An immigrant visa shall be valid for such period, not exceeding four months, as shall be by regulations prescribed, except that any visa issued to a child lawfully adopted by a United States citizen and spouse while such citizen is serving abroad in the United States Armed Forces, or is employed abroad by the United States Government, or is temporarily abroad on business, shall be valid until such time, for a period not to exceed three years, as the adoptive citizen parent returns to the United States in due course of his service, employment, or business. A nonimmigrant visa shall be valid for such periods as shall be by regulations prescribed. In prescribing the period of validity of a nonimmigrant visa in the case of nationals of any foreign country who are eligible for such visas, the Secretary of State shall, insofar as practicable, accord to such nationals the same treatment upon a reciprocal basis as such foreign country accords to nationals of the United States who are within a similar class. An immigrant visa may be replaced under the original number during the year in which the original visa was issued for an immigrant who establishes to the satisfaction of the consular officer that he was unable to use the original immigrant visa during the period of its validity because of reasons beyond his control and for which he was not responsible: *Provided,* the consular officer is in possession of the duplicate signed copy of the original visa, the immigrant is found by the consular officer to be eligible for an immigrant visa and the immigrant pays again the statutory fees for an application and an immigrant visa.

(d) Prior to the issuance of an immigrant visa to any alien, the consular officer shall require such alien to submit to a physical and mental examination in accordance with such regulations as may be prescribed. Prior to the issuance of a nonimmigrant visa to any alien, the consular officer may require such alien to submit to a physical or mental examination, or both, if in his opinion such examination is necessary to ascertain whether such alien is eligible to receive a visa.

(e) Each immigrant shall surrender his immigrant visa to the immigration officer at the port of entry, who shall endorse on the visa the date and the port of arrival, the identity of the vessel or other means of transportation by which the immigrant arrived, and such other endorsements as may be by regulations required.

(f) Each nonimmigrant shall present or surrender to the immigration officer at the port of entry such documents as may be by regulation required. In the case of an alien crewman not in possession of any individual documents other than a passport and until such time as it becomes practicable to issue individual documents, such alien crewman may be admitted, subject to the provisions of this title, if his name appears in the crew list of the vessel or aircraft on which he arrives and the crew list is visaed by a consular officer, but the consular officer shall have the right to exclude any alien crewman from the crew list visa.

(g) No visa or other documentation shall be issued to an alien if (1) it appears to the consular officer, from statements in the application, or in the papers submitted therewith, that such alien is ineligible to receive a visa or such other documentation under section 212, or any other provision of law, (2) the application fails to comply with the provisions of this Act, or the regulations issued thereunder, or (3) the consular officer knows or has reason to believe that such alien is ineligible to receive a visa or such other documentation under section 212, or any other provision of law: *Provided,* That a visa or other documentation may be issued to an alien who is within the purview of section 212(a)(7), or section 212(a)(15), if such alien is otherwise entitled to receive a visa or other documentation, upon receipt of notice by the consular officer from the Attorney General of the giving of a bond or undertaking providing indemnity as in the case of aliens admitted under section 213: *Provided further,* That a visa may be issued to an alien defined in section 101(a)(15)(B) or (F), if such alien is otherwise entitled to receive a visa, upon receipt cf a notice by the consular officer from the Attorney General of the giving of a bond with sufficient surety in such sum and containing such conditions as the consular officer shall prescribe, to insure that at the expiration of the time for which such alien has been admitted by the Attorney General, as provided in section 214(a), or upon failure to maintain the status under which he was admitted, or to maintain any status subsequently acquired under section 248 of the Act, such alien will depart from the United States.

(h) Nothing in this Act shall be construed to entitle any alien, to whom a visa or other documentation has been issued, to enter the United States, if, upon arrival at a port of entry in the United States, he is found to be inadmissible under this Act, or any other provision of law. The substance of this subsection shall appear upon every visa application.

(i) After the issuance of a visa or other documentation to any alien, the consular officer or the Secretary of State may at any time, in his discretion, revoke such visa or other documentation. Notice of such revocation shall be communicated to the Attorney General, and such revocation shall invalidate the visa or other documentation from the date of issuance: *Provided,* That carriers or transportation companies, and masters, commanding officers, agents, owners, charterers, or consignees, shall not be penalized under section 273(b) for action taken in reliance on such visas or other documentation, unless they received due notice of such revocation prior to the alien's embarkation.

APPLICATIONS FOR VISAS

Sec. 222. [8 U.S.C. 1202] (a) Every alien applying for an immigrant visa and for alien registration shall make application therefor in such form and manner and at such place as shall be by regulations prescribed. In the application the immigrant shall state his full and true name, and any other name which he has used or by which he has been known; age and sex; the date and place of his birth; present address and places of previous residence; whether married or single, and the names and places of residence of spouse and children, if any; calling or occupation; personal description (including height, complexion, color of hair and eyes, and marks of identification); languages he can speak, read, or write; names and addresses of parents, and if neither parent living, then the name and address of his next of kin in the country from which he comes; port of entry into the United States; final destination, if any, beyond the port of entry; whether he has a ticket through to such final destination; whether going to join a relative or friend, and, if so, the name and complete address of such relative or friend; the purpose for which he is going to the United States; the length of time he intends to remain in the United States; whether or not he intends to remain in the United States permanently; whether he was ever arrested, convicted or was ever in prison or almshouse; whether he has ever been the beneficiary of a pardon or an amnesty; whether he has ever been treated in an institution or hospital or other place for insanity or other mental disease; if he claims to be an immediate relative within the meaning of section 201(b) or a preference or special immigrant, the facts on which he bases such claim; whether or not he is a member of any class of individuals excluded from admission into the United States, or whether he claims to be exempt from exclusion under the immigration laws; and such additional information necessary to the identification of the applicant and the enforcement of the immigration and nationality laws as may be by regulations prescribed.

(b) Every alien applying for an immigrant visa shall present a valid unexpired passport or other suitable travel document, or document of identity and nationality, if such document is required under the regulations issued by the Secretary of State. The immigrant shall furnish to the consular officer with his application two copies of a certification by the appropriate police authorities stating what their records show concerning the immigrant; two certified copies of any existing prison record, military record, and record of his birth; and two certified copies of all other records or documents concerning him or his case which may be required by the consular officer. One copy of each document so furnished shall be permanently attached to each copy of the application and become a part thereof. In the event that the immigrant establishes to the satisfaction of the consular officer that any document or record required by this subsection is unobtainable, the consular officer may permit the immigrant to submit in lieu of such document or record other satisfactory evidence of the fact to which such document or record would, if obtainable, pertain.

(c) Every alien applying for a nonimmigrant visa and for alien registration shall make application therefor in such form and manner as shall be by regulations prescribed. In the application the alien shall state his full and true name, the date and place of birth, his nationality, the purpose and length of his intended stay in the United States; personal description (including height, complexion, color of hair and eyes, and marks of identification); his marital status; and such additional information necessary to the identification of the applicant and the enforcement of the immigration and nationality laws as may be by regulations prescribed.

(d) Every alien applying for a nonimmigrant visa and alien registration shall furnish to the consular officer, with his application, a certified copy of such documents pertaining to him as may be by regulations required.

(e) Except as may be otherwise prescribed by regulations, each copy of an application required by this section shall be signed by the applicant in the presence of the consular officer, and verified by the oath of the applicant administered by the consular officer. One copy of the application for an immigrant visa, when visaed by the consular officer, shall become the immigrant visa, and the other copy shall be disposed of as may be by regulations prescribed. The application for a nonimmigrant visa or other documentation as a nonimmigrant shall be disposed of as may be by regulations prescribed. The issuance of a nonimmigrant visa shall, except as may be otherwise by regulations prescribed, be evidenced by a stamp placed by the consular officer in the alien's passport.

(f) The records of the Department of State and of diplomatic and consular offices of the United States pertaining to the issuance or refusal of visas or permits to enter the United States shall be considered confidential and shall be used only for the formulation, amendment, administration, or enforcement of the immigration, nationality, and other laws of the United States, except that in the discretion of the Secretary of State certified copies of such records may be made available to a court which certifies that the information contained in such records is needed by the court in the interest of the ends of justice in a case pending before the court.

* * *

Chapter 4.   Provisions relating to Entry and Exclusion

* * *

TEMPORARY REMOVAL FOR EXAMINATION UPON ARRIVAL

Sec. 233.   [8 U.S.C. 1223] (a) Upon the arrival at a port of the United States of any vessel or aircraft bringing aliens (including alien crewmen) the immigration officers may order a temporary removal of such aliens for examination and inspection at a designated time and place, but such temporary removal shall not be considered a landing, nor shall it relieve vessels or aircraft, the transportation lines, or the masters, commanding officers, agents, owners, or consignees of the vessel or aircraft upon which such aliens are brought to any port of the United States from any of the obligations which, in case such aliens remain on board, would, under the provisions of this Act bind such vessels or aircraft, transportation lines, masters, commanding officers, agents, owners, or consignees. A temporary removal of aliens from such vessels or aircraft ordered pursuant to this subsection shall be made by an immigration officer at the expense of the vessels or aircraft or transportation lines, or the masters, commanding officers, agents, owners, or consignees of such vessels, aircraft or transportation lines, as provided in subsection (b) and such vessels, aircraft, transportation lines, masters, commanding officers, agents, owners, or consignees, shall, so long as such removal lasts, be relieved of responsibility for the safekeeping of such aliens: *Provided,* That such vessels, aircraft, transportation lines, masters, commanding officers, agents, owners, or consignees may with the approval of the Attorney General assume responsibility for the safekeeping of such aliens during their removal to a designated place for examination and inspection, in which event, such removal need not be made by an immigration officer.

(b) Whenever a temporary removal of aliens is made under this section, the vessels or aircraft or transportation lines which brought them, and the masters, commanding officers, owners, agents, and consignees of the vessel, aircraft, or transportation line upon which they arrived shall pay all expenses of such removal to a designated place for examination and inspection or other place of detention and all expenses arising during subsequent detention, pending a decision on the alien's eligibility to enter the United States and until they are either allowed to land or returned to the care of the transportation line or to the vessel or aircraft which brought them. Such expenses shall include maintenance, medical treatment in hospital or elsewhere, burial in the event of death, and transfer to the vessel, aircraft, or transportation line in the event of deportation, except where such expenses arise under section 237(d) or in such cases as the Attorney General may prescribe in the case of aliens paroled into the United States temporarily under the provisions of section 212(d)(5).

(c) Any detention expenses and expenses incident to detention incurred (but not including expenses of removal to the place of detention) pursuant to sections 232 and 233 shall not be assessed under this Act against the vessel or aircraft or transportation line or the master, commanding officer, owner, agent, or consignee of the vessel, aircraft, or transportation line in the case of (1) any alien who arrived in possession of a valid unexpired immigrant visa, or (2) any alien who was finally admitted to the United States pursuant to this Act after such detention, or (3) any alien other than an alien crewman, who arrived in possession of a valid unexpired nonimmigrant visa or other document authorizing such alien to apply for temporary admission to the United States or an unexpired reentry permit issued to him, and (A) application for admission was made within one hundred and twenty days of the date of issuance of the visa or other document, or in the case of an alien in possession of a reentry permit, within one hundred and twenty days of the date on which the alien was last examined and admitted by the Service, or (B) in the event application for admission was made later than one hundred and twenty days of the date of issuance of the visa or other document or such examination and admission, if the vessel, aircraft, or transportation line or the master, commanding officer, owner, agent, or consignee of the vessel, aircraft, or transportation line establishes to the satisfaction of the Attorney General that the ground of exclusion could not have been ascertained by the exercise of due diligence prior to the alien's embarkation, or (4) any person claiming United States nationality or citizenship and in possession of an unexpired United States passport issued to him by competent authority, or (5) any person claiming United States nationality or citizenship and in possession of a certificate of identity issued pursuant to section 360(b) of this Act, or any other document of identity issued or verified by a consular officer which shows on its face that it is currently valid for travel to the United States and who was allowed to land in the United States after such detention.

(d) Any refusal or failure to comply with the provisions of this section shall be punished in the manner specified in section 237(b) of this Act.

PHYSICAL AND MENTAL EXAMINATION

Sec. 234. [8 U.S.C. 1224] The physical and mental examination of arriving aliens (including alien crewmen) shall be made by medical officers of the United States Public Health Service, who shall conduct all medical examinations and shall certify, for the information of the immigration officers and the special inquiry officers, any physical and mental defect or disease observed by such medical officers in any such alien. If medical officers of the United States Public Health Service are not available, civil surgeons of not less than four years' professional experience may be employed for such service upon such terms as may be prescribed by the Attorney General. Aliens (including alien crewmen) arriving at ports of the United States shall be examined by at least one such medical officer or civil surgeon under such administrative regulations as the Attorney General may prescribe, and under medical regulations prepared by the Surgeon General of the United States Public Health Service. Medical officers of the United States Public Health Service who have had special training in the diagnosis of insanity and mental defects shall be detailed for duty or employed at such ports of entry as the Attorney General may designate, and such medical officers shall be provided with suitable facilities for the detention and examination of all arriving aliens who it is suspected may be excludable under paragraphs (1), (2), (3), (4), or (5) of section 212(a), and the services of interpreters shall be provided for such examination. Any alien certified under paragraphs (1), (2), (3), (4), or (5) of section 212(a) may appeal to a board of medical officers of the United States Public Health Service, which shall be convened by the Surgeon General of the United States Public Health Service, and any such alien may introduce before such board one expert medical witness at his own cost and expense.

INSPECTION BY IMMIGRATION OFFICERS

Sec. 235.   [8 U.S.C. 1225] (a) The inspection, other than the physical and mental examination, of aliens (including alien crewmen) seeking admission or readmission to, or the privilege of passing through the United States shall be conducted by immigration officers, except as otherwise provided in regard to special inquiry officers. All aliens arriving at ports of the United States shall be examined by one or more immigration officers at the discretion of the Attorney General and under such regulations as he may prescribe. Immigration officers are hereby authorized and empowered to board and search any vessel, aircraft, railway car, or other conveyance, or vehicle in which they believe aliens are being brought into the United States. The Attorney General and any immigration officer, including special inquiry officers, shall have power to administer oaths and to take and consider evidence of or from any person touching the privilege of any alien or person he believes or suspects to be an alien to enter, reenter, pass through, or reside in the United States or concerning any matter which is material and relevant to the enforcement of this Act and the administration of the Service, and, where such action may be necessary, to make a written record of such evidence. Any person coming into the United States may be required to state under oath the purpose or purposes for which he comes, the length of time he intends to remain in the United States, whether or not he intends to remain in the United States permanently and, if an alien, whether he intends to become a citizen thereof, and such other items of information as will aid the immigration officer in determining whether he is a national of the United States or an alien and, if the latter, whether he belongs to any of the excluded classes enumerated in section 212. The Attorney General and any immigration officer, including special inquiry officers, shall have power to require by subpoena the attendance and testimony of witnesses before immigration officers and special inquiry officers and the production of books, papers, and documents relating to the privilege of any person to enter, reenter, reside in, or pass through the United States or concerning any matter which is material and relevant to the enforcement of this Act and the administration of the Service, and to that end may invoke the aid of any court of the United States. Any United States district court within the jurisdiction of which investigations or inquiries are being conducted by an immigration officer or special inquiry officer may, in the event of neglect or refusal to respond to a subpoena issued under this subsection or refusal to testify before an immigration officer or special inquiry officer, issue an order requiring such persons to appear before an immigration officer or special inquiry officer, produce books, papers, and documents if demanded, and testify, and any failure to obey such order of the court may be punished by the court as a contempt thereof.

(b) Every alien (other than an alien crewman), and except as otherwise provided in subsection (c) of this section and in section 273(d), who may not appear to the examining immigration officer at the port of arrival to be clearly and beyond a doubt entitled to land shall be detained for further inquiry to be conducted by a special inquiry officer. The decision of the examining immigration officer, if favorable to the admission of any alien, shall be subject to challenge by any other immigration officer and such challenge shall operate to take the alien, whose privilege to land is so challenged, before a special inquiry officer for further inquiry.

(c) Any alien (including an alien crewman) who may appear to the examining immigration officer or to the special inquiry officer during the examination before either of such officers to be excludable under paragraph (27), (28), or (29) of section 212(a) shall be temporarily excluded, and no further inquiry by a special inquiry officer shall be conducted until after the case is reported to the Attorney General together with any such written statement and accompanying information, if any, as the alien or his representative may desire to submit in connection therewith and such an inquiry or further inquiry is directed by the Attorney General. If the Attorney General is satisfied that the alien is excludable under any of such paragraphs on the basis of information of a confidential nature, the disclosure of which the Attorney General, in the exercise of his discretion, and after consultation with the appropriate security agencies of the Government, concludes would be prejudicial to the public interest, safety, or security, he may in his discretion order such alien to be excluded and deported without any inquiry or further inquiry by a special inquiry officer. Nothing in this subsection shall be regarded as requiring an inquiry before a special inquiry officer in the case of an alien crewman.

EXCLUSIONS OF ALIENS

Sec. 236. [8 U.S.C. 1226] (a) A special inquiry officer shall conduct proceedings under this section, administer oaths, present and receive evidence, and interrogate, examine, and cross-examine the alien or witnesses. He shall have authority in any case to determine whether an arriving alien who has been detained for further inquiry under section 235 shall be allowed to enter or shall be excluded and deported. The determination of such special inquiry officer shall be based only on the evidence produced at the inquiry. No special inquiry officer shall conduct a proceeding in any case under this section in which he shall have participated in investigative functions or in which he shall have participated (except as provided in this subsection) in prosecuting functions. Proceedings before a special inquiry officer under this section shall be conducted in accordance with this section, the applicable provisions of sections 235 and 287(b), and such regulations as the Attorney General shall prescribe, and shall be the sole and exclusive procedure for determining admissibility of a person to the United States under the provisions of this section. At such inquiry, which shall be kept separate and apart from the public, the alien may have one friend or relative present, under such conditions as may be prescribed by the Attorney General. A complete record of the proceedings and of all testimony and evidence produced at such inquiry, shall be kept.

(b) From a decision of a special inquiry officer excluding an alien, such alien may take a timely appeal to the Attorney General, and any such alien shall be advised of his right to take such appeal. No appeal may be taken from a temporary exclusion under section 235(c). From a decision of the special inquiry officer to admit an alien, the immigration officer in charge at the port where the inquiry is held may take a timely appeal to the Attorney General. An appeal by the alien, or such officer in charge, shall operate to stay any final action with respect to any alien whose case is so appealed until the final decision of the Attorney General is made. Except as provided in section 235(c) such decision shall be rendered solely upon the evidence adduced before the special inquiry officer.

(c) Except as provided in subsections (b) or (d), in every case where an alien is excluded from admission into the United States, under this Act or any other law or treaty now existing or hereafter made, the decision of a special inquiry officer shall be final unless reversed on appeal to the Attorney General.

(d) If a medical officer or civil surgeon or board of medical officers has certified under section 234 that an alien is afflicted with a disease specified in section 212(a)(6), or with any mental disease, defect, or disability which would bring such alien within any of the classes excluded from admission to the United States under paragraphs (1), (2), (3), (4), or (5) of section 212(a), the decision of the special inquiry officer shall be based solely upon such certification. No alien shall have a right to appeal from such an excluding decision of a special inquiry officer. If an alien is excluded by a special inquiry officer because of the existence of a physical disease, defect, or disability, other than one specified in section 212(a)(6), the alien may appeal from the excluding decision in accordance with subsection (b) of this section, and the provisions of section 213 may be invoked.

IMMEDIATE DEPORTATION OF ALIENS EXCLUDED FROM ADMISSION OR ENTERING IN VIOLATION OF LAW.

Sec. 237. [8 U.S.C. 1227] (a) (1) Any alien (other than an alien crewman) arriving in the United States who is excluded under this chapter, shall be immediately deported, in accommodations of the same class in which he arrived, unless the Attorney General, in an individual case, in his discretion, concludes that immediate deportation is not practicable or proper. Deportation shall be to the country in which the alien boarded the vessel or aircraft on which he arrived in the United States, unless the alien boarded such vessel or aircraft in foreign territory contiguous to the United States or in any island adjacent thereto or adjacent to the United States and the alien is not a native, citizen, subject, or national of, or does not have a residence in, such foreign contiguous territory or adjacent island, in which case the deportation shall instead be to the country in which is located the port at which the alien embarked for such foreign contiguous territory or adjacent island. The cost of the maintenance including detention expenses and expenses incident to detention of any such alien while he is being detained shall be borne by the owner or owners of the vessel or aircraft on which he arrived, except that the cost of maintenance (including detention expenses and expenses incident to detention while the alien is being detained prior to the time he is offered for deportation to the transportation line which brought him to the United States) shall not be assessed against the owner or owners of such vessel or aircraft if (A) the alien was in possession of a valid, unexpired immigrant visa, or (B) the alien (other than an alien crewman) was in possession of a valid, unexpired nonimmigrant visa or other document authorizing such alien to apply for temporary admission to the United States or an unexpired reentry permit issued to him, and (i) such application was made within one hundred and twenty days of the date of issuance of the visa or other document, or in the case of an alien in possession of a reentry permit, within one hundred and twenty days of the date on which the alien was last examined and admitted by the Service, or (ii) in the event the application was made later than one hundred and twenty days of the date of issuance of the visa or other document or such examination and admission, if the owner or owners of such vessel or aircraft established to the satisfaction of the Attorney General that the ground of exclusion could not have been ascertained by the exercise of due diligence prior to the alien's embarkation, or (C) the person claimed United States nationality or citizenship and was in possession of an unexpired United States passport issued to him by competent authority.

(2) If the government of the country designated in paragraph (1) will not accept the alien into its territory, the alien's deportation shall be directed by the Attorney General, in his discretion and without necessarily giving any priority or preference because of their order as herein set forth, either to—

(A) the country of which the alien is a subject, citizen, or national;

(B) the country in which he was born;

(C) the country in which he has a residence; or

(D) any country which is willing to accept the alien into its territory, if deportation to any of the foregoing countries is impracticable, inadvisable, or impossible.

(b) * * *.

* * *

Chapter 5. Deportation; Adjustment of Status

GENERAL CLASSES OF DEPORTABLE ALIENS

Sec. 241. **[8 U.S.C. 1251]** (a) Any alien in the United States (including an alien crewman) shall, upon the order of the Attorney General, be deported who—

(1) at the time of entry was within one or more of the classes of aliens excludable by the law existing at the time of such entry;

(2) entered the United States without inspection or at any time or place other than as designated by the Attorney General or is in the United States in violation of this Act or in violation of any other law of the United States;

(3) hereafter, within five years after entry, becomes institutionalized at public expense because of mental disease, defect, or deficiency, unless the alien can show that such disease, defect, or deficiency did not exist prior to his admission to the United States;

(4) is convicted of a crime involving moral turpitude committed within five years after entry and either sentenced to confinement or confined therefor in a prison or corrective institution, for a year or more, or who at any time after entry is convicted of two crimes involving moral turpitude, not arising out of a single scheme of criminal misconduct, regardless of whether confined therefor and regardless of whether the convictions were in a single trial;

(5) has failed to comply with the provisions of section 265 unless he establishes to the satisfaction of the Attorney General that such failure was reasonably excusable or was not willful, or has been convicted under section 266(c) of this title, or under section 36(c) of the Alien Registration Act, 1940, or has been convicted of violating or conspiracy to violate any provision of the Act entitled "An Act to require the registration of certain persons employed by agencies to disseminate propaganda in the United States, and for other purposes", approved June 8, 1938, as amended [see 22 U.S.C. 618(c)], or has been convicted under section 1546 of title 18 of the United States Code;

(6) is or at any time has been, after entry, a member of any of the following classes of aliens:

(A) Aliens who are anarchists;

(B) Aliens who advocate or teach, or who are members of or affiliated with any organization that advocates or teaches, opposition to all organized government;

(C) Aliens who are members of or affiliated with (i) the Communist Party of the United States; (ii) any other totalitarian party of the United States; (iii) the Communist Political Association; (iv) the Communist or any other totalitarian party of any State of the United States, of any foreign state, or of any political or geographical subdivision of any foreign state; (v) any section, subsidiary, branch, affiliate, or subdivision of any such association or party; or (vi) the direct predecessors or successors of any such association or party, regardless of what name such group or organization may have used, may now bear, or may hereafter adopt: *Provided*, That nothing in this paragraph, or in any other provision of this Act, shall be construed as declaring that the Communist Party does not advocate the overthrow of the Government of the United States by force, violence, or other unconstitutional means;

(D) Aliens not within any of the other provisions of this paragraph who advocate the economic, international, and governmental doctrines of world communism or the establishment in the United States of a totalitarian dictatorship, or who are members of or affiliated with any organization that advocates the economic, international, and governmental doctrines of world communism or the establishment in the United States of a totalitarian dictatorship, either through its own utterances or through any written or printed publications issued or published by or with the permission or consent of or under the authority of such organization or paid for by the funds of, or funds furnished by, such organization;

(E) Aliens not within any of the other provisions of this paragraph, who are members of or affiliated with any organization during the time it is registered or required to be registered under section 7 of the Subversive Activities Control Act of 1950, unless such aliens establish that they did not have knowledge or reason to believe at the time they became members of or affiliated with such an organization (and did not thereafter and prior to the date upon which such organization was so registered or so required to be registered have such knowledge or reason to believe) that such organization was a Communist organization;

(F) Aliens who advocate or teach or who are members of or affiliated with any organization that advocates or teaches (i) the overthrow by force, violence, or other unconstitutional means of the Government of the United States or of all forms of law; or (ii) the duty, necessity, or propriety of the unlawful assaulting or killing of any officer or officers (either of specific individuals or of officers generally) of the Government of the United States or of any other organized government, because of his or their official character; or (iii) the unlawful damage, injury, or destruction of property; or (iv) sabotage;

(G) Aliens who write or publish, or cause to be written or published, or who knowingly circulate, distribute, print, or display, or knowingly cause to be circulated, distributed, printed, published, or displayed,or who knowingly have in their possession for the purpose of circulation, publication, distribution, or display, any written or printed matter, advocating or teaching opposition to all organized government, or advocating or teaching (i) the overthrow by force, violence, or other unconstitutional means of the Government of the United States or of all forms of law; or (ii) the duty, necessity, or propriety of the unlawful assaulting or killing of any officer or officers (either of specific individuals or of officers generally) of the Government of the United States or of any other organized government, because of his or their official character; or (iii) the unlawful damage, injury, or destruction of property; or (iv) sabotage; or (v) the economic, international, and governmental doctrines of world communism or the establishment in the United States of a totalitarian dictatorship;

(H) Aliens who are members of or affiliated with any organization that writes, circulates, distributes, prints, publishes, or displays, or causes to be written, circulated, distributed, printed, published, or displayed, or that has in its possession for the purpose of circulation, distribution, publication, issue, or display, any written or printed matter of the character described in paragraph (G);

(7) is engaged, or at any time after entry has engaged, or at any time after entry has had a purpose to engage, in any of the activities described in paragraph (27) or (29) of section 212(a), unless the Attorney General is satisfied, in the case of any alien within category (C) of paragraph (29) of such section, that such alien did not have knowledge or reason to believe at the time such alien became a member of, affiliated with, or participated in the activities of the organization (and did not thereafter and prior to the date upon which such organization was registered or required to be registered under section 7 of the Subversive Activities Control Act of 1950 have such knowledge or reason to believe) that such organization was a Communist organization;

(8) in the opinion of the Attorney General, has within five years after entry become a public charge from causes not affirmatively shown to have arisen after entry;

(9) was admitted as a nonimmigrant and failed to maintain the nonimmigrant status in which he was admitted or to which it was changed pursuant to section 248, or to comply with the conditions of any such status;

(10) entered the United States from foreign contiguous territory or adjacent islands, having arrived there on a vessel or aircraft of a nonsignatory transportation company under section 238(a) and was without the required period of stay in such foreign contiguous territory or adjacent islands following such arrival (other than an alien described in section 101(a)(27)(A) and aliens born in the Western Hemisphere);

(11) is, or hereafter at any time after entry has been, a narcotic drug addict, or who at any time has been convicted of a violation of, or a conspiracy to violate, any law or regulation relating to the illicit possession of or traffic in narcotic drugs or marihuana, or who has been convicted of a violation of, or a conspiracy to violate, any law or regulation governing or controlling the taxing, manufacture, produc-

tion, compounding, transportation, sale, exchange, dispensing, giving away, importation, exportation, or the possession for the purpose of the manufacture, production, compounding, transportation, sale, exchange, dispensing, giving away, importation, or exportation of opium, coca leaves, heroin, marihuana, any salt derivative or preparation of opium or coca leaves or isonipecaine or any addiction-forming or addiction-sustaining opiate;

(12) by reason of any conduct, behavior or activity at any time after entry became a member of any of the classes specified in paragraph (12) of section 212(a); or is or at any time after entry has been the manager, or is or at any time after entry has been connected with the management, of a house of prostitution or any other immoral place;

(13) prior to, or at the time of any entry, or at any time within five years after any entry, shall have, knowingly and for gain, encouraged, induced, assisted, abetted, or aided any other alien to enter or to try to enter the United States in violation of law;

(14) at any time after entry, shall have been convicted of possessing or carrying in violation of any law any weapon which shoots or is designed to shoot automatically or semiautomatically more than one shot without manual reloading, by a single function of the trigger, or a weapon commonly called a sawed-off shotgun;

(15) at any time within five years after entry, shall have been convicted of violating the provisions of title I of the Alien Registration Act, 1940 [18 U.S.C. 2385, 2387];

(16) at any time after entry, shall have been convicted more than once of violating the provisions of title I of the Alien Registration Act, 1940; or

(17) the Attorney General finds to be an undesirable resident of the United States by reason of any of the following, to wit: has been or may hereafter be convicted of any violation or conspiracy to violate any of the following Acts or parts of Acts or any amendment thereto, the judgment on such conviction having become final, namely: an Act entitled "An Act to punish acts of interference with the foreign relations, the neutrality, and the foreign commerce of the United States, to punish espionage, and better to enforce the criminal laws of the United States, and for other purposes", approved June 15, 1917, or the amendment thereof approved May 16, 1918; sections 791, 792, 793, 794, 2388, and 3241, title 18, United States Code; an Act entitled "An Act to prohibit the manufacture, distribution, storage, use, and possession in time of war of explosives, providing regulations for the safe manufacture, distribution, storage, use, and possession of the same, and for other purposes", approved October 6, 1917 [50 U.S.C. 121–143]; an Act entitled "An Act to prevent in time of war departure from and entry into the United States contrary to the public safety", approved May 22, 1918 [22 U.S.C. 223–226b]; section 215 of this Act [8 U.S.C. 1185]; an Act entitled "An Act to punish the willful injury or destruction of war material or of war premises or utilities

used in connection with war material, and for other purposes", approved April 20, 1918 [50 U.S.C. 101–106]; sections 2151, 2153, 2154, 2155, and 2156 of title 18, United States Code; an Act entitled "An Act to authorize the President to increase temporarily the Military establishment of the United States", approved May 18, 1917, or any amendment thereof or supplement thereto [50 U.S.C. App. 201–211]; the Selective Training and Service Act of 1940 [50 U.S.C. App. 301–318]; the Selective Service Act of 1948; the Universal Military Training and Service Act [50 U.S.C. App. 451–471a]; an Act entitled "An Act to punish persons who make threats against the President of the United States", approved February 14, 1917 [18 U.S.C. 871]; section 871 of title 18, United States Code; an Act entitled "An Act to define, regulate, and punish trading with the enemy, and for other purposes", approved October 6, 1917, or any amendment thereof; the Trading With the Enemy Act [50 U.S.C. App. 1]; section 6 of the Penal Code of the United States; section 2384 of title 18, United States Code; has been convicted of any offense against section 13 of the Penal Code of the United States committed during the period of August 1, 1914, to April 6, 1917, or of a conspiracy occurring within said period to commit an offense under said section 13 or of any offense committed during said period against the Act entitled "An Act to protect trade and commerce against unlawful restraints and monopolies", approved July 2, 1890 [15 U.S.C. 1–7], in aid of a belligerent in the European war; section 960 of title 18, United States Code;

(18) has been convicted under section 278 of this Act [8 U.S.C. 1328] or under section 4 of the Immigration Act of February 5, 1917; or

(19) during the period beginning on March 23, 1933, and ending on May 8, 1945, under the direction of, or in association with—

(A) the Nazi government of Germany,

(B) any government in any area occupied by the military forces of the Nazi government of Germany,

(C) any government established with the assistance or cooperation of the Nazi government of Germany, or

(D) any government which was an ally of the Nazi government of Germany,

ordered, incited, assisted, or otherwise participated in the persecution of any person because of race, religion, national origin, or political opinion.

(b) The provisions of subsection (a)(4) respecting the deportation of an alien convicted of a crime or crimes shall not apply (1) in the case of any alien who has subsequent to such conviction been granted a full and unconditional pardon by the President of the United States or by the Governor of any of the several States, or (2) if the court sentencing such alien for such crimes shall make, at the time of first imposing judgment or passing sentence, or within thirty days thereafter, a recommendation to the Attorney General that such alien not be deported, due notice having been given prior to making such recommendation to representatives of the interested State, the Service, and prosecution authorities, who shall be granted an opportunity to make representations in the matter. The provisions of this subsection shall not apply in the case of any alien who is charged with being deportable from the United States under subsection (a)(11) of this section.

(c) An alien shall be deported as having procured a visa or other documentation by fraud within the meaning of paragraph (19) of section 212(a), and to be in the United States in violation of this Act within the meaning of subsection (a)(2) of this section, if (1) hereafter he or she obtains any entry into the United States with an immigrant visa or other documentation procured on the basis of a marriage entered into less than two years prior to such entry of the alien and which, within two years subsequent to any entry of the alien into the United States, shall be judicially annulled or terminated, unless such alien shall establish to the satisfaction of the Attorney General that such marriage was not contracted for the purpose of evading any provisions of the immigration laws; or (2) it appears to the satisfaction of the Attorney General that he or she has failed or refused to fulfill his or her marital agreement which in the opinion of the Attorney General was hereafter made for the purpose of procuring his or her entry as an immigrant.

(d) Except as otherwise specifically provided in this section, the provisions of this section shall be applicable to all aliens belonging to any of the classes enumerated in subsection (a), notwithstanding (1) that any such alien entered the United States prior to the date of enactment of this Act, or (2) that the facts, by reason of which any such alien belongs to any of the classes enumerated in subsection (a), occurred prior to the date of enactment of this Act.

(e) An alien, admitted as a nonimmigrant under the provisions of either section 101(a)(15)(A)(i) or 101(a)(15)(G)(i), and who fails to maintain a status under either of those provisions, shall not be required to depart from the United States without the approval of the Secretary of State, unless such alien is subject to deportation under subsection (a)(6) or (7) of this section.

(f) (1)(A) The provisions of this section relating to the deportation of aliens within the United States on the ground that they were excludable at the time of entry as aliens who have sought to procure or have procured visas or other documentation, or entry into the United States, by fraud or misrepresentation, whether willful or innocent, may, in the discretion of the Attorney General, be waived for any alien (other than an alien described in subsection (a)(19) of this section) who—

  (i) is the spouse, parent, or child of a citizen of the United States or of an alien lawfully admitted to the United States for permanent residence: and

  (ii) was in possession of an immigrant visa or equivalent document and was otherwise admissible to the United States at the time of such entry except for those grounds of inadmissibility specified under paragraphs (14), (20), and (21) of section 212(a) which were a direct result of that fraud or misrepresentation.

(B) A waiver of deportation for fraud or misrepresentation granted under subparagraph (A) shall also operate to waive deportation based on the grounds of inadmissibility at entry described under subparagraph (A)(ii) directly resulting from such fraud or misrepresentation.

(2) The provisions of subsection (a)(11) of this subsection as relate to a single offense of simple possession of 30 grams or less of marihuana may, in the discretion of the Attorney General, be waived for any alien (other than an alien described in subsection (a)(19) of this section) who—

(A) is the spouse or child of a citizen of the United States or of an alien lawfully admitted for permanent residence, or

(B) has a child who is a citizen of the United States or an alien lawfully admitted for permanent residence,

if it is established to the satisfaction of the Attorney General that the alien's deportation would result in extreme hardship to the United States citizen or lawfully resident spouse, parent, or child of such alien and that such waiver would not be contrary to the national welfare, safety, or security of the United States.

Apprehension and Deportation of Aliens

Sec. 242. **[8 U.S.C. 1252]** (a) Pending a determination of deportability in the case of any alien as provided in subsection (b) of this section, such alien may, upon warrant of the Attorney General, be arrested and taken into custody. Any such alien taken into custody may, in the discretion of the Attorney General and pending such final determination of deportability, (1) be continued in custody; or (2) be released under bond in the amount of not less than $500 with security approved by the Attorney General, containing such conditions as the Attorney General may prescribe; or (3) be released on conditional parole. But such bond or parole, whether heretofore or hereafter authorized, may be revoked at any time by the Attorney General, in his discretion, and the alien may be returned to custody under the warrant which initiated the proceedings against him and detained until final determination of his deportability. Any court of competent jurisdiction shall have authority to review or revise any determination of the Attorney General concerning detention, release on bond, or parole pending final decision of deportability upon a conclusive showing in habeas corpus proceedings that the Attorney General is not proceeding with such reasonable dispatch as may be warranted by the particular facts and circumstances in the case of any alien to determine deportability.

(b) A special inquiry officer shall conduct proceedings under this section to determine the deportability of any alien, and shall administer oaths, present and receive evidence, interrogate, examine, and cross-examine the alien or witnesses, and as authorized by the Attorney General, shall make determinations, including orders of deportation. Determination of deportability in any case shall be made only upon a record made in a proceeding before a special inquiry officer, at which the alien shall have reasonable opportunity to be present, unless by reason of the alien's mental incompetency it is impracticable for him to be present, in which case the Attorney General shall prescribe necessary and proper safeguards for the rights and privileges of such alien. If any alien has been given a reasonable opportunity to be present at a proceeding under this section, and without reasonable cause fails or refuses to attend or remain in attendance at such proceeding, the special inquiry officer may proceed to a determination in like manner as if the alien were present. In any case or class of cases in which the Attorney General believes that such procedure would be of aid in making a determination, he may require specifically or by regulation that an additional immigration officer shall be assigned to present the evidence on behalf of the United States and in such case such additional immigration officer shall have authority to present evidence, and to interrogate, examine and cross-examine the alien or other witnesses in the proceedings. Nothing in the preceding sentence shall be construed to diminish the authority conferred upon the special inquiry officer conducting such proceedings. No special inquiry officer shall conduct a proceeding in any case under this section in which he shall have participated in investigative functions or in which he shall have participated (except as provided in this subsection) in prosecuting functions. Proceedings before a special inquiry officer acting under the provisions of this section shall be in accordance with such regulations, not inconsistent with this Act, as the Attorney General shall prescribe. Such regulations shall include requirements that—

(1) the alien shall be given notice, reasonable under all the circumstances, of the nature of the charges against him and of the time and place at which the proceedings will be held;

(2) the alien shall have the privilege of being represented (at no expense to the Government) by such counsel, authorized to practice in such proceedings, as he shall choose;

(3) the alien shall have a reasonable opportunity to examine the evidence against him, to present evidence in his own behalf, and to cross-examine witnesses presented by the Government; and

(4) no decision of deportability shall be valid unless it is based upon reasonable, substantial, and probative evidence.

The procedure so prescribed shall be the sole and exclusive procedure for determining the deportability of an alien under this section. In any case in which an alien is ordered deported from the United States under the provisions of this Act, or of any other law or treaty, the decision of the Attorney General shall be final. In the discretion of the Attorney General, and under such regulations as he may prescribe, deportation proceedings, including issuance of a warrant of arrest, and a finding of deportability under this section need not be required in the case of any alien who admits to belonging to a class of aliens who are deportable under section 241 if such alien voluntarily departs from the United States at his own expense, or is removed at Government expense as hereinafter authorized, unless the Attorney General has reason to believe that such alien is deportable under paragraph (4), (5), (6), (7), (11), (12), (14), (15), (16), (17), (18) or (19) of section 241(a). If any alien who is authorized to depart voluntarily under the preceding sentence is financially unable to depart at his own expense and the Attorney General deems his removal to be in the best interest of the United States, the expense of such removal may be paid from the appropriation for the enforcement of this Act.

(c) When a final order of deportation under administrative processes is made against any alien, the Attorney General shall have a period of six months from the date of such order, or, if judicial review is had, then from the date of the final order of the court, within which to effect the alien's departure from the United States, during which period, at the Attorney General's discretion, the alien may be detained, released on bond in an amount and containing such conditions as the Attorney General may prescribe, or released on such other conditions as the Attorney General may prescribe. Any court of competent jurisdiction shall have authority to review or revise any determination of the Attorney General concerning detention, release on bond, or other release during such six-month period upon a conclusive showing in habeas corpus proceedings that the Attorney General is not proceeding with such reasonable dispatch as may be warranted by the particular facts and circumstances in the case of any alien to effect such alien's departure from the United States within such six-month period. If deportation has not been practicable, advisable, or possible, or departure of the alien from the United States under the order of deportation has not been effected, within such six-month period, the alien shall become subject to such further supervision and detention pending eventual deportation as is authorized in this section. The Attorney General is hereby authorized and directed to arrange for appropriate places of detention for those aliens whom he shall take into custody and detain under this section. Where no Federal buildings are available or buildings adapted or suitably located for the purpose are available for rental, the Attorney General is hereby authorized, notwithstanding section 3709 of the Revised Statutes, as amended (41 U.S.C. 5), or section 322 of the Act of June 30, 1932, as amended (40 U.S.C. 278a), to expend, from the appropriation provided for the administration and enforcement of the immigration laws, such amounts as may be necessary for the acquisition of land and the erection, acquisition, maintenance, operation, remodeling, or repair of buildings, sheds, and office quarters (including living quarters for officers where none are otherwise available), and adjunct facilities, necessary for the detention of aliens. For the purposes of this section an order of deportation heretofore or hereafter entered against an alien in legal detention or confinement, other than under an immigration process, shall be considered as being made as of the moment he is released from such detention or confinement, and not prior thereto.

(d) Any alien, against whom a final order of deportation as defined in subsection (c) heretofore or hereafter issued has been outstanding for more than six months, shall, pending eventual deportation, be subject to supervision under regulations prescribed by the Attorney General. Such regulations shall include provisions which will require any alien subject to supervision (1) to appear from time to time before an immigration officer for identification; (2) to submit, if necessary, to medical and psychiatric examination at the expense of the United States; (3) to give information under oath as to his nationality, circumstances, habits, associations, and activities, and such other information, whether or not related to the foregoing, as the Attorney General may deem fit and proper; and (4) to conform to such reasonable written restrictions on his conduct or activities as are prescribed by the Attorney General in his case. Any alien who shall willfully fail to comply with such regulations, or willfully fail to appear or to give information or submit to medical or psychiatric examination if required, or knowingly give false information in relation to the requirements of such regulations, or knowingly violate a reasonable restriction imposed upon his conduct or activity, shall be fined not more than $1,000 or imprisoned not more than one year, or both.

(e) Any alien against whom a final order of deportation is outstanding by reason of being a member of any of the classes described in paragraphs (4), (5), (6), (7), (11), (12), (14), (15), (16), (17), (18) or (19) of section 241(a), who shall willfully fail or refuse to depart from the United States within a period of six months from the date of the final order of deportation under administrative processes, or, if judicial review is had, then from the date of the final order of the court, or from the date of the enactment of the Subversive Activities Control Act of 1950 [50 U.S.C. 781, note], whichever is the later, or shall willfully fail or refuse to make timely application in good faith for travel or other documents necessary to his departure, or who shall connive or conspire, or take any other action, designed to prevent or hamper or with the purpose of preventing or hampering his departure pursuant to such order of deportation, or who shall willfully fail or refuse to present himself for deportation at the time and place required by the Attorney General pursuant to such order of deportation, shall upon conviction be guilty of a felony, and shall be imprisoned not more than ten years: *Provided*, That this subsection shall not make it illegal for any alien to take any proper steps for the purpose of securing cancellation of or exemption from such order of deportation or for the purpose of securing his release from incarceration or custody: *Provided further*, That the court may for good cause suspend the sentence of such alien and order his release under such conditions as the court may prescribe. In determining whether good cause has been shown to justify releasing the alien, the court shall take into account such factors as (1) the age, health, and period of detention of the alien; (2) the effect of the alien's release upon the national security and public peace or safety; (3) the likelihood of the alien's resuming or following a course of conduct which made or would make him deportable; (4) the character of the efforts made by such alien himself and by representatives of the country or countries to which his deportation is directed to expedite the alien's departure from the United States; (5) the reason for the inability of the Government of the United States to secure passports, other travel documents, or deportation facilities from the country or countries to which the alien has been ordered deported; and (6) the eligibility of the alien for discretionary relief under the immigration laws.

(f) Should the Attorney General find that any alien has unlawfully reentered the United States after having previously departed or been deported pursuant to an order of deportation, whether before or after the date of enactment of this Act, on any ground described in any of the paragraphs enumerated in subsection (e), the previous order of deportation shall be deemed to be reinstated from its original date and such alien shall be deported under such previous order at any time subsequent to such reentry. For the purposes of subsection (e) the date on which the finding is made that such reinstatement is appropriate shall be deemed the date of the final order of deportation.

(g) If any alien, subject to supervision or detention under subsections (c) or (d) of this section, is able to depart from the United States under the order of deportation, except that he is financially unable to pay his passage, the Attorney General may in his discretion permit such alien to depart voluntarily, and the expense of such passage to the country to which he is destined may be paid from the appropriation for the enforcement of this Act, unless such payment is otherwise provided for under this Act.

(h) An alien sentenced to imprisonment shall not be deported until such imprisonment has been terminated by the release of the alien from confinement. Parole, probation, or possibility of rearrest or further confinement in respect of the same offense shall not be a ground for deferral of deportation.

COUNTRIES TO WHICH ALIENS SHALL BE DEPORTED; COST OF DEPORTATION

Sec. 243. [8 U.S.C. 1253] (a) The deportation of an alien in the United States provided for in this Act, or any other Act or treaty, shall be directed by the Attorney General to a country promptly designated by the alien if that country is willing to accept him into its territory, unless the Attorney General, in his discretion, concludes that deportation to such country would be prejudicial to the interests of the United States. No alien shall be permitted to make more than one such designation, nor shall any alien designate, as the place to which he wishes to be deported, any foreign territory contiguous to the United States or any island adjacent thereto or adjacent to the United States unless such alien is a native, citizen, subject, or national of, or had a residence in such designated foreign contiguous territory or adjacent island. If the government of the country designated by the alien fails finally to advise the Attorney General within three months following original inquiry whether that government will or will not accept such alien into its territory, such designation may thereafter be disregarded. Thereupon deportation of such alien shall be directed to any country of which such alien is a subject, national, or citizen if such country is willing to accept him into its territory. If the government of such country fails finally to advise the Attorney General or the alien within three months following the date of original inquiry, or within such other period as the Attorney General shall deem reasonable under the circumstances in a particular case, whether that government will or will not accept such alien into its territory, then such deportation shall be directed by the Attorney General within his discretion and without necessarily giving any priority or preference because of their order as herein set forth either—

(1) to the country from which such alien last entered the United States;

(2) to the country in which is located the foreign port at which such alien embarked for the United States or for foreign contiguous territory;

(3) to the country in which he was born;

(4) to the country in which the place of his birth is situated at the time he is ordered deported;

(5) to any country in which he resided prior to entering the country from which he entered the United States;

(6) to the country which had sovereignty over the birthplace of the alien at the time of his birth; or

(7) if deportation to any of the foregoing places or countries is impracticable, inadvisable, or impossible, then to any country which is willing to accept such alien into its territory.

(b) If the United States is at war and the deportation, in accordance with the provisions of subsection (a), of any alien who is deportable under any law of the United States shall be found by the Attorney General to be impracticable, inadvisable, inconvenient, or impossible because of enemy occupation of the country from which such alien came or wherein is located the foreign port at which he embarked for the United States or because of reasons connected with the war, such alien may, in the discretion of the Attorney General, be deported as follows:

(1) If such alien is a citizen or subject of a country whose recognized government is in exile, to the country in which is located that government in exile if that country will permit him to enter its territory; or

(2) if such alien is a citizen or subject of a country whose recognized government is not in exile, then to a country or any political or territorial subdivision thereof which is proximate to the country of which the alien is a citizen or subject, or, with the consent of the country of which the alien is a citizen or subject, to any other country.

(c) If deportation proceedings are instituted at any time within five years after the entry of the alien for causes existing prior to or at the time of entry, the cost of removal to the port of deportation shall be at the expense of the appropriation for the enforcement of this Act, and the deportation from such port shall be at the expense of the owner or owners of the vessels, aircraft, or other transportation lines by which such alien came to the United States, of if in the opinion of the Attorney General that is not practicable, at the expense of the appropriation for the enforcement of this Act: *Provided,* That the costs of the deportation of any such alien from such port shall not be assessed against the owner or owners of the vessels, aircraft, or other transportation lines in the case of any alien who arrived in possession of a valid unexpired immigrant visa and who was inspected and admitted to the United States for permanent residence. In the case of an alien crewman, if deportation proceedings are instituted at any time within five years after the granting of the last conditional permit to land temporarily under the provisions of section 252, the cost of removal to the port of deportation shall be at the expense of the appropriation for the enforcement of this Act and the deportation from such port shall be at the expense of the owner or owners of the vessels or aircraft by which such alien came to the United States, of if in the opinion of the Attorney General that is not practicable, at the expense of the appropriation for the enforcement of this Act.

(d) If deportation proceedings are instituted later than five years after the entry of the alien, or in the case of an alien crewman later than five years after the granting of the last conditional permit to land temporarily, the cost thereof shall be payable from the appropriation for the enforcement of this Act.

(e) A failure or refusal on the part of the master, commanding officer, agent, owner, charterer, or consignee of a vessel, aircraft, or other transportation line to comply with the order of the Attorney General to take on board, guard safely, and transport to the destination specified any alien ordered to be deported under the provisions of this Act, or a failure or refusal by any such person to comply with an order of the Attorney General to pay deportation expenses in accordance with the requirements of this section, shall be punished by the imposition of a penalty in the sum and manner prescribed in section 237(b).

(f) When in the opinion of the Attorney General the mental or physical condition of an alien being deported is such as to require personal care and attendance, the Attorney General shall, when necessary, employ a suitable person for that purpose who shall accompany such alien to his final destination, and the expense incident to such service shall be defrayed in the same manner as the expense of deporting the accompanied alien is defrayed, and any failure or refusal to defray such expenses shall be punished in the manner prescribed by subsection (e) of this section.

(g) Upon the notification by the Attorney General that any country upon request denies or unduly delays acceptance of the return of any alien who is a national, citizen, subject, or resident thereof, the Secretary of State shall instruct consular officers performing their duties in the territory of such country to discontinue the issuance of immigrant visas to nationals, citizens, subjects, or residents of such country, until such time as the Attorney General shall inform the Secretary of State that such country has accepted such alien.

(h)(1) The Attorney General shall not deport or return any alien (other than an alien described in section 241(a)(19)) to a country if the Attorney General determines that such alien's life or freedom would be threatened in such country on account of race, religion, nationality, membership in a particular social group, or political opinion.

(2) Paragraph (1) shall not apply to any alien if the Attorney General determines that—

(A) the alien ordered, incited, assisted, or otherwise participated in the persecution of any person on account of race, religion, nationality, membership in a particular social group, or political opinion;

(B) the alien, having been convicted by a final judgment of a particularly serious crime, constitutes a danger to the community of the United States;

(C) there are serious reasons for considering that the alien has committed a serious nonpolitical crime outside the United States prior to the arrival of the alien in the United States; or

(D) there are reasonable grounds for regarding the alien as a danger to the security of the United States.

SUSPENSION OF DEPORTATION; VOLUNTARY DEPARTURE

Sec. 244. [8 U.S.C. 1254] (a) As hereinafter prescribed in this section, the Attorney General may, in his discretion, suspend deportation and adjust the status to that of an alien lawfully admitted for permanent residence, in the case of an alien (other than an alien described in section 241(a)(19)) who applies to the Attorney General for suspension of deportation and—

(1) is deportable under any law of the United States except the provisions specified in paragraph (2) of this subsection; has been physically present in the United States for a continuous period of not less than seven years immediately preceding the date of such application, and proves that during all of such period he was and is a person of good moral character; and is a person whose deportation would, in the opinion of the Attorney General, result in extreme hardship to the alien or to his spouse, parent, or child, who is a citizen of the United States or an alien lawfully admitted for permanent residence; or

(2) is deportable under paragraphs (4), (5), (6), (7), (11), (12), (14), (15), (16), (17), or (18) of section 241(a); has been physically present in the United States for a continuous period of not less than 10 years immediately following the commission of an act, or the assumption of a status, constituting a ground for deportation, and proves that during all of such period he has been and is a person of good moral character; and is a person whose deportation would, in the opinion of the Attorney General, result in exceptional and extremely unusual hardship to the alien or to his spouse, parent, or child, who is a citizen of the United States or an alien lawfully admitted for permanent residence.

(b) The requirement of continuous physical presence in the United States specified in paragraphs (1) and (2) of subsection (a) of this section shall not be applicable to an alien who (A) has served for a minimum period of twenty-four months in an active-duty status in the Armed Forces of the United States and, if separated from such service, was separated under honorable conditions, and (B) at the time of his enlistment or induction was in the United States.

(c)(1) Upon application by any alien who is found by the Attorney General to meet the requirements of subsection (a) of this section the Attorney General may in his discretion suspend deportation of such alien. If the deportation of any alien is suspended under the provisions of this subsection, a complete and detailed statement of the facts and pertinent provisions of law in the case shall be reported to the Congress with the reasons for such suspension. Such reports shall be submitted on the first day of each calendar month in which Congress is in session.

(2) In the case of an alien specified in paragraph (1) of subsection (a) of this section—

> if during the session of the Congress at which a case is reported, or prior to the close of the session of the Congress next following the session at which a case is reported, either the Senate or the House of Representatives passes a resolution stating in substance that it does not favor the suspension of such deportation, the Attorney General shall thereupon deport such alien or authorize the alien's voluntary departure at his own expense under the order of deportation in the manner provided by law. If, within the time above specified, neither the Senate nor the House of Representatives shall pass such a resolution, the Attorney General shall cancel deportation proceedings.

(3) In the case of an alien specified in paragraph (2) of subsection (a) of this section—

> if during the session of the Congress at which a case is reported, or prior to the close of the session of the Congress next following the session at which a case is reported, the Congress passes a concurrent resolution stating in substance that it favors the suspension of such deportation, the Attorney General shall cancel deportation proceedings. If within the time above specified the Congress does not pass such a concurrent resolution, or if either the Senate or the House of Representatives passes a resolution stating in substance that it does not favor the suspension of the deportation of such alien, the Attorney General shall thereupon deport such alien in the manner provided by law.

(d) Upon the cancellation of deportation in the case of any alien under this section, the Attorney General shall record the alien's lawful admission for permanent residence as of the date the cancellation of deportation of such alien is made, and unless the alien is an immediate relative within the meaning of section 201(b) the Secretary of State shall reduce by one the number of immigrant visas authorized to be issued under section 203(a)(7) for the fiscal year then current.

(e) The Attorney General may, in his discretion, permit any alien under deportation proceedings, other than an alien within the provisions of paragraph (4), (5), (6), (7), (11), (12), (14), (15), (16), (17), (18), or (19) of section 241(a) (and also any alien within the purview of such paragraphs if he is also within the provisions of paragraph (2) of subsection (a) of this section), to depart voluntarily from the United States at his own expense in lieu of deportation if such alien shall establish to the satisfaction of the Attorney General that he is, and has been, a person of good moral character for at least five years immediately preceding his application for voluntary departure under this subsection.

(f) The provisions of subsection (a) of this section shall not apply to an alien who—

(1) entered the United States as a crewman subsequent to June 30, 1964;

(2) was admitted to the United States as a nonimmigrant alien as defined in section 101(a)(15)(J), or has acquired the status of such a nonimmigrant exchange alien after admission, in order to receive graduate medical education or training, regardless of whether or not the alien is subject to or has fulfilled the two-year foreign residence requirement of section 212(e); or

(3)(A) was admitted to the United States as a nonimmigrant exchange alien as defined in section 101(a)(15)(J) or has acquired the status of such a nonimmigrant exchange alien after admission other than to receive graduate medical education or training, (B) is subject to the two-year residence requirement of section 212(e), and (C) has not fulfilled that requirement or received a waiver thereof.

ADJUSTMENT OF STATUS OF NONIMMIGRANT TO THAT OF PERSON ADMITTED FOR PERMANENT RESIDENCE

Sec. 245. [8 U.S.C. 1255] (a) The status of an alien who was inspected and admitted or paroled into the United States may be adjusted by the Attorney General, in his discretion and under such regulations as he may prescribe, to that of an alien lawfully admitted for permanent residence if (1) the alien makes an application for such adjustment, (2) the alien is eligible to receive an immigrant visa and is admissible to the United States for permanent residence, and (3) an immigrant visa is immediately available to him at the time his application is filed.

(b) Upon the approval of an application for adjustment made under subsection (a), the Attorney General shall record the alien's lawful admission for permanent residence as of the date the order of the Attorney General approving the application for the adjustment of status is made, and the Secretary of State shall reduce by one the number of the preference or nonpreference visas authorized to be issued under section 202(e) or 203(a) within the class to which the alien is chargeable for the fiscal year then current.

(c) The provisions of this section shall not be applicable to (1) an alien crewman; (2) an alien (other than an immediate relative as defined in section 201(b) or a special immigrant described in section 101(a)(27)(H)) who hereafter continues in or accepts unauthorized employment prior to filing an application for adjustment of status; or (3) any alien admitted in transit without visa under section 212(d)(4)(C).

RESCISSION OF ADJUSTMENT OF STATUS

Sec. 246. [8 U.S.C. 1256] (a) If, at any time within five years after the status of a person has been adjusted under the provisions of section 244 of this Act or under section 19(c) of the Immigration Act of February 5, 1917, to that of an alien lawfully admitted for permanent residence, it shall appear to the satisfaction of the Attorney General that the person was not in fact eligible for such adjustment of status, the Attorney General shall submit to the Congress a complete and detailed statement of the facts and pertinent provisions of law in the case. Such reports shall be submitted on the first and fifteenth day of each calendar month in which Congress is in session. If during the session of the Congress at which a case is reported, or prior to the close of the session of the Congress next following the session at which a case is reported, the Congress passes a concurrent resolution withdrawing suspension of deportation, the person shall thereupon be subject to all provisions of this Act to the same extent as if the adjustment of status had not been made. If, at any time within five years after the status of a person has been otherwise adjusted under the provisions of section 245 or 249 of this Act or any other provision of law to that of an alien lawfully admitted for permanent residence, it shall appear to the satisfaction of the Attorney General that the person was not in fact eligible for such adjustment of status, the Attorney General shall rescind the action taken granting an adjustment of status to such person and cancelling deportation in the case of such person if that occurred and the person shall thereupon be subject to all provisions of this Act to the same extent as if the adjustment of status had not been made.

(b) Any person who has become a naturalized citizen of the United States upon the basis of a record of a lawful admission for permanent residence, created as a result of an adjustment of status for which such person was not in fact eligible, and which is subsequently rescinded under subsection (a) of this section, shall be subject to the provisions of section 340 of this Act as a person whose naturalization was procured by concealment of a material fact or by willful misrepresentation.

* * *

CHANGE OF NONIMMIGRANT CLASSIFICATION

Sec. 248. [8 U.S.C. 1258] The Attorney General may, under such conditions as he may prescribe, authorize a change from any nonimmigrant classification to any other nonimmigrant classification in the case of any alien lawfully admitted to the United States as a nonimmigrant who is continuing to maintain that status, except in the case of—

(1) an alien classified as a nonimmigrant under subparagraph (C), (D), or (K) of section 101(a)(15),

(2) an alien classified as a nonimmigrant under subparagraph (J) of section 101(a)(15) who came to the United States or acquired such classification in order to receive graduate medical education or training, and

(3) an alien (other than an alien described in paragraph (2)) classified as a nonimmigrant under subparagraph (J) of section

101(a)(15) who is subject to the two-year foreign residence requirement of section 212(e) and has not received a waiver thereof, unless
such alien applies to have the alien's classification changed from
classification under subparagraph (J) of section 101(a)(15) to a classification under subparagraph (A) or (G) of such section.

RECORD OF ADMISSION FOR PERMANENT RESIDENCE IN THE CASE OF
CERTAIN ALIENS WHO ENTERED THE UNITED STATES PRIOR
TO JULY 1, 1924 OR JUNE 30, 1948

Sec. 249. [8 U.S.C. 1259] A record of lawful admission for permanent
residence may, in the discretion of the Attorney General and under such
regulations as he may prescribe, be made in the case of any alien, as of
the date of the approval of his application or, if entry occurred prior to
July 1, 1924, as of the date of such entry, if no such record is otherwise
available and such alien shall satisfy the Attorney General that he is not
inadmissible under section 212(a) insofar as it relates to criminals, procurers and other immoral persons, subversives, violators of the narcotic
laws or smugglers of aliens, and he establishes that he—

(a) entered the United States prior to June 30, 1948;

(b) has had his residence in the United States continuously since
such entry;

(c) is a person of good moral character; and

(d) is not ineligible to citizenship.

* * *

Chapter 6. Special Provisions Relating To Alien Crewmen

* * *

CONDITIONAL PERMITS TO LAND TEMPORARILY

Sec. 252. [8 U.S.C. 1282] (a) No alien crewman shall be permitted to
land temporarily in the United States except as provided in this section,
section 212(d)(3), section 212(d)(5), and section 253. If an immigration
officer finds upon examination that an alien crewman is a nonimmigrant
under paragraph (15)(D) of section 101(a) and is otherwise admissible and
has agreed to accept such permit, he may, in his discretion, grant the
crewman a conditional permit to land temporarily pursuant to regulations
prescribed by the Attorney General, subject to revocation in subsequent
proceedings as provided in subsection (b), and for a period of time, in any
event, not to exceed—

(1) the period of time (not exceeding twenty-nine days) during
which the vessel or aircraft on which he arrived remains in port, if
the immigration officer is satisfied that the crewman intends to
depart on the vessel or aircraft on which he arrived; or

(2) twenty-nine days, if the immigration officer is satisfied that
the crewman intends to depart, within the period for which he is

permitted to land on a vessel or aircraft other than the one on which he arrived.

(b) Pursuant to regulations prescribed by the Attorney General, any immigration officer may, in his discretion, if he determines that an alien is not a bona fide crewman, or does not intend to depart on the vessel or aircraft which brought him, revoke the conditional permit to land which was granted such crewman under the provisions of subsection (a)(1), take such crewman into custody, and require the master or commanding officer of the vessel or aircraft on which the crewman arrived to receive and detain him on board such vessel or aircraft, if practicable, and such crewman shall be deported from the United States at the expense of the transportation line which brought him to the United States. Until such alien is so deported, any expenses of his detention shall be borne by such transportation company. Nothing in this section shall be construed to require the procedure prescribed in section 242 of this Act to cases falling within the provisions of this subsection.

(c) Any alien crewman who willfully remains in the United States in excess of the number of days allowed in any conditional permit issued under subsection (a) shall be guilty of a misdemeanor, and upon conviction thereof shall be fined not more than $500 or shall be imprisoned for not more than six months, or both.

* * *

Chapter 7.   Registration of Aliens

[omitted]

Chapter 8.   General Penalty Provisions

* * *

UNLAWFUL BRINGING OF ALIENS INTO UNITED STATES

Sec. 273.   [8 U.S.C. 1323] (a) It shall be unlawful for any person, including any transportation company, or the owner, master, commanding officer, agent, charterer, or consignee of any vessel or aircraft, to bring to the United States from any place outside thereof (other than from foreign contiguous territory) any alien who does not have an unexpired visa, if a visa was required under this Act or regulations issued thereunder.

(b) If it appears to the satisfaction of the Attorney General that any alien has been so brought, such person, or transportation company, or the master, commanding officer, agent, owner, charterer, or consignee of any such vessel or aircraft, shall pay to the collector of customs of the customs district in which the port of arrival is located the sum of $1,000 for each alien so brought and, except in the case of any such alien who is admitted, or permitted to land temporarily, in addition, a sum equal to that paid by such alien for his transportation from the initial point of departure, indicated in his ticket, to the port of arrival, such latter sum to be delivered by the collector of customs to the alien on whose account the assessment is made. No vessel or aircraft shall be granted clearance pending the determination of the liability to the payment of such sums or while such sums remain unpaid, except that clearance may be granted prior to the determination of such question upon the deposit of an amount sufficient to cover such sums, or of a bond with sufficient surety to secure the payment thereof approved by the collector of customs.

(c) Such sums shall not be remitted or refunded, unless it appears to the satisfaction of the Attorney General that such person, and the owner, master, commanding officer, agent, charterer, and consignee of the vessel or aircraft, prior to the departure of the vessel or aircraft from the last port outside the United States, did not know, and could not have ascertained by the exercise of reasonable diligence, that the individual transported was an alien and that a visa was required.

(d) The owner, charterer, agent, consignee, commanding officer, or master of any vessel or aircraft arriving at the United States from any place outside thereof who fails to detain on board or at such other place as may be designated by an immigration officer any alien stowaway until such stowaway has been inspected by an immigration officer, or who fails to detain such stowaway on board or at such other designated place after inspection if ordered to do so by an immigration officer, or who fails to deport such stowaway on the vessel or aircraft on which he arrived or on another vessel or aircraft at the expense of the vessel or aircraft on which he arrived when required to do so by an immigration officer, shall pay to the collector of customs of the customs district in which the port of arrival is located the sum of $1,000 for each alien stowaway, in respect of whom any such failure occurs. Pending final determination of liability for such fine, no such vessel or aircraft shall be granted clearance, except that clearance may be granted upon the deposit of a sum sufficient to cover such fine, or of a bond with sufficient surety to secure the payment thereof approved by the collector of customs. The provisions of section 235 for detention of aliens for examination before special inquiry officers and the right of appeal provided for in section 236 shall not apply to aliens who arrive as stowaways and no such alien shall be permitted to land in the United States, except temporarily for medical treatment, or pursuant to such regulations as the Attorney General may prescribe for the ultimate departure or removal or deportation of such alien from the United States.

BRINGING IN AND HARBORING CERTAIN ALIENS

Sec. 274. [8 U.S.C. 1324] (a) Any person, including the owner, operator, pilot, master, commanding officer, agent or consignee of any means of transportation who—

(1) brings into or lands in the United States, by any means of transportation or otherwise, or attempts, by himself or through another, to bring into or land in the United States, by any means of transportation or otherwise;

(2) knowing that he is in the United States in violation of law, and knowing or having reasonable grounds to believe that his last

entry into the United States occurred less than three years prior thereto, transports, or moves, or attempts to transport or move, within the United States by means of transportation or otherwise, in furtherance of such violation of law;

(3) willfully or knowingly conceals, harbors, or shields from detection, or attempts to conceal, harbor, or shield from detection, in any place, including any building or any means of transportation; or

(4) willfully or knowingly encourages or induces, or attempts to encourage or induce, either directly or indirectly, the entry into the United States of—

any alien, including an alien crewman, not duly admitted by an immigration officer or not lawfully entitled to enter or reside within the United States under the terms of this Act or any other law relating to the immigration or expulsion of aliens, shall be guilty of a felony, and upon conviction thereof shall be punished by a fine not exceeding $2,000 or by imprisonment for a term not exceeding five years, or both, for each alien in respect to whom any violation of this subsection occurs: *Provided, however*, That for the purposes of this section, employment (including the usual and normal practices incident to employment) shall not be deemed to constitute harboring.

* * *

(c) No officer or person shall have authority to make any arrest for a violation of any provision of this section except officers and employees of the Service designated by the Attorney General, either individually or as a member of a class, and all other officers whose duty it is to enforce criminal laws.

ENTRY OF ALIEN AT IMPROPER TIME OR PLACE; MISREPRESENTATION AND CONCEALMENT OF FACTS

Sec. 275. [8 U.S.C. 1325] Any alien who (1) enters the United States at any time or place other than as designated by immigration officers, or (2) eludes examination or inspection by immigration officers, or (3) obtains entry to the United States by a willfully false or misleading representation or the willful concealment of a material fact, shall, for the first commission of any such offenses, be guilty of a misdemeanor and upon conviction thereof be punished by imprisonment for not more than six months, or by a fine of not more than $500, or by both, and for a subsequent commission of any such offenses shall be guilty of a felony and upon conviction thereof shall be punished by imprisonment for not more than two years, or by a fine of not more than $1,000, or both.

REENTRY OF DEPORTED ALIEN

Sec. 276. [8 U.S.C. 1326] Any alien who—

(1) has been arrested and deported or excluded and deported, and thereafter

(2) enters, attempts to enter, or is at any time found in, the United States, unless (A) prior to his reembarkation at a place outside

the United States or his application for admission from foreign contiguous territory, the Attorney General has expressly consented to such alien's reapplying for admission; or (B) with respect to an alien previously excluded and deported, unless such alien shall establish that he was not required to obtain such advance consent under this or any prior Act,

shall be guilty of a felony, and upon conviction thereof, be punished by imprisonment of not more than two years, or by a fine of not more than $1,000, or both.

* * *

JURISDICTION OF DISTRICT COURTS

Sec. 279. [8 U.S.C. 1329] The district courts of the United States shall have jurisdiction of all causes, civil and criminal, arising under any of the provisions of this title. It shall be the duty of the United States attorney of the proper district to prosecute every such suit when brought by the United States. Notwithstanding any other law, such prosecutions or suits may be instituted at any place in the United States at which the violation may occur or at which the person charged with a violation under section 275 or 276 may be apprehended. No suit or proceeding for a violation of any of the provisions of this title shall be settled, compromised, or discontinued without the consent of the court in which it is pending and any such settlement, compromise, or discontinuance shall be entered of record with the reasons therefor.

* * *

Chapter 9.   Miscellaneous

* * *

POWERS OF IMMIGRATION OFFICERS AND EMPLOYEES

Sec. 287. [8 U.S.C. 1357] (a) Any officer or employee of the Service authorized under regulations prescribed by the Attorney General shall have power without warrant—

(1) to interrogate any alien or person believed to be an alien as to his right to be or to remain in the United States;

(2) to arrest any alien who in his presence or view is entering or attempting to enter the United States in violation of any law or regulation made in pursuance of law regulating the admission, exclusion, or expulsion of aliens, or to arrest any alien in the United States, if he has reason to believe that the alien so arrested is in the United States in violation of any such law or regulation and is likely to escape before a warrant can be obtained for his arrest, but the alien arrested shall be taken without unnecessary delay for examination before an officer of the Service having authority to examine aliens as to their right to enter or remain in the United States;

(3) within a reasonable distance from any external boundary of the United States, to board and search for aliens any vessel within

the territorial waters of the United States and any railway car, aircraft, conveyance, or vehicle, and within a distance of twenty-five miles from any such external boundary to have access to private lands, but not dwellings for the purpose of patrolling the border to prevent the illegal entry of aliens into the United States; and

(4) to make arrests for felonies which have been committed and which are cognizable under any law of the United States regulating the admission, exclusion, or expulsion of aliens, if he has reason to believe that the person so arrested is guilty of such felony and if there is likelihood of the person escaping before a warrant can be obtained for his arrest, but the person arrested shall be taken without unnecessary delay before the nearest available officer empowered to commit persons charged with offenses against the laws of the United States. Any such employee shall also have the power to execute any warrant or other process issued by any officer under any law regulating the admission, exclusion, or expulsion of aliens.

(b) Any officer or employee of the Service designated by the Attorney General, whether individually or as one of a class, shall have power and authority to administer oaths and to take and consider evidence concerning the privilege of any person to enter, reenter, pass through, or reside in the United States, or concerning any matter which is material or relevant to the enforcement of this Act and the administration of the Service; and any person to whom such oath has been administered (or who has executed an unsworn declaration, certificate, verification, or statement under penalty of perjury as permitted under section 1746 of title 28, United States Code), under the provisions of this Act, who shall knowingly or willfully give false evidence or swear (or subscribe under penalty of perjury as permitted under section 1746 of title 28, United States Code) to any false statement concerning any matter referred to in this subsection shall be guilty of perjury and shall be punished as provided by section 1621, title 18, United States Code.

(c) Any officer or employee of the Service authorized and designated under regulations prescribed by the Attorney General, whether individually or as one of a class, shall have power to conduct a search, without warrant, of the person, and of the personal effects in the possession of any person seeking admission to the United States, concerning whom such officer or employee may have reasonable cause to suspect that grounds exist for exclusion from the United States under this Act which would be disclosed by such search.

* * *

BURDEN OF PROOF

Sec. 291. [8 U.S.C. 1361] Whenever any person makes application for a visa or any other document required for entry, or makes application for admission, or otherwise attempts to enter the United States, the burden of proof shall be upon such person to establish that he is eligible to receive such visa or such document, or is not subject to exclusion under any provision of this Act, and, if an alien, that he is entitled to the nonimmigrant, immigrant, special immigrant, immediate relative, or refugee status claimed, as the case may be. If such person fails to establish to the satisfaction of the consular officer that he is eligible to receive a visa or other document required for entry, no visa or other document required for entry shall be issued to such person, nor shall such person be admitted to the United States unless he establishes to the satisfaction of the Attorney General that he is not subject to exclusion under any provision of this Act. In any deportation proceeding under chapter 5 against any person, the burden of proof shall be upon such person to show the time, place, and manner of his entry into the United States, but in presenting such proof he shall be entitled to the production of his visa or other entry document, if any, and of any other documents and records, not considered by the Attorney General to be confidential, pertaining to such entry in the custody of the Service. If such burden of proof is not sustained, such person shall be presumed to be in the United States in violation of law.

RIGHT TO COUNSEL

Sec. 292. [8 U.S.C. 1362] In any exclusion or deportation proceedings before a special inquiry officer and in any appeal proceedings before the Attorney General from any such exclusion or deportation proceedings, the person concerned shall have the privilege of being represented (at no expense to the Government) by such counsel, authorized to practice in such proceedings, as he shall choose.

* * *

TITLE III—NATIONALITY AND NATURALIZATION

Chapter 1. Nationality at Birth and by Collective Naturalization

NATIONALS AND CITIZENS OF THE UNITED STATES AT BIRTH

Sec. 301. [8 U.S.C. 1401] The following shall be nationals and citizens of the United States at birth:

(a) a person born in the United States, and subject to the jurisdiction thereof;

(b) a person born in the United States to a member of an Indian, Eskimo, Aleutian, or other aboriginal tribe: *Provided*, That the granting of citizenship under this subsection shall not in any manner impair or otherwise affect the right of such person to tribal or other property;

(c) a person born outside of the United States and its outlying possessions of parents both of whom are citizens of the United States and one of whom has had a residence in the United States or one of its outlying possessions, prior to the birth of such person;

(d) a person born outside of the United States and its outlying possessions of parents one of whom is a citizen of the United States who has been physically present in the United States or one of its outlying possessions for a continuous period of one year prior to the birth of such person, and the other of whom is a national, but not a citizen of the United States;

(e) a person born in an outlying possession of the United States of parents one of whom is a citizen of the United States who has been physically present in the United States or one of its outlying possessions for a continuous period of one year at any time prior to the birth of such person;

(f) a person of unknown parentage found in the United States while under the age of five years, until shown, prior to his attaining the age of twenty-one years, not to have been born in the United States;

(g) a person born outside the geographical limits of the United States and its outlying possessions of parents one of whom is an alien, and the other a citizen of the United States who, prior to the birth of such person, was physically present in the United States or its outlying possessions for a period or periods totaling not less than ten years, at least five of which were after attaining the age of fourteen years: *Provided*, That any periods of honorable service in the Armed Forces of the United States, or periods of employment with the United States Government or with an international organization as that term is defined in section 1 of the International Organizations Immunities Act (59 Stat. 669; 22 U.S.C. 288) by such citizen parent, or any periods during which such citizen parent is physically present abroad as the dependent unmarried son or daughter and a member of the household of a person (A) honorably serving with the Armed Forces of the United States, or (B) employed by the United States Government or an international organization as defined in section 1 of the International Organizations Immunities Act, may be included in order to satisfy the physical-presence requirement of this paragraph. This proviso shall be applicable to persons born on or after December 24, 1952, to the same extent as if it had become effective in its present form on that date.

* * *

NATIONALS BUT NOT CITIZENS OF THE UNITED STATES AT BIRTH

Sec. 308. [8 U.S.C. 1408] Unless otherwise provided in section 301 of this title, the following shall be nationals, but not citizens of the United States at birth:

(1) A person born in an outlying possession of the United States on or after the date of formal acquisition of such possession;

(2) A person born outside the United States and its outlying possessions of parents both of whom are nationals, but not citizens, of the United States, and have had a residence in the United States, or one of its outlying possessions prior to the birth of such person; and

(3) A person of unknown parentage found in an outlying possession of the United States while under the age of five years, until shown, prior to

his attaining the age of twenty-one years, not to have been born in such outlying possession.

CHILDREN BORN OUT OF WEDLOCK

Sec. 309. [8 U.S.C. 1409] (a) The provisions of paragraphs (c), (d), (e), and (g) of section 301, and of paragraph (2) of section 308, of this title shall apply as of the date of birth to a child born out of wedlock on or after the effective date of this Act, if the paternity of such child is established while such child is under the age of twenty-one years by legitimation.

(b) Except as otherwise provided in section 405, the provisions of section 301(g) shall apply to a child born out of wedlock on or after January 13, 1941, and prior to the effective date of this Act, as of the date of birth, if the paternity of such child is established before or after the effective date of this Act and while such child is under the age of twenty-one years by legitimation.

(c) Notwithstanding the provision of subsection (a) of this section, a person born, on or after the effective date of this Act, outside the United States and out of wedlock shall be held to have acquired at birth the nationality status of his mother, if the mother had the nationality of the United States at the time of such person's birth, and if the mother had previously been physically present in the United States or one of its outlying possessions for a continuous period of one year.

Chapter 2. Nationality Through Naturalization

JURISDICTION TO NATURALIZE

Sec. 310. [8 U.S.C. 1421] (a) Exclusive jurisdiction to naturalize persons as citizens of the United States is hereby conferred upon the following specified courts: District courts of the United States now existing, or which may hereafter be established by Congress in any State, District Court[s] of the United States for the District of Columbia and for Puerto Rico, the District Court of the Virgin Islands of the United States, and the District Court of Guam; also all courts of record in any State or Territory now existing, or which may hereafter be created, having a seal, a clerk, and jurisdiction in actions at law or equity, or law and equity, in which the amount in controversy is unlimited. The jurisdiction of all the courts herein specified to naturalize persons shall extend only to such persons resident within the respective jurisdiction of such courts, except as otherwise specifically provided in this title.

(b) A person who petitions for naturalization in any State court having naturalization jurisdiction may petition within the State judicial district or State judicial circuit in which he resides, whether or not he resides within the county in which the petition for naturalization is filed.

(c) The courts herein specified, upon request of the clerks of such courts, shall be furnished from time to time by the Attorney General with such blank forms as may be required in naturalization proceedings.

(d) A person may be naturalized as a citizen of the United States in the manner and under the conditions prescribed in this title, and not otherwise.

(e) Notwithstanding the provisions of section 405(a), any petition for naturalization filed on or after the enactment of this subsection shall be heard and determined in accordance with the requirements of this title.

ELIGIBILITY FOR NATURALIZATION

Sec. 311. [8 U.S.C. 1422] The right of a person to become a naturalized citizen of the United States shall not be denied or abridged because of race or sex or because such person is married. Notwithstanding section 405(b), this section shall apply to any person whose petition for naturalization shall hereafter be filed, or shall have been pending on the effective date of this Act.

REQUIREMENTS AS TO UNDERSTANDING THE ENGLISH LANGUAGE, HISTORY, PRINCIPLES, AND FORM OF GOVERNMENT OF THE UNITED STATES

Sec. 312. [8 U.S.C. 1423] No person except as otherwise provided in this title shall hereafter be naturalized as a citizen of the United States upon his own petition who cannot demonstrate—

(1) an understanding of the English language, including an ability to read, write, and speak words in ordinary usage in the English language: *Provided*, That this requirement shall not apply to any person physically unable to comply therewith, if otherwise qualified to be naturalized, or to any person who, on the date of the filing of his petition for naturalization as provided in section 334 of this Act, is over fifty years of age and has been living in the United States for periods totaling at least twenty years subsequent to a lawful admission for permanent residence: *Provided further*, That the requirements of this section relating to ability to read and write shall be met if the applicant can read or write simple words and phrases to the end that a reasonable test of his literacy shall be made and that no extraordinary or unreasonable conditions shall be imposed upon the applicant; and

(2) a knowledge and understanding of the fundamentals of the history, and of the principles and form of government of the United States.

PROHIBITION UPON THE NATURALIZATION OF PERSONS OPPOSED TO GOVERNMENT OR LAW, OR WHO FAVOR TOTALITARIAN FORMS OF GOVERNMENT

Sec. 313. [8 U.S.C. 1424] (a) Notwithstanding the provisions of section 405(b), no person shall hereafter be naturalized as a citizen of the United States—

[the omitted paragraphs describe at length various classes of anarchists, Communists, and other totalitarians, using language similar to that of § 212(a)(28)]

* * *

(c) The provisions of this section shall be applicable to any applicant for naturalization who at any time within a period of ten years immediately preceding the filing of the petition for naturalization or after such filing and before taking the final oath of citizenship is, or has been found to be within any of the classes enumerated within this section, notwithstanding that at the time the petition is filed he may not be included within such classes.

(d) Any person who is within any of the classes described in subsection (a) solely because of past membership in, or past affiliation with, a party or organization may be naturalized without regard to the provisions of subsection (c) if such person establishes that such membership or affiliation is or was involuntary, or occurred and terminated prior to the attainment by such alien of the age of sixteen years, or that such membership or affiliation is or was by operation of law, or was for purposes of obtaining employment, food rations, or other essentials of living and where necessary for such purposes.

* * *

REQUIREMENTS AS TO RESIDENCE, GOOD MORAL CHARACTER, ATTACHMENT TO THE PRINCIPLES OF THE CONSTITUTION, AND FAVORABLE DISPOSITION TO THE UNITED STATES

Sec. 316. [8 U.S.C. 1427] (a) No person, except as otherwise provided in this title, shall be naturalized, unless such petitioner, (1) immediately preceding the date of filing his petition for naturalization has resided continuously, after being lawfully admitted for permanent residence, within the United States for at least five years and during the five years immediately preceding the date of filing his petition has been physically present therein for periods totaling at least half of that time, and who has resided within the State in which the petitioner filed the petition for at least six months, (2) has resided continuously within the United States from the date of the petition up to the time of admission to citizenship, and (3) during all the periods referred to in this subsection has been and still is a person of good moral character, attached to the principles of the Constitution of the United States, and well disposed to the good order and happiness of the United States.

(b) Absence from the United States of more than six months but less than one year during the period for which continuous residence is required for admission to citizenship, immediately preceding the date of filing the petition for naturalization, or during the period between the date of filing the petition and the date of final hearing, shall break the continuity of such residence, unless the petitioner shall establish to the satisfaction of the court that he did not in fact abandon his residence in the United States during such period.

Absence from the United States for a continuous period of one year or more during the period for which continuous residence is required for admission to citizenship (whether preceding or subsequent to the filing of the petition for naturalization) shall break the continuity of such residence except that in the case of a person who has been physically present and residing in the United States after being lawfully admitted for permanent residence for an uninterrupted period of at least one year and who thereafter, is employed by or under contract with the Government of the United States or an American institution of research recognized as such by the Attorney General, or is employed by an American firm or corporation engaged in whole or in part in the development of foreign trade and commerce of the United States, or a subsidiary thereof more than 50 per centum of whose stock is owned by an American firm or corporation, or is employed by a public international organization of which the United States is a member by treaty or statute and by which the alien was not employed until after being lawfully admitted for permanent residence, no period of absence from the United States shall break the continuity of residence if—

(1) prior to the beginning of such period of employment (whether such period begins before or after his departure from the United States), but prior to the expiration of one year of continuous absence from the United States, the person has established to the satisfaction of the Attorney General that his absence from the United States for such period is to be on behalf of such Government, or for the purpose of carrying on scientific research on behalf of such institution, or to be engaged in the development of such foreign trade and commerce or whose residence abroad is necessary to the protection of the property rights in such countries of such firm or corporation, or to be employed by a public international organization of which the United States is a member by treaty or statute and by which the alien was not employed until after being lawfully admitted for permanent residence; and

(2) such person proves to the satisfaction of the court that his absence from the United States for such period has been for such purpose.

The spouse and dependent unmarried sons and daughters who are members of the household of a person who qualifies for the benefits of this subsection shall also be entitled to such benefits during the period for which they were residing abroad as dependent members of the household of the person.

(c) The granting of the benefits of subsection (b) of this section shall not relieve the petitioner from the requirement of physical presence within the United States for the period specified in subsection (a) of this section, except in the case of those persons who are employed by, or under contract with, the Government of the United States. In the case of a person employed by or under contract with Central Intelligence Agency, the requirement in subsection (b) of an uninterrupted period of at least one year of physical presence in the United States may be complied with by such person at any time prior to filing a petition for naturalization.

(d) No finding by the Attorney General that the petitioner is not deportable shall be accepted as conclusive evidence of good moral character.

(e) In determining whether the petitioner has sustained the burden of establishing good moral character and the other qualifications for citizenship specified in subsection (a) of this section, the court shall not be limited to the petitioner's conduct during the five years preceding the filing of the petition, but may take into consideration as a basis for such determination the petitioner's conduct and acts at any time prior to that period.

(f) Naturalization shall not be granted to a petitioner by a naturalization court while registration proceedings or proceedings to require registration against an organization of which the petitioner is a member or affiliate are pending under section 13 or 14 of the Subversive Activities Control Act of 1950 [50 U.S.C. 792, 793].

* * *

PREREQUISITE TO NATURALIZATION; BURDEN OF PROOF

Sec. 318. [8 U.S.C. 1429] Except as otherwise provided in this title, no person shall be naturalized unless he has been lawfully admitted to the United States for permanent residence in accordance with all applicable provisions of this Act. The burden of proof shall be upon such person to show that he entered the United States lawfully, and the time, place, and manner of such entry into the United States, but in presenting such proof he shall be entitled to the production of his immigrant visa, if any, or if other entry document, if any, and of any other documents and records, not considered by the Attorney General to be confidential, pertaining to such entry, in the custody of the Service. Notwithstanding the provisions of section 405(b), and except as provided in sections 328 and 329 no person shall be naturalized against whom there is outstanding a final finding of deportability pursuant to a warrant of arrest issued under the provisions of this or any other Act; and no petition for naturalization shall be finally heard by a naturalization court if there is pending against the petitioner a deportation proceeding pursuant to a warrant of arrest issued under the provisions of this or any other Act: *Provided*, That the findings of the Attorney General in terminating deportation proceedings or in suspending the deportation of an alien pursuant to the provisions of this Act, shall not be deemed binding in any way upon the naturalization court with respect to the question of whether such person has established his eligibility for naturalization as required by this title.

MARRIED PERSONS AND EMPLOYEES OF CERTAIN NONPROFIT ORGANIZATIONS

Sec. 319. [8 U.S.C. 1430] (a) Any person whose spouse is a citizen of the United States may be naturalized upon compliance with all the requirements of this title except the provisions of paragraph (1) of section 316(a) if such person immediately preceding the date of filing his petition for naturalization has resided continuously, after being lawfully admitted for permanent residence, within the United States for at least three years, and during the three years immediately preceding the date of filing his petition has been living in marital union with the citizen spouse, who has been a United States citizen during all of such period, and has been physically present in the United States for periods totaling at least half of that time and has resided within the State in which he filed his petition for at least six months.

(b) Any person, (1) whose spouse is (A) a citizen of the United States, (B) in the employment of the Government of the United States, or of an

American institution of research recognized as such by the Attorney General, or of an American firm or corporation engaged in whole or in part in the development of foreign trade and commerce of the United States, or a subsidiary thereof, or of a public international organization in which the United States participates by treaty or statute, or is authorized to perform the ministerial or priestly functions of a religious denomination having a bona fide organization within the United States, or is engaged solely as a missionary by a religious denomination or by an interdenominational mission organization having a bona fide organization within the United States, and (C) regularly stationed abroad in such employment, and (2) who is in the United States at the time of naturalization, and (3) who declares before the naturalization court in good faith an intention to take up residence within the United States immediately upon the termination of such employment abroad of the citizen spouse, may be naturalized upon compliance with all the requirements of the naturalization laws, except that no prior residence or specified period of physical presence within the United States or within the jurisdiction of the naturalization court or proof thereof shall be required.

(c) Any person who (1) is employed by a bona fide United States incorporated nonprofit organization which is principally engaged in conducting abroad through communications media the dissemination of information which significantly promotes United States interests abroad and which is recognized as such by the Attorney General, and (2) has been so employed continuously for a period of not less than five years after a lawful admission for permanent residence, and (3) who files his petition for naturalization while so employed or within six months following the termination thereof, and (4) who is in the United States at the time of naturalization, and (5) who declares before the naturalization court in good faith an intention to take up residence within the United States immediately upon termination of such employment, may be naturalized upon compliance with all the requirements of this Title except that no prior residence or specified period of physical presence within the United States or any State or within the jurisdiction of the court, or proof thereof, shall be required.

(d) Any person who is the surviving spouse of a United States citizen, whose citizen spouse dies during a period of honorable service in an active duty status in the Armed Forces of the United States and who was living in marital union with the citizen spouse at the time of his death, may be naturalized upon compliance with all the requirements of this title except that no prior residence or specified physical presence within the United States, or within the jurisdiction of the naturalization court shall be required.

* * *

PETITION FOR NATURALIZATION; DECLARATION OF INTENTION

Sec. 334. [8 U.S.C. 1445] (a) An applicant for naturalization shall make and file in the office of the clerk of a naturalization court, in duplicate, a sworn petition in writing, signed by the applicant in the applicant's own handwriting, if physically able to write, which petition shall be on a form prescribed by the Attorney General and shall include averments of all facts which in the opinion of the Attorney General may be material to the applicant's naturalization, and required to be proved upon the hearing of such petition.

(b) No person shall file a valid petition for naturalization unless (1) he shall have attained the age of eighteen years and (2) he shall have first filed an application therefor at an office of the Service in the form and manner prescribed by the Attorney General. An application for petition for naturalization by an alien shall contain an averment of lawful admission for permanent residence.

(c) Petitions for naturalization may be made and filed during the term time or vacation of the naturalization court and shall be docketed the same day as filed, but final action thereon shall be had only on stated days, to be fixed by rule of the court.

(d) If the applicant for naturalization is prevented by sickness or other disability from presenting himself in the office of the clerk to make the petition required by subsection (a) such applicant may make such petition at such other place as may be designated by the clerk of court or by such clerk's authorized deputy.

(e) Before a petition for naturalization may be made outside of the office of the clerk of the court, pursuant to subsection (d) above, or before a final hearing on a petition may be held or the oath of allegiance administered outside of open court, pursuant to sections 336(a) and 337(c) respectively of this title, the court must satisfy itself that the illness or other disability is sufficiently serious to prevent appearance in the office of the clerk of court and is of a permanent nature, or of a nature which so incapacitates the person as to prevent him from personally appearing in the office of the clerk of court or in court as otherwise required by law.

(f) Any alien over eighteen years of age who is residing in the United States pursuant to a lawful admission for permanent residence may, upon an application prescribed, filed with, and approved by the Service, make and file in duplicate in the office of the clerk of court, regardless of the alien's place of residence in the United States a signed declaration of intention to become a citizen of the United States, in such form as the Attorney General shall prescribe. Nothing in this subsection shall be construed as requiring any such alien to make and file a declaration of intention as a condition precedent to filing a petition for naturalization nor shall any such declaration of intention be regarded as conferring or having conferred upon any such alien United States citizenship or nationality or the right to United States citizenship or nationality, nor shall such declaration be regarded as evidence of such alien's lawful admission for permanent residence in any proceeding, action, or matter arising under this or any other Act.

INVESTIGATION OF PETITIONERS; PRELIMINARY EXAMINATIONS ON PETITIONS

Sec. 335. [8 U.S.C. 1446] (a) At any time prior to the holding of the final hearing on a petition for naturalization provided for by section

336(a), an employee of the Service, or of the United States designated by the Attorney General, shall conduct a personal investigation of the person petitioning for naturalization in the vicinity or vicinities in which such person has maintained his actual place of abode and in the vicinity or vicinities in which such person has been employed or has engaged in business or work for at least five years immediately preceding the filing of his petition for naturalization. The Attorney General may, in his discretion, waive a personal investigation in an individual case or in such cases or classes of cases as may be designated by him.

(b) The Attorney General shall designate employees of the Service to conduct preliminary examinations upon petitions for naturalization to any naturalization court and to make recommendations thereon to such court. For such purposes any such employee so designated is hereby authorized to take testimony concerning any matter touching or in any way affecting the admissibility of any petitioner for naturalization, to administer oaths, including the oath of the petitioner for naturalization and to require by subpena the attendance and testimony of witnesses, including petitioner, before such employee so designated and the production of relevant books, papers, and documents, and to that end may invoke the aid of any court exercising naturalization jurisdiction as specified in section 310 of this title; and any such court may, in the event of neglect or refusal to respond to a subpoena issued by any such employee so designated or refusal to testify before such employee so designated issue an order requiring such person to appear before such employee so designated, produce relevant books, papers, and documents if demanded, and testify; and any failure to obey such order of the court may be punished by the court as a contempt thereof. The record of the preliminary examination authorized by this subsection shall be admissible as evidence in any final hearing conducted by a naturalization court designated in section 310 of this title.

(c) The record of the preliminary examination upon any petition for naturalization may, in the discretion of the Attorney General, be transmitted to the Attorney General and the recommendation with respect thereto of the employee designated to conduct such preliminary examination shall when made also be transmitted to the Attorney General.

(d) The recommendation of the employee designated to conduct any such preliminary examination shall be submitted to the court at the hearing upon the petition and shall include a recommendation that the petition be granted, or denied, or continued, with reasons therefor. In any case in which the recommendation of the Attorney General does not agree with that of the employee designated to conduct such preliminary examination, the recommendations of both such employee and the Attorney General shall be submitted to the court at the hearing upon the petition, and the officer of the Service in attendance at such hearing shall, at the request of the court, present both the views of such employee and those of the Attorney General with respect to such petition to the court. The recommendations of such employee and of the Attorney General shall be accompanied by duplicate lists containing the names of the petitioners, classified according to the character of the recommendations, and signed by such employee or the Attorney General, as the case may be. The judge to whom such recommendations are submitted shall, if he approve[s] such recommendations, enter a written order with such exceptions as the judge may deem proper, by subscribing his name to each such list when corrected to conform to his conclusions upon such recommendations. One of each such list shall thereafter be filed permanently of record in such court and the duplicate of each such list shall be sent by the clerk of such court to the Attorney General.

(e) After the petition for naturalization has been filed in the office of the clerk of court, the petitioner shall not be permitted to withdraw his petition, except with the consent of the Attorney General. In cases where the Attorney General does not consent to withdrawal of the petition, the court shall determine the petition on its merits and enter a final order accordingly. In cases where the petitioner fails to prosecute his petition, the petition shall be decided upon its merits unless the Attorney General moves that the petition be dismissed for lack of prosecution.

(f)(1) A petitioner for naturalization who removes from the jurisdiction of the court in which his petition for naturalization is pending may, at any time thereafter, make application to the court for transfer of the petition to a naturalization court exercising jurisdiction over the petitioner's place of residence, or to any other naturalization court if the petition was not required to be filed in a naturalization court exercising jurisdiction over the petitioner's place of residence: *Provided,* That such transfer shall not be made without the consent of the Attorney General, and of the court to which the petition is transferred.

(2) Where transfer of the petition is authorized the clerk of court in which the petition was filed shall forward a certified copy of the petition and the original record in the case to the clerk of court to which the petition is transferred, and proceedings on the petition shall thereafter continue as though the petition had originally been filed in the court to which transferred, except that the court to which the petition is transferred may in its discretion, require the production of two credible United States citizen witnesses to testify as to the petitioner's qualifications for naturalization since the date of such transfer.

FINAL HEARING IN OPEN COURT UPON PETITIONS FOR NATURALIZATION; FINAL ORDER UNDER THE HAND OF THE COURT ENTERED UPON RECORD; EXAMINATION OF PETITIONER AND WITNESSES BEFORE THE COURT

Sec. 336. [8 U.S.C. 1447] (a) Every final hearing upon a petition for naturalization shall be had in open court before a judge or judges thereof, and every final order which may be made upon such petition shall be under the hand of the court and entered in full upon a record kept for that purpose, and upon such final hearing of such petition the petitioner, except as provided in subsection (b) of this section, shall be examined under oath before the court and in the presence of the court. If the petitioner is prevented by sickness or other disability from being in open court for the final hearing upon a petition for naturalization, such final hearing may be had before a judge or judges of the court at such place as may be designated by the court.

(b) The requirement of subsection (a) of this section for the examination of the petitioner under oath before the court and in the presence of the court shall not apply in any case where an employee designated under section 335(b) has conducted the preliminary examination authorized by subsection (b) of section 335; except, that the court may, in its discretion, and shall, upon demand of the petitioner, require the examination of the petitioner under oath before the court and in the presence of the court.

(c) The Attorney General shall have the right to appear before any court in any naturalization proceedings for the purpose of cross-examining the petitioner and the witnesses produced in support of the petition concerning any matter touching or in any way affecting the petitioner's right to admission to citizenship, and shall have the right to call witnesses, including the petitioner, produce evidence, and be heard in opposition to, or in favor of, the granting of any petition in naturalization proceedings.

(d) The clerk of the court shall, if the petitioner requests it at the time of filing the petition for naturalization, issue a subpoena for the witnesses named by such petitioner to appear upon the day set for the final hearing, but in case such witnesses cannot be produced upon the final hearing other witnesses may be summoned upon notice to the Attorney General, in such manner and at such time as the Attorney General may by regulation prescribe.

(e) It shall be lawful at the time and as a part of the naturalization of any person, for the court, in its discretion, upon the bona fide prayer of the petitioner included in the petition for naturalization of such persons, to make a decree changing the name of said person, and the certificate of naturalization shall be issued in accordance therewith.

OATH OF RENUNCIATION AND ALLEGIANCE

Sec. 337. [8 U.S.C. 1448] (a) A person who has petitioned for naturalization shall, in order to be and before being admitted to citizenship, take in open court an oath (1) to support the Constitution of the United States; (2) to renounce and abjure absolutely and entirely all allegiance and fidelity to any foreign prince, potentate, state, or sovereignty of whom or which the petitioner was before a subject or citizen; (3) to support and defend the Constitution and the laws of the United States against all enemies, foreign and domestic; (4) to bear true faith and allegiance to the same; and (5)(A) to bear arms on behalf of the United States when required by the law, or (B) to perform noncombatant service in the Armed Forces of the United States when required by the law, or (C) to perform work of national importance under civilian direction when required by the law. Any such person shall be required to take an oath containing the substance of clauses (1) through (5) of the preceding sentence, except that a person who shows by clear and convincing evidence to the satisfaction of the naturalization court that he is opposed to the bearing of arms in the Armed Forces of the United States by reason of religious training and belief shall be required to take an oath containing the substance of clauses (1) through (4) and clauses (5)(B) and (5)(C), and a person who shows by clear and convincing evidence to the satisfaction of the naturalization court that he is opposed to any type of service in the Armed Forces of the United States by reason of religious training and belief shall be required to take an oath containing the substance of clauses (1) through (4) and clause (5)(C). The term "religious training and belief" as used in this section shall mean an individual's belief in a relation to a Supreme Being involving duties superior to those arising from any human relation, but does not include essentially political, sociological, or philosophical views or a merely personal moral code. In the case of the naturalization of a child under the provisions of section 322 of this title the naturalization court may waive the taking of the oath if in the opinion of the court the child is unable to understand its meaning.

(b) In case the person petitioning for naturalization has borne any hereditary title, or has been of any of the orders of nobility in any foreign state, the petitioner shall in addition to complying with the requirements of subsection (a) of this section, make under oath in open court in the court in which the petition for naturalization is made, an express renunciation of such title or order of nobility, and such renunciation shall be recorded in the court as a part of such proceedings.

(c) If the petitioner is prevented by sickness or other disability from being in open court, the oath required to be taken by subsection (a) of this section may be taken before a judge of the court at such place as may be designated by the court.

CERTIFICATE OF NATURALIZATION; CONTENTS

Sec. 338. [8 U.S.C. 1449] A person admitted to citizenship by a naturalization court in conformity with the provisions of this title shall be entitled upon such admission to receive from the clerk of such court a certificate of naturalization, which shall contain substantially the following information: Number of petition for naturalization; number of certificate of naturalization; date of naturalization; name, signature, place of residence, autographed photograph, and personal description of the naturalized person, including age, sex, marital status, and country of former nationality; title, venue and location of the naturalization court; statement that the court, having found that the petitioner intends to reside permanently in the United States, except in cases falling within the provisions of section 324(a) of this title, had complied in all respects with all of the applicable provisions of the naturalization laws of the United States, and was entitled to be admitted a citizen of the United States of America, thereupon ordered that the petitioner be admitted as a citizen of the United States of America; attestation of the clerk of the naturalization court; and seal of the court.

* * *

REVOCATION OF NATURALIZATION

Sec. 340. [8 U.S.C. 1451] (a) It shall be the duty of the United States attorneys for the respective districts, upon affidavit showing good cause therefor, to institute proceedings in any court specified in subsection (a) of section 310 of this title in the judicial district in which the naturalized citizen may reside at the time of bringing suit, for the purpose of revoking and setting aside the order admitting such person to citizenship and canceling the certificate of naturalization on the ground that such order and certificate of naturalization were illegally procured or were procured by concealment of a material fact or by willful misrepresentation, and such revocation and setting aside of the order admitting such person to citizenship and such canceling of certificate of naturalization shall be effective as of the original date of the order and certificate, respectively: *Provided*, That refusal on the part of a naturalized citizen within a period of ten years following his naturalization to testify as a witness in any proceeding before a congressional committee concerning his subversive activities, in a case where such person has been convicted for contempt for such refusal, shall be held to constitute a ground for revocation of such person's naturalization under this subsection as having been procured by concealment of a material fact or by willful misrepresentation. If the naturalized citizen does not reside in any judicial district in the United States at the time of bringing such suit, the proceedings may be instituted in the United States District Court for the District of Columbia or in the United States district court in the judicial district in which such person last had his residence.

(b) The party to whom was granted the naturalization alleged to have been illegally procured or procured by concealment of a material fact or by willful misrepresentation shall, in any such proceedings under subsection (a) of this section, have sixty days' personal notice, unless waived by such party, in which to make answer to the petition of the United States; and if such naturalized person be absent from the United States or from the judicial district in which such person last had his residence, such notice shall be given either by personal service upon him or by publication in the manner provided for the service of summons by publication or upon absentees by the laws of the State or the place where such suit is brought.

(c) If a person who shall have been naturalized after the effective date of this Act shall within five years next following such naturalization become a member of or affiliated with any organization, membership in or affiliation with which at the time of naturalization would have precluded such person from naturalization under the provisions of section 313, it shall be considered prima facie evidence that such person was not attached to the principles of the Constitution of the United States and was not well disposed to the good order and happiness of the United States at the time of naturalization, and, in the absence of countervailing evidence, it shall be sufficient in the proper proceeding to authorize the revocation and setting aside of the order admitting such person to citizenship and the cancellation of the certificate of naturalization as having been obtained by concealment of a material fact or by willful misrepresentation, and such revocation and setting aside of the order admitting such person to citizenship and such canceling of certificate of naturalization shall be effective as of the original date of the order and certificate, respectively.

(d) If a person who shall have been naturalized shall, within five years after such naturalization, return to the country of his nativity, or go to any other foreign country, and take permanent residence therein, it shall be considered prima facie evidence of a lack of intention on the part of such person to reside permanently in the United States at the time of filing his petition for naturalization, and, in the absence of countervailing evidence, it shall be sufficient in the proper proceeding to authorize the revocation and setting aside of the order admitting such person to citizenship and the cancellation of the certificate of naturalization as having been obtained by concealment of a material fact or by willful misrepresentation, and such revocation and setting aside of the order admitting such person to citizenship and such canceling of certificate of naturalization shall be effective as of the original date of the order and certificate, respectively. The diplomatic and consular officers of the United States in foreign countries shall from time to time, through the Department of State, furnish the Department of Justice with statements of the names of those persons within their respective jurisdictions who have been so naturalized and who have taken permanent residence in the country of their nativity, or in any other foreign country, and such statements, duly certified, shall be admissible in evidence in all courts in proceedings to revoke and set aside the order admitting to citizenship and to cancel the certificate of naturalization.

(e) The revocation and setting aside of the order admitting any person to citizenship and canceling his certificate of naturalization under the provisions of subsection (a) of section 338 of the Nationality Act of 1940 shall not, where such action takes place after the effective date of this Act, result in the loss of citizenship or any right or privilege of citizenship which would have been derived by or been available to a wife or minor child of the naturalized person had such naturalization not been revoked: *Provided*, That this subsection shall not apply in any case in which the revocation and setting aside of the order was the result of actual fraud.

(f) Any person who claims United States citizenship through the naturalization of a parent or spouse in whose case there is a revocation and setting aside of the order admitting such parent or spouse to citizenship under the provisions of subsection (a) of this section on the ground that the order and certificate of naturalization were procured by concealment of a material fact or by willful misrepresentation shall be deemed to have lost and to lose his citizenship and any right or privilege of citizenship which he may have, now has, or may hereafter acquire under and by virtue of such naturalization of such parent or spouse, regardless of whether such person is residing within or without the United States at the time of the revocation and setting aside of the order admitting such parent or spouse to citizenship. Any person who claims United States citizenship through the naturalization of a parent or spouse in whose case there is a revocation and setting aside of the order admitting such parent or spouse to citizenship and the cancellation of the certificate of naturalization under the provisions of subsection (c) or (d) of this section, or under the provisions of section 329(c) of this title on any ground other than that the order and certificate of naturalization were procured by concealment of a material fact or by willful misrepresentation, shall be deemed to have lost and to lose his citizenship and any right or privilege of citizenship which would have been enjoyed by such person had there not been a revocation and setting aside of the order admitting such parent or spouse to citizenship and the cancellation of the certificate of naturalization, unless such person is residing in the United States at the time of the revocation and setting aside of the order admitting such parent or spouse to citizenship and the cancellation of the certificate of naturalization.

(g) When a person shall be convicted under section 1425 of title 18 of the United States Code of knowingly procuring naturalization in violation of law, the court in which such conviction is had shall thereupon revoke, set aside, and declare void the final order admitting such person to citizenship, and shall declare the certificate of naturalization of such person to be canceled. Jurisdiction is hereby conferred on the courts having jurisdiction of the trial of such offence to make such adjudication.

(h) Whenever an order admitting an alien to citizenship shall be revoked and set aside or a certificate of naturalization shall be canceled, or both, as provided in this section, the court in which such judgment or decree is rendered shall make an order canceling such certificate and shall send a certified copy of such order to the Attorney General. In case such certificate was not originally issued by the court making such order, it shall direct the clerk of court in which the order is revoked and set aside to transmit a copy of such order and judgment to the court out of which such certificate of naturalization shall have been originally issued. It shall thereupon be the duty of the clerk of the court receiving such certified copy of the order and judgment of the court to enter the same of record and to cancel such original certificate of naturalization, if there be any, upon the records and to notify the Attorney General of the entry of such order and of such cancellation. A person holding a certificate of naturalization or citizenship which has been canceled as provided by this section shall upon notice by the court by which the decree of cancellation was made, or by the Attorney General, surrender the same to the Attorney General.

(i) The provisions of this section shall apply not only to any naturalization granted and to certificates of naturalization and citizenship issued under the provisions of this title, but to any naturalization heretofore granted by any court, and to all certificates of naturalization and citizenship which may have been issued heretofore by any court or by the Commissioner based upon naturalization granted by any court, or by a designated representative of the Commissioner under the provisions of section 702 of the Nationality Act of 1940, as amended, or by such designated representative under any other Act.

(j) Nothing contained in this section shall be regarded as limiting, denying, or restricting the power of any naturalization court, by or in which a person has been naturalized, to correct, reopen, alter, modify, or vacate its judgment or decree naturalizing such person, during the term of such court or within the time prescribed by the rules of procedure or statutes governing the jurisdiction of the court to take such action.

* * *

Chapter 3. Loss of Nationality

LOSS OF NATIONALITY BY NATIVE-BORN OR NATURALIZED CITIZEN

Sec. 349. [8 U.S.C. 1481] (a) From and after the effective date of this Act a person who is a national of the United States whether by birth or naturalization, shall lose his nationality by—

(1) obtaining naturalization in a foreign state upon his own application, upon an application filed in his behalf by a parent, guardian, or duly authorized agent, or through the naturalization of a parent having legal custody of such person: *Provided*, That nationality shall not be lost by any person under this section as the result of the naturalization of a parent or parents while such person is under the age of twenty-one years, or as the result of a naturalization obtained on behalf of a person under twenty-one years of age by a parent, guardian, or duly authorized agent, unless such person shall fail to enter the United States to establish a permanent residence prior to his twenty-fifth birthday: *And provided further,* That a person who shall have lost nationality prior to January 1, 1948, through the naturalization in a foreign state of a parent or parents, may, within one year from the effective date of this Act, apply for a visa and for admission to the United States as a special immigrant under the provisions of section 101(a)(27)(E); or

(2) taking an oath or making an affirmation or other formal declaration of allegiance to a foreign state or a political subdivision thereof; or

(3) entering, or serving in, the armed forces of a foreign state unless, prior to such entry or service, such entry or service is specifically authorized in writing by the Secretary of State and the Secretary of Defense: *Provided*, That the entry into such service by a person prior to the attainment of his eighteenth birthday shall serve to expatriate such person only if there exists an option to secure a release from such service and such person fails to exercise such option at the attainment of his eighteenth birthday; or

(4)(A) accepting, serving in, or performing the duties of any office, post, or employment under the government of a foreign state or a political subdivision thereof, if he has or acquires the nationality of such foreign state; or (B) accepting, serving in, or performing the duties of any office, post, or employment under the government of a foreign state or a political subdivision thereof, for which office, post, or employment an oath, affirmation, or declaration of allegiance is required; or

(5) making a formal renunciation of nationality before a diplomatic or consular officer of the United States in a foreign state, in such form as may be prescribed by the Secretary of State; or

(6) making in the United States a formal written renunciation of nationality in such form as may be prescribed by, and before such officer as may be designated by, the Attorney General, whenever the United States shall be in a state of war and the Attorney General

shall approve such renunciation as not contrary to the interests of national defense; or

(7) committing any act of treason against, or attempting by force to overthrow, or bearing arms against, the United States, violating or conspiring to violate any of the provisions of section 2383 of title 18, United States Code, or willfully performing any act in violation of section 2385 of title 18, United States Code, or violating section 2384 of said title by engaging in a conspiracy to overthrow, put down, or to destroy by force the Government of the United States, or to levy war against them, if and when he is convicted thereof by a court martial or by a court of competent jurisdiction.

(b) Any person who commits or performs any act specified in subsection (a) shall be conclusively presumed to have done so voluntarily and without having been subjected to duress of any kind, if such person at the time of the act was a national of the state in which the act was performed and had been physically present in such state for a period or periods totaling ten years or more immediately prior to such act.

(c) Whenever the loss of United States nationality is put in issue in any action or proceeding commenced on or after the enactment of this subsection under, or by virtue of, the provisions of this or any other Act, the burden shall be upon the person or party claiming that such loss occurred, to establish such claim by a preponderance of the evidence. Except as otherwise provided in subsection (b), any person who commits or performs, or who has committed or performed, any act of expatriation under the provisions of this or any other Act shall be presumed to have done so voluntarily, but such presumption may be rebutted upon a showing, by a preponderance of the evidence, that the act or acts committed or performed were not done voluntarily.

Sec. 350. [Repealed.]

RESTRICTIONS ON EXPATRIATION

Sec. 351. [8 U.S.C. 1483] (a) Except as provided in paragraphs (6) and (7) of section 349 of this title, no national of the United States can expatriate himself, or be expatriated, under this Act while within the United States or any of its outlying possessions, but expatriation shall result from the performance within the United States or any of its outlying possessions of any of the acts or the fulfillment of any of the conditions specified in this chapter if and when the national thereafter takes up a residence outside the United States and its outlying possessions.

(b) A national who within six months after attaining the age of eighteen years asserts his claim to United States nationality, in such manner as the Secretary of State shall by regulation prescribe, shall not be deemed to have expatriated himself by the commission, prior to his eighteenth birthday, of any of the acts specified in paragraphs (2), (4), and (5) of section 349(a) of this title.

Sections 352 to 355. [Repealed.]

Nationality Lost Solely From Performance of Acts or Fulfillment of Conditions

Sec. 356. [8 U.S.C. 1488] The loss of nationality under this chapter shall result solely from the performance by a national of the acts or fulfillment of the conditions specified in this chapter.

Application of Treaties; Exceptions

Sec. 357. [8 U.S.C. 1489] Nothing in this title shall be applied in contravention of the provisions of any treaty or convention to which the United States is a party and which has been ratified by the Senate upon the effective date of this title: *Provided, however,* That no woman who was a national of the United States shall be deemed to have lost her nationality solely by reason of her marriage to an alien on or after September 22, 1922, or to an alien racially ineligible to citizenship on or after March 3, 1931, or, in the case of a woman who was a United States citizen at birth, through residence abroad following such marriage, notwithstanding the provisions of any existing treaty or convention.

* * *

Appendix B

PROTOCOL RELATING TO THE STATUS OF REFUGEES

Selected Provisions

Done January 31, 1967

Entry into force, October 4, 1967

606 U.N.T.S. 267, 19 U.S.T. 6223, T.I.A.S. No. 6577

Article I. General provision

1. The States Parties to the present Protocol undertake to apply Articles 2 to 34 inclusive of the Convention to refugees as hereinafter defined.

2. For the purpose of the present Protocol, the term "refugee" shall, except as regards the application of paragraph 3 of this Article, mean any person within the definition of Article 1 of the Convention as if the words "As a result of events occurring before 1 January 1951 and . . ." and the words ". . . as a result of such events", in Article 1A(2) were omitted.

3. The present Protocol shall be applied by the States Parties hereto without any geographic limitation, save that existing declarations made by States already Parties to the Convention in accordance with Article 1B(1)(a) of the Convention, shall, unless extended under Article 1B(2) thereof, apply also under the present Protocol.

Article II. Co-operation of the national authorities with the United Nations

1. The States Parties to the present Protocol undertake to co-operate with the Office of the United Nations High Commissioner for Refugees, or any other agency of the United Nations which may succeed it, in the exercise of its functions, and shall in particular facilitate its duty of supervising the application of the provisions of the present Protocol.

2. In order to enable the Office of the High Commissioner, or any other agency of the United Nations which may succeed it, to make reports to the competent organs of the United Nations, the States Parties to the present Protocol undertake to provide them with the information and statistical data requested, in the appropriate form, concerning:

(a) The condition of refugees;

(b) The implementation of the present Protocol;

(c) Laws, regulations and decrees which are, or may hereafter be, in force relating to refugees.

* * *

Appendix C

CONVENTION RELATING TO THE STATUS OF REFUGEES

Selected Provisions
Done at Geneva, July 28, 1951
Entry into force, April 22, 1954
189 U.N.T.S. 137

CHAPTER I. GENERAL PROVISIONS

Article 1. Definition of the term "Refugee"

A. For the purposes of the present Convention, the term "refugee" shall apply to any person who:

(1) Has been considered a refugee under the Arrangements of 12 May 1926 and 30 June 1928 or under the Conventions of 28 October 1933 and 10 February 1938, the Protocol of 14 September 1939 or the Constitution of the International Refugee Organization;

Decisions of non-eligibility taken by the International Refugee Organization during the period of its activities shall not prevent the status of refugee being accorded to persons who fulfil the conditions of paragraph 2 of this section;

(2) As a result of events occurring before 1 January 1951 and owing to well-founded fear of being persecuted for reasons of race, religion, nationality, membership of a particular social group or political opinion, is outside the country of his nationality and is unable or, owing to such fear, is unwilling to avail himself of the protection of that country; or who, not having a nationality and being outside the country of his former habitual residence as a result of such events, is unable or, owing to such fear, is unwilling to return to it.

In the case of a person who has more than one nationality, the term "the country of his nationality" shall mean each of the countries of which he is a national, and a person shall not be deemed to be lacking the protection of the country of his nationality if, without any valid reason based on well-founded fear, he has not availed himself of the protection of one of the countries of which he is a national.

B. (1) For the purposes of this Convention, the words "events occurring before 1 January 1951" in Article 1, Section A, shall be understood to mean either (*a*) "events occurring in Europe before 1 January 1951"; or

(*b*) "events occurring in Europe or elsewhere before 1 January 1951", and each Contracting State shall make a declaration at the time of signature, ratification or accession, specifying which of these meanings it applies for the purpose of its obligations under this Convention.

(2) Any Contracting State which has adopted alternative (*a*) may at any time extend its obligations by adopting alternative (*b*) by means of a notification addressed to the Secretary-General of the United Nations.

C. This Convention shall cease to apply to any person falling under the terms of section A if:

(1) He has voluntarily re-availed himself of the protection of the country of his nationality; or

(2) Having lost his nationality, he has voluntarily re-acquired it; or

(3) He has acquired a new nationality, and enjoys the protection of the country of his new nationality; or

(4) He has voluntarily re-established himself in the country which he left or outside which he remained owing to fear of persecution; or

(5) He can no longer, because of circumstances in connexion with which he has been recognized as a refugee have ceased to exist, continue to refuse to avail himself of the protection of the country of his nationality;

Provided that this paragraph shall not apply to a refugee falling under section A(1) of this Article who is able to invoke compelling reasons arising out of previous persecution for refusing to avail himself of the protection of the country of nationality;

(6) Being a person who has no nationality he is, because the circumstances in connexion with which he has been recognized as a refugee have ceased to exist, able to return to the country of his former habitual residence;

Provided that this paragraph shall not apply to a refugee falling under section A(1) of this Article who is able to invoke compelling reasons arising out of previous persecution for refusing to return to the country of his former habitual residence.

D. This Convention shall not apply to persons who are at present receiving from organs or agencies of the United Nations other than the United Nations High Commissioner for Refugees protection or assistance.

When such protection or assistance has ceased for any reason, without the position of such persons being definitively settled in accordance with the relevant resolutions adopted by the General Assembly of the United Nations, these persons shall *ipso facto* be entitled to the benefits of this Convention.

E. This Convention shall not apply to a person who is recognized by the competent authorities of the country in which he has taken residence as having the rights and obligations which are attached to the possession of the nationality of that country.

F.   The provisions of this Convention shall not apply to any person with respect to whom there are serious reasons for considering that:

(*a*) he has committed a crime against peace, a war crime, or a crime against humanity, as defined in the international instruments drawn up to make provision in respect of such crimes;

(*b*) he has committed a serious non-political crime outside the country of refuge prior to his admission to that country as a refugee;

(*c*) he has been guilty of acts contrary to the purposes and principles of the United Nations.

Article 2.   General obligations

Every refugee has duties to the country in which he finds himself, which require in particular that he conform to its laws and regulations as well as to measures taken for the maintenance of public order.

Article 3.   Non-discrimination

The Contracting States shall apply the provisions of this Convention to refugees without discrimination as to race, religion or country of origin.

* * *

Article 7.   Exemption from reciprocity

1.   Except where this Convention contains more favourable provisions, a Contracting State shall accord to refugees the same treatment as is accorded to aliens generally.

2.   After a period of three years' residence, all refugees shall enjoy exemption from legislative reciprocity in the territory of the Contracting States.

3.   Each Contracting State shall continue to accord to refugees the rights and benefits to which they were already entitled, in the absence of reciprocity, at the date of entry into force of this Convention for that State.

4.   The Contracting States shall consider favourably the possibility of according to refugees, in the absence of reciprocity, rights and benefits beyond those to which they are entitled according to paragraphs 2 and 3, and to extending exemption from reciprocity to refugees who do not fulfil the conditions provided for in paragraphs 2 and 3.

5.   The provisions of paragraphs 2 and 3 apply both to the rights and benefits referred to in Articles 13, 18, 19, 21 and 22 of this Convention and to rights and benefits for which this Convention does not provide.

* * *

Article 9.   Provisional measures

Nothing in this Convention shall prevent a Contracting State, in time of war or other grave and exceptional circumstances, from taking provisionally measures which it considers to be essential to the national security in the case of a particular person, pending a determination by the Contracting State that that person is in fact a refugee and that the continuance of such measures is necessary in his case in the interests of national security.

* * *

CHAPTER II.   JURIDICAL STATUS

Article 12.   Personal status

1.   The personal status of a refugee shall be governed by the law of the country of his domicile or, if he has no domicile, by the law of the country of his residence.

2.   Rights previously acquired by a refugee and dependent on personal status, more particularly rights attaching to marriage, shall be respected by a Contracting State, subject to compliance, if this be necessary, with the formalities required by the law of that State, provided that the right in question is one which would have been recognized by the law of that State had he not become a refugee.

* * *

Article 16.   Access to courts

1.   A refugee shall have free access to the courts of law on the territory of all Contracting States.

2.   A refugee shall enjoy in the Contracting State in which he has his habitual residence the same treatment as a national in matters pertaining to access to the Courts, including legal assistance and exemption from *cautio judicatum solvi.*

3.   A refugee shall be accorded in the matters referred to in paragraph 2 in countries other than that in which he has his habitual residence the treatment granted to a national of the country of his habitual residence.

CHAPTER III.   GAINFUL EMPLOYMENT

Article 17.   Wage-earning employment

1.   The Contracting State shall accord to refugees lawfully staying in their territory the most favourable treatment accorded to nationals of a foreign country in the same circumstances, as regards the right to engage in wage-earning employment.

2.   In any case, restrictive measures imposed on aliens or the employment of aliens for the protection of the national labour market shall not be applied to a refugee who was already exempt from them at the date of entry into force of this Convention for the Contracting State concerned, or who fulfils one of the following conditions:

   (a) He has completed three years' residence in the country,

   (b) He has a spouse possessing the nationality of the country of residence. A refugee may not invoke the benefits of this provision if he has abandoned his spouse,

(c) He has one or more children possessing the nationality of the country of residence.

3. The Contracting States shall give sympathetic consideration to assimilating the rights of all refugees with regard to wage-earning employment to those of nationals, and in particular of those refugees who have entered their territory pursuant to programmes of labour recruitment or under immigration schemes.

* * *

CHAPTER IV. WELFARE

* * *

Article 22. Public education

1. The Contracting States shall accord to refugees the same treatment as is accorded to nationals with respect to elementary education.

2. The Contracting States shall accord to refugees treatment as favourable as possible, and, in any event, not less favourable than that accorded to aliens generally in the same circumstances, with respect to education other than elementary education and, in particular, as regards access to studies, the recognition of foreign school certificates, diplomas and degrees, the remission of fees and charges and the award of scholarships.

Article 23. Public relief

The Contracting States shall accord to refugees lawfully staying in their territory the same treatment with respect to public relief and assistance as is accorded to their nationals.

Article 24. Labour legislation and social security

1. The Contracting States shall accord to refugees lawfully staying in their territory the same treatment as is accorded to nationals in respect of the following matters:

(a) In so far as such matters are governed by laws or regulations or are subject to the control of administrative authorities: remuneration, including family allowances where these form part of remuneration, hours of work, overtime arrangements, holidays with pay, restrictions on home work, minimum age of employment, apprenticeship and training, women's work and the work of young persons, and the enjoyment of the benefits of collective bargaining;

(b) Social security (legal provisions in respect of employment injury, occupational diseases, maternity, sickness, disability, old age, death, unemployment, family responsibilities and any other contingency which, according to national laws or regulations, is covered by a social security scheme), subject to the following limitations:

(i) There may be appropriate arrangements for the maintenance of acquired rights and rights in course of acquisition;

(ii) National laws or regulations of the country of residence may prescribe special arrangements concerning benefits or portions of benefits which are payable wholly out of public funds, and concerning allowances paid to persons who do not fulfil the contribution conditions prescribed for the award of a normal pension.

2. The right to compensation for the death of a refugee resulting from employment injury or from occupational disease shall not be affected by the fact that the residence of the beneficiary is outside the territory of the Contracting State.

3. The Contracting States shall extend to refugees the benefits of agreements concluded between them, or which may be concluded between them in the future, concerning the maintenance of acquired rights and rights in the process of acquisition in regard to social security, subject only to the conditions which apply to nationals of the States signatory to the agreements in question.

4. The Contracting States will give sympathetic consideration to extending to refugees so far as possible the benefits of similar agreements which may at any time be in force between such Contracting States and non-contracting States.

CHAPTER V.   ADMINISTRATIVE MEASURES

* * *

Article 26.   Freedom of movement

Each Contracting State shall accord to refugees lawfully in its territory the right to choose their place of residence and to move freely within its territory, subject to any regulations applicable to aliens generally in the same circumstances.

Article 27.   Identity papers

The Contracting States shall issue identity papers to any refugee in their territory who does not possess a valid travel document.

Article 28.   Travel documents

1. The Contracting States shall issue to refugees lawfully staying in their territory travel documents for the purpose of travel outside their territory unless compelling reasons of national security or public order otherwise require, and the provisions of the Schedule to this Convention shall apply with respect to such documents. The Contracting States may issue such a travel document to any other refugee in their territory, they shall in particular give sympathetic consideration to the issue of such a travel document to refugees in their territory who are unable to obtain a travel document from the country of their lawful residence.

2. Travel documents issued to refugees under previous international agreements by parties thereto shall be recognized and treated by the

Contracting States in the same way as if they had been issued pursuant to this article.

* * *

Article 31.   Refugees unlawfully in the country of refuge

1.   The Contracting States shall not impose penalties, on account of their illegal entry or presence, on refugees who, coming directing from a territory where their life or freedom was threatened in the sense of Article 1, enter or are present in their territory without authorization, provided they present themselves without delay to the authorities and show good cause for their illegal entry or presence.

2.   The Contracting States shall not apply to the movements of such refugees restrictions other than those which are necessary and such restrictions shall only be applied until their status in the country is regularized or they obtain admission into another country. The Contracting States shall allow such refugees a reasonable period and all the necessary facilities to obtain admission into another country.

Article 32.   Expulsion

1.   The Contracting States shall not expel a refugee lawfully in their territory save on grounds of national security or public order.

2.   The expulsion of such a refugee shall be only in pursuance of a decision reached in accordance with due process of law. Except where compelling reasons of national security otherwise require, the refugee shall be allowed to submit evidence to clear himself, and to appeal to and be represented for the purpose before competent authority or a person or persons specially designated by the competent authority.

3.   The Contracting States shall allow such a refugee a reasonable period within which to seek legal admission into another country. The Contracting States reserve the right to apply during that period such internal measures as they may deem necessary.

Article 33.   Prohibition of expulsion or return ("refoulement")

1.   No Contracting State shall expel or return ("refouler") a refugee in any manner whatsoever to the frontiers of territories where his life or freedom would be threatened on account of his race, religion, nationality, membership of a particular social group or political opinion.

2.   The benefit of the present provision may not, however, by claimed by a refugee whom there are reasonable grounds for regarding as a danger to the security of the country in which he is, or who, having been convicted by a final judgment of a particularly serious crime, constitutes a danger to the community of that country.

Article 34.   Naturalization

The Contracting States shall as far as possible facilitate the assimilation and naturalization of refugees. They shall in particular make every effort to expedite naturalization proceedings and to reduce as far as possible the charges and costs of such proceedings.

* * *

Index

References are to Pages

LANGUAGE, 48, 123, 861

LAW ENFORCEMENT
See also Discretion, Prosecutorial.
Generally, 82, 352, 403, 434–448, 466, 481, 547, 768, 789, 811, 815, 832.
Border, 84, 271, 746, 758, 771.
Detention, 234, 253, 278, 293–314, 318, 354, 403, 603, 609, 722.
Fraud (including sham marriages), 138, 149, 174, 399, 470, 557, 647, 774–776, 793, 855, 874, 877, 880.
Interdiction of boats, 724.

MORAL FOUNDATIONS AND CONSTRAINTS
Citizenship, 835–839, 933.
Due process, 455–457.
Family reunification, 113.
Immigration policy generally, 61–80.
Refugee programs, 635.
Undocumented aliens, 181, 826–832.

NATIONAL ORIGINS QUOTAS
See History.

NONIMMIGRANTS
Generally, 97, 103, 283, 577, 582, 606.
Adjustment to immigrant status, 282–291.
Admission procedures, 271, 276.
Bracero program, 52, 175, 182, 746, 748–752, 758, 800, 804, 831.
Categories, 98.
Temporary workers, 175–181, 748–753, 769, 798–826.
Work authorization, 272, 400.

PAROLE, 97, 102, 232–236, 301, 305, 308, 316, 337

PREFERENCE SYSTEM
See also Immigrants, Refugees and Political Asylum.
Generally, 55, 101, 106–114.
Adopted children, 146.
Family reunification preferences, 106–109, 113, 125–154.
Illegitimate children, 125, 135–145.
Marriage, 146–154.
Nonpreference immigration, 114.
Occupational preferences, 107–108, 154–175.
Stepchildren, 135.

PROFESSIONAL RESPONSIBILITY, 86, 149–151, 470, 485, 617

REFUGEES AND POLITICAL ASYLUM
See also Evidence and Evidentiary Standards; Parole.
Generally, 53, 57–59, 102, 118, 235, 419, 558, 570, 615–743.
Adjustment to lawful permanent resident status, 626, 641.
"Bootstrap", 668.
Cubans, 235, 294–306, 621.
De facto refugees, 740.
Definition, 615–616, 619, 624, 626–638, 656, 660.
Deterrent measures, 314, 619, 720–726.

REFUGEES AND POLITICAL ASYLUM
—Cont'd
Diplomatic asylum, 640.
Discretionary nature of asylum, 644–649, 660–668, 709.
Economic migrants, 637, 644.
Exceptions, 642, 671–682.
Extended voluntary departure (and other safe haven), 469, 726–743.
Extradition, 638, 677, 682.
"Firmly resettled", 626.
Haitians, 235, 294, 319, 594, 616–618, 632, 637, 682–686.
Hearing, asylum case (transcript), 686–700.
Indochinese, 622, 637.
Judicial review, 700.
Kudirka incident, 640, 725.
Notice of asylum rights, 711–720.
Overseas refugee programs, 618, 620–638.
Political asylum, generally, 619, 638–726.
Procedures for asylum applications, 640–645, 661, 706–708.
Refoulement and nonrefoulement, 639, 649, 658.
Salvadorans, 710, 729–739.
Sanctuary movement, 739.
Seventh preference (conditional entry), 622, 639, 658, 663.
Standards for adjudication, 640, 644, 649–682, 700, 741.
State Department role, 642, 644, 701–708.
UNHCR, 615, 653, 655, 670.
Withholding of deportation, 641–649, 654–667, 709.

REGISTRATION OF ALIENS (including "green cards"), 261, 272, 276, 440, 445, 463

RELIEF FROM DEPORTATION
See also Refugees and Political Asylum.
Generally, 403, 409, 464–559, 570.
Adjustment of status,
See Admission Procedures.
Deferred action (nonpriority status), 474.
Estoppel, 281, 554–558.
Judicial review, 570.
Private bills, 547–552.
Registry, 552–554.
Stay of deportation, 484, 570, 576.
Suspension, 487–537, 600.
Voluntary departure, 403, 438, 443, 464–473, 578, 713.

RESIDENCE, DOMICILE, PHYSICAL PRESENCE, 545–546, 852, 859–861

SHAM MARRIAGES
See Law Enforcement, Fraud.

STATUTORY CONSTRUCTION, 231, 330, 333, 335, 372, 383, 387–391, 490–508, 541, 573, 665

STOWAWAYS, 282

UNDOCUMENTED ALIENS AND ILLEGAL MIGRATION
Generally, 102, 119, 376, 744–832.

MCMLXXXVI

I. Federal agencies, appellate structure, etc.
  A. INS - determine (part of justice dept.)
    1. aliens eligibility to immigrate
    2. hiring alien as temporary workers
    3. admissability of alien under 33 grounds of exclusion
    4. aliens deportability under 19 grounds of deportation
    5. waiver of excludability or deportability
    6. asylum & refugee status
    7. eligibility for naturalization or denaturalization
  B. Dept. of Labor — certifies unavailability of American workers
  C. State dept.
    1. determines eligibility for visa under grounds of exclusion
    2. some waiver of excludability
  D. Appellate structure
    1. order of excludability appealable to Attorney general
      by the Board of Immigration appeals
    2. Associate Commissioner of examinations
    3. Judicial review

II. non-immigrants - p. 98
III. Immigrants
  A. numerical & non-numerical preferences p. 104~114
IV. Standard test for sham marriage - whether bride & groom planned to have a life together
V. Labor certification
  A. First, actual job offer must be made to alien
  B. must characterize job - according to Dict. of occupational Titles
  C. must place ad, usually in paper of general circulation and post notice at office where job is offered
VI. Excludability §212
  A general grounds - p. 185-192
  B. When it may be waived p. 184
VII. Waiver of excludability - p. 192 & §212(b)-(i)
VIII. Parole - unacceptable aliens allowed to go free but still subject to finding of excludability
IX. Procedures in exclusion
  A. order to show cause
  B. hearing before immigration judge
  C. Appeal to Board of Immigration appeals
  D. may seek habeas corpus review in district court must request stay of exclusion

X. Visa process
  A. application at American Consulate
  B. alien sent "packet three"
  C. notice of appointment
  D. Consular officer conducts interview — has full discretion whether or not to grant visa

XI. Basis for denying permanent residence:
  A. intent to reside permanently
  B. fraud concerning identity and citizenship
  C. must approach a immigration inspection station
  D. nonimmigrants + J non-immigrants
  E. must not have be in unauthorized employment
  F. must not be subject to grounds of exclusion
  G. Pre-conceived intent to adjust

XII. Entry + re-entry doctrine
  A. Entry: 3 requirements
    1. physical presence
    2. inspection or avoidance of inspection
    3. freedom from official restraint
  B. Re-entry — a permanent resident returning from a trip abroad makes a new entry, and is subject to burden of excludability

XIII. Distinction between deportation and exclusion
  A. From notes:
    1. Rights in deportation proceeding:
      a. standard of proof — clear, unequivocal and convincing proof of alienage
      b. alien has burden of proving legal entry
      c. alien must be Mirandized after OSC
      d. have 5th amend. rights
    2. 2 issues
      a. whether alien is subject to deport. as in O.S.C
      b. whether alien can be excused from deportation
  B. from Book: ("Immigration primer")
    1. automatic stay of depo deportation upon review
    2. alien has more rights in deportation, but still:
      a. no right to attorney
      b. no necessity to be present
      c. no presumption of innocence
      d. no exclusionary rule, or requirement of due process

XIV. Grounds of deportation — p. 372 – 378

XV. Judicial review — either appellate or district

XVI. Asylum
  A. Applying:
    1. go to dist. director
    2. fill out application
    3. get interviewed
    C. state dept. issue advisory decision
    2. may appeal to immigration judge who judges by standard of clear probability of particularized persecution

XVII. Extended Voluntary departure

Grounds of exclusion are raised when:
1. at American consulate
2. immigration officer at border
3. where alien makes appl. for permanent status
4. resident alien brought up for deportation
5. naturalized citizen if ground is found in naturalization
(albeit only after denaturalization proceedings)